THE OXFORD HANDB(

CHRISTOLOGY

THE OXFORD HANDBOOK OF

CHRISTOLOGY

Edited by

FRANCESCA ARAN MURPHY

Assistant Editor

TROY A. STEFANO

OXFORD

UNIVERSITY PRESS

Great Clarendon Street, Oxford, OX2 6DP,
United Kingdom

Oxford University Press is a department of the University of Oxford.
It furthers the University's objective of excellence in research, scholarship,
and education by publishing worldwide. Oxford is a registered trade mark of
Oxford University Press in the UK and in certain other countries

Published in the United States of America by Oxford University Press
198 Madison Avenue, New York, NY 10016, United States of America

British Library Cataloguing in Publication Data
Data available

Library of Congress Cataloging in Publication Data
Data available

ISBN 978–0–19–964190–1 (Hbk.)
ISBN 978–0–19–880064–4 (Pbk.)

CONTENTS

PART III MEDIAEVAL CHRISTOLOGY

PART IV REFORMATION AND CHRISTOLOGY

PART V MODERN AND POSTMODERN CHRISTOLOGY

PART VI IMAGINING THE SON OF GOD IN MODERNITY

List of Figures

LIST OF CONTRIBUTORS

Khaled Anatolios is Associate Professor of Historical Theology at the Boston College School of Theology and Ministry. His most recent monograph is *Retrieving Nicaea: The Development and Meaning of Trinitarian Doctrine* (2011). He is on the board of directors of the Pappas Patristic Institute of Holy Cross Greek Orthodox School of Theology.

Robert Barron received his Master's degree in Philosophy from the Catholic University of America in Washington, DC, in 1982 and was ordained to the priesthood for the Archdiocese of Chicago in 1986. He received his doctoral degree from the Institut Catholique de Paris, with a *mention* of *très honorable* in June of 1992. In 1996 his book *Thomas Aquinas: Spiritual Master* was published by Crossroad. This text was given the Catholic Press Association First Prize in Spirituality. In 1998 his book *And Now I See: A Theology of Transformation* was published by Crossroad. Between 2000 and 2008 he published *Heaven in Stone and Glass: Experiencing the Spirituality of the Great Cathedrals* (2002), *The Strangest Way: Walking the Christian Path* (2002), *Bridging the Great Divide: Musings of a Post-Liberal, Post-Conservative, Evangelical Catholic* (2004), *The Priority of Christ: Toward a Postliberal Catholicism* (2007), *The Word on Fire: Proclaiming the Power of Christ* (2008), and *Eucharist* (2008). In 2005 he published a DVD entitled *Untold Blessings: The Three Paths of Holiness*, and this was followed in 2006 by a DVD entitled *Conversion* and in 2007 by another called *Seven Deadly Sins; Seven Lively Virtues*. His outstanding DVD series *Catholicism* has been widely acclaimed. In 2008 Fr. Barron was named the first holder of the Francis Cardinal George chair of Faith and Culture at University of Saint Mary of the Lake/Mundelein Seminary outside of Chicago. In 2012, Francis Cardinal George appointed Fr. Barron President of the University of Saint Mary of the Lake and tenth rector of Mundelein Seminary.

Richard J. Bauckham is currently a senior scholar at Ridley Hall, Cambridge. He taught for fifteen years at the University of Saint Andrews, and for fifteen years before that at the University of Manchester. He won the Michael Ramsey Award and the Christianity Today Book Award for his 2006 masterpiece *Jesus and the Eyewitnesses: The Gospels as Eye-Witness Testimony* (2006). In 2010 Richard Bauckham was honoured with the Franz-Delitzsch Award for his book *The Jewish World Around the New Testament*.

Markus Bockmuehl is Professor of Biblical and Early Christian Studies at the University of Oxford, where he has also served as Associate Head of the Humanities Division. His books include *The Epistle to the Philippians* (1998), *Seeing the Word: Refocusing New Testament Study* (2006), and *Simon Peter in Scripture and Memory* (2012). Among his recent edited volumes are *Redemption and Resistance* (2007), *Scripture's Doctrine and Theology's Bible* (2008), and *Paradise in Antiquity* (2010).

Lawrence S. Cunningham is John A. O'Brien Professor of Theology (Emeritus) at the University of Notre Dame. The author or editor of over twenty-six books, he has written widely on Christian spirituality and has contributed a number of essays and book chapters on Christian art, architecture, and photography.

Brian E. Daley, S.J. is Catherine F. Huisking Professor of Theology at the University of Notre Dame. Father Daley was recently awarded the 'Ratzinger Prize'. He is the author of *The Hope of the Early Church: A Handbook of Patristic Eschatology* (1991) and *On The Dormition of Mary: Early Patristic Homilies, Gregory of Nazianzus* (2006). He gave the D'Arcy Lectures at Oxford on *God Visible: Patristic Christology Reconsidered* and is currently turning these lectures into a book. Father Daley is the editor of the Patristic journal *Traditio*.

Gavin D'Costa is Professor of Catholic Theology at the University of Bristol. He is author of seven books, most recently: *Christianity and the World Religions: Disputed Questions in the Theology of Religions* (2009) and *Vatican II and the World Religions* (Oxford University Press, 2014). He is an advisor to the Vatican, the Roman Catholic Bishops in England and Wales, and to the Church of England, Board of Mission on matters related to other religions.

Mark W. Elliott is Reader in Church History at the University of St Andrews. He is the author of *The Heart of Biblical Theology: Providence Experienced* (2012), *Engaging Leviticus: Reading Leviticus Theologically with Its Past Interpreters* (2012), *The Reality of Biblical Theology* (2007), *Isaiah 40–66* (Ancient Christian Commentary Series) (2007), *Postmodernism and Theology* (1998), and *The Song of Songs and Christology in the Early Church, 381–451* (2000). He has also edited three books and written numerous scholarly articles.

Simon Gathercole is Senior Lecturer in New Testament Studies at the University of Cambridge. He is Fellow and Director of Studies in Theology at Fitzwilliam College, and the author of *Where is Boasting? Early Jewish Soteriology and Paul's Response in Romans 1–5* (2002), *The Preexistent Son: Recovering the Christologies of Matthew, Mark, and Luke* (2006), *The Gospel of Judas: Rewriting Early Christianity* (Oxford University Press, 2007), and *The Composition of the Gospel of Thomas* (2012). He is co-editor of the journal *Early Christianity*.

Raymond Gawronski, S.J. is currently Visiting Scholar at the Dominican School of Philosophy and Theology in Berkeley and adjunct Professor of Theology at St. Patrick's Seminary. After many years as Professor of Dogmatic Theology at Marquette University, he moved into full-time spiritual direction and retreat work at the St. John Vianney Seminary in Denver, where he was also full Professor of Theology for eight years. He has specialized in the mission of Hans Urs Von Balthasar, focusing on his vision of a contemplative theology. Author of *Word and Silence: Hans Urs von Balthasar and the*

Spiritual Encounter of East and West (1995), Fr. Gawronski has also published widely on the *Spiritual Exercises* (*A Closer Walk with Christ*) and on various cultural issues, especially as regards spiritual traditions.

Gregory Glazov has a DPhil from Oxford. His doctoral dissertation, 'The "Bridling of the Tongue" and the "Opening of the Mouth" in Biblical Prophecy', was published by Sheffield Academic Press in 2001. He is currently Professor of Biblical Studies at Seton Hall University. He has published articles on the book of Job, Vladmir Solovyov, and biblical anthropology in *Vetus Testamentum, Communio*, and for the Linacre Centre. His most recent book is *The Burning Bush: Vladimir Solovyov's Writings on Judaism: Texts and Commentary* (2015). Dr. Glazov serves as Coordinator of the Great Spiritual Books program of ICSST's Institute for Christian Spirituality.

Michael J. Gorman holds the Raymond E. Brown Chair in Biblical Studies and Theology at St. Mary's Seminary & University in Baltimore, Maryland, USA, where he was previously Dean of its Ecumenical Institute of Theology. He is the author of ten books, including *Cruciformity: Paul's Narrative Spirituality of the Cross* (2001), *Inhabiting the Cruciform God: Kenosis, Justification, and Theosis in Paul's Narrative Spirituality* (2009), and *The Death of the Messiah and the Birth of the New Covenant: A (Not So) New Model of the Atonement* (2014).

Kevin Hector is Assistant Professor of Theology and of the Philosophy of Religions at the University of Chicago, and the author of *Theology Without Metaphysics* (2011).

David S. Hogg is Associate Dean of Academic Affairs and Associate Professor of Divinity at Beeson Divinity School, Samford University. Professor Hogg is the author of *Anselm of Canterbury: The Beauty of Theology* (2004).

Andrew Louth is Emeritus Professor of Patristic and Byzantine Studies at the Durham University, UK. His most recent book is *Introducing Eastern Orthodoxy* (2013).

Brian Lugioyo is Associate Professor of Theology and Ethics at Azusa Pacific University and an ordained elder in the Free Methodist Church. He is the author of *Martin Bucer's Doctrine of Justification* (2010).

Paul Mankowski, S.J. is scholar-in-residence at the Lumen Christi Institute, Chicago.

Bruce McCormack is the Charles Hodge Professor of Systematic Theology at Princeton Theological Seminary and Director of the Center for Barth Studies. In 1998 he was awarded the prestigious Karl Barth Prize and in 2004 was awarded a Dr.theol.h.c. from the Friedrich Schiller University. He is the author of *Karl Barth's Critically Realistic Dialectical Theology: Its Genesis and Development, 1909–1936* (Clarendon Press, 1997) and numerous essays on Barth.

Alison Milbank is Associate Professor of Literature and Theology at the University of Nottingham, where she lectures on various aspects of religion, culture and aesthetics. She is the author of *Daughters of the House: Modes of the Gothic in Victorian Fiction* (1992),

Dante and the Victorians (1998), *Chesterton and Tolkien as Theologians: The Fantasy of the Real* (2009), and co-author (with Andrew Davison) of *For the Parish: A Critique of Fresh Expressions* (2010). She edited *Beating the Traffic: Josephine Butler and Anglican Social Action on Prostitution Today* (2007).

Francesca Aran Murphy is Professor of Systematic Theology at the University of Notre Dame. She is the author of numerous books, including *Christ the Form of Beauty* (1995), *God is Not a Story* (Oxford University Press, 2007), and a theological commentary on *I Samuel* (2010). She is currently editing a new series for Bloomsbury Academic called *Illuminating Modernity*. The first book in the series, of which she is a co-author, is called *Illuminating Faith*.

Gilbert Narcisse, O.P. is Prior Provincial of the Toulouse Dominicans. He is President of the Collège Universitaire Saint-Dominique (CUSD), where he holds a chair in theology. Professor Narcisse is the author of *Le Christ en sa beauté: Hans Urs von Balthasar, Saint Thomas d'Aquin* (2005), *Le Christ en sa beauté: Hans Urs von Balthasar, Saint Thomas d'Aquin. II Textes annotés* (2005), *Premiers pas en théologie* (2005), and *Les raisons de Dieu: argument de convenance et esthétique théologique selon saint Thomas d'Aquin et Hans Urs von Balthasar* (1997).

Aidan Nichols, O.P. is Prior of Blackfriars, Cambridge, and the author of fifty books on different aspects of Christian theology.

Rik van Nieuwenhove lectures in theology at Mary Immaculate College, Limerick, Ireland. He is the author of *Introduction to Medieval Theology* (2012) and *Jan van Ruusbroec: Mystical Theologian of the Trinity* (2003), co-author of *Introduction to the Trinity* (2011), and co-editor of *Late Medieval Mysticism of the Low Countries* (2008) and *The Theology of Thomas Aquinas* (2005). His research interests include mediaeval theology and spirituality, the theology of the Trinity, and soteriology.

Kenneth Oakes is currently a postdoctoral scholar at the University of Notre Dame, having previously been a postdoctoral fellow at the University of Tübingen. He is the author of *Karl Barth on Theology and Philosophy* (Oxford University Press, 2012) and *Reading Karl Barth: A Companion to the Epistle to the Romans* (2011), co-author of *Illuminating Faith: An Invitation to Theology* (2015), and editor of *Captive to Christ, Open to the World: On Doing Christian Ethics in Public* (2014).

Gabriel Said Reynolds is Professor of Islamic Studies and Theology at Notre Dame. His research is focused above all on the Qur'an and Muslim–Christian relations. He wrote a dissertation on the Islamic history of Christianity of ʿAbd al-Jabbar (d. 1025) which won the Field Prize at Yale and was published as *A Muslim Theologian in the Sectarian Milieu* (2004). Reynolds also prepared an introduction and translation of this history published as *The Critique of Christian Origins* (2008). At Notre Dame Reynolds has organized two international conferences (2005, 2009) on the Qur'an, and edited the acts of the conferences as *The Qur'ān in Its Historical Context* (2008) and *New Perspectives on the Qur'ān: The Qur'ān in Its Historical Context 2* (2011). In 2012–13 Prof. Reynolds directed 'The Qur'ān Seminar' a year-long project with a team of twenty-eight international scholars to produce a collaborative scholarly commentary on the Qur'an. He is co-director of *The International Qur'anic Studies Association* (iqsaweb.org). Reynolds' principal work on the Qur'an is *The Qur'ān and Its Biblical Subtext* (2010). He has also published *The Emergence of Islam* (2012).

Norman Russell is an honorary research fellow of St Stephen's House, Oxford, and sometime tutor in early Church history at Heythrop College, London.

Michele M. Schumacher is a mother of four and a private docent at the University of Fribourg, Switzerland, Department of Moral Theology, and Professor of Theological Anthropology at the European Institute of Anthropological Studies, Philanthropos. Other than her work of formulating a 'new feminism' (cf. *Evangelium Vitae*, no. 99), she has published in the areas of theological anthropology, redemption, mediation, sexual ethics, and Christian marriage. Her most recent work is entitled *A Trinitarian Anthropology: Adrienne von Speyr and Hans Urs von Balthasar in Dialogue with St. Thomas Aquinas* (2014), and she is currently working on a manuscript on the natural desire for God.

Calvin Stapert is Professor of Music Emeritus at Calvin College where he taught for thirty-eight years. He is author of *My Only Comfort: Death, Deliverance and Discipleship in the Music of J. S. Bach* (2000), *A New Song for an Old World: Musical Thought in the Early Church* (2007), *J. S. Bach* (2009), *Handel's* Messiah: *Comfort for God's People* (2010), and *Playing Before the Lord: The Life and Work of Joseph Haydn* (2013). He has also published many articles, mainly dealing with matters at the junction of music and theology, and is a founding member of the Society for Christian Scholarship in Music.

Troy A. Stefano is a doctoral student at the University of Notre Dame. His first book, forthcoming from Fortress Press, is called *The Trinity in Modern Catholic Theology*. He has published various chapters and articles in the areas of historical and systematic theology, and is currently working on three book translations.

Diane B. Stinton is Associate Professor of Mission Studies and Dean of students at Regent College, Vancouver. Professor Stinton specializes in theological developments in the global South. She taught theology for many years in Kenya, where she helped launch two new programs: an M.Th. in African Christianity at Daystar University, and an M.Th./Ph.D. in World Christianity at the Nairobi Evangelical Graduate School of Theology (NEGST). She is the author of *Jesus of Africa: Voices of Contemporary Christology* (2004), which is a benchmark work in its field, and the editor of *African Theology on the Way: Current Conversations* (2010). She is also a general editor for the Ecumenical Symposium of Eastern Africa Theologians (ESEAT) series on African Christianity.

Olivier-Thomas Venard, O.P. is Professor of New Testament and Vice-Director of the École biblique et archéologique française de Jérusalem. Fr. Venard is the author of a three-volume work entitled *Thomas d'Aquin Poète Théologien* (2002–9). He is engaged in major ecumenical research on the literal meaning which the Hebrew Bible has for Christians.

Joseph Wawrykow teaches in the Department of Theology at the University of Notre Dame, where he is also a fellow of the Medieval Institute. He is the author of *God's Grace and Human Action* (1995) and *The Westminster Handbook to Thomas Aquinas* (2005), and co-editor of *Christ Among the Medieval Dominicans* (1998) and *The Theology of Thomas Aquinas* (2005). He currently serves his Department as its Director of doctoral studies.

John Webster is Professor of Divinity at the University of St Andrews. He is the author of a number of books on the theology of Karl Barth and on topics in Christian doctrine. Recent publications include a collection of essays, *The Domain of the Word* (2012). He is currently writing a five-volume systematic theology.

Thomas G. Weinandy, O.F.M., Cap. is currently the Executive Director of the Secretariat for Doctrine at the United States Conference of Catholic Bishops in Washington, DC. Fr. Thomas Weinandy is a Capuchin/Franciscan. He obtained a doctorate in Historical Theology from King's College, University of London, UK. He has taught theology at a number of colleges and universities in the United States and was a tutor and lecturer in History and Doctrine at the University of Oxford from 1991 to 2004. He has written or edited sixteen books and has published numerous articles in theological journals and pastoral periodicals. He is a member of The Catholic Theological Society of America, The Fellowship of Catholic Scholars, The Academy of Catholic Theology, and The North American Patristics Society. He was the Executive Director for the Secretariat for Doctrine at the United States Conference of Catholic Bishops, from January 2005 to August 2013. He is now teaching at the Dominican House of Studies in Washington, DC, and at the Gregorian University in Rome.

Rowan Williams is currently Master of Magdalene College, Cambridge. He was Lady Margaret Professor of Divinity in Oxford from 1986 to 1992. He was Bishop of Monmouth from 1991 until 2000 when he was enthroned as Archbishop of Canterbury. A leading light in contemporary theology, Williams is the author of many books, including *The Edge of Words: God and the Habits of Language* (2014) and *The Wound of Knowledge: Christianity Spirituality from the Bible to Saint John of the Cross* (2014).

Robert J. Woźniak was ordained in the Archdiocese of Krakow in 1999. He wrote his dissertations in the University of Navarre on Bonaventure's theophenomenology of natural desire (2003) and on his theology of God the Father (published as: *Primitas et plenitudo. Dios Padre en la teología trinitaria de San Buenaventura*, 2007). He taught at the Pontifical and Civil Faculty of Theology in Lima, Peru. He is currently Professor of Systematic Theology at the Pontifical Academy of Theology in Krakow. He has written several books in Polish, and his first English language book appeared in 2012 as *Rethinking Trinitarian Theology*.

K. K. Yeo is Harry R. Kendall Professor of New Testament at Garrett-Evangelical Theological Seminary (Illinois) and Visiting Professor at Peking University and Zhejiang University in China. He was inducted into the Society of New Testament Studies in 1998, and is a Lilly as well as Luce Fellow. He is the author of numerous works in Chinese, and co-edited the Biblical Library Series in Shanghai (China). His works in English include *Rhetorical Interaction in 1 Corinthians 8 and 10: A Formal Analysis with Implications for a Cross-Cultural, Chinese Hermeneutic* (1995), *What Has Jerusalem to Do with Beijing? Biblical Interpretation from a Chinese Perspective* (1998), *Chairman Mao Meets the Apostle Paul: Christianity, Communism, and the Hope of China* (2002), *Cross-Cultural Paul: Journeys to Others, Journeys to Ourselves* (2005), and *Musing with Confucius and Paul: Toward a Chinese Christian Theology* (2008).

Randall C. Zachman is Professor of Reformation Studies at the University of Notre Dame. He is the author of *Reconsidering John Calvin* (2012), *Image and Word in the Theology of John Calvin* (2007), *John Calvin as Teacher, Pastor, and Theologian: The Shape of his Writing and Thought* (2006), and *The Assurance of Faith: Conscience in the Theology of Martin Luther and John Calvin* (2005).

Philip G. Ziegler is Senior Lecturer in Systematic Theology at the University of Aberdeen. He is the author of *Doing Theology When God is Forgotten: The Theological Achievement of Wolf Krötke* (2007), and co-editor of *The Providence of God* (2009) and *Explorations in Christian Theology and Ethics: Essays in Conversation with Paul L. Lehmann* (2009).

INTRODUCTION

FRANCESCA ARAN MURPHY

THREE years ago, the editor of this volume wrote to thirty-nine or forty scholars inviting them to write for a handbook on Christology which, she opined with naïve optimism, could be a classic work on the topic, to which theology students and their teachers would refer for half a century to come. You are holding the book which she wanted to see in your hand. The professors gave generously of their scholarship, and brought it off. This is indeed a classic, comprehensive textbook on Christology whose value will be evident for many decades to come.

Handbooks are made to be used, not merely contemplated for pleasure. This handbook is in one sense no exception. The luminous and thorough chapters on Christ in the Bible, the scintillatingly brilliant sections on patristic and mediaeval Christology, the solid and refreshing section on the Reformation, the outstanding section on modern and postmodern Christology, the flashes of genius in the section on the modern Christological imaginary, and the powerful section on the 'grammar' of Christology today—all these will help many a student through their essays and exams on specific topics. They can and should be used for that purpose, just as many a young theology professor, fresh out of PhD specialization, will be able to use individual sections to brush up their Christology before they must teach it. I am immensely proud of this book in too many ways to number, and one is certainly that it is fit for purpose and useful to pragmatic inquirers. Just about everything one needs for a paper on the Christology of the Old and New Testaments, the Fathers and the Schoolmen, the early, late, and post-moderns is here for the edification of the student. My only warning on this front is not to try plagiarizing it, because the pieces are too well written to be readily disguised as the work of anyone other than masters in the art of theology. Real scholars love dictionaries, encyclopaedias, and other repositories of knowledge both concise and comprehensive, and this book will easily claim a place in their libraries.

And yet, this book has too much scholarly grace and breadth of imagination to be a merely utilitarian 'how to' manual of Christology. When I invited the authors to contribute their chapters I specified the kind of 'classic' I imagined was the unpretentious biblical and patristic-mediaeval scholarly work which Anglican dons seemed to effortlessly produce in the mid-twentieth century. The contributors to this book have gone one better than my mental project of 'The Wandering Christologists' by Dorothy Sayers. It is in fact a work of lasting scholarship for our own time, a very different time in imaginative, religious, and ecclesiological terms. They have produced a rigorous work, made to be handled, and certainly a book, but somehow much more than a handbook.

I have two pieces of advice for the reader, and the first, as I said, is simply to use and deploy it. The second is to treat it like a library, and to wander from the chapter you came to read to others about things you have no use for by authors you may not know. If you came to read the section on 'Imagining the Son of God in Modernity' then stop a while and reflect on Paul Mankowski's opening chapter, and let his defense of 'truth' as the deepest meaning of the Logos question your own theological aesthetic assumptions. If you came to read the 'systematics' essays on 'The Grammar of Christology', then consider also Daley, Louth, and Russell's classic pieces of Patristic scholarship. If you came for Reformation Christology do not go away until you have read, highlighted, and inwardly digested Wawrykow and Nieuwenhove on Aquinas and Bonaventure. If Reynolds on 'The Islamic Christ' brought you in, consider, in the same section, Hogg's 'Christology: The *Cur Deus Homo*', and interrogate yourself about the connections between Anselm, the Crusades, and Islam. If you came for the biblical studies, then you are in for a feast, but try to save some room for the systematics section, where you will find Gathercole and Webster on the top of their form. This is perhaps not the place to recall in detail a great debate between Murphy, Gathercole, and Webster about whether the incarnate Christ had a creaturely human nature: suffice it to say that one of the trio lost.

The book naturally opens with 'The Bible', but it does not leap straight into the Christology of the New Testament. Before we can think straight about that very ambiguous topic, we need first to consider the modes of God's self-communication to us. Paul Mankowski argues that 'God's incarnate voice to us' in the Bible is that of a reasonable chap making truth claims which transcend their linguistic medium. Olivier-Thomas Venard develops the same theme in his chapter on 'Christology from the Old Testament to the New', arguing that Christ's first, most original incarnation is in the language of the Hebrew Bible. Read the two in conjunction and you may find that what that does to your head unravels your original project of a quick scan followed by an overnight paper-writing session. Representing a bridge between these two exercises in the theological interpretation of the language of Christology and several chapters about the historical Jesus stands Gregory Glazov's philological analysis of Romans 9–11, explaining through an analysis of Paul's words about God's 'casting off' his people, why it is that Christ's suffering cannot be extricated from the suffering of the Jewish people. There follow three set pieces of Anglican-Evangelical New Testament scholarship, condensing and crystallizing many years of historical-biblical reflection on the person of Jesus by Bauckham, Gorman, and Bockmuehl. These chapters sum up the stable product of in-depth Christological-biblical research, initiating the novice into the givens in the field as it now stands, whilst simultaneously showing the old timers how much and how irreversibly the field has changed in the past quarter century. Never say never again, but we may say that it will be a long time before Christology is once again dominated by one single historical-critical model, as it was from the end of the nineteenth to the late twentieth century.

The second section takes us to Patristics. The author of the recent, highly acclaimed *Retrieving Nicaea*, Khaled Anatolios, opens with a lucid explanation of the origins and evolution of the controversy about whether Christ is indeed the one God, or merely one of the many subordinate gods in a polytheistic pantheon. The Nicene 'homoousios' answered that question. There follows one of the many 'classics within a classsic' which make up this book: Brian Daley on the debates between moralizing Antiochene Christologists and Alexandrian sacramentalizing Christologists. These debates culminated in the Chalcedonian formula, which dogmatically defined Christ as two unconfused and undivided natures in one single, divine Person. Andrew Louth's piece is historical but takes us into one of the deep questions of contemporary Christology: what precisely does it mean to say, with Severus of Antioch, that 'one of the Trinity suffered in the flesh'? Norman Russell reminds us of the great range of Patristic atonement theories, from moral exemplarism to deification and a defeat of the devil: we cannot understand the concerns of the first seven Ecumenical Councils without a good grasp of the soteriology laid out here. The anthropology which flowed from the Fathers' soteriology is also irreparable for understanding Nicaea I, Constantinople, Ephesus, Chalcedon I–III, and Nicaea II. In the Fathers' eyes, baptized Christians are, as Russell says, 'deified rational animals'.

Our third section is about Mediaeval Christology. Aidan Nichols has written about every corner of theology; we are lucky to have caught him here, on his best suite and first love, theological aesthetics. Readers will not easily find a more succinct and accessible account of the Iconoclastic controversies and their Christological meaning than Nichols' essay on 'Image Christology in the Age of the Second Council of Nicaea'. In an interesting pair of essays, Gabriel Reynolds shows how little relation the Islamic Christ bears to the canonic Christ, while David Hogg argues persuasively that Anselm's *Cur Deus Homo* was not so much passively influenced by 'mediaeval feudalism' as it was actively aimed at influencing Muslims. Alison Milbank's chapter on 'The Crucified Christ in Western Mediaeval Art' will be repeatedly re-read for its profound meditation on the meaning of the artistic representations of Christ in the Middle Ages. Joseph Wawrykow's piece is no mere exercise in the historical description of Thomas' Christology, but rather takes us right into the question of whether it can make sense for modern systematics today. So, too, does Rik van Nieuwenhove's broader piece, on atonement theology between Bonaventure and Ockham. Nieuwenhove shows how Ockham's non-sacramental and voluntaristic atonement theory opens the path to Reformation theories of forensic justification. Calvinists should read this essay with great care.

Our fourth section on 'Reformation and Christology' traces the path of the Reformation from Luther to Bultmann. We are very pleased here to front two rising young voices: on the one hand, Brian Lugioyo examines Martin Luther's Christology through the lens of his Eucharistic theology; on the other hand, at the opposite end of the spectrum from this liturgical approach, Kevin Hector deftly handles the

Christologies of Kant, Schleiermacher, and Hegel as treatises in the philosophy of religion. Our other Reformation historians have deserved renown: Zachmann on Calvin, Elliott on the Christologies of the seventeenth century, and the silver-granite Ziegler on Christology from Strauss to Käsemann are each persuasive and eloquent; for these authors have not only an historical narrative to plod through but complex Christological assertions to present. Most of what happened of any theological importance between 1518 and 1890 is captured in this section.

Part V leads us into 'Modern and Postmodern Theology'. Here, as befits modernity, the content and perspective become much more varied and decentered. Troy Stefano presents us with Bulgakov and von Balthasar reacting to Schleiermacher while Bruce McCormack shows why modern Kenoticism failed because it was not big enough to comprehend God. K. K. Yeo tackles the huge topic of Chinese Christology, in a chapter which will be required reading for anyone hoping to grasp the problems and opportunities posed by Christianity's greatest growth area in the world today. Diane Stinton's chapter is of a piece with Yeo's, showing how the great questions of future Christologies will relate to power and culture as much as they do to the relation between the two natures of Christ. Michele Schumacher somehow manages to produce a perfect and sympathetic snapshot of the major concerns of feminist Christologists. Part V is about questions and problems: how can Christ be fully human alongside his divine nature and 'Logos-person', how can Christ be fully human without also being Chinese, female, African, as well as a Jewish man from Bethlehem in Judaea? With the calm that descends upon some denizens of a hermitage, Raymond Gawronski points us in the direction of a very difficult answer by reminding us that our science of Christ, how well we know Christ, is measured only by our experience of him.

Thus pastoral and practical questions impinge deeply upon Christology. Although the doctrinal questions cannot be properly understood unless they are theoretically articulated, still, there is a special fruitfulness for modernity in the artistic and imaginative representation of Christ. A handbook on Christology would be a torso without a section on 'Imagining the Son of God in Modernity'. How Beethoven and Dostoevsky have imagined Christ, as very ably described here by Stapert and Williams, tells us at least as much, and perhaps more, about 'modern Christology' as nineteenth-century lives of Jesus and twentieth-century meditations on his consciousness. When the theologians of the future write their histories of the doctrine of Christ, 'musical Christologies' and studies of 'Christ in Cinema' (Barron) will help them as much as textbooks. The Christ of modern art (Cunningham) is the imagined Christ who resides in most modern believers' hearts. If you assign Hector, do not neglect to assign Stapert; it would be pedagogically wise to read Cunningham alongside Ziegler.

Our seventh and final section tackles 'The Grammar of Christology: Christological Norms'. Here again I am especially happy to introduce some figures who are deserving of equal recognition in an Anglo-Saxon context to that which they deservedly have in their own countries. Writing from Poland, Robert Woźniac makes a sturdy case that Christology is the foundation stone of all the theological loci, without which they lose their centered meaning. Gilbert Narcisse, Provincial of the Toulouse Dominicans, lays out with an unerring hand the principles which must necessarily guide Roman Catholic Christology. Readers will appreciate the profound spirituality which undergirds the wit and rigor of these Polish and French priests. They will also be interested to weigh the analogies and differences between Narcisse's claims and what Kenneth Oakes has to say about normative Protestant Christology. Simon Gathercole shows with his customary vigor and dispatch that the Christ of the Canonical Gospels is more primitive and thus more historically plausible than the Gnostic Christ. Thomas Weinandy, in yet another classic piece, reiterates the fundamental meaning of Nicaea and Chalcedon, that in the Incarnation, *God* truly is human, and God truly is *human*, and, most headbangingly of all, God *truly is* human. D'Costa writes of the place of Christ in relation to world religions. And to top it all, John Webster, in fine fettle, pronounces that Christology is not, in fact, the summit of theology: we should place there, he affirms, the doctrine of the immanent Trinity. His essay resounds 'backwards' through much of the book, because the heart of his argument is that, at the end of the day, the economy and even the Incarnation itself, must take second place before the eternal reality of God himself, Father, Son, and Holy Ghost.

PART I

THE BIBLE

CHAPTER 1

···

LANGUAGE, TRUTH, AND *LOGOS*

···

PAUL MANKOWSKI, S.J.

In the Old Testament, God reveals himself through his deeds—especially those wrought in the history of his chosen people—but he is made present to man preeminently as a *voice*. Other sensory phenomena (fire, smoke, thunder) accompany his manifestations, but are kept distinct from his godhead. His voice moreover is a *speaking* voice. God does not roar.

What is spoken by God's speaking voice is language, which is to say that language is the paramount medium of *discursive* communication of God to man. Foregrounding its derivation from the Latin *lingua*, or 'tongue', the term 'language' will henceforth be restricted to that mode of communication originating in acoustical/auditory transmission of thought, that is, to what we know as human speech. Language is not God's exclusive means of interaction with man, but it is the primary modality by which God makes himself understood—and that in such a way that one receptor can reliably transmit his understanding to other men. To claim that God has elected language for this task is not, or not necessarily, a tautology. God's communication with angels need not be constrained by corporeal limitations and preconditions imposed by acoustics (e.g., possession of lungs, articulatory organs, ears), or by memory, or by the capacity to recombine words so as to generate new utterances. What is communicated by language, however, must obviously limit itself to the sphere of linguistic possibility, and the mapping of those limits is the burden of this chapter.

LOGOS AND CREATION

···

Divine communication to man is perfected in the person of Jesus Christ, who is both the mediator and the fullness of revelation—a revelation effected by deeds and words having an inner unity—*gestis verbisque intrinsece inter se connexis* (*Dei Verbum* #2).

Revelation, while including it, is broader than language. This is given striking expression in the prologue to the Gospel of John, wherein the evangelist identifies Christ as the *logos*—the *logos* that is at once God and 'in the presence of' God.

John's employment of the term *logos* was a departure from the Jewish discourse of Messianic expectation and puts into play theological categories only indirectly operative in the Old Testament. In this doctrine, *logos* is not something Christ *has* but something Christ *is*. The semantic range of the Greek term is large (saying, reason, speech, calculation, account, story, language itself all occupy part of the territory), but ancient authors from Plato onward distinguish its general notions of (1) ratiocination, and (2) expression of what has been reasoned or reckoned. Christ, as *logos*, is at once (in some sense) divine reason and (in some sense) the projection, expression, or communication of that reason.

The primordial projection of the *logos* is in the activity of creation: *omnia per ipsum facta sunt, at sine ipso factum est nihil quod factum est.* In the first place, the opening verse of the prologue to John consciously echoes the incipit of Genesis—'in the beginning'—and furthermore the role of the *logos* in the coming-to-be of all things makes oblique reference to the six 'words' that God utters on the six days of creation. Whereas in the second creation narrative the Lord God silently formed man and so forth (Gen. 2:7 ff.), in the first creation account (Gen. 1:1–2:4) God gives voice to his will as indicated in the repeated expression, 'and God said'. Following each occurrence of the phrase is an injunction of the form 'let there be *x*'. The Hebrew verbs here are not commands (imperatives) but forms that are conventionally called jussives but more precisely (in the categories of irrealis modality) volitives: they express the will or desires of the speaker. It is noteworthy that the Hebrew creation story, although conceptually pre-metaphysical, avoids many of the conceptual pitfalls that Greek metaphysics will later identify. Unlike imperatives, which notionally require an addressee to be commanded ('O light, come to be!'), a volitive requires no preexistent auditor or receptor but focuses on the intentions of the speaker who employs it. It should further be stressed that the words of creation in Genesis are not mere examples of the 'performative language' of analytic philosophy (by which, e.g., the words 'I promise' bring about for the speaker the obligation they express) but an unparalleled act of discourse by which God speaks and *eo ipso* that which he speaks comes from non-being into being. Syntactically as well as narratively the first chapter of Genesis underlines God's supreme sovereignty over and radical apartness from all that he created.

To return to the *logos* of John 1:3, it is *through him* that all things come to be—both a divine intention and a projection or expression of that intention. The Second Vatican Council's dogmatic constitution on revelation *Dei Verbum* says, 'God, who through the Word creates all things and maintains them in existence, gives men a lasting witness to Himself in created realities' (*Dei Verbum* #3). Here again the prologue to John is striking in that the Word's self-manifestation to man is not in the first instance acoustic or lexical: 'in him was life, and the life was the *light* of men'. The metaphor is optical rather than linguistic (significantly, the same is true of the cardinal term ἀποκάλυψις—revelation—which means uncovering, unveiling, disclosure). Two inferences suggest themselves: first, the imagery employed by the sacred author implies that the *logos* is not subject to the limitations of human discourse; considered as God's thought, the ceaseless creative activity of *logos* is infinitely larger than that which can be comprehended by language. Second, considered as the communication of God's thought, its receptors are not restricted to those persons with developed language skills. Those who can neither hear nor understand speech—the very young, the very old, the deaf, or cognitively deficient—may still be able to see this light, and so be instructed or succored by the divine Word. The *logos* is universal as to that which it expresses, *omnia facta*, and universal as to whom it is addressed. Kittel perceptively remarks, 'Jesus is not just the One who brings the Word but the One who incorporates it in His person, in the historical process of His speech and action, of His life and being' (Kittel 1964: vol. 4, 126). That said, it should be remembered that it is the same *logos* bearing witness in what *Dei Verbum* calls 'created realities' (*res creatae*) as well as 'the works done by God in the history of salvation' (*Dei Verbum* ## 2, 3).

LOGOS AND TRUTH

Christ, then, is the fullness of revelation and is also the mediator of revelation to man, including that particular channel of revelation which is language. Language makes use of meaning-conveying phrases including commands, exclamations, questions, and assertions, all of which operate in Sacred Scripture but among which the last has an important peculiarity. Assertions (or statements or propositions) are sentences that can be believed or doubted, judged true or false. The truths that God communicates to man about himself will have their definitive form in assertions. Truth is not the only value of assertions, even within the sphere of revelation. In particular instances beauty, intelligibility, translatability, vividness, and memorability may also be pertinent—as also for commands, exclamations, and questions. But the truth or falsehood of an assertion is never irrelevant to its function. The consequences for revelation are immense. In the first place, the understanding grasped by the person who assents to an assertion has the potential to be transmitted to another person. The philosophical jargon by which propositions are termed 'sharable objects'—sc. of 'propositional attitudes' such as belief and doubt—points to this characteristic. Whereas a command ('sit down!') or a question ('who's in charge?') might be repeated by an auditor, the content of neither utterance can be shared in the sense of appropriated assent. Of course a true assertion ('Jesus is Lord') might likewise be repeated perfunctorily by its receptor as a meaningless act of parroting, but the most natural speech act by which a person should give voice to the transmitted assertion would indicate that he himself both understood it and assented to it. Thus the primarily good of an assertion (its truth) is diffusive of itself, and that in a way in which the transmitter cooperates with the *logos* as a co-*creator*: something new—expressed by, but greater than, a linguistic act—has been brought into the world, namely, the profession of a true conviction by a person who did not profess it earlier. Recast in a performative mode such that the propositional attitude is placed in a first-person declaration, the phrase 'I believe in Christ' if uttered by the apostle Philip and, because of him, by the Ethiopian eunuch (cf. Acts 8:27–38) would not be two tokens of a single sentence but assertions of distinct true realities.

It may be objected that the truth of revelation is wrongly narrowed if we limit it to well-formed assertions about God. After all, the biblical divine commands ('You shall have no gods before me' and 'You shall not oppress the sojourner in your midst') teach us truths about God by revealing the goodness of the being who issued them, and, by their directive character, they change us so as to become more receptive of godly truths generally. Even the psalmist, moreover, says 'the *ordinances* [i.e., injunctions] of the Lord are truth' (Ps. 19:9; cf. also Ps. 119:151). Similarly, many of the questions directed at men by the Lord may be said to be instructive, and for that very reason conveyors of truth ('Why do you spend your money for that which is not bread?' and 'Why do you see the mote that is in your brother's eye?'). In the case of these speech forms the revelation of truth operates anagogically, that is to say, those who allow themselves to be provoked by God's questions or commands may thus discover and assent to assertions about God from whom they issue. While only utterances in the form of assertions can be judged true (or false) in the strict sense, those non-propositional speech forms that, in their narrative context, play a heuristic role in leading (*anagōgē*) the reader or addressee to acknowledge such assertions may themselves be termed true in this secondary anagogical sense.

The function that assertions have as *sharable* truth-bearers give them an indispensable role as criteria of orthodoxy—that is, assertions are not only a means of God's instruction of his people but his people's means of identifying itself, namely, by shared beliefs. While the fullness of revelation is a person, and not a collection of assertions about that person, the sharable objects of belief and doubt must be commonly intelligible, whence the deposit of faith understood as *fides quae* (cf. 1 Tim. 6:20) must be asseverative, and to this extent linguistic. Speaking of the Church's Magisterium, *Dei Verbum* says, 'it draws from this one deposit of faith everything which it presents for belief as divinely revealed' (*ea omnia … quae tamquam divinitus revelata credenda proponit*) (*Dei Verbum* #10). The gerundive force of *credenda* here is not simply predictive/desiderative but obligative, and *ea omnia* can only refer to teachings in the form of assertions. The self-identification of the Church—including but not limited to determination of orthodoxy and heterodoxy—must be predicated on the *assent* of her members to these publicly proposed linguistically transmitted *credenda*.

LANGUAGE AND
THE EXTRA-LINGUISTIC TRUTH

Again it may be objected that limiting orthodoxy to discursive formulations misleadingly narrows the criteriology of faith. The Church both East and West has a long history of graphic representation of sacred objects, including the persons of the Trinity, within which some traditions have conventionalized the schemata of representation to such a degree that individual portrayals (of, e.g., Jesus Christ) are judged true or false, valid or invalid by experts in the representational guild as well as by the lay faithful. Further, such images have been used in certain circumstances as catechetical tools as well as aids to devotion. Can it be claimed then that a crucifixion by Cranach or a Pantocrator by the Rublev school or a window of Chartres cathedral might also be a 'truth-bearer', and as such an object of belief or doubt, and thus a vehicle of orthopathy (if we may so designate the 'right response' to a non-linguistic statement) or its contrary?

In his essay *Art and Illusion*, E. H. Gombrich recounts the story of 'a small girl who became worried and pensive when many Christmas cards began to arrive at her home. How could one tell which was the 'correct' rendering of the Holy Night?' (Gombrich 1960: 109). Gombrich himself insists that a picture 'can no more be true or false than a statement can be blue or green' (Gombrich 1960: 59). Yet in the same essay he introduces the instructive notion of 'captioning': in simplest terms, judgment about what a particular image is an image *of* depends on a claim external to the image itself—'this is an image of a man'; 'this is an image of Jesus Christ'; 'this is an image of Jesus Christ in the manger' (Gombrich 1960: 59). Captioning, in this sense, is more than a simple label but refers to the necessary content of understandings at least implicitly shared by the image-maker and image-viewer such that identifications conveyed are the identifications received. Very often, this captioning takes the form of a lengthy education by which, for example, one becomes able to 'read' the attributes associated with sacred persons in the iconic tradition or more generally to recognize biblical persons or events in reference to the narrative qualities of the image. Captioning, then, is the entire historical-didactic context in terms of which an image may have a shared meaning.

Granted that a shared meaning or reading of an image is possible, can it ever be *obligatory*? It is striking that the Church proposes no image—not even the Cross—as an object of faith that must be accepted in a particular way; the Christian is not, for example, required to say of any particular representation, *this* is a *true* image of Christ. Transmitters of 'false' images are not faulted the way propounders of false doctrines are, nor are those who refuse to recognize a 'true' image faulted as are those who refuse to acknowledge a true doctrine. Even where the intention of the image-maker is that orthodox conviction may be abandoned or subjected to ridicule by means of his image, it is not in the image itself but in the captioning—that is, the asseverative linguistic content external to the image but performatively connected to it—that the kinds of identifications can be made on which judgments of orthodoxy and heterodoxy are based. Consider the case of a mediaeval catechist, explaining the sacred imagery in the stained glass window of a church to unlettered catechumens; any misidentifications will be ultimately attributable to captioning (the narrative) rather than to the image in the window. More suggestively, consider the case of the Alexamenos graffito, found in the Domus Gelotiana on the Palatine in Rome. This displays a crucified figure with the head of a donkey, with a human figure to the side of the cross, accompanied by a Greek inscription reading 'Alexamenos worships [his] God'. The intentions of the original captioner (and, if different, of the image-maker as well) were almost certainly derisive of the worshiper and his cult. Yet this graffito (probably dating to the early third century) is one of the earliest images of the crucifixion of Christ, mockery notwithstanding, and for that reason has become cherished by Christians. In a manner of speaking, the graffito has been given a second, broader frame, along with a secondary caption: while we still see an act of risible donkey-worship we see within a larger field an act of mild aggression against an ancient believing Christian, such that the originally intended scorn both remains and is paradoxically dissolved in the poignancy of the depicted Crucifixion. Here too it is finally the linguistically expressed assertions indexically connected to the image that serve as objects of belief or doubt. Even in circumstances where a particular tradition of sacred art has developed a finely articulated and rigorously enforced iconology such that component graphic symbols can be termed an ideographic 'language' readily and unambiguously decoded by trained receptors, this pictorial language will in every case be parasitic on one or more natural languages by means of which the meanings are assigned and shared. In sum, the only assertions a graphic language can make are assertions of a natural language.

Yet how are we to understand the activity of the *logos* as directed at human beings who lack language entirely? The light belonging to the *logos*—in the terms of John 1:4 and 1:9—is radiated to men without restriction or qualification. In addition to the unborn and infants there exist persons blind and deaf from birth, who live into their adult years with no evidence of post-partum intellectual development, who give no indications of using or understanding language. Their smiles and frowns may be interpreted by others as in some sense communicative as well as responsive, but in such cases there is no way to identify an intended message distinct from the observer's purely subjective projections, and thus we have no natural empirical access to their mental life. (St. Elizabeth's reading of the stirring of the unborn John may be taken as supernaturally assisted.) Yet we are obliged on doctrinal grounds to acknowledge that persons who lack language can be infused with the habit or virtue of faith. The Council of Trent anathematizes those who would assert that baptized infants, since they lack the act of belief, are not to be numbered among the faithful—*parvulos eo, quod actum credendi non habent, suscepto baptismo inter fideles computandos non esse* (Denzinger 2012: 1626). We can aggregate all language-lacking human beings under the same condemnation, since they share with infants the pertinent characteristic, and therefrom draw a positive conclusion: however we may come to understand the connection between, say, brain function and human intellection, or between human intellection and the virtue of faith, the *logos* through which each human person was created can also communicate to that person what is necessary for salvation, even if the person cannot himself transmit that awareness to us. Augustine would have it that it is his mind in virtue of which every man—of whatever intellectual endowment—is made in the image of God and in virtue of which he is actually *capax Dei* and potentially *particeps Dei* (*De trinitate* 14.8.11); this suggests that mind considered in itself has a radical simplicity quite distinct from the complexities of human cognition, and that the true light that enlightens all men has, antecedently to bringing its creature into divine communion (as *particeps*), already in its creative operation made it receptive (as *capax*) (see also Aquinas, *Quaestiones disputatae de veritate* q.14, a.XI, ad1). The human embryo and the human idiot are in no sense disadvantaged as *imagines Dei*.

In Christological terms, God's adoption of human language is part of his divine condescension. This linguistic condescension is already evident in the Old Testament—for example, in the formula of prophetic declamation, 'the word of the Lord came to me, saying …' (giving the divine quotation in the prophet's own dialect of Hebrew)—and it is fully realized in the Incarnation, when the Word spoke to man by taking on the particularities of Galilaean Aramaic. The Word was made flesh, and what we here understand by the 'flesh' must include the human capacity for speech (considered as a *proprium* of *Homo sapiens*) as well as one or more specific human languages, with their own concrete and historically determined limitations of syntax, morphology, lexicon, and so forth.

LOGOS AND LANGUAGES

God communicates to man discursively not only in language but in *languages*. No single natural language or language family enjoys a divinely privileged position. The Bible makes this plain in Genesis 11, the account of the Tower of Babel. We are told (Gen. 11:1) that the earth once knew the same words and a single pronunciation. Thwarting man's prideful ambition to lift himself by his own artifice from his rightful abode into the heavens, God mixed up this language (Gen. 11:9) and dispersed man over all the earth. What is important to grasp is that no exception is made for the language of narration, Hebrew. It too must be understood, within the terms of the biblical text, as one of the secondary corrupted languages derived from the calamity of dispersal and confusion. We are thus forbidden, by the Bible itself, to imagine that God spoke Hebrew in the Garden of Eden or indeed before the Flood, which obliges us to acknowledge that the divine utterances, the human (and serpentine) speeches, as well as the narrative passages of the first eleven chapters of the Bible are a *translation*—a translation, moreover, of a lost and irrecoverable 'original'.

One of the philosophical consequences of this truth is the corollary recognition that the meaning of a sentence can be extracted from its expression in one language so as to be expressed equivalently in another. Those who accept the Bible as authoritative must assent to the proposition that cognitively reliable translation is *possible*, because the Bible claims in and by its own realization that translation is *actual*. The salvific meanings of Scripture—or indeed of any other assertion—are not confined to the language in which they were first uttered but are notionally universal.

That the Bible gives us God's discourse in a language other than God's leads to the distinct theological recognition that translation is not only possible but *permissible*. There is a pointed contrast here with, for example, the traditional Muslim treatment of the Qur'an, which is revered as the actual spoken words of God preserved with incomparably perfect fidelity (in Muslim terminology, *'i'jāz al-qur'ān*). Rendering these vocables into any other language is viewed as a violation of the divine nature of the text (whence non-Arabic versions are piously termed interpretations rather than translations), nor can an edition lacking the original Arabic words be properly called a Qur'an. No parallel limitation operates in Judaism or Christianity. Not only is the so-called Hebrew Bible actually polyglot (including extended passages in Aramaic and brief expressions in other languages) but the Gospels, being written in Greek, have effectively denied us the Lord's *ipsissima verba* and definitively abolished any temptation to limit what we call the word of God to particular privileged languages. While the evangelists preserve a very few Aramaic words of Jesus that must be taken as verbatim transcriptions of his speech, it is noteworthy that most are wholly without doctrinal significance and the longest is itself an Aramaic *translation* of Scripture: 'Eli, Eli, lama sabachthani?' (Ps. 22:1). The Bible—Old Testament and New—calls for its own Pentecostalization (omnilingual rendering, universal dispersion) independently of extra-biblical theological commitments.

The possibility and permissibility of biblical translation have the effect of disinclining Christians from employing the sacred text in magic. In cults where particular vocables are received as unmediated and direct divine utterance, they may become regarded as having a divine power in themselves, whereas their humanly-determined meaning becomes of secondary importance—if not a sacrilegious and hubristic assault on the mystery of the godhead. The use of such words (prised out of narrative context) in incantations and curses, or inscribed on materials so as to be hidden rather than read (as in certain kinds of amulets), are examples of magical treatment. While the intra-biblical stress on translation does not of itself preclude extra-narrative employment (numerological exegesis, for example, has a long if sterile history), its focus on meaning, and especially *sharable* sentence meaning, continually steers attention away from magical and esoteric byways onto the conventional linguistic readings of the text.

LINGUISTIC LIMITATIONS OF TRANSLATION

It is a truism that no two languages stand in relation to each other such that there can be a one-to-one mapping of word to word, syntagma to syntagma; for this reason the translator must adapt the resources of the receptor language so as best to approximate the meanings given in the donor language. In areas where the donor language is richer than the receptor—that is, more finely gradated, supplied with distinctions not recognized in the receptor—the translation ignores contrasts or variations operative in the original. In areas where the receptor is richer than the donor, the translation may put into play distinctions that are not operative in the donor language and, in some circumstances, cannot do other than resolve ambiguities that are irreducibly equivocal in the original text. That is to say, the translator may be confronted by a fork in the road presented by the refinements of receptor language such that he must make a choice between interpretative options of which the original text was unaware or toward which it was indifferent. The former dilemma might be called the predicament of underdetermination and the latter the predicament of overdetermination. The terms cannot usefully be applied to one language in general in contrast with another language in general. Regardless of the languages selected as donor and receptor each will show areas of grammar and lexicon in which it is cruder than the other and in which it is more refined.

Taking up the predicament of underdetermination, this may be readily illustrated in terms of verbal syntax. In the expression of a positive command, biblical Greek distinguished perfective aspect (instantaneous and terminative) and imperfective aspect (iterative-continuous). Thus the fourth petition of the Lord's Prayer ('give us our bread') is expressed by aorist imperative at Matthew 6:1 (δὸς ἡμῖν) and by the present imperative at Luke 11:3 (δίδου ἡμῖν). The former beseeches a single punctive action, the latter a repeated activity. English imperatives do not reflect this aspectual contrast, whence our translators' 'give' underdetermines the rendering of both Matthew and Luke. (Paradoxically, inasmuch as the Aramaic of Jesus' time, like English, lacked this aspectual contrast in positive imperatives, the variant renderings of Matthew and Luke may themselves be cases of *over*determination from Aramaic to Greek, each being forced to choose between perfective and imperfective alternatives irrelevant to their original.)

Likewise every translation must confront the predicament of overdetermination. To take an example of, perhaps, more didactic than practical interest: the languages of Polynesia have a system of personal pronouns in which the first-person plural distinguishes an inclusive form (we = I and others and you) and an exclusive form (we = I and others but not you). In this case English and Greek and the other Indo-European languages concur with Aramaic and Hebrew and the other Semitic languages in having a common first-person plural form (we/us) for which the inclusive or exclusive extension can only be determined by context. Were we rendering Mark 4:38 ('Teacher, do you not care that we are perishing?') into Maori, however, would we use first-plural inclusive *tatou* ('... that you, Lord, and we are perishing'), implying that the disciples believed Jesus also near death, or first-person exclusive *matou* ('... that we, but not you, are perishing'), implying the contrary? The same ambiguity touches Peter's exclamation on the mount of the Transfiguration (e.g., Mark 9:5): 'Master, it is good for us to be here'. The Maori translator must decide whether Peter's *us* includes or excludes Jesus. It is important to see that overdetermination cuts off possible interpretations that are left open to the reader in the original.

In ordinary circumstances the epistemic limitations of under- and overdetermination are not of great consequence in translation, either resolved by the larger narrative context or compensated by adjustments in diction. When the work to be translated is a sacred (or otherwise doctrinally authoritative) text, these common limitations have important theological consequences. The general principle is that, where an assertion is doctrinally valid, no entailment consequent on a *translation* of that assertion is valid if this entailment hinges on an under- or overdetermination of the original. Underdetermination erases claims (explicit or implicit) made in the original, while overdetermination creates 'ghost claims' that are not.

The perils of overdetermination are illustrated in a recently-proposed Tamil translation of the Bible. A member of the Dravidian language family, Tamil has honorific

and non-honorific word forms used of persons. The biblical languages lack comparable honorifics, whence as a receptor language Tamil will overdetermine the original
honor-marking. Departing from the actual usage of spoken Tamil—wherein the honorific distribution is based on social markers such as family status and gender—the
translation committee decided to use the honorific for all biblical personages with the
exceptions of Satan and Judas. Yet this protocol introduces into the scriptural message
a foreign didacticism that equates honor with moral virtue, as well as a highly arbitrary moral cipher by which the reader is invited, for example, to infer that Manasseh
or Jezebel or Simon Magus share some excellence with Jesus that they do not with
Judas—a highly dubious 'ghost claim' that puts the integrity of the entire translation
at risk.

Where the donor language makes distinctions the receptor language does not,
translations will produce ambiguities alien to the original. Some neo-Gnostic theologians have exploited these ambiguities in order to mythologize aspects of scriptural
revelation in ways congenial to their extra-biblical commitments. For example, the
biblical Hebrew verb is morphologically inflected for gender in the second and third
person, that is, the verb is spelled differently when its subject is masculine and when it
is feminine. This is not the case in English (or other Indo-European languages), which
therefore underdetermines verbal gender in rendering Hebrew. Those who would
advance the reading She Who Is as a translation of the tetragrammaton (the divine
name YHWH) can only do so in ignorance of, or by affecting not to know, the fact
that this reading is excluded by the specifically masculine inflection of the original
(cf. the Hebrew of Exod. 3:14f.). The danger lies not so much in the receptor's erasure
of the donor's distinctions—adequately compensated by other grammatical and lexical devices—but in the heterodox inference speciously derived from a translational
equivocation that the original does not permit.

Logos, Truth, and Other Values

Over and above the truth of revelation, what can be said of its beauty? If He who is
revealed is acknowledged to be beautiful (as well as true and good) Himself, is it not permissible to look for beauty in the media of revelation, in particular in its language? If and
where beauty is found in Sacred Scripture, should a translation be expected to transmit
this beauty with the same fidelity that it transmits its truth?

Here again it is notable that the Church does not oblige us to confess our conviction
that any particular part or aspect of Scripture is beautiful in the way that she obliges
us to confess that it is true. No one is condemned as a 'heteropath' or otherwise cen-
sured for failing to take pleasure in passages in whose melody or pathos the greatest
saints exulted. Nor is the Bible self-conscious of its beauties the way it is self-conscious
of its truth. While it is the case that a very large portion of the Old Testament consists
of poetry, the 'engine' of Hebrew verse is not tied to its musicality but is almost wholly

conceptual, the device called augmentative parallelism: 'Three things are too wonderful for me, four I do not understand' (Prov. 30:18). Providentially, perhaps, this means that what is specifically poetic in Hebrew poetry can be conveyed, without remainder, into any other language of translation—and, what is more, by a translator wholly lacking in extraordinary artistic gifts. This raises the question of whether those translators who infuse biblical texts with sensual beauties are faithful or unfaithful in so doing. In his famous Cambridge lecture *The Name and Nature of Poetry*, A. E. Housman speaks of his being transported by Coverdale's Psalter:

> As for the seventh verse of the forty-ninth Psalm in the Book of Common Prayer, 'But no man may deliver his brother, nor make agreement unto God for him', that is to me poetry so moving that I can hardly keep my voice steady in reading it. And that this is the effect of language I can ascertain by experiment: the same thought in the bible version, 'None of them can by any means redeem his brother, nor give to God a ransom for him', I can read without emotion.
>
> (Housman 1933: 11)

Granted that Housman's reaction was the effect of language, it remains to decide whether the beauty of this language is something that exists in the original or something with which Coverdale gratuitously endowed his translation. Few if any commentators have noted conspicuous elegance in the Hebrew passage, but the more pertinent question is rather: where the original is drab, is beauty in the translation a betrayal? Does it make the hearer of God's word a dilettante where he would have a disciple, or should it be seen rather as faithful to the *pragmatics* of biblical poetry—namely, by making the text more memorable, and thus a more fecund object of study and contemplation and transmission to further generations? In either case it would seem that original beauty, considered as beauty, is peripheral to the Bible's own concerns.

Paradoxically, the same cannot be said of the ugliness in the Bible, which is self-aware in a way the beauties are not. Ugliness here refers not to depiction of abhorrent acts, but to provocatively uncouth and repellent language, including Hebrew vulgarisms—even those issuing from the mouth of God—so coarse as to be judged unpronounceable by the Masoretes, who inserted a euphemistic substitute (*qere*) in the margin of the Bible manuscripts to be voiced out loud in place of the obscenity recorded on the sacred page. In the case of this ugliness the shock effect was undoubtedly intended by the sacred author, and the translator's hesitancy concerns not whether the semantic value of the ugly word is transmittable—it is—but whether and to what extent the unseemliness may, in concrete circumstances, risk the smirching of the divine author. Here again the condescension of the *logos* into human language is attended by all-too-human entailments from which a monkish piety may wish to avert its eyes. It is arguable that the harvesters and shepherds who first heard the hard words were less dismayed by their earthiness than were their later translators, and that this delicacy (still almost universally operative today in biblical translation) reinforces a kind of linguistic docetism that distances the reader from the incarnate voice of God.

LOGOS AND CO-CREATION

The notion linking Christology to human language is that of Christ as *logos*, in particular, *logos* as *expressive* of its own activity. This expression is realized primordially in the act of creation, which includes divine self-communication to that which is created, of which language is one medium and the message recorded in Sacred Scripture a uniquely privileged transmission, polyglot in form and ordered to continual omnilingual re-expression and dispersion. *Dei Verbum* (#11) emphasizes that God's revelation is both fully realized in the Word, Jesus Christ, and that the part of revelation contained in Scripture is written *Spiritu Sancto inspirante*, whence the books of the Bible have God as their author. At the same time the men chosen by God used their own capacities and powers (*facultatibus ac viribus suis utentes*) in writing the sacred books so that in what they conveyed they too are true authors (*ut veri auctores scripto traderent*). Considered as a whole, Scripture is at once an annunciation and an instantiation of the co-creative work by which man participates in the life-giving activity of the *logos*.

SUGGESTED READING

Dei Verbum (1965).

BIBLIOGRAPHY

Dei Verbum: Constitutio dogmatica de divina revelatione, ex actis SS oecumenici concilii Vaticani II (1965) (Rome: Typis Polyglottis Vaticanis).

Denzinger, H. (2012), *Enchiridion Symbolorum: A Compendium of Creeds, Definitions, and Declarations on Matters of Faith and Morals*, ed. R. Fastiggi and A. Englund Nash (San Francisco: Ignatius Press).

Gombrich, E. H. (1960), *Art and Illusion: A Study in the Psychology of Pictorial Representation* (Oxford: Phaidon Press).

Housman, A. E. (1933), *The Name and Nature of Poetry* (Cambridge: Cambridge University Press).

Kittel, G. (1964), *Theological Dictionary of the New Testament*, trans. G. Bromiley (Grand Rapids, Mich.: Eerdmans).

CHAPTER 2

···

CHRISTOLOGY FROM THE OLD TESTAMENT TO THE NEW

···

OLIVIER-THOMAS VENARD, O.P.
TRANSLATED BY FRANCESCA ARAN MURPHY

INTRODUCTION

···

WHAT makes modern theology shy away from a Christology of the Old Testament? 'Then … he expounded to them in all the scriptures the things concerning himself' (Luke 24:27). Luke does not describe the contents of Jesus' exposition to his two followers on the road to Emmaus: that job has been carried out within Christian tradition. From the entwined double entendres of Gothic stained glass which impose types upon antitypes—the Manna and the Last Supper, the brass serpent and the crucifix, Jonah regurgitated and Christ resurrected— down to the post-Vatican II weekly lectionaries which displayed the OT and NT as a diptych, Christians have been taught that Christ acts throughout the Scriptures, in both the Old and New Testament as one.

Throughout the round of feast days Christians pick out the typological and allegorical correspondences between Christ and the OT heroes; they grasp that although he goes about it in unexpected ways, still, Christ fulfills the promises which the OT makes. When in the week before Christmas they sing the O Antiphons they can see how Christ is portrayed as the star who pulls together the motley crew of prophetic actors. In the Good Friday reproaches they meet the voice of Christ who reproves the Israelites for their ingratitude for all he did for them during the Exodus; in the course of the seven readings which unfold from creation on, participants in the Easter Vigil meditate upon his ever more intimate embrace of humanity. The Christological unity of the first and second Testament is so essential to Christian faith that the Marcionite denial of it is the very first heresy. One can see why, even in the documents which lend their approbation to modern historical-critical exegesis, the Magisterium never ceases to encourage us to read the whole of Scripture Christologically. Nonetheless, apart from a few, rare geniuses (de Lubac, Beauchamp, and more recently, Lefebvre, Pentiuc), most Catholic biblical scholarship completely ignores this way of reading Scripture.

The idea of an OT Christology draws fire from two sides. On the one hand, the Church wants us to respect Judaism for itself, and on the other we are advised to study Scripture scientifically.

Is an OT Christ anti-Jewish? A controversy which has been around almost as long as Christianity sets it at odds with Judaism in the interpretation of the biblical books which they share. From the time of Justin de Naplouse's *Dialogue with Trypho* the controversy has focused on the prophecies and the promises, especially those of a 'messiah', or 'anointed one'. Messianism is a core theme of the OT, because what kings, prophets, and priests have in common is that all of them were anointed. The Christian apologetic is simple: with many tiny brush strokes, the divine promises and prophecies created a composite portrait of the Messiah; but when he came to his own, they blindly rejected him, and he was acclaimed not by them but by the pagans.

For centuries Jews have regarded the idea of an OT Christology as underwritten by the desire to make their Scriptures say something other than they really do, thereby taking their Scriptures away from them. Jews today can easily refute the Christian reconfiguration of the biblical idea of Messianic hope through the lens of a more rational and historical exegesis, and the NT itself. Far from reconstructing the notion of what a Messiah should be, the historical Jesus barely registers on the Messianic scale. Indeed, perhaps the most sympathetic view of Jesus adopted by some Jews today is of Jesus as a failed Messiah. Furthermore, the identity of the Messiah, his precise function, and even how many of them there were supposed to be are subjects of debate. That makes the notion of an OT 'Christology' at best an (over)interpretation of the Hebrew Bible by people driven into making Jesus the expected Messiah. In the context of Jewish-Christian dialogue, then, the idea of an OT Christology sounds like an 'unresolved problem' (Commission for Religious Relations with the Jews 1985: 2, 3). If one wants to excise supersessionism, it is difficult not to see OT Christology as endangering that intention.

Is a Christology of the OT anti-modern? The more a Christology conflicts with contemporary ideas about time, God, and language, the more unbelievable it appears to modern people. Their historical consciousness is offended by the chronological effects of the pre-incarnational activity of Christ. As defined by modernity, the past is *other* than the present. Christ's presence in the OT, however, is revealed as a temporal movement composed of moments which are *analogous* to each other, underneath the sign of the *eschaton* and a divine eternity which transcends them. Typology rests upon structural and semantic analogies between facts and persons, and these analogies presuppose, in contrast to modern agnosticism (Cahill 1982: 275), a Creator God who acts and speaks throughout the historical process. Finally, where the ancients thought that truth resides in the thick meaning of texts, moderns want to reduce language to an ideally transparent token of the noetic reality-broker which the concept represents. Moderns aim for scientific precision, which in this case means philological precision, not the poetic or mystical imagination. They seek the one single meaning of texts, their most primitive meaning, not the play of multiple meanings. Contemporary biblical exegesis which accepted the thought that there could be a Christology of the OT would orient it toward a history of the variations of the Messianic idea in ancient history, right down to its ultimate transformation which Jesus set in motion.

The idea that all we are doing is 're-reading' the texts is seductive to those who want an OT Christology which avoids polemical issues. We then say that one and the same text can contain many different truths, all of which constitute equally valid perspectives. So the first Jews who believed in Jesus 're-read' the corpus of Scripture 'in the light' of the resurrection and their own belief that he was the Messiah, and, in fact, their faith in his divinity. Others, however, continued to read the Scriptures differently, and actually denied their Christological or Messianic interpretation as they had different agendas, such as the pressing and important issue of the preservation of the Jewish people.

The NT certainly does stress that interpretation plays an important role in the acknowledgment of Christ's active presence before the Incarnation. There is something unprecedented at the heart of the Gospel (1 Cor. 2:9–10a) and it takes a special light to perceive Christ's work. Paul's famous metaphor about the veil over Moses' face and the Christian unveiling (2 Cor. 3:12–18) aptly expresses how sweeping it is and how much the Christian understanding of the Scriptures is tied to a mediation which changes how one sees everything. John insists on the resurrection and the gift of the Spirit for grasping that the Scripture speaks of Christ, taking them to be catalysts for memory and understanding. 'Until the Spirit is given, the meaning cannot appear. And the gift of the Spirit presupposes that Christ has achieved his mission. Thus the veil is destroyed with one blow' (de Lubac 1959: 403–4).

The New Testament realizes that reading the OT Christologically requires a hermeneutic. This must begin with the reader acting on the text (Luke 24:27: *diermeneuein*). The text has to act on the reader as well. The Scriptures 'speak of a living and active God', exercising a performative role in the psyche of the believer (Heb. 4:12–13). The prophets supply light to the believer's heart (2 Peter 1:19). Finally, the reader has to act on himself, for we are asked to hear the Scriptures with an interior disposition of faith if we want to recognize the true Joshua prophetically envisaged by the Scriptures (Heb. 4:1–5).

In reality, the Christian tradition has developed a particular hermeneutic for Scripture. Since the origins of typological and allegorical readings with St. Paul, the Christological reading of Scripture has developed down to the well-known system of the 'four senses' of Scripture—the historical, typological, moral, and eschatological—unified by the overarching figure of Christ. This system embraces the dialectic of the believer and the Scriptures: it corresponds to an intellectual discipline and to a spiritual journey on the part of readers which Gregory the Great encapsulated in the fine phrase, '*divina eloquia cum legente crescunt*' (*Homilia in Ezechielem*, 1, 7, 8: *PL* 843D).

It is incontestable, then, that the Christology of the Old Testament has a hermeneutical dimension. It follows from a 'retrospective perception' such that 'one should not say that the Jew does not see that which the texts proclaim' (Commission Biblique

Pontificale 2001: 54). But it also has an objective reality within the text: 'in the light of Christ and of the Holy Spirit, the Christian uncovers *in the texts themselves* a surplus of meaning which is already concealed within it' (Commission Biblique Pontificale 2001: 54). Thus one should not reduce the Christology of the Old Testament to an a posteriori hermeneutic. This is the case not least because the NT claims that the texts of the OT come to fruition in the Christology of the Gospel.

THE CHRISTOLOGY OF THE NEW TESTAMENT IS AN OLD TESTAMENT CHRISTOLOGY

Each of the NT authors developed 'his' Christology in his own unique way. Yet all of them have something in common: they say who Christ is in the language of the Scriptures. The phrase 'according to the Scriptures' is present in the most ancient creed (1 Cor. 15), showing that it is impossible to separate the word of Jesus, the word of the evangelists, and the word of God as given in Scripture.

The NT offers a robust picture of Christ acting in sacred history before the Incarnation. When they allude to Christ's presence in the Scriptures before the Incarnation, the New Testament authors do not just say, 'this is our interpretation of it', they say, 'the rock *was* Christ'. Their texts

> always give the impression that the concrete and historical person of Jesus whom they had met on earth did not wait until that moment to exist in reality, even on a different plane from the earthly one ... He was present in the Old Testament acting in the formation of the chosen people and laying the ground work for his coming among us. And it is not simply the second person of the Trinity in his eternal and transcendent existence who gets involved in our history: it is Jesus Christ himself who is already at work.
>
> (Benoit 1982: 29)

The equation is simple. John 1:18 states that 'no one has ever seen God' but Jesus Christ has made him known. Thus the OT theophanies are the closest possible encounters with Jesus Christ as the visible face of God. The most outstanding NT statements about Christ in the OT are as follows.

There is a claim that Jesus Christ exists before his Incarnation. The New Testament uses several metaphors relating to change of place to express who Jesus is: sending (Gal. 4:4; John 4:34; 5:24; 6:29; 7:29, etc.), coming out or coming forth (Mark 1:38; John 16:28), descent (Rom. 10:6; Eph. 4:9 ff.; John 3:13; 6:33, 38), 'bringing' (Heb. 1:6), manifesting or appearing (1 Tim. 3:16; 2 Tim. 1:10; Titus: 2:11; 3:4; 1 Pet. 1:20), or simply 'coming' (1 Tim. 1:15; Heb. 10:7; John 1:9; 12:46, etc.). Even such *logia* or sayings as 'I have come' in the Synoptics indicate a prophetic awareness of being sent on a mission, and have again today been recognized as allusions to Christ's pre-existence (Gathercole 2006). Paul also mentions changes of state: from rich to poor (2 Cor. 8:9), from the free-born son to being born of a woman under the law (Gal. 4:4), from the sinless to the sin-bearer (2 Cor. 5:21; Rom. 8.3), and from glory to crucifixion (1 Cor. 2:8) (Benoit 1982: 25).

The New Testament also claims that Christ is present at the creation of the world and in primeval history. Over the course of the development of the apostolic preaching, he is increasingly aligned to diverse originary (*reshit*) figures without limiting him to any of them. He is *speech*. In the Synoptic tradition, Jesus appears able to reveal secrets that have been hidden since the foundation of the world (Matthew 13) and as a language which is more lasting than the creation itself (Matt. 24:34; cf. Baruch 4:1). The Word in John's prologue is much more the Hebrew *devar* than the Alexandrian *logos*. He is the tangible speech of the Creator God, operating in the world before the Incarnation (Isa. 55:10–11; Baruch 3:29, echoing Deut. 30:12 ff. which already alludes to a word coming down from heaven). The same Jewish conception of a word which creates, and thus contains, the world returns in John's epilogue, which impresses that the word of Jesus comprehends the world rather than being comprehended by it (John 21:25).

He is *Torah*. Romans 10:16 applies Deut. 20:12 ff. to the Gospel, by way of Sirach 23:26; John projects onto Jesus features which Judaism would later on ascribe to the Torah. He contains the treasures of *wisdom* (Col. 2:3). He is himself the wisdom of God (1 Cor. 1:24–31; 2:6 ff.). The prologue to John's Gospel resonates with Genesis 1, Proverbs 8:22–36, and Wisdom 7:22. Christ also appears as the *archetype* in reflections on the double creation (interior and exterior) evoked by the double-narrative of Genesis 1 and Genesis 2 in Alexandrian Judaism, such as those of Philo. Colossians 1:15 ff. take a Stoic formula about God's cosmic supremacy and builds it into a statement about Christ's soteriological supremacy, as the *protokos*, begotten in view of the creation, as the prototype of all which will be created through him, especially humanity. In 1 Cor. 15:45, and in Romans 5:12 ff., Christ is the new Adam, the primordial man descending from his heavenly pre-existence.

The NT affirms that Jesus Christ is present in the history of the Patriarchs. Christ was at work in Abraham. Abraham saw his 'day' (John 8:56; cf. Amos 5:18) and rejoiced in it (a play on Isaac in Gen. 17:1–17). Even more so than Isaac, Christ is Abraham's offspring (Gen. 12:7; Gal. 3:16). In the Passion narrative, which echoes the binding of Isaac at many points (Genesis 22), and in Paul's preaching (Rom. 8:32), Christ is the new Isaac who offers himself in sacrifice.

According to Hebrews 7–8, it is Christ who appeared to Abraham in Genesis 14, more than the historically shadowy Melchisedech (cf. Gen. 14:14–18). Finally, Christ supersedes Abraham (John 8:53, 58).

The NT claims that Jesus Christ is present in the Exodus history. Jesus is, for instance, presented as the new Moses proclaimed in Deuteronomy 18:18. Moses was the only person ever to have seen God and whose passing away remained mysterious (Deut. 34:1–12) so that even if the purpose of Deuteronomy 18:18 was to show the institution of prophecy, the belief in the incomparability of Moses (cf. Acts 6:11) made him the prophet of the advent of an unsurpassable mediator like himself; it even made people believe he would return (Acts 3:22). Jesus Christ also emulates and surpasses Moses because he is the son while Moses was the servant (Heb. 3:2 ff.). In Acts 7:35 Stephen lists the commonalities between Jesus and Moses the persecuted prophet. Matthew narrates Jesus as a new Moses persecuted from infancy on (Matthew 1–2) who journeys down into Egypt and comes up again. Hebrews 11:25 ff. has Moses bear the hatred which was directed at Christ (Exod. 3:7 ff.), especially through the people's endless complaining. The repeated refrain, 'Moses has said unto you, but I say unto you' indicates that when he promulgates the Law a second time (Matt. 5:2; Deut. 18:18), he takes it to a new level. Jesus Christ is also the one of whom Moses wrote. Moses himself attests that he wrote about Jesus in all his texts (John 5:46). In John 1:45, Philip tells Nathaniel that he has literally found 'the one of whom Moses wrote in the law and the prophets'. Paul acknowledges that Christ was at work in the Exodus miracles: 'And did all drink the same spiritual drink: for they drank of that spiritual Rock that followed them: and that Rock was Christ' (1 Cor. 10:4). It is he who is immolated in the Paschal lamb (Exod. 12:1; cf. 1 Pet. 1:20; John 1:29). He is raised even higher than the bronze serpent (Num. 21:4 and John 3:15). He is the manna (Exod. 16:4–6; cf. John 6:31, 39 ff.) and the water supplied by Moses, or by God. Following one variant on Jude 5, it is *Iêsous kyrios* who rescued Israel from Egypt (Metzger 1971: 723–4). This indicates that Moses did not just prefigure Jesus, but previewed, foresaw, and prophesied him.

The NT affirms that Christ spoke with Moses. John often presents Jesus as the one who shows humanity the Name, taking up Moses' task (Exod. 3:14–16). But he also suggests that upon seeing the tabernacle, Moses saw the preexistent Christ, 'full of grace and truth' (Exod. 34:6; John 1:14). The one who 'and did tabernacle among us' (John 1:14, Young's literal translation of ἐσκήνωσεν) is the κύριος with whom Moses went head to head in the tabernacle (*skene* Exod. 25:9; Num. 12:4–8). Jesus takes over for himself the divine name Moses received at the burning bush (Exod. 3:14; John 5:58 and passim).

The NT sees Christ present in the history of the kings. In the psalms of which he is the presumed author, David prophesies the death and resurrection of Christ (Acts 2:31, citing Ps. 16:8–11 and Ps. 132:11 with an allusion to 2 Sam. 7:12; Acts 13:33 ff. cites Ps. 2:7 and then Isa. 55:3, 'I will give you the holy and sure blessings of David').

Christ is more the speaker of the psalms than David. Psalm 22:2 is placed in the dying Jesus' mouth by the earliest Passion narrative. In 589, the third synod of Toledo condemned Theodore of Mopsuestia for having said that in a literal sense David is the author of this psalm: for ancient Christian thought the Christian message beats out chronology because it transcends it (Aquinas 1996: 256).

Christ outperforms David. 'For David did not ascend into the heavens; but he himself says, "The Lord said to my Lord, Sit at my right hand, till I make thy enemies a stool for thy feet"' (Acts 2:34–5). He counts himself above David, who names the Messiah or Christ as 'Lord', thinking that he will be one of his descendants (Matt. 22:42). This Christ who is greater than Solomon is the son of David (Matt. 9:27), born in Bethlehem. Fitting the Magna Carta of Davidic royal Messianism in the intertexts of the stories of annunciation (2 Sam. 7; 1 Chr. 17), he calls God his Father and God calls him his son. He builds the house of God and inaugurates his kingdom.

The NT also states that Christ is present in the prophets. The prophets spoke of him in words and in deeds. They had symbolized the meeting between God and his people as a marriage, and Jesus seems to honor this in his actions (John 2:1–11) and in nuptial parables in which he has the role of the bridegroom.

The prophets had symbolized his ministry. Jesus performed miracles like those of Elijah (Luke 4:25–6; 7:11–16), and is borne up to the heavens as Elijah was (Luke 25:51; Brodie 2000). They prefigured his tragic fate: in Jeremiah and Ezekiel a 'son of man' represents the human condition in its frailty, persecuted for having presumed to intimacy with God, or as the suffering servant of Isaiah's hymns. The early Church Fathers alluded to the sufferings of Christ through paraphrases of the prophets and the psalms of dereliction more often than they cited the evangelical Passion narratives.

They *saw* him. In relation to the rejection of Christ, John 12:38 cites Isaiah 53:1 ('Who hath believed our report? and to whom is the arm of the Lord revealed?'). John goes on to say 'These things said Isaiah, when he saw his glory, and spake of him' (John 12:41, alluding to the theophany in the Temple in Isa. 6:1–4, read as a prophetic vision of the glory of Christ).

Christ is likewise the one who speaks through them. For example, does 'you have burdened Me with your sins' make more sense coming from incandescent God of armies or from the crucified Christ (Bauckham 1999)?

What for the NT authors are the signs in the OT that Christ is at work? Their Christology of the OT does not give preeminence to structural correspondences or to formal analogies between types of person, or a posteriori evidence for situational analogies, of the kinds to which later Christians were so fondly attached and which left them continually teetering on the verge of allegory. The NT authors looked rather for the continuous flow of an historical process within the unifying design of the divine wisdom (Matt. 11:13–14). The manifestations of Christ in the history of salvation are the ascending stages of the condescension of divine benevolence, and Christ's ministry is *literally* the final link in a chain of ancient theophanies.

The manifestations of Christ in the history of salvation are created and manifested in the literal details of Scripture. Genesis' *omission* of a genealogy for Melchisedech (Gen. 14:17–19) allows Hebrews 7:3 to 'assimilate' him to the eternal divine priest. But conversely, it is *the presence of a word* (*kurios*) which allows Paul and NT writers to see the pre-existent Christ in many of the OT passages in which he figures (Benoit 1982: 46). Often it is the repetition or variation of known 'trademark' words for God which sets in motion the discovery of Christ in the Old Covenant. In 1 Corinthians 10:6, when Paul uses the adverb *typikos*, the typology does not bear so much upon Christ's action through the manna or the rock as on the moral counterexample supplied by the Israelites. The identification of Christ in the scenes mentioned by 1 Corinthians 10:1–4 is drawn from textual details: the contrast between *aggelos tou theou* (Exod. 14:19) and *theos* (Exod. 14:31; 17:2). A similar case is where the 'two-sidedness' of the divine agency (e.g. Gen. 19:24; G.P. 109:1; G.P. 44:7–8) allows Justin further to elaborate upon the

Christology of the OT: the 'second God' produced by the letter of the text preserves the transcendence of the first who can neither move nor be manifest amongst human beings (Trakatellis 1976).

There again, the use of idiosyncrasies occasioned by a translation, for instance the singular (which is collective in Hebrew) rather than the plural in Genesis 12:7 allows Paul to limit the promise to the one single heir who is Christ. Another way of finding Christ acting in the Old Testament is through a word's having a double meaning when taken literally. The most spectacular example is Joshua, which in Hebrew is the same name as Jesus and allows the author of Hebrews to move from one to the other, as interchangeable. Likewise a literal reading of Deuteronomy 18:18 ('I will raise up for them a prophet like you from among their brothers') works even better in Hebrew than in Greek to uphold belief in a Moses *redivivus* (Nodet 2003: 226).

The possibility that Moses will return alive is cemented by the anomalies in the story of his death (Deut. 34:1–12). He dies in great shape, just because he has reached the statutory 120 years (Gen. 6:3), he is buried, but by God in an unmarked grave! Matters are similar with Elijah, as the biblical tradition appears to 'hold him in reserve' for the arrival of the plenary revelation (he is assumed into heaven without having died: in 2 Chr. 21:12–15 he writes after his death!). Both of them are thus *alive and kicking* for the transfiguration scene. Such narrative ambiguities are threaded through a Christology which ties Jesus and the prophets together. In the case of the relationship to Elijah the mere narrative ambivalence is sufficiently evoked by the opaque double-sidedness of a messenger, or an angel of the Lord, or of the Lord himself (Mal. 3:1; Exod. 3:2; 23:20; Gen. 16:7).

There can also be a certain editorial dynamic. Thus the figure of the 'son of David' comes to be recognized as Jesus as a result of the rewriting of the memory of the rather unremarkable historical king that Solomon actually and historically was, so that by the time of Josiah he had morphed into a wise and wealthy king, by the time of the Exile he was perceived as a scourge of idolatry, and in the era of Darius he had positively become a sun-king. The Chronicler, stubbornly open to the future, transforms Nathan's oracle: the house and kingdom of David of 2 Samuel 7:16 becomes under his pen the house and kingdom of *God* (1 Chr. 17:14, cf. 28:5; 29:5; 2 Chr. 9:8; Lichtert 2008).

Another mobilizer for Christology in the OT is in the recognition of a certain kind of linguistic positioning in Christ's speech. We also find this in prophetic speech, or in that of He in whose name they speak. An enmeshing of sayings is common amongst the prophets and in the psalms. For instance, the speakers and the referent of Isaiah 52:13–53 are enigmatic (cf. Acts 9:34). 'The "voices" do not reveal where they come from: it is left to the reader to figure out who is speaking. But the true meaning of the text is the drama engendered by the exchange of voices' (Beauchamp 1989: 325). One speaker can hide behind another, and a divine speaker could be hiding himself behind a human saying. This logic makes sense of Jesus' evocation of the paradoxical 'divine name' (I AM) of Exodus 3:14. When he uses the name, John has the tautological reticence of Exodus 3:14

to start from, which itself had already been reshaped in its probing by a prophetic 'voice' (Isa. 51:12 responding to Isa. 40:1, 3.6: 'a voice cries' and yet that voice remains unknown). John builds upon this, taking the ironic pedagogy of the name to a logical conclusion. Just like earlier prophets, Jesus in his preaching assumes the first-person singular of the divine voice. It becomes ever more ambiguous throughout his ministry, however, as to who is really speaking when he speaks. Who is actually saying his lines? Is it the prophet whom Jesus cites? Is it the God in whose name the prophet or Jesus speaks? Or is it Jesus himself (Neusner 1993)? The Synoptics settle for one simple question, 'Who do you say I am?' (Matt. 16:14–16).

What all these Christological mobilizers have in common is that they put the ontology of the text below that of 'reality'. Diverse textual facts are the foundation for a Christology which is neither allegorical nor typological. They appear as *witnesses* for the coming of Christ, relayed by the prophets and by the promises to speak properly.

The continuity between the OT and Christ was discovered on the basis of belief in the promises which God makes in Scripture. The identification of Jesus as the son of David (Acts 2:30; cf. Heb. 6:13) is less about typology than about the prophecy and the promises carried out. The written words into which they are crystallized present a dynamism between God, time, and language. Providence is here perceived as something very real and actual.

In its identification of Jesus with Moses, Joshua, or Melchisedech, the author of Hebrews draws the perpetual present of proclamation out of the spatio-temporal text ('as long as it is called "today"', Heb. 3:13). He can reopen what is implicit in the text in the *hic et nunc* because God's 'today' is the same at any time when he might write or read. His experience of reading is such that the sacred writing grasps its hearer-reader before being grasped by him. One is hardly surprised that Hebrews expresses admiration for the word of God, calling it a true transcendental (Heb. 4:11–13). A genuine sacramentality emerges in the text. Writing transcends space and time. God is discovered in Scripture in such a way that this writing becomes a real symbol, concretely symbolizing the divine in and of itself. Inspired by God (2 Tim. 3:16: θεόπνευστος), this text seems to be the personal embodiment of the word of God: 'Scripture says', 'speaks' (Rom. 9:17; 10:11), 'foresees' (Gal. 3:8).

The Scriptures come across as a witness of God to God (1 John 5:9–11), or as God's oath to himself (Heb. 6:13–14 reminds us 'God swears by himself because there is no one greater than he'). This resonates with an echo of the divine tautology ('I am that I am'): 'εἰ μὴν εὐλογῶν εὐλογήσω σε καὶ πληθύνων πληθυνῶ σε'.

Jesus Christ takes over the 'Mosaic economy of the book' (Sonnet 2002). Moses writes the words of the Torah as a substitute for his own presence and as a means for the Israelites to cross the Jordan into the Promised Land, which he himself will not cross. In the Mosaic economy, it is due to the living word of the book that life is propagated in space and time. 'This word is your life' (Deut. 32:47). The book is thus the principle of a life of its own, distinct from but also engraphed into genealogical propagation (Sonnet 2002: 522–3).

These things are thus bound together: the reading and writing of the book, the life and death of Moses, entering into life in the Promised Land for his disciples. For the Jews the text thus becomes a portable homeland (Heine 1968: 483). It is in this homeland, where language determines reality, that the Christology of the Old Testament goes into action.

The assumption of this conception of the book is especially striking in the first Gospel. Beginning as 'the book of the genealogy of Jesus Christ' (Matt. 1:1), it concludes by including everything within this book: 'Make disciples of all nations … teaching them to observe all that I have commanded you' (Matt. 28:20), centering upon the revelation of a 'kingdom', addressed to his real family, defined as those who hear the word of God and obey it (Matt. 13), it sets itself up as a kind of manual for the generation of brothers and sisters of Jesus by the seed which is the word intended *in the book itself* (Matt. 10:7; 24:14; and 28:20; John 1:12; 1 Pet. 1:23), the gateway to the kingdom (Sonnet 2005).

In sum, a Christology is biblical insofar as it witnesses to and encapsulates the encounter between God and humanity mediated by language and by texts. Well before the various anti-types later developed by Christian exegesis, Scripture itself is an anti-type of Christ.

What Did Scripture Mean
in First-Century Judaism?

What can come across as an a posteriori hermeneutic is actually a movement which begins from within Scripture itself. To understand the objective force of this Christology, it is necessary to grasp how Jews related to Scripture in the first century.

There was not *an* OT, but rather, a diverse variety of Scriptures. At the time of the NT, the idea of a canon and the dynamism toward one had been around for a long time, as is implied by the Pentateuch. But there did not yet exist what can properly be called a biblical canon, as is indicated by the existence of one, two, or even three variants on the ending of the Lukan narrative, reflecting the state of play at that time in synagogue libraries (Blanchard 2002: 41). Given their diversity, the Scriptures functioned less as a doctrinal corpus than as a language in which first-century Jews expressed and developed their 'narrative identity'.

Scripture is constructed out of successive re-readings of itself. Chronicles rewrites Samuel and Kings, with daring variations (cf. 2 Sam. 24 and 1 Chr. 21). The 'deutero-canonical' writings are in many respects a Jewish re-reading of Scripture multiplied to the 'n-th power' (Bogaert 2007: 484). Typology is in many ways present in the texts themselves (Kuntzmann 2002), as if it were in fact a Jewish style of writing well before it became a Hellenistic style of reading: it is a manner of composition which is consubstantial with the biblical text. The stories about the Garden of Eden roll like a watermark through the Patriarchal narratives and the Exodus (von Rad 1952–3; Römer 2002). The Exodus themes are repeated by Deutero-Isaiah and by Jeremiah (Isa. 43:16–21; Jer. 23:7–8).

In the first century the Scriptures were the linguistic materials which framed emotions and events. It was a vast reservoir of stories, with their repeated motifs, and of expressions, preserved at more or less of a distance from their original context and open to being used to descry and to verbalize the action of God in one's own time (Longenecker 1987; Beale 1994). In some contexts, such as Qumran, it aroused a kind of literary genre called the *pesher*, an interlinear commentary on the authoritative texts which elucidates present historical reality through the words of the Scriptures.

Nor was the possibility of composing new Scriptures written off. Amongst the Dead Sea Scrolls, the Temple Scroll (11Q19) presents itself as a new book of Moses: sixty-six columns rewrite the Pentateuchal laws, using the voice of God in the first person with complete abandon, and at times even correcting the biblical text itself.

In short, for first-century Judaism, the Scriptures were sufficiently fixed to be a code, and sufficiently elastic to allow for new combinations. They had a transcendental quality, structuring the person's relation to reality. So clearly the massive presence of Scripture in the apostolic witness to Christ is not necessarily something tacked on to the testimony later on.

Their ways of reading were diverse. The Jewish relationship to Scripture consisted in simultaneously actualizing and transmitting them. Even if during the Diaspora, Alexandrian Judaism established a reflexive and philological relation to the text, Greek translations were also the occasion of lesser or greater variations in the text itself, whilst the Hellenistic style of reading was developed, with its allegorical methods. In the *Gola*, the art of actualizing the Scriptures is preserved alongside the practice of targums. In Palestinian Judaism, right down to the first century, there was at Qumran still no clear separation between the text and its commentary. Transmission and actualization came together to the extent that it is often difficult to distinguish between the exegetical re-reading of a biblical text and a manuscript variant (e.g., 4Q365 according to Tov and Sidnie 1994). The difference between the editorial process and the interpretative process is not of kind but of quantity.

The communities of readers were divided amongst themselves: the various Jewish camps of Sadduccees, Pharisees, and Essenes did not recognize the same corpus of inspired texts, and diverged in the interpretation of the texts which they did have in common. These disparities did not produce skepticism or irreligion, but rather a growth of faith in the texts themselves. After so many hopes for the fulfillment of the promises or of the prophets had been let down by the historical realities, the text of Scripture itself had achieved comprehensive prophetic quality. Beyond their disparity, people sought their principle of intelligibility, looking for what held the Scriptures together. Daniel had already looked to the 'end of time' (Dan. 12:4) as the moment of the ultimate unveiling of the book. The Essenes also appeared to have sought the ultimate secret (the *ras* of Hodayyot 13 (= 5) 11.12; or the qetz ha-aron (1QpHab VII.7–8) which would enable them to reinterpret the Torah, a revelation which would be hidden until the appearance of the Master of Justice. Although these diverse first-century Judaisms had a common belief in the Temple, they did not agree on who should be responsible for it: they disagreed over the high priests. This could not but sharpen their disagreements over the issue of authority.

Christ's Causal Effect
on the Scriptures

'By what authority are You doing these things? And who gave You this authority to do these things?' (Mark 11:28). So far as we know from treating the Gospels as the only Jewish examples of *bioi* of the founder (Burridge 1992), creating an undeniable historical footprint, Jesus exercised an outstanding personal authority. This led to the use of his name in acts of thaumaturgy (Acts 3:11; 9:34; 16:18; 19:13; Matt. 7:22; 24:5; cf. jAvod. Zar. 2.40d–41a), and even in rites of exorcism (Puech 2009). Only an exceptional possession of authority on Jesus' part can explain how Paul, who had been a pharisaic scourge of idolatry, could have unhesitatingly included the concrete person of Christ within his adoration of the Holy One of Israel in 1 Cor. 8:6 ('yet for us *there is* one God, the Father, of whom *are* all things, and we for Him; and one Lord Jesus Christ, through whom *are* all things, and through whom we *live*') (Hurtado 2005).

Jesus' ministry initiated a dialectic between historical events and scriptural texts. He was in many respects a disconcerting Messiah. In keeping with the apocalypticism of his time, he laid a trail to help his hearers understand his words and gestures, by deliberately inscribing them in the pre-given scenarios which existed in the shared biblical memory, such as the destiny of the 'son of man' (Dan. 7:10–25), the return of the ancient prophets (Matt. 17:11–12), the symbol of the Twelve, and so on.

The NT foregrounds two moments in the process of the scriptural clarification of Christ's ministry. There is, first of all, a partial comprehension, where the Scriptures which people already have stocked in their memory shed light on the words and gestures of Jesus (John 2:17). This is followed by a fuller comprehension both of the Scriptures and of Jesus' words (John 2:22). Just as the disciples already knew or understood the Scriptures during Jesus' ministry so the profound bond between what they said and what happened could only be brought to light with the resurrection and the faith to which it gave birth.

The 'mystery' of the death and resurrection of Christ shows itself as the ultimate secret, the point of anamnesis which draws the scattered and dispersed Scriptures up into a single book. In the scene of the journey to Emmaus (Luke 24:44), Luke suggests that the first Jewish disciples, like other first-century Jewish writers, created anthologies of ancient scriptural texts, in order to try to grasp the ministry and the person of

Jesus. They created many 'lists of achievements' (Schuchard, Van Segbroeck): 'As it is written of him', καθὼσ γὲγραπται (e.g. Matt. 26:24), translates the expression *ka'ăsher katŭb* which is common in the Dead Sea Scrolls.

The dialectic between the historical facts and the Scriptures can be seen clearly in the memory of his Passion. The death of a 'Messiah' on the Cross, which would have constituted an impenetrable enigma for first-century Jews, is taught in advance by the Scriptures, so much so that the Passion of Jesus already alludes to Psalm 22 and Second Zechariah.

The armoire of citations and biblical allusions which the Passion narratives create are understood as the consequences of 'stubborn historical facts' which they elucidate (Yarbro-Collins 1994: 482), not as a fiction, which would not have made sense within Jewish or Graeco-Roman literary codes (Auerbach 1959; Taylor 2011). Of course the scriptural references accumulated over the course of many readings, performances, and editions, but in line with a special scriptural *synkrisis* which permits the narrators to elaborate it from within Jesus' perspective by highlighting a citation or primitive scriptural allusion (Dodd 1952; Aletti 1999).

Christ taught a creative reception of the Scriptures and of his words. Jesus did not only show his authority by thaumaturgical words. He also spoke of the Scriptures (Meier 2005: 134). He promoted a specific kind of reception. For him, the Scriptures were less a pretext for disputation (or snares: Matt. 22:15.34–5 and passim) than they were occasions to put the word of the living God into practice (Matt. 5:18). He taught them to read the Scriptures literally: 'God has said' (Matt. 15:4–9); 'have you not read?' (Matt. 19:4; 21:15, 42; 22:31, 43–4).

He sometimes seems to elicit an attachment to Scripture as a fixed totality (Matt. 5:18: 'till heaven and earth pass away, one jot or one tittle will by no means pass from the law till all is fulfilled'). But he does not envisage a fixed body of texts. In reality, by emphasizing literality, he reminds us that literary space is the occasion of practice and of hands-on experience (Matt. 5:19).

This attachment to the *experience* of the letter is confirmed in the single Gospel scene in which Jesus writes (with his finger in the sand and confronting the accusers of the woman taken in adultery, John 8:8). The narrator does not tell us what Jesus wrote in the sand. It is the gesture and the way of writing which he accentuates. While the accusers reduce the Word to a binary logic, taking a text and making reality apply to it, Jesus shows what the law is through his own attitude. He exhibits what it means for writing to be writing; it is an 'earth' with its own given consistency to delve into and cultivate, not a reservoir of meanings which can immediately be projected upon reality. This correlates with the Jewish relation to Scripture in those times.

Jesus does not just comment on the Scriptures. He authoritatively promulgates Scripture. He soars straight over the oral law, overturning it. 'It is written / Moses has told you / and I tell you'. This presumption—which people could see as impiously putting himself into competition with the one sole Judge (Deut. 4:2; 2:37), or as sparklingly fresh vindication of free speech in the face of a God who shows himself

(Deut. 29:28), or as a daring claim to be the new Moses (Deut. 18:18)—puts the words of Scripture and Jesus' own words on the same plane, the one serially following on from the other.

A fortiori, the relation to Scripture will be transformed by his own resurrection, which demands a new attitude to the Scriptures: not only of 'knowing' but of 'believing' them (John 3:2–3, 10–11; 5:39–40). So it is not surprising when finally in John's Gospel Christ takes up the dialectic of the oral and the written into that of knowledge and of faith. In order to recognize the word (*logos*) of God in the writings (*graphes*) which carry it (John 5:38 ff.), and thus to be brought to life by them, it is necessary to believe *that it speaks about him* (John 5:46 ff.).

The turning of Scripture and the words of Christ into a single series reaches its apex in the witnesses to his resurrection, which is simultaneously proclaimed as being 'according to the Scriptures', a frequent leitmotif of the primitive kerygma (cf. 1 Cor. 15:1–7) and as fulfilling Jesus' own words: 'He is resurrected as he said he would' (Matt. 28:6). There is here a striking intermeshing of causes, like in Neoplatonic causality: it is only by first knowing the resulting effect that one can know the preceding cause. Jesus' resurrection is the catalyst for the unification of the Scriptures into a single book, but it is only thanks to these Scriptures that the resurrection can be expressed and known (John 20:9).

At the completion of the apostolic tradition, by the time for instance of the canonical editions of John, the outcome is that in thirty-six occurrences of leximes deriving from *grapho* or *gramma*, it is often impossible to know what it is intended: a precise scriptural reference, or a general one, or a passage from the Synoptics, or from the traditions which they contain, or the word of Jesus himself (Moloney 2006).

It is as the word of God that Jesus unifies the Scriptures. Once the Scriptures are put into a single series with the words of Jesus, he seems to become their true author, or the authority behind them. In its opening lines Hebrews emphasizes the defining character of the word of Christ in comparison to all the words which came before it in earlier Scripture (Heb. 1:1–3). Christ's authority is such that he alone perfects the era of faith of the Patriarchs and ancient heroes, ensuring and fulfilling the salvation of these legendary figures (Heb. 11:39–40). In the light of the resurrection, the memory of the crucifixion becomes such a powerful key for integrating the Scriptures that the NT authors end up reversing the hermeneutical movement, and affirm that Jesus' immolation on the Cross is the cornerstone of the book of Scripture. In Revelation, it is because he has passed through the Cross that Jesus is the only one who can open the book (Rev. 5:4–8).

Ultimately there is a reciprocal relation between faith in the risen Christ and the *com*-prehension of the Scriptures as *the* Bible. 'It is difficult to present clear examples of the divine inspiration of the ancient Scriptures from before the advent of Christ; but the coming of Jesus has brought those who thought the Law and the Prophets were not divine to see the evidence that they were written with the help of heavenly grace' (Origen, *De Principiis*, IV.1.6–7).

'Ignoratio Scripturarum est Ignoratio Christi'

Jerome's famous formula (*Commentary on Isaiah*, Prologue, *PL* 24.17) is not a merely moralistic exhortation to pious studiosity. It rests on an ontological identification between Christ and the Scriptures. The 'superior mode of existence' (Benoit 1982: 29) thanks to which Christ engaged in human business before his incarnation is that of the literary history of the Jewish people. This proclaims, realizes, and contains the encounter between God and humanity as mediated by the word.

We need to think about God more realistically in order to recover a Christology of the OT. The Christology of the OT is not drawn out of non-existent intentions in the mind of God; they do not relate to the ideal and non-real. Divine thoughts, designs, and plans are actually 'the sovereign reality, of which human events are the mere reflections' (Benoit 1982: 32).

In the Scriptures, language is not just representation, but also potency and force. It is not just a phantom delegate for reality, but precedes reality. Far from the 'modern' dissociation of noetics and ontology, Scripture integrates the word and the thing (*davar*), the vision and the event, phenomenology and metaphysics (Balthasar 1960), metalanguage and language (Sonnet 2002: 510). Right down to the New Testament, the scriptural citations of Scripture show that there is no adequate distinction between a scriptural text and its 'historical' or 'prophetic' referent. The Christology of the OT requires us to rethink the place of literary development in Judaeo-Christian revelation, showing us that revelation is not only in history, but also in language itself (*Dei Verbum* #2: *gestis verbisque intrisesce inter se connexis*).

In order make a Christology of the OT conceivable, we need to change our ideas about causation and about time. The relation between Christ and the inspired Scriptures is one of causation, with the word 'cause' being taken in its fullest sense and without reducing it to efficient causality, which is what modernity thinks is all there is. He exercises a formal and final causality which is only manifested in the realization of its effect.

The Christology of the OT invites us to rethink our Christological apophaticism. It invites us to rediscover the identity of Christ as divine language, and his multiple ways of approaching humanity: the embodiment in Scripture is no less concrete than the incarnation as a human person. This is the crown of the *admirabile commercium* of the divine *Verbum* and the human *verba*, the crossroads which found the interplay of divine and human words in Scripture.

Once the OT is entirely 'Christologized', the Christ whom we rediscover is closer to us and more transcendent than ever, escaping the grasp of those who know him the best. The Christology of the OT gives new life to Christological apophaticism and reclaims the Christian faith as a 'doctrine of ignorance'. The Christology of the OT does not reduce either to hermeneutics or to ontology: beyond intellectual and spiritual experience, it derives from a 'metaphysics of conversion' (Gilson 1929: 299).

Suggested Reading

Catholic Church et al. (1984); Commission for Religious Relations with the Jews (1985); de Lubac (1959).

Bibliography

Aletti, J.-N. (1999), 'Le Christ raconté. Les Évangiles comme littérature?', in F. Mies (ed.), *Bible et littérature. L'homme et Dieu mis en intrigue* (Brussels: Lessius), 29–53.

Aquinas, T. (1996), *Commentaire sur les Psaumes*, ed. J.-É. Stroobant de Saint-Éloy (Paris: Cerf), 255–83.

Auerbach, E. (1959), *Mimesis. Dargestellte Wirklichkeit in der abendländischen Literatur*, 2nd edn. (Bern: Francke).

Balthasar, H. R. von (1960), 'Révélation et beauté' ['Offenbarung und Schönheit', in *Verbum Caro: Skizzen zur Theologie I* (Einsiedeln: Johannes Verlag, 1960), 100–34], trans. Faculté de théologie of Lille, *Mélanges de science religieuse* 55 (1998): 5–32.

Bauckham, R. (1999), *God Crucified: Monotheism and Christology in the New Testament* (Grand Rapids, Mich.: Eerdmans).

Bauckham, R. (2006), *Jesus and the Eyewitnesses: The Gospels as Eyewitness Testimony* (Grand Rapids, Mich.: Eerdmans).

Beale, G. K. (ed.) (1994), *The Right Doctrine from the Wrong Text? Essays on the Use of the Old Testament in the New* (Grand Rapids, Mich.: Baker).

Beauchamp, P. (1989), 'Lecture et relectures du quatrième chant du serviteur, d'Isaïe à Jean', in J. Vermeylen (ed.), *The Book of Isaiah. Le livre d'Isaïe: Les oracles et leurs relectures, unité et complexité de l'ouvrage* (Leuven: Leuven University Press), 325–55.

Benoit, P. (1982), 'Préexistence et incarnation', in *Exégèse et théologie IV* (Paris: Cerf), 11–61.

Blanchard, Y.-M. (2002), 'Naissance du Nouveau Testament et canon biblique', in J.-M. Poffet (ed.), *L'autorité de l'Écriture* (Paris: Cerf), 23–50.

Bogaert, P.-M. (2007), 'Les compléments deutérocanoniques dans la Bible. Un "intertestament" canonique', *Revue théologique de Louvain* 38: 473–87.

Brodie, T. L. (2000), *The Crucial Bridge: The Elijah-Elisha Narrative as an Interpretive Synthesis of Genesis-Kings and a Literary Model for the Gospels* (Collegeville, Minn.: Liturgical Press).

Burridge, R. A. (1992), *What Are the Gospels? A Comparison with Graeco-Roman Biography* (Cambridge: Cambridge University Press).

Cahill, J. (1982), 'Hermeneutical Implications of Typology', *Catholic Biblical Quarterly* 44: 268–81.

Catholic Church, Commission Biblique Pontificale, and H. Cazelles (eds.) (1984), *Bible et Christologie* (Paris: Cerf).

Collins, J. J. (ed.) (1998), *The Encyclopedia of Apocalypticism*, vol. 1: *The Origins of Apocalypticism in Judaism and Christianity* (New York: Continuum).

Commission Biblique Pontificale (2001), *Le peuple juif et ses saintes Écritures dans la Bible chrétienne* (Vatican City: Libreria Editrice Vaticana).

Commission for Religious Relations with the Jews (1985), *Notes on the Correct Way to Present the Jews and Judaism in Preaching and Catechesis in the Roman Catholic Church.* <http://www.vatican.va/roman_curia/pontifical_councils/chrstuni/relations-jews-docs/rc_pc_chrstuni_doc_19820306_jews-judaism_en.html> (accessed July 22, 2014).

de Lubac, H. (1959), *Exégèse medievale, les quatre sens de l'Écriture*. Théologie 41, vol. 1 (Paris: Aubier).

Dodd, C. H. (1952), *The Old Testament in the New*. The Ethel M. Wood Lecture delivered before the University of London on 4 March 1952 (London: Athlone Press).

Gathercole, S. J. (2006), *The Preexistent Son: Recovering the Christologies of Matthew, Mark, and Luke* (Grand Rapids, Mich.: Eerdmans).

Gilson, É. (1929), *Introduction à l'étude de saint Augustin* (Paris: Vrin).

Goshen-Gottstein, A. (1997), 'Hillel and Jesus: Are Comparisons Possible?', in J. H. Charlesworth and L. L. Johns (eds.), *Hillel and Jesus: Comparative Studies of Two Major Religious Leaders* (Minneapolis: Fortress), 31–55.

Heine, H. (1968), *Sämtliche Schriften in zwölf Bänden*, vol. 11: *Schriften 1851–1855*, ed. K. Briegleb (Munich: Hanser Verlag).

Hurtado, L. W. (2005), *How on Earth Did Jesus Become a God? Historical Questions about Earliest Devotion to Jesus* (Grand Rapids, Mich.: Eerdmans).

Kubis, A. (2012), *The Book of Zechariah in the Gospel of John* (Pendé: Gabalda).

Kuntzmann, R. (ed.) (2002), *Typologie biblique. De quelques figures vives* (Paris: Cerf).

Lichtert, C. and D. Nocquet (eds.) (2008), *Le Roi Salomon un héritage en question. Hommage à Jaques Vermeylen* (Brussels: Lessius).

Longenecker, R. (1987), ' "Who is the Prophet Talking About?" Some Reflections on the New Testament's Use of the Old', *Themelios* 13: 4–8.

Martin, F. (1996), *Pour une théologie de la lettre. L'inspiration des Écritures*. Cogitatio fidei 196 (Paris: Cerf).

Meier, J. P. (2005), *Un certain Juif, Jésus. Les données de l'histoire*, vol. 2: *Les paroles et les gestes* (Paris: Cerf).

Metzger, B. M. (1971), *A Textual Commentary on the Greek New Testament* (New York: United Bible Societies).

Moloney, F. J. (2006), 'What Came First: Scripture or Canon? The Gospel of John as a Test Case', *Salesianum* 68: 7–20.

Neusner, J. (1988), *Why No Gospels in Talmudic Judaism?* (Atlanta: Scholars Press).

Neusner, J. (1993), *A Rabbi Talks with Jesus: An Intermillenial, Interfaith Exchange* (New York: Doubleday).

Nodet, É. (2003), *Histoire de Jésus? Nécessité et limites d'une enquête* (Paris: Cerf).

Paul, A. (1987a), 'Genèse de l'apocalyptique et signification du canon des Écritures', in *La vie de la Parole: De l'Ancien au Nouveau Testament. Études offertes à Pierre Grelot* (Paris: Desclée), 421–33.

Paul, A. (1987b), *Le judaïsme ancien et la Bible* (Paris: Desclée).

Puech, É. (2009), 'Les manuscrits de Qumran et Jésus', *Kephas* 27: 23–31.

Römer, T. (2002), 'Typologie exodique dans les récits patriarcaux', in R. Kuntzmann (ed.), *Typologie biblique. De quelques figures vives* (Paris: Cerf), 49–76.

Sonnet, J.-P. (2002), 'Lorsque Moïse eut achevé d'écrire' (Dt 31, 24): Une "théorie narrative" de l'écriture dans le Pentateuque', *Revue des Sciences Religieuses* 90: 509–24.

Sonnet, J.-P. (2005), 'De la généalogie au "Faites disciples" (Mt 28,19). Le livre de la génération de Jésus', in C. Focant and A. Wénin (eds.), *Analyse narrative et Bible, deuxième colloque international du RRENAB, Louvain-La-Neuve, avril 2004* (Leuven: Leuven University Press), 199–209.

Taylor, J. (2011), *The Treatment of Reality in the Gospels: Five Studies* (Pendé: Gabalda).

Tov, E. and S. White (1994), '4Q Reworked Pentateuch^c', in H. Attridge et al., in consultation with J. Van der Kam, *Qumran Cave 4. VIII: Parabiblical Texts, Part 1*. Discoveries in the Judaean Desert XIII (Oxford: Clarendon Press), 265–318.

Trakatellis, D. C. (1976), *The Pre-existence of Christ in Justin Martyr: An Exegetical Study with Reference to the Humiliation and Exaltation Christology* (Missoula: Scholar Press).

Trebolle Barrera, J. C. (1998), *The Jewish Bible and the Christian Bible: An Introduction to the History of the Bible*, trans. W. G. E. Wilson (Leiden: Brill).

von Rad, G. (1952–3), 'Typologische Auslegung des Alten Testaments', *Evangelische Theologie* 12: 17–33.

Yarbro-Collins, A. (1994), 'From Noble Death to Crucified Messiah', *New Testament Studies* 40: 481–503.

CHAPTER 3

JEWISH SUFFERING AND CHRISTOLOGY IN PAULINE AND RECENT PAPAL THOUGHT

GREGORY GLAZOV

THIS study examines the relevance of Jesus' Jewishness to Christology via Romans 9–11. The examination is catalyzed by reflection at the crossroads of two sets of questions. The first set relates to an anecdote reported by Hans Henrix about Pinchas Lapide once asking Karl Rahner whether one can ignore Jesus' Jewishness in reflecting on the Incarnation. Rahner, puzzling over the question, replied that 'Jesus' rootedness in the history and reality of Israel was an arbitrary coincidence without any theological value.' Henrix labeled Rahner's position quasi-docetic (Henrix 2011). The anecdote yields the first set of questions catalyzing this study: Is Jesus' Jewishness important to the Incarnation? Is it quasi-docetic to say no? If so, how so? The second set of questions relates to papal criticism of Holocaust denial and whether this criticism is based on faith or morals. Many people, noting that Holocaust denial is a lie, assume the latter. However, since papal pronouncements about Jew-hatred and Holocaust denial are grounded in creation theology, election theology, and Christology/soteriology, faith is also involved. The Christological and soteriological themes arise because of links drawn between the suffering of the Jewish people and the suffering and death of Christ. I will attempt to show how Romans 9–11, the scriptural touchstone of post-Vatican II Catholic–Jewish rapprochement, provides scriptural grounds for this connection.

HOLOCAUST, JEW-HATRED, AND
CATHOLIC CHRISTOLOGY

In January 2009, Benedict XVI lifted the excommunication of four bishops of the St. Pius X Society (SSPX) to help that society heal its schism with the Catholic Church, whereupon it emerged that one of the bishops was a Holocaust denier. In the ensuing public furor, the Vatican implied that prior knowledge of this denial would have obstructed the lifting of the excommunication. Traditionalists rushed to mock the implication that Holocaust denial should be deemed a heresy. I will argue that the Vatican indeed condemned Holocaust denial not just on the basis of morals but also on that of faith but was right, orthodox, for doing so.

Benedict, following the papal precedent, condemned Holocaust denial and the Jew-hatred that informs it, on the grounds of both faith and morals. Morals are evident in the emphasis on the importance of remembering the anguish of the Jewish people and not lying about or belittling it. Faith is involved in the emphasis on how Jew-hatred, which underlies such lies and revisionism, violates three levels of theology: those of creation, election, and Christology. Being a crime against humanity, Holocaust denial offends the Christian faith because Christian Scriptures hold humanity to be created in the image and likeness of God (Gen. 1:26–7). Benedict emphasized this point via John Donne's poem 'No man is an island'. In doing so, he also echoed Abraham Joshua Heschel's thought that as an affront to biblical creation theology, the Nazi attack on the Jewish people and attempts to deny, minimize, or forget their crime was/is also an attack on the God of Abraham (Heschel 1991: 4; Vereb 2006: 119; Benedict XVI 2009). This in turn entails biblical covenantal or election theology, the precedent for which was articulated in Pope Pius XI's condemnation of Nazism on September 6, 1938, when he declared that 'it is impossible for a Christian to take part in anti-Semitism' because 'through Christ and in Christ we are the spiritual progeny of Abraham'; 'Spiritually, we are all Semites' (Pius XI 1938) (Secretary of State Pacelli used this same language in a speech in Rome; Lapide 1968: 118; Rychlak 2010: 123, 476, n. 118). More recent popes developed this level of reflection by stressing the necessity of relating the Holocaust to reflection on the historical faith of the Jewish people. Pope John Paul II, for example, said the following on June 24, 1988 when addressing the Jewish community of Vienna:

> You (Jews) and we (Christians) are still weighed down by memories of the *Shoah*, the murder of millions of Jews and Christians in camps of destruction … An adequate consideration of the suffering and martyrdom of the Jewish people is impossible without relating it in its deepest dimension to the experience of faith that has characterized Jewish history, from the faith of Abraham to the Exodus to the covenant on Mount Sinai. It is a constant progression in faith and obedience to the loving call of God. As I said last year before representatives of the Jewish community in Warsaw, *from these cruel sufferings may arise even deeper hope, a warning call to all of*

humanity that may serve to save us all. Remembering *Shoah* means hoping that it will never happen again, and working to ensure that it does not. Faced with this immeasurable suffering we cannot remain cold. *But faith teaches us that God never forsakes those who suffer persecution but reveals himself to them and enlightens through them all peoples on the road to salvation.*

(John Paul II 1988; Klenicki 2006: 21)

The address declares that Jewish suffering is revelatory and salvific. If one were to look for Old Testament passages that might ground this declaration, the Servant Songs of Isaiah 40–55, which identify Israel as a Suffering Servant, would quickly come to mind. John Paul II avoided making such association explicit, perhaps out of a sensitivity that Jews would take it as a form of Christian theological imperialism. Having demonstrated such sensitivity earlier in ordering the removal of a Carmelite convent and cross from Auschwitz, he may on this occasion have indicated that reflections on the level of faith should be grounded first of all on Jewish faith experience.

Commencing his pontificate by going to Auschwitz-Birkenau, Benedict XVI reflected and developed this same sensitivity by grounding reflection about the Shoah on one of Israel's national psalms of lament, Psalm 44:

The rulers of the Third Reich wanted to crush the entire Jewish people, to cancel it from the register of the peoples of the earth. Thus the words of the Psalm: *"We are being killed, accounted as sheep for the slaughter"* (Ps. 44:11) were fulfilled in a terrifying way. Deep down, those vicious criminals, by wiping out this people, wanted to kill the God who called Abraham, who spoke on Sinai and laid down principles to serve as a guide for mankind, principles that are eternally valid. If this people, by its very existence, was a witness to the God who spoke to humanity and took us to himself, then that God finally had to die and power had to belong to … those men, who thought that by force they had made themselves masters of the world. By destroying Israel, by the *Shoah*, they ultimately wanted to tear up the taproot of the Christian faith.

(Benedict XVI 2006)

The statement represents Jew-hatred as an attack on Christian salvation history, founded on God's calls of Abraham, Moses, and Israel. As with John Paul II, explicit linkage between Israel's suffering and the suffering of Christ is avoided. Instead, the attempt to understand this suffering commences with an attempt to relate it to its own Scriptures, in this case as a terrifying fulfillment of Ps. 44:11, according to which Israel is still to be understood as a witness to God before the nations. Also noteworthy is the reversal of the traditional Christian deicide charge against the Jews. But by speaking of the Nazi desire to kill God and to destroy Israel and the Christian faith, the passage hints at a connection between the Shoah and Christ's Passion. The question is whether such a connection is allowed or intended in papal thinking and whether such thinking can advance Roman Catholic doctrine on this point.

Catholic theological touchstones for linking Christ's Passion with Jewish suffering in the past century may be noted in Jacques Maritain's reflections on Chagall's *White Crucifixion* and in the life and writings of St. Edith Stein (John Paul II 1999: para. 9). Elie Wiesel's *Night* contains reflections suggestive of this theme. Ultimately, such reflections demand scriptural grounding. As Romans 9–11 provides the richest New Testament resource for Christian reflection on Jewish–Christian relations, its contents are key in this regard, not least because it contains imagery and concepts over which parties engaged in Jewish–Christian dialogue often stumble.

ROMANS 9–11 AS STUMBLING BLOCK

Romans 9–11, with its declarations at 11:1 and 11:26 that 'God has not rejected his people' and that 'all Israel will be saved', provides Vatican II with the principal scriptural ground for repudiating supersessionism and guiding Catholic–Jewish relationships. The verses in between, Rom. 11:8–14 and 25, speak of a divine blinding and hardening of Israel, portraying Israel as veiled at 2 Cor. 3:14. In ages past, these verses paved the way to Christian representations of the Jews and the Synagogue as blind. These representations are registered in the Latin Good Friday prayer of 1570, and also in its amended post-1962 versions, for, although the 1962 version lacked term *perfideis*, the petition for the Lord 'to illuminate their hearts', remained. These verses from Romans 11 also sandwich an extended metaphor which compares the 'hardened', 'blinded' portion of Israel to hardened, dead olive branches. Being the favorites of supersessionists and anti-Semites, they often complicate Jewish–Christian dialogue, as may be briefly illustrated. Philip Cunningham, for example, reflects the difficulties on the Christian side by writing that:

> the Council did not intend for twenty-first-century Christians to be bound by the Pauline metaphor that Jews not 'in Christ' are like dead branches that have been lopped off from God's holy olive tree. The Council clearly wished to discourage this sort of negative perspective when it declared that 'Jews should not be spoken of as rejected or accursed as if this followed from Holy Scripture.' The question is how to account hermeneutically for this disallowance of Paul's 'unfriendly' ideas. In addition to the pruned olive branches of unbaptized Jews, these most notably include the 'veiled' Jewish reading of Israel's Scriptures in 2 Cor. 3, descriptions of the Torah as mediating a curse in Gal. 3.10–14, and the claim that God is angry with 'the Jews, who killed both the Lord Jesus and the prophets' in 1 Thess. 2.14–16.
>
> (Cunningham 2012: 143, citing *Nostra Aetate* 4 and the Pontifical Biblical Commission, *The Interpretation of the Bible in the Church* [1993] IV, A, 3)

Amy Jill Levine, on the other hand, reflects how Jews find Paul's explanation that the Jews 'failed' to recognize Jesus because a divine 'hardening' is 'not altogether a model of good Jewish–Christian relations ... since Paul does identify those hardened Jews as "enemies of God" and as lopped off the root of Israel (Romans 11)' (Levine 2006: 218, 82–4; Foxman 2007). Like Cunningham Levine also wonders 'how to account her-meneutically for this disallowance of Paul's "unfriendly" ideas' (Levine 2006: 218). Effectively, these veterans of Jewish–Christian dialogue share the traditionalist impression that Romans 9–11 contains ideas that are extremely unfriendly to the Jews.

The questions demand clarifying first the meaning which the images of hardening, blinding, and veiling carry in Romans 9–11. This may be done by discerning their biblical background and Paul's rhetorical use of it. For example, studies of biblical punishments and curses, especially in Deuteronomistic strata, indicate that divine curses are often purgative and rehabilitative of a covenantal relationship. Consequently, it needs to be clarified whether the curses and the hardening in Romans 9–11 signify not the break of a relationship but a stage in its renewal and purification.

One focal point in this discussion is the meaning of the 'spirit of stupefaction' in Rom. 11:8. The term *katanuxis* (κατανύξις, derived from νύγμα, 'prick') plays a key role in the LXX as term of choice for conveying the phenomenon of burning, heart-piercing, silence or stupefaction which attends the process of compunction frequently indicated in Hebrew biblical depictions of divine–human confrontations by versions of the root *dāmam* (cf. M.T. and LXX on Gen. 27:33, 38; Lev. 10:3, Ps. 4:5, and cf. Pss. LXX 30:12, 32:4b, 73:21–4, and 109:16, where the 'broken-hearted' are seen by the LXX (108:16) as 'pricked of heart' (κατανενυγμένον τῇ καρδίᾳ; Vulg *conpunctum corde*) or Ps. 35:15 where the M.T.'s ungodly slander 'without silence' *wᵉlo' dāmmû*) is read by the LXX (= 34:15) as 'without heart-piercing/remorse' (οὐ κατενύγησαν; Vulg = *nec conpuncti*)).

In prophetic call narratives this phenomenon is intended to work healing, wonder, and amazement in the human individual or corporate partner of this confrontation. The phenomenon is central in the call narrative of Isaiah (Isa. 6:6–12) and its development in Isa. 29:9, 10, 18; 32:3; 35:5, important here because vv. 29:9, 10 constitute a background for Rom. 11:8. Thus Isaiah, after seeing the Seraphim in Isa. 6:5, cries *nidmêtî* (Niphal of *dāmam*) 'I have been silent' or 'I have been silenced' (so α, θ, σ = [*esiōpēsa*], Vulg [*tacui*] and Targ. which the LXX renders as κατανένυγμαι [cf. Lev. 10:1–3]). In light of the presence of the 'hot coals' in Num. 16:46; and the way in which the *trishagion* echoes Num. 14:21, 27, 29, the Seraphim here are best interpreted as the burning serpentine genii reminiscent of (a) the *hannᵉḥāšîm hāśᵉrāpîm*, the 'burning serpents' of Num. 21:6 which stung the Israelites who murmured in the wilderness and (b) Nehushtan, the bronze serpent which Moses made in Num. 21:8–9 to heal those who were being stung by the former (Glazov 2001: 120–1, 132–8). Consequently, the Seraphic coal which cleanses Isaiah's lips, after he experiences *katanuxis* (6:1–8), impacts upon him as Nehushtan did upon the murmurers who looked upon him with repentance (cf. Wis. 16:6.11) and thereby explains and anticipates the burning which the Lord prescribes for Isaiah's people in Isa. 6:12 in conclusion to a retributive taunt against idolatry (cf. Glazov 2001: 126–30 on Isa. 6:9–12 and Pss. 115, 135) and thus being relegated to experience a burning that will eventually work *katanuxis* within them (Glazov 2001: 142–9). Jer. 1:9 and 5:14 reinterpret these coals as the word of God by which the prophet is to set the people on fire, while Ezekiel 10:2 envisions the fulfillment of the prophecy in the distribution of the coals from the divine throne upon the people by the man in linen (Glazov 2001: 153, 192–4, 350–1). Since this figure is identical with the one commissioned in 9:4 to mark with a *taw* those who mourn or show compunction, this identity also links the *taw* to the *coals*. Either they are identical or the coals are used to inscribe the *taw* (cf. 4 Ezra 14:40 which combines the features of the coal of Isa. 6:5 with the word of Jer. 1:9; 5:14).

The prophecy of Isa. 6:6, 9–12 is also developed in the later chapters of Isaiah, beginning with 29:9, 10 which announce that God will pour over the people a spirit of deep sleep (*rûaḥ tardēmâ*, interpreted by the LXX as πνεῦμα κατανύξεως). In this vein, Isa. 29:9–24 interprets the heart, lips, eyes, and stupefaction of Isa. 6:9–12 corporately as a prophecy for Israel's body politic. The cup/spirit which the people are to experience betokens an experience of calamity, blindness, and staggering. But it also serves to astonish and amaze (29:14a), and so work a marvelous reversal of Judah's fortune and in turn that of its Chaldean enemies by reducing the latter to silence, i.e., compunction (registered in the Hebrew of 47:5 adverbially by *dûmām*, and in the LXX by κατανενυγμένη) (Glazov 2001: 142–8). This spirit of stupefaction is also described in Psalm 60:3 = LXX Ps. 59:5 as a 'wine of reeling' (οἶνον τανύξεως, Vulg = *vino conpunctionis*). Evidently, then, *katanuxis* plays a unifying role in Isaiah, from its first appearance in 6:9–12, where God commissions the prophet to blind, deafen, and stupefy Israel in response to its worship of blind, deaf, and silent idols, to its reappearance in later chapters where this blinding, deafening, and stupefaction (29:9, 10, 18; 32:3; 35:5; cf. Rom. 11:8) become metaphors for the dark night of Israel's Exile. In this night, Israel is, as it were, reduced to a worm, the weakest of eyeless creatures. Blind, spoiled, and dispersed (Isa. 41:14, cf. Ps. 22:6; Job 17:14), it nonetheless clings to God and becomes in the process His Servant to dispense light and life to the nations (Isa. 42:67, 18–19, 24–5; 49:6–7; 53:11).

Turning now to the New Testament, the reappearance of the linkage between the spirit of God and *katanuxis* in Acts 2:37 suggests that Luke envisions the people's experience of *katanuxis* in listening to Peter's preaching at Pentecost (κατενύγησαν τὴν καρδίαν) [*conpuncti sunt corde*]) and consequent reception of the Holy Spirit to signify the coming realization of Israel's mission to the Gentiles announced by Isaiah. In light of this, his depiction of St. Paul's conversion as a process involving a period of blindness before the reception of the Spirit, also suggests that *katanuxis* plays a role in this conversion. One version of Paul's call narrative reveals that he was 'kicking against the goads (κέντρα)' (Acts 26:14). This piercing, coupled with the subsequent blindness, return of sight, and reception of the Holy Spirit conform Paul to the pattern of Isaiah in Isaiah 6 and of the people of Israel in Isa. 29:10 ff. All that has been said so far suggests, therefore, that when Romans 11 cites Isa. 29:10 ff. to explain Israel's blindness, this blindness also need not be interpreted in a negative way but rather as a phase in a cathartic process that prepares the one who experiences it to become a Servant of the Lord called, in turn, to bring *katanuxis*, light and salvation to the Gentiles. The next stage in this inquiry is to clarify that this is the meaning which Paul intends his reference to Israel's blindness and hardening in Romans 9–11 to carry.

One may begin by following Michel Remaud in noting that the use of the word 'mystery' in 11:25 to explain Israel's rejection of the Gospel as the result of a divinely sponsored 'rejection' and 'hardening' (11:7, 15, 25) hardly negates the idea that Israel remains for-ever dear to God (11:28) but allows it to play a providential role in the salvation of the Gentiles. Internal textual evidence for Paul's belief in this role is further suggested by the parallels between 11:12–15 and 5:10 evident in the role played in both by the terms καταλλάσσω (*reconciliation*) and ζωή (life). The first, 5:10, reads:

> For if, while we were enemies, we were *reconciled* (καταλλάγημεν) to God through the death of his Son, how much more can we be sure that, being now reconciled, we shall be saved through his *life* (ζωῆ)!

The second, 11:15, reads:

> Since their rejection meant the *reconciliation* (καταλλαγή) of the world, do you know what their re-acceptance will mean? Nothing less than *life* (ζωή) from the dead! (11:15).

(Remaud 2003: 29).

Remaud argues that as the world does not get reconciled twice, these moments of Christ's and Israel's rejection and restoration must be interrelated. Accordingly, the *rejection* and cutting off of the Servant, Christ and Israel, brings *reconciliation* to the world, while the lifting up of the Servant, in the resurrection of Christ and in the re-acceptance of Israel will bring *life* and *salvation*. The lifting up has begun with the resurrection of Christ, and its fruits bestowed secretly and germinally to humanity through the mystery of faith, but the goal of this uplifting and salvation has not yet been openly achieved, and Israel's tragic history is the bitter witness to this shortfall (Remaud 2003: 28–30).

Seeing a parallel between Christ's suffering at the hands of ancient Romans and Jews and Israel's suffering at the hands of Christians and Gentiles, Remaud proposes that, as all are shown to be guilty, those who contemptuously deem Israel to have 'stumbled so as to fall' and think that it has been rejected and accursed by God conform to the people Isaiah described as coming to understand in shame (Isa. 37:27; 41:11; 45:16–17) and dumbfounded astonishment or *katanuxis* (Isa. 47:5; 52:15), that the one whom they deemed to be forsaken by God in fact bore their iniquities (cf. Isa. 52:13–53:12). Remaud proceeds to explore how this reading resonates with the intuitions of Chagall and Maritain. One key issue here is whether the intuition, including the perception that Paul's thought is rooted in Isaiah, reflects Paul's own understanding.

The question can be resolved with the help of two fairly recent monographs on Paul's use of Scripture in Romans (Wagner 2002) and rhetorical, structural, and midrashic strategy in Romans 9–11 (Gadenz 2009).

Gadenz's study corroborates Remaud's idea that the correlation between 5:10 and 11:15 is intentional by highlighting a second parallel between Christ and Israel in the echo of 8:32 ('He who did not spare his own Son but gave him up for us all, will he not also give us all things with him?') at 11:21 ('For if God did not spare [οὐκ ἐφείσατο] the natural branches, neither will he spare you'). Weighing the arguments of scholars who suggest on the basis of this parallel that Israel, like Christ, suffers vicariously for the world (Hays 1993: 61–2; Donaldson 1993: 94, 1997: 223) and authors who think that the primary parallel in Romans 11:21 concerns hardened Israel and potentially backsliding Gentile Christians (e.g. Moo 1996: 706; Wright 2002: 685; Jewett 2007: 689), Gadenz adds weight to the former by noting that the 'life from the dead' image for Israel's restoration in 11:15 suggests that Israel's 'not being spared' at 11:21, together with its coming back to 'life from the dead', follows the pattern of Christ's death and resurrection.

To be sure, Paul first applied this pattern to the individual baptized Christian at Rom. 6:31 but this point corroborates that Paul's correlation of Christ's and Israel's suffering and resurrection, respectively, was intentional. For as Gadenz shows, 8:32 is part of a longer explanation in 8:31–7 that believers who suffer do so with Christ (8:17–18; cf. Gal. 3:13) on their way to glorious victory with Him (8:37). This passage strengthens further the links between Christ's and Israel's suffering because 8:35 lists the roots of six of the seven terms associated with the curses of Deut. 26–8, 30–2 (Münderlein 1965: 136–42; Waters 2006: 251; Gadenz 2009). Cognates of the term that cannot be traced to Deuteronomy, 'danger' (κίνδυνος), appeared in 1 Cor. 15:30–1 (see also 2 Cor. 11:26). This passage, by explaining Paul dies daily (καθ᾽ ἡμέραν ἀποθνῄσκω) on account of these dangers, anticipated the progression of thought in Romans where, after the tribulation list of 8:35, Paul cites the phrase 'we are slain all the day long' (θανατούμεθα ὅλην τὴν ἡμέραν) from the national psalm of lament (Ps. 43:23 LXX; M.T. 44:22). This is the psalm which Benedict used at Auschwitz-Birkenau. Consequently, like the individual Christians who share in Christ's sonship (Rom. 8:15) but nonetheless 'die' with Christ in Rom. 8:17, 35 (cf. 1 Cor. 15, 31), so in Romans 9–11, during the interval time between its current experience of the Exile and other Deuteronomic curses and its restoration, Israel shares in the sonship along with Christ (Rom. 9:4), is not spared like him (Rom 8:32; 11:21), but in this way arrives like him at life from the dead (11:15). By citing the national lament Psalm 44 (LXX 43), 8:36 provides further scriptural context for understanding how Romans 9–11 presents Israel's hardening. To cite Hays: 'If exilic Israel's suffering is interpreted by the psalmist not as punishment but as suffering for the sake of God's name, then perhaps even the temporary unbelief of Israel can be understood as part of God's design to encompass Jews and Gentiles alike with his mercy' (Hays 1993: 57–61).

Wagner's work on Paul's use of Scripture in Romans 9–11 and the relevant part of the epilogue in 15:7–13, demonstrates that Paul invoked all three parts of the canon, and key figures therein, but especially Moses and Isaiah and clarifies his intentions in doing so by identifying how he personally altered his citations of the LXX text. Six sets of these alterations may be summarized here.

(1) The first set, the citations in Rom. 9:13 of Mal. 1:23 (᾽Ιακὼβ ἠγάπασα τὸν δὲ ᾽Ησαῦ ἐμίσησα) and in Rom. 9:25 of Hosea 1:9–10; 2:1, 23, explains the relationship between the Gentiles and Jews in divine providence. Paul cites Malachi to explain that the Gentiles, represented by Esau, were formerly rejected vis-à-vis the Jews, represented by Jacob, and then cites Hosea to announce the reversal of their rejection, geographically universalizing Hosea's prophecy in the process by changing Hosea 1:10 to read 'wherever (οὗ ἐάν)

(rather than "in the place where") it was said to you are not my people ... they will be called sons of God ...'.

(2) Rom. 10:15, 16 repeats this good news by broadening the announcement in Isa. 52:7 of the redemption heralded at Isa. 40:1–9 to include the Gentiles. The broadening techniques involve omitting the link with the mountains of Jerusalem, sounding the word gospel, not sounded since 2:16, and pluralizing 'herald' to interpret Isaiah as a prophet of Paul's own mission, a device repeated at 10:16 by citing Isa. 53:1; 'Who Has believed *our* message?' These alterations of Isaiah make Christ the fulfillment of the Servant Song of 52:13–53:12 and stress that Israel's unbelief was prophesied and is part of God's design.

(3) Even more radically, the conclusion of the second section, at 10:19–21, states that Moses and Isaiah both witness that Israel knew from Scripture that the Gentiles would obtain *righteousness* first. The Song (Deut. 32), placed by Moses in Israel's mouth, teaches that the curses for rebellion are a fait accompli and compares Israel to both an unfaithful wife and contemptuous children who make God jealous and angry and prompt him in turn to provoke Israel for the sake of its salvation with jealousy for 'no-people' (32:21). Having noted earlier in 1 Cor. 10:20–2 that Deut. 32:21 is of interest to Isaiah (65:1), Paul cites the latter here to observe that Israel resists the grace which God shows the Gentiles.

(4) Isaiah's importance grows in ch. 11, where vv. 7–10, 12, 15 stress how Moses (Deut. 29:4; 32:21), and Isaiah (Isa. 29:10), reversing the hardening oracle of Isa. 6, declare that the purpose of the blinding and hardening will be to bring grace to the Gentiles and lead to a full reconciliation and renewal of creation (11:12, 15). Rom. 11:25–7 broadens the ambit of covenantal grace by changing Isa. 59:20 to read not 'to Zion' but 'from Zion' and by working in the promise of an abiding spirit into the echo of the little Apocalypse of Jer. 31–7.

(5) Finally, within the summation of the epistle's message, in 15:21, Paul cites Isa. 52:15b and 53:1. The former verse completes the prologue to the Servant Song, and follows the announcement in 52:15a that 'many Gentiles will be amazed at him and kings shall shut their mouths'. The latter verse commences the Servant Song itself (53:1–12), building thereby on 10:15–16 but also on 4:25, and 8:32 where Paul spoke of Jesus being 'handed over for us/for our transgressions', corroborating that Isaiah's Servant Song is central to Paul.

(6) The relative absence of citations between 11:14 and 11:25 is deemed by Wagner to be a function of Paul's extended exposition of the unusual agricultural metaphor about the branches. This is a point of significant disagreement between him and Gadenz. Noting that the term 'mystery' in the proto-Pauline letters always refers to something previously hidden but now revealed by God and belonging to the end times, Gadenz sides with scholars who deem that the 'mystery' which Paul announces in v. 25 is not anticipated by Scripture, not grounded on scriptural prophecy but is something new, belonging to Christian revelation, and revealed, specifically, via Paul (vv. 25b–26a) (for extensive list of scholars, see Gadenz 2009: 210–11, nn. 149, 150).

In response to scholars who trace Paul's mystery in 11:25 to his study of Israel's Scriptures (again, see extensive n. 149 in Gadenz 2009: 210) and/or adduce parallels from Isaiah and Qumran (including Isa. 44:21; 45:17.25 and 1QpHab VII, 4–5), Gadenz contends that the scriptural text in question should support all three clauses of the mystery (2009: 210, n. 149). Accordingly, the text must announce (a) Israel's total salvation (b) after a period of hardening that (c) ends with the attainment of the fullness of the Gentiles. Gadenz next underscores that Pauline references to 'mystery' (in the singular) are never otherwise supported by Scripture, a phenomenon with parallels at Qumran, but conceptually traceable to Daniel 2 and 4:6 (9) (cf. Wis. 2, 22; 6, 22) which declares that God has kept some mysteries hidden. Gadenz then concludes that the purpose of the Scriptures cited must not, ultimately, reveal or witness to the mystery he is presenting but lend authority to his testimony (Gadenz 2009: 209–13).

The point that Paul's announcements of the revelation of 'mystery' are elsewhere unattested by Scripture seems sound, and such usage may be dependent on Daniel and Qumran. However, revelation of mysteries in dreams in Daniel 2 and 4, like *pesher* exegesis at Qumran is a two-stage process: The first stage is the presentation of the mystery in a bound and sealed form; the second is their opening, which is the meaning of *pesher*. This concept accords with Paul's frequent references to Isa. 8:16 and 29:11, verses which speak of the sealing and binding of revelation and of Israel's current inability to see it. Consequently, if Paul's concept of the mystery is dependent on Daniel and Qumran, it may be anticipated in Scripture but in a hidden, bound form whose opening requires another stage of inspired revelation. As for the demand that the text in question must contain all three elements of the mystery, it falls before Wagner's demonstration that Paul adduces witnesses from each part of the canon to underscore that Israel *has heard and known* the message. Moses, in Deuteronomy, announced the temporary hardening via jealousy of the nations. Isaiah announced temporary hardening and blinding for the sake of bringing light to the nations. Given Paul's work in coordinating these verses, and insistence that *having heard* them Israel knows the message, there is no need to find one verse that contains all of these ideas. Moreover, if the function of the Scriptures is simply to authenticate the messenger, the mode by which all the Scriptures cited accomplish this must be clarified.

This issue relates to the question why the long passage preceding the announcement of the mystery in v. 25 lacks citations of Scripture. Gadenz thinks it's because the revelation of which Paul speaks is not in Scripture but in Paul's own life. If this were so, the contents of this passage should relate to a revelatory experience of Paul's. The section is one extended simile concerning what Wagner characterizes as pertaining to 'the Lord's unorthodox husbandry'. It does seem rather mysterious, and unattested by Scripture. For this very reason it seems a better candidate for the hypothetical revelation unattested by Scripture than the concepts of Israel bringing light to the nations whilst being hardened and blind, all of which have scriptural antecedents. Despite this difference, however, both sets of images share the 'hardening' theme because the 'hardening and blinding' of Israel is comparable to the 'hardened and dead' branches and the purpose of both is to vivify and graft in the Gentiles prior to the regrafting and revivification of Israel. This thematic connection suggests that the mystery which the demonstrative τοῦτο denotes in v. 25 refers not just to the announcements of vv. 25 and 26, ideas anticipated and explained by Scripture, but to the shocking and novel idea presented in the preceding extended metaphor of dead branches being restored to life. Moreover, if Paul really did use the term 'mystery' to speak of things newly and personally revealed, the unorthodox image of dead branches being revivified must have been given to Paul by personal revelation.

The argument implies that Paul's comparison of Israel's hardening and restoration to dead and regrafted branches is prompted both by Scripture and personal experience. This inference is appropriate to the context given the presence of two autobiographical *exempla* highlighted by Gadenz at 11:1b and 11:13–14. In the first Paul illustrates that hardened Israel can be saved because he, an Israelite who was formerly hostile to the Gospel, experienced God's mercy. In the second he develops his parallel between the manner of his salvation at the height of his zeal (Gal. 1:14–16), and that of the hardened part of Israel (Rom. 11:14; cf. 10:2). Gadenz concludes: 'As the verses represent Paul as a type of hardened Israel, they announce that salvation will ultimately come to hardened Israel (11:26) as it did for Paul on the road to Damascus, with the Lord Jesus appearing from the heavenly Zion' (Gadenz 2009: 217, n. 163).

This proposal begs for comparisons to details in accounts of Paul's call. If one searches among his own accounts, an interesting correspondence is offered by the call verse in 1 Cor. 15:8 as interpreted by Matthew W. Mitchell (2014) who stresses that the term ἔκτρωμα there means not 'untimely birth' but abortion or miscarriage, i.e., something dead, that was then brought back to life through his experience of the risen Christ. The correspondence between his being like an ἔκτρωμα in 1 Cor. 15:8 and his comparison of Israel to 'dead branches' in Romans 11 is thus very close. The contents of this correspondence are indeed a mystery which Paul claims he experienced through personal revelation but its contours and purpose are corroborated and illuminated by Scripture. Consequently, Pauline writings internal and external to Romans witness that his picture of Israel in Romans 9–11 is modeled on his own biography.

Another autobiographical narrative which contains piercing imagery suggestive of *katanuxis* and which may further explain the relationship between Paul's encounter with the divine and his Gentile mission is 2 Cor. 12:1–12. The mention of 'boasting' at the outset suggests the passage is autobiographical. The piercing imagery is that of the 'thorn in the flesh' (σκόλοψ τῇ σαρκί) alias an 'angel of Satan' (2 Cor. 12:7) given to 'make strength perfect in weakness'. The 'thorn' and the 'angel' could be interpreted as an idiom for an enemy (cf. Ezek. 2:6), but the theme of heavenly ascent prompts Morray-Jones to suggest a link with the Hekhalot tradition according to which the angel would be an angelic gatekeeper of the divine throne tasked with attacking those deemed unworthy to ascend to it (Morray-Jones 1980: 33–40; cf. Windisch 1924: 382–90). This explanation identification correlates with the imagery of Isaiah 6 since the Seraphim may be identified with serpentine genii-guardians of the divine throne. Echoes of Isaiah 6 are indeed present in references to 'seeing the Lord', 'being sent' 'far away' to people who 'will not accept your testimony' (Morray-Jones 1980: 296 citing Betz 1970). Of interest here also is Morray-Jones' observation that the pattern of experiencing the divine conforms to Paul's concept of glorification through suffering (Rom. 8:29; 2 Cor. 3:18), according to which, the inner, heavenly, personality is conformed to the image of Christ-as-*kabod*/glory, characterized by *power*, while the earthly personality is conformed to that of the earthly Jesus, characterized by *weakness* (2 Cor. 12:9–11) as also echoed in passages such as 2 Cor. 4:18 ('while we live, we are always being given up to death for Jesus' sake, so that the life of Jesus may be made visible in our mortal flesh'; cf. Gal. 2:20; Eph. 2:6 and 4:24). Noting the Temple link and the theme of ascent, Morray-Jones steers away from proposals to identify it with the Damascus experience (Tabor 1986: 32–4; Segal 1992: 34–71) and directs his attention to Acts 22 which describes a vision Paul had during his first post-conversion visit to Jerusalem, dated by Galatians to three years after the conversion (1:18) and fourteen years prior to his second visit (Gal. 2:1).

> In the context of this speech (Acts 22), the implied reference to these verses of condemnation of Israel (Isaiah) and predicted destruction of the Jewish state amounts to a statement that the divine glory (Christ) has abandoned Israel in favor of the nations. Thus, whereas Isaiah was sent to Israel, Paul is sent to the Gentiles. This radical interpretation of the prophetic account explains the anger of his listeners (Acts 22:22), and it is intriguing to note that this anger is expressed in the language reminiscent of *m. Hag.* 2.1C: 'And whoever is not careful about the glory of his creator, it were fitting for him that he had not come into the world.'
>
> (Morray-Jones 1993: 287)

He concludes that Acts 22 contains an autobiographical layer including the account of the outraged response of a Jewish, probably Pharisaic audience, and that it was his intense frustration with them on this occasion, and not the Damascus road event, that drove him to develop such a radical interpretation of Isaiah 6. However, the reasoning is circular. If Paul angered his audience by his radical interpretation of Isaiah, he must have developed it earlier on the basis of parallels between some earlier revelatory experience and his understanding of Isaiah (and perhaps Ezekiel, again cf. Ezek. 2:6). The theme of going to the Gentiles is common to the Damascus experience.

Luke's account of the Damascus event at Acts 26:14 contains an even clearer instance of *katanuxis* in the declaration that Paul has been 'kicking against the goads', in the description of his subsequent blindness, reception of the Spirit at baptism, and recovery of sight, a pattern that echoes the linkage between *katanuxis* and the reception of the Holy Spirit at Acts 2:37.

Were I allowed a moment of speculation on the nature of the goads against which Paul was kicking, I would propose that, in the context of Acts, these relate to Paul's jealousy of Stephen and consternation over his role in Stephen's death. For Luke's comparison of Stephen's face to that of an angel at the time of his martyrdom is told from his persecutors' point of view, the ultimate source of which eyewitness memory for the Christian community and Luke should have been Paul. The grace and glory of the visage of Christ on Stephen's face, reflected in Stephen's plea for forgiveness of his persecutors, must have incited Paul to jealous anger and burned within him like hot coals and pierced him like sharp goads, whereby he discovered that God's strength was made perfect in weakness and that doing good to one's enemies is like heaping burning coals upon their heads (Rom. 12:20).

This exploration may now be concluded. Remaud's attempt to ground the intuitions and reflections expressed by Chagall, Maritain, or Edith Stein regarding the interconnection of Christ's redemptive suffering with the suffering of Israel is borne out by the latest biblical scholarship on Romans 9–11. As argued by Paul, Christ's suffering, death, and resurrection fulfills the mission of Israel prophesied in all three parts of the canon. Accordingly, every individual disciple of Christ is given to receive eternal life and glory by uniting himself to Christ through suffering, *katanuxis*/compunction, and reception of the Holy Spirit, but Israel as a people is also intimately connected with this saving mission. If its hardening and blindness signifies the experience of Deuteronomic curses, this experience is also redemptive for the world. Jesus Christ came to accomplish Israel's mission in his body, and Israel in its body completes and advances the mission of Christ. For this reason, all attempts to read Paul's description of Israel as blind, hardened, and stupefied in a supersessionistic manner are offensive to Pauline Christology.

Why Jesus' Jewishness Matters

This chapter has formulated an argument based on Romans 9–11 explaining what Rahner *should* have said in response to Lapide's question about the significance of Jesus' Jewishness. Instead of saying that Jesus' rootedness in Israel's history was an arbitrary coincidence without any theological value (on account of the deficiency in the development of this doctrine), Rahner *could* have said that Christ's Jewishness is important Christologically and soteriologically because Christ fulfills Israel's soteriological role in history and because Israel, in turn, advances Christ's mission. This answer may therefore illuminate the explanation furnished by Fr. Lombardi, the papal secretary, after Benedict had condemned Holocaust denial, as to why this denial fails to grasp the mystery of Christ's suffering:

> Before this double mystery—of the horrible power of evil and the apparent absence of God—the only response of the Christian faith is the passion of the Son of God . . .. These are the most profound and decisive questions of man and of the believer before the world and history. We can't, and shouldn't avoid them, and much less deny them. On the contrary, our faith would become deceitful and empty . . .. Those who deny the Holocaust don't know anything about the mystery of God, nor of the cross of Christ. It's even more grave when the denial comes from the mouth of a priest or bishop, that is, from a Christian minister, be he united or not to the Catholic Church.
>
> (Zenit.org 2009)

Fr. Lombardi's stress on the need to relate the Holocaust to the Cross of Christ should be understood in the context of the faith reflections on Jewish suffering by John Paul II, probably, as argued in this chapter, grounded on Isaiah 53, and by Benedict XVI, explicitly grounded on Psalm 44. These statements develop the intuitions of Maritain and Edith Stein that Jewish suffering is Messianic and intimately connected with the suffering of Christ. Michel Remaud provided scriptural backing for this intuition on the strength of Romans 9–11, on the strength of two parallel verses in Romans, and on the presumption that this parallelism was grounded on the theology of Israel and Christ as both fulfilling the type of Isaiah's Suffering Servant for Paul. The latter half of this study develops this argument by showing, on the strength of more recent scholarship, further intertextual evidence suggesting that Paul intentionally correlated the death of Christ with Israel's hardening, grounding the argument on the Song of Moses in Deuteronomy, Isaiah's Servant Songs, and Psalm 44. He was prompted to do so, moreover, on account of his personal experience of the resurrected and glorified Christ. Paul's dead and revived-branches metaphor to explain the mystery of Israel's mission in history is thus rooted in and modeled on his own personal experience of death and resurrection in Christ. In Romans, Paul stresses that Christ's suffering is bound up with the suffering of all human beings, with all individual Christians who suffer knowingly with him, but also with the corporate suffering of his people, experienced darkly and unknowingly. That dark suffering fulfills prophecy and touches deeply on Christology. Consequently, when Christians engage in Holocaust denial and revisionism they express a Jew-hatred that fails to be touched and humanized by Christ's Passion and offends Christian Christology.

Suggested Reading

Pius XI (1938); Remaud (2003).

Bibliography

Aletti, J.-N. (1998), *Israël et la Loi dans la Lettre aux Romains* (Paris: Cerf).

Bell, R. (1994), *Provoked to Jealousy: The Origin and Purpose of the Jealousy Motif in Romans 9–11* (Tübingen: Mohr Siebeck).

Bell, R. (2005), *The Irrevocable Call of God: An Inquiry into Paul's Theology of Israel* (Tübingen: Mohr Siebeck).

Benedict XVI (2006), 'Pastoral Visit of his Holiness Pope Benedict XVI in Poland: Address by the Holy Father: Visit to the Auschwitz Camp'. <http://www.vatican.va/holy_father/benedict_xvi/speeches/2006/may/documents/hf_ben-xvi_spe_20060528_auschwitz-birkenau_en.html> (accessed July 14, 2014).

Benedict XVI (2009), 'Address of His Holiness Benedict XVI to Members of the Delegation of the "Conference of Presidents Of Major American Jewish Organizations"'. <http://www.vatican.va/holy_father/benedict_xvi/speeches/2009/february/documents/hf_ben-xvi_spe_20090212_jewish-organizations_en.html> (accessed July 14, 2014).

Betz, O. (1970), 'Die Vision des Paulus im Tempel von Jerusalem: Apg. 22.17–21 als Beitrag zur Deutung des Damaskuserlebnisses', in O. Böcher and K. Haacker (eds.), *Verborum Veritas, FS Gustav Stählin zum 70. Geburtstag* (Wuppertal: Brockhaus), 113–23.

Butticaz, S. (2012), '"Has God Rejected His People?" (Romans 11.1). The Salvation of Israel in Acts: Narrative Claim of a Pauline Legacy', in D. P. Moessner, D. Marguerat, M. C. Parsons, and M. Wolter (eds.), *Paul and the Heritage of Israel: Paul's Claim upon Israel's Legacy in Luke and Acts in the Light of the Pauline Letters* (London: T. & T. Clark), 148–64.

Cunningham, P. A. (2012), 'Paul's Letters and the Relationship between the People of Israel and the Church Today', in R. Bieringer and D. Pollefeyt (eds.), *Paul and Judaism: Crosscurrents in Pauline Exegesis and Study* (London: T. & T. Clark), 141–62.

Donaldson, T. L. (1993), '"Riches for the Gentiles" (Rom 11:12): Israel's Rejection and Paul's Gentile Mission', *Journal of Biblical Literature* 112: 81–98.

Donaldson, T. L. (1997), *Paul and the Gentiles: Remembering the Apostle's Convictional World* (Minneapolis: Fortress).

Foxman, A. (2007), 'Latin Mass Cause for Concern'.<http://www.adl.org/press-center/c/latin-mass-cause-for-concern.html> (accessed July 14, 2014). Originally appeared in Jewish Telegraphic Agency on July 11, 2007.

Gadenz, P. (2009), *Called From the Jews and the Gentiles: Pauline Ecclesiology in Romans 9–11* (Tübingen: Mohr Siebeck).

Glazov, G. (2001), *The Bridling of the Tongue and the Opening of the Mouth in Biblical Prophecy* (Sheffield: Sheffield Academic Press).

Hays, R. B. (1993), *Echoes of Scripture in the Letters of Paul* (New Haven: Yale University Press).

Henrix, H. H. (2011), 'The Son of God Became Human as a Jew: Implications of the Jewishness of Jesus for Christology', in P. A. Cunningham, J. Sievers, M. Boys, H. H. Henrix, and J. Svartvik (eds.), *Christ Jesus and the Jewish People Today: New Explorations of Theological Relationships* (Grand Rapids, Mich.: Eerdmans), 114–43.

Heschel, A. J. (1991), 'No Religion Is an Island', in H. Kasimow and B. L. Sherwin (eds.), *No Religion Is an Island: Abraham Joshua Heschel and Interreligious Dialogue* (Maryknoll, NY: Orbis Books), 3–22.

Hofius, O. (1986), 'Das Evangelium und Israel. Erwägungen zu Römer 9–11', *Zeitschrift für Theologie und Kirche* 83: 297–324.

Jewett, R. (2007), *Romans: A Commentary* (Minneapolis: Hermeneia).

John Paul II (1988), 'Meeting with the Representatives of the Jewish Communities in the Apostolic Nunciature in Vienna [24 June 1988]' [In German and Italian]. <http://www.vatican.va/holy_father/john_paul_ii/speeches/1988/june/> (accessed July 14, 2014).

John Paul II (1999), 'Apostolic Letter Issued *Motu Proprio* Proclaiming Saint Bridget of Sweden Saint Catherine of Sienna and Saint Teresa Benedicta of the Cross Co-Patronesses of Europe [1 October 1999]'. <http://www.vatican.va/holy_father/john_paul_ii/motu_proprio/documents/hf_jp-ii_motu-proprio_01101999_co-patronesses-europe_en.html> (accessed July 18, 2014).

John Paul II (2006), 'Visit to Jordan, Israel and the Palestinian Authority: A Pilgrimage of Prayer, Hope and Reconciliation, ADL'. <http://www.adl.org/interfaith/JohnPaul_II_Visit.pdf> (accessed July 30, 2014).

Klenicki, L. (2006), 'Pope John Paul II: Visit to Jordan, Israel, and the Palestinian Authority: A Pilgrimage of Prayer, Hope and Reconciliation'. <http://archive.adl.org/interfaith/johnpaul_ii_visit.pdf> (accessed July 30, 2014).

Lapide, P. E. (1968), *Three Popes and the Jews* (New York: Hawthorn Books).

Levine, A.-J. (2006), *The Misunderstood Jew: The Church and the Scandal of the Jewish Jesus* (New York: HarperCollins).

Mitchell, M. W. (2014), *Abortion and the Apostolate: A Study in Pauline Conversion, Rhetoric and Scholarship* (Piscataway, NJ: Gorgias Press).

Moo, D. J. (1996), *The Epistle to the Romans* (Grand Rapids, Mich.: Eerdmans).

Morray-Jones, C. R. A. (1993), 'Paradise Revisited (2 Cor 12:1–12): The Jewish Mystical Background of Paul's Apostolate*: Part 1: The Jewish Sources', *Harvard Theological Review* 86: 177–217.

Munck, J. (1959), 'Paulus Tanquam Abortivus', in A. J. Brockhurst (ed.), *New Testament Essays: Essays in Memory of T. W. Manson, 1893–1958* (Manchester: Manchester University Press), 180–93.

Münderlein, G. (1965), 'Interpretation einer Tradition. Bemerkungen zu Röm 8,35f', *Kerygma und Dogma* 11: 136–42.

Oesterreicher, J. M. (1986), *The New Encounter Between Christians and Jews* (New York: Philosophical Library).

Pius XI (1938), 'Speech to Belgian Pilgrims 1938'. Originally published in French in *La Libre Belgique* (September 14, 1938) and *La Documentation Catholique*, 39 (1938): cols. 1459–60. Available online as 'Spiritually We Are Semites'. <http://www.ccjr.us/dialogika-resources/ primary-texts-from-the-history-of-the-relationship/1255-pius-xi1938sept6> (accessed July 14, 2014).

Remaud, M. (2003), *Chrétiens devant Israël serviteur de Dieu* (orig. Paris: Cerf 1983). Trans. Margaret Ginzburg and Nicole François as *Israel, Servant of God* (London: T. & T. Clark).

Rychlak, R. J. (2010), *Hitler, the War, and the Pope: Revised and Expanded* (Huntington, Ind.: Our Sunday Visitor).

Segal, A. F. (1992), *Paul the Convert: The Apostolate and Apostasy of Saul the Pharisee* (New Haven: Yale University Press).

Tabor, J. D. (1986), *Things Unutterable: Paul's Ascent to Paradise in Its Graeco-Roman, Judaic and Early Christian Contexts* (New York: University Press of America).

Theobald, M. (2009), 'Unterschiedliche Gottesbilder in Röm 9–11? Die Israel-Kapitel als Anfrage an die Einheit des theologischen Diskurses bei Paulus', in U. Schnelle (ed.), *The Letter to the Romans* (Leuven: Leuven University Press), 135–77.

Vereb, J. M. (2006), *"Because He Was a German!": Cardinal Bea and the Origins of Roman Catholic Engagement in the Ecumenical Movement* (Grand Rapids, Mich.: Eerdmans).

Wagner, R. (2002), *Heralds of the Good News: Isaiah and Paul in Concert in the Letter to the Romans* (Leiden: Brill).

Waters, G. (2006), *The End of Deuteronomy in the Epistles of Paul* (Tübingen: Mohr Siebeck).

Windisch, H. (1924), *Der zweite Korintherbrief* (Göttingen: Vandenhoeck & Ruprecht).

Wright, N. T. (2002), 'The Letter to the Romans: Introduction, Commentary, and Reflections', *New Interpreter's Bible* 10: 393–770.

Zenit.org (2009), 'Father Lombardi Denounces Holocaust-Deniers', January 30. <http:// www.zenit.org/en/articles/father-lombardi-denounces-holocaust-deniers> (accessed July 14, 2014).

CHAPTER 4

THE GOSPELS AS TESTIMONY TO JESUS CHRIST

A Contemporary View of their Historical Value

RICHARD J. BAUCKHAM

HISTORY AS A CHRISTOLOGICAL ISSUE

THE figure whom Christians call Jesus the Messiah (Christ), the man whose teaching and example they seek to follow, the man in whom they find God manifest and whom they therefore include in their worship of God, the incarnate divine Son in whom they believe, is the Jesus presented to us in the New Testament. The four Gospels tell the story of his earthly life in human history and indicate that he is not merely a figure of the past but also the living Lord, risen from death, exalted to share God's rule over the cosmos. Over the centuries, creeds and traditional doctrine have sought to clarify understanding, but the Gospels remain indispensable because they recount the history of Jesus.

In the process that led to the Church's acceptance of these four Gospels as authentic and to the exclusion of other gospels, the principal criterion of selection was apostolicity. This did not mean that all the authors were apostles (Mark and Luke were not) but that they were all 'apostolic persons', people who, if not themselves apostles, were close to the followers of Jesus, the eyewitnesses of his history. These Gospels were valued because they embodied the testimony of those who were close to Jesus and participated in his history. These apostolic eyewitnesses were understood to be reliable both as witnesses to the events and as witnesses to the meaning of the events. As in all historiography, so also in the Gospels fact and interpretation are interwoven. Christians have always recognized this. It is because the Gospels are regarded as apostolic testimony about Jesus' historicity and his meaning that Christians have trusted them as reliable portrayals of Jesus.

As historiography, albeit history with a message, the Gospels make historical claims that cannot be immune from historical investigation. Theologians in the early centuries, such as Augustine, were not oblivious to historical issues in the Gospels. It was only with the eighteenth-century Enlightenment that some intellectuals began to use historical enquiry to reconstruct a historical figure different from the Jesus the Gospels portray. This was the beginning of the so-called 'quest of the historical Jesus', which, through many vicissitudes, has continued down to the present day. It was the result of two developments. One was the rise of critical historiography, with its propensity to interrogate historical records in the attempt to reconstruct 'what really happened'. The other was the Enlightenment's rejection of traditional authority, including that of the Church. For many of those engaged in the quest, its goal was to strip away the early Christian interpretation of Jesus in order to discover a 'real Jesus' quite different from the Christ of the Church's dogma. For many of these scholars, such as the German liberals of the nineteenth century, Jesus was a figure of religious inspiration for faith and practice, but one who is a purely human example and ethical teacher, a Jesus they found credible, unlike the divine Christ of traditional belief. While others have joined the quest expecting to verify the historical basis for the Christ of traditional faith, the quest for a more credible or congenial Jesus has taken ever-changing forms down to the present. It is just as easy to attribute anti-dogmatic or anti-conservative bias to those who find a Jesus different from the Gospels' portrayal as it is to attribute conservative bias to those who find a Jesus compatible with the Gospels.

The question the quest raises for Christian faith and theology is how to deal with the distinction between 'the Jesus of history' and 'the Christ of faith'. Here 'the Christ of faith' refers to Jesus as he is presented to us in the New Testament, Jesus as the object of Christian faith. The Gospels' account of the earthly Jesus, with its obvious historical claims, belongs essentially to who the Christ of faith is. The 'Jesus of history' or 'historical Jesus' refers to the Jesus whom historians reconstruct, using historical methods to get back behind the way the Gospels portray him. The reconstructions of the historical Jesus that the quest has produced are so enormously varied that 'the historical Jesus' has to be defined as: whatever sort of Jesus any particular historian reconstructs. If the quest is to be judged by its success in establishing even a minimal, generally agreed account of the historical Jesus, then it must be judged a failure.

For all history involves interpretation. This is not to deny that historians can establish beyond reasonable doubt some basic facts about Jesus, for example, that he died on a Roman cross, that his home town was Nazareth in Galilee, that he was a teacher with disciples, and so forth. (History can deal only in probabilities, not certainties, but sometimes the probabilities are so high as to be beyond reasonable doubt.) But such facts are of no real interest unless they form the framework for an account that answers such questions as why he was put to death, what he taught, what he understood his mission to be, how he was related to his context (social, political, economic, religious). Only answers to such questions can give us a historical Jesus, but answering such questions entails judgements on which historians will differ for various reasons.

We should not emphasize the subjective element in historical reconstruction to the point of supposing that historical Jesus scholars necessarily find merely the sort of Jesus they want to find. Even when this happens, it does not preclude the possibility that they could be right, and, as in all historical enquiry, it is the arguments that matter. Arguments can be assessed on their merits, irrespective of the motives of the scholar who presents them. Nevertheless, it remains the case that every historical reconstruction of Jesus is an interpretation of him, unavoidably influenced both by different judgements of the evidence and by different approaches to faith and life. For almost all historical Jesus scholars, the stakes in this particular historical enquiry are high, whether in relation to their own religious faith or to that of others. Most of them are not trained historians as such, but trained biblical scholars, who have learned their practice of history only from others who work in this particularly specialized field.

The quest has usually entailed attempts to distinguish between historically reliable and historically unreliable material in the Gospels. It has been assumed that, because the Gospels are Christian interpretations of Jesus, they must incorporate material that reflects only that interpretation, not the history of Jesus. The way to get closer to history therefore seems to be to filter out the reliable material from the mass of unreliable. There is a close relationship between the selection of reliable material and the overall interpretation of Jesus a particular historian propounds. By comparison with the Jesus of the Gospels, any such historical reconstruction of Jesus will appear both reductive (taking account only of some of the contents of the Gospels) and also an interpretation rivalling those of the Gospel writers.

Faced with an ever-changing assortment of historical Jesuses, there are theologians and biblical scholars who conclude simply that the quest of the historical Jesus is of no relevance to the Church, whose Jesus is the Christ of faith, to be found in the New Testament and the Creeds (e.g., Johnson 1996; McKnight 2012). It is also possible to agree that the Jesus in whom Christians believe is the Jesus of the Gospels, and that no historical reconstruction of Jesus can be a substitute for the Christ of faith, but also to allow some place for historical reconstruction. What is sought here is a minimal historical reconstruction that is *compatible* with the Jesus of the Gospels. This might at least show that what historians can establish about Jesus is *open to* the interpretation of Jesus the Gospels give (cf. Bock and Webb 2009). While there may be some value in this approach, it is doubtful how far it can progress beyond a small collection of facts about Jesus without issues of interpretation colouring the reconstruction and precluding general agreement on it.

In my book *Jesus and the Eyewitnesses* (Bauckham 2006) I suggested that there is a way beyond the alternative of 'the Jesus of history' and 'the Christ of faith'. The category that does better justice to how the Gospels combine history and theology is 'the Jesus of testimony'. I propose that we can return to the original and traditional view of the Gospels as apostolic testimony, but in a way that takes up the challenge of modern historical approaches to the Gospels by arguing that the Gospels are a particular kind of historiography. Diverging from what has been the dominant paradigm in Gospel studies since the early twentieth century, I see the Gospels as embodying the eyewitness testimony of those who had known Jesus and interpreted him in a way that grew out of their own experience of him and his history. To explain this view, I first portray the dominant paradigm—a view of the transmission of the Gospel traditions that understood the Gospel texts to be remote from the testimony of the eyewitnesses.

THE DOMINANT PARADIGM: FORM CRITICISM AND ITS CONSEQUENCES

The approach to the Gospels known as form criticism (*Formgeschichte*) was pioneered by Rudolf Bultmann and Martin Dibelius around 1920 (Dibelius 1919; Bultmann 1921). For the form critics the Gospels were folk literature, which they compared with the material studied by the folklorists of their day. They maintained that this type of oral tradition was formed and transmitted by the folk, not by individuals, and that the communities that valued such folklore had no interest in history. The Jesus traditions, they held, by analogy, were anonymous community traditions, not connected to individuals who had been eyewitnesses of Jesus' history, but only to the community itself. They were transmitted not by people concerned to relate past history, but for purposes oriented to the communities' present, and could therefore be freely modified or even created *de novo* in accordance with the community's present needs. It was in the form of this kind of tradition that the Jesus traditions reached the Gospel writers.

For many of the form critics there could be no quest for the historical Jesus. There was no means of reaching back to him behind the oral tradition. Bultmann opined that Christian faith is in the Christ of the apostolic kerygma and would be compromised by knowledge of a Jesus reconstructed by historians. Most scholars were not content to know so little about Jesus. Those who looked at it theologically were not so sure as Bultmann that Christian faith needed to know nothing about the Jesus who lived in Palestine except that he existed. But the form critical view of the way the Gospel traditions reached the Gospels hindered a new quest. Because the tradition was supposed to be oriented to the present and unconcerned with preservation of Jesus traditions, anything of historical value would have survived in spite of the tendencies of the tradition. So extremely rigorous criteria were needed to identify 'authentic' material. Moreover, because form criticism held that all the traditions about Jesus were passed on as single units (one story or one saying), it seemed that each unit had to be assessed individually.

This was the situation that the 'criteria of authenticity' were designed to meet. The two criteria of dissimilarity were crucial. Anything Jesus did or said that was uncharacteristic of both early Judaism and of early Christianity could be judged authentic. Anything early Christians would have felt uncomfortable saying about Jesus could be judged authentic. These were intended as extremely rigorous criteria, designed for the task of isolating indubitably authentic material in the mass of untrustworthy traditions. Only when these criteria made it possible to break through the barrier form criticism erected between the tradition and Jesus could other criteria (such as the criterion of coherence) come into play.

The criteria-based quest was unrealistic from the perspective of historical method. Faced with nothing but a mass of atomized units of tradition, not to be distinguished by the literary source from which they come and unaccompanied by any indications of their derivation, how is it conceivable that the 'authentic' and the 'inauthentic' could be distinguished? The results of such an approach to reconstructing the historical Jesus have been unsurprisingly diverse. Their application has proved too subjective to produce any consensus. There have been attempts to adjust or to reformulate the criteria (e.g., Wright 1996: 86, 131–3; Theissen and Winter 2002; Casey 2010: 101–41), but scholars have begun to acknowledge that the criteria are just not fit for purpose and the criteria-based quest has failed (see especially Keith and Le Donne 2012; also Rodríguez 2009; Dunn 2013: 282–5). An important strand of thought in this abandonment of the criteria-based approach is the recognition that the distinction between 'authentic' and 'inauthentic' material is simplistic. Since all Jesus traditions have reached us through the early Christians, we do not have any uninterpreted traditions (even a saying of Jesus memorized *verbatim* by the disciples and translated literally into Greek would have been selected as significant for handing on), but, on the other hand, it is a mistake to see interpretation as necessarily hindering our access to the 'real Jesus'. The traditions can be understood as witness to the 'impact' Jesus made on his followers (Dunn 2003) or as the way Jesus was interpreted in the memory of his disciples (Dunn 2003; Le Donne 2009).

The form critical paradigm was fatally flawed as a model of the way Jesus traditions reached the Gospels. The criteria-based quest has failed not because of the criteria but because of the view of the nature of the sources that form criticism bequeathed. In fact, form criticism's model of oral tradition has been discredited for compelling reasons (Dunn 2003: 193–5; Bauckham 2006: 241–9; Tuckett 2009). I have argued that the New Testament evidence points to a formally controlled tradition, such as can be found in many oral societies, but also that, in the period up to the writing of the Gospels, we must also reckon with the eyewitnesses. While the events of Jesus' story were within living memory, the eyewitnesses, many of whom were well known in the Christian movement, are likely to have been regarded as the accessible sources and authoritative guardians of the traditions that they themselves had formulated at the beginning (see also Gerhardsson 2001, 2005).

Paul, writing his first letter to the Corinthians around the year 53, little more than twenty years after the event, recites a well-known catalogue of people to whom Jesus appeared after the resurrection. Among them he mentions an appearance to five hundred believers at the same time, 'many of whom', he adds, 'are still alive' (1 Cor. 15:6). This comment would be pointless unless he meant, 'If you don't believe me, check it out with some of those people'. If he could say that with regard to minor eyewitnesses, as most of the five hundred must have been, how much more would it have been true of the major eyewitnesses, people such as the twelve apostles and James the brother of Jesus, whom Paul also includes in his list. He did not need to say that they were still alive and kicking at the time of writing because his readers knew it. That many eyewitnesses were not alive and accessible is taken for granted.

WHAT ARE THE GOSPELS?

Probably most scholars are convinced that the literary genre to which the Gospels belong is the Graeco-Roman biography (*bios*, the life of a famous person). Burridge (1992) has shown most fully that the Gospels share the major features of this genre, which must be distinguished from modern kinds of biography. But little attention has been paid to this in recent scholarship on Jesus and the Gospels. (Burridge's work and the Gospels as biography get scant attention in Dunn 2003: 184–6; Casey 2010: 184–5; Allison 2010: 441–4. Scholars advocating the use of social memory theory in historical Jesus studies seem uninterested in considering ancient biographies as embodiments of social memory with which the Gospels should be compared [Le Donne 2009; Keith 2011]. Watson's elaborate study of Gospel writing [Watson 2013] entirely ignores the biographical genre of the canonical Gospels. On the other hand, see Keener 2003: 3–52, 2009: 73–125, 2011; Eddy and Boyd 2007: 309–61.) But it is with the genre of the Gospels that we should start in considering the nature of their testimony to Jesus.

The biographical genre indicates the genuine interest of early Christians in the past of Jesus, although naturally this would be an interest in the past as relevant to the present. Moreover, as contemporary biographies, written within living memory of their subject or not long afterwards, they would be expected to share the best practice of contemporary historiography with regard to sources. The relative lack of documentary sources for ancient historians meant that good history could really only be written while eyewitness sources were accessible. A historian, preferably an eyewitness himself, should at least have been able to interview eyewitnesses face-to-face. This ancient historiographical practice resembled modern oral history. It was not always employed but it was regarded as historiographical best practice, to which historians at least paid lip service. It suggests that the relationship between the Jesus traditions in their oral form and their incorporation in the Gospels might be expected to resemble the relationship between eyewitness sources and their incorporation in ancient historiographical works, as Byrskog (2000) has argued. If some of the eyewitnesses themselves were accessible when the Gospel writers were collecting material for their Gospels then we should expect the Gospel writers to have treated them as their best available sources.

Literary genre conditions reader expectations, and so the first readers or hearers of the Gospels are likely to have expected them, as contemporary biographies, to embody eyewitness testimony. But here we should also take account of a specific notion about eyewitnesses that seems to have been current in the early Christian movement. In the first chapter of Acts, Luke tells the story of how Judas Iscariot was replaced by Matthias to make up the number of the twelve apostles. The qualification to be one of the twelve was that such a person must (as Peter says in the narrative) 'have accompanied us during all the time that the Lord Jesus went in and out among us, beginning from the baptism of John until the day that he was taken up from us' (Acts 1:21–2). The twelve apostles were the official body of eyewitnesses of Jesus, but the narrative also indicates that there were others beside the twelve who fulfilled that qualification. In the preface to his Gospel, Luke says that he has recorded traditions as they were transmitted by those 'who were eyewitnesses from the beginning' (Luke 1:2). (For the convention of beginning the story of Jesus from the time when John was baptizing, see also Acts 10:37; 13:23–5.) We also find the same principle in John's Gospel. In John 15:27 Jesus speaks to his disciples about the way they are to give testimony about him in the future: 'you are to testify because you have been with me from the beginning'. This idea that the best qualified eyewitnesses would be those who had followed Jesus from the beginning of his ministry to the end in fact coincides with the kind of qualification that mattered in ancient historiography that depended on eyewitness testimony (Bauckham 2009: 27). It shows that Gospel writers were intended to meet the expectations of readers who understood their work to be historical biography and would therefore look for indications of its sources in eyewitness testimony.

It does not follow that all the content of the Gospels derives from those who had been 'eyewitnesses from the beginning'. I have suggested that the use of personal names in the Gospels may preserve the identity of the eyewitnesses who first told some of the particular stories (Bauckham 2006: 39–55). There is an aspect of the occurrence of personal names in the Gospels that seems puzzling at first sight. It is not surprising that well-known public persons, such as Pontius Pilate the Roman governor and the high priest Caiaphas, are named in the Gospels. Nor is it surprising that disciples of Jesus who play a major part in the stories—Peter, Mary Magdalene, Thomas, and so on—are named. Nor perhaps is it very surprising that most of the more minor characters are anonymous. The Gospels are full of unnamed individuals who come into contact with Jesus on just one occasion. There is no reason why their names should have been remembered or regarded as particularly important. What is more difficult to explain is why just a few of these minor characters *are* given names. Why is it that in Mark's Gospel Jairus and Bartimaeus are named (Mark 6:3; 10:46), while all other recipients of Jesus' healings are anonymous? Why does Luke, in his narrative of the two disciples who met the risen Jesus on the way to Emmaus, name one of the two (Cleopas) (24:18) but not the other? Why does Mark go to the trouble of naming not only Simon of Cyrene, who carried Jesus' cross to Calvary, but also his two sons, Alexander and Rufus (15:21)? Why does Luke name Zacchaeus the tax collector and Simon the Pharisee (19:2; 7:40)? Given that a large majority of the minor characters in all the Gospels are anonymous, why do they name specifically those few who are named?

The only hypothesis I know that accounts for the evidence is that in most of these cases the named persons became members of the early Christian communities and themselves told the stories in which they appear in the Gospels. These traditions were transmitted under their names. It was from Bartimaeus himself that Mark's narrative of his healing came, and from Cleopas that Luke's story of the walk to Emmaus derived.

However, such names account for only a few passages in the Gospels. The persons in the Gospels who most obviously fall into the more important category of eyewitnesses, those who had been with Jesus 'from the beginning', are the twelve. All three of the Synoptic Gospels provide a full list of the members of this group (Matt. 10:2–4;

Mark 3:16–19; Luke 6:13–16). The lists seem carefully preserved, providing not only the bare personal names of the twelve (Simon, Judas, James, etc.), but also patronymics (such as 'sons of Zebedee') and nicknames (such as Peter) and other epithets (such as 'the Zealot'). Most of the personal names were extremely common ones and in some cases more than one of the twelve bore the same personal name. There had to be other ways of distinguishing one from another, and the various ways this is done in the lists correspond to Palestinian Jewish naming practices in this period. The lists appear to preserve the way each of the twelve was known within their circle during the ministry of Jesus. They are setting out the credentials of the eleven men (because the twelfth man in the lists is Judas Iscariot) who were regarded as the official body of witnesses, those who could vouch for the most important material incorporated by these three Gospels (Bauckham 2006: 93–113).

It is likely that the twelve, as the official body of eyewitnesses, at an early stage formulated a body of traditions deriving from their collective memories of Jesus, probably also drawing on the memories of other disciples of Jesus, especially the women disciples. The lists of the twelve in the Synoptics acknowledge their indebtedness to their common testimony. There is good reason to suppose that Mark's Gospel largely reflects Peter's particular version of the traditions of the twelve, a version in which he naturally prioritized his own personal memories.

Mark's Gospel as Peter's Testimony

Two of the Gospels explicitly claim to be based on eyewitness testimony. The conclusion to John's Gospel identified its author as the disciple it calls 'the disciple Jesus loved' (21:24). Alone among the Gospel writers, Luke provides the kind of historiographical preface in which an author might speak of his sources (Aune 2002; Adams 2006). Against the background of historiographical practice, his claim to record the events 'just as they were handed on to us by those who from the beginning were eyewitnesses and ministers of the word' (1:2) most naturally refers to his direct contact with the eyewitnesses, though it can also plausibly include his dependence on Mark's Gospel if he understood it as a record of eyewitness testimony.

By contrast, Mark's Gospel does not, to the average modern reader, appear to claim a basis in eyewitness testimony. But here is where the expectations of ancient readers or hearers of a historical biography, written within living memory of its subject, come into play, along with their probable knowledge of the Christian principle of 'eyewitnesses from the beginning'. Such readers/hearers would soon hear of the beginning of Jesus' ministry and then of Jesus' call of the first disciples. The first disciple of all, the first one to be mentioned in the Gospel, is the fisherman Simon, who later comes to be called also Peter. Mark lays special emphasis on Simon by repeating his name: 'Simon and Simon's brother Andrew' (1:16). It would have been more natural to say, 'Simon and his brother Andrew', as most modern English translations render it. The repetition of the name

Simon is no more natural in Greek than in English. It is repeated for emphasis. Mark is drawing special attention to the fact that Simon Peter is with Jesus 'from the beginning'. He also appears in the Gospel narrative more frequently than any other character except Jesus. He is the last disciple to be named in the Gospel, in fact the last person to be named (16:7).

This pattern of reference—first and last disciple to be named, with many appearances in between those two endpoints—marks Peter out as the character in the Gospel from whom Mark received most of his recorded traditions about Jesus. Another feature of Mark's narrative confirms this. There is a key part of the story from which all of the twelve, including Peter, are absent and could not have served as Mark's eyewitness sources. This part of the narrative, including the story of the crucifixion and death of Jesus, his burial and the discovery of the empty tomb, is such an important part of the whole Gospel narrative that eyewitness sources matter here more than anywhere. If not the twelve, who were they? The first readers or hearers would expect to know. This is where Simon of Cyrene comes in, along with his sons, through whom, presumably, his story reached Mark (15:21). Even more important are the women disciples, who in Mark appear only here. Three of them are carefully named (Mary Magdalene, Mary the mother of James and Joses, Salome). All three are said to be present at the Cross, two of these at the burial, and all three at the empty tomb. Mark specifies which of the women are present at each of the events (15:40, 47; 16:1). They are the subject of verbs of seeing: they 'were looking on' when Jesus was crucified and died; they 'saw' where he was laid in the tomb; they 'saw' the stone rolled away; they 'saw' the young man sitting on the right side; and he invites them to 'see' the empty place where Jesus' body had lain (15:40, 47; 16:4, 5, 6). They scarcely do anything else except watch and observe. It could hardly be clearer that it is as eyewitnesses that they have their place in the narrative.

The role of the women disciples confirms the impression that Peter, who is present through most of the Gospel apart from the clearly emphasized gap between 14:72 and 16:7, is Mark's major eyewitness source for most of the Gospel. The internal evidence of the Gospel is thus consistent with the early external evidence about the Gospel provided by Papias, bishop of Hierapolis, at the beginning of the second century (Bauckham 2006: 202–39). In a statement echoed by later writers in the early Church, Papias claimed that Mark had worked as Peter's interpreter and wrote down the Gospel traditions as Peter had recounted them. There was a time when most scholars thought this a plausible view of Mark's Gospel, but recently most have dismissed it. The form critical way of conceiving of Gospel origins forbids it. Now that the form critical paradigm is seen as defective, one can reconsider Papias' credibility.

Papias was collecting traditions about Jesus originating from named disciples of Jesus, a few of them still alive and resident not far from his home town, in the late first century, around the time when the Gospels of Matthew, Luke, and John were being written. He wrote (or completed) his book some years later, but it was in the late first century that he assembled his material (Bauckham 2006: 12–38). So he really was in a position to know something about how the Gospels originated, and his evidence about Mark's Gospel deserves to be taken more seriously than it has been in recent scholarship. But the plausibility of Papias' account emerges particularly strongly now that we can corre-late it with indications in Mark's Gospel that Peter is the key to its traditions.

John's Gospel as the Testimony of the Beloved Disciple

Despite its apparent claim to authorship by the disciple who appears in its narrative anonymously as 'the disciple Jesus loved' (21:24; cf. 1:14), many modern scholars find it inconceivable that this Gospel, so different from the Synoptics, could even be based on eyewitness testimony, let alone have an eyewitness as its author. This Gospel belongs no less evidently to the genre of ancient biography than do the others. Indeed, to early read-ers or hearers it would probably have appeared more like historiography than the other Gospels, especially in its much greater precision with regard to chronology and geogra-phy (Bauckham 2007: 93–112). The fact that this Gospel appears to be a more interpre-tative work than the others, the product of theological reflection, is not an obstacle to recognizing in it the eyewitness testimony of a disciple who claims intimacy with Jesus. His closeness may have made him feel authorized to interpret Jesus more profoundly than the other Gospel writers. At several points in the narrative where this disciple's presence is noted, he appears alongside Peter in a way that acknowledges Peter's eyewit-ness role but claims a greater perceptiveness as to the meaning of the events on the part of the Beloved Disciple (13:23–9; 20:4–9; 21:7).

The Gospel's eyewitness claim becomes more credible if we abandon the tradi-tional identification of the author as John the son of Zebedee, which is not what the earliest patristic evidence really proposes (Bauckham 2006: 412–71; 2007: 33–72), and follow the view that the Beloved Disciple is not as one of the twelve, but as a disciple normally resident in Jerusalem, who did not travel around with Jesus. This makes the differences in the narrative of events between this Gospel and the Synoptics intelligible. Unlike the Synoptics, John has no list of the twelve in his Gospel. This Gospel makes no claim to relay the official tradition of the twelve, like Mark and the two Gospels that incorporate much of Mark. Instead, if we consider the disciples who are prominent in John's narrative, we find that, apart from Peter and Mary Magdalene, they are disciples who are not prominent in the other Gospels (for example, Thomas, Philip, Martha, and Mary of Bethany) or who do not appear at all in the other Gospels (such as Nathanael, Nicodemus, Lazarus). This may indi-cate that this Gospel reflects the eyewitness testimony of a different circle of dis-ciples, the circle in which the Beloved Disciple moved. His own testimony would include what he learned from other disciples who were present at events at which he himself, as a Jerusalem resident, was not. This provides a plausible explanation of the fact that John portrays events that do not appear in the Synoptic Gospels or takes a different perspective on the same events.

History as a Christological Issue

The Psychology of Eyewitness Memory

In everyday life, we normally value eyewitness memory (our own or that of others) more highly than second-hand reports. But we also know that, while memory is generally reliable, it can occasionally deceive us. Supposing the Gospels to be close to the testimony of those who had known Jesus, should we rely on their memories? There is now a large body of research in cognitive psychology relating to autobiographical memory (memory of personally experienced events) that helps us assess this. My chapter on this topic in *Jesus and the Eyewitnesses* (Bauckham 2006: 319–57) was the first attempt to make use of this resource for study of the Gospels (see now also McIver 2011). I was concerned only with memory for events (which psychologists call episodic memory), not with the transmission of the sayings of Jesus independently of stories about him.

Some historical Jesus scholars have concluded, from an acquaintance with the literature on memory research, that memory is generally rather unreliable, grossly distorted by present concerns, and unstable (Allison 2010: 1–9). However, while this impression may be given by some of the research, the reason is that the psychologists often focus on memory's failings. They do so because understanding when and how memory sometimes fails may assist understanding of how it manages to be usually very reliable (Cohen 1989: 222; Hoffman and Hoffman 2006: 282; Schacter 2007: 6). The importance of memory research for the study of the Gospels is not that it shows memory to be generally unreliable or always reliable, but that it shows what sort of events are remembered well, what aspects of those events are likely to be remembered, and what conditions help to ensure accurate and stable preservation of memories. The following is a summary of the conclusions I reached through a study of the research:

First, what would events have to be like in order for them to be remembered well? Unique and unusual events are remembered best; consequential or salient events are remembered better than less significant ones; events in which the eyewitness is emotionally involved are remembered better than others. These criteria illustrate why eyewitness testimony in court can be seriously unreliable, because witnesses are asked to remember things that did not concern them at the time. But, conversely, by these same criteria the events of the story of Jesus score well as events their participant eyewitnesses would likely remember well.

Second, what aspects of events are remembered well? Recollected events seldom include dates other than temporal indications integral to the story. The gist is often accurately recalled while details are not and may well vary in different tellings. Again these criteria throw some doubt on testimony in court, where it is often peripheral details of an event that witnesses are asked to recall. But in the Gospels, where variation in details can easily be observed in parallel versions of a story (e.g., the four accounts of Peter's denials), it is the core narrative that counts and the variations of detail should not discredit it.

Third, preservation of memories is assisted by rehearsal, which also gives them stability. When memories are told, they often acquire a standard narrative form, which they retain. It is correctly observed that the narrativization of experience, which occurs even in the selectivity entailed by the act of remembering, is interpretive. The eyewitnesses could not remember their experiences of Jesus without conveying the meaning these events had for them. Memory research confirms the tendency in recent historical Jesus study to reject the equation of 'authentic' material in the traditions with 'uninterpreted' facts. The coinherence of fact and meaning in testimony is not just inevitable but a key aspect of its value.

There is currently a surge of interest in memory in historical Jesus studies. But for the most part it is not in psychological research into autobiographical memory, but in the social-scientific theory of social memory (Le Donne 2009; Rodríguez 2010; Keith 2011; Dunn 2013: 230–47; cf. Bauckham 2006: 310–18). While this includes a claim that even individual memory is not separate from its social context, the most common use of social memory in historical work is to speak of the way societies remember historic events with a view to the needs of the present, often long after the events. For some Gospels scholars this functions as an equivalent to form criticism in stressing the creativity of communities who freely adapt versions of the past for present use. However, Le Donne argues against a stress on creative as opposed to retentive memory, and insists that, when dealing with a period within one or two generations of an event, the historian cannot ignore the initial perceptions and interpretations of the event by witnesses and contemporaries (Le Donne 2009: 60–4).

There are problems with the use of social memory theory. As a theoretical approach, it tends to erase the special quality of recollected memories of personally experienced events, flattening out the differences between different kinds of memory. Moreover, it provides no criteria for judging the relative weight of, on the one hand, personal memory's continuity with past experience and, on the other, the shaping of memory by the context in which remembering takes place. It seems a matter of preference how far practitioners allow for the former. If we are to take eyewitness memory in the Gospels seriously, social memory is probably less helpful than research into autobiographical memory.

Psychologists distinguish between episodic memory (recollections of experienced events) and semantic memory, which is memory for information. The traditions of the sayings of Jesus must fall largely into the latter category (except where a saying is integral to a story). In this case, it is vital to reckon with the probability that the disciples of Jesus deliberately memorized his sayings. Most of the Synoptic teaching of Jesus is cast in mnemonic forms designed to be easily remembered. As Gerhardsson (2005: 11) puts it, 'The most characteristic feature of Jesus' sayings is their laconicism and brevity.' The variations in the versions of sayings of Jesus in our sources do not show that they were not memorized, only that they were probably not memorized *verbatim*. In the ancient context, it is hardly conceivable that a teacher like Jesus would expect his disciples to remember his teaching without deliberately committing it to memory (Bauckham 2006: 280–7; Keener 2009: 145–52). (It is also notable that in the

Gospels the variation in sayings of Jesus is generally much less than the variation in stories.) It is not at all clear that modern experiments to test semantic memory (e.g. DeConick 2008) reproduce the remembering process that Jesus' disciples would have employed.

Testimony as a Historical and Theological Category

Throughout this essay I have used the category 'testimony' as the most appropriate one for describing the kind of evidence about Jesus that we have in the Gospels. In this final section we need to examine more closely what kind of evidence testimony is.

First, philosophical studies show that reliance on testimony is a normal and proper feature of human knowing. We know all kinds of things because other people tell us them, and we rightly doubt what we are told only when there is reason to do so. We do not refuse to believe until we can verify something for ourselves. Testimony is as basic a means of knowledge as perception, memory, and inference (Coady 1992).

By its very nature testimony asks to be trusted. This trust need not be uncritical. We may have reasons for judging a witness to be reliable or unreliable. In courts of law, judges and juries have various ways of deciding whether they can trust a particular witness or not. Historians have ways of assessing the reliability of historical sources. But usually what we consider are general reasons for trusting or not trusting a witness's testimony as a whole. We cannot verify for ourselves everything the witness claims. If we judge a witness to be trustworthy, then we have to trust that witness to be telling us the truth about much that we cannot verify otherwise.

So testimony is irreducible. We cannot go behind it and make our own autonomous verification. We cannot establish the truth of testimony for ourselves as though we stood where the witnesses stood. It would be impossible to write history without constant reliance on testimony. This does not require historians to engage in naïve credulity, any more than our reliance on testimony in everyday life requires this. Critical historiography engages in a dialectic of trust and critical assessment of witnesses. For those who seek an unattainable degree of certainty it may seem that historians take a risk in trusting their sources. But historical knowledge is never more than a judgement of probabilities and the risks involved are no different from those we all take in trusting testimony every day of our lives.

This is what follows for the historical study of the Gospels. The form critical approach required a distrustful attitude to the sources, such that only by testing each individual unit of tradition with rigorous criteria could anything of historical value be rescued from the traditions. Historical Jesus scholars have thereby acquired the habit of requiring a kind of verification of testimony that is not commonly required in everyday life, in law courts, or in the work of most historians. Now that we have moved beyond the form critical view of the Jesus tradition, we should be able to apply a more ordinary method of assessing the sources. The appropriate way to proceed is to evaluate the trustworthiness of each Gospel as a whole. (If we are confident that a whole category of material in a

Gospel can be attributed to a single source, then we may proceed also to the assessment of that source as a whole.)

There are various approaches to this. For example, we can consider how far the Gospel accounts of Jesus are coherent with everything we now know about early first-century Jewish Palestine. It is not so much a matter of judging whether the figure of Jesus presented in each of the Gospels is historically credible within the Judaism of his time (a difficult matter to judge), but more a matter of judging whether all the traces of Jesus' context that abound in the Gospel traditions reflect their supposed time and place. One should acknowledge that the kind of evidence the Gospels present is testimony and historical study of them needs to be appropriate to this kind of evidence.

A second feature of testimony as evidence is that, in historiography, as in general human experience, testimony can provide us with insider knowledge from involved participants. This is what the historians of the ancient world valued. They did not value the testimony of some accidental bystander with no interest in what they observed, but rather the engaged testimony of participants in the events. Modern people have become suspicious of evidence of this kind. They value the supposedly more objective evidence of the disengaged observer, and suspect the participant of subjective bias. But it is arguable that ancient historians had a better view of this. They realized that the best way of understanding what really went on was to listen to those who had been insiders. Such people are affected by the events they witnessed, and they will talk about the significance the events had for them. We cannot neatly detach fact from meaning in their testimony. But should we want to?

The need for testimony from participants who cannot speak of what they lived through without conveying the meaning and significance it had for them is especially the case with events for which we have few good parallels in history. The events of the life, ministry, death, and resurrection of Jesus were events of that kind, at least if the witnesses are to be believed. They were not just run-of-the-mill historical events, but history-making events. Exceptional events require testimony from involved and engaged participants—exactly what I believe we have in the Gospels. This does not mean that testimony is to be trusted uncritically (Bauckham 2006: 502; Byford 2013). But assessment must respect the exceptionality of the events to which testimony is borne and the unique access that insider testimony offers to it.

Third, in testimony fact and meaning coinhere, and witnesses who give testimony do so with the conviction of a significance that requires to be told. Witnesses of significant events speak out of their own ongoing attempts to understand. Paul Ricoeur speaks of the two inseparable aspects of testimony: on the one hand, its quasi-empirical aspect, the testimony of the senses, the report of the eyewitness as to facts, and, on the other hand, the interiority of testimony, the engagement of the witness with what he or she attests (Ricoeur 1981). The faithful witness is not merely accurate, but faithful to the meaning and demands of what is attested. This applies to everything we have in the Gospels. It is partly what it means to call them *apostolic* testimony. The witnesses are people whose ongoing engagement with what they had witnessed qualified them to speak with authority about its significance.

In conclusion, reading the Gospels as testimony differs from attempts at historical reconstruction behind the texts. It takes the Gospels seriously as they are; it acknowledges the uniqueness of what we can know only in this testimonial form. It honours the form of historiography they are, but at the same time we can now recognize that testimony is the appropriate category with which to read the Gospels in faith and for theology. These eyewitness testimonies speak to us from the inside of the events, experienced by those who recognized the disclosure of God in them. Beyond the dichotomy of the Jesus of history and the Christ of faith, they offer us the Jesus of testimony.

SUGGESTED READING

Allison (2009); Bauckham (2006); Dunn (2003); Fowl (2006); Keener (2009).

BIBLIOGRAPHY

Adams, S. A. (2006), 'Luke's Preface and its Relationship to Greek Historiography: A Response to Loveday Alexander', *Journal of Greco-Roman Christianity and Judaism* 3: 177–91.

Allison, D. C. (2009), *The Historical Christ and the Theological Jesus* (Grand Rapids, Mich.: Eerdmans).

Allison, D. C. (2010), *Constructing Jesus: Memory, Imagination, and History* (London: SPCK).

Aune, D. (2002), 'Luke 1.1–4: Historical or Scientific *Prooimion?*', in A. Christopherson, C. Claussen, J. Frey, and B. Longenecker (eds.), *Paul, Luke and the Graeco-Roman World: Essays in Honour of Alexander J. M. Wedderburn.* Journal for the Study of the New Testament Supplement Series 217 (Sheffield: Sheffield Academic Press), 138–48.

Bauckham, R. (2006), *Jesus and the Eyewitnesses: The Gospels as Eyewitness Testimony* (Grand Rapids, Mich.: Eerdmans).

Bauckham, R. (2007), *The Testimony of the Beloved Disciple: Narrative, History, and Theology in the Gospel of John* (Grand Rapids, Mich.: Baker).

Bauckham, R. (2009), 'The Eyewitnesses in the Gospel of Mark', *Svensk Exegetisk Årsbok* 74: 19–39.

Bauckham, R. (2012), 'The Gospel of Mark: Origins and Eyewitnesses', in M. F. Bird and J. Maston (eds.), *Earliest Christian History: History, Literature, and Theology—Essays from the Tyndale Fellowship in Honor of Martin Hengel.* Wissenschaftliche Untersuchungen zum Neuen Testament 2/320 (Tübingen: Mohr Siebeck), 145–69.

Bock, D. L. and R. L. Webb (eds.) (2009), *Key Events in the Life of the Historical Jesus: A Collaborative Exploration of Context and Coherence.* Wissenschaftliche Untersuchungen zum Neuen Testament 247 (Tübingen: Mohr Siebeck; reprinted Grand Rapids, Mich.: Eerdmans, 2010).

Bultmann, R. (1921), *Die Geschichte der Synoptischen Tradition* (Göttingen: Vandenhoeck & Ruprecht). English translation: *The History of the Synoptic Tradition*, trans. J. Marsh (Oxford: Blackwell, 1963; 2nd edition 1968).

Burridge, R. A. (1992), *What Are the Gospels? A Comparison with Greco-Roman Biography.* SNTS Monograph Series 70 (Cambridge: Cambridge University Press; expanded edition: Grand Rapids, Mich.: Eerdmans, 2004).

Byford, J. (2013), 'Testimony', in E. Keightley and M. Pickering (eds.), *Research Methods for Memory Studies* (Edinburgh: Edinburgh University Press), 200–14.

Byrskog, S. (2000), *Story as History—History as Story: The Gospel Tradition in the Context of Ancient Oral History* (Tübingen: Mohr Siebeck; reprinted Leiden: Brill, 2002).

Casey, M. (2010), *Jesus of Nazareth: An Independent Historian's Account of his Life and Teaching* (London: T. & T. Clark).

Coady, C. A. J. (1992), *Testimony: A Philosophical Study* (Oxford: Clarendon Press).

Cohen, G. (1989), *Memory in the Real World* (Hove and London: Lawrence Erlbaum).

DeConick, A. (2008), 'Human Memory and the Sayings of Jesus: Contemporary Experimental Exercises in the Transmission of Jesus Traditions', in T. Thatcher (ed.), *Jesus, the Voice, and the Text: Beyond the Oral and the Written Gospel* (Waco, Tex.: Baylor University Press), 135–79.

Dibelius, M. (1919), *Die Formgeschichte des Evangelium* (Tübingen: Mohr Siebeck). English translation: *From Tradition to Gospel*, trans. B. L. Woolf (London: Nicholson and Watson, 1934).

Dunn, J. D. G. (2003), *Jesus Remembered* (Grand Rapids, Mich.: Eerdmans).

Dunn, J. D. G. (2013), *The Oral Gospel Tradition* (Grand Rapids, Mich.: Eerdmans).

Eddy, P. R. and G. A. Boyd (2007), *The Jesus Legend: A Case for the Historical Reliability of the Synoptic Jesus Tradition* (Grand Rapids, Mich.: Baker).

Fowl, S. E. (2006), 'The Gospels and "the Historical Jesus"', in S. C. Barton (ed.), *The Cambridge Companion to the Gospels* (Cambridge: Cambridge University Press), 76–96.

Gerhardsson, B. (2001), *The Reliability of the Gospel Tradition* (Peabody, Mass.: Hendrickson).

Gerhardsson, B. (2005), 'The Secret of the Transmission of the Unwritten Jesus Tradition', *New Testament Studies* 51: 1–18.

Hengel, M. (2005), 'Eye-witness Memory and the Writing of the Gospels', in M. Bockmuehl and D. A. Hagner (eds.), *The Written Gospel* [Festschrift for Graham N. Stanton] (Cambridge: Cambridge University Press), 70–96.

Hoffman, A. M. and H. S. Hoffman (2006), 'Memory Theory: Personal and Social', in T. L. Charlton, L. E. Myers, and R. Sharpless (eds.), *Handbook of Oral History* (Lanham, MD: AltaMira Press), 275–96.

Johnson, L. T. (1996), *The Real Jesus: The Misguided Quest of the Historical Jesus and the Truth of the Traditional Gospels* (San Francisco: HarperCollins).

Keener, C. S. (2003), *The Gospel of John: A Commentary*, 2 vols. (Peabody, Mass.: Hendrickson).

Keener, C. S. (2009), *The Historical Jesus of the Gospels* (Grand Rapids, Mich.: Eerdmans).

Keener, C. S. (2011), 'Assumptions in Historical-Jesus Research: Using Ancient Biographies and Disciples' Traditioning as a Control', *Journal for the Study of the Historical Jesus* 9: 26–58.

Keith, C. (2011), *Jesus' Literacy: Scribal Culture and the Teacher from Galilee*. Library of New Testament Studies 413 (London: T. & T. Clark).

Keith, C. and A. Le Donne (eds.) (2012), *Jesus, Criteria, and the Demise of Authenticity* (London: T. & T. Clark).

Le Donne, A. (2009), *The Historiographical Jesus: Memory, Typology, and the Son of David* (Waco, Tex.: Baylor University Press).

McIver, R. K. (2011), *Memory, Jesus and the Synoptic Gospels*. SBL Resources for Biblical Studies 59 (Atlanta: Society of Biblical Literature).

McKnight, S. (2012), 'Why the Authentic Jesus Is of No Use for the Church', in C. Keith and A. Le Donne (eds.), *Jesus, Criteria, and the Demise of Authenticity* (London: T. & T. Clark), 173–85.

Ricoeur, P. (1981), 'The Hermeneutics of Testimony', in *Essays on Biblical Interpretation*, ed. L. S. Mudge (London: SPCK), 123–30.

Rodríguez, R. (2009), 'Authenticating Criteria: The Use and Misuse of a Critical Method', *Journal for the Study of the Historical Jesus* 7: 152–67.

Rodríguez, R. (2010), *Structuring Early Christian Memory: Jesus in Tradition, Performance and Text*. Library of New Testament Studies 407 (London: T. & T. Clark).

Schacter, D. L. (2007 [2001]), *How the Mind Forgets and Remembers: The Seven Sins of Memory* (London: Souvenir Press).

Theissen, G. and D. Winter (2002), *The Quest for the Plausible Jesus: The Question of Criteria*, trans. M. Eugene Boring (Louisville: Westminster/John Knox).

Tuckett, C. (2009), 'Form Criticism', in W. Kelber and S. Byrskog (eds.), *Jesus in Memory: Jesus in Oral and Scribal Perspectives* (Waco, Tex.: Baylor University Press), 21–36.

Watson, F. (2013), *Gospel Writing: A Canonical Perspective* (Grand Rapids, Mich.: Eerdmans).

Wright, N. T. (1996), *Jesus and the Victory of God* (London: SPCK).

CHAPTER 5

THE WORK OF CHRIST IN THE NEW TESTAMENT

MICHAEL J. GORMAN

'THE work of Christ' is standard theological shorthand for the saving activity of Jesus of Nazareth—a vast topic, with nearly every verse of the NT and every work of NT scholarship relating to it. Thus this chapter will necessarily be selective. We begin with some important preliminary observations about approach and method before exploring aspects of Christ's work itself.

SOME INITIAL OBSERVATIONS

Firstly, the phrase 'the work of Christ' is something of a misnomer in two important ways. To use an analogy from daily life, the NT does not portray Jesus as an independent contractor, but as part of a family business. Sent by God the Father to effect salvation, Jesus does what he does as God's representative, or in (free) obedience to his Father, or both, doing so by the power of God's Spirit. Thus to speak of the work of Christ is to speak simultaneously of the work of the Father and of the Spirit, and thus to speak almost necessarily of Christ's work in what would later be called Trinitarian terms. This does not mean that there is nothing distinctive or unique about his work: for example, only Jesus died on the Cross, and only Jesus reigns as Lord at the Father's 'right hand'. But Jesus' saving activity as a whole cannot be understood or appropriately articulated apart from his relationship to the Father and the Spirit, and therefore to their activity. In particular, there has been a growing scholarly recognition that the NT 'links Jesus with virtually every purpose and main activity of God' (Hurtado 2006: 621), including creation, salvation, judgment and more. In both Testaments, God (YHWH) is Savior and Lord, and in the NT so also is Jesus.

Moreover, throughout the NT Jesus' work is not limited to his own heavenly commissioned and Spirit-empowered activity, but it is shared, first with his disciples during his earthly ministry (e.g., Henderson 2006), and then with his apostles and the entire Church after his resurrection. Again, this is not to deny a distinctive and unique character to Jesus' saving work, but merely to say that aspects of it continue beyond his own activity. The NT writers insist that Jesus remains active in and through the Church, usually by the Spirit. The RSV translation of Acts 1:1 captures this well: 'In the first book, O Theophilus, I have dealt with all that Jesus *began* to do and teach' (emphasis added).

Secondly, we cannot separate Christ's 'work' from Christ's 'person', despite some efforts to do so from each side (e.g., Fee 2007, focusing on Christ's person/divinity; the many attempts to brand Jesus only as a human teacher or liberator). Jesus liberated the captive and died for the sins of the world as the Messiah, Suffering Servant and Lamb of God, and so on; he is active in the Church and the world as Lord; he will come again to save and to judge as Son of Man.

Accordingly, if Jesus does God's work, and if his work cannot be separated from his person, then raising the question of the 'work' of Christ automatically raises the question of his identity vis-à-vis God. Leander Keck argues that the content of NT Christology is 'the work of Christ grounded in the person [or identity] of Christ' (Keck 2005: 274), and that their inseparability is due to the connection between Christ's relationship with God and the human situation in need of repair—the theological and the anthropological/soteriological correlates (271–2). Keck warns that, throughout history, whenever Jesus is separated from Christology, 'the separated Jesus always agrees with those who do the separating' (269). Moreover, a 'low' Christology assumes a 'superficial anthropology', whereas 'the deeper the human dilemma is, the "higher" the Christology must be to deal with it' (272).

Such a 'high' NT Christology need not detract from Jesus' full humanity. Even the Gospel of John has a fully human Jesus (Thompson 2001), and in the hyper-symbolic Apocalypse, Jesus is both sharer in God's identity and activity *and* a fully human, faithful witness, yielding 'the narrative embodiment of proto-Chalcedonian Christology' (Hays 2012: 81).

The claims of Keck and Hays, echoed by others, remind us that the NT writings bear at least implicit witness to the later Christological questions and affirmations associated with Nicaea and Chalcedon. But, as N. T. Wright has repeatedly noted in commenting on the creeds, the NT never separates Christ's identity from his mission.

Thirdly, the work of Christ (understood in this thick way as the activity of the human Jesus related to both God's mission and the Church's witness) is an astonishingly multifaceted reality in the NT, as even a single gospel or letter reveals. This is true in part because the NT's Christological claims reflect the writers' varying perceptions of Israel's and humanity's need, its 'brokenness'. What Christ does is a response to that which people need but cannot do for themselves. Thus NT soteriology, the purpose and consequence of Christ's work, will also necessarily be both diverse and complex (Middleton and Gorman 2009). Furthermore, Christ's work in the NT is a complex set of activities, rather than one act (e.g., his death). Though Christ's work certainly centers on his redemptive death and resurrection, it is not limited to that pivotal moment; the older idea that 'the work of Christ' refers only to his death is misguided.

Also misguided is an approach to the NT that would limit, or nearly limit, the atonement to a single 'model', namely some form of penal substitution. Mistaken as well is the idea that the Cross is only the work of *Christ*. The NT's interpretation of his crucifixion as a gracious act of *God*, even a divine self-revelation, is among the most shocking and influential hermeneutical and epistemological moves in human history.

Accordingly, a trend in recent interpretation of Jesus' death is to stress the variety of NT interpretations of atonement, even in Paul, the traditional source of penal-substitution theory (Carroll and Green 1995; Hooker 1995; Harrisville 2006; McKnight 2007). The three traditional theological models (*Christus victor*, satisfaction/substitution, moral influence) do not fully capture the NT's theological diversity and depth. Christ's death is depicted as the fate of a prophet and/or martyr; as the means of redeeming others from slavery; as an act of enemy-love and reconciliation; as victory over various powers; and as sacrifice—and more, an event that disturbs every status quo but creates new life and realities (Harrisville 2006).

Despite this Christological variety, many NT scholars posit a certain commonality of basic convictions and interests within the various NT writings (e.g., Matera 1999), and this chapter reflects that position.

Fourthly, in the NT, Christ's diverse-yet-unified work is greater than his earthly ministry and his death, for it stretches from preexistence to arrival/incarnation and all the way to resurrection/exaltation and finally *parousia*. There is a kind of narrative continuity in the story of Jesus' person and activity. The exalted Lord remains the crucified Messiah, as Luke (Luke 24:13–48), John the evangelist (John 20:19–29), Paul (Gal. 2:15–21), and John the seer (Rev. 5) each tells us in their own way. And Paul, at least, sees continuity between Christ's (divine) self-emptying in the Incarnation and his (human) self-humbling in the crucifixion (Phil. 2:6–8). In other words, Jesus not only *is* but also *does* 'the same yesterday and today, and forever' (Heb. 13:8). The centerpiece, the Cross, stands in continuity with all that precedes and follows.

Fifthly, the meaning of the term 'Christ' in our chapter title is controverted. Is it basically a name? Does it (sometimes? ever?) retain its significance as a title ('Messiah'), especially outside the Gospels? Regarding Paul the question is sharply debated, some finding Christ to be largely a name (e.g., Matera 2012), others arguing that Paul's entire theology is dependent on *Christos* meaning 'Messiah' (Novenson 2012; Wright 2013).

Whatever one's answer to the question of *Christos* in the NT, however, it is clear to nearly all interpreters that the NT writers saw Jesus in terms of the scriptural story of Israel, either as the fulfillment of Scripture, the climax of the covenant, or the turning point of salvation history. Of particular importance for the portrayal of Jesus were (1) the book of Isaiah, especially the servant songs of Isaiah 40–55 and nearby texts (e.g., 52:7; 52:13–53:12; 61:1–2), which, taken together, depict one who brings good news and peace, liberates the oppressed, and offers himself for the sins of others; (2) Daniel 7 (the Son of Man); and (3) certain psalms (e.g. Psalm 22). *For the NT writers, then, Jesus brings the promised eschatological salvation and beneficent rule of God.* It is here! Not in its fullness, but nonetheless here and now. This divine salvation and sovereignty has come *in* Jesus *to* Israel and *through* Israel *to* the rest of the world. Judaism, then, is the womb of all NT Christology, though it was nurtured in the cultural and political realities of the Roman Empire in which Judaism (and therefore earliest Christianity) existed.

Lastly, as a subset of NT theology, NT Christology has been subject to the directions in which the parent field has moved. Two pairs of recent scholarly trends, one literary in nature and the other historical, bear mentioning.

First is the turn to narrative and intertextuality. For example, no longer are Christological titles studied only with respect to alleged sources but also, and even more so, with respect to their connection to a particular Christology developed within a narrative that contains echoes of various texts ('intertexts'), especially scriptural texts. Nor are passages deemed to be of Christological import read in isolation (as in form criticism), or even primarily vis-à-vis alleged sources (as in redaction criticism), but as part of a narrative and/or rhetorical whole. Thus critical titles (e.g., Messiah, Son of God, Lord) and texts are interpreted as symbols of and contributors to the unfolding narrative of a gospel (e.g., Kingsbury 1983 and Watson 2010 on Mark) or a letter (e.g., Kirk 2008 on Romans). The Christological significance of Phil. 2:6–11 and Col. 1:15–20 is now sought primarily from the text itself and its use in a particular letter (and beyond), not from alleged sources or history-of-religions research. This does not mean that such passages should be read in historical isolation, but outside texts and realities are now seen less as controlling sources than as fruitful connections—intertexts—within a creative authorial enterprise. This turn to intertextuality was provoked, at least in part, by Richard Hays (1989), and both he and his students have stressed intertextuality in their own work on 'narrative Christology' in the Gospels, too (Rowe 2006; and a forthcoming major volume from Hays).

Another major development has been the turn to cultural realities and politics; the former is manifest in social-scientific studies of NT Christology, and the latter situates NT theology in the context of first-century Jewish and imperial politics. Regarding the social sciences, two illustrative examples will have to suffice. John Barclay (Barclay 2015) argues that our understanding of Christ as divine gift and as self-gift can be enhanced by social-scientific studies of gift-giving. David Watson, attempting to solve a longstanding critical problem in Markan studies, interprets Mark as a narrative that reconfigures the meaning of honor and shame for Jesus and his followers (Watson 2010). Here we see the integration of critical methods as well as the symbiosis of Christology and ecclesiology noted above. Thus these new directions in method, though not always utilized by the same scholars, are not necessarily at odds.

We turn now to the actual content of Christ's work in the NT.

SOME ASPECTS OF THE WORK OF CHRIST
IN THE NEW TESTAMENT

The question of how to structure a discussion of the work of Christ in the NT is itself complex. Many treatments highlight the particular Christologies of specific NT documents or writers (e.g. Matera 1999; Longenecker 2005). Another approach, which we will adopt, is to proceed topically, permitting us to follow the essay title's implicit Christological grammar by positing a series of Christ's activities, with a sort of narrative continuity from preexistence to *parousia*. We will also note some of the connections between Christ's work as both God's and the Church's work.

We begin with the fundamental unity in NT Christology: *Jesus brings the promised eschatological salvation and beneficent rule of God.* All of the following actions are aspects of this conviction. (For simplicity, the subject, or actor, in each activity is 'Jesus'.)

Jesus mediates creation and new creation. This startling claim (e.g. John 1:1–10; Col. 1:15–20; Heb. 1:2) immediately raises the question of Christ's identity. He cannot be the agent of creation unless he 'preexists', that is, he is with God before he becomes human, as the Fourth Gospel puts it. There is a hint of preexistent Wisdom (Wisdom of Solomon 7; Proverbs 8) in such texts, though there is debate about precisely how NT writers perceived the status of that Wisdom and its relationship to Jesus. It is clear, however, that the NT implies continuity in Christ's work. As Colossians puts it, as the image of God he was the agent of the creation of all things, and as the one in whom God's fullness dwelled he was the agent of the redemption of all things—a new creation. Thus Paul says, 'if anyone is in Christ, new creation!' (2 Cor. 5:17; my translation). The new creation promised in Isaiah has been inaugurated in Christ, God's apocalyptic, salvific intervention. Its culmination is therefore the presence of both God and the Lamb among humans in that new creation (Rev. 21:1–22:5).

Jesus freely and fully identifies with humanity. Christ's preexistent activity, at least according to Paul, includes his caring for the needs of Israel in the wilderness (1 Cor. 10:1–4). But for both Paul and John, it is the Incarnation that reveals Christ's full and voluntary identification with all humanity: 'the Word became flesh and lived among us' (John 1:14); 'though [Jesus] was in the form of God, [he] did not regard equality with God as something to be exploited, but emptied himself, taking the form of a slave, being born in human likeness'—a freely chosen kenosis followed by a similar self-humbling in death (Phil. 2:6–8). (The same writers freely employ 'sending formulae' to indicate God's initiative [John 3:16–17; Rom. 8:3; Gal. 4:4].) The Gospels portray Jesus' ministry as his identifying with all people in baptism, seeking the lost, associating with sinners, and welcoming the outcast. Hebrews reminds us that, despite Jesus' own sinlessness, in both his past, earthly ministry and his present, exalted high-priestly ministry, Jesus identifies with, and assists, sinful, weak, and suffering people (Heb. 2:14–18; 4:14–16). Similarly, the exalted Christ is present among his people in the seven churches of the Apocalypse, loving them and assuaging them of their fears (Rev. 1:5, 12–20). Paul adds that Jesus now intercedes for believers (Rom. 8:34; cf. Acts 7:55–6).

Jesus inaugurates and embodies God's beneficent rule. The Synoptic Gospels recount Jesus' essential message: 'The kingdom (or reign, or rule) of God is at hand', meaning 'it has begun'. This is not merely a report about a new teaching, but a claim about what Jesus is *doing*. His ministry—healing and liberating, reversing the status quo, welcoming the poor and rejected—is his action as God's servant, especially as portrayed in Isaiah 40–55. Paradoxically, it is in such service that God's sovereignty is being established. As Messiah and Son of God, both royal titles, Jesus embodies that sovereignty in himself, even, implicitly, on the Cross (e.g., Mark 15 par.).

A similar perspective, in a different idiom, emerges in John and Paul as the rule or lordship of Christ. In John, Jesus' kingdom originates not from the world (John 18:36) but from God, who sent the Son to save the world. Jesus is explicitly lifted up and glorified as king on the Cross (e.g. John 3:14; 18:19), the emblem of his voluntary self-gift (John 10:7–18) and his servant-love (John 13). In Paul, Jesus is the Lord, identified with the κύριος (YHWH) in Scripture and contrasted with the κύριος in Rome. As in John, Christ's rule as Lord is inseparable from his self-giving love (Phil. 2:1–11).

Jesus welcomes the poor and weak. Expressing his identification with humanity and his embodiment of God's beneficent, status-reversing rule, Christ welcomes the needy, especially those disregarded or outcast by others (e.g. Matt. 11:4–5; Mark 1:40–4; Luke 19:1–10; John 7:53–8:11). This prominent motif in the Gospels is highlighted also by Paul: in the crucified Messiah God chose what is foolish, weak, and despised to shame the wise and powerful, and therein revealed true divine power and wisdom (1 Cor. 1:18–31). Those 'in Christ' must also welcome the weak (Rom. 15:1–4; 1 Cor. 8:1–11:1). Paul therefore castigates the Corinthians for barring the risen Jesus from their 'Lord's supper' because they have failed to welcome the poor (1 Cor. 11:17–34). In contrast, but in continuity with the earthly Jesus, the exalted Christ of Revelation invites the (spiritually) 'wretched, pitiable, poor, blind, and naked' Laodicean believers to renewed communion with him (Rev. 3:14–22).

Jesus forgives, heals, delivers, and conquers. Throughout the Gospels, Jesus forgives people and frees them from sin's effects, heals them from illness, and delivers them from Satan and the demons; he is victorious over these evil powers by God's power: 'God anointed Jesus of Nazareth with the Holy Spirit and with power … [and] he went about doing good and healing all who were oppressed by the devil' (Acts 10:38, summarizing the Gospel accounts). Acts also tells how that power continues in the apostles—who forgive and heal in *Jesus'* name and power (Acts 2:38; 3:6, 16; etc.). In his gospel Luke names this critical aspect of Jesus' ministry ἄφεσις: release or liberation from any oppressive power and the evil practices such powers generate. With liberation comes participation in God's kingdom, with new, topsy-turvy values or, in John's terms, simply 'life'.

Both Luke and Matthew connect this liberation to Jesus' role as God's Messiah and servant from Isaiah 40–55, especially Isa. 61:1–2 (Matt. 11:4–5; Luke 4:16–21; 27:22; Acts 10:38; 26:18), but also, in Matthew, Isaiah 53 (Matt. 8:16–17). Texts in Matthew's Passion narrative that may allude to Isaiah 53 (Matt. 26:63; 27:12, 14) suggest that Matthew, at least, sees continuity between Jesus' healing ministry and his death for sins.

Forgiveness and liberation is one interpretation of Jesus' death in the Pauline tradition. Christ liberates people from sin as power, the curse of the law, bondage and slavery, divine wrath, death, and cosmic powers (e.g. Rom. 6:6–7; Gal. 1:4; 3:13–14; 1 Thess. 1:10; Col. 2:13–15). Christ brings about a new Exodus and perhaps also deliverance from exile (so esp. Wright 1991, 2013). Participation in Christ's death and resurrection is the means to experience this liberation, and some suggest that justification is itself participation in God's apocalyptic liberation (Campbell 2009). Both Hebrews and Revelation also associate Jesus' death with liberation (Heb. 2:14–15; Rev. 1:5). As liberator Jesus is also in some sense conqueror, and the *Christus victor* interpretation of his death finds its roots in that image (esp. Col. 2:13–15).

Jesus brings God's shalom. The NT writers believe that the life, death, and resurrection of Jesus inaugurated the prophetically promised eschatological age of shalom, the reign of God's peace and justice. But despite the efforts of some scholars (e.g. Swartley 2006), this dimension of Christ's work has been often relatively neglected.

Luke presents Jesus' birth (Luke 2:1–20) as the birth of the age of peace in distinction to the alleged good news of peace brought by the emperor Augustus. Shalom, the restoration of wholeness in the created order, is realized in Jesus' ministry of healing and liberation. In the Gospels Jesus is the one who both embodies God's eschatological shalom and teaches others to be makers of shalom, which will be evidence of their identity as God's offspring (Matt. 5:9). Luke especially stresses that on the Cross, Jesus practices the peace he has been preaching (Luke 23:32–43), and Stephen imitates him before being stoned (Acts 7:59–60).

The Pauline tradition portrays Jesus' death as God's means of effecting peace and reconciliation between humans and God and also among humans (Rom. 5:1–11; Eph. 2:11–22; Col. 1:19–22). N. T. Wright argues that reconciliation is the center of Pauline theology (Wright 2013: 3–74, 1473–1519), which coheres with his view that the Gospels present Jesus' earthly mission as actualizing God's will on earth as in heaven (Wright 2012).

In the Pauline tradition, Christ is the Lord of peace (2 Thess. 3:16; cf. Eph. 2:14) who, with God the Father, remains the giver of grace and peace (cf. Rom. 1:7; 1 Cor. 1:3, etc.). Christ shapes those 'in him' into a peace-seeking, non-retaliatory, non-violent people both within the Church and in relations with outsiders (Rom. 12:9–21; 1 Cor. 6:1–11; 1 Thess. 5:11–15), in anticipation of the coming fullness of peace and security from God, not Rome (1 Thess. 5:3). Peace themes surface occasionally in other epistolary literature, too (e.g., Heb. 12:11, 14; 13:20; 1 Pet. 3:11; 2 Pet. 3:14).

Jesus offers himself in faithful obedience and sacrificial love. Jesus' compassion, mercy, and love are attested by all four Gospels. The Fourth Gospel explicitly interprets Jesus' death, both as the means of forgiveness from sins and as ethical example, as the culmination of his love (John 13). Paul does the same (Rom. 8:37; Gal. 2:20; cf. Phil. 2:1–8), and implies that Christ continues that love in the present (Rom. 8:35). Christ's present love is made explicit in Revelation (Rev. 1:5). Both John and Paul insist that Jesus' love is simultaneously God's love (e.g., John 3:16; Rom. 5:6–8).

It seems likely that Paul, and perhaps other NT writers, envisions Jesus' death as both his faithfulness to God and God's faithfulness to Israel (various interpretations in Bird and Sprinkle 2009). Numerous studies of certain Pauline texts propose that they refer to the Messiah's faith/faithfulness, especially in the Greek phrase πίστις Χριστοῦ, faith 'in' or 'of' Christ (esp. Hays 2002, though James Dunn [Dunn 2008] and others remain opposed). Messiah's faithfulness in Paul and elsewhere would refer especially to his death as the culmination of a life of freely chosen faithful obedience and as the paradigm of believers' 'obedience of faith' (Rom. 1:5; 16:26). His faithful death stands in continuity, for Paul, with his incarnation (Phil. 2:6) and, especially for the evangelists, with his entire life. In Revelation, Jesus is, paradoxically, both co-eternal with God and exemplary 'faithful witness' to God (Hays 2012).

Similarly, Jesus lived and died, especially according to Luke, as God's ultimate prophet. For some interpreters, this means *not* as a sacrifice for sins. There has been a strong reaction against the sacrificial understanding of Jesus' death as penal substitution (is it 'divine child abuse'?), many denying its presence in the NT, but others defending it, often in a more nuanced form (e.g. Marshall 2007: 1–67). Alternatives to traditional interpretations of Jesus' death as atoning sacrifice include the claim that the NT portrays atonement in terms of the scapegoat (following René Girard) and that Paul, at least, depicts Jesus' death as a martyrdom, and only as such possibly also an atoning sacrifice (survey in Williams 2010: 1–26). Others (e.g. Brondos 2006) deny that the death itself had any salvific value, but is 'for us' only as a manifestation of Jesus' absolute faithfulness to God, leading to his Roman crucifixion.

However, numerous NT texts interpret Jesus' death in terms of Isaiah 53 (e.g., Rom. 4:25; 1 Cor. 15:3b–5; 2 Cor. 5:21; 1 Pet. 2:22–5; Heb. 9:28; Rev. 5:6, 12; Janowski and Stuhlmacher 2004), which means that it must be seen, in some sense (though not exclusively) as a form of sacrifice 'for sins' and 'for us', meaning at least 'on account of sins' and 'for our benefit', and probably also as a kind of substitution or representation. The issue, however, remains contested.

A constructive way forward, particularly in Paul, is the notion of 'interchange' (Hooker 1990: 13–69), which resembles the patristic view that 'Christ became what we are so that we could become what he is' (see Gal. 3:13; 2 Cor. 5:21; 8:9). This approach rightly understands Christ's death in Paul as both redemptive and transformative, and it maintains the narrative and soteriological connection between atonement and incarnation.

Jesus effects the new covenant and creates the community of the new covenant. Another theme in the study of Jesus' death is the corporate—rather than merely individual—character of the event's purpose and effect. Moreover, the theme of new covenant seems to suggest a central aspect of the atonement throughout the NT, perhaps even another 'model' (Gorman 2011; cf. Carroll and Green 1995: 69). Such an interpretation of the atonement in the NT is both more communal and more participatory than traditional models; believers share the 'cup' of Jesus (suffering) and the κοινωνία of the promised Spirit (Ezek. 11:17–20; 36:23–8; cf. Jer. 31:31–4).

This sort of reading of the atonement coheres with the synoptic witness that Jesus called a group of twelve to symbolize the covenantal renewal of Israel. It also coheres with the Pauline language of being 'in' the Messiah, in which Jesus' present work by the Spirit is ongoing transformation of the Church into his likeness, which includes suffering (e.g., 2 Cor. 4:8–12; Col. 1:24). Similarly, 1 Peter notes that the new 'chosen race … royal priesthood … holy nation' (1 Pet. 2:9) shares in Christ's suffering (1 Pet. 4:12–19).

The Pauline and Johannine (esp. Rom. 8:1–11 and John 15) language of mutual indwelling that exists between Christ/the Spirit and the Church should be understood in light of the new covenant. The promised Spirit has come to indwell the community and each member so that they may individually and corporately embody the 'law of Christ', which is the 'new commandment' of Christlike love (Gal. 6:2; cf. 1 Cor. 9:21; John 13:1–17, 34–5; cf. 1 John 3:16; 4:10).

Thus for most NT writers, Christ's past activity of covenantal faith/faithfulness/obedience toward God and love toward others constitutes the essential structure of the moral life. This can be articulated in terms of discipleship and imitation, or in terms of indwelling and participation. In either case, the goal is the expression of Jesus-like activity in the present.

Jesus enables resurrection and participation in the life of God, even as he acts as both humanity's judge and its savior. The Gospel accounts of Jesus' raising the dead indicate that he brings God's power and life into human darkness and death (e.g., John 11). In order to describe the ongoing life-giving activity of God in Christ by the Spirit, several recent NT interpreters, especially of Paul, have reintroduced such terms as *theosis*, or divinization (becoming like God), and *Christosis* (Blackwell 2011; Gorman 2009; Litwa 2012). Relevant texts include such classic passages as 2 Pet. 1:4 and 2 Cor. 3:18, but other less explicit texts are also being explored.

Theosis, like 'interchange', implies that salvation means restoration of humanity's original Godlike qualities such as righteousness and immortality. This is achieved by a process of becoming conformed to Christ the Son, especially now in his godly character (even in suffering) and later in his resurrection life. Since throughout the NT Christ is both the image of God and the obedient Son, 'Christification is divinization, and divinization is humanization' (Gorman 2009: 37).

Even those who do not find theosis per se in the NT increasingly acknowledge the centrality of participation in Christ as absolutely central at least to Pauline soteriology and Christology. Participation, of course, implies Christ's resurrection and living presence; and, for many recent interpreters, it is the context for the right interpretation of justification: 'Justification is the result of the believer's participation in Jesus' resurrection life' (Powers 2001: 122). Resurrection life is not confined to the future in Paul (Kirk 2008). Indeed, resurrection is a critical part of justification for Paul (Rom. 4:25), and possibly also of the high-priestly Christology and soteriology of Hebrews (Moffitt 2011).

Paradoxically, however, for Paul the risen Christ's present activity is to reenact, by the Spirit, his own life and death of *cruciform* faithfulness and love (e.g., . 2:19–20; 5:6). Baptism is entry into that new, resurrection but cruciform life (Romans 6), while the Lord's Supper (1 Cor. 10; 11:17–34) is the reaffirmation of Jesus' ongoing presence in the community, continuing his identification with the poor and weak. When Paul calls for cruciform existence, he is calling his communities to allow the risen Jesus to re-embody his own life and death in his body, the Church (Gorman 2001). The body of Christ is not a metaphor but is Christ's ongoing identity and activity in the world.

It would be incomplete to speak of Christ's life-giving activity without considering his role as judge. Throughout the NT his work constitutes both an offer and a demand, and he is portrayed as the one who thereby divides humanity during his earthly ministry (e.g. Luke 12:49–53) and who will execute divine judgment at his future coming, or presence (παρουσία; e.g., Matt. 25:31–46; 2 Cor. 5:10; Rev. 19:11–21; anticipated, at least in John 5, in the present). Those who fail to embrace Jesus' message and mission may be viewed as being in a state of self-exclusion and self-condemnation, as the Gospel of John suggests (John 3:14–22).

Nevertheless, the thrust of the NT's portrayal of Jesus is his compassionate desire to rescue and restore all, not to condemn. Christ's saving work culminates in the future participation of redeemed humanity in 'the renewal of all things' (Matt. 19:28), which means in his glory, which is also God's glory, God's radiant presence (Mark 10:35–40; Acts 7:55; Rom. 8:17; Phil. 3:21; 1 Pet. 1:3–21; Rev. 21:1–22:5).

Words such as 'glory', 'life', and 'resurrection'—both present and future—arguably sum up NT soteriology, with texts like John 3:16–17, John 10:10, 2 Cor. 3:18, and 2 Tim. 1:10 functioning as succinct summaries, and the entire Gospel of John serving as a full-length narrative account of that claim. Such texts also require us to ask, 'Who precisely is this Jesus who brings God's glorious life to humans?' We conclude with two NT answers to this question.

Jesus reigns as Messiah/Son of God and (counter-imperial) Lord. One of the most significant recent developments in NT Christology has been the turn to more politically oriented interpretations. Jump-started by John Howard Yoder's *Politics of Jesus* (Yoder 1972), which took seriously the socio-political dimensions of Jesus and the NT, this development has both matured and been challenged. Nonetheless, nearly all NT scholars agree that first-century politics and religion were inseparable, and they have mined the NT for its potential social and political Christologies.

This effort has gone in two different, though related, directions. One has focused on the NT's portrayal of Jesus as the Jewish Messiah. The other has focused on Jesus as the counter-imperial Lord who offers an alternative politic to Caesar's. The new interest in Jesus and empire moves beyond the obvious texts (e.g., Revelation) and spans the whole NT, creating a subdiscipline of empire studies with a vast bibliography (e.g. Porter and Westfall 2011). The main thesis of these scholars is that the NT portrays Jesus as one who came to inaugurate a different empire, resulting in a network of communities, each intended to be an alternative *polis* with values and practices commensurate with Jesus' identity as the world's true Lord. Much of the early energy in this area was focused on

Paul, but it quickly expanded to include the Gospels, Acts, and other writings. Some scholars (e.g., Carter 2000) speak of Jesus as the bringer of 'the empire of God'. Even the Gospel of John has been interpreted in this way. In John, Jesus may be portrayed not only as greater than Moses, but also as God's subversion of Caesar (Thatcher 2009). For Thatcher, the Cross as a 'tale of terror' (Rome's perspective) becomes a tale of triumph as the true Son of God dethrones Caesar and creates an 'inversion of empire'.

Seeing Jesus as Messiah and seeing him as alternative Lord are not unrelated. The Gospels' portrayal of Jesus establishing God's kingdom, or reign, and the common NT language of Jesus' lordship make similar claims about all forms of power other than that of God in Christ. As N. T. Wright has often said to summarize this perspective, if Jesus is Lord, Caesar is not.

Not everyone is convinced by these sorts of political interpretations (e.g., Kim 2008), and it is possible that certain interpreters have made excessive claims. Nonetheless, understanding the Christology of the NT writings requires attention to the NT's imperial context, and it is virtually certain that the person/work of Christ the Lord is at least implicitly portrayed in contrast to the identity/activity of Caesar the lord. Furthermore, simply to use the title 'Lord' (κύριος) of Jesus inevitably raises the question of Jesus and YHWH, the κύριος of the Septuagint.

Jesus participates in the divine identity. As noted above, throughout the NT (not only in John, where it is most explicit), what Jesus does is often what God is said to do in the OT. All of the topics we have considered, from creation of the world to liberation of the oppressed to death by crucifixion, raise questions about the relationship between Christ's work and God's, and therefore between Christ's person, or identity, and God's. For Paul, Mark, John, and Revelation at least, the Cross appears to be not only a Christophany, but also a theophany. Thus Richard Bauckham uses the language of 'divine identity' to express the relationship between Christ the Son and God the Father implied in many parts of the NT (Bauckham 2008).

Bauckham bases his work on an examination of the nature of Second Temple Jewish monotheism and of the NT writers' interpretation of such texts as Isaiah 40–55. He argues that NT Christology is the highest imaginable Christology: Christological monotheism, or 'divine identity Christology': 'the inclusion of Jesus in the unique divine identity' (Bauckham 2008: 19)—which does not mean that Jesus *exhausts* the divine identity. With respect to Christ's work, this means that the preexistent Christ participated in the divine activity of creation, and that the risen Jesus shares in God's sovereignty and is thereby worthy of worship. As for the earthly Jesus, Bauckham argues that the earliest Christians interpreted Jesus through Isaiah 53 as a figure both human and divine in his earthly humiliation and his exaltation, each revealing Jesus' divine identity; that is, Jesus reveals God's identity as God crucified (see also Gorman 2009: 9–39; Hays 2012). The cry of desolation on the Cross (Mark 15:34; Matt. 27:46) is therefore 'God's self-identification with the Godforsaken', the ultimate act of divine love and self-revelation (Bauckham 2008: 254–68).

A number of interpreters have seen divine identity and mission more broadly in the Gospels, and not merely at the Cross or in the Gospel of John. N. T. Wright has argued that all four Gospels portray Jesus as the embodiment of YHWH returning to Zion to effect the end of exile and eschatological salvation, both for Israel and for all peoples (Wright 2012). Simon Gathercole has argued that the 'I have come' + purpose formulae in the Synoptics indicate the advent of the preexistent Son, who heals, calls sinners, exorcises demons, and dies not merely as a prophet or as the personification of preexistent divine Wisdom, but as the incarnation of God's Son (Gathercole 2006; similarly Marcus 1992: 72). Jesus therefore appropriately receives worship. Kavin Rowe (Rowe 2006) examines Luke's allegedly 'low' Christology and concludes that 'Jesus' and 'God' both maintain distinctive narrative identities but function as an indissoluble unity, as the one 'Lord'. Accordingly, the narrative of Jesus' activity is the revelation of God.

What was the source of this early inclusion of Jesus in the divine identity? The most common answer, drawing especially on Paul, has been the experience of the resurrected Jesus in worship, leading to the attribution of divine language to Jesus as creator, incarnate one, and redeemer, as poetic, liturgical texts like Phil. 2:6–11 and Col. 1:15–20 suggest (Hurtado 2003; Bauckham 2008). Chris Tilling (Tilling 2012), however, argues that Paul's letters portray Jesus' divinity as relational, meaning that Christ-believers now relate to Christ the way that Judaism says people relate to God.

Not everyone has been content with this direction in NT Christology. James McGrath (McGrath 2009), for example, argues that because the earliest (Jewish) Christians did not offer sacrifices to Jesus and God, they did *not* include Jesus in the divine identity. Because temple sacrifice plays such a minimal role in early Christianity, however, McGrath's view is unlikely to replace the stronger, if not flawless, arguments of Bauckham/Hurtado or Tilling. More trenchant has been the longstanding critique of such views by McGrath's teacher, James Dunn (Dunn 1980, 2010), who questions the language of divine identity while affirming that for the earliest Christians Jesus 'embodied ... the divine presence' and 'the outreach of God himself' (Dunn 2010: 146). That is, Jesus is not, and does not act as, an 'independent contractor' but is part of a 'family business' in bringing God's salvation.

CONCLUSION

We have surveyed trends in the study of NT Christology and considered some of the main aspects of Christ's work in the NT. We emphasized that Jesus brings God's promised eschatological salvation and beneficent rule. We have seen that Christ's work is inseparable from his person, or identity, and that his identity is revealed in his activity. We have also seen significant continuity in his work from creation to *parousia*. And we have seen that his work is inseparable as well from God's work and, in a different sense, from the Church's mission.

The benefits of Christ's work for humanity are manifold, and they are both present and future. They can be summarized, as we have seen, in words such as liberation, life, resurrection, and glory—or simply salvation. In a word, then, to speak of the work of Christ in the NT is to say, 'Jesus saves'. Which is to say that in Jesus, God saves.

SUGGESTED READING

Carroll and Green (1995); Harrisville (2006); Hays (2002); Longenecker (2005); Matera (1999).

BIBLIOGRAPHY

Barclay, J. M. G. (2015), *Paul and the Gift* (Grand Rapids, Mich.: Eerdmans).

Bauckham, R. (2008), *Jesus and the God of Israel: God Crucified and Other Studies on the New Testament's Christology of Divine Identity* (Grand Rapids, Mich.: Eerdmans).

Bird, M. F. and P. M. Sprinkle (2009), *The Faith of Jesus Christ: The Pistis Christou Debate* (Peabody, Mass.: Hendrickson).

Blackwell, B. C. (2011), *Christosis*. WUNT2/314 (Tübingen: Mohr Siebeck).

Brondos, D. A. (2006), *Paul on the Cross: Reconstructing the Apostle's Story of Redemption* (Minneapolis: Fortress).

Campbell, D. A. (2009), *The Deliverance of God: An Apocalyptic Rereading of Justification* (Grand Rapids, Mich.: Eerdmans).

Carroll, J. T. and J. B. Green (1995), *The Death of Jesus in Early Christianity* (Peabody, Mass.: Hendrickson).

Carter, W. (2000), *Matthew and the Margins: A Sociopolitical and Religious Reading* (Maryknoll, NY: Orbis).

Dunn, J. D. G. (1980), *Christology in the Making: A New Testament Inquiry into the Origins of the Doctrine of the Incarnation* (London: SCM; 2nd edn. 1989).

Dunn, J. D. G. (2008), ʹΕΚ ΠΙΣΤΕΩΣ: A Key to the Meaning of ΠΙΣΤΙΣ ΧΡΙΣΤΟΥ', in J. R. Wagner, C. K. Rowe, and A. K. Grieb (eds.), *The Word Leaps the Gap: Essays on Scripture and Theology in Honor of Richard B. Hays* (Grand Rapids, Mich.: Eerdmans), 351–66.

Dunn, J. D. G. (2010), *Did the First Christians Worship Jesus? The New Testament Evidence* (London: SPCK).

Fee, G. D. (2007), *Pauline Christology: An Exegetical-Theological Study* (Peabody, Mass.: Hendrickson).

Gathercole, S. J. (2006), *The Preexistent Son: Recovering the Christologies of Matthew, Mark, and Luke* (Grand Rapids, Mich.: Eerdmans).

Gorman, M. J. (2001), *Cruciformity: Paul's Narrative Spirituality of the Cross* (Grand Rapids, Mich.: Eerdmans).

Gorman, M. J. (2009), *Inhabiting the Cruciform God: Kenosis, Justification, and Theosis in Paul's Narrative Soteriology* (Grand Rapids, Mich.: Eerdmans).

Gorman, M. J. (2011), 'Effecting the New Covenant: A (Not So) New, New Testament Model for the Atonement', *Ex Auditu* 26: 26–59.

Harrisville, R. A. (2006), *Fracture: The Cross as Irreconcilable in the Language and Thought of the Biblical Writers* (Grand Rapids, Mich.: Eerdmans).

Hays, R. B. (1989), *Echoes of Scripture in the Letters of Paul* (New Haven: Yale University Press).

Hays, R. B. (2002), *The Faith of Jesus Christ: The Narrative Substructure of Gal 3:1–4:11*, 2nd edn. (Grand Rapids, Mich.: Eerdmans).

Hays, R. B. (2012), 'Faithful Witness, Alpha and Omega', in Hays and S. Alkier (eds.), *Revelation and the Politics of Apocalyptic Interpretation* (Waco, Tex.: Baylor University Press), 69–83.

Henderson, S. W. (2006), *Christology and Discipleship in Mark*. SNTSMS 135 (Cambridge: Cambridge University Press).

Hengel, M. (1981), *The Atonement: The Origins of the Doctrine in the New Testament*, trans. J. Bowden (London: SCM).

Hooker, M. D. (1990), *From Adam to Christ: Essays on Paul* (Cambridge: Cambridge University Press).

Hooker, M. D. (1995), *Not Ashamed of the Gospel: New Testament Interpretations of the Death of Christ* (Grand Rapids, Mich.: Eerdmans).

Hurtado, L. W. (2003), *Lord Jesus Christ: Devotion to Jesus in Earliest Christianity* (Grand Rapids, Mich.: Eerdmans).

Hurtado, L. W. (2006), 'Christology', in K. D. Sakenfeld (ed.), *The New Interpreter's Dictionary of the Bible* (Nashville: Abingdon), vol. 1, 612–22.

Janowski, B. and P. Stuhlmacher (eds.) (2004), *The Suffering Servant: Isaiah 53 in Jewish and Christian Sources*, trans. D. P. Bailey (Grand Rapids, Mich.: Eerdmans).

Keck, L. E. (2005), 'The Task of New Testament Christology', *Princeton Seminary Bulletin* 26: 266–76.

Kim, S. (2008), *Christ and Caesar: The Gospel and the Roman Empire in the Writings of Paul and Luke* (Grand Rapids, Mich.: Eerdmans).

Kingsbury, J. D. (1983), *The Christology of Mark's Gospel* (Philadelphia: Fortress Press).

Kirk, J. R. D. (2008), *Unlocking Romans: Resurrection and the Justification of God* (Grand Rapids, Mich.: Eerdmans).

Litwa, M. D. (2012), *We are Being Transformed: Deification in Paul's Soteriology*. BZNW 187 (Berlin: de Gruyter).

Longenecker, R. N. (ed.) (2005), *Contours of Christology in the New Testament* (Grand Rapids, Mich.: Eerdmans).

McGrath, J. F. (2009), *The Only True God: Early Christian Monotheism in Its Jewish Context* (Champaign, IL: University of Illinois Press).

McKnight, S. (2007), *A Community Called Atonement* (Nashville: Abingdon).

Marcus, J. (1992), *The Way of the Lord: Christological Exegesis of the Old Testament in the Gospel of Mark* (Louisville: Westminster/John Knox).

Marshall, I. H. (2007), *Aspects of the Atonement: Cross and Resurrection in the Reconciling of God and Humanity* (London: Paternoster).

Matera, F. J. (1999), *New Testament Christology* (Louisville: Westminster/John Knox).

Matera, F. J. (2012), *God's Saving Grace: A Pauline Theology* (Grand Rapids, Mich.: Eerdmans).

Middleton, J. R. and M. J. Gorman (2009), 'Salvation', in K. D. Sakenfeld (ed.), *The New Interpreter's Dictionary of the Bible* (Nashville: Abingdon), vol. 5, 45–61.

Moffitt, D. M. (2011), *Atonement and the Logic of Resurrection in the Epistle to the Hebrews*. NovTSup 141 (Leiden: Brill).

Novenson, M. (2012), *Christ among the Messiahs: Christ Language in Paul and Messiah Language in Ancient Judaism* (Oxford: Oxford University Press).

Porter, S. E. and C. L. Westfall (eds.) (2011), *Empire in the New Testament* (Eugene, Oreg.: Wipf and Stock).

Powers, D. G. (2001), *Salvation through Participation: An Examination of the Notion of the Believers' Corporate Unity with Christ in Early Christian Soteriology*. CBET 29 (Leuven: Peeters).

Rowe, C. K. (2006), *Early Narrative Christology: The Lord in the Gospel of Luke.* BZNW 139 (Berlin: de Gruyter; repr. Grand Rapids, Mich.: Eerdmans, 2009).

Swartley, W. M. (2006), *Covenant of Peace: The Missing Peace in New Testament Theology and Ethics* (Grand Rapids, Mich.: Eerdmans).

Thatcher, T. (2009), *Greater than Caesar: Christology and Empire in the Fourth Gospel* (Minneapolis: Fortress).

Thompson, M. M. (2001), *The God of the Gospel of John* (Grand Rapids, Mich.: Eerdmans).

Tilling, C. (2012), *Paul's Divine Christology.* WUNT 2/323 (Tübingen: Mohr Siebeck).

Watson, D. F. (2010), *Honor Among Christians: The Cultural Key to the Messianic Secret* (Minneapolis: Fortress).

Williams, J. J. (2010), *Maccabean Martyr Traditions in Paul's Theology of Atonement: Did Martyr Theology Shape Paul's Conception of Jesus's Death?* (Eugene, Oreg.: Wipf and Stock).

Wright, N. T. (1991), *The Climax of the Covenant: Christ and the Law in Pauline Theology* (Edinburgh: T. & T. Clark; Minneapolis: Fortress, 1993).

Wright, N. T. (2003), *The Resurrection of the Son of God* (London: SPCK; Minneapolis: Fortress).

Wright, N. T. (2012), *How God Became King: The Forgotten Story of the Gospels* (New York: HarperCollins).

Wright, N. T. (2013), *Paul and the Faithfulness of God* (London: SPCK; Minneapolis: Fortress).

Yoder, J. H. (1972), *The Politics of Jesus: Behold the Man! Our Victorious Lamb* (Grand Rapids, Mich.: Eerdmans; 2nd edn. 1994).

CHAPTER 6

THE GOSPELS ON THE PRESENCE OF JESUS

MARKUS BOCKMUEHL

DEAD or alive? Absent or present? These are among the most fundamental questions surrounding the ongoing significance of Jesus in the decades after his death.

The first seems easy: all known early Christian groups believed Jesus did not stay dead but rose again. From Scriptures to Creeds via most intervening debates, this entailed his 'bodily' resurrection along with exaltation into the immediate presence of God. From the earliest days of the Church, that conviction in turn guaranteed the acclamation and worship of the risen Messiah as empowered Son of God (for a definitive account of this dynamic, see Hurtado 2003).

Answers to the second question, by contrast, often remain opaque. Was the risen Jesus of the Gospels present or absent to the early Christian believer? Is Jesus personally here with me and with us, or is he away elsewhere until he returns as ruler and judge?

This has been a live question since antiquity, and remains so now. Contemporary Christians of a traditional Catholic mind-set might reply that Jesus is most concretely present in the Eucharist; Lutherans, in Word and Sacrament; most other Protestants, in the reading or proclamation of Scripture; evangelicals and charismatics, in the experience of the heart and the Holy Spirit. It seems the temporarily absent Jesus is sublimated to popular Christian experience in a bewildering variety of ways, mutually incompatible and dependent on diverse factors of theological, denominational, and perhaps—dare we say—temperamental preference.

The Creeds and much of the dogmatic tradition tend to be silent or negative about the experiential presence of Jesus. 'From there he shall come to judge the living and the dead' clearly does not give much encouragement to a pietistic or mystical assurance that 'he walks with me and he talks with me … he lives within my heart'.

Official Church doctrine does sometimes try to nuance these things more carefully. Vatican II, for example, specified five ways in which Jesus is present: (1) in the sacrament, priests act in the person of Christ. This pertains, above all, (2) in the consecrated bread and wine; but (3) whenever baptism or any other sacrament is administered, Christ is also personally and effectively present. This is also the case (4) through the reading of the word of God and the preaching of the Gospel, and most comprehensively (5) in the worshipping community (O'Collins 2012; on the Eucharist, see also *Sacrosanctum Concilium* 1963: §7; Lash 1968: 138–67; and O'Collins 1999).

Recent decades of New Testament research have paid welcome fresh attention to the Christological *identity* of Jesus and thereby provided a richer soil in which to understand the growth of Trinitarian thought. Abandoning some of the historically minimalist and gradualist certainties of an earlier generation, English-speaking, twenty-first-century New Testament scholarship has tended to show that even the earliest sources assume an articulate Christology pretty much from the start. The faithfulness of the Jewish Jesus in his life, crucifixion, and resurrection was always messianically redemptive: it opened a way for his followers to participate in his union with God as Father—a union first known and understood in worship (e.g., Hurtado 2003) to include Jesus in the identity of God himself (e.g., Bauckham 2008). However simple or (more likely) complex its construal may have been in practice, the road from the Christologies of the Jesus movement to those of the second and third centuries looks today less pot-holed and unpassable than it did twenty-five years ago.

Yet enhanced understanding of 'early high Christology' has not generated a comparable interest in the question of *how* the risen Jesus was in fact experienced or conceived as either personally present or indeed personally absent. Sometimes New Testament scholarship has deemed the question to be inappropriate. In systematic theology, debates about the nature of the Ascension, or indeed of 'presence' in Catholic sacramental theology, have not exhausted this question (see, for example, Farrow 1999: 165–254, 2011: 63–88; and Burgess 2004: 135–61). Even leading reference works may have no entry for either 'presence' or 'absence' of Christ (compare, however, Thomson 1988; Schilson 1995; and Gowan 2007; for Old Testament dimensions, see also Wilson 1995 and, more recently, de Hulster and MacDonald 2013): the latest edition of *Die Religion in Geschichte und Gegenwart* seems ironically emblematic for this state of affairs when precisely for the entry 'Gegenwart' it lists only a cross-reference to 'Zeit'—but has nothing to say about presence, divine or otherwise.

Thus, the question of a continued presence of Jesus *as Jesus* has not generated prominent interest in New Testament study. Three classic reference points may suffice to illustrate this.

When Rudolf Bultmann (1884–1976) wrote his landmark *Jesus* book in 1926, he could still afford to do so in a slender volume of just 50,000 words—a feat of economy that has spectacularly eluded his more recent successors. That achievement was fuelled by his certainty that virtually nothing of historical significance could be known about Jesus, let alone bear any contemporary consequence. Jesus is, for Bultmann, knowable precisely *not* as a personal presence but exclusively through the Word that calls forth the hearer's existential response (Bultmann 1926: 180–2). Yet if Christ is not personal, then Christ is not Jesus—who in turn cannot be either present or (alive but) absent *qua Jesus*, and must be merely dead.

Albert Schweitzer's (1875–1965) paradigm-shifting work on *The Mysticism of Paul the Apostle* (1953; originally published 1930) found that Paul's Gospel concentrated on the notion of participation in Christ—his Christ mysticism. For Schweitzer's Paul, this Christ is not *personally* present or absent, but primarily mediates an impersonal divine power. And far from locating Christ in the Eucharist, Paul and all other Christians believed Christ to be in heaven with God and nowhere else (thus, Schweitzer 1953: 33).

Ernst Käsemann (1906–1998) did stress a more concrete and personal Lordship of the exalted Christ who is at work on earth through the Spirit, above all in the Church as his body but also in individual believers. Once again, however, this is not in an obvious sense the personal presence of Jesus *qua* Jesus. Christ is no longer primarily continuous with Jesus of Nazareth: the supreme Lord is not primarily a 'person'. (See, for example, Käsemann 1969; compare further documentation in Orr 2011: 20–36, who notes New Testament scholarship's continuing neglect of any genuine dimension of Christ's absence in Paul; see also Orr 2014.)

THE GOSPELS

Here, we will explore the presence or absence of the living Jesus more specifically in the Gospels. How far did the evangelists deliberately distinguish between the pre-Easter Jesus, the post-Easter Jesus, and the situation of their own time? Form criticism's historical minimalism encouraged the view that in the Gospel tradition the presence of Christ is experienced through the voice of Christian prophets who freely articulate words of the risen Jesus that are then woven into the Gospel texts—especially in Q (see, notably, Boring 1991). This primarily mid-twentieth-century approach subsequently fell on harder times, due partly to its flawed historical presuppositions about early Christian prophecy.

The View from Q

Which brings us to the critical but newly precarious place of the Q hypothesis. If this sayings source existed, and if its purpose was really to offer a complete and free-standing account of Jesus, then it could indeed be significant that Q appears to skip both the Passion and the resurrection. If furthermore that undying, unrising Jesus were a deliberate creation rather than the fruit of compositional circumstance, we might infer some sort of present existential access to Jesus from his recorded teaching—perhaps as the seemingly transcendent and abiding Son of Man who reveals the Father to those he chooses (Q 10.22), and who discloses in himself the divine presence that longs to gather Jerusalem's children as a hen gathers her chicks (Q = Luke 13:33–4; on this passage, see Kirk 1998: 313–14 as cited in Hurtado 2003: 250). If this in turn holds true, then one might wish to consider the merit of analogies with the more timeless and panentheistic Saviour of the *Gospel of Thomas* (e.g., 30, 77) or, indeed, the Nag Hammadi discourses—analogies that in the later twentieth century were often foregrounded in publications sympathetic to the so-called 'Jesus Seminar'.

The succession of 'ifs' in the preceding paragraph highlights the problematic concatenation of hypotheses in such arguments about Q. Even assuming this source did exist, many scholars rightly regard attempts to construct a distinctive 'Q theology' or a 'Q community' in isolation as mired in speculation. Our question about the four Gospels will here be more usefully pursued in relation to their extant canonical form. The four Gospels' discrete narrative frames attest what the most influential Jesus narratives believed about his absence or continued presence in their own day.

Jesus Then and Now

Even from this viewpoint, however, our task is not straightforward. Any miracle or word of assurance has interpretative potential to be projected homiletically into an account of the Redeemer's continuing presence to the believer. But does the text intend this or not? Christian homilists through the ages have extrapolated pastorally from the powerful sense of Jesus' presence in the pre-Easter narrative—as healer and preacher, but also as the beloved Son, or indeed as the one whom even demons and storms obey. This is a perfectly understandable and valid mode of application. Methodologically, however, it runs a potentially limitless risk of pious eisegesis, and in the absence of clear textual indicators can offer little exegetical evidence for the text's intention one way or the other.

The text's overwhelmingly liturgical performance and congregational reception necessarily means that every ecclesial Gospel reading performs for the hearers an approximation and re-presentation of Jesus' own narrated speaking and acting in their midst (cf. McDonald 2005: 68). In that sense we may say that the public Gospel comes quasi-sacramentally to mediate something of the very Jesus of which it speaks.

In order to limit the potential for eisegesis, we will do well to recognize the evangelists' respect for the narrative pastness of their account, which by and large does *not* engage in indiscriminate aggiornamento for their own times (cf. Lemcio 1991).

Nevertheless, in some cases the Gospels *themselves* in fact encourage such homiletical extension of the presence of Jesus into the time of the reader: that too is an important feature of the historical phenomenology. Such cases might be said to include heightened Pharisaic enmity in Matthew (*passim*), Mark's potentially abolitionist interpretation of the hand-washing dispute (7:19), Luke's Roman synagogue benefactor at Capernaum (7:5), or John's envisaged expulsions from the synagogue (9:22; 12:42), among others. But in fact not one of these texts functions self-evidently along such lines; it remains the case that they constitute exceptions rather than the norm. Jesus recruits no Gentile disciples and appears not to baptize anyone; his followers eat no forbidden food and contest no sacrifices, tithing, or circumcision—all of which might seem fair game if the evangelists allowed themselves editorial 'relevance'.

So just because the texts may tolerate or invite homiletical re-application, it does not follow that they therefore *document* the experienced presence of the post-Easter Jesus in the life of the early communities. We will do well to proceed more cautiously, even at the risk of somewhat slimmer initial pickings.

The Gospel of Mark

Such caution is immediately pertinent in Mark. Jesus has of course a dramatic and divinely powerful narrative presence here as a manifest healer, exorcist, and teacher who is certainly present to his disciples and to all to whom he ministers.

Jesus repeatedly announces not only his death but also his resurrection and a future mission (8:31; 9:9–10; 14.9, 28; 16.7; etc.). But Mark is taciturn about what that post-Easter age might look like or what Jesus would personally have to do with it. The 'I have come' sayings at 2:17 or 10:45 talk about his mission but say nothing about the future beyond it, whether or not one deems them to hint at pre-existence (as does Gathercole 2006). The bridegroom with whom his friends cannot fast (2:19–20) is evidently the earthly Jesus rather than the risen Lord present to the post-Easter Church (so rightly Yarbro Collins 2007 ad loc. [contra Bultmann]). 'Who is this, that the wind and sea obey him?' (4:41) is of course a homiletically powerful rhetorical question; but while Matthew (14:28–30) and texts like the *Odes of Solomon* (39:8–13) richly capitalize on that opportunity for application, Mark himself does not.

Similarly, whether the transfiguration narrative is originally a displaced resurrection appearance or (as I think) not, the angelically transformed Jesus on the mountain does perhaps hint at how the post-Easter Church is to think of his glorified presence, since the disciples may not speak of it until after the resurrection (9:9). But Mark himself does not follow up, and the disciples puzzle about what this 'resurrection' might mean (9:10). For the post-Easter disciples it is perhaps the Spirit rather than Jesus himself who will be present: when they are persecuted and on trial, it is the Spirit who will give them the words to speak (13:11).

After 2:18–20 the theme of absence resurfaces implicitly in Jesus' anointing for burial (14:3–9): what Mary of Bethany has done will be told wherever the gospel is preached throughout the world (14:9). Yet Jesus says nothing about his own future presence, except perhaps inasmuch as 'the gospel' presumably represents him. And Mark's Last Supper envisages no future repetition of that meal until it resumes with Jesus himself in the kingdom of God (14:22–25).

One tantalizing hint that Mark intends more than this is the promise in 14:28 that after the resurrection Jesus will 'go before' the disciples to Galilee, deliberately reiterated by the angels in 16:7 with the assurance that 'there you will see him'. From an intra-Marcan perspective this promise might offer an assurance that the presence of Jesus will be with the disciples in the Galilee from which they have come and where they began to exercise the mission on which Jesus sent them (6:7–12) (somewhat speculatively on this point, compare Best 1981: 200–1).

Commentators sometimes make a virtue of necessity by invoking supposed ancient 'standard literary practice' of merely alluding to events later than the main narrative (thus, for example, Yarbro Collins 2007). Yet in a case like the resurrection appearances the reader surely has every reason to want to know more—unless, perhaps, he or she knows the answer already in the form of a tradition like that related in Matthew 28 (where some have conjectured the expansion of a lost Marcan ending).

Without either the hypothetically lost or the canonical longer ending, Mark's omission of eyewitness encounters with the risen Jesus does appear rhetorically to underscore what one leading commentator calls 'the absence of Jesus in the time of the author and audiences' (Yarbro Collins 2007 ad loc.), an absence explicitly anticipated in 2:19–20. This is, to be sure, an argument largely from silence, mitigated in any case by the Son of Man's exaltation to God's right hand and powerful future coming with the clouds of heaven (9:1; 13:24–7). Nevertheless, Mark offers little explicit assurance about the continuity of Jesus' active presence with his followers on earth (*pace* Karrer 1998: 307).

Strikingly the promised Galilean narrative sequel is absent not only from Mark's extant base text but from its canonical supplementation (16:9–20) and every other known variant. Perhaps that is because by the time of the supplementor such sequels had already been supplied in two other Gospels (Matthew and John) on which the canonical longer ending depends. What we do learn from this early second-century conclusion is that, after commissioning the disciples, the risen Jesus was exalted to God's right hand in heaven where presumably he is now—though the concluding writer nevertheless insists that 'the Lord Jesus' himself 'worked with' the apostles and 'confirmed' their evangelistic message by performing accompanying signs (16:19–20). The editor does not make clear if such activity continues to the present day, but neither does he say that it has ceased.

The Gospel of Matthew

Where Mark remains ambivalent or unresolved on our question, Matthew is clearer. He does not keep us guessing about an unfulfilled Galilean resurrection encounter or about the Messiah's abiding presence—a theme that links Jesus' earthly ministry to his risen life, and the Gospel story to the everyday life of the Church.

Three passages are widely agreed to point strongly in this direction. Matthew 1:23 introduces Jesus not only as the promised Messiah representing God's presence but as carrying the name which personifies that presence—Emmanuel.

This affirmation famously meets its matching *inclusio* in the risen Messiah's promise that 'I am with you to the end of the age' (28:20)—he whom the disciples see in Galilee is none other than Jesus, continuous in person (and by name, v. 16) with the earthly Jesus (cf. Kupp 1996: 230). Matthew reports no ascension: his Jesus is *already* exalted to the divine exercise of 'all power in heaven and on earth'; he does not leave the disciples but remains 'with you', present rather than absent. The context of his presence in Matthew 28 is in discipleship and worldwide evangelism, baptism, and keeping of his commandments—the Torah of Jesus. This all-sovereign Jesus is 'with us' as his *name* is 'God with us' (1:23; 28:20). Baptism is in the 'name' of the triune God who is present (28:19): the Father opens access to the presence of the Son and the Son to that of the Father (compare, already, 11:27), just as Father and Spirit already accompanied the birth and baptism of the Son (1:18, 20; 3:16) (compare, similarly, Karrer 1998: 308).

Further in relation to Matthew 28, some have seen an important connection between Torah, presence, and community formation that continues from the pre-Easter to the post-Easter Jesus and evokes Pentateuchal themes. At Sinai, the giving of the Law similarly connects both to the covenantal constitution of the *qahal*/ἐκκλησία of Israel and to the presence of YHWH on the mountain and in the tabernacle (Kupp 1996: 216–17), while Moses goes on to pass the baton of God's commissioning presence to Joshua-'Jesus' in the books of Deuteronomy and Joshua (see McDonald 2005: 83–4). But, while the Old Testament Joshua receives the divine promise of presence from Moses, the New Testament Joshua-Jesus issues it himself. Matthew came to be the evangelist who, more than any other, nourished the powerful patristic and mediaeval idea of Christ as the new lawgiver.

This theme of Emmanuel's presence, sustained by the *inclusio* between chapters 1 and 28, comes to expression in several other passages. Chapter 18 affirms an ecclesial locus of the Messiah's presence: wherever two or three gather in his name, there Jesus is among them (18:20). In context, this promise focuses on Jesus' ratification of the community's juridical decision-making, but recent studies have rightly questioned attempts to restrict the saying's reach to that immediate context without reference to Jesus' presence more generally (see Kupp 1996 and Surlis 2011: 88–9). Ratification by Jesus functions as an aspect of his more far-reaching presence promised for the mission of the Church in 28:20 (see, for example, Pokorny 1999).

A widely cited saying in the Mishnah finds God's presence (Shekhinah) dwelling wherever two or three gather over words of the Torah (M. *Abot* 3.2, ביניהם שרויה שכינה תורה דברי ביניהם ויש שיושבים שנים, [Hananiah b. Teradion]). Parallels like these suggest that Matthew is unlikely to be concerned strictly with 'the regulation of disputatious church members' (Kupp 1996: 199). In our passage, then, Matthew's Jesus assures his followers of divine ratification and ecclesia-constituting presence. This contrasts starkly with 23:38 where the Jerusalem Temple is being left 'desolate' as a place of absence. (It seems at least conceivable that Hananiah ben Teradion's saying promises analogous compensation for the Shekhinah's catastrophic absence from the Temple; Pokorny [1999: 479–80] infers that, for Matthew by contrast, every Christian gathering can therefore become the place of presence.)

Matthew 18:20 thus may be said to constitute together with 1:23 and 28:20 the core trio of passages that define and energize this evangelist's theme of the presence of Jesus (Kupp [1996: 175] refers to 1:23 as the 'masthead' over the whole Gospel).

But Matthew does also resume certain Marcan themes of absence. These include his passages about fasting in the bridegroom's company and about the presence of false Messiahs and of the poor when Jesus is absent (9:15; 24:3–5; 26:11). Whether or not such residual Marcan themes of absence are due to what some Synoptic critics like to call 'editorial fatigue' (Goodacre 1998), they complicate Matthew's assurance of Jesus' abiding presence in chapter 28. Despite its emphatic affirmation, Matthew retains a 'rhetorical sense of ambiguity' (Kupp 1996: 199) about how precisely that presence works.

Matthew's ambiguity proves to be surprisingly complex and diffuse, as two examples may illustrate. A few verses before 18:20, Jesus has assured the disciples that 'Whoever receives one such child in my name receives me' (18:5). More memorably still, in the eschatological scenario of chapter 25 one of the key criteria of judgement is failure to care for the king's needs when he was hungry, thirsty, a foreigner, destitute, ill, or in prison (25:35–6).

'Finding Jesus in the poor' is a laudably popular and well-loved trope of Christian homiletics and praxis, and might seem to hold considerable promise for our topic. Nevertheless, there are telling uncertainties and paradoxes about the logic of this identification, not least because those who truly encounter him are unaware of it (cf. Coakley 2008: 316). Matthew 25 affirms a clear bond between Jesus and those deprived of clothes, food, health, friendship, or freedom, even if commentators rightly note that the 'least' among Jesus' brothers and sisters are here in the first instance the poor among his disciples (25:40, 45).

In some sense, then, to serve the 'least' is indeed to serve Jesus himself. But to say that still leaves unclear if this is for Matthew an ontological or a relational calculus: does the presence of Jesus attach intrinsically and sacramentally to the poor *themselves*? Though this is often asserted, Matthew's Jesus seems in the next chapter to *deny* any intrinsic identity: 'you always have the poor with you, but you will not always have me' (26:11). Evidently there is no ontological equation in the sense that the poor person *as such* represents or mediates Jesus. Relational and analogical puzzles remain about precisely whether and how Jesus is present in the act of serving the poor.

A similar ambiguity pertains at 18:5: is Jesus present in the child, or is the act of receiving the child vicariously to receive Jesus by way of some analogy? (Compare the force of the rabbinic term כאילו, for example, in *M. Abot* 3.3 immediately after the previously cited passage: three who sit and talk about Torah are 'as if' כאילו they ate God's own table.) Once again Matthew disrupts any straightforward correlation in the very next verse by identifying the children not with Jesus but with his followers—'these little ones *who believe in me*' (18:6).

These are difficult questions, and Matthew is less troubled by them than are his modern interpreters. Jesus does exercise a powerful salvific presence in the Gospel narrative as the one who stills the storm (8:23–7), who steadies the hand of the believer to walk on the turbulent waves (14:28–31), who heals 'all' of those who even touch the hem of his garment (14:36). He is the gentle one whose burden is light and who refreshes the weary (11:28–30). In these and other passages, Matthew happily projects his narrative forward into the life of faith. The voice of the exalted Jesus also speaks powerfully to the reader's own experience in 23:34–6: Jesus it is who has sought in vain maternally to gather Jerusalem's children together until her house was left desolate; he it is who now sends (present tense! but compare 10:16) the prophets, sages, and scribes persecuted by their enemies; and he it is who will return to be greeted by Jerusalem's welcome.

Matthew's Last Supper, finally, formulates a liturgically richer setting than Mark, complementing the Passover meal's interpreted bread of affliction with the bread and wine as the broken body and shed covenant blood of Jesus. For Matthew this is specifically 'for the forgiveness of sins' (26:26–8). Unlike Paul (1 Cor. 11:25) and perhaps Luke (22:19), however, Matthew like Mark makes no suggestion that this meal is to be repeated or that it conveys a post-Easter presence of Jesus (though compare 26:29).

Matthew is thus the most unwavering of the evangelists in affirming the presence of the living Jesus in and with the Church in its life and its mission after Easter. That affirmation is for him not hedged about with Marcan question marks nor sublimated by narratives of departure and substitution by the Spirit. Matthew is aware of the dialectic of absence, but remains content to affirm Jesus as always present. He never articulates precisely how this is, and refuses to materialize or localize that presence with any narrowly sacramental focus. Nevertheless, between the two endpoints of his great *inclusio* of 'God with us' (1:23–28:20), the cumulative effect of his narrative delivers an affirmation of presence far stronger and richer than the religious commonplace of anonymous divine providence or assistance (see also McDonald 2005: 85–6). The same Jesus who was Emmanuel as Mary's child promises his abiding presence in the Church's internal discernment and outreach to the world, and especially in their welcome and service of the least of his brothers and sisters.

Luke's Gospel and Acts

Unlike Mark and Matthew, Luke places the geographic focus of post-Easter continuity quite emphatically not in Galilee but in and around Jerusalem, the city that rejected Jesus. It is here that his life has its beginning and end, here that he is exalted to heaven, here that he will return, and here that the Church is born. Luke is also structurally and narratively more candid about the departure of Jesus than either Mark or Matthew. As in John and of course in Acts, Jesus leaves the disciples after the resurrection but the Spirit comes to take his place for the interim; indeed, Acts is explicit in seeing the Spirit as the Spirit of Jesus (16:7; cf. 2:38; 5:9; 8:39).

Yet Luke's conception of Jesus' departure nevertheless calls for clarification. Ascensions as such have good precedent in biblical and ancient Jewish accounts of Enoch, Moses, and Elijah. Though ascended, they are intermittently present in contemporary experience—as indeed in the Synoptic transfiguration accounts. Similarly, Luke's idea of the exaltation of Christ as ascent or movement from earth to heaven finds certain parallels in other New Testament writers (e.g., 1 Tim. 3:16; 1 Pet. 3:22; Eph. 4:8–10; Heb. 7:26). The risen Jesus of Nazareth thus becomes a heavenly actor in the unfolding narrative (see Zwiep 1997 and 2001; I am less persuaded by the view that this is a device to help resolve post-70 tensions over the delayed parousia). Nevertheless, the uniquely spatial nature of Luke's ascension account does distinctively visualize the explicit challenge of presence and absence, which particularly occupies both Luke and John. (Depending on one's text-critical judgement this is perhaps only hinted at in Luke 24, but it is certainly explicit in Acts 1. See, for example, the discussion in Parsons 1987.)

Luke is alone among the Gospels in articulating the post-resurrection exaltation of Jesus in a narrative of visible space-time movement. (Note also that Justin, *Apol.* 1.67.8, and *Barn.* 15.9 continue to assume that resurrection and exaltation narratively coincide, as do several Pauline texts; Mark 16:9–20 apparently does the same.) The result graphically impresses upon the reader that in this event Jesus has 'departed' (διέστη ἀπ᾽ αὐτῶν, Luke 24:51; cf. Acts 1:9–11) and must now in some sense be 'there' rather than 'here'. The Son of Man *will be revealed* on a day in the future (17:30), and on that day the disciples will eat and drink at Jesus' table in his kingdom (22:30).

In his narrative conceptualization of the exaltation of Jesus, Luke partly parallels the Johannine association of Jesus' departure with the promise of the Spirit. Jesus leaves and the Spirit arrives—not to replace him, but ostensibly to represent him and continue his work by empowering the disciples, as especially Acts goes on to suggest. Significantly, the charge of the departing Jesus is to proclaim his message to all nations specifically *in his name* (24:47; contrast more broadly Matt. 28:19). And even in the face of his departure, the risen Jesus nevertheless employs the present tense in assuring the disciples that he himself is 'sending the promise of my Father' to them—presumably a promise that is not straightforwardly exhausted with the arrival of the 'power from on high' (24:49) ten days later at Pentecost.

In a handful of passages Luke picks up from Matthew or Q the theme of a sapiential Jesus who speaks as if already ascended. Where in Matthew (23:34) it is Jesus who sends prophets, sages, and scribes, in Luke's parallel (11:49) it is explicitly the Wisdom of God who sends prophets and apostles. In Luke 13:34 as in Matthew, Jesus laments over Jerusalem's rejection of his desire to gather her children as a hen gathers her chicks under her wings. In a third passage, unique to Luke, Jesus promises that in the coming persecution he himself will give the disciples 'words and wisdom' that their enemies cannot resist (21:15; contrast Mark 13:11).

Like Matthew and Mark, Luke does not identify the Eucharist as a locus of the abiding presence of Jesus, although like Paul he does imply its repetition (22:19); the text neither encourages nor prohibits any homiletical application of the fact that the disciples on the Emmaus road recognize Jesus in his breaking of the bread (24:35; *not* 'in the bread', as popular Catholic piety sometimes has it).

Just as Luke's Jesus receives the Spirit in birth and baptism (1:3; 3:22) and is impelled by the Spirit in his ministry (4:1), so in death he surrenders his Spirit to his Father (14:46) while as the risen one he sends the Father's promise and predicts the coming of power from on high (24:49)—identified in Acts 2:33 as the Spirit poured out at Pentecost. Whether earthly or ascended, Jesus mediates and is mediated by the Spirit of God. Eloquent attention has also been drawn in recent Christological work to Luke's use of the term ὁ κύριος for Jesus (note especially Rowe 2006): from the felt encounter with the unseen Lord in Mary's visit to Elizabeth (1:43) (thus Nassauer 2012), to the dynamic action of 'the Lord' as protagonist in Acts, this encapsulates Luke's sense of a continuing presence of Jesus. This casts doubt on periodic assertions of an 'absentee christology' in Acts (Buckwalter [1996: 21–2] detects this in Moule 1966, though it is later tempered in Moule 1977: 104–5; compare, also, MacRae 1973), or of a Christ who is 'absent yet curiously present' (Parsons 1987: 160), perhaps neither in heaven nor on earth but in 'thirdspace' (Sleeman 2009: 91 and *passim*; contrast O'Toole 1984, 2004; Buckwalter 1996: 173–5; and others.)

Luke is clearly deliberate about the theme of departure, and the ascension marks for him the cessation of resurrection appearances. No exception is made in Acts even for Paul, although the Jesus he persecutes is the Jesus who calls him (9:4; 22:8; 26:14) and who later appears to him in a unique visionary encounter (22:18; cf. 7:56). Luke finds Jesus' continued divine presence guaranteed by the Spirit.

The Gospel of John

The Fourth Gospel perhaps reflects most articulately and acutely on the tension between the present and the absent post-Easter Jesus; indeed on one account nearly half the Gospel is concerned with the topic of Jesus' departure (thus, Eckstein 2011: 162 [#13101] with reference to 13:1–20:31 and 21:25). His powerful theme of the Incarnation as mediating the divine presence compels John to confront the question of whether and how believers experience the ongoing presence of Jesus. And it seems counterproductive to try and dissolve the deliberate tension of presence and departure by relativizing measures of either literary criticism or comparison with the Johannine letters (so, rightly, Eckstein 2011: 163–7 [#13101]).

More often than in the other Gospels, Jesus repeatedly announces that he has to 'go away' (e.g., 7:33; 8:14, 21–3; 13:3, 33, 36; 14:2–3, 28; 16:5, 7, 17, 19; 17:11, 13; cf. 20:17)—a point not lost on a quizzical audience wondering if he is going to the Greeks (7:35). In this Gospel Jesus tackles the problem of his departure from the disciples while he is still with them, rather than after Easter (as he does in Luke). Specifically, the Farewell discourses dwell extensively on the question of presence and communion with Jesus once he is no longer there. It is precisely the fact that he 'goes away' that alone makes it possible for him to 'come again' (πάλιν ἔρχομαι: cf. 14:3, 18, 28) in order to take his disciples to the apartments he has prepared for them in his Father's house. This may seem on the surface a puzzling and disturbing rationale: why inflict the absence of the interim on the disciples just for the sake of being able to return?

The first point to note is that John engages the theme of absence as the necessary consequence of a temporally bounded incarnation. This strikingly separates his approach from that of the timeless Saviour of the Nag Hammadi Gospels, who never stoops to take flesh and never ceases his disembodied instruction of the gnostic mind exalted above the world.

John's solution is similar to Luke's, but developed in considerable depth and complexity. Jesus promises that while he himself will 'go away', Father and Son will send 'another' advocate or ombudsman, the Spirit, who will in fact be 'with' and 'in' the believers forever (14:16–17; 14:25–6; 15:26).

This Johannine promise of 'another' Paraclete famously lent hostages to fortune, which both Mani (CMC 64.8–65.18) and Mohammed (Qur'an 61.6 and commentaries) put to welcome use in their own cause. That said, John's correlation between Jesus and the Paraclete is so inextricably close that the Paraclete in fact embodies the love and living presence of Jesus himself. 'Another' appears not to mean 'other' but more of the same: their distinctive unity is the reason Jesus can paradoxically claim to be absent without leaving the disciples orphaned. Even in the absence of Jesus, the Spirit's task and teaching is what Jesus does and teaches; he did speak only what he hears (16:13). The Spirit acts to remind the disciples of Jesus, to teach them and lead them into all truth, and it is through the Spirit that Jesus is able to leave his peace with them (14:16–17, 25). In the Spirit's coming, the disciples will know that they are in Jesus and he in them; indeed by keeping his commandments they love him and he will love them and manifest himself to them (14:20–1). The Spirit is the presence of the living Jesus, who is present even while absent and who will come to them even though he is going away (14:18, 28; cf. 14:3). (Sproston North [2013] links this dynamic especially to the Lazarus narrative of chapter 11, which textual and artistic sources show to have exercised a powerful influence on the early Christian imagination.)

The question of whether the Paraclete is the *same* or *another* is contested even between the Gospel of John and the First Letter of John, where he is emphatically identified as Jesus Christ the Righteous (1 John 2:1). But 1 John also confirms that the Spirit in fact mediates assurance of the abiding presence of Jesus: it is through the Spirit that we know the Son abides in those who keep his commandments (3:23–4). (Of course, the interpretation of the successive pronouns in 3:24 is notoriously contested.)

A theological development of the Paraclete's role in the presence has been suggested not only for 1 John but also within the resumptive and somewhat circular prose of the Farewell discourses themselves. Scholarship on these discourses has at times attempted to resolve the compositional tensions of John 15–16 by interpreting them as a *relecture* of chapters 13–14. (See, for example, Dettwiler 1995: 293–9 and *passim*. Outside John 14–16, the Gospel foregrounds a more traditional conception of the Spirit without reference to the Paraclete [cf. 1:32–4; 3:34; 7:39; 20:22].)

A basic theological challenge throughout is the absence of Jesus: how can salvation possibly be mediated if the incarnation of divine salvation is now absent? Rather than affirming a Matthean idea of continued presence, the Johannine Jesus here foregrounds his departure (beginning with 13:33–8). But for John this absence is packaged in such a way that the Paraclete as the present manifestation of God's love overcomes the challenge, mediating his joy and presence to disciples who are thus not left abandoned. (Exegetically less convincing is Migliasso 1979: 261 and *passim*; the problem of absence raised by Jesus' physical death is overcome by his perennial presence brought about in the disciples through the 'mystery' of his death.)

John 13:34–5 and 15:1–17 point to a second, ethically oriented pair of concepts that draw on an abiding and quasi-mystical union with Jesus. These twin themes arise from the image of the vine and its fruit-bearing and from the love of Jesus for the disciples as his friends. The theme of union arguably presupposes a notion of abiding presence, perhaps along the similarly timeless-sounding lines of 14:23: 'If anyone loves me, he will keep my word, and my Father will love him, and we will come to him and make our home with him.'

A fuller discussion could take further account of the influential language of Christ's body as the new temple, addressed in 2:21 (cf. 1:14), although in truth John himself does not greatly develop this theme. A more difficult question often raised in this connection is the force of the strongly Eucharistic language in 6:51–8. The fourth evangelist wants to affirm that to consume Jesus' body and blood is to receive the life of the living Father and Son and to participate in their union. But the text does not relate this directly to the repetition of a liturgical action involving bread and wine—indeed no wine is mentioned, and arguably only metaphorical bread.

Many of John's passages appear *before* Easter, where much of the discourse material develops its Christological reference to Jesus in the present tense—and famously there is scope for confusion about whether in addition to *descending* from heaven Jesus has also already *ascended* (e.g., 3:13). Similarly the so-called High Priestly prayer of Chapter 17, with its timeless language of the Son's intercession as well as union with the Father, makes the reader wonder if the narrative camera is located in any actual moment of the earthly life of Jesus or rather eternally in the Son's union with the Father. This ambiguity is deeply rooted in John's subtle eschatology, which Johannine scholars often consider to be mostly of the 'realized' variety (compare the recent discussion in Eckstein 2011: 152–5). The experience of the disciples often appears deliberately construed to bear on that of the readership and the Johannine community.

Finally, and rather like Luke, John envisages a delay between Jesus' resurrection and his departure to be with the Father. During that period Jesus is still intermittently present, but Mary Magdalene *may* not touch him—and Thomas *need* not (20:17, 27). Before the appearance to Thomas, Jesus bestows the Holy Spirit by breathing on the disciples—implying graphically that here too as Jesus departs his place is literally taken by his own πνεῦμα (20:22). The concluding chapter supplements discourse about Jesus' presence in the Paraclete by juxtaposing the possibility of the Beloved Disciple's continuing witness to Jesus with the authorization of the restored Simon Peter as the one who will now vicariously continue the good Shepherd's care and feeding of his flock (21:15–25). By extension a similar thought may be present in the Synoptic suggestion that those who receive the Apostles receive Jesus himself (Matt. 10:40; Luke 10:16; cf. John 13:20).

Conclusion

The dialectic of the risen Jesus' absence and presence appears for the evangelists to become more articulate and more pressing as time passes. Mark's largely apocalyptic mediation of the issue seems not to problematize the question of whether Jesus is in any sense present here and now. Perhaps this Gospel was intended from the start as it was certainly received in the early Church, primarily as a sourcebook of (Petrine) 'memoirs' of the Spirit-filled life of Jesus rather than as a complete and definitive free-standing gospel in its own right. Matthew resolves the tension firmly in favour of Jesus' abiding presence in the Church and its mission: there is no departure at all, and therefore presumably no genuine problem of absence. Luke is the first evangelist to deal explicitly with the end of resurrection appearances and the reality of departure; for him, as for John, this means that the departed Jesus sends his Spirit to continue his work. In Luke–Acts the gift of the Spirit allows the same 'Lord' Jesus to remain the 'teaching and doing' protagonist in the apostolic mission (cf. Acts 1:1). John, finally, wrestles with the departure and absence of Jesus most explicitly of all, and develops a powerfully eschatological and sacramental vision of union with the Son as a way to assure believers of his continued presence. It is at least worth considering if the Fourth Gospel's realism about the tension between departure and presence makes possible its strongly mystical and sacramental emphasis. For Matthew, Luke, and John that presence is at times sublimated or otherwise proximate, but in all three there are at least instances of continued encounter with Jesus himself. The subtlety and diversity of sacramental, corporate, and visionary experience bears testimony to a continued Christian confidence that the One to Come is indeed present in our midst.

Suggested Reading

Bauckham (2008); Gathercole (2006); Hurtado (2003).

Bibliography

Bauckham, R. (2008), *Jesus and the God of Israel: God Crucified and Other Studies on the New Testament's Christology of Divine Identity* (Grand Rapids, Mich.: Eerdmans).

Best, E. (1981), *Following Jesus: Discipleship in the Gospel of Mark*. JSNTSup 4 (Sheffield: JSOT Press).

Boring, M. E. (1991), *The Continuing Voice of Jesus: Christian Prophecy and the Gospel Tradition* (Louisville: Westminster/John Knox).

Buckwalter, H. D. (1996), *The Character and Purpose of Luke's Christology*. SNTSMS 89 (Cambridge: Cambridge University Press).

Bultmann, R. (1926), *Jesus* (Tübingen: Mohr Siebeck).

Burgess, A. R. (2004), *The Ascension in Karl Barth* (Burlington, Vt.: Ashgate).

Coakley, S. (2008), 'Finding Jesus Christ in the Poor', in B. R. Gaventa and R. B. Hays (eds.), *Seeking the Identity of Jesus: A Pilgrimage* (Grand Rapids, Mich.: Eerdmans), 301–19.

de Hulster, I. J. and N. MacDonald (eds.) (2013), *Divine Presence and Absence in Exilic and Post-Exilic Judaism. Forschungen zum Alten Testament* (Tübingen: Mohr Siebeck).

Dettwiler, A. (1995), *Die Gegenwart des Erhöhten. Eine exegetische Studie zu den johanneischen Abschiedsreden (Joh 13,31–16,33) unter besonderer Berücksichtigung ihres Relecture-Charakters*. FRLANT 169 (Göttingen: Vandenhoeck & Ruprecht).

Eckstein, H.-J. (2011), 'Die Gegenwart des Kommenden und die Zukunft des Gegenwärtigen. Zur Eschatologie im Johannesevangelium', in H.-J. Eckstein, C. Landmesser, and H.Lichtenberger (eds.), *Eschatologie–Eschatology: The Sixth Durham–Tübingen Research Symposium: Eschatology in Old Testament, Ancient Judaism and Early Christianity.* Wissenschaftliche Untersuchungen zum Neuen Testament 272 (Tübingen: Mohr Siebeck), 149–69.

Farrow, D. (1999), *Ascension and Ecclesia: On the Significance of the Doctrine of the Ascension for Ecclesiology and Christian Cosmology* (Grand Rapids, Mich.: Eerdmans).

Farrow, D. (2011), *Ascension Theology* (London: T. & T. Clark).

Gathercole, S. J. (2006), *The Pre-existent Son: Recovering the Christologies of Matthew, Mark, and Luke* (Grand Rapids, Mich.: Eerdmans).

Goodacre, M. (1998), 'Fatigue in the Synoptics', *New Testament Studies* 44: 45–58.

Gowan, D. E. (2007), 'Divine Presence', in in K. D. Sakenfeld (ed.), *The New Interpreter's Dictionary of the Bible* (Nashville: Abingdon), vol. 2, 146–9.

Hurtado, L. W. (2003), *Lord Jesus Christ: Devotion to Jesus in Earliest Christianity* (Grand Rapids, Mich.: Eerdmans).

Karrer, M. (1998), *Jesus Christus im Neuen Testament.* Grundrisse zum Neuen Testament 11 (Göttingen: Vandenhoeck & Ruprecht).

Käsemann, E. (1968), *The Testament of Jesus: A Study of the Gospel of John in the Light of Chapter 17*, trans. G. Krodel (London: SCM Press).

Käsemann, E. (1969), *Jesus Means Freedom*, trans. F. Clarke (London: SCM Press).

Kirk, A. (1998), *The Composition of the Sayings Source: Genre, Synchrony, and Wisdom Redaction in Q.* NovTSup 91 (Leiden: Brill).

Kupp, D. D. (1996), *Matthew's Emmanuel: Divine Presence and God's People in the First Gospel.* SNTSMS 90 (Cambridge: Cambridge University Press).

Lash, N. (1968), *His Presence in the World: A Study in Eucharistic Worship and Theology* (London: Sheed and Ward).

Lemcio, E. E. (1991), *The Past of Jesus in the Gospels* (Cambridge: Cambridge University Press).

McDonald, P. (2005), ' "I Am With You Always, to the End of the Age": Presence in the Gospel according to Matthew', *Proceedings of the Irish Biblical Association* 28: 66–86.

MacRae, G. W. (1973), 'Whom Heaven Must Receive Until the Time: Reflections on the Christology of Acts', *Interpretation* 27: 151–65.

Migliasso, S. (1979), 'La presenza dell'Assente. Saggio di analisi letterario–strutturale e di sintesi teologica di Gv. 13,31–14,31' (Doctoral dissertation, Pontifical Gregorian University, Rome).

Moule, C. F. D. (1966), 'The Christology of Acts', in L. E. Keck and J. L. Martyn (eds.), *Studies in Luke–Acts* (Nashville: Abingdon), 159–85.

Moule, C. F. D. (1977), *The Origin of Christology* (Cambridge: Cambridge University Press).

Nassauer, G. (2012), 'Gegenwart des Abwesenden. Eidetische Christologie in Lk 1.39–45', *New Testament Studies* 58: 69–87.

O'Collins, G. (1999), 'The Risen Jesus: Analogies and Presence', in S. E. Porter, M. A. Hayes, and D. Tombs (eds.), *Resurrection.* JSNTSup 186 (Sheffield: Sheffield Academic Press), 195–217.

O'Collins, G. (2012), 'Vatican II on the Liturgical Presence of Christ', *Irish Theological Quarterly* 77: 3–17.

O'Toole, R. F. (1984), *The Unity of Luke's Theology: An Analysis of Luke–Acts.* Good News Studies 9 (Wilmington, Del.: M. Glazier).

O'Toole, R. F. (2004), *Luke's Presentation of Jesus: A Christology.* Subsidia Biblica 25 (Rome: Editrice Pontificio Istituto Biblico).

Orr, P. (2011), 'Christ Absent and Present: A Study in Pauline Christology' (Doctoral dissertation, Durham University, Durham).

Orr, P. (2014), *Christ Absent and Christ Present: A Study in Pauline Christology*. WUNT 2 (Tübingen: Mohr Siebeck).

Parsons, M. C. (1987), *The Departure of Jesus in Luke–Acts: The Ascension Narratives in Context*. JSNTSup 2 (Sheffield: JSOT).

Pokorny, P. (1999), ' "Wo zwei oder drei versammelt sind in meinem Namen …" (Mt 18,20)', in B. Ego et al. (eds.), *Gemeinde ohne Tempel/Community without Temple. Zur Substituierung und Transformation des Jerusalemer Tempels und seines Kults im Alten Testament, antiken Judentum und frühen Christentum*. WUNT 118 (Tübingen: Mohr Siebeck), 477–8.

Rowe, C. K. (2006), *Early Narrative Christology: The Lord in the Gospel of Luke* (Berlin: de Gruyter).

Sancrosanctum Concilium, Constitution on the Sacred Liturgy, promulgated by Pope Paul VI, 4 December 1963.

Schilson, A. (1995), 'Gegenwart Christi', *Lexikon für Theologie und Kirche* 4: 352–3.

Schweitzer, A. (1953), *The Mysticism of Paul the Apostle* (London: A. & C. Black).

Sleeman, M. (2009), *Geography and the Ascension Narrative in Acts*. SNTSMS 146 (Cambridge: Cambridge University Press).

Sproston North, W. E. 2013. ' "Lord, if you had been here …" (John 11.21): The Absence of Jesus and Strategies of Consolation in the Fourth Gospel', *Journal for the Study of the New Testament* 36: 39–52.

Surlis, T. J. (2011), *The Presence of the Risen Christ in the Community of Disciples: An Examination of the Ecclesiological Significance of Matthew 18:20*. Tesi Gregoriana Serie Teologia 188 (Rome: Pontificia Università Gregoriana).

Thomson, J. G. S. S. (1988), 'The Presence of God', *Encyclopedia of the Bible* 2: no. 1750–2.

Wilson, I. (1995), *Out of the Midst of the Fire: Divine Presence in Deuteronomy* (Atlanta, Ga.: Scholars Press).

Yarbro Collins, A. (2007), *Mark: A Commentary*. Hermeneia (Minneapolis, Minn.: Fortress).

Zwiep, A. W. (1997), *The Ascension of the Messiah in Lukan Christology*. NovTSup 87 (Leiden: Brill).

Zwiep, A. W. (2001), 'Assumptus est in caelum: Rapture and Heavenly Exaltation in Early Judaism and Luke–Acts', in F. Avemarie and H. Lichtenberger (eds.), *Auferstehung—Resurrection: The Fourth Durham-Tübingen Research Symposium on Resurrection, Transfiguration and Exaltation in Old Testament, Ancient Judaism and Early Christianity*. WUNT 135 (Tübingen: Mohr Siebeck), 323–49.

PART II

PATRISTIC CHRISTOLOGY

CHAPTER 7

CHRISTOLOGY IN THE FOURTH CENTURY

KHALED ANATOLIOS

WITH Galerius' Edict of Toleration in 311, followed by Constantine's and Licinius' Edict of Milan in 313, Christians began a migration from the margins towards the center of political and social life in the Roman Empire. At the same time, the Church of the fourth century was racked by internal divisions caused by tumultuous doctrinal debates that struck at the heart of its identity as a community dedicated to the confession of Jesus Christ as Lord. Modern scholars often characterize these disputes as 'Trinitarian' inasmuch as they were concerned with divergent assessments of Christ's divinity as it related to the Father and the Spirit. A narrative of the development of Christian doctrine is then constructed which tells how Christ's divinity was controverted in the fourth century and, once that was more or less settled through the triumph of the Nicene ὁμοούσιος, questions about Christ's humanity and the relation between his humanity and divinity were then taken up in the Christological debates of the fifth century. Although it is true that the boundaries between the debated doctrinal positions in the fourth century are typically drawn by pointing to distinct standpoints regarding Christ's divinity, the underlying logic of these positions included assessments of Christ's humanity and its relation to divinity. Moreover, both with regard to particular questions about the divine–human identity of Jesus Christ and more general questions of the intelligibility and plausibility of Christian faith, fourth-century Christians were often preoccupied with how the humanity and divinity of the crucified and risen Lord were to be conceived in light of the Christian proclamation of the unfathomable and endlessly surprising mystery of divine goodness. This chapter will present the legacy of fourth-century Christology in terms of an accumulating vision of Jesus Christ as the ultimate revelation and enactment of divine goodness. I present some fundamental elements of the fourth-century construction of this Christological vision: (1) Christological apologetics in the fourth century; (2) the Nicene–'Arian' debates about the status of Christ's divinity; (3) the Apollinarian controversy about Christ's human soul; and (4) Christological proclamation in fourth-century preaching.

CHRISTOLOGICAL APOLOGETICS

One way Christians reacted to their enhanced social and political status after the Constantinian settlement was by attempting to communicate to their fellow citizens the intelligibility of Christian faith. In an earlier epoch, Christian apologists had to deal with objections that Christians were atheists, since they rejected the prevailing syncretistic religious culture; or that they practiced immorality and violence in their cultic rituals; or were not good citizens. But the official imperial endorsement of Christianity and the consequent public visibility of Christians rendered such objections and suspicions largely obsolete. Nevertheless, accusations of the sheer irrationality and unintelligibility of Christian claims persisted well after political and social critique had subsided. Some of the important treatments of Christology in the fourth century are constructed in terms of this apologetic concern. Athanasius' classic *On the Incarnation* declares its intention to counter the objection that Christian faith is 'irrational' (ἄλογον) because it proclaims as Lord a man who was crucified and died. Eusebius of Caesarea, in his *Proof of the Gospel*, sets himself against 'the mob of slanderers flooding us with the accusation that we are unable logically to present a clear demonstration of the truth we hold ... [T]hey say that we only teach our followers like irrational animals to shut their eyes and staunchly obey what we say without examining it at all, and call them therefore "the faithful" because of their faith as distinct from reason' (*Proof* 1.10; Ferrar 1920: 6). Towards the end of the century, Gregory of Nyssa's *Catechetical Orations* is offered as a guide for Christian catechists to enable them to respond to 'those who are searching for the rational basis of our religion' (*Cat. Or.* 15; Hardy 1954: 291).

These apologetic treatises of the fourth century employed strategies inherited from earlier eras, such as the argument from Old Testament prophecies and retaliatory denunciations of Greek mythology and idolatry. But the most distinctive feature of fourth-century Christian apologetics is an effort to present the reasonability of Christian faith in terms of the efficacy of the Christological proclamation to generate a coherent and compelling view of reality as a whole. This strategy is displayed in two works of the fourth century: Athanasius' *On the Incarnation* (*c.*328–5) and Gregory of Nyssa's *Catechetical Orations* (composed in the early 380s). In both treatises, the intelligibility of confessing an incarnate, crucified, and risen Lord is seen to reside in the logic of a consistent narrative of divine goodness, which is manifest in God's special love for humanity, φιλανθρωπία. The Christian newness of the doctrine of the Incarnation is rendered intelligible by being presented as a maximal confirmation and dramatization of the more universally accepted principle of the generosity of divine goodness, such as we find in Plato's *Timaeus* (*Tim* 29e). However, the distinctly Christian narrative of divine goodness begins with a doctrine of creation in which the world was not simply always there, even just as formless matter, but rather was brought into being from nothing through the sovereign will of an omnipotent and benevolent God. God intentionally brings about what previously did not exist in order that 'light may not remain unseen or glory unwitnessed, or goodness unenjoyed, or that any other aspect we observe of the divine nature should lie idle with no one to share or enjoy it' (Gregory of Nyssa, *Cat. Or.* 5; Hardy 1954: 276).

Such an articulation of the logic of creation as based on the divine will to self-communication prepares the way for presenting the Incarnation as an intensification of the very same logic. This point is rhetorically reinforced by Athanasius when he transfers the language of divine compassion associated with God's redemptive work to the divine work of creation. God's act of creation is already a merciful condescension (*Inc.* 3). Athanasius presents human sinfulness as an obstacle not only to human flourishing but also to the divine goodness itself: 'It was not worthy of the goodness of God that those created by him should be corrupted ... The weakness, rather than the goodness of God, is made known by neglect, if, after creating, he abandoned his own work to be corrupted' (*Inc.* 6; Behr 2011: 63). In the face of pervasive human evil, the Incarnation and redemptive work of Christ are presented as consistent with the logic of God's benevolence in the act of creation and as manifesting the higher logic of the perseverance of divine generosity in the face of human sinfulness. Divine transcendence, goodness, and power must be newly conceived in terms of this higher logic: 'God's transcendent power is not so much displayed in the vastness of the heavens ... as in his condescension to our weak nature' (Gregory of Nyssa, *Cat. Or.* 24; Hardy 1954: 301).

The intelligibility of the Incarnation is thus presented as exemplifying the invincible goodness of the divine nature, which was already manifest in the act of creation but has been even more lavishly displayed in the work of redemption. At the same time, the proclamation of the God–human was made more plausible by being correlated with a theological anthropology which emphasizes that the radical structure and content of the human being lies precisely in its intrinsic likeness to God, its status as *imago Dei*. Gregory of Nyssa understands the *imago Dei* precisely as the capacity to participate in divine goodness (*Cat. Or.* 5; SC 453, 164) and uses the common terminology of 'mingling' (κρᾶσις) to describe the synthesis of material and spiritual elements in the human constitution as well as the union of human and divine in Christ. This terminological overlap emphasizes the point that the material–spiritual mingling that is constitutive of human nature also constitutes its intrinsic readiness for the Christological mingling of human and divine that will be its fulfillment.

Athanasius and Gregory of Nyssa thus present the intelligibility of the Incarnation in terms of its consistency with both divine goodness and the intrinsic human disposition to share in that goodness. The Incarnation, death, and resurrection of Christ thus realize the triumph of the self-communication of divine goodness, even in the face of human evil. In response to the persisting objection that such a unity of divinity and humanity compromises the integrity of divine impassibility, both employ a conception of the relation between God and creation that echoes the Stoic cosmological framework, namely that the divine active principle of *logos* pervades the passivity of matter. Transposed into a Christological key, this notion is used to explain that just as God is active and humanity receptive in divine–human interactions in general, so also in the unity of divinity and humanity in Christ. The result of this dialectic is a transformative relation between the human and the divine such that the human is assimilated to the divine without the divine being compromised by the human. In Christ, God transformatively appropriates to himself human weaknesses, to the point of death, but this brings about not the diminishment of God but the death of death itself, resurrection and deification.

This Christological narrative of the triumph of divine goodness in the face of human limitations and evil, which both Athanasius and Gregory of Nyssa offer as part of a defense of the intelligibility of Christian faith, was nevertheless not ready-made for the use of fourth-century theologians. It was constructed not only in the midst of struggles with non-Christians, but also among Christians themselves, regarding the way in which this narrative of divine philanthropy relates to the questions of the identity of Jesus Christ, his divinity and humanity, and the relation between the two. Throughout the fourth-century debates about the status of Jesus' divinity, all sides considered the point at issue to be not merely some esoteric speculations describing the divine being, but rather the Christian vision of reality itself. That Jesus Christ, in his divinity and representative humanity, enabled humanity's access to divine goodness was at the center of this vision.

THE NICENE–'ARIAN' CONTROVERSY

The fourth-century Church was dominated by the doctrinal debates that erupted in Egypt, around 320, between Alexander, the Patriarch of Alexandria, and Arius, an Egyptian presbyter, and only began to arrive at a definitive resolution at the Council of Constantinople of 381. A synoptic view of these debates can be gained by identifying the central agitating issue as that of reconciling an intensified sense of God's absolute primacy, as uncaused and unoriginated (ἀγέν(ν)ητος), with the confession of Jesus Christ as Lord. The intensified emphasis on God's transcendence as 'uncaused' was partly a reaction to Origen's speculation that God's eternal almightiness necessitated that there always be a creation over which God is almighty through his Word (*First Principles* 1.2.10). This Origenian hypothesis seemed to be a regression to a Hellenistic worldview in which the world itself always existed and was unoriginated (cf. Aristotle, *de caelo* 1.3.270b). By the beginning of the fourth century, there was a general consensus among Christians that God alone is uncaused, while creation was brought into being from non-existence as an effect of his sovereign will. For some, it was merely tautological to say that God alone is uncaused and to say that being uncaused was in fact what it meant to be God. The problem then became how to reconcile this Christian reassertion of the sovereignty of the uniquely self-existent and uncaused God with the proclamation that Jesus Christ is Lord, despite the scriptural attestations that Christ was both a human creature and originated from the Father as his only-begotten Son (cf. John 1:14).

Assessments of Christ's Divinity

Throughout the tumultuous interplay of various factions, alliances, and competing Church councils that pervaded the fourth-century debates, two main approaches could be discerned to the problematic posed above. One approach, exemplified by a trajectory of thinkers including Arius, Asterius, and Eunomius, was based on the premise that the primary criterion of absolute divinity was precisely God's self-existence as uncaused and unoriginated (ἀγέν(ν)ητος). In this schema, Christ's lordship and divinity were conceded and designated by such scriptural titles as Word, Wisdom, and Power of God. But these titles were interpreted as indicating a lower level of divinity than the one absolutely transcendent and unoriginated God. If even in his divinity, this Word and Wisdom was caused—inasmuch as he was 'begotten'— then he is in the last analysis a creature. Moreover, to say that he was altogether caused was to say that he came into existence from non-being, like all other creatures, through the sovereign will of the one uncaused God. In Arius' infamous slogan, 'there was once when the Son was not'. Nevertheless, he was unique as the first and highest creature, who was created to be the obedient instrument of all of God's subsequent creative activity. His unity with the God he called 'Father' is therefore a unity of will and activity, not a unity of substance. Christ's creaturely divinity nevertheless represented the ideal and unsurpassable mode of relation between creation and the sovereign God, which is epitomized by his perfect obedience: 'obedient with regard to the ordering and creation of all existing things, obedient with regard to all governance ..., obedient in his words, mediator in doctrine, mediator in law ... He became obedient unto the cross and unto death' (Eunomius, *Confession of Faith*; Vaggione 1987: 155).

In this account of Christ's divinity, his being is not identifiable with absolute divine goodness. Expounding Jesus' rejoinder to the rich young man, 'Why do you call me good? No one is good but God alone' (Luke 18:19), Eunomius asserts that it is only the Uncaused God who is properly good, 'the cause of his own goodness and of all goodness' (Gregory of Nyssa, *Against Eunomius* 3.9.1; GNO II, 264). For Eunomius, it is necessary to acknowledge the Son's ontological inferiority so that we may not acquiesce in his created divinity but employ it as a vantage point from which to give glory to the only uncaused God. Indeed, the Son represents divine goodness precisely because he was brought into being as a benevolent mitigation of divine transcendence which is necessary for mediating between the only uncaused God and creation. As Asterius put it, apart from this attenuation, creation could 'not withstand the immediate hand of God' (Fragment 26; Vinzent 1993). Eusebius of Caesarea explains that since created things were not capable of approaching God, the Father's philanthropy established his only-begotten Son and entrusted him with the constitution and governance of the universe (*Ecclesiastical Theology* 1.13). This interpretation of Christ's mediatorial divinity thus reinforces a view of divine transcendence in which the highest level of divinity is conceived in terms of otherness with respect to creation, while Christ represents the activity of divine goodness in bringing about a mediatorial being between the one uncaused God and the rest of creation.

If one option in the assessment of Christ's divinity in the fourth century was to qualify that divinity by reference to the standard of being-uncaused as the marker of absolute divine transcendence, the alternative trajectory redefined divine transcendence by the standard of Christ's relation to the Father. Eventually, as discussion extended to the status of the Spirit, the eternal relations between Father, Son, and Spirit were conceived as intrinsic to and constitutive of divine being (Gregory Nazianzus, *Or.* 31.9). In this account, divine goodness was fully shared within the Father–Son relation, and the content of divine goodness and love consisted in the Father's perfect sharing of his own being with the Son. Hilary of Poitiers puts it thus: 'God does not know how to be ever anything else than love, nor to be anything else than Father. He who loves does not envy and he who is a father is at the same time wholly a father … Hence, in so far as He is the Father, He must be the whole Father of all His own attributes which are in the one whom He has begotten from Himself, while the perfect birth of the Son, with all of these attributes, completes Him as the Father' (*Trin.* 9.61; McKenna 1954: 383–4). The Son's 'perfect birth' from the Father means that he is not just the product or mediator of the Father's goodness but a full sharer in that goodness. Gregory of Nyssa describes Christ as 'the fullness of all good' (*Against Eunomius* 3.6.7; GNO II, 188), 'equal in every conception of existent or conceivable good to the majesty of the Father's goodness' (*Against Eunomius* 1.339; GNO 1, 127). The same is true of the Holy Spirit: 'Everyone knows that the person of the Son and that of the Holy Spirit do not lack anything of perfect goodness, perfect power, and every such quality' (*Against Eunomius* 1.167; GNO 1, 77).

This is the trajectory represented by the Council of Nicaea of 325, which declared the Son to be 'one in being' (ὁμοούσιος) with the Father. A few decades later, in response to the teachings of Marcellus and Photinus that the Father and Son are ultimately identical and without distinction in the eternity of divine being, Basil of Caesarea proposed the terminological distinction between the common being of Father, Son, and Spirit as sharing the same essence (οὐσία) and the particular mode of being by which each of them shared in the single essence as distinct 'persons' (ὑποστάσεις). Thus, the Son shared all the perfections of the Father in the distinct particularity of his receiving them from the Father as only-begotten Son. With this distinction in place, the Council of Constantinople reaffirmed the Nicene ὁμοούσιος, which was now taken to mean that the Son was both eternally distinct from the Father in his personal particularity and yet fully and equally shared in the being of the Father.

The Divinity and Humanity of Christ in Trinitarian Debate

The fourth-century debates about the proper way to speak about Christ's divinity were always bound to different conceptions of just how this divinity was related to and disclosed by the humanity. From that point of view, the two trajectories outlined above can be distinguished in terms of whether they conceived the relation between Christ's divinity and humanity within a continuum of Christ's mediatorial function or, more dramatically, in terms of the humanity bringing about a kenotic reversal of divine attributes even while paradoxically maintaining these divine attributes. These distinct Christological options also projected two different conceptions of how Christ's humanity and divinity manifested divine goodness.

Christologies which attributed to Christ an inferior divinity argued to this conclusion partly on the basis of his human limitations. At the beginning of the controversy, Alexander identifies this style of reasoning on the part of Arius and his followers: 'Recalling all the words about the salvific suffering, humiliation, self-emptying, "poverty", and other attributes that the Savior took on for our sake, they pile these up to impugn the supreme deity that was his from the start' (Optiz, 1936: *Urk* 14.37). These Christologies tended to posit continuity between his humanity and divinity, as both encompassed within his primordial function of mediating between creation and the utterly transcendent and uncaused God. Indeed, in some cases, not only is Jesus' divinity reduced so as to approximate his humanity, but his humanity is elevated so as to approach the status of his mediatorial divinity. In Eusebius of Caesarea's Christology, for example, we encounter in Christ's divinity both a mitigated transcendence and also a mitigated humanity, inasmuch as Jesus is conceived as lacking a human soul (*Ecclesiastical Theology* 1.20). In these Christologies of continuity, the unity of Christ is easily ascertained, while the soteriological function of Christ 'for us' (*pro nobis*) is applied to the very origin of his being. From the perspective of Nicene theologies, the fatal flaw of such Christologies of continuity was that they separated the divinity and humanity of Christ from the putatively superior divinity of the uncaused God. Moreover, they seemed to make the very being of Christ, even in his divinity, a means to human flourishing, in contrast to the scriptural teaching that not only were all things made through Christ but for him (cf. Col. 1:16). Finally, the most potent and visceral accusation leveled against such a Christology by its opponents was that it made the Christian worship of Christ into idolatry, worship directed to a being who is other than the one true God.

On the other hand, theologies which asserted the full and equal divinity of the Son interpreted Christ's humanity not as part of a continuum that includes his creaturely and attenuated divinity but rather as a dramatic act of divine self-emptying. In this perspective, the disclosure of the shared divinity of the Father and Son through Christ's kenotic humanity had a paradoxical logic. On the one hand, the limitations of this humanity constituted a certain negation or abandonment of divine perfections with respect to the assumed humanity: the Immortal became mortal, the one who was in the form of God took on the form of a servant (cf. Phil. 2). On the other hand, this self-emptying was consistent with the divine goodness and love for humanity that characterized the shared divine nature of both Father and Son. For these Christologies of reversal, the activity of divine goodness is manifest not in the ontologically middle status of the Son but rather in the activity of his self-humbling and suffering. So, against Eunomius' insistence that only the uncaused God is good, Gregory of Nyssa points to Christ's self-emptying as the decisive sign of his divine goodness: 'What more bitter malice can one find than to deny that he is good who "being in the form of God did not regard equality with God as something to be exploited" (Phil. 2:6) but lowered himself to the abasement of the human nature and did so only for the love of humanity?' (*Against Eunomius* 3.9:8; GNO II, 266).

One of the strongest criticisms leveled against these Christologies of kenotic reversal was that they effectively posited 'two Christs', one who was no less transcendent and impassible than the Father, and another who was the subject of human limitations and suffering. The labors of Nicene theologies in rebutting this charge required balancing the differentiation between Christ's humanity and divinity with the assertion of a single subject of both. The fruits of these labors set the stage for the Christological formulas of the later Christological councils, and may arguably be seen to anticipate the logic, if not the terminological precision, of these formulas. We may profitably analyze this logic as it was constructed in relation to three important Christological issues: (1) the Christological shape of Scripture; (2) Christ's relation to the Spirit; and (3) the suffering of Christ.

The Christological Shape of Scripture

Anti-Nicene theologies referred to the human limitations of Christ as evidence of his inferior divinity. They also capitalized on any language that designated Christ's exalted status as 'received', and took special advantage of the description of Wisdom in Prov. 8:22 as 'created' ('The Lord created me as the beginning of his ways, for his works', LXX). In general, this exegetical procedure attributed all scriptural language understood to be referring to either the Incarnate or pre-existent Christ as indifferently applicable to and expressive of the mediatorial being of the created Word and Son. Nicene theologies, however, insisted that the Scriptures posited two distinct dramatic stages in the career of the Word, which had to be properly differentiated in order to be correctly applied to the Word who became Incarnate. This two-act Christological metanarrative of Scripture was seen to be presented in condensed from in Scripture itself, as in the double affirmation in John 1 that the Word was with God in the beginning and that the Word became flesh or in the Philippians hymn that speaks of the transition from the form of God to the form of a servant. When these condensed summaries of the Christological narrative are applied to Scripture as a whole, they yield, in Athanasius' words, 'a double account of the Savior' (*Orations* 3.29; AW I.I/3, 340). The recognition of this double account discloses the necessity for correctly assigning any Christological predications to one or other of these acts in the Christological drama, whether to the pre-existent divinity or to the Incarnate state. This yields the basic Christological rule of interpreting Scripture, which Gregory of Nazianzus articulates thus: 'Apply what is more elevated to the divinity, the nature that is superior to passivities and corporeality, and what is more abased to the composite one who for your sake emptied himself and became enfleshed … and then was exalted' (*Oration* 29.18). Thus, the distinction between Christ's divinity and humanity is seen to be inscribed in the first place in the Christological narrative of Scripture, while there is one subject who is posited as the protagonist of this two-act drama. Moreover, both acts of this drama are disclosive of the goodness of God: the exalted correlativity of Father and Son discloses that goodness as an intra-divine generosity whereby the Father shares his being fully with the Son, while the humiliation of the Son manifests that goodness as love for humanity, φιλανθρωπία.

Christ and the Spirit

Non-Nicene theologies typically designated the Spirit as created by the Son and third in the ontological hierarchy that begins with the uncaused God. At the same time, scriptural language about Christ's being 'anointed' (cf. Ps. 45:7: 'Therefore God, your God, has anointed you with the oil of gladness beyond your companions', NRSV) or 'sanctified' was used as evidence that the divinity of Christ was something he acquired, rather than being connatural to him. In dealing with such texts, defenders of Nicene theology applied the Christological hermeneutic outlined above with reference to Christ's relation to the Spirit. The result is a 'Spirit Christology' in which Christ's giving of the Spirit is assigned to his divinity, while his reception or being anointed by the Spirit is assigned to his humanity. The salvific import of this transaction is that humanity now has the capacity to receive the fullness of the Spirit by being incorporated into Christ's humanity. The fact that it is the same one who both gives and receives the Spirit guarantees that humanity's reception of the Spirit will be indefectible for those who are in Christ:

> Just as the apostle's words indicate that we would not have been freed and 'highly exalted' if it were not that 'he who is in the form of God took the form of a servant', (Phil. 2:6, 7) so also David shows that in no other way would we have partaken of the Spirit and been sanctified if it were not that the Giver of the Spirit, the Word himself, spoke of himself as anointed by the Spirit for our sakes. Therefore we have received securely in that he is said to be anointed in the flesh.
>
> (*Or.* 1:50; Anatolios 2004: 108)

The Suffering of Christ

The complex ways in which estimations of Christ's divinity were bound up with interpretations of his humanity are manifest with particular intensity in different understandings of how Christ's suffering discloses both his divinity and humanity, as well as the relation between them. This complexity is manifest in the polemical exchanges between Eunomius and the Cappadocian brothers, Basil of Casearea and Gregory of Nyssa, which involved reciprocal accusations that each side was ashamed of the Cross. On this occasion, the question of how the crucifixion of Christ was related to his divinity was contested in reference to Acts 2:36: 'God has made him both Lord and Messiah, this Jesus whom you crucified' (NRSV). A significant element in the logic of

theologies that attributed a reduced divinity to the preexistent Christ was the principle that susceptibility to suffering and death could not be ascribed to the highest level
of divinity. Theologies that affirmed that the Son's divinity is equal to the Father dealt
with the problematic of Christ's suffering by attributing it to the *kenotic* condition of
his humanity, while maintaining that, in his divinity, the Son fully enjoyed an unmiti-
gated divine impassibility. It was in reaction to this logic that Eunomius accused Basil of
being ashamed of the Cross inasmuch as he did not allow the suffering of the Cross to be
attributed to Christ's divinity. Eunomius challenged the whole logic of a differentiation
of divine and human attributions as inconsistent with the notion of Christological *kenosis*. According to Eunomius, ascribing Christ's human limitations and sufferings exclusively to the humanity makes the humanity of Christ both the subject and the object of
the self-emptying, as if it was the humanity that emptied itself to be human (Nyssen,
Against Eunomius 3.3.26; GNO II, 117).

In clarifying his own position on the interpretation of Acts 2:36, Gregory of Nyssa
is forced by this polemical exchange to balance the differentiation of the humanity and divinity, on the one side, with the attribution of both to a single subject, on
the other. Gregory's subsequent exposition of this exegetical approach is comprised
of three main elements. First, the divinity and humanity are clearly differentiated,
principally along the lines of an active/passive distinction. In this regard, Gregory
explains that 'our contemplation of the respective properties of the flesh and the
divinity remains unconfused (ἀσύγχυτος) as long as each is contemplated in itself
… The flesh is of a passible nature (παθητικῆς ἐστι φύσεως), while the Word is active
(ἐνεργητικῆς δὲ ὁ λόγος). The flesh is not the Creator of existent things nor is the
power of the divinity passive' (*Against Eunomius* 3.3.64; GNO II, 130). While this
principle of differentiation serves to protect the impassibility and thus genuine divinity of the Incarnate Word, it is also vulnerable to the accusation that the supporters
of Nicaea teach a doctrine of 'two Christs'. The second element of Gregory's treatment of Christ's suffering responds to that charge by reasserting the unity of Christ
by recourse to the principle of the sharing of properties: 'the Master takes to himself the bruisings of the servant while the servant is glorified with the honor of the
Master' (*Against Eunomius* 3.3.66; GNO II, 131). In order to see why this principle of
the communication of properties does not annul the distinction of natures, we have
to keep in mind Gregory's active/passive distinction. There is an asymmetrical dynamism to the contact and 'mingling' between Christ's divinity and humanity, such that
the divinity remains operative and transformative in this contact while the humanity is receptive and transformed unto deification. The third element of Gregory's
treatment of Christ's suffering is to posit a single subject of this dynamic exchange of
divine and human properties. Thus, the references to the crucifixion and the lordship
of Christ in Acts 2:36 are described as two states (δύο πράγματα) that nevertheless
belong to one person (ἓν πρόσωπον) (*Against Eunomius* 3.3.42; GNO II, 122). The
Word Incarnate is the same one (ὁ αὐτός) as the eternal Word even if the humanity that he actively assumes and deifies is other than the humanity that receives the
transformative power of his divinity (*Against Eunomius* 3.3.62; GNO II, 130).

THE APOLLINARIAN CONTROVERSY

Gregory of Nyssa's analysis of the suffering of Christ was part of his effort to argue for the full divinity of the Son despite Christ's human sufferings, without positing 'two Christs'. The Nicene vulnerability to the accusation of teaching 'two Christs' was central to the problematic of the second main controversy that animated the development of Christological doctrine in the fourth century, that surrounding the teaching of Apollinaris of Laodicea (c.315–92). Apollinaris was a staunch supporter of Nicene Trinitarian theology whose sensitivity to the possible distortions of that theology was awakened especially by the teaching of another supporter of Nicaea, Marcellus of Ancyra. Marcellus interpreted the Nicene teaching on the consubstantiality of the Father and the Son as meaning that there was ultimately no distinction between Father and Son in God's internal and eternal being. For Marcellus, the primary name to designate the divinity of Christ was Word (λόγος) and this Word was eternally immanent in God until it was extrapolated and made subsistent in view of the act of creation. Once Christ's salvific work is completed, the Word will be retracted back into the eternal divine singularity. Marcellus read this doctrine into Paul's remark that Christ in the end will hand over his kingship to God the Father (1 Cor. 15:24). Marcellus' teaching was condemned by various Church councils, stretching from 336 to the Council of Constantinople. The confession in the Constantinopolitan Creed that Christ's kingdom will not end is directed against this Marcellan teaching. Marcellus' approach confirmed some of the worst fears of those suspicious of Nicaea. Not only did he seem to be teaching a kind of modalism, but his emphatic assertion of divine singularity did not allow him to find any place for Christ's humanity in the eschatological retraction of the Word into the divine oneness. Marcellus admitted that he simply did not know what would become of Christ's humanity once the economy of salvation is consummated. His Trinitarian modalism thus led directly to an emphasis on the difference and separation between the eternal Word and Christ's economic identity. The accusation of 'two Christs' seemed entirely warranted in the case of the modalist pro-Nicene theology of Marcellus.

In reaction to Marcellus, as well as to other pro-Nicenes who seemed content with a divisive Christology, such as the Antiochian, Diodore of Tarsus, Apollinaris was intent on shoring up the unitive dimension of Nicene Christology. His drastic strategy for accomplishing this goal was to insist that the Word took the place of the human mind of Christ. Nevertheless, Apollinaris anticipated Chalcedonian language by speaking of Jesus Christ as ὁμοούσιος with both God and humanity (*On the Union in Christ* 8; Leitzmann 1904: 188). His consubstantiality with humanity resides in his assumption of human flesh, which was perfectly obedient to the divine Word. Just as a human being is composed of flesh and spirit, so is Christ, even if in his case, the spiritual or intellectual component is the divinity itself (*Fragment* 89; Leitzmann 1904: 227)! But, contrary to the later Chalcedonian formula, for Apollinaris the double consubstantiality of Jesus

Christ with humanity and God does not result in two substances but in a single essence (οὐσία), composed of the combination of divine mind and human flesh (*Fragment* 117; Leitzmann 1904: 236).

Three main motives impelled Apollinaris to this conclusion. First, he was concerned about the integrity of Christian worship directed to Christ, which must have only one object (*Fragment* 9; Leitzmann 1904: 206–7). Second, for Apollinaris the reliability of human salvation required that the immutable divinity be solely in charge of the work of human salvation and not share that responsibility with a changeable humanity. This element of Apollinaris' reasoning seems to invoke the active/passive distinction that we have encountered previously. According to this reasoning, the human mind is structurally active with respect to the passibility of the body. Inasmuch as human sanctification and deification comes about through the divinity actively transforming the passive humanity, this transformation can only be secured if the active principle that governs this process is the immutable divinity and not a changeable humanity (*Fragment* 76; Leitzmann 1904: 222). A third motivation for Apollinaris' position is also explicable in terms of the active/passive distinction. Apollinaris argues that the supposition that Christ did have a human mind would actually result in the destruction of human freedom and thus of human nature (*Fragment* 87; Leitzmann 1904: 226). That is because the combination of the two active principles of divine and human intellects would naturally result in the divine active principle overruling the activity of the human principle and extinguishing self-rule. However, in Apollinaris' understanding, the supposition that the divine mind replaces the human soul succeeds in retaining the natural dynamism of the immanent interaction of activity and passivity in the human being. The passible flesh is perfected in its passivity through Eucharistic communion with Christ's flesh, while the active human intellect retains its self-standing integrity and achieves perfect governance over the flesh by freely assimilating itself to Christ (*Fragment* 74; Leitzmann 1904: 222).

With regard to the development of Christian doctrine, the significance of Apollinaris' Christology arguably lies not so much in its intrinsic contents as in the reactions it generated. It was articulated in the midst of a polemical confrontation with Diodore of Tarsus that sounded the opening salvoes in the antagonism between 'Alexandrian' and 'Antiochian' Christologies. Diodore rejected Apollinaris' model of the divinity and humanity constituting a single essence and spoke rather of the indwelling of the humanity by the divine Word. The union between the two was one of grace and honor, rather than nature, and it was on the basis of this association by grace that Christ was to be worshiped, rather than on a unity of essence between his divinity and humanity. Despite some modern anachronistic interpretations, Diodore's principal concern was not to safeguard the full humanity of Christ but rather to avoid making Christ's divinity itself the subject of the limitations and passibilities of the humanity. Diodore's polemic against Apollinaris was taken up by his student, Theodore of Mopsuestia, and later by Nestorius, thus generating an Antiochian anti-Alexandrian style of Christological reasoning. Although later Alexandrians disowned Apollinaris' teaching on the lack of a human soul in Christ, Cyril's insistence that the Word was the subject of human predications in Christ would call forth a similar critique by later Antiochians as was directed by Diodore against Apollinaris.

A different approach to refuting Apollinaris, one that would have a more formative legacy in the later tradition, was generated by the Cappadocians Basil of Caesarea, Gregory of Nazianzus, and Gregory of Nyssa. The Cappadocian response could accommodate the full humanity of Christ without diluting the affirmation of a single ontological subject. Gregory of Nazianzus' *Epistle* 101, composed in the early 380s, is a model of this approach. After the customary expressions of shock and dismay at Apollinaris' 'innovation', Gregory puts forth a synthetic Christological confession that posits a single subject of a twofold dramatic plot in which the first act belongs to the eternity of his divinity and the second describes his self-humbling on humanity's behalf:

> We do not separate the human being from the divinity, but we confess as dogma one and the same, who before was God and not human, the only Son before all ages, unmingled with body or anything bodily; but who at the consummation of the ages has assumed humanity for our salvation, passible in his flesh, impassible in his divinity; circumscribed in the body, uncircumscribed in the Spirit. The same one is earthly and heavenly … so that by one and the same, who was a complete human being and also God, the entire humanity that had fallen through sin might be refashioned.
>
> (*Epistle* 101.13–15; SC 208)

Gregory could be seen to be reaching for a way to apply the developing precision of Trinitarian formulation to the description of Christ. He explains that the latter case is the reverse of the former; in the Trinity, there are three 'he's' (ἄλλος καὶ ἄλλος) but only one 'it', whereas in Christ, there are different 'it's' (ἄλλο καὶ ἄλλο) but only one 'he'. Gregory explicitly designates the two 'it's' of Christ as two natures (φύσεις δύο; *Epistle* 101.19; SC 208), though he insists that this does not amount to 'two sons'. He uses the analogy of the unity of soul and body, which was to become prominent in later Christological debates, to insist on the 'unity and identity' of Christ. Against the objection that positing a complete humanity as well as a complete divinity in Christ would inevitably lead to two juxtaposed wholes, Gregory seems to transpose Apollinaris' active/passive framework in a way that both affirms a human active principle and renders it receptive to divine activity. He explains: 'So our mind is complete and a governing principle, but only in relation to soul and body; not complete in an absolute way; rather it is a servant of God and subject to God' (*Epistle* 101.43; SC 208). In this way, Gregory manages to uphold Christ's complete humanity while enfolding that humanity within a dynamic unity in which it is subservient to the divinity. But the most historically significant element in Gregory's response to Apollinaris is his famous articulation of the fundamental principle that binds together Christology and soteriology: 'What is not assumed is not healed' (*Epistle* 101.32; SC 208). Stated positively, this principle stipulates that the unity of Christ, whose motive and goal is human salvation, is to be conceived as the union of the entirety of human being with the divine: 'Keep the whole humanity and mingle it with God so that you may benefit me completely' (*Epistle* 101.36; SC 208).

CHRIST PROCLAIMED: PREACHING CHRIST
IN THE FOURTH CENTURY

Modern students of ancient Christianity are often puzzled by the passion with which ordinary people of that time seem to have engaged the sophisticated doctrinal debates that pervaded the fourth century. Surely, a good part of the explanation for the popular participation in these debates must be that their import was communicated through skillful preaching. A brief overview of an exemplary instance of such preaching can be gained from a homily commemorating the birth of Christ, delivered by Gregory of Nazianzus, around 380. The central motifs of this homily can provide a summary of some of the main elements of fourth-century Christology, as well as demonstrate how the concrete significance of these doctrinal elements was communicated to ordinary Christians.

Gregory begins by exhorting his congregation to Christological joy. This joy consists in being caught up in the exaltation that results from Christ's loving condescension: 'Christ is born—give praise! Christ comes from heaven—rise up to meet him! Christ is on the earth—be lifted up' (Daley 2006: 117). This distinctly Christian joy is to be differentiated from pagan frivolity; it is properly celebrated not by carousing and dissipation but by recounting the Christian story of reality which finds its principle and climax in the mystery of Christ: 'As for us who worship the Word, if we must live luxuriously, let us luxuriate in the word, and in the law and in the narratives of God' (Daley 2006: 119). The author of this story is God, identified as Trinity, a conception of God as dynamic and self-contemplating Goodness which is to be distinguished from that held by those who are 'stingy with divinity' and admit only divine singularity. The latter are explicitly identified as the Jews, but his listeners are surely meant to associate this stinginess with Christian anti-Nicenes as well. The Triune Goodness communicates itself in creation because 'the Good needs to be poured out … that there might be more beings to receive its benefits' (Daley 2006: 121). The summit of God's goodness, however, is manifest especially in the creation of the human being as a 'mixed' worshiper, constituted of both matter and spirit, and innately oriented towards deification. In response to human sinfulness, God's generosity was not diminished but rather stretched to the unfathomable point of the Incarnation. Gregory's account of the Incarnation pointedly contains an anti-Apollinarian thrust: the Word 'came to his own proper image and bore flesh for the sake of flesh, and mingled with a rational soul for my soul's sake, wholly cleansing like by like' (Daley 2006: 123). 'O new mixture! O unexpected blending!' sings Gregory (Daley 2006: 123), yet he has deftly prepared us precisely to expect this blending by depicting humanity itself as originally constituted by a similar blending. Nevertheless, it is the divine self-humbling in the Christological economy that is a higher manifestation of divine goodness than the original act of creation: 'How rich is his goodness? … He establishes a second communication, far more amazing than the first: just as then he gave us a share in what was better, so now he takes on a share of what is worse. This is more godlike than the first gift' (Daley 2006: 124). Gregory concludes his homily with a doxology that is the rhetorical climax of an exhortation to appropriate Christ's union with humanity through concrete imitation:

> Walk uncomplainingly through all the ages and miracles of Christ, as Christ's disciple. Be purified, be circumcised … And in the end, be crucified with him, die with him, be buried eagerly with him, so that you may also rise with him and be glorified with him and reign with him, seeing God, so far as that is attainable, and being seen by him: the one who is worshipped and glorified in a Trinity, who we pray might be revealed to us even now … in Christ Jesus our Lord, to whom be glory and power for the ages of ages. Amen.

(Daley 2006: 127)

The Christian narrative of God's self-communicating goodness in Christ, proclaimed homiletically by Gregory, was what was fundamentally at stake both in the apologetic self-presentation of Christians in the fourth century and throughout the doctrinal debates of that period.

Suggested Reading

Anatalios (2011); Grillmeier (1965/75); Young and Teal (2010).

Bibliography

Anatolios, K. (1998), *Athanasius: The Coherence of His Thought* (London and New York: Routledge).

Anatolios, K. (2004), *Athanasius. The Early Church Fathers* (London and New York: Routledge).

Anatolios, K. (2011), *Retrieving Nicaea: The Development and Meaning of Trinitarian Doctrine* (Ann Arbor, Mich.: Baker Academic).

Ayres, L. (2006), *Nicea and Its Legacy: An Approach to Fourth-Century Trinitarian Theology* (New York: Oxford University Press).

Behr, J. (2004), *The Nicene Faith* (Crestwood, NY: St. Vladimir's Seminary Press).

Behr, J. (2011), *Saint Athanasius the Great of Alexandria: On the Incarnation. Greek Original and English Translation* (Yonkers, NY: St. Vladimir's Seminary Press).

Daley, B. (2003), 'Divine Transcendence and Human Transformation: Gregory of Nyssa's Anti-Apollinarian Christology', in S. Coakley (ed.), *Re-Thinking Gregory of Nyssa* (Oxford: Blackwell), 67–76.

Daley, B. (2006), *Gregory of Nazianzus. The Early Church Fathers* (London and New York: Routledge).

Ferrar, W. J. (1920), *Eusebius: The Proof of the Gospel*, 2 vols. (London: SPCK).

Gallay, P. (ed.) (1974), *Grégoire de Nazianze. Lettres théologiques*. SC 208 (Paris: Cerf).

Grillmeier, A. (1965/75), *Christ in Christian Tradition* (London and Oxford: Mowbrays).

Hardy, E. (ed.) (1954), *Christology of the Later Fathers* (Philadelphia: Westminster Press).

Jaeger, W. (ed.) (1960), *Contra Eunomium Libri*. GNO 1–2 (Leiden: Brill, 1960).

Leitzmann, H. (1904), *Apollinaris von Laodicea und Seine Schule. Texte und Untersuchungen* (Tübingen: Möhr Siebeck).

Lienhard, J. (1999), *Contra Marcellum: Marcellus of Ancyra and Fourth-Century Theology* (Washington, DC: Catholic University of America Press).

McKenna, S. (trans.) (1954), *Saint Hilary of Poitiers. The Trinity*. FOC 25 (Washington, DC: Catholic University of America Press).

Metzler, K. and Savvidis, K. (eds.) (2000), *Athanasius Werke I.I/3. Oratio III Contra Arianos* (Berlin and New York: de Gruyter).

Mühlenberg, E. (ed.) (2000), *Grégoire de Nysse. Discours Catéchétique*, introduction, translation, and notes by Raymond Winling. SC 453 (Paris: Cerf).

Opitz, H.-G. (1936), *Athanasius Werke. Band 3. Teil 1. Urkunden zur Geschichte des Arianischen Streites 318–328. 1. Lieferung* (Berlin: De Gruyter). And: NPNF (2nd series): 3:35–41.

Robertson, J. M. (2007), *Christ as Mediator: A Study of the Theologies of Eusebius of Caesarea, Marcellus of Ancyra, and Athanasius of Alexandria*. Oxford Theological Monographs (Oxford: Oxford University Press).

Spoerl, K. M. (1994), 'Apollarian Christology and the Anti-Marcellan Tradition', *Journal of Theological Studies* 45: 545–68.

Vaggione, R. P. (1987), *Eunomius: The Extant Works* (Oxford: Clarendon Press).

Vinzent, M. (1993), *Asterius von Kappadokien. Die Theologischen Fragmente: Einleitung, kritischer Text, Übersetzung und Kommentar*. Supplements to *Vigiliae Christianae* 20 (Leiden: Brill).

Young, F. and A. Teal (2010), *From Nicaea to Chalcedon: A Guide to the Literature and its Background*, 2nd edn. (Ann Arbor, Mich.: Baker Academic).

CHAPTER 8

ANTIOCH AND ALEXANDRIA

Christology as Reflection on God's Presence in History

BRIAN E. DALEY, S.J.

EVERY beginning student of theology knows at least something of the opposition between 'Antiochene' and 'Alexandrian' approaches to Christology and to biblical interpretation in the decades leading up to the councils of Ephesus and Chalcedon. The usual way of characterizing their differences is to say, in Grillmeier's terminology, that the theologians of the 'school of Antioch' who flourished in the late fourth and early fifth centuries—Diodore of Tarsus, Theodore of Mopsuestia, Nestorius of Constantinople, Theodoret of Cyrus—represented, with a variety of modulations, the classic 'Word–human being' (λόγοςἄνθρωπος) approach to conceiving of the person of the Savior: God's divine Logos, who shares fully in the divine substance, has 'taken up' a full human being to be his 'Temple', his dwelling place, and bestows his favor on this human being to such a unique degree that the man represents him in the world, reveals the 'face' (πρόσωπον) of the Word as his own, shares even in divine honor and status; yet this indwelling of the Word in the man does not reduce or substantially alter the full operation of the man's human faculties, and never blurs the natural boundaries between the creator and the creature, God and the human. Along with this approach to Christology, it is usually said, scholars from the 'school of Antioch' were known for their skills in interpreting Scripture, and especially for their aversion to the allegorical or figural style of exegesis—seeing every incident and every phrase as a cipher for the human person's salvation in Christ or for spiritual growth—which had dominated ancient Scripture scholarship since Origen. Antiochene exegetes are seen as showing a greater respect for the 'historical' or 'literal' meaning of the biblical text, an interest that corresponded with their emphasis on the humanity of Jesus. The 'school of Alexandria' on the other hand—drawing on the powerful legacy of Athanasius, influenced by the Origenist tradition of biblical scholarship, as represented by the late fourth-century exegete Didymus the Blind, and nourished by the Christology of Apollinarius of Laodicaea and his loyal followers—were dominated by the towering ecclesiastical, exegetical, and theological figure of Cyril of Alexandria. Their biblical interpretation remained in the allegorical camp, which reached the heights of baroque fantasy at Didymus' hands; and their picture of Christ was unworldly, representing him as God the Word owning, transforming, and irradiating human flesh and even a human mind, to such an extent that Jesus could no longer be called a human being on his own, but formed 'one nature', one living organism with the Word, who was the source and master of all his human acts.

Like all caricatures, this picture has a good deal of truth to it, but it is not the whole story, and so can be misleading. Recent studies of the work of Antiochene and Alexandrian exegetes in the period have tended to conclude that it is hard to speak of differences in 'method' or even in hermeneutical principles between scholars in the two 'schools'; although interpreters from Antioch were deliberately less ingenious in finding spiritual significance in every passage of the Bible than their Alexandrian contemporaries were. They were also committed to the early Christian assumption that the Bible, as a continuous narrative of God's history with the world, finds its climactic and unifying meaning in the saving acts of Jesus Christ, and recognized the need for ἀναγωγία, the quest for a 'higher meaning' in a text, when such interpretation seemed warranted (see Diodore, *Commentary on the Psalms*, Prologue, CCSG6, 7.123–8.162; cf. Young 2002). For Diodore and his pupils, the key to good exegesis was never to let the interpretation of individual texts slip out of their context in the story of salvation history, as they understood it. While they did not share our modern understanding of historical investigation, they did begin their interpretations of texts with an overarching narrative of the history of God's promises as they move towards fulfillment, in Israel and the Church, and insisted that every scriptural passage be interpreted in the context of its presumed original location within that narrative. Influenced, perhaps, by the tradition of rhetorical training at Antioch, they were on the lookout for practical, moral applications of the texts they studied—a tendency most obvious in the exegesis of John Chrysostom. Exegetes in Alexandria, on the other hand, such as Didymus and Cyril, although interested in the events of Israel's past, seem to have taken greater interest in finding the ways in which a given text might nourish their readers' spiritual and theological growth, or deepen their grasp of the full meaning of the Mystery of Christ. They tended to be grammarians rather than rhetoricians—seekers for meaning, rather than for moving examples—and to read the Scripture contemplatively rather than kerygmatically (cf. Wessel 2004: 183–252).

As far as their respective understandings of the person of Christ are concerned, however, it is an over-simplification to suggest that the Antiochene theologians of the fourth and fifth centuries were primarily concerned with promoting a sense of the full humanity of Jesus, or that the Alexandrians gave that full humanity only lip-service; it is here, perhaps, that Grillmeier's typology of word–flesh and word–human being Christology loses its usefulness and becomes misleading, under the influence of mid-twentieth-century concerns (see McGuckin 1994: 205–7). Diodore himself, for instance, occasionally uses the traditional terminology of 'the Logos and his flesh', without suggesting thereby any diminution of Jesus' humanity (see Greer 1966); and Cyril is insistent, throughout his increasingly bitter controversy with Nestorius, that the 'flesh' which he speaks of as forming 'one nature' with the Word, in the Incarnation, included a complete and functioning rational human soul. Even if he made use of terms and formulas popularized by Apollinarius and his followers, Cyril was no Apollinarian in his understanding of the humanity of Christ. Neither 'school' was interested in seeking to recover a 'historical Jesus' who was thought to be more real, more foundational to faith, more like ourselves, than the Jesus presented in the Gospel narrative; and neither 'school' understood the 'person' of Christ to be identified in any privileged way with his human consciousness (see McGuckin 1994: 134, 207). These are modern concerns, remote from the general world of ancient philosophical and theological discourse.

Two things separated the theological thought-patterns of the theologians we label as 'Antiochenes' and 'Alexandrians'. One is a different sense of the relevance of *time* to human salvation in Christ. The Antiochenes seem to have thought of the fullness of human salvation as an eschatological state, characterized by the gift of unchangeability and stability, by freedom from sin and passion, and by the incorruptibility and immortality of the risen body; these graces are fully realized now only in the risen Jesus, who lives eschatologically already, in a different 'state' (κατάστασις) or world than the world of space and time we inhabit. Theodore of Mopsuestia and Theodoret emphasize that salvation is given to us at present only as a promise, in the 'pledge' of the Holy Spirit and in the 'types' or anticipatory symbols of the Church's sacraments; when we move on from this κατάστασις to the next, at the end of history, we will share in the state of transformation now revealed in the glorified human Christ (see Koch 1965: 141–79; Dewart 1971: 30–48; Koch 1974; Daley 1991). Secondly, the Antiochene theologians emphasize the *boundaries* between God and creation, between God's sphere of being and activity and that of the concrete, historical world we inhabit.

> It is well known that the one who is eternal and the one whose existence has a beginning are greatly separated from each other, and the gulf found between them is unbridgeable.
>
> (Theodore of Mopsuestia, *On the Nicene Creed*,
> Catechetical Homily 4; Mingana 1932: 45)

Unlike Athanasius, who also emphasized God's otherness than creation but who laid an equal, coordinate emphasis on the divine Logos' personal, substantial presence within creation, the Antiochenes were concerned to maintain only God's distance—out of an underlying concern not to promote any idea of creation or salvation that might compromise the transcendent qualities of the three divine Persons. 'Divinization' of the fallen human being is rarely mentioned by either Theodore or Theodoret (see Koch 1965: 150; Koch 1974: 235–8). In contrast to their interest in biblical 'history', perhaps, Antiochene theologians tend to begin their treatments of theological issues, including salvation in Christ, by discussing God's being in the more general terms of the unity of the divine substance and its common attributes, as understood from the Greek philosophical tradition, rather than in terms of the scriptural narrative (see Koch 1974: 235; Theodoret, Ep. 145; cf. Bergjan 1993: 192–5). So in his so-called Sermon 'against the Theotokos', which opened his controversy with Cyril of Alexandria, Nestorius treats the person and saving work of Jesus within the context of God's general providence: because God, who transcends the world, never ceases to care for the world he has created—because God is 'untouched by change', yet 'benevolent and just'—he finally has 'dignified it with a gift which was furthest away and yet nearest to hand', and has taken up a human being, Jesus, to 'bring about the revival of the human race' (Nestorius' *First Sermon Against the Theotokos* in Norris 1980: 124, 126; also see 123–31). These ideas were heavy with implications for their understanding of the person of Christ.

Apart from his commentary on the Psalms, Diodore's work survives mainly in small fragments, mostly preserved by hostile sources. Diodore was a prolific writer of vast learning; he is supposed to have produced commentaries on the entire Old Testament, as well as works on natural science and polemical treatises directed against the Jews, Neoplatonist philosophy, and a number of Christian sects. Many of the fragments dealing with the person of Christ are taken from his work *Against the Synousiasts*, which was apparently an anti-Apollinarian treatise, attacking the portrait of Christ as 'the man from heaven', an organic unity of the divine Logos with living human flesh, which the Apollinarians had popularized (see Greer 1990). It is understandable that Diodore should have emphasized the distinctness of the Logos from the human being in which he has revealed himself in our midst (Diodore of Tarsus, Fragment 36; Abramowski 1949: 51–3). What worried his later critics was that Diodore, in his anti-Apollinarian work seems to have insisted on the distinction of 'two Sons' in Christ: the son of Mary, who, as 'temple' of God the Word, can be called 'Son of God' by *grace*, and the one who is Son of God by *nature*, ὁμοούσιος with the Father, and who is God the Logos. With the subsequent Antiochene tradition, Diodore was very concerned with theological precision; so he writes:

> If anyone, speaking inexactly, also wants to call the Son of God, God the Word, son of David because of the temple of God the Word that was taken from David, let him call him so. And let him call the one descended from David's seed Son of God, by grace but not by nature—as long as he is not unaware of his natural ancestors and does not reverse the order, or say that the one who is incorporeal and before the ages *is* both from God and from David, both passible and impassible.
>
> (Diodore of Tarsus, *Against the Synousiasts*, Frag. 4, as in Leontius of Byzantium, *Deprehensio et Triumphus super Nestorianos* [*DTN*])

Diodore is willing to apply the title 'Son of God' to Jesus as a conventional, non-literal way of pointing out that he was the bearer or dwelling-place of the eternal Son of God, but he insists on the abiding distinction between what Jesus and the Word are in themselves, and what Jesus has become, by God's gracious action, in the divine economy. In another fragment, he denies preaching 'two sons' in any way that would be harmful to Trinitarian or Christological doctrine:

> We urge you to be safe in being precise about doctrine. The Son, perfect before the ages, assumed a perfect descendant of David: the Son of God took the Son of David. You say to me, 'Then you are proclaiming two sons?' I do not speak of two sons of David; for

I did not say that God the Word is David's son, did I? Nor do I say there are two Sons of God in essence; for I do not say there are two produced from God's essence, do I? I say that God the eternal Word dwelt in him who is from the seed of David.

(Diodore of Tarsus, *Against the Synousiasts*, Frag. 1,
in Leontius of Byzantium, *DTN*)

The point seems almost a pedantic one, but one can see here the sense of the boundary between the divine nature and the historical order in which God has worked salvation, the sense that God's transcendence must be protected from pious imprecision, which would characterize both Diodore and his heirs.

Perhaps the most gifted and influential of those heirs was Theodore of Mopsuestia. Diodore's pupil spent ten years as a presbyter and scriptural commentator in Antioch, in the 380s, before becoming bishop of Mopsuestia, sixty miles north of the city, in 392. His exegesis, which has earned him the title 'the Interpreter' in the Assyrian Church of the East, follows the same analytical, sparingly figural approach Diodore had developed; it also seeks—as Diodore's did—to situate biblical passages in their place within the longer narrative of God's people, as they are drawn towards eschatological salvation. Theodore has also left catechetical and doctrinal works of great interest, such as fragments of a large treatise *On the Incarnation*, directed against Arian and Apollinarian conceptions of Christ as Diodore's work had been.

Theodore is deeply concerned to draw a sharp, bright line between the transcendent, triune God—separated from creation by an 'unbridgeable gulf' of being—and the 'human nature', the 'form of a human being', which God the Son 'put on' to reveal himself in the human world (Theodore of Mopsuestia, *Cat. Hom.* 5; Mingana 1932: 50–1; cf. *Cat. Hom.* 5; Mingana 1932: 36ff.). Theodore's usual way of speaking about the relation of the divine Son to the man Jesus is in terms of 'indwelling', of presence as in a temple (alluding to Jesus' words in John 2:19), or of the Son's 'clothing' himself in the 'form of a servant' (as suggested by Phil. 2.7). More important for him seems to have been the precise *mode* of the Son's presence in a visible, created human being. In a fragment of his treatise *On the Incarnation*, Theodore distinguishes between God's presence in essence (οὐσία), in operation or activity (ἐνέργεια), and in 'good pleasure' or 'favor' (εὐδοκία). As the transcendent ground and source of all created being, and the provident guide of the universe in its continued functioning, God must be present to all creatures equally in essence and in operation; so Theodore argues that the only way in which he can be particularly present or absent to individuals must be in the third way of 'good pleasure', of love and grace. The Word's indwelling in Jesus, then, must be conceived along these lines, as representing a unique degree of divine election and good pleasure, a unique identification of this man with the Word, by God's prior choice and action, which has enabled Jesus to reveal the Word uniquely to the world and to share uniquely in God's glory and work as judge and savior of human history. Theodore concludes:

The indwelling took place in [Jesus] as in a son; it was in this sense that [God] took pleasure in him and indwelt him. But what does it mean to say 'as in a son'? It means that having indwelt him, he united the one assumed as a whole to himself and equipped him to share with himself in all the honor in which he, being Son by nature, participates, so as to be counted one person (πρόσωπον) in virtue of the union with him and share with him all his dominion, and in this way to accomplish everything in him, so that even the examination and judgment of the world shall be fulfilled through him and his advent. Of course, in all this the difference in natural characteristics is kept in mind.

(On the Incarnation VII, Frag. 2; Norris 1980: 117)

Theodore is willing to accept the Church's traditional language of 'incarnation' to describe the presence of the Word in Jesus, provided one understands it as meaning the Word became actually visible in human terms, and 'assumed a complete man, who was a man not only in appearance but a man in a true human nature' (*Cat. Hom.* 5; Mingana 1932: 60; cf. 54). To take incarnation any more literally than this—to identify 'the Son of the seed of David according to the flesh', of Romans 1:3, with the eternal Son—is incorrect: 'Indeed it is not God who became flesh, nor was it God who was formed from the seed of David, but the man who was assumed for us' (*Cat. Hom.* 8; Mingana 1932: 91). Theodore's favorite way of speaking about this 'assumption', it seems, is in terms of *union*: it is a 'close union' or 'precise union' (ἄκρα ἕνωσις; e.g. *Cat. Hom.* 3, 6, 8; Mingana 1932: 36ff.; 66ff.; 84; 91), an 'ineffable union' (ἄρρητος ἕνωσις; e.g., *Cat. Hom.* 8; Mingana 1932: 86ff.), a 'perfect union (τελεία ἕνωσις) between the one who was assumed and the one who assumed' (*Cat. Hom.* 6; Mingana 1932: 64). Theodore insists that this union between Word and man is not transitory: 'the human form can never and under no circumstances be separated from the divine nature which put it on' (*Cat. Hom.* 8; Mingana 1932: 89). Jesus the man has always been 'precisely united' with God the Word. But Theodore is reluctant to speak of what it is that binds the divine Son and the man Jesus together in other than functional terms: the man was so led by the Holy Spirit that 'he had the Logos of God working within him and throughout him in a perfect way, so as to be inseparable from the Logos in his every motion' (*On the Incarnation* VII, Frag. 3l; Norris 1980: 117); and they are unified, most strikingly and most visibly, in the honor they receive, both from God the Father and from the rest of creation, as the man Jesus is glorified (e.g. *Cat. Hom.* 6, 7; Mingana 1932: 65, 78, 80). Seizing on the biblical axiom that a husband and wife are 'no longer two, but one flesh' (Gen. 2:24; Matt. 19:6), Theodore observes that a married couple clearly are not impeded from this unity by their being two people (*Cat. Hom.* 8; Mingana 1932: 90; cf. *On the Incarnation* VIII, Frag. 7; Norris 1980: 120).

Theodore's careful picture of the 'perfect union' of two different acting beings in Christ the Savior affects his way of theologically interpreting the activities of Christ, as they are reported in the Gospels. In 'assuming the fashion of a human being' and dwelling in him, the Logos 'hid himself at the time in which he was in the world, and conducted himself with the human race in such a way that those who beheld him in a human way, and did not understand anything more, believed him to be simply human' (*Cat. Hom.* 6; Mingana 1932: 65). All the events of Jesus' life, guided by the indwelling Word, were intended by God to be saving Mysteries, Theodore goes on to suggest, that is, models of the growth towards immortality which we also hope to share.

> It was easy and not difficult for God to have made him at once immortal, incorruptible and immutable as he became after his resurrection, but because it was not he alone whom [God] wished to make immortal immutable, but us also who are partakers of his nature, he rightly, and on account of this association, did not so make the first-fruits of us all, in order that, as the blessed Paul said, 'He might have the pre-eminence in all things' (Col. 1.18). In this way, because of the communion that we have with him in this world, we will, with justice, be partakers with him of the future good things.
>
> (*Cat. Hom.* 6; Mingana 1932: 69, 70)

In such reflections, Theodore sounds like Gregory of Nyssa. Yet he emphasizes, too, that Jesus the man had to pursue virtue himself, even though

> he fulfilled virtue more exactly and more easily than was possible for other people, since God the Logos ... had united Jesus with himself in his very conception and furnished him with a fuller cooperation for the accomplishment of what was necessary.
>
> (*On the Incarnation* VII, Frag. 5; Norris 1980: 119)

Theodore also emphasizes the reality of the sufferings and death of Jesus: a natural death whose public character served to emphasize the physical reality of his resurrection, 'by which death was abolished' (*Cat. Hom.* 7; Mingana 1932: 74). Jesus' passion and death raise the ultimate difficulties to our accepting a literal understanding of the Word's incarnation. Alluding to a version of Hebrews 2:9, which was known by Origen—'Apart from God (χωρὶς θεοῦ) he tasted death for everyone'—Theodore emphasizes that Jesus was only able to die because the Godhead kept himself 'cautiously remote' from him in that time, 'yet also near enough to do the needful and necessary things for the nature he had assumed'. He continues:

> He himself [i.e., the Word] was not tried with the trial of death, but he was near to him and doing to him the things that were congruous to his nature as the maker who is the cause of everything. That is, he brought him to perfection through sufferings and made him forever immortal, impassible, incorruptible, and immutable for the salvation of the multitudes who would be receiving communion (κοινωνία) with him.
>
> (*Cat. Hom.* 8; Mingana 1932: 87)

In all of his reflections on the experiences of Jesus and their significance in the economy of salvation in the *Catecheses*, at any rate, Theodore tends to speak of the Logos and the man in whom he dwelt, or even of the 'natures' of divinity and humanity, as two agents, two 'he's, without much precision on the way in which they can be thought of as one. Occasionally, he uses the terminology of *person* (πρόσωπον)—the dynamic concept of a 'speaker' or dramatic 'role' associated with a theatrical 'mask' or 'face' (πρόσωπον)—to suggest that it is in their permanent association of action and appearance that the Word and the man Jesus find their inseparable unity. So Theodore writes, in a fragment of *On the Incarnation*:

> When we try to distinguish the natures, we say that the 'person' of the human being is complete and that that of the Godhead is complete. But when we consider the union, then we proclaim that both natures are one 'person', since the humanity receives from the divinity honor surpassing that which belongs to a creature, and the divinity brings to perfection in the human being everything that is fitting.
>
> (*On the Incarnation* VIII, Frag. 8; Norris 1980: 120–1)

Theodore's most famous pupil, undoubtedly, was the monk Nestorius. Nestorius was brought to Constantinople as bishop in the spring of 428. The contemporary ecclesiastical historian Socrates characterizes him as vain, quarrelsome, and intolerant of other opinions (*Ecclesiastical History* 7.29), and hazards the judgment that Nestorius was 'disgracefully illiterate' in the theological tradition (*Ecclesiastical History* 32). In the sermon which provoked the outbreak of hostilities between himself and Cyril of Alexandria, Nestorius gives voice to a more rigid version of Theodore's conception of Christ than we find in Theodore's own works. Nestorius is mainly concerned here to draw clear distinctions between the divine Logos, who has saved us all in Christ, and the human Jesus, the Son of Mary, who was his 'temple', 'the instrument of his godhead' (*First Sermon 'against the Theotokos'*; Norris 1980: 125). God cannot be born, God cannot die, he insists: but God, who is above all change, is also active in the world, benevolent towards his creatures (*First Sermon 'against the Theotokos'*; Norris 1980: 125–6). So the Son, in Paul's words, 'emptied himself, taking the form of a slave' (Phil. 2.7); he 'assumed a person (πρόσωπον), of the same nature [as ours]' (*First Sermon 'against the Theotokos'*; Norris 1980: 127) in order to pay to God the debt our nature had incurred through sin (*First Sermon 'against the Theotokos'*; Norris 1980: 126f.). In this human 'person', which now belongs to the Son of God, our nature or common reality, Nestorius argues, was able to plead its case before God against the devil, who brought charges against it going back to Adam. Pointing to the innocence of Jesus, the new Adam, human nature itself calls out for release from the punishment of corruption and mortality:

> Our nature, having been put on by Christ like a garment, intervenes on our behalf, ... This was the opportunity which belonged to the assumed man, as a human being: to dissolve, by means of the flesh, that corruption which arose by means of the flesh.
>
> (*First Sermon 'against the Theotokos'*; Norris 1980: 128)

Human nature can make this claim on God because it now belongs to 'the Christ, who is at once God and man' (*First Sermon 'against the Theotokos'*; Norris 1980: 129). The human being, who is the created instrument of the Word, is honored and worshiped and followed by the faithful because the Word is 'within' him and has 'assumed' him as his 'instrument' (*First Sermon 'against the Theotokos'*; Norris 1980: 129, 130). The very difference between the deity and humanity that have come together in Christ is what makes possible his uniquely exalted position as Savior.

Later on in the 430s and 440s, the exiled Nestorius labored to defend his own orthodoxy in a series of tracts and letters, some of which have come down to us in a collection known as the *Book of Heracleides*. There Nestorius attempts to develop a whole Christology based on the idea of 'union by *persona* (or πρόσωπον)', in order to clear himself from the reputation of having taught that the Word and Jesus were 'two Sons'. The conception behind Nestorius' argument seems to be based on the familiar text Philippians 2:6–7, where Christ is said to have put aside the 'form of God' (μορφὴ θεοῦ) and have taken up the 'likeness of a slave' (μορφὴ δούλου), so that he 'came to be in human likeness (ὁμοιώματι), and was found, in shape, as a human being (σχήματι ὡς ἄνθρωπος)'. Probably drawing on Neoplatonic theory as well as on earlier Antiochene usage, Nestorius speaks of these various 'forms' or 'appearances' as πρόσωπα: 'faces' or 'personae'. Every natural substance, he suggests in the *Book of Heracleides*, has its own πρόσωπον, its external form or self-presentation, formed from its intrinsic natural properties, which allows it to be known by others. Since the Word of God and the historical man Jesus are irreducibly distinct in their own fundamental realities, and since any suggestion of a blending of the two inevitably would imply compromising either the transcendence of the Word or the humanity of Jesus—making him into an Arian or an Apollinarian Son of God—what the Incarnation really means, in Nestorius' scheme, is that each of these two realities in Christ has conferred its own 'face' on the other, forming a single, externally perceptible whole, which acts and appears as one. Nestorius insists this exchange of πρόσωπα is more than a matter of simple behavior, of 'acting as if'; by conferring their 'faces' on each other, the Word and the man actually 'form' each other into something new. So he writes, alluding to Philippians 2:

> For he [the Word] exists in his hypostasis and has made it [the flesh?] the likeness of his likeness, neither by command nor by honor nor simply by the equality of grace, but he has made it his likeness in its natural likeness [= form], in such a way that it is none other than that very thing which he has taken for his own πρόσωπον, so that the one might be the other and the other the one, one and the same in the two substances: a πρόσωπον fashioned by the flesh and fashioning the flesh in the likeness of its own Sonship in the two natures, and one in the two natures—the one fashioned by the other and the other by the one, the same unique likeness of the πρόσωπον.
>
> (Nestorius, *Book of Heracleides*; Driver and Hodgson 2002: 159, trans. modified)

Nestorius wants to affirm a genuine and lasting unity between the eternal Word and the human Jesus; but he insists on conceiving it in terms of an exchange of perceptible forms, the Word shaping the human Jesus into someone who reveals God, and Jesus giving the Word of God human words and a human face. He is opposed to any way of conceiving the unity of Christ in terms of 'substance'. To see Christ's unity as substantial or natural unity implies for Nestorius inevitably that either the Word is himself capable of change and suffering, and therefore less than fully God, or that the humanity of Jesus is incomplete, simply a matter of appearance. Nestorius writes:

> [W]e shun those who speak of the Incarnation apart from this union: either by a change only in likeness, which is the view of the pagans, or in hallucinations, or in a form (σχῆμα) without hypostasis which 'suffers impassibly' [Nestorius' caricature of Cyril's view]; or in predicating natural sufferings of God the Word, as being either hypostatically united to the flesh or in the flesh as a rational or irrational soul [text uncertain]; or, finally, in asserting that the union resulted in a natural hypostasis and not a voluntary πρόσωπον. For we may not make the union of God the Word corruptible and changeable, nor call it passible and necessary, but it is a voluntary union in πρόσωπον and not in nature.
>
> (Nestorius, *Book of Heracleides*; Driver and Hodgson 2002: 181, trans. modified)

For Nestorius as for Theodore, what was most to be feared in speaking of the Incarnation as substantial or natural, or as the hypostatic or concretely realized union of the Word and a man, was that it compromised the transcendent qualities of God: his impassibility, his unchangeability, his freedom. God reveals himself in Christ, but not as being himself part of our world.

Theodoret of Cyrus was a contemporary and a defender of Nestorius, a bitter critic of Cyril of Alexandria, yet also the most moderate of the Antiochenes in his understanding of the unity of Christ, the most ready to work towards a conciliatory position. In his late work, the *Eranistes*, Theodoret mounts an elaborate refutation of what he understands to be the weakness of the Alexandrian approach to Christ: that it so emphasizes the identity of God and the human in him, that it takes John 1:14, 'The Word *became* flesh and dwelt among us', so literally, that it inevitably suggests the Word, as God, underwent change, rather than simply being the saving agent of change in humanity—for Theodoret, such an assertion that would contradict 'the incorporeal, illimitable character of the divine nature' (*Eranistes*, Dialogue 1; Ettlinger 1975: 66.4–68.12).

Theodoret insists, throughout this work, that an accurate theology, faithful to the Christian tradition, must distinguish between the human Jesus, who underwent change and suffering and who received the gift of incorruptibility in his resurrection, and the divine Word who had made the human Jesus his own. Theodoret constantly stresses that it was the man and not 'the divine nature' that suffered on the Cross, and that the two sets of properties are united only in the πρόσωπον, the one acting figure formed by the two utterly different individuals, the two ὑποστάσεις, of the Word and Jesus, indivisibly united now in their saving actions as the Christ (*Eranistes*, Dial. 3; Ettlinger 1975: 209.26–30). So Theodoret affirms, through the mouth of his 'Orthodox' speaker:

> It behooves us to say that the flesh was nailed to the tree, but to hold that the divine nature even on the cross and in the tomb was inseparable from this flesh, though

from it derived no sense of suffering, since the divine nature is naturally incapable of undergoing both suffering and death and its substance is immortal and impassible ... And when we are told of passion and of the cross, we must recognize the nature which submitted to the passion; we must avoid attributing it to the impassible one, and must attribute it to that nature which was assumed for the distinct purpose of suffering.

(Ettlinger 1975: 227.2–6; 228.23–5; trans. Blomfield Jackson, NPNF II, 3.233–4)

The task of orthodox theological language, Theodoret assumes, is to keep this distinction of the divine and the human constantly before the Church's eyes, along with their wonderful unity in the economy of salvation.

The main opponent of Nestorius and Theodoret, from the late 420s until his death in 446, was Cyril of Alexandria, the most thoughtful and prolific spokesman for the Alexandrian tradition. Cyril's opposition rested on a different way of conceiving and speaking about the Mystery of Christ and about salvation: different terminology, different priorities, a different rhetoric. The non-negotiable axion of Cyril's Christology is not the *otherness* of the divine nature with respect to circumscribed, mutable, passible creatures, but the *involvement* of God the Son, the second hypostasis of the divine Trinity, in the historical process of salvation we call God's 'management' of things—his 'economy' (McGuckin 1994: 184; see also O'Keefe, 1997: esp. 58). So Cyril underlines the continuity in the narrative of the Scriptures and the Creeds, by emphasizing the singleness of the subject of the acts that have saved us: it is God the Word, God the Son, who is born of a Virgin, who receives his own Holy Spirit in baptism for our sakes, who heals the sick and raises the dead by his human touch, who dies in his own body on the Cross and reunites that body with his own soul on the morning of the resurrection. Cyril is careful to distinguish his own understanding of the person of Christ from that of Apollinarius: the 'one nature' or real, living agent, the Word, who has 'been made flesh' in time, includes in that biblically named 'flesh' a complete human mind, a 'rational soul'. Cyril agrees with his Antiochene critics that the Logos, as God, does not undergo change or limitation or suffering in his own divine nature, even while he insists that it is this very Logos as agent, as subject, who experiences precisely these things in what has become, by incarnation, his own passible, changeable human flesh.

In his first statement of this Christological approach within a context of controversy—his so-called 'second letter' to Nestorius, in which he takes the Constantinopolitan bishop to task for the deficiencies in his formulation of the Mystery—Cyril expresses his position concisely yet completely; citing the Nicene Creed as the guide for what must be said of Christ, and for how one must say it, he explains:

We do not say that the Logos became flesh by having his nature changed, nor for that matter that he was transformed into a complete human being composed out of soul and body. On the contrary, we say that in an unspeakable and incomprehensible way, the Logos united to himself, in his hypostasis, flesh enlivened by a rational soul, and in this way became a human being and has been designated 'Son of man'. He did not become a human being simply by an act of will or 'good pleasure' (εὐδοκία), any more than he did so by merely taking on a 'person' (πρόσωπον).

Furthermore, we say that while the natures which were brought together into a true unity were different, there is, nevertheless, because of the unspeakable and unutterable convergence into unity, one Christ and one Son out of the two. This is the sense in which it is said that, although he existed and was born from the Father before the ages, he was also born of a woman in his flesh … It is not the case that first of all an ordinary human being was born of the holy Virgin and that the Logos descended upon him subsequently. On the contrary, since the union took place in the very womb, he is said to have undergone a fleshly birth by making his own the birth of the flesh which belonged to him. We assert that this is the way in which he suffered and rose from the dead. It is not that the Logos of God suffered in his own nature, being overcome by stripes or nail-piercing or any of the other injuries; for the divine, since it is incorporeal, is impassible. Since, however, the body that had become his own underwent suffering, he is—once again—said to have suffered these things for our sakes, for the impassible one was within the suffering body.

> (Cyril of Alexandria, *Second Letter to Nestorius*; Norris 1980: 132–3)

In reading this text, it is important to attend to the particular terms and expressions Cyril chooses to signify the personal unity of Christ. As in the Nicene Creed, the subject of the narrative is God the Logos; *he* is the one who became a human being, experienced true birth from a human mother, suffered in the way only humans can suffer. Christology is not about 'divinity' and 'humanity', first of all, but about what the Son of God did for our sakes. Secondly, the verbs reveal a sense of the importance of time, of narrative sequence: 'the natures he brought together *were* different, yet there *is* now convergence … one Son out of the two'; what *were* different *are* now, in a new sense altogether, 'one and the same'. And thirdly, Cyril speaks here and elsewhere of this new unity in Christ as 'union in hypostasis' (ἕνωσις καθ' ὑπόστασιν), in the concreteness of an individual existence, and later even as 'union in nature' (ἕνωσις κατὰ φύσιν), understanding 'nature', too, as the living actuality of an organic individual being (*Third Letter to Nestorius*, §4, 5, and anathema 3; Wickham 1983: 19, 29). The Word can be said to have 'made fleshly birth his own' (οἰκειοῦσθαι), so that the flesh, its sufferings and even its death are now 'his' (see also *First Letter to Successus*, 6).

The implications of this picture of Christ are both linguistic and substantive. Linguistically, Cyril delights in using the somewhat shocking turns of phrase that we usually classify as 'the communication of properties', predicating human experiences directly of God the Word and divine qualities directly of the man Jesus. In his celebrated 'Third Letter to Nestorius', for instance—a piece meant to stake out the boundaries between his own approach and that of the Antiochenes as confrontationally as possible—he refers to the Eucharistic species as 'the personal, truly vitalizing flesh of God the Word himself' (*Third Letter to Nestorius*, 7; Wickham 1983: 23; cf. anathema 11), and later goes on to anathematize those who 'do not acknowledge God's Word as having suffered in flesh, been crucified in flesh, tasted death in flesh and been made first-born from the dead, because as God he is Life and life-giving' (*Third Letter to*

Nestorius, anathema 12; Wickham 1983: 33; also see Chadwick 1951; Gebremedhin 1977).
Just like the title θεοτόκος for Mary, which first moved Nestorius to impose some distinctions in the interest of Nicene orthodoxy, phrases like these are deliberately meant as
'limit-cases', hard sayings that test the extent to which we are willing to affirm that God
the Word is really the one who has saved us in the person and works of Jesus, that God
the Word is really the one we encounter in Jesus' humanity and even in his sacramental
presence in the Church. But the Christological debate, for Cyril, is clearly not simply a
debate over how we think and talk about the Savior; it is also a consideration of what we
actually understand God to have done for us, with us, in Christ.

For Cyril and his Antiochene interlocutors, the most challenging substantive aspect
of the paradox of Christ's person was his suffering: must Christians affirm that God the
Son is the one who suffered, in his own flesh, on the Cross, or must one make a strict
distinction between the suffering one and the one who raised him? Cyril insists most
emphatically, in many of his later works, that the first of these statements is in fact a
central affirmation of Christian faith. So he asks, in his third *Tome against Nestorius*, 'By
faith in whom, then, are we justified? Is it not in him who suffered death according to
the flesh for our sake? Is it not in one Lord Jesus Christ? Have we not been redeemed by
proclaiming his death and confessing his resurrection?' (*Against Nestorius* 3.2, in ACO I,
1, 6.61; Russell 2000: 165). Cyril is willing to concede, by the mid-430s, that the humanity
and the divinity that belong to Christ can be distinguished as two separate natures during his earthly life, by a kind of exercise in thought 'at the merely speculative level' (κατὰ
μονὴν τὴν θεωρίαν), as long as one recognizes that in fact 'they belong to one individual,
so that the two are two no more, but one living being is brought to its full realization
through both' (*Second Letter to Succensus*, 5, trans. mine; cf. Wickham 1983: 92–3). And
it is this 'one living being'—God the Word, who has taken on our 'flesh' in time—who is
the subject of his flesh's passion:

> The passion therefore will belong to the economy, God the Word esteeming as his
> own the things which pertain to his own flesh, by reason of the ineffable union,
> and remaining external to suffering as far as pertains to his own nature, for God is
> impassible.
>
> (Scholia on the Incarnation 36; Pusey 1881: 225)

Cyril repeatedly affirms that Christ, as the Word with his 'flesh', 'suffered impassibly'—a paradox that excited the amazement and scorn of his Antiochene opponents,
and even some modern scholars (Cyril, *To the Royal Ladies, On Right Faith* 2.164; PG
76.1393B; *On the Creed*, 24; *That Christ is One*; McGuckin 1995: 117; see Theodoret,
Eranistes, 3; Ettlinger 1975: 218.29–34; see also Cyril, *Second Letter to Succensus*, 4–5; cf.
Hallman 1991).

In some of these passages Cyril suggests that the 'impassible suffering' of Christ is
more than simply a paradox that tests our grasp of the Mystery of his person; Cyril also
presents it as 'an example (ὑποτύπωσις) for us in human fashion ... so that we might
follow in his steps' (*To the Royal Ladies, on Right Faith* 2.164; see Smith 2002). If one

remembers that suffering, like all human 'passions' or passivities, was understood in the Hellenistic world as an experience that normally destroyed the harmony and integrity of a natural organism, Jesus' 'impassible suffering', seen as human vulnerability freely taken on and 'owned' by the life-giving Word of God in his human body and soul, becomes the means by which he heals *our* passions and destructive weaknesses in his own humanity, and turns our suffering into a means of growth. So Cyril writes of the death of Christ, the climax of his sufferings, in his *Letter to the Monks*, during the summer of 431:

> As one of us, though he knew not death, he went down into death through his own flesh, in order that we might also go up with him to life. For he came to life again, having despoiled the nether world, not as a human like us but as God in flesh, among us and above us. Our nature was greatly enriched with immortality in him first, and death was crushed when it assaulted the body of life as an enemy. For just as it conquered in Adam, so it was defeated in Christ.
>
> (*Letter to the Monks of Egypt*, 38; McInery 1987: 33)

What was really at stake for Cyril, however, in the question of the suffering of the incarnate Word and in all the other issues surrounding that of the unity of subject in Christ, was the economy itself; to attribute the acts and words and even the sufferings of Christ to anyone but God the Son, to anything but the Word's own flesh, is for him to lessen the message of the Gospel. Quoting John 3:16—'God so loved the world that he gave his only-begotten Son'—Cyril asks plaintively:

> When God the Father so exalts his love for the world, explaining how immensely great and vast it is, then why do our opponents so belittle it, saying that it was not the true Son who was given for us? They introduce in place of the natural Son someone else who is like us, and has the sonship as a grace; but it really was the Only-begotten who was given for our sake ... What will then be left of the great and admirable love of the Father, if he only gave up a part of the world for its sake, and a small part at that? Perhaps it would not even be wrong to say that the world was redeemed without God's help, since it was served in this respect from within its own resources?
>
> (*That Christ is One*; McGuckin 1995: 120–1)

If it is God who has redeemed the world, and if he has done it in Christ, who is God's own Son, then Cyril insists we must see the story of Christ as nothing less than a story about God himself.

Perhaps the real issues that divided the theologians of Antioch and Alexandria in the fourth and fifth centuries could be expressed in broader questions such as these:

(1) *What is theological language really about?* For Nestorius and Theodoret, at least, its purpose was to prevent us from making dangerous mistakes about God: it needed to be precise, self-conscious, and technically sophisticated if it was to avoid the pitfalls of Arianism, Apollinarianism, or pagan myth. For Cyril, its

purpose was to express and elicit reverence and wonder at the great things God has done for us; it was evocative, deliberately paradoxical, redolent of the atmosphere of liturgical prayer; and the great danger to be avoided was speaking of Christ in overly secular terms.

(2) *How should one read the Scriptures?* Both the Antiochene and the Alexandrian traditions of theology were rooted in highly developed cultures of scholarly biblical interpretation; both 'schools' recognized in the Christian Bible a single witness to a single story of salvation that culminated in the person and work of Christ, a story summed up in Creeds like that of Nicaea (cf. Wessel 2004: 268–9). But the Antiochenes insisted on the need for a certain degree of hermeneutical sophistication if one were to read the Bible in a way worthy of God—a hermeneutic based on the Greek philosophical tradition about what the divine nature is and is not. Cyril was aware of these philosophical traditions, too, and was willing to use them to the degree that they did not obscure the shocking originality of the biblical message; but Scripture itself, not philosophy, for him had to be the starting point of Christian theology. So on the question of the suffering of the Word in his flesh, he concludes his argument by saying: 'Inspired Scripture tells us he suffered in "flesh", and we would do better to use those terms than to talk of his suffering "in a human nature"' (*Second Letter to Succensus*, 5; Wickham 1983: 93). Philosophical language always brought with it the subtle tendency to place human reasoning about what God must be like above the Gospel message about who and what God is.

(3) *How does God save us?* The Antiochene theologians tend to understand salvation in terms similar to Gregory of Nyssa's: as growth in moral virtue and stability, coupled with freedom from physical corruptibility, both of which are presently visible in the risen Christ but are promised to us only in the age to come. They speak a good deal of the work of grace and of the presence of the Holy Spirit in the Church, but are noticeably reluctant to use the language of 'divinization'. In fact, the Antiochenes tend to conceive of grace, to use Augustine's terminology, more in cooperative than in operative terms, more as assistance than as the creation of new freedom: God clearly has begun the work of redemption among us, but—as in Jesus—God clearly expects us to 'grow in grace by pursuing the virtue which is attendant upon understanding and knowledge' (Theodore of Mopsuestia, *On the Incarnation* VII, Frag. 5; Norris 1980: 119; also see Dewart 1971: 49–73). For Cyril, on the other hand, grace is God's work, just as the story of salvation is the story of God's action, not ours. Nestorius, in fact, criticizes Cyril by saying, 'You take as the starting point of your narrative the maker of the natures [in Christ], and not the πρόσωπον of union' (*Book of Heracleides*; Driver and Hodgson 2002: 153): Cyril begins with God, he suggests, not with the Christ who is a balanced union of what is divine and what is human. And while tacitly accepting this criticism, Cyril also sees God as the end of the narrative, frequently drawing on 2 Peter 1:4 to remind his readers that salvation in Christ implies we are to become 'sharers in the divine nature'. In his *Commentary on John*, for instance—a

work that antedates the Nestorian controversy by as much as five years—Cyril reflects on the Mystery of Christ's person as the foundation of the Church's unity:

> He came to be at once God and a human being, so that by joining together in himself things that are widely separate in nature and have diverged from all kinship with each other, he might reveal humanity as a participant and 'sharer in the divine nature' ... So the Mystery of Christ has come into being as a kind of beginning, a way for us to share in the Holy Spirit and in unity with God: all of us are made holy in that Mystery.
>
> (*Commentary on John*, 11:11; Pusey 1872: 998a–1000a)

(4) *How is God related to this created order?* How *real* is God's presence in this world of space and time? The Antiochenes were concerned to emphasize God's *otherness* with regard to creation, God's freedom from all the limitations and vulnerabilities that classical philosophy saw as part of contingent existence; they feared that a Christology that one-sidedly emphasized the single subject of Christ's person and acts might lead to the 'confusion' of God and a creature, might lose its sense of God's transcendence. Cyril, and the Alexandrian tradition since Athanasius, on the other hand, while also aware of the otherness of God, were even more concerned to emphasize God's intimate presence in and to creation: this was in their view the paradox on which biblical faith turned. Cyril's fear was of losing a sense of the divine authorship of salvation. The Antiochenes saw God and creation as for now related synchronically, dialectically; the most interesting part of the narrative of salvation, for them, lay in the eschatological future, when the promise present in the Gospel, and in the symbolic 'types' of the Church's liturgy, would come to fulfillment for humanity. Their Christology made room for a created order that possesses real autonomy, for real independence in human action; but the danger was of driving a wedge between God and the created order that would eventually make God remote from, even irrelevant to, everyday life. Cyril saw God's role in creation and redemption rather in diachronic, dramatic terms (see e.g., *On the Creed*, 7–15); the turning-point in the history of salvation lay already in the past, in the Word's taking on our human flesh and our human experiences to be his own. The fulfillment of the promise was available to the believer, in Jesus' gift of the Holy Spirit to the disciples, and through them to the Church; in the Church's unity, centered on the personal, substantial Eucharistic presence of Christ; in the incipient realization, even now, of our human participation in the life of God. Cyril's Christology took God's reality in Christ, and so in the life of the Christian disciple, with the utmost seriousness; the risk was that this reality might so overshadow ordinary, mundane reality—in Jesus and in our day-to-day religious life—that the Gospel might lose its credibility altogether and become a Gnostic myth.

Christology is always the affirmation of paradox. The theologians of both Antioch and Alexandria recognized that both sides of the paradox of Christ, as 'Emmanuel', had to be maintained if the Gospel message of his coming was to be proclaimed fully. The fact that subtle differences in their terminology, their rhetorical emphasis, their imagery and argument concerning the person of Christ, were able to grow into different theological, exegetical, and spiritual traditions, and ultimately to lead to ruptures within the Christian body that still exist today, ought to remind us just how deep the paradox of his person runs, and how urgent it is for all of us still to engage it faithfully.

SUGGESTED READING

Grillmeier (1988); McInery (1987); Norris (1980).

BIBLIOGRAPHY

Primary Sources

Diodorus Tarsensis (1980), *Commentarii in Psalmos* I, ed. J.-M. Olivier. Corpus Christianorum Series Graeca, vol. 6 (Turnhout: Brepols).

Driver, G. R. and L. Hodgson (trans.) (2002), *Nestorius The Bazaar of Heracleides* (Eugene, Oreg.: Wipf and Stock; reprint, previously printed by Oxford University Press, 1925).

Ettlinger, G. H. (trans. and ed.) (1975), *Eranistes (English and Greek Edition)* (Oxford: Oxford University Press).

Leontius of Byzantium, 'Deprehensio et Triumphus super Nestorianos', in J.-P. Migne (ed.), *Patrologia Graeca*, vol. 86 (Paris: Migne), 1357B–1385B.

McGuckin, J. (trans.) (1995), *On the Unity of Christ* (Crestwood, NY: St. Vladimir's Press).

McInery, J. L. (trans.) (1987), *St. Cyril of Alexandria: Letters 1–50*. Fathers of the Church 76 (Washington, DC: Catholic University of America Press).

Mingana, A. (trans.) (1932), Theodore of Mopsuestia, *On the Nicene Creed*. Woodbrooke Studies 5 (Cambridge: W. Heffer & Sons).

Norris, R. A., Jr. (trans. and ed.) (1980), *The Christological Controversy* (Minneapolis: Fortress).

Pusey, P. E. (ed.) (1872), *Sancti patris nostri Cyrilli archiepiscopi Alexandrini in D. Joannis evangelium*, 3 vols. (Oxford: Clarendon Press).

Pusey, P. E. (trans.) (1881), *Scholia on the Incarnation* (London and Oxford: Parker and Rivingtons).

Schwartz, E. (ed.) (1927), *Acta Conciliorum Oecumenicorum* [ACO] (Berlin and Leipzig: de Gruyter).

Theodoret (1892), *Dialogues*, trans. B. Jackson, in P. Schaff and H. Wace (eds.), *Nicene and Post-Nicene Fathers* [NPNF] Series II, Volume 3 (Grand Rapids, Mich.: Eerdmans; reprinted Peabody, MA: Hendrickson Publishers, 1995).

Secondary Sources

Abramowski, R. (1949), 'Der theologische Nachlass des Diodor von Tarsus', *Zeitschrift für die neutestamentliche Wissenschaft* 42: 51–3.

Bergjan, S.-P. (1993), *Theodoret von Cyrus und der Neunizänismus* (Berlin: de Gruyter).

Chadwick, H. (1951), 'Eucharist and Christology in the Nestorian Controversy', *Journal of Theological Studies* 2: 145–64.

Daley, B. E. (1991), *The Hope of the Early Church: A Handbook of Patristic Eschatology* (Cambridge: Cambridge University Press).

Dewart, J. M. (1971), *The Theology of Grace of Theodore of Mopsuestia* (Washington, DC: Catholic University of America Press).

Gebremedhin, E. (1977), *Life-giving Blessing: An Inquiry into the Eucharistic Doctrine of Cyril of Alexandria* (Uppsala: Uppsala University Press).

Greer, R. A. (1966), 'The Antiochene Christology of Diodore of Tarsus', *Journal of Theological Studies* 17: 327–41.

Greer, R. A. (1990), 'The Man from Heaven: Paul's Last Adam and Apollinaris' Christ', in W. S. Babcock (ed.), *Paul and the Legacies of Paul* (Dallas: Southern Methodist University Press), 165–82.

Grillmeier, A. (1988), *Christ in Christian Tradition: From the Apostolic Age to Chalcedon (451)*, 2nd edn. (Louisville: Westminster/John Knox).

Hallman, J. M. (1991), *The Descent of God: Divine Suffering in History and Theology* (Minneapolis: Fortress).

Koch, G. (1965), *Die Heilsverwirklichung bei Theodor von Mopsuestia*. Münchener theologische Studien 31 (Munich: Max Hueber Verlag).

Koch, G. (1974), *Strukturen und Geschichte des Heils in der Theologie des Theodoret von Kyros. Eine dogmen- und theologiegeschichtliche Untersuchung*. Frankfurter theologische Studien 17 (Frankfurt: Knecht Verlag).

McGuckin, J. (1994), *St. Cyril of Alexandria: The Christological Controversy* (Leiden: Brill).

O'Keefe, J. J. (1997) 'Impassible Suffering? Divine Passion and Fifth-Century Christology', *Theological Studies* 58: 39–60.

Russell, N. (2000), *Cyril of Alexandria* (London: Routledge).

Smith, J. W. (2002), ' "Suffering Impassibly": Christ's Passion in Cyril of Alexandria's Soteriology', *Pro Ecclesia* 11: 463–83.

Wessel, S. (2004), *Cyril of Alexandria and the Nestorian Controversy: The Making of a Saint and a Heretic* (Oxford: Oxford University Press).

Wickham, L. R. (1983), *Cyril of Alexandria: Select Letters* (Oxford: Clarendon Press).

Young, F. M. (2002), *Biblical Exegesis and the Formation of Christian Culture* (Grand Rapids, Mich.: Baker).

CHAPTER 9

CHRISTOLOGY IN THE EAST FROM THE COUNCIL OF CHALCEDON TO JOHN DAMASCENE

ANDREW LOUTH

THE Fathers of the Council of Chalcedon (451) issued a Definition of faith (Ὅρος Πίστεως: Tanner 1990: 83–7), which recapitulated the declarations of faith at the three Œcumenical Councils already recognized, citing the symbol of faith (the Creed) of the Councils of Nicaea (325) and Constantinople (381: the first clear evidence we have of such a creed) and, for the Council of Ephesos (431), endorsing two of Cyril's letters (the second synodal letter to Nestorios, and the letter to John of Antioch and the Oriental bishops, which affirmed the 'Formula of Union', securing agreement over the decisions of Ephesos), and then added the so-called Tome of Leo, the pope's letter in support of Flavios, archbishop of Constantinople, concluding with its own epitome of the Faith. This final epitome affirmed that in the one Person of Christ, there were united the divine nature, consubstantial with the Father, and the human nature, consubstantial 'with us' through his mother, the Virgin Mother of God (Θεοτόκος), 'without confusion, change, division, or separation' (ἀσυγχύτως, ἀτρέπτως, ἀδιαιρέτως, ἀχωρίστως).

Older treatments of the history of Christian doctrine have usually presented the Definition of Chalcedon (often reduced, wrongly, to the final epitome) as the culmination of patristic Christology, but it is better seen as a watershed, for much water was still to flow after the council. The extent and importance of post-Chalcedonian Christology has become more widely known with the publication of the first four parts of volume II of Grillmeier's *Christ in Christian Tradition*, as well as a deeper appreciation of the Christological reflection of the seventh-century Maximos the Confessor and the eighth-century John Damascene.

Although the aim of the Fathers of the Council of Chalcedon was to secure unity, the result was the opposite: the council opened divisions in the Church that have never been healed between those who accepted the council (who called themselves Orthodox or Catholic, but were called by their opponents dyophysites, if not 'Nestorians') and those who rejected the council (who also called themselves Orthodox or Catholic, and were called by their opponents monophysites, if not 'Eutychians', and by modern scholars 'miaphysites'—a barbarous coinage). Owing to misunderstanding between the two sides, sometimes wilful, not to mention non-theological issues, it is difficult to make clear the nature of the difference between them in theological terms, and it is perhaps more helpful to say that those who accepted Chalcedon did so because they believed that the Definition was faithful to the teaching of Cyril of Alexandria, while those who rejected the Definition did so because they felt that it betrayed his true teaching. The problem, however, with such a criterion as the faithfulness of Chalcedon to Cyril's teaching lay in the writings of Cyril himself. As Grillmeier remarked, 'The historical development of Cyril was in fact so ambivalent that his works could become a common arsenal for contrary christologies depending on what one sought in them' (Grillmeier 1995: 23). The supporters of Chalcedon looked for the Cyril who agreed with John of Antioch over the 'Formula of Union' which brought the Council of Ephesos to a successful conclusion, while the detractors of Chalcedon looked for the strident opponent to Nestorios, as manifest in his third synodal letter, to which were appended the uncompromising Twelve Anathemas (Tanner 1990: 50–61). So long as Cyril was alive, he was able to preserve some semblance of unity, but by the time the Council of Chalcedon was called he had been dead for seven years.

The years after Chalcedon saw different attempts to recover the unity that Chalcedon appeared to have relinquished. The lead was taken by emperors and ecclesiastical politicians. After initial support for Chalcedon, it seemed that the most likely way ahead was to abandon Chalcedon, and affirm the teaching of the three earlier Œcumenical Councils. This was the policy advanced in the *Henotikon*, the work of Akakios, Patriarch of Constantinople, and Peter Mongos, Patriarch of Alexandria, issued by Emperor Zeno in 482 (Coleman-Norton 1966: 924–33). This affirmed what it presented as the faith of the first three councils, and anathematized those who taught anything contrary 'either in Chalcedon or in many synod whatever': Chalcedon was not condemned, rather abandoned. In its summary of the Faith, the *Henotikon* affirmed that 'one of the Trinity' became incarnate: a phrase that was to become a key term in later Christological reflection. Pope Felix III condemned the *Henotikon*, as Rome was keen to support the Council of Chalcedon, which had endorsed the Tome of Leo, and anathematized Patriarch Akakios, initiating the 'Acacian schism' which lasted until the death of Emperor Anastasios I, Zeno's successor, in 518.

SEVEROS OF ANTIOCH

Engagement with the aftermath of Chalcedon at a serious theological level began to take place as Severos, Patriarch of Antioch 512–18, came on the scene in the early sixth century. He was the greatest theologian of his generation; his attacks on Chalcedon shaped the Christological debate in the sixth century (see Grillmeier 1995: 21–173). Severos stands in the tradition of Christological reflection represented by the patriarchs of Alexandria, Athanasios and Cyril, who laid stress on the unity of Christ: Christ was to be acknowledged as the Word made flesh, the Word of God living a human life, which was his human life. The later Cyril had come to believe that this was best expressed by the formula, μία φύσις τοῦ θεοῦ λόγου σεσαρκωμένη, 'one nature incarnate of God the Word', a phrase he believed (wrongly) to have the authority of Athanasios; this phrase became the rallying cry of Severos and his followers. It was an ambiguous phrase, for the word φύσις, nature, could be used to mean *what* something is, and in that sense Christ derived from two natures—divine nature, consubstantial with the Father, and human nature, consubstantial 'with us'—something that Cyril, and following him Severos, was keen to affirm. But it is clear that, though φύσις could have this meaning for Cyril, it could have a meaning closer to the verb from which it is derived: φύω, to spring forth—like a plant or growing thing (φυτόν). Cyril uses the present participle of the verb in his second book *Against Nestorios*, when he says, outlining his Nicene faith: 'following the confessions that have been passed down to us by the holy Fathers concerning these things, we affirm the same Word, which has essentially sprung forth (φύντα) from God the Father, to have come into being for us; he has become incarnate and human, that is, has taken for himself a body from the holy Virgin, and made it his own' (Pusey 1875: 93): that is, it is this very φύσις derived from the Father that has become incarnate. Here, I think, lies Cyril's fondness for the so-called *mia physis* formula: it emphasizes not just the unity of Christ, but the rootedness of the Word Incarnate in the being of the Godhead. It is this sense of the unity of Christ that Severos affirmed; it is not so much a matter of describing the make-up of Christ (where the language of two natures is possible, though Severos is too much opposed to Chalcedon to countenance it), but a matter of making clear the divine-human activity of Christ, where the divine and human elements could not be separated. An example Severos gives frequently is that of Christ's walking on the water:

> For how will anyone divide the walking upon the water? For to run upon the sea is foreign to the human nature, but it is not proper to the divine nature to use bodily feet. Therefore that action is of the incarnate Word, to whom belongs at the same time divine character and humanity indivisibly.
>
> (Severos, *Ep.* 1 to Sergios; Torrance 1988: 154)

This sense of the indivisibility of the activity of the Incarnate Word goes back to Athanasios, and is warmly embraced by Severos. Chalcedon's language of 'in two natures', as opposed to 'out of two natures' of the original draft (an alteration insisted on by the papal legates, to accommodate the language of the Tome of Leo), as well as its vagueness about the identity of the one person in Christ, was enough to render the Chalcedonian Definition inadequate in Severos' eyes.

Other elements in Severos' Christology stem from this radical stress on the unity of Christ. The 'one person' of Christ is unambiguously identified with the second Person of the Trinity, so that Severos speaks of 'one of the Trinity' assuming human nature (terminology used in the *Henotikon*, equally anathema to Severos). This means that it can be said that 'one of the Trinity suffered in the flesh', and for this reason there was added to the *Triagion* hymn in Antioch the phrase 'who was crucified for us', for in Antioch the hymn of the Seraphim of Isa. 6, of which the *Trisagion* is an expansion, was understood to be addressed to Christ (as suggested by John 12:41): 'Holy God, Holy Strong, Holy Immortal, who was crucified for us, have mercy on us'. If, however, the *Trisagion* was understood as addressed to the Trinity, as in Constantinople, such an addition suggested that the Godhead itself was passible. Such misunderstanding lay behind the riots in Constantinople in 512, which so amused Gibbon (Gibbon, *History*, ch. 47).

NEO- OR CYRILLINE CHALCEDONIANISM

Severos' attacks on the inadequacies of the Chalcedonian Definition provoked responses from its defenders. Theologians such as Nephalios and John of Caesarea in the early sixth century sought to show how the Definition drew on citations from Cyril of Alexandria in formulating its teaching. Severos, with his deep knowledge of the Alexandrian theologian, had little difficulty in demonstrating how terms and phrases from Cyril in the Definition were taken out of context. As they sought to defend Chalcedon, theologians found themselves clarifying the unclarities on which Severos had laid his finger, and in doing so often found themselves in effect conceding the case to Severos, as they argued that Chalcedon must be interpreted in the light of the Alexandrian doctor, who came to be known as the 'seal of the Fathers'.

This response to Severos has been called 'Neo-Chalcedonianism' (by Joseph Lebon; see Moeller 1951) or, perhaps more fairly, 'Cyrilline Chalcedonianism' (by John Meyendorff; see Meyendorff 1969: 33–57). It is important in the sixth century, because it came to be embraced by the Emperor Justinian I (emperor: 527–65; see Grillmeier 1995: 317–475) in his attempts to create common ground between the defenders and detractors of Chalcedon. These efforts, though nearly successful, were eventually frustrated. They left their mark on the Christological tradition of the Church by being incorporated in the decisions of the Fifth Œcumenical Council, held at Constantinople in 553 (Constantinople II).

Fundamentally, Cyrilline Chalcedonianism, in seeking to interpret the Chalcedonian Definition in the light of Cyril, conceded the core of Severos' case (while continuing to use the language of Chalcedon). First of all, it is made clear that the one person of the Definition is the Word or Son of God, 'one of the Trinity'; secondly, this means that suffering can be attributed to the Incarnate Word, who is 'one of the Trinity'—there is an orthodox theopaschism, it can be affirmed that 'one of the Trinity suffered in the flesh'; thirdly, the phrase, so beloved of the later Cyril, 'One incarnate nature of God the Word', is capable of an orthodox interpretation; furthermore, for these Cyrilline Chalcedonians, both of the expressions, 'out of two natures' of the original draft of the

Definition, and 'in two natures' of the final version, are acceptable: Christ is known ἐκ δύο φύσεων and ἐν δύο φύσεσιν.

The Influence of Philosophy

Cyrilline Chalcedonianism, which began with attempts to clarify Chalcedon in response to monophysite arguments and led, under imperial pressure, to efforts to find common ground with the monophysites, is the central trend in Christological discussion in the sixth century. Other factors affected the development of Christological reflection. First of all, there were developments in the philosophical culture of the Greek-speaking world. Initiated by the third-century philosopher Plotinos, what is now known as Neoplatonism reached its zenith in the fifth century in the philosophical system of Proklos, who was the Platonic Successor (διάδοχος) in the Academy of Athens from c.437 to 485. Although his philosophy is expressly pagan in inspiration, his ideas came to influence Christian theology, especially through writings ascribed to Dionysios the Areopagite, Paul's Athenian convert, which belong, probably, to the first quarter of the sixth century. The influence of Dionysios on Christian theology seems to have been a slow process. Initially interest focused on his discussion of Christology in *ep.* 4, in which, in the course of an abstractly philosophical account of the Incarnation, he uses the phrase 'a certain new theandric activity' (καινήν τινα τὴν θεανδρικὴν ἐνέργειαν) of the actions of Christ. This was picked up by the monophysites and cited at the discussions held by Justinian in 532 (though in the form 'one theandric [divine-human] activity': μία θεανδρικὴ ἐνέργεια). This phrase fits with the stress on the unity of Christ so dear to Severos, but Dionysios' Christology cannot be confidently classified as monophysite; there are also apparent echoes of the Tome of Leo in *ep.* 4. The notion of θεανδρικὴ ἐνέργεια was to play an important role in the controversies of the seventh century. More important, however, for the history of Byzantine theology was the way in which the Areopagite placed all his theology, including his Christology, in a cosmic and liturgical context. All theology, all attempts to name or praise God, are placed in the context of the liturgy. Furthermore, his notion of hierarchies, through which the created order is united with God and deified, gives his theology a cosmic dimension. Jesus is called 'the principle of all hierarchy, sanctification, and divine activity' (*Ecclesiastical Hierarchy* I. 1): the whole assimilation of the created order to God is focused on Jesus, in whom the uncreated and the created are united. Individual Christians are led to union with God, deification, through a process of purification, illumination, and perfection—a union that is based on the union of divine and human in Christ. Christology, then, for Dionysios has cosmic dimensions and finds expression in liturgical celebration and personal ascetic endeavour (see Grillmeier 2013: 298–342). This is a theme that will later be developed by Maximos the Confessor. Seeing Christology in a liturgical context opens up another way of Christological reflection: that of liturgical poetry. Liturgical poetry begins to flourish in the sixth century, not least in the kontakia of Romanos the Melodist, a Greek from Syria, who found himself in Constantinople for roughly the reign of the Emperor Justinian (527–65). The Christology of the kontakia of Romanos is Chalcedonian, and is expressed through meditation on biblical narratives, drawing together the prefigurations of the Old Testament and the fulfilment of the New. So, in his kontakion on the Nativity of Christ, he represents the Virgin Mary addressing God in these terms:

> High King, what have you do to with beggars?
> Maker of Heaven, why have you come to those born of earth?
> Did you love a cave or take pleasure in a manger?
> See, there is no place for your servant in an inn,
> I do not say a place, not even a cave,
> for that too belongs to another.
> To Sara, when she bore a child,
> a vast land was given as her lot. To me, not even a fox's hole.
> I used the cavern where willingly you made your dwelling,
> a little Child, God before the ages.
>
> (Lash 1995: 4)

Severos, too, expressed his theology in liturgical poetry, as well as in homilies and theological tracts.

The Commentators on Aristotle

As well as the developments of philosophical culture represented by the elaborate Neoplatonism of Proklos, in the sixth century we see the blossoming of commentary on the works of Aristotle, by then associated especially with the philosophical schools of Alexandria, which, in contrast to Athens, was less stridently pagan (some of the commentators, Elias and David, for example, were most likely Christians). Most of this commentary is concerned with the nature of argument, but some of it concerns the meaning of terms such as substance and quality. Such discussion influenced the efforts of Christian theologians in their attempts to clarify the terminology that had become traditional in both Trinitarian theology and in Christology: terms such as substance (οὐσία), person (πρόσωπον and/or ὑπόστασις), nature (φύσις). The clarification tended to be very technical; a kind of theological jargon is evolving. This dominant Byzantine tradition accepted the way in which Chalcedon, by transferring the terminology of person and nature from Trinitarian theology (where it had been used by the Cappadocian Fathers) to Christology, seems to endorse a common terminology for both Trinitarian theology and Christology. Those who rejected Chalcedon tended to be unhappy with both these tendencies: unhappy both with the technical language, and what seemed to them an attempt to collapse into a single discourse *theologia* (that is, Trinitarian theology) and *oikonomia* (God's dealings with the created order, especially the Incarnation). These misgivings lay behind other issues that emerged.

Byzantine theologians who were involved in this clarification of theological terminology include the two greatest theologians of the sixth century: Leontios of Byzantium, who kept more or less to a strict Chalcedonianism (see Grillmeier 1995: 181–229), and Leontios of Jerusalem, who inclined more to Cyrilline Chalcedonianism (see Grillmeier 1995: 271–312; Gray 2006). Other developments in Christology in the sixth century concern the monophysites, whose writings are less well preserved (in Greek, at least). One of the Aristotelian commentators was John Philoponos, whose understanding of Aristotle's logic led him to find fault with the Chalcedonian distinction between person and substance/nature (Aristotle simply makes a distinction between first substance, which is concrete, and second substance, which is abstract); Philoponos used the same term, nature, for what different beings shared (nature, substance, in Chalcedonian terms) and who or what they were (person, individual). The *mia physis* formula for Christ was therefore a natural expression, though he found it difficult to express what it was that united the three persons of the Trinity, and was consequently accused of tritheism, both by the Byzantines and by some of his fellow monophysites (see Chadwick 1987; Grillmeier 1996: 107–46). Though the problem was Trinitarian, not Christological, it was rooted in the *mia physis* formula for Christ, as Byzantine theologians were quick to note (the memory of John Philoponos remained live in the memory of the Byzantine Orthodox: John Damascene is referring to him when he says that the monophysites' problems go back to their introducing 'St Aristotle' as the 'thirteenth apostle': see Louth 2002: 159). Philoponos' problems seem to have been a matter of terminology. Other monophysites appear to have had deeper problems: Julian of Halikarnassos seems to have believed that the one nature of Christ so united Godhead and manhood, that Christ's human nature, even before the resurrection was incorruptible; his teaching, called aphthartodocetism, was opposed not only by the Byzantine Orthodox, who regarded it as a natural consequence of monophysitism, but also by Severos himself (Grillmeier 1995: 79–111). Also troubling in monophysite circles was a controversy about the ignorance of Christ. Attempts to account for Christ's confession of ignorance of the Second Coming (cf. Mark 13:32) by those who affirmed Christ to be one nature seem to have led to the notion that Christ was truly ignorant, not just 'economically' in his human nature; again this was a controversy that split the monophysites, though we hear about it from their opponents, too (see Wickham 1993).

The schism in the Church caused by the Council of Chalcedon continued to trouble the Church and the Empire. After Justinian's attempts at reconciliation failed (though they were very nearly successful: see Brock 1980), the monophysites established a hierarchy separated from that of the Church of the Empire (Jacob Baradaeus was secretly consecrated Bishop of Edessa in about 542 and spent the rest of his life—he died in 578—establishing a separate, clandestine hierarchy for those who rejected Chalcedon); the Byzantine emperors resorted to persecution, not always without success.

MONENERGISM AND MONOTHELETISM

The seventh century saw, first of all, the Persian invasion of the eastern provinces of the Byzantine Empire, which exploited the divisions in the Church, especially deep in Syria and Palestine, which led to renewed attempts on the part of the Byzantines to heal the schism caused by Chalcedon. This issued, first of all, in the 'ecumenical' success of Kyros, the newly appointed Patriarch and Augustal Prefect of Alexandria, in 633, when he secured reconciliation between the supporters and detractors of Chalcedon in the so-called Pact of Union (*Acta conciliorum oecumenicorum* II.2, pp. 594, 17–600, 20). The key to the Pact of Union was the acceptance of the Chalcedonian Definition of one Person and two integral natures, with the 'clarification' that there was only a single divine-human activity (Dionysios' notion of a θεανδρικὴ ἐνέργεια being [mis-] quoted): a doctrine called monenergism. This was immediately opposed by Sophronios, newly elected Patriarch of Jerusalem; a few years later a refinement of monenergism, called monotheletism, was proposed, according to which Christ was one person in two natures, but with a single (divine) will—teaching lent imperial authority in the Ekthesis of 638. By this time the Persian invasion had been repelled, only to make way for the Arab conquest of the Empire in the middle years of the 630s, which proved to be permanent. Reconciliation with the monophysites became even more imperative. From the end of the 630s onwards, the opposition to monotheletism was led by a monk, by then living in North Africa, a former high-ranking civil servant in the Imperial Chancery, Maximos, whose opposition to monotheletism led eventually to his arrest, trial, mutilation, and death in exile in 662, for which he is known as the 'Confessor'. By that time, Maximos had written extensively in opposition to monotheletism and persuaded Pope Martin to call a synod in Rome, the Lateran Synod of 649 (regarded as the sixth Œcumenical Council by Maximos' followers in the succeeding decades), which condemned both monenergism and monotheletism, and the hierarchs involved in these heresies (see Winkelmann 2001).

The impulse behind monenergism and monotheletism was political: anxiety at the way in which the schism in the Church weakened the eastern provinces of the Byzantine Empire, where the schism was most evident. It was, however, theologically astute, and simply developed the stress on the unity of Christ's activity found both in Severos and his Neo-Chalcedonian opponents. What was meant by the refinement known as monotheletism is quite obscure: we have no real expositions of monotheletism from those alleged to have maintained it, and it is not impossible (indeed, quite likely) that monotheletism, the denial of Christ's human will, was the entailment in the mind of Maximos and his followers of the so-called monotheletes' attempt to play down the role of the human will in Christ in the interests of a coherent understanding of the psychological structure of Christ's willing (see Price 2010). Maximos' presentation of the orthodox position seems to be tentative, and to try out various ways of understanding how Christ willed both divinely and humanly.

Maximos the Confessor

Maximos' understanding of the way the Godman willed turned on the episode of the Agony in the Garden in which Christ prayed, 'not my will (θέλημα), but yours, be done' (Luke 22:42). What Christ called 'your will', as he addressed the Father, was his divine will, as the persons of the Trinity have one will in common; what he called 'my will' was his human will. Much of the controversy over monotheletism turned on the interpretation of this episode in the Gospels; at both the Lateran and the Sixth Œcumenical Councils, the Fathers spent a session hearing read expositions by various Fathers of the Agony in the Garden: a gratifyingly edifying spectacle! One can well imagine that the monotheletes thought Christ's human will quiescent, silently ceding to the divine will. Maximos pressed more deeply. Our redemption turned on Christ's human will willing our salvation; to think it quiescent would seem strange, but to admit any friction, or worse disagreement, between the divine and human wills of Christ would lead to an incredible picture of Christ's moral activity. Maximos tried to solve the problem (essentially his problem, caused by his insistence on the integrity of both Christ's human will and his divine will) by distinguishing in the process of human will between those elements that are there because of the fallen human condition, and those elements that are part of the very process of willing and making a moral decision. To consider the role of the will was something new in Greek philosophy, indeed the use of the term θέλημα in this context is mostly likely because of the centrality of the interpretation of the Agony to the question of Christ's willing. Although Maximos' reflection on the nature of willing is largely original, he presents it as deriving from earlier patristic reflection on willing. He appeals a couple of times to the fifth-century Diadochos of Photiki (maybe one of the Fathers of Chalcedon); he also finds definitions of willing in Clement of Alexandria (which are not to be found in any works that have reached us). Thence he presents the idea that willing is natural, the natural desire of a rational creature (see *Opusc.* 26: PG 91: 276C). As a result of the Fall, it is often necessary for the human, rational creature to consider what it is that is naturally desired; a process of deliberation is required. It is in this process of deliberation that the mind seems to move this way and that, to exhibit a frailty of purpose, that, if present in Christ, would seem to threaten the unity of his person. For Maximos, this process of deliberation, leading to the forming of an intention, or opinion about the choice facing us, in Greek γνώμη, is simply due to the Fall, to the moral darkness that has fallen on us as a result; it is not part of Christ's moral experience which is free from this moral darkness. Maximos therefore makes a distinction between the natural will and the gnomic will: Christ has a natural human will—he wills as a human being—but no gnomic will, as his willing does not emerge from moral uncertainty, and Christ also has a natural divine will, which is united to his natural human will. The Agony in the Garden bears testimony to the cost to the human will of Christ's 'voluntary passion'; it is not evidence of any reluctance to fulfil the divine will.

The *opuscula* written in defence of Chalcedonian orthodoxy against the monotheletes are concerned with exploring the nature of Christ's moral activity, which was an important aspect of the process of working through the entailments of Chalcedonian Christological orthodoxy finally endorsed by the Sixth Œcumenical Council (Constantinople III: 680–1). This, often highly technical, defence of Chalcedon does not exhaust Maximos' contribution to Christology. In his earlier writings we find an approach to Christology, equally derived from Chalcedon, that explores the wider resonances of the Chalcedonian Definition, rather than defending a particular point.

A striking example of this is found in Maximos' consideration of the transfiguration of Christ in *Amb.* 10 (PG 91: 1125D–1169B). Maximos begins by seeing the disciples' ascent of the Mount Thabor with Christ is terms of their spiritual ascent (Mount Thabor is, as it were, assimilated to Mount Sinai/Horeb, associated with both Moses and Elias). There, on the summit of the mountain, Christ is transfigured: his face (Greek πρόσωπον), which they behold, is a symbol of his divinity, beyond human understanding (the object, then, of apophatic theology); the whitened garments are symbols of the words of Holy Scripture, or of the *logoi* of creation itself, in which God reveals himself (corresponding to kataphatic theology): the terminology of apophatic/kataphatic is drawn from Dionysios, but transferred to Christology. In another treatise, his *Questions and Doubts*, Maximos says that 'the face/person of the Word … is the characteristic hiddenness of his being' (*Q&D* 191.48: Declerck 1982: 134). In the Transfiguration, the disciples see revealed in the face/person of Christ the ineffable face/person of God. This cosmic vision of Christ, containing the whole of creation, summing up in himself the whole of Scripture, the goal of the spiritual life, shifts the attention of theology from the formulae of dogma to the contemplation of the manifestation of God in Christ (see Louth 2008). The role of dogma is not at all diminished—Maximos himself gave up his life for Orthodox dogma—for it is the role of dogma to safeguard our contemplation of Christ against any distortion. One aspect of this cosmic vision is worth underlining: because creation is through the *Logos*, each individual creature is determined by its own *logos*, and all these *logoi* of creation are summed up in Christ. These *logoi* are therefore inviolate; the Fall does not distort the Creator's plan at an ontological level, only at the level of the way, τρόπος, in which creatures exist. This sense of the inviolability of the *logoi* of creation underlies Maximos' conviction of the error of monotheletism: if Christ were without a human will, the *logos* of his human nature would be defective, which would frustrate the purpose of the Incarnation to restore human nature.

Clarification and Defence of the Faith: John Damascene

Maximos was vindicated at the Sixth Œcumenical Council of 680–1, in its condemnation of monenergism and monotheletism, though he was not mentioned by name (nor, indeed, was Pope Martin), and thereafter the doctrine of two wills in Christ became part of orthodox doctrine (with a brief lapse under Emperor Philippikos at the beginning of the next century). With the establishment of the Islamic Umayyad Empire in 661, Christians in the former eastern provinces of the Byzantine Empire, from Syria to Egypt, and later North Africa, too, found themselves in a different religious climate.

The Muslims had no great desire to convert Christians, nor did they make any distinction between the different confessions; Chalcedonian Christians found themselves on a par (or even at a disadvantage compared) with those who rejected Chalcedon (as well as those who rejected the Council of Ephesos, who had settled in Persia as the Church of the East), and indeed with other religious groups such as Jews and Samaritans. This equality of opportunity encouraged argument between the religious groups, each seeking to defend their own religious tradition, and there survives from this period evidence of extensive polemical literature (what survives is entirely Orthodox, as they had the opportunity to preserve it). As the differences between the Christian groups—Byzantine Orthodox, monophysite (or Jacobite, after Jacob Baradaeus), monothelete, and 'Nestorian'—were Christological, much of this literature was concerned with Christology. A good deal of it is concerned with assembling patristic proof texts, a practice which goes back to the fifth century, or providing arguments for those engaged in defending their own position (soon there would be Christian defences against Islam, intended not primarily for Muslims, but for Christians attacked for their beliefs by Muslims; Christological issues were raised here, too). Such argument led to a process of clarifying the Orthodox position (each group thought of their position as Orthodox), and the most important figure among those who defended imperial Orthodoxy in what was now the *dar al-Islam* was John Damascene.

John Damascene was a native of Damascus, born around 675, then the capital of the Umayyad Empire, and probably followed his father and grandfather is serving in the fiscal administration of the Empire. Probably in the early years of the eighth century, he left the civil service and became a monk in or near Jerusalem (traditionally the Monastery of Mar Sava, though this tradition is late and unreliable). There he devoted himself, under the shadow of the domes of the mosques on the Temple Mount, to defending the Orthodox Christianity of the imperial Byzantine tradition. His most famous work is *On the Orthodox Faith*, which he probably much later incorporated into a three-part work called *The Fountain of Knowledge*, Πήγη Γνώσεως, as the final section. It contains a long series of chapters on Christology (the work takes the form of a century of chapters, a monastic genre already used by Maximos). Besides that he also wrote a number of treatises against the various Christological heresies: monophysitism (the 'Jacobites' or 'akephaloi'), monotheletism, and Nestorianism. The treatment of Christology in the polemical writings is inevitably technical, concerning the terminology of substance, person, and nature, and, in the case of the monotheletes, the nature of Christ's moral experience, his willing. The same is true of many chapters in *Exposition of the Orthodox Faith*.

It is striking, then, that John begins the Christological section of *On the Orthodox Faith* by placing the Incarnation in the context of the biblical history of salvation, the divine *oikonomia*. Leading on from the account of the human Fall at the end of chapter 44, chapter 45 begins by describing the human fallen state: stripped of grace and deprived of the open converse (παρρησία) with God that humans had known in Paradise, they were clothed with the 'roughness of a wretched life' (symbolized by the fig leaves), their bodies became mortal and coarse (symbolized by the garments of skin), they were excluded from Paradise, condemned to death and subject to corruption. But God, in his compassion, did not abandon human beings in their fallenness, on the contrary he endeavoured in many ways to educate them and call them to conversion: by their life of groaning and trembling, by the flood, by the confusion of tongues at Babel, 'by the care of angels, by the conflagration of cities, by prefigurative theophanies, by wars, by victories, by defeats, by signs and wonders and various miracles, by the Law, by prophets' (*Expos.* 45.14–16; Kotter 1973: 107). In this way John characterizes the saving history of the Old Testament, all of which was intended 'to destroy sin in its many forms … and to restore human kind to a state of well being' (45.16–19; Kotter 1973: 107). Since, however, human sin had brought about death, 'it was necessary for the one who was to redeem human kind to be sinless and thus not subject to the death of sin, and also for human nature to be strengthened and renewed and by his example educated and taught the way of virtue, that turns away from corruption and leads to eternal life' (45.20–4; Kotter 1973: 107). What was needed was not simply the conquering of death, but at the same time the education of human kind to benefit from this redemption: in this John echoes (probably at some distance) the same dual emphasis we find in Athanasius, when he says, 'for in two ways the Saviour showed his love for human kind through the incarnation, because he both rid us of death, and renewed us' (*inc.* 16.21–3: Thomson 1971: 172). With this, John introduces the Incarnation itself: 'at last, the great ocean of his loving kindness towards human kind was manifest. For the creator and Lord himself took up the struggle on behalf of his own creation and became a teacher in deed' (45.24–7; Kotter 1973: 107).

> By the good pleasure of God the Father, the only-begotten Son and Word of God and God, who is in the bosom of the Father, consubstantial with the Father and the Holy Spirit, before eternity, without beginning, who is in the beginning, and is with God the Father, and is God, he who is in the form of God inclined the heavens and came down, that is he lowered, without lowering, his inalienable exaltedness, and descended to be among his slaves in an ineffable and incomprehensible descent (for that is what descent means), and being perfect God he became perfectly human and accomplished the newest of all new things, the only new thing under the sun.
>
> (45.36–45; Kotter 1973: 108)

'The newest of all new things, the only new thing under the sun': thus John characterizes the radical innovation of the Incarnation. God as human became the mediator between God and human kind, and in his human life 'he became obedient to the Father and healed our disobedience by that which is ours and from us, and became an example to us of that obedience, without which there is no salvation' (45.51–3; Kotter 1973: 108).

The next chapter returns to the history of salvation, giving an account of the Annunciation to the holy Virgin, following this with a careful statement of the virginal conception and the Incarnation. Once the Virgin had given her consent,

> the Holy Spirit came upon her … purified her, and gave her at once the power to receive the Godhead of the Word and to beget. Then the subsistent (ἐνυπόστατος)

Wisdom and Word of God Most High, the Son of God, consubstantial with the Father, overshadowed her and, in the manner of a divine seed, from her chaste and most pure blood compacted for himself flesh animated with a rational and intellectual soul, the first fruits of our compound nature, not by seed, but by creation through the Holy Spirit, the form not being put together bit by bit, but perfected all at once. The Word of God himself became the *hypostasis* of the flesh ... So there was at once flesh, at once the flesh of God the Word, at once animate, rational and intellectual flesh, at once the animate, rational and intellectual flesh of God the Word. Therefore we do not speak of a deified human being, but of God become human; for, being by nature perfect God, the same became by nature a perfect human being, not changing his nature nor simply appearing to be incarnate, but being hypostatically united without confusion, change or division to the rationally and intellectually animated flesh assumed from the Virgin, which possesses its existence in him, neither changing his divine nature into the substance of flesh, nor changing the substance of his flesh into his divine nature, nor bringing about one composite nature out of his divine nature and the human nature he had assumed.

(46.14–42; Kotter 1973: 109–10)

This is the careful language of the Cyrilline Chalcedonian tradition that John fully embraced.

This brief summary shows how John combines a sense of the meaning of the Incarnation, with a grasp of the technical language evolved to preserve the faith from misunderstanding. It is important to realize this, as, for all the skill in technical language demonstrated in the later Byzantine tradition, it is John's account, with its clear kerygmatic purpose, that became the most valued epitome of the patristic tradition among the Byzantines (as well as being the most direct recourse to the Greek patristic tradition for Western scholasticism, and indeed later Western theology).

John's polemical works against what he regarded as Christological heresy show that he regarded the different heresies in rather different lights. In his work *On Heresies*, John has a chapter on the monophysites. It begins thus: 'Egyptians, also called schematics [meaning unclear] or monophysites, who, on the pretext of the document, the Tome [of Leo, presumably], agreed at Chalcedon, have separated themselves from the Orthodox Church. They have been called Egyptians, because it was the Egyptians who began this form of thought under the Emperors Marcian and Valentinian; but in every other respect they are orthodox' (*Hæres.* 83.1–5; Kotter 1981: 49). This is surprisingly mild, and the mildness is borne out in the three treatises John composed against the monophysites; for the most part, John argues that the Orthodox and monophysites believe the same thing, but that the monophysites express their belief in clumsy and ambiguous terminology. His attitude to the monotheletes, on the contrary, is quite different: because they deny that Christ has a human will, they are treated as virtual Apollinarians. If what they believe were true, then human salvation would be put in jeopardy. Similarly with his treatises against the Nestorians; they are not just muddled, but in error. John's tone, however, suggests that they are for him not heretics he has met in flesh and blood.

John's theology, as expressed in *On the Orthodox Faith*—including his Christology, to which he devotes many chapters—was to be influential, both in the East and the West (and maybe even, to judge from translations, among Oriental Christians). His greatest influence, however, among Orthodox Christians has been through his liturgical poetry, of which he was a pioneer, especially in the form of the canon. His liturgical poetry is dense with precisely expressed doctrine; much of it is known by heart by Orthodox Christians.

Christology was central to his defence of icons. For John, images were essential to human (as opposed to angelic) thought: the human being was created in God's image, and was an image-maker, both literally and in his modes of thought. The Incarnation authenticated this use of images: in the Incarnation, Christ 'placed himself in the order of signs', to use the expression from Maurice de la Taille, much beloved by the Anglo-Welsh poet, David Jones, who understood what John meant by images (De La Taille 1934: 212).

SUGGESTED READING

Bathrellos (2004); Blowers and Wilken (2003); Grillmeier (1995, 1996, 2013); Louth (2002: 144–79).

BIBLIOGRAPHY

Acta conciliorum oecumenicorum II.2 (1932), ed. Eduard Schwartz (Berlin and Leipzig: de Gruyter).

Acta Conciliorum Oecumenicarum Concilium Universale Constantinopolitanum Tertium. Series secunda, vol. I, II/1, ed. R. Riendinger (Berlin and New York: de Gruyter, 1990–2).

Bathrellos, D. (2004), *The Byzantine Christ* (Oxford: Oxford University Press).

Blowers, P. M. and R. L. Wilken (trans.) (2003), Maximus the Confessor, *On the Cosmic Mystery of Jesus Christ* (Crestwood, NY: St. Vladimir's Seminary Press).

Brock, S. (1980), 'The Orthodox–Oriental Orthodox Conversations of 532', in *Apostolos Varnavas* XLI (Nicosia), Vol. XI of *Syriac Perspectives on Late Antiquity* (London: Variorum Reprints, 1984), 219–27.

Chadwick, H. (1987), 'Philoponus the Christian Theologian', in R. Sorabji (ed.), *Philoponus and the Rejection of Aristotelian Science* (London: Duckworth), 41–56.

Coleman-Norton, P. J. (1966), *Roman State and Christian Church*, 3 vols. (London: SPCK).

Declerck, J. H. (1982), *Maximi Confessoris Quaestiones et Dubia.* CCSG 10 (Turnhout: Brepols).

De La Taille, M. (1934), *The Mystery of Faith and Human Opinion Contrasted and Defined* (London: Sheed and Ward; first published 1930).

Gray, P. T. R. (2006), *Leontius of Jerusalem, Against the Monophysites: Testimonies of the Saints and Aporiae* (Oxford: Oxford University Press).

Grillmeier, A. (1995), in collaboration with T. Hainthaler, *Christ in Christian Tradition*, vol. II/part 2, trans. J. Cawte and P. Allen (London: Mowbray).

Grillmeier, A. (1996), in collaboration with Theresia Hainthaler, *Christ in Christian Tradition*, vol. II/part 4, trans. O. C. Dean (London: Mowbray).

Grillmeier, A. (2013), in continuation of his work by T. Hainthaler, *Christ in Christian Tradition*, vol. II/part 3, trans. M. Ehrhardt (Oxford: Oxford University Press).

Kotter, B. (1973), *Die Schriften des Johannes von Damaskos*, vol. II: *Expositio Fidei*. Patristische Texte und Studien 12 (Berlin: de Gruyter).

Kotter, B. (1981), *Die Schriften des Johannes von Damaskos*, vol. III: *Liber de Haeresibus. Opera polemica*. Patristische Text und Studien 22 (Berlin: de Gruyter).

Lash, E. (trans.) (1995), St. Romanos the Melodist, *On the Life of Christ: Kontakia* (San Francisco: Harper.

Louth, A. (2002), *St John Damascene: Tradition and Originality in Byzantine Theology* (Oxford: Oxford University Press).

Louth, A. (2008), 'From the Doctrine of Christ to the Person of Christ: St Maximos the Confessor on the Transfiguration of Christ', in P. W. Martens (ed.), *In the Shadow of the Incarnation: Essays on Jesus Christ in the Early Church in Honor of Brian E. Daley, S.J.* (Notre Dame, Ind.: University of Notre Dame Press), 260–75.

Meyendorff, J. (1969), *Le Christ dans la théologie byzantine* (Paris: Cerf).

Moeller, C. (1951), 'Le chalcédonisme et le néo-chalcédonisme en Orient de 451 à la fin du VIᵉ siècle', in A. Grillmeier and H. Bacht (eds.), *Das Konzil von Chalkedon*, Band I (Würzburg: Echter-Verlag), 637–720.

Price, R. (2010), 'Monotheletism: A Heresy or a Form of Words?', *Studia Patristica* 48: 221–32.

Pusey, P. E. (ed.) (1875), *Cyrilli Archiepiscopi Alexandrini Epistolae Tres Œcumenicae, etc.* (Oxford: Parker).

Tanner, N. P. (ed.) (1990), *Decrees of the Ecumenical Councils*, 2 vols. (London: Sheed and Ward).

Thomson, R. W. (ed. and trans.) (1971), Athanasius, *Contra Gentes* and *De Incarnatione* (Oxford: Clarendon Press).

Torrance, I. R. (1988), *Christology after Chalcedon: Severus of Antioch and Sergius the Monophysite* (Norwich: Canterbury Press).

Wickham, L. (1993), 'The Ignorance of Christ: A Problem for Ancient Theology', in Lionel Wickham, C. P. Bammel, and E. C. D. Hunter (eds.), *Christian Faith and Greek Philosophy in Late Antiquity* (Leiden: Brill), 213–26.

Winkelmann, F. (2001), *Der monenergisch–monotheletische Streit*. Berliner Byzantinische Studien 6 (Bern: Peter Lang).

CHAPTER 10

THE WORK OF CHRIST IN PATRISTIC THEOLOGY

NORMAN RUSSELL

THE distinction between the person of Christ and the work of Christ is a comparatively modern one, going back to the scholastic mind-set of the sixteenth-century Protestant Reformers. It nevertheless conveniently isolates for our consideration the patristic understanding of the soteriological benefits achieved for believers by Christ's incarnation, death, and resurrection. These benefits include what Western scholars have traditionally called the atonement, which focuses on the reconciliation brought about by Christ's expiatory sacrifice on the Cross, but were much broader in scope, taking in the whole of salvation history from the world's creation to its eschatological fulfilment at the end of time. It was the experience of Christ in the Church rather than purely theoretical considerations that drove the complex debate on the person of Christ. From the earliest confession, 'Jesus is Lord', to the Chalcedonian definition and beyond, the Fathers of the Church sought to give expression to who Christ was on the basis of their shared experience of what he had accomplished for humankind. Responding in the earlier period to pastoral and apologetic needs and from the fourth century especially to the demands of Christological controversy, they set out their understanding of Christ's work in a rich variety of concepts and images. None of the Fathers wrote a systematic treatise on the topic, but their teaching did not lack coherence. One way of approaching it is through the schematization offered by Athanasius of Alexandria who saw a fundamentally twofold character in the work that Christ accomplished. 'For in two ways', he says, 'our Saviour had compassion through the incarnation: he both rid us of death and renewed us' (*De Inc.* 16; Thomson 1971: 173). These two ways may be characterized as the one backward-looking (what was lost in Adam was regained in Christ) and the other forward-looking (what Christ is, we shall be), or put more analytically, the one focusing on recapitulation and restoration, the other on participation and deification. These four components of Athanasius' two ways will provide us with a framework for our discussion.

RECAPITULATION

The idea of recapitulation goes back to the primitive Christian kerygma. We find it in the Pauline corpus with the claim of Ephesians that it is the will of God that all things in the fullness of time should be gathered up (ἀνακεφαλαιώσασθαι) in Christ (Eph. 1:10). It remained an important theme throughout the patristic era. Recapitulation, in Eric Osborn's words, 'declares the unity of God and the unity of saving history' (Osborn 1993: 148). It is the central idea in Justin Martyr's writings. As the Logos, the first-born of God, Christ is the fullness of divine wisdom and truth in whom all who teach the truth share, because truth is one. Not only the sages of ancient Greece, but also the Hebrew patriarchs and prophets were Christians before the incarnate life of the Logos (1 *Apol.* 46). Christ is also the fullness of divine goodness as the one who bestows the new covenant. This is why in the *Dialogue with Trypho* Justin Martyr can present the Christian community as the new Israel. It is not so much the supersession of the old that concerns him as the inclusion and completion of the old in the new, the true spiritual Israel.

Justin Martyr's insights are picked up by Irenaeus of Lyon who develops them in new directions. Irenaeus' first mention of recapitulation is to counter a Gnostic exegesis of Ephesians 1:10 (*Haer.* 1.1.5). Against the Valentinians who taught otherwise, Irenaeus insists that the Logos who became incarnate for us is identical with the Logos through whom God created the world. It was necessary for our salvation that Christ should have recapitulated all things in himself—and therefore humankind as well—'making the invisible visible, the incomprehensible comprehensible and the impassible passible' (*Haer.* 3.17.6; trans. mine). Without the human solidarity expressed by such a recapitulation, Irenaeus cannot see how the redemption won by Christ's obedience even to the point of death could be transmitted to the human race as a whole.

Christ's saving recapitulation of humanity is symbolized by many details in the Gospel narratives. The genealogy in Luke, for example (Luke 3:23–8), recapitulates in Jesus all the generations going back to Adam (*Haer.* 3.32 1). The Virgin birth, while marking a new beginning for the human race, also represents a strong element of continuity—it was 'our' flesh that Jesus took from Mary (*Haer.* 3.3.11). The human events recounted of his life, when Jesus suffered pain, wept, and experienced other emotions, indicate the completeness of the humanity he assumed: 'For they are all symbols of the flesh taken from the earth, which he recapitulated in himself, saving his own creation' (*Haer.* 3.31.2; trans. mine). Anticipating Gregory of Nazianzus' aphorism, 'What is not assumed is not healed' (*Ep.* 101.32; trans. mine), Irenaeus insists that if God aimed to empty death of its potency and restore humanity to life, he had to recapitulate in himself his original creation of humankind. Without that common inheritance, the real human substance, there would have been nothing for the Logos to work on.

The recapitulation theme continued to play an important role in the thinking of later Fathers. It is, for example, the background against which we should interpret Origen's controversial universalism, as expressed in his theory of ἀποκατάστασις, the final restoration of all rational creatures (with the exception of Satan) to loving union with God. But for the most part it led to ideas that were not later judged to be heterodox. On the level of human nature no one discusses the implications of the Incarnation for humanity with greater sensitivity than Cyril of Alexandria. Writing in the second decade of the fifth century, Cyril identifies three models of recapitulation, a moral one (the condemnation of sin), a physical one (the overcoming of death), and a spiritual one (the making of believers to be children of God). He bases his classification not on a priori considerations but on a detailed study of Paul and John. Indeed, biblical exegesis lies at the heart of all his writings, and it is his close scrutiny of the text in his commentaries that leads him to some of his most striking insights. When he considers, for example, why the sinless Christ should have submitted to baptism, he concludes that Christ, as the second Adam, the representative of a new humanity, is the *recipient* as well as the *agent* of redemption. 'For he receives his own Spirit and partakes of it, insofar as he was man, but gives it to himself as God' (*In Jo.* 11.9; Keating 2004: 29, 37). The baptism of Christ reveals the fundamental thrust of the divine economy. Christ is himself the first-fruits of redemption, raising our humanity by his resurrection and ascension to a heavenly throne. For 'in Christ we see human nature, as if experiencing a new beginning of the human race, enjoying freedom of access to God' (*Adv. Nest.*, Prooem. 1; Russell 2000: 135).

The cosmic dimension of salvation does not appear to have been relevant to Cyril's Christological concerns, but he would not have been unaware of it. His uncle and episcopal predecessor, Theophilus, had developed this aspect of recapitulation impressively in his homilies. Taking his cue from Paul's vision of creation longing for freedom from bondage to decay (Rom. 8:19–23; cf. Eph. 1 and Col. 1), Theophilus paints a vivid picture of the cosmic repercussions of the crucifixion, an event which marks the climax of divine intervention in the created world as Christ reigns from the Cross: 'All the air is in motion because the body of the Creator is suspended on high. All the earth rejoices because the blood of its king is sprinkled upon it' (*Hom. in Cruc.*; Russell 2007: 37, 68). The whole of creation is exhorted to rejoice because the effects of Christ's sacrifice permeate the whole of material reality, remedying its disorder and healing its suffering. These salvific effects are appropriated symbolically by the individual Christian through the sacraments.

All these aspects of recapitulation were brought together magnificently by Maximus the Confessor in the seventh century. The Incarnation marks the union of created and uncreated. It was not a response to sin but 'the divine purpose conceived before the beginning of created beings' (*Thal.* 60; Blowers and Wilken 2003: 124). Human sin did result in the Incarnation becoming 'another beginning, a second nativity for human nature' but did not determine it, for it is 'the preconceived goal for which everything exists, but which itself exists on account of nothing' (*Thal.* 61; Blowers and Wilken 2003: 135). It was not for human conduct to determine the divine economy. But Man is a microcosm, and the Fall therefore had cosmic dimensions. The Word of God by recapitulating in himself all the things he had created without himself undergoing any change, and thus *becoming* 'the "sin" that I caused, in terms of possibility, corruptibility and mortality' without himself becoming passible, corruptible, and mortal (*Thal.* 44; Blowers and Wilken 2003: 121), leads the whole of creation triumphantly back to its intended fulfilment in God.

RESTORATION

The Fathers treat the theme of restoration from two perspectives: the human, in terms of what we lost in the Fall, and the divine, in terms of Christ's expiatory sacrifice and victory over the demonic. What we lost in the Fall was the affinity to the divine expressed by our creation 'according to the image and likeness of God' (Gen. 1:26). This is a theme that was to grow in importance in later patristic literature. Irenaeus discusses it at length, making a distinction, as do his successors, between image and likeness. Such a distinction is necessary because Man was made 'like the invisible Father through the visible Son' (*Haer.* 5.16.1; trans. mine). The image is intrinsic to our createdness, but the likeness lies in our rationality and is recovered through the Spirit. Irenaeus declares that it was not only the Incarnation but also the Passion that restored the likeness. Using the patterning that so appealed to the patristic mind, he points out the correspondences between the Fall and the crucifixion, the latter undoing the effects of the former, 'remedying the disobedience accomplished through a tree by the obedience accomplished through a tree' (*Haer.* 5.16.2; trans. mine). Finally, the recovery by believers of the likeness re-established by Christ is a gradual process which can only be achieved in a fully Trinitarian context, 'the Father being pleased and commanding, the Son doing and creating, and the Spirit nourishing and giving increase' (*Haer.* 4.63.2; trans. mine).

The lead given by Irenaeus was followed by Origen, who raised the discussion to a new level of theological and philosophical subtlety by taking the two versions of creation in Genesis as accounts of two separate creations. The first spiritual creation and first Fall resulted in the descent of souls into material bodies created for them to make possible an ascent back to communion with God through the recovery of the divine likeness as a result of the mediation of the Logos. The dual creation, with the pre-existence of souls that it entailed, was rejected as heretical at the beginning of the fifth century, but the second half of the narrative, the ascending movement to God through the recovery of the likeness, proved very influential—writers such as Evagrius of Pontus and others in the Origenian tradition holding that Christ mediates between the Trinity and the individual soul.

Not all the Fathers were happy to take this approach. Augustine, for example, accepts the idea of gradual progress in the renewal of the image but for him the divine image in the soul is directly that of the Trinity, as reflected in the memory, will, and understanding (*De Trin.* 14.17.23). The great Alexandrians, Athanasius and Cyril, followed a somewhat different path, making a distinction not between image and likeness but between Christ who is the Image itself and Man who is merely 'in the image' (Athanasius, *Ar.* 2.67; Cyril, *Juln.* 1.29). Athanasius overcame the subordinationist risks implicit in such an approach by locating the image firmly on the divine side of the gulf separating the created from the uncreated. Cyril, drawing on a more developed understanding of the role of the Holy Spirit, emphasizes the Trinitarian context of our growth in the image, insisting that 'we are conformed to the true and exact image of the Father, that is to the Son, and that his divine beauty is impressed on our souls through participation in the Holy Spirit' (*Juln.* 1.33; trans. mine). In these fourth- and fifth-century treatments of the image we move beyond the backward-looking recovery through the Incarnation of what was lost in Adam to how human fulfilment is to be ultimately achieved through assimilation to the glorified Christ.

Closely connected with the recovery of the image is the therapeutic model of salvation. Origen held that the Logos undertook the Incarnation to heal the wounds caused in our souls by the Fall (*Cels.* 8.72). Athanasius refers to the Cross as the θεραπεία of creation (*Gent.* 1). Augustine speaks eloquently of Christ as the 'healer and medicine both in one' (*De Doct. Chr.* 13; trans. mine). But the therapeutic model is overshadowed by the theme of *Christus Victor*. It is striking even on a cursory reading of the Fathers how great a role Christ's victory over the powers of the underworld plays in their narrative of salvation. From Justin Martyr, who claims that 'Jesus derives his name from the saving power he exhibits in his conquest of the devil' (*Dial.* 125; Osborn 1993: 169) to Maximus the Confessor, who explains how Jesus 'inaugurated a complete restoration' by winning a victory over the demonic, 'putting to death the very power that expected to seduce him just as it had Adam in the beginning' (*Thal.* 21; Blowers and Wilken 2003: 11), the Fathers were convinced that even if evil as a privation of good lacked real existence, there was nevertheless a powerful, malevolent will at work in the world that could not be defeated by merely human or even angelic means. This was a conviction shared equally by the Latin Fathers: Augustine declares in the *City of God* that the power of the demons who had 'sought to seduce human beings into misery by the boast of immortality' (*De Civ. Dei* 9.15; trans. mine) was destroyed by Christ. 'For just as the devil through pride led humankind through pride to death; so Christ through humility led humankind back through obedience to life' (*De Trin.* 4.10.13; trans. mine).

The rhetorical style of these passages, with their neat balancing of antitheses, should not tempt us to think that the demons symbolize disordered human impulses. They were real objects of terror, who figure prominently in homiletic literature as bands of evil spirits massing against the angelic forces at the point of a person's death in order to seize the soul that dies in sin and drag it down to their own region. In Origen's speculative mind the question seems to have arisen whether the devil and his angels would not eventually be saved at the ἀποκατάστασις. That, at least, is how his detractors construed certain passages in the *De Principiis*. But the salvation of the devil was rejected by a broad spectrum of writers, by Augustine on the one hand as incompatible with biblical testimony (*De Civ. Dei* 21.23), and by Theophilus on the other as logically requiring that Christ should be crucified a second time on behalf of the demons (*Ep. Fest.* 16.12; Russell 2007: 110, 140). Although Christ had proved victorious, the devil still had some room to manoeuvre so as to threaten believers. The divine economy could not ultimately be thwarted, but neither was salvation automatic.

How Christ's definitive victory was compatible with the continuing resilience of the vanquished enemy of the human race was explained by the fact that the victory was not won by force. Paul had spoken of a ransoming or redemption (ἀπολύτρωσις) effected by Christ through the sacrificial shedding of his blood (Rom. 3:25–6; 1 Cor. 1:30). In his *Commentary on Romans* Origen speculated that if a ransom was paid, it must have been paid to someone, and that someone could only have been Satan who had acquired dominion over humankind as a result of the Fall. Satan could not in fact have overcome the sinless Christ, so he must have been deceived into thinking he could do so (*Com. Rom.* 3.8). This argument proved very influential, particularly in the West, where it was taken up by Ambrose of Milan. Ambrose sets it out for one of his correspondents in transactional terms: 'The devil had purchased and owned the services of our sinful race, and required a price for releasing from his service those whom he held in bondage. The price of our liberation was the blood of the Lord Jesus, which had to be paid to the devil to whom we were sold by our sins' (*Ep.* 72.8; Homes Dudden 1935: 607). As a trained lawyer and administrator, Ambrose felt comfortable with a legal model of redemption from slavery. Not only did the devil receive the payment owed to him, but the claims of divine justice were satisfied. Christ was sacrificed in our stead, not so much recapitulating humanity in the Irenaean manner as substituting himself for the true malefactor, namely, ourselves, in order to satisfy the norms of justice (*De Fuga* 44). Christ died that 'since the divine decrees cannot be broken, the person punished and not the sentence of punishment should be changed' (*Expos. Ev. Luc.* 4.7; Homes Dudden 1935: 609). Augustine was much more circumspect. Although he accepts that humanity had been enslaved to the devil through sin, he says nothing about a ransom paid to him (Portalié 1909: 2371–4). The devil had no rights over us (*De Trin.* 4.16). Christ's victory over him was a by-product of his reconciliation of humanity with God through his death and resurrection, thus becoming the fount of grace for us (*Enchiridion* 108). Nevertheless, it was the forensic model that became dominant in the West for reasons that have not yet been adequately investigated.

In the East, Gregory of Nazianzus objected to the idea of a ransom paid to the devil. Among the appellations of Christ, he describes as 'redemption' (ἀπολύτρωσις) Christ's freeing of us because we had come under the dominion of sin, and as 'ransom' (λύτρον) his giving of himself for the purification of the world (*Or.* 30.20). But the ransom, which was God himself, could not have been paid to the devil—an outrageous idea in Gregory's view. The ransom was paid to the Father, not because he asked for it, but 'for the sake of the economy and to proclaim the sanctification of Man by the humanity of God' (*Or.* 45.22; trans. mine). Gregory of Nyssa, however, was prepared to accept the idea of a ransom paid to the devil and to develop it with the help of the image of the fishhook. The devil would not have dared 'to engage with the untempered presence of God', he claimed, so the weak human flesh of Christ was offered as a bait concealing the fishhook of his divinity so that the devil might be tricked into gulping it down 'and thus with life allowed entry into death and light having shone in darkness, what is understood as the opposite of light and life might vanish' (*Or. Catech.* 24; trans. mine). Modern theologians are often scandalized by this image (Ludlow 2007: 108–24) but it sits well with the concern of the Fathers to emphasize that Christ's victory was not imposed by force. Indeed, Maximus the Confessor finds the element of deceit useful in allowing him to draw a neat theological parallel between the Fall and salvation. Just as Adam was deceived by the expectations of becoming divine (Gen. 3:5), so the devil was deceived by the expectation of becoming human (*Thal.* 64; Blowers and Wilken 2003: 160). Nevertheless, although Gregory's fishhook image also commended itself to John Damascene (*De Fid. Orth.* 3.27), sacrifice and ransom never became in the East the major themes that they became in the West. More important to the Eastern Fathers were the themes of participation and deification.

PARTICIPATION

'Where unity is central to salvation', Osborn has observed, 'the theme of participation or communion becomes prominent' (Osborn 1993: 170). Irenaeus puts it at its simplest: 'Communion with God is light and life … Separation from God is death' (*Haer.* 5.27.2; trans. mine). The philosophical elaboration of this theme begins with Origen. In the Platonic tradition participation had long been used to express how the contingent was related to that which exists of itself. Origen brings to it a new dynamic dimension, a human response to the operations of the Trinity with the power to transform the participant. Participation in the Spirit results in spiritualization, and participation in the Son leads to filiation. Such sharing in the sonship of the Son is possible because the Logos took on himself the whole of human nature, thus mediating in his own person between the simplicity of God and the multiplicity of the world. His multiplicity is expressed in his ἐπίνοιαι, or titles, namely, Son, Logos, wisdom, life, God, and so on; the participant in these becomes a son or daughter, a rational, wise, and living being, and a god 'by participation'—in a dependent and derivative sense—as distinct from Christ, who possesses these titles 'by nature'.

Yet for Origen the Son's mediatorial role meant that, although the Son was God 'by nature', he was the recipient of deity in relation to the Father just as he was the one who bestows deity in relation to the believer. In the following generation this view became increasingly unacceptable. So far as Athanasius was concerned, to maintain that Christ had his being from the Father 'by participation' was incompatible with regarding him as Saviour, 'for it is not possible that he who merely possesses from participation should impart of that partaking to others since what he has is not his own but the Giver's' (*De syn.* 51; trans. mine). Only a Saviour who was on the uncreated side of the now firmly established ontological divide could save us, because salvation now entailed the transformation of the human nature which had first been transformed in the person of Christ himself. For when the Logos assumed a human body, he became the single subject by the *communicatio idiomatum* of all that his body experienced. It therefore follows that by participating in the deified humanity of the Logos (brought about by baptism and the Eucharist and maintained by imitation, or the moral life) we also participate in his impassable divinity, because his flesh has been endowed with divinity just as his divinity has been endowed with humanity. As a result of this communication of divine life, we advance from the corruptibility and mortality of the created to share in the incorruption and immortality of the uncreated, and so arrive at the contemplation of the Father.

After Athanasius, any Christology that maintained the full divinity of Christ entailed a radical discontinuity between uncreated and created, divine and human, that was bridged only by the participation of the divine in the human through the kenotic self-emptying of the Logos and the participation of the human in the divine in the person of Christ through the *communicatio idiomatum*. There were different narrations of how the Christian believer could benefit from this. Augustine gives us one widely accepted version. The Word of God is the mediator 'in whom we can participate and by participation reach our felicity' (*De Civ. Dei* 9.15; Bettenson 1972: 361). He is our mediator in that although divine he shares in our nature: 'God himself, the blessed God who is the giver of blessedness, became partaker of our human nature and thus offered us a short cut to participation in his own divine nature' (*De Civ. Dei* 9.15). His liberating us from mortality and misery does not simply raise us to the angelic state; it brings us to that very Trinity 'in which the angels themselves participate, and so achieve their felicity' (*De Civ. Dei* 9.15). This, says Augustine, was the purpose of the Incarnation.

Another approach is found in Gregory of Nazianzus, who prefers to speak of the imitation of Christ rather than participation in him. Yet this imitation is transformative, not imitative in an external sense. The Christian becomes like the incarnate Son through the reception of the sacraments and the practice of 'philosophy'—a disciplined ascetic life—with the result that the Christian becomes 'mingled' with the divine light. The language of mingling was also important to Gregory of Nyssa. It expressed how a lesser reality could be interpenetrated by a greater without loss of its own identity, much in the same way as participation. In a famous image, Gregory compares the human in Christ to a drop of vinegar absorbed in a boundless ocean, which, however much diluted, still continues to exist. The Incarnation marks the beginning of a new glorified humanity in which the believer can share through baptism and the Eucharist. It is thus that participation in the divine attributes is made possible—in beatitude, mercy, φιλανθρωπία, and incorruption, not in the nature of God—a participation that restores in us the divine likeness. The concept of participation in the divine attributes enables Gregory of Nyssa to speak of an ever-deepening intimacy with God without compromising God's fundamental unknowability and transcendence.

In Cyril of Alexandria participation becomes a key concept for understanding how human beings are able to appropriate the divine life (Keating 2004: 144–90). There are two kinds of participation, he says, one natural the other relative. In illustration of what he means by natural participation he offers the analogy of a flower and its fragrance. 'What is signified is a natural relationship, not a participation in something separate' (*Dial. Trin.* 6, 593b; trans. mine). In this sense, the Son may be described as the fragrance of the Father. The other kind of participation is on an external and moral level. It is illustrated by a person imitating an example. Our participation in Christ is of this second kind, and yet it does not simply remain on the moral level. It enables us, as Cyril is fond of repeating, to 'mount up to a dignity above our nature' (cf. *Comm. Jn.* II, *inter alia*). To express this idea Cyril frequently appeals to 2 Peter 1:4, 'partakers of the divine nature', a verse rarely referred to by any previous Christian author, but usable by Cyril because of the distinctions he makes in the sense of the word 'participation'. The way we become 'partakers of the divine nature' is through Christ, in virtue of his being the 'common frontier' (μεθόριον) between the divine and the human, the meeting-point between the uncreated and the created. The divine nature may be totally other from us in essence but it has entered into our world through the Incarnation in order to enable us to share in the divine life in a relative or external sense. The Word made humanity his own, having appropriated it by his taking flesh from the Theotokos and having deified it by his suffering, death, and resurrection. In Christ the Word has appropriated human nature in a manner that became an irreversible part of his identity. Our corresponding appropriation of the divine nature as Christian believers is 'relative' and 'by grace'. The agent of this participation is the Spirit. Our dynamic participation in the divine nature through Christ in the Spirit is initiated by baptism and maintained by sharing in the Eucharist and obeying the commandments. We share in the divine attributes through participating in the new life which the incarnate Word inaugurated. The corporate dimension is vitally important—participation is not a private activity. And through the action of the Spirit, the Eucharist transforms us even corporeally. 'For it was absolutely necessary not only that our soul should be recreated into newness of life by the Holy Spirit, but also that this coarse and earthly body should be sanctified by an analogous participation and called to incorruption' (*In Jo.* 4.2, 362b; trans. mine). Because in Christ the Word, who is the Son of God 'by nature', has appropriated human nature in its completeness and endowed it with divine life, he has become the frontier between the created and the uncreated, with the result that we have the possibility of appropriating 'relatively', 'by participation', and 'by grace' the divine life that hitherto had been inaccessible to us on the other side of the divide. Our appropriation must be effected sacramentally through the Holy Spirit. As Cyril puts it in his dispute with Nestorius, by the Eucharist 'the Son does not change the least thing belonging to the created order into the nature of his own deity ... but there is imprinted in some way in those who have become partakers of the divine nature through participating in the Holy Spirit a spiritual likeness to him, and the beauty of the ineffable deity illuminates [them]' (*Adv. Nest.* 3.2; trans. mine). Because what Christ accomplished is the work of the Word of God, our participation in him raises us to a new level of being.

DEIFICATION

Deification has several senses in patristic literature, but at its most profound it refers to the *transformative* effect of participation in Christ. Of the various terms the Fathers use to express the work of Christ—salvation, redemption, reconciliation, recapitulation, recreation, restoration, and so forth—deification is the one that seems least rooted in the language of the New Testament. The word first appears as θεοποίησις in the late second century, and in its most familiar form, θέωσις, only in the mid-fourth century. Yet what the word expresses lies at the heart of the early Church's kerygma, namely, that 'God sent his only Son into the world that we might live through him' (1 John 4:9).

In John's Gospel there is a report of a critical debate between Jesus and 'the Jews' that took place in the Temple at Jerusalem, in the portico of Solomon (John 10:22–39). In the course of the debate (at verse 34), Jesus quotes Psalm 82:6, 'I said, you are gods', to demonstrate a fortiori that if those to whom the word of God came in the past could be addressed as gods, he could call himself the unique Son of God without blasphemy. This verse was later used by Justin Martyr who adapts a Rabbinic exegesis of Psalm 82:6 (the 'gods' are those who obey the Torah) to argue that in fact they are those who obey the commandments of Christ. Not long afterwards this exegesis was taken up by Irenaeus who identified the gods specifically with those who had put on Christ through baptism, thus launching the verse on its career as a key text supporting the notion of deification. Irenaeus was prompted by his exegesis of the 'gods' as the baptized to enunciate the 'exchange' formula: the Son of God 'became what we are in order to make us what he is himself' (*Haer.* 5, Praef.; trans. mine). The rich implications of this two-way traffic were to influence Christological thinking. Both the self-emptying of the divine without loss of divine impassibility and the deification of the human without loss of human finitude are required for Christ to fulfil his salvific role.

These implications were not fully drawn out until the Christological debates of the fourth and fifth centuries. In the third century Origen presents a different Christology, one of continuity between the human and the divine. The purpose of the Incarnation was to mediate between the simplicity of God and the multiplicity of the world, to reach down to the level of created being and endow it with divine life. This happens first in the person of Christ, his flesh being deified by his soul and his soul by the Logos. We can share in this ascending movement up the hierarchy of being through our participation in Christ. Such participation is not primarily sacramental, although it is assumed that baptism is the starting point of Christian discipleship. Participation, as a response to the divine initiative, is achieved by 'proceeding along the steep path of virtue' (cf. Origen, *Prin.* 4.31) and by sharing in Christ's ἐπίνοιαι, thus imitating him morally and intellectually; for the Holy Spirit actively makes us holy and spiritual so that the divine Son can make us gods and sons. Only as gods who have recovered the divine likeness can we come to share in the intimacy that the Logos enjoys with the Father. Participation in the life of the Trinity makes us spirits, christs, and gods living henceforth with the life of God. There is no confusion between the essence of God and the human soul because the relationship of participation ensures that the distinction persists between a dependent reality and that which is self-existent. The Logos, though deified in relation to the Father, is nevertheless 'God by nature', in contrast to the perfected Christian who is 'a god by participation' (*Sel. in Psalm.* 135).

A century later, Athanasius presents a different perspective on the relationship between God and all else, a perspective dominated by a disjunction that is alien to Origen's thinking. In his struggle with Arius who stood more squarely in the Origenian tradition than he did himself, Athanasius insisted that the Son could not be a participant in divinity and still be our Saviour (*Ar.* 1.9). The world had been created out of nothing with the purpose of finding fulfilment in God. As a result of the Fall, humanity had a tendency to sink back into nothingness. The salvation brought by Christ was the power of reversing the momentum and restoring the ascent of humanity towards the divine. God and nothingness are the two poles of reality. The reverse of the natural process of corruption is the process of deification. But the Saviour could not be the one who bestows deification if he was himself deified. The disjunction of uncreated and created was overcome in his own person as a simultaneous 'otherness' and 'nearness' that draws humanity to the 'otherness' of the uncreated (Anatolios 1998: 35–8). The created and uncreated converge in Christ, not without tension. The humanity that Christ assumed therefore has a representative significance. Human nature as such has become the Word's 'own'. There is a human solidarity in Christ. Divine life has been communicated to the flesh and human nature has been exalted. This reality is appropriated by the believer sacramentally. Dynamic participation in the Word is effected through baptism and the Eucharist. In the *Epistle to Serapion* deification is synonymous with baptism (*Ep. Serap.* 1). The fulfilment of the deified state is eschatological when 'we shall sit on thrones' (Rev. 3:21) with Christ. This is an approach markedly different from Origen's intellectualism. We do not transcend human nature through shedding the flesh and becoming pure minds. The representative humanity assumed by the Word is transformed and endued with divine life. We begin to share in this transformation through participating in Christ sacramentally.

After Athanasius this becomes the dominant account of Christ's redemptive work. Gregory of Nazianzus, in particular, keeps coming back to it in his *Orations*. We are structured for the divine life, deified rational animals with a movement towards the divine pole by 'an inclination towards God' that was interrupted by the Fall (*Or.* 30.11; trans. mine). Christ as the Second Adam is 'a union of two opposites' of flesh and spirit, the latter deifying and the former being deified (*Or.* 38.13; trans. mine). The higher nature prevailed 'that I might become a god in the same measure that he became a man' (*Or.* 29.19; trans. mine). Christ makes us gods 'by the power of the Incarnation' (*Or.* 30.14; trans. mine), restoring the lost image in his own person so that we can share in it. The basis of this sharing is baptism and the Eucharist. But Gregory lays much more emphasis than Athanasius on spiritual ascent through the contemplative life. In fact it is in this context that the word 'theosis' is first used (*Or.* 3.1; 4.71). The 'gods' are those who through the Holy Spirit in baptism have begun to appropriate the deified humanity of the Son and who through the practice of ascetic discipline are consolidating their ascent to their eschatological fulfilment.

This was not an approach that was shared universally in the Greek-speaking world. Antiochene theologians in the tradition of Diodore of Tarsus and Theodore of Mopsuestia do not speak of deification because they conceive of salvation in purely eschatological terms. For the Cappadocians, however, the eschatological fulfilment may be initiated even in this life. Augustine, too, shared the same perspective. This is evident in his sermons and treatises, though because references to deification are a good deal sparser than in Gregory Nazianzus, the theme has not been much noticed until comparatively recently (Meconi 2013). For Augustine, as for all his predecessors, the gods of Psalm 82:6 are the baptized, for 'if we have been made sons of God, we have also been made gods'—deified by grace, that is, adopted by baptism, so as to become fellow heirs with Christ (*Enar. in Ps.* 49.2; trans. mine). Christ is the agent of a new creation, remodelling human nature to conform once again to the divine image (*De Trin.* 14–15). Like Gregory, Augustine also speaks of a spiritual ascent within the human heart. In this context deification is eschatological: 'We experience mortality, we endure infirmity, we look forward to divinity' (*Mainz Sermon* 13.1; trans. mine).

The fullest development of Gregory of Nazianzus is in Maximus the Confessor. That the economy of salvation is about the penetration and transformation of the human by the divine is the subject of profound meditation by Maximus. The purpose of the Incarnation is not only to restore what was lost in the Fall, but also to endue humanity with divine life as 'an additional advantage through theosis over the first creation' (*Thal.* 54; trans. mine). The humanization of the divine and the divinization of the human meet in the person of Jesus Christ (*Thal.* 22). The reciprocity of kenosis and theosis is frequently emphasized: 'God and man are paradigms of each other that as much as God is humanized to man through love for mankind, so much is man able to be deified to God through love' (*Ambig.* 10; Louth 1996: 101). What enables the human and the divine to converge is the unifying function of love. By participating in the mystery of love the believer participates in Christ himself. For the first time the spiritual ascent is fully integrated with the Incarnation and participation in the Eucharist. The mystery of Christ is the context in which the spiritual transition is made from the limitations of this life to the glory of the next. Theosis, the salvific goal for which humanity was created, is inaugurated in this life by fully appropriating the mystery of Christ. For a person who has ascended to the highest levels of unity in Christ out of the multiplicity of the world has already attained the Eighth Day and become a god by deification (*Cap. Theol.* 1.54).

THE 'TWO WAYS'

Athanasius' assertion that there are two ways of compassion by which Christ both rid us of death and renewed us is thus extraordinarily rich in its implications. Under the inspiration of Cyril and Maximus, we could reinterpret these two ways as three kinds of inclusiveness, three modes by which Christ brings creation from multiplicity to unity. In the first mode Christ overcomes the divisiveness of sin. As the second Adam, the representative of our renewed humanity, he is both the giver and the receiver of salvation. He 'became the "sin" that I caused', taking our damaged humanity and healing it in his own person. There is no exclusive vicariousness in patristic teaching. In the second mode Christ overcomes the arrow of time. His salvific work encompasses the past and the future, undoing the effects of the Fall on the one hand and inaugurating the eschatological age on the other. In the third mode Christ overcomes the fundamental division between created and uncreated, inserting us through his work of compassionate love into the life of the Trinity itself. The deification of the Christian is the ultimate purpose of the Incarnation.

SUGGESTED READING

Keating (2004); Osborn (1993); Russell (2004); Turner (1952).

BIBLIOGRAPHY

Anatolios, K. (1998), *Athanasius: The Coherence of his Thought* (London: Routledge).

Beeley, C. A. (2008), *Gregory of Nazianzus on the Trinity and the Knowledge of God* (Oxford: Oxford University Press).

Bettenson, H. (1972), *Augustine Concerning The City of God against the Pagans* (Harmondsworth: Penguin Books).

Blowers, P. M. and R. L. Wilken (2003), *On the Cosmic Mystery of Christ: Selected Writings from St Maximus the Confessor* (Crestwood, NY: St. Vladimir's Seminary Press).

Fairbairn, D. (2003), *Grace and Christology in the Early Church* (Oxford: Oxford University Press).

Homes Dudden, F. (1935), *The Life and Times of St Ambrose*, 2 vols. (Oxford: Clarendon Press).

Keating, D. A. (2004), *The Appropriation of Divine Life in Cyril of Alexandria* (Oxford: Oxford University Press).

Keating, D. A. (2007), *Deification and Grace* (Naples, Fla.: Sapientia Press).

Louth, A. (1996), *Maximus the Confessor* (London: Routledge).

Louth, A. (2002), *St John Damascene: Tradition and Originality in Byzantine Theology* (Oxford: Oxford University Press).

Ludlow, M. (2007), *Gregory of Nyssa, Ancient and (Post)modern* (Oxford: Oxford University Press).

Meconi, D. V. (2013), *The One Christ: St. Augustine's Theology of Deification* (Washington, DC: Catholic University of America Press).

Osborn, E. (1993), *The Emergence of Christian Theology* (Cambridge: Cambridge University Press).

Portalié, E. (1909), 'Augustin (Saint)', in A. Vacant and E. Mangenot (eds.), *Dictionnaire de Théologie Catholique* (Paris: Letouzey), vol. 1, 2268–472.

Russell, N. (2000), *Cyril of Alexandria* (London: Routledge).

Russell, N. (2004), *The Doctrine of Deification in the Greek Patristic Tradition* (Oxford: Oxford University Press).

Russell, N. (2007), *Theophilus of Alexandria* (London: Routledge).

Thomson, R. (trans.) (1971), Athanasius, *Contra Gentes* and *De Incarnatione* (Oxford: Clarendon Press).

Turner, H. E. W. (1952), *The Patristic Doctrine of Redemption: A Study of the Development of Doctrine during the First Five Centuries* (London: Mowbray).

Winslow, D. F. (1979), *The Dynamics of Salvation: A Study in Gregory of Nazianzus* (Cambridge, Mass.: The Philadelphia Patristic Foundation).

PART III

MEDIAEVAL CHRISTOLOGY

CHAPTER 11

IMAGE CHRISTOLOGY IN THE AGE OF THE SECOND COUNCIL OF NICAEA (787)

AIDAN NICHOLS, O.P.

INTRODUCTION

IN the Christian tradition, the Christological significance of sacred art does not turn exclusively on the iconographic content of that art—the question of which particular themes should be depicted—for the very existence of such an art is itself theologically delicate. Against a largely, but by no means entirely, aniconic background in Judaism, the legitimacy of a sacral art requires some justification before proceeding to discussion of how it chooses and handles its own motifs. What kind of conceptual connection is needed if visual art and Christology are to be linked? This was the most difficult, though not the only, question that faced the 'Council of the Icon', Nicaea II, in 787.

The term 'icon', at its Christian origins, signifies not simply portable images of holy figures, in whatever medium, but any sacred image on whatever scale—including, then, in the form of murals: painting or mosaic-work on walls. At the 'Council of the Icon' it was not only images of Christ, in these various sizes and media, which were at stake. The veneration, and indeed the making, of images of the *Theotokos*, the Mother of Christ, and the saints, had been called into question as well. For orthodox Christianity the realm of the holy is populated, if also focused on a single figure. This combination makes the imaginative world of the Great Church a Christocentric constellation.

The fuller emergence of an iconography suited to this 'world'—for Iconophiles an altogether appropriate consequence of the Incarnation of the Word—had followed seemingly spontaneously from the development of a more ample material culture once the Church acquired legal status in the Roman Empire. 'Iconomachia', the battle against all such images, stemmed from the conviction that certainly their veneration but probably also their sheer existence was, to the contrary, doctrinally intolerable. Occasional rumblings of episcopal disapproval, whether in the fourth century or in the eighth, heralded the advent of organized Iconophobia. The catalyst of the latter was a mood of anxiety in Byzantine officialdom (and the army): did the Christian empire, successor of ancient Israel, lie under divine judgement (and thus exposure to its enemies) on account of a new version of the 'idolatry' so often excoriated by the prophets?

The heresy 'born in the purple' (Gerö 1973: 131)—generated, that is, in the mind of the emperor Leo III—began, in the late 720s, as a policy decision about the removal of images from public prominence but it culminated, owing to the efforts of his son, Constantine V, in a theoretically based Iconoclasm where the Christological issue became central to the debate (Gerö 1977a).

Iconophile theology was stimulated by this challenge to focus more sharply on the icon of Christ. Though the implications of the Incarnation for the rise of a Christian art had already been sifted in the period of the 'first Iconoclasm', between 726/730 and 787, notably by Germanus of Constantinople and, from the safe distance of the Caliphate, John of Damascus, apologists for the icons had to come to terms with Constantine V's specifically Christological objections, whether in the Council sessions, or, more fully, during the period of the 'second Iconoclasm', which lasted from 813 to 843. In that later period, the body of reflection left by Nicephorus of Constantinople and Theodore of Studios would make them the most prominent of the Iconodule doctors, in relation, above all, to the icon of Christ (Parry 1996: 99).

In what follows I shall concentrate on the four above-named Iconophile doctors and the Second Council of Nicaea, while recognizing that other, if less crucial, figures might have been selected for discussion (notably Leontius of Neapolis, before the crisis, the Arabic writer Theodore Abu Qurrah during its course, and the patriarch Photius after its ending). Issues of possible interpolations into relevant documents will not be raised here since, as is admitted by critics of more traditional scholarship, the (hypothetical) interpolators remain witnesses to the theological understanding current in the later eighth and ninth centuries, that is, within the parameters of the age of Byzantine Iconoclasm and its resultant literature (Brubaker and Haldon 2001, 2011).

GERMANUS OF CONSTANTINOPLE

Germanus I was patriarch of Constantinople as the Iconoclast crisis broke. In his earlier career, when confronted with the issue of monothelitism, he appears to have blown with a changing imperial wind. Contrastingly, his letters to or about a scattering of Iconophobe bishops in Asia Minor on the eve of the first Iconoclasm embody the firmness of mind he was to maintain in the teeth of opposition from his civil masters. The three letters in question, to Constantine of Nikoleia, Thomas of Claudiopolis, and John of Synada (not himself an opponent of icons but Constantine's metropolitan), convey a strong sense of the full congruence between the Incarnation event and a Christological (and by extension Mariological and hagiological) visual art. In the words of the letter to

John, 'We form in images the portrait of [Christ's] holy flesh; we salute it [the portrait] and discern in it all the cultus and honour that is appropriate; we recall by this means his divine, life-giving and ineffable Incarnation' (cited in Grumel 1922: 171). The same letter makes some attempt to indicate the suitability of images of Mary and the saints without managing to achieve a full Christological rationale for these subsidiary cases: 'If we salute the images of our Lord and Saviour, of his spotless Mother who is truly Mother of God, and of the saints, we do not, however, have in their regard an equal affection and faith … We recognize … him as the Master who distributes the blessings of salvation, her as praying for us in her quality as Mother, and all the saints as our co-servants who, in the same nature as us, have been pleasing to God' (cited in Grumel 1922: 174).

Rebutting the accusation that the image cult was a new idolatry, Germanus stressed that the outward similarity of the repertoire of gesture shared by that cult with pagan worship should not be made the basis of faulty inference. The interior sentiment that dictates the actions in question is utterly different. In the words of the letter to Thomas of Claudiopolis, 'The rapid end of idols, pronounced by Wisdom (cf. Wis. 14:12–14), that is, their permanent disappearance and abolition, has no other cause than the appearance of Jesus Christ, our great God and Saviour, whom holy Church, redeemed from all the confines of the earth, confesses and glorifies unceasingly in piety' (cited in Grumel 1922: 171). For Germanus, the images are an aid to right worship which could in abstract principle proceed perfectly well without them. The Iconophobe question has not, however, been posed in the abstract, for, de facto, the Church is in possession of images and makes use of their cultus. The lengthy 'Narration of Heresies and Synods', traditionally ascribed to Germanus (if correctly, then possibly its writing was the occupation of his enforced retirement after 730) heralds the view of the modern Eastern Orthodox that the defence of the icons belongs properly with the ever more amply defined Christological doctrine of the Church.

John of Damascus

John of Damascus was already dead by the time Constantine V's Iconophobe Council concluded its business at Hiereia in 754. His life belongs, therefore, to the early decades of Iconoclasm whose growth he surveyed with alarm from the safe distance of the Umayyad caliphate of which, before embracing monastic life in Palestine, he had been a civil servant.

By way of defending the images, John wrote three short treatises, each ending with a *florilegium* (a collection of patristic texts), and these fill out what is said in the chapter on this topic in his systematic survey of Christian theology *The Fount of Knowledge*, the central, dogmatic section of which became known in the Latin West as 'On the Orthodox Faith'.

The first *Treatise on the Holy Images* is especially fine, and might well be judged the most wide-ranging apologia produced by an Iconophile doctor, notably through John's exploration of what can be called the *generally imagistic* character of biblical revelation at large. His account has room for Christological elements without, however, attaining the sharp Christological focus of the kind we shall find in writers after Nicaea II, notably Nicephorus and Theodore.

Despite some overlap of material, the three treatises differ significantly in their manner of approach. The first, which coincides with the first rumblings of official Iconoclasm in east Rome, seeks to show the enormous analogical range of the concept of image as exhibited in biblical revelation. It also investigates the plurality of senses that can be given the term 'veneration', προσκύνησις, which both etymologically and ritually denotes a 'bowing down [to the ground]'). This, John points out, need not express λατρεία, the 'exclusive worship' of God (Louth 2003: 11) but may also stand for respect—including, very importantly, respect for persons and things *for the sake of the honour of God*.

These two etymological enquiries are presupposed in his account of the Christological icon. John ends this first defence of the icons with a commented (and therefore unusual) *florilegium*. The second treatise, seemingly prompted by the deposition of Germanus I, is a simplified and more pugnacious version of the first, while the third opens in the much the same spirit as the second before transmuting into a serene and systematic account of icon theology. The *florilegia* attached to these second and third treatises are, in contrast to the first, simply *catenae* of passages—but important ones since they seem to have guided the patristic enquiries pursued at Nicaea II.

Christologically, Damascene (like Germanus) founds the image cult on the Incarnation of the Word. 'I am emboldened to depict the invisible God, not as invisible but as he became visible for our sake, by participation in flesh and blood' (I.4; Louth 2003: 22). If a divine precept forbade all making of images in the Old Testament dispensation (which John denies, restricting that command to image-making that confused the created with the Uncreated), in the New Testament, by contrast, God furnished for humankind an image of himself. By 'transcending his own nature', the incorporeal One took on the 'form of a slave': so, 'depict him on a board and set up to view the One who has accepted to be seen' (I.8; Louth 2003: 24–5). In that context, John encourages images of the annunciation, the nativity, the baptism of Christ, his transfiguration, the miracles worked in the public ministry, the Passion, death and burial, the resurrection and ascension.

John's treatment of the Incarnation as the entry of the Logos into visible 'imageability' in no way diminishes his commitment to the notion of the pre-existent Son as uncreated invisible Image of the Father, as that teaching was forged by Athanasius in the course of the Arian controversy. (In John's third *Treatise* Athanasius' pneumatology is invoked in the same context: for by his procession from the Father the Spirit is the natural image of the Son [III.18, cf. Athanasius, *To Serapion*, I.24].) John manages with ease the simultaneous use of these two distinct registers of language thanks to his analogical concept of imagehood, which includes both the natural image and the artistic image—and also extends beyond them, to the way in which the counsels of God are 'imaged' in the anticipation of the trends or events of cosmic history in the divine mind; to the metaphorical texture of much of Scripture, especially when it speaks of God or the angelic powers; to the 'types' that foreshadow later realizations of the divine plan in salvation history; and, not least, to memorials of the past of salvation history, whether these be literary records or physical artefacts.

Curiously, in the first *Treatise* Damascene does not include in this inventory the creation of man in the divine image (Gen. 1:26–7)—though he gives it pride of place in the comparable list in *On the Orthodox Faith* (ch. 89), and adds it to the similar catalogue in the last of the *Treatises on the Divine Images* (III.20; cf. also II.20 for an honourable mention of the theme).

These 'lists' embody John's understanding of how 'reality echoes reality', for 'the image, in its differing forms, is always mediating, always holding together in harmony' (Louth 2002: 216). This wider context in a cosmology, at once philosophical and revelation-indebted, for which imagehood is a ubiquitous feature of the real obviously helped John to formulate a theological apologia for the icon of Christ.

Within this context, his stress on the Logos' assumption of materiality was essential to John's strategy of underscoring the continuity between Incarnation and the exhibition of the Incarnate One in iconic art. It generates a high doctrine of matter, as used not only in the original flesh-taking but also in the continuing post-Pentecost economy of Son and Spirit. 'I reverence therefore matter and I hold in respect and venerate that through which my salvation has come about. I reverence it not as God, but as filled with divine energy and grace' (II.14; Louth 2003: 71).

Damascene makes a spirited attempt to yoke together the issue of icons of Christ with that of the images of the saints (and, by implication, Mary), arguing that the Saviour cannot be sundered from those most manifestly saved. 'To make an image of Christ as glorified but to spurn the image of the saints as without glory' is tacitly to deny his saving work. It is to reject the Pauline principle of the co-glorification of those who co-suffer with Christ, and the Johannine prediction that 'we shall be like him' (1 John 3:2, cited in I.19).

THE SECOND COUNCIL OF NICAEA

From the point of view of the practitioner of 'Church dogmatics', the crucial contribution of the Seventh Ecumenical Council lies in its ὅρος or dogmatic definition as promulgated in its seventh session (Nichols 1988). This is a brief text which while, to be sure, it can boast a Christological component has principally in view the fuller range of iconic representation of whose legitimacy Iconophobes were sceptical (including, then, the images of Mary and the saints).

To the historical theologian, however, the ὅρος ought not to be sundered from the corpus of Conciliar speeches found in the *Acta* of Nicaea II, seven sessions of which were held, in late September and the first half of October, 787, in the cathedral of Hagia Sophia at Nicaea (now Iznik) and the eighth in the Magnaura palace in Constantinople in the presence of the emperor, Constantine VI, and his mother, the empress Irene, who, acting jointly, signed the decrees of the Council into civil law.

While the first three sessions, like the eighth and last, were chiefly taken up with necessary formalities, the fourth and fifth sessions examined the biblical and patristic evidence for the making and veneration of images, a task which spilled over into the sixth session whose official purpose was the refutation of the claim of the 754 Iconoclast Council to be counted among the right-believing (orthodox) synods. Inevitably, then, much of the time of the Council was taken up with exegetical questions and the examination of patristic *florilegia* (Dumeige 1978).

Iconophile speakers (chiefly bishops, but abbots and other monks also participated) sought to establish a fundamental iconic continuity joining Israel and the Church of later times. While by no means discounting the seismic shift of the Incarnation, they stressed how images 'made by hands' to the honour of God were already known in patriarchal times (see Jacob's stele), at Sinai (compare the accoutrements of the desert tabernacle) and to the mind of the prophets (for example in Ezekiel's imagining of the renewed Temple), and thus formed a constitutive part of the divine outreach in salvation history. With the Incarnation, when the entry of the Logos into the material realm gave even greater prominence to the role of sight in the apprehension of divine working, the making of sacred images continued and intensified, being counted among the 'unwritten traditions' stemming from the preaching of the apostles—though, judiciously, allowance might also be made for a time-lag, since 'whatever in the course of time seemed good to our fathers of blessed memory to build upon the foundation of the apostles and prophets that, we accept' (Mansi 1960: 328E).

Iconophile spokesmen at the Council were the more willing to affirm the origin of icons in the first apostolic generation owing to their conviction that the mimetic or pictorial icon reproduces the mode in which revelation in Christ was primarily given. This mode was a visual mode, since, in a rather obvious sense, the hearers of the incarnate Word saw him before they listened to his teaching, while many of his most striking revelatory acts were gestures rather than words (in his birth and infancy, his public ministry, Passion, death, and resurrection). Thus ' "faith comes from the sense of hearing", says the apostle [Rom. 10:17], but it is already stamped in the understanding of those who see through the sense of sight, and by its power they proclaim the mystery that God has been manifested in the flesh and has been believed in the world, a mystery which will be found the most conducive of all to sanctification and salvation' (Mansi 1960: 249E).

True, like the saints—but pre-eminently so—Christ is not living now within earthly parameters but is in glory. Yet he retains his bodiliness, and if iconographers seek to express his glorified body by the use of brilliant gold this does not contravene the proper limits of representation since it 'depicts no more than the biblical words used to express this same indescribable reality' (Giakalis 2005: 85). Whereas those who by θέωσις have attained the immediate vision of Christ in his glory do not need images, the earthly faithful 'need some bodily confirmation of what they have heard' (Mansi 1960: 116A).

Since the Council not only post-dated the Hiereia synod but was also required to reverse its findings, it was inevitable that thought be given to the Constantinian

Christology of the image which Hiereia had made its own. In his 'Enquiries' Constantine had sought to show that the making and veneration of icons naturally solicited either a Nestorian or a monophysite interpretation. Either what was depicted was the human nature of Christ only, thus separating the natures, which went against the mind of Chalcedonian orthodoxy, or what was portrayed there sought to picture the divine nature through the human with which it was not just indissolubly conjoined (so much was perfectly orthodox by the criteria of previous Councils), but, rather, hopelessly con-fused. If the 'monophysizing' objection were less clearly put than its 'Nestorianizing' counterpart, Iconophiles at Nicaea II could at least respond that the *simultaneous* accu-sation of both Nestorianism and monophysitism was inherently implausible (Giakalis 2005: 95). More positively, they could, and did, go on to argue that what the icon of Christ shares with its subject is neither of his natures but his *name*. It 'participates in the name of the archetype' (i.e., Christ himself in his divinity and humanity), not in his being as such (Mansi 1960: 252CD).

Adopting Constantine V's Christological objection to the icons carried with it a major disadvantage for Iconophobes. His argument had no purchase in regard to the images of Mary and the saints. They could only insinuate (but on what grounds?) the pertinence of an a fortiori approach. 'With the first [i.e., arguments for the legitimacy of icons of Christ] refuted, there is no need of these [i.e., arguments against the lawfulness of icons of the Theotokos and saints]' (Mansi 1960: 273CD).

As if by compensation, however, Hiereia had taken from Constantine the sugges-tion that Christ had instituted an icon of himself, namely the Eucharistic species: 'the God-given icon of his flesh, the divine bread, along with the life-bearing blood from his side' (Mansi 1960: 1264C). This 'true icon of the dispensation of Christ our God' had the advantage of not claiming to represent pictorially what it iconized and opening the road to idolatry. (The Iconophobe bishops, however, tacitly abandoned Constantine's claim that the Eucharist was consubstantial with Christ, sensing, it would seem, the difficulty of maintaining at one and the same time both this claim and the claim to iconic status. If the Eucharist were an image of Christ [Gerö 1975: 10] as a consequence of his institution of a sacramental convention, it could only be, surely, a 'thetic' image, rendered such by his will, not a 'natural' one, a consequence of ontology.) Iconophiles could reply that the Lord had not said at the institution. 'This is the image of my body', but 'This is my body'. If the Eucharist is only an icon of the body, it cannot be that body itself—as the liturgies maintain.

What is surprising—and required the attention of the new generation of Iconodule doctors after Nicaea II—was the absence of any reference to this crucial circle of Christological issues in the Conciliar ὅρος, its dogmatic definition, which contents itself with a straightforward affirmation of the reality of the Incarnation as the one element Christology can bring to the defence of the icons, declaring that representational art provides confirmation that 'the becoming man of the Word of God was real and not just imaginary' (τῆς ἀληθείας καὶ οὐ κατὰ φαντασίαν τῆς θεοῦ λόγου ἐνανθρωπήσεως, Tanner 1990: vol. 1, 135). In this sense, Nicaea II does not go beyond the first signs of an Iconophile response to episcopal critics under Leo III, namely, the letters of Germanus.

THEODORE OF STOUDIOS

Theodore of Stoudios was not a dogmatic thinker in the organized manner of John of Damascus who preceded him or of Nicephorus of Constantinople who succeeded him. That did not diminish the spirited quality of the defence of the icons by this highly influential reformer of monasteries and 'theo-political' critic of the *modus operandi* of the imperial office, notably in his *Refutations of those who fight against Images*, the *Antirrhetici*. In Theodore's catecheses and copious correspondence less than might be expected is said about the role of the icons, though they are saluted as ways of commemorating the mysteries of the life of Christ in the feasts of the liturgical year (Cholij 2009: 158).

Theodore's *Antirrhetici* belong to the period of the 'Second Iconoclasm', after Nicaea II, even if, surprisingly, he refers more frequently to Justinian II's 692 'Council *in Trullo*' (which formulated canons to be added to the dogmatic definitions of the Fifth and Sixth Ecumenical Councils) than to the 787 Synod (Cholij 2009: 56).

The first of these three discourses touches on a number of the issues that Iconoclasm had raised from the beginning: notably, the accusation of idolatry (I.2), the proper interpretation of the Mosaic commandment (I.5–6), and the significance of matter in the divine economy (I.7). Theodore interweaves with this rehearsal of 'arguments which he inherited from the previous generation [of Iconophile doctors]' (Roth 1981: 11), the treatment of topics aired at Hiereia as a consequence of the more sophisticated Iconophobia that gained ground under Constantine V: the relation between image and original (I.8–9), the status of the Eucharist as an image of Christ (I.10–12), the place of representations of the Cross (I.15), and the possibility that worship or veneration admits of a variety of modes or degrees (I.19). But what is especially striking about the first *Refutation* is the speed with which Theodore reaches the neuralgic issue of Christology—almost at the outset of the treatise (I.3–4), immediately after the preamble of the text and discussion of the accusation of idolatry.

Here Theodore deals with the claim that in the making of icons of Christ either the uncircumscribable divinity is confused with the circumscribable humanity (in the manner of monophysites) or the two natures are separated (in the manner of Nestorians). In this first brief rebuttal, Theodore points out that to deny the pertinence of such terms as 'visible', 'tangible', 'graspable', to the revelation of the divinity in the humanity is in effect to deny that the Word became flesh (I.3). It may be true to say that what the Word took on was 'the whole human nature' but he did not for that reason fail to become circumscribed. After all, had that nature, as it existed in him, not been 'contemplated in an individual manner' he simply could not have been seen by others (I.4). And, Theodore stresses, it is 'he'—the Logos incarnate—who is thus seen. For Theodore, the unity of the hypostasis of Christ (the typical emphasis of Cyrilline Chalcedonianism) guarantees that what is shown to human eye in the humanity assumed discloses what is true of the divinity which in no way is laid aside.

Neither confusion nor separation follows, then, 'for this is the novel mystery of the dispensation, that the divine and human natures came together in the one hypostasis of the Word, which maintains the properties of both natures in the indivisible union' (I.4). Theodore subsequently asks: since, owing to the union, the divinity of Christ is always found conjointly with his humanity, is it then to be said that his divine being is 'present in' the icon (I.12)? He responds, not in any univocal sense, for the 'deified flesh' is absent (there is a contrast here with the Holy Eucharist, the subject principally at stake in this passage). *Both* divinity *and* humanity can be said to be 'in' the icons only by a 'relative participation, since they share in the honour and glory' of their prototype, the incarnate Word (I.12).

Moreover (here Theodore touches on a further Christological objection from the Iconophobe side), the way in which, in Church practice, Christ is shown forth iconographically in multitudinous images does not imply Iconophiles posit a multiplicity of Christs (even though each icon is *named* 'Christ')—any more than the way in which in the language of Scripture the threesome of the divine Persons are each called 'Lord' means Bible Christians must accept a (polytheistic) multiplicity of gods (I.9).

In the second *Refutation* which is laid out as a dialogue between 'Orthodox' and 'Heretic', Theodore presumes that Iconoclasts have been in part persuaded by its predecessor—at least to the extent that they admit the legitimacy of *making* images of Christ. (Actually, the end of the second *Refutation* will record a significant qualification to the moderate Iconoclast's admission that image-making is acceptable: see below.) But they continue to refuse any *venerating* of such images. The biblical injunction is to worship God alone, and there is no mention here of One, himself God, who is understood as the 'prototype' of an image (II.3). In his retort, Theodore insinuates that neither is there in Israel's Scriptures mention of worshipping in an at least binitarian manner—that is, of adoring the Son along with the Father. But now that the Incarnation of the Father's only-begotten One has occurred, he (the Son) has 'entered into circumscription', becoming like us in all things but sin, and *by that very fact* has revealed himself as the prototype of any images that are made of him (II.5). He has thus in effect made himself venerable, the object of worship, in a new mode.

The problem for the Heretic that this principle is nowhere explicitly stated in Scripture still remains. Theodore concedes as much, but he insists that it *is* stated in the Fathers. 'Many teachings which are not written in so many words, but have equal force with the written teachings, have been proclaimed by the holy fathers' (II.7). Examples Theodore can cite are the ὁμοούσιος of the Son with the Father, the Godhead of the Holy Spirit, the identity of Mary as the *Theotokos*, as he remarks, 'and other doctrines too many to list'. These doctrines were confessed in response to the emergence of heresies, and without that confession 'our worship is denied'. Iconomachy is a case in point: the emergence of the Iconoclast heresy both imperilled the integrity of worship and called forth the doctrine that Christ is related to the icons as prototype to image.

The image–prototype relation in images of Christ occupies much of the rest of the second *Refutation*. The comparison between, on the one hand, the Father and the Son, and, on the other hand, the emperor and his image, which the (first) Nicene controversy had made popular (not least in the version offered by St Basil the Great, in his treatise *On the Holy Spirit* [18.45]), is acceptable to the Iconoclast—who, after all, is no Arian—where the natural imagehood of the invisible Son is concerned. The Heretic agrees that worship shown to the Son also attains the Father, just as honour paid to the image of the emperor attains its prototype, the emperor himself (II.24). But he will not admit the pertinence of Basil's analogy when it comes to comparing the icon of Christ (the mimetic image of the Son), on the one hand, and the Son himself (the Father's natural image) on the other. Theodore replies that the emperor comparison is even more germane to the case under discussion, since, like the emperor and his image, the incarnate Son and his image are 'things in our world' (II.26), and moreover, owing to the divinity he shares with the Father, the Son made man is in his own way 'an emperor'. (One thinks of the *Pantokrator* images in east Roman art.)

The second *Refutation* does not close without recording a certain backtracking on the Heretic's part. He doubts whether the circumscription of Christ's flesh can be said to be maintained after the resurrection (II.41). Thus the possibility of pictorial representation ends with the death of Christ. But, replies Theodore, what of the anti-docetic features in the narratives of the Resurrection appearances? 'See my hands and my feet that it is I myself' (Luke 24:39). Evidently, the risen Christ 'had not lost the properties of his human nature' (II.43). If he retained those properties in a way utterly in contrast with the manner in which we possess them, how could St Paul assert the 'concorporeality' of the Corinthian Christians to whom he was writing, who were certainly in the body, and the risen Lord (II.47)?

Theodore's third and last *Refutation* confirms the importance of themes already sounded in the previous two: the centrality of single hypostasis thinking in his Christology of the icon, along with the continuing pertinence to the debate of the circumscription concept, the notion of Christ's 'concorporeality' with the members of his Church-body, the distinction yet affinity between the 'natural' and the 'mimetic' image, and the crucial role of the prototype–image relationship. In discussion of the second of four Iconophile theses by which this quadripartite final *Refutation* is structured, Theodore adds an argument from the Genesis creation account of man as in the image and to the likeness of God (Gen. 1:26, with a possible tacit allusion to the Colossians description of Christ as the image par excellence, Col. 1:15).

> The fact that man is made in the image and likeness of God shows that the work of iconography is a divine action. But since an image can be copied from an image, inasmuch as Christ is man though also God, he can be portrayed in an image not in spirit but in body. But if he is portrayed in one of the two, then obviously he has an image exactly resembling him which reveals the shared likeness.
>
> (III.B.5)

Recognizing the difference of nature (but not of hypostasis) between Christ and his image leads Theodore, especially in correspondence, to distinguish a 'relative', σχετική, and an 'adoring', λατρευτική, version of veneration, προσκύνησις: a use of language congruent with the ὅρος of Nicaea II but which the mediaeval Latin scholastics abandoned (in favour of a distinction between 'relative' and 'absolute' λατρεία), to the dismay of some Eastern Orthodox (Grumel 1921: 260–8).

NICEPHORUS OF CONSTANTINOPLE

Nicephorus' corpus furnishes the richest, or at any rate, the most extensive, material for appreciating the nexus that joins Christology with the icon. Nicephorus' Christology is a Chalcedonianism consciously refined by the nuances added at the Fifth and Sixth Ecumenical Councils (his view of the Seven Councils, at the last of which he was spokesman for Irene and Constantine VI, was set out in his late work *The Twelve Chapters*). In the first of his *Antirrhetici* or *Discourses against the Iconoclasts* he stresses that the Word's taking on of human nature in the hypostatic union, undertaken as this was for the 're-formation' of our species, does not deprive that nature of its proper attributes and yet 'the whole is transfigured toward the better through the power of the Logos' (I.26). The Iconoclast denial of circumscription (owing to the divine nature of the One whose humanity is here invoked), and hence of the possible pictorial representation of the Word, robs the humanity of Christ of a key property of all who live in our nature, thus rendering it a defective example of our kind.

By itself, however, affirmation of the continuing integrity of the humanity assumed, in its essentially 'circumscribed' reality, does not fully answer the developed Iconoclast case. In the wake of Constantine V's challenge, Nicephorus realized that 'the real issue to be proved is that the divine-human hypostasis as hypostasis can be pictorially represented, and not just its human nature' (Travis 1984: 69). In Nicephorus' eyes, the Iconoclast denial of this claim betrays the belief that even with the Incarnation the divine retains a fundamental incompatibility with human nature. This was for him the wider Christological import of icon theology.

In *Discourse against the Iconoclasts* I Nicephorus contends that the icon of Christ enjoys a defining similarity with its archetype *so far as* the divine–human hypostasis (the composite hypostasis of the incarnate Word) is concerned. It is owing to the hypostatic union of both natures that the whole hypostasis can be described as 'circumscribed' and, consequently, the divine nature 'co-circumscribed' albeit only (for this was a peculiarly audacious formulation) in reference to the singularity of the hypostasis, not as taken in itself. The name 'Christ' denotes 'the duality of the natures presented to us in the one hypostasis' (I.46). To affirm the Incarnation is to state that the hypostasis of the Word has visibly appeared—and when he appeared, he did not do so without the divine nature.

Only by separating the soul of Christ from his body could the imperial theology justify the claim that the incarnate Word was a non-circumscribable existent—but then that Word would not be, actually, in the flesh. If, though, Christ in the visibility of his hypostasis, has 'form and character' (I.38), then an icon can characterize, represent, depict, him. *Pace* Iconoclast respect for the symbol of the Cross, though the Cross is indeed venerable, its veneration is altogether misused when made an excuse for desecrating the icon of the Crucified. Of the two artefacts, the latter is the more honourable since it does not merely 'point out the manner of his Passion to us' but 'is that which manifests Christ himself to us' (*Discourses against the Iconoclasts* III.35).

Nicephorus' invocation of Aristotelian ontology assisted his efforts to point up the essentially relative or relational nature of the icon. Its Christological value lies in the *relation* it sets up to Christ, appealing to one of the fundamental terms—namely, relationship or the πρὸς τί—by whose means Aristotle had carved into 'categories' the being of what is (Alexander 1958).

Like Theodore, Nicephorus was well aware of the provision of the 692 Council *in Trullo* that in future Christ should for preference be depicted in his human form and not simply symbolically (more specifically in the form of a lamb, but this may be taken as an instance of a wider range of possible symbols). That could be relevant to the development not just of artistic practice but of the Christian life itself since for Nicephorus 'divine longing and the Spirit' (*Discourses against the Iconoclasts* II.19) lie behind the making of representations of Christ and the figures who belong with him in constellation.

Conclusion

The quarrel over the images was by no means entirely Christological in character. The arguments deployed on either side ranged far more widely in their scanning of the sources of revelation in Scripture and tradition, and the proponents of those arguments were motivated by broad considerations of spiritual aspiration and pastoral prudence, rather than an exclusively intellectual concern with the coherence of Christological doctrine. Just so, the images whose making and veneration were the subject of the debate were icons of the saints and the Mother of the Lord and not simply of the person of the Saviour or the narrative scenes of his redemptive work.

And yet the Christological issue became the controversy's central focus. If from the viewpoint of Iconophile writing this was apparent only in the 'Second Iconoclasm', after 787, it had already been more than hinted in the 'First Iconoclasm' whose entirely temporary *coup de grâce* was provided at the Seventh Ecumenical Council. Indeed it could be argued that, theologically speaking (the political history is another matter), it is the second phase of the 'First Iconoclasm', dating from the 'reception' of the 'Constantinian' Christology of the image at the 754 Council of Hiereia, that marks the decisive turn in the movement, for that was when Constantine V's more Christologically focused attack on the images took centre-stage.

In that sense there might be said to be three 'Iconoclasms'—726/30–54, 754–87, 813–43—with the Christological aspect predominating in the second and third phases, though without obliterating the importance of other themes (Gerö 1977b: 52). Using that terminology, then: whereas in the *first* Iconoclast period, Germanus of

Constantinople and John of Damascus already signal the crucial role of appeal to Incarnation in the debate over icons, only Theodore and Nicephorus, writing in the *third* Iconoclast period, frame that appeal in terms of the technical Christology of their time. This was for the very good reason that only in the *second* Iconoclastic period had that distinctively contemporary Christology surfaced in the 'circumscription' thinking of the gifted—if, from the standpoint of the Great Church, misguided—imperial theologian whose name, by the end of the whole controversy, was synonymous with Iconophobia and the destruction of the images. The Second Nicene Council sought to address the wider spectrum of arguments as comprehensively as possible, but the failure of the bishops to rise to the Constantinian challenge made a resurgence of Byzantine Iconoclasm as likely as its intellectual liquidation in the work of the last Iconophile doctors was desirable.

For, arguably, the ability to represent Christian revelation accessibly was at stake.

> The issue of representation was central: if Christianity could not be adequately expressed by logical means, resort must be had to image, and, where words failed, to the visual image. Thus the religious image, justified in the early stages as a way of educating the ignorant and illiterate, became the staple of Christian society and attracted its own sophisticated theology of representation. Religious images—icons—stand at the logical end of Christian representation. From Christology—the attempt to define the nature of Christ—the passage of debate to the theory of the image was utterly predictable, and if images were to acquire such significance, the exact manner of their representation must be settled.
>
> (Cameron 1991: 226)

This was the goal of the Christology of the icon. The early Byzantine theology of the icon, thanks to its combined Hellenic and biblical inheritance, had one great advantage in pursuing this goal: unlike most modern aesthetics, it did not lack 'the courage of a "theory", θεωρία which bore within itself a speculation and a contemplation, and discovered the invisible in the visible' (Grillmeier 1975: 74).

SUGGESTED READING

Dumeige (1978); Giakalis (2005); Parry (1996).

BIBLIOGRAPHY

Alexander, P. J. (1958), *The Patriarch Nicephorus of Constantinople: Ecclesiastical Policy and Image-Worship in the Byzantine Empire* (Oxford: Oxford University Press).

Brubaker, L. and Haldon, J. (2001), *Byzantium in the Iconoclast Era, c.680–850: The Sources. An Annotated Survey* (Cambridge: Cambridge University Press).

Brubaker, L. and Haldon, J. (2011), *Byzantium in the Iconoclast Era, c.680–850: A History* (Cambridge: Cambridge University Press).

Cameron, A. (1991), *Christianity and the Rhetoric of Empire: The Development of Christian Discourse* (Berkeley: University of California Press).

Cholij, R. (2009), *Theodore the Studite: The Ordering of Holiness* (Oxford: Oxford University Press; reprint, originally published 2002).

Dumeige, G. (1978), *Nicée II* (Paris: Éditions de l'Orante).

Gerö, S. (1973), *Byzantine Iconoclasm during the Reign of Leo III, with Particular Attention to the Oriental Sources* (Louvain: Peeters).

Gerö, S. (1975), 'The Eucharistic Doctrine of the Byzantine Iconoclasts and its Sources', *Byzantinische Zeitschrift* 68: 4–22.

Gerö, S. (1977a), *Byzantine Iconoclasm during the Reign of Constantine V, with particular attention to the Oriental sources* (Louvain: Peeters Publishers).

Gerö, S. (1977b), 'Byzantine Iconoclasm and the Failure of a Medieval Reformation', in J. Gutmann (ed.), *The Image and the Word: Confrontations in Judaism, Christianity and Islam* (Missoula, Mont.: Scholars Press), 49–62.

Giakalis, A. (2005), *Images of the Divine: The Theology of Icons at the Seventh Ecumenical Council*, revised edn. (Leiden: Brill).

Grillmeier, S. J. A. (1975), 'Die Herrlichkeit Gottes auf dem Antlitz Jesu Christi. Zur Bildtheologie der Väterzeit', in Grillmeier, *Mit Ihm und in Ihm. Christologische Forschungen und Perspektiven* (Freiburg: Herder), 19–75.

Grumel, V. (1921), 'L'iconologie de S. Theodore Studite', *Echos d'Orient* 20: 251–68.

Grumel, V. (1922), 'L'iconologie de S. Germain de Constantinople', *Echos d'Orient* 21: 165–79.

Louth, A. (2002), *St John Damascene: Tradition and Originality in Byzantine Theology* (Oxford: Oxford University Press).

Louth, A. (2003), *John of Damascus: Three Treatises on the Divine Images* (Crestwood, NY: St. Vladimir's Seminary Press).

Mansi, J. D. (ed.) (1960), *Sacrorum conciliorum nova et amplissima collectio* (Florence, 1758–98, reprinted Graz), Vol. XIII.

Mondzain-Baudinet, M.-J. (trans.) (1989), *De notre bienheureux père et archêveque de Constantinople Nicéphore discussion et refutation des bavardages ignares, athées et tout à fait creux de l'irreligieux Mamon contre l'Incarnation de Dieu et le Verbe notre Sauveur. Discours contre les iconoclastes* (Paris: Klincksieck).

Nichols, A. (1988), 'The *Horos* of Nicaea II: A Theological Evaluation', *Annuarium Historiae Conciliorum* 20: 171–81.

Parry, K. (1996), *Depicting the Word: Byzantine Iconophile Thought of the Eighth and Ninth Centuries* (Leiden: Brill).

Roth, C. P. (1981) 'Introduction', in Roth (trans.), St Theodore the Studite, *On the Holy Icons* (Crestwood, NY: St. Vladimir's Seminary Press).

Tanner, N. P. (ed.) (1990), *Decrees of the Ecumenical Councils*, 2 vols. (London: Sheed and Ward).

Travis, J. (1984), *In Defense of the Faith: The Theology of the Patriarch Nicephorus of Constantinople* (Brookline, Mass.: Hellenic College Press).

CHAPTER 12

···

THE ISLAMIC CHRIST

···

GABRIEL SAID REYNOLDS

ISLAMIC teaching is shaped by the conviction that God has communicated his will to humans through a series of prophets (Ar. *anbiya*' or *rusul*), a series that begins with Adam, includes Jesus, and ends with Muhammad. Prophets pass on divine revelation in two ways: first, they proclaim the very words of God which they receive from an angel (and which may be recorded in a scripture such as the Qur'an); second, since prophets are protected from error and sin, everything else they say and do sets an example—or *sunna*, in Arabic—for believers to imitate.

As regards incidental matters of religious practice or ceremony the message of these prophets may differ, yet as regards essential religious matters it is the same. From this perspective Islam is an eternal religion, the only religion ever willed by God. In Sura 3 the Qur'an proclaims: 'God's religion is *islam*' (Q 3. 19). In Arabic *islam* means 'submission', and this verse seems to mean that God desires all humans to be submissive to him. But inasmuch as *islam* was later taken as the name of Muhammad's religion, not a few Muslim scholars understand the verse to mean, 'God's religion is Islam'.

While all of the prophets brought the same essential (Islamic) message, Muhammad is nevertheless a prophet like no other. He is the last of the prophets (a doctrine supported with reference to Qur'an 33. 40, which calls Muhammad the 'seal' of the prophets), the one whom earlier prophets predicted. The scripture he brought, the Qur'an, rendered all earlier scriptures superfluous. His *sunna*—preserved in literary reports known as 'hadith'—replaced that of earlier prophets. On the importance of imitating Muhammad's *sunna*, the theologian and mystic Abu Hamid al-Ghazali (d. 1111) writes:

> Know that the key to happiness is to follow his *sunna* and to imitate the messenger of God—blessings and peace be upon him—in how he begins and end things, in how he moves or remains still, and even in the way he eats, stands, sleeps and speaks.
>
> (Ghazali, n.d.: 85)

Thus at the center of Islam is Muhammad, and all Islamic thought begins with the message he brought. Thus is true with Islamic thinking on Christ no less than with any other topic.

ISLAMIC TEACHING ON THE BIBLE

As for the Bible, most Muslim scholars consider it to be a corruption of Islamic revelations once given to Moses and Jesus. Picking up on Qur'anic vocabulary, Muslim scholars argue that God gave a divine scripture to Moses, a scripture like the Qur'an, known as the Tawrat (cf. Hebrew *torah*), and a scripture to Jesus, known as the Injil (cf. Greek *euangélion*). These scriptures were lost, or intentionally altered, and the Bible was written in their place. Thus Muslims generally do not think of the Bible as a book with the textual elements as known to Jews (Torah, Prophets, Writings) or to Christians (Old and New Testaments, Major and Minor Prophets, Pauline and Catholic Epistles, etc.). Instead they think of the Bible as a falsified vestige of a once pristine revelation.

This concept of scriptural falsification, known to Muslim scholars by the Arabic term *tahrif*, implies that the Qur'an is the only true scripture in existence today. The idea of *tahrif* emerged in part from Qur'anic passages which condemn Jews and Christians for hiding, misinterpreting, or fabricating divine revelation: 'Do not cover up the truth with falsehood and conceal the truth, for you know [it]' (Q 2. 42; cf. Q 2. 140, 146, 159, 174; 3. 71, 187); 'Those who were in error exchanged the declaration with one which they were not told' (Q 2. 59a; cf. Q 7. 162); 'Woe to those who write revelation with their hands and then say, "This is from God"' (Q 2. 79).

The hadith, which tend to reflect the sectarian milieu of a later period, include more specific declarations on the unreliability of the Bible. One well-known hadith exhorts Muslims not to trust the reports of Jews and Christians:

> Ibn ʿAbbas said, 'O Muslims? How do you ask the people of the Scriptures, though your Book (i.e. the Qur'an) which was revealed to His Prophet is the most recent information from Allah and you recite it, the Book that has not been distorted? Allah has revealed to you that the people of the scriptures have changed with their own hands what was revealed to them.'

> (Bukhari 1981: 3. 850)

Now this hadith also suggests that early Muslims were curious about the Bible (otherwise there would have been no point in warning them about it). In fact throughout Islamic history individual Muslim scholars—including Yaʿqubi (d. 897/8), Abu Hatim al-Razi (d. 934), and al-Biqaʿi (d. 1480)—have studied the Bible. Yet most Muslim scholars of the classical period, and still today, do not encourage believers to read the Bible (unless they do so for the sake of proselytizing Jews and Christians). On this question a fatwa promulgated on March 3, 2004, on *islamonline.net* (the website of the influential Egyptian Mufti Yusuf al-Qaradawi) explains:

> The Prophet [Muhammad] (peace and blessings be upon him) disclosed that *iman* [faith] necessitates belief in the previous Divine Books ... However, belief in the fact that Allah sent Books prior to the Qur'an does not imply that the extant books of the other religions are not corrupted. We Muslims believe in what was originally revealed to the prophets before Muhammad ... not in what remains of those revelations.

> (Hecker 2011: 41)

Yet if the Bible was corrupted, the Qur'an and the hadith do not explain *how* it became so. This matter was left to the speculation of later Muslim scholars such as 'Abd al-Jabbar (d. 1025), who discusses the origins of the New Testament in his work the *Critique of Christian Origins*. 'Abd al-Jabbar relates an account in which some of the first followers of Jesus ask their pagan Roman overlords to support them in a conflict that has broken out with the Jews. The Romans agree to do so provided that the followers of Jesus embrace Roman religious practices, and abandon those of Moses and Jesus. This condition caused a split among the followers of Jesus: those who refuse to take the Roman deal flee, taking the true scripture of Jesus (the 'Injil') with them; those who agree gather together to write a new book in its place, and thus the first Christian Gospel was composed ('Abd al-Jabbar 2010: 92–4).

Yet even Muslim scholars who do not have an explanation for the corruption of the Bible generally avoid relying on it as a source for their thought on Christ. Indeed, most classical Muslim scholars interpret the Qur'anic material on Jesus with a concern to distinguish, or better, distance, Islamic teaching on Christ from that of Christianity. In other words, the history of Islamic thought on Christ is fundamentally independent from the study of the Bible and the tradition of Christological thought of the Church.

JESUS IN THE QUR'AN

Instead the Islamic Christ is above all the product of Islamic reflection on the Qur'an, an Arabic work about two-thirds the length of the New Testament. The Qur'an is divided into 114 chapters, or Suras, which are organized (with some notable exceptions) from longer to shorter. While the exact date of its composition remains a matter of debate, the Qur'an is certainly the earliest Islamic text. The first Qur'anic manuscripts dates to the late seventh century (the traditional date of Muhammad's death is 632), while subsequent Islamic works date to the late eighth century. If some of those works, such as hadith collections, are presented as traditions passed down orally from Muhammad himself, these traditions often prove to be anachronistic, or reliant on material in the Qur'an. In other words, the Qur'an is a unique witness to an early stage of Islamic thought, a stage which predates the formation of standard Islamic doctrine.

It is telling, then, that the Qur'an shows an unusual concern with Jesus, including the circumstances and meaning of his virgin birth (Q 3. 45–59; 19. 16–36; 21. 91), the miracles he accomplished (Q 3. 49; 5. 110), and the crucifixion and his ascension to heaven (Q 4. 157–9; 5. 117). Indeed on several occasions the Qur'an seems to elevate Jesus above other prophets, as in Q 2. 253a:

> These messengers, some We have preferred over others. Of their number, there are some to whom God spoke and He raised some in rank. And We bestowed clear wonders upon Jesus son of Mary and strengthened him with the Holy Spirit ...
>
> (Q 2. 253a; all Qur'an translations are from Khalidi 2001)

According to Islamic tradition Muhammad proclaimed the Qur'an in western Arabia, first (AD 610–22) in the pagan city of Mecca, and then (AD 622–32) in Medina, a city with Arab converts to Islam and three important Jewish tribes. These cities, according to Islamic tradition, were far removed from significant Christian populations, even if individual Christians, or small groups of Christians, occasionally wandered by. Yet the Qur'an's frequent use of Christian traditions (including, in Sura 18, the Seven Sleepers of Ephesus and the Alexander Romance) suggests that the tradition is wrong on this point, and that the Qur'an's historical milieu was above all Christian.

A sign of the Qur'an's close conversation with Christianity is its association of Jesus with the Holy Spirit. The Qur'an mentions the Holy Spirit (in Qur'anic Arabic, *ruh al-qudus*, a form which reflects Syriac *ruha d-qudsha*) on four occasions. Three of these occasions (Q 2. 87, 153; 5. 110) involve Jesus. Elsewhere the Qur'an describes Jesus simply as 'a spirit from [God]' (Q 4. 171), and describes how he was conceived by God's spirit: 'Remember also she who preserved her virginity, and We breathed into her of Our Spirit, and made her and her son to be a wonder for mankind' (Q 21. 91). Yet if there is something distinctly Christian about the association of Christ with the Holy Spirit, the way in which the Qur'an presents this association suggests that it means to contradict Christian teaching. There is nothing here, for example, of John 20, where the resurrected Christ breathes upon the disciples and declares 'Receive the Holy Spirit'.

Indeed much of the Qur'an's material on Christ reflects a concern to use Christian tradition against Christians. For example, like Paul and Syriac Christian texts such as the *Cave of Treasures*, the Qur'an compares Christ to Adam. However, while Christian authors use this comparison to illustrate the divinity of Christ, the Qur'an seems to do so in order to illustrate his humanity: 'The likeness of Jesus in God's sight is like Adam. He created him of dust then said to him "Be!" and he was' (Q 3. 59). And whereas the *Cave of Treasures* has God command the angels to bow before Adam as a prophetic anticipation of the angelic prostration before Christ (an idea inspired in part by Philippians 2:6–11), the Qur'an includes the story of the angels' bowing to Adam (Q 2. 34; 7. 11–12; 15. 28–33; 17. 61–2; 18. 50; 20. 115–16; 38. 71–8), but makes this incident only a lesson on obedience to God's command.

In a similar way the Qur'an has Jesus create a bird from clay and breathe into it, bringing the bird to life (Q 3. 49; 5. 110). In Christian texts such as the Infancy Gospel of

Thomas this miracle is an allusion to the divine nature of Jesus; it puts him in the place of God, who created man from clay and brought him to life with His breath (Genesis 2:7). The Qur'an, however, relates that Jesus accomplished this miracle only 'by God's leave', and thus suggests that he was incapable of doing so on his own.

This sort of explicit transformation of Christian tradition suggests that the Qur'an means to make a conscious critique of Christian Christology. On the Qur'anic portrayal of Jesus Tarif Khalidi comments: 'Jesus is a controversial prophet. He is the only prophet in the Qur'an who is deliberately made to distance himself from the doctrines that his community is said to hold of him' (Khalidi 2001: 12). In other words, the Qur'an tells stories about Jesus not only in order to teach religious lessons, but also to teach a lesson about Jesus. In places it explicitly reprimands Christians for their teaching on Christ, as in Q 5. 75 (cf. Q 4. 171; 9. 21):

> Christ the son of Mary is only a messenger, and messengers have come and gone before him. His mother was a saintly woman and they both ate food. Consider how We make clear Our revelations to them, and then consider how they pervert the truth!
>
> (Q 5. 75)

Elsewhere the Qur'an has Christ himself explain that he is not to be worshiped:

> I confirm what lies before me of the Torah and to make licit for you some of what had been made illicit. I come to you with a sign from your Lord. So fear God and obey me. God is my Lord and your Lord; so worship Him, for here lies a path that is straight.
>
> (Q 3. 50–1; cf. Q 5. 72, 116–17; 61. 6)

The Qur'an's interest in distancing Christ from Christian doctrine reflects above all its teaching on God. The God of the Qur'an is a jealous God who insists above all that no one belittle Him by worshiping someone or something else. Indeed the association of someone or something else with God is the Qur'an's unforgivable sin: 'God forgives not that He be the associate of anyone, but forgives what is less than this to whomsoever He pleases' (Q 4. 48, 116). The jealousy of the Qur'an's God shapes passages on Christ, such as Q 4. 171:

> O People of the Book, do not be excessive in your religion. Do not say about God anything but the truth. The Christ Jesus son of Mary is indeed the prophet of God and his Word which He cast into Mary, and a spirit from Him. So believe in God and his messengers, and do not say: 'Three!' Desist, for this would be best for you. God in truth is One—glory be to Him, that He should have a child! To Him belongs what is in the heavens and what is on earth. God suffices as All-Worthy of trust.

Here the Qur'an does not offer a logical refutation of Christian doctrine, let alone an argument based on the Bible. Instead it implies that the things which Christians say belittle its God. To this it adds a threat: 'Desist, for this would be best for you'.

Now a Christian might contend that Christian doctrine does not belittle God. Christians, after all, do not argue that Christ is a second God, but rather that he is God incarnate, and indeed they maintain that the Incarnation is a manifestation of God's greatness. The Qur'an shows no concern for this sort of Christological argument, and little interest generally in the way that Christians articulate the doctrines of Trinity and Incarnation. Instead the Qur'an seems to attribute simplistic views to Christians, views which might be easily refuted. From this perspective the Qur'an's Christology is shaped by a concern with religious apologetics.

Telling the Story of a Muslim Christ

This concern with apologetics is evident as well in the presentation of Christ in later Islamic texts. An interest in religious apology explains the salient concern in early Islamic traditions to articulate the standing of Muhammad vis-à-vis Christ. For example, a hadith found in the collection of Bukhari (870) has Muhammad recount his ascension to heaven with the angel Gabriel, and his meeting with Jesus (and John) along the way:

> When we reached over the second heaven, I saw Yahya (i.e. John) and Jesus who were cousins. Gabriel said, 'These are John (Yahya) and Jesus, so greet them'. I greeted them and they returned the greeting saying, 'Welcome, O Pious Brother and Pious Prophet'!
>
> (Bukhari 1981: 4. 640)

This hadith makes Jesus (along with John) a brother to Muhammad, but it continues by describing Muhammad's ascension up through the levels of heaven, above Jesus and all other prophets, to the seventh level of heaven and, according to some versions, to the very throne of God. A second hadith makes proper Islamic belief in Muhammad and Christ a requirement for admission into paradise:

> The Prophet said, 'If anyone testifies that None has the right to be worshipped but Allah Alone Who has no partners, and that Muhammad is His Slave and His Apostle, and that Jesus is Allah's Slave and His Apostle and His Word which He bestowed on Mary and a Spirit created by Him, and that Paradise is true [cf. Q 4. 171], and Hell is true, Allah will admit him into Paradise with the deeds which he had done even if those deeds were few.'
>
> (Bukhari 1981: 4. 644)

Yet early Muslims were not only concerned with apologetics. They were also eager to tell their own story about Christ, as the Qur'an has little to say about his life or his character. This interest in telling the story of the Muslim Christ (or, as Tarif Khalidi names it, in proclaiming a 'Muslim Gospel') explains the spread of traditions about Jesus in collections of hadith (such as that of Bukhari, cited above), Qur'an commentaries, and historical chronicles (including those works known as 'Stories of the Prophets').

Many of these traditions are the product of the creative speculation of storytellers on a Qur'anic passage or turn of phrase. One of the best-known hadith on Jesus has the Prophet declare that Satan touches all children at the moment of their birth *except for Mary and Jesus*. This hadith might seem to work against the apologetical concerns of Muslims, inasmuch as it gives a privilege to Mary and Jesus that Muhammad does not share (Bukhari 1981: 4. 641; 6. 71). Indeed the hadith is not a product of apologetics at all, but rather of haggadic exegesis. It explains Q 3. 36, which has Mary's mother dedicate Mary to God, declaring: 'I seek refuge in You for her and her progeny from Satan' (Mary's 'progeny' is understood to be none other than Jesus). This hadith, meanwhile, became the source of later traditions which tell the story of the futile attempts of the devil (Iblis) to touch Jesus:

> Iblis tried to get at Jesus from above; but lo, the heads and shoulders of the angels reached the sky. He tried to get at him form under the earth; but lo, the feet of the angels were anchored firmly. He tried to enter between them, but they prevented him.
>
> (Tha'labi 2002: 644; cf. Tabari 1987: 115)

Many other early Islamic traditions on Jesus appear to be the stuff of haggadic exegesis. A passage in Sura 19 (Q 19. 30–3; cf. Q 3. 46) has Jesus speak, miraculously, as a child (a miracle known from the Infancy Gospel of Thomas). A tradition found in the *Stories of the Prophets* of Tha'labi (d. 1035) adds detail to this passage: 'When Mary brought Jesus to her people, they took stones and wanted to stone her. When Jesus spoke, they let her be. It was said that he did not speak any more until he had reached the level of other boys' (Tha'labi 2002: 646; cf. Tabari 1987: 120).

In Sura 3 the Qur'an has Jesus proclaim: 'I shall reveal to you what you eat' (Q 3. 49). A tradition in Tha'labi explains this proclamation with a long story about Jesus and a dishonest Jew who refuses to admit to that he has swallowed a loaf of bread (Tha'labi 2002: 661–3; the story ends with the earth opening up and swallowing the Jew). Such tales are evidently meant to be entertaining, yet some traditions also include elements meant to counter Christian teaching. This is the case with a tradition in Tha'labi meant to explain the Qur'an's reference to Jesus' creating a bird from clay (Q 3. 49; 5. 111):

> He specialized in bats because the bat is the most perfect of all the birds. It has breasts and teeth, gives birth and menstruates, and flies. [The Muslim scholar] Wahb said that Jesus' bird flew only as long as people were looking at it. When it passed out of sight it fell dead, to distinguish the work of mortal man from the work of God, and to teach that perfection belongs only to God.
>
> (Tha'labi 2002: 656)

Now in their concern to tell the story of an Islamic Christ, Muslim authors did not only weave tales with Qur'anic threads. They also looked to New Testament accounts (known to them mostly through oral transmission, and not from the New Testament itself), which they reshaped into Islamic traditions. For example, both Tha'labi and Tabari tell the story of the gifts of the magi given to the baby Jesus, a story not found in the Qur'an; Tha'labi has the magi explain that they have brought incense to Jesus because God will raise Jesus into heaven (Q 3. 55; 4. 156) as 'the smoke of incense enters heaven' (Tha'labi 2002: 644–5; Tabari 1987: 116). Tha'labi also retells the Gospel story of Peter's attempt to walk on water. However, he refers to Peter only as 'a short fellow', has him sink immediately, and has Jesus declare that God 'hates him' for trying to act like a prophet (Tha'labi 2002: 660).

The interest of early Muslims in both storytelling and religious competition with Christians is evident in traditions on the crucifixion. The point of departure for these traditions is Q 4. 157, which includes the declaration: '[The Israelites] killed him not, nor did they crucify him, but so it was made to appear to them (*shubbiha la-hum*).' Most Muslim scholars (but not all, cf. the tradition on Jesus' crucifixion and death in Tabari 1987: 122) see this declaration as a denial of Jesus' death, and explain the phrase *shubbiha la-hum* to mean that someone other than Jesus appeared to the Jews on the Cross. This explanation is found, among other places, in the commentary attributed to Muqatil b. Sulayman (d. 150/767). This commentary explains that Judas Iscariot was made to look like Jesus and crucified, a just punishment for his betrayal of a prophet (*Tafsir Muqatil*, n.d.: 1.420, on Q 4. 157).

In other Islamic crucifixion traditions Jesus asks his disciples for a volunteer to die in his place. When one of them (sometimes identified as Peter, as in Tabari 1987: 121) agrees to do so he is promptly changed into the appearance of his master. Jesus is then taken to heaven, while the faithful disciple is taken off to the Cross (see, e.g., Qummi, 1412/1991: 1.111, on Q 3. 55; Zamakhshari, 1365/1946: 1.586–7, on Q 4. 153–9; and Ibn Kathir, 1424/2004: 1.550, on Q 4. 156–9). For his part 'Abd al-Jabbar has a less fantastic explanation: as Judas is on his way to betray Jesus he meets a friend whom he thoughtlessly greets with a kiss. The Jewish guards following Judas grab this unsuspecting fellow and crucify him ('Abd al-Jabbar 2010: 72–5).

The teaching that Jesus escaped death on the Cross is connected to a teaching that he will return in the end times. After reporting various traditions on the crucifixion Tabari reports a tradition on Jesus' ascension. According to this tradition Jesus 'was given the wings of an angel', in heaven that he might fly around the divine throne until the moment of his return to earth (Tabari 1987: 122–3). The idea that Jesus will return to earth is in part a response to Q 43. 61, which describes Jesus as 'a portent of the Hour', and to Q 4. 159 ('Among the People of the Book none there are but shall believe in him before his death …'), often understood to mean that all Jews and Christians will accept the Islamic teaching on Jesus before he dies.

This understanding shapes the eschatological traditions on Jesus' return, one of the principal features of which is the report that he will destroy the symbols of Christianity, and bring all people into the fold of Islam. Tha'labi cites a tradition in which Muhammad himself reports these things about Jesus (and adds some suggestions on how to recognize Jesus upon his return):

> When you see [Jesus] you will recognize him, for he is a man of medium build, tending towards ruddiness and paleness, with lank hair, as if something had been dripped on it, not that moisture was poured on it. He will descend between two scepters and will break the cross, slay the pig, establish the head-tax, and make wealth abundant ... He will do battle with people about Islam until he destroys all the sects of his time except Islam, and prostration will be made to Allah along, the Lord of all beings. In his time, God will destroy the messiah of error, of lying [the anti-Christ], al-Dajjal. Security will spread in the Earth so that lions will graze with cattle, wolves with sheep. Boys will play with animals and they will not harm one another. Then he will remain on Earth for forty years. He will marry and have children, then he will die, and the Muslims will pray over him and bury him in Medina next to 'Umar.
>
> (Tha'labi 2002: 675–6; cf. Tabari 1408/1988: 3.289;
> cf. Qummi 1.165, on Q 4. 159; Ibn Kathir, 1.553, on Q 4. 159)

Such traditions help explain why a space is kept reserved in the Prophet's mosque in Medina for Jesus' tomb, something noted by the English explorer Richard Burton (1893: 1.325) during his undercover pilgrimage in the nineteenth century.

While the traditions on the crucifixion and return of Jesus reflect a concern with anti-Christian apologetics, other traditions (found mostly, although not exclusively, in works dedicated to asceticism or Sufism) involving Christ are concerned not with religious competition with Christians but rather with the moral reformation of Muslims. In these traditions Jesus becomes a spiritually enlightened master who teaches renunciation of the world:

> Jesus said, 'Blessed is he who guards his tongue, whose house is sufficient for his needs, and who weeps for his sins'.
>
> (Khalidi 2001: 51)

> Jesus said, 'O Disciples, which of you can build a house upon the waves of the sea?' They said, 'Spirit of God, who can do that?' He said, 'Beware the world and do not make it your abode'.
>
> (Khalidi 2001: 53; cf. Matthew 7:24–7)

> Jesus used to prepare food for his followers, then call them to eat and wait upon them, saying: 'this is what you must do for the poor'.
>
> (Khalidi 2001: 79; cf. John 13)

> The day that Jesus was raised to heaven, he left behind nothing but a woolen garment, a slingshot, and two sandals.
>
> (Khalidi 2001: 94)

A pig passed by Jesus. Jesus said, 'Pass in peace'. He was asked, 'Spirit of God, how can you say this to a pig?' Jesus replied, 'I hate to accustom my tongue to evil'.

(Khalidi 2001: 123)

Some of these traditions are related to the New Testament, yet they do not render the biblical material Islamic, or use biblical material against Christians. Such traditions are not meant to defend Islam or attack Christianity, but rather to convince Muslims to embrace a life of moral rigor.

The appearance of Jesus in these traditions seems to reflect a certain fascination with Jesus' celibacy. According to Islamic teaching other prophets married (some traditions have Jesus marry after his return to earth in the end times); indeed Islamic law forbids Muslims to consecrate themselves to a celibate life. Accordingly the report that Jesus was celibate must have suggested to many scholars that he had unusual qualities of auster-ity and self-mortification. The common epithet given to Jesus, 'Spirit of God' (related to Q 4. 171 and 21. 91), must have contributed to the idea that he favored the spirit over the body.

While some of the above traditions include biblical material, they do not reflect an interest in the Bible per se. This sort of interest is found, however, among exceptional Muslim authors. Both the Isma'ili Shi'ite Abu Hatim al-Razi (d. 934) and, centuries later, Biqa'i (d. 1480), argue that the Bible is a licit source of religious knowledge. The early historian Ya'qubi (d. 897/898) dedicates a section of his work to the biography of Jesus according to the New Testament. Ya'qubi describes the Gospel accounts in detail, including the nativity, the temptation of Jesus in the wilderness, and the Beatitudes. Now Ya'qubi employs phrases (such as 'according to what the Christians maintain' or 'as the Gospel authors state') meant to signal his intention only to recount the contents of the Bible, and not to affirm its veracity. Nevertheless it is noteworthy that he does not couch that recounting in a refutation of the Bible. Nor does he withhold details which contradict the Islamic story of Jesus. He describes, for example, the blood and water that flowed from the side of Jesus, and Mary Magdalene's vision of the risen Christ on Sunday morning at the tomb.

THE ISLAMIC CRITIQUE OF
CHRISTIAN CHRISTOLOGY

Most classical Muslim scholars were more interested in arguments which show why Christians are wrong about Christ. Works explicitly dedicated to the refutation of Christians (*radd 'ala l-nasara*) appear from almost the very beginnings of Islamic lit-erature. Perhaps the most important tradition of anti-Christian polemic consists of theological treatises. The tradition of Islamic theology (*kalam*) was from the beginning dedicated to the rational defense of Islam, and most Islamic theological treatises are not philosophically-minded reflections on God and His attributes in the light of revelation, but rather rational refutations of an opponent's doctrine or rational defenses of one's own. Treatises on Christianity are no exception.

Among the earliest extant anti-Christian theological treatises are those of the Zaydi Shi'ite al-Qasim b. Ibrahim al-Rassi (d. 860) and Abu 'Isa al-Warraq (d. c.861), a controversial figure accused of apostasy from Islam. Warraq's irreligious reputation led to the destruction of most of his works, but his refutation of Christians was preserved by the Jacobite Christian philosopher and theologian Yahya b. 'Adi (d. 972), who quotes Warraq's work in his response to it. In his anti-Christian polemic Warraq presents to the reader a series of logical strategies that can be used to demonstrate the irrationality of the Christian doctrines on the Trinity and the Incarnation. To this end he discusses Christian teaching on the death and resurrection of Christ:

> So say to them all: If the Messiah died, then who revived him after death? If they say: He revived himself, say to them: So the deceased revive themselves. But how can someone with no control, knowledge or power revive himself? If they say: Another revived him, they attest that some other than the Messiah revives the deceased ... but according to their principles it then follows that the Messiah was not divine and that the Divinity was another than him.
>
> (Warraq 2002: 121)

Warraq's question and answer style is typical as well in later theological refutations of Christianity, including those of Maturidi (d. 944), of the Mu'tazili 'Abd al-Jabbar in his *Mughni*, and of 'Abd al-Jabbar's Ash'ari contemporary Baqillani (d. 403/1013).

A second, and distinct, tradition of early Islamic anti-Christian polemic is centered instead on the validity of the Bible and the Qur'an, and on claims of miracles made by Christians and Muslims. In his *Kitab al-din wa l-dawla*, the Christian convert to Islam 'Ali al-Tabari (d. 240/855) argues that the Old Testament prophets, and Christ himself, predict the coming of Muhammad. Al-Jahiz (d. 868/69) contends in an anti-Christian letter (written at the request of the caliph al-Mutawakkil [r. 847–247/861]), that Christian teaching is confusing and Christians are confused: 'How can one succeed in grasping this doctrine, for if you were to question concerning it two Nestorians, individually, sons of the same father and mother, the answer of one brother would be the reverse of the other' (Jahiz, trans. Finkel, 1927: 333). Perhaps the most extraordinary work in this second, scripture-based, tradition of anti-Christian polemic is 'Abd al-Jabbar's *Critique of Christian Origins*. It argues, on the basis of biblical passages, that Jesus was a Muslim prophet. 'Abd al-Jabbar provides an Islamic key to reading the Bible.

A third tradition of early anti-Christian polemic is made of texts which describe debates between Christians and Muslims, or which purport to be the record of an exchange of controversial letters between them. Among these are a series of texts which purport to be records of an exchange between the Umayyad Caliph Umar II (r. 717–720) and the Byzantine emperor Leo III (r. 717–740), but which likely date to a later period (see Gaudeul 1984). A number of early Shiʿite texts recount stories in which one of the twelve Shiʿite imams (including ʿAli, cousin of the Prophet and first of the imams) masterfully refutes Christians in a public debate over Christ (see Bertaina 2011: 106–17, 171–6, 191–3).

Perhaps the best-known exchange of epistles is that which began with *A Letter to a Muslim Friend*, written by Paul of Antioch, bishop of Sidon (dates uncertain). Muslim responses to Paul's letter were written by the Egyptian al-Qarafi (d. 1285) and the famous Syrian jurist and polemicist Ibn Taymiyya (d. 1328). Paul's letter subsequently became the basis of a new apologetical letter in the fourteenth century, written by an anonymous Christian in Cyprus, who sent his letter to a Syrian Muslim named Ibn Abi Talib al-Dimashqi (d. 1327), and to the same Ibn Taymiyya. Both recipients wrote polemical responses to the Christian letter (see Ebied and Thomas 2005: 1–35) in which they counter a wide range of Christian apologetical arguments and suggest that Christian teaching is ridiculous. Their rhetoric is at times aggressive, at times sarcastic, and often humorous. At one point Dimashqi, feigning exasperation, exclaims:

> How can it be right for [Jesus] to be worshipped when he was a man and the Son of Man, and all his actions were the actions of a man in inner and outer make-up, growing, development, being nourished, sleeping, being drunk with wine, high spirits, fear, alarm, running away, hunger, thirst, learning lowly trades such as cloth dyeing, and so on?
>
> (Ebied and Thomas 2005: 383)

Dimashqi's rhetorically clever polemical arguments anticipate the manner in which modern Muslim apologists present the figure of Christ.

CHRIST IN MODERN ISLAMIC THOUGHT

If the modern Islamic representation of Christ is informed by classical sources, it is also distinguished by a new argument, namely that Jesus is a prophet whose character reflects one aspect of Islam only. The most distinctive example of this idea might be *Children of the Alley* (also translated under the title *Children of Gebelawi*), a 1959 Arabic novel by Nobel laureate Naguib Mahfouz (d. 2006). Therein Mahfouz tells the story of a Cairo neighborhood and three men who, one after another, deal with its problems through the years. The first of these men, Gabal ('mountain'—a reference to Sinai), punishes troublemakers in the neighborhood firmly and meticulously. The second, Rifaʿa (an allusion to the ascension of Jesus), seeks to resolve disputes by teaching lessons of forgiveness and compassion. The third, Qasim ('the divider'), is a perfect balance of the first two. *Children of the Alley* is an allegory which makes

Moses the prophet of law, Jesus, the prophet of mercy, and Muhammad the prophet of both.

The portrayal of Jesus as the prophet of (only) mercy and compassion draws on the traditions in mediaeval Islamic works which speak of Jesus as 'the spirit of God' and make him into an ascetic moral reformer. At the same time this portrayal is meant to make Jesus into something less than Muhammad, into a prophet who compensated for the way in which Moses emphasized the law, but who did not have the complete prophetic character of Muhammad. Only Muhammad perfectly integrated justice and mercy, and only Muhammad could be the final prophet whose example all future generations were to follow. A vivid example of this modern portrayal of Christ is found in the 2007 Iranian film of Nader Talebzadeh, *The Messiah*. Talebzadeh makes Jesus into a something like a Muslim hippie, a soft-spoken, long-haired wandering prophet who condemns Jewish leaders for their abuse of the law (*The Messiah* also includes two endings, one in which Jesus is crucified and one in which Judas, transformed into the likeness of Jesus, is crucified).

The modern period has also seen the founding of Islamic institutions dedicated to spreading Islam, and the rise of professional Islamic apologists, many of whom are dedicated to making the case that Christian teaching on Christ is unacceptable. This task has led to an unprecedented level of studies which are meant to show how the Bible can be read with an Islamic key, or that the Bible cannot be trusted because it is incoherent or offensive (or both). The Indian Rahmatullah Kairanawi (d. 1891) is still remembered with reverence by Muslims concerned with proselytism (*da'wa*) for his 1854 public debate in India with the German Protestant Karl Gottlieb Pfander in Agra and for his book on the Bible: *Izhar al-haqq* ('The Exposition of Truth').

The South African Ahmed Deedat (d. 2005) is a household name in much of the Islamic world because of his debates with numerous Protestant missionaries. Deedat wrote a wide range of apologetic booklets (including 'Is the Bible God's Word?', 'Desert Storm: Christ in Islam', and 'Crucifixion or Cruci-fiction?'), which resemble the tracts of Christian missionaries in form, but which are meant to show that those missionaries are all wrong. The approach of Deedat (and, more recently, that of the Indian Zakir Naik) is distinctive inasmuch as it privileges apologetics above the development of a coherent doctrine rooted in a traditional Islamic science. Deedat, for example, mocks the Bible on the one hand as a lewd and indecent book (most famously in a debate with Jimmy Swaggert). On the other hand he cites the Bible approvingly for its predictions of Muhammad, or for its signs that Islam is the true religion. To this end he cites Romans:

'For as many as are led by the Spirit of God, they are the *sons of God*' (Romans 8:14).
     Can't you see that in the language of the Jew, every righteous person, every Tom, Dick and Harry who followed the Will and Plan of God, was a 'Son of God'. It was a metaphorical descriptive term commonly used among the Jews.

(Deedat 1983: 28)

In a footnote here, Deedat comments regarding Paul's statement in this verse: 'Let us give the devil his due. He is talking sense here.'

The concern of Muslims in the modern period with apologetics helps explain the enthusiastic response of the publication of the Gospel of Barnabas, an Italian text which dates from late mediaeval Europe and which recounts the story of Jesus' life from an Islamic perspective. For example, it tells the story of a leper who longs to be healed by Jesus, and calls out to him 'I know that you, Lord, are a man, but a holy one of the Lord, so pray to God, and he will give me health' (*Gospel of Barnabas*, ch. 222; Ragg 1907). The work (perhaps written by a Spanish Muslim who fled from the Reconquista to Venice) is attributed to Barnabas, no doubt because in Acts Barnabas (an 'apostle' [Acts 14:14]) first acts as Paul's sponsor (Acts 9:26–7) but then later clashes with him before the two part ways (Acts 15:35–9). The anti-Pauline message of the *Gospel of Barnabas* is explicit in the conclusion, when Barnabas warns those (i.e., Christians) who have been led astray by Paul: 'Others preached, and yet preach, that Jesus is the Son of God, among whom Paul is deceived. But we, as much as I have written, that preach we to those who fear God, that they may be saved in the last day of God's Judgment. Amen' (*Gospel of Barnabas*, ch. 222; Ragg 1907). Although the *Gospel of Barnabas* was first published only in 1907, it has been translated into most Islamic languages, and is available in most Islamic bookstores, something that cannot be said for the canonical Gospels.

Indeed in the Islamic world it is unusual for educational or religious institutions to encourage Muslims to read the Bible, and most Muslims are unfamiliar with its contents. This unfamiliarity helps explain in part the great success of *The Genius of Christ*, published in 1955 by the prolific Egyptian Muslim author Abbas Aqqad. While Aqqad defends Islamic teaching on Christ therein, he also introduces his Muslim readers to the biblical story of Christ. A similar interest in the Christ of the Gospels shapes *City of Wrong*, published one year earlier by another Egyptian Muslim author, Muhammad Kemal Hussein. Hussein tells the story of Jesus' last day from the perspective of the characters of the Gospel accounts who knew him. While Hussein does not include an account of the crucifixion itself, neither does he deny it. Moreover, he shows a distinct interest in problems which arise from the Gospels. For example, he has Caiaphas, in an internal dialogue, struggle to find fault with the way in which Jesus dealt with the woman caught in adultery (John 8), an interesting example inasmuch as the standard Islamic punishment for an adulterous woman is stoning.

Thus Muslim interest in the biblical presentation of Christ has risen dramatically in the modern period. Some Muslims have found in the Bible a new tool for the defense of Islam. Others have found therein a new material with which to tell the story of an Islamic Christ.

Suggested Reading

'Abd al-Jabbar (2010); Khalidi (2001); Michel (1985).

BIBLIOGRAPHY

'Abd al-Jabbar (2010), *The Critique of Christian Origins*, ed. S. K. Samir, trans. G. S. Reynolds (Provo, Ut.: BYU Press).

Aqqad, 'Abbas (2001), *The Genius of Christ*, trans. F. P. Ford (Binghamton, NY: Global Publications).

Bertaina, D. (2011), *Christian and Muslim Dialogues: The Religious Uses of a Literary Form in the Early Islamic Middle East* (Piscataway, NJ: Gorgias).

al-Bukhari (1981), *The Translation of the Meanings of Sahih al-Bukhari*, trans. M. M. Khan (Medina: Dar al-Fikr) [references are to volume and number of hadith].

Burton, R. (1893). *Pilgrimage to al-Madinah and Meccah* (London: Tylston and Edwards).

Deedat, A. (1983), *Christ in Islam* (Minna, Nigeria: Islamic Education Trust).

Ebied, R. and D. Thomas (ed. and trans.) (2005), *Muslim–Christian Polemic During the Crusades: The Letter from the People of Cyprus and Ibn Abi Talib al-Dimashqi's Response* (Leiden: Brill).

Gaudeul, J.-M. (1984), 'The Correspondence between Leo and 'Umar: 'Umar's Letter Re-discovered', *Islamochristiana* 10: 109–57.

al-Ghazali (n.d.), *Kitab al-arba'in fi usul al-din* (Cairo: Al-Maktaba al-Tijariyya al-Kubra).

Hecker, D. (2011), 'Fatwa aus dem Internet', *Zeitschrift des Instituts für Islamfragen* 1: 41–2.

Hussein, M. K. (1959), *City of Wrong*, trans. K. Cragg (New York: Seabury Press).

Ibn Kathir (1424/2004), *Tafsir*, ed. Muhammad Baydun (Beirut: Dar al-Kutub al-'Ilmiyya).

Ibn Taymiyya (1984), *A Muslim Theologian's Response to Christianity, Ibn Taymiyya's Al-Jawab al-Sahih*, trans. T. Michel (Delmar, NY: Caravan Books).

al-Jahiz, Abu 'Uthman 'Amr (1962), 'Fi al-Radd 'ala al-Nasara', in J. Finkel (ed.), *Three Essays of al-Jahiz* (Cairo: Salafiyah Press) [partially translated and introduced in J. Finkel, 'A Risala of al-Jahiz', *Journal of the American Oriental Society* 47 (1927): 311–34].

Khalidi, T. (2001), *The Muslim Jesus: Sayings and Stories in Islamic Literature* (Cambridge, Mass.: Harvard University Press) [citations of sayings or stories are to Khalidi's translations; precise references to Islamic sources are found following the translation].

Michel, T. (1985), *A Muslim Theologian's Response to Christianity: Ibn Taymiyya's al-Jawab al-sahih* (Delmar, NY: Caravan Books) [an introduction to, and an abridged translation of, the fourteenth-century anti-Christian polemic of the influential Muslim scholar Ibn Taymiyya].

Muqatil b. Sulayman (ed.) (n.d.), 'Abdallah Muhammad al-Shihata* (Cairo: Mu'assasat al-Halabi).

al-Qummi, Abu l-Hasan (1412/1991), *Tafsir* (Beirut: Mu'assasat al-A'llami li-l-Matbu'at).

Ragg, L. and L. Ragg (trans.) (1907), *Gospel of Barnabas* (Oxford: Clarendon Press).

al-Tabari, Abu Ja'far (1408/1988), *Jami' al-bayan fi ta'wil al-Qur'an*, ed. Muhammad 'Ali Baydun (Beirut: Dar al-Fikr) [references are to part and page].

al-Tabari, Abu Ja'far (1987), *The History of al-Tabari, Volume 4: The Ancient Kingdoms*, trans. M. Perlmann (Albany, NY: State University of New York Press).

al-Tabari, 'Ali b. Rabban (1982), *Kitab al-Din wa-l-dawla*, ed. 'Adil Nuwayhid (Beirut: Dar al-Afaq al-Jadida); English trans.: *The Book of Religion and Empire*, trans. A. Mingana (Manchester: Manchester University Press, 1922).

al-Tha'labi, Abu Ishaq (2002), 'Ara'is al-majalis fi qisas al-anbiya' or 'Lives of the prophets', trans. W. M. Brinner (Leiden: Brill).

Thomas, D. (ed. and trans.) (2008), *Christian Doctrines in Islamic Theology* (Leiden: Brill).

al-Warraq, Abu Isa (1992), *Anti-Christian Polemic in Early Islam: Abu 'Isa al-Warraq's 'Against the Trinity'*, ed. and trans. D. Thomas (Cambridge: Cambridge University Press).

al-Warraq, Abu Isa (2002), *Early Muslim Polemic Against Christianity: Abu 'Isa al-Warraq's 'Against the Incarnation'*, ed. and trans. D. Thomas (Cambridge: Cambridge University Press).

Ya'qubi, Ahmad b. Abi Ya'qub (1379/1960), *Ta'rikh Ya'qubi* (Beirut: Dar Sadir).

al-Zamakhshari, Muhammad (1365/1946), *Al-Kashf 'an haqa'iq ghawamiḍ al-tanzil*, ed. Muhammad Husayn Ahmad (Cairo: Matba'at al-Istiqama).

CHAPTER 13

···

CHRISTOLOGY

The Cur Deus Homo

···

DAVID S. HOGG

JUST over 500 years ago, Matthias Grünewald completed the *Isenheim Altarpiece*. This is probably among Grünewald's most famous works in which John the Baptist is depicted pointing to Christ as he hangs on the Cross. Among the points worthy of comment is the fact that Grünewald was satisfied to let the anachronism of John the Baptist standing next to the dying Christ remain because the purpose was not to convey chronology or a snapshot in time, but to make a theological point. John, the last and greatest prophet not only directed attention to Christ, but directed attention away from himself. This desire is summed up for Grünewald in the biblical citation he includes from John, 'He must increase, but I must decrease'.

What was true for John the Baptist is true for all who come after him in believing Jesus is the Messiah. We point to Jesus. Christians do this in many ways, and one is through the doctrines we formulate and profess. Presently, we are concerned with the Christology of Anselm of Canterbury in his *Cur Deus Homo*. This seminal addition to the Church's unending task of refining theology in changing contexts has received as much adulation as detraction. There are three well-trodden areas of dispute and disagreement that deserve mention for those interested in grappling with Anselm's Christology.

CENTRAL ISSUES OF CONTENTION

···

First, Jasper Hopkins, while adding much to our understanding of Anselm, has argued that the *Cur Deus Homo* is indebted to the mediaeval feudal context. His view diminishes the abiding significance of Anselm's theology of the atonement (Hopkins 2007 [1972]: 197–8). Protagonists can be found arguing both sides of this both before and after Hopkins' articulation of this concern (Cohen 2004). The most convincing rejection of this criticism remains in John McIntyre's classic *St. Anselm and his Critics: A Reinterpretation of the* Cur Deus Homo (McIntyre 1954).

Second, a significant refutation of the *Cur Deus Homo* was launched by Gustav Aulén in his seminal work, *Christus Victor* (Aulén 1978). According to Aulén, Anselm veered from the orthodox explanation of the atonement that had been set out by the Church Fathers who had emphasized the cosmic drama of redemption that was resolved through Christ's ransom. Despite a positive reception, Aulén's argument has not fared so well over the long term. As numerous theologians have pointed out, Aulén's narrow reading of the Church Fathers neglected to account for the multiplicity of explanations they gave for the atonement (e.g., freedom from sin, establishing the new covenant, penal substitution, reconciliation, etc.), to say nothing of the multifaceted presentation of the atonement in Scripture. Furthermore, despite Aulén's insistence that Luther reoriented the Church to this so-called classic view of the atonement, interpreters of Luther have not always agreed with Aulén's presentation of Luther's view (Letham 1993). In his defense, it should be acknowledged that both Scripture and the Fathers address atonement as Jesus' victory over Satan, even if this perspective is not as dominant as Aulén contends.

Third, some theologians have struggled with the idea that God should demand satisfaction from sinful humanity to the point that his only son should be sacrificed in such a gruesome and unseemly manner (Gorringe 1996), amounting to divine child abuse (LaChance 2004). This criticism has been tied to the foregoing point that Anselm veered away from the Church's position by accentuating satisfaction. It seems inevitable that an emphasis on satisfaction, perhaps influenced by a mediaeval feudal society, should lead to a portrayal of God as ruthless and vengeful (Noble 2012: 50–9). David Bentley Hart, among others, has cogently and carefully pointed out that such a reading has failed to appreciate Anselm on his own terms. What lies at the heart of Anselm's atonement theology is not law or vengeance, but grace (Hart 1994: 341). This is not to suggest that Anselm has offered the final word on the atonement, but that he advanced the Church's understanding and more gratitude than criticism is warranted.

A litany of theologians throughout the centuries have both built upon the foundation laid by Anselm and interacted with the tenets of his argument. Thomas Aquinas draws on Anselm when he states that Christ's death was both necessary and the best means by which humanity could be delivered from sin (*ST* III, q.46, a.1; Anselm 1998: 276–9). Duns Scotus engages the *Cur Deus Homo*, but this time in disagreement. Scotus' quarrel with Anselm is twofold. First, he disagrees that the offense cause by humanity is infinite, regardless of the nature of the one against whom the offense was given. Directly following this first point, Scotus believes that not all works are owed to God, and thus some of them can be applied to the satisfaction we must give God. Scotus contends that Christ's atoning work was not of infinite value because it was not born out of free will, but that is not a problem because human guilt is not infinite and we all have the ability to add to the work of Christ through our works (Cross 1999: 129–32).

Perhaps the most famous mediaeval theologian to interact with Anselm's theology of the atonement is Peter Abelard. This debate is fraught with difficulty. The difficulty is not so much in the intricacies of the arguments, but in the history of interpretation. The work of Hastings Rashdall has influenced the way many have understood Abelard's position (Rashdall 1919). Unfortunately, Rashdall was more interested in using ancient sources to support his own view of the atonement than in reading them carefully (Rayner 2012). Many have followed Rashdall's interpretation that Abelard did not hold to a satisfaction or substitutionary view of the atonement; rather, he espoused an exemplary view. This interpretation rests on reading a long excursus in Abelard's commentary on Romans where he says that believers are spurred on to greater obedience as they are inspired by Christ's example (Abelard 1969: 117–18). The misunderstanding comes when this comment is read out of context. The careful reader will note that Abelard spends no little time at the beginning of the commentary affirming the necessity of Christ's death and resurrection as the only means of salvation. Abelard held to what we now call an objective view of the atonement. The footnote he later adds should be understood within this context. Abelard's point is not that redemption is effected in people when they are inspired by Christ's example, but that Christians, who already have the Holy Spirit operating in their life, should be all the more inspired to live obediently when they consider the sacrifice and cost of their salvation accomplished and applied at the Cross and in the empty tomb. Abelard's point in this excursus is not to address the move from unbeliever to believer, but to stress the ongoing transformative work effected in the believer by their ever growing love and appreciation for what Christ has done on their behalf.

Every reader of the *Cur Deus Homo* must bear in mind that Anselm never intended his work be the *locus* of redemption, but, to extend the analogy with Grünewald, a long tapering finger *pointing* to the Savior who *is* redemption (Sumner 2013: 34–5). There is a fine line between demanding great care in formulating an orthodox Christology and recognizing that the doctrine itself does not impart salvation. Christ saves, Christology does not. If the great achievement of the *Cur Deus Homo* is that it ignited debate about doctrinal formulation or spurred on disagreements over which atonement paradigm is most foundational, then we have missed his point entirely.

THEOLOGICAL METHOD

The *Cur Deus Homo*, like the much contested *Proslogion*, is a work in which faith provides the context in which reason operates. Faith and reason in Anselm's thought were neither a dichotomy to be reconciled nor dialogue partners needing compromise. Anselm's theological method guided by the principle of *fides quaerens intellectum* is no less operational in the *Cur Deus Homo* than it was years before in the *Proslogion*. How else could he take up the challenge of talking about atonement through Christ, *remoto christo*? Christology does not begin *tabula rasa* and proceed on the basis of reason anymore than the existence and nature of God can be argued that way. Granted, Anselm may not have been as keenly self-conscious about his presuppositions; nevertheless, he was aware of the necessity of grounding his theology in the immanent deposit of revelation delivered by a transcendent God. The theological method that gives rise to *fides quaerens intellectum* rests on the conviction that Christian doctrine lives in the tension between the immanent and the transcendent. Faith is possible because it is reasonable, which is why probing the rationality of faith is vital; yet faith is also plausible because its divine object lies beyond human reason in the realm of the ineffable.

The *remoto christo* principle in the *Cur Deus Homo* is less a statement about the rationality of Christology and the atonement than it is a conviction that when faith is the presupposition of reason, the task of doctrinal formulation and expression (the immanent) is placed in right relationship to the object of that doctrine (the transcendent). Anselm's primary concern is not that he should find a single way to explain the atonement, but that he should find another way to explain the atonement. His students were capable of rehearsing accepted doctrines and substantiating them with scriptural support and ancient witnesses. What they were less adept at doing, it would seem, was translating that knowledge to a world not their own. In the *Cur Deus Homo*, Anselm takes up the mantle of pastor in the Pauline sense of doing the work of an evangelist (cf. 2 Tim. 4:5).

That this is his immediate intention is clear from the Preface in which he states that the work is divided into two parts and both parts are directed towards those who do not believe. Such a work is not, however, devoid of utility to the believer, as he states in his commendation of the work to Pope Urban II, since whenever reasons are given to elucidate the faith already held, they become nourishment to those with 'cleansed hearts' (Anselm 1998).

Anselm's interest in relating reason to faith has led to a very long tradition, particularly in the last century or so, of considering how he fits into a larger discussion of the connection of faith and reason. There are no signs of this conversation ending (Sweeney 2012), but over the last couple of decades this same material in Anselm has undergone renewed scrutiny with respect to its relation to contexts beyond Western Europe. What if Anselm's reference to faith and reason, especially in the second part of the *Cur Deus Homo* where he says, 'the supposition is made that nothing were known about Christ', is a reference to people belonging to a different faith? Could Anselm have had in mind Muslims or, more plausibly, given what he says at the end of the *Cur Deus Homo*, Jews? Even while the *Cur Deus Homo* redirected thinking about the atonement in a number of ways within the Church, is it possible that he was also prodding Christian thinking to take a multi-faith world more seriously?

The *Cur Deus Homo* as Apologetic

The literature on this facet of the *Cur Deus Homo* is growing (Sweeney 2012: 277), but not large in comparison to other areas of response to Anselm's atonement theology, and there is disagreement over how much Anselm might have known of Islamic belief or to what degree he cared to engage Jewish tradition. A consensus on this subject lies in the future. To date, the easier issue to address is the relationship of the *Cur Deus Homo* to the Jewish context. Despite beginning his work with a rather bland reference to refuting the objections of 'unbelievers' (Anselm 1998: 261), he ends the discourse with Boso thanking Anselm for providing an argument 'which would satisfy not only Jews, but even pagans' (Anselm 1998: 355). It is curious that Anselm should have differentiated at the end what he left generic at the beginning. Anselm begins by noting that the subject of the necessity of the incarnation, death, and resurrection of Christ is not only one with which unbelievers have struggled, but also one which has caught the attention of believers as well as the learned and unlearned (Anselm 1998: 265). It appears that Anselm opens his investigation with the broadest of audiences in mind. That the pagans to which Anselm refers at the end, and at other places throughout the *Cur Deus Homo*, may include Muslims, though not only Muslims, is a point to which we will return; but to begin with, we will pick up the more well-trodden path of the relationship between the *Cur Deus Homo* and Jewish influence.

A JEWISH CONTEXT?

Anna Sapir Abulafia is well known for her work on Christian–Jewish relations in the mediaeval period, and though much of her work focuses on social, political, and economic contexts, when dealing with the theological aspect of this interfaith dynamic, she has noted that Anselm's *Cur Deus Homo* is an important theological work (Abulafia 1992). Following R. W. Southern's assessment, Abulafia argues that Gilbert Crispin's popular work of the time, *Disputatio Iudei et Christiani*, borrowed ideas from Anselm even before he managed to finish the *Cur Deus Homo* (Abulafia 1992: 24). Abulafia contends that, 'Jewish rejection of Christianity may well have stimulated the composition of the *Cur Deus Homo*', but that the unbelievers to which Anselm refers, 'are not specifically Jews and pagans, and that the *Cur Deus Homo* was not, in the first instance, addressed to them' (Cohen 1999: 178). G. R. Evans had written much earlier that 'when Anselm refers to the *infideles* in the *Cur Deus homo* he means those who dispute the doctrine of the redemption: he gives no other details of their opinions, because he intends to meet the objections of every dissident on this point' (Evans 1980: 144).

It seems from these arguments that Anselm was not particularly interested in debating Jews, per se. Jeremy Cohen, who is not entirely convinced by Abulafia's position, offers the explanation that if Anselm was writing against Jewish belief he probably conceived of this position in a stylized manner and in conjunction with a larger compendium of convictions and attitudes. Whether intentionally or not, by the late eleventh century, argues Cohen, Jewish arguments against an orthodox Christology may have been folded into a larger set of refutations leveled against Christian theology (Cohen 1999: 178–9). Thus, Anselm has no need to identify Jews specifically in his introduction but, on reflection at the end of his work, he notes how much of what he has said could apply to an apologetic against the Jews. Consequently, the many-pronged argument given for the Incarnation and atonement were deemed broad enough to cover the gamut of popular unbelieving positions, yet sufficiently detailed to prove helpful against specific iterations of unbelief. Such a position comports well with the idea that Anselm early identified that the question why God became a man is a preoccupation of all sorts of people (unbelievers, believers, learned, and unlearned), including Jews.

F. B. A. Asiedu maintains two salient points. First, that Anselm was the one to borrow from Gilbert's *Disputatio Iudei et Christiani*, rather than the other way around as Abulafia believes; second, that Anselm had Jews specifically and intentionally in mind when he wrote the *Cur Deus Homo*, and not just a distant, stylized version of Jewish refutations as Cohen asserts. With over nine hundred years past since Gilbert and Anselm wrote their works, adjudicating this disagreement is not straightforward. In favor of Asiedu's first concern, though, is that Gilbert's work was published in late 1092 or early 1093, which predates the time Anselm likely began writing his *Cur Deus Homo*. Furthermore, Anselm's interest in Jewish objections to Christology is evident in his earlier work, *On the Incarnation of the Word* (Anselm 1998: 238; Asiedu 2001: 534). In light of the known presence and active debates between Jews and Christians at Westminster where Anselm visited Gilbert, to say nothing of the fact that these two were good friends, it is reasonable to assume that Anselm was neither simply folding Jewish objections in with a larger group of arguments against Christology, nor that his reference to unbelievers at the beginning of the *Cur Deus Homo* or expressly to Jews at the end, should be taken at less than face value. This interpretation of Anselm based on external evidence is further corroborated by what we read from the pen of his companion Eadmer.

It is no secret that Eadmer sought to make William Rufus look as evil as possible in his *Historia Novarum in Anglia*, and for this reason we should be careful about any inferences we draw from his descriptions of William's beliefs and behaviors. Still, there is a noteworthy point that can be drawn from two stories in this polemicized work. The first story is about a group of Jews who asked King William to help convince Jewish converts to Christianity to return to the faith of their fathers. William agreed to do this, but for a price (Eadmer 1964: 103). A second story is like the first, except that it has to do with a single family rather than a group (Eadmer 1964: 104–5). In a work intended to denigrate Rufus, Eadmer reveals a rare glimpse of compassion. Surely this description more closely approximates the reality of mediaeval Jewish experience. That is, that while attacks were being perpetrated, some, even at the highest levels, sought to act kindly and with at least a modicum of concern for their fellow countrymen. As Asiedu points out, Anselm's much more temperate and compassionate approach in the *Cur Deus Homo* is striking. Anselm is not afraid of hard questions, and treats them seriously and carefully. There is no anger or frustration in him, but a genuine desire to persuade, convince, and convert (Asiedu 2001: 544–6). Anselm was no quixotic figure opposing fearsome foes of fancy. As any monk worth his station knows, the consequences of unbelief are no trifling matter. The *Cur Deus Homo* was no Christology for a general audience, but a serious attempt to address real questions from real unbelievers, and it is to a second type of unbeliever that we must now turn.

THE PAGAN CONTEXT

When Anselm was writing his *Cur Deus Homo* there was rapid change on several fronts, and these shifts may have had more of an impact on Anselm's thought and work than has been realized (Asiedu 2001: 531).

In 1095 Pope Urban II called the Council of Claremont at which he officially launched the First Crusade. Anselm was not present at that council, sending Boso, his interlocutor for the *Cur Deus Homo*, as representative (Southern 1990: 203). Little attention has been given to the overlap between Anselm's life and the First Crusade, though we must take care not to overplay it. The primary reason for neglecting this context is that Anselm wrote so little that clearly reflects an interest or comment on the crusades. There are, however, significant hints about this.

In a letter to a young man named William, Anselm implores him not to travel to Jerusalem and fight (Anselm 1990–4, vol. 1: 278–81). In mounting his case, Anselm declares that,

> it is to wickedness and wicked deeds that you are hastening with such fondness, my beloved. It is to wickedness and wicked crimes that your impetuosity for seething worldly destruction is dragging you, my longed for friend. For the bloody confusion of wars is wickedness; the proud ambition of worldly vanity is wickedness; the insatiable greed for hollow honors and hollow riches is wickedness.

Although this letter was written in the spring of 1086, before the First Crusade as a serious papal directive was a rumor, Anselm's opinion of war and pilgrimage to Jerusalem is revealing. Is it any wonder he did not travel to the Council of Claremont in 1095, but sent a student in his place? Anselm finds war distasteful at best, and sinful at worst. It does not matter to him that this young man was traveling to the holy city of Jerusalem. The purpose was inexcusable, and the activity abominable. Lest we think that Anselm is speaking about war in general and abstract terms, it is worth noting that toward the end of the letter he beseeches William to 'abandon that Jerusalem which is now a vision not of peace but of tribulation, and the treasures of Constantinople and Babylon now being pillaged by cruel hands …' (Anselm 1990–4, vol. 1: 280). Terse though this description may be, it implies that Anselm was not arguing against war in a generic sense, but with a knowledge of current events in Palestine. These were the events that led up to the First Crusade. It appears that William's brother had joined an expedition to aid the Byzantine Empire in their clash with Islamic-Turkish armies that had captured Jerusalem and were continuing to press their advantage. By 1086 the situation had become desperate (Southern 1990: 169). Anselm may have despised warfare and had little appreciation for the First Crusade, but it is short-sighted to conclude from this that his knowledge of Islam was negligible and played no part in his thinking. Not only is it clear that Anselm had a degree of awareness about the wider world around him, we cannot afford to overlook the fact that Boso was his representative at Clarement. Given that the *Cur Deus*

Homo was not finished until 1098, and that, presumably, most of it was written after 1095 (it having been started no earlier than 1094) (Vaughn 2012: 107), and that Boso helped in writing the book and is the only named interlocutor in all of Anselm's works, and given that Boso had direct knowledge of the Christian–Islamic situation in Palestine on account of his presence at Claremont, we should take great care before assuming that references in the *Cur Deus Homo* to unbelievers were either abstract (that is, an unbeliever living in Western Europe/stylized as per above) or only describing Jews.

After the First Crusade had begun, Anselm wrote another letter, this time to the bishop of Salisbury (Anselm 1990–4, vol. 1: 126–7). We do not learn anything about Anselm's knowledge of Islam from this letter, but we do find the same sentiments about war and the Crusade. It appears that the Abbot of Cerne had purchased a ship and persuaded other monks to travel with him to Jerusalem so that they could join the effort. This action is condemned in strong terms. The Abbot, 'should not be permitted to roam around so inordinately or to send his monks or to go himself to Jerusalem—indeed to confusion and damnation'. Although this decree came from the Archbishop, it had the added authority of both king and pope. On its own, this information may appear to be little more than an interesting footnote to contemporary events, but as part of a larger nexus of clues that point to Anselm's awareness of international affairs, a cumulative case can be made for the relevance of external factors in interpreting what is meant by 'unbelievers' in the *Cur Deus Homo*.

There is also a group of letters written to and from Anselm in the years immediately following the successful completion of the First Crusade. In these letters, we discover that Anselm wrote to King Baldwin I of Jerusalem as a friend.

> Mindful of the great love and generosity shown to me by your father and mother and their children I do not know how to express in writing how much I rejoice about the grace of God which he has revealed in your brother and you by choosing you for that honor.
>
> (Anselm 1990–4, vol. 2: 210)

Even allowing for Anselm's usual florid language that may give us an unintentionally inflated impression of the relationship he enjoyed with the family, he is still able to write to Baldwin as a friend. At the end of the letter, Anselm commends its bearer to Baldwin's service as a mutual friend who was well known to Baldwin's family and had spent a long time serving in Anselm's court (Anselm 1990–4, vol. 2: 210, 62–3, note 3). Not long after this missive, Anselm received a letter from Hugh, archbishop of Lyon, wishing to thank him for his prayers while he took a pilgrimage to Jerusalem and to express his eagerness to tell him about his travels. Contemporary with this correspondence, Anselm had to deny a request by Diacus, bishop of Santiago di Compostella, who had requested that soldiers be sent to help with the armed struggle against the Saracens (Anselm 1990–4, vol. 2: 261). Just prior to this request, Anselm received a letter from his brother-in-law informing him of his desire to go on pilgrimage to Jerusalem in the wake of the First Crusade (Anselm 1990–4, vol. 2: 262–3, 268–9).

We should also pay more attention to his whereabouts and activities during his first exile. The details of Anselm's departure from the tyrannical and ungodly oppression of William Rufus are well documented in Eadmer's accounts, as well as in more modern biographies and histories. Anselm finished his *Cur Deus Homo* while in Italy. He visited Rome and Capua and, most importantly, attended the Council of Bari in 1098. It would be very odd indeed if Anselm lived in these places during the First Crusade and never thought about Christian–Muslim dialogue, especially when we consider that Bari was among the key cities through which crusaders passed. It is this time in exile and the potential influence it had on Anselm's view of the world that Asiedu brings out through looking more closely at Eadmer's account of Anselm's movements during this time (Asiedu 2001: 542–8).

All these events and conversations show us that Anselm was aware of the wider world in which he lived, especially as it pertained to Islamic presence and influence. We also see how much the rest of Western Europe was aware of the situation in Jerusalem, which makes it all the more plausible that Anselm was neither ignorant nor uninterested in developments and interactions between Christians and Muslims. This context makes Anselm's statements all the more enticing, that he wrote the *Cur Deus Homo* in response to a request, and that he finished it hastily and left much unsaid that he would have liked to include. We will, in all likelihood, never know exactly what prompted Anselm to write on the Incarnation and atonement, but since he is careful to inform us that both parts of the *Cur Deus Homo* are primarily for unbelievers and to help believers in their conversations with unbelievers, we are left with the unavoidable impression that the *Cur Deus Homo* has a missional purpose.

THE MISSIONAL CHARACTER OF THE *CUR DEUS HOMO*

In Sally Vaughn's new biography of Anselm she takes some time to consider the community at Bec where Anselm received his formative training. After making the convincing case that Bec was a considerable force in the Anglo-Norman world, she moves on to suggest that the monks of Bec, 'may well have seen themselves as missionaries in a barbarian land' (Vaughn 2012: 32). Drawing on Gilbert Crispin's *Vita Herluini*, she argues that Lanfranc is portrayed as a missionary sent from Normandy to England as its new archbishop. The Church in England was, according to Gilbert, in such dire straits that nothing short of missionary work and deep reform was demanded. No doubt Anglo-Saxon Church leadership disagreed with this description of their situation (Vaughn 2012: 35), just as modern scholarship is not persuaded by the Norman account of their new subordinates. Nevertheless, if Gilbert's presentation of Lanfranc as missionary is representative, then it is an important piece for understanding Anselm's context. Vaughn proposes that with respect to his earlier works such as the *Monologion* and *Proslogion*, 'Anselm was writing at least partly for the unconverted, suggesting that he was seeing himself at least partly as fulfilling a missionary role in his first theological writings' (Vaughn 2012: 41).

The unbelievers with which Anselm was concerned in his early days at Bec were not likely the same group or even type of unbelievers to which he addressed himself as archbishop. The recognition that Anselm was writing to address specific points of unbelief, if not specific unbelievers, highlights an overlooked point in Anselmian studies: Anselm had a missionary outlook. The missional character in Anselm's writings is most apparent in the *Proslogion* and the *Cur Deus Homo*, the works that deal with the person and work of God respectively. To say that the *Proslogion* is about the existence of God alone is to miss the point. Anselm was never interested in a God about whom we could say little more than that he exists. For the believer, the work of explaining the faith to an unbelieving world is about pointing to a personal God, a God who creates and sustains because he is love. Anselm's early life was wrapped up in communicating that truth to all who would hear through his little treatise (Hogg 2004: 89–98).

As the years passed, however, Anselm became aware of the need to move on to explain the work of God in Christ as well. For a monk, exploring Christ's work of atonement could only be encouraging, but to a world lost in unbelief it seems confusing, even offensive. It is this aspect of Anselm's Christology, and especially his theology of the atonement, that is just beginning to get more attention, and deservedly so. For some time, the conversation has been largely in-house. The last few centuries have been preoccupied with discussing the relative merits and relationship of satisfaction, honor, and justice as parts of a larger doctrinal scheme. Both those who praise Anselm's approach and those who decry it have failed to consider its place, not simply as one part of a theological system, but as one part of an apologetic effort. Just as Jesus came to save sinners, so Christology must be related to unbelief. Anselm understood this. Perhaps it is time we stopped asking how much of Anselm's culture he imbibed and embedded into his Christology, and started inquiring how Anselm saw his Christology engaging the unbelievers at the center and circumference of his culture. Maybe Anselm was savvier than the stereotype of a cloistered monk; maybe Anselm understood more of the purpose and place of Christology than has heretofore been recognized. Whether seeking to engage thoughtful unbelief in some form of atheistic context, Jewish objections to different facets of Christology or Muslim rejections of atonement, Anselm cared to 'give satisfaction to all who ask the reason for the hope that is in us' (Anselm 1998: 265). What, then, were those reasons and do they comport with the external evidence we have so far garnered?

INTERNAL INDICATORS OF
EXTERNAL INTEREST

The first issue that must be addressed is one that is also commonly leveled against the *Proslogion*, namely, how can this work be considered apologetic if it assumes a biblical or Christian worldview? In other words, if the claim is that the treatise will rely on and progress through reason, then it is inconsistent to presuppose the very faith that is being proved. As we read through the *Cur Deus Homo*, however, it becomes abundantly clear that *remoto christo* does not mean *remoto fide*. Anselm understood faith as the larger context in which reason worked, not the other way around. Reason is not independent of faith, but reliant on it. Prior commitments guide our reasoning regardless of whether or not they are identified with a larger, formal or explicitly religious system. The issue is not the reasoning itself, but the faith that grounds and guides the rational process. Anselm's purpose is not to search out naked reason as though that were common ground free of convictions and presuppositions, but to show how consistent and rational are the reasons for his faith not only in themselves, but also in how they relate to the world around us.

Turning to the specific objections presented by Boso, the first is that unbelievers cannot accept that God would demean himself so as to take on human flesh by being born of a woman and then suffer at the hands of the very creatures he made culminating in scourging and crucifixion (Anselm 1998: 268). This objection could be made by many outside the Church, and probably is intended as a kind of soft start to the conversation; nevertheless, Anselm's response is intriguing insofar as he ties together information from the OT and NT, showing how NT theology is a fitting and appropriate counterpart to OT theology (Anselm 1998: 268–9). He calls our attention to the fact that just as sin entered humanity through a man's disobedience (recalling Gen. 3), so humanity's restoration has been affected through a man's obedience. For anyone who knows their Pauline epistles, it is obvious Anselm is drawing on Rom. 5:19, which is, coincidentally or not, part of an argument made to a group that included a significant Jewish presence.

Part two of Anselm's answer is that just as the sin that caused the damnation of humanity originated with a woman (recalling Gen. 3 again), so it is fitting that the one who would save us from condemnation should originate, after a fashion, from a woman. Finally, Anselm adds that just as the devil beguiled humanity through what hung on a tree, so it is appropriate that the devil should be defeated by one who hung on a tree. To this three-part answer, Boso complains that this is all well and good, but the problem remains that unbelievers do not agree that Jesus 'humbled himself for the purposes we proclaim' (Anselm 1998: 269). Boso asks why salvation could not have been accomplished by another being (Anselm 1998: 270). Anselm responds that were humanity saved by a non-divine being, humanity could not be restored to its proper dignity, but he waits until book two to elaborate on this further. Anselm mounts the case that humanity could only be restored by someone who partakes of human nature for where there is no identity in nature, there could be no representation (Anselm 1998: 321–4). This part of his argument relies heavily on the presumption that Adam was not only real, but the representative head of humanity. This is a point that would require much more elaboration than Anselm supplied were he addressing unbelievers who knew nothing of the biblical story of creation. As it is, he can assume a shared knowledge, if not belief, in the beginnings of the human race—an assumption that makes the most sense if Jews and Muslims are his intended audience.

Perhaps the most obvious way in which the *Cur Deus Homo* would connect with a Jewish audience or help a Christian apologist engage a Jew is through the preponderant emphasis on the need for a sacrifice. Anselm draws the reader's attention to the fact that no one can be saved without recompense for sin. This conversation comes immediately on the heels of the now famous discussion of whether or not the redeemed make up the number of the fallen angels. This is important because the sum total of that argument is that, 'humans in that heavenly city ... ought to be of like character to those who were to be there, whose substitutes they are to be, that is, the same in character as the good angels now are' (Anselm 1998: 300–3). This plays into Anselm's next argument which is that recompense for sin is necessary to make sinners blessed or pure.

Anselm tells a parable in which a pearl is knocked out of a man's hand into the mud by a malicious person. Would that person simply pick up the muddy pearl and place it in his treasure box in that soiled state? Would he not clean it first? So it is with humanity. Satan knocked humanity out of the hand of God and now God, who will not let his creation languish in the filth of sin, must not only pick us up, but clean us up. But how does God clean us? He does this by providing recompense to God for our sin, by taking our debt upon himself, and, most significantly, paying that debt in full according to the proportion of the one to whom it is owed (Anselm 1998: 303–5).

In consideration of this explanation, Richard Campbell is surely right when he states that, 'Anselm's use of terms such as *justitia, honor* and *debitum* would have had resonances with the legal and social structures of his day, and thereby would have seemed readily understandable and relevant to his contemporary audience' (Campbell 1996: 256–8). I would add that these are also terms that are common currency in Judaism and Islam. This is not to suggest that either group were still offering sacrifices in mediaeval Europe, but that their sacred texts are replete with such notions. We cannot forget that Anselm's background was comprised of more than a feudal system. An argument could be made that an equal or greater influence for a monk would have been the OT. Here, quite obviously, we find the most overlap between Christianity and Judaism. The pages of the OT are saturated with the blood of sacrifices that speak to the need for recompense, but recompense that is not sufficient to the proportion of the guilt, otherwise the sacrificial system would have been abolished. As it is, the presentation of Christ in the NT is as the Lamb of God who takes away the sin of the world, not just the sin of the one who offered him up. Anselm's theology of the atonement is not foreign to Christianity or Judaism; rather, it touches on the very heart of what matters most to the writers of both the OT and NT. A denial of a feudal or mediaeval cultural influence on Anselm is not warranted, but neither is ignoring the profound impact of major biblical themes and their effectiveness in simultaneously teaching Christians about the reasons for their faith and explaining to Jews how the Christ is the fulfillment of all they've been looking for.

One last example that needs further investigation as to its inter-faith value is the time Anselm spends addressing the question of Jesus' free will in dying. Amidst the discussion on the will of the Father and the Son, Boso asks Anselm about the justice of the innocent Son dying for guilty humanity. He inquires:

> For what justice is it for the man who was of all the most just to be put to death for a sinner? What man would not be judged worthy of condemnation, if he were to condemn someone innocent and release the guilty party? … If God could not save sinners except by condemning a just man, where is his omnipotence?
>
> (Anselm 1998: 275)

Again, we cannot say that this question was solely that of a group of unbelievers, but then Anselm seems most interested in both the *Cur Deus Homo* and the *Proslogion* to present arguments that serve a dual purpose. They aim to help the faith of the Christian to grow as well as provide reasons to the unbeliever's concerns. Among the religions that are concerned with justice and guilt is Islam. One of the difficulties Muslims have with Christianity is this very idea that a just person should die on behalf of the guilty.

In light of this material, one might ask why this perspective on Anselm has remained peripheral. In responding to this query, it is important in the first place to remember the seminal influence of Eadmer on Anselm's memory. Eadmer wrote the first biography of Anselm, the *Vita Anselmi*, the purpose of which is hagiographic. The point was not to consider worldly influences, but divine direction. This meant that the compass for future biographies was set in a provincial direction, even if the scope of that provincial focus included England, France, and Rome. Eadmer also wrote the widely read and influential *Historia Novarum in Anglia*. As the title suggests, his attention was fairly firmly fixed on England. Once again, the early direction of thinking about Anselm did not seek to engage with influences foreign to Western Europe.

It is also worth repeating that Anselm himself did not make Islam a significant or even obvious dialogue partner. This may have been because Islam, though known to Western Europeans, was still at arm's length, and thus not sufficiently interesting to warrant special attention. It also may have been that in the political and social climate of the late eleventh and early twelfth century when Seljuk Turks were causing mayhem and hardship, that identifying Muslims as a people needing to be engaged in civil, theological discussion was frowned upon. In the end, however, how often are we aware of the influences that are at work in our thinking, let alone consciously ensuring that we identify them so future readers will have greater clarity in understanding why we wrote what we did?

In all of this, it should come as no surprise that Anselmian scholarship has, with some minor exceptions, largely neglected the presence of a multi-faith context for the *Cur Deus Homo*, and especially as that relates to an Islamic influence. Given that Christology speaks to both the Church and to unbelievers, and given that there is good reason to suspect Anselm treated Christology in this way, we cannot continue to neglect this aspect of Anselm's seminal work. We must continue the effort to connect Anselm's formulation of Christology to an ever broader and deeper understanding of Christian apologetics and inter-faith dialogue, all while self-consciously remaining aware of the world in which we live.

THE ABIDING WITNESS OF
THE *CUR DEUS HOMO*

The significance and influence of the *Cur Deus Homo* shows no signs of abating. As Christians continue to seek for wisdom from the past that might inform their present circumstances, Anselm's theology at large and his Christology in particular provide a well to which we may return repeatedly. This has to do with the fact that he was a careful thinker who also sought to apply wisdom from the past to contemporary issues, but also that he wrote his theology as a churchman. This means that he understood his responsibility to the Church, but it also means that he understood that such a responsibility included a mission to the lost. To be an effective churchman means stooping alongside the Lord of glory to serve, rather than to be served.

Insofar as this describes Anselm's heart, there should be no surprise that he fashioned his Christology in the *Cur Deus Homo* so as to help the Church better understand its confession so that it could better engage unbelief. A theologian who has the humility to stay in and serve the Church is a theologian who cannot ignore the needs of those who are on the periphery of new experiences, no matter how distant or foreign they may seem.

The biographies of Anselm reveal a complex man of depth and many talents. Reflection on his theology proves no different. The *Proslogion* caused a stir in his own day and has yet to stop fascinating and frustrating. His prayers and meditations were popular throughout his life, and have continued to encourage, correct, concern, and confound Christians to the present day. His other works also have an abiding quality to them, but none quite like the *Cur Deus Homo*. Just as Christ spoke to disciples and dissenters alike, so has Anselm. Just as Christ spoke of the holiness of God and the sinfulness of humanity, so has Anselm. Just as Christ has been loved and hated, so has Anselm. Anselm is not the Christ, but he spent his life pointing to him in the hopes that Christ might increase even as he decreased.

SUGGESTED READING

Asiedu (2001); Deme (2003); Hart (1994); Hogg (2004); McIntyre (1954).

BIBLIOGRAPHY

Abelard, P. (1969), *Opera Theologica* (Turnhout: Brepols).
Abulafia, A. S. (1992), 'Theology and the Commercial Revolution: Guibert of Nogent, St Anselm and the Jews of Northern France', in D. Abulafia, M. Franklin, and M. Rubin (eds.),

Church and City, 1000–1500: Essays in Honour of Christopher Brooke (Cambridge: Cambridge University Press), 23–40.

Abulafia, A. S. (1998), *Christians and Jews in Dispute: Disputational Literature and the Rise of Anti-Judaism in the West (c.1000–1150)* (Aldershot: Ashgate).

Anselm (1973), *The Prayers and Meditations of Saint Anselm with the Proslogion*, trans. B. Ward (London: Penguin).

Anselm (1990–4), *The Letters of Saint Anselm of Canterbury*, 3 vols., ed. and trans. Walter Fröhlich (Kalamazoo, Mich.: Cistercian Publications).

Anselm (1998), *Anselm of Canterbury, The Major Works*, ed. and trans. B. Davies and G. R. Evans (Oxford: Oxford University Press).

Asiedu, F. B. A. (2001), 'Anselm and the Unbelievers: Pagans, Jews, and Christians in the *Cur Deus Homo*', *Theological Studies* 62: 530–48.

Aulén, G. (1978), *Christus Victor*, trans. A. G. Hebert (London: SPCK).

Campbell, R. (1996), 'The Conceptual Roots of Anselm's Soteriology', in D. E. Luscombe and G. R. Evans (eds.), *Anselm, Aosta, Bec and Canterbury: Papers in Commemoration of the Nine-Hundreth Anniversary of Anselm's Enthronement as Archbishop, 25 September 1093* (Sheffield: Sheffield Academic Press), 256–63.

Cohen, J. (1999), *Living Letters of the Law: Ideas of the Jew in Medieval Christianity* (Berkeley: University of California Press).

Cohen, N. (2004), 'Feudal Imagery or Christian Tradition? A Defense of the Rationale for Anselm's *Cur Deus Homo*', *The Saint Anselm Journal* 2: 22–9.

Cross, R. (1999), *Duns Scotus*. Great Medieval Thinkers (New York: Oxford University Press).

Deme, D. (2003), *The Christology of Anselm of Canterbury* (Aldershot: Ashgate).

Eadmer (1962), *The Life of St Anselm*, ed. and trans. R. W. Southern (Oxford: Clarendon Press).

Eadmer (1964), *History of Recent Events in England*, ed. and trans. R. W. Southern (Oxford: Clarendon Press).

Evans, G. R. (1980), *Old Arts and New Theology: The Beginnings of Theology as an Academic Discipline* (Oxford: Oxford University Press).

Gasper, G. E. M. (1999), 'Anselm's *Cur Deus Homo* and Athanasius' *De Incarnatione*: Some Questions of Comparison', in *Cur Deus Homo, Atti del Congresso Anselmiano Internazionale* (Rome: Pontificio Ateneo S. Anselmo), 147–78.

Gasper, G. E. M. and I. Logan (eds.) (2012), *Saint Anselm of Canterbury and His Legacy* (Toronto: Pontifical Institute of Mediaeval Studies).

Gorringe, T. (1996), *God's Just Vengeance* (Cambridge: Cambridge University Press).

Hart, D. B. (1994), 'A Gift Exceeding Every Debt: An Eastern Orthodox Appreciation of Anselm's *Cur Deus Homo*', *Pro Ecclesia* 7: 333–49.

Hogg, D. S. (2004), *Anselm of Canterbury: The Beauty of Theology* (Aldershot: Ashgate).

Hopkins, J. (2007 [1972]), 'God's Sacrifice of Himself as a Man', in K. Finsterbusch, A. Lange, and K. F. Diethard Römheld (eds.), *Human Sacrifice in Jewish and Christian Tradition* (Leiden: Brill), 237–57.

LaChance, P. J. (2004), 'Understanding Christ's Satisfaction Today', *The Saint Anselm Journal* 2: 60–6.

Letham, R. (1993), *The Work of Christ* (Downers Grove, Ill.: IVP).

Luscombe, D. E. and G. R. Evans (eds.) (1996), *Anselm: Aosta, Bec and Canterbury* (Sheffield: Sheffield Academic Press).

McIntyre, J. (1954), *St. Anselm and his Critics: A Re-interpretation of the* Cur Deus Homo (Edinburgh: Oliver & Boyd).

Noble, I. (2012), 'The Gift of Redemption: Vladimir Lossky and Raymond Schwager on Anselm of Canterbury', *Communio Viatorum* 52: 48–67.

Rashdall, H. (1919), *The Idea of the Atonement in Christian Theology* (London: Macmillan).

Rayner, M. J. (2012), 'Rashdall's Doctrine of Atonement', *Modern Believing* 53: 273–84.

Southern, R. W. (1990), *Saint Anselm: A Portrait in a Landscape* (Cambridge: Cambridge University Press).

Sumner, G. (2013), 'Why Anselm Still Matters', *Anglican Theological Review* 95: 25–35.

Sweeney, E. (2012), *Anselm of Canterbury and the Desire for the Word* (Washington DC: Catholic University of America Press).

Vaughn, S. (1987), *Anselm of Bec and Robert of Meulan: The Innocence of the Dove and the Wisdom of the Serpent* (Berkeley: University of California Press).

Vaughn, S. (2012), *Archbishop Anselm 1093–1109: Bec Missionary, Canterbury Primate, Patriarch of Another World* (Farnham: Ashgate).

CHAPTER 14

··

SEEING DOUBLE

The Crucified Christ in Western Mediaeval Art

··

ALISON MILBANK

> And since, on this account he wished to suffer, even though he was beyond the power of suffering in his nature as God, then he wrapped himself in flesh that was capable of suffering, and revealed it as his very own, so that even the suffering might be said to be his because it was his own body which suffered and no one else's.
>
> (Cyril of Alexandria, On the Unity of Christ)

ALTHOUGH an Eastern icon from the ninth century may be almost indistinguishable in style from one made a thousand years later, there is a seismic shift in the portrayal of Christ in Western art of the same period, especially in the way Christ's suffering on the Cross is represented. Both East and West are, together, responding to the Council of Chalcedon of 451, which left the Church to work out the implications of a Christology of the union of two complete natures, human and divine, 'without confusion of substance, but by unity of person' as the creed attributed to St Athanasius puts it (Schaff 1877: 69). Cyril of Alexandria, quoted in the epigraph above, offered one of the most profound and subtle early responses to Nestorius' challenge to that union of natures by linking the Word's enfleshing to the redemption and deification of the Christian believer, so that the mortal may be able to put on immortality, just as Christ 'wrapped himself in flesh'. This mystical exchange is central to Cyril's theology and animates his discussion of Christ's suffering in his human nature, so that 'what he was by nature, we might become by grace' (Cyril 2000: 35). Throughout Cyril's essay *On the Unity of Christ*, and despite his aim to question Nestorian separation of human and divine natures, he nevertheless keeps all the antitheses in play—passible/impassible; suffering/glory; divine/human; body/soul—while arguing that it is by assuming and integrating these antinomies that Christ saves humanity.

The theology of the icon developed in Eastern Christianity was a way of making this deificatory transformation into a religious practice; it was enacted through an image which was written so as to transport the one venerating it into another, transcendent realm. Western art—or rather, image-making as we should call it in the mediaeval period—is often seen as moving away from the dispassion and *theosis* of the icon towards increasing naturalism and emotional empathy, as the Carolingian *Christus Victor*, judging the world from the Cross, gives way to the agonized, tortured body of the Man of Sorrows. This chapter, however, will seek to complicate this narrative by arguing that in every period of Western mediaeval art there is some attempt to realize a Cyrilline union of the two natures, and that where this is successfully achieved, there remains a potential for that redemptive transformation and participation in the divine life of the icon tradition. Moreover, the moves towards increasing realism of representation can be the catalyst for a truly dynamic communication of idioms, in which the two natures are paradoxically juxtaposed. Following Augustine, the Middle Ages loved to dwell on the deformity of Christ's body on the Cross, but in the greatest art, this ugliness of the suffering servant can become beautiful, calling the viewer into the Passion mystery of redemptive transformation, so that Christ's deformity can make humanity whole again.

EARLY MEDIAEVAL *CHRISTUS TRIUMPHANS*

Although there exist representations of the crucifixion on ampullae and gems dating from the third century, it was not until the Empress Helena's archaeological investigations in the Holy Land and discovery of the true Cross that representation of Christ crucified became common (Viladesau 2005: 42–3). Its introduction seems to be coterminous with the discovery also of icons-not-made-with-hands, such as the Mandylion of Edessa, which came to prominence in the sixth century, and which claimed to be in some way the mark of the face of Christ himself, miraculously printed or copied from life by Nicodemus (Belting 1994: 305). With no description even attempted in the Gospels, up to now Christ had been represented either as akin to Dionysus, with curly hair, young and beardless, or as a philosopher, bearded. From the Mandylion icon and certain supposedly contemporary descriptions, Christ took on the features that would remain constant for a thousand years: reddish chestnut hair, curling at the ends, a forked beard and long nose. Such an iconography is common to Eastern icon and Western sculptural crucifix, as can be seen in the Holy Face of Lucca (Figure 14.1), which survives in the form of a thirteenth-century copy of an eighth-century original. Its importance was international, so that the Battló Majesty from Catalonia (Figure 14.2), like many other Spanish crucifixes shows its influence (Mann 1993: 322–4).

Although early images of the crucified Saviour occasionally show him wearing nothing but a loincloth, in many early wooden crucifixes he wears the *colobium*, a priestly garment also worn by kings to show their sacerdotal role of service to their people. When painted in red as in the Battló example, the kingly aspect is emphasized, and the authority of Christ over death and sin. Such images stress therefore both the historical Jesus whose facial image is reproduced, and the divine Son, whose divinity, shrouded

FIGURE 14.1 *Volto Sacro*/Holy Face of Lucca, wooden figure of Christ, early-thirteenth century copy of an earlier figure, Cathedral of San Martino, Lucca, photograph by Juanbanjo.

in flesh, tricked the unseeing Satan to exceed his authority, and thus lose his putative 'rights' over fallen humanity (Aulén 2010). The robe in such images is both revelation of kingship and representation of that Cyrilline wrapping in flesh and blood. In the same way the image itself both shows Christ—as an image—but also hides within it a relic (Schiller 1972: 141). The Luccan crucifix once held a relic of Christ's blood, for example, while others might hold a fragment of the Cross.

In these early mediaeval images of the crucifixion, the eyes of Christ remain open, as if he were alive. His arms are actively outstretched upon the Cross and the palms are often opened, so that he seems to be offering himself, rather than passively suffering. Indeed, often as in Lucca and the Battló examples, his face is calm and peaceful. Combined with the robe, this suggests an eternal image of Christ's redemptive action, rather than a representative account of the historical scene of his suffering. Indeed, scholars argue that what is being imaged here is the Last Judgement, and the Christ portrayed is the 'Son of Man' of the first chapter of Revelation, 'clothed with a long robe and with a golden sash across his chest' (Rev. 1:13). In the same chapter there is reference to the Second Coming of Christ, when 'every eye will see him, even those who pierced him' (Rev. 1:7). Many early crucifixion pictures, such as the ivory book cover from Reims (Figure 14.3) include Longinus with his spear and Stephaton with the vinegar on a long stick, representing two responses to Christ's suffering. The former, according to the apocryphal

FIGURE 14.2 Battló Majesty, painted wooden crucifix, mid-twelfth century, Museu Nacional de Catalunga, Barcelona.

Acts of Pilate, was healed from his blindness by the blood and water released from the side of Christ, which he pierced as the soldier in John 19:34, while the latter is equated with the unknown person who offered the vinegar in John 19:29 (Ehrman and Pleše 2011: 465–90). They represent therefore, the response of life-giving faith and that of bitter rejection to the offer of salvation.

Paradoxically, it will be the one who pierced Christ who will be saved, whose sight is the gift of grace. He who offered vinegar is interpreted according to Psalm 69:21: 'for my thirst they gave me vinegar to drink' and 69:23: 'Let their eyes be darkened so that they cannot see'. In the inclusion of Longinus and Stephaton, therefore, the early crucifixions make their own act of representation part of a salvific process, and an anticipation of the Last Judgement. Nicodemus, who came to visit Jesus by night in John 3, and provokes the words about the brazen serpent, is a figure also associated with salvific sight: 'as Moses lifted up the serpent in the wilderness, even so must the Son of man be lifted up: that whoever believes in him should not perish, but have eternal life' (John 3:14–15). Christ elevated on the Cross, like the brazen serpent which healed the Israelites, is the source of healing. Rachel Fulton emphasizes the importance of the Cross as a catalyst of judgement, and cites an eleventh-century bishop, Gerard of

FIGURE 14.3 Ivory book cover panel of the Crucifixion, Rheims, *c.*860–70. © Victoria and Albert Museum no. 303-1867.

Arras and Cambrai, who uses the brazen serpent as a justification for the use of images in churches:

> And we, travelling from the Egypt of carnal conversation through the desert of earthly exile to the land of celestial promise, are rid from our hearts of the venom of the ancient enemy through the sight (*respectum*) of the Mediator hanging on the cross. For whoever will have gazed (*conspexerit*) upon Christ through the image and passion of the son of God (*per imaginem filii Dei ac passionem*), that one will be able to evade the ancient enemy.
>
> (Fulton 2002: 85)

Thus we see how by means of Revelation and St John's Gospel and the original brazen serpent of the Exodus story the representation of the crucified Christ is not only justified but rendered salvific in itself just as the carved snake once was. This seeing, however, is receptive: it enables grace to flow just as the lance of Longinus once opened the side of Christ. Following the science of Aristotle's *De Anima*, touch is the basis of all sensation that allows the world to manifest itself to us (Aristotle 1995: 200–1). Longinus' lance then opens the flow of redemptive love to bathe and heal his sight, and reorder his body and soul together. It is no accident that the wound on nearly every mediaeval crucifix lies just below the breast for it is nutritive—the water and blood of the Eucharist, which Carolingian and earlier Christian theology saw as a form of medicine, as well as salvation from death. In many early mediaeval crucifixes, instead of Longinus, the figure of Mary or Ecclesia holds a chalice to receive the blood. In this ninth-century ivory book-cover, the Virgin and Longinus are included in a salvific crescendo of death, where angels stretch down to receive Christ's soul, while the graves open below, sun and moon bear witness, and Ecclesia/Mary stretches to catch the saving blood.

Although we can never fully recover exactly how earlier ages saw these images, it is clear that their seeing was a complex activity, and that the images presented to them were not simple, even though they have a powerful affective force as objects. It is clear also that to make sense of these images it is necessary to see doubly: to view a scene as both memorial of a particular moment in time but also as ultimate and ahead of time, at the Last Judgement, and as a moment that is itself generative of eternal life through grace and the sacraments that literally flow from it. Such images distance and judge the viewer while almost beckoning him or her into an embrace. We know that participation could be quite extreme in that the Holy Face of Lucca was almost destroyed and had to be recarved because people kissed or chipped at it too enthusiastically.

This seeing doubly in terms of iconography was paralleled by discerning the double nature of Christ made manifest in its extremity on the Cross. Celia Chazelle demonstrates how it was debates about adoptionism at the court of Charlemagne and his successors that led to the development of images of the crucifixion, despite Carolingian caution about artistic representation (Chazelle 2001: 14–71). Familiar as we are with the idea that the suffering of Christ shows his humanity, it is sometimes difficult to remember that Alcuin and others viewed the crucifixion as an event that revealed above all his divinity and had recourse to it to refute any view that Christ was adopted as God after his resurrection. The blood is central to this assertion of his divinity. What might seem a piece of gory realism is common to crucifixions throughout the whole mediaeval period: the free-flowing blood from hands, side, and feet. The blood as proof that Christ really suffered (thus avoiding Docetism) is equally 'his blood, through whom all things are created [which is] poured for the salvation of all' (Chazelle 2001: 62). Where we might see vulnerability the early mediaeval eye saw creative power, which alone could reunify humanity to its Creator. The open hands and calm expression of Christ in these images testify also to his voluntary suffering, which is an index of the sinlessness of his human nature, so a symbol of his divinity works equally to reveal the humanity. His suffering, writes Alcuin, is 'voluntary but true', unified by his will, which is in complete union with his Father.

THE IMITATIVE TURN AND THE *CHRISTUS PATIENS*

The huge artistic shift in representation of Christ's Passion in the twelfth century onwards should not conceal the fact of a great deal of continuity. St Bonaventure, whose life of St Francis was instrumental in developing his founder's life as that of a continuous Passion, also writes in *The Tree of Life* of Christ's 'priestly robe of red', and here the red comes from his own blood rather than an actual vestment. Cyril's wrapping image continues in the 'sacred garment, artistically woven by the Holy Spirit from [the Virgin's] chaste body' (Bonaventure 1978: 157). Although the role of the blood in removing personal sin is important earlier, in Bonaventure the individual reader is central addressee. And there is no doubt of the central role of the Franciscan movement in this turn to the individual, the personal, and the affective. Francis, who prayed constantly to his crucified Lord, also made himself into a living work of art representing Christ's suffering. Having had a vision of a seraph bearing between his wings 'the figure of a man crucified', Francis finds his own body marked with Christ's wounds. It is a vision that calls out paradoxical emotions—joy and sorrow—and opens a space of contradiction, as he seeks to reconcile seraphic immortality and 'the weakness of Christ's passion' (Bonaventure 1978: 305). The answer to the paradox lies in himself: his weakness will be transformed into Christ's likeness by seraphic love. It seems as if he embraces an Abelardian theory of atonement, in which it is the overflowing charity of God that is revealed on the Cross and which effects our redemption by calling out love in response (Abelard 2011). Francis thus becomes another image-not-made-with-hands, 'depicted not on tablets of stone or on panels of wood by the hands of a craftsman, but engraved in the members of his body by the finger of the living God' (Bonaventure 1978: 307).

Moreover, not only does Francis display throughout his life a love of the Cross but he has a particular devotion to the crucifix, including the one in St Damian's church, which addresses him, and still exists in Santa Chiara in Assisi. It conforms to twelfth-century style. Christ wears a loincloth, has open eyes and arms carefully open, while the sections beside his body contain smaller figures of disciples, Longinus/centurion and Stephaton. Above the resurrected Christ is welcomed by wondering angels. Although flat and with no place to hold relics, this was an image displayed above the chancel and later incorporated into the rood screen, where it was an important part of the Holy Week liturgy. Franciscan piety, however, would lead to a new portrayal of Christ's suffering.

By the time of the celebrated Florentine figural crosses of Cimabue (1280–5) and Giotto (before 1312), a great deal has changed. The body of Christ bends outwards into

FIGURE 14.4 Giotto di Bondone, Crucifix, painted wood, 1290–1300, Sante Maria Novella, Florence.

an 'S' shape in Cimabue but inwards in the case of Giotto (Figure 14.4), for whom the weight of the body pulls the arms down. The head too is bent and the eyes closed. This is the dead Christ of Good Friday, whose fingers are at rest because there is no more life in them and whose body is thin and even yellowish in tone, with defined ribs and only one nail holding the feet in place.

For writers like Bruce Cole 'the remote, heroic Son of God has been replaced by a very human image of a dead man divested of all the old associations of hierarchical grandeur which date back to the very beginning of Florentine art' (Cole 1976: 40). And yet, despite the deadness of the body the blood flows freely, not just oozing down from gravity but flowing out in a full arc in a manner that is not realistic but is wholly theological, since it is the death of Christ that allows us life. Moreover, the little figures from beside the body have gone, to be replaced by a patterned cloth. There is little critical discussion about the meaning of this background, which could so easily have been narrowed, now that it serves no representational function. Yet its Byzantine pattern echoes the style of the *colobium* on the Battló Christ in majesty, almost as if it were a royal robe laid out in one piece as in a shroud. The shroud cloth of Charlemagne still survives in the Cluny in Paris, and is made of patterned silk in red and gold. It seems therefore that Giotto is not necessarily abandoning the 'hierarchical grandeur' of the earlier Christ Triumphant but opening his kingly shroud to offer Christ to our view almost in the manner of the winding-cloth in the later deposition paintings. What is different about the kingship in Giotto's image is that it is not so much that of Christ reigning *from* the Cross as the king of glory reduced *to* the Cross. The halo with its tripartite sections is another indicator of his divine status but it does not radiate out from his head—indeed it is given a perspectival flatness and material positioning behind the cloth. If one were to continue the circle down, it should appear between Christ's arm and body, but it does not. There is therefore a tension between naturalism and the symbolic within the image, just as there is between the active kingly and the passive victim. With the eyes closed, the challenge to the viewer to see the truth of Christ's self-offering is muted. Instead of a judgement leading to participation, there is a compassionate response. No longer under the shower of blood, the Virgin Mary and St John are caught in gestures of grief at the far ends of the Cross, so that they too are primarily mourners whose gaze moves along the arms to centre the focus upon the face and down to the side wound.

I have stressed the awkwardness and ambiguity of Giotto's presentation in order to qualify the usual readings of his portrayal as simply towards naturalism and as being proto-Renaissance in character. Instead, like Francis seeking to make sense of immortal angel and suffering Christ, Giotto employs his realist technique to interrogate the problematic of identification and compassion that was now so to the fore in religious art and practice. Similarly in his fresco portrayals of the Passion story in the Scrovegni Chapel in Padua, his ability to render forms monumental, weighty, and rounded is used quite histrionically to portray intense emotion and to lay out a scene almost as if in a dramatic tableau, opening a space for the viewer's involvement. Yet by the reserve and hiddenness of the figures now fully suggested by his mastery of embodied form, he suggests something exceeds our comprehension. Rather than simple naturalism, it is this contradiction that energizes his work and makes it great religious art because it too, like the Romanesque examples, forces us to see double, although the focus shifts from Christ himself somewhat towards the perspective of the viewers and their surrogates in the characters portrayed. Barbara Raw claims that the figure of Mary is a witness to Christ's humanity, while that of St John verifies his divinity, especially when he holds the Gospel book (Raw 2009: 98). In the arm of this crucifix, however, he holds no book. Instead, the mystery of the event is held within the rounded folds of John's own person, but reserved, unlike the visibility of Francis' stigmata.

THE LATER MIDDLE AGES: THE EUCHARIST AND THE MAN OF SORROWS

Every crucifix in the Middle Ages was to be understood as in some sense a Eucharistic image. Hence the importance of St John at the scene because of his witness to the mixed flow of blood and water, representing baptism and the Eucharist, as well as the mystical exchange between humanity and Christ. From the inclusion of the word 'transubstantiated' in the articles of faith at the Fourth Lateran Council of 1415 onwards, the identification of the suffering Christ with the Eucharistic elements took on a new force. As Thomas's Eucharistic hymn, *Adoro Te Devote* emphasized, Christ was hidden, and it required discernment to see the truth of the body and blood behind what came to be called the 'accidents' of bread and wine. Miracles such as that of St Anthony of Padua, for whom an ass discerned the real presence of Christ in the host, abounded. Although in Thomas it is the whole and risen Christ who is received, stories such as the mass of St Gregory became popular in the later Middle Ages which involved the bleeding body of Christ appearing on the altar at the consecration rather than a resurrected figure (Schiller 1972: 226–8). The rising popularity of such images is due to controversies about transubstantiation that seem to have put pressure on the delicate balance of distance and intimacy in Thomas' Eucharistic devotion.

From the fourteenth century onwards, the compassionate identification with the suffering humanity of Christ is combined with an increasing collapse of distance in the act of vision. Where once it was necessary for faith to discern the God reigning from the tree, now to adore the all-too-visible image of the gory, bloody corpse of the Redeemer is important in order to assert his real though hidden presence in the Mass. So paradoxically, blood becomes the indicator of divinity once again, although this may not readily be apparent to a modern gaze. Just as worshippers focused on the elevation of the host at Mass, so viewers of holy images began to gaze at a figure of the crucified Christ called the Man of Sorrows (Figure 14.5).

This German version from about 1430 by Master Franke, is typical of the northern style. 'Man of sorrows' is a quotation from Isaiah 53's description of the suffering servant: 'when we see him there is no beauty that we should desire him. He is despised and rejected of men: a man of sorrows, and acquainted with grief' (Isa. 53:2–3). Here is the ugly Christ whose lack of comeliness is a sign that he bears the transgressions of us all. These words had long been part of liturgical and private meditation but now they took on a new literality. Cimabue's Christ was perfect in mathematical ratio and Giotto's too had a pure, pale beauty. Yet here the pink hands of the angel accentuate the

FIGURE 14.5 Master Franke, Man of Sorrows, painted wood, *c.*1420, Museum der Bildenden Künste, Lepzig.

ghastly yellow of the dead body of Christ, which has to be propped up by angelic hands. The sickly eyes look up from the lowered head seeking our pity, while the arms stuck out akimbo with ungainly agency seek to point out the flowing blood and the chastising whip. Each object in the scene is part of the now expanded narrative of the Passion and each has its typological anticipation in the Old Testament, mainly in Isaiah and the Psalms. What happens in response to the *devotio moderna* of intense affective identification with Christ's suffering in the later Middle Ages is that, just like the actualization of transubstantiation in the Mass of St Gregory, the allegorical distance of figurative reading of the Old Testament is crossed, so that type and fulfilment are closed up into one image. In the tight, crowded structure of Franke's painting, formal style and content mirror this closure and the lack of mediation. The image is also influenced by the mystical visions of those like Birgitta of Sweden, who found themselves at the historical scene of Christ's chastisement, and added iconographical details to the narrative. Here, St Birgitta's *Revelations* seem to be in the artist's mind: 'He was crowned with thorns. Blood trickled over his eyes, his ears, his beard' (Schiller 1972: 147).

The presence of the angels and the fact that they hold the body suggests the Mass, when the angels are invoked in order to take the sacrifice to the heavenly altar at the consecration. They handle the body through the winding sheet, just as the ministers use a cloth to handle the sacrament. Thomas Aquinas writes of this *Supplices* prayer in the *Summa*: 'The priest does not pray that the sacramental species may be borne up to heaven; nor that Christ's true body may be borne thither, for it does not cease to be there; but he offers this prayer for Christ's mystical body, which is signified in this sacrament, that the angel standing by at the Divine mysteries may present to God the prayers of both priest and people' (Aquinas 2006: 163). If a Thomist theology lies behind the image, then the Christ presented is the Church, the mystical body, and the image opens to include the viewer as part of that entity. But although the angels put their fingers into the actual wounds to draw our attention to them, their hands and gaze actually get in the way of any entrance by the Christian viewer. The angel at the back of Christ forces our gaze forward and allows no movement beyond. Christ's own hand, indeed, partly covers the flow of blood from his side, which seeps down into his loincloth, rather than out as a regenerative fountain. Only the central attention to the navel, that guarantor of Christ's true humanity, offers some possibility of a mystical exchange, but even that is fronted by the whip.

The Italian versions of the image of the Man of Sorrows are much more restrained than their Low Country or German equivalents. The painter and Dominican friar, Fra Angelico, included a Man of Sorrows as one of the simple frescos he made for the cells of his brothers in the San Marco community in Florence around 1440. As in many Man of Sorrows images, this shows the dead Christ after his deposition and yet still within the tomb. A winding cloth is invisibly held, presumably again by angels, behind the figure of Christ, who is also shown with the Cross, as well as a number of the *arma Christi*, that is, the objects or events of the Passion narrative, which are here seen as the instruments by which Christ achieves his victory. Particularly interesting here is the fact that people and events are foregrounded, rather than simple objects: the betraying kiss of Judas; the hand taking the pieces of silver; Peter's denial; the hand that hits the blindfolded Saviour. In contrast to the awkwardness of the Franke example, here the multiple objects form a unity, as the eye is taken in a circle formed partly by the cloth, and guided by the disembodied hands and heads. Angelico's mastery of geometry is very evident.

The image is less obviously naturalistic than the angelic holding of the Franke Christ, in that it is wholly meditative in character, as befits its location in the private cell of a friar. The objects are not held by figures but engendered from the background, or even from the devoted contemplation of the Virgin and St Thomas Aquinas. Our Lady sits in the classic pose of pensive thought, while Thomas kneels, quill at the ready to record his visions. The Christ upon whom they meditate is much more active than in

Franke: standing, not propped, so that his resurrection is assumed. Even in his humiliation, on the upper right of the picture, he is tranquil behind the blindfold, with the reed held lightly as befits a king. The wooden board announcing his kingship is also prominent. Most importantly, he stands with hands outstretched, opening his hands towards the two saints. As befits an image which contains Thomas Aquinas, this unites the believers in the redemptive action of self-offering; it is not merely an image of pity calling forth compassion. Rather the human figures of contemplation together with those involved in the *arma Christi* become part of the divine action. For the tranquillity and dignity of the figure of Christ emphasize his divine activity. He is shown thrice, as if to indicate the fact that the Passion is the work of the entire Trinity. The image requires interpretation, and thus the collapsing of exegetical levels in Franke is here avoided. The contemplative pose of the two saints implies a hermeneutical distance, as does the centring of a tilted square stone on the sarcophagus. Georges Didi-Huberman has convincingly argued that the prevalence of such focus on stones and pillars in Angelico's painting is a meditative device based on the mystical theology of Dionysius the Areopagite, in which the blockage to the movement of the eye enforced by the stone is akin to the movement from positive (*kataphatic*) to negative (*apophatic*) in the movement to divine union (Didi-Huberman 1995: 69–80). Realizing the limitation of a name or quality to define the divine is the springboard to a deeper understanding of the mystery of God. For Didi-Huberman, the background of these convent frescos is a representation of the unknowable depths of God. The figure of Christ therefore, as the Logos, both reveals and conceals, but this dialectic calls the meditative viewer into the journey towards union. Here Angelico employs what is usually conceived of as a humanist device—perspective—for theological and Christological meditation.

THE TURN TO THE GROTESQUE

For a last example of the late mediaeval period, which by very different means enables this double seeing, I shall examine the famous Isenheim Altarpiece by Matthias Grünewald, painted in 1512–15 (Figure 14.6).

This may seem a complete antinomy to Fra Angelico's tranquil harmony, for this is one of the most grotesque representations of the crucifixion, in which Christ's body is not tranquil but in rigid agony. Not only does the blood flow profusely but red is the keynote colour throughout all the wings of the outer tryptych, and even the tomb below is livid scarlet. The grief of those beside the Cross is extreme and ugly; only the flanking saints, Anthony and Sebastian, have any tranquillity, and even that is somewhat rendered problematic by a demon blowing through the broken window behind St Anthony, while an arrow transfixes St Sebastian and emerges from his back.

The many wounds upon the body of Christ begin to make sense when one includes the fact that the altarpiece was made for the Antonine order, who cared for sufferers of plague and skin diseases (Mellinkoff 1988: 3). It had become common, following the

FIGURE 14.6 Matthias Grünewald, Isenheim Altarpiece, painted wood, 1512–16, Unterlinden Museum, Colmar.

visions of St Brigitta of Sweden and St Gertrude of Hefta, to count the wounds inflicted throughout Christ's Passion in the thousands, and here the many marks stand also for the boils and marks on the bodies of those the monks cared for. So implicitly, this was a Christ in whose sufferings the believer might find a share. Yet does not the abjection of this tortured figure prevent his divinity being manifested in any way? Does the relative realism of the pain and pus render the image realist and individualized, without any universal significance?

In fact, this image is far from naturalistic. It is not a representation of an actual historical scene, or not entirely, for although the Virgin falls into the arms of St John the evangelist, St John the Baptist stands on the other side, although he was long dead by the time of the crucifixion. A symbolic lamb, also an element in the Baptist's proclamation of Jesus as Messiah—'behold the lamb of God' (John 1:36)—stands bleeding into a chalice like the lamb of Revelation 13:8, 'slain from the beginning of the world'. John quotes his own words—'he must increase but I must decrease' (John 3:30)—and this idea is rendered bizarrely literal in the greater size of the body of the Saviour in comparison to the other figures. The feet reach right down almost to the ground in opposition to the increasing practice in this period of raising the Cross well above the heads of those attending the event.

The verse that follows John 3:31, helps to interpret this positioning: 'he that comes from above is above all: he that is of the earth is earthly and speaks of the earth'. The great Cross in the painting roots Christ in the earth, while his arms seem taut, raising his fingers, albeit nailed, to heaven. It is the enfleshing in pus and blood that renders Christ's suffering redemptive for mortal human kind. The tension and energy of his passion reveals its divine character. The lamb peacefully gazing upon him, while holding the resurrection Cross of victory, shows the union of Christ with the Father that renders him paradoxically impassible while in torment. Indeed, the poised Anthony and the Sebastian unhurt by the arrow, show how God's grace through this central act of redemptive love makes healing possible, Anthony saving from St Anthony's Fire and Sebastian from the plague.

Moreover, both crucifixion and the entombment below open up: the former twice—first, to reveal the annunciation, the Virgin delighting in her Son, and the resurrection, and secondly to reveal a sculpted group of St Anthony and other saints, with wings showing his desert temptations on one side, and his friendly meeting with St Paul on the other. It is the side of the Cross that opens to reveal these inner mysteries, just as the death of Christ opens the way to glory. The centrality of St Anthony, who was tormented mentally as well as physically, makes him the friend of the sick, and calls them into relation. Moreover, the entombment opens to show a sculpture of the Last Supper, so that communion, friendship, and service are revealed as the heart of Christian and brotherly living. The entire artwork enacts a theology of participation in the body of Christ, whose power is revealed in his weakness, so that the mystical exchange of Godhead and humanity may be achieved. Like Angelico, Grünewald achieves his effect by double seeing rather than simple affective identification. He too has his techniques of dissimilitude, akin to Angelico's stonework, first in the Baptist and the lamb, but secondly in the portrayal of the two flanking saints, who are realistically rendered as if alive but who are positioned on stone plinths, with architectural decoration, as if they were statues in niches. Sebastian's arrow seems to turn to stone as it meets the column. Are they statues or people? Perhaps the idea is that the statue can act for the saint, especially, of course, when it contains a relic. But the ambiguity, like the grotesque style of the crucified body, allows the distance between viewer and image, which mirrors and imitates the analogical distance between human creature and Creator, and which once acknowledged is the beginning of the operation of grace and the understanding of the Incarnation. In the Isenheim altarpiece, this lies within, as that to which the crucifixion is the key. Purified by the acceptance of forgiveness offered by the Cross, illumined by the joyful and glorious mysteries of Incarnation and resurrection, the viewer is drawn into union, thus enacting the threefold mystical ascent at the heart of mediaeval spiritual practice. And the seeming antinomies of stone and flesh, God and Man, body and soul, are what work through a Dionysian mystical theology to bring the viewer into communion: to taste and see.

This short essay has sought to demonstrate that there is much more continuity throughout the mediaeval period in the portrayal of Christ than might normally be assumed. Just as loinclothed figures with eyes closed can be found in the Anglo-Saxon period, and the *Christus Triumphans* of the holy face of Lucca keeps its crown until today, so artists in every period sought to see doubly: to portray a divine victim. It has to be admitted that the later examples represent the best of the age in theological exploration of the crucifixion, since there is ample material that shows a perverse delight in the infliction of suffering. Very often, as James Marrow has argued, what seems like an almost sadistic proliferation of torments in late mediaeval Northern European art is due to a refusal of interpretative distance, so that elements and details from prophecy and the Psalms used figuratively in the liturgy and in manuscript illumination come to be rendered literally (Marrow 1979: 199). There was a parallel in the biblical hermeneutics of Nicolas of Lyra, who reduced the four levels of interpretation to a double literal, while Jacques Lefèvre d'Etaples (Faber Stapulensis) went even further by subsuming all meanings to Christ, who alone is the subject of Scripture (Smalley 1964: xvi). This prepared the way for Luther's Christic reading of the Psalms, which goes much further than the allegorical figuration of earlier periods. So when the ninth-century Stuttgart Psalter illustrates Psalm 22:18–22 as prefiguring Christ, actual soldiers mocking are united in one image with the communion chalice and with an allegorical lion and unicorn (from verse 21, 'unicornis' in the Vulgate). A range of levels of interpretation are at play here, whereas in Bosch's *The Crowning with Thorns* of 1490–1500, much of its sinister power comes from the literalizing of figurative elements.

So the man on the right wears a dog-collar to fulfil Psalm 22:16: 'for dogs have compassed me'; the man with the crossbow bolt in his hat is a rendering of Psalm 11:2: 'for behold the wicked bend their bow'. There are, indeed, a number of other significations in the painting: secular and sacred powers of the day, Islam and Judaism; the four humours and so on (Foster and Tudor-Craig 1986: 60). The emphasis, however, is less on the mystery of the Passion, and more on contemporary political critique, particularly of Pope Julius II, whose oak leaves are worn by the dog-collared man. All are materialized in an uncanny, brutal naturalism in which the strongest light is reflected on the armoured fist about to push the crown on the head of the docile Christ, who lacks all life and energy in comparison with his lively tormentors. Perhaps this is not Christ so much as his suffering body, the Church, her only halo the crown of thorns. Seeing double like this can no longer be a means of salvific participation but a mode of sorrowful recognition of the distance between humanity and God, Christ and his earthly body, which a few years later would provoke the German Reformation.

SUGGESTED READING

Didi-Huberman (1995); Marrow (1979); Viladesau (2005).

BIBLIOGRAPHY

Abelard, P. (2011), *Commentary on Romans*, trans. S. R. Cartwright (Washington, DC: Catholic University of America Press).

Aquinas, T. (2006), *Summa Theologiae, Volume 59, 3a, Holy Communion*, ed. Thomas Gilby (Cambridge: Cambridge University Press).

Aristotle (1995), *On the Soul. Parva Naturalia, On Breath*, trans. W. H. Hett. Loeb Classical Library (Cambridge, Mass: Harvard University Press).

Aulén, G. (2010 [1930]), *Christus Victor: A Historical Study of the Three Main Types of the Idea of Atonement*, trans. A. G. Herbert (London: SPCK).

Belting, H. (1994), *Likeness and Presence: A History of the Image before the Era of Art* (Chicago: University of Chicago Press).

Bonaventure (1978), *The Journey of the Soul into God, The Tree of Life, The Life of St Francis*, trans. E. Cousins. Classics of Western Spirituality (London: SPCK).

Chazelle, C. (2001), *The Crucified God in the Carolingian Era: Theology and Art of Christ's Passion* (Cambridge: Cambridge University Press).

Cole, B. (1976), *Giotto and Florentine Painting, 1280–1375* (New York: Harper & Row).

Cyril of Alexandria (2000), *On the Unity of Christ*, trans. J. A. McGuckin (Crestwood, NY: St Vladimir's Seminary Press).

Didi-Huberman, G. (1995), *Fra Angelico: Resemblance and Figuration* (Chicago: University of Chicago Press).

Ehrman, B. and Z. Pleše (2011), *The Apocryphal Gospels* (New York and Oxford: Oxford University Press).

Foster, R. and P. Tudor-Craig (1986), *The Secret Life of Paintings* (Woodbridge: Boydell Press).

Fulton, R. (2002), *From Judgement to Passion: Devotion to Christ and the Virgin Mary, 800–1200* (New York: Columbia University Press).

Kitzinger, E. (1954), *The Cult of Images in the Age before Iconoclasm* (Cambridge, Mass.: Harvard University Press).

Mann, J. (1993), *Majestat Batlló: The Art of Medieval Spain AD 500–1200* (New York: Metropolitan Museum of Art).

Marrow, J. H. (1979), *Passion Iconography in North European Art of the Late Middle Ages and Early Renaissance: A Study of the Transformation of Sacred Metaphor into Descriptive Narrative* (Kortrijk: Von Ghemmot).

Melinkoff, R. (1988), *The Devil at Isenheim: Reflections of Popular Belief in Grünewald's Altarpiece* (Berkeley: University of California Press).

Raw, B. (2009), *Anglo-Saxon Crucifixion Iconography and the Art of the Monastic Revival*. Cambridge Studies in Anglo-Saxon (Cambridge: Cambridge University Press).

Schaff, P. (1877), *The Creeds of Christendom, with a History and Critical Notes*, vol. 2 (New York: Harper).

Schiller, G. (1972), *Iconography of Christian Art*, vol. 2: *The Passion of Jesus Christ*, trans. Janet Seligman (London: Lund Humphries).

Smalley, B. (1964), *The Study of the Bible in the Middle Ages* (Notre Dame, Ind.: University of Notre Dame Press).

Viladesau, R. (2005), *The Beauty of the Cross: The Passion of Christ in Theology and the Arts from the Catacombs to the Eve of the Reformation* (Oxford: Oxford University Press).

CHAPTER 15

··

THE CHRISTOLOGY OF THOMAS AQUINAS IN ITS SCHOLASTIC CONTEXT

··

JOSEPH WAWRYKOW

Aquinas offers comments on Christ in several writings, across a range of genres: in biblical commentaries (as in the expositions of Matthew and of John); in such systematic writings as the *Scriptum on the Sentences* of Peter Lombard, the *Summa contra Gentiles*, and the *Compendium of Theology*; in several of the academic sermons; and even in a disputed question (in five articles), on the incarnation of the Word. Aquinas' fullest discussion of Christ is found in his final major systematic writing, the *Summa theologiae*. The *Summa*'s 'treatise' on Christ is in its third part (the tertia pars) and contains fifty-nine questions (*ST* III, qq.1–59). The tertia pars aspires to comprehensiveness in Christological topics addressed, and the organization and writing display considerable skill. The *Summa*'s prima pars has been devoted to God (and the procession of creatures from the triune God); its second part, to the movement of the rational creature to God as beatifying end, in general (prima secundae) and with particular concern for the principal virtues involved in that movement to God (in the secunda secundae), the theological virtues (II–II, qq.1–46), and the cardinal (qq.47–170). The Christology of the tertia pars draws on those earlier discussions in presenting Jesus, true God and true human; in this integration of the theo-logy and the theological anthropology of the earlier parts, the Christology of the tertia pars in turn completes those discussions, in the light of revelation in Christ. The Christology of the tertia pars is a masterful achievement, testimony to Aquinas' lifelong encounter with Christ; his fidelity to Scripture and to the theological traditions, both West and East; and his skills as a theologian, intent on teaching Christ most adequately.

The present chapter, focusing on the Christology of the *Summa*, proceeds in three stages. The first presents the Christology in broad strokes, noting what Aquinas stresses in teaching the incarnate Word, the place of Jesus in God's saving plan, and the principal sources of this teaching on Christ. The second looks more closely at the teaching about the humanity of Christ, attending to the co-assumed, to what is taken up by the Word in becoming incarnate along with the human nature itself. This discussion of select questions in the treatise will allow opportunity to reflect on the teaching in a double sense: not only what is taught, when it comes to the Word as incarnate and as this human, but how that is taught. The chapter concludes with an assessment of Aquinas' mature Christology, by considering criticisms made of this teaching by those unsettled by an incarnational approach.

MAIN FEATURES OF THE CHRISTOLOGY OF THE *SUMMA*

Aquinas's Christology is incarnational, and explicitly in conformity with what has been determined by the Church meeting in council, at Ephesus (431), Chalcedon (451), and II Constantinople (553) (*ST* III, q.2, aa.1–2, 6). Incarnation involves an act: the second person of God has taken up human nature and come to express that, to instantiate it. In taking up human nature and becoming human, there is no change to the Word. What is true of the second person from eternity, continues to be true in incarnation. The Word/Image/Son is a distinct person in the Godhead, not to be confused with the Father, from whom the Word eternally proceeds, or the Holy Spirit, who proceeds from the Father and the Son; the Word is one and the same God as the Father and the Spirit. By the act of incarnation the divine second person is also human. Whatever is true of being human is now also asserted of the incarnate Word. Aquinas is attentive to the mystery: this union, in which a second nature is united to the first in the divine person, is unique, due to the power of God and not to be conflated with whatever other unions to which we have direct access.

The account of incarnation as act in turn provides a grammar for speaking of Christ (cf. *ST* III, q.16). In Christ, there is a union of two natures, the divine nature which is the Word eternally, and, human nature, taken up in incarnation. The two natures remain in their integrity. But, they are united in one and the same person; and that person has both natures, wholly and without confusion. The subject of the divine nature in the case of Christ, is the Word; the Word in the case of Christ is the subject of the human nature, instantiating that nature and expressing it as well. The union is personal or hypostatic (synonymous terms for Aquinas; *ST* III, q.2, aa.2–3), and whether it is the divine or the human nature that is under consideration, there is the same subject: the Word. The person of Jesus is the Word; in the conciliar formula, 'one person, two natures', the Word is the person. By virtue of the hypostatic union of the two natures, there are things that can be said of the Word precisely as God (whatever falls under divine nature, such as God's eternal perfections); there are other things that can be said of the incarnate Word precisely as human (whatever falls under human nature). Actually, there is a third set of predications that can be asserted of the Word: what pertains to the Word as, precisely, that divine person (and not another). Thus, Aquinas' is a single subject Christology, which takes seriously the two natures, and admits of a triple predication: statements made of the Word as Word; others, made of the Word as God; and, others that take account of the becoming incarnate, made of the Word as human.

In conformity with the Eastern Fathers (cf. *ScG* IV, ch. 41.10), not least John of Damascus, Aquinas invokes instrumental causality in figuring the relation between the human and divine natures in Christ (Tschipke 2003; Blankenhorn 2010). The humanity stands to the divinity as the personal and conjoined, and animate, instrument. By 'personal and conjoined', Aquinas is repeating that the union of the natures is in the person of the Word, who is the subject of all of the doings ascribed to Christ, human as well as divine. By 'animate', Aquinas is reminding us that in taking up human nature, the incarnate Word has everything essential to being human—the human body and the human soul, including a human intellect and will. And, in Christ, these are fully operational: the incarnate Word knows and wills as human. That human willing and acting is central to Christ's saving work. Of itself, no human acting could be causal of spiritual effect. But, as the personal, conjoined, and animate instrument, by the Word's assumed humanity the incarnate Word can cause grace and bring about salvation, spiritual gifts that have their origin in God; the divine Word does this through the characteristic actions of its own instantiated humanity, through the instrumentality of the operations of knowing and love of the Word as human.

There is a close link between Christology and soteriology in Aquinas. In the *Summa*, this is evident from the treatise's first question, on the fittingness of the incarnation. In *ST* III, q.1, salvation has a positive cast. God has brought human beings into existence in order to share God's own life with humans. Humans are called to beatitude, which will come in the next life, when those who have lived as God wills reach God Godself, and by God's elevating gift are able to know and love God directly. Aquinas is also aware of the obstacle posed by sin. People haven't lived as God intends, and so haven't prepared for eternal beatitude. To reach that end set for people by God—itself transcending our natural capacities—the problem of sin must be overcome, and so people set right with God, reordered to God as to their beatifying end, and acting in accordance with God's salvific will. Christ is the way to that beatifying end. Aquinas has made that point early in the prima pars, when he explains the organization of the *ST*. So the fittingness of the incarnation is asserted on soteriological grounds. *ST* III, q.1, a.2c offers a detailed account of the place of Christ in human salvation and God's salvific plan. That the incarnation of the Word is fitting, he states, can be seen both in terms of promoting progress in the good, and, helping in moving away from evil. Under each heading Aquinas notes five ways in which the incarnation of the Word works for good, and moves others away from evil. The incarnation of the Word promotes the good because the incarnation incites the journeyer to faith in God, and hope in God, and love of God; and as incarnate the Word provides a model for emulation, as well as announces the end of the journey, eternal life itself. As for moving away from evil, the incarnation warns against the key sins that obstruct the fulfillment of God's will for humans (e.g., pride, presumption); as incarnate, the Word also makes up for the sin that separates people from the God who is their end, by satisfying for sin.

Aquinas repeats the link between Christology and soteriology throughout the tertia pars. He makes his own an Anselmian interest in asking about the 'why' of incarnation, put in soteriological terms, while making good use of his single subject, triple predication Christology. The Savior needs be God, because God saves, only God can provide salvation, a share of God's own life, and all that brings one to salvation (grace and the attendant virtues and gifts). The Savior needs to be human, because it is humans who are called to eternal life, humans who have put themselves off track and need to be brought back on track and reconciled to God, and shown by one who shares their nature how to live and so become readied for the end of eternal life. And, that it is the second divine person who becomes human and provides for salvation also makes eminent sense. *ST* III, q.3 is about the person who assumes human nature. It is not strictly necessary that it be the Word who becomes human; it lies within the divine power for another of the persons to be the term of the assumption of human nature (*ST* III, q.3, a.5), or even all three persons to be the term of the assumption (a.6). But, that in fact the assumption of human nature has terminated in the second divine person shows God's wisdom especially well. *ST* III, q.3., a.8 alleges reasons for that fittingness. Perhaps the simplest is the one connecting salvation to creation. All things are made according to the Word, who is the Wisdom of God and so the plan of all creation. Who better then to become incarnate, to remake fallen humans, to enable them to attain to the God who beatifies (ad 2)?

In discussing God's plan for humans and the place of Christ in that plan, Aquinas is trading on a view of human existence as a journey. Life in this world can be seen as a path, which should lead to the end, in the next world, of eternal life. Sin takes one off the path; correct human operation, with the aid of Christ, keeps one on the path and progressing to the end of the journey. That end is variously described by Aquinas: beatitude or beatific vision; the direct knowing and loving of God. But, in the tertia pars Aquinas also puts the end in a way that foregrounds the centrality of Christ in God's saving plan and action. Eternal life can be viewed as an inheritance, given to those who are children of God. Human beings are adopted into sonship through Christ; and by attaining to eternal life, by entering into the life of the triune God, what pertains naturally to the second divine person as divine Son is extended to others, to God's adopted children (e.g., *ST* III, q.24, a.3c; Somme 1997), through the instrumentality of the assumed humanity. Here, Romans 8, a passage to which Aquinas turns increasingly in the mature writings, is receiving its due.

One can identify in the tertia pars two sets of post-scriptural Christian interlocutors with whom Aquinas is in conversation. The first set takes its rise from the Christology of Book Three of the *Sentences* of Peter Lombard, and runs through the scholastic commentarial tradition. It is not simply that the Lombard had identified issues that warrant inclusion in a Christology, or recounted the views of patristic theologians (mainly Western, and in particular Augustine) on them. In addition, the Lombard reported the main currents of Christological opinion at mid-twelfth century in Paris, and in developing their own Christologies, later scholastics took full account of the main twelfth-century positions. *Sentences* III, d.6 has in fact an iconic status. Here, the Lombard notes that his contemporaries have advanced three positions on how the divine and the human come together in Christ. The first opinion, *homo assumptus*, asserts that the Word takes up a *homo* at the moment of that *homo*'s conception; the Word shares its person with that *homo*, and in tandem the Word with its *homo* goes about the work of salvation. The third of the Lombard's opinions, the habitus theory, is worked out in opposition to *homo assumptus*. In this view, the Word takes up the ingredients of human nature, separately, such that the Word has a body, and has a soul; but the two, body and soul, are not themselves united, lest a second person (a 'human person') come to be in addition to the divine person. The second opinion, the composite person or subsistence theory, posits that the Word in becoming human takes up human nature and comes to express that, without loss to itself as fully divine Word. Whereas *homo assumptus* would seem to be asserting a single person, and two natures but two supposits as well (one for each of the natures), in the second opinion, supposit and person are the same, and only one; in the person or supposit the two natures are united. The three opinions provided the springboard for much of Western scholastic Christology for the rest of the Middle Ages. The third opinion was condemned as heretical later in the twelfth century, and no thirteenth-century scholastic wanted to hold it. Most professed an affinity for the second opinion, although some were open to the charms of *homo assumptus* (especially when nature was viewed as itself a subject). As for Aquinas, he makes mention of the three opinions throughout his career, from his *Scriptum on the Sentences* (obviously) through the *Summa contra Gentiles* (IV, chs. 37–38), to the *Summa theologiae* (e.g., III, q.2, aa.3–5). He consistently expressed his preference for the second opinion, as more adequate to the reality of the union of the natures, and always rejected outright the third opinion. He never affirmed the first opinion, but his attitude towards it was less severe early in his career. In the *Scriptum* (*In III*, d.VI, q.I, a.II, resp.), he explicitly denies that it is heretical, although he thinks it inadequate. By the *ScG* and then the *ST*, however, his position has hardened.

It is through his engagement with another set of texts and interlocutors that Aquinas' mature Christology is marked off from that of his contemporaries. Aquinas is unparalleled in the thirteenth century for the depth and extent of his knowledge of early patristic debates and determinations about Christ (Backes 1931; Morard 1997, 2005; Emery 2007). After the first Parisian regency (1256–9), while back in Italy as he worked on building up the educational structure of his Order, Aquinas had come across, in Latin translation, the acts and proceedings of the early ecumenical councils, with their supporting documentation. Through the study of this foundational material, which had passed out of general theological circulation in the West after the Carolingian period, Aquinas' Christology became sharper and more focused in its expression. Aquinas had always favored a single subject Christology, but now Aquinas could do that with the explicit support of the early councils from Ephesus on and of Cyril of Alexandria, and with a keener sense of the failings of Nestorius, now known at first hand. Corresponding with this new knowledge and the enhanced importance for him of the early, Greek, Christological tradition, the other context receded in importance, and was evaluated against the standard of early Christian orthodoxy. Thus, in the *Summa* (III, q.2. a.6 c.), the Lombard's three opinions are no longer 'opinions'. The first and the third are in fact 'heresy', lapsing into errors long ago condemned by the Church meeting in council (the lapse, Aquinas adds, is unwitting, due to the low level of twelfth-century knowledge of the early councils); and the second opinion is not opinion, but orthodox truth, conforming to what the Church has defined, beginning with Ephesus, and continuing through Chalcedon and II Constantinople, councils much under Cyril's spiritual sway. There is justification for calling the Christology of the mature Aquinas 'Cyrillian' (e.g., Blankenhorn 2010: 148), although Aquinas has learned from others as well. With Cyril, it matters greatly that the natures are united in the divine person, and that the humanity is indeed the humanity of the Word, as incarnate.

THE STRUCTURE OF THE *SUMMA*'S TREATMENT OF CHRIST (*ST* III, QQ.1–59)

Aquinas was hardly the first to offer a systematic account of Christ. Several models, when it came to inclusion of topics and their ordering, were available to him and he learned from such writings as the Lombard's *Sentences* and the subsequent commentaries on the Christological distinctions (Bk. III, dd.1–23); John of Damascus' Christological chapters in *de fide orthodoxa*, already partly translated by the time of the *Sentences* and fully available by the end of the twelfth century; and the *Summa fratris alexandri*, a work by Franciscan theologians at mid-thirteenth century drawing on the writings of Alexander of Hales as well as their own. But, the organization of *ST* III, qq.1–59 does not replicate any one of these precedents. Aquinas has in the execution added considerable material to the typical scholastic presentation on Christ. *ST* III, qq.1–59 fall into two main parts, each of which is further divided into sections or groups of questions. In the first main part, Aquinas discusses, as he puts it in the prologue to the tertia pars, the mystery of the Incarnation, whereby God was made man for our salvation. The first main part itself falls into three sections. The first of these sections is constituted by the opening question on the fittingness of the Incarnation. That is followed by a section on the mode of union, progressing in turn from an account of the union in general (q.2), through a consideration of the person who assumes (q.3), to an examination of the nature that is assumed, both in itself (qq.4–6) and then in terms of what is 'co-assumed' with that nature (qq.7–15; more on this below). That Aquinas gives only a single question to the person who assumes is not worrisome: that question in effect picks up the thread of the account of God in the prima pars; it is not possible to follow the analyses of III, q.3, without first studying I, qq.2–26 (on the divine essence, including the essential divine operations of knowing and willing), and the trinity of persons (qq.27–43), especially those questions that are on the second divine person (I, qq.34–5). The third section of the first main part of the treatise on Christ looks at the 'consequences of the union'

(III, qq.16–26), with regards to the incarnate Word in itself (qq.16–19), in relation to the Father (qq.20–4), and then in relation to others (qq.25–6), especially as mediator between God and humans.

The second main part of the treatise on Christ (III, qq.27–59) falls into four sections: the entry into the world (qq.27–39), Christ's life, doctrine, and miracles (qq.40–5), his Passion and death (qq.46–52), and, finally, the resurrection and post-resurrection (qq.53–9). Although some questions on the Passion and death would make their way into a typical scholastic treatise on Christ (as in the Lombard), as well as some questions on his resurrection (as in the commentarial tradition, but not in the Lombard himself), the second main part of the treatise on Christ is quite distinctive. Prior to the *Summa*, it was not the practice to include the retelling of Christ's story from beginning to end, and beyond, in the scholastic treatise on Christ; that inclusion is Aquinas' innovation with the *Summa* (Scheffczyk 1985).

The ordering of the two main parts may at first glance seem puzzling: modern readers may have expected the telling of the story of Christ before getting into the finer points of incarnational Christology, as in the treatise's first main part. Aquinas could assume in his intended readers a knowledge of Christ and did not need to engage in such preliminary proclamation to set the stage. The ordering of the treatise makes pedagogical sense, given Aquinas' intentions for his intended readers. Assuming a basic knowledge of Christ, won through study of the Bible and liturgical practice, Aquinas can work through the technical issues and state forcefully his single subject Christology (with due attention to the different kinds of statement that are made about the Word who is the person of Jesus), as he does in the treatise's first main part, before turning anew to the Gospel account in the treatise's second main part. The exercises of the first main part will have prepared the reader for a refined appreciation of the Gospel proclamation as recounted in the second main part of the treatise; the questions of the second main part of the treatise are to be read in the light of the earlier questions.

TEACHING CHRIST: ON THIS HUMAN, JESUS

Aquinas' skill as a teacher can be illustrated by looking at particular questions on Christ, in this case from the second section of the treatise's first main part; this will make apparent Aquinas' appreciation of the genuine humanness of the Word incarnate. Much of that second section (III, qq.2–15) is given over to what is taken up by the Word (qq.4–15). The Word in incarnation has taken up human nature (qq.4–6). The incarnate Word can be classified as truly human (although more than merely human; the Word is also fully divine), having everything needed to make some being, human: the human body; the human soul, which gives a human the capacity for sensation and movement, and for rational thought and willing. To ascribe a nature to something is to say what it essentially is, what makes it the sort of thing that it is. The Word in incarnation also takes up the co-assumed, those features of human existence that are particular to a given human.

The co-assumed go beyond, as it were, the nature (common to all beings classified as human), allowing the distinctiveness of this particular human, Jesus (the Word incarnate), to receive its due.

The questions on the co-assumed fall into two groups. Qq.7–13 reflect on the perfections that are co-assumed by the Word in becoming human. Aquinas begins with questions on Christ's grace: q.8 is on his grace as head of the Church, which grace is identical with the grace that renders him holy, treated in q.7. He then looks (qq.9–12) at Jesus' knowledge as human (this knowledge is multiple); and concludes the treatment of the co-assumed perfections by treating Christ's humanly power, viewed in the instrumental relation of the humanity to the divinity (q.13). Among the knowledges ascribed to Christ is beatific knowledge (q.10), possessed by Christ throughout his earthly life; an infused knowledge by which he knows God and all things in related to God as their beginning and end (q.11); and an experiential knowledge. By the time of the *Summa* such experiential knowledge is affirmed as real of Christ, and at III, q.12, a.2c, Aquinas explicitly acknowledges that on this, his position has changed from what he taught in the *Scriptum on the Sentences*. Christ did grow in knowledge, comes to know things, although he also possesses from his conception the beatific vision and the infused knowledge crucial to his saving mission. The remaining two questions on the co-assumed ask about the defects that have been taken up, both the defects of body (q.14) and of soul (q.15).

In asserting given perfections and defects of the Word incarnate, Aquinas observes certain guidelines. First, the treatment is governed by the scriptural witness, as mediated by the Christian traditions. There is usually overt scriptural support for this or that co-assumed perfection or defect. Scripture is clear that Christ did will the good, did have the passions of soul which were moved properly, did suffer, did die, and Aquinas will quote Scripture as needed, in making his point. Secondly, Aquinas keeps in mind the link between the person and natures of Christ, and salvation. The Word becomes incarnate so that by his human actions humans might attain to God; and for that the incarnate Word will needs be susceptible, for example, to suffering and death, tailored to overcoming the sin that separates humans from the God who is their beatifying end.

Q.7, on the grace and attendant virtues and gifts possessed by Christ, and qq.14–15 are illuminating. In q.7, Aquinas asks about the grace of Christ (aa.1; 9–13); his virtues (aa.2–4), his possession of the gifts of the Holy Spirit (aa.5–6), and his gratuitous graces (aa.7–8). In the background of this discussion of Christ is the teaching of the secunda pars, on the movement of the rational creature to God as beatifying end. All of these—grace, virtues (especially infused), gifts, even the gratuitous graces—are important for an account of humans in correct relationship to God and acting as God wills humans to act. Grace elevates humans beyond the merely natural capacities, orienting them and their acts to God as beatifying end. For fallen humans, grace also heals, addressing the disruption in the self brought by sin. By sin, the lower self is put at odds with the higher self; and the whole person is put at odds with God. The grace that justifies brings forgiveness, puts the person right before God, and heals the self, reordering the lower to the higher as subordinate and subject to it. Those who are justified and elevated by grace are set on a journey whose end will come in the next life, in the immediate knowing and loving of God. What a graced person wills and does moves the person ever closer to the eternal end. In the conversion to God, the person receives grace construed as habitual; God prepares the person for that infusion by the grace of *auxilium*; and remains active in the person's life by moving the person, anew by *auxilium*, to acts that are good and pleasing to God (*ST* I–II, q.109). For Aquinas, along with the habitual grace that justifies and elevates a human, other virtues are infused: the theological virtues of faith, hope, and charity; infused moral virtues (paralleling, but at a higher level, the cardinal virtues); the gifts of the Holy Spirit. These good habits provide new capacity: they mark the transformation of a person into someone capable of actions that are pleasing to God, and as aided by God's other gifts, the *auxilia* that reduce that person, of heightened potential, to morally good and meritorious actions that bring one to the God who is the beatifying end of human existence. The theological virtues establish a capacity for the believing, and the hoping, and the loving, that relate a person properly to God; the infused moral virtues make possible the acts of justice and the other virtues that are good and sought by God from creatures made by and for God; and the gifts of the Holy Spirit render their possessor docile to the promptings of the Holy Spirit, involved in the actualization by God of the new potential of the justified, sanctified self. (As for the gratuitous gifts (I–II, q.111, aa.1, 4–5): while habitual grace and *auxilium*, and the theological and infused moral virtues, and the gifts, are involved in the individual's own spiritual progress, the gratuitous gifts have to do with that person's work on behalf of others in their movement to God as end.)

In III, q.7, grace, virtue, and gift (and gratuitous graces) are affirmed of Christ. The incarnate Word is justified and elevated by grace, established in right relationship with God; the humanity of the Word incarnate is perfected as well by the virtues infused with grace, and by the gifts of the Spirit that render their possessor docile to the promptings of the Spirit. The Spirit factors into the account of Jesus' life, actions, and suffering, as leading, guiding, prompting him in his good actions, actions which are ordered to spiritual effect. Just as other human beings need God's gifts to accomplish the moral and supernatural good, so does the Word incarnate. When Aquinas discusses the humanity standing to the divinity as instrumental cause and asserts that it is via the actions of the Word as human that human salvation is worked out, he is thinking of that personal, conjoined, and animate instrument as marked by the grace and virtue and gift affirmed in q.7.

But, are such gifts really necessary, for someone who is God? And, if grace gives a participation in the divine nature, what need would someone who is God (and so isn't 'participating' in God) have for grace? Aquinas' response to these queries in the objections of article one in q.7 sets the tone for the rest of the question. At bottom, the objections reduce a single subject Christology to a single predication Christology, in ascribing to the Word as fully divine Word what applies in fact to the Word precisely as incarnate, as truly human. But, the incarnate Word's moral perfection is not due to the fact that the Word is God; it is due to the perfecting of the Word in the Word's assumed humanity by grace and virtue and gift. The pattern in play for other humans who are correctly related and oriented to God and acting in a way pleasing to God, is in play with Christ. Whatever good any human wills and does owes much to God; and that is true of Christ.

Yet, this human is unlike other humans in several ways, and q.7 is intent on pointing that out, to do justice to this particular human. Aquinas' identification of those differences, however, hardly undercuts his main point, about the need of the Word incarnate for grace and the like. These differences have to do with the purpose of the Incarnation, and so the distinctiveness of this human, what sets him apart from other humans. Other humans are not the savior; Jesus is; and by the actions of this human, others can attain to God as their beatifying end. And so, in keeping with his saving purpose, Jesus is marked with a fullness—of grace, of virtue, of gift—that is unique to him. And that fullness is quite apt, given the closeness of his humanity to his divinity (*ST* III, q.7, a.1c). Other humans are sinners. So in their justification, they are forgiven their sins as they are made pleasing to God. Jesus, as Scripture reminds us, was without sin (any sinning on his part would subvert his saving work); and so in his justification, there is no movement from sin towards God; but there is a justification (*ST* III, q.7, a.9, ad 2). That he is pleasing to God is due to God's grace.

It is another difference between this human as graced and others that is the most remarkable, and considerably debated in the scholarship. The teaching of the prima secundae is that grace is ordered to glory, that actions in this life, aided by grace and the like, bring one to eternal life in the next. People live now by grace, and out of faith, hope, charity; in the future, when in the immediate presence of God, people will know and love God face to face. What has been hoped for will give way to comprehension, and so hope passes away; what has been believed, will give way to vision itself (I–II, q.67, aa.3–4). Of the theological virtues, only charity will remain (a.6), intensified in conjunction with the vision. In this life, a human being is a journeyer (*viator*), in the next, *comprehensor*.

Was Christ a journeyer during his time in the world? The questions on the co-assumed culminate in an article that directly asks this question (q.15, a.10); but Aquinas' position informs the teaching even in q.7, on the grace of Christ (e.g., q.7, a.1 ad 2; a.3c), and winds its way throughout the discussion of the co-assumed. For Aquinas, what marks the culmination for others of their journey and comes in the next life, was possessed by Christ throughout his time on earth. From the moment of his conception, he enjoyed the direct vision of God as beatifying; even in this world, he was a *comprehensor*. In the final question on the co-assumed, Aquinas adds some detail to this depiction: this beatitude was restricted to *soul* while Christ was active in the world. It was not extended to the body, as it will be for others when they attain heaven. Extending beatitude to his body prior to the Passion would have rendered the Passion impossible—an incorrupt, immortal body cannot suffer or die. Full beatitude, as extended to the body, would have frustrated Christ's saving work. Yet, Christ in the world was not only *comprehensor*. He could be a *viator* as well. His good actions as meritorious were of great benefit to others, for whom he worked, throughout his life and on the Cross; but they could also merit for himself the bodily notes that mark full beatitude, and which he received in the resurrection, as his reward.

Several of the articles in q.7 follow on the affirmation that Christ was *comprehensor*, beatified in soul, throughout his earthly existence, that by God's gift, his human operations of knowing and loving were perfect. In a.2, Aquinas asserts that Christ had the full range of virtues, infused with the grace that he had received in its fullness. In aa.3 and 4, he adds that Christ didn't have the virtues of faith or of hope. By faith, one sees now in a glass darkly, by hope, one aspires to a future good; as beatified in soul, Christ would lack such imperfection (that is, aspiring to is lesser than having). Does that mean that Jesus lacked the gifts of the Holy Spirit, which perfect someone who has the virtues, including the virtues of faith and hope? In particular, since fear is associated with the virtue of hope, does his lack of that virtue mean that he didn't have the gift of fear (a.6)? In the prima secundae, among the ways that Aquinas distinguishes the habits that are gifts from those habits that are these theological virtues is to refer to duration. The virtues of faith and hope pass away; they do not remain in heaven. But, the gifts remain, even in heaven (I–II, q.68, a.6). By the gifts, a person is made docile to the promptings of the Holy Spirit; even in heaven, the Holy Spirit is active, in a way appropriate to beatific vision. And so someone enjoying now the beatitude of soul would lack the virtue of faith or hope, but not the gifts associated with those virtues.

Qq. 14 and 15 in the tertia pars turn from the perfections to the defects, of body and of soul, that are to be ascribed to this human and that figure into his saving work. Several defects come under consideration: hunger and thirst; inclination to sin, and difficulty in doing the good; ignorance; and, of course, death. The view of Christ in these questions on defects is recognizably scriptural. Jesus was without sin, a point made several times in the NT. So he was not born in original sin; nor did he actually sin. He is thus not by necessity subject to the gamut of consequences that follow on sin. Aquinas notes, Jesus did not have some of those consequences: his lower self was not in rebellion against the higher self, nor was he inclined to sin. He was not subject to internal temptations (although as active in a fallen world, he was subject to external temptation, a point discussed at length at III, q.41). Nor was he subject to any ignorance that would cloud his mental operations. But, while without sin, he did have the chief of the consequences of sin, death, the physical death that marks the end of one's time in the world. Death is the due penalty for sin; since there is sin, there is death. Someone who lacks sin, need not die. But Jesus did die. Here, the second of the guiding principles in treating the co-assumed is fully at play, the soteriological purpose of the Incarnation. Sin separates other human beings from the God who beatifies; Christ's death meets that problem; so Christ must be able to die. He does die, although he as sinless is not subject to such necessity. The Word in becoming incarnate has freely taken up that consequence of sin. Since dying presupposes an ability to change, to undergo diminution, Christ has the possibility that accompanies sin and leads to death. The discussion of the defects that are, and are not, co-assumed is thoroughly and insistently economic (III, q.14, 4 ad 2: *defectus nostros dispensative assumpsit*). The Word in becoming incarnate willingly took up those defects that would promote the incarnate Word's saving work, and were compatible with the perfections, also co-assumed, involved in that saving work.

In depicting the defects of Christ, Aquinas makes skillful use of a basic distinction, between what pertains to the nature itself (as limned in qq.4–6) and different states in which the nature might be found. The following states can be identified: prior to the Fall; after the Fall; after the Fall and under grace; and, the final state, heaven or final beatitude. Each of these states has its own characteristics, and it is worthwhile to limn them in detail. For Aquinas, the first people were endowed with their nature and created in grace. Thus, while as corporeal there is an inclination to dissolution, that inclination need not have been actualized; and only was, because of sin, as the penalty for sin. And, prior to the Fall, people need not have sinned. They could sin, because of the will, which is part of their nature; it was open to them to misuse the will, in sinning. But, they need not have misused the will: sinning is not essential to being human. So prior to the Fall, human beings did not need to sin, and did not need to die. If they had not sinned, they would have been confirmed in grace and would have been granted the fullness of beatitude.

After the Fall, grace is removed, sin becomes a feature added on to human nature; original sin is passed on, putting humans at odds with God, and introducing an inclination to sin to the exercise of will and a difficulty in doing good (although some of the good natural to a person as human still remained within the scope of human capacities; see I–II, q.109, a.2c). Hunger and thirst enter the scene, as does ignorance. In this state, people had to die: death is the principal penalty owed the sinner. In the third of the states, after the Fall and under grace, some of the problems established by human sin are met and overcome: graced humans are forgiven and justified, elevated to God's level and ordered to God as beatifying end; the opposition within the self is in principle overcome, although moral transformation and growth into God remains a lifelong process. People still hunger and thirst. They die physically, as a reminder of the seriousness of their sin, although as in grace they are no longer subject to spiritual death. In the final state, in the immediate presence of God, all physical and spiritual limitations are removed; irrevocably confirmed in the good, the human person now flourishes fully, sharing in the life for which God has intended such rational beings. Here, there is beatitude of both soul and body.

Aquinas is not assigning this human, Jesus, to any one of these states, nor is he ascribing all of the characteristics of any one of these states to him. Rather, in Jesus the co-assumed characteristics are taken from each of these states. In light of the scriptural witness, about his defects (some, not all) and his saving purpose, this does not seem arbitrary; nor is the result garish. In retrospect, the invocation of the states is present even in the discussion of Christ's grace (in q.7). In affirming of Christ the grace, virtue, and gift that render possible the acts that are meritorious, sacrificial, satisfying, Aquinas is attending to what holds of the state after sin and as under grace, echoing as well the first state. In affirming of Christ from the moment of conception the beatitude of soul, he is ascribing to Christ something that pertains to the heavenly state. In the subsequent consideration of the defects, the invocation of the different states is more sustained and explicit, to render the depiction of this human, who is Savior, more adequate.

The inclusion of the category of the co-assumed in the scholastic treatise is clever, and suitable to the presentation of Christ. The talk about the co-assumed does not detract from the genuine humanity; it adds texture to the depiction of the human who is the Savior of the world. In general terms, a human may be under one or another of these states, subject to the attributes of that state; but the person remains human. A person who is subject to sin and its consequences and lacks grace, remains human; so too does the person who is subject to grace; and so too does the person who attains the vision of God ('grace does not destroy nature, but perfects it'; *ST* I, q.1, a.8, ad 2). The difference among states has to do with human flourishing, or the absence of it due to the difficulties wrought by sin. This is true as well of Jesus, the one who is not under any one of these states alone and is not subject to all the attributes of a given state. This human receives from each of these states, as is appropriate for the human whose function is to save.

More on the Humanity: Assessment

Does Aquinas offer a credible depiction of Christ in his humanity and humanness? Some doubt the ability of any incarnational Christology to uphold the full humanity, whatever the good intentions of its author. Doesn't the divinity inevitably overwhelm the humanity, so that the heavy-lifting when it comes to Christ is to be ascribed to the fact that he is God? In the case of Aquinas, that concern misses the mark. The Word incarnate has a full human nature. Aquinas shows exquisite care in attending to which aspect of the Word (Word as Word; as God; as human) is in play, and steadfastly refuses to conflate the three.

That concern might be expressed by arguing that in the case of Jesus incarnationally-construed, there is something crucial to being human that ends up missing from Christ: a human person, in the usual sense, someone (a creature) who comes to be as a particular actualization of the potential constituted by the nature (cf. *ScG* IV, ch. 40.9–12). One of the attractions of an adoptionist Christology, or of a Nestorian Christology, is that it posits a human person in the usual sense; and that one (a creature) has been brought into an intimate connection with the Word, whether at conception or later on. Jesus in such Christologies is exactly like other humans, not just in nature but also in person. And, 'what is not assumed, is not redeemed …' Yet, granted that there is not a 'human person' in the ordinary sense in Aquinas' Christology (there isn't), this criticism too seems not especially telling. While not created, there is nonetheless a person in Christ, and Aquinas has a great deal to say about that person, not least as incarnate. And, as incarnate, without loss to itself as the eternal Word of the Father, this person is indeed human. The divine person as incarnate is fully human. It is this person who realizes the potential constituted by the nature for a human form of life, acts and suffers as human, and is raised as human for human salvation. A human person in exactly the same way that I am a human person? No; but a human person, nonetheless.

This stress on the identity of the person of Jesus provides a depiction of unity, of one-ness, that is impossible in an adoptionist, or in a Nestorian, Christology. Who lives, acts, and suffers in the earthly sojourn? Who dies on the Cross? In these other Christologies, a (merely) human subject, who has partnered with the divine person. In Aquinas, fol-lowing Cyril and the great councils, it is the divine second person who as incarnate, is also, truly, human. That identification with humanity, that assertion of oneness and identity, without confusion of the natures, trumps the worry about a lack of a created person in Christ. God loves humans so much that God has become one of us.

Some claims peculiar to this Christology may also seem problematic, arguably under-cutting the true humanness of Jesus. Aquinas claims that Jesus lacked faith (and hope) and that throughout his earthly sojourn he enjoyed the beatific vision. The denial of faith, and ascription of beatitude (of soul) initially seems at odds with the claim about Jesus as model, who shows others how to live authentically. Faith is central to relation to God; surely beatitude is best reserved for the next life, something to aspire to but not yet possessed. Even here, however, there is something to be said for Aquinas' teaching. For one thing, he does not deny faith (or hope) simply; he denies to Christ the *virtues* of faith, of hope, because of what is imperfect in them: to believe is to see in a glass darkly; that gives way to vision; to hope is to hope for something future that one does not now possess. Aquinas grants to Jesus the perfections associated with faith and hope (obe-dience, and trust in God, respectively) (*Quaestio disputata de spe*, a.1 ad 12 and ad 4; Wawrykow 2012b: 302–3).

While Jesus is for Aquinas undoubtedly model, he is not simply or principally model. He is, rather, the Savior, whose coming has as its end true human flourishing and in the end full human flourishing (with God). The teaching about Jesus as model is sub-ordinate to, and shaped by, the affirmation that he is Savior. That is the guiding insight, expressed repeatedly in the linking of Christology and soteriology. Each of the appar-ently problematic claims noted above bespeak the fullness of Christ's grace, and that is a fullness that is connected with his saving work. 'He was full of grace; from his fullness all have received' (John 1:14, 16). He lacks what is imperfect in the virtues of faith, and of hope, because he stands in the most intimate relation to God: he knows and loves God directly, which is appropriate, for Aquinas, to the fulfilled human who is Savior.

The assertion that Jesus enjoyed the beatific vision from the moment of his con-ception, stands among the most controversial in this Christology. Even Aquinas' most insightful readers have expressed reservations about this (Torrell 2000). There is, nonetheless, a soteriological dimension to the affirmation. In the *Summa contra Gentiles*, Aquinas brackets consideration of Christ's own beatific vision. To make the soteriological point, that through Christ others can attain to the end of eternal life, Aquinas looks to the Incarnation itself, to the coming together of divine and human in the Word becoming human (*ScG* IV, ch. 54.2). That ontological unity points to and anticipates the unity that will come for others in the beatific vision, where humans and God come to be together. That comparison is not exact: the one (incarnation) is an ontological unity, the other (beatific vision) is an operational unity. In the bea-tific vision, someone is united to God in the sense that by God's elevating action, a human knows and loves God directly, face to face. In the *Summa theologiae*, on the other hand, Aquinas will repeat the comparison of ontological union in incarnation and the beatific vision of others (e.g., *ST* III, q.1, 2c), grounding the latter in the former. In the more robust Christology of the *ST*, Aquinas adds another comparison, by bringing in Christ's own beatific vision, throughout his earthly life. By this vision, the incarnate Word is himself, as human, united to God operationally; and his beatifying vision grounds that of others, who reach God as beatifying through him. The Savior gives what he himself has, provides to others spiritual effects: as God, authoritatively, as human, instrumentally (cf. *ST* I–II, q.112, a.1 ad 1). What holds of the graced acts that merit and satisfy and are sacrificial, Aquinas is saying here, holds of the ultimate spiritual effect, beatific vision itself.

SUGGESTED READING

Barnes (2012); Gondreau (2005); McCord Adams (1999); Morard (2005); Wawrykow (1998); Wawrykow (2012a).

BIBLIOGRAPHY

Works by Aquinas

Compendium theologiae, Sancti Thomae de Aquino *Opera Omnia* iussa Leonis XIII P. M. Edit, Tomus XLII (Rome: Editori di San Tommaso, 1970), 77–205.
Quaestio disputata de spe, in *Quaestiones Disputatae*, vol. II, ed. P. Bazzi et al. (Turin: Marietti, 1949), 803–12.
S. Thomae Aquinatis Doctoris Angelici Liber de veritate Catholicae fidei contra errores infidelium, qui dicitur Summa contra gentiles, ed. P. Marc with the help of C. Pera and P. Caramello, 3 vols. (Turin: Marietti, 1961).
S. Thomae de Aquino Ordinis Praedicatorum Summa Theologiae cura et studio Instituti Studiorum Medievalium Ottaviensis, 5 vols. (Ottawa: Studii Generalis O. Pr., 1941).
Scriptum super libros sententiarum magistri Petri Lombardi Episcopi Parisiensis, 4 volumes. Vols. 1–2 edited by P. Mandonnet, vols. 3–4 edited by M. F. Moos (Paris: Lethielleux, 1929–47).
Super Evangelium S. Ioannis Lectura, ed. R. Cai (Turin: Marietti, 1951).
Super Evangelium S. Matthaei Lectura, ed. R. Cai (Turin: Marietti, 1951).

Secondary Sources

Backes, I. (1931), *Die Christologie des hl. Thomas v. Aquin und die griechischen Kirchenväter* (Paderborn: Schöningh).
Barnes, C. (2012), *Christ's Two Wills in Scholastic Thought* (Toronto: Pontifical Institute of Mediaeval Studies).
Blankenhorn, B. (2010), 'The Place of Romans 6 in Aquinas's Doctrine of Sacramental Causality: A Balance of History and Metaphysics', in R. Hütter and M. Levering (eds.),

Ressourcement Thomism: Sacred Doctrine, the Sacraments, and the Moral Life. Essays in Honor of Romanus Cessario, O.P. (Washington, DC: Catholic University of America Press), 136–49.

Boyle, J. (1996) 'The Twofold Division of St. Thomas's Christology in the *Tertia Pars*', *The Thomist* 60: 439–47.

Emery, G. (2007), 'A Note on St. Thomas and the Eastern Fathers', in Emery, *Trinity, Church, and the Human Person: Thomistic Essays, Faith and Reason: Studies in Catholic Theology and Philosophy* (Naples, Fla.: Sapentia Press), 193–207.

Geenen, G. (1952), 'En marge de Concile de Chalcédoine. Les textes du Quatrième Concile dans les oeuvres de Saint Thomas', *Angelicum* 29: 43–59.

Gondreau, P. (2005), 'The Humanity of Christ, the Incarnate Word', in R. Van Nieuwenhove and J. Wawrykow (eds.), *The Theology of Thomas Aquinas* (Notre Dame: University of Notre Dame Press), 252–76.

Gondreau, P. (2009), *The Passions of Christ's Soul in the Theology of St. Thomas Aquinas* (Scranton: University of Scranton Press).

Laporte, J.-M. (2003), 'Christ in Aquinas's *Summa theologiae*: Peripheral or Pervasive?', *The Thomist* 67: 221–48.

McCord Adams, M. (1999), *What Sort of Human Nature? Medieval Philosophy and the Systematics of Christology* (Milwaukee: Marquette University Press).

Morard, M. (1997), 'Une source de saint Thomas d'Aquin. Le deuxième concile de Constantinople (553)', *Revue des sciences philosophiques et théologiques* 81: 21–56.

Morard, M. (2005), 'Thomas d'Aquin lecteur des conciles', *Archivum Franciscanum Historicum* 98: 211–365.

Ruello, F. (1987), *La christologie de Thomas d'Aquin* (Paris: Beauchesne).

Scheffczyk, L. (1985), 'Die Stellung des Thomas von Aquin in der Entwicklung der Lehre von den Mysteria Vitae Christi', in M. Gerwing and G. Ruppert (eds.), *Renovatio et Reformatio. Wider das Bild vom "finisteren" Mittelalter; Festschrift für Ludwig Hödl zum 60. Geburstag* (Münster: Aschendorff), 44–70.

Schenk, R. (1990), ' "Omnis Christi actio nostra est instructio": The Deeds and Sayings of Jesus as Revelation in the View of Thomas Aquinas', in L. Elders (ed.), *La doctrine de la révélation divine de Saint Thomas d'Aquin* (Vatican City: Pontificia Accademia di S. Tommaso d'Aquin, Libreria Editrice Vaticana), 103–31.

Somme, L.-T. (1987), *Fils adoptifs de Dieu par Jésus Christ. La filiation divine par adoption dans la théologie de saint Thomas d'Aquin* (Paris: Vrin).

Torrell, J.-P. (1999-), *Le Christ en ses Mystères. La vie et l'oeuvre de Jésus selon saint Thomas d'Aquin* (Paris: Desclée).

Torrell, J.-P. (2000), 'S. Thomas d'Aquin et la science du Christ', in Torrell, *Recherches thomasienne* (Paris: J. Vrin), 198–213.

Tschipke, T. (2003), *L'humanité du Christ comme instrument de salut de la divinité* [translation of 1939 German original] (Fribourg: Academic Press).

Wawrykow, J. (1998), 'Wisdom in the Christology of Thomas Aquinas', in K. Emery and J. Wawrykow (eds.), *Christ Among the Medieval Dominicans* (Notre Dame: University of Notre Dame Press), 175–96.

Wawrykow, J. (2005), 'Hypostatic Union', in R. Van Nieuwenhove and J. Wawrykow (eds.), *The Theology of Thomas Aquinas* (Notre Dame: University of Notre Dame Press), 222–51.

Wawrykow, J. (2007), 'Christ and the Gifts of the Holy Spirit in Aquinas', in T. Prügl and M. Schlosser (eds.), *Kirchenbild und Spiritualität: Ekklesiologie aus dem Anspruch des mendikantischen Ordensideals* (Festschrift für Ulrich Horst) (Paderborn: Ferdinand Schoeningh), 43–62.

Wawrykow, J. (2012a), 'Jesus in the Moral Theology of Thomas Aquinas', *Journal of Medieval and Early Modern Studies* 42: 13–33.

Wawrykow, J. (2012b), 'Theological Virtues', in E. Stump and B. Davies (eds.), *The Oxford Handbook of Aquinas* (Oxford: Oxford University Press), 287–307.

Weinandy, T. (2004), 'Jesus' Filial Vision of the Father', *Pro Ecclesia* 13: 189–201.

Weinandy, T. (2006), 'The Beatific Vision and the Incarnate Son: Furthering the Discussion', *The Thomist* 70: 605–15.

White, T. J. (2005), 'The Voluntary Action of the Earthly Christ and the Necessity of the Beatific Vision', *The Thomist* 69: 497–534.

CHAPTER 16

LATE MEDIAEVAL ATONEMENT THEOLOGIES

RIK VAN NIEUWENHOVE

In this chapter I will attempt to outline late mediaeval theologies of salvation, from Bonaventure and Thomas Aquinas to Duns Scotus and William of Ockham. While a discussion of only a handful of authors may appear a modest enough enterprise, given the richness of late mediaeval theology, it will nonetheless allow us to detect some important shifts, which will come to fruition in the theology of major Protestant thinkers.

Peter Lombard discusses the salvific value of Christ's life and death in Book III, distinctions 15–22 of his *Sentences*. Other distinctions, such as those dealing with the theological virtues (dist. 23–32), the cardinal virtues (dist. 33), and the gifts of the Holy Spirit (dist. 34) are also of some significance. An in-depth discussion of mediaeval theories of salvation should therefore examine more than what authors write about the Cross of Christ. Indeed, as we will see, scholastic theologians of the thirteenth century operated with an integrative vision of salvation. This means a number of things. First, to recall a popular distinction (Fiddes 2007) it implies that those thirteenth-century theories of salvation are both objective and subjective, which means that they discuss the repercussions of salvation for the relation between creation and God—this is the objective aspect; and they also deal with the transformative effect on the Christian believer through the operation of grace—this is the subjective aspect. It further means that the saving meaning of the life, death, and resurrection of the Word can only be theologically understood in its entirety from the perspective of intra-Trinitarian dynamics, which, in turn, moulds their theology of creation and their views on sacramental economy. I will further suggest that this kind of integrative vision is usually undergirded by a Christian-Neoplatonist worldview, and when this crumbles, the integrative vision is weakened or dissipates altogether. While this occurs in some nominalist authors, something of the older vision lingers on in some late mediaeval mystical authors. By way of example I will examine Ruusbroec's contribution.

BONAVENTURE AND THOMAS AQUINAS

St Bonaventure's Christology offers an outstanding example of the kind of integrative view I have alluded to. The mediating role the Son assumes between humanity and God finds its origin in the fact that he is the middle Person within the Trinity (generated by the Father, he co-spirates the Holy Spirit) (*Breviloquium* IV, 2.6). But this centrality extends further than that. In *Collationes in Hexaemeron* I, 11, quoting Colossians 2:3 ('Christ, in whom are hidden all the treasures of wisdom and knowledge'), Bonaventure claims that the Son of God, as the central Person of the Trinity (I *Sent.* d. 2, a. u., q. 4; Hayes 2000a: 192–214), is also the centre of our metaphysical, ethical, and theological worlds, amongst others. In *metaphysical* terms Bonaventure's exemplarist worldview centres around the Word, in whom the Father expresses himself within the Trinity and, in doing so, provides the metaphysical foundation of the created world, which is the material expression of the archetypal exemplars which reside in the Second Person of the Trinity (I *Sent.* d. 6, a. u., q. 3). Thus, like Thomas Aquinas, Bonaventure considers the creation of the world as the material expression of the generation of the Word from the Father; and the intelligibility of the world, as well as its sacramentality, are founded on the divine exemplars which dwell in the Word. In the words of Zachary Hayes:

> Exemplarity has a critical role to play in Bonaventure's thought both at the philosophical and at the theological levels. It is only exemplarity that can unlock the deepest meaning of created reality to the human mind, for it is only when we perceive the world in its symbolic nature as the objectification of the self-knowledge of God that we know it in its true reality.
>
> (Hayes 2000b: 46)

This is, incidentally, why St Bonaventure prefers the name 'Word' to 'Son', for the name 'Word' implies a reference, not just to the Father, but also to creation, the Incarnation, and Christ's teaching. This is well expressed in his *Commentary on John* I, 6: 'And since the Son of God had to be described ... not only in relationship to the Father, from whom he proceeds, but also to creatures, which h made, and to the flesh which he took on, and to the teaching that he communicated, he had to be described in a most excellent and fitting manner with the term Word. For that term relates to all these matters.'

Christ is also the foundation of *morality*. In terms stronger than those of Thomas Aquinas (*Summa Theologiae* II–II, q. 23, a. 7; *ST* II–II, q. 10, a. 4), Bonaventure will argue that genuine virtue is impossible without charity and faith in Christ. Christ is at the heart of our *theological* endeavours, which focus on the work of reconciliation (*opera reconciliationis*). The Incarnation and Cross of Christ are the central source of grace, which branches out in the theological and cardinal virtues, the gifts and fruits of the Holy Spirit, the habit of the beatitudes (*Brevil.* V) and the sacramental economy (*Brevil.* VI).

Within the confines of this contribution I cannot develop all aspects of Bonaventure's multi-faceted Christology. I will focus on his soteriology in the strictest sense, namely his views on the salvific meaning of the death of Christ. As a preliminary remark, I need to point out that in Bonaventure's view, however, the Incarnation perfects creation, 'bringing the entire universe to full perfection by uniting the first and the last, the Word of God, which is the origin of all things, and human nature, which was the last of all creatures' (*Brevil.* IV, 1.2). It can therefore not be understood solely in terms of reparation of sin. John Duns Scotus was further to develop this idea.

Bonaventure adopts the Anselmic theory of satisfaction but supplements it in a number of ways (as did Thomas Aquinas). He will, for instance, pay more attention to the question of how exactly Christ is the fountainhead of grace and merit for humankind. Although Anselm's argument hinges on the sinlessness of Christ (as the holy representative of humanity) he did not sufficiently probe the question of how Christ's headship was a source of grace, nor did he ponder the significance of the organic link between Christ and his members, the Church. Both Bonaventure and Thomas were to correct this. As has become clear from the chapter by David Hogg in this volume, Anselm's theory of satisfaction should not be interpreted in terms of a vindictive God who needs retribution of the Cross to appease his divine anger. Rather, sin distorts the created world, and the sacrifice, or self-gift, of the God-man repairs the brokenness of creation and restores its glory. Anselm's notion of satisfaction is not indebted to the world of feudalism (as is often claimed), but it is rather similar to the sacrament of penance, in which the sinful person expresses his sorrow by making a sacrifice, which thus becomes satisfactory (it restores the relationship with God from whom we had alienated ourselves) (Van Nieuwenhove 2003b).

When discussing the traditional view that the Incarnation occurred to redeem humankind, Bonaventure adopts the Anselmic language of satisfaction:

> Humanity could not recover its excellence through any other redeemer than God. For if this redeemer had been a mere creature, then humanity would have become subject to another creature, and thus would not have regained its state of excellence. Nor could humanity have recovered its state of friendship with God (*amicitiam quoque Dei recuperare non poterat*) except by means of a suitable mediator, who could touch God with one hand and humanity with the other, who could be the likeness and friend of both: God-like in his divinity, and like us in his humanity. Nor, again, could humankind have recovered purity of soul (*innocentia mentis*) if its guilt had not been removed, which divine justice could not fittingly remit unless suitable satisfaction had been made (*per satisfactionem condignam*). But only God could make such satisfaction for the whole human race, while humanity alone was bound to make it because it had sinned. Therefore it was most appropriate (*congruentissimum*) that humanity should be restored by a God-man, born of Adam's stock.
>
> (*Brevil.* IV, 1.4; cf. also III *Sent.* d. 20, a. u., q. 2)

A number of points are worth noting. Firstly, Bonaventure argues that salvation through the Incarnation, life, death, and resurrection of Christ was the most fitting manner of redeeming humankind. He does not claim that it is the only possible way—but it has a certain aesthetic appeal. Secondly, while *satisfactio* is intrinsically linked with Christ's suffering (III *Sent*. d. 16, a. 1, q. 1), the source of merit of Christ's atoning work is not suffering itself but his love and obedience which find expression in that suffering (III *Sent*. d. 18, a. 1, q. 3). Thirdly, as Bonaventure explains in III *Sent*. d. 20, a. u., q. 2 (inspired by St Anselm's *Cur Deus Homo*, II.20) *satisfactio* is deeply alien to a vindictive understanding of God, for the key presupposition of *satifactio* is the fact that it harmonizes divine mercy and justice. A restoration of our relationship with God without *satisfactio*, by mere divine *fiat*, would not be in accord with justice (for it would be a whitewash of sin, unacceptable in light of the profundity of evil committed by humankind); again, if God demanded retribution without the atoning activity of the God-man, he would be lacking in mercy. Fourthly, it is important to note what 'satisfaction' effects: it is the cause of our purification from sin, allowing us to regain our 'innocence'. Thus, the satisfaction Christ offers changes our relationship with God, allowing us to recover our state of friendship with God; it does not change God; it changes us—a perspective that Anselm had shared, following St Augustine's Book Ten of *De Civitate Dei*. Thus, through the self-gift of God in Christ we who were guilty before God become righteous, and our miserable condition becomes transformed into a glorious one. This transformation of humankind is an ongoing process, which implies our participation in the life of the Church and its sacraments, which are filled with the merit of Christ's Passion (III *Sent*. d. 20, a. u., q. 4)—the topic of the Fourth Book of the *Sentences*.

When arguing that no other sinless creature (*creatura pura*) could make satisfaction or atone, Bonaventure (again following Anselm) claims that the offence against God—given his infinite dignity—is so large that even a sinless creature that is not divine could not possibly make recompense (III *Sent*. d. 20, a. u., q. 3). Duns Scotus was to question the notion that Christ's merit has an infinite value on account of his divine Personhood. He will also dispute whether the Word Incarnate was necessary for our salvation. Before we deal with Duns Scotus' views we will examine the soteriology of St Thomas Aquinas.

Thomas Aquinas' Christology is to be found mainly in the Third Part of his *Summa Theologiae*. Like Bonaventure, he operates with an integrative vision, which situates soteriological issues in a broader Trinitarian perspective, and connects them with sacramentology, ecclesiology, and the life of Christian virtues. Like Bonaventure, Thomas draws an explicit connection, for instance, between the generation of the Word from the Father within the Trinity, and the acts of creation and salvation. In relation to creation: in generating the Son the Father expresses himself and the whole of creation (*ST* I, q. 34, a. 3). Every created thing, therefore, has traces of the Trinity written in the core of its being. The Word is reflected in the very form inherent in a created thing, 'as the form of the thing made by art is from the conception of the craftsman (*ex conceptione artificis*)' (*ST* I, q. 45, a. 7)—a perspective indebted to Augustine's Christian Neoplatonism. There is both a visible sending of the Son (Incarnation), and an invisible sending in the soul resulting in 'a certain experimental knowledge' or loving wisdom (*ST* I, q. 43, a. 5, ad 2). These missions are the temporal 'extensions', if you like, of the eternal generation of the Son from the Father. We acquire this loving wisdom by becoming incorporated in Christ through grace and charity, becoming adoptive sons. Thus we are likened to the Eternal Word, reflecting, and participating in, the oneness between the Father and his Son (*ST* III, q. 23, a. 3).

Scholars (Torrell 1999) have noted that Thomas pays more attention than his predecessors to the life of Christ (*ST* III, q. 35–45), before considering his death, resurrection, and ascension into heaven. When discussing the saving meaning of Christ's death, Thomas adopts the notion of satisfaction from Anselm, and he shares his view that the infinity of sin required a God-man whose divine Personhood bestowed an infinite dignity upon his saving work (*ST* III, q. 1, a. 2, ad 2)—a view Duns Scotus was to challenge. I wrote 'required' because Thomas holds the view that, strictly speaking, God could have saved humanity in a different way, without the Incarnation of his Son (*ST* III, q. 1, a. 2). Again, in relation to the question whether God would have become human if sin had not occurred, he appears to have a preference for the view that God would have become incarnate anyhow, although he acknowledges that the biblical witness favours the other view (*ST* III, q. 1, a. 3).

With Anselm and Bonaventure, Thomas argues that *satisfactio* harmonizes God's mercy and justice (*ST* III, q. 46, a. 1, ad 3), and he draws a distinction (*ST* I–II, q. 87, a. 7) between punishment in the strict sense (which is inflicted upon us against our will), on the one hand, and making satisfaction on the other. We freely undertake the latter to restore our relationship with God, through Christ, as in acts of penance. This distinction also applies to the Cross of Christ (which must be understood in terms of penance by the sinless representative of humanity, rather than in terms of punishment by an angry God). Thus, given this link between penance and making satisfaction, Thomas' soteriology cannot possibly be understood in penal terms, or meeting the demands of vindictive justice but should be seen in terms of 'the reconciliation of friendship' (*reconciliatio amicitiae*) (*ST* III, q. 90, a. 2).

Thomas makes clearer than Anselm had done that one person can make satisfaction for another if they are united in charity (*ST* I–II, q. 87, a. 8). This explains why Thomas emphasizes the organic unity between Christ and the members of his Body: 'The Head and members are as one mystic person; and therefore Christ's satisfaction belongs to all the faithful as being his members' (*ST* III, q. 48, a. 2, ad 1). This is a theological view which is closely linked with his more developed notion as to how Christ can be the source of grace as the Head of the Church (*ST* III, q. 8): 'Grace was bestowed upon Christ, not only as an individual, but inasmuch as he is the Head of the Church, so that it might overflow into his members' (*ST* III, q. 48, a. 1). This intimate link between Christ and his Church, the community of believers, further suggests that Thomas does not subscribe to a theory of substitution but sees salvation in terms of participation (we participate in, and appropriate, the salvation Christ effected).

While retaining the notion of satisfaction in the key question on the efficiency of Christ's Passion (*ST* III, q. 48), Thomas introduces many other central terms, such as merit (*ST* III, q. 48, a. 1) and redemption (*ST* III, q. 48, a. 4), the 'buying back' from our servitude to sin—although it must be said that Thomas reverts back to language of *satis-factio* to describe *redemptio* throughout the article. Another key term is sacrifice, which has the advantage of being more explicitly biblical than *satisfactio*, and which allows Thomas to develop a rich theology of how the Old Testament ceremonies prefigured the sacrifice of Christ (*ST*, I–II, q. 102). Let's discuss this notion of sacrifice in some more detail, as it will allow us to recapitulate a number of issues. First, sacrifices are offered to God, not for his benefit, but for that of ourselves and our neighbour (*ST* II–II, q. 30, a. 4, ad 1)—which again illustrates that Thomas does not subscribe to a theory of divine propitiation or appeasement (*ST* III, q. 49, a. 4, ad 2). Secondly, Thomas states that every external sacrifice derives its value from an inner or invisible sacrifice. Drawing on Book Ten of *De Civitate Dei*, he repeatedly quotes (*ST* III, q. 22, a. 2; *ST* III, q. 48, a. 3, obj. 3) Augustine's dictum that 'a visible sacrifice is a sacrament—that is, a sacred sign—of an invisible sacrifice'. An outward or visible sacrifice can be any action performed for God's sake; but this outward action is only an expression of an inner sacrifice, which is our gift of self to God in devotion and love (cf. *ST* II–II, q. 85, a. 4). Thus, the 'invisible sacrifice' which finds expression in visible sacrifices we perform, is our sanctification, whereby we offer ourselves up to God (*ST* III, q. 22, a. 2; *ST* II–II, q. 85, a. 2, quoting Ps. 51:19; *ST* II–II, q. 85, a. 4; *ST* III, q. 48, a. 3, ad 2). This view of sacrifice has a number of implications.

Firstly, it entails that the sufferings of Christ are not the primary source of our salvation, but rather what they denote ('invisibly'), namely his love and obedience to the Father (*ST* III, q. 47, a. 4, ad 2; *ST* III, q. 47, a. 2, ad 3). While later mediaeval piety relished suffering and the power of the blood (Bynum Walker 2004), this is not Thomas' primary concern.

Secondly, it establishes an intimate link between Christ's self-gift in his life and death, and the self-gift of the Christian believer throughout his life. For every deed performed for the sake of God acquires a 'sacrificial' dimension, uniting us to God and Christ (*ST* II–II, q. 85, a. 3, ad 1). This brings us to an important aspect of Thomas' soteriology, namely the way he emphasizes how we need to appropriate Christ's saving work, by becoming members of his Body, the Church, in faith, hope, and love and participation in the sacraments (*ST* III, q. 49, a. 3, ad 1). For the fact that Christ is the Head of the Church cuts both ways: it means that Christ's merits can be shared with us, but it also means that we are called to become Christ-like through sharing in his sacrificial life. Indeed, Thomas, when acknowledging that afflictions and death still remain although Christ has redeemed us, states that this is as it should be, for our afflictions in this life allow us to become conformed to Christ's sufferings (*ST* I–II, q. 85, a. 5, ad 2), allowing us to bear the marks of Christ's Passion in us (Van Nieuwenhove 2005: 291). Commenting on Romans 8:17, he writes that we can only partake in Christ's glory through sharing in suffering, allowing us to grow in likeness to Christ (*Ad Rom.* no. 651; *ST* III, q. 49, a. 3, ad 3; *ST* I–II, q. 85, a. 5, ad 2). The least one can say is that Thomas' understanding of salvation does not fail to face up to the realities of life's afflictions.

Thirdly, the link Augustine established between 'sacrifice' and 'sacrament' proves very fruitful too. Sacrifice, so Thomas informs us, is etymologically derived from the notion of making holy (*facit sacrum*; cf. *ST* II–II, q. 85, a. 3, ad 3). It is no surprise that Thomas, when beginning to explain the nature of sacraments in general, again quotes Augustine's saying that the visible sacrifice is the sacred sign, or sacrament, of an invisible sacrifice (*ST* III, q. 60, a. 1, *sed contra*). A sacrament is defined in general terms as a sign of something holy which sanctifies us (*signum rei sacrae inquantum est sanctificans homines*; *ST* III, q. 60, a. 2), or, in popular scholastic parlance, it effects what it signifies (*efficiunt quod figurant*; *ST* III, q. 62, a. 1, ad 1)—and what it effects is our sanctification, which is exactly what constituted the nature of the invisible sacrifice in Augustine's dictum. The 'something holy' a sacrament refers to is ultimately Christ's saving work. Indeed, because Christ's humanity is the instrument of his divinity—a notion Thomas borrowed from John Damascene—all aspects of Christ's life and death acquire a saving significance (*ST* III, q. 48, a. 6). The link between sacrifice and sacrament can be clarified by mentioning Thomas' insight—inspired by St Paul—that Christ's passion is the sacrament of our salvation, for through Christ's death and resurrection we die to sin and attain new life in and for God (*Ad Rom.* 6:11, no. 491; *ST* III, q. 56, a. 2, ad 4).

The sacraments in the strict sense (baptism, Eucharist, and so forth) are specific signs and instrumental causes of the continuing efficacy of Christ's salvific work. They derive their saving power from Christ's passion, as was symbolized by the water and blood flowing from the side of the crucified Christ (*ST* III, q. 62, a. 5). Baptism, 'the door of the sacraments' (*ST* III, q. 73, a. 3), makes us conformable to Christ's Passion and resurrection, insofar as we die to sin and begin a new life of righteousness (*ST* III, q. 66, a. 2). This illustrates, again, that Thomas sees our justification in intrinsicist terms: it is not a mere imputation of justice but requires an inner transformation, caused by Christ's Passion (in the past), effected (in the present) in us through grace and virtues, and pointing towards our future participation in eternal life with God (*ST* III, q. 60, a. 3). Similarly, in an article in which Thomas discusses the different names of the Eucharist (*ST* III, q. 73, a. 4), he points out that it recalls the *sacrifice* of Christ's Passion (past), establishes unity or *communion* amongst the faithful (present), and anticipates our future enjoyment of God, sharing in the good grace (*Eucharist*) of life ever-lasting (cf. Rom. 6:23).

Thomas' soteriology is a very rich one indeed. It is a vision spanning the whole spectrum of his theology—from its origins in the heart of the Trinity to his sacramentology and eschatology. It permeates every aspect of his theology and spirituality. Shunning all extrinsicism, for him salvation is a call to participation and transformation in Christ, which explains why Thomas' discussions of different virtues in the Second Part of the *Summa Theologiae* are often crowned by a reference to the beatitudes (*ST* I–II, q. 69) and gifts of the Holy Spirit (*ST* I–II, q. 68), indicating that the Christian life of virtue needs to be understood from within Christological and pneumatological perspectives (Pinckaers 1995: 154–5). Given the centrality of his notion of the Church as the Mystical Body of Christ, implying an intimate link between Christ and the faithful, I am reluctant to call his soteriology a 'theory' of salvation but rather an invitation to live and die in Christ.

While Thomas' soteriology is not legalistic, forensic, penal, or substitutionary, some modern scholars might object to the fact that Thomas refuses to attribute suffering to the divine nature (*ST* III, q. 46, a. 12)—unlike many twentieth-century theologians who argue that a God who is immune to suffering cannot love (Moltmann 1974: 219–27).

Thomas, deeply imbued with a sense of the otherness and transcendence of God, argues that the Word suffers, not in his divine nature, as God, but in his human nature, as man. While this theological position may not satisfy modern theologians it seems to me a sound one. As Thomas Weinandy made clear, the view that God suffers as God—whatever that could possibly mean—does not do justice to the radical nature of the Incarnation. What matters is not that God suffers as God, but that the Word suffers as a human being:

> This is what humankind is crying out to hear, not that God experiences, in a divine manner, our anguish and suffering in the midst of a sinful and depraved world, but that he actually experienced and knew first hand, as one of us—as a man—human anguish and suffering within a sinful and depraved world. This is what a proper understanding of the Incarnation requires and affirms.
>
> (Weinandy 2000: 206)

DUNS SCOTUS AND WILLIAM OF OCKHAM

Duns Scotus wrote after the Condemnations of 1277, which led to an increasing separation of faith and theology, on the one hand, and reason and philosophy, on the other, which in turn resulted in a growing voluntarist understanding of God, rather than the other way around (Van Nieuwenhove 2013). This voluntarism was to have important ramifications for both his own and later scholastic soteriology, such as Ockham's.

Duns Scotus is mainly remembered for his defence of the immaculate conception of the Virgin Mary—a doctrine which had been rejected by the major thirteenth-century scholastics as it appeared to undermine the universality of Christ's salvific activity, which is why they argued that Mary's sanctification occurred *in utero* sometime after her conception. Duns Scotus also explicitly argued that the Incarnation and the predestination of Jesus would have taken place, even if sin had not occurred (*Lect. Par.* III, 19, 7)—thus radicalizing the views on this issue of his predecessors.

Duns Scotus is in some ways an innovator, and in other ways a transitional figure: while he retains a realist outlook (as distinct from Ockham's later nominalism) he does introduce a moderate voluntarism in theology. This voluntarism is aimed at safeguarding God's utter freedom and transcendence: 'no other good, apart from God himself, functions as a reason for God's willing' (*Rep. Par. I-A*, d. 41, sol. q., no. 55), and if something is right or good it is such 'not simply on account of right reason, but insofar as it is willed by God' (*Rep. Par. I-A*, d. 44, q. 2, no. 31). This perspective has implications for soteriology. Duns Scotus adopts the theory of satisfaction (*Lect. Par.* III, 20; *Ord.* III, d. 20 un., n. 3, 10; *Ord.* IV, d. 15, q. 1), but he takes issue with Anselm on a number of issues. First, Duns Scotus denies that the offence caused by Adam's sin is intrinsically infinite—which was a key presupposition of Anselm and his followers. He further denies (*Lect.* III, d. 20, q. 1, no. 39) that satisfaction for sin could only have occurred through a

God-man (again aiming to safeguard God's utter freedom). In contrast to his predecessors Duns Scotus is of the view that a pure creature could have made satisfaction for humanity. This does not take anything away from the glory of God; on the contrary. As Rosato puts it: 'Knowing that God became incarnate and died on the Cross, when something other or lesser would have been able to merit grace for the fallen, should enkindle a deep love for God in man because it reveals the lengths to which God will go to bring his fallen creatures back to him' (2009: 175).

Scotus pays particular attention to the question of how Christ's atonement is the source of merit. Christ's saving work is only considered meritorious because God deems it such (*Ord*. III, d. 19, q. un., no. 7). This does not mean that, for Duns Scotus, divine *acceptatio* is utterly arbitrary. The divine acceptance of Christ's merit is based, not on his divine Personhood (a theological position which Scotus considers problematic, if only because it downplays the role of Christ's human will), but it is grounded on the created will and created grace of the God-man (Rosato 2009: 165ff.). Yang has made clear that *acceptatio* is a 'broad theological term' that does not simply refer to the fact that God passively accepts our good acts performed at the stirring of the infused habit of charity. It can also refer, in a more active sense, to the divine ordination to accept such acts as meritorious in accordance with his eternal will, which provides the ontological basis for the passive acceptance. Duns Scotus' notion of divine *acceptatio* thus aims to underscore that ultimately the divine will, rather than secondary causes, is the cause of merit:

> [It] means that there is a higher cause of God's passive acceptance of X than the fact that X is of such meritorious worth, and that this cause is none other than the *acceptatio* by which God has preordained X as an act meritorious of a certain reward and has promised to passively accept it in the future as such. Therefore, Scotus' voluntarism is not as extreme as some scholars allege.
>
> (Yang 2009: 432–3)

Scotus' moderate voluntarism further extends to his understanding of sin (where he adopts a forensic notion) and his view on sacraments (where he refuses to attribute instrumental causality), and ethics (his rejection of eudaimonistic ethics) (Van Nieuwenhove 2013: 240). Thus, while Scotus' voluntarism is not as radical as is often alleged, the integrative dimension begins nonetheless to crumble in his theological outlook. The emphasis shifts to questions of merit and divine acceptance, while the intrinsic connections between theology of the Trinity, soteriology, and sacramentology are beginning to wane. It is, however, in the theology of William of Ockham that we find a more radical exponent of this approach.

William of Ockham is best remembered for his nominalist position, namely, the philosophical view that universals are nothing but names, and every mind-independent thing is particular. Universality is a feature of our cognitive acts and does not refer to anything outside the mind. This nominalism is a departure from the realist stance of Duns Scotus and his thirteenth-century predecessors (Bonaventure, Thomas Aquinas).

William further radicalizes Duns Scotus' voluntarism and his aversion to Neoplatonism. Like Duns Scotus, Ockham operates with a strong understanding of divine freedom and omnipotence. This also implies a rejection of divine ideas.

It is here, perhaps, that William's main contribution lies (rather than in his nominalism as such): If the world consists solely of individual items, and universals have no real ontological status, the Christian Neoplatonic world loses its rational foundation. There are no longer any divine ideas (for they were, of course, universals), or rather: divine ideas operate no longer as exemplars of created beings but are nothing but the immediate knowledge God has of creatures themselves. This rules traditional exemplarism out, and with its demise the world loses its intrinsic ontological intelligibility, which explains why Ockham is often portrayed as a philosopher who prepares the way for both a more empiricist or experiential approach, and a more fideist one. Moreover, as I argue elsewhere (Van Nieuwenhove 2013: 256–63), the rejection of divine ideas implies the demise of the mediaeval sacramental worldview in which creation is a pointer towards God and makes him present. Accordingly, it will also do away with the transcendental thrust of mediaeval theology, opening the way for a more *diesseitig* approach to the world.

We have only a fragmentary *Reportatio* of William's comments on Book III of the *Sentences*, consisting of only 12 questions. Of these only questions 8 (on grace in the soul of Christ) and 10 (on the Incarnation) have a general Christological rather than soteriological relevance in the strict sense. The reader will search in vain for a profound discussion of Anselm's theory of salvation in any of Ockham's writings. This is not surprising: if the distinction between divine mercy and justice is a merely conceptual one, Anselm's concern to harmonize them must look rather futile (McGrath 1985: 189).

While he shares voluntarism with Duns Scotus, Ockham's version of voluntarism is fairly radical: 'If God wants it, by that very fact it is just' (IV *Sent.* qq. 10–11). This has implications for his theory of salvation. For instance, Ockham will argue that 'a human being is able by the absolute power of God to be saved without created charity' (*Quodlib.* VI, q. 1, a. 2). Ockham radicalizes Duns Scotus' divine *acceptatio* theory. Only God decides the worth of a person or an action, and nothing is meritorious save by God's acceptance. On the other hand, the point should not be over-emphasized: Ockham is happy enough to state (*Quodlib.* VI, q. 1, a. 2) that 'according to the laws now ordained by God, no human being will ever be saved ... without created grace'. Thus, the contrast between ordained and absolute power aims to stress the radical contingency of everything that is not God, and that the world as we know it is not necessary. Such a view does not necessarily imply the concept of an arbitrary God. Indeed, rather than construing it in terms of an arbitrary God, the distinction between God's *potentia absoluta* and *potentia ordinata* marks 'the voluntary self-limitation of the omnipotent God and hence the non-necessary contingent nature of the established order of creation and redemption' (Oberman 1987: 460).

What is more worrying than voluntarism as such, I think, is the fact that the world has lost its inner intelligibility (the rejection of divine ideas embedded in creation) and its sacramental character, resulting in a loss of the transcendental thrust of mediaeval scholastic thought in the fourteenth century and, in general terms, the espousal of a more extrinsicist understanding of the world. Henceforth, 'a purely natural' understanding of the world develops, and the integrative vision that permeated scholastic theology in the thirteenth century dissolves. Thus, Ockham operates not only with a strong acceptation-theory, but also with an extrinsicist and forensic understanding of grace and sin (Aers 2009: 31). Mortal sin, for instance, cannot be defined in real terms but only in nominal terms: it is that which is forbidden by God, or that which we omit to do although it has been ordered by God (IV *Sent.* qq. 10–11). Again, salvation depends solely on divine acceptance, and downplays the role of infused habits or the virtue of charity. In the words of one scholar, sympathetically disposed towards Ockham's outlook:

> Ockham's point is that nothing in the natural world dictates the order of salvation. Beatific vision and damnation do not depend on the intrinsic nature of things but solely on the will of God. Hence the rules of salvation are an external order not unlike the legal systems of human rulers, who regulate rewards and punishments by statute.
>
> (Wood 1997: 268–9)

Given his individualism Ockham further fails to develop the notion of the Church as the Body of Christ; and the connection effected by charity between the virtues becomes weakened.

It is not difficult to see Ockham as a precursor of Protestant theology which will consider sin and salvation mainly in forensic terms. Mediaeval theologians, in contrast, had considered sin as a distortion of created reality. Through their critique of the divine ideas and rejection of exemplarism—a move that was inspired by their espousal of a voluntarist God whose power and freedom could not possibly be limited by a rationality outside of himself—Ockham and his followers inaugurated a world which has lost its transcendental intelligibility. Sin, too, comes to be understood mainly in terms of an offence against God (that is, a forensic notion) which can be dealt with through an extrinsicist justification. Similarly, the merit of Christ, also, is imputed by God (divine *acceptatio*)—an idea John Calvin was to adopt in his *Institutes of Christian Religion* II, 17.1–5.

Jan van Ruusbroec

The more integrated vision of salvation was not to disappear altogether. Indeed, it continued to find expression in the writings of some of the fourteenth-century mystical theologians. Due to constraints of space, a number of brief references to one mystical theologian, Jan van Ruusbroec, will have to suffice.

While Ruusbroec appears to adopt the Anselmic theory of salvation, his main contribution lies elsewhere. He is more interested in describing our transformation through the modelling of our life on that of Christ, enabling us to participate in the intra-Trinitarian dynamics. In his first book, *The Realm of Lovers*, Christocentric and Trinitarian emphases are further enriched by weaving the gifts of the Holy Spirit and angelic hierarchies into a complex picture that forms the backdrop for an outline of our transformation. I will first deal with the Trinitarian aspect; then I will consider the role of the Word Incarnate, and finally I will mention, by way of example, how one of the gifts of the Holy Spirit is integrated into Ruusbroec's outline of our transformation.

For Ruusbroec, the acme of the Christian life is the 'common life' (*ghemeyne leven*), perhaps best translated as the Catholic or universal life. In order to understand its meaning, I need first to sketch his theology of the Trinity.

Ruusbroec adopts the Bonaventurean doctrine, according to which the Father generates his Word from the fruitfulness of his paternal nature, and from the mutual contemplation of Father and Son the Holy Spirit proceeds as their Bond of Love. Ruusbroec calls this (the generation of the Son and the procession of the Holy Spirit) the 'out-going' aspect of the Trinity. He then makes an original move: he claims that the Holy Spirit, as the Bond of Love of Father and Son, is the principle of the return of the divine Persons into their shared perichoretic unity. This is the 'in-going' dimension of the Trinity—where the divine Persons then find 'rest'—this is the moment of fruition or rest. From here the process starts all over again, in its threefold dynamic ('going-out'; 'going-in'; 'fruition'), allowing him to describe the Trinity in highly dynamic terms as 'an ebbing, flowing sea' (Van Nieuwenhove 2003a).

The significance of this original Trinitarian theology is the way it shapes the life of the Christian: the Christian is called to share in the 'out-going' dimension (a life of charity, engaging actively with the external world); in the 'in-going' aspect (a life of devotion and interiority); and in a life of contemplation and fruition of God (in the Augustinian sense of 'enjoying God', namely God as the ultimate concern in life). The contemplative life, however, is not the highest for Ruusbroec. As indicated, his ideal is the common life, which combines all three dimensions in a harmonious synthesis (charitable activity, interiority, contemplation).

If Ruusbroec's ideal is deeply Trinitarian, it is no less Christocentric for that. For Christ is, of course, 'the common person', the one who is without cease contemplative and active:

> Christ is, in accordance with his humanity, the greatest contemplative that ever was, for he was one with Wisdom, and he himself was the Wisdom with which we contemplate. Yet he was also actively meeting the needs of people in his works of charity, while contemplating the countenance of the Father without cease. And this is the nobility of this gift: to be active and contemplative, and remain unhindered, as much as one can.
>
> (*Realm*, 2158–64)

The 'nobility of this gift' refers to the gift of understanding (Latin: *intellectus*), one of the gifts of the Holy Spirit. Ruusbroec further relates it to the beatitude of the pure of heart who will see God—for these people have become so like Christ, the Wisdom and Image of God, that they do not become distracted (*onverbeeldet*) by earthly temptations.

From this brief outline it will have become clear that Ruusbroec adopts the exemplarism of the Augustinian–Bonaventurean tradition but he develops it in a more theological-anthropological manner. While acknowledging that the sacramentality and intelligibility of the world is due to its ideal existence as divine exemplars (*Realm*, 2076–103), he pays particular attention to how the soul is attuned to union with the Image of God, the second Person of the Trinity. He ends his book by describing how the Christian becomes transformed (*ghetransformeert*)

> by the eternal Image, the Wisdom of the Father, who is an Image and Exemplar of all creatures. In this Image all material and spiritual things have their life. Through this Image all creatures flow into their created being, and receive a likeness to God … But the noble, common person is most alike [to God], for he flows out with virtues, and in this he resembles God, who flows out with his gifts; and he remains in eternal enjoyment, and there he is one with God beyond all gifts. This is an enlightened common person in a most noble fashion.
>
> (*Realm*, 2749–56)

Thus, Ruusbroec is one of the last heirs to a Christian-Neoplatonist tradition in which exemplarism grounds the sacramentality and intelligibility of creation, and moulds the human person in such a way as to be naturally attuned to becoming transformed in Christ, the Image and Exemplar of God, through whom we come to participate in the intra-Trinitarian dynamics of activity and fruition.

Suggested Reading

Emery (2010); Hayes (2000a); Oberman (1987); Rosato (2009); Van Nieuwenhove (2013).

Bibliography

Primary Sources

Aquinas, T. (1955), *Summa Theologiae* (Rome: Marietti).

Aquinas, T. (1981), *Summa Theologica*, trans. Fathers of the English Dominican Province (Westminster, Md.: Christian Classics).

Bonaventure (1881–1902), *Opera Omnia*, ed. Fathers of the Collegium S. Bonaventurae, Ad Claras Aquas, 10 vols. (Quaracchi).

Bonaventure (2005), *Breviloquium*, vol. IX: *The Works of St Bonaventure*, trans. D. V. Monti (New York: The Franciscan Institute).

Bonaventure (2007), *Commentary on the Gospel of John*, vol. XI: *The Works of St Bonaventure*, trans. R. Karris (New York: The Franciscan Institute).

Ruusbroec, J. van (2002), *Opera Omnia*, vol. IV: *Dat Rijcke der Ghelieven* [The Realm of Lovers], ed. G. De Baere. CCCM 104 (Turnhout: Brepols).

Scotus, John Duns (1639), *Opera Omnia*, ed. L. Wadding, 12 vols. (Lyons: Durand).

Scotus, John Duns (1950–), *Opera Omnia*, ed. C. Balić et al. (Vatican City: Typis Polyglottis Vaticanis).

Scotus, John Duns (2004–8), *The Examined Report of the Paris Lecture: Reportatio I-A*, ed. A. B. Wolter and O. V. Bychkov, 2 vols. (New York: The Franciscan Institute).

William of Ockham (1967–88), *Opera Philosophica et Theologica*, ed. G. Gál et al. (New York: The Franciscan Institute).

William of Ockham (1991), *Quodlibetal Questions*, vols. 1 and 2, trans. A. Freddoso and F. E. Kelley (New Haven: Yale University Press).

Secondary Sources

Aers, D. (2009), *Salvation and Sin: Augustine, Langland, and Fourteenth-Century Theology* (Notre Dame: University of Notre Dame Press).

Bynum Walker, C. (2004), 'The Power in the Blood: Sacrifice, Satisfaction, and Substitution in Late Medieval Soteriology', in S. Davis, D. Kendall, and G. O'Collins (eds.), *The Redemption: An Interdisciplinary Symposium on Christ as Redeemer* (Oxford: Oxford University Press), 177–204.

Emery, G. (2010), *The Trinitarian Theology of St Thomas Aquinas* (Oxford: Oxford University Press).

Fiddes, P. S. (2007), 'Salvation', in K. Tanner, I. Torrance, and J. Webster (eds.), *The Oxford Handbook of Systematic Theology* (Oxford: Oxford University Press), 176–96.

Hayes, Z. (2000a), *The Hidden Center: Spirituality and Christology in St. Bonaventure* (St. Bonaventure, NY: The Franciscan Institute).

Hayes, Z. (2000b), 'Introduction' to Saint Bonaventure's *Disputed Questions on the Mystery of the Trinity* (St. Bonaventure, NY: The Franciscan Institute).

McGrath, A. (1985), 'Some Observations Concerning the Soteriology of the Schola Moderna', *Recherches de Théologie Ancienne et Médiévale* 52: 182–93.

Moltmann, J. (1974), *The Crucified God* (London: SCM Press).

Oberman, H. (1987), 'Via Antiqua and Via Moderna: Late Medieval Prolegomena to Early Reformation Thought', in A. Hudson and M. Wilks (eds.), *From Ockham to Wyclif* (Oxford: Blackwell), 445–63.

Pinckaers, S. (1995), *The Sources of Christian Ethics* (Edinburgh: T. & T. Clark).

Rosato, A. V. (2009), 'Duns Scotus on the Redemptive Work of Christ' (Doctoral dissertation, University of Notre Dame, Notre Dame).

Torrell, J. P. (1999), *Le Christ en ses mystères: Tome I. La Vie et l'Oeuvre de Jésus selon Thomas d'Aquin* (Paris: Desclée).

Van Nieuwenhove, R. (2003a) *Jan van Ruusbroec, Mystical Theologian of the Trinity* (Notre Dame: University of Notre Dame Press).

Van Nieuwenhove, R. (2003b), 'St Anselm and St Thomas Aquinas on "Satisfaction": or how Catholic and Protestant Understandings of the Cross Differ', *Angelicum* 80: 159–76.

Van Nieuwenhove, R. (2005), 'Bearing the Marks of Christ's Passion: Aquinas's Soteriology', in R. Van Nieuwenhove and J. Wawrykow (eds.), *The Theology of Thomas Aquinas* (Notre Dame: University of Notre Dame Press), 277–302.

Van Nieuwenhove, R. (2012), 'The Saving Work of Christ', in B. Davies and E. Stump (eds.), *The Oxford Handbook of Aquinas* (Oxford: Oxford University Press), 436–47.

Van Nieuwenhove, R. (2013), *An Introduction to Medieval Theology* (Cambridge: Cambridge University Press).

Weinandy, T. (2000), *Does God Suffer?* (Edinburgh: T. & T. Clark).

Wood, R. (1997), *Ockham on the Virtues* (West Lafayette, Ind.: Purdue University Press).

Yang, A. S. (2009), 'Scotus' Voluntarist Approach to the Atonement Reconsidered', *Scottish Journal of Theology* 62: 421–40.

PART IV

REFORMATION
AND CHRISTOLOGY

CHAPTER 17

MARTIN LUTHER'S EUCHARISTIC CHRISTOLOGY

BRIAN LUGIOYO

DOXOLOGICAL CHRISTOLOGY

THE primary locus for Christological reflection has always been the Church's worship. Nowhere was this truer than in the sixteenth century. The Protestant Reformation had its Christological controversy at the altar. Protestants have often forgotten this Christological location. But for Martin Luther, this was the appropriate place, for here, again and again, Jesus Christ confronted his Church in the present. Luther's Christology was thoroughly doxological.

The worship of God in Jesus Christ permeates Luther's work. However, it seems that the lacuna of a systematic treatise on Christology within his corpus has led some to conjecture that Christology was for him a secondary theme (Holl 1948). It was not secondary but diffused. The ad hoc nature of his theology and the size of his work make his Christology difficult to articulate systematically, but not hard to observe. Luther's Christology acts as the foundation for his theology. Faith in Christ was his presiding doctrine, 'from it, through it, and to it all my theological thought flows and returns day and night' (*WA* 40.1: 33).

The academy's imperative to systematize makes articulating Luther's occasional theology a Herculean task. Theodosius Harnack (1886), Paul Althaus (1966), and Theobald Beer (1980), are among those who have attempted to give Luther's Christological themes a coherent shape. Others have taken the long historical route in articulating his Christology. Ian Siggins (1970) and Marc Lienhard (1982) articulate Luther's Christological thought within its proper setting. Lienhard remains the essential guide to Luther's Christology. Still others have focused on particular aspects of Luther's Christological reflections. One of the most modern popular themes was Luther's doctrine of the atonement (e.g., Aulén 1931). (For a concise summary of recent research on Luther's Christology, see Arnold 2014.)

Some scholars have provided valuable insight into Luther's Christology by focusing on the Lord's Supper. The works of Hermann Sasse (1959) and Albrecht Peters (1966) have been helpful in illuminating Luther's emphasis on the presence of Christ in worship (cf. Jensen 2014). Within his Eucharistic writings, Luther profoundly articulated his most radical Christological themes. Paul Gennrich (1929) saw that for Luther an attack on the real presence resulted in annihilating Jesus Christ, the chief article of his theology. So for him, Luther's Christology could be said to emerge from his doctrine of the Eucharist (Gennrich 1929: 3; cf. Congar 1962, 1982). That the battle over the Supper became integral to Luther's Christology was not because of its absence in his thought prior, but because during these battles Luther launched his Christological thought in a certain direction (Lienhard 1982: 195–6; cf. Lienhard 1985).

That Christ at the altar was central to Luther's Christology is evident in how his theological heirs crystallized his Christology Eucharistically. The *alter Martinus*, Martin Chemnitz developed his Christology predominantly from Luther's Eucharistic reflections (Valčo 2012). The Christological article in the *Formula of Concord* (1577) drew principally from Luther's Eucharistic writings—over ten citations alone come from Luther's *Confession Concerning Christ's Supper* (1528) (Kolb and Wengert 2000: 616–35). Such emphases from the second generation of Wittenberg theologians show that Luther's Christology emanated from a life of worship at the altar.

Luther's Christology was about worshiping a God who had come near and stayed near. On that basis this chapter will limit itself to presenting Martin Luther's Christology as found within his understanding of the Eucharist. Luther said much more about Christ apart from the controversies (cf. Siggins 1970; Lienhard 1982; Arnold 2014); nevertheless, Luther's most insightful Christological discoveries surfaced while defending the sacrament of the true body and blood of Christ (cf. Gennrich 1929; Congar 1962; Lienhard 1982; Steinmetz 2008). Starting with Luther's mediaeval context, this essay will demonstrate how Luther's Eucharistic Christology describes the work of Christ in his arguments against the sacrifice of the mass, and describes the person of Christ in his arguments for the bodily presence of Christ against Huldrych Zwingli and Johannes Oecolampadius.

THE MEDIAEVAL MASS: LUTHER'S CONTEXT

The mediaeval mass evoked a reverent, at times crippling, fear in the hearts of many in the sixteenth century. During this period it was common to hear tales of visions of bleeding morsels of flesh miraculously appearing in place of the host. These 'bleeding host' tales reveal that the presence of Christ could be a convicting presence (Duffy 2005: 103–4). Adding to the deep sense of awe was the common view that in the mass the believer confronted Christ not solely as savior but as a demanding judge. This latter aspect of mediaeval piety was true for Martin Luther.

From his first mass in 1507 and throughout his career in the Erfurt monastery, Luther was terrified of holding mass (Brecht 1985: 71–6). Nothing could repress his distress.

I almost fasted myself to death, for again and again I went for three days without taking a drop of water or a morsel of food. I was very serious about it. I really crucified the Lord Christ. I wasn't simply an observer but helped to carry him and pierce [his hands and feet]. God forgive me for it, for I have confessed it openly! This is the truth: the most pious monk is the worst scoundrel. He denies Christ is the mediator and high priest and turns him into a judge.

(WA Tr 4: no. 4422, 305–6; *LW* 54: 339–40)

Luther was before a demanding judge—a judge who had instituted a more demanding interior righteousness 'greater than that of the scribes and the Pharisees' (Matt. 5:20). Christ was both judge and legislator. These Christological motifs heightened Luther's anxiety to work out his salvation.

The mediaeval system of salvation offered Luther a righteousness of Christ (*iustitia Christi*) that was incomplete for salvation. As Gabriel Biel put it 'if our merits would not complete those of Christ, the merits of Christ would be insufficient, yes, *nihil*' (quoted in Oberman 1992: 117). The demands of the righteousness of God (*iustitia Dei*) were only met when one's works were added to the righteousness of Christ. 'The *iustitia Dei* is the standard according to which the degree of appropriation and the effects of the *iustitia Christi* are measured and will be measured in the Last Judgment. The *iustitia Dei* is the eternal immutable Law of God' (Oberman 1992: 120). Luther came to see this system as making 'both Christ and the Father as terrible judges and tyrants, and the Holy Spirit as a taskmaster, since we have been taught nothing else than that God must be reconciled by our works' (*WA* 45: 567; *LW* 24: 116). It was partially against this adversarial paradigm that Luther made his reformation discovery in 1515. Justification was alone by the grace of God, who gave the sinner both the *iustitia Christi* and *iustitia Dei* simultaneously (Oberman 1992: 120; cf. McGrath 2011: 125ff.). Christ came to set Christians free from the law, not to set up a new one.

This system of theology, for Luther, had thrown Christology into an arena of fear and works, rather than comfort and grace. Rejecting Christ for our good works doglegged the Gospel and emphasized an angry God as judge, rather than a suffering Savior come near. Such a system displayed that the Church had not taken the gracious coming of God in the flesh for our salvation seriously (Brecht 1985: 78–9).

And yet, for Luther the Incarnation was taking on a more pivotal role. In 1518 at the Heidelberg Disputation, Luther displayed his new theological program emphasizing the Incarnation and the Cross. A year later, while exegeting the fifth Psalm, he summarized this program, stating that the 'Crux sola est nostra theologia' (*WA* 5: 176). It was the revealed, incarnate God—which the late mediaeval theologians had discarded—that became his starting point. Theology could not begin with the divinity of Christ; it had to begin with his humanity. This emphasis became the foundation for his later Christological developments in the controversy over the Eucharistic presence (Lienhard 1982: 155).

His early experience of Christ in the Eucharist shifted from one of fear to one of love. Christ was his mediator and Savior, not a terrifying legislator, judge, and tyrant. Two major issues became the impetus of Luther's Christological particularities. The first issue was the sacrifice of the mass that spurred him to articulate his view of the work of Christ. The second concerned the presence of Christ in the Eucharist that goaded him to refine his view on the person of Christ.

The Sacrifice of the Mass: The Work of Christ

[I]n the mass the papists do nothing but continually ride the words 'we offer up, we offer up', and 'these sacrifices, these gifts'. They keep completely quiet about the sacrifice that Christ has made. They do not thank him. Indeed, they despise and deny his sacrifice and try to come before God with their own sacrifice.

(*WA* 18: 23–4; *LW* 36: 313)

Blasphemy, idolatry, the devil's work were some of the slurs Luther used to describe this view of the sacrifice. He shuddered at the idea that in the mass priests were crucifying Christ again as if God needed continuously to be appeased (*WA* 8: 493; *LW* 36: 147). Luther saw this diminishing of Christ's sole sacrifice as the chief of all abominations in the mass. Rather than the mass being a sacrifice, good work, and meritorious, Luther demanded it be seen as a testament and gift (Leaver 1983: 125; Hunsinger 2008: 100–5). What was especially reprehensible was that the word of promise in the mass was made unintelligible by mumbled whispers, keeping from the people the words that, if proclaimed aloud, would be the greatest comfort (*WA* 6: 362; *LW* 35, 90).

Two Christological motifs become apparent in Luther's assault on the sacrifice of the mass. The first called attention to the proper view of the words of institution. These words were Christ's last will and testament. In issuing his new testament he became a testator. The second Christological theme he accentuated was that Christ was our chief priest. As our chief priest, it was he who made atonement for sin through his once-and-for-all sacrifice at Calvary. Luther's Christology would not make his Savior's work cheap.

'Verba Testamentum'—Christ our Testator

At the sacring, with the host elevated, the priest would whisper 'Hoc est enim Corpus Meum'. Here 'the priest had access to mysteries forbidden to others: only he might utter the words which transformed bread and wine into the flesh and blood of God incarnate' (Duffy 2005: 110). In the mass the priest put on display God's inenarrable power, a power that could only be handled through preparing oneself properly to recite the mass.

Within this liturgical atmosphere the sacrament was seen as an *opus operatum*—a work that conferred grace regardless of faith when properly performed. These powerful five words, along with the words of institution, remained inaudible and foreign to the congregation, in part, because faith in the words of promise was no longer necessary (*WA* 6: 513; *LW* 36, 37). 'Has not the devil here in a masterly way stolen from us the chief thing in the mass and put it to silence?' (*WA* 6: 362; *LW* 35: 90). Reforming the Church meant retrieving these words' power, not in a priest's mutterings, but in Christ and his promise.

The words of institution, Luther believed, proclaimed the whole Gospel. In his *Treatise on the New Testament, that is, The Holy Mass* (1520), he stated that:

> [T]he mass was instituted to preach and praise Christ, to glorify his sufferings and all his grace and goodness, so that we may be moved to love him, to hope and believe in him ... And had there been no preaching, Christ would never have instituted the mass. He is more concerned about the word than about the sign. For the preaching ought to be nothing but an explanation of the words of Christ, when he instituted the mass and said 'This is my body, this is my blood', etc. What is the whole gospel but an explanation of this testament? Christ has gathered up the whole gospel in a short summary with the words of this testament or sacrament.
>
> (*WA* 6: 373–4; *LW* 35: 105–6)

Christ as the preached Word was the heart of his Eucharistic theology and theology in general (Davis 2008: 45–8). The promises of forgiveness and eternal life were made in the testament proclaimed by Christ, the Testator. Christ as testator bequeathed the inheritance of forgiveness and eternal life to his disciples, saying 'This is my blood of the new testament, which is shed for many for the remission of sins' (Matt. 26:28). With these words Christ made a solemn promise of righteousness and salvation to his heirs, the Church (*WA* 6: 357; *LW* 35: 84). In the sacrament was the clearest articulation of Christ's last will and testament (Forde 2007: 146–51; Schwarz 2009: 198–210).

Because the maker of a will must die for the will to take effect, the theme of Christ as testator was linked to Luther's ideas of the Incarnation and the Cross. In *The Babylonian Captivity of the Church* (1520) he stressed this stating:

> Hence the words 'compact', 'covenant', and 'testament of the Lord' occur so frequently in the Scriptures. These words signified that God would one day die. 'For where there is a testament, the death of a testator must necessarily occur' (Heb. 9[:16]). Now God made a testament; therefore, it was necessary that he should die. But God could not die unless he became man. Thus the incarnation and the death of Christ are both comprehended most concisely in this one word, 'testament'.
>
> (*WA* 6: 514; *LW* 36: 38; cf. *WA* 6: 358, 513–14; *LW* 35: 85, *LW* 36: 38)

In his death, Christ put into motion the new testament in the mass that assures the Church of its reception of forgiveness and eternal life. Luther recognized six distinct aspects in this Eucharistic theme of a testament.

There is, first, the testator who makes the testament, Christ. Second, the heirs to whom the testament is bequeathed, we Christians. Third, the testament itself, the words of Christ—when he says, 'This is my body which is given for you. This is my blood which is poured out for you, a new eternal testament', etc. Fourth, the seal or token is the sacrament, the bread and wine, under which are his true body and blood. For everything that is in this sacrament must be living. Therefore Christ did not put it in dead writing and seals, but in living words and signs which we use from day to day ... Fifth, there is the bequeathed blessing which the words signify, namely, the remission of sins and eternal life. Sixth, the duty, remembrance, or requiem, which we are to do for Christ; that is, that we should preach his love and grace, hear and meditate upon it, and by it be incited and preserved unto love and hope in him.

(*WA* 6: 359; *LW* 35: 86–7)

The sixth aspect of the testament is tied to faith. Faith was strengthened in the sacrament, the objective seal of God's forgiveness. This faith in the testament ensures the reception of the bequest 'even though you were scaly, scabby, stinking, and most filthy' (*WA* 6: 361; *LW* 35: 88).

Faith in the testament was the vehicle that united the individual to Christ, the testator. Using the metaphor of a wedding ring in his treatise *The Freedom of a Christian* (1520), Luther spoke of a joyful exchange (*admirabile commercium*) between Christ and sinner. Faith intimately unites the believer to Christ. Faith attaches itself to the promise of God and makes what is Christ's now, the believers' and what is the believers' now, Christ's (*WA* 7: 25–6; *LW* 31: 349–52). Through faith in Christ's new testament proclaimed in the mass, Luther saw the benefits won by Christ distributed to the Church (Steinmetz 2008: 279).

Luther eliminated sacrificial language when writing *An Order of Mass and Communion for the Church at Wittenberg* (1523) (*WA* 12: 211; *LW* 53: 26). All that remained were the words of institution, which, rather than a whispered prayer to God, were to be a vernacular proclamation to the people.

AN ATONING SACRIFICE—CHRIST OUR HIGH PRIEST

In *The Misuse of the Mass* (1521), Luther stated that 'We have only one single priest, Christ, who has sacrificed himself for us and all of us with him' (*WA* 8: 486; *LW* 36: 138). Luther would emphasize the sole atoning sacrifice of the high priest, Jesus Christ, in his Eucharistic writings (cf. *WA* 18: 23; *LW* 36: 313; *WA* 8: 493–4, 506; *WA* 18: 29; *LW* 36: 147, 162, 320). Luther held that as our high priest at the mass Christ offers up our praises and thanksgiving to the Father, something that later Lutheran theologians would call his intercessory sacrifice (Aulén 1958: 151–2). We will look at both the atoning and intercessory sacrifices of Christ in Luther's thought in turn.

Trusting in the sacrificial work of the mass, which had elevated the role of the priest-hood, watered down the atoning blood of Christ's sole sacrifice. In *Concerning the Ministry* (1523), he wrote:

> The gospel and all of Scripture present Christ as the high priest, who alone and once for all by offering himself has taken away the sins of all men and accom-plished their sanctification for all eternity. For once and for all he entered into the holy place through his own blood, thus securing an eternal redemption [Heb. 9:12, 28; 10:12, 14]. Thus no other sacrifice remains for our sins than his, and, by putting our trust altogether in it, we are saved from sin without any merits or works of our own.
>
> *(WA* 12: 175; *LW* 40: 14)

Luther held that on the Cross Jesus Christ appeased God's wrath and made satis-faction for our sins. Contrary to Gustav Aulén's thesis that Luther had distanced him-self from Anselm's atonement theory (Aulén 1931: 101–22), we see how he alludes to Anselmian notions, when writing about the mass. That is not to say that Luther's theory of the atonement is exclusively Anselmian. Luther's view of the atonement cannot be easily systematized (see Althaus 1966: 202–3; Lienhard 1982: 181–2; Lohse 1999: 225–8; Arnold 2014: 275, 284–5). Nevertheless, in his Eucharistic writings, Luther underlines that the incarnate Son made satisfaction for us once and for all through his death. Again in his *The Misuse of the Mass* (1521), he stated:

> There are not several ways to reconcile God, but one way alone … The body of Christ is given and his blood is poured out, and thereby God is reconciled, for it was given and poured out for you—as he says: 'for you'—so that he may avert from us the wrath of God which we by our sins have deserved. And if the wrath is gone then the sins are forgiven. Therefore he says it shall be given and poured out for the forgiveness of sins. If the body were not given and the blood not poured out, then the wrath of God would remain upon us and we would retain our sins … Here you see clearly that no work of satisfaction or sacrifice or reconciliation is of any use; only faith in the given body and the shed blood reconciles. Not that faith does the reconciling which Christ has performed for us.
>
> *(WA* 8: 518–19; *LW* 36, 176–7)

Luther highlights that in Christ the wrath of God is appeased. In his catechisms, espe-cially, Luther goes further than Anselm, showing that Jesus Christ does this not only through his humanity, but also in his divinity (Arnold 2014: 284). Lienhard sees Luther positing an inter-divine conflict where there is 'a struggle within God himself, a combat between the Father and the Son become human, the Son offering himself to the wrath of the Father in order to let love triumph and open the way to forgiveness' (Lienhard 1982: 182). However, in Luther's Eucharistic writings he emphasizes the substitution-ary work that wins forgiveness as predominantly tied to the humanity of Christ and his priestly office.

Luther allowed for a sacrificial sense in the mass through Christ's priestly work as intercessor (Lienhard 1982: 127–30; Hunsinger 2008: 100–5). '[T]his sacrifice of prayer, praise, and thanksgiving, and of ourselves as well, we are not to present before God in our own person. But we are to lay it upon Christ and let him present it for us' (WA 6: 368; LW 35: 99). Through Christ we offer our sacrifices of prayer to the Father; we do not offer Christ to the Father, rather 'Christ offers us' (WA 6: 369; LW 35: 99). Christ as our High Priest 'receives our prayer and sacrifice, and through himself, as a godly priest, makes them pleasing to God' (WA 6: 368; LW 35: 99). The sacrament is not a work that gains forgiveness for Luther, but it can be said to be a sacrifice of praise and thanksgiving achieved through Christ's intercessory sacrifice.

The work of Christ is not a passive sacrifice repeated on the altar. His high priestly sacrifice was accomplished once and for all, and the inheritance won through his death has been ratified 'for you' in the New Testament, that is, his body and blood. These Christological themes of testator and high priest provide insight into Luther's Eucharistic Christology.

THE BODILY PRESENCE IN THE MASS: THE PERSON OF CHRIST

Protestants were united in opposing the sacrifice of the mass. Protestants were divided over Christ's presence in the Eucharist. Where the sacrifice of the mass minimized Christ's work, the real presence of Christ in the bread and wine, for Luther, threatened the Incarnation (Nagel 1953).

During the 1520s, Luther, Zwingli, and Oecolampadius would publish multiple treatises and sermons over the presence of the body of Christ in the Eucharist. Zwingli and Oecolampadius were not content with disregarding the doctrine of transubstantiation; they wanted to demonstrate that Christ was present in a spiritual way as a result of Christ's ascension. They presented three arguments that would guide Luther's reflections on the Eucharist, and on the person of Christ. How was one to understand the phrase 'This is my body'? And how could one articulate the location of the body of Christ at the 'right hand of God'? The final question was whether the physical body of Christ was of benefit, since according to John 6:63 'the flesh avails not'. Let's start with the first question.

'This is my Body'—The Word of Christ

At the Marburg Colloquy, Luther took a piece of chalk and wrote on the desk 'Hoc est corpus meum'. From a literal interpretation of these words he would not be moved. Luther's theology of Christ's presence in the Eucharist was tied to his theology of the

Word, particularly the words of institution. He believed that God's Word can be trusted, though it be folly to reason.

Andreas Karlstadt, Zwingli, and Oecolampadius offered differing solutions to the phrase, each looking at a different word. Karlstadt believed that when Jesus spoke 'this', he pointed to his physical body. Zwingli held that the 'is' was to be understood as 'represents', employing the concept of *alleosis*. Oecolampadius believed that 'body' should be understood as 'sign of my body'. To Luther these were tortured attempts by reckless fanatics (*leichtfertige Schwermer*) who 'juggle and play the clown with the words of the Supper according to their fancy' (*WA* 23: 85; *LW* 37: 27; cf. *WA* 23: 107; *LW* 37: 41). He saw their hermeneutical manipulations as excrement (*dreck*) (*WA* 23: 97; *LW* 37: 34). These arguments stank, for when Christ said 'This is my Body', he meant what he said (Steinmetz 2008: 279).

As Davis notes, 'For Luther, the whole issue of Christ's presence in the Eucharist was controlled by his view of the Words of Institution as God's Word of power' (Davis 2008: 46). Davis highlights the importance again of the word of promise to effect Christ's presence in the bread. Luther states that 'as soon as Christ says: "This is my Body", his body is present through the Word and the power of the Holy Spirit' (*WA* 19: 491; *LW* 36: 341). He states that Christ 'has put himself into the Word, and through the Word he puts himself into the bread also' (*WA* 19: 493; *LW* 36: 343). For Luther, Christ, the Word, settles the exegetical debate (Davis 2008: 44–8).

'The Right Hand of God'—The Two Natures of Christ

The second argument against Christ's bodily presence was tied to the idea that Christ currently sits 'at the right hand of God'. Oecolampadius and Zwingli took the phrase 'right hand of God' to mean that the resurrected body of Christ was localized in heaven and therefore could not be in two places at once. But if the humanity of Christ was at the right hand of God, where was this?

Luther gathered that Zwingli and Oecolampadius had dreamed up 'an imaginary heaven in which a golden throne stands, and Christ sits beside the Father in a cowl and golden crowns, the way artists paint it' (*WA* 23: 131; *LW* 37: 55). But, which Scripture had limited the 'right hand of God' in this manner? Listing various passages, Luther demonstrates that the 'right hand of God' is not 'a golden throne, but is the almighty power of God, which at one and the same time can be nowhere and yet must be everywhere' (*WA* 23: 133; *LW* 37: 57). Appealing to the right hand of God as a specific location for Christ's body was foolish.

The ascension had become the center of dispute. David Steinmetz notes 'the ascension did not mean for Luther, as it did for Zwingli, that Christ had left the world's space and time but only that the mode of his continuing presence in the world had changed. The problem for Luther's Eucharistic theology was not distance from the world, but inaccessible immanence within it' (Steinmetz 2002: 279). For Zwingli, Christ's humanity was finite and after the resurrection remained finite, thus limiting the way in which the body of Christ could be present. On the one hand, with the ascension, Zwingli believed that Christ's body was now locally present in heaven, at the right hand of God (Steinmetz 2008: 275). On the other hand, for Luther, something remarkable happened to Christ's body after the resurrection, demonstrated in its ability to walk through doors. The body of Christ had taken on new properties that it did not have prior to the resurrection (Steinmetz 2002: 278). This new body became the basis for how Luther would understand the *communicatio idiomatum*. The risen body of Christ now participates in the omnipresence of God and so can be present to the Church in multiple ways.

Borrowing from the scholastics (William of Ockham and Gabriel Biel), Luther described three ways in which an object can be present. The first mode of presence was circumscribed or local. An object is locally present when 'the space and the object occupying it exactly correspond and fit into the same measurement, such as wine or water in a cask' (*WA* 26: 327; *LW* 37: 215). The second way an object can be present, he called definitive or uncircumscribed. This is when a 'body is not palpably in one place and is not measurable according to the dimensions of the place where it is, but can occupy either more room or less' (*WA* 26: 327–8; *LW* 37: 215). This manner describes the presence of angels in a room, demons in a body, Christ's presence passing through a wooden door when he entered the upper room. It is this mode of presence that Christ utilizes to be present in the Eucharist. The last mode of presence is the repletive mode. It allows for an object to be everywhere simultaneously 'in all places whole and entire' (*WA* 26: 329; *LW* 37: 216). This presence is God's alone, associated with the right hand of God and his omnipresence.

The unity of the divine and human natures in one person, for Luther, led him to say that Christ's human nature takes on the attribute of omnipresence or ubiquity—what later theologians would term the majestic properties or *genus maiestaticum*. In his *Confession Concerning Christ's Supper* (1528), he describes the relationship between the two natures of Christ as follows:

> Our faith maintains that Christ is God and man, and the two natures are one person, so that this person may not be divided into two; therefore, he can surely show himself in a corporeal, circumscribed manner at whatever place he will, as he did after the resurrection and will do on the Last Day. But above and beyond this mode he can also use the second, uncircumscribed mode, as we have proved from the gospel, that he did at the grave and the closed door.
>
> But now, since he is a man who is supernaturally one person with God, and apart from this man there is no God, it must follow that according to the third supernatural mode, he is and can be wherever God is and that everything is full of Christ through and through, even according to his humanity—not according to the first corporeal, circumscribed mode, but according to the supernatural divine mode. Here you must take your stand and say that wherever Christ is according to his divinity he is there as a natural, divine person and he is also naturally and personally there, as his conception in his mother's womb proves conclusively … Wherever this person is, it is the single, indivisible person, and if you can say, 'Here is God', then you must also say, 'Christ the man is present too'.

> And if you could show me one place where God is and not the man, then the person is already divided and I could at once say truthfully, 'Here is God who is not man and has never become man'. But no God like that for me! … No, comrade, wherever you place God for me, you must also place the humanity for me. They simply will not let themselves be separated and divided from each other. He has become one person and does not separate the humanity from himself.
>
> (*WA* 26: 332–3; *LW* 37: 218–19)

Here, there is a strong Alexandrian Christological tendency in Luther's demand that the two natures stay united in the one person of Christ, against what he sees in Zwingli and Oecolampadius as the Nestorian tendency to split the person (*WA* 50: 589–90; *LW* 41: 103; see Ngien 2004).

In the Church's tradition the concept of the *communicatio idiomatum* was used to demonstrate that the attributes were exchanged from the natures to the person. But here, in what can be termed a hyper-Alexandrian move, Luther implements the concept between the two natures themselves (Arnold 2014: 282). Some scholars fear that Luther's Christ has become docetic, monophysite, a *tertium quid*, perhaps even modalist (Congar 1962: 484–6; Lienhard 1982: 171, 344–5; Lohse 1999: 230). Does a human nature that participates in omnipresence remain human or become a mixed thing? Others have argued against these claims, emphasizing that the *communicatio idiomatum* is the basis for refuting docetism and monophysitism in Luther's thought (Bayer 2007: 15–16; Hinlicky 2007: 140–4).

The controversy over Luther's teaching of the ubiquity of Christ's human nature and thus his body has tended to miss the structure of Luther's thought, where the Word is central (Quere 1985: 65–6; Jorgenson 2004: 358–9; Davis 2008: 15). Ralph Quere argues that, 'Even when Luther's doctrine of ubiquity … is introduced as a further argument for and basis of Christ's eucharistic presence, that presence remains tied to the Word' (Quere 1985: 65). Hence Luther states:

> He is present everywhere, but he does not wish that you grope for him everywhere. Grope rather where the Word is, and there you will lay hold of him in the right way. Otherwise you are tempting God and committing idolatry … He is present through the Word, although not in the same way as here in the Sacrament, where through the Word, he binds his body and blood so that they are received corporeally in the bread and wine. If we believe the one, it is easy also to grasp and believe the other. Heaven and earth are his sack; as corn fills the sack, so he fills all things. And as a seed bears a stalk, an ear, and many kernels … much more is Christ able to distribute himself whole and undivided into so many particles.
>
> (*WA* 19: 492–3; *LW* 36: 342–3)

Because Christ tells us that he is present through his Word in the bread and wine, the doctrine of ubiquity becomes a necessary possibility against those who say Christ cannot be present. For Luther the priority is always the Word.

Similarly, if the *communicatio idiomatum* in Luther's thought can seem to divinize the human nature, it also seems to humanize the divine nature. The *communicatio idiomatum* moves in both directions. Here Luther's theology of the Cross comes to the fore in the Eucharistic debate. The Cross has placed suffering into the life of God—what later theologians would call the humble properties or the *genus tapeinoticon* (Ngien 1995, 2004). 'Now if the old witch, Lady Reason, *alleosis*' grandmother should say that the Deity surely cannot suffer and die, then you must answer and say: That is true, but since the divinity and humanity are one person in Christ, the Scriptures ascribe to the divinity, because of his personal union, all that happens to the humanity, and vice versa' (*WA* 26: 321; *LW* 37: 210). It is important that God both suffer and die for Luther, since it was only the divinity of God that could overcome death (Arnold 2014: 288). Though statements like these seem to make Luther a patripassian, it is more accurate, with Lienhard, to call his position 'Dei-passianism', since patripassianism was a modalist heresy open to the idea that the Father was crucified (Lienhard 1982: 171). The suffering of God is an early and important theme in Luther in which 'the depth of Luther's christology is revealed' (Lienhard 1982: 171).

The *communicatio idiomatum* can be said to be the 'hermeneutical motor of his whole theology' (Steiger 2000: 125). The desire to keep the unity of the natures in the one person of Christ was foundational for him. Even though some see Luther's description of the communication of the *genus maiestaticum* as a metaphysical conundrum, his idea of the communication of the *genus tapeinoticon* has inspired Karl Barth, Dietrich Bonhoeffer, and Jürgen Moltmann. Luther worshiped God incarnate, not naked. A naked deity, for him, was of no benefit. The flesh of Christ avails.

'The Flesh Avails Not'—The Benefit of Christ's Flesh

Zwingli's appeal to John 6:63 in the discussion about the presence of Christ's body revealed the distance between the two reformers' anthropologies and, hence, how they approached the relationship between the two natures of Christ. Zwingli understood the dichotomy here between 'flesh' and 'spirit' as a dichotomy between physical reality and non-physical reality, hence holding to a radical dualism. Luther maintained a psychosomatic unity and understood 'flesh' and 'spirit' in this passage as a dichotomy between the self-centered life and the God-centered life (*WA* 26: 349–54; *LW* 37: 235–8; cf. Steinmetz 2002: 75–6).

When Zwingli appealed to John 6:63 as an argument against the benefit of Christ's bodily presence in the bread and wine, he highlighted the degree to which he was willing to distinguish the two natures of Christ. Salvation came from Christ's divine nature, not his human nature, though it was necessary that through his human nature he suffer and die (*ZW* 3: 779; cf. *ZW* 4: 827–8; *LCC* 24: 212–13). Zwingli emphasized the divine nature of the Christ over his human nature, and in so doing, Luther saw Zwingli as dividing the person of Christ.

Luther emphasized the unity of the two natures in the one person of Christ. In his sermon on John 6:45–7 (1531), he states at length:

> Thus our fanatics—Zwingli and others—also declare Christ's human nature must be excluded here, that it is His divinity and not His humanity which imparts eternal life. In this way they divide Christ. But who teaches them to tear Christ asunder, to fashion out of Christ, the Son of the Virgin Mary, another person, one who is also the Son of God? They divorce Mary's Son from God's Son, and in defense they quote Christ's own words (John 6:63): 'The flesh is of no avail'. They aver that Scripture points to the fact that one must not place trust in man, but in God alone. Therefore they conclude, the passage which declares that he who believes in Christ has eternal life must refer to His divinity to the exclusion of His humanity.
>
> We are not that smart; we must believe that our God sent His Son, Jesus Christ, who was born of the virgin Mary, as we also confess in our Creed: … In Him I believe; and I believe, therefore, in the Son of God without severing Him from the Son born of Mary. My faith adheres not only to the Son of God or to His divinity but also to Him who is called Mary's Son; for they are identical. I am determined to know nothing of a Son of God who is not also Mary's Son who suffered, the God enveloped in humanity who is one Person. I dare not separate the one from the other and say that the humanity is of no use, but only the divinity.
>
> (*WA* 33: 154–6; *LW* 23: 101–2)

The humanity of Christ could not be discarded for his divinity. To posit that the presence of Christ's body in the bread and wine would 'avail not', was for Luther a sign of heresy.

For Luther it was in the humanity of Christ that humans were able to benefit from his person and work. Without the humanity of Christ, there was no salvation. 'The fundamental position that God's presence is salutary only where connected with the humanity of Jesus Christ is central to Luther's theology' (Lohse 1999: 231). It was crucial for Luther to demonstrate that the humanity of Christ was not only accessible in the bread and wine, but also beneficial.

Luther believed that Christ had instituted the Supper in order to distribute the power of his suffering and thus that the forgiveness of sins was in the bread and wine (*WA* 18: 200). Luther believed that the forgiveness won by Christ's sacrifice on the Cross was distributed in the sacrament. In the sacrament Christ has distributed the benefit of his sacrifice through his testament attached to the bread and wine (Quere 1985: 58–60). The Word is foundational to the distribution of the benefit in the bread and wine, because it is the Word that promises that the body and blood are in the bread and wine.

In *That These Words of Christ, 'This is my Body', Etc., Still Stands Firm Against the Fanatics* (1527), he outlines three benefits of the presence of Christ's humanity in the bread and wine. The first benefit in the bread and wine is that it makes the proud blind and shows worldly reason to be folly (*WA* 23: 255; *LW* 37: 131). The second benefit of the real presence is a bodily benefit in which 'our body is fed with the body of

Christ, in order that our faith and hope may abide and that our body also may live eternally from the same eternal food of the body of Christ which it eats physically … As we eat him, he abides in us and we in him. For he is not digested or transformed but ceaselessly he transforms us, our soul into righteousness, our body into immortality' (*WA* 23: 255; *LW* 37: 132). The third benefit is the 'forgiveness of sins', since God's powerful Word is in it (*WA* 23: 257; *LW* 37: 133). Because the Word says that the bread and wine are the body and blood and that these are given for our forgiveness of sins, it is so.

For Luther, Zwingli's spiritualizing of the Supper removed Christ from the church. Luther's Eucharistic Christology would not allow for this. At the Supper, one encounters Christ himself, fully and not divided. At the altar, 'One either loses Christ completely, or has him completely' (*WA* 23: 253; *LW* 37: 131). The gestalt of Luther's Christology was Eucharistic. A distant Christ was of no benefit. Luther conceived of a metaphysical substructure that made the presence of Christ in the bread and wine through the Word a possibility. As Robert Jenson notes, Luther's focus on the words of institution and the unity of Christ present to us 'a rule controlling all the church's liturgical practice' (Jenson 2003: 278).

Concluding Thoughts

The doxological nature of Luther's Christology warrants reflection. In addition to those who have mined Luther's Christology Eucharistically (Gennrich 1929; Congar 1962, 1982; Lienhard 1985), further work on Luther's doxological Christology is needed. The exploration of Luther's Christology in his hymns by Klaus Burba (1956) and Robin Leaver (2007) have been promising, but more work needs to be done. Research into the liturgical ordering of Luther's mass and the Christological theology within will no doubt bear much fruit.

Another trajectory into Luther's Christology should be tied to the ecumenical mandate. Perhaps a greater understanding of the manner in which we worship Christ will reveal what we believe of him. Here the works by George Hunsinger (2008) and Robert Croken (1991) on the Eucharist are invaluable. Unfortunately, what has divided Christianity is the very body that was meant to unite us.

Luther's Eucharistic Christology places us before Christ present on the altar. In, with, and under bread and cup, as Luther reminds us, we partake of Christ's body, our greatest treasure.

Suggested Reading

Jensen (2014); Jenson (2003); Lienhard (1982); Lohse (1999); Mühlen (1996); Sasse (1959); Steinmetz (2008); Yeago (1996).

BIBLIOGRAPHY

Primary Sources

Luther, Martin, *D. Martin Luthers Werke: Kritische Gesamtausgabe* (Weimar: H. Böhlau, 1883); cited as *WA* (Weimarer Ausgabe). English translation published in Martin Luther, *Luther's Works*, ed. J. Pelikan and H. T. Lehman, American edn., 55 vols. (St. Louis/Philadelphia: Concordia/Fortress, 1955–72); cited as *LW*.

The major works by Luther cited are: *A Treatise on the New Testament, that is, The Holy Mass* (1520) (*WA* 6: 353–78; *LW* 35: 75–112); *The Babylonian Captivity of the Church* (1520) (*WA* 6: 497–573; *LW* 36, 11–126); *The Misuse of the Mass* (1521) (*WA* 8: 477–563; *LW* 36: 127–230); *The Abomination of the Secret Mass* (1525) (*WA* 18: 22–36; *LW* 36: 307–28); *The Sacrament of the Body and Blood of Christ—Against the Fanatics* (1526) (*WA* 19: 482–523; *LW* 36: 329–61); *That These Words of Christ, 'This is My Body', etc, Still Stand Firm Against the Fanatics* (1527) (*WA* 23: 64–283; *LW* 37: 3–150); *Confession Concerning Christ's Supper* (1527) (*WA* 26: 261–509; *LW* 37: 151–372).

Secondary Sources

Althaus, P. (1966), *The Theology of Martin Luther*, trans. R. Schultz (Philadelphia: Fortress).

Arnold, M. (2014), 'Luther on Christ's Person and Work', in R. Kold, I. Dingel, and L. Batka (eds.), *The Oxford Handbook of Martin Luther's Theology* (Oxford: Oxford University Press), 274–93.

Aulén, G. (1931), *Christus Victor: An Historical Study of Three Types of the Idea of Atonement*, trans. A. Herbert (London: SPCK).

Aulén, G. (1958), *Eucharist and Sacrifice*, trans. E. Wahlstrom (Philadelphia: Muhlenberg Press).

Bayer, O. (2007), 'Das Wort ward Fleisch. Luthers Christologie als Lehre von der Idiomenkommunikation', in O. Bayer and B. Gleede (eds.), *Creator est Creatura. Luthers Christologie als Lehre von der Idiomenkommunikation* (Berlin: de Gruyter), 5–34.

Bayer, O. (2008), *Martin Luther's Theology: A Contemporary Interpretation*, trans. T. Trapp (Grand Rapids, Mich.: Eerdmans).

Beer, T. (1980). *Der fröhliche Wechsel und Streit. Grundzüge der Theologie Martin Luthers* (Einsiedeln: Johannes Verlag; first published by Benno: Leipzig, 1974).

Brecht, M. (1985), *Martin Luther: His Road to Reformation 1483–1521*, trans. P. Schaff (Minneapolis: Fortress).

Burba, K. (1956), *Die Christologie in Luthers Liedern* (Gütersloh: Carl Bertelsmann Verlag).

Chemnitz, M. (1578; ET 2008), *The Two Natures of Christ*, trans. J. Preus (St. Louis, Mo.: Concordia Publishing).

Congar, Y. (1962), 'Regards et réflexions sur la christologie de Luther', in A. Grillmeier (ed.), *Das Konzil von Chalkedon. Geschichte und Gegenwart* (Würzburg: Echter), vol. 3, 457–86.

Congar, Y. (1982), 'Lutherana. Théologie de l'eucharistie et christologie chez Luther', *Revue des sciences philosophiques et théologiques* 66: 169–97.

Croken, R. (1991), *Luther's First Front: The Eucharist as Sacrifice* (Ottawa: University of Ottawa Press).

Davis, T. (2008), *This Is My Body: The Presence of Christ in Reformation Thought* (Grand Rapids, Mich.: Baker).

Duffy, E. (2005), *The Stripping of the Altars: Traditional Religion in England 1400-1580*, 2nd edn. (New Haven: Yale University Press).

Forde, G. (1997), *On Being a Theologian of the Cross: Reflections on Luther's Heidelberg Disputation* (Grand Rapids, Mich.: Eerdmans).

Forde, G. (2007), *The Preached God: Proclamation in Word and Sacrament* (Grand Rapids, Mich.: Eerdmans).

Gennrich, P. (1929), *Die Christologie Luthers im Abendmahlsstreit 1524–1529* (Königsberg: Buch und Steindruckerei von O. Kümmel).

Harnack, T. (1886), *Luthers Theologie mist besonderer Beziehung auf siene Versöhnungs- und Erlösungslehre*, vol. 2 (Erlangen: Verlag von Andreas Deichert).

Hinlicky, P. (2007), 'Luther's Anti-Docetism in the *Disputatio de divinitate et humanitate Christi* (1540)', in O. Bayer and B. Gleede (eds.), *Creator est Creatura. Luthers Christologie als Lehre von der Idiomenkommunikation* (Berlin: de Gruyter), 139–85.

Holl, K. (1948), *Gesammelte Aufsätze zur Kirchengeschichte* (Tübingen: Mohr Siebeck).

Hunsinger, G. (2008), *The Eucharist and Ecumenism: Let us Keep the Feast* (Cambridge: Cambridge University Press).

Jensen, G. (2014), 'Luther and the Lord's Supper', in R. Kold, I. Dingel, and L. Batka (eds.), *The Oxford Handbook of Martin Luther's Theology* (Oxford: Oxford University Press), 322–32.

Jenson, R. (2003), 'Luther's Contemporary Theological Significance', in D. McKim (ed.), *The Cambridge Companion to Martin Luther* (Cambridge: Cambridge University Press), 272–88.

Johnson, M. (2013), *Praying and Believing in Early Christianity: The Interplay between Christian Worship and Doctrine* (Collegeville, Minn.: Liturgical Press).

Jorgenson, A. (2004), 'Luther on Ubiquity and a Theology of the Public', *International Journal of Systematic Theology* 6: 351–68.

Kolb, R. and Wengert, T. (eds.) (2000), *The Book of Concord: The Confessions of the Evangelical Lutheran Church*, trans. C. Arand et al. (Minneapolis: Fortress).

Leaver, R. (1983), ' "Verba Testamenti" versus Canon: The Radical Nature of Luther's Liturgical Reform', *Churchman* 97: 123–31.

Leaver, R. (2007), *Luther's Liturgical Music: Principles and Implications* (Grand Rapids, Mich.: Eerdmans).

Lienhard, M. (1982), *Luther, Witness to Christ: Stages and Themes of the Reformer's Christology*, trans. E. Robertson (Minneapolis: Augsburg Publishing).

Lienhard, M. (1985) 'Luthers Abendmahlslehre im Kontext seiner Christologie und Ekklesiologie', in P. Manns (ed.), *Martin Luther. 'Reformator und Vater im Glauben'— Referate aus der Vortragsreihe des Instituts für Europäische Geschichte Mainz* (Stuttgart: F. Steiner Verlag Wiesbaden), 154–69.

Lohse, B. (1960), 'Luthers Christologie im Ablasstreit', *Luther-Jahrbuch* 27: 51–63.

Lohse, B. (1986), *Martin Luther: An Introduction to His Life and Work*, trans. R. Schultz (Philadelphia: Fortress).

Lohse, B. (1999), *Martin Luther's Theology: Its Historical and Systematic Development*, trans. R. Harrisville (Minneapolis: Fortress).

McGrath, A. (2011), *Luther's Theology of the Cross: Martin Luther's Theological Breakthrough* (Chichester: Wiley-Blackwell).

Mühlen, K. (1996), 'Christology', in H. Hillerbrand (ed.), *The Oxford Encyclopedia of the Reformation* (Oxford: Oxford University Press), vol. 1, 314–22.

Nagel, N. (1953), 'The Incarnation and the Lord's Supper in Luther', *Concordia Theological Monthly* 24: 625–52.

Ngien, D. (1995), *The Suffering of God According to Martin Luther's 'Theologia Crucis'* (Bern: Peter Lang).

Ngien, D. (2004), 'Chalcedonian Christology and Beyond: Luther's Understanding of the *Communicatio Idiomatum*', *Heythrop Journal* 45: 54–68.

Oberman, H. (1989), *Luther: Man Between God and the Devil*, trans. E. Walliser-Schwarzbart (New Haven: Yale University Press).

Oberman, H. (1992), *The Dawn of the Reformation: Essays in Late Medieval and Early Reformation Thought* (Edinburgh: T. & T. Clark).

Peters, A. (1966), *Realpräsenz. Luthers Zeugnis von Christi Gegenwart im Abendmahl* (Berlin: Lutherisches Verlagshaus).

Quere, R. (1985), 'Changes and Constants: Structure in Luther's Understanding of the Real Presence in the 1520s', *The Sixteenth Century Journal* 16: 45–78.

Sasse, H. (1959), *This is My Body: Luther's Contention for the Real Presence in the Sacrament of the Altar* (Minneapolis: Augsburg Publishing).

Schwarz, R. (2009), 'The Last Supper: The Testament of Jesus', in T. Wengert (ed.), *The Pastoral Luther: Essays on Martin Luther's Practical Theology* (Grand Rapids, Mich.: Eerdmans), 198–210.

Siggins, J. (1970), *Martin Luther's Doctrine of Christ* (New Haven: Yale University Press).

Steiger, J. (2000), 'The *communicatio idiomatum* as the Axle and Motor of Luther's Theology', *Lutheran Quarterly* 14: 125–58.

Steinmetz, D. (2002), *Luther in Context* (Grand Rapids, Mich.: Baker).

Steinmetz, D. (2008), 'The Eucharist and the Identity of Jesus in the Early Reformation', in B. Gaventa and R. Hays (eds.), *Seeking the Identity of Jesus: A Pilgrimage* (Grand Rapids, Mich.: Eerdmans), 270–84.

Valčo, M. (2012), '*Sedes Doctrinae* in the Eucharistic Christology of Martin Chemnitz', *E-Theologos* 3: 52–67.

Wandel, L. (2005), *The Eucharist in the Reformation: Incarnation and Liturgy* (Cambridge: Cambridge University Press).

Yeago, D. (1996), 'The Catholic Luther', in C. Braaten and R. Jenson (eds.), *The Catholicity of the Reformation* (Grand Rapids, Mich.: Eerdmans), 13–34.

CHAPTER 18

··

THE CHRISTOLOGY OF
JOHN CALVIN

··

RANDALL C. ZACHMAN

JOHN Calvin frames his understanding of the person and work of Christ in light of three sets of distinct but inseparable realities. The first reality is the self-revelation of God, first as Creator and then as Redeemer. God is revealed as the author and fountain of every good thing both in the universe and in Christ, and Christ is sent to reunite us with the Creator in eternal life, thereby fulfilling the purpose of our creation. The second reality is the self-disclosure of Jesus Christ first in the Law given to Israel, and then in the Gospel proclaimed to all nations. The Law is distinct from the Gospel, but Jesus Christ reveals himself and his work in both, and the two forms of Christ's self-disclosure confirm and enrich each other, even as the Gospel brings the time of the Law to its end and fulfillment. The third reality is the knowledge of God and the knowledge of ourselves. We can only truly appreciate and understand who Christ is and what he does for us when we know ourselves as sinners lying under the wrath of God. Much of what God does in Christ would offend us if we did not keep in mind our own predicament before the judgment seat of God.

Calvin grounds his understanding of the self-revelation of God in Christ in the self-disclosure of God in creation. According to Calvin, God reveals Godself by means of God's powers or perfections. 'For the Lord manifests himself by his powers, the force of which we feel within ourselves and the benefits of which we enjoy' (*Institutes of the Christian Religion* I.v.9; McNeill 1960: 1:62). These powers or perfections reveal the nature of God, and therefore include God's goodness, wisdom, power, mercy, justice, and life. Our awareness of the powers of God gives birth to piety and religion. 'For this sense of the powers of God is for us a fit teacher of piety, from which religion is born' (*Inst.* I.ii.1; McNeill 1960: 1:41). The powers of God are themselves portrayed in the works of God throughout the universe, including those works God does within each one of us. 'We must therefore admit in God's individual works—but especially in them as a whole—that God's powers are actually represented as in a painting' (*Inst.* I.v.10; McNeill 1960: 1:63). The self-portrayal of God's powers in the works that God does in the universe leads Calvin to call the universe the living image of God, or the theater of God's glory. The original purpose of creation involved our contemplation of the powers of God in the universe, so that we might feel their force within us and enjoy their benefits in our hearts in order to be united to God in eternal life. 'The natural order was that the frame of the universe should be the school in which we were to learn piety, and from it pass over to eternal life and perfect felicity' (*Inst.* II.vi.1; McNeill 1960: 1:341).

However, because our judgment is perverted by sin, we misunderstand the works of God, and do not rightly contemplate the powers of God represented in them. If we do come to some awareness of the powers of God, our ingratitude keeps us from acknowledging God to be the author and source of those powers, and thus the fountain of every good thing. We need the Word of God, represented first in the teaching of Moses, so that we might rightly apprehend the self-revelation of God in the works of God in the universe. 'It is therefore clear that God has provided the assistance of the Word for the sake of all those to whom he has been pleased to give useful instruction because he foresaw that his likeness imprinted upon the most beautiful form of the universe would be insufficiently effective. Hence, we must strive onward by this straight path if we seriously aspire to the pure contemplation of God' (*Inst.* I.vi.3; McNeill 1960: 1:72–3). The Word of God acts as spectacles to correct our vision, so that we rightly contemplate the works of God and the powers of God represented therein.

The self-revelation of God in Christ will follow the same trajectory, for the same God who is revealed in Christ is first revealed in the most beautiful fabric of the universe. Just as the powers of God are portrayed in the works of God in the universe, so are the powers of God represented in the person and work of Christ. However, Christ reveals himself to be the source of these powers, unlike the works of God in the universe, which reveal God to be the author and source of every good thing. 'By this we are taught not only that by the Son's intercession do those things which the Heavenly Father bestows come to us but that by mutual participation in power the Son himself is the author of them' (*Inst.* I.xiii.13; McNeill 1960: 1:138). Just as our awareness of the powers of God leads to the knowledge of God the Creator, so our experience of the powers of God in Christ leads us to the self-revelation of God in him. 'This practical knowledge is doubtless more certain and firmer than any idle speculation. There, indeed, does the pious mind perceive the very presence of God, and almost touches him, when it feels itself quickened, illumined, preserved, justified, and sanctified' (*Inst.* I.xiii.13; McNeill 1960: 1:138).

Even though the powers of God present in Christ reveal him to be their author and source, along with the Father, Calvin insists that the self-revelation of God in Christ takes place by means of the works done in his humanity, for his divine nature per se is as inaccessible to us as is the Father's. Thus it is the humanity of Christ in particular that makes Christ the image of the invisible God. 'For Christ, so far as his secret divinity, is no better known to us than the Father. But he is said to be the express image of God, because in him God has entirely revealed himself, inasmuch as his infinite goodness, wisdom and power appear in him substantially' (*Commentary on John 14:10*; Torrance and Torrance 1959–72: 5:78). Christ not only makes the invisible God somewhat visible in his humanity, but he may also be said to be the way the infinite God makes himself finite, so that we might be able to come to know God. 'In this sense Irenaeus writes that the Father, himself infinite, becomes finite in the Son, for he has accommodated himself to our little measure lest our minds be overwhelmed by the immensity of his glory' (*Inst.* II.vi.4; McNeill 1960: 1:347). Just as we cannot come to know the invisible God directly, but only by means of our contemplation of the works of God in the universe, so we cannot come to know the divine nature of Christ directly, but only insofar as God has accommodated Godself to us in the humanity of Christ. 'First, the greatness of the divine glory must be taken into account, and at the same time the littleness of our capacity. Our acuteness is very far from being capable of ascending so high as to comprehend God. Hence all thinking about God without Christ is a vast abyss which immediately swallows up all our thoughts' (*Comm. 1 Peter 1:20*; Torrance and Torrance 1959–72: 12:250).

The coordination of Christ with the self-revelation of God the Creator not only means that the self-revelation of God will be similar in both images, but it also means that Christ has as his goal the completion of God's work of creation. Human beings were created in the image of God that they might be united to God in eternal life. Christ not only reveals the invisible God in his humanity, making him the image of the invisible God, but he also restores the image of God in humanity, so that we might be united to God in eternal life. He does this by means of his humanity in particular. 'Christ is not only, as the eternal Word of God, his lively image, but even on his human nature, which he has in common with us, the imprint of the Father's glory has been engraved, that he might transform his members to it' (*Comm. John 17:22*; Torrance and Torrance 1959–72: 5:149). Once Christ transforms his members completely into the image of God, so that they may be united to God, the humanity of Christ will no longer be the medium of divine self-revelation, for the children of God will see God face to face. 'But when as partakers in heavenly glory we shall see God as he is, Christ, having discharged the office of Mediator, will cease to be the ambassador of his Father, and will be satisfied with that glory which he enjoyed before the creation of the world' (*Inst.* II.xiv.3; McNeill 1960: 1:485). This is why, according to Calvin, Paul speaks of Christ handing the kingdom back to the Father at the end of his reign (1 Cor. 15:28). 'So then will he yield to the Father his name and crown of glory, and whatever he has received from the Father, that "God may be all in all" [1 Cor. 15:28]' (*Inst.* II.xiv.3; McNeill 1960: 1:485).

The self-representation of God in the universe is ineffective without the witness of the Word, acting as spectacles so that we might rightly judge the works set before us. In a similar way, Christ as the image of the invisible God must be set before us in the Word, so that we might come to the knowledge of him. The Word that sets forth Christ comes in two distinct but inseparable forms, first as the Law and then as the Gospel. Calvin makes this distinction foundational to the knowledge of God the Redeemer in the title he gives to the book of the *Institutes* that takes up this theme: 'The knowledge of God the Redeemer in Christ, first disclosed to the fathers under the Law, and then to us in the Gospel' (*Inst.* II; McNeill 1960: 1:239). The Law and the Gospel both reveal Christ, but they do so in different ways, following different dispensations. 'It was not in vain that God of old willed, through expiations and sacrifices, to attest that he was Father, and to set apart for himself a chosen people. Hence, he was then surely known in the same image in which he with full splendor now appears to us' (*Inst.* II.ix.1; McNeill 1960: 1:423). The Law sets forth Christ in a shadowy manner, whereas the Gospel reveals him with present clarity. The Law reveals Christ in types and symbols, whereas the Gospel shows Christ to be the antitype and reality of the types and symbols. The Law reveals Christ as the one still to come, whereas the Gospel reveals Christ as having already come. The Law reveals Christ only to Israel and the Jews, whereas the Gospel reveals Christ to all nations.

Once the Gospel arrives, the dispensation of the Law comes to an end. However, the Law remains as a valuable source of knowledge of Christ, and in that sense it is indispensable even after the arrival of the Gospel. 'But the gospel did not supplant the entire law as to bring forward a different way of salvation. Rather, it confirmed and satisfied whatever the law had promised, and gave substance to the shadows' (*Inst.* II.ix.4; McNeill 1960: 1:427). Calvin is convinced that we only truly come to know Christ when we seek the self-disclosure of Christ in the Law as well as in the Gospel. 'It yet greatly assists our faith to compare the reality with the types, so that we may seek in the one what the other contains' (*Comm. 1 Peter* 1:19; Torrance and Torrance 1959–72: 12:248). Calvin will seek a deeper understanding of the person and work of Christ in the Law than he could acquire from the Gospel alone. Christ is only truly known when he is seen to be the reality symbolized in the all priests and kings of Israel. 'From this it follows that both among the whole tribe of Levi and among the posterity of David, Christ was set before the ancient folk as in a double mirror' (*Inst.* II.vii.2; McNeill 1960: 1:350). The self-disclosure of Christ in the Law and the Gospel will confirm the self-revelation of God in Christ himself, namely, that God has revealed himself in Christ to be the author and fountain of every good thing. 'This is what we should in short seek in the whole of Scripture: truly to know Jesus Christ, and the infinite riches that are comprised in him and offered to us by him from God the Father. If one were to sift thoroughly the Law and the Prophets, he would not find a single word which would not draw and bring us to him' ('*A tous amateurs de Iesus Christ, et de son S. Evangile, salut*'; Haroutunian 1958: 70).

The self-disclosure of Christ in the Law and the Gospel can only rightly be understood if it is combined with the knowledge of ourselves as sinners. If the Law and the Gospel reveal that Christ has been set forth by the Father as the one in whom we are to find every good thing offered to us by God, the knowledge of ourselves reveals to us that these gifts are offered to sinners who lost every good thing that God had initially given them in Adam. 'With this we ought to be content: that the Lord entrusted to Adam those gifts which he willed to be conferred upon human nature. Hence Adam, when he lost the gifts received, lost them not only for himself but for us all' (*Inst.* II.i.7; McNeill 1960: 1:249). However, the loss of every good thing we were meant to receive from Adam is compounded by the fact that every evil thing has flooded in to take its place. 'Therefore, after the heavenly image was obliterated in him, he was not the only one to suffer this punishment—that, in place of wisdom, virtue, holiness, truth, and justice, with which adornments he had been clad, there came forth the most filthy plagues, blindness, impotence, impurity, vanity, and injustice—but also entangled and immersed his offspring in the same miseries' (*Inst.* II.i.5; McNeill 1960: 1:246). God in turn responds to the presence of evil in us by turning against us in wrath, and by revealing that wrath in creation. 'But after man's rebellion, our eyes—wherever they turn—encounter God's curse. This curse, while it seizes and envelops innocent creatures through our fault, must overwhelm our souls with despair' (*Inst.* II.vi.1; McNeill 1960: 1:341). The knowledge of ourselves makes us feel in our consciences the reason why God sent Christ to be our Mediator and Redeemer, for we sinners need to be reconciled to God, and God in his wrath needs to be reconciled to us. 'In this ruin of mankind no one now experiences God either as Father or as Author of salvation, or favorable in any way, until Christ the Mediator comes forward to reconcile him to us' (*Inst.* I.ii.1; McNeill 1960: 1:40).

Calvin describes the person and work of Jesus Christ in three ways: in light of his office as Mediator, in light of his threefold office as Christ, and in light of his obedience, which includes his life, death, resurrection, ascension, and coming in glory. These three ways correlate clearly with the three sets of distinct but related realities with which we began. The office of Mediator is related to the purpose of human creation in Adam. The office of Christ is grounded in the disclosure of Christ in the Law given to Israel. The obedience of Christ is related to the knowledge of ourselves, and our status before the judgment seat of God.

In order to fulfill the office of Mediator, it was of greatest importance that Christ be both true God and true human (*Inst.* II.xii.1; McNeill 1960: 1:464). Sinful human beings on their own cannot reconcile themselves to God, nor can they approach God until God has been reconciled to them. Hence only God could descend to become human to mediate between God and sinful humanity, and reunite the estranged parties. Although Christ must be truly divine, Calvin stresses the fact that Christ is also truly human, and claims that Scripture emphasizes this reality to show that God has truly come to dwell with us as one of us. 'Therefore, lest anyone be troubled about where to seek the Mediator, or by what path we must come to him, the Spirit calls him "man", thus teaching us that he is near us, indeed touches us, since he is our flesh' (*Inst.* II.xii.1; McNeill 1960: 1:465). As the truly divine and truly human Mediator, Christ has as his task the restoration of the good things we lost in Adam, and the removal of the evil things we acquired from Adam. Both tasks will be fulfilled through the human nature of Christ. The Son of God will make what is his by nature—to be God's Son—and impart it to us by grace, so that in him we might become children of God. 'Therefore, relying on this pledge, we trust that we are sons of God, for God's natural Son fashioned for himself a body from our body, flesh from our flesh, bones from our bones, that he might be one with us' (*Inst.* II.xii.2; McNeill 1960: 1:465). This means that Christ must be the natural Son of God even according to his humanity, even if it is only by reason of his divine Sonship (*Inst.* II.xiv.4; McNeill 1960: 1:486). The bestowal of divine Sonship on his humanity makes possible our adoption as children of God, and our hope of inheriting eternal life: 'we are assured of the inheritance of the Heavenly Kingdom; for the only Son of God, to whom it wholly belongs, has adopted us as his brothers' (*Inst.* II.xii.2; McNeill 1960: 1:465–6).

The Mediator also has the task of removing every evil from us, and he does this by taking our place before God. If the transfer of Sonship to us reconciles us to God, then taking the place of Adam before God reconciles God to us. In particular, Christ reconciles God to us by offering our flesh as the price of satisfaction to God's justice, and by paying the penalty we owed. 'He offered as a sacrifice the flesh he received from us, that he might wipe out our guilt by his act of expiation and appease the Father's righteous wrath' (*Inst.* II.xii.3; McNeill 1960: 1:466–7). On the one hand, the offering of our flesh to God in the death of Christ wipes out our sin in an act of expiation. 'Here he clearly indicates why he assumed flesh: that he might become a sacrifice and expiation to abolish our sins' (*Inst.* II.xii.4; McNeill 1960: 1:468). On the other hand, the death of Christ clearly offers our flesh to God in a way that appeases God's righteous wrath and makes it possible for God to love us, where before God could only hate us. 'In short, the only reason given in Scripture that the Son willed to take our flesh, and accepted this commandment from the Father, is that he would be a sacrifice to appease the Father on our behalf' (*Inst.* II.xii.4; McNeill 1960: 1:468). Calvin is consistently at pains to claim that the death of Christ appeases the wrath of God and changes God's attitude towards us from hatred and anger to love and mercy. 'For unless Christ had made satisfaction for our sins, it would not have been said that he appeased God by taking upon himself the penalty to which we were subject' (*Inst.* II.xvii.4; McNeill 1960: 1:532). However, Calvin never specifies what we owed to God's justice by way of satisfaction, or what the penalty is that Christ paid for us in our flesh. He simply insists that this is what Christ had to do to fulfill the office of Mediator. 'Accordingly, our Lord came forth as true man and took the person and the name of Adam in order to take Adam's place in obeying the Father, to present our flesh as the price of satisfaction to God's righteous judgment, and, in the flesh, to pay the penalty that we had deserved' (*Inst.* II.xii.3; Mc Neill 1960: 1:466).

If Jesus must be truly divine and truly human to fulfill the office of Mediator, he must also be anointed by the Holy Spirit to fulfill the threefold office of 'Christ'. If the office of Mediator involves Jesus taking the place of Adam so that he might restore us to the original goal of our creation, then the office of Christ connects Jesus to Israel so that he might fulfill all the promises of God made to them. Once again, we see that the way Christ does this is by freely giving to us all the good things we lack and by taking upon himself all the evil things that are ours, that he might thereby reconcile God and humanity. Christ bestows the good things we lack in his office as king. God promised David that his son would be enthroned as king of Israel forever, and this promise is fulfilled when Jesus Christ ascends to the right hand of God in heaven. From there, he richly bestows the Spirit on those who belong to him, so that they might receive from him all that they lack. 'For the Spirit has chosen Christ as his seat, that from him might abundantly flow the heavenly riches of which we are in such need. The believers stand unconquered through the strength of their king, and his spiritual riches abound in them. Hence they are justly called Christians' (*Inst.* II.xv.5; McNeill 1960: 1:500). Calvin insists that the kingdom of Christ is spiritual, and hence lies in eternal life, and not in this life, which must instead be lived under the hardship of the Cross. The goal of Christ's kingship is union with God in eternal life, and he enriches and defends those who belong to him until he leads them safely to this goal. Once this goal is attained, Christ will no longer be our king, but God will be all in all. 'Thus Paul rightly infers: God will then of himself become the sole Head of the church, since the duties of Christ in defending the church will have been accomplished' (*Inst.* II.xv.5; McNeill 1960: 1:501). However, Calvin increasingly came to see earthly rulers as foster fathers and nurses of the Church, who are appointed by Christ to care for the Church in its pilgrimage to eternal life. Those kings who do not 'kiss the Son' by allowing the Gospel to be preached and published in their lands will be deposed by Christ. 'For where David urges all kings and rulers to kiss the Son of God [Ps. 2:12], he does not bid them lay aside their authority and retire to private life, but to submit to Christ the power with which they have been invested, that he alone may tower over all' (*Inst.* IV.xx.5; McNeill 1960: 2:1490).

If Christ as king is the source of the Spirit enriching the faithful unto eternal life in union with God, then Christ as priest is the one who makes the expiatory sacrifice to God that appeases God's wrath and makes it possible for sinners to approach God in prayer. 'But God's righteous curse bars our access to him, and God in his capacity as judge is angry towards us. Hence, an expiation must intervene in order that Christ as priest may obtain God's favor for us and appease his wrath. Thus Christ to perform this office had to come forward with a sacrifice' (*Inst.* II.xv.6; McNeill 1960: 1:501). Christ as priest offers the sacrifice for sin that truly blots out our guilt and makes satisfaction for sin, and thereby fulfills the priesthood and sacrifices of Israel. Now that Christ has come, there can be no more priesthood, and no more sacrifices, because the reality symbolized by priesthood and sacrifice has been fulfilled in his death. 'The priestly office belongs to Christ alone because by the sacrifice of his death he blotted out our own guilt and made satisfaction for our sins [Heb. 9:22]' (*Inst.* II.xv.6; McNeill 1960: 1:502). This claim lays the foundation for Calvin's categorical rejection of the Roman priesthood, as well as of the sacrifice of the Mass, for he sees both as denying the fulfillment of priestly sacrifice in the death of Christ. 'The more detestable is the fabrication of those who, not content with Christ's priesthood, have presumed to sacrifice him anew! The papists attempt this each day, considering the Mass as the sacrificing of Christ' (*Inst.* II.xv.6; McNeill 1960: 1:503).

Christ is anointed by the Spirit to be the prophet who brings to fulfillment the prophecies to Israel. Since Christ is the one represented, portrayed, and symbolized by the Law given to Israel, his coming brings the Law to completion. Now that Christ has come, prophecy is at an end. 'This, however, remains certain: the perfect doctrine he has brought has made an end to all prophecies' (*Inst.* II.xv.2; McNeill 1960: 1:496). Christ as prophet proclaims himself as the fountain of every good thing given to us by God, and gives us his Spirit so that we might share in this preaching. '[H]e received anointing, not only for himself that he might carry out the office of teaching, but for his whole body that the power of the Spirit might be present in the continuing preaching of the gospel' (*Inst.* II.xv.2; McNeill 1960: 1:496). In this sense Christ as prophet continues to preach and teach through the teaching and preaching of the Church, even as the Church must add nothing to the doctrine first revealed to it by Christ, which brings to fulfillment the prophecy revealed to Israel.

When Calvin turns to the question of how Jesus, as Mediator and Christ, brings about our salvation, he asks about our knowledge of ourselves. We can only profit from the examination of the life, death, resurrection, and ascension of Christ when we remember who we are before God and how hopeless our condition would be apart from Christ. 'No one can descend into himself and seriously consider what he is without feeling God's wrath and hostility toward him. Accordingly, he must anxiously seek ways and means to appease God—and this demands a satisfaction. No common assurance is required, for God's wrath and curse always lie upon sinners until they are absolved of guilt' (*Inst.* II.xvi.1; McNeill 1960: 1:504). Calvin highlights the knowledge of ourselves because he is aware that the narration of the life and death of Jesus has much in it that would offend us and drive us away, or render us without hope. Even though Christ shows his divine power at times in his life, especially in his miracles and in his transfiguration, Calvin claims that the divinity of Christ comes to be increasingly hidden, until it seems to disappear completely in his suffering and death. 'That dreadful appearance of ignominy and malediction which is seen in the death of Christ, not only obscures His glory, but removes it altogether from our sight' (*Comm. John 12:23*; Torrance and Torrance 1959–72: 5:37).

Calvin appeals to the teaching of Paul that Christ had emptied himself, and understands this claim via Irenaeus, that the divinity of Christ increasingly came to be hidden and at rest, so that only a suffering and dying human being can be perceived. 'Christ, indeed, could not renounce his divinity, but He kept it concealed for a time, that under the weakness of the flesh it might not be seen. Hence He laid aside His glory in the view of men, not by lessening, but by concealing it' (*Comm. Phil. 2:7*; Torrance and Torrance 1959–72: 11:248). This concealment is seen from the beginning of Christ's life, when Luke tells us that he grew in knowledge. Far from seeing this as undermining faith in Christ's divinity, Calvin sees this as clearly establishing Christ's genuine humanity, while his divine power was concealed. 'The words of Irenaeus, that he suffered, while his Godhead remained at rest, I may interpret not only of his bodily death, but of his incredible grief and torment of mind, as is expressed in his complaining cry, "My God, why hast thou forsaken me?" In short, unless we wish to deny that Christ was made true man, we shall not be ashamed to admit that he freely took what cannot be separated from human nature' (*Comm. Luke 2:40*; Torrance and Torrance 1959–72: 1:107). Since Christ is making satisfaction for Adam's disobedience, his sacrifice of himself will only be efficacious if it is offered voluntarily and freely, on the basis of his human nature, and not by means of his divine power. 'And we must hold fast to this: that no proper sacrifice to God could have been offered unless Christ, disregarding his own feelings, subjected and yielded himself wholly to his Father's will' (*Inst.* II.xvi.5; McNeill 1960: 1:508).

Calvin especially appeals to the knowledge of ourselves when he comes to the condemnation and execution of Jesus at the hands of Pontius Pilate. 'The curse caused by our guilt was awaiting us at God's heavenly judgment seat. Accordingly, Scripture first relates Christ's condemnation before Pontius Pilate, governor of Judea, to teach us that the penalty to which we were subject had been imposed upon this righteous man' (*Inst.* II.xvi.5; McNeill 1960: 1:508–9). He does this to show that Christ increasingly takes upon himself all the evil that afflicts us, in order to free us from it. When Calvin narrates the trial and execution of Jesus, he makes it clear that the language of satisfaction and the payment of the penalty refers not to something positive that Jesus pays to God on our behalf, but rather refers to the way Christ takes from us all the evil he finds in us in order to do away with it in himself. 'To take away our condemnation, it was not enough for him to suffer any kind of death: to make satisfaction for our redemption a form of death had to be chosen in which he might free us by transferring our condemnation to himself and by taking our guilt upon himself' (*Inst.* II.xvi.5; McNeill 1960: 1:509). The same must be said of Christ's death as a sacrifice for sin. Christ dies on the Cross, which is cursed by God, to show that the curse of God that lay on us has been transferred to him. 'That is, he who was about to cleanse the filth of those iniquities was covered with them by transferred imputation' (*Inst.* II.xvi.6; McNeill 1960: 1:510). The full extent of the transfer of our sin to Christ is revealed in his cry from the Cross, 'My God, my God, why have you forsaken me?' Christ frees us from the wrath of God by taking that wrath upon himself, so that he might be said to descend into hell in our place. 'And surely no more terrible abyss can be conceived than to feel yourself forsaken and estranged from God, and when you call upon him, not to be heard. It is as if God himself had plotted your ruin' (*Inst.* II.xvi.11; McNeill 1960: 1:516). Thus, when Calvin describes in detail the way Christ makes satisfaction for sin by his suffering and death, he does not speak of Christ paying God the price of our satisfaction to appease God's wrath and render God propitious towards us, but rather speaks of God laying on Christ all the evil things which we have brought upon ourselves, in order to free us from them. 'This is our acquittal: the guilt that held us liable for punishment has been transferred to the head of the Son of God [Isa. 53:12]. We must, above all, remember this substitution, lest we tremble and remain anxious throughout life—as if God's righteous vengeance, which the Son of God has taken upon himself, still hung over us' (*Inst.* II.xvi.5; McNeill 1960: 1:509–10).

If God frees us from sin and wrath by transferring our sin, guilt, curse, death, and damnation to Christ, then the death of Christ does not propitiate God's righteous wrath, but is rather the effect of God's limitless and free love for sinners. How then can Calvin repeatedly insist that God loves us only because Christ died for us to appease God's wrath, when he knows that Christ died for us, and took our sin, guilt and condemnation upon himself, because God already loved us? How can Calvin describe the death of Christ as the cause of God's love for us, when he also knows that it is the effect of God's love, and is therefore the clearest proof of God's love? Does God love us because Christ died for us? Or did Christ die to show how much God already loves us?

Calvin thinks that the language of Scripture gives rise to this apparent contradiction. On the one hand, Scripture says that God sent the Son out of God's prior love (John 3:16, 1 John 4:9–10). On the other hand, Scripture says that we were enemies of God when Christ died for us, and Calvin takes this to mean that God was our enemy as well. 'The Spirit usually speaks in this way in the Scriptures: "God was men's enemy until they were reconciled to grace by the death of Christ" [Rom. 5:10]' (*Inst.* II.xvi.2; McNeill 1960: 1:504). Calvin attempts to reconcile this apparent contradiction in various ways. He will suggest that the language of Scripture describing Christ's death as reconciling God to us and appeasing God's wrath is accommodated to our capacity, so that we might clearly recognize our misery apart from Christ, and embrace the mercy of God in Christ more ardently (*Inst.* II.xvi.2; McNeill 1960: 1:505). Calvin also claims that God's prior love for sinners is hidden in God's electing will, and is only revealed when Christ is seen to propitiate God for us (*Comm. Romans 5:10*; Torrance and Torrance 1959–72: 8:110). Finally, the knowledge of ourselves gives rise to this problem, for when our consciences become aware of sin, they cannot but conclude that God is wrathful towards us, until God's mercy appears in the death of Christ. 'God interposed his own Son to reconcile himself to us, because he loved us; but this love was hid, because we were in the meantime enemies to God, continually provoking his wrath. Besides, the fear and terror of an evil conscience took away from us all enjoyment of life. Thence as to the apprehension of our faith, God began to love us in Christ' (*Comm. 1 John 4:10*; Torrance and Torrance 1959–72: 5:292).

If the death of Christ and his descent into hell represent the extent of his willingness to take our sin and curse upon himself, then his resurrection and especially his ascension represent his willingness to give us all the good things that we lack, to lead us to union with God in eternal life. 'To the resurrection is quite appropriately joined the ascent into heaven. Now having laid aside the mean and lowly state of mortal life and the shame of the cross, Christ by rising again began to show forth his glory and power more fully. Yet he truly inaugurated his Kingdom only at his ascension into heaven' (*Inst.* II.xvi.14; McNeill 1960: 1:522). Calvin again insists that the ascension of Christ, as witnessed by the apostles, reveals the genuine humanity of Christ even after his resurrection. For the glorified humanity of Christ, and especially his flesh, is the source of our hope and the fountain from which every good thing flows from God to us. Since Christ has entered the heavenly kingdom in our own flesh, we can hope to inherit eternal life with him. Now that Christ has ascended, he can intercede with God on our behalf, and provide access to the throne of God. Finally, we can now seek in Christ all that we need to lead us to eternal life, since God has lavished every good thing on his humanity, so that it might flow from him to us. ' "When he ascended into heaven he led captivity captive" [Eph. 4:8, cf. Vg.; cf. Ps. 68:18], and despoiling his enemies, he enriched his own people, and daily lavishes spiritual riches upon them' (*Inst.* II.xvi.16; McNeill 1960: 1:525).

If the life and death of Christ introduces a dialectic of revelation and concealment for Calvin, which he develops in light of Irenaeus, Christ's resurrection and ascension introduce a dialectic of absence and presence, which Calvin develops in conversation with Augustine. As human, Christ is absent from us in heaven. Yet by his Spirit, Christ is more present to us now than he was when he walked on earth, and the riches God abundantly bestows upon his ascended humanity flow to the faithful by the power of the Holy Spirit. This dialectic of absence and presence is foundational for Calvin's teaching on the Holy Supper of the Lord, for he wants the faithful to be assured that Christ really does offer to feed them with spiritual food when the bread and wine are presented to them, but he wants the faithful to rise to heaven to seek the source of that food in the ascended humanity of Christ, and not in the bread and wine offered to them on earth. Calvin thought that both the Roman Church, and the Lutherans, violated this understanding of the genuine ascended humanity of Christ by speaking of the body and blood of Christ as either being contained in or offered under the bread and wine. Calvin was especially distressed by the Lutheran teaching that by the unity of divinity and humanity in the person of the Son of God, the flesh of Christ is present wherever his divinity is present, and is therefore able to be offered to the faithful in the bread and wine of the Supper. Calvin did not see himself as divorcing the humanity of Christ from his divinity by insisting that the humanity of Christ is present in heaven, for he thought that the unity of Christ's person made it possible for the good things of God to flow from the Father to us through the genuine humanity of Christ, even as a spring flows through channels to water fields. 'In like manner, the flesh of Christ is like a spring and inexhaustible fountain that pours into us the life springing from the Godhead into itself. Now who does not see that communion of Christ's flesh and blood is necessary for all who aspire to heavenly life?' (*Inst.* IV.xvii.9; McNeill 1960: 2:1369).

If the dialectic of revelation and concealment is resolved in the resurrection and ascension of Christ, then the dialectic of absence and presence will be resolved on the Last Day when Christ will descend from heaven to judge the living and the dead. 'It is right, therefore, that faith be called to ponder that visible presence of Christ which he will manifest on the Last Day. For he will come down from heaven in the same visible form in which he was seen to ascend [Acts 1:11; Matt. 24:30]' (*Inst.* II.xvi.17; McNeill 1960: 1:525). The visible appearance of Christ, in full manifestation of his divinity, will constitute the last act of his reign as king, when he will separate the godly from the reprobate, and lead the godly to eternal life in union with God. After this, as we have previously seen, Christ will hand the kingdom back to the Father, and will no longer be the Mediator between God and humanity. The faithful will be completely transformed into the image of God, and so they will no longer see God manifested in the flesh of Christ, but will see God face to face, so that God will be all in all (*Inst.* II.xiv.3; McNeill 1960: 1:486).

The glory of Christ revealed in the resurrection and ascension not only points us to the future when we shall enjoy eternal life with God, but also illuminates the Cross of Christ itself with the light of God's glory. The manifestation of divine power in the risen Christ reveals that Christ voluntarily emptied himself of that power so that he might offer himself as the sacrifice and expiation of our sins in his death. The glory of God's power may be hidden in his death, but the glory of God's love shines forth quite clearly. 'The fact that the Son of God suffered himself to be reduced to such ignominy, yea, descended even to hell, is so far from obscuring, in any respect, his celestial glory, that it is rather a bright mirror from which is reflected his unparalleled grace towards us' (*Comm. Psalm 22:7*; Torrance and Torrance 1959–72: 8:366). When Jesus seeks to sustain the faith of the disciples in light of the shocking nature of his approaching death, he tells them of his coming glory, which will not be revealed apart from his death, but will rather be revealed in his death. 'And this was accomplished: for in the death of the cross which Christ suffered, so far from obscuring his honor, there shines the brightest, since there his incredible love to mankind, his infinite righteousness in atoning for sin and appeasing the wrath of God, his wonderful power in overcoming death, subduing Satan, and, indeed, opening up heaven, put forth it full brightness' (*Comm. John 13:32*; Torrance and Torrance 1959–72: 5:69). The Cross of Christ is therefore an even brighter manifestation of the goodness and love of God than is the theater of God's glory in creation. For in the Cross, God has not only lavished every good thing upon us, but has also taken every evil thing away from us. 'For in the cross of Christ, as in a splendid theater, the incomparable goodness of God is set before the whole world. The glory of God shines, indeed, in all creatures on high and below, but never more brightly than in the cross, in which there is a wonderful change of things—the condemnation of all men was manifested, sin blotted out, salvation restored to men; in short, the whole world was renewed and all things restored to order' (*Comm. John 13:31*; Torrance and Torrance 1959–72: 5:68).

Thus we are to learn of the free love of God for us both in creation and in Christ. For the goodness of God revealed in the universe reveals the free love of God for us, and we should contemplate this with gratitude. 'For if it is asked why the world was created, why we have been put in it to have dominion over the earth, why we are preserved in this life to enjoy innumerable blessings and are endowed with light and understanding, no reason can be given but the free love of God towards us' (*Comm. 1 John 4:9*; Torrance and Torrance 1959–72: 5:290). However, the sending of the eternal Son of God to die for us so that we might live is for Calvin the chief representation of God's love that transcends all others, for it reveals not only that God loves us, but that God is love itself. 'For it was not only the infinite love of God which did not spare his own Son, that by his death he might restore us to life, but it was a more wonderful goodness which ought to ravish our minds with amazement. Christ is such a shining and remarkable proof of the divine love toward us that, whenever we look at him, he clearly confirms the doctrine that God is love' (*Comm. 1 John 4:9*; Torrance and Torrance 1959–72: 5:290).

SUGGESTED READING

Edmondson (2004); Jansen (1956); Muller (2012); Peterson (1983); Van Buren (1957); Willis (1966).

BIBLIOGRAPHY

Primary Sources

Haroutunian, J. (ed. and trans.) (1958), *Calvin: Commentaries* (Philadelphia: Westminster).
McNeill, J. T. (ed.) (1960), *Calvin: Institutes of the Christian Religion*, trans. F. L. Battles, 2 vols. (Philadelphia: Westminster).
Torrance, D. W. and T. F. Torrance (eds.) (1959–72), *Calvin's New Testament Commentaries*, 12 vols. (Grand Rapids, Mich.: Eerdmans).

Secondary Sources

Edmondson, S. (2004), *Calvin's Christology* (Cambridge: Cambridge University Press).
Jansen, J. F. (1956), *Calvin's Doctrine of the Work of Christ* (Cambridge: J. Clarke).

Muller, R. (2012), *Calvin and the Reformed Tradition: On the Work of Christ and the Order of Salvation* (Grand Rapids, Mich.: Baker).

Peterson, R. A. (1983), *Calvin's Doctrine of the Atonement* (Philipsburg, NJ: Presbyterian and Reformed Publishing).

Van Buren, P. (1957), *Christ in our Place: The Substitutionary Character of Calvin's Doctrine of Reconciliation* (Grand Rapids, Mich.: Eerdmans).

Willis, E. D. (1966), *Calvin's Catholic Christology* (Leiden: Brill).

CHAPTER 19

CHRISTOLOGY IN THE SEVENTEENTH CENTURY

MARK W. ELLIOTT

INTRODUCTION: THE OMISSION OF CHRISTOLOGY

THE seventeenth century has often been considered a forgettable one for Christian theology. It was the time of the birth-pangs of the modern world and liberal society. Also, in terms of the history of doctrine, the century has lurked in the shadows, known more for its 'fringe activities' (Deism, Scholasticism, Socinianism, Hypercalvinism, Jansenism, eccentric Mysticism) rather than for constructive advances in the mainstream. With Christology the situation is arguably worse, in that many of the recent textbooks relate the period between 1400 and 1800 as a time of *plus ça change, plus c'est la même chose* for that doctrine, with 1600 marking the nadir of creativity. This verdict has been reinforced by studies of the early modern era being quick to assume that Reformation theologies were variations on themes established by the late Middle Ages. Early modern Christology then: a case of *Nichts Neues im Westen*. Therefore, whether one looks at Pelikan's *Jesus through the Centuries* (1985) or Grillmeier's *Chalkedon* (1954) (except for the essay by J. Ternus in 'Chalkedon im Gespräch zwischen Konfessionen und Religionen'), the omission of the seventeenth century from these treatments encourages such a verdict. One is disappointed by the paucity of Christology in R. D. Preus' *Theology of Post-Reformation Lutheranism* (1970) and in Richard Muller's *Post-Reformation Reformed Dogmatics* (2003). The Protestant *Handbuch der Theologie und Dogmensgeschichte* has hardly anything on early modern Christology, focusing on the doctrine of Scripture and 'epistemology'. Even the *Theologische Realenzyklopädie* article by Walther Sparn (1988) though adequate on Lutheran positions, is brief on other traditions (Catholic, Reformed, Non-Conformist). The Catholic 'equivalent' by Courth (2000) covers the early modern material in under thirty pages, and devotes most attention to the French Oratorians. We will trace the distinctive features and commonalities across Reformed, Lutheran and Catholic early modern Christologies.

THE REFORMED: CHRISTOLOGY, TRINITY, AND ATONEMENT

The seventeenth century is theologically infamous for Deism and Socinianism. It was around questions of the Providence of God and the Trinity that battles raged, although a denial of the pre-existence of Christ was included in the Socinian 'package', expressed in the Racovian Confession (1604) of Fausto Sozzini himself. Socinus distinguished between the humbled man from Nazareth and the resurrected man who could be called a secondary God according to a 'two-state' (Phil. 2:6) or 'before and after' Christology (Gerber 1969: 49; Gomes 2009). One may speak of 'nice, hot disputes' (Dixon 2003): the controversies around the Second Person of the Trinity became intricate and passion-fuelled. Whether the Son was to be called αὐτόθεος ('God in himself') was a sensitive point in Reformed circles. William Perkins had argued for the aseity of the divine Persons, as had the mature Calvin (Muller 2003: 4, 326; Muller 2008: 31). Yet Maccovius would say the Son was αὐτόθεος *only* in terms of essence but not in terms of his mode of subsistence ('eternally begotten of the Father') (Bell 2011: 118). During the Westminster Assembly in 1645 Thomas Goodwin wrote that the Father was the fountain of Deity and the Son was 'very God *of* very God' (O'Collins and Jones 2010: 115; cf. Van Dixhoorn 2012). Francis, the elder Turretin, explained around 1679 that the Son could be called God of himself according to his essence, for he has *aseitas essentialis*, but not according to his *person* whose divinity was in some sense 'derived' (Turretin, *Institutes of Elenctic Theology* [Geneva, 1685] III, xxviii.40). Thus there were Trinitarian sensitivities to be aware of for anyone attempting Christology. Turretin argued that the Incarnate Christ exercised faith (*Inst.* III, xiii.12–14), since his human nature only received fullness after suffering and, *contra* the Catholic Bellarmine, during his life Christ's soul was that of a 'traveller', one that was continuously ascending, even while in terms of bodily fortune Christ 'descended'. Turretin devoted much space to 'The Mediatorial Office' (*Inst.* III, xiv). Adoration is due to 'the person of the Mediator' (*Inst.* III, xiv.18) as θεάνθρωπος (again, *contra* Bellarmine) mediating between the human race and God properly understood as the Father (III, xiiv.2), as the divine nature makes the human suffering worth a great price. The human nature manifests his exalted glory. At *Institutes* xiv.8 Turretin speaks of Christ meriting faith for the Elect, and the extent of his atonement, satisfaction, and intercession is one and the same. In this he was fairly typical of mid-century Reformed theology.

Socinians believed that God could have pardoned sin without the satisfaction of Christ, and indeed they did not like any idea of atonement achieved through the sufferings of an innocent man (as Christ was), which seemed to them unjust. Goodwin pointed to Mark 14:36 'all things are possible unto thee'—to suggest that there was no ontological necessity for the work of Christ, but rather it was God's *chosen* way; and it was chosen because penal substitutionary atonement was the chosen way to show all God's attributes, including justice. Further, one should not think of a satisfaction in terms of an exact price merited. This was largely a Trinitarian theological question, but it showed how Christology was positioned between the Doctrine of God and the soterio-logical question of what the Cross achieved and how.

Controversies around the theory of penal substitution and satisfaction theory were launched by numerous Arminians, who wanted some loosening of the doctrines of Calvinist Reformed theology. Hugo Grotius in his *De satisfactione Christi* (1617) regarded the death of Christ as a public warning and a demonstration of divine right-eousness. There was no objective, quantifiable value to what Christ did, but it was in accordance with the Father's valuation (*juxta Dei patris aestimationem*), as Philip van Limborch put it during the 1660s. Yet the Reformed Johann Piscator (d. 1625) criticized his former pupil Vorstius for the latter's Arminianism, for his denial of the imputation of Christ's active as well as his passive righteousness to believers (Mühling 2009: 123), a denial which the likes of Thomas Goodwin would approve. By nature passive, the death on the Cross erased original sin; it was the blood and not the previous activity of Christ (active obedience) that covers all sin, according to 1 John 1:7. However the School of Saumur, as defined by Moses Amyraut in the mid-1630s, insisted that Christ's active obedience must be regarded as imputed and this would have a strong influence on the Genevan 1675 *Formula consensus ecclesiarum Helveticarum* (Sparn 1988: 4). This can be seen as providing resistance to Christian moralism by affirming a Christological moral-ism, as Jesus Christ fulfilled the covenant of works through his entering into the cov-enant of grace. The Savoy Declaration of 1653 made the position of double imputation explicit, where Westminster six years earlier had been unclear. Now Christ's active obe-dience was asserted against those, following Piscator, who denied it.

Thomas Goodwin made it clear that Christ and his mission came from heaven. The idea of an eternal covenant (*pactum salutis*) between Father and Son was a bulwark against Socinianism; and Goodwin was happy to say that all of three divine Persons cooperated in the deal struck to work salvation on behalf of the Elect, given the Spirit's involvement. He found in Isaiah 49 and Psalm 2 covenantal dialogues between Father and Son. Goodwin's Christology posited that the divine nature acts not immediately, by virtue of the hypostatic union, but mediately through the work of the Spirit' (O'Collins and Jones 2010: 225).

The Scottish divine Samuel Rutherford preferred not to envisage a Trinitarian cov-enant within Christ (*The Covenant of Life Opened* 305): for him the Spirit's place was 'merely' in the application of the covenant of grace. The great Johannes Cocceius at Leiden in the 1650s believed the Spirit was involved, but only as a facilitator, not as a legal partner in the eternal covenant between Father and Son. The Savoy Declaration (1653) avows covenantal Christology: 'God in his eternal purpose, to choose and ordain the Lord Jesus his only begotten Son ... according to a covenant made between them'. Reconciliation is primarily to the Father, although the whole Trinity is in on it.

(See Patrick Gillespie, *Ark of the Covenant* [1677] where Psalm 2:7 is a hinge for this doctrine of 'covenant of redemption'.)

For the Reformed theologians the unity of the Person is indeed a dwelling of the Logos in his humanity (Col. 2:9). This event added nothing to the Logos other than a relationship, or a second modus of finite substance, so that he could exist in his humanity as well as out of it (John 3:13) (Sparn 1988: 3). Only in the concrete case of Christ could there be any communication of idioms, so the Incarnation did not mean that some 'universal humanity' was thenceforth attached to the universal Logos. The Reformed preferred to emphasize the activities of both natures, which produced a common effect (the so-called *genus apotelesmaticum*). Unlike the Lutherans, Christ's *status exaltationis* began only with the resurrection: the *kenosis* was the humiliation of the human servant form that the Word or Son assumed. The humanity was the obedient instrument of Logos. It is not so much a case of properties of natures that became communicated as of gifts that became exchanged.

Just as important were the offices of Christ, or the threefold office (Prophet, Priest, and King). This was a theme that had existed in mediaeval theology from at least Aquinas but in the hands of Calvin it became a structuring principle, since Calvin and followers thought Scripture favoured a Christology which was more functional than metaphysical. For Polanus at Basel in the first decade of the century, the economy of salvation mirrored the Trinity (Muller 2008: 130). The office of 'priest' applied to Christ could be viewed as the presupposition of forensic justification. What was communicated (and this only in the concrete case of Christ) were the gifts of divinity and humanity. Arminian theologians too would keep the three offices long after they had dismissed talk of the three *genera*. Philippians 2 became central in the discourse, although Polanus seems to have imported this from the Lutherans. 'In this sense, then, incarnation needs be viewed as *pars humiliationis Filii Dei*: it is the point at which the transcendent, infinite God enters the human sphere for the sake of our salvation' (Muller 2008: 136). Although not clear in Perkins, there does seem to be a unity in Christ which is supplied by the office of the Mediator as determined for him by the eternal decision of the Trinity, with a Christology that is 'not so much "from above" as it runs along the historical line of the covenant promise' (Muller 2008: 172).

Christian faith presupposed Christ's resurrection, and Grotius seemed to advocate some sort of subjectivizing 'pisteology'. It was Christ regarded anew that mattered: first in God's pre-fixing his mission rather than his having any real pre-existence *qua* man, and second with regard to how Christ was received on earth (Gerber 1969: 55). For John Owen, Christ was not so much the subject of the beatific vision but the object, the content of it in a way that distinguished him from Turretin's (and Aquinas') intellectualist notion of it (McDonald 2012). Owen emphasized the Holy Spirit's transformative work on the human being assumed by the Word, even as the rational soul guided Christ's actions (Spence 2007: 56–9 with reference to the 1679 *Pneumatologia*). Yet '[t]he covenant of redemption is the foundation of the economy of salvation and of the Incarnation and it is this, therefore, that should be the starting point of any discussion of the person of Jesus Christ in Owen's theology' (Trueman 2007: 80). Owen read back the economic work of the Spirit (which operated even to preserve the hypostatic union through Good Friday) into the covenant operating in eternity, making it fully Trinitarian: 'the role of the Logos is restricted in direct relation to the human nature to that of providing hypostasis' [to the anhypostatic humanity] (Trueman 2007: 94; cf. Owen, *Works* 160–1, 180). Karl Barth was correct to see the classic Reformed opinion as rejecting the synthetic view of Lutherans on the grounds that it would limit the freedom of God. 'We shall look in vain for a statement like that of Quenstedt, that the divine-human person arises in the union of the two natures' (Barth 1958: 68). The relationship of the two natures was asymmetric. Owen's pneumatological and dynamic version seems an improvement on Bucanus' notion of an infusion of habitual grace (Barth 1958: 90). It also encouraged the idea that it takes one (an elect soul) to know one (Christ as federal and fraternal soul). Here the humanity of Jesus as distinct from the Word yet reliant on the Spirit comes to expression.

Towards the end of the century, in a development that would have a wide-ranging effect on subsequent theology, John Locke insisted in a historical, not metaphysical, reading of Christ, whereby his Jewish Messiah-ship became all important for one's understanding of who he was. This included the facticity of his bodily resurrection and ascension and return in judgement as marks of the Messiah (Pitassi 1994: 106). This differed from the Orthodox view only in the sense of a development of covenantal-historical categories that gradually left ontological ones behind.

LUTHERAN CHRISTOLOGY: FROM EUCHARIST TO METAPHYSICS AND BEYOND

An associated doctrine that was already *famously* controversial, even before the end of the sixteenth century, stood on the far side of Christology from the doctrine of the Trinity, in the sense of its being a practical doctrine: this was the Eucharist. The Schwabian theologians from Johannes Brenz and his south German successors through to David Hollaz (at Wittenberg until 1707) would contend: if the exalted human Christ is really all powerful and omnipresent in the Eucharist, then that must have been also the case when he was Jesus of Nazareth, as one who was on intimate terms with the universe even as he walked through Galilee. One of the architects of the binding confessional definition, the *Formula of Concord* (1580), Nikolaus Selnecker, had asserted that it was *humana natura in abstracto* which as ubiquitous had been raised with Christ and hence existed everywhere through the encounter of God in Jesus. This tendency contained echoes of Luther's *De servo arbitrio* and the somewhat 'violent' theology of Flacius, which would view our nature as killed and buried, with Christ as providing a totally new humanity. Around 1600 there was even a sense that humanity in its sinfulness was in fact 'nothing', which was more extreme than Luther's verdict of 'vanity'. Lutheran theology went on to provide a remedy in the freeing of human beings and through this, nature and the cosmos—by the majestic, new humanity of Christ.

The great Martin Chemnitz, whose crowning achievement was the *Formula of Concord* (1580) had reversed the flow of ideas, and turned the spotlight on the Incarnation as having priority over 'Eucharist': the third *genus* (*maiestaticum*) (see below) is what makes Christ's real presence possible in the Eucharist (Mahlmann 1969: 230). Chemnitz emphasized the *action* of God in Jesus rather than the *being* of the man Jesus in participation in God. The idioms are not to be considered in themselves, but simply attributed to his person. In the sentence 'God as man', 'God' and 'man' are still preserved. The Son of God could be mediator of salvation.

There was an understandable reaction to the rather nihilistic view of Jesus' humanity among the Schwabians, of a mystical theology that seemed to imply that since the risen Christ was everywhere, he was also nowhere. As early as 1595 the Helmstadt and Braunschweig theologians were telling their southern cousins that Jesus was going to be present in mysterious ways only where he promised to be, that is, in the Eucharist but nowhere else, and had certainly not been ubiquitous during his earthly life.

The extent to which Luther and Lutherans were replacing a traditional metaphysics with one of their own has been a topic of some discussion in modern scholarship, at least with A. Ritschl in the 1870s, and this continued with H. E. Weber (1908), then W. Sparn (1976). After 1600 there was some unravelling of this close connection between the Eucharist and Christology, with attention shifting to the latter. This anti-metaphysical position can be seen as early as Hafenreffer's *Loci* of 1600 where he, like Brenz and Luther, but in a more deliberate way denied that metaphysics and logic held absolute sway in theology. After all, he contested, *Et verbum caro factum est* is a great mystery (Baur 1977: 226). In Wittenberg, Balthasar Meisner in his *Christologiae Sacrae disputationes* (1624) made it clear that the communication between God and humanity in Christ was neither substantial nor accidental, but beyond these categories: Theodor Thumm and Lucas II Osiander came to Tübingen in 1618–19 and built on Hafenreffer's legacy, provoking a final showdown. The Tübingen theologians spoke of a *perichoresis* of natures. Thumm's *Majestas Jesu Christi θεανθρώπου* (1621) was followed by his *ταπεινοσιγραφία Sacra de exinanitione Christi* (1628)—the *magnum opus* of Schwabian Christology.

In the Incarnation there was clearly some elevation of Christ's humanity, that which since Martin Chemnitz had been known as the *genus maiestaticum* ('genus of majesty'; that the divine attributes can be predicated of the human nature), that distinguishing mark of Lutheran Christology, which went along with the *genus apotelesmaticum* (the cooperation of natures in the work: 'the blood of Jesus his Son purifies us from all sin' [1 John 1:7]); and the *genus idiomaticum* which, as representing the patristic consensus on Christology was accepted in large part by the Reformed Churches. This *genus maiestaticum* (that the humanity of Jesus was elevated to a glorious state of being through sharing in divine power) was what the Reformed (and Catholics) baulked at. The Lutheran J. Gerhard wrote (*Loci* III, 1, q.45): '*Filius Dei maiestatem suam divinam assumptae carni communicavit*' and did not hesitate to call this the deification of Christ's human essence.

For Chemnitz, John 3:34 ('Christ ... given Spirit without measure') had meant 'not only the communication of the highest possible finite gifts to the human nature of Christ, but also the communication of divine attributes themselves' (Hoogland 1966: 33). But the Tübingen theologians went further by insisting on a *genus tapeinoticum* ('genus of humility'; from the Greek, ταπεινωσις; that the human attributes can be predicated of the divine nature) that the divine nature was, not as applying to the Logos (as had been rejected by the Formula of Concord), but to Christ's humanity. Christ Incarnate had the *genus maiestaticum* during his life, but it was progressively qualified and overlapped by the *genus tapeinoticum* in his humanity (hence not touching his divine nature), hiding his majesty. So they viewed the Incarnate Christ as a king abdicating his royal powers and retreating into the priestly and sacrificial function (*munus sacerdotale*) through an occultation or κρύψις of his divine power, which he as man did not use (Breidert 1977: 23). Nevertheless, God's power was still shared by his majestic humanity although in a progressively disguised way (hence: κρύψις), for example, in the humanity's ruling the universe even during Christ's life. Only in the state of exaltation did full and uninterrupted revelation of his human majesty become possible for Christ (Wiedenroth 2011: 18). Tübingen theology took John 5:17 ('the Father is at work ... and I too am working') to indicate that the Father was at work through Christ's own work, rather than alongside him, supplying it.

Their opponents from Giessen objected: in Christ there was a use and manifestation of power, but Christ never did have use of that power as man, for the Logos' divine power bypassed the weakened humanity. To those in Tübingen this appeared like a withdrawal of the Logos from the Incarnation's personal union. By the Giesseners' refusing to countenance participation between the two until after the Ascension, Christ's cry of dereliction on the Cross seemed not so absurd. Giessen followed a salvation-historical pattern of weakness then exaltation, rather than trying to hold majesty and *kenosis* in tension, as at Tübingen. At Wittenberg in the 1590s Hunnius had tried to make the ubiquity of Christ respectable by limiting it to a inner presence ('prasentia intima') of the humanity to the universal Word (not a geographical range extending out into the cosmos)—and Balthasar Mentzer learned from him. Mentzer taught (thesis 31) that the Word could be present in Christ to creatures, not as a quality (omnipotence) of God that would be immeasurable, but only as divine action of Christ present among creatures, as a gracious intensification of God's presence to all creatures in providence (thesis 16). This meant that Christ achieved a fullness of all things which was necessary for the salvation of each person, a fullness in which we are perfected (Col. 1:19; 2:9–10). It did *not* mean that his humanity expanded so as to be wherever the Logos was.

Mentzer insisted that the active presence of God in the Incarnation was a special form of providence (Baur 1977: 235). He developed this so as to insist on divine personal presence as active, and advanced four theses which Hafenreffer (who had crossed swords with him over the question of divine passibility) and others would condemn in 1622. Mentzer claimed that the personal union is only the remote foundation of the ubiquity of Christ's humanity: the immediate foundation is rather the promise. Yet this ubiqiuity is only for Christ's exalted state, and even then is just a presence of divine action. This had already been challenged in 1617 by the combative Lucas Osiander II, who argued that in the Incarnation God wagered his power by falling under the wheels of fortune, so committed was he to being joined to humanity (Baur 1977: 246).

In 1621 the protégé of Osiander Melchior Nicolai insisted on a Christology where Christ's humanity rules the world even as the Logos suffered. For Tübingen, the ubiquity of Christ's humanity relied on the conjunction in the Incarnation and the *perichoresis* of natures, and the divine promise fixed only the manner of the presence as a sacramental, gracious or glorious. The ubiquity belonged to the incarnate, humble state as well and the exalted state builds on the union established there. The state of grace on the way to glory did not constitute the ubiquity of Christ's humanity as such, for that was already a given from the womb, but rather constituted it as glorious and should not be described in terms of action but of being (Wiedenroth 2011: 72).

The Giessen theologians then insisted that the Logos on earth continued to rule the world, although not via his humanity (*non mediante carne*). To Tübingen ears this sounded too much like the Reformed *extra calvinisticum* as did the emphasis on asymmetry in the union between Word and humanity. The Giessen position was that his humanity used no such power of its own, such was the extent of the kenosis, where the human nature as the one of the natures fit to suffer became quite distinct from the operations and being of the Word. Therefore Christ as man did not use that power: there was an emptying of using (κένωσις τῆς χρήσεως) and not even a hidden use of it, yet there was still that intimate presence on the inside of Jesus, as it were (Breidert 1977: 23). Majesty occurred to the humanity only after the resurrection. This meant that his exaltation was an event, a real change for the flesh.

Both sides were in agreement that the *subjectum quo* of kenosis is the Person, but the *subjectum quod* is the exalted humanity in the Incarnation. He received majesty as a human being in order to lay it down. There was no real *kenosis* of *logos incarnandus*, i.e., the Word as becoming flesh (as it would be in the nineteenth century) in order to become human, but a kenosis of the *Logos incarnatus*, of the One found *as man*. Seventeenth-century Lutherans would hardly have thought that the Logos as such could lose any of his divine properties. But Lutheran Christology of that time was just as interested in God's humanity, not least in all the discussion of the *genus maiestaticum*. There was a Lutheran emphasis on the extent of *revelation* of the veiled glory in Christ as an object of faith not sight, with which one could contrast the functional approach of the Reformed: what did Christ *do*? Controversial was the Tübingen insistence on 'omnipraesentia indistans carnis Christi exinanitae', that is, that even in the state of kenosis he was nevertheless all-present everywhere as a human being. However, this speculation gradually gave way to a pietism-inspired gaze on the mystery of Jesus' humanity in a state of humiliation, yet with some amount of majesty.

The leader of the Swiss Reformed Heinrich Bullinger in 1557 had written to Martin Borrhaus in Basel about Lutheran innovation ('*hoc dogma novum Brentianum*'). Were he and the Reformed right to see Lutherans leaving the patristic tradition of doctrine? Lutheran scholars like Werner Elert thought so and believed that this was a good thing, even a return to a biblical Christology (Elert 1957). If God truly was Jesus of Nazareth, then Christ was true God. Yet in what did the personal unity consist? Was it in actions rather than essence? If so was that soteriology driving Christological definition, or put philosophically, *agere* determining *esse*?

Abraham Calov made it clear that it was not enough to know the Bible, as say his bête noire, Grotius did: one must also interpret it correctly, through the prism of the Revelation of God that was and is Jesus Christ (Jung 1999: 93). Accordingly mid-century theologians such as J. König took Psalm 110:7 ('drink from the stream'), as Lutherans had before him, to mean Christ's humiliation. The Christological union found in the being of Jesus was formed from the complete coming together of natures (Stegmann 2006: 93). Most Lutherans did not think that the humanity of Christ shared in the Word's universal dominion when on earth, but did believe he was somehow universally present to all creatures (*Confessio brevis*, 1621; *Decisio saxonica* 1624; Calov was one of the few dissenters). J. Gerhard's influence would advance the popularity of the *genus tapeinoticum*. With the victory for Giessen, 'the two-states doctrine entered Lutheran systematic theology as a more or less settled category of Christological thought' (Hoogland 1966: 44).

For the Reformed there was no question of 'the form of God' applying to Christ's humanity. Hence the divine nature played a role at beginning, middle, and end of Christ's life (Hoogland 1966: 50; Polanus, *Syntagma* VI, 26), but the glorious humanity only came to be after Christ's ascension. J. Heidegger described the movement from resurrection to session as progressing in stages of exaltation, as if to reassure that the humanity stayed in continuity with what it had been (*Corpus* II, 18.47), with Van Mastricht (*Theologiae* II, V, 17.13–14) insisting on four steps (Hoogland 1966: 61–4). Glory is restored to Christ as divine, but introduced to the Christ as human, as Turretin saw (*Inst.* II, 13.9.6), although Van Mastricht conceived of this glory as new and not just the reflected glory of the divine nature. The Reformed did stress the moral supremacy of the lowly Christ, as well as his humanity's cooperation in the works (*communicatio apotelesmatum*) and that, since believers adore the person of Christ, the nature is adorable by association or communion, of gifts or graces: holiness, wisdom, and power-authority (Hoogland 1966: 87; Van Mastricht, V.8.16). Polanus (as Calvin) denied that 'merit' or anything at all causal was to be read into Phil. 2:9's διό-, 'therefore'; yet later in the century, when the idea that Christ was fulfilling the covenant of works grew stronger, then we find in (e.g.) Van Mastricht a clear sense of Christ's 'merit and reward'.

REACTION

In all this, perhaps Christology became just another doctrine among others to be believed, as pietists in the following generations would claim (Schröder 1983: 97). The Reformed focus on the natures made discussion too abstract to appeal to those of an experiential piety (Hoogland 1966: 92). Borrowing between the two major Protestant traditions worked both ways. J. Gerhard took over from Calvin the 'threefold office' motif, which could be made to correspond to the downwards (prophet) and upwards (priest) movements of the two states. Later Lutherans would pick and choose their orthodoxies. With Buddeus at Jena (1667–1729) and his Lutheran version of Reformed federal theology, as it was mediated by pietist influences, Christ restored human beings to a rational existence through the effects of the divine nature working on the human. Buddeus refused the Tübingen doctrine of a hidden use of the powers, but held that Christ made a freely willed decision not to use them, while retaining as man the property of omniscience, with occasional use of it, and more was his frequent use of omnipotence in the miracles, and some ubiquity of presence by his energies, although in a limited way, especially to all humans in their weakness (Nüssel 1996: 108–14). Christ's prophetic office (*munus propheticus*) became interpreted in a moral sense (Rohls 1998: 75) as performed by a man of sorrows making his life a satisfaction and in death a prayer to forgive his enemies. This was a step on the way to an Enlightenment 'Christology from below' (Nüssel 1996: 124–6). Jesus showed how human beings can find the spiritual goal they were made for, as immortal beings. From a valuing of the functional, it was a short step to disdaining the metaphysics of the *communicatio idiomatum* as of no practical use. In terms of Dogmatics, L. von Mosheim (at Helmstedt from 1723) judged that Christ's 'Sonship' could be dealt with in the doctrine of God so as to free up Christology to be about a human being with a full human personality (Mosheim 1772: 621). By then the metaphysics of the natures seemed outworn, and the message was that one must not take the *communicatio idiomatum*, hence the *genus idiomaticum* too seriously. Jesus as founder of a religion was the teacher of the true path of salvation. Where the Bible speaks of 'eternal covenant', this meant an eternal priesthood that was easily translated into prophetic terms (Mosheim 1772: 671).

Like many pietists Spener regarded the kenosis as the core of the mystery of the Incarnation (Gerber 1969: 69) Like the Reformed, his Christology moved to interpret who Christ was by considering what he achieved. The state of humiliation began with Christ's birth, as he emptied out the form of divinity (Spener 1760: 193; Gerber 1969: 71). Christ could learn to be a moral man, owing to the vacuum left by the divinity which withdrew only to gleam out from its hiddenness, in his soul as well as his mighty deeds. This anticipated nineteenth-century versions of kenotic theory.

CATHOLIC CHRISTOLOGY: SCHOLASTICISM AND SPIRITUALITY

According to Congar (1954: 258), Protestant Christology became heterodox when it lost its moorings from the Church and drifted from belief in the Trinity. It tended to lose sight of 'persons' and the ecclesiological reality. Within the body of Christ, as persons members also participate in His Person, in a dependent relationship where believers are given His Personal identity. Wilhelm Dantine (1984: 238) concludes that although the Council of Trent's Christology was conservative, Christ's divinity seemed to become so abstract that theological grasping of Christ was directed to his human nature. Jesus Christ as mediator in his humanity became the central point of Trent's whole theology.

In a way that was indebted to Scotist tradition the Jesuit Gabriel Vasquez (d. 1604) viewed the Sonship of the Word of God in Christ as distinct in Christ from the human Christ. Following Aquinas, Suarez regarded Christ's humanity as participating in that Sonship to the point of the Word being located as it were within the humanity (Aquinas, *ST* III q.2, a.9: *homo potius est in Filio Dei, quam Filius in Patre*; Ternus 1954: 146). To Agostino Berbal S.J. in his *De Divini Verbi incarnatione* (Zaragoza 1630, disp. 66) it seemed that the Scotist position could verge towards 'two sons' in Christ at a certain 'distance' from each other, although this portrayal seems somewhat alarmist.

According to Bellarmine, since God is pure being and pure act, any movement of his is a moving in and on the creation: in the case of the Incarnation this meant on and in Christ's humanity. Second, a mediator really ought to be a third party. Bellarmine could not risk saying that the Son was only semi-divine, so he prefers to say that Jesus was created as we are but without sin as the Righteous One (Sedelaar 1937: 50–2). It is for that reason that he seemed to focus exclusively on *the man Jesus* so as, in the eyes of the Reformed, to approximate to the position of the Polish heretic Stancaro who denied the role of the Word of God in mediation. Bellarmine was not withholding a role from the Word, but the latter's role was seen as a sustaining and empowering role, not that of performing mediation as such. Bellarmine was interested in the mediating function of the religion of Jesus Christ, with the result of viewing that mediation as intersubjective (Bellarmine I: 436, in Deville 1987: 41). What Bellarmine called the *principium a quo* of the works of mediatorship was Christ's human nature. Communication of *operations* was emphasized, and the Holy Spirit was seen to play his part here in effecting that. Bellarmine disliked the Reformed's tendency to argue that the *communicatio idiomatum* was merely verbal or that the 'descent into hell' was only a metaphor for suffering dereliction. (Calvin had seen this *theologoumenon* as extending the work of Christ to something not dissimilar to what von Balthasar would later explicitly denote as the experience of human despair.) For Bellarmine and much of the tradition Christ's descent to Hades was more like a preaching mission than the final dark step in his work of atonement. The humanity was the mediator and this humanity earned its exaltation; and that not as an instrument separated from the divinity but in 'perichoretic' union with it. Grace made the Incarnation possible, but in Christ's career on earth, merit had to be achieved (*Disputations* III, 8; V, 1–10; Tylenda 1973: 15).

Suarez saw things similarly: one cannot say that the Word *as God* is mediator. The divinity merely sustained the humanity in the job of mediation (Suarez, *Comm. in Summa Theol.* III, q.26, a2 and Bellarmine, *De Christo* I, V, cII–VIII). Hence the humanity was not a 'nothing' (if there was essence there had to be existence) to which the Word joined, but the humanity *did* lack a mode of existence, since every human being needs personhood to fulfil it (Kaiser 1968: 103; Suarez *DI*, disp. 36, s1, m17), and complete its existence; and in the case of Jesus it was no different. Suarez writing in the last decade of the sixteenth century and the first decade of the seventeenth was following Aquinas in holding that only in Christ (outwith God himself) is there an *esse substantiale completum et perfectum* to be found. But in doing so, as Scotus and Durandus wanted, Suarez allowed for a union that had room for many 'existences', and hence for the participation of the members of the Church. Yet the main point is that in the Incarnation there is a union in *being* in which there is a kind of *enhypostasis*. Any created personality is 'lost' in the Incarnation. Any created *personalitas* supplies merely a modus of being human before being replaced *qua* person (Kaiser 1968: 117; disp. 31, s11). Accordingly, it is to an individual humanity (not 'Humanity', nor an individual human person) that something happened, or changed in a substantial and real way in the Incarnation. The mode of union is a formal, not a substantial connection, and the humanity is dependent on the Word's subsistence to exist, and on the power of God passing through it in a work of Trinitarian action. Hence it is not Being but Union that was the foundation of the Incarnation. Suarez was not so focused on the purpose of the Incarnation, but more about the possibility of a union in the first place. Franz Courth seems to accuse Suarez of not tarrying to look at Christ because he was desperate to relate the events of salvation history to ultimate universal philosophical truth (Courth 2000: 38; *De Incarn.* Disp. XXXVI sect. I, ed. Vives XVIII, 270). However, the life of Jesus was discussed by Suarez in the context of pious and theological discussion of mysteries of Mary. The historical one, who is not to be lost sight of in theological disputation, is also the Son of God predestined in respect of his human nature: the humanity predestined to be joined with the Son of God. On that event of union the salvation of the world was hinged.

Gabriel Vasquez mostly agreed with his fellow Jesuit Suarez on this point, but emphasized that this new modus that humanity experienced in Christ was also a relation. It was the blessing of humanity that was the formal purpose of the operation, not a hypostatic union for its own sake. It is the person of the Word who achieved this union and provided humanity with a gift of grace by that very union. He also distinguished himself from Suarez in believing that the Word was united with the whole of the humanity in one union, not needing to enter into composite of unions with different members of Humanity. The Incarnation thus is the meeting of the Word with 'Humanity'. Here Vasquez struck a Christological tone more akin to that of Cyril, while Suarez's approach was more reminiscent of that of John of Damascus.

Vincent de Paul's favourite verse seems to have been 'It is no longer I who live, but it is Christ who lives in me' (Gal. 2:20), even if the motto of the Daughters of St Vincent de Paul's motto became 'Given to God for the Service of the Poor'. Christocentric spirituality can also be detected in the emphases of the Salamanca Carmelites, who offered a great commentary on Thomas' *Summa Theologiae*. The two volumes devoted to the Incarnation of 1687 and 1691 introduced discussion of the Incarnation as a covenant, or the union of the Word with the whole humanity as only taking place after the creation of the human soul. The union, although substantial, has the sense of the Word causing effects that operated on the humanity. There was in the Franciscan tradition a view that, in the moment of Incarnation, nothing was taken away from Christ's humanity but something exalted was added (Kaiser 1968: 19). Unlike the Thomists who saw the incarnating Logos as also creating the humanity, for the Franciscans the humanity was created, but did not lose anything at the moment of Incarnation. The real difference from

Scotus was in his evaluation of 'person'. For Scotus 'person' had been defined only in a creature's relation to God. The Jesuit Clement Stephanus (d. 1641) saw 'person' more as the wholeness of an individual human being.

There was an emphasis on the two natures in Roman Catholic Christology, with a note of 'dependence' of the human on the divine (power) as joining the two in the One Person according to the order of being, but also foregrounding the human nature of Jesus introducing the faithful devotionally to 'God in Christ', with Augustinian echoes of *'per Christum ad Deum'*. By the middle of the century one finds Petavius (*Opus de theologicis dogmatibus*, 1644–50) as a positive theologian drawing more on Scripture and tradition than on scholastic metaphysics. As a result of his reading in the Eastern Fathers he emphasized a substantial union of God achieved by the Holy Spirit in believers as *the* thing effected by Christ's mission, with Christ as the perfect human who could pass the Spirit on to others (Binninger 2011; Hofmann 1976). It seemed easier to make Christology in Spirituality's image, that is, to infer something about Christ's divine Sonship from examining the adoptive sonship of believers, than to start with Trinitarian doctrine and theological anthropology (Ternus 1954: 148).

A less scholastic version of this appeared with the *École française* of spiritual writing: Pierre de Bérulle was able to say that, while miraculous, the Incarnation was not unnatural and that it showed us how human natural capacity for God has been increased through Jesus, who held in himself the Word's divine essence (Bérulle 1844: 81). Christ took a servant-like position in order to place man to God as his final end. Here there should be no discriminating between the two textual variants in Hebrews 10:5: the body as offering and the ear or soul in service were both devoted. The divine life remained what it was, and it did annul the human life through absorption (Bérulle 1844: 93), and it will do the same to the lives of believers, as they consent to have theirs hidden with Christ in God (Col. 3:3).

This concurred with an emphasis on any divine–human mediation being that of a priestly sort, in a human-Godward movement. Interestingly Bérulle replaced 'prophet' in the prophet–priest–king triad with 'offering'. 'His call for a renewal of the ministerial priesthood was deeply Trinitarian and thoroughly centered on Christ the High Priest ... For Bérulle, the heart of the matter was the sanctification of the clergy' (O'Collins and Jones 2010: 185). The order of knowing (and spirituality) takes precedence over the order of being. In the 1640s, the following generation, '[f]or [Jean-Jacques] Olier, permanently offering sacrifice, and not merely making intercession, qualifies the heavenly life of Christ and its impact on the Church on earth' (O'Collins and Jones 2010: 193)—this is what the eternal Melchizedek does. Christ today offers himself and Church as holocaust to God in the odour of his sweetness (*L'esprit des cérémonies de la messe*, 1657). Even on the very day of the Incarnation he offered himself to the Father with all the faithful. In heaven he is eternally consumed in communion with the Father. Now, whereas Hebrews used active verbs for Christ ascending—Olier adapts these to the passive voice: Christ was lifted, received, consumed by the satisfied Father. As Olier observed: 'the religion of Jesus Christ was a perfect religion because he annihilated himself utterly in his father, and in this way returned to God completely as religion demands' (*Traité des Saints orders*; Olier 1984: 232f.; cf. *L'esprit des cérémonies*; Olier 2004: 7, 2). He adds that God knew about the Incarnation even when creating and concludes that there would have been an Incarnation without sin. Christ came not just as redeemer but adorer. Jesus came so that a human could adore God: Jesus the mystic was 'le religieux de Dieu par excellence' (Krummenacker 1998: 168).

Priestly power and annihilationist spirituality both in terms of self-abnegation and Eucharistic theory went hand in hand, reflecting a Christology where Christ's kenosis extended to a self-humiliation with its apogee or nadir on the Cross, an experience which while not touching the divinity, affects fine humans like Paul and Jesus 'pouring oneself [one's human self] out as an offering'. Robert Daly writes: 'Bellarmine's typically Western emphases on the words of consecration and on the christological aspects of the Eucharist to the detriment of its trinitarian, pneumatological and ecclesiological aspects is … the line that contemporary magisterial teaching has chosen to follow' (Daly 2000: 247). 'Annihilationism' in all its forms (Christological, Eucharistic, mystical) might be viewed as an unhappy over-reaction against Protestant polemics, to affirm the actuality of sacrifice on the altar. But Daly's is not the only cogent explanation. The intensity of self-offering is convincing.

Bérulle stated that the human Christ himself worshipped God. When they do the same, believers become divinized like him. Vincent de Paul and Olier followed in this line, but even the Jansenist Pascal would move in the direction of a Christianity based on the humanity of Christ (De Nadaï 2008). Pascal may have started from the position of emphasizing the Word of God, but certainly in the *Apologie* and perhaps earlier in the *Pensées* there is a meditation on the name of Jesus as distinct from 'Christ'. There are later fragments which reinforce this, as Sellier has noted, between October 1651's *Lettre aux Périer* ('On the death of his father') and 1660's *Prière pour demander à Dieu le bon usage des maladie*s: there was not just an analogical but a common grace shared between Jesus' humanity and 'ours', and the act of sacrifice and perpetual self-offering in heaven amount to one human act, in contradistinction to Augustine's view.

Formed by the Oratorians and Descartes in turn, N. Malebranche considered Christ to be a cosmic mediator and Christ as touchstone of all principles, including the natural world—as it appeared as the object of Descartes' study. The Incarnation was the purpose of creation, and soteriology was thus placed within the Father–Son relationship (Baur 2000: 572). God's actions could be filed under his attributes. God works his way into everything. Bérulle had claimed that it took the Incarnation to justify creation: Malebranche did well to oppose this, arguing that nature has done well in its regularity, so that it was not only in the Incarnation and *Heilsgeschichte* where God could be at work. Yet in Christ God shows what this looks like and makes it possible for particulars to receive grace, once the 'coordinates' for that to happen have been established by God in the Incarnation (Baur 2000: 588). The interceding human Jesus makes a contribution by receiving from the Father even as he emptied himself.

The Incarnation was about a relationship between two individuals, the Father and Jesus, not between classes or species. Malebranche avoided the issue of natural/ supernatural or created versus uncreated grace. Instead he talked about a connection in the Incarnation from the finite to infinite. It is not a matter of grace doing things to nature, but of cooperation between divine and human, which would be to the *greater* glory of God, than it would be were all to be taken monergistically. The emphasis on the humanity of Christ being the motor of salvation kept Catholic Christology anchored, ecclesial, to a large degree concrete and with its own Eucharistic herme-neutic. Malebranche shows how much he belonged to the *Oratoire*: as original Man Christ needed more light, and we can recognize the rational man in Christ. This is en route to Enlightenment Christology.

CONCLUDING REFLECTIONS

Against those who consider much of these later developments as theology too much driven by philosophy and spirituality, one might want to contend: does the problem not lie with the professional and Protestant systematic theologian, informed by historical criticism, who wants to find reflection on Christ objectively with reference to who he was, and not at all subjectively in the sense of who he has continued to be and be for us? One reason why eventually (from Spener onwards) a kenosis might have become acceptable was some version of the *extra Calvinisticum*, which meant that the kenosis of the Word would not have amounted to a total loss of the Son's divine power and knowl-edge. The Word remained to direct creation, world history, and God's people, even while Jesus gave him bodily form.

So the Reformed could be happy to think of the life of Jesus in terms which seemed like a story of retreat to the priestly office (*munus sacerdotale*) and perhaps to the office of proclamation (*munus propheticum*), through his veiling the divinity, because while Jesus reveals who God is, he is not 'all there is' to God. The spiritual writers of Catholic, Lutheran, and Reformed traditions shone light on how there could be mystery behind this unique human being. The one who announced rather than brought the Kingdom of God in its fullness, yet inaugurated it in his Person was one whose presence was mediated in the devotion of believers, Eucharistically and otherwise. David Hollaz in 1710 was able to write that from the moment of con-ception onwards, divine power was present to Christ's humanity: this meant that Christ was a super saint, who lived by the inspiration of the Holy Spirit (Schmid 1979: 222).

SUGGESTED READING

Gomes (2009); Heppe (1950); Muller (2008); Schmid (1979).

Bibliography

Almost all primary texts can easily be found at the Post-Reformation Digital Library <http://www.prdl.org>.

Barth, K. (1958), *Church Dogmatics* IV/2, trans. G. W. Bromiley (Edinburgh: T. & T. Clark).

Baur, F. J. (2000), *Erlöste Endlichkeit. Malebranches Christologie als Antwort auf die neuzeitliche Problematik von Natur und Gnade* (St Ottilien: EOS).

Baur, J. (1977), 'Auf dem Wege zur klassischen Tübinger Christologie. Einführende Überlegungen zum sogenannten Kenosis-Krypsis-Streit', in M. Brecht (ed.), *Luther und seine klassischen Erben* (Tübingen: Mohr Siebeck), 195–269.

Bell, M. D. (2011), 'Maccovius (1588–1644) on the Son of God as αὐτόθεος', *Church History and Religious Culture* 9: 105–19.

Bérulle, P. (1844), *L'apôtre du Verbe Incarné Ou Élévations sur les Grandeurs de Jésus-Christ dans le Mystère de l'incarnation. Sommaire des Oeuvres du Cardinal de Bérulle* (Paris: Baracand/Mellier).

Binninger, C. (2011), 'Die pneumatologisch-anthropologischen Ansätze in der Trinitätslehre des Dionysius Petavius und ihr Einfluss auf die "Römische Schule" um Carlo Passaglia und Johann Baptist Franzelin', *Münchener theologische Zeitschrift* 62: 343–55.

Breidert, M. (1977) *Die kenotische Christologie des 19. Jahrhunderts* (Gütersloh: Mohn).

Congar, Y.-M. (1954), 'Dogme christologique et Ecclésiologie', in A. Grillmeier and H. Bacht (eds.), *Das Konzil von Chalkedon. Geschichte und Gegenwart*, vol. 3: *Chalkedon heute* (Würzburg: Echter), 239–68.

Courth, F. (2000), *Christologie: Von der Reformation bis ins 19. Jahrhundert* (Freiburg: Herder).

Daly, R. J. (2000), 'Robert Bellarmine and Post-Tridentine Eucharistic Theology', *Theological Studies* 61: 239–60.

Dantine, W. (with Eric Hultsch) (1984), 'Lehre und Dogmenentwicklung im Römischen Katholizismus', in C. Andresen (ed.), *Handbuch der Dogmengeschichte und Theologiegeschichte* (Göttingen: Vandenhoeck & Ruprecht), vol. 3, 289–423.

De Nadaï, J.-C. (2008), *Jesus selon Pascal* (Paris: Desclée).

Deville, R. (1987), *L'école français e de spiritualité* (Paris: Desclée de Brouwer).

Dixon, P. (2003), *Nice and Hot Disputes: The Doctrine of the Trinity in the Seventeenth Century* (London: T. & T. Clark).

Elert, W. (1957), *Der Ausgang der Altkirchlichen Christologie* (Berlin: Lutherisches Verlag-Haus).

Gerber, U. (1969), *Christologiache Entwürfe* (Zürich: EVZ-Verlag).

Gomes, A. W. (2009), 'The Rapture of the Christ: The "Pre-Ascension Ascension" of Jesus in the Theology of F. Suarez (1539–1604)', *Harvard Theological Review* 102: 75–99.

Heppe, H. (1950), *Reformed Dogmatics Set Out and Illustrated from the Sources* (London: Allen & Unwin).

Hofmann, M. (1976), *Theologie, Dogma und Dogmenentwicklung im theologischen Werk Denis Petau*. Regensburger Studien zur Theologie 1 (Munich: Herbert Lang).

Hoogland, M. P. (1966), *Calvin's Perspective on the Exaltation of Christ in Comparison with the Post-Reformation Doctrine of the Two States* (Kampen: J. H. Kok).

Jung, V. (1999), *Das Ganze der Heiligen Schrift. Hermeneutik und Schriftauslegung bei Abraham Calov* (Stuttgart: Calwer theologische Monographien).

Kaiser, P. (1968), *Die Gott-menschliche Einigung in Christus als Problem der spekulativen Theologie seit der Scholastik* (Munich: Hueber).

Krummenacker, Y. (1998), *L'école française de spiritualité. Des mystiques, des fondateurs, des courants et leurs interprètes* (Paris: Cerf).

McDonald, S. (2012), ' "Beholding the Glory of God in the Face of Jesus Christ": John Owen and the "Reforming" of the Beatific Vision', in E. Tay (ed.), *The Ashgate Research Companion to John Owen's Theology* (Aldershot: Ashgate), 141–58.

Mahlmann, T. (1969), *Das neue Dogma der lutherischen Christologie. Problem und Geschichte seiner Begründung* (Gütersloh: Mohn).

Mosheim, J. L. von (1772), *Einleitung die Wahrheit und Göttlichkeit der christlichen Religion. Gründlich zu beweisen und gegen die Ungläubigen und Deisten zu vertheidigen* (Erlangen: Wolfgang Walther).

Mühling, A. (2009), 'Arminius und die Herboner Theologen. Am Beispiel von Johannes Piscator', in M. van Leeuwen (ed.), *Arminius, Arminianism and Europe* (Leiden: Brill).

Muller, R. (2003), *The Triunity of God*, vol. 4: *Post-Reformation Reformed Dogmatics* (Grand Rapids, Mich.: Baker).

Muller, R. (2008), *Christ and the Decree: Christology and Predestination in Reformed Theology from Calvin to Perkins* (Grand Rapids, Mich.: Baker).

Nüssel, F. (1996), *Bund und Versohnung. Zur Begrundung der Dogmatik bei Johann Franz Buddeus* (Göttingen: Vandenhoeck & Ruprecht.)

O'Collins, G. and M. K. Jones (2010), *Jesus Our Priest: A Christian Approach to the Priesthood of Christ* (New York: Oxford University Press).

Olier, J.-J. (1984), *Le traité des Saints Ordres, comparé aux écrits authentiques de Jean-Jacques Olier*, ed. G. Chaillot, P. Cochois, I. Noye (Paris: Procure de la Compagnie de Saint-Sulpice).

Olier, J.-J. (2004), *L'Esprit des cérémonies de la messe*, ed. C. Barthe (Perpignan: Le Forum).

Pitassi, M.-C. (1994), 'Le Christ lockien à l'épreuve des textes. De la Reasonableness aux Paraphrase and Notes', in Pitassi (ed.), *Le Christ entre Orthodoxie et Lumières, Actes du Colloque tenu à Genève en août 1993* (Geneva: Droz), 101–22.

Preus, R. (1970), *The Theology of Post-Reformation Lutheranism, Volumes I and II* (St Louis: Concordia).

Ratschow, C. H. (1964–6), *Lutherische Dogmatik zwischen Reformation und Aufklärung*, 2 vols. (Gütersloh: Gütersloher Verlagshaus G. Mohn).

Rehnman, S. (2002), *Divine Discourse: The Theological Methodology of John Owen*. Texts and Studies in Reformation and Post-Reformation Thought (Grand Rapids, Mich.: Baker).

Rohls, J. (1998), *Protestantische Theologie der Neuzeit* (Tübingen: Mohr Siebeck).

Schmid, H. H. (1979), *Die Dogmatik der evangelisch-lutherischen Kirche. Dargestellt und aus den Quellen belegt*, vol. 9. (Gütersloh: Gütersloher Mohn); English translation from German, 6th edn.: *Lutheran Dogmatics* (Philadelphia: Lutheran, 1899).

Schröder, R. (1983), *Johann Gerhards Lutherische Christologie und die Aristotelische Metaphysik* (Tübingen: Mohr Siebeck).

Sedelaar, L. (1937), *Die Lehre von der Mittlerschaft Christi nach dem heiligen Bellarmin* (Würzburg: Echter).

Sparn, W. (1976), *Wiederkehr der Metaphysik. Die ontologische Frage in der lutherischen Theologie des frühen 17. Jahrhunderts* (Stuttgart: Calwer Verlag).

Sparn, W. (1988), 'Jesus Christus V Vom Tridentinum bis zur Aufklärung', *Theologische Realenzyklopedie* 17: 1–16.

Spence, A. (2007), *Incarnation and Inspiration: John Owen and the Coherence of Christology* (London: Continuum).

Stegmann, A. (2006), *Johan Friedrich König. Seine theologia positiuca acroamatica(1664) im Rahmen des frühneuzeitlichen Theologiestudiums* (Tübingen: Mohr Siebeck).

Tay, E. (2012), 'Christ's Priestly Oblation and Intercession: Their Development and Significance in John Owen', in Tay (ed.), *The Ashgate Research Companion to John Owen's Theology* (Aldershot: Ashgate), 159–70.

Ternus, J. (1954), 'Das Seelen- und Bewußtseinsleben Jesu', in A. Grillmeier and H. Bacht (eds.), *Das Konzil von Chalkedon. Geschichte und Gegenwart*, vol. 3: *Chalkedon heute* (Würzburg: Echter), 81–237.

Trueman, C. (2007), *John Owen: Reformed Catholic, Renaissance Man* (Aldershot: Ashgate).

Tylenda, J. (1973), 'Christ the Mediator: Calvin Versus Stancaro', *Calvin Theological Journal* 8: 5–16.

Van Dixhoorn, C. (2012), *The Minutes and Papers of the Westminster Assembly, 1643–1652* (Oxford: Oxford University Press).

Weber, H. E. (1908), *Der Einfluß der protestantischen Schulphilosophie auf die orthodox-lutherische Dogmatik* (Darmstadt: Wissenschaftl. Buchges., 1969; 1st edn., Leipzig).

Weber, H. E. (1937–51), *Reformation, Orthodoxie und Rationalismus* (Gütersloh: Gütersloher Mohn).

Wiedenroth, U. (2011), *Krypsis und Kenosis*. Studien zu Thema und Genese der Tübinger Christologie im 17. Jahrhundert (Tübingen: Mohr Siebeck).

CHAPTER 20

CHRISTOLOGY AFTER KANT

KEVIN HECTOR

THERE are at least two respects in which a Christology could be 'after Kant': either by taking Immanuel Kant's critical philosophy as establishing the boundaries within which candidate Christologies must operate, or by elaborating a Christology that plays a key role in rethinking the critical philosophy itself. Kant's own Christology nicely exemplifies the former possibility, while Friedrich Schleiermacher's and G. W. F. Hegel's Christologies exemplify the latter.

KANT'S CRITICAL PHILOSOPHY RETHINKING CHRISTOLOGY

To understand these possibilities, something must first be said about Kant's critical philosophy itself. The key steps of Kant's argument for this philosophy are as follows: (1) that space and time are not 'out there', in the world, but rather are the subjective conditions that we necessarily apply to our sensible impressions of what *is* out there, from which it follows that we have no perceptual access to objects apart from these conditions, that is, as they are 'in themselves'; (2) that, for such perceptions to amount to knowledge, one must set them in a ruled relationship to one another by conceptualizing them; (3) that concepts, as a kind of judgment, must be governed by the rules of logic, especially by logical categories of cause and effect, substance and accident, etc.; (4) that concepts and perceptions must be one and all recognizable as one's own, that is, as the concepts and percepts of a single self-consciousness, and can be so recognizable only if set in logical relation to one another, from which it follows that the categories must govern perception, too; (5) that one's perceptions, and thus the realm of sensible experience, must thus be governed by universal and necessary principles, most importantly the principle of causation, which explains why the empirical world operates in accordance with causal laws; (6) that these laws do not necessarily govern objects 'in themselves', such that it is at least possible that the latter, supersensible realm is a realm of freedom; and (7) that the latter is indeed a realm of freedom, as evidenced by the fact that our wills can be governed by a moral law to such an extent that natural forces, including especially those involving our self-interest, no longer determine our will.

Kant claims, accordingly, that human freedom is a matter of our wills being governed by the moral law, and, given that the will is, by definition, a kind of cause, that one's being so governed is a matter of bringing about effects that conform to that law. To be governed by the moral law, therefore, and so to be free, is to will, first, that one's will would itself be brought into conformity with that law, and, second, because one acts within the realm of sensible experience, that the latter realm, too, would be brought into such conformity. This raises two serious problems, however. On the one hand, Kant earlier claimed that the sensible realm is governed by the laws of nature, including a more or less mechanistic law of natural causation. It is not clear, then, how one could so much as hope that the moral law would be effective in this realm, such that it is not clear how one could reasonably will the moral law—assuming, that is, that one cannot reasonably will that which one knows to be impossible. On the other hand, insofar as our wills are not merely imperfect but radically evil, as Kant maintains, it would appear that the moral law cannot be effective even in relation to one's own will. Once again, it would seem that in willing the moral law, one would be willing that which one knows to be impossible, from which it would follow that one cannot reasonably will it.

Kant insists, however, that it must be reasonable to will the moral law, and that one is accordingly warranted in postulating whatever conditions are necessary to the establishment of such reasonableness. Kant thus claims that it is reasonable to have faith in the existence of a God, on the basis of the following argument: 'the acting rational being in the world', he writes,

> is not also the cause of the world and of nature itself. Consequently, there is not the least ground in the moral law for a necessary connection between the morality and the proportionate happiness of a being belonging to the world as part of it and hence dependent upon it, who for that reason cannot by his will be a cause of this nature and, as far as his happiness is concerned, cannot by his own powers make it harmonize thoroughly with his practical principles. Nevertheless, in the practical task of pure reason, that is, in the necessary pursuit of the highest good, such a connection is postulated as necessary: we *ought* to strive to promote the highest good (which must therefore be possible). Accordingly, the existence of a cause of all nature, distinct from nature, which contains the ground of this connection, namely the exact correspondence of happiness with morality, is also *postulated*.
>
> (Kant 1996a: 5:124–5; cf. Kant 1998: §87, 5:450, 452–3; §88Z, 5:458)

Kant's idea here is that if (a) one can will the moral law only if one can reasonably hope that one's so willing will be effective; (b) one can so hope only if the laws of nature can be brought into harmony with the moral law; and (c) the laws of nature can be brought into such harmony only if they are governed by a supreme cause which is itself moral in nature, then (d) if one *must* will the moral law, one must assume the existence of such a supreme cause.

Kant thus appeals to faith in order to address the apparent disconnect between that which one wills in willing the moral law, and the sensible realm in which that will is to be effective. He follows a similar approach to the other problem mentioned above, namely that it seems impossible that one could actually bring one's will into conformity with the moral law. To address this problem, Kant claims that it must be reasonable to hope (that is, one would be *justified* in holding) that one would be regarded as so conformed by an all-knowing moral lawgiver, yet because we are radically evil by nature—where this means that our will is fundamentally determined by self-interest rather than by pure respect for the moral law—such hope is itself reasonable only if two conditions are met: first, that one becomes a new person, morally speaking, and second, that one's guilt be atoned for. This is where Christology seems to play an important role in Kant's thought, though his argument here is admittedly a bit obscure. A plausible reconstruction would go something like this: (a) given that we are radically evil by nature, we can reasonably hope to be regarded as righteous by an all-knowing moral lawgiver only if our nature undergoes a revolution; (b) given that our moral nature is ours, Kant thinks, only if it is due to our free choice, it follows that this revolution must itself be due to our free choice; (c) given that we are radically evil, however, it would appear that we cannot freely change our moral nature, since all of our acts are grounded in, and so consequent upon, our fundamental self-interestedness; (d) a revolution in one's moral nature thus turns out to depend upon [a] Christ, that is, one who sacrifices his or her welfare for the sake of following the moral law, for in the face of such a Christ, one beholds a pure commitment to the moral law, unmixed with any natural incentive, one can thus hold such a commitment in esteem unmixed with one's self-interest, and one can therefore commit oneself to the moral law on the basis of this respect alone.

Again, Kant does not clearly and straightforwardly elaborate such an argument, but it seems plausible—based on his understanding of Christ, of moral exemplars, and of the problem that needs to be addressed—that this is what he had in mind. He comes close to saying as much, in fact, when he claims that exemplars can play a key role in one's moral development, especially when the former are portrayed as suffering for the sake of morality; he thus suggests that a moral teacher should

> represent him [the example] at a moment when he wishes that he had never lived to see the day that exposed him to such unutterable pain and yet remains firm in his resolution to be truthful, without wavering or even doubting; then my young listener will be raised step by step from mere approval to admiration, from that to amazement, and finally to the greatest veneration and a lively wish that he himself could be such a man (though certainly not in such circumstances); and yet virtue is here worth so much only because it costs so much, not because it brings any profit. All the admiration, and even the endeavor to resemble this character, here rests wholly on the purity of the moral principle, which can be clearly represented only if one removes from the incentive to action everything that people reckon only

to happiness. Thus morality must have more power over the human heart the more purely it is presented. From this it follows that if the law of morals and the image of holiness and virtue are to exercise any influence at all on our soul, they can do so only insofar as they are laid to heart in their purity as incentives, unmixed with any view to one's welfare, for it is in suffering that they show themselves most excellently.

(Kant 1996a: 5:156; cf. 5:77)

If we have this passage in mind when we read Kant's suggestion that Christ is significant precisely as '*an example to be emulated*', and especially his characterization of Christ as 'a human being willing not only to execute in person all human duties ... but also, though tempted by the greatest temptation, to take upon himself all sufferings, up to the most ignominious death, for the good of the world', it seems plausible that what one is here supposed to emulate is Christ's pure commitment to the moral law (even when such commitment runs contrary to all natural incentives), and that the emulation of this commitment can itself embody such purity, since his example elicits in one a respect for the moral law that is likewise contrary to natural incentives (Kant 1996b: 6:64, 62). In such a case, one whose moral nature had been self-interested could freely commit him- or herself to the moral law on a basis other than that self-interest, and could therefore become a new person, morally speaking (see Kant 1996b: 6:48, 66–7).

Kant claims that one thus regenerated could reasonably hope to be regarded as righteous by God, since the moral law is now his or her ground-maxim and new nature. By itself, however, regeneration is a necessary but not sufficient condition of such hope, for a serious impediment remains, namely, the guilt one accrued in one's former life. That is to say, even though a person has become a new creature,

he nevertheless started from evil, and this is a debt which is impossible for him to wipe out. He cannot regard the fact that, after his change of heart, he has not incurred new debts, as equivalent to his having paid off the old ones. Nor can he produce, in the future conduct of a good life, a surplus over and above what he is under obligation to perform each time; for his duty is to do all the good in his power.

(Kant 1996b: 6:72)

Kant's point, obviously indebted to Anselm's *Cur Deus Homo*, is that one cannot do something more than one is morally obliged to do, and so accrue a moral surplus with which to repay those debts, since one is every moment obligated to do one's duty, and one cannot do more than one's duty. No one can pay these debts on one's behalf, moreover, since guilt is 'the *most personal* of all liabilities, namely a debt of sins which only the culprit, not the innocent, can bear' (Kant 1996b: 6:72). Given one's guilt for sin, accordingly, and the apparent impossibility of one's doing anything to discharge that guilt, it seems impossible yet again that one could reasonably hope to be counted righteous by God, and so impossible to will the moral law.

Kant's resolution of this issue is complicated, but it goes something like this: he argues, first, that the old person deserves infinite punishment, but that this punishment was not visited upon him or her, yet given that the new person 'now leads a new life and has become a "new man", the punishment cannot be considered appropriate to [him or her]' (Kant 1996b: 6:72–3). So: the old person owes a debt that he or she did not pay, but the new person, qua new, owes nothing, since he or she is a different person, morally speaking, from the one who incurred the debt. This provides us with a possible solution to our problem, namely, that 'the punishment must be thought as adequately executed in the situation of conversion itself' (Kant 1996b: 6:73). So then: if 'conversion' is 'an exit from evil and an entry into goodness', how does this count as the taking-on of punishment? Kant's answer is that 'the emergence from the corrupted disposition into the good is in itself already sacrifice … and entrance into a long train of life's ills which the new human being undertakes … simply for the sake of the good, yet are still fitting *punishment* for someone else, namely, the old human being (who, morally, is another human being)' (Kant 1996b: 6:74). To be converted, accordingly, is to enter on a life characterized by pain and suffering, namely, the pain consequent upon one's putting off one's old self and experiencing this *as* a sacrifice of self. This counts as payment for the debts one has previously incurred, since, 'considered in his empirical character as a sensible being, he is still the same human being liable to punishment, and he must be judged as such before a moral tribunal of justice and hence by himself as well' (Kant 1996b: 6:74). Because the new person is numerically identical with the old person, in other words, there is a sense in which the new person can be thought liable for the old person's debts. But because the new person is *morally* a different being, he or she does *not* owe these debts, from which it follows that qua new being he or she can 'bear as *vicarious substitute* the debt of sin for [the old person]', which is precisely 'that surplus over the merit from works for which we felt the need earlier' (Kant 1996b: 6:74–5). One's guilt is thereby atoned for, Kant claims, in consequence of which one can reasonably hope, once again, to be regarded by God as righteous.

Kant argues, accordingly, that one can reasonably will the moral law only if one can reasonably hope to be justified; that one can reasonably hope to be justified only if one's moral nature has been regenerated and one's guilt has been atoned for; and that christology—with a small 'c', as it were—plays a key role in enabling one to meet the latter conditions. Kant's own philosophy thus includes a christology 'after Kant', since, for him, christological claims are warranted just insofar as they lend plausibility to, and so fit neatly within, the more basic principles of his philosophy.

CHRISTOLOGICAL RETHINKING OF KANT'S CRITICAL PHILOSOPHY

Kant's is not the only Christology 'after Kant', however. As noted earlier, many theologians responded to Kant not by trying to fit theological claims into the boundaries of his philosophy, but by rethinking some of his most basic contentions.

F. Schleiermacher

Schleiermacher's theology exemplifies such a response. Like several of his contemporaries, Schleiermacher was dissatisfied with certain aspects of Kant's thought, particularly with what he perceived as the distance Kant introduces between human beings and nature, and his sense that Kant's emphasis on laws cannot account for, and may in fact discourage, individual self-expression. Schleiermacher saw these as theological problems, to which a theological—and specifically Christological—answer was needed.

Schleiermacher thus begins his argument by reframing the relationship between the realm of freedom and the realm of nature or 'dependence', claiming that these realms seem to stand at odds with one another, or at a remove from one another, only insofar as one fails to recognize that freedom and dependence are both absolutely dependent, and insofar as one therefore fails to harmonize them by bringing both realms into attunement with the Whence of this absolute dependence. Simply stated, then, Schleiermacher's claim is that freedom and dependence seem to stand in an antithesis precisely insofar as we do not bring them properly into relationship with God—insofar, that is, as we are sinful.

To bring the realms of freedom and dependence into harmony, accordingly, they must be brought into attunement with the one upon whom they depend absolutely, but because we are sinful, we cannot bring about such attunement, for such efforts would necessarily, and so self-defeatingly, treat our relationship to the Whence of absolute dependence as if it could be due to our freedom. Our only hope, accordingly, is for the Whence itself to bring us back into attunement, which, Schleiermacher claims, is precisely what the Whence does in Christ.

This brings us to Schleiermacher's Christology, where he argues that Jesus Christ is God incarnate or, more precisely, that every moment of Jesus' life perfectly apprehends and reproduces the loving activity in which God eternally subsists, in consequence of which 'every moment of [Christ's] existence, so far as it can be isolated, presents just such a new incarnation and incarnatedness of God, because always and everywhere all that is human in him springs from the divine' (Schleiermacher 2011: §96.3, 397). To ward off a common misreading, it is important to note that for Schleiermacher God-consciousness is the creaturely organ, so to speak, through which Jesus apprehends God's being-in-act; hence, when Schleiermacher asserts that 'to ascribe to Christ an absolutely powerful God-consciousness, and to attribute to him an existence of God in him, are exactly the same thing' (§94.2, 387), he means that Christ's perfectly potent God-consciousness is the instrument through which God's being-in-act is perfectly reproduced in Christ's life, such that God is present in and through, and not just to, him.

Schleiermacher claims, moreover, that this perfectly-potent God-consciousness could not have arisen through 'normal' human history, because everyone in that history is tainted by corporate sinfulness, such that their God-consciousness was invariably subordinated to their sensible self-consciousness. Christ's God-consciousness, then, 'cannot be explained by the content of the human environment to which he belonged' (§93.3, 381), but must be 'newly implanted' by God: 'since the whole human race is included in this sinful corporate life', Schleiermacher contends, 'we must believe that this God-consciousness has a supernatural origin' (§88.4, 365). Hence, given that Christ possessed a perfectly receptive God-consciousness, in spite of the fact that sinful human history could not produce such a consciousness, we must conclude that Christ's God-consciousness is the result of a creative act of God (or, more precisely, the result of *the* creative act of God; see §89.1, 367, and §109.3, 501). Schleiermacher concludes, therefore, that 'anyone who assumes in the Redeemer a native sinlessness and a new creation through the union of the divine with the human, postulates a supernatural conception as well' (§97.2, 405).

This implanting of the God-consciousness is only the beginning, however—or, better, only the precondition of the beginning—of Christ's incarnation of God. Because God is pure activity, God's union with humanity in Christ can never be 'done', in the sense of a completed, static state of unitedness, but must rather be a continual act of uniting. Accordingly, 'every activity of Christ must exemplify the same relation as that which marks the act of union (which, indeed, is only a union for such activities), that is, that the impulse springs from the divine nature; so also conversely the act of union must exemplify the same relation as that through which every activity of Christ exists (since every activity is only an individual manifestation of this union)' (§97.1, 399). The state of union between Christ's divinity and humanity is thus due to a continuous uniting, inasmuch as the pure act of God's being is continually united with and reproduced in Christ's life. The union of divine and human is new every moment, therefore, not because Christ is not fully divine, but because this is precisely the way a human can be fully united with divinity-as-pure-act.

For Schleiermacher, accordingly, the decisive thing about Christ is not merely that he is perfectly God-conscious (and so perfectly attuned to the Whence of absolute dependence), but that this perfect God-consciousness is the means through which God's being is incarnated. On this account, then, Christ is the very incarnation of God's being-in-act, because at every moment Christ perfectly apprehends and reproduces that act as his own. And because the act in which God eternally subsists is redeeming love, it follows that Jesus incarnates God precisely by apprehending that love and reproducing it as his own, in relationship to God and all other creatures (see §§166–7; also §93.3, 381; §93.4, 383; §66.2, 272).

It is not enough, however, for Christ to have lived a life of perfect God-consciousness, for if we are to be redeemed, the power of this life must somehow be communicated to us. Christ accomplishes this, Schleiermacher argues, by drawing us into the activity of his life—he not only acts upon every circumstance of his own life, he also acts upon us, in such a way that his activity becomes our activity. Schleiermacher asserts, therefore, that 'the activity by which he assumes us into fellowship with him is a creative production in us of the will to assume him into ourselves, or rather—since it is only receptiveness for his activity as involved in the impartation—only our assent to the influence of his activity' (§100.2, 426). More specifically, Schleiermacher argues (a) 'that whatever in human nature is assumed into vital fellowship with Christ is assumed into the fellowship of an activity solely determined by the power of the God-consciousness, which

God-consciousness is adequate to every new experience and extracting from it all it has to yield'; (b) 'That each assumption of this sort is simply a continuation of the same creative act which first manifested itself in time by the formation of Christ's person'; (c) 'that each increase in the intensity of this new life relatively to the disappearing corporate life of sinfulness is also such a continuation'; and (d) that in this new life man achieves the destiny originally appointed for him, and nothing beyond this can be conceived or attempted for a nature such as ours' (§101.4, 437).

Schleiermacher then claims that one's assumption into fellowship with Christ is mediated through the Spirit of the community he founded, in such a way that we freely receive his influence, and his receptivity to God becomes our own. As such, 'he stands to the totality of believers in exactly the same relation as the divine nature in him does to the human, animating and taking it up into the fellowship of the original life [that is, Christ's]' (§105.1, 468). Christ is perfectly receptive to God's pure act and perfectly reproduces it as his own action; in redeeming us, Christ makes us receptive to his receptivity so that it becomes ours. On this account, then, Christ's work is a repetition of his person. Schleiermacher argues, accordingly, that 'In him the passivity of his human nature was nothing but a lively susceptibility to an absolutely powerful consciousness of God, accompanied by a desire to be thus seized and determined, which became changed through the creative act into a spontaneous activity constituting a personality. In the same way our desire is heightened in conversion by the self-communication of Christ till it becomes a spontaneous activity of the self that constitutes a coherent new life' (§108.6, 495). Christ redeems us, therefore, by continuing the pure activity that constitutes his person, namely, the act of receiving and reproducing God's act. Our conversion, therefore, 'may be said to be just the evocation of this spontaneous activity in union with Christ' in which the 'lively susceptibility passes into quickened spontaneous activity' (§108.6, 495). Hence, Christ redeems us, and can redeem us, by continuing to incarnate God's pure activity.

For Schleiermacher, then, Christ is perfectly receptive to God's being-in-love and perfectly reproduces it as his own, and in redeeming us, Christ makes us receptive to his receptivity so that we, too, can receive and reproduce God's love. There is, then, a sort of transitive property at work here, which Schleiermacher understands as (and, in turn, uses to explain) the work of Christ's Spirit. To explain how this works, Schleiermacher takes as his model Christ's disciples, since he sees in them exactly the transformation he is trying to explain, namely one where they were initially merely receptive to Christ, but were eventually transformed so that Christ's receptivity (and activity) became their own. Schleiermacher claims, accordingly, that the disciples first had to become susceptible to Christ's activity: 'in spending time together with Christ', he writes, 'the disciples' receptivity developed, and by perceiving what he held before them, a foundation was laid for their future effectiveness for the kingdom of God'. During their time with Christ, then, the disciples watched what Jesus said and did, and from this they began to learn what it meant to follow him. Through such training, the disciples grew in their susceptibility to Christ's influence, but his receptivity had not yet become their own, for they had not yet internalized this influence. A crucial step in their development occurred, therefore, when Jesus recognized them as competent to assess others' recep-tivity, since, Schleiermacher notes, 'the right binding and loosing of sin is essentially just an expression of a fully cultivated receptivity for what pertains to the kingdom of God' (§122.1, 566). Jesus' recognition of the disciples' authority to bind and loose thus meant that the disciples had learned what it meant to follow him, which meant, in turn, that Jesus' influence on them was no longer merely external (see §122.3). This recogni-tion also meant that the disciples were now in a position to confer this same recogni-tion upon others, such that Jesus' influence was now fully transitive: the disciples had internalized Jesus' influence through becoming receptive to him, and once they had become sufficiently receptive, he recognized them as competent recognizers of such receptivity; once others had become sufficiently receptive, they too would be recog-nized as such, and so on.

From this, Schleiermacher thus extrapolates a more general model according to which a 'multifarious community of attunement' is carried on: first, those who have been attuned to Christ express that attunement through their gestures, words, actions, and recognition-laden responses *to* such expressions; if others recognize this person's expressions as properly receptive of Christ's influence, they may imitate them in similar circumstances until they have become reliably disposed to do so, at which point these expressions become part of their own attunement; still others may then recognize the latter's expressions as attuned to Christ, imitate those expressions, become reliably dis-posed to repeat them, and so on. In this way, the Spirit of Christ's own receptivity is car-ried forward through a chain of intersubjective recognition.

For Schleiermacher, then, God redeems one by attuning one to Godself, and God does this by incarnating such attunement in Christ and conveying it through his Spirit. And because the loving God to whom one is attuned is also the Whence upon whom all things depend absolutely, it follows that the realms of freedom and dependence can be harmonized through this same attunement. Schleiermacher thus offers a theologi-cal diagnosis of, and theological solution to, certain problems he sees in Kant's philoso-phy; hence, instead of elaborating a Christology within the bounds of that philosophy, as Kant himself had done, Schleiermacher looks to Christology in order to reconceive its basic terms.

G. W. F. Hegel

Like Schleiermacher, Hegel was dissatisfied with certain aspects of Kant's philosophy, though their diagnoses differed in important respects. Hegel agreed with Kant that human knowledge depends upon our application of categories (or, in Hegel's preferred idiom, 'universals') to objects, just as human action depends upon the application of such universals to one's will. The problem, Hegel thought, was that Kant construed these universals in such a way that the particulars to which they were meant to apply—objects, situations, ourselves—remained external to them, which is why Kant's philosophy remained susceptible to various skeptical and anti-positivist worries. Hegel's solution, therefore, was to defend an alternative account of universals, according to which the latter are fully reconciled or at home with particulars.

One of Hegel's most basic arguments, then, is that human knowing is essentially self-conscious, involving the application of universals to particulars, but that we must become self-conscious of our self-consciousness—that is, that we must become *for* ourselves what we are *in* ourselves. For this to be the case, Hegel claims, one's self-consciousness must itself become an object to one, and one must see oneself in, and accordingly be at home with, the self-consciousness one thus beholds. Hegel writes, accordingly, that self-consciousness

> is that which *relates itself to itself* and is *determinate*, it is *other-being* and *being-for-self*, and in this determinateness, or in its self-externality, abides within itself; in other words, it is *in and for itself.*—But this being-in-and-for-itself is at first only for us, or *in itself*, it is spiritual *Substance*. It must also be this *for itself*, it must be the knowledge of the spiritual, and the knowledge of itself as Spirit, i.e. it must be an *object* to itself, but just as immediately a sublated object, reflected into itself. It is *for itself* only for *us*, insofar as its spiritual content is generated by itself. But insofar as it is also for itself for its own self, this self-generation, the pure notion, is for it the objective element in which it has its existence, and it is in this way, in its existence for itself, an object reflected into itself.

> (Hegel 1976: §25, 14; cf. §36, 21)

One's self-consciousness can thereby be mediated to one, yet as a self-conscious subject, one can simultaneously mediate it to oneself, as when one recognizes another's recognition of one *as* such a subject. A self-consciousness that thus mediates objects, and itself *as* an object, to itself, and is therefore at home with itself, is what Hegel terms 'spirit'.

This brings us to Hegel's treatment of religion, since one's relationship to God plays an essential role in one's ability to be fully at home with oneself and all other particulars. Hegel's argument here, simply stated, is that religion is fundamentally a matter of (divine) spirit being for (human) spirit, though he thinks that particular religions usually portray Spirit's relationship to spirit one-sidedly, in consequence of which either divine Spirit is reduced to human spirit (as in Roman religion—as Hegel understands it), or the particularities of human spirit are excluded from the divine (as in most Eastern religions, on Hegel's understanding). By contrast, Hegel sees in Christianity a particular religion in which Spirit is truly for spirit, and vice versa, such that Christianity is for him the *consummate* or *revelatory* religion. ('Revelatory', for if a particular religion corresponds to that which religion is, then in beholding *this* religion, one simultaneously beholds religion itself.) In Christianity, that is to say, God reconciles us to Godself, and we can thus behold ourselves as God beholds us and so be fully at home with ourselves precisely in that reconciliation.

Thus reconciliation, as well as Christology, lie at the heart of Hegel's account. Reconciliation is necessary, on this account, because of the cleavage that exists between us and *God*, inasmuch as we fail to correspond with our truth or what we ought to be, and between us and the *world*, inasmuch as we experience the world as a hostile, or at least indifferent, environment. Hegel terms the former cleavage 'evil', the latter, 'misery'. This is not how things should be, however, since both sorts of cleavage indicate that we have fallen short of our truth, or have become what Hegel calls an abstraction from our actuality. We thus live in a sort of contradictory state—vis-à-vis God and the world—but God overcomes this contradiction by contradicting it, that is, by taking even this cleavage into unity with Godself. This is the fundamental meaning of Christ's life, death, and resurrection, namely, that in Christ God has brought that which is opposed to God—even evil and death—into unity with God and thus overcome that opposition. Hegel claims, accordingly, that in Christ

> the abstraction of humanity, the immediacy of subsisting singularity, is sublated, and this is brought about by death. But the death of Christ is the death of this death itself, the negation of negation ... It is their finitude that Christ has taken [upon himself], this finitude in all its forms, which at its furthest extreme is evil ... This finitude, on its own account (as against God), is evil, it is something alien to God. But he has taken it [upon himself] in order to put it to death by his death. As the monstrous unification of these absolute extremes, this shameful death is at the same time infinite love.
>
> (Hegel 2006: 324–5 n.199)

In this movement of reconciliation, that is to say, we see that there is nothing outside of God's infinite love, since it is capacious enough to embrace even its opposite.

This infinite love, in turn, must characterize God's very being, since God is able to take up and so negate this negation. Hegel claims, accordingly, that in this movement of reconciliation, we see the triune movement in which God eternally subsists, for

> the reconciliation in Christ, in which one believes, makes no sense if God is not known as the triune God, [if it is not recognized] that God *is*, but also is as the other, as self-distinguishing, so that this other is God himself, having implicitly the divine nature in it, and that the sublation of this otherness, and the return of love, are the Spirit.
>
> (Hegel 2006: 327)

In God's act of reconciling us to Godself, then, we see 'the eternal history, the eternal movement, which God himself is' (Hegel 2006: 327). Hegel thus understands God as an eternal movement in which God distinguishes Godself from Godself and then sublates the distinction, such that in reconciling us to Godself, God simply includes us in the overcoming of distinction by which God's eternal being is characterized.

In Christ, then, God has overcome our would-be negation of unity with God by taking that negation itself into unity with God, and the Spirit progressively transforms our lives so that 'this truth should become ever more identical with one's self, with the human will, and that this truth should become one's volition, one's object, one's spirit' (Hegel 2006: 337). In beholding and being conformed to this truth, accordingly, we see that humanity is included in God's infinitude, and can thus stand in a new relationship to ourselves: conscious of ourselves as reconciled to God, we see that there is nothing in heaven or on earth with which we cannot be at home and with respect to which, therefore, we cannot be free. That is to say, if finitude and negation have been reconciled to God, then insofar as we identify with our selves as so reconciled, we can likewise see all else as included in that reconciliation, and can ourselves be reconciled with it, too.

Religion, and Christianity in particular, thus play a key role in Hegel's thought, for in Christianity we behold not only a particular religion that is one with its concept, but a universal (Spirit) that includes all particulars, including even humanity's would-be negation of that universal, such that universality and particularity no longer fall apart. In beholding this divine Spirit, therefore, and one's reconciliation to it, one can thereby stand in a different relationship to oneself and everything else, since one can now be at home with oneself in each of these relationships. Hegel thus takes himself to have addressed the most significant problem facing Kant's philosophy, and Christology plays a key role in his strategy for doing so.

CONCLUSION

Kant, Schleiermacher, and Hegel are not the only theologians to have elaborated and defended a Christology 'after Kant', though their respective approaches are surely among the most influential on those who have attempted to do so. Think here of their influence on Ludwig Feuerbach, Isaak Dorner, A. E. Biedermann, Albrecht Ritschl, Wilhelm Herrmann, Karl Barth, Paul Tillich, Eberhard Jüngel, Jürgen Moltmann, Dorothee Sölle, and Oswald Bayer, to name just a few. Given the significant differences among their Christologies, it should be evident that there is more than one way of understanding Christ 'after Kant', and, in the case of Schleiermacher and Hegel, that an understanding of Christ can even contribute to one's understanding of Kant's philosophy itself.

SUGGESTED READING

Kant (1996: 133–272); Kant (2005: 39–216); Schleiermacher (2011: 374–475).

BIBLIOGRAPHY

Hegel, G. W. F. (1976), *Phenomenology of Spirit*, trans. A. V. Miller (New York: Oxford University Press).

Hegel, G. W. F. (2006), *Lectures on the Philosophy of Religion One-Volume Edition: The Lectures of 1827*, trans. and ed. P. C. Hodgson (New York: Oxford University Press).

Kant, I. (1996a), 'Critique of Practical Reason (1788)', in P. Guyer and A. W. Wood (trans. and eds.), Immanuel Kant, *Practical Philosophy*. The Cambridge Edition of the Works of Immanuel Kant (New York: Cambridge University Press), 133–272.

Kant, I. (1996b; repr. 2005), 'Religion within the Boundaries of Mere Reason (1793)', trans. G. di Giovanni, in A. W. Wood and G. di Giovanni (eds.), Immanuel Kant, *Religion and Rational Theology*. The Cambridge Edition of the Works of Immanuel Kant (New York: Cambridge University Press), 39–216.

Kant, I. (1998; repr. 2007), *Critique of Pure Reason*, trans. and ed. P. Guyer and A. W. Wood. The Cambridge Edition of the Works of Immanuel Kant (New York: Cambridge University Press).

Schleiermacher, F. (2011), *The Christian Faith* (Berkeley, CA: Apocryphile Press).

CHAPTER 21

......

THE HISTORICAL JESUS AND CHRISTOLOGY FROM DAVID FRIEDRICH STRAUSS TO KÄSEMANN

......

PHILIP G. ZIEGLER

INTRODUCTION

......

CHRISTOLOGY is the discursive expansion of the evangelical confession of the identity of Jesus as the Christ of God. It seeks to elucidate the meaning, basis, and entailments of this confession and to bring these insights to bear upon the understanding and ordering of all other aspects of Christian faith, thought, and practice. In this task, the New Testament witness to the identity of the man Jesus of Nazareth has ever played a central part. Beginning in the late eighteenth century a new and distinctly modern problem arose with respect to the role of the New Testament witness generally, and the Gospels in particular, in the business of Christology. The diversity of biblical portraits of Jesus assumed a new and different significance in view of modern historical critical study of the origins of the New Testament, research which cared little for their presumptive supernatural origin and canonical unity. The problem of the 'historical Jesus' and the unsettled question of its significance for Christology are abiding legacies of the rise and development of historical criticism of the Bible over the last two centuries.

By the start of the nineteenth century, Enlightenment philosophies had long been raising searching questions about the intelligibility of ancient Christological dogma. The contingency and historically parochial character of Christian claims were criticized by thinkers like Lessing and Kant who argued that deductive rationality and universal accessibility were necessary marks of any religious claims worthy of the allegiance of modern women and men. The religious and moral value of the historical per se was assailed. Christological doctrines were rendered further suspect by the role they were said to play in the ideological mystifications of ecclesiastical priest-craft against which the emerging natural and human sciences and associated political cultures set their face. Traditionalist authority and the dehumanizing consequences of the invocation of ideas of the supernatural and the miraculous suffered sustained attacks in the work of figures like Hume, Rousseau, and again, Kant. The traditional figure of Jesus Christ stood precisely at the intersection of these two lines of modern critique: the incarnate Son of God—*vere deus et vere homo*—a figure at once miraculous and historical, contingent and supernatural, now doubly dubious.

Already a node of critical pressure on conceptual grounds then, the emergence of historical criticism of the Gospels themselves opened up the prospect that the canonical portrait of Christ—together with the doctrines which depended upon it—were not only an unfit vehicle for the 'necessary truths of reason' as had previously been worried, but were also seriously deficient even as regards the 'accidental truths of history' (Lessing 1972: 53). Reimarus' *ad hominem* dismissal of Jesus' disciples as self-serving fabricators proved typical in the questions raised, if not in the answers ventured. His *Fragments* staked the essential methodological claim that the Church's dogmatic account of its Scriptures be supplanted by a *naturalistic* one, and 'announced all the *motifs* of the future historical treatment of the life of Jesus' (Schweitzer 1968: 26). The subsequent 'quest of the historical Jesus' concentrated scholarly attention throughout the nineteenth century on the question of just what could be known of Jesus of Nazareth by means of historical science. The humanity of Jesus Christ became a pivot point of theological debate during this entire period (Welch 1965: 8).

While the motivations and aims of scholars varied, matters of Christological importance were inevitably at stake. For some, the aim of such research was a better orthodoxy: by insisting that future Christology would be marked by 'a full and unreserved recognition of His human nature as "*homo-ousios*" with our own', the unprecedented emphasis on understanding the humanity of Christ promised to correct deep seated monophysite reflexes in the tradition that effectively discounted the significance of the reality of the life Jesus lived (Baillie 1948: 10). The flourishing of *kenotic* Christology in this period is also indicative of this emphasis. In this movement the humanity of the man Jesus—understood as an autonomous willing subject and agent and, crucially, a historically developing personality—exercised a defining constraint upon Christology. Theologians working in this vein asked, 'How ought we to re-conceive of the nature of divinity in Christ given the incontrovertible integrity of his human nature and existence?' That someone like Thomasius was willing to run the risk of reducing the meaning of 'incarnation' to something like 'theophany' (Baillie 1948: 96) in deference to the integrity of Jesus' humanity indicates how seriously the matter had come to be taken.

Other scholars pursued the more radical and revisionist aim of unearthing the 'real' historical figure of Jesus purportedly buried beneath centuries of Christian piety and the obfuscations of ecclesiastical dogma. While for some this could be a work of progressive piety, for others it was an exercise in scientific *sang-froid* that undermined both theological dogmaticism and the passions of the pious imagination. David Friedrich Strauss was one of the most influential of these 'anti-dogmatists'.

DAVID FRIEDRICH STRAUSS

Strauss' *Life of Jesus Critically Examined* first appeared in 1835, a 'spark by which the long-accumulated fuel burst into bright flame' as F. C. Baur remarked (Strauss 1977: xxvi). Forswearing both supernaturalist and rationalist defences of the historical character of the events attested in the Gospels, Strauss proposes a *mythical* reading of the accounts of Jesus' ministry, death, and resurrection. 'Myth' is a heuristic category by means of which Strauss purports to identify and explain the fictitious elements in the Gospel stories. To designate something as mythical is not to cast it as a conscious fabulation or authorial deception. Strauss proposes that features of the Gospel narratives which *prima facie* are unhistorical—because they (negatively) break the known laws of nature, causality, human psychology, or are self-contradictory, or (positively) are poetical, trade in prevalent religious ideas, or reflect narrative conventions—are to be explained on the basis of the shared cultural consciousness out of which they grew. To categorize such unhistorical elements in the Gospel as 'myths' is to understand them as the imaginative products of 'unconscious folk poeticizing' which give voice not so much to the mind of any one individual author, as to the consciousness of a whole religious culture (Frei 1985: 235). Without denying that the Gospels may contain some historical facts despite themselves, Strauss adjudged that most of the Gospel texts were mythical in this sense, expressions of the *social imaginary* of the religious world in which the New Testament was composed. As such they were largely disqualified as sources of *historical* information about Jesus. What Strauss says of one passage may be extended to his view of the whole: the Gospels offer up 'no particular fact in the life of Jesus, but only a new proof of how strong was the impression of his messiahship left by Jesus on the minds of his contemporaries' (Strauss 1973: 177). The overall effect of such a mythical reading is, as Strauss saw it, to 'have apparently annihilated the greatest and most valuable part of that which the Christian has been wont to believe concerning his Saviour Jesus, have uprooted all the animating motives which he has gathered from his faith, and withered all his consolations' (Strauss 1973: 757).

Nevertheless, the *Life of Jesus* ended with a 'concluding dissertation' in which Strauss surprisingly angles 'to re-establish dogmatically that which has been destroyed critically' in such a way as to show that 'the dogmatic significance of the life of Jesus remains inviolate' (Strauss 1973: 757, lii). This trick—in which Strauss himself soon lost confidence—draws heavily on aspects of Hegel's speculative philosophy of religion. Strauss argues that historical criticism renders untenable traditional doctrines of Christ in which absolute significance was 'annexed to the person and history of one individual'. Yet the Christological *idea* might still be salvaged if its object were no longer taken to be the single man Jesus, but rather the human race as such wherein are resolved the many contradictions predicated of 'the Christ' (Strauss 1973: 780). Like Feuerbach, Strauss suggests that anthropology provides the secret key to the rational meaning of Christology: the future of Christology can be secured by its transposition into a poetics of human self-description. When Strauss later abandoned the attempt to salvage Christological doctrine philosophically, he concluded more simply that 'the critical investigation of the life of Jesus is the test of the dogma of the person of Christ' (Strauss 1977: 5), a test which traditional Christology could not pass. To the extent that Christological doctrines traded upon the factuality of the Gospels—claims Strauss felt he had demonstrated *in fine* to be almost entirely mythical and so unhistorical—those doctrines were fatally compromised. Even in his most mature work, he deployed the category of myth to a single, rigidly critical end and did not exploit other possibilities it might have afforded (beyond the Hegelian conceit) as a 'potentially rich hermeneutical device' for Christological reconstruction or reinterpretation (Frei 1985: 242).

What Strauss accomplished shaped subsequent debates surrounding the Christological significance of the question of the historical Jesus. Two divergent paths opened up from this juncture. The first option was to admit the materially decisive connection between the Jesus of critical history and the Christ of Christian faith such that the deliverances of historical scholarship bore more or less directly on the tenability of Christological claims. Both revisionist and conservative possibilities exist along this route: one could continue to argue, like Strauss, that critical scholarship delivered negligible historical knowledge and no surety concerning the man Jesus, and that what little it did establish undermined, rather than buttressed, the claims of classical Christology. Alternately, one could contend that critical research could deliver up a wide and defensible core of historical facts upon which renewed understandings of these same Christological doctrines could in fact be sustained. The story Albert Schweitzer tells in the latter half of *The Quest of the Historical Jesus* is largely that of the extensive exploration of these possibilities up to the turn of the twentieth century. Below we will briefly consider the positions of von Harnack and Troeltsch as influential examples of the constructive wing of this line of development.

The second option after Strauss was to contest the claim that there is a materially significant connection between the historical Jesus and the Christ of Christian faith, and to argue instead that historians' reconstructions should have no bearing on faith's grasp—and theology's conception—of the identity of Christ the Saviour. The various considerations adduced in support of this view distil into arguments for the *historical impossibility* of attaining to the 'real' Jesus by *wissenschaftliche* means, and the *theological illegitimacy* of appealing to reconstructions of the historical Jesus 'behind' the scriptural portrait as a source and norm for Christological doctrine or as the proper object of Christian faith. We will look to the work of Kähler, Herrmann, and Bultmann for articulations of these contentions.

THE NECESSITY OF THE HISTORICAL JESUS FOR MODERN CHRISTOLOGY

Maurice Wiles remarked that even as it undermined traditional doctrine, historical criticism has 'the potential to bring new life to the figure of Jesus for Christian experience in our own times' (Wiles 1979: 22). The first trajectory we can trace beyond Strauss seized upon this possibility. Despite Strauss' limited yield, the continued application of the tools of historical discovery, it was wagered, could deliver an intellectually credible and religiously vibrant portrait of Jesus of Nazareth unfettered from the 'stony rocks of ecclesiastical doctrine' (Schweitzer 1968: 399). As befits the methods and fascinations of the age, portraits produced in this mode emphasized the inner motivations, natural psychological development, and moral character of Jesus. They aimed to convey a complete impression of him as a powerful personality, a man of compelling religious genius. In this they owed less to Strauss than to Schleiermacher, whose posthumously published *Life of Jesus* advocated for the central place of Jesus' supreme God-consciousness in accounting for his person and actions. Ernst Renan's infamous, if less technical, contribution to the genre is not atypical with its combination of critical historical observation and rhapsodic commendation of the 'great soul' of Jesus: even his ignorance and mistaken worldview—namely, his exaggerated belief in God's concern for humanity and reliance upon special providence—are but 'beautiful errors' that have proved and remain 'the secret of his power' (Renan 1864: 60). The power of Jesus to save was reconceived on such terms as that of an exemplary human existence controlled by a pure and profound moral-religious vision. Talk of the divine translates into talk of the sublime; talk of the condescension of God into talk of human ascent to greatness: 'Let us place, then, the person of Jesus at the highest summit of human greatness' (Renan 1864: 305). Such studies could be accused of trafficking in accounts of the man Jesus more persuasively *ideal* than historically real; their ideality actually standing surrogate for displaced deity. When they sought to correct for this, later practitioners of this biographical art 'at its height' would reaffirm and intensify—rather than leave off—its overarching aim and techniques.

Adolf Von Harnack

In a famous exchange of public letters in 1923, Harnack scorned as irresponsible Karl Barth's suggestion that the Christ of faith could be known *otherwise* than as the historical person of Jesus whose identity was available to objective scholarly investigation. He asked rhetorically, 'If the person of Christ stands at the centre of the gospel, how else can the basis for reliable and communal knowledge of this person be gained but through critical-historical study so that an imagined Christ is not put in place of the real one?' To deny this would lay Christology open to 'every suitable fantasy and to every theological dictatorship which dissolves the historical ingredient of our religion' (Rumscheidt 1972: 31, 39). On Harnack's view, commitment to historical scholarship is no alien imposition but arises from the substance of Christian faith itself: 'as this religion teaches that God can only be truly known in Jesus Christ, it is inseparable from historical knowledge' (Harnack 1989: 108). To confess that Jesus Christ was *vere homo* licenses and demands scientific investigation of his individual personality and character in its contingent historical context.

Harnack explains that Jesus, as anyone, 'can think, speak, and do absolutely nothing at all in which his peculiar disposition and his own age are not coefficients' (Harnack

1989: 82–3). Only the historian can win objective access to these essential 'coefficients', rationally sifting out the kernel of reality from the husks of ancient testimony with its prophecy, mythology, and miracle. Harnack's own work portrays Jesus once again as a supreme religious personality, 'a man who has rest and peace for his soul, and is able to life and strength to others' because 'his gaze penetrated the veil of the earthly, and he recognised everywhere the hand of the living God' (Harnack 1901: 37–8). Jesus' identity is fused with the teaching at the heart of the religion he founds: the universal governance and benevolence of God, the supreme value of the human soul, and the summons to a higher morality motivated by love. We must rely upon the best deliverances of historical science if Christian faith and theology are to be delivered from the caprice of subjective piety and the unwarranted scepticism of faithless *Wissenschaft*. Harnack's conclusion is clear: historical Jesuology can and must provide the entire substance of any credible modern Christology, transforming the latter radically indeed.

Ernst Troeltsch

Ernst Troeltsch elaborated a further defence of the necessity of the historical Jesus for a vital modern Christian faith (Troeltsch 1990: 183ff.). The intelligibility of classical Christological dogma disintegrated under the assaults of historical criticism such that the 'eternal, timeless, unconditioned and supra-historical' Christ of the ancient faith bears no real relation to the 'finite and conditioned' portrait of Jesus now firmly set back into history by modern scholarship. In view of the progressively more 'devastating answers' returned to the question of our historical knowledge of Jesus, continued embrace of classical Christology becomes obscurantist, intellectually dishonest, and Christianly irresponsible. It is irresponsible because it alienates present-day Christianity from any credible portrait of the one who is and must remain the centre and 'rallying point' of its 'community and cult' if it is to have a future. Troeltsch conceives of the contemporary meaning of Jesus and his necessity in social-psychological rather than metaphysical terms, namely, the 'need a religious community has for a support, centre and symbol of its religious life'. Faith must insist upon Jesus as a 'holy reality' and not merely a beautiful myth, and so relies on critical historical analysis to establish and display the 'factuality of the total historical phenomenon of Jesus and the basic outline of his teaching and his religious personality' (Troeltsch 1990: 202, 197–8). Troeltsch invests in the possibility of overcoming the problems raised by modern historical consciousness with more and better history.

Such an account of Jesus' identity will eschew all metaphysical predicates, content to demonstrate 'the foundational meaning of the *personality* of Jesus as the *revelation* of God, the head of the community, and the effective symbol of saving and healing religious power, for as long as the Christian life-world endures' (Troeltsch 1991: 91). To replace traditional Christology with a Jesuology of this kind is the *sine qua non* of any properly *modern* Christianity, i.e., one which admits the claims of modern rationality and wants to retain the humanly valuable religious forces carried by Christianity in the West. The strategy is classically liberal in its isolation of the role of Jesus' personality and its beneficial impact upon piety as the basis for a renewal of Christianity; only a Jesus freed from the dead hand of dogma can enliven modern faith and thought. Distinctive, however, is Troeltsch's suggestion that the historic significance of Jesus' person should be parsed in sociological and psychological terms in recognition of the role 'cult and community' play in religious life. Such a strategy is exposed to the peril of evacuating Jesus' person into his *beneficia* understood naturalistically, and is invested in an historicism which might be regarded as inimical to essential features of Christian faith. Yet, others have suggested that it may hold untapped promise for Christological renewal underwritten by creative engagement with the social sciences (Coakley 1988: 193f.).

Doing Without the Historical Jesus: The Pursuit of Kerygmatic Christology

The sceptical conclusions Albert Schweitzer drew concerning the modern attempts to write the life of the historical Jesus are well known: the figure of the historical Jesus proves endlessly plastic. With the dual aim of demonstrating both the past facts about Jesus and his contemporary relevance, biographies of Jesus inevitably produced a hybrid figure—a 'half-historical, half-modern, Jesus' (Schweitzer 1968: 398)—situated in two worlds and a betrayal of both. The primary cure for this ill was a better history that eschewed modernization and held Jesus firmly in his own historical era. We need a prosecution of the quest that gets it right. The portrait of Jesus as a man saturated with Jewish apocalyptic expectation and submerged in eschatological modes of thinking and manners of life is Schweitzer's own contribution to ensuring that 'the true historical Jesus should overthrow the modern Jesus' (Schweitzer 1968: 403, 399). These were the features of the historical Jesus commonly suppressed in modern portraiture because they alienated Jesus from modernity, rendering him humanly remote and useless to morals and enlightened piety. They seemed to demand that we moderns part company with Jesus 'at the most decisive point' (Weiss 1971: 135).

But Schweitzer also seems to suggest that the results of critical history can be circumvented altogether in a present experience of Christ. He proposes that alongside the alien historical figure of the apocalyptic radical from Nazareth we are met by *another* Jesus: namely, a 'mighty spiritual force' whose own spirit reaches into the present by way of his simplicity, whose imperious teaching moves us by an immediate influence (Schweitzer 1968: 399, 401). Here the decisive material connection between the Jesus of history and the Christ of faith is unwinding. The identity and significance of Jesus here and now is distinct and insulated from that of the historical figure of Jesus then and there. As Schweitzer concludes, 'the truth is, it is not Jesus as historically known, but Jesus as spiritually arisen within men, who is significant for our time and can help it' (Schweitzer 1968: 401).

In the suggestion that the Jesus discovered by critical history should not only be distinguished but also substantially decoupled from the Christ of faith, we meet a hallmark of the second overarching trajectory beyond Strauss. Along this line of thinking, the critical reconstruction of the life of the historical Jesus is adjudged historically impossible, Christologically irrelevant, theologically illegitimate, or some combination of the three. Soundings in the work of Kähler, Herrman, and Bultmann will delineate these claims.

Martin Kähler and Wilhelm Herrmann

In a short set of pugnacious and influential essays published in 1896 as *The So-Called Historical Jesus and the Historic Biblical Christ of Faith*, Martin Kähler repudiated attempts to renew Christology on the basis of critical study of the historical Jesus and to 'set limits to the learned pontificating of the historians' (Kähler 1988: 73). Kähler argues that the very nature of the Gospels scuttles the historian's enterprise. The texts which tell of Jesus are, as to their origin, the confessions and testimonies of those who have believed upon him as the Christ; as to their content and ordering, they bespeak the interests and demands of faith; and as to their aim, they intend the promulgation and direction of that same faith in future generations. Arising from faith, ordered in faith, and keyed to the advancement of faith, the Gospels provide next to nothing of biographical interest but record instead the primitive and normative patterns of Christian proclamation. Indeed, they are the antithesis of the 'embellishing, rationalising, and psychologising rhetoric of recent biographies of Jesus' not because they represent some deficient antique species of the genre, but because they are in point of fact not historical biographies at all, but rather are 'already a form of dogmatics'. The paucity of historical source material to hand means that 'human creativity' must remain the primary motor driving attempts to write the life of Jesus (Kähler 1988: 93, 44, 43).

The person of whom the Gospels do tell us something is, Kähler asserts, the *historic biblical Christ*. The adjective 'biblical' signals acknowledgement that the canonicity of the Gospels is relevant to their substance and form. The adjective 'historic' has the force of 'effective across time' or 'history-making'; indeed it is synonymous with 'Saviour' since Kähler understands Jesus' saving work to be 'his person in its historic-suprahistoric effect' (Kähler 1988: 95). We should say that 'the real Christ, that is, the Christ who has exercised an influence on history … *this real Christ is the Christ who is preached*' and is delivered into the present 'without the midwifery of historical research' (Kähler 1988: 66, 121). Faith arises from the experience of 'being "overpowered" by Christ as he encounters us in the picture the Bible paints of him … the picture of Christ preached from and in faith' (Kähler 1988: 77).

To identify the truth of the biblical portrait of Jesus with its evangelical effectiveness across time is to court charges of subjectivism and pragmatism (i.e., it's true because it works). Alert to such worries, Kähler argues that the objective and backward referent for the biblical picture of Christ is the saving work of God in Christ. The formation of the apostolic witness itself is a primal work of Jesus *qua* Saviour: '*Christ himself is the originator of the biblical picture of the Christ*', a picture which bears the 'ineffaceable impress' of his own 'self-attestation' (Kähler 1988: 87, 79). Kähler expounds this claim:

> One might say … that the Christ of the Gospels is 'the transparency of the Logos', with the qualification that this diaphanous medium is not a nebulous legend but a tangible human being, portrayed in a rich and concrete though brief and concise manner. This is, of course, not enough for a complete biography of Jesus of Nazareth; but it is sufficient for preaching and dogmatics.
>
> (Kähler 1988: 95)

Kähler can relax about the problem of the historical Jesus because he conceives of the biblical witness as intrinsic to the outworking of the divine economy of salvation, something as he says, 'intrinsically interwoven with the creative means of grace, with the Word of God as it has arisen in history and done its work there' (Kähler 1988: 139). The question of how 'diaphanous' the earthly man Jesus can become and still be Christologically relevant remains.

In reasserting the divine origin and purpose of the Gospels and their portrait of Jesus he pushes back against the critical challenge posed by positive history in an attempt to shift the discussion into an explicitly dogmatic register. Kähler's concept of the '*historic* Christ' introduces into the debate something akin to the suggestive notion of *Wirkungsgeschichte*—'effective history'—and his emphasis on the missionary *preaching* of the primitive Church as the sole carrier of the memory of Jesus also anticipates Bultmann's appeal to the sole theological legitimacy of the *kerygmatic* Christ.

Wilhelm Herrmann—Bultmanns's formative teacher—treats the problem of the historical Jesus in his influential work, *The Communion of the Christian with God*, in a manner akin to Kähler. Christian faith arises from the conviction that 'God makes Himself know to us, so that we may recognise Him, through *a fact, on the strength of which we are able to believe on Him*', namely, 'the appearance of Jesus in history' (Herrmann 1906: 65, 59). But does not the 'fact' of Jesus recede into the past, leaving us with only a storied tradition which, *qua* history, is shrouded in the 'mist of probability' (Herrmann 1906: 70)? Against Harnack and Troeltsch, Herrmann denies that 'fair confidence' in the judgements of the historians can dispel such fatal uncertainty. There can be no overcoming of history by history; indeed such an attempt is 'a fatal error' and 'misuse of science' (Herrmann 1906: 76–7). Instead, the certainty of faith is attained only when 'Jesus Himself becomes a real power to us when He reveals His inner life to us' in a present and overwhelming experience of the *beneficia Christi* which recapitulates the first disciples' own experience of his messianic power. Herrmann conceives of a personal encounter in which the figure of Jesus previously mediated by the 'mere record' becomes immediate as the agent of his own presence, the 'Living One' (Herrmann 1906: 74). Anchored to this, Christian faith and theology can 'allow the historical criticism of the New Testament writings to have full play', for the ever-shifting results of historical research serve only to 'destroy certain false props of faith' and to afford fresh occasions for the believer to lay hold of 'that portrait of Jesus which he carries within him as absolute truth' (Herrmann 1906: 77). Herrmann concludes:

> When we speak of the historical Christ we mean that personal life of Jesus which speaks to us from the New Testament, as the disciples' testimony to their faith, but which, when we perceive it, always comes home to us as a miraculous revelation. That historical research cannot give us this we *know*. But neither will it ever take this from us by any of its discoveries. This we *believe*, the more we experience the influence that this picture of the glory of Jesus has upon us.
>
> (Herrmann 1906: 77–8)

The suggestion that the problem of the historical Jesus is overcome on the basis of a *contemporary* experience of faith occasioned by the portrait of Christ attested in the New Testament closely resembles Kähler's proposal. Yet Herrmann's account is more subjective, personal, and undogmatic in form than the more ecclesial, public, and doctrinally articulated position advanced by Kähler. Where Herrmann is content to speak of the 'fact' of Jesus at the origin of the Gospel witness, Kähler expounded more fully the claim that an act of divine self-attestation stands at the origin of the Gospel portrait as well as at the present point of its proclamation and reception in faith. Taken together these accounts display many of the features of the position which will be radicalized in the next generation by Rudolf Bultmann.

Rudolf Bultmann and Beyond

The key to Bultmann's position on the matter of the historical Jesus is the conviction that the New Testament materials are *kerygmatic* to the core: even in the earliest layers of tradition accessible within the Gospel texts, what is met is the faith and proclamation of the Church. The *kerygma* is the product of the Easter faith of the earliest Christians, a declaration of their trust and assurance in the Cross of Christ as God's own saving act. Its content is essentially paradoxical for it identifies a finite and contingent human destiny—namely that of Jesus of Nazareth—as at one and the same time the eschatological event of divine salvation. He is, echoing Herrmann, 'the fact of salvation' (Bultmann 1969b: 284). The historicity of this event is ingredient in the *kerygma* as one of the poles of the paradox of the Gospel. As Bultmann insists, 'he in whom God presently acts, through whom God has reconciled the world, is a real historical human being ... [an] historical occurrence in space and time' (Bultmann 1984: 41). Though our historical spades turn at the *kerygma*, that message itself gestures insistently towards the historical reality of Jesus as the one in whom the eschatological crisis of divine judgement and forgiveness has come.

In light of this, one might expect critical historical study of the life of Jesus to be essential to Christology. Bultmann argues otherwise. All the essential moves are made in the introduction to his early work *Jesus and the Word* and confirmed in later essays up into the 1960s (Bultmann 1934 and 1964). First, he argues that in disclosing the composite, layered, and kerygmatic character of the Gospels, form and redaction criticism have corroded the prospects of a credible reconstruction of the life and personality of Jesus. Plainly stated: 'we can now know almost nothing concerning the life and personality of Jesus, since the early Christian sources show no interest in either, are moreover fragmentary and often legendary; and other sources about Jesus do not exist' (Bultmann 1934: 8, 14). He observes that this work of radical historical criticism is a salutary iconoclasm: whereas conservative scholars were 'perpetually engaged in salvage operations', Bultmann said, 'I calmly let the fire burn, for I see that what is consumed is only the fanciful portraits of Life-of-Jesus theology, and that means nothing other than "Christ after the flesh". But "Christ after the flesh" is no concern of ours' (Bultmann 1969a: 132). Bultmann's interest in the historical identity of Jesus is concentrated solely upon him as the purposed 'bearer of a message' destined to become himself the content of the new Christian message. He admits he would be untroubled should the name of Jesus only appear in quotation marks as a cipher and 'abbreviation for the historical phenomenon with which are concerned' (Bultmann 1934: 8, 14). Such a gesture would reflect not only historical scepticism, but also—crucially—the attitude of Christian faith. Bultmann understands himself to be reproducing the disposition of the New Testament itself: 'Paul and John each in his own way indicate that we do not need to go beyond the *"that"*' (Bultmann 1964: 20). He explains:

> The proclaimer must become the proclaimed, because it is the fact *that* he proclaimed which his decisive. The decisive thing is his person (not his personality), *here* and *now*, the event, the commission, the summons. When the primitive community called him Messiah they were confessing he was the decisive event, the act of God, the inaugurator of the new world. The definitive element in the concept of the Messiah is not the kind of nature which may be ascribed to him. The Messiah is he who in the final hour brings salvation, God's salvation, the eschatological salvation which brings to an end all human ways and wishes.
>
> (Bultmann 1969b: 284)

The historical is only materially relevant as a constituent of the eschatological, that is, as the affirmation *that* Jesus Christ is the occasion and locus of God's ultimate saving activity. It is the historicity (*that*) and not the history (*what* or *how*) of Jesus that is Christologically relevant. As Bultmann puts it, the Christ of the *kerygma* is not an historical figure, but 'the *kerygma* presupposes the historical Jesus, however much it may have mythologised him' (Bultmann 1964: 18). If Christology is a properly eschatological discourse—and hence can only view Jesus *kata pneuma*—then it has no stake in the elaboration of an account of the Jesus of history. For the historian *qua* historian has no access to this reality as it can only be verified in and by the existential decision of faith itself. The logic of this position had been anticipated and made pellucid by Kierkegaard in his *Philosophical Fragments* (Kierkegaard 1985: 103).

Bultmann thoroughly rejects the Christological significance of critical reconstructions of the life of Jesus. Pursuit of the historical Jesus, in as much as it looks to validate belief in the Gospel, is a distraction—indeed a defection—from the *kerygma* wherein Jesus Christ, the saving Word of God, is in fact present to be encountered and grasped in and by faith. Bultmann's programme of 'demythologising' the New Testament is—in contrast to Strauss' work with the same concept—a *constructive* hermeneutical undertaking in the service of what Kähler called the 'transparency' of Jesus to the Logos. The interpretation of ancient mythical devices thus aims at clarification of contemporary proclamation of the *Christus praesens* rather than any exhumation of a Jesus of history.

A number of questions attend Bultmann's proposal: how 'transparent' can Jesus become before being nullified? What does it mean to affirm Jesus as a 'person' without 'personality' as Bultmann does? How coherent is the notion of a historical *that* without any meaningful extension, substance, and form? Is this actually what the New Testament witness presents? Does the meaning of the Pauline 'κατὰ σάρκα' map onto the critical historical perspective upon the figure of Jesus?

Already in 1935, fellow form critic, Martin Dibelius had signalled the need to redress an imbalance, arguing that 'the Gospels seek to give more than mere reports ... they seek to report historical facts as well as to engage in Christology. In the synthesis of these two tendencies lies their secret, and he who honestly engages in Gospel criticism must endeavour to explain this secret' (Dibelius 1935: 97). The generation after Bultmann attempted to deliver dogmatic Christology 'a better solution than the historical life-of-Jesus theology and the dehistoricizing kerygmatic theology' (Dahl 1991: 109). Various strategies were essayed to thicken the historical element of the *kerygma* by reference to a body of traditional and authentic *didache* concerning Jesus which either encompassed the *kerygma*, ran parallel to it, or was properly ingredient within it. A distinctive intervention came from Ernst Käsemann.

While continuing to affirm that the Gospels are *kerygmatic*, Käsemann rejects a radical historical scepticism which he considers theologically dangerous. The Gospels themselves provide the lynchpin, insisting as they do that their eschatological message of salvation concerns 'the earthly Jesus' and is 'bound to *this* man from Nazareth, to the arena of Palestine and to a concrete time with its special circumstances' (Käsemann 1964: 25, 31). Their very literary form reflects a conviction that 'the life history of Jesus has its relevance for faith'—indeed as Käsemann observes, 'if one has absolutely no interest in the historical Jesus then one does not write a Gospel' (Käsemann 1964: 25; 1969: 41). The Gospels embody a countermovement of *Historisierung* (historicizing) of the mythical subject of the primitive *kerygma*, a movement of which dogmatic Christology must take account (Käsemann 1964: 24). If it is exegetically illegitimate to conceive of Jesus apart from the perspective of Easter faith in his eschatological lordship, it is similarly problematic to conceive of him as Lord and Saviour apart from his identity as the earthly Jesus. In this we see how the New Testament message considers 'the historical Jesus among the criteria of its own validity', as a canon for resisting any drift toward Docetism, and a check upon spiritualist enthusiasm. Käsemann is worried that the emphases of the Kähler/Herrmann/Bultmann line reduced the identity of Jesus to a mathematical singularity whose abstraction allows 'Christ' to become a 'mytho-logical cipher' of uncertain referent (Käsemann 1969: 43–4). Käsemann sees both the eschatological content of Jesus' preaching of the Kingdom of God, and the course of his obedience to the Cross—the pattern of his life of self-humbling—as materially decisive historical elements of Jesus' identity. In Christological terms, Käsemann suggests that the Gospels commit the theological tradition to a concern for the integrity of the singular subject of the *status exaltationis* and *status exinanitionis*, the paradoxical identity of the exalted and the humiliated Lord (Käsemann 1964: 46).

A primary theological concern animating Käsemann is the need to resist the ideological captivity and self-justifying conceit into which Christian faith can lapse. Too thoroughgoing a historical scepticism and too complete an identification of Christ as present in the *kerygma* enfeebles faith's capacity for discernment:

> The question as to what is prior to faith in the sense that itupplies the criteria of faith can in the last resort only be answered christologically; and answered in such a way as to keep Christology distinct from ecclesiology and anthropology and in no circumstances to substitute either for it. Christ alone is the Ground, the Lord and Judge of faith ... the *kerygma* which is worthy of the name does not, then, simply make Christ present; it creates at the same time a proper distance between him and the hearer.
>
> (Käsemann 1969: 60)

One of the functions of the question of the historical Jesus in relation to Christology is to help to secure this distance. Acknowledgement of the individuality and otherness of the man from Nazareth—the mortified shape of his life and the uniqueness of his message of the advent of the Kingdom of God—is intrinsic, then, to the way in which the Christian community 'puts its faith beyond its own power to manipulate'. The particularity of the earthly Jesus is ingredient in the *extra nos* to which the *kerygma* testifies, and aids in discerning the spirits and resisting the transmutation of the preached Christ into the sublime object of religious ideology (Käsemann 1969: 61, 63). The Gospels themselves embody and bequeath to the Church this dynamic of inner Christological critique ensuring that, 'the function of recalling the historical Jesus is, within the framework of the Gospel, a permanent necessity' (Käsemann 1969: 64).

CONCLUDING REMARKS

Since it was raised in the nineteenth century, the question of the historical Jesus and its significance for Christology has become a permanent feature of the theological land-scape. The transit of this question from Strauss' *Leben Jesu* to the inauguration of the 'New Quest' after the Second World War has proven to be paradigmatic: many current debates read as variations on themes first worked through during this long-century of enquiry and debate. We conclude this discussion with two summary observations.

First, there is a sense in which the question of the historical Jesus and the Christ of faith mirrors—sometimes closely, oftentimes more remotely—aspects of traditional treatments of the relation of the human and divine natures. The ease with which modern thinkers deploy the language of ancient heresy in diagnosing the contemporary Christological problems at which they take aim—think, for example, of Käsemann's repeated invocation of Docetism—is telling in this regard. One could further argue that Bultmann's minimalist approach to the historical life of Jesus within the eschatological *kerygma*—a 'person without a personality'—echoes the logic of the *anhypostatic* character of Christ's humanity as conceived neo-Chalcedonian thinkers. Traditional concern for the unity of Christ's person and its coherence as the single subject of all Christological predication is reiterated (albeit in a different idiom) in debates concerning whether the *kerygma* of the Christ as Saviour and Lord derives from the man Jesus himself, his teaching, activity, and person. What is to be made of such parallels? Are they so many dogmatic ghosts not yet exorcized from modern historical conceptualities? Or do they signal the abiding and formative power of the eschatological grammar of the New Testament to press upon and mould ancient metaphysical and modern historical discourse alike?

Second, beginning with the comprehensive application of the notion of 'myth' by Strauss, modern historical scholarship has seen that the depictions of Jesus in the New Testament—and by extension their distillation, restatement, and conceptual expansion in the subsequent doctrines of the Church—are intrinsically *hermeneutical* in character. Critical analysis of how various literary conventions, poetical forms, typology, prophecy, symbolism, etc., function in the Gospels as *theologoumena* not only honours the essentially dogmatic or kerygmatic nature of the texts, it also invites reflection on their specifically Christological significance. For such mythical devices as are ingredient in the Gospels are not simply the literary and conceptual detritus of an antique worldview now alien to us. They are themselves hermeneutical devices, 'the means used to express the significance of the person, Jesus, as the decisive, eschatological saving act of God' (Bultmann 1969b: 284; 1984: 33–5). Pushing further we may reflect upon their more specifically *historiographical* function. John Marsh observes that the writing of history, whether ancient or modern, involves not only chronicling *that* and *how* a thing happened but also discerning and displaying *why* it happened, that is, it involves discursive strategies for pressing beyond simply recording 'what took place' in order to represent 'what was going on in what took place'. The Gospels are fundamentally concerned to relate *what took place* in the life and death of Jesus so that others may come to learn by the way these stories are told just *what was going on* that constitutes them as the Gospel of God (Marsh 1968: 18, 49). On such a view the thoroughly dogmatic and kerygmatic form of Gospels is seen to be integral to their character *as history* rather than being played off against history in a false positivist dichotomy. Bultmann's contention that critical study of the New Testament involved the work of *Geschichte* rather than mere *Historie*—that is, required an 'interpretation of history based on the historic (that is, on the existential) encounter with history' itself—arises from an appreciation of the mutual entanglement of the theological and historiographical in these texts (Bultmann 1964: 31).

It has recently been argued that classical Christological categories were neither imposed upon nor deduced from the biblical witness, but rather should be understood to redescribe patterns of judgements actually 'present *in* the texts' (Yeago 1994: 153). To approach to the biblical portrait of Jesus Christ as the subject of the evangelical *kerygma* with a view to perceiving how it operates *historiographically*, invites the thought that the analysis, repetition, and conceptual expansion of this portrait in Christological doctrine could be apprehended as an exercise in historiographical redescription, an expression of the need in every era to discern and to say again *what went on* in *what took place* in the life and death of man, Jesus of Nazareth.

Suggested Reading

Coakley (1988); Frei (1974); Hanson (1966); Morgan (1982).

Bibliography

Baillie, D. M. (1948), *God was in Christ* (London: Faber & Faber).

Barth, K. (1959), 'David Friedrich Strauss', in Barth, *Protestant Theology in the Nineteenth Century*, trans. J. Bowden (London: SCM Press), 527–54.

Bultmann, R. (1934), *Jesus and the Word*, trans. L. Pettibone Smith and E. Huntress Lantero (New York: Charles Scribner's Sons).

Bultmann, R. (1964), 'The Primitive Christian Kerygma and the Historical Jesus', in C. E. Braaten and R. A. Harrisville (eds.), *The Historical Jesus and the Kerygmatic Christ* (Nashville: Abingdon Press), 15–42.

Bultmann, R. (1969a), 'On the Question of Christology', in Bultmann, *Faith and Understanding*, trans. L. Pettibone Smith (New York: Harper & Row), 116–44.

Bultmann, R. (1969b), 'The Christology of the New Testament', in Bultmann, *Faith and Understanding*, trans. L. Pettibone Smith (New York: Harper & Row), 262–85.

Bultmann, R. (1984), 'New Testament and Mythology', in Bultmann, *New Testament and Mythology and Other Basic Writings*, trans. S. M. Ogden (Philadelphia: Fortress), 1–44.

Coakley, S. (1988), *Christ Without Absolutes: A Study of the Christology of Ernst Troeltsch* (Oxford: Clarendon Press).

Conzelmann, H. (1973), *Jesus* (Philadelphia: Fortress).

Dahl, N. A. (1991), *Jesus the Christ: The Historical Origins of Christological Doctrine*, trans. D. Juel (Minneapolis: Fortress).

Dibelius, M. (1935), *Gospel Criticism and Christology* (London: Ivor Nicholson & Watson).

Frei, H. (1974), *The Eclipse of Biblical Narrative: A Study of Eighteenth and Nineteenth Century Hermeneutics* (New Haven: Yale University Press).

Frei, H. (1985), 'David Friedrich Strauss', in N. Smart, J. Clayton, P. Sherry, and S. T. Katz (eds.), *Nineteenth Century Religious Thought in the West* (Cambridge: Cambridge University Press), vol. 1, 215–60.

Hanson, A. (1966), *Vindications: Essays on the Historical Basis of Christianity* (London: SCM Press).

Harnack, A. von (1901), *What is Christianity?* (New York: Putnam & Sons).

Harnack, A. von (1989), *Liberal Theology at its Height*, ed. H. M. Rumscheidt (London: Collins).

Harvey, A. E. (1982), *Jesus and the Constraints of History: The Brampton Lectures, 1980* (London: Duckworth).

Harvey, V. A. (1966), *The Historian and the Believer* (New York: Macmillan).

Herrmann, W. (1906), *The Communion of the Christian with God*, trans. J. S. Stanyon (London: Williams & Norgate).

Horton Harris, H. (1973), *David Friedrich Strauss and his Theology* (Cambridge: Cambridge University Press).

Kähler, M. (1988), *The So-Called Historical Jesus and the Historic Christ of Faith*, trans. C. E. Braaten (Philadelphia: Fortress).

Käsemann, E. (1964), 'The Problem of the Historical Jesus', in Käsemann, *Essays on New Testament Themes*, trans. W. J. Montague (London: SCM Press), 15–47.

Käsemann, E. (1969), 'Blind Alleys in the "Jesus of History" Controversy', in Käsemann, *New Testament Questions of Today*, trans. W. J. Montague (London: SCM Press), 23–65.

Kay, J. F. (1994), *Christus Praesens: A Reconsideration of Rudolf Bultmann's Christology* (Grand Rapids, Mich.: Eerdmans).

Kierkegaard, S. (1985), *Philosophical Fragments: Johannes Climacus*, ed. and trans. with introduction and notes by H. V. Hong and E. H. Hong (Princeton: Princeton University Press).Published Princeton, N.J.: Princeton University Press, c1985. >

Law, D. R. (2010), 'Kenotic Christology', in D. Fergusson (ed.), *The Blackwell Companion to Nineteenth Century Theology* (Oxford: Wiley-Blackwell), 251–80.

Lessing, G. E. (1972), *Lessing's Theological Writings*, trans. H. Chadwick (Stanford: Stanford University Press).

Mackintosh, H. R. (1912), *The Doctrine of the Person of Jesus Christ* (New York: Charles Scribner's Sons).

Marsh, J. (1968), *Saint John* (Harmondsworth: Penguin).

Massey, M. C. (1983), *Christ Unmasked: The Meaning of* The Life of Jesus *in German Politics* (Chapel Hill: University of North Carolina Press).

Morgan, R. (1982), 'Historical Criticism and Christology: England and Germany', in S. Sykes (ed.), *England and Germany: Studies in Theological Diplomacy* (Frankfurt am Main: Peter Lang), 80–112.

Renan, E. (1864), *Vie de Jésus* (Paris: Michel Lévy).

Robinson, J. M. (1959), *The New Quest of the Historical Jesus* (London: SCM Press, 1959).

Rumscheidt, H. M. (1972), *Revelation and Theology: An Analysis of the* Barth–Harnack Correspondence *of 1923* (Cambridge: Cambridge University Press).

Schweitzer, A. (1968), *The Quest of the Historical Jesus: A Critical Study of Its Progress from Reimarus to Wrede*, introduction by James M. Robinson, trans. W. Montgomery (New York: Macmillan).

Strauss, D. F. (1973), *The Life of Jesus Critically Examined*, trans. G. Eliot, ed. P. C. Hodgson (London: SCM Press).

Strauss, D. F. (1977), *The Christ of Faith and the Jesus of History: A Critique of Schleiermacher's* The Life of Jesus, trans. L. Keck (Philadelphia: Fortress).

Troeltsch, E. (1990), 'The Significance of the Historical Existence of Jesus for Faith', in Troeltsch, *Writings on Theology and Religion*, trans. R. Morgan and M. Pye (Louisville: Westminster/ John Knox), 182–207.

Troeltsch, E. (1991), *The Christian Faith*, trans. G. E. Paul (Minneapolis: Fortress).

Weiss, J. (1971), *Jesus' Proclamation of the Kingdom of God*, trans. R. H. Hiers and D. L. Holland (London: SCM Press).

Welch, C. (ed. and trans.) (1965), *God and Incarnation in Mid-Nineteenth Century German Theology: G. Thomasius, I. A. Dorner, A. E. Biedermann* (New York: Oxford University Press).

Wiles, M. (1976), 'Does Christology Rest on a Mistake?', in Wiles, *Working Papers on Doctrine* (London: SCM Press), 122–31.

Wiles, M. (1979), *Explorations in Theology 4* (London: SCM Press).

Wiles, M. (1994), 'Can We Still Do Christology?' in Wiles, *A Shared Search: Doing Theology in Conversation with One's Friends* (London: SCM Press), 164–75.

Yeago, D. (1994), 'The New Testament and the Nicene Dogma: A Contribution to the Recovery of Theological Exegesis', *Pro Ecclesia* 3: 152–78.

PART V

MODERN AND POSTMODERN CHRISTOLOGY

CHAPTER 22

CHRISTOLOGY FROM LESSING TO SCHLEIERMACHER

TROY A. STEFANO

DEFINING THE PROBLEMATIC: LESSING'S DITCH

WHETHER expressed in the dramatic form of a Lessing, the frigid constraints of a Kant, the Olympian serenity of a Goethe, or the Dionysiac fury of a Nietzsche, the contempt for incarnate divinity has been ubiquitous. The eighteenth century was a period of unprecedented epistemological and ontological legislation against such a belief: 'rules' were established, 'judges' were appointed, and 'violators' were prosecuted with the full power of one's brow. The belief that Jesus—an historic and contingent figure, receding into the abyss of history—is the Christ of God, the center of all history, the one in whom God reveals himself and makes present his eschatological fullness, is a capital offense. This is a violation of the separation of event and truth as two distinct genera, which Lessing dubbed 'the ugly, broad ditch', and summarized in the phrase: 'Accidental truths of history can never become the proof of necessary truths of reason' (Lessing 1956: 53). The implication of this 'ditch' is that there are two orders that cannot be traversed: that of events, the historical, the ontic, the existential, the categorical, the particular; and that of truth, the metaphysical, the ontological, the essential, the transcendental, the universal; and there cannot be any Christological 'intermingling' of the two. Historical processes and events are immanent, contingent, and relative.

After all, how can an individual point in the stream of history have an absolute and unconditional meaning (Ratzinger 2004: 194–5; Schönborn 2010: 39)? Can the figure of Nazareth tip the entire scale of history in his favor, considering that he is outweighed by the two thousand years that have passed since his death, not to mention the full weight of the future (Von Balthasar 1992: 25)? If history itself has not passed a sufficient judgment, then the Enlightenment philosophers certainly have: *all* historical events are relative, and this includes the life of Jesus. And thus, any attempt to find in Jesus the definitive self-revelation of God was marked out of bounds a priori. One could classify the way in which Lessing's ditch formed the scope of the Christological problematic in the late eighteenth century in three ways:

1. *Epistemological-horizontal dimension ('the elliptical problem'):* It was with Lessing's 'ditch' in mind that Reimarus began the history of Protestant biblical criticism, in which the 'simple figure of Nazareth' was divested of the 'ceremonial robes' of dogma (see Schweitzer 2005: 13–26), leading to the separation of the 'Jesus of history' (the categorical, immanent, historical) and the 'Christ of faith' (the transcendental, rational, ideal). Jesus could no longer claim any ultimate uniqueness: he was a figure in history, and like all historical figures and events, his significance was relative. He should be subject to historical-critical inquiry and any excess claims should be excised. There can be no ontological continuity between the pre-Easter Jesus and the post-Easter Jesus, whether understood in terms of the early Christian witness-testimony or the continuation of that testimony in the community of today. Severed from the Jesus of history, the Christ of faith became a free-radical, in need of both explanation and, if its significance is to be retained, a surrogate attachment (cf. Strauss' attempt to secure an anthropological surrogate, as well as that of Feuerbach: Strauss 1973: 780).

2. *Vertical-ontological dimension ('the Chalcedonian problem'):* Lessing's 'ditch' called into question the sufficiency and plausibility of faith as the mediator between the transcendental and the categorical. He regarded the Chalcedonian claim that Jesus is God and man as a confusion of genus ('if that is not a μετάβασις εἰς ἄλλο γένος, then I do not know what Aristotle meant by this phrase', Lessing 1956: 54; cf. Aristotle, *De Caelo*: Book 1, Cap. 1, 268b 1). *Tertium non datur.* But it was only after Lessing that non-plausibility and non-sufficiency became impossibility (cf. Reimarus 1985; and afterwards, Kant 2005a: 6:119; Schleiermacher 2011: §94). The 'ditch' became concretized into ontological legislation: the a priori presupposition of the incommunicability of the transcendental and categorical gave rise to the premise of historical immanentism, operative in historical-critical exegesis. The traditional doctrine of Jesus as 'one person in two natures' is rendered impossible a priori, for that would entail, respectively, (a) the communication of the two incommunicable orders (by way of hypostatic union in one person); and (b) a violation of exclusively intra-historical processes.

3. *Eschatological-theological dimension ('the Trinitarian problem'):* The consequence of this Christological dissolution is the separation of Christology from the doctrine of God. Once there is the a priori legislation that between the transcendental and categorical there cannot be any true communication or identity, Jesus cannot be the eschatological self-disclosure of God as he is in himself—the presupposition that led to the formation of the doctrine of the Trinity by the early Church. With one decree, God as Trinity and Jesus as eternally pre-existent Son must be rejected. If Jesus is to retain any significance after such a separation, it is on immanentist terms.

The Landscape of Nineteenth-Century Solutions: The Place of Schleiermacher

The late eighteenth to mid-nineteenth century witnessed various approaches to this 'gap', which inevitably also entails corresponding reformulations of the three dimensions of the Christological problematic. Broadly speaking, there were two categories: those which attempted to 'close' the gap by arguing that it can be overcome by a higher-order knowledge and those which attempted to preserve the relation between the categorical and transcendental by faith.

'Closing' the Ellipse by Higher-Order Knowledge

Such diverse philosophical approaches as those of Kant and Hegel could be brought together analytically under this category insofar as they attempted to 'embrace' the horizontal-epistemological ellipse within a philosophical 'circle' of higher knowledge, whether in the form of 'a moral idea of reason' (Kant) or 'absolute knowledge' (Hegel). For Kant, the God-man, at best, is a temporal vehicle for a timeless truth. Kant makes a clear distinction between an *empirical* (historical) faith' and a *rational* faith' (Kant 2005a: 6:119; cf. the contrast between an 'ecclesiastical faith' and a 'pure moral faith' in 6:117). The one begins with the given of history; the other with the postulates of reason. For Kant, 'in the appearance of the God-man, the true object of the saving faith is not what in the God-man falls to the senses, or can be cognized through experience, but the prototype lying in our reason which we put in him (since, from what can be gathered from his example, the God-man is found to conform to the prototype), and such a faith is all the same as the principle of a good life conduct' (6:119). Thus, the relationship between the 'moral idea of reason' (the surrogate for the Christ of faith) and the 'non-real ideal' (*Urbild*) or 'prototypical example' (the surrogate for the Jesus of history) is one of exemplarity and non-identity. The Trinity, which presupposes the transcendental identity of God and Jesus, is considered an *adiaphora* (cf. Kant 2005a: 6:140–7, 2005b: 7:39).

Hegel tries to overcome the 'gap' by calling into question the intrinsic incommunicability of the two orders. For Hegel, the categorical *is* the transcendental in the mode of antithesis, and thus, it is a function of the transcendental's ('the Absolute's') self-othering and self-actualization. Hegel's *idea* contains the structure of thesis–antithesis–synthesis, in which one can traverse Lessing's gap both epistemologically and ontologically through a logic of dialectical and teleological development. In Hegel, unlike Kant, the relationship between 'the Absolute' (the surrogate for the Christ of faith) and the 'historical actualization of the idea' (the surrogate for the Jesus of history) is one of ontological identity, and not merely one of exemplarity (Hegel 1956: 318–36, 1977: §748–78). But like Kant, he attempts to 'close' the gap by establishing a purview that makes the dictates of the ideal and rational—which serve as the surrogate for the Christ of faith—dominant, and makes the function of the historical realization of the 'idea' recessive by relation. The 'gap' in both cases is not overcome by faith, but by a 'closed' philosophical circle (Hegel 1977: §788–808, 1991: §214). As Schelling realized, this resolution may deal successfully with Lessing, but it eviscerates the Christian theological and soteriological drama. For acts, both human and divine, must be grounded in freedom, and so can never be established by reason, but only received by faith (Staudenmaier 1840: §391–6; Schelling 1977: 160, 162).

'Mediating' the Ellipse by Faith

Of those who engaged this problematic within the ellipse of faith, there are four analytically distinguishable groups:

1. *Those who 'resolve' the dilemma by reducing the transcendental to the categorical— 'Christology from below' and the question of transcendental limits:* Strauss had made the 'critical investigation of the life of Jesus' the test which traditionally Christology must pass for retainability and, as Strauss was quick to point out, once the Christ of faith was made to siphon through historical critical analysis, there was nothing of substance left: 'We are no longer Christians' (Strauss 1903: 61). Some theologians, however, were more optimistic. While agreeing with Strauss that the Jesus of history is the standard and criterion for all claims of faith, theologians disagreed widely about what kind of claims such a Jesuology could license. For some, he was a 'great soul' (Renan 1863), whose significance rests in embodying an ideal. He was a (pacifist-universalistic) 'religious personality' (Harnack 1972: 36–43) who is a 'holy reality' that stands as the source of and symbol for the Christian community (Troeltsch 1991: 88–91). His significance was in his 'ethical profession' (Ritschl 1874: 412–13). In these cases, there is a definitive disjunction between the transcendental and the categorical as in Strauss, but there is attributed to Jesus a certain uniqueness, largely understood in terms of the intra-historical influence of his personality and example, which becomes the surrogate for the Christ of faith. Such a uniqueness is established in the relationship between the historically-critically established figure and the sociologically-psychologically established community that he influenced. The heights of his uniqueness—whether he is *merely* a 'great soul' among a history of great figures, as in Renan, or the ethical revelation of the Kingdom of God, as in Ritschl, for example—vary widely; nonetheless, they never broach the divine.

The other direction taken during this period was that of German (Thomasius and Gess) and British (Forsyth and Mackintosh) Kenoticism. These kenoticists are united in the way in which they reject not only Christ's dyophysitism, but more importantly, his dyothelitism; however, unlike the first path taken by Renan, Harnack, and others, which creates an ideal surrogate for the displaced divinity, the kenoticists siphoned the transcendental into the categorical by changing the traditional doctrine of morphological kenosis—that God changed his 'form' of glory into the 'form' of humility in the Incarnation, based on Phil. 2:6's ὅς ἐν μορφῇ Θεοῦ ὑπάρχων—into a doctrine of substantial kenosis. God as divine is stripped of his attributes and becomes the human Jesus. The kenoticists attempt to overcome the epistemological-horizontal and the vertical-ontological gaps by reducing the transcendental to the categorical to the point of ontological identification. A 'gap' now appears between whatever the divine was before Jesus and whatever the divine is as a result of its substantial change in order to become categorical in Jesus. Because of this newly inserted 'gap', Isaak Dorner rightly characterizes such an approach as turning the Incarnation into a mere theophany (Dorner 1853: 1270; cf. Baillie 1948: 94–8); since Incarnation and a doctrine of Revelation traditionally presuppose the revelation of God *as he is in himself*.

2. *Those who reinterpret the dilemma by turning the gap into a theological positive—the non-historic and the transcendental encountered existentially*: In a section entitled 'something about Lessing', Kierkegaard writes that 'Lessing opposes what I would call quantifying oneself into a qualitative decision' (Kierkegaard 1992: 95). Kierkegaard engages in an important hermeneutical shift: unlike Reimarus and the ensuing tradition of liberal Protestant criticism, Kierkegaard reads Lessing as claiming the a priori 'incommensurability' rather than 'incommunicability' of the two genera. This has three important consequences: the first is that Lessing's own word, *der Sprung* ('the leap'), which was used to express his inability to travel between 'accidental truths of history' and the 'necessary truths of reason' now became a term freighted with immense existential weight to express an act of isolation for which there is no mediation (cf. Ferreira 2006: 213). For Kierkegaard, 'the leap is a category of decision' (Kierkegaard 1992: 99; cf. 2010: 22). The second consequence is that the Incarnation, as a metaphysical claim, is no longer ruled out a priori: for, it is no longer a question of the impossibility of communication between genera, but of their incommensurability (and thus now a question of existential and cognitive urgency). The question now becomes how a Christian understands God revealed in Christ. Kierkegaard observes that our 'leap' is not from the homogeneous to the non-homogeneous; rather, all of our leaps are within a relative degree of homogeneity, since the Christian paradox is 'Christ's entry into the world': that is, the qualitatively different (non-homogeneous) leap is 'the one made by God coming into Time, *not by us*. On *our* side a transition may be a leap (that is, a qualitative transition) even if homogeneous in contrast to the leap made by God into the world' (Ferreira 2006: 218; cf. Kierkegaard 2010).

The third consequence of transferring Lessing's ditch into an existential register is that for Kierkegaard, 'there is no "objective" means of access, in the sense of modern historical "objectivity", to an adequate understanding of Jesus Christ, not even of his crucifixion' (Kierkegaard 1992: 386). Seen as the God-man, who suffered both humanly and superhumanly, Christ is 'an extremely unhistorical person' in the 'situation of contemporaneity' (Kierkegaard 1992: 60). Since Christ is not accessible through historical means, Kierkegaard lays an emphasis on the 'form' (*Gestalt*) of the New Testament depiction of Christ, and not on the historical Jesus, as the basis for our qualitative 'leap'. There is a 'continuity of form' between the New Testament Christ and our experience of him through personal relation, but only retrospectively from the vantage point of existential belief (Kierkegaard 2010: 399–400). Kierkegaard leaves open the gap between the historical Jesus and the biblical Christ. Thus, Kierkegaard can at once criticize aesthetic theology (cf. Kierkegaard 1987; Von Balthasar 2009: 48–52), and at the same time be an aesthetic theologian by grounding the urgency of decision in an encounter with the 'form' of Christ in the New Testament. For Kierkegaard, faith does not mediate between the categorical and the transcendental by allowing the historical Jesus to become diaphanous to the Son of God; rather, faith presents one with a transcendental encounter that is aesthetic and non-historic precisely because it is pan-(or supra-)historic ('contemporaneous', in Danish, *Samtidighed*). Emanuel Hirsch makes a good point that an 'historical simultaneity' is needed aside Kierkegaard's 'subjective-theoretical' simultaneity, to make an encounter with Jesus Christ truly possible (Hirsch 1978: 48).

3. *Those who 'resolve' the dilemma by positing the Christ of faith with minimal historicity—the kerygmatic Christ and the formal limits of historicity*: The second trajectory after Strauss is to prioritize the Christ of faith, with a minimal connection to the Jesus of history. While Martin Kähler and Wilhelm Herrmann present relatively 'thicker' historical grounding of the Christ of faith in the Jesus of history, Rudolf Bultmann minimizes the historical connection to a merely formal claim *that* Jesus existed, and radicalizes the bipolarity between that Jesus and the kerygmatic Christ (Bultmann 1969: 284). And he explains the 'gap' between the Jesus of history (stimulus) and the Christ of faith through a process of mythologization, wherein the revelatory worth of Christology takes place. In the case of the first group, the Christ of faith was severed from the Jesus of history, in order to allow the latter as established by historical-critical analysis to keep Christ-talk in check. The second category is the opposite to the first: the Christ of faith is affirmed, whereas the Jesus of history as established by historical-critical method is rejected; and the only connection between the Christ of faith and its ground is aesthetic (the 'form' of Christ in the Gospels), but not the Jesus of history. Christ is only known qualitatively and existentially, but cannot be known quantitatively or historically. This third category, as represented by Bultmann, differs from the second insofar as it posits the formal existence of the historical Jesus. But it differs from the first not only insofar as it preserved the Christ of faith, but also insofar as it was sufficient *that* Jesus existed, but how he existed, or his personality and influence was of no concern. For Bultmann, the continuity between the pre-Easter Jesus and the post-Easter Jesus was bridged by a process of mythologization. The figure of Nazareth, that is the subject of historical-critical analysis, was 'dressed' up with 'forms' (expressions, categories, and so forth) that were not intrinsic developments of his own 'form' but 'impositions', albeit existentially meaningful ones. There is no continuity of subject between Jesus and Christ. 'Jesus Christ', as a totality, is a bipolar phenomena.

4. *Those who 'resolve' the dilemma by forming a theory of correlation*: While Schleiermacher precedes and was a formative influence for many of the figures described above, analytically he presents a distinct pathway in the nineteenth century that, in light of his influence, has proven to be the richest of these solutions. The challenge faced by the third category is that it does not have the ability to form a coherent and/or substantial connection between Jesus and Christ, person and personality, figure

and influence. This point helps to shed light on Schleiermacher's innovation and signifi-cance: taking advantage of historicism's displacement of the Kantian emphasis on the exact sciences, he argues regressively from historical effect to pyscho-personal cause. The logic of his argument could be presented thus:

- Schleiermacher begins with the philosophical and historical presupposition that any historic figure exercises a certain degree of influence; and that a person's personality is mediated in and through that influence, in such a way that, by looking at that influ-ence, one could establish a posteriori and retrospectively certain claims about the personality that would give rise to such an influence. Thus, there is a qualitative cor-respondence across history between personality and influence, and the magnitude of the former determines the scope of the latter; and the scope of the latter, conversely, can disclose the magnitude of the former. Inverting the logic of Melanchthon's 'to know Jesus is to know his effect', Schleiermacher argues, 'to know his effects is to know Jesus', thereby beginning with the *experience* of Jesus in the community of faith, and a posteriori attempting to establish the historical conditions for such an experi-ence and influence in Jesus' personality (Schleiermacher 2011: §87, 3; §91, 2).
- The function of Christianity is to draw historical being through the mediation and influence of Jesus into the ground of its existence by the experience (*Ankündigung*) or feeling (*Gefühl*) of Absolute Dependence (*schlechthinniger Abhängigkeit*), which is also called God-consciousness (§11; cf. §94, §100).
- Looked at retrospectively, the personality of Jesus must be such that he is able to have that kind of effect (i.e., effect that kind of God-consciousness in us) (§92). From this, Schleiermacher concludes that he must be the prototypical God-man, who has perfect God-consciousness, and who can spread (effect) that conscious-ness to others in and through history (§92). Looked at progressively, the person of Jesus radiates a personal influence that is historical, but at every moment, can only be explained by direct divine causality (§91.1; §94.2; §13).

The heart of Schleiermacher's insight is the continuity (of person, personality) amidst discontinuity (historical and geographical disparities) between the pre-Easter and post-Easter Christ. On the one hand, Schleiermacher defeats Kant at his own 'game' by using subjective consciousness as the basis for establishing a categorical truth. On the other hand, he uproots Lessing's axiom by showing how a categorical figure could be the mediator of a transcendental truth (i.e., God-consciousness).

Within the landscape of those who mediate the ellipse by faith, by comparison to the first group, Schleiermacher is able to utilize his theory of 'the historical impact of per-sonality' to establish an historical Jesus that both evades the historical-critical critique of Jesus in the Gospels, while forming a basis for the Christ of faith. He is able to retain the Christ of faith as Kierkegaard does, but he does not ground Christ in the Gospel text aesthetically, since the biblical text was largely the subject of the Enlightenment criticisms like those of Reimarus and Strauss. Instead he grounds that faith in the personality of Jesus himself. Schleiermacher's Jesus is not bipolar, but a charismatic and God-filled man, whose person and personality are so intimately wed that his influence on the community of faith today cannot be explained apart from the historical life and person of Jesus and a direct divine causality in mediating his religious influence on us (§91.1; §94.2). Apart from the Tübingen theologians—whose legacy in the twentieth century cannot be separated from the overpowering shadow of Schleiermacher's influence (e.g., Walter Kasper, Joseph Ratzinger, Hans Urs von Balthasar)—it seems that Schleiermacher's negotiation was the best available: despite Strauss' quibbles (Strauss 1977: 159–69), we gain 'back' a basis for faith in Jesus … but it comes at the cost of replacing Chalcedonian orthodoxy with a historically immanent surrogate—a perfected human being with 'God-consciousness'. Furthermore, Schleiermacher's impact outside of the elitist ranks of theology lends to the task of engaging him a certain existential urgency. (Christoph Cardinal Schönborn observes a widespread 'neo-Arianism' that sees Jesus as a man accredited by God, but nonetheless as radically immanent; Schönborn 2010: 41–2.) Notwithstanding, within the tradition of liberal Protestantism, Schleiermacher is the closest to the mediaeval synthesis in which the faith of the community (i.e., 'form') corresponded to the Object of revelation (i.e., 'content'). Schleiermacher's own lack of determinacy amplifies his possibilities. But it is here that we see Schleiermacher as both promise and problem.

SCHLEIERMACHER AS PROMISE AND PROBLEM

Schleiermacher has the proverbial wax nose. His own thought, while providing many solutions to the Enlightenment's challenges, presents an even greater challenge to the doctrines and dogmas of traditional Christology. As a Christian theologian who wrestles with these questions from within the community of faith, Schleiermacher represents the internalization of the Enlightenment's challenges within the bosom of theology. Unlike a Lessing or a Kant, or even a Reimarus or a Strauss, Schleiermacher does not bring an extrinsic standard against which to measure the Christian faith, but develops a Christomorphic standard that measures all other claims (cf. Niebuhr 1964: 210–14). But for every solution, he posed a new challenge; and thus, the history of theology's dealings with Lessing after the nineteenth century became transfigured into a history of the affirmative or negative reception of Schleiermacher.

The Schleiermachian Transfiguration of the 'Elliptical Problem'

In order to establish Jesus' historicity and personality apart from the Gospel texts and only according to the 'impact factor' of the subjective experience of the Christian community, Schleiermacher limits himself to a naturalistic understanding of historical causality that can serve the function of establishing an historical cause as a result of an historical effect. 'The appearance of the Redeemer in history is, as divine revelation, neither an absolutely supernatural nor an absolutely supra-rational thing' (Schleiermacher 2011: §13). The upside of his solution is that Schleiermacher argues that what the Christian community says about Jesus is grounded in Jesus himself. His claim of historical influence provides a thread that weaves together the Jesus of history and the Christ of faith. The downside is that this requires the reduction of Jesus to what can be transmitted as a matter of historical influence and to what therefore the Christian community experiences.

This has two consequences. First, the relationship between the Jesus of history and the Christ of faith is established qualitatively, by a value judgment in the subjective religious experience of the Christian community. Schleiermacher's difference here from Kierkegaard and Bultmann is that he takes this qualitative claim as positing a quantitative and historical condition, essentially by-passing the New Testament texts. For, 'faith in Jesus as redeemer was not based on details, but develops out of a total impression—from which it follows only that there are no details in existence which could have prevented that impression' (§99, *Postscript*). Second, the traditional separation between Jesus' person and work is now conflated into a single reality: soteriology retrospectively posits, a posteriori, Christ's essence (his personality). For, 'The peculiar activity and the exclusive dignity of the Redeemer imply each other and are inseparably one in the self-consciousness of believers' (§92). The full significance of soteriology must be enfolded within the physical and personal influence of Jesus' personality, that is, within his public ministry, leading up to and including the Passion. The result is that the traditional locus of Christ's soteriological work in the *Triduum*—definitively including his death, descent into Hades, and resurrection—is marked as irrelevant for Christological consideration, since they are factors that cannot be transmitted historically as part of Jesus' influence. The process of enfolding the traditional significance of the *Triduum* into Jesus' personality entailed an irretrievable reduction of the scope and meaning of Christ's work.

The result these two aspects have for traditional Christology can be seen in the way they pan out in those whom he influenced. Schleiermacher is vague regarding the extent to which the figure of Jesus is open to quantitative investigation. His thought can go in the direction of Barth, for example, and imply a 'closed' ellipse between community and person that sits 'above' historical analysis, and which is content with the formal assertion of the Redeemer's historical existence and personality; but conversely, his thought can go in the direction of Kasermann, or even Drey and Möhler, in the nineteenth century, or Pannenberg, Kasper, Ratzinger, and Von Balthasar, in the twentieth, among others, in positing the true quantitative immersion of Jesus as a condition for his qualitative effect, and as such, the hospitality of (kerygmatic) Christology to historical inquiry. The latter figures are quick to point out that what is at stake is not simply historical curiosity or an obsession with the Kantian exact sciences, but the internal coherence of Jesus himself as an historic being. Furthermore, the extent to which Jesus is deemed quantitative is the extent to which the New Testament texts themselves would have a bearing on understanding his person and personality.

As the nineteenth century came to a close, and for the period leading up to the Second World War (before the so-called 'Second Quest'), an increased optimism became prevalent regarding the transparency of the New Testament texts to the historical figure of Jesus. The course of this discussion in the twentieth century will take the form of asking the extent to which Jesus was himself conscious of his significance (as established by the New Testament texts) as the measure for the continuity between personality and community (the original Schleiermachian ellipse). With Johannes Weiss' *Die Predigt Jesu vom Reiche Gottes* (1892), the original Schleiermachian ellipse, which proposed a timeless, ethical 'impact' by Jesus' personality, came to a close and the ellipse was expanded into new categories: Schleiermacher's relationship between Jesus' personality and the community of faith became the relationship between Jesus' self-understanding of the apocalyptic significance of his own life in relation to the horizon of the totality of history (the universal, pan- and meta-historic scope of his work). Such a 'stretching' of Schleiermacher's ellipse threatened to 'snap' the thread, and render Jesus, once again, into a duality.

The Schleiermachian Transfiguration of the 'Chalcedonian Problem'

For Schleiermacher, regardless of the authority associated with any specific confession, whatever discourse does not serve the task of shedding light upon a *direct* aspect of the collective and personal experience of Christ should be dispensed with as useless and inexpedient (Schleiermacher 2011: §15–19; §95; cf. §92.2). Chalcedon gets the axe, along with Constantinople III and Nicaea I. Whatever Schleiermacher says about Christ, he is always on '*this* side' of the Creator–creature divide, and he tolerates no piercing of those barriers.

The potency of Schleiermacher's own Christology is the way in which it is able to overcome Lessing's ditch, as well as make fuller use of the philosophical development of the term 'person' in the direction of self-consciousness and subjectivity—a development that occurred largely after and only in indirect dependence on the original theological context of personhood (i.e., *hypostasis*, and eventually, *prosopon* and *personae* as Trinitarian terms). Schleiermacher begins, like Aquinas, by positing that God as the Absolute must be *purus actus*; but unlike Aquinas, he sees this as signifying that God can only be communicated to the world through 'vital receptivity' in feeling and cognition, and that no 'substantial' presence can be asserted (§94). The world, as a whole, has the same degree of passivity and dependence upon God; and thus, God's omnipresence, grounded in God as *pure act*, must be ubiquitous and the same. The only factor that can license the claim of God having 'a greater presence' is the 'vital receptivity' and consciousness of the world's relation to God in a rational self-consciousness, which Schleiermacher calls 'God-consciousness'. The consciousness of one's absolute dependence on God becomes the surrogate for the traditional language of God's substantial presence. This means that he opposes Lessing, much like Kierkegaard, by claiming that the 'gap' is not one defined by incommunicability, but by incommensurability. '[F]or to ascribe to Christ an absolutely powerful God-consciousness, and to attribute to Him an existence of God in Him, are exactly the same thing' (§94.2). The point is that for Schleiermacher, one's actions and personality flow out of one's personhood; and one's personhood is identified with one's self-consciousness; and if in the person of the Redeemer his self-consciousness is one and the same as his consciousness of God, then it follows that his person, personality, and actions have a revelatory value at 'every moment', and could be called the 'indwelling of the Supreme Being as His peculiar being and His inmost self' (§94.2).

The fact that Schleiermacher frames the Christological question in terms of gradations of God-consciousness means that Jesus becomes a humanist *par excellence*. Schleiermacher develops the theme (perhaps in a way unprecedented since Irenaeus) that Jesus' life is the 'completed creation of human nature' (§94.3). Christology becomes the summit of anthropology, and the source for the fullest human realization. By bearing 'God-consciousness' in such an unprecedented way, Jesus not only developed humanity's potency for God-consciousness, but fulfilled and perfected human nature (§94.2). What results is a Jesus who is a humanist *par excellence*, insofar as he embodies the human 'ideal' (*Urbild*) historically (§93). But, the cost of attaining this fully self-conscious and exclusively human Jesus is the thoroughgoing rejection of Chalcedonian dogma and a radical reinterpretation of its meaning.

In §96, Schleiermacher sets forth seven specific attacks on the Chalcedonian definition, all of which are governed by his overall constriction of Christological meaning to an immanent frame:

- *Contra pre-existence*: He attacks the idea of a *Logos endiathetos* by claiming that the subject of reference in the Gospels (and in our faith) is the *unified* (incarnate) person of Jesus. And thus, the subject cannot be transferred to a pre-existent being.
- *Contra 'one person in two natures'*: We cannot claim that Jesus is 'one person in two natures', since that would be to presuppose that divine nature and human nature are two species under one broader genus of 'nature'. 'Nature', as such, cannot be attributed to God. 'Nature' can only be predicated of finite existence; and a true understanding of God recognizes that the Absolute is 'beyond all existence and being'.
- *Contra Chalcedon's dyophysitism*: If 'person' means 'an Ego which is the same in all the consecutive moments of its existence', how can Jesus be 'one person' and preserve a 'unity of life' if he has a duality of natures? Either one nature gives way to the other for the sake of the unity of life, or the unity of life gives way to the duality of natures.
- *Contra Constantinople III's dyothelitism*: The same thing occurs with the 'two wills' in Christ: if there are two wills, there is no unity of person, even if the wills always 'agree'. But if there is unity of person, then one will must give way to the other.
- *Contra two minds/consciousnesses*: Again, the same is true regarding the 'two reasons': either he can see things omnisciently and simultaneously with divine reason, or he can see things one after another with human reason.

- *Contra use of the term 'nature' in Christology*: Considering that Trinitarian talk has 'three persons' in 'one nature', or more often, 'one essence' and Christology has 'one person' in 'two natures', there is an imprecise and limited use of the terms insofar as they have different meanings as pertains to Jesus and as pertains to God.
- *Contra the use of the term 'person' in Christology*: The same goes for 'person'. On the one hand, there is 'one person' who 'bears two natures'; on the other, there is 'one nature' that is shared by 'three persons'.

The main point of Schleiermacher's dogmatic critique is that Jesus is *homoousios* with us, and that means that he must have a truly human personality and a fully human self-consciousness. Jesus' peculiar relation to God can only be considered after that *fact*. For Schleiermacher, this means the end of Chalcedon, Constantinople III, and ultimately, Nicaea. The result of such a critique for the twentieth century is that theologians who wish to make use of Schleiermacher's ellipse as a solution to the Enlightenment critiques, albeit in modified or 'stretched' forms, were faced with a dilemma: Either they accept the cost of radically reinterpreting the fundamental Christian proclamation that it is God who saves us in Jesus in the way that Schleiermacher did. Or they are faced with the task of thinking through Christology on the basis of his critiques. The fate of Chalcedon—and with it, the full meaning that God saves in Jesus—now largely rests with engaging Schleiermacher.

The Schleiermachian Transfiguration of the 'Trinitarian Problem'

Bracketing Schleiermacher's detailed critique of the doctrine of the Trinity (Schleiermacher 2011: §171), there are three key points regarding the relationship between his Christology and theology: the first is that he recognizes that the traditional doctrine of the Trinity depends upon an ontological identification of Jesus (as Son) with God (as Father). Second, while excluding such an identification a priori, based on the arguments outlined above, Schleiermacher seeks the underlying Christological experience that gave rise to such an explanation: it is the way in which Jesus as fully human person brings personhood to realization in others through himself; and to be a person is to be fully conscious of God. Third, the experience, therefore, of Jesus' own absolute dependence on God was interpreted as the Father–Son relation, in which God was made present in him; our experience of absolute dependence on God (the Father), is mediated through him (the Son), and thus, entails God's presence in us (the Spirit). These are the tradition's names for variations in the Christian consciousness of God as it has unfolded in Christ; but ontologically speaking, these variations cannot be inscribed eschatologically in God. Schleiermacher offers a phenomenological analysis of the Trinity, and then proceeds to reduce it to its underlying Christian experience, in which the difference between Sabellius and Athanasius seems irrelevant (§172). Any eschatological distinctions in God's self are out of bounds. The immanent Trinity is thus rendered superfluous and illegitimate, since what is perceived as the economic Trinity (that God, through Christ, creates persons) is disconnected ontologically from God's self. If there is to be any saving of the Trinity, God's presence in Christ must pierce the iron wall of the Creator–creature divide in the manner of Chalcedon. Thus, once again, the reception of Chalcedon after Schleiermacher bears ultimate, if not eschatological, weight.

The Twentieth Century—Living within and beyond Schleiermacher: Testing Limits

Considering Schleiermacher's constriction of the correlation between personality and community to an intra-historical and naturalistic mediation, he restricted the Christian understanding of salvation to an intra-historical event and state ('God-consciousness'), and correspondingly restricted Christology as the efficient cause for such an end. Schleiermacher seems to float 'between' quantitative history and the transcendental, in a domain that neither touches the transcendental nor is fully immersed in the histori-cal: it is the special domain of qualitative history, the unique Schleiermachian correla-tion between believing community and believed figure. The questions that permeated twentieth-century reception of Schleiermacher pertain to the outer limits of his ellipse and the possibility of Chalcedon after such a critique. Can his ellipse be expanded ver-tically into the transcendent (upwards) and quantitative history (downwards) without rupturing? Can there be a way of conceiving of Jesus as having a fully human personality and self-consciousness while preserving Chalcedonian dyophysitism?

SUGGESTED READING

Lessing (1956: 51–6); Ratzinger (2004: 193–270); Reimarus (1985); Schleiermacher (2011); Schweitzer (2005); Von Balthasar (1992: 25–121).

BIBLIOGRAPHY

Baillie, D. M. (1948), *God Was in Christ: An Essay on Incarnation and Atonement* (New York: Charles Scribner's Sons).

Bultmann, R. (1969), 'The Christology of the New Testament', in Bultmann, *Faith and Understanding*, trans. L. Pettibone Smith (New York: Harper & Row), 262–85.

Dorner, I. A. (1853), *Entwicklungsgeschichte der Lehre von der Person Christi von den ältesten auf die neueste*; Zweiter Teil, 'Die Lehre von der Person Christi vom Ende des vierten Jahrhunderts bis zur Gegenwart' (Berlin: Verlag von Gustav Schlawitz).

Ferreira, M. J. (2006), 'Faith and the Kierkegaardian Leap', in A. Hannay and G. Marino (eds.), *The Cambridge Companion to Kierkegaard* (New York: Cambridge University Press), 207–34.

Harnack, A. (1972), *The Mission and Expansion of Christianity: The First Three Centuries*, trans. J. Moffatt (Gloucester, Mass.: Peter Smith).

Hegel, G. W. F. (1956), *The Philosophy of History*, trans. J. Sibree (Mineola, NY: Dover Publications).

Hegel, G. W. F. (1977), *Phenomenology of Spirit*, trans. A. V. Miller (New York: Oxford University Press).

Hegel, G. W. F. (1991), *The Encyclopaedia of Logic: Part I of the Encyclopedia of Philosophical Sciences with the Zusätze* (Indianapolis: Hacket Publishing).

Hirsch, E. (1978), *Christliche Rechenschaft*, Vol. 1, in *Werke, B. III*, ed. H. Gerdes (Berlin: Verlag Die Spur).

Kant, I. (2005a), 'Religion within the Boundaries of Mere Reason' (1793), trans. G. di Giovanni, in A. Wood and G. di Giovanni (eds.), *Religion and Rational Theology*. The Cambridge Edition of the Works of Immanuel Kant (New York: Cambridge University Press).

Kant, I. (2005b), 'The Conflict of the Faculties' (1798), trans. M. J. Gregor and R. Anchor, in A. Wood and G. di Giovanni (eds.), *Religion and Rational Theology*. The Cambridge Edition of the Works of Immanuel Kant (New York: Cambridge University Press).

Kierkegaard, S. (1987), *Either/Or*, Part I. Kierkegaard's Writings, III, trans. H. Hong and E. Hong (Princeton, NJ: Princeton University Press).

Kierkegaard, S. (1992), *Concluding Unscientific Postscript to Philosophical Fragments*, Vol. 1. Kierkegaard's Writings, XII, trans. H. V. Hong and E. H. Hong (Princeton, NJ: Princeton University Press).

Kierkegaard, S. (2010), *Kierkegaard's Journals and Notebooks: Volume 3: Notebooks 1–15*, ed. N. J. Cappelørn, A. Hannay, B. H. Kirmmse, and D. Kangas (Princeton, NJ: Princeton University Press).

Lessing, G. E. (1956), 'On the Proof of the Spirit and of Power', trans. and ed. Henry Chadwick, *Lessing's Theological Writings*. A Library of Modern Religious Thought (Stanford, Calif.: Stanford University Press).

Niebuhr, R. R. (1964), *Schleiermacher on Christ and Religion: A New Introduction* (Eugene, Oreg.: Wipf and Stock Publishers).

Ratzinger, J. (2004), *Introduction to Christianity*, trans. J. R. Foster (San Francisco: Ignatius Press).

Reimarus, H. S. (1985), *Fragments from Reimarus: Brief Critical Remarks on the Object of Jesus and his Disciples as seen in the New Testament*, trans. and ed. G. E. Lessing and C. Voysey (London and Edinburgh: Williams and Norgate).

Renan, E. (1863), *The Life of Jesus* (London: Watts & Co.).

Ritschl, A. (1874), *Die christliche Lehre von der Rechtfertigung und Versöhnung. 3 Bände: Die positive Entwickelung der Lehre* (Bonn: Marcus).

Schelling, F. W. J. (1977), *Philosophie der Offenbarung*, ed. Manfred Frank (Frankfurt: Suhrkamp Taschenbuch Verlag).

Schleiermacher, F. (2011), *The Christian Faith* (Berkeley, Calif.: Apocryphile Press).

Schönborn, C. (2010), *God Sent His Son: A Contemporary Christology*, trans. H. Taylor (San Francisco: Ignatius Press).

Schweitzer, A. (2005), *The Quest of the Historical Jesus: A Critical Study of Its Progress from Reimarus to Wrede* (Mineola, NY: Dover Publications).

Staudenmaier, F. A. (1840), *Encyklopädie der theologischen Wissenschaften als System der gesammten Theologie, mit Angabe der theologischen Litteratur* (Mainz; 2nd edn. 1 vol. only).

Strauss, D. F. (1903), *Der alte und der neue Glaube*, 15th edn. (Leipzig).

Strauss, D. F. (1973), *The Life of Jesus Critically Examined*, trans. G. Eliot, ed. P. C. Hodgson (London: SCM Press).

Strauss, D. F. (1977), *The Christ of Faith and the Jesus of History: A Critique of Schleiermacher's The Life of Jesus*, trans. L. E. Keck (Philadelphia: Fortress).

Troeltsch, E. (1991), *The Christian Faith: Lectures Delivered at the University of Heidelberg in 1912 and 1913*, trans. G. E. Paul. Fortress Texts in Modern Theology (Minneapolis: Fortress).

Von Balthasar, H. U. (1992), *Theo-Drama: Volume III. The Dramatis Personae: The Person in Christ*, trans. Graham Harrison (San Francisco: Ignatius Press).

Von Balthasar, H. U. (2009), *Glory of the Lord: A Theological Aesthetics: Volume I: Seeing the Form*, trans. E. Leiva-Merikakis (San Francisco: Ignatius Press).

CHAPTER 23

CHRISTOLOGY AFTER SCHLEIERMACHER

Three Twentieth-Century Christologists

TROY A. STEFANO

THERE are three main paths after Schleiermacher: there are those who retain a 'closed' ellipse between person and community, floating 'above' history and yet not touching the transcendental (e.g., Ritschl, Herrmann); there are those who attempt to open Schleiermacher's ellipse vertically towards the transcendental, but not descending to the quantitative (e.g., Dorner, Kahler, and Barth); and finally, there are those who attempt to stretch the ellipse to its limits by opening it vertically towards the transcendental *and* descendingly towards the quantitative. Among this last group one finds Käsemann and the Catholic Tübingen theologians in the nineteenth century, and in the twentieth, there are Wolfhart Pannenberg, Sergius Bulgakov, and Hans Urs von Balthasar as three of the greatest representatives of the legacies of Wittenberg, Byzantium, and Rome, united in their resolve to find a modern approach to Chalcedon that spans Lessing's ditch and rethinks Schleiermacher's transpositions.

WOLFHART PANNENBERG (1928–2014)

Wolfhart Pannenberg's greatest contribution to modern theology is the way he deploys the concept of revelation to hurtle Lessing's ditch and to pierce the horizontal, vertical, and eschatological limits of Schleiermacher's ellipse. In *Revelation as History* (1968), he continues the line that flows through Kierkegaard to Schleiermacher that rejects Lessing and his heirs' claim of 'incommunicabilty' between the two orders. He criticizes Schleiermacher's eliding revelation with God-consciousness by claiming that revelation cannot be adequately understood as the disclosure of truths *about* God

('God-consciousness'), but must be interpreted as the self-revelation of God (Schwöbel 2005: 130; Pannenberg 1968).

The key notion of God's self-revelation—philosophically taken from Hegel, but received in its theological form through Karl Barth and Karl Rahner—functions as the theoretical apparatus by which the transcendental can make itself both known and present in the categorical. The heart of his argument is that if there is any revelation, there can only be a single unique revelation in which God is both the author and medium of revelation; indeed, that 'form' and 'content' are one in God, and thus, mode and content are equally revelatory (Pannenberg 1968: 129–33). But here Pannenberg parts ways with Rahner, Barth, and Kasper, and is joined only by Balthasar: God's full self-revelation can only be placed at the end of history, in relation to which the totality of history and all of reality is illuminated and receives meaning (Pannenberg 1968: 127–9; cf. Von Balthasar 1998: 19–54). This universal, pan-, and meta-historical self-revelation means that God can be seen in all things, but only *indirectly*, because all of God's acts in history can only have their full meaning insofar as they are seen in light of the fullness of God's eschatological self-revelation. The distinctively Christian claim, for Pannenberg, is that God's eschatological self-revelation is proleptically actualized in the destiny, particularly in the resurrection, of Jesus Christ (Pannenberg 1977: 53–65, 135–41, 108, 157, 406).

Pannenberg and the 'Elliptical Problem'

Pannenberg has 'stretched' Schleiermacher's correlation that 'floated' in the 'in-between' of personality and community to a dialectic between 'history' (quantitative) and 'eschaton' (vertical-eschatological-theological). The claim of *indirect* revelation is Pannenberg's version of the ellipse: faith is the act by which one engages in the 'reflexive action' of interpreting historical acts by reference to God's eschatological self-disclosure (cf. Pannenberg 1968: 144–61). The *indirectness* of revelation is what allows Pannenberg to claim that while the acts and words brought about by God in history are immersed in quantitative history to such an extent that they are 'open to anyone who has eyes to see' (Pannenberg 1968: 135–58, 2009: 249), they are only seen as revelatory insofar as the seer, moved by faith, can reflexively interpret those truly quantitative events in the horizon of God's eschatological self-revelation (cf. Pannenberg 2009: 249–57; especially, 1998: 144–61, wherein, like Von Balthasar, he sees this 'interpreting function' in the context of pneumatology). The believer, therefore, must not begin with the vantage point of the reflexive interpretation of the community (as did Schleiermacher); rather, the believer must begin with the domain of quantitative history, in which God's acts take place, and then—only then—see to what extent those acts are diaphanous to God's eschatological truth.

Pannenberg therefore inverses Schleiermacher's method: 'Christology is concerned ... not only with *unfolding* the Christian community's confession of Christ [cf. Schleiermacher's regressive argument], but above all with *grounding* it in the activity and fate of Jesus in the past' (Pannenberg 1977: 28). 'Thus the task of Christology is to establish the true understanding of Jesus' significance from his history' (1977: 30). But, by returning to a Jesus that is fully immersed in quantitative history, considered apart from our experience of him, as the standard against which our claims of faith must be made, Pannenberg is stepping outside of the 'safety zone' that Schleiermacher's 'floating' ellipse had attained from the hammer of historical-critical investigation. But for Pannenberg, it is only when we 'ask and show the extent to which this history substantiates faith in Jesus' that we truly claim that Christ is not a product of our desires or a development in religious myth (1977: 47–9), but truly, the protological 'in-breaking' of God's self-revelation into history (1977: 128–9).

If one begins with quantitative history, then the doctrines of the Incarnation and pre-existence of Jesus cannot form the starting point for theological reflection; rather, those are claims about Jesus' unity with God that stand at the conclusion of one's inquiry (1977: 33–7). One must begin with the pre-Easter Jesus and ask how the early Christian community arrived at such a belief (1977: 21–9). To this extent, Pannenberg, much like Walter Kasper, forms a 'mini-ellipse' between Jesus (as historical figure) and the first eyewitnesses/early Christian communities—they both proceed via a 'history of traditions' approach. The pre-Easter Jesus, admittedly, spoke with a claim to authority, perhaps even divine authority, but such a claim was not sufficient to elicit (or at least, to justify) faith in him (Pannenberg 1977: 66). Pannenberg argues that it is *only* Jesus' resurrection that could explain the almost immediate interpretation of his life and death as having transcendental, indeed, eschatological meaning. Within the milieu of late Jewish apocalypticism, in which God's actions in history receive a universal significance by reference to the end of history as the definitive moment of the revelation of God's glory (*kabod*), Jesus' resurrection radiated forth an immediate significance: in him, the end of the world has begun and God himself has confirmed the pre-Easter activity of Jesus (1977: 66–88). Indeed, the *diaphanous* quality of Jesus' resurrection in that milieu freights it with the radiant meaning that 'God is ultimately revealed in Jesus' (1977: 73).

Pannenberg and the 'Chalcedonian Problem'

Does the resurrection, as an event, license the discourses of ontological identity, traditionally conveyed in the concepts of incarnation, pre-existence, and dyophysitism? Pannenberg believes that claims such as 'incarnation' and 'pre-existence' may be used to express the eschatological character of God's self-revelation in Christ in light of the resurrection. But, Pannenberg believes, the problems associated with dyophysitism—regarding which he reiterates Schleiermacher's critiques (Pannenberg 1977: 283–307)—derive from beginning with the premise of the Incarnation or pre-existence and then trying to establish his humanity, rather than beginning with his humanity and then establishing his divinity (through the resurrection). Like Schleiermacher, he rejects the language of two substances or natures, claiming, again like Schleiermacher, that they destroy the unity of subject and thus his true humanity.

Pannenberg's alternative to Chalcedonian discourse is the idea of 'revelational presence', which tries to navigate the narrow path between adoptionism and identity of essence. His concept of revelation is able to overcome not only Lessing's incommunicabilty, but also Schleiermacher's incommensurability by the (Hegelian–Barthian–Rahnerian) idea of God's self-differentiation and self-revelation. His logic can be presented in four points:

1. *Reconsidering 'becoming' and 'sameness' in God:* 'God in all his eternal identity is still to be understood as a God who is alive in himself, who can become something and precisely in so doing remain true to himself and the same' (Pannenberg 1977: 320). Pannenberg reconciles 'becoming' and 'sameness' in God by claiming that if we conceive of eternity in an un-Platonic way in which eternity contains and includes time, then God does not 'change' (the equivalent to 'becoming in general') in the Incarnation, but 'becomes one' with something different from himself (1977: 321).

2. *The unity with the other within God as the ground for God's unity with the other outside of God (creation):* Pannenberg invokes Rahner's formulation of the Hegelian dialectic of self-differentiation, in which God as creator 'constitutes the differentiation to himself by retaining it as his and, conversely, because he truly wants to have the other as his own, he constitutes it in its genuine reality' (Rahner 1961: 148). Self-differentiation *within* God grounds God's self-differentiation *with* creation: 'God remains himself precisely in the other, but also that he becomes something, thus that God establishes the other as his own reality precisely by emptying *himself*, giving *himself* away through this.' For Rahner, however, this meant the immanent Trinity (Rahner 1998: 98–103), whereas for Pannenberg this refers to the concept that 'the "intention" of the incarnation had been determined from all eternity in God's decree' (1977: 321).

3. *Unity with the other within God extended to encompass the Incarnation:* If God's self-differentiation within God's self can account for creation, and if therefore eternity can include time, then 'an element of God's becoming and being in the other, in the reality differentiated from himself, is one with his eternity requires that what newly flashed into view from time to time in the divine life can be understood at the same time as having always been true in God's eternity' (Pannenberg 1977: 321). Henceforth, Pannenberg has laid the groundwork for the claim that Jesus can *truly* be God as a modality of God's self-otherness. This is a reinterpretation of the simultaneity implied in dyophysitism in the direction of a unity by way of the dialectic of self-differentiation.

In these three steps, Pannenberg links up with Rahner (and Bulgakov and Von Balthasar) regarding the premise of grounding the unity of God and man in Jesus with God's own self-differentiation. However, Pannenberg breaks company with these figures in that his concept of self-differentiation relies on his unique view of eschatology. For Pannenberg, God protologically has an 'eternal decree' that is a sufficient basis for claiming a self-differentiation in God. That decree becomes 'actualized' when God 'decides' to be revealed in Jesus of Nazareth. In the resurrection, that relation between God and Jesus is made. The result for God is eschatological: God is a Trinity in the end, as a result of that 'decision'. God's Triune-ness is 'inscribed' eschatologically. God therefore is (now, always was) a Trinity.

Pannenberg attempts to bridge the gap between God protologically and God eschatologically with an understanding of the eschaton whose main precedent is Blaise Pascal's doctrine of predestination, in which God can eschatologically choose 'damnation' or 'salvation', while holding that decision in suspense while a person's life is panning out, although that eschatological decision becomes retrospectively true. Applying this to God, Pannenberg says that God was always a Trinity, *but* ... as a result of an eschatological decision. The question is how, if eschatological becomes sempiternal, that was not the case protologically in the full, ontological sense, and not merely in a notional or intentional form. Furthermore, any language of the Triune God or the (divine) Son creating the world would seem to be little more than semantics (1977: 390–9). (Pannenberg qualifies this issue in his later *Systematic Theology*.)

The next step, then, is the meeting point between his 'Christology from below' and his theology from the eschaton: the resurrection.

4. *The connection between 'grounding' the unity of Jesus and God within God's self-differentiation, on the one hand, and the actual 'establishing' of Jesus as the self-revelation of God, on the other, happens only in Jesus' resurrection.* The height of the tension between 'grounding' and 'establishing' comes forward in this passage:

> Jesus' unity with God—and thus the truth of the incarnation—is also *decided* only retroactively from the perspective of Jesus' resurrection for the whole of Jesus' human existence on the one hand and thus also for God's eternity, on the other. Apart from Jesus' resurrection, it would not be true that from the beginning of his earthly way God was one with this man. That is true from all eternity *because* of Jesus' resurrection. Until his resurrection, Jesus' unity with God was hidden not only to other men but above all, which emerges from a critical examination of the tradition, for Jesus himself also. *It was hidden because the ultimate decision about it had not been given.* One could speak differently only by depriving the event of the resurrection of its contingency, of its element of newness, by means of some sort of theological or physical determinism, or if one wants to deny the significance of Jesus' resurrection in general for the question of Jesus' unity with God. The confirmation of Jesus' unity with God in the retroactive power of his resurrection makes the hiddenness of this unity during Jesus' earthly life comprehensible and thus makes room for the genuine humanity of his life.
>
> (Pannenberg 1977: 321–2; italics mine; cf. 364)

There is a degree of internal coherence in his position: the retroactive dimension of identity is not merely characteristic of the relationship of Jesus' resurrection to his pre-Easter life, but also the template that governs the relationship between the eschaton and history. But the seemingly voluntarist language of 'ultimate decision'—reminiscent of Schleiermacher and Barth's doctrine of the eternal decree, by virtue of which there is an eternal aspect in God that is constitutively related to a temporal event—treads a line that is closer to adoptionism than it is to identity of essence. Despite this internal consistency, there is a methodological 'rift'. On the one hand, Pannenberg is committed to a 'Christology from below' in which claims, such as the Incarnation or eternal pre-existence of the Son are marked out *de iure* as starting points. On the other hand, Pannenberg requires the work of God's eschatological self-revelation—a non-'from below' starting point—to retrospectively 'break into history' to lend to the resurrection its revelatory value.

It seems that Pannenberg's critiques of the tradition's readings of Jesus' origins from God protologically (i.e., Virgin birth, Incarnation, eternal pre-existent Son) is recapitulated into Jesus' origins from God eschatologically (i.e., retrospectively by eschatological self-revelation in the resurrection). Both approaches claim sempiternal meaning, except the latter presupposes a slight voluntarism if taken exclusively. The key questions are (a) whether there is a difference in God as God protologically and eschatologically as a result of the drama of salvation, and (b) whether Jesus could truly have not only pointed to the 'beginning of the end' but embody the 'end of the world' and the 'renewal of all things' in himself if he were not the eschaton in history. Is Jesus 'out-measured' by the eschaton's final self-revelation, or is the eschaton's final self-revelation the transposition into world-time of what was already achieved in Christ?

Pannenberg and the Trinitarian Problem

'In his revelational unity with God, which constitutes Jesus' own divinity, Jesus at the same time remains distinct from God as his Father' (Pannenberg 1977: 115). The beginning of the doctrine of the Trinity, Pannenberg claims, lies in this. Based on the constitutively eschatological dimension of God's self-revelation, wherein the temporal aspects of the eternal decree already become constitutive of God's self-revelation, Pannenberg can claim that God is a Trinity of persons without any modalistic softening. He also sees the eternal decree as guarding against the Moltmannian collapse of God *in se* and God *ad extra* that leads to the idea of God 'becoming' a Trinity. For, God *in se*, by virtue of the eternal decree, is none other than what is revealed *ad extra*, even if the event of the resurrection is what vindicates and establishes such an eschatological self-revelation. In his later works, particularly his *Systematic Theology*, Pannenberg moves towards seeing in Jesus' 'revelational identity' a greater degree of ontological identity, in order to substantiate a 'thicker' Trinitarianism (cf. 1998 20–34; 2009: 259–336), though he maintains an 'economic' form that is inscribed only eschatologically (Pannenberg 2009: 259–336). 'Already the concept of revelation which is developed by the trinitarian understanding of God rests on anticipation of the end of history in the person and history of Jesus Christ' (Pannenberg 2009: 332).

SERGIUS BULGAKOV (1853–1900)

It would be difficult to find two modern theologians who are more distinct in form and in substance than Bulgakov and Pannenberg. One crucial factor is that the encounter of tradition and Enlightenment occurred in different ways in Germany and Russia. The German problematic was the separation of 'event' and 'truth', whereas the Russian problematic was governed by the dialectic of 'created' and 'uncreated'. This means that the criticisms of Lessing, and the philosophies of religion of Hegel and Schelling, have a much greater reception in Russian thought (e.g., Solyviev) than the issues of historical criticism, raised by Reimarus and Strauss. Bulgakov writes that the entire history of religion could be narrated in terms of the tension between the transcendent and the immanent (2012: 20–38). What is common, however, to twentieth-century German and Russian theologians is the attempt to shed the legacy of idealism in philosophy, and to break free from a psychologizing, moralizing, or 'naturalizing' of faith, so as to recover a sense of the givenness, the historical and punctiliar character, of a revelation that reconstructs the whole of human knowing and relating (Williams 2005: 574; cf. Bulgakov 2012: 1–102).

The task of restoring to revelation its supernatural character is for Bulgakov the prerogative of dogmatics; and it presupposes not only the truth of dogmas but that the inspired form of Scripture mediates the revelatory events it discloses. Bulgakov affirms the Son's immersion in quantitative history in the Incarnation (Bulgakov 2008: 274). But, as with Schleiermacher, this is a formal claim that is not pursued further, for such is not the task of theology. Following the Käsemannian line after Schleiermacher, he writes that 'The Gospels are doctrinal books, not "historical" ones. The history enters into the doctrine, into the teaching of the faith, and is subordinated to its goals' (2008: 275; cf. Käsemann 1964: 25; 1969: 41). His Christological task is to establish the dogmatic basis in which the immanentism that pervades the modern period could be overcome, while attempting to clarify and present a coherent picture of Jesus' unity of life amidst his duality of natures. While Bulgakov does not single out Schleiermacher directly, the phenomena that he identifies for critique are thoroughly Schleiermachian. First, apologetically, he singles out a conception of Christianity that is regulated by an immanent framework; second, dogmatically, he takes up the challenge of engaging Apollinarius' critique that in Christ, there cannot be two active principles, since one will always give way to the other (Bulgakov 2008: 1–18, 444). The point is that Bulgakov's engagement with Apollinarius has relevance only because he finds in Apollinarius the 'same' critique that Schleiermacher promoted. We can read Bulgakov's task as a response to Schleiermacher. In this sense, we can see Bulgakov and Pannenberg as both engaged in the broader conversation of Schleiermachian reception.

Bulgakov on the 'Elliptical Problem'

Rather than using Lessing's original categories, Bulgakov's version of the elliptical problem is transposed into the dialectic of Creator–creature: 'The Word-God (without ceasing to be the Word and God) became not-God; *the Creator became a creature*' (Bulgakov 2008: 213). What are the conditions for this possibility, indeed, actuality? Bulgakov's argument could be presented thus:

1. *'The Word'*: Bulgakov makes the traditional move of interpreting John 1:14 according to Phil. 2:9–11: 'First of all, this passage talks about the descent from heaven of the *supramundane* God; that is, it talks not only about the Incarnation itself but also about the act that preceded it in heaven: the decision or the will to enact the Incarnation.' The non-traditional aspect to his interpretation is that in this passage he reads that the Word's descent is based on an intra-Trinitarian obedience/kenosis, that 'in the cross of the earthly path is realized the cross of heavenly kenosis' (Bulgakov 2008: 217).

2. *'Became'*: The meaning of kenosis, therefore, is not that God changes his substance or nature (*pace* Gess et al.), but his 'form'. Such a distinction presupposes that in God there is a difference between 'nature' and 'form' (or, 'state of life'). Bulgakov asserts that in God there is a distinction between 'the life of God *according to* Himself, as He is in His unchangeable essence, and His life *for* Himself, as He lives out His essence for Himself in the living act. Here He has the power to change for Himself the *mode* of the living out of this essence' (Bulgakov 2008: 221–2). Thus, the intra-Trinitarian obedience of the Son is constitutive according to nature and accompanied with glory according to form. When this obedience becomes the kenosis of the Son in the Incarnation, the nature remains but what changes is its accompanying glory.

3. *'Flesh'*: As opposed to the idea of divinity taking on humanity, or the inhabitation of divinity in human flesh, Bulgakov is guided by the idea of 'the descent of Divinity down to man, the self-diminution of Divinity, His humiliation or kenosis' (Bulgakov 2008: 219). 'In becoming man, God does not stop being God; even after descending from heaven, He remains in heaven. Likewise, man does not stop being man after he receives God into himself. In voluntary self-humiliation, God renounces something, abandons something, in order to become accessible to man, in order to make possible the approach to man. And man, in opening himself up to receive God, transfigures himself, without the possibilities implanted in this essence being destroyed' (Bulgakov 2008: 220).

Bulgakov is aware of Schleiermacher's challenge to such a position, which he sees as anticipated in Apollinarius' 'it is impossible with intelligence and volition to be united into one principle' (L., frag. 2; quoted, 6): if we have the duality of natures, then we lose the unity of person; if we have the unity of person, then we lose the duality of natures. Bulgakov calls into question the presupposition of both of these critiques: namely, the incommensurability of the two principles.

The conventional opinion is that there can be no mediation between God and creature: *tertium non datur*. But in reality there *is* such a mediation between God and the creature: *tertium datur*, and this *tertium* is Sophia, the true Wisdom of God, eternal and creaturely. Creaturely sophianicity, however, is only the bridge for, or the onto-logical possibility of, the movement of God and the creature toward one another.

(Bulgakov 2008: 220)

Bulgakov concretizes the 'in-between' of God and creation as Sophia, distinguishing between divine Sophia (equivalent with the divine nature, the richness of possibilities in God from which creation derives) and creaturely Sophia (the indestructible 'imago Dei' in creation). The ontological gap, traditionally understood only apophatically and as a barrier, now bears positive content. It serves as 'a mediation, an ontological bridge to effect this union—a ladder on which this ascent-descent can be accomplished' (2008: 220). Sophia is Bulgakov's answer to modernity's immanence after Lessing—this is the thesis of Paul Valliere's *Modern Russian Theology* (2000: 271). How does this solve the problem of the 'one person and two natures' in Christ? If God becomes this man, how can he continue to truly be man? If this man is God, then how can God continue to be God? And, how can both happen simultaneously and in the same 'being' and 'person'?

Bulgakov on the 'Chalcedonian Problem'

Bulgakov perceptively targets the particularly modern form of the Chalcedonian prob-lem in the question of consciousness. Chalcedon addressed the duality of being or nature, Constantinople III addressed the duality of wills; the modern installment of the question is the duality of consciousnesses in Christ. The force of this question is that the modern human being is defined by the singularity of his or her I-consciousness. To say that in Jesus, there are two I's or two personalities is to destroy the unity of person. Bulgakov's sophiology is saturated with the modern (especially Hegelian and Schellingian) develop-ments regarding subjectivity and consciousness, and it is in these developments that he sees a way forward for Chalcedonian Christology. He distinguishes in Sophia two aspects from Scripture: 'She is, properly, Sophia (Hokhma), as the revelation of the Wisdom of God; and she is also Glory, as the revelation of God's Beauty and All-blessedness' (Bulgakov 2008: 107). He finds his solution in an interpretation of the first aspect as 'the consciousness of self of the trinitarian God' (2008: 108). The relationship between the eternal Son and human nature, with a human self-consciousness, is not such a crazy thing after all, since there is a precedent of that kind of relation in God's self—namely, the relationship between the eternal Son and the divine Sophia as the 'consciousness of self of the Trinitarian God'. Bulgakov sees these parallel relations—eternal Son–divine Sophia as divine self-consciousness and eternal Son–creaturely Sophia as human self-consciousness—as the meaning of 'the Heavenly Man' of 1 Cor. 15:49 (2008: 242). Thus, Bulgakov's point can be demonstrated by using a tripartite anthropology (9):

Adam: *pneuma* (created Sophia as consciousness of self); soul (psyche); body (soma).
   Christ: Logos (divine Sophia as consciousness of self); soul (psyche); body (soma).

His claim is that the 'continuum' between creaturely Sophia and divine Sophia means that there has always been a potential—an eternally decreed and onto-logically inscribed hospitality—within the human (soul and body) for the Logos. Bulgakov justifies this claim by saying that the 'World came to be through Him', and thus, takes a creaturely form that reflects its Prototype, including the Word's relation to Sophia (2008: 242). Bulgakov believes he has solved the Chalcedonian problem by showing, on the one hand, 'The Divine Sonhood is precisely Jesus' Divine I, His self-consciousness as Divine consciousness' (2008: 264); and, on other hand, in the kenotic state that receives its measure by his human essence, 'He becomes progres-sively conscious of His divinity, not through His own, direct hypostatic consciousness, but through the Father' (2008: 279). For, 'It is only through the Father that He comes to know His divine hypostasis, His Divine Sonhood. The Son's divine consciousness is therefore *mediated* by the knowledge of the Father being revealed in Him, that is, by *divine knowledge*' (2008: 279). In his kenotic state, the Son's self-identity as eternal Son is given to him through his unique relation to the Father; therefore, his personal relation with the Father is established, in his consciousness, logically prior to his con-sciousness of his own divinity. Bulgakov sees this as the 'affirmative' or 'positive' side implied in Chalcedon's No's (unconfusedly, unchangeably, indivisibly, inseparably; Bulgakov 2008: 1–73, 443–8).

This provides a powerful solution, but also some concerns. First, one must wonder whether the replacement of the human I-consciousness with the Son's I-consciousness does not lead to a form of Docetism, in which Jesus seems human but isn't fully 'like us in all things except sin'. On the other hand, wouldn't Pannenberg's Jesus, given God's self-decree to make *this* man his self-revelation, be faced with a similar prob-lem after Jesus' resurrection? How would Pannenberg's post-resurrected Jesus' self-consciousness relate to the divine self-consciousness which has chosen to reveal itself in Jesus? Second, from Pannenberg's standard, he pays insufficient detail to the historical aspect, or more particularly, to the centrality of Jesus' resurrection. Third, while Pannenberg and Bulgakov both agree that Jesus' consciousness of himself as Son of the Father is mediated through his human consciousness, Bulgakov argues that his divine consciousness unfolds in accordance with the psycho-corporeal measure allotted to it by his humanity development, whereas Pannenberg locates this specifi-cally in (after) the resurrection. This reveals a fundamental point of tension between the two figures: the relation between dogmatics and exegesis. Bulgakov chooses 'form' over 'history', whereas Pannenberg chooses 'history' over 'form'. This creates exegetical differences in terms of what can be claimed regarding the pre-Easter Jesus' self-consciousness.

Bulgakov on the 'Trinitarian Problem'

Despite the obvious difference between Bulgakov and Pannenberg, there are certain formal similarities. Pannenberg's concept of self-revelation functions analogously to Bulgakov's sophiology insofar as both attempt to depict a ground in God for God's ability to remain God's self while in another. The concept of self-revelation, admittedly, does more justice to the ontological gap and to grounding the Incarnation in the Trinitarian relations of (or self-differentiation within) God as opposed to the divine being as such. But, conversely, Pannenberg's protological deity only has an intentional fullness, whereas Bulgakov's has an ontological fullness that overflows from divine Sophia into creation, and surges climactically in the Incarnation.

Thus, for Bulgakov Christology regulates eschatology (2008: 410–42), but for Pannenberg, eschatology regulates Christology. These hermeneutical commitments are reflected in their respective stances on Chalcedon. Bulgakov is able to offer a viable, if not powerful, depiction of Chalcedonian Christology that includes the full weight of ontological identity without introducing the cumbersome process of moving from eternal decree (world created for Incarnation and God's self-revelation in the Incarnation), to temporal realization (the Incarnation itself, actualized by Jesus' resurrection), and finally to eschatological inscription of that temporal actualization in God's self-revelation (God as Trinity). If God truly reveals himself as he is in himself, and if revelation occurs within the freedom to disclose himself as such, then a doctrine of the immanent Trinity is more suitable than a doctrine of the eternal decree.

Barring the obvious differences in exegetical preferences and practices, we should ask if there is any way of preserving the unambiguous ontological identity between Father and Son asserted by Bulgakov *and* the definitive significance of the historical in general, and the resurrection in particular, argued by Pannenberg? Is there any way of achieving both of their goals—namely, preserving Jesus' 'unity of life' while affirming a divine identity—without the cost of an un-human seeming God-Man (Bulgakov) or an absent pre-Easter ontological identity (Pannenberg)? Can we preserve the importance of the final, eschatological 'in-breaking' and revelation of God, while also maintaining that Jesus is himself the eschaton, and thus, Christ is not governed by any measure greater than himself? For these answers, we turn to the most integrated, or, quite literally, 'concerted' Christological and Trinitarian theology of the past 200 years.

HANS URS VON BALTHASAR (1905–1988)

The structure of Von Balthasar's treatment of Christ is closer to that of Pannenberg than that of Bulgakov; but the content of his thought is nearer to that of Bulgakov. Von Balthasar is committed to beginning with Jesus, as we encounter him (*Theo-Drama III*), and then moving to the Trinity (*Theo-Drama IV–V*). But, the Jesus that we encounter is always the eternal Son. Von Balthasar overcomes Schleiermacher and Lessing's ditch at the intersection of the Son's self-emptying mission and faith's vision.

Von Balthasar on the 'Elliptical Problem'

For Pannenberg, to begin from 'below' means to begin with the historical critically reconstructed Christ and to move, through an analysis of the formation of tradition, to the initial Christian testimony to Christ. The initial testimony itself is not a non-reducible form, but a penultimate form that can be broken down and analyzed to access a more primordial, reconstructed Jesus. Bulgakov begins by positing the existence of Jesus and proceeds to reinterpret an incarnational Christology. Von Balthasar argues that to begin 'from below' does not mean to begin with the historical-critical approach, but rather, from the 'form of beauty'. For Von Balthasar, the eyes of faith grant the believer the ability to see in Christ a wholeness that makes the love of the Father shine through him. Von Balthasar does not deny the quantitative immersion of the Son, that is, the true historicity of the Incarnate One; but he denies that the way to approach this is through dissecting Jesus. He argues, in a way that is reminiscent of Schleiermacher, that the passage of the 'form' of Jesus to the 'form' of Christ is intrinsic to Jesus himself. And any transmission of this 'form' cannot sunder it to analyze its pieces, but must preserve its wholeness. He thus establishes a theory of Christian experience, by which there can be simultaneously qualitative and quantitative transmission of Christ throughout history. Nonetheless, Von Balthasar posits the objectivity of Jesus as revelation as the condition for that experiential transmission. It is the scope of Jesus' mission that provided the point of continuity between the man of Nazareth and the universalized Object of faith.

Von Balthasar on the 'Chalcedonian Problem'

Von Balthasar uses the concept of mission to avoid both the dissecting prongs of the historical-critical method and Bulgakov's non-historical approach. It is a key concept in the Gospel of John, but also rooted in the Synoptics, and it provides Von Balthasar with the connection between the Jesus of history and early incarnational hymns in Scripture as well as the inner bond between the doctrine of the immanent Trinity and the three persons revealed in the economy (Von Balthasar 1992: 515). In the Gospels, Jesus identifies himself with his mission. Jesus is aware that he has received a mission from the Father and is its complete embodiment in the world (1992: 187). His awareness of his mission has no conceivable beginning (1992: 177, 178, 197, 268, *inter alia*). In a way that is true of no other human being, he *is* this mission (1992: 167–8, 509). He has identified himself in complete inner freedom with a task that has been given to him (1992: 517). The tension seen between Jesus' free embrace of his mission (the active dimension) and his obedience to that mission (the receptive/passive dimension) expresses how his mission did not begin after the Incarnation. Rather, the Incarnation, including its constitutive humility, is the active undertaking of the Son. The Son's mission, insofar as it is free, is co-determined by the Father and Son from all eternity; but insofar as it is given to him and received obediently, the Son hands himself over to receive his mission from Another, namely the Holy Spirit (1992: 183).

The soteriological dimension of the mission as it was co-determined freely from all of eternity calls for the Son's obedience (cf. Heb. 5:8)—an obedience undertaken on behalf of sinners in order to redeem their disobedience (1992: 187, 517–18). If the Son freely and actively undertakes his mission in the Incarnation, and thus takes on the form of obedience and receptivity as a result of his own activity, then obedience is the economic expression of the Son's active and eternal co-determination with the Father to save the world. The other soteriological dimension of the mission is that the Father gives the entire responsibility for the world's salvation to the Son (cf. John 5:22–30). This has two implications: first, that Jesus' mission is itself the embodiment of the Father's self-pouring love in the mode of sending. This explains how the loving disposition of the one-who-sends (the Father) shines forth in the one-who-is-sent (the Son) (1992: 515). Insofar as the Son is entrusted by the Father to reveal and share the love of the Father for the world, this means that the Father's love itself, which is not something he has, but what he is, is given to the Son.

> For, if he-who-is-sent has essentially to reveal the love of him-who-sends, and if he is identical with his divine mission, he must (as the personal bearer of this mission of love) be the divine, that is, eternal Offspring of him-who-sends, whom he himself calls 'Father' in a sense that bursts all analogies. We begin to discern the meaning of 'fatherhood' in the eternal realm when we consider the Son's task, which is to reveal the Father's love: such 'fatherhood' can only mean the giving away of everything the Father is, including his entire Godhead (for God, as God, 'has' nothing apart from what he 'is'); it is a giving-away that, in the Father's act of generation—which lasts for all of eternity—leaves the latter's womb 'empty': in God, poverty and wealth (that is, wealth and giving) are one and the same ... As God, however, the Son must be equal to the Father, even though he has come forth from the Father. And since the Father has expressed his whole love—which nothing can hold back—in the Son, the Son is the perfect image of the Father, apt to represent the Father's self-giving in his creation in every respect.
>
> (Von Balthasar 1992: 518–19)

In the same way that the Father hands over his self to the Son by begetting him and entrusting him with the task of embodying his love for the world in his mission, so also does the Son hand himself over to the world, thereby mirroring the Father's self-gift and allowing the Father's love to shine through him (1992: 515–19). The second implication is that this demonstrates that Jesus is not a finite subject entrusted with a task that can only be carried out by the infinite God, since 'the bearer of such responsibility in this subject can be none other than a divine Person. Only a divine Person can measure up to "God's cause" and be God's "agent" on earth' (1992: 509–10). It is Jesus' identity with his mission that allows us to say truly that God himself saves in Jesus Christ.

By redefining God's 'substance' as self-giving love, and by reinterpreting the Son's con-substantiality with the Father in terms of the Father giving the Son his being as self-gift, Von Balthasar has set up the apparatus to fulfill Bulgakov's aspirations without the latter's restraints. Bulgakov wanted to ground the I-consciousness of Jesus in the eternal Son, but could only do so by claiming that the I-consciousness of the Son was limited by the measure of his humanity. Von Balthasar holds that the Incarnation begins with the intra-Trinitarian obedience of the Son to empty himself. The connection between the I-consciousness of the Son as eternal Son and the I-consciousness of the Son as the man Jesus is only in the knowledge of his mission which he received from the Father through the Spirit. Thus, to know that he is sent into the world to bear the weight of the world is the necessary *and* sufficient condition for claiming a continuity of subject between the eternal Word and Jesus of Nazareth. For it is in this humility that he embodies the Father's self-emptying love.

This structure offers Von Balthasar the opportunity to make full use of the resurrection. Rather than seeing it as the *transitus* for ontological identification, as with Pannenberg, Von Balthasar sees in the resurrection a *transitus* in the directionality of the salvific drama. The function therefore of the resurrection is not mainly ontological but soteriological and epistemological. Von Balthasar invokes the distinction between the *status exinanitionis* and *status exaltationis* to separate two directionalities in the 'task' of the Son: the pre-resurrected state centers upon the Son's incarnation, death, and descent into Hell, depicting the depths of the Son's obedience and solidarity with Godless humanity. The post-resurrected Christ ascends to the right hand of the Father, now bearing those depths, and taking them into the inner life of God (1992: 522–3). Since for Von Balthasar, as for Bulgakov, Christology regulates eschatology, the resurrection has a cosmic-universal scope. We can see the significance of this *transitus* in Von Balthasar's poetically-theological dramatization of the Son's incarnate prayer to the Father:

> Earlier on, Father, you and I were one, and they stood outside of us as enemies, and from a distance we took counsel to see how they might be helped. Today I stand in the midst of our enemies; I have become a traitor to your justice, and if you want to strike out at them, strike first at me … I take their place … For, O my Father! What else is your justice than your love for me, and what the wrathful glance of your eye other than the most glorious revelation of your love for me? … And so look: even your enemies here, my friends, are yours. And I do not place myself as a protective wall before them to shield them from your fury. Rather, I take them into my hand like the celebrant takes his paten and I raise them up to you … And when I now go and sacrifice myself for them, to whom should I entrust them if not to you, Father, as my precious inheritance, as my Incarnation's fruit of sorrows and as the grapes on my vine? For whom have I ripened them if not for you, so that, once I have conquered death and hell, I might place them on your eternal table in the perfected vessel of the Kingdom?
>
> (Von Balthasar 1979: 85–6)

Von Balthasar on the 'Trinitarian Problem'

Von Balthasar's Trinity is eschatological as with Pannenberg. But it is eschatological only soteriologically, not ontologically. This means that the final 'stage' for the drama of salvation is within God's inner life. Here we see the ultimate stretching of Schleiermacher's ellipse. The ascension of the Son entails the 'taking up to the Father' of reconciled creation. The transformation of the world is the playing out of the Son's victory in Trinitarian terms.

THE TWENTY-FIRST CENTURY

Fifteen centuries after the Council of Chalcedon (451), Karl Rahner's article on Chalcedon as end or beginning set the tone for the second half of the twentieth century (Kasper 1985: 17). Rahner wrote that every conciliar statement is not only the end of a dispute, in which truth becomes unambiguous and victorious, but also the beginning of a search for deeper insight (Rahner 1954). With Pannenberg, Bulgakov, and Von Balthasar, there is a special engagement with the Enlightenment in general, and with Schleiermacher in particular. For them, Rahner poses more of a challenge than a solution; but insofar as he defined the form of the received problematic, he exercised an influence that should never be underestimated. They each stretched the limits of his 'correlation' to encompass the heights of heaven, the fragmentation of critical history, and the harrowing depths of hell. In fact, some would argue that they stretched his correlation to the point of rupture, and that we are facing anew the challenge of the bipolarity of the Jesus of history and the Christ of faith; and yet, these three figures each in their own way hold a new promise and problem for us, as we meditate upon the possibilities for Chalcedonian Christology in our own time.

SUGGESTED READING

Bulgakov (2008); Pannenberg (1977, 2009); Rahner (1954); Von Balthasar (1992, 1998, 2009).

BIBLIOGRAPHY

Bulgakov, S. (2004), *The Comforter*, trans. B. Jakim (Grand Rapids, Mich.: Eerdmans).
Bulgakov, S. (2008), *Lamb of God*, trans. B. Jakim (Grand Rapids, Mich.: Eerdmans).
Bulgakov, S. (2012), *Unfading Light: Contemplations and Speculations*, trans. T. A. Smith (Grand Rapids, Mich.: Eerdmans).
Käsemann, E. (1964), 'The Problem of the Historical Jesus', in Käsemann, *Essays on New Testament Themes*, trans. W. J. Montague (London: SCM Press), 15–47.
Käsemann, E. (1969), 'Blind Alleys in the "Jesus of History" Controversy', in Käsemann, *New Testament Questions of Today*, trans. W. J. Montague (London: SCM Press), 23–65.
Kasper, W. (1985), *Jesus the Christ* (Mahwah, NJ: Paulist Press).
Pannenberg, W. (1968), 'Dogmatic Theses on the Doctrine of Revelation', in Pannenberg (ed.), *Revelation as History*, trans. E. Quinn (New York: Macmillan), 125–58.

Pannenberg, W. (1977), *Jesus—God and Man*, trans. L. L. Wilkins and D. A. Priebe, 2nd edn. (Philadelphia: Westminster).

Pannenberg, W. (1998), *Systematic Theology, Volume 3*, trans. G. W. Bromiley (Grand Rapids, Mich.: Eerdmans).

Pannenberg, W. (2009), *Systematic Theology, Volume 1*, trans. G. W. Bromiley (Grand Rapids, Mich.: Eerdmans).

Rahner, K. (1954), 'Chalkedon—Ende oder Anfang?', in A. Grillmeier and H. Bacht (eds.), *Das Konzil von Chalkedon. Geschichte und Gegenwart* (Würzburg: Echter-Verlag), 3–49.

Rahner, K. (1961), *Theological Investigations, Volume 4: More Recent Writings*, trans. K. Smith (Baltimore, Md.: Helicon Press).

Rahner, K. (1998), *The Trinity*, trans. J. Donceel (New York: Crossroad Publishing Company).

Schleiermacher, F. (2011), *The Christian Faith* (Berkeley, Calif.: Apocryphile Press).

Schwöbel, C. (2005), 'Wolfhart Pannenberg', in D. F. Ford with R. Muers (eds.), *The Modern Theologians: An Introduction to Christian Theology since 1918* (Malden, MA: Blackwell), 129–46.

Valliere, P. (2000), *Modern Russian Theology: Bukharev, Soloviev, Bulgakov—Orthodox Theology in a New Key* (Grand Rapids, Mich.: Eerdmans).

Von Balthasar, H. U. (1979), *Heart of the World*, trans. E. S. Leiva (San Francisco: Ignatius Press).

Von Balthasar, H. U. (1992), *Theo-Drama, Volume III. The Dramatis Personae: The Person in Christ*, trans. G. Harrison (San Francisco: Ignatius Press).

Von Balthasar, H. U. (1994), *Theo-Drama, Volume IV. The Action*, trans. G. Harrison (San Francisco: Ignatius Press).

Von Balthasar, H. U. (1998), *Theo-Drama, Volume V. The Last Act*, trans. G. Harrison (San Francisco: Ignatius Press).

Von Balthasar, H. U. (2009), *Glory of the Lord: A Theological Aesthetics, Volume I. Seeing the Form*, trans. E. Leiva-Merikakis (San Francisco: Ignatius Press).

Williams, R. (2005), 'Eastern Orthodox Theology', in D. F. Ford with R. Muers (eds.), *The Modern Theologians: An Introduction to Christian Theology since 1918* (Malden, MA: Blackwell), 572–88.

CHAPTER 24

....

KNOWING ABOUT JESUS, KNOWING JESUS

Christology and Spirituality

....

RAYMOND GAWRONSKI, S.J.

TERTULLIAN's question: 'What has Athens to do with Jerusalem?' (*De Praescriptione*, vii) might serve as the classical articulation of the polarity we face when asking about Christology and spirituality. Jesus was a Palestinian Jew whose religion was centered in Jerusalem. Though it is believed that he would have known Greek, and though the vast bulk of the New Testament is composed in Greek, nothing in the Gospels leads us to think that he was formed in the Greek tradition. In Tertullian's terms, he himself was all Jerusalem, and virtually no Athens.

Christology—the reasoned, at least as classically understood, 'scientific' study of Christ—has come to mean the product of thoughtful reflection on the content of revelation. As practiced in the Western academy of the past several hundred years, it has come to exclude the rest of the human faculties of perception. Moreover with the highly textual orientation of traditional Protestant and recent Catholic theology, the approach to Christ has been limited to biblical studies. This phenomenon is most clearly articulated by Hans Urs Von Balthasar in his programmatic essay 'Theology and Sanctity' where he laments that the most significant development of the history of Christianity has been the 'divorce' between a 'kneeling' and a 'sitting' theology, between what has come to be known as 'spirituality' and what became 'dogmatic theology' (Balthasar 1989). It is, in simplest form, a divorce between heart and head.

Writing from the concerns of spirituality, our question is: 'what is it to know Jesus Christ?' where 'know' has the intimate connotation of the biblical sense—Jerusalem—but also the more limited sense of modern European scholarship—Athens. 'They knew Him in the breaking of the bread' (Luke 24:35) indicates how they 'knew Him' after the Resurrection—apart from privileged apparitions. So our question must be: what is it to 'know Jesus'? Knowing 'about Jesus' is part of this, to be sure, but just as surely it cannot supplant the reality of encountering—'knowing'—Jesus.

Von Balthasar traces this development back through the Scholastics, observing that it is highly noteworthy that in the first millennium, all great theologians were saints. Let it be noted, that in the Western Church, perhaps as it moved further from the ancient tradition still maintained in the East, the criteria for sanctity—or at least for canonization—have become concerned with 'heroic virtue' rather than with charismatic or pneumatological gifts. The way to discern if a Christian 'knows' Christ has become to assess the moral fruit of the life of the candidate, as judged by the Catholic Church as worthy to be held up to others as a standard.

But what then is theology? Why is St. John called 'the theologian'? No one reading a theologian of the past thousand years or more would confuse that writing with that of St. John the Evangelist. And yet, he is called 'the theologian'. One might call theology 'reasoned reflection on the truths of faith'. The central reality these 'truths' articulate is the person of Jesus, called the Christ—Messiah—for that title is itself a statement of faith, that is, a theological, and Christological, statement.

Jesus left us no writings. The power of his presence—personal encounter—characterizes the heart of his mission. For St. Mark, at least, Jesus himself is the Gospel, the Good News. And yet, he also taught and the Gospels claim to present his teachings as well as his actions. St. Paul's writings are eminently theological, and supply perhaps the greatest single source for the formation of Christology. Like the other writers of the New Testament, Paul created what Christians believe is an inspired portrait and articulation—and then reflection upon—this person who is seen as the definitive revelation of the unseen God, and who also—in a more contemporary phrase—'reveals man to man'. From the point of view of spirituality, Christology offers the code, the official description, for painting—de-picting—for re-creating in this world the face of the one whom Christians are called to imitate. Spirituality is the tree from which the fruit—the saint, the one conformed to Christ—can be formed as conformed to Christ, or not. An inadequate description will create a less than adequate face, hence the crucial importance of a correct—orthodox—description.

Yet in each age after the life of Jesus, different aspects of the one mystery have been highlighted, leading to the formation of different types of disciples, with a different model of—sense of—discipleship and sanctity, and with it a different sort of prayer: and, again, behind this, different understandings of who Christ is, that is, different Christologies.

THE NEW TESTAMENT

In the New Testament itself, two main strands of Jewish tradition come together: the wisdom and the apocalyptic/prophetic. The earliest NT writings are those of the Jewish scholar named Paul, who focuses on the spirituality of the Cross. Christ is 'made the Son of God', Lord, at his resurrection. The disciples are to imitate Paul as he imitates Christ, who 'emptied Himself' to become man. The Kenosis is central here. Paul was a founder of communities, and he writes much of 'the body'—what much later was called the 'mystical body'. Christ is a 'sacrifice for sin'. Christ 'died for our sins'—a death in atonement, a death which is a birth into new life. The Christian is to enter into Christ's resurrection by sharing in Christ's atoning suffering and death (Col. 1:24). He is to be a 'new creation'. A 'Pauline spirituality' is one of mystical encounter—Paul himself had explicitly mystical experience. It is both free of adherence to the Jewish ritual observance, and yet insistent upon a strict moral code, especially in sexual matters. Paul may have fostered a break from rabbinic practice, but he was no antinomian. Yet he did not begin with moral behavior, but rather saw moral behavior as the key to discernment whether one was 'in Christ'. Thus, the oft-repeated sentiment that: 'Those who are in Christ do not do such things' (e.g., Rom. 8). Jesus Christ is Lord, and the important thing is to be 'in Christ'.

The Gospel of St. John, generally seen as the most spiritual of the Gospels, focuses on the 'Beloved Disciple' and the opening of the heart of Christ to his beloved for a mutual indwelling. Christ is the Word of God made flesh: the highest mystical view is combined with a radical insistence on the corporeal reality of the Incarnation. Perhaps because Gnostic movements which devalued the corporeal life in the name of a heightened spirituality were influential at the time, John in his writings, highlights the material—the flesh, σάρξ—even as he emphasizes the contemplative and spiritual. John's relation with Mary—both at the foot of the Cross, and later at Ephesus—serves as model for the contemplative yet hierarchical Church. John presents Jesus as the very temple, his own body replacing the Jerusalem Temple. This leads to a new liturgical sense, as we also see in the Letter to the Hebrews.

There is a special relation with women in the Gospel of John. The image of the 'Beloved Disciple' laying his head on the breast of Jesus serves as basic image for the contemplative life, as does the story of Martha and Mary, where Mary, seated at the feet of Jesus, is depicted as the model of contemplative life, which will become for Origen and much of the tradition the goal of discipleship. Service also figures largely here: whereas the Synoptic Gospels highlight the institution of the Eucharist at the Last Supper, John—who places the extensive Last Supper discourse at that meal—does not explicitly mention the institution of the Eucharist, but rather focuses on the washing of the feet of the disciples. The notion of 'abiding' is central to John, the mutual indwelling which is the heart of the Trinity, and into which the disciple is initiated by Jesus. Love alone emerges as the summit of the teaching.

In the Synoptics, the disciples are shown as gradually coming to an understanding of who Christ is. Jesus is portrayed as a teacher—a rabbi—who gathers a group of disciples whom he instructs in more intimate detail than the teaching he is giving to the multitudes. Jesus is shown as in the prophetic tradition, engaging in symbolic actions, in purifying words and deeds as regards the practice of religion, as preaching the Kingdom of God, and its imminence. Gradually he leads others to see that he is the Messiah, the Christ, as Peter proclaims—but who this Christ is, and what that means, is newly articulated in him, and only fully revealed by the Holy Spirit. There had been one strong and strongly developing understanding of this in the 'Suffering Servant' of Isaiah, but nothing had pointed to this 'son of David' being a martyr, let alone one who 'died for our sins' as St. Peter will write (1 Pet. 2:24) and Paul elsewhere (1 Cor. 15:3 *inter alia*). Jesus most commonly identifies himself with the figure from Daniel—the 'Son of Man'. He is addressed as teacher, and shown as being addressed as 'Lord'. He is also called the 'Son of God' and at least in Mark's Gospel, in the Passion, he himself accepts this title.

Throughout the New Testament there is an expectation of the Parousia, of the 'coming of the Kingdom of God in power'—and of the return of the Lord. The last word of the Testament is 'Μαρανα θα', variously translated, but 'Come Lord' seems to convey it.

The spirituality to emerge from the encounter with Jesus was seen in Acts' description of the life of the most primitive Christian community, which is sometimes seen as a charter for monasticism. The Dead Sea Scrolls—identified with the Essene community—speak of a Teacher, a Master, of a communal meal, and share the apocalyptic spirit of the New Testament. The emphasis on community is noteworthy as is the 'breaking of the bread'—the sacramental meal at the center of the life of the community. This was balanced, from early times, by a move into the desert: first in Palestine, then in Egypt and Syria, eventually in Europe itself. The book of Acts also shows the power of imitating Christ in death: Stephen's vision of Christ at his stoning speaks both of the faith in who Jesus is—the Son of Man of Daniel—and the way of being united with him spiritually, by dying a martyr's death in union and imitation of him. The 'spiritual life' of the early Christians could be characterized as a longing to 'bear witness to Christ' in suffering martyrdom: to renounce the world—hence the high value placed on virginity—and to 'imitate Jesus' by being killed unjustly. Stephen, the first martyr, showed the way, his death portrayed as a close imitation of the death of Jesus, similarly with Paul's final journey to Jerusalem.

THE EARLY CHURCH

What we have come to know as Christology was hammered out in debates between leading centers of Greek learning in the eastern Mediterranean world in the centuries after Christ. The intellectual life of the nascent Christian Church began to take place in Alexandria, where, building on the work of the Jewish Platonist Philo, Clement and Origen began a famous catechetical school, showing that the true 'Gnostic'—the true 'philosopher'—was the Christian. This built on the Greek tradition which valued contemplation above all things: and the way to contemplation was through an intellectual ascent, that is, through ideas. In Origen we see an intertwining of the spiritual and the intellectual, for he was the son of a martyr, and was himself eager for a martyr's death, but he was also profoundly intellectual. Christ was seen as 'the good shepherd' in these early times, and also as a teacher.

It was in the intellectual center of Alexandria then that the first great controversies began, for it was there that the first intellectual articulation of who Christ is was attempted. It was the debate as to the relation of Christ to God (the Father) centered on the Platonically/Hellenistically educated priest Arius that triggered the first great, lasting intellectual crisis in the Church. Arius claimed that Christ was the greatest of God's creatures, but was not equal to God. The relation of the Father to the Son, and later of what came to be called 'persons' in the Trinity, would take the Christian Church centuries to hammer out. Council after council met, carefully if also passionately articulating what came to be known as the 'Faith of the Church', or orthodoxy. Jesus Christ, true God and true man, one in substance/being, with the Father (ὁμοούσιος). Three persons in One God. The Holy Spirit proceeding from the Father (later, in the West, 'and from the Son'—'Filoque').

These 'Christological' articulations of the faith were seen as essential to the reality of discipleship in a culture where cerebral activity was the defining activity of the human being. However, there were two limits to this, on either side. On the one hand, there was the 'contemplative ideal' at the heights of the intellectual life itself (namely, Neoplatonism) and on the other, there was the emerging monastic practice.

As Christianity went from being a persecuted, underground movement of 'house churches' in which people gathered for mutual support in awaiting the coming of the Kingdom and living godly lives in a morally turpid world, hoping for (or sometimes seeking to avoid) the grace of martyrdom which was seen as the peak of the spiritual life, to a religion of the state, in which clear definitions were needed for the faith the state required of its subjects, the phenomenon of monasticism began to emerge as the preferred way to live the spiritual life. The sacramental life of the settled Christian communities might be the ordinary means of salvation, but the extraordinary—ascetical—life of the desert called those who wanted to live the spiritual life. In doing this, they were continuing a tradition that went back to the Jerusalem community, but also incorporating elements that were not likely as present. So the radical solitude of much of desert monasticism—μοναχός—would seem to contrast strongly with the communal emphasis of the early Church. Still, even in writings of the Desert Fathers, communal meetings do stand out. But the sacramental, and ecclesial, life receded in favor of the direct search for and encounter with God in the solitude of the desert. Thus began what has remained a formative tension in Christian life.

At the same time as the Church Fathers were developing their articulations of Christology, they were often linked with others who were living lives of radical contemplation in the desert, such as Athanasius and Antony. Other figures stand out: Jerome, Cassian, Irenaeus, Evagrius Ponticus and Diadochus, Maximus, Augustine, the Cappadocians, Dionysius. There was no insistence on 'experience': it was taken for granted and permeated the conceptual articulation of their theology. Yet what is surprising is that our contemporary sense of 'relationship' with Jesus—or of a warm, personal presence—is largely absent in these ages, with the notable exception of Augustine, whose integrated intellectual spirituality played a defining role for the Western Church.

In Origen, it is true, a bridal mysticism appears. Bridal mysticism was found articulated most clearly in the Song of Songs in the Old Testament, and appears in the New as well ('The Spirit and the Bride say, Come'; Rev. 22:17). With Origen, the commentary on the Song of Songs, which became a staple of monastic spirituality, first appears.

The Christological controversies of these early centuries found two poles in Alexandria (λόγος/σάρξ) and then Antioch (λόγος/ἄνθρωπος). The school of Alexandria represented a Greek, that is, Platonic, tradition, which eventually veered towards monophysitism. Alexandria had been the home of Arius, himself heavily Platonist. There was a tendency here to a great abstraction, to seeing Christ as more an 'essence' than a person. And as always in the Platonic world there was a central move inwards and upwards, from the 'less real' (and physical) to the 'more real' (and incorporeal/immaterial). In Antioch, home to Nestorius, the opposite tendency emerged: that of sacrificing the divinity of Christ to his humanity. These two tendencies in Christology have remained marked in the Church's life, and spirituality, ever since.

Christ in these early centuries was often depicted as Pantocrator—and in its earthly sense, as cosmic Emperor. As the Church emerged from the catacombs and in fact became the religion of the Empire, it was only natural that the Risen Christ—Teacher, Good Shepherd—should also be seen as the cosmic emperor. And, again, it was in these centers of learning and culture that the theological debates were at their most fierce. The articulation of who Christ was, the attempt to place into language—to articulate in thought—the whole picture of reality, of orthodoxy. Spiritual health depended upon this, even as the description of a picture could be correct or seriously distorted and distorting. Orthodoxy was the key to spiritual health, while spiritual sickness, or distortion, was called 'heresy' and attempts were made to cut such sickness from the body of the faithful. Since the event of the resurrection was central to all reality, and the 'cosmic Christ' was who the Risen Jesus was, and as the Church found itself embodying access to his reality on earth, the divine liturgy itself became the locus of encounter with God on earth. If in the Gospel the Risen Christ was shown as encountered and known 'in the breaking of the bread', ever more glorious liturgical articulations of this presence formed a spirituality of worship which was at the heart of the Christian experience, East and West, for the first millennium. He was known 'where two or three were gathered in His Name', where the 'Word' was proclaimed and heard, where the 'bread was broken and shared'. St. John Chrysostom and St. Basil the Great are especially noted for their contributions in the liturgy.

In the desert—Egypt, Syria, Palestine—the other main tradition in the Church, namely, the monastic tradition, kept growing apace. Here, it was the inner battle for purity of heart, and so battle with the demons that was the main struggle of the Christian soul and with it, the development of the discernment of spirits. In later Hesychasm a search for the inner light began. St. Antony the Great and Pachomius, Evagrius Ponticus, Diadochus of Photike, and a host of Desert Fathers were laying the foundations of that monasticism which would be central in the Church's experience of God for the next millennium. At its heart was the practice of prayer which centered on the recitation of the psalms and on 'ejaculatory' prayers. From monasticism, the practice of confession of sins began to grow and spread beyond the monasteries, deepening the conversion begun for all the faithful at baptism.

Mediterranean Christianity had begun as an outgrowth of Jewish thought and practice and—more to our point—mysticism/apocalypticism, and spread among various strata of people in the Roman Empire. It early became a religion of cultured people, living in a high civilization. It took root among some of the intelligentsia, who, as in Alexandria and Antioch, began articulating their knowledge of Christ in terms of Greek thought, as well as among others, who—perhaps for ethnic reasons, like the Copts of Egypt—either were not part of the Graeco-Roman civilization or who, like Jerome, chose to flee that civilization in its latter days.

THE MIDDLE AGES

With the collapse of the Roman Empire, new peoples emerged from the north and east of Europe, storming the very gates of Hippo where the Roman theologian and mystic Augustine lay dying. The invasion of the 'barbarians' roughly coincided with the rise of Islam in the ancient homeland of Christianity. It is no doubt a factor in the dramatic rise of Islam that Christianity had been weakened by internal struggles, most notably the iconoclastic controversy—that is, the question of whether or not representations should be made of holy subjects. This had much to do with the development of subsequent spirituality in the East, where 'knowing Christ' became a matter of contemplating Christ both in the liturgy and especially in his inspired iconic representation, where the icons as locus of divine presence came to be comparable to the reserved Eucharist in the Western Church. The twin pillars of liturgical contemplation and monastic spirituality would come to characterize the Eastern Church and be bearers of the faith, as the centers of Greek intellectuality became swamped by Islam, and the Church retreated to the monasteries and churches.

Islam represented a rejection of the iconic tradition, a Docetic Christology and also perhaps a radical expression of monophysitism. It was also an embodiment of the 'desert spirituality' which had characterized Israel prior to its occupation of Canaan as well as some of the early spirituality of the Church: that is, non-sacramental and non-liturgical yet also non-monastic, radically focused on 'the One God' and so also in the end radically non-Christological. Christianity had become a religion of the cities, and vast stretches of the countryside of the Middle East and North Africa were lost to it as Islam absorbed them.

But in Europe, as Roman civilization re-emerged and was spread, the Church herself found new life among the 'barbarian peoples'. The vehicle for the spread of the faith was monasticism, identified in Western Europe with St. Benedict, and in the East, though to a lesser degree, with Sts. Cyril and Methodius. With the loss of urban centers of study, for the next thousand years, monasticism would be the home of both Christian reflection and spiritual practice.

The West had been evangelized at the same time as the Eastern Empire, but the West did not have the tremendous intellectual tradition that characterized the Greek-speaking world, and the Latin tradition developed more slowly, and more simply, than the Greek. Still, it is France that is considered the 'eldest daughter of the Church', with claims that Gospel peers of Jesus himself—Mary Magdalene, Lazarus—traveled to France. Early Christian Fathers—Athanasius in Trier, Irenaeus of Lyons, Vincent of

Lerins, Martin of Tours, Hilary of Poitiers, Ambrose of Milan—were present in the far western European regions of the Roman Empire. Less speculative and more practical, the Western Church emphasized the role of the Son in the procession of the Holy Spirit, and so added the 'Filioque' to the Creed of Nicaea, thus emphasizing what was initially an unspoken but commonly agreed upon understanding—but as a unilateral addition, this would do much mischief in coming centuries.

The understanding of who Christ was had been hammered out in the seven great councils of the early Church, councils that took place in the East and were mostly staffed by representatives of the Eastern Church—yet with Western participation, most particularly through representatives of the Roman pontiff. Throughout the late first millennium, most of Europe was experiencing a deepening of the evangelizing work of the monks. Models of sanctity—of deep imitation of Christ—were offered by the saints. The monastic ideal was to the fore, with the eremitical life both at its roots and fringes. St. Bernard renewed the ancient impulse of spousal mysticism and deepened the warm, personal devotion to Jesus.

With the crowning of Charlemagne, a new manifestation of the Roman Empire occurred. The ancient Roman civilization was being brought back to life in the forests of the north, this time, under Christian tutelage—hence 'Holy Roman Empire'. For the traveling warrior nations of Northern Europe, a new sort of spirituality emerged, one of the warriors for Christ. If Christ was the king, then the disciple was to be his good knight. Military orders emerged, and with them, at the turn of the millennium, a great impetus to imitate Christ by traveling to the Holy Places in the Holy Land—but that Holy Land must be freed from its occupiers, the 'infidels' who had departed from orthodox Christianity and returned to a non-Trinitarian non-incarnational religion. Templars, Crusaders, Teutonic Knights were attempts at priestly-military brotherhoods in the service of Christ the king. Pilgrimage—a people moving toward God—played a great role in this spirituality of movement.

Throughout this period—moving into the High Middle Ages—there continued a flourishing of monastic life. There had been great saints in the British Isles, most notably in Ireland, which was the westernmost outpost of the great tradition of Egyptian monachism, and its ascetical-mystical heart. From there, the monastic movement re-invigorated Europe, and there was a flowering of Benedictine monasticism and mysticism, most notably among the women mystics of Germany. Hildegard, Gertrude, Mechthilde, Walburga, and Elizabeth of Hungary all experienced an intimacy with Jesus which was glowing in its realism. There was a 'northern Thebaid' in the hermitages across all of Europe, where people would go to fast and pray and live hidden lives—often as anchorites walled up alongside churches—seeking the experience of God. One went into solitude to encounter Christ—along with Bruno and Romuald and an army of other solitaries. So on the one hand there were the Crusades, attempts to give one's life in the service of the heavenly king by lengthy pilgrimage and actual combat, there were saintly kings and queens serving Christ above all in their service of the poor, and on the other, the peaceful work of the monks and nuns, taming the soil, maintaining the civilizing work of prayer and study, centered on the adoration of Christ in contemplative prayer.

Toward the end of the first and beginning of the second millennium in the West the monastic spiritual ideal gradually began to take on more scholastic elements. The sense-based philosophy of Aristotle began to penetrate the West, replacing the mystically oriented thought of Plato. For Plato, and the ancient world formed by him, this world is but a participation in the only real world, the unseen world of the forms—of the ideas. For Aristotle, there is no knowledge which is not based in the senses. Aristotle's philosophy helped Western Christians articulate the centrality of the Incarnation and its physicality: that there is nothing in the mind that was not first in the senses, as the scholastic maxim would have it. This combined with the insistence on the role of human reason perhaps encouraged by the 'filioque' would have profound effects on Western spirituality, focusing on the incarnation of the Logos.

There gradually arose, in the West, a world of the schools. Emerging from the monasteries, these came to have a life of their own, as the mind began to declare its autonomy from the heart, as the inquiring intellect began to move away from the communal mind—and leadership—of the hierarchical Church. In this world of ideas, the Son tended to become 'mind incarnate'—and as for even St. Bonaventure, there was 'The ascent of the mind to God'. The privileged way to God was the way of the consecrated life, the life of what were called 'the religious' as distinct from the secular clergy and the laity. The 'religious' followed what were called the 'counsels of perfection'.

As the Church in mediaeval Europe became more powerful, there was a need to bridge the gap between the wisdom and holiness of the monasteries and the world outside their walls, and so there emerged the new communities of mendicants. In a newly rich world, in which the Church herself was wealthy and powerful, poverty emerged as an ideal in the following of Christ—and so St. Francis and his movement. St. Francis had roots in the Benedictine tradition, but introduced a more personal note in his devotion to the infant Jesus, and in his experience of the stigmata, that is, literally sharing in the wounds of Jesus.

The need to share the wisdom of the contemplative cloister with the world, combined with the need to combat heresies which would distort the true image of the face of Christ and so of his disciple, led to the movement of St. Dominic. These two movements, bringing the cloister into the world, began to bring an 'imitation of Christ' more clearly into practice. Whereas earlier—in the first millennium—the Church was, as it were, intoxicated with the glorious event of the resurrection, where the universe was transformed by the resurrection of Christ, and it was only a matter of time before its effects could be known in the Christian emperor and the kingdoms under him, by the second millennium, this began to wear thin, and a closer following of Christ, with a new focus on his Passion, emerged as a hunger. Mary had been known as the mother of the faithful, ever since she was given to John as the beloved disciple's mother at the foot of the Cross, and went to live with John at Ephesus. Now, in the Middle Ages, Mary herself came to a cosmic status and was honored as Queen of Heaven: the images of her coronation by her Son complete, in a way, the Christological debates of the first centuries. Adoration of Christ in the Eucharist also emerged as a locus of encounter in the Western Church.

Thus the monasticism of the first millennium was supplemented by another sort of monasticism, a much more mobile monasticism, which sought to serve Christ not just in choir and in chant and in daily work, but much more concretely, in this world, by identification with the poor, the peace-makers, the teachers. The universities began seeking an autonomy, leaving the primarily contemplative, transformative interest of monastic theology, and moving into the world of thought itself, a thought that was increasingly unrelated to the movements of the heart, and so, increasingly cut off from contemplation. The life of the mind climbed to ever greater, more abstract heights in its articulation and understanding of the truths of the faith—but philosophy tended to replace and absorb a more practical spiritual life, and led to the reaction called the *Devotio Moderna*. This devotion, centered in the northwest of Europe, the Rhineland countries of Germany, Flanders, and Holland, produced the classic of *The Imitation of Christ*. Christ was no longer seen primarily as the Cosmic Christ—the Pantocrator—and there now emerged, in line with the earlier Franciscan movement, a Jesus 'meek and humble of heart'. A religion of inwardness, an emphasis on evangelical simplicity emerged to balance the rapidly degenerating sterility of late scholasticism. Whereas the world of thought focused on the more abstract qualities of Christ, the world of prayer had to find Jesus in his humanity. For Thomas Aquinas the two came together in his love of the 'broken bread', in his devotion to the Eucharist, and is reflected in his Eucharistic hymns.

There had been a flourishing of mysticism in the late Middle Ages. With Meister Eckhart in Germany and *The Cloud of Unknowing* in Britain, the apophaticism of the early Christian East returned and urged the soul to go beyond the world of thoughts, words, and images into the formless silence which opens onto God.

The Society of Jesus broke upon the scene in Europe just around the time that the northwestern European nations were discovering Jesus in his word alone, and turning away from both sacramental life and ascetical/mystical life as known in monasticism, both of which had become perhaps as much obstacles as openings to the encounter with Christ. There had long been a devotion to the person of Jesus, and handbooks of meditation on his life. St. Ignatius focused devotion to the person of Christ in a way that made the fruit of the hermit's cell accessible to the believer in the world, through the use of time (a month's retreat, hours of meditation), space (isolation), and a systematic insertion into deep currents of contemplation, supplemented with the rediscovery of the ancient practice of the discernment of spirits. This mysticism of the person of Jesus was to be buttressed by study of the theological tradition of the Church, in the spirit of obedience to Church authority. The tradition formed by St. Ignatius insisted on the humanity of Christ as entry point into his divinity, and was radically cataphatic, insisting on the use of the imagination, in unique contradistinction to much of the tradition, most notably of the East.

THE REFORMATION

The Reform movement in northwestern Europe moved along different lines. A shared devotion to the person of Jesus yet did not lead to a deep personal encounter with him in the contemplative tradition nor yet in the community of the wider Church, but rather in smaller groups of fervent disciples who were focused on the experience of the Word, with a steadily weakening tie to sacrament, hierarchy, and scholastic reflection. A theological tradition began developing which was reminiscent of rabbinic study of the Scriptures, where 'sola Scriptura' meant that the text of Scripture itself became the locus of incarnation, largely replacing the Eucharist or mystical encounter, though these remained present in varying degrees. Various understandings of theology and of who Christ was began appearing, and with them, various spiritualities emerged as well. In general, the majesty and otherness of God was stressed (Calvin), though a warm piety of the heart might balance this, most notably in the Lutheran tradition. There was a relation to Jesus as 'friend of my soul'—a non-imperial, non-ecclesial Jesus—especially in what became Pietism. For Calvin, the image of Christ as priest-prophet-king spoke of a majestic presence, though the majesty of God was highlighted, along with God's awesome, yet terrifying, power as seen in predestination. For Luther and his spiritual progeny, the dialectic spirit guaranteed no rest, for the Cross became so central as to effectively block all access to 'glory'—that glory most celebrated in ancient and Eastern Christianity, but also not lacking in Baroque Catholicism. Indeed, Luther's protest was a thoroughgoing rejection of all that was philosophical ('the whore reason'), and though he respected mystical saints like Bernard, there was also a rejection of the contemplative, insofar as it was not clearly evangelical. The magnificent choral meditations of J. S. Bach and others brought Luther's theology of the Cross and warm personal devotion to Jesus into the heart of Christian experience in the new communities.

While the new Protestant ideas were distancing the northwest of Europe from the community of traditional Christianity, Spain produced a century of tremendous mystics, in St. John of the Cross, St. Teresa of Avila, and St. John of Avila, all considered doctors of the Church. St. Teresa especially insisted that there was no leaving behind the humanity of Christ in ascent to God. Both she and John of the Cross had heavily introspective and psychological understandings, which yet were relatively weak doctrinally. Spirituality began to take an inner turn, a self-reflective, psychological turn, and though the person of Jesus remained absolutely central, there was no real Christological reflection present in their works.

SEVENTEENTH CENTURY TO THE MODERN PERIOD

With the seventeenth century, we begin moving into the modern world of Europe. Monasticism had long been in decline. The spiritual life was largely represented by religious orders, in the Catholic world; monasticism in the Orthodox; and by pietistic movements of fervor in the Protestant world. The seventeenth century was the century of tremendous spiritual life in France—the 'Grand siècle', largely formed by the Jesuits—but it was also the century in which the seeds of Enlightenment rationalism were being spread. The devotion to the Sacred Heart—a particularly Catholic devotion—countered that rationalism. Blaise Pascal wrote of 'reasons of the heart'—and the tension as between the rigidity of Jansenism and the magnanimity of the Jesuits developed.

Modernity emerged as a reaction to the mediaeval/spiritual worldview, a declaration of autonomy by the world from the things of God, hence, 'secularism'. The Catholic Church and her institutions were increasingly beleaguered throughout the eighteenth century in Western Europe as the institution of monasticism in particular, and its child in religious life, was attacked throughout the Catholic world by a new understanding of 'enlightenment' in which reason, cut off from traditional wisdom and the Logos revealed in the Scriptures, declared its autonomy. Monasticism continued its decline, indeed, was generally suppressed, and the religious life which had pervaded entire societies—most notably the French—was radically ripped out. That is, the heart was ripped out by the head, a head which no longer recognized Jesus as Lord, nor God as his Father. Rather, 'God' became a Deist idea, disincarnate, represented by the autonomous 'reason' let loose upon the world: what Pascal called the 'god of the philosophers' triumphed over the 'God of Abraham, Isaac, and Jacob'. Rather than the Christian heart—spirituality and its asceticism—sensuality and sentimentality in various forms began to increase, notably in the arts.

The nineteenth century was the great century of 'progress' in the West. Religion had been dealt a most serious blow in the revolutions of the late eighteenth and early nineteenth centuries, and though a 'reactionary' order had been restored in Europe, autonomous reason, cut off from tradition, faith, or hierarchical authority continued its work creating a new world. There were periods of growth throughout the Catholic world in particular: seen most notably in the Carmelite saints of the late nineteenth and early twentieth centuries, with their strong relations with the person of Jesus.

In the Germanic world, a search for Jesus was begun, which has continued to this day. No longer looking in the heart nor in the contemplative tradition, this search is exclusively a textual search, trying to find Christ as an idea that was instantiated—or was not—in the man Jesus of Nazareth.

Other images of Jesus emerged in the twentieth century. In the heavily Marxist world of that century, Jesus was seen as liberator in liberation and feminist theology. Christ was seen as prophet—in what was criticized by some as a return to Old Testament theology. Balancing this were new spiritualities of service, as seen in figures like Dorothy Day and Mother Teresa. As historically much of Christianity had been a state religion, gradually identified with the wealthy classes, the Worker Priest movement in Europe sought to bring to life Christ's identification with the working man, while in the US there was the Catholic Worker movement. Liberation theology later produced martyrs especially in Latin American countries where nominal Christians were seen as scandalous oppressors of God's 'little ones', and this prophetic dimension of Christ's ministry emerged within the Church itself.

A spirituality of Christian service came much to the fore then, along with a new awareness of human suffering. Perhaps Matthew 25 more than any other chapter—the

Last Judgment scene, narrated by Jesus—came to characterize this age above all. This was central to the witness of Mother Teresa of Calcutta, declared a saint of the Catholic Church, whose spirituality was focused on this Gospel scene, while living an inner life characterized by 'dark nights' which bore fruit in joyful service.

Yet monasticism also experienced a new life both through the new ecumenical center of Taize and through the work of the great American monk-writer Thomas Merton, whose witness to the monastic impulse highlighted the transcendental witness of Christ in an all-claiming world, without losing the prophetic dimension.

Dialogue with the great traditions of Asia has singularly characterized this age, and along with it, in an age which is without form—as the great Anglican poet T. S. Eliot observed—a return to apophatic mysticism. Merton, Benedictine Bede Griffiths, and others pioneered the contemplative encounter with Asia. The ancient practice of spiritual direction and interest in retreats has also flourished. It is the Buddhist tradition above all that has been a dialogue partner, and has quietly but profoundly influenced many in the West. But the move to a formless absolute and away from the revealed person of Christ has also provoked a strong reaction, especially from Church hierarchy, concerned lest moving away from Greece—and toward India especially—the Church is not in danger of losing the biblical God of Israel as well, and with him, of course, the form and figure of the historical Jesus of Nazareth.

Perhaps balancing this, further East, the teaching of Jesus in the Beatitudes profoundly formed the Hindu saint Mohandas Gandhi, and Christian values have brought a previously unknown awareness of and concern for social justice to Asian traditions in phenomena like 'Engaged Buddhism'.

The Eastern Churches began producing figures of Christian witness in forms beyond the monastic and liturgical. Largely lacking a philosophically based theological tradition in the second millennium, the East tended to articulate its further witness through literature and music. Writers like Dostoevsky and Tolstoy brought Christian concerns into the world. Prince Myshkin—'The Idiot'—is considered a prima facie expression of the kenotic Christ, Christ the humiliated fool, who is a central figure of Russian literature. Greek writer Nikos Kazantzakis explored difficult Christian themes revealed in profound human situations.

There was a revival of Hesychasm on Mount Athos, in which the search for the experience of the Taboric Light built on the tradition of the Desert Fathers, focusing it on this particular transformative experience, issuing from the transfiguration of Christ. Russo-Canadian Catholic mystic Catherine de Hueck Doherty brought this spirituality to life in North America through the poustinia movement while Serafim Rose, Orthodox mystic in Northern California, became an influential writer in Russia itself. The eremitical vocation has been experiencing a quiet reappearance in the West as well.

In the twentieth century, Pentecostalism and the related charismatic movement claimed to bring back the Spirit of Pentecost into a church which had become suspicious of the ostensible gifts of the Holy Spirit at the time of Montanus. It was claimed that the charisms of the early Church were being poured out again. Along with this, came a 'Spirit Christology'.

In light of the tremendous secularization of modernity, during the long pontificate of Pope John Paul II, there was a call for a 'new evangelization'. In the teaching, Christ the preacher came to the fore, now a humanist Christ who 'reveals man to man'. Having experienced the great horrors of the godless twentieth century in the heart of tortured Europe, that papacy brought to the consciousness of many the spiritual revelations of St. Faustina Kowalska, whose spiritual diary is replete with encounters with Jesus—her mission of 'mercy' has touched millions worldwide. The Church also saw figures like St. Benedicta of the Cross (Edith Stein) and St. Maximilian Kolbe giving their lives in union with Christ in the concentration camps which became a symbol for the godlessness of the twentieth century. Walter Ciszek's *He Leadeth Me*, a spiritual classic based on reflections of the author's decades in Soviet prisons, and Alexander Solzhenitsyn's *Gulag Archipelago* both offer profound reflections and a spirituality for what has been to date the century of greatest Christian martyrdom.

In the Lutheran tradition, Pastor Dietrich Bonhoeffer shared in this witness of confronting radical evil, and dying a death in martyrdom. For Bonhoeffer, the world in its 'worldliness' became the place of encounter with Christ, especially as he experienced the 'official' Church as much compromised with the world. Later, the 'Death of God' movement—building on the profound insights of Nietzsche, himself son of a pastor—sought to find God in a world stripped of the sacred.

Returning to Von Balthasar's concern about the integration of theology and spirituality, twentieth-century dogmatic theologian Karl Rahner famously observed: 'The Christian of the future will be a mystic or he will not exist at all' (Rahner 1981: 149). This leaves us with the question: how does one know Christ—where does one find Christ today? As always, formed by meditation on the portraits of the Gospels and teaching of the Epistles, emboldened by the vision of Revelation, guided by the dogmas articulated in the Creeds, Christ is to be found where he said he would be found: among the least of his brethren, among the little ones, among the children, and, as his brethren noted, in the breaking of the bread, where two or three are gathered in his name. Ultimately, he will be encountered where—being Lord—he wants to reveal himself, and where he finds a receptive heart.

SUGGESTED READING

Kereszty and Roch (2002); Pourrat (1953); Von Balthasar (1982, 1989).

BIBLIOGRAPHY

Bouyer, L. (1963), *History of Christian Spirituality*, 3 vols., trans. M. P. Ryan (New York: Desclee).
Bouyer, L. (1978), *The Eternal Son*, trans. S. Inkel and J. F. Laughlin (Huntington, Ind.: Our Sunday Visitor Press).
Holmes III, U. T. (1980), *A History of Christian Spirituality* (New York: Seabury Press).

Jones, C., G. Wainwright, and E. Yarnold (eds.) (1986), *The Study of Spirituality* (New York: Oxford University Press).

Kereszty, O. and A. Roch (2002), *Jesus Christ, Fundamentals of Christology* (New York: Alba House).

McIntosh, M. A. (1996), *Christology from Within* (Notre Dame: University of Notre Dame Press).

Pourrat, P. (1953), *Christian Spirituality*, 4 vols., trans. W. H. Mitchell and S. P. Jacques (Westminster, Md.: Newman Press).

Rahner, K. (1981), *Theological Investigations: Concern for the Church*, vol. 20, trans. E. Quinn (New York: Crossroads).

Thompson, W. M. (1991), *Christology and Spirituality* (New York: Crossroads).

Viller, M. (ed.) (1974), 'Jesus Christ', in *Dictionnaire de Spiritualité Ascétique et Mystique: Doctrine et Histoire* (Paris: Beauchesne).

Von Balthasar, H. U. (1982), *The Glory of the Lord, Volume 1: Seeing the Form*, trans. E. Leiva-Merikakis (San Francisco: Ignatius Press).

Von Balthasar, H. U. (1989), 'Theology and Sanctity', in Von Balthasar, *Explorations in Theology, Volume 1: The Word Made Flesh*, trans. A. V. Littledale (San Francisco: Ignatius Press), 181–209.

CHAPTER 25

CHINESE CHRISTOLOGIES

Images of Christ and Chinese Cultures

K. K. YEO

UNDERSTANDING the identity of Jesus Christ in the Scriptures has been a difficult question ever since Jesus asked of his disciples: 'Who do you say that I am?' (Matt. 16:15; Mark 8:29; Luke 9:20), and the question becomes even more challenging if approached from diverse cultures. All Christologies have soteriological significance: how will Christ fulfill various human needs or predicaments? Philipp Melanchthon says, 'To know Christ is to know his benefits' (Pauck 1969: 21; see also Pelikan 1999; Kärkkainen 2003). To respond to this Christological and hermeneutical question, the chapter will first survey from historical and typological perspectives what Chinese Christian Christologies have to say concerning which Christology saves, and which destroys, China. Then, we will attempt to construct, first, a distinctive Chinese Christology of *dao* (way) that attempts to demonstrate the mutually transformative power between Christology and language, and, secondly, a Chinese Christology of *renren* (a person who loves) that attempts to demonstrate Christ(ians) as the glorious image(s) of God. The implication is that such a biblical, contextual, and global Chinese Christology has the aspiration of ordering the world with beauty.

CHINESE CHRISTIAN CHRISTOLOGIES: AN HISTORICAL PERSPECTIVE

Our first task is to survey the historical landscape of Chinese Christologies, noting how the images of Christ relate to and impact specific cultural contexts.

From Tang to Ming Dynasties: Christ and Chinese Religions

Nestorian Christianity interpreted the Virgin Mary to be the mother of Jesus (Χριστοτόκος), but not the mother of God (Θεοτόκος), and held to the dyophysite Christology (the disunion between the divine and human natures of Jesus Christ—the divine λόγος and human Jesus). It was condemned as heresy at the Council of Ephesus in 431 (Hickley 1980: 6). A few centuries later, some of the Syrian Nestorians came to north China at the political height of the Tang Dynasty (618–906), when China was steeped in the Buddhist ethos. Therefore, much of the Chinese rendition of Nestorian Christology was expressed through Buddhist terminologies, and was theologically similar to Nestorian adoption Christology (that is, Christ was born a human and later adopted as God's Son). On the top of the Nestorian tablet found in Xian in 1652, there is a carving of two dragons holding a pearl, a cross (not a crucifix) that surmounts a lotus (the emblem for Buddhism), and a cloud (the emblem for Daoism), but a text on it reads, 'He hung up in the shining sun in order to triumph over the realm of darkness' (Cary-Elwes 1957: 34–5).

During the Northern Sung Dynasty (960–1125), Buddhism was declining, and Confucianism was gaining in strength. The Neo-Confucian orthodoxy of the Ming Dynasty (1368–1643) developed its Sinocentrism, and that posed a challenge to the work of the Jesuit missionaries. Confucianism, under the revival of Wang Yangming (1472–1529), argued for unity of self and society, knowledge (*zhi*) and action (*xing*), mind-heart (*xing*) and universal principle (*li*). Philosopher Wang believed that innate knowledge of right and wrong in every individual should lead one to public life driven by love (*ren*). The Jesuit missionaries were quick to use the principle of accommodation and an indigenous approach in their Christology, such as in the work of Matteo Ricci (1552–1610). Ricci's missionary strategy was to supply the needs of China, as he discerned them, to reach out to the most influential groups in Chinese society, that is, the intelligentsia. He introduced Christ to the Chinese via Western mathematics, science, and cartography, and he reached out to the emperor and the official elite. Ricci's image of a Christ who dressed in the silk robes of the literati attracted the Chinese intelligentsia. Ricci interpreted Confucius to be a moralist and Christ to be a morally perfect Savior. Ricci understood sanctification to be the spiritual-moral discipline of Chinese Christians. The Jesuits' Christology granted blessings for Chinese Christians to worship *Tian* (heaven) and their ancestors. When the French Jesuits healed Kangxi (1654–1722), the emperor returned his royal favor to them and wrote a Christological poem, using aesthetic language to express biblical truth:

> When the work was accomplished, blood formed a creek.
> Grace from the west was thousand feet deep.
> He who lowered himself for us stepped on the midnight trip.
> Before the rooster crowed twice, betrayed thrice was He.
> Five hundred slashes torn every inch of his skin.
> Two thieves at six feet high hanged besides him.
> The sadness was greater than anything seen by anyone.
> This poem is for You, the Holy one.

(Kanxi 2013)

Not all the Jesuit fathers, however, agreed with Ricci's view on the Rites of Confucius. It was during the Rites controversy (1644–1721) that both the Jesuits and the Chinese themselves were unprepared to deal with the complex relationship between the Law (Old Testament laws, or laws in any culture or religion) and Christ. A pertinent Christological question in this period was: What have the laws of Europe or those of China (e.g., astronomy and calendar) to do with Christ? The key missionary concern has been Christ and culture: What has Jerusalem and the Bible to do with Beijing and culture? (My book, *What Has Jerusalem to Do with Beijing? Biblical Interpretation from a Chinese Perspective* [1998], is one example of the continuous quest of Chinese Christians hoping to find some answers.) Most Protestants, up to the present, saw these Rites (of reverencing ancestors and *Tian*) as idolatrous, while Catholics are now more open. (I have attempted to deal with this issue in my Chinese book, *Ancestor Worship: Rhetorical and Cross-Cultural Hermeneutical Response* [1996].) Many Chinese Christians live in an oxymoronic state where they want to be faithful believers of Christ and also filial pietists. Many live in an impossible world of embracing the teaching of both Confucius and Christ. Does Christ, the New Law, annul or supplement and fulfill the Old Law, such as that of Confucian teachings (Whyte 1988: 71–2)?

Qing Dynasty: Chinese Christ and Violence (Inner and Outer Person, Fully Divine and Fully Human)

A set of problems for the Qing Dynasty (1721–1911) government was its foreign policy and power equation with the West. The image of Christ that impacted China through the form of scientific technology or intellectual encounter with the literati of the previous centuries was long gone. Rather, it came to China violently through the opium trade (as early as c.1720, but mostly in the 1800s) to the common people. It came at a time when the vulnerable Chinese soul was on the brink of collapse due to violence within and without the country. Much of the violence was conveyed to the Chinese via the Cross of Christ.

It was a challenge for missionaries themselves to understand the complexity of China so as to make the whole Gospel of Christ incarnational in the real socio-political and cultural contexts of China. The way the 'fully divine and fully human' Christ was translated into the 'fully spiritual and fully social' of Chinese personhood became the crux of Christology at that time. A distorted Christology might have encouraged a confused and psychotic Chinese Christian toward a bizarre apocalyptic salvation of China, such as that of Hong Xiuquan (1813–64), the leader of the Taiping Rebellion (1850–64). Hong saw himself chosen by God to be the Chinese Messiah, 'God's Chinese Son' (Spence 1996) in order to exorcize the Manchu demons from China and lead the elect Chinese to usher in God's kingdom on earth. He claimed to share the same nature with Christ, to be as it were Christ's brother (Cary-Elwes 1957: 193; Cheng 1963: 82–3). He envisioned a Christian theocracy on Chinese soil. Understanding Christ's kingdom on earth was a significant Christological issue for the Chinese. Hong's millenarian idea was expressed in Christian form (*tianguo*, i.e., Heavenly Kingdom) and infused with the traditional Chinese secret society structure (*taiping*, i.e., Realm of Great Peace and Equity).

One significant issue that arose in the history of Chinese Christology was whether the Gospel of Christ calls for social transformation or is concerned primarily with individual salvation. The disunion between Christ's divinity and humanity, thus, heaven and earth, is ill-suited to traditional Chinese ways of thinking about the harmonious relationship between the individual and society. A proper understanding of Christ's fully divine and fully human nature could help the Chinese come to terms with the healthy tension between the social and spiritual dimensions of the Gospel, between the inner and outer selves of a person.

From the Republic of China to the Recent Past: Christ and State, Theology and Politics

The rise of nationalism and Maoism in the Republic of China (1900–49) impacted the Chinese Christology of the time, continuing the old question of Christ and the state. Sun Yat-sen's (1866–1925) Christology is expressed in the revolutionary movement he spearheaded, which gained support from overseas Chinese and Christians abroad. Sun was a Christian who embraced the Christian truth as well as the truth of socialism. The idea of a righteous nation (reign of God in Christ) and the politics of people's democracy and socialism, according to Sun Yat-sen, could work hand in hand. Thus, Sun had high hopes for the Communist world revolution and the Soviet Union, and his intention was to harmonize his Three Principles with Marxism. (This is evident in his *Principle of the People's Livelihood*, but his lecture in 1924 seeks to offer a constructive critique and differentiation between Communism and the Min-sheng principle; see Bauer 1976: 348.) However, the Nationalists and Chiang Kai-shek (1887–1975), even with the help of some Christians, could not win the heart of the Chinese people. Most Chinese, Christians or not, asked the challenging questions: How can Christ be the head of the church *and the state*? Is a *Christian* head of state in a better position than an atheist ruler to restore the sovereignty of China? These are questions about the relationship between Christ and the state, theology and politics.

As history has it, it was Chinese Communists who, like the prophets of the Old Testament, started out as a social revolution for land-reform against landlords, and ended up with a continuous revolution on economic, political, and even religious levels which formed trajectories that led to the People's Republic of China under Mao (1949–76). The peace and prosperity of Christ seemed to reign through a righteous atheist government until the ten-year period of the Cultural Revolution (1966–76), ironically called 'Cultural Destruction', 'Ten Years of Calamity', or 'Ten Years of Madness' (Feng 1996). The hope of Christ was sucked out of the air in China during those ten years. In response, Chinese Christians sought to present Christ in two ways: first, the

Three-Self Patriotic Movement (TSPM) (Zhang 1996: 175–202), Chinese Christians who wished to love Christ *and* socialist China; and, secondly, independent family-church Christians who wished to love Christ *only*.

Under Mao, all churches were legally required to 'register' with the state: not all complied so there were registered and unregistered churches. Both the Three-Self (self-support, self-government, self-propagation) and the registered and the unregistered family churches struggled with indigenous Christologies and their salvific or destructive effects. For example, Watchman Nee (1903–72) founded 'Christian Assembly' (Little Flock) in 1922, arguing that a church as the body of Christ is headed not by full-time local pastors, but by apostles (similar to the apostle Paul). Even though the Christian Assembly did not neglect altogether the social concerns of the day, Nee's Gnostic-like Christology, and therefore dualistic anthropology, tended to contrast the flesh with the spirit, thus inculcating a militant sanctification process of self-denial (against whatever he deemed carnal) and escapism into the spiritual realm. He was preoccupied with sanctification, concerning himself with such things as the 'second blessing', 'baptism of the Spirit', and 'spiritual illumination'. He distinguished the spiritual Christian from the 'carnal Christian' who spent time in the world (see Nee 1998). Although this doctrine of sanctification is more an extra-biblical, Greek understanding than a biblical view, Chinese who despaired of combining the Confucian ethics of social selves with a vivid spirituality found Nee's teaching promising.

Wang Ming-dao's (1900–88) Christology was also a spiritual and charismatic one, as Wang continued to preach the born-again message at the Christian Tabernacle (Shijia Hutong) he founded in Beijing in 1936. His message emphasized spiritual regeneration and ultimate trust in God despite daily suffering and persecution.

Greater hermeneutical sensitivity to the demands of indigenous Christologies is found in the works of Wu Leiquan (1870–1944) and T. C. Chao (1888–1979). Operating out of the spirit of the May Fourth Movement (1916), with its critique of traditional Chinese society and Western imperialism, Wu Leiquan's Christology was tied to the national salvation of China. According to Wu, it would be 'only futile for Christianity to identify itself with traditional Chinese culture' (Wu 1936: 71–2). Wu found a common cause between the new impulses toward socialism in China and what he saw as socialist dimensions of Jesus' teaching (Wu 1936: 90–2). For Wu, Jesus' kingdom is a combination of idealism and materialism, a prototype of the socialist society, the communal sharing of property. Jesus, according to Wu, offers a socialist kingdom of freedom, justice, and equality (Wu 1936: 97). Wu argued that the perfect personhood of Jesus, who exemplified unity in his words and deeds, reveals to humanity a radically new and holistic form of existence. This new way of being truly human is what the 'kingdom of God' means.

Wu found affinities between Jesus' vision of the kingdom of God and Confucianist ideals. In Wu's view, Jesus was concerned for the peace of the whole universe, including social justice for the poor and outcast. Wu saw a connection here with the Confucianist ideal of *ren* (love), and he thought that Jesus' kingdom ethic could therefore be positively linked with the Confucian idea of self-cultivation for the purpose of maintaining a harmonized family, ruling a nation, and bringing about peace to the universe.

T. C. Chao's Christology is different from Wu's, although he also sought a contextual theology. Early on, Chao rejected his Confucianist culture and adopted a Western reading of the biblical Christ. Later, he developed a more indigenous Chinese approach. In his 1935 book, *The Biography of Jesus*, Chao rejected the idea that Jesus' message is political, much less revolutionary (in his preface [1965: 6–8], Chao does not see Jesus as eschatological or apocalyptic; see also his critical view of socialism on pp. 674–5). Although he sought to work out a Christian social ethic that was not individualistic, ultimately, he did not embrace socialism. He lamented that so many of the youth of his time were attracted to Communism; he also attacked the individualistic 'selfish' gospel of much popular Christian faith. Chao's Christology struggled with the question of reconciling the Confucian impetus to transform society through self-cultivation with a Protestant soteriology based on accepting the free grace of God through Christ. He rejected the Confucian teaching about self-perfection, as well as the liberal Protestant idea of atonement as moral example. Chao's ethic is rooted in dying and rising with Christ, a mystical interpretation (of the book of Romans) on the death and resurrection of Christ.

Is Christ fully divine *and* fully human? Nee and Wang seemed to underline the fully divine Christ, while Wu and Chao tried to hold to the 'both-and'. The Christological debate at this time indicates that those Chinese Christians who supported the TSPM chose the common ground between Christianity and Communism, thereby proclaiming Christ to be divine *and* human. Julia Ching calls this alternative way 'that of collaboration in the humanist cause ... a faith in humanity which can be acceptable to Christians, in so far as it is open to God' (1976: 1:26). Julia Ching articulates further: 'Faith is directed toward that which is beyond history, dogma or myth, to a God who Himself transcends theism, since, if He exists, it will be so independently of people's affirmation and negations' (Ching 1976: 1:31; see also Woo 1973). Chinese Christians in New China began to reflect Christologically on the relationship between God's *creative* work and God's *redemptive* work. The Gospel of Christ is concerned not only with the reconciliation of people to God; it also has a mission for the state and society.

Recent Typology of Chinese Christologies

Four Interpretative Models

Most Chinese biblical scholarship, including research into Christology, has long betrayed the assumption that biblical interpretation can be a-cultural (naïvely or deliberately). In order to take seriously the composite contexts of Scripture and the complex horizons of the Chinese (whether in China or overseas) world—which consist of multiple nationalities, regional groups and dialects, diverse cultures, pluralistic religions, and socio-political realities—Chinese Christologies must read their cultures biblically and read the biblical texts in their own languages. Below I briefly mention the works of John P. Keenan, Kwok Pui-lan, Enoch Wan, and Jonathan Tan to introduce recent typologies of Chinese Christologies.

John P. Keenan has worked to some extent on a Christology in dialogue with a Buddhist Mahāyāna worldview and Scripture (see Keenan 1992: 86–91, 1993: 48–63, 1999: 453–77, 2004: 89–100; see also Lai 2004: 209–28). Very early on, the work of Zhang Chunyi (1871–1955), a baptized Anglican who later became a Buddhist, utilized the same interpretation. Both Zhang and Keenan are critical of the distortions in Western Protestantism with regard to Chinese Christianity. Especially in Zhang's prolific exploration of 'Mahāyāna theology', we see his elaboration of 'Buddhicizing Christianity' (*fohua jidujiao*) so as to indigenize the Gospel (before his conversion to Buddhism, he read the Bible through Chinese philosophical lenses) and to reform distortions of Chinese Christianity as a 'foreign religion' (after his conversion to Buddhism, he used Buddhism to rectify misrepresentations and limitations in the Bible and misinterpretations of Chinese preachers, so that authentic Christianity could be realized). (I am indebted to the excellent article and bibliographical details of Lai Pan-chiu and So Yuentai [2007]; see particularly their balanced critiques of Zhang on pages 80–4.) While Zhang is critical of the influence of Judaism on biblical faith, Keenan is critical of the influence of Greek ontology on biblical faith. Keenan opts for the mystical tradition and apophatic theology of early Christianity, and reconstructs a Mahāyāna Christology of emptiness (*sunyata*) (Keenan 1993: 53–9; see also, Keenan 1989: 225–35). Keenan uses profusely the wisdom tradition of both the Old and New Testaments, and argues that 'wisdom is a mode of conscious awareness and the wisdom of theology issues from minds familiar with the emptiness and understanding of all doctrines in their co-arising articulation' (Keenan 1989: 7–44, 225). Keenan's Christology emphasizes 'the constant motif of the Gospels to call for conversion away from a sign-clinging mind ... to a mind that is receptive of the Spirit and aware of Abba ... The Easter experience is one of disclosure and enlightenment' (Keenan 1989: 228; see also Keenan 2004: 97–8).

Kwok Pui-lan's feminist ecological model for Christology uses natural metaphor and wisdom tradition, which 'proposes to see Jesus as one epiphany of God. It accents Jesus' teachings about right living, his relation with the natural environment and other human beings, his subversive wisdom on ecojustice, and his promise of God's compassion for all humankind' (Kwok 2000: 93). Using these lenses to expand the works of Christ, Kwok creatively sees that Christ's death and Passion must be interpreted 'within the larger context of his struggle for justice for all—humans and all of creation. His resurrection can be seen as a rebirth, a regeneration that gives new hope' (Kwok 2000: 93). Kwok raises a critical question on theological method as she assumes that Chinese Christology should be comfortable and compatible with the Chinese linguistic pattern and worldview:

> The Christ figure, interpreted as the savior of humankind redeeming believers from sin and depravity, is quite foreign to Chinese thinking ... the Chalcedonian controversy of whether Jesus is fully human or divine would not have taken place in China, which has a different philosophical system ... That the Father would demand the

death of the Son as a ransom or as a sacrifice would be unthinkable in the Confucian symbolic structure.

(Kwok 2000: 90)

Chalcedon corrected the error of the Nestorian division of Christ's two natures and the Eutychean error that Christ had only one nature (see Cross and Livingstone 2005: 318). The Chalcedonian language may be foreign to the Chinese worldview, yet a cross-cultural hermeneutic requires that one does theology not simply out of convenience or familiarity, but also by allowing otherness and strangeness to transform, or even save, us.

Enoch Wan proposed a Sino-Christology with a balanced approach inclusive of three aspects: (1) Jesus Christ as 'heaven-human-unite-one-*dao*' ('*tian-ren-he-yi-de-dao*')— the incarnate Jesus and the resurrected Christ is both personal being and theological *dao*); (2) Jesus Christ as 'grace-passion-true-Lord' ('*en-qing-zhen-zhu*')—the relational (*guan-xi*) theologizing of Jesus' work (salvation) as the reconciling of humanity to God and to fellow human beings as mediator, redeemer, and reconciler; and (3) eschatologically, Jesus as 'perfect-beauty-revered-honor-Lord' ('*wan-mei-jun-rong-zhu*')—Jesus' work to Chinese 'is both shame-bearer for sinners and honor-winner for believers' (Wan 2000: 13–20; Wan 2003; see also Wan's Chinese work [1998]). Wan's Christology is attempting to be indigenous in its translation but also, by doing so, seeking to allow biblical Christologies to fulfill the Sino-language.

From the death and resurrection of Christ, one can discern the necessity of eschatological critique in one's Christological construction. Jonathan Tan Yun-ka, in his article 'Jesus, the Crucified and Risen Sage: Constructing a Contemporary Confucian Christology' (2002: 1481–1513), serves as an example. Tan writes:

> Jesus the sage is one who listens to or discerns what he has heard … Just as a *sheng* [sage] discerns the 'Way of Heaven' (*tiandao*) and then manifests it to others, so too, Jesus *discerns* the Way of his Father, the Lord of Heaven (*tianzhudao*), which is described in the Gospels as the nearness of the Reign of God, proclaims it in his preaching and manifests it in his life to all peoples … [T]he earliest followers of Jesus in the Acts of the Apostles were referred to as 'followers of the Way' (Acts 9:2), before being subsequently called 'Christians' (Acts 11:26).
>
> (Tan 2002: 1506)

Similar to the Confucian sage of moral perfection that is to be imitated by others, Jesus is to be imitated by Christians (Tan 2002: 1507). But the similarities do not make Confucian Christology unique; it is the cross(ing over)-cultural aspect that makes Chinese theology Christian. Tan articulates this point well:

> There is nothing uniquely Christian in saying that Jesus is a perfect and divine sage. Hence, it is submitted that for Confucian East Asian Christians, Jesus is best seen as the crucified and risen sage, an image that *juxtaposes* the paschal mystery (i.e.,

the suffering, death, and resurrection of Jesus) within a Confucian-Christian under-standing of Jesus as sage *par excellence* ... [For] historically many Confucian literati had great difficulty accepting the crucifixion of Christ.

(Tan 2002: 1509)

The Chinese image of Jesus for Tan is therefore inclusive of the sage *and* the son of the Lord of Heaven. Tan's Christology portrays Jesus as: (1) the embodiment of perfect humanity and divinity; (2) discerning and proclaiming the nearness of the Way of the Lord of Heaven; (3) demonstrating by his life, suffering, and death on the Cross what this Way of the Lord of Heaven entails for us; and (4) 'inviting us to imitate him and his preferential option for the poor and marginalized by joining God in embracing and walking along this Way from its beginning to its end' (Tan 2002: 1513).

Reflections

The hermeneutics of the four typologies above is warranted by the New Testament Christologies, as any contextual Christology will need to embrace also other Christologies of the global Church. The global Church will then return to the richness and variety—thus the *catholicity*—of New Testament Christologies and the expan-sive nature of biblical hermeneutics evident in the fourfold Gospels, as well as Pauline Christologies.

Among those current Chinese writings that attempt to be aware of the dual-nature-in-one person identity, it is noteworthy that particular biblical texts and topics are favored in Christological studies. For example, the Chinese palate on Christology favors John's Gospel over the Synoptics (see multiple essays addressing this hermeneutic in He and Yeung 2009; see also Lai and Lam 2010). If Synoptic Christologies are discussed, they are linked to the kingdom-of-God discourse pertaining to the socialist socio-political reality of modern China. Paul's writings are preferred over Jewish documents (Hebrews, James) in the New Testament, as Chinese scholars are preoccupied with Pauline Christology that speaks to a moral self or Confucian morality.

CONSTRUCTIVE CHINESE CHRISTOLOGIES

Let me conclude with two examples of *constructive* Chinese Christologies, one of *dao* (Word) and the other of *renren* (a person who loves). The first Christology of *dao* will be described briefly to exemplify the uniqueness of Chinese language in its portrayal of Christ, demonstrating that both Christology and language need each other. More extensively dealt with is the second Christology of *renren*, shedding light on a uniquely Chinese Christology regarding Christ and Christians as image(s) of God, suggesting the saving power of an *aesthetic* Chinese Christology.

Chinese Christology of Dao

The Greek word *logos* in the Gospel of John is translated as *dao* in the Chinese Bible. The Chinese word *dao* has three meanings: first, the cosmic or creative principle; second, the personal truth or embodied wisdom; and third, the verbal word (speech) or communal dialogue. In other words, to Chinese readers:

(1) Jesus is portrayed in John's Gospel as the Creator of the cosmos, the foundation of truth and the principle that holds all things together. God/Jesus is the Creator of order from chaos, light from darkness, and meaning from void. The notion of *dao* speaks of wholeness and integrity in the Chinese understanding of the universe. Indeed, Jesus as the creative *dao* takes human form and keeps on working and performing miracles. These works and miracles are called 'works' (ἔργα in Greek) and 'signs' (σημεία in Greek) in John's Gospel (e.g., 2:11; 11:40; 12:23).

(2) Jesus is the personified wisdom, as the word *dao* means wisdom, truth, and knowledge that has the character and vitality of life. Jesus as the wisdom-λόγος-*dao* comes to us through the Hebrew tradition of wisdom (*hokmah* in Hebrew) as exhibited in Proverbs 8. Understood in a patriarchal setting, the use of female imagery is certainly a creative and cross-cultural endeavor. The wisdom-*dao* Christ has personhood; he is not just an abstract principle. Thus, Jesus Christ the personal *dao* has to be an *incarnated logos*. 'In the *dao* was *life*, and the *life* was the light of humanity' (cf. John 1:4). Truth (ἀλήθεια) is equivalent to wisdom in John's Gospel, a personified wisdom with which one can interrelate. So the *dao* was 'full of grace and truth' (John 1:14), 'grace and truth came through Jesus Christ' (John 1:17).

(3) Jesus as the rhetorical-*dao* speaks of communal dialogue, as the Chinese Catholic Bible translates: 'In the beginning was the speech [the Protestant Bible in Chinese uses *dao*] …' The creation is more than *ex nihilo* (out of nothing); it also is a creation of meaning from meaninglessness via God's saying, 'let there be …' (Gen. 1). Jesus is the Word of God that makes sense of human language. Jesus is the rhetoric of God that allows the Holy One and human beings to communicate with him. Jesus manifests God by means of what he says. The direct speech of Jesus in John's Gospel is imperative because the revelation of this *dao*-Christology of God is happening from Jesus' own lips. So the self-claims of Jesus ('I am the …' in 6:35–40; 8:12; 9:15; 10:7; 10:11; 11:20–7; 14:6; 15:1) appear only in the Johannine Gospel.

John is aware that, while words have their creativity, they also have limitations—especially mono-linguistic understanding. When the limitation of words is evidenced, John uses two ways to express the meaning of God:

(1) Silence is used in John, for example, 8:24: 'If you [pl.] do not believe "I am", you will die in sin'. The question is: 'I am' what? The Greek text is silent. (Erroneously,

some of the English and Chinese translations say, 'If you do not believe I am the Christ' or 'If you do not believe I am he', but the addition of 'the Christ' or 'he' is unwarranted. Silence is a better expression here.) Words cannot really express and reveal who 'I am' is. (Also, the twofold ending of John 20:30 and 21:25 hints at the same meaning. John 20:30, 'Jesus did many signs … that are written in this book', and John 21:25, 'so many other things that Jesus did if recorded in the books, the world could not contain them', are not stating the obvious; they are the acknowledgment that Jesus the Word of God cannot fully be expressed by our words. Thus, Jesus is the great 'I am' mentioned in Exodus 3:14 ['I am who I am'].)

(2) That words cannot adequately express who God is does not mean that speech is useless. It is all the more necessary to use words. John, the master of language, uses irony, metaphor, and dialogue as ways to transcend the limitations of language.

Although language has its limitations, it still is the best medium by which to express the mystery of the unknown and to be in constant conversation with truth within a community. The Johannine Jesus is in constant conversation with God and people. For example, Jesus talks to God the Father in John 17.

Chinese Christology (*Renren*) and *Imago Dei*

One of the challenging issues in Chinese Christological discussion is holding to the tension of 'fully divine fully human' Christology, so that the glory of Christ can save Chinese cultures. The proposed Chinese Christology of *renren* assumes that Jesus comes not to abolish the old, but to fulfill and to order it with beauty. This section offers a Christian Chinese Christology (and soteriology; see Yeo 2012: 102–15) that explains Jesus as the fulfillment of the Confucian ritual-ideal of 'being human' (*ren*) (on the Confucian ritual theory and virtue, see Yeo 2008: 35–40).

Confucius' 'soteriological concern' is that people do not know how to coexist, and that rituals or ceremonies (*li*) that socialize us to be human have declined, and music (*yue*) that beautifies our souls is corrupted. According to Confucius, the greatest danger is that people thought they could love heaven without loving people. So Confucius teaches people to actualize the mandate of heaven (*Tianming*) by committing themselves to love (*ren*, which is human-relatedness), for what makes human beings (*ren*) is love (*ren*; see *Analects* 12:22), thus the term *renren* (literally, *human beings* who love; see Fung 1948: 69–73). The similar biblical concept is love (ἀγάπη). 'Virtue does not exist in isolation; there must be neighbors', says Confucius (*Analects* 4:25). 'In order to establish oneself, one helps others to establish themselves; in order to enlarge oneself, one helps others to enlarge themselves' (*Analects* 6:28). Therefore, the 'lostness' of humanity is primarily brokenness, isolation, and de-humanization. Here I am going beyond the Confucian anthropology and soteriology toward that of a Christian, or better still, a Christian Chinese anthropology: the salvation Jesus offers and epitomizes is that of wholeness and worthiness of humanity—human beings are created *as* the image of God (1 Cor. 11:7; Jas. 3:9).

Humans represent God in managing the earth and reflecting God's glory in the world (they are the light of the world). The image (Hebrew *tselem*, Greek εἰκών, Latin *imago*) and likeness (Hebrew *demuth*, Greek ὁμοίωσις, Latin *similitudo*) of God is the ideal/fully human mentioned in the Bible (Gen. 1:26; 5:2; 9:6) having similar denotations of royal lordship (Ps. 8:5; cf. Heb. 2:6–8), esteem (rather than as slaves to gods, as some ancient Near Eastern creation myths propose), and physical-spiritual uniqueness (immanence representative of the transcendent Creator God on earth) as that of the Confucian understanding of the aesthetic, ideal human (*junzi*) (on the Genesis text, see Westermann 1984: 146; on human beings as 'God's vice-regent on earth', see Wenham 1987: 31). Jesus has revealed for us what it means to be fully human, both in his being with God and with people. Jesus' openness and empathy toward sinners, outcasts, the separated, the disowned, and the rejected reveals the extent of his full divinity encountering his full humanity. Christ is fully human, and together in one person he is also the *imago Dei* (Col. 1:15; Heb. 1:3) who lives and gives his life totally for others and for God, not himself. In doing so, he has not lost but has fully encountered himself and the Triune God.

The Christological anthropology of the Scriptures (Gen. 1:26–7, 5:1–3, 9:6) speaks of humanity as created in/as *imago Dei* (Hebrew *beth*). The two dimensions of *imago Dei* are rendered as *ren*/ἀγάπη (love). The first dimension is reflected in humanity's corporeal-animated creatureliness that encounters God, his Word, and his presence. It is that gifted ability to enter into an aesthetic relationship with God (with all we are—mind, heart, soul, will, body) that allows human creatures *to be* God's image in the world (Westermann 1984: 156). Secondly, the image of God as seen in the creation account, with the phrase 'male and female he created them', not only emphasizes that both male and female are created 'as our image' and 'as our likeness', but also explains 'image' and 'likeness' as the social self (or *co*-humanity of male and female in the first *pair* of humanity characterized by love) relating and encountering each other in psychosomatic wholeness, intimacy and fulfillment, glory and dignity (see Wolff 1974: 159; as Clines writes, 'It is the *homo* [*human*], not the *animus* or the *anima*, that is the *imago Dei*' [1968: 86]).

The human predicament is that one tends to live apart from God's presence (not for God's glory) and subsequently lives a narcissistic life that leads to the shameful loss of self (John 12:25; Luke 9:24; Matt. 10:39). The alienation between I and self, between self and other, between other and the world, between humanity and God is called the distortion or corruption of the *imago Dei*. That constitutes sin, falling short of the glory of God (Rom. 3:23). Jesus is the Christ precisely because in his incarnation, life, death, and resurrection he lives fully *as* the *imago Dei* (2 Cor. 4:4; Col. 1:15) and thus reconciles and restores the broken *imago Dei* to be the new humanity and creation (Rom. 8:29; Eph. 2:15; 4:22–4; Col. 3:9–11) for us. Christians living as the new humanity are being changed into the likeness of Christ from one degree of glory to another (2 Cor. 3:18).

The 'fully human' language in both Confucian ethics and biblical Christology emphasizes complete love for others (Rom. 13:8). Through the power of righteousness, justice, and glory, only the fully human Jesus can restore and save 'less-than-human' humanity from the power of sin. Thus the *unity* of Jesus' divinity *and* humanity is an aesthetic-relational category. The Divine can enter the sphere of humanity and become 'fully human', *yet* Jesus is *still fully divine*, and eschatologically, the 'all in all' (1 Cor. 15: 28; Eph. 1:23; Col. 3:10; Gal. 3:28). No human being can be fully divine and 'all in all', but the unity and communion we (the fully human) can have with God (the fully divine) is a divine gift and invitation to us all to live in the glory and beauty of God—already an in-Christ reality.

Christ manifests most perfectly the I–Thou relationship with God and with human beings. This line of thought is close to Confucius' understanding of the transcendence of heaven, best known in its representation of immanence in ethical life. According to Confucius, it is the virtue of human beings that reveals the beauty, order, and sacredness of heaven. The mandate of heaven has endowed us and is calling us to be moral-spiritual selves, to receive thankfully God's indwelling Spirit in us. As God's image, human beings are called to be free expressions and diverse representations of our oneness with God, with one another, and in harmony with God's world.

Conclusion

Chinese Christology is grounded in both Scripture and Chinese cultures. As the vernacular expresses the beauty of Christ, the language is transformed to reflect God's glory. A contextual Christology, such as that of the Chinese, not only speaks to the Chinese but also to the global Church who must listen to what they find strange. The God of the Bible is Christ-like; creation has Christ as the firstborn; and humanity created as God's image is re-created as *imago Christi*. Therefore, God's creation of cultures is Christocentric in its logic and beauty. Almost countless kinds of sea creatures and animals and plants are created, according to Genesis 1, and God affirms the goodness of his work of diversity and beauty. No wonder we see that which is creative and redemptive is always clothed with God's glory and beauty. (The creation of the human race, people-groups [*nations*, see Gen. 10, 17] and God's blessing of different languages [Acts 2:4] are seen as reflections of God's *glory*. This glory of God is manifested in various tongues, different musical instruments, and diverse style of worship, thus the global Church is envisioned in Revelation as complementary in diversity [Rev. 7:9].) God's world, after all, is first and foremost Christocentric—in creation, redemption, and consummation.

Suggested Reading

Brown (1994); Cosgrove, Weiss, and Yeo (2005); England and Lee (1993); Green, Pardue, and Yeo (2014); He and Yeung (2009); Kärkkainen (2003); Pelikan (1999); Yeo (1998).

Bibliography

Bauer, W. (1976), *China and the Search for Happiness: Recurring Themes in Four Thousand Years of Chinese Cultural History* (New York: Seabury Press).

Brown, R. E. (1994), *An Introduction to New Testament Christology* (New York: Paulist Press).

Cary-Elwes, C. (1957), *China and the Cross: A Survey of Missionary History* (London: Longmans).

Chao, T. C. (1965), *The Biography of Jesus* (in Chinese) (Hong Kong: Christian Literature Publisher; originally published 1935).

Cheng, J. C. (1963), *Chinese Sources for the Taiping Rebellion in China 1850–1864* (Hong Kong: Hong Kong University Press).

Ching, J. (1976), 'Faith and Ideology in the Light of the New China', in Lutheran World Federation (ed.), *Christianity and the New China* (South Pasadena, Calif.: Ecclesia), 15–36.

Clines, D. J. A. (1968), 'The Image of God in Man', *Tyndale Bulletin* 19: 53–103.

Cosgrove, C., H. Weiss, and K. K. Yeo (2005), *Cross-Cultural Paul: Journeys to Others, Journeys to Ourselves* (Grand Rapids, Mich.: Eerdmans).

Cross, F. L. and E. A. Livingstone (eds.) (2005), *The Oxford Dictionary of the Christian Church*, 3rd rev. edn. (Oxford: Oxford University Press).

England, J. C. and A. C. C. Lee (eds.) (1993), *Doing Theology with Asian Resources: Ten Years in the Formation of Living Theology in Asia*. The Programme for Theology and Culture in Asia 1983–1993 (Auckland: Pace).

Feng, J. (1996), *Ten Years of Madness: Oral Histories of China's Cultural Revolution* (San Francisco: China Books).

Fung, Y. (1948), *A Short History of Chinese Philosophy*, ed. and trans. D. Bodde (New York: Macmillan).

Green, G., S. Pardue, and K. K. Yeo (eds.) (2014), *Jesus Without Borders: Christology in the Majority World* (Grand Rapids, Mich.: Eerdmans).

He, G. and D. H. N. Yeung (eds.) (2009), *Sino-Christian Theology Reader* (in Chinese), 2 vols. (Hong Kong: Institute of Sino-Christian Studies).

Hickley, D. (1980), *The First Christians of China: An Outline History and Some Considerations Concerning the Nestorians in China During the Tang Dynasty* (London: China Study Project).

Kangxi, 'The Poem of the Cross'. <http://www.yutopian.com/religion/christian/Kangxi.html> (accessed July 27, 2014).

Kärkkainen, V.-M. (2003), *Christology: A Global Introduction* (Grand Rapids, Mich.: Baker).

Keenan, J. P. (1989), *The Meaning of Christ: A Mahayana Theology* (Maryknoll, NY: Orbis Books).

Keenan, J. P. (1992), 'Mahayana Theology', in A. Harrak, K. Kopperdryer, B. Steben, and B. H.-K. Luk (eds.), Steben *Literature and Humanities*, vol. 3: *Contacts Between Cultures* (Lewiston, NY: Edwin Mellen Press), 86–91.

Keenan, J. P. (1993), 'The Emptiness of Christ: A Mahayana Christology', *Anglican Theological Review* 75: 48–63.

Keenan, J. P. (1999), 'What Can Buddhism Add to Christianity?', *Japanese Journal of Religious Studies* 17: 453–77.

Keenan, J. P. (2004), 'A Mahāyāna Theology of the Real Presence of Christ in the Eucharist', *Buddhist-Christian Studies* 24: 89–100.

Kwok, P. (2000), *Introducing Asian Feminist Theology* (Cleveland, Ohio: Pilgrim Press).

Lai, P. (2004), 'A Mahāyāna Reading of Chalcedon Christology: A Chinese Response to John Keenan', *Buddhist-Christian Studies* 24: 209–28.

Lai, P. and J. Lam (eds.) (2010), *Sino-Christian Theology: A Theological Qua Cultural Movement in Contemporary China* (Frankfurt: Peter Lang).

Lai, P. and Y. So (2007), 'Mahāyāna Interpretation of Christianity: A Case Study of Zhang Chunyi (1871–1955)', *Buddhist-Christian Studies* 27: 67–87.

Nee, W. (1998), *The Spiritual Man* (Anaheim, Calif.: Living Stream Ministry; originally published 1928).

Pauck, W. (ed.) (1969), *Melanchthon and Bucer*. Library of Christian Classics 19 (Philadelphia: Westminster).

Pelikan, J. (1999), *Jesus through the Centuries: His Place in the History of Culture* (New Haven: Yale University Press).

Spence, J. D. (1996), *God's Chinese Son: The Taiping Heavenly Kingdom of Hong Xiuquan* (New York: W. W. Norton).

Tan, J. Y. (2002), 'Jesus, the Crucified and Risen Sage: Constructing a Contemporary Confucian Christology', in R. Malek (ed.), *The Chinese Face of Jesus Christ*, vol. 3b. Monumenta Serica Monograph Series (Sankt Augustin, Germany: Institut Monumenta Serica and China-Zentrum).

Wan, E. (1998), *Banishing the Old and Building the New: An Exploration of Sino-Theology* (Ontario: Christian Communication).

Wan, E. (2000), 'Jesus Christ for the Chinese: A Contextual Reflection', *Chinese Around the World* (November): 13–20.

Wan, E. (2003), 'Practical Contextualization: A Case Study of Evangelizing Contemporary Chinese', Global Missiology English 1. <http://ojs.globalmissiology.org/index.php/english/issue/view/27> (accessed July 27, 2014).

Wenham, G. J. (1987), *Genesis 1–15* (Waco, Tex.: Word).

Westermann, C. (1984), *Genesis 1–11: A Commentary*, trans. J. J. Scullion (London: SPCK).

Whyte, B. (1988), *Unfinished Encounter: China and Christianity* (London: Collins).

Wolff, H. W. (1974), *Anthropology of the Old Testament*, trans. M. Kohl (London: SCM Press).

Woo, F. J. (1973), 'Another China Visit: Religion, the Religious Dimension and Religious Surrogates', *China Notes* 11: 42–4.

Wu, L. (1936), *Christianity and Chinese Culture* (in Chinese) (Shanghai: Youth Association Bookstore).

Yeo, K. K. (1996), *Ancestor Worship: Rhetorical and Cross-Cultural Hermeneutical Response* (in Chinese), 2nd edn. (Hong Kong: Chinese Christian Literature Council).

Yeo, K. K. (1998), *What Has Jerusalem to Do with Beijing? Biblical Interpretation from a Chinese Perspective* (Harrisburg, Pa.: Trinity Press International).

Yeo, K. K. (2008), *Musing with Confucius and Paul: Toward a Chinese Christian Theology* (Eugene, Oreg.: Cascade Books).

Yeo, K. K. (2012), 'Christian Chinese Theology: Theological Ethics of Becoming Human and Holy', in J. P. Greenman and G. L. Green (eds.), *Global Theology in Evangelical Perspective: Exploring the Contextual Nature of Theology and Mission* (Downers Grove, Ill.: IVP Academic), 102–15.

Zhang, R. X. Y (1996), 'The Origin of the "Three Self"', *Jian Dao* 5: 175–202.

CHAPTER 26

FEMINIST CHRISTOLOGIES

MICHELE M. SCHUMACHER

MISOGYNY AMONG THE FATHERS AND MEDIAEVAL CHURCHMEN

> It is still not unusual for Christian priests and ministers, when confronted with the issue of women's liberation, to assert that God 'become incarnate' uniquely as a male and then to draw arguments for male supremacy from this. Indeed the Christological tradition itself tends to justify such conclusions. The underlying—and often explicit—assumption in the minds of theologians down through the centuries has been that the divinity could not have deigned to 'become incarnate' in the 'inferior' sex, and the 'fact' that 'he' did not do so of course confirms male superiority.
>
> (Daly 1985a: 70)

Any such statement coming from a post-Christian theologian of the stature of Mary Daly tends to be regarded by traditional theologians with 'a hermeneutics of suspicion' running cross-courant to the use of the same term as developed by E. Fiorenza: that of 'a critical feminist interpretation for liberation ... that places on all biblical texts the warning "Caution—could be dangerous to your health and survival"' (Fiorenza 2001: 175). Similarly, traditional theologians easily shun the still more direct feminist portrayal of the idea 'deeply ingrained in the Catholic theological tradition' that women have 'a humanity inferior to men', so as to 'relate to God only under men "as their head"' (Børresen 1981: 30–5, 171–8; Ruether 1987: 281; cf. Ruether 1993a: 12; Carr 1998: 164–5). The biblical affirmation that both men and women are created in the image of God, it is argued, has been 'obscured by the tendency to correlate femaleness with the lower part of human nature in a hierarchical scheme of mind over body, reason over passion' (Gudmundsdottir 2010: 10; cf. Ruether 1974, 1993a: 10–12, 1993b: 93–9; Mulder 1997; Carr 1998: 136–7, 162ff.; Beattie

2003: 114ff.; Legrand 2006), or by her difference from the male norm (Børresen 1981; Fulkerson 1997; Ruether 1993a: 9–12, 1993b: 19–20). Yet, many so-called 'new feminists', who seek to remain faithful to Church tradition (cf. John Paul II 1995: §99; Schumacher 2004a), recognize that it is 'hardly difficult to gather texts charging the Fathers with a negative, scornful image of woman, which is as disgraceful for those who uphold it as for the one whom they denigrate' (Pelletier 2001: 50–1). These new feminists likewise point to the Fathers as looking upon woman 'as the inferior sex by nature', of associating her body 'with sense and matter', and of likewise condemning her to intellectual and moral inferiority with respect to men, due to the limitations of her physical sex; and this moral inferiority accounts for the 'more likely a priori that women personified in Eve would be the cause of Original Sin' (Miller 1995: 28). Similarly, it is admitted that the Aristotelian model of sexual polarity, which attributes to women weaker intellects than those of men, as well as disordered wills and a natural subservience to men (Allen 2002: 145), was 'fully integrated into the study of theology' through the commentaries on Lombard's *Sentences* by St. Bonaventure and St. Thomas (Allen 1997: 469); and it is this notion of her 'natural' inferiority which accounts for the idea—common to the Fathers as well as to St. Thomas—that her submission to man is for her own benefit and not simply for man's utility (Pesch 1988: 220–1; Pelletier 2001: 54; cf. Aquinas, *ST* I, q.92, a.1, obj.2 and ad.2; *SCG* III, ch.123, §3). Furthermore, 'since man can be more efficiently helped by another man in other works', Thomas reasons, it is uniquely in the act of generation that she is regarded by him as a helpmate to man (*ST* I, q.92, a.1; cf. q.98, a.2).

On the other hand, precisely because St. Thomas insists upon woman's importance for generation, he is exonerated by some (Pesch 1988: 219; Nolan 1994, 2000) of the feminist charge (cf. Børresen 1981: 173, 330, 340; Ruether 1987: 281, 1993a: 11, 1993b: 96; Ranke-Heinemann 1990: 185ff.; McLaughlin 1993: 120; Johnson 1994: 24–5; Hilkert 2005: 193; Young 2010: 187) of conceiving of woman as a 'misbegotten male' (*mas occasionatus*) (cf. *ST* I, q.92, a.1, obj.1). For what is true of a particular instance of nature—*not*, as many incorrectly read St. Thomas and Aristotle, the particular nature *of the female*, but rather the particular nature (or power) of the male semen, which was thought to be solely responsible for the human form (Nolan 2000: 60)—is not true, Thomas and Aristotle reason, of 'human nature in general': woman 'is included in nature's intention as directed to the work of generation'. And because 'the general intention of nature depends on God, Who is the universal Author of nature', it follows that 'in producing nature, God formed not only the male but also the female' (*ST* I, a.92, a.1, ad.1). In short, 'The male semen (*natura particularis*) may not intend to produce a female child, but Natura (*natura universalis*) intends that female children should be produced. So the female may be accidentally caused vis-à-vis the male semen, but she is no accident so far as Nature is concerned' (Nolan 1994: 159). 'Her existence, therefore, conforms to the divine will' (Børresen 1981: 159).

THE PROBLEMATIC IDENTIFICATION OF THE MALE AND THE DIVINITY

Herein, however—in the relation in anthropology between the particular and the general—is, ironically enough, inverted the 'problem' of Christology from a feminist point of view: the 'scandal' (cf. Daly 1985a: 79) posed by the particularity of Christ's human nature as sexed, such that the fundamental question of Christology—*Cur Deus homo?*—is replaced by the question *Cur Deus vir?* In contrast to fifth-century consciousness, wherein the doctrine of Chalcedon was formulated, our own cultural climate is one wherein 'it is not divinity-humanity, but the male-female dualism which bedevils' (McLaughlin 1993: 129). It is thus asked: how is it possible that one sex—the male—is capable of representing and redeeming both sexes? Can 'a symbol which would appear to be necessarily male ... be said to be inclusive of all humanity' (Hampson 1992: 51)? And, in reverse, how can a woman see herself 'as made in the image of a male God, a God whose human face is seen in the man Jesus' (McLaughlin 1993: 140)? 'The image itself is one-sided, as far as sexual identity is concerned, and it is precisely on the wrong side, since it fails to counter sexism and functions to glorify maleness' (Daly 1985a: 72). Women 'are called to honor a male savior sent by a male God whose legitimate representatives can only be male, all of which places their persons precisely as female in a peripheral role. Their femaleness is judged to be not suitable as metaphor for speech about God' (Johnson 1994: 26). Feminist theologians 'must question', therefore, E. Fiorenza reasons, 'whether the historical man, Jesus of Nazareth, can be a role model for contemporary women' (Fiorenza 1984: 60).

It is thus not surprising that Ruether should present 'more than half of the membership of the Christian churches' as finding themselves 'rendered inferior and excluded by Christology' (Ruether 1993a: 8–9; cf. Hampson 1992: 53). It is ironic, however, that within the context of the same volume, another feminist theologian frustratingly acknowledges: 'It is not only conservatives, but most women in the pew who join academic theologians in an impatient rejection of the feminist complaint that women cannot find a "savior" in this God-Man Jesus.' The difficulty in getting 'this conversation about the gender of Jesus going' is caused, she explains, by the fact that we have 'all' been 'shaped by the teaching that Jesus Christ is the Representative Man [sic], the Second Adam, the Man for Others, *Ecce Homo*, and therefore beyond or inclusive of all sexuality' (McLaughlin 1993: 120). Indeed, precisely because traditional theology is androcentric, its texts are recognized by women as 'gender inclusive' (Hopkins 1995: 32). 'Women have studied the Christologies of Anselm, Aquinas, Luther, Calvin, Schleiermacher, Barth, Bultmann, Tillich, Rahner, and Schillebeeckx and assumed they are included in the fully human that is Christ' (Carr 1998: 161).

While it remains disputed whether women are perceived by the tradition as misbegotten and defective, many feminists (cf. Børresen 1981; Ruether 1993a: 9, 1993b: 19–20; Johnson 1994: 23–5; Hopkins 1995: 32; Agacinski 2005; Gundmundsdottir 2010: 11–12) since Simone de Beauvoir (1949; cf. English translation 1989) as well as new feminists (cf. Allen 1997, 2002; Schumacher 2004b, 2013) point to the normative nature of the male sex throughout much of Western history; whence the traditional emphasis upon the supreme fittingness—if not the necessity—of the maleness of the human nature assumed by Christ. Aquinas is recognized by Ruether as providing the 'clearest formulation' of the 'anti-woman use of Christology' (Ruether 1981: 45). Because 'Christ came to restore human nature by his very assumption', St. Thomas reasons that 'it was necessary that he assume everything following upon human nature, namely, all the properties and parts of human nature, among which is sex [*omnes proprietates et partes humane nature, inter quas est etiam sexus*]' (III *Sent.*, d.12, q.3, a.1, qc.1 co.). Despite the so-called 'fragility' of the female sex (III *Sent.*, d.12, q.3, qc.2, arg.2) and the logic of redemption in virtue of which Christ is said to heal our infirmities by taking them on (III *Sent.*, d.12, q.3, qc.1, co.; III *Sent.*, d.12, q.3, qc.1s. c.2; and *ST* III, q.5, a.4), it was not necessary, Thomas holds, that Christ assume *all* infirmities of human nature (and thus the female sex in the case at hand), 'but only those befitting the purpose (*ad finem*) of the assumption, namely, the work of redemption' (III *Sent.*, d.12, qc.2, ad.2). The 'more noble sex' (*ST* III, q.31, a.4, ad.1) is said, moreover, to correspond better to his roles as perfect victim for sacrifice (cf. I–II, q.102, a.3, ad.9), as head of the Church (III *Sent.*, d.12, q.3, a.1, qc. 2s., c.1), and as teacher, governor, and defender of the human race. These are roles for which woman is judged 'incompetent' (qc.2 co.).

So some feminists recognize that 'All efforts to marginalize women in the Church and Christian society, to deprive them of voice, leadership, and authority, take the form of proclaiming that Christ was male and so only the male can "image" Christ' (Ruether 1985c: 106; cf. Ruether 1987: 28, 1993b: 126; Hampson 1992: 45; Ross 1993: 202; Hilkert 2005: 202). The reasoning of Aquinas, for whom the superiority of the male sex points to the fittingness of Christ's masculinity, is turned on its head: the masculinity of Christ is used by a patriarchal culture to reinforce the normative function of masculinity and to simultaneously justify the subordination of women (cf. Daly 1985a, 1985b; Ruether 1981: 45–6, 1993a: 8–13, 1993b: 126; Johnson 1993a: 118–19; Fiorenza 1995: 47; Carr 1998: 163), for Christology gives a male human being 'a status which is given to no woman' (Hampson 1992: 35), whence the question 'whether Christianity is ethical ... Is it not the case that such a religion is by its very nature harmful to the cause of human equality?' (Hampson 1992: 53).

Still more regrettable, the maleness of Christ is used to draw arguments of male supremacy (cf. Daly 1985a: 70–2; Johnson 1993a: 119) and is used to draw the theologically unjustifiable identification of masculinity with divinity. 'As visible image of invisible God, the human man Jesus is used to tie the knot between maleness and divinity very tightly' (Johnson 1992: 35; cf. Ruether 1981: 45–7), while simultaneously reinforcing, as other feminists observe, the patristic identification of women and sin (cf. Daly 1985a: 72, 76–7, 89; Ruether 1993b: 19, 159–72; Carr 1998: 47; McReynolds and Graff 2005).

All of this is—some feminists believe (cf. Hampson 1992: 59)—symptomatic of the 'inescapable' uniting of the two natures of Christ, especially in our present philosophical framework, so far removed from that wherein patristic Christology developed. Today, it is observed, 'many people tend to collapse the distinction between the two natures' of Christ (Hampson 1992: 57). Hence Daly's denouncing of 'Christolatry' (Daly 1985a: 69; Heyward 2010: 167) as a reaction to what she presents as patriarchal reasoning: 'if God is male, then the male is God' (Daly 1985b: 38; cf. Daly 1985a: 72; Fiorenza 1995: 47). Heyward faults the doctrines of Nicaea and Chalcedon for having produced 'a Platonic image of a divine man whose humanity is incredible' (Heyward 2010: 32), whence her willingness to sacrifice Christ's divinity for the sake of his more credible humanity and his modeling of 'a praxis of relational particularity and cooperation' (Heyward 1989: 21). Her own Christ is 'fully and only human' (Heyward 2010: 31), and 'the christological task of Christian feminism' is envisioned in the radical terms of relaying the foundations of Christology: away 'from the ontology of dualistic opposition towards the ethics of justice-making' (Heyward 1989: 21; cf. Ruether 1993a: 23).

As these examples serve to illustrate, the feminist challenge occasioned by the so-called patriarchal image of Christ leads to the following dilemma:

> If one emphasizes that God was incarnate as male, the particularities of Jesus' embodied existence are respected, but it is difficult to argue that the bodies of women are included in that Incarnation. In other words, this approach to the Incarnation shows the compatibility of Divinity with the male way of being in the world, but not with the female. If one argues that what God assumed in the Incarnation was human nature, a nature whose maleness is inconsequential to his mission, one risks a return to the Docetism and Gnosticism of earlier centuries through an attenuation of Jesus' very embodiment. Respecting the reality of Jesus' body excludes women from the Incarnation. Including women in the Incarnation leads to unreal claims about Jesus' body.
>
> (O'Neill 2002: 39; cf. Hopkins 1995: 86)

CHALLENGING THE INTERPRETATIVE FRAMEWORK OF THE MALENESS OF CHRIST

While some feminists have responded to this challenge by admitting the incompatibility of Christianity and feminism so as to opt out of the former (cf. Daly 1985b: xi–xxx; Hampson 1992: 53, 76), others have simply changed the terms of the debate. Recognizing that the 'primary reason' for the rejection of Christology as 'irredeemable' is the 'insurmountable block of a male Christ who fails to represent women' (Ruether 1985c: 106; cf. Ruether 1987: 281), or one whose 'name has been wielded as a bludgeon' against them (Hewyard 2010: 31), they suggest that the real problem posed by Christ's masculinity is *functional* rather than ontological: it is 'lifted up and made essential for his christic function and identity, thus blocking women precisely because of the female sex from participating in the fullness of their Christian identity as images of Christ' (Johnson 1993a: 119; cf. Hampson 1992: 45; Ruether 1993a: 12, 1993b: 19–20), whence also—it bears repeating—their inability to represent Christ in the ordained priest-hood (cf. Ruether 1987: 281, 1993b: 126; Johnson 1994: 153; Fiorenza 1995: 39; Hopkins 1995: 85; McReynolds and Graff 2005: 169). A 'patriarchal anthropology' has, in other words, given birth to a patriarchal Christology (cf. Ruether 1987: 281; Ruether 1975: 618, 1993a: 21; Carr 1998: 164), with the result that 'Jesus' maleness has not functioned in the same way as the "particularity" of his Semitic identity or of his youth' (Daly 1985a: 79; cf. Johnson 1993a: 119; Ruether 1981: 47, 1993a: 23). Unlike these and other particularities of Jesus' humanity, his maleness is portrayed as 'essential' to his human nature (Ruether 1987: 281) in view of legitimizing 'men's superiority over women' (Johnson 1993a: 119; cf. Stevens 1993: 1; Hopkins 1995: 83), of justifying 'male dominance and female subor-dination' (Johnson 1994: 151) and of denying women full participation in the Church. Still more lamentable, 'To make the maleness of Jesus Christ a christological principle' is said 'to deny the universality of salvation' (Johnson 1994: 73; cf. Ruether 1993a: 12) thus 'jeopardiz[ing] women's salvation' (Johnson 1993a: 119). The presentation of a man as 'the unique self-revelation of God and the universal Redeemer of the whole world' risks, it is reasoned—particularly within the context of a 'patriarchal and androcentric culture and faith community'—the 'further theological and practical devaluation of women' (Strahm 1991: 12; cf. Daly 1985a: 72; Bernet 1991: 178–9).

The 'crucial question' for feminist theology thus becomes whether sexual differences 'ought to carry the theological significance they have come to bear' (Ross 1993: 186; cf. Johnson 1991). Indeed, 'the classic doctrine of the Incarnation speaks of the divinity and humanity of Christ, *not* his maleness' (Carr 1998: 161 and cf. 23; Johnson 1994: 164); whence the feminist effort to circumvent 'a fixation on the "maleness" of Christ as a decisive factor in Christology' (Hinga 1995: 186). '[T]heologically speaking', it is said to have 'no ultimate significance' (Ruether 1993b: 137; Johnson 1991: 116, 1994: 156; Hopkins 1995: 32; Carr 1998: 109, 112). Or, to be more specific, it 'says nothing of importance about Jesus, but speaks volumes about the Church's investment in the category of maleness as a way to control "Appropriate" [sic] gender roles and licit sexuality' (Young 2010: 194; cf. Fulkerson 1997: 108). Feminist theology is said to expose 'the idolatry which occurs when preliminary or conditional concerns are elevated to unconditional significance; something finite (maleness, sexuality) is lifted to the level of the infinite' (Carr 1998: 102). '[A]ndrocentric stress on the maleness of Jesus' humanity' is thus said to 'fully warrant the charge of heresy and even blasphemy currently being leveled against it' (Johnson 1994: 167; cf. Carr 1998: 15). In its most radical form, feminist theology reasons that 'a serious Christian response' to the androcentric symbols of Christianity 'will have to show' that these symbols do 'not have the effect of reinforcing and legitimating male power and female submission, or it will have to transform Christian imagery at its very core' (Christ 1977: 205).

Few feminist theologians join Carol Christ and Mary Daly in maintaining that the symbols of Christianity are intrinsically patriarchal (Christ 1977; Daley 1985a). Because, however, Christ's maleness is 'used theologically, ethically, and ecclesiastically against women', mainstream feminist theologians affirm it 'only after a series of negations of traditional interpretations and uses of the symbol' (Carr 1998: 112). The '*effects*' of the

traditional male symbols and doctrines of Christianity must be 'transformed' or purified of the influence of patriarchy, therefore, before these symbols can be made available
to women (Carr 1998: 109; emphasis mine).

For some feminists, however, it is not enough to question the theological *interpretation*, or the pastoral *use* of the Christ symbol as male, because the question itself is
'contextualized in a frame of reference that assumes that femininity and masculinity are
ontologically predetermined natural or revealed differences' (Fiorenza 1995: 45). 'Not
only traditional teaching (exegesis and doctrinal formulation), but also its very scriptural basis have been developed in a society whose structure is patriarchal and therefore
male-centred' (Børresen 1981: 341; cf. Ruether 1975: 611f.). Suspect, therefore, are the categories that are presupposed to the theological task: 'maleness' and 'femaleness' are recognized as categories that are *already* charged with patriarchal meaning before they are
further interpreted by patriarchal theologians in view of reinforcing 'patriarchal politics'.

> The Chalecdonian doctrine of Christology ... is political. It shaped and was shaped by
> the imperial politics of meaning that legitimated kyriarchal domination and exploita-
> tion ... Its kyriocentric formulation of the dual nature of Christ attributes his divinity
> to the 'eternal begetting of the Father' and his humanity to the temporal birth by the
> Virgin mother of G*d [sic] (*Theotokos*). This Christological doctrine thereby inscribes
> into Christian orthodox self-understanding and identity the 'mysterious economy' of
> kyriarchal relations and imperial domination. By associating fatherhood/masculinity
> with divinity and eternity and by firmly placing motherhood/femininity in the tem-
> poral realm of humanity, it introduces not only gender dualism but also the dualism
> between church and world, religion and nature, heaven and earth.
>
> (Fiorenza 1995: 22)

Similarly, Ruether recognizes in the Christological vision of Nicea (325), an 'imperial Christ' in whom 'patriarchy, hierarchy, slavery, and Graeco-Roman imperialism
have all been taken over and baptized by the Christian church' (Ruether 1981: 48–9).
Classical Christology is thus viewed as a 'history of Christian power relations': 'the
history of how the church, in its doctrine, discipline, and worship, has legitimated
the use of ecclesial, civil, and social power either to exercise coercive control or to
elicit voluntary cooperation' (Heyward 1989: 14). Both the Jesus-of-history theologians and the Christ-of-faith theologians are 'in search of the Jesus Christ of his own
politic' (Heyward 1989: 18). 'Dogmatic absolutism' and the requirement of 'doctrinal
conformity' are thus considered 'dangerous': they encourage 'the abuse of power' by
denying 'the necessary openness for internal criticism and reform which a living faith
requires' (Hopkins 1995: 13).

Some feminist theologians go further than 'destabilizing the patriarchal politics
of Christology', as Fiorenza suggests (Fiorenza 1995: 45). They opt for a postmodern
approach (cf. Butler 1990; Fulkerson 1991, 1997) to the 'problem' posed by Christ's maleness: one that challenges not only its political meaning or its theological interpretation,
but even its ontological reality:

> Jesus is not 'male'. Rather, the Christian tradition has read him as 'male' in order to create and reinforce a social order wherein males are seen as more important than females. Such a social order also has the effect of insisting on sexual complementarity, which disadvantages women, who must be joined to men in order to gain the privileges of maleness, and which disallows all sexual relationships that are not part of the patriarchal, heterosexual, potentially procreative marriage. Jesus' 'maleness' is an instrument of control in the Christian tradition.
>
> (Young 2010: 185)

Admittedly few feminist theologians actually deny Christ's maleness. In drawing attention to the Christa symbol, for example, their intention is not to question whether 'Christ *was* a woman' but whether he might have been: 'Whether there *could have been* a Christa'. 'Why', it is asked, 'should redeemers always be men?' (Bernet 1991: 172; cf. Daly 1985a: 77). Many feminists admit that Christ was male, while simultaneously addressing his person in terms that are symbolically female. In an attempt to 'relieve the monopoly of male images of Logos and Son' and to 'untie the knot of sexist Christology', Johnson (1994: 165; cf. Johnson 1993b: 106, 109), for example, and Ruether (1993b: 117; 1993a: 14) address Christ as personified Wisdom. '[T]he male hegemony must be deconstructed such that the image of God made Flesh is seen and experienced as female as well as male. We need a Jesus as "like me", a woman' (McLaughlin 1993: 121). While Johnson, not unlike McLaughlin, presents this option as 'removing the male emphasis that so quickly turns to androcentrism' (Johnson 1994: 157; cf. Børresen 1981: 332), it is nonetheless illustrative of the tendency among recent theologians, and feminist theologians in particular (cf. Ruether 1975: 611, 1993b: 18f; Fiorenza 1984: 2ff.; Ross 1993: 194), to 'substitute gynocentrism for androcentrism' (Legrand 2006: 75).

This is apparent in McLaughlin's search for 'gender-bending images' in the tradition that might serve to resolve her personal 'dilemma': that of having a sense of self 'as woman' which would not allow her to entertain a 'call to priesthood'; for 'there were no words or icons which gave permission to see that new thing under the sun' (McLaughlin 1993: 131). That 'new thing' she proposes is a 'gender-bending' Christ symbol. Calling upon 'female Jesus-naming' in the works of Clement of Alexandra, St. Anselm, Julian of Norwich, and others, on the one hand, and upon the example of the second-century martyr, Blandina, in whose female person was recognized the crucified Christ, on the other, McLaughlin reasons: if a woman (Blandina) might be recognized as revealing God, then 'the God who is incarnate must be seen as neither essentially male, nor essentially female, but as both, and therefore as a Third One, who opens the eyes of the beholder to something more than the expected' (McLaughlin 1993: 136). It is 'not', she clarifies, that 'Jesus is a "feminine" or androgynous man. Rather, Jesus who was and is both "historical fact" and symbol, a man, is like a "cross-dresser," one not "caught" by the categories' (McLaughlin 1993: 141). In a manner similar to Pamela Young, who calls for a 'queer' Jesus, who 'does not conform to the conventional or normative categories' (Young 2010: 188), McLaughlin's 'transvestite' Jesus 'makes a human space where

no one is out of place because the notion of place and gender has been transformed'
(McLaughlin 1993: 144).

Questioning the Meaning
of Redemption

Many feminists think the redemption wrought by Christ is this transformation of gender.
This fits the 'impetus' that drives their 'critical theology', namely the goal of 'making real'
(Ruether 1975: 619) the 'Magna Charta' of Christian feminism (Fiorenza 1984: 61): 'There
is neither Jew nor Greek, there is neither slave nor free, there is neither male, nor
female; for you are all one in Christ Jesus' (Gal. 3:28). For some feminists this means,
as McLaughlin disapprovingly remarks, moving 'beyond sexuality' (cf. Daly 1985a: 15,
26, 50; Young 2010) and seeking a solution 'in the extra-canonical Gnostic texts where
androgynous spiritualities ... offer attractive models for re-formed, non-hierarchical
Christian community' (McLaughlin 1993: 125). Others take the difference of the sexes
as 'the starting point for a feminist incarnational Christology' (Hopkins 1995: 93) and
grant priority to 'the discovery of women-self, woman-voice and woman-in-relation as
woman made in God's image' (McLaughlin 1993: 125). Presupposed in both cases is the
breaking out of patriarchy's hold upon woman's conception of herself and of the authentically human: the 'exorcism of the internalized patriarchal presence, which carries with
it feelings of guilt, inferiority, and self-hatred that extends itself to other women' (Daly
1985a: 50). Patriarchy, or sexism, is thus recognized by some feminists as 'the sin of our
time' (Carr 1998: 113)—even of *all* time: indeed, 'the original sin' (Daly 1985a: 49–50, 72;
cf. Fulkerson 1991; Ruether 1993b: 173ff.)—and 'women's religious protest and affirmation' are understood as 'grace for our time' (Carr 1998: 113). Or, to put it more objectively,
grace is the 'infusion of liberating empowerment from beyond the patriarchal cultural
context', which allows women 'to critique and stand out against ... androcentric interpretations of who and what they are' (Ruether 1985a: 115). Conversion is thus the process
'of turning away from trivialization and defamation of oneself as a female person' and
of 'turning toward oneself as worthwhile' (Johnson 1994: 62; cf. Ruether 1993b: 183ff.).
As for men, they come to conversion by entering into 'real solidarity with women in
the struggle for liberation' (Ruether 1993b: 190), even at the risk of the 'loss of male
economic status and privilege' and of being 'repudiated or scorned by other males as
"unmanly"' (Ruether 1993b: 191).

   In short, feminist theology is widely understood as a form of liberation theology
(cf. Ruether 1975, 1993b: 193ff.; Heyward 1989: 21ff.; Hopkins 1991: 44; Fulkerson 1997:
102), wherein liberation is understood in terms of 'the struggle of women to free
themselves from all internalized male norms and models' (Fiorenza 1984: 60). Christ,
however has been 'presented to women as the reenforcer of their oppression, not as
their redeemer' (Ruether 1987: 281), and 'the *imago dei*/Christ paradigm' has been 'an

instrument of sin rather than a disclosure of the divine and an instrument of grace'
(Ruether 1993b: 19–20; cf. Daly 1985a: 72), whence the now classic question of feminist
theology: 'Can a male savior save women?' (Ruether 1993b: 116; cf. Carr 1998: 161). For
many feminists, the maleness of Christ appears *at best* to get in the way of his liberating function.

On the other hand, it is precisely *as male* that Jesus is recognized by other feminists as particularly well suited to renounce 'this *system* of domination' and 'patriarchal privilege' and to manifest 'the *kenosis of patriarchy*, the announcement of the new
humanity through a lifestyle that discards hierarchical caste privilege and speaks on
behalf of the lowly' (Ruether 1993b: 137; cf. Coakley 2002: 61). A woman would not be
able to renounce power and privilege nor to assume the redemptive act of taking the
place (*stellvertreten*) of the lowly and denigrated, because she is *already* in that place
(cf. Bernet 1991: 174). Ironically, still other feminists denounce the very ideals that the
kenosis entails—obedience, subjection, self-denial, sacrifice—as leading to the 'harm
(*Unheil*), terror and oppression' of women, precisely because they are proposed as salvific (*heilig*) by way of imitation (Strobel 1991: 57; cf. Daly 1985a: 77; Hopkins 1991, 1995:
51ff.; Ruether 1993b: 186; McReynolds and Graff 2005; Gudmundsdottir 2010: 143ff.). Sin
and salvation are 'simply two diverse symptoms of the same disease' (Daly 1985a: 72).
Some Christian feminist theologians have thus 'called into question the very foundations of Christian tradition, all of which represent a view which sees self-denial and
self-sacrifice as the defining attributes of Christian love' (Ramsay 2000: 123). These
attributes are said to correspond to a male-centered notion of redemption, because they
reverse the particularly male sin of 'pride, will-to-power, exploitation, self-assertiveness,
and the treatment of others as objects rather than persons' (Saiving 1979: 35). Women,
on the other hand, are said to sin by way of their 'underdevelopment or negation of the
self' (Saiving 1979: 37) and consequently of their 'complicity in self destruction' (cf. Daly
1985a: 51): they collaborate 'with sexism in lateral violence toward themselves and other
women' (Ruether 1993b: 165 and cf. 180).

Of course, not all feminists agree with the oppressor–victim alignment according to
the division of the sexes (cf. Coakley 2002; West 2000), nor are they all willing to sacrifice the notion of self-denial or self-gift as intrinsic to Christian perfection (cf. Greene-
McCreight 1997; West 2000; Coakley 2002; Beattie 2006: 72–3). Still less are they all
willing to reduce the meaning of Christian salvation to liberation from sexism and
patriarchy. Because, however, Christology is recognized as 'a function of soteriology'
(Strahm 1991: 14), and because feminists are not in agreement over the content of salvation and how it is to be achieved, 'a universal dogmatic christology' is thought by some
to be impossible (cf. Hopkins 1995: 12). The 'reference point for a feminist Christological
concept is not', from this perspective, '*the* Christology in its dogmatic form, but the
question what salvation/liberation/redemption ... means concretely for women in different contexts' (Kalsky 1991: 226).

As differing from the patriarchal sin of 'idolatry', which projects one's own self-image
upon the Godhead (cf. Daly 1985a: 69, 79; Heyward 1989: 19; Heyward 2010: 33), the
temptation of Christian feminism is that, therefore, of projecting upon Christ one's

own 'salvific aspirations' (cf. Hopkins 1995: 77). Indeed, Susan Parsons has good reason to remind other feminists that 'redemption cannot be something fabricated for the sake of the world'. Rather, it is 'the possibility for human beings, women and men, to be themselves the birthplace of the divine' (Parsons 2002: 131). This need not mean that the uniqueness and universality of Jesus Christ 'as Logos, Lord, Son of God, New Adam and Pantocrator' might simply be 'replaced by the uniqueness and universality of the christic experience' of 'justice-making relationships' (Hopkins 1995: 87; cf. Heyward 1989: 20; Heyward 2010: 166), or that the Chalcedon formula of 'truly God and truly man' might be reduced to a 'symbolic' function of pointing to 'the incarnational of the divine in our embodied selves' (Hopkins 1995: 57 and cf. 97). The point is nonetheless well made that 'the hymn of Phil. 2 was, from the start, an invitation to enter into Christ's extended life in the Church, not just to speculate dispassionately on his nature' (Coakley 2002: 34).

From the Historical Christ to the Mystical Christ

In thus drawing attention to the 'pneumatological reality' of Christ, which 'cannot be restricted to the historical person Jesus or to certain select members of the community' (Johnson 1993a: 129; cf. Ruether 1993b: 138), the invitation is also launched to surpass a 'naïve physicalism', which 'collapses the totality of the Christ into the human man Jesus' (Johnson 1991: 113, 115). Instead, we are reminded that 'the whole Christ is a corporate personality, a relational reality, redeemed humanity' (Johnson 1994: 72). '[M]embers of the community of disciples are *en Christo*, and their own lives assume a christic pattern' (Johnson 1993a: 128; cf. Heyward 1989: 84; Hilkert 2005: 203).

The question nonetheless remains whether we can simply bypass the 'scandal' caused by the concrete particularity of the incarnate Christ—including his maleness—without denying his unique mediating role and his unique importance in the redemption of the world. The maleness of Christ is thought to place 'limits on what human experiences Jesus can have had', and therefore also, it is reasoned, 'on what dimensions of human existence he can be said to sanctify' (O'Neill 2002: 53; cf. Johnson 1994: 73). The God-man is thus recognized as one 'partial' model of redeemed humanity that 'needs to be joined by other models, other memories' (Ruether 1993b: 115; cf. Mulder 1997: 19, n. 29).

These statements stand in contrast to what other feminists recognize as the 'particularity of the Christian confession', namely the attribution of 'definitive, absolute, and universal significance to the particular, historical man—the Jewish itinerary preacher, Jesus of Nazareth—for our understanding of God (*the* incarnation of God) and for the salvation of all of history and humanity (*the* Redeemer of humanity)' (Strahm 1991: 11). 'For there is one God, and there is one mediator between God and men (ἄνθρωπον), the man (ἄνθρωπος) Christ Jesus' (2 Tim. 2:5). It appears impossible, from the perspective of the Christian faith itself, to speak of the continued Incarnation of Christ (*corpus mysticum*) in the absence of the historical Incarnation that we celebrate in the event of the Annunciation (*corpus natum*) and thus also in the absence of the corporeal body of Christ that serves—not excluding his sacramental body (*corpus eucharisticum*)—as the point of union (cf. Eph. 2:16) between the fullness of the Godhead (cf. Col. 1:19) and the Church as the mystical body of Christ (cf. Eph. 1:23; Col. 1:18, 24). As the instrument of his divinity, his sacred humanity is simultaneously 'sanctified and sanctifier' (*ST* III, q.34, a.1, ad. 3; cf. q.8, a.5).

On the other hand, Christ's descending mediation (his assimilation of himself to humankind by way of the Incarnation) might be understood as ordered to the ascending mediation of his return to the Father along with his Body-Bride: his assimilation of humanity to himself, not withstanding our willing cooperation. This means that the salvific exchange (*admirabile commercium*) of the Incarnation is not simply realized between the two natures of Christ, but also and most specifically between his divine person and the persons of each of his members, beginning with his Mother who, as Aquinas teaches (*ST* III, q.30, a.1), received him by her fiat for all humankind. 'Rightly therefore the Fathers see Mary not merely as passively engaged by God, but as freely cooperating in the work of man's salvation ... For as St. Irenaeus says, she "being obedient, became the cause of salvation for herself and for the whole human race" ... "[T]he knot of Eve's disobedience was untied by Mary's obedience: what the virgin Eve bound through her disbelief, Mary loosened by her faith" ' (Vatican Council II 1964: §56).

Feminist theologians have good reason to argue that the patristic formulation *quod non est assumptum non est sanctum* should be complemented by the biblical image of the Pauline metaphor of the body of Christ (1 Cor. 12:12–27), which 'expand[s] the reality of Christ to include potentially all of redeemed humanity' (Johnson 1993a: 128). Similarly, the patristic presentation of Christ's humanity as the instrument (*organon*) of his divinity might be complemented by the Thomistic presentation of an exchange between Head and members (*ST* III, q.8, a.5, ad.1). In both cases, the particular humanity of Christ, including his maleness, points to the relational and communitarian dimension of his human nature (cf. Moltmann-Wendel 1991: 108). This has important implications for a doctrine of redemption that points to the participation of each of his members, who make up for what is 'lacking' in his suffering 'for the sake of his Body the Church' (cf. Col. 1:24). Christ's members are not just passively assimilated to him, but rather become like him in the act of becoming one *with* him: in their gift of themselves in response to his absolutely primary gift of self to each and to all. 'There is', therefore, 'no male hero who stands alone, but one whose mother is hailed as Co-Redeemer, along with his mixed rag-bag of "friends", those proclaimed as saints—and those whose memories have no clear herstory' (D'Costa 2000: 199; cf. O'Neil 1993, 2002).

In conclusion (as I have argued elsewhere, within the context of formulating a new feminism):

> In his assumption of human nature, the eternal Son ... also assumed the complementary and communal value (i.e., as sexed and gendered) of this same nature: Christ

is not only man (*homo*) but also male (*vir*). As such (fully human and fully male), he is 'naturally' and 'obediently' orientated to woman as his partner in humanity. The standard and 'measure of everything human in all its dimensions', Christ exists within what Hans Urs von Balthasar calls 'a human constellation', including, most especially, his mother Mary. Born of a woman, as are all human beings, he also subjected himself to her in filial obedience (cf. Luke 2:51) and willingly depended upon her 'spousal' collaboration (i.e., as archetype of the church) for the accomplishment of his mission; a mission which began with her fiat granting him 'entry', through the flesh, therein. The bridal obedience and submission of Mary is, on the other hand, dependent upon the filial obedience (cf. John 14:31) and spousal sacrifice of Christ (cf. Eph. 5:25), which is to say that her own immaculate fiat is, as it were, formed within his own. More specifically, her Immaculate Conception—that which 'equips' her for her extraordinary bridal (i.e., virginal) and maternal vocation—is itself the fruit of his redemptive merit. In the filial-maternal relationship of Mary and Jesus and in the spousal relationship of Christ and the church there is thus revealed the fact that we can have 'no adequate hermeneutic of man, of what is "human," without appropriate reference to what is "feminine." ' More specific to our context, 'we cannot omit' from the mystery of Christ 'the mystery of "woman": virgin-mother-spouse [John Paul II 1988: no. 22]'.

(Schumacher 2004b: 49–50; cf. Miller 1995: 31ff.; Schumacher 2004c)

SUGGESTED READING

Gudmundsdottir (2010); Hopkins (1995); Johnson (1991, 1993a); Miller (1995); O'Neill (1993, 2002); Ruether (1981, 1993b); Stevens (1993).

BIBLIOGRAPHY

Agacinski, S. (2005), *Métaphysique des sexes. Masculin/Féminin aux sources du christianisme* (Paris: Éditions du Seuil).

Allen, P. (1997), *The Concept of Woman*, vol. 1: *The Aristotelian Revolution, 750 BC–AD 1250* (Grand Rapids, Mich.: Eerdmanns).

Allen, P. (2002), *The Concept of Woman*, vol. 2: *The Early Humanist Reform, 1250–1500* (Grand Rapids, Mich.: Eerdmanns).

Aquinas, T. (1933), *Scriptum Super Sententiis Magisatri Petri Lombardi*, III, ed. M. F. Moos (Paris: Lethielleux).

Aquinas, T. (2009), *Summa Contra Gentiles* III–2, trans. V. J. Bourke (Notre Dame: University of Notre Dame Press).

Aquinas, T. (2012), *Summa Theologiae*, vols. 13–20 of Latin/English Edition of the Works of St. Thomas Aquinas, trans. L. Shapcote, ed. J. Mortensen and E. Alarcon (Lander, Wyo.: The Aquinas Institute for the Study of Sacred Doctrine).

Beattie, T. (2003), *Woman: New Century Theology* (London: Continuum).

Beattie, T. (2006), *New Catholic Feminism: Theology and Theory* (London and New York: Routledge).

Bernet, S. (1991), 'Die grössten Unmenschlichkeiten hat man im Namen eines schönen Heilskonzeptes begangen (Inge Merkel). Universale Erlösungsvorstellungen und ihr Hang zum Totalitären', in D. Strahm and R. Strobel (eds.), Vom Verlangen nach Heilwerden. Christologie in feministisch-theologischer Sicht (Fribourg/Luzern: Exodus), 81–99.

Børresen, K. (1981), Subordination and Equivalence: The Nature and Role of Women in Augustine and Thomas Aquinas (Washington, DC: University Press of America).

Butler, J. (1990), Gender Trouble: Feminism and the Subversion and Identity (London: Routledge).

Carr, A. (1998), Transforming Grace: Christian Tradition and Women's Experience, 2nd edn. (New York: Continuum).

Christ, C. (1977), 'The New Feminist Theology: A Review of the Literature', Religious Studies Review 3: 203–12.

Coakley, S. (2002), Powers and Submissions: Spirituality, Philosophy and Gender (Malden, Mass.: Blackwell).

Daly, M. (1985a), Beyond God the Father: Toward a Philosophy of Women's Liberation, 2nd edn. (Boston: Beacon Press).

Daly, M. (1985b), The Church and the Second Sex, 3rd edn. (Boston: Beacon Press).

D'Costa, G. (2000), Sexing the Trinity: Gender, Culture and the Divine (London: SCM Press).

de Beauvoir, S. (1989), The Second Sex, trans. and ed. H. M. Parshley, 3rd edn. (New York: Vintage Books).

Fiorenza, E. (1984), Bread Not Stone: The Challenge of Feminist Biblical Interpretation (Boston: Beacon Press).

Fiorenza, E. (1995), Jesus, Miriam's Child, Sophia's Prophet: Critical Issues in Feminist Christology (New York: Continuum).

Fiorenza, E. (2001), Wisdom Ways: Introducing Feminist Biblical Interpretation (Maryknoll, NY: Orbis Books).

Fulkerson, M. (1991), 'Sexism as Original Sin: Developing a Theacentric Discourse', Journal of the American Academy of Religion 59: 653–75.

Fulkerson, M. (1997), 'Contesting the Gendered Subject: A Feminist Account of the Imago Dei', in R. Chopp and S. Greeve (eds.), Horizons in Feminist Theology: Identity, Tradition and Norms (Minneapolis: Fortress), 99–115.

Greene-McCreight, K. (1997), 'Gender, Sin and Grace: Feminist Theologies Meet Karl Barth's Hamartiology', Scottish Journal of Theology 50: 415–32.

Gudmundsdottir, A. (2010), Meeting God on the Cross: Christ, the Cross, and the Feminist Critique (Oxford: Oxford University Press).

Hampson, D. (1992), Theology and Feminism, 3rd edn. (Oxford: Blackwell).

Heyward, C. (1989), Speaking of Christ: A Lesbian Feminist Voice (New York: Pilgrim Press).

Heyward, C. (2010), The Redemption of God: A Theology of Mutual Relation, 2nd edn. (Eugene, Oreg.: Wipf & Stock).

Hilkert, M. (2005), 'Cry Beloved Image: Rethinking the Image of God', in A. O. Graff (ed.), In the Embrace of God: Feminist Approaches to Theological Anthropology, 2nd edn. (Eugene, Oreg.: Wipf & Stock), 190–205.

Hinga, T. (1995), 'Jesus Christ and the Liberation of Women in Africa', in M. A. Oduyoye and M. Kanyoro (eds.), The Will to Arise: Women, Tradition and the Church in Africa, 2nd edn. (Maryknoll, NY: Orbis Books), 183–94.

Hopkins, J. (1991), 'Christologie oder Christolatrie? Feministische Einwände gegen die traditionelle Modelle von Jesus dem Christus', in D. Strahm and R. Strobel (eds.), Vom

Verlangen nach Heilwerden. Christologie in feministisch-theologischer Sicht (Fribourg/Luzern: Exodus), 37–51.

Hopkins, J. (1995), *Towards a Feminist Christology: Jesus of Nazareth, European Women, and the Christological Crisis* (Grand Rapids, Mich.: Eerdmanns).

John Paul II (1988), Apostolic Letter, *Mulieris dignitatem.*

John Paul II (1995), Encyclical Letter, *Evangelium Vitae.*

Johnson, E. (1991), 'The Maleness of Christ', in *The Special Nature of Women? Concilium* 6: 108–16.

Johnson, E. (1993a), 'Redeeming the Name of Christ—Christology', in C. LaCugna (ed.), *Freeing Theology: The Essentials of Theology in Feminist Perspective* (San Francisco: Harper), 115–37.

Johnson, E. (1993b), 'Wisdom was Made Flesh and Pitched her Tent Among Us', in M. Stevens (ed.), *Reconstructing the Christ Symbol: Essays in Feminist Christology* (Mawah, NJ: Paulist Press), 95–117.

Johnson, E. (1994), *She Who Is: The Mystery of God in Feminist Theological Discourse* (New York: Crossroads).

Kalsky, M. (1991), 'Vom Verlangen nach Heil: Eine feministische Christologie oder messianische Heilsgeschichten?', in D. Strahm and R. Strobel (eds.), *Vom Verlangen nach Heilwerden. Christologie in feministisch-theologischer Sicht* (Fribourg/Luzern: Exodus), 208–33.

Legrand, H. (2006), 'Les femmes sont-elles à l'image de Dieu de la même manière que les hommes? Sondage dans les énoncés de quelques Pères grecs', in O. Pesch and J.-M. Van Cangh (eds.), *L'homme, image de Dieu. Données bibliques, historiques et théologiques* (Brussels: Académie Internationale des Sciences Religieuses), 49–77.

McLaughlin, E. (1993), 'Feminist Christologies: Re-Dressing the Tradition', in M. Stevens (ed.), *Reconstructing the Christ Symbol: Essays in Feminist Christology* (Mawah, NJ: Paulist Press), 118–49.

McReynolds, S. and A. Graff (2005), 'Sin: When Woman are the Context', in A. Graff (ed.), *In the Embrace of God: Feminist Approaches to Theological Anthropology*, 2nd edn. (Eugene, Oreg.: Wipf & Stock), 161–72.

Miller, M. (1995), *Sexuality and Authority in the Catholic Church* (Scranton, Pa.: University of Scranton Press).

Moltmann-Wendel, E. (1991), 'Beziehung—die vergessene Dimension der Christologie', in D. Strahn and R. Strobel (eds.), *Vom Verlangen nach Heilwerden. Christologie in feministisch-theologischer Sicht* (Fribourg/Luzern: Exodus), 100–11.

Mulder, A. (1997), 'Thinking about the *Imago Dei*—Minimalizing or Maximalizing the Difference Between the Sexes: A Critical Reading of Rosemary Radford Ruether's Anthropology Through the Lens of Luce Irigaray's Thought', *Feminist Theology* 14: 9–33.

Nolan, M. (1994), 'The Defective Male: What Aquinas Really Said', *New Blackfriars* 75: 156–66.

Nolan, M. (2000), 'The Aristotelian Background to Aquinas's Denial that "Woman is a Defective Male"', *The Thomist* 64: 21–69.

O'Neill, M. (1993), 'The Mystery of Being Human Together', in C. M. LaCugna (ed.), *Freeing Theology: The Essentials of Theology in Feminist Perspective* (San Francisco: HarperCollins), 139–60.

O'Neill, M. (2002), 'Female Embodiment and the Incarnation', in F. Eigo (ed.), *Themes in Feminist Theology for the New Millennium (I)* (Villanova, Pa: Villanova University Press), 35–66.

Parsons, S. F. (2002), 'Feminist Theology as Dogmatic Theology', in Parsons (ed.), *The Cambridge Companion to Feminist Theology* (Cambridge: Cambridge University Press), 114–32.

Pelletier, A.-M. (2001), *Le Christianisme et les femmes. Vingt siècles d'histoire* (Paris: Cerf).

Pesch, O. (1988), *Thomas von Aquin. Grenze und Grösse mittelalterlicher Theologie. Eine Einführung* (Mainz: Matthias-Grünewald-Verlag).

Ramsay, K. (2000), 'Losing One's Life for Others: Self-Sacrifice Revisited', in S. F. Parsons (ed.), *Challenging Women's Orthodoxies in the Context of Faith* (Aldershot: Ashgate), 121–33.

Ranke-Heinemann, U. (1990), *Eunuchs for the Kingdom of Heaven: Women, Sexuality, and the Catholic Church*, trans. P. Heinegg (New York: Penguin Books).

Ross, S. (1993), 'God's Embodiment and Women: Sacraments', in C. M. LaCugna (ed.), *Freeing Theology: The Essentials of Theology in Feminist Perspective* (San Francisco: HarperCollins), 185–209.

Ruether, R. (1974), 'Misogynism and Virginal Feminism in the Fathers of the Church', in Ruether (ed.), *Religion and Sexism: Images of Woman in the Jewish and Christian Tradition* (New York: Simon & Schuster), 150–84.

Ruether, R. (1975), 'Feminist Theology as a Critical Theology of Liberation', *Theological Studies* 36: 605–26.

Ruether, R. (1981), *To Change the World: Christologies and Cultural Criticism* (New York: Crossroads).

Ruether, R. (1985a), 'Feminist Interpretation: A Method of Correlation', in L. M. Russell (ed.), *Feminist Interpretation of the Bible* (Philadelphia: Westminster), 111–24.

Ruether, R. (1985b), 'The Future of Feminist Theology in the Academy', *Journal of the American Academy of Religion* 53: 703–13.

Ruether, R. (1985c), *Womanguides: Readings Toward a Feminist Theology* (Boston: Beacon Press).

Ruether, R. (1987), 'John Paul II and the Growing Alienation of Women from the Church', in H. Küng and L. Swindler (eds.), *The Church in Anguish: Has the Vatican Betrayed Vatican II?* (San Francisco: Harper & Row), 279–83.

Ruether, R. (1993a), 'Can Christology be Liberated From Patriarchy?', in M. Stevens (ed.), *Reconstructing the Christ Symbol: Essays in Feminist Christology* (New York and Mahwah, NJ: Paulist Press), 7–29.

Ruether, R. (1993b), *Sexism and God-Talk: Toward a Feminist Theology*, 2nd edn. (Boston: Beacon Press).

Saiving, V. (1979), 'The Human Situation: A Feminine View', reprinted in C. Christ and J. Plaskow (eds.), *Womanspirit Rising: A Feminist Reader in Religion* (San Francisco: Harper & Row, 1992), 25–42.

Schumacher, M. (ed.) (2004a), *Women in Christ: Toward a New Feminism* (Grand Rapids, Mich.: Eerdmans).

Schumacher, M. (2004b), 'The Nature of Nature in Feminism, Old and New: From Dualism to Complementary Unity', in Schumacher (ed.), *Women in Christ: Toward a New Feminism* (Grand Rapids, Mich.: Eerdmans), 17–51.

Schumacher, M. (2004c), 'The Unity of the Two: Toward a New Feminist Sacramentality of the Body', in Schumacher (ed.), *Women in Christ: Toward a New Feminism* (Grand Rapids, Mich.: Eerdmans), 201–31.

Schumacher, M. (2013), 'A Woman in Stone or in the Heart of Man? Navigating between Naturalism and Idealism in the Spirit of *Veritatis Splendor*', *Nova et Vetera* 11: 1249–86.

Stevens, M. (1993), 'Introduction', in Stevens (ed.), *Reconstructing the Christ Symbol: Essays in Feminist Christology* (Mawah, NJ: Paulist Press), 1–5.

Strahm, D. (1991), 'Für wen haltet ihr mich?', in Strahm and R. Strobel (eds.), *Vom Verlangen nach Heilwerden. Christologie in feministisch-theologischer Sicht* (Fribourg/ Luzern: Exodus), 11–36.

Strobel, R. (1991), 'Feministische Kritik an traditionellen Kreuzestheologien', in D. Strahm and R. Strobel (eds.), *Vom Verlangen nach Heilwerden. Christologie in feministisch-theologischer Sicht* (Fribourg/Luzern: Exodus), 52–64.

Vatican Council II (1964), Dogmatic Constitution on the Church, *Lumen Gentium*, in A. Flannery (ed.), *Vatican Council II: The Conciliar and Post Conciliar Doctuments* (Collegeville, Minn.: Liturgical Press, 1975).

West, A. (2000), 'Justification by Gender: Daphne Hampson's *After Christianity*', in S. F. Parsons (ed.), *Challenging Women's Orthodoxies in the Context of Faith* (Aldershot: Ashgate), 33–52.

Young, P. (2010), 'Neither Male nor Female: Christology beyond Dimorphism', in E. Leonard and K. Merriman (eds.), *From Logos to Christos: Essays on Christology in Honour of Joanne McWilliam* (Waterloo, Ont.: Wilfrid Laurier University Press), 181–96.

CHAPTER 27

JESUS CHRIST, LIVING WATER IN AFRICA TODAY

DIANE B. STINTON

> Jesus ... cried out, 'Let anyone who is thirsty come to me, and let the one who believes in me drink. As the scripture has said, "Out of the believer's heart shall flow rivers of living water"'.
>
> (John 7:37–8; NRSV)

Jesus' great proclamation at the Feast of Tabernacles (John 7:37–8) offers a vivid image for envisioning Christological development down through the ages. At the very culmination of this great Jewish feast in the Temple courts in Jerusalem, Jesus draws upon the water symbolism of the Feast to publicly invite anyone thirsty to come to him to receive rivers of living water. A profound symbol for first-century Jews in the arid land of Israel, 'living water' signified springs or fountains of genuine life which only God could provide (Isa. 12:3; Jer. 2:13; cf. Isa. 44:3–5; 55:1; 58:11; Ps. 36:8, 9). In Old Testament prophetic tradition, it also signified the Spirit that would flow forth from the Messiah (Zech. 14:8; Ezek. 47:8–10). The very ambiguity in the text of John 7:38, whether the streams of living water flow from Christ himself or from the believer, actually serves the present purpose since both readings bear import. The ultimate source, Jesus Christ, the Messiah of God, gives himself, the 'living water', through the Holy Spirit to all who believe in him. That living water then springs up into eternal, abundant life within the believer (John 4:10) and flows out of the believer like streams of living water to the world. Thus both readings coalesce to portray a vista of the great river of Christological tradition throughout history, both prior and subsequent to this event in the life of Jesus. B. W. Johnson observes,

> [T]he promise takes a wider sweep. He who drinks shall not only never thirst but becomes himself a running fountain, an unfailing supply of the waters of life. Meyer says: 'The mutual and inspired intercourse of Christians from Pentecost downward, the speaking in psalms, and hymns, and spiritual songs, the mutual edification of

Christian assemblies by means of inspired gifts, even to the speaking of tongues, the entire work of the apostles, and the early evangelists, furnish an abundant commentary on this text'. Christ is the living water; he who believes upon Christ has Christ formed within him, and hence must become a fountain to dispense the living water wherever he goes.

(Johnson 1886)

This early Christ-devotion and Christ-talk soon spread through the Spirit-empowered witness of Christ-followers 'in Jerusalem, in all Judea and Samaria, and to the ends of the earth' (Acts 1:8). Textual and non-textual evidence from the apostolic era attests to widespread reflection on the identity and significance of Jesus Christ, or Christology, not only throughout Israel, Syria, Asia Minor, and northwest into Europe, but also southwards into North Africa, Egypt, Ethiopia, and Nubia. Indeed, early African theologians, such as Tertullian, Origen, Cyprian, Athanasius, and Augustine, played a decisive role in the very formation of Christian theology and practice (Oden 2007). The subsequent story of Christianity in Africa, from these earliest traditions of the ancient churches—whether Roman Latin, Hellenistic, Orthodox, or indigenous—through the waves of Catholic and Protestant European mission in Africa from the fifteenth century, to the twentieth-century rise of Pentecostal and African Instituted Churches (AICs), creates a complex of Christological reflection as extensive as the waterways of the Nile delta.

Against this broad backdrop, the purpose of this chapter is to explore emerging African Christology of the twentieth and twenty-first centuries in its own right, and in its relation to the wider, historic streams of Christian tradition. Where does it cohere with biblical, historical, and systematic reflection on Jesus the Christ? Where and why does it diverge? And are such divergences best interpreted as tributaries, new streams forging distinctive channels of Christological reflection from African perspectives, which nonetheless continue to feed into the main river of ongoing Christian tradition? Or are they more like distributaries, diverting away from the main stream of Christian tradition, possibly to dry up into wadis that no longer carry the living water from its source in Christ?

Definitive conclusions are ill advised given the wide range of Christological reflections across Africa today. Indeed, the pluriformity of Christological expression warrants the common use of the plural 'Christologies'. Nonetheless, the thesis presented here is that overall, emergent African Christologies reflect creative, contextual engagement with the central question of Jesus' identity and significance by interpreting and appropriating biblical revelation and Christian tradition in the light of African realities both past and present. Within the present scope, the discussion is limited to Christianity in tropical Africa, focusing primarily on churches derived from the modern missionary movement. Three African proverbs serve as rubrics for exploring the overarching themes of coherence and contextuality in twentieth- and twenty-first-century African Christologies.

'WHERE A RIVER FLOWS, THERE IS ABUNDANCE' (NILOTIC PROVERB)

Without a doubt, the African Christologies delineated above stand squarely in the river of biblical, historical, and systematic Christian tradition, thereby nourishing the spiritual lives of hundreds of millions of African believers. Jean-Marc Éla, a leading African theologian from Cameroon, begins his Christological reflections by citing the Apostle Paul: 'I decided to know nothing among you except Jesus Christ, and him crucified' (1 Cor. 2:2). Drawing upon Walter Kasper's observations that the contents of the Gospel can be summarized in one word, 'Jesus Christ', and that Christology is essentially the elucidation of the core affirmation, 'Jesus is Lord', Éla asserts, '[I]f the eyes of the New Testament are focused on Jesus Christ, every theological reflection begins and ends with Jesus of Nazareth. In a sense, Christology is theology itself, its center of gravity, its motive and its basic theme' (Éla 1994: 17). Likewise, two prominent theologians from Eastern Africa, J. N. K. Mugambi from Kenya and Laurenti Magesa from Tanzania, introduce their co-edited anthology of Christological essays as follows:

> Christology is, in the final analysis, the most basic and central issue of Christian theology. The faith, the hope and the praxis of love that Christian theology attempts to explicate, and which Christians endeavour to witness to by their life, must have Christ as their foundation and goal ... In fact, to be precise, theology is not Christian at all when it does not offer Jesus Christ of Nazareth as the answer to the human quest, and as the answer to people who ask the reason for the hope that all Christians hold through faith (cf. 1 Peter 3:15).
>
> (Mugambi and Magesa 1989: x)

Not only the centrality but also the fundamental content of Christology, as African theologians articulate it, aligns squarely with historic Christian tradition. For example, John Mbiti, often deemed the father of African theology, originally built his Christology on the New Testament. Mbiti interpreted the key moments in Jesus' life through the framework of the significance of rites of passage in most African societies. Because Jesus, in his birth, baptism, entry into Jerusalem, death and resurrection, underwent 'rites of passage' understandable to African cultures, it makes sense to think of Jesus as 'a perfect man' and as someone who achieves 'everything which constitutes a complete, corporate member of society' (Mbiti 1972: 56). Mbiti argued that Christ's resurrection from the dead is the most fascinating of these moments, and the one with the greatest magnetism for Christians in Africa. So for him the victorious Christ, *Christus Victor* must be the centrepiece of an African Christology. Mbiti claimed that Christ the Victor is the image of Christ which most immediately touches the sensibilities of Africans and their spiritual and cultural needs: 'The greatest need among African peoples', Mbiti wrote, 'is to see, to know, and to experience Jesus Christ as the victor over the powers and forces from which Africa knows no means of deliverance' (Mbiti 1972: 55).

Another early proponent of African theology, Ghanaian John Pobee, likewise examined NT teaching on the humanity of Jesus, working exegetically from the text and also interpretatively from his native Akan anthropology. He further outlined key aspects of Jesus' divinity as revealed in the biblical text: his sinlessness, despite temptation; his divine power and authority, demonstrating through his teaching and miracles the reign of God in their midst; his identity as creator and judge of the world; and his pre-existent and eternal nature (Pobee 1979). While noting that biblical faith encompasses different kinds of Christologies, whether derived from the plurality of New Testament perspectives on Christ or the ensuing development of historical and systematic expressions, Pobee concluded:

> Nevertheless, the diverse Christologies converge and agree on two points: 'Jesus is truly man and at the same time truly divine.' It is these two ideas that any Christology, whether African or European, American or Chinese, Russian or Australian, Akan or Ga, Ewe or Dagbani, Yoruba or Igbo, is concerned to capture, even if the imageries or terminologies may change. All the Christological titles come back to these same two ideas. The humanity and the divinity of Jesus are the two nonnegotiables of any authentic Christology.
>
> (Pobee 1979: 83)

In affirming this core Christian doctrine, African Christians—like believers of any era and locale—wrestle to comprehend and convey the great paradoxes concerning Jesus the Christ: his transcendence and immanence; his coinherence with the Triune God and his Incarnation as a human, reflecting unity and diversity within the Godhead; his particularity as a first-century Jew and his universality as the Risen Christ. In all these fundamental Christological queries, Christians in Africa are clearly aligned with those from other parts of the globe and from previous eras of the faith.

Finally, African Christians certainly stand in the great river of Christian tradition by honouring the Bible as the essential matrix for Christological formulation and the plumb line for any valid expression of Christology. As Teresa Okure asserts, '[T]he question of the global Jesus needs to be situated first and foremost within the context of biblical history and faith where it rightly belongs, and from which it derives its fundamental identity' (Okure 2001: 237). Indeed, scholars within and beyond the continent of Africa acknowledge the paramount place of the Bible for African Christians, as well as their tendency to accord it greater respect and authority than do Christians in the global North (Jenkins 2006: 4–5).

While acknowledging room for various interpretations of Scripture, according to the historical and cultural context of the interpreter, Pobee articulates widespread conviction among African Christians:

The African like the European is using his cup to draw from 'the same river', which is the Good News of 'Jesus Christ and him crucified', to gain life (1 Cor. 2:2). The African's cup may be made of seemingly crude and simple material; the European's cup may be china. Both cups draw from 'the same river', the Gospel of God. For this reason the Bible is of crucial importance for the statement of the African's vision on Christ; the Bible remains the charter document of the church.

(Pobee 1983: 6)

If twentieth- and twenty-first-century African Christology coheres closely with these 'non-negotiables' of the Christian faith throughout history, then what makes it distinctively 'African'? An early statement from Mbiti sums up the present section and segues into the next proverb:

The final test for the validity and usefulness of any theological contribution is Jesus Christ. Since His Incarnation, Christian Theology ought properly to be Christology, for Theology falls or stands on how it understands, translates and interprets Jesus Christ, at a given Time, Place and human situation.

(Mbiti 1971: 190)

'A RIVER FOLLOWS THE SLOPE' (BATEKE PROVERB)

As the surrounding terrain channels the flow of a river, so the various contexts of Africa—historical, geopolitical, socio-economic, and religio-cultural—shape the course of Christological development in Africa. Hence the key concept of 'contextuality' provides contours for interpreting the various streams of Christ's living water in contemporary African Christianity. While the term 'contextuality' and its cognates are relatively recent, coined in 1972 by Shoki Coe within the circles of the Theological Education Fund, the process is not. Coe defines 'contextuality' as 'that critical assessment of what makes the context really significant in the light of the *Missio Dei*. It is the missiological discernment of the signs of the times, seeing where God is at work and calling us to participate in it' (Coe 1976: 21). In Coe's view, theologizing entails a dialectic between 'contextuality', this awareness and participation in God's agenda, and 'contextualization', or the critical interaction between the eternal, transcendent Word of God and the particular, ever-changing circumstances of humankind. While the terms 'contextuality' and 'contextualization' have spawned extensive scholarly debate over the past decades, the core concepts are constructive here to explain the distinctive contours of African Christology. For in line with what Mbiti advocated above, African Christians do indeed seek to understand, translate, and interpret Jesus Christ in their particular contexts of time, place, and situation.

Rationale for doing so is found in biblical and historical precedent. Biblical scholars account for the very diversity of NT Christological expression in terms of the different contexts and theological perspectives of the authors, as well as the evangelistic and didactic strategies of the early disciples. As I. Howard Marshall makes clear,

> Terms that were intelligible to Jews, such as Son of man, were not the most suitable when speaking to Gentiles who had not read the book of Daniel. Any missionary worth his salt would use terms and concepts familiar to his hearers which could be used to re-express the Christian message, and the use of the term 'Lord', familiar in pagan ruler and mystery cults, to apply to the 'one Lord Jesus Christ' (1 Cor. 8:6) was an obvious development of this kind.
>
> (Marshall 1990: 38–9)

Ever since these earliest Christological developments witnessed in the NT, believers have continued to translate Jesus into new contexts of faith and to reflect on his identity and significance midst changing cultural contexts. Hence Jaroslav Pelikan's exploration of what each historical era brought to its portrayal of Christ:

> For each age, the life and teachings of Jesus represented an answer (or, more often, *the* answer) to the most fundamental questions of human existence and of human destiny, and it was to the figure of Jesus as set forth in the Gospels that those questions were addressed.
>
> (Pelikan 1999: 2)

Despite the wealth of biblical, historical, and systematic expressions of Christology that span the centuries, producing the 'kaleidoscopic variety' of images of Jesus today (Pelikan 1999: 2), the corresponding process within African Christianity is relatively recent. Certainly, on the one hand, Christians born in Africa have always interacted with an 'African Christ' and have always envisaged Christ 'through African eyes': this has been so since Christianity came to Africa. Christology has both formal, academic expressions and informal expressions in song, ritual, art and iconography, homiletics, and prayer. Especially amongst African Instituted Churches, informal African expressions of belief in Christ, in prayer, hymns, art, liturgy, and sermons bear witness to the African *consensus fidelei*: most believers spontaneously see Jesus both through their own culture and traditions and through the Bible. It's not a matter of either/or but of both/and. African Christians know Christ both through the Bible and through the lens of their own culture. But nonetheless on the other hand, it has come to light in the past forty or fifty years that African believers need to make much more use of specifically African theories of knowledge in their critical reflection on Christ; it has been belatedly recognized that they need to do more to integrate their systematic Christology into African metaphysics and African cosmologies (and vice versa, to integrate specifically African metaphysics into Christology). Their Christology does not take systematic advantage of their culture, does not sufficiently 'baptize' African culture and thought and draw it into Christology.

So for instance, in the late 1960s, Mbiti lamented that 'African concepts of Christology do not exist', and began to present those of Jesus' features which are indeed congruent with African worldviews (Mbiti 1972: 51). Back in 1963, British missionary John V. Taylor pinpointed the problem of Christianity being perceived in Africa as a 'white man's religion', in these oft-quoted words:

> Christ has been presented as the answer to the questions a white man would ask, the solution to the needs that Western man would feel, the Saviour of the world of the European world-view, the object of adoration and prayer of historic Christendom. But if Christ were to appear as the answer to the questions that Africans are asking, what would he look like? If he came into the world of African cosmology to redeem Man as Africans understand him, would he be recognizable to the rest of the Church Universal? And if Africa offered him the praises and petitions of her total, uninhibited humanity, would they be acceptable?
>
> (Taylor 1963: 16)

In response to these felt needs for an authentic, relevant African Christology, a surge of Christological reflections ensued, primarily in key anthologies and journal articles, with some monographs in addition—to the point that by the end of the twentieth century, African Christologies came to occupy the heart of Christian theology in Africa (Manus 1998).

Within this swell of literature, theologians regularly acknowledge that there are risks involved in talking about 'Africa' in broad, stereotypical terms, without acknowledging that many different peoples, languages, histories, and cultures inhabit this one great continent. Nonetheless, many assume enough homogeneity in the African experience to warrant the term 'African' Christology, while also grounding their theological reflections in a particular people group. Consequently, the plural form 'Christologies' is widely used, as noted above, to reflect the multiplicity of local perspectives. Thus the universality of the Gospel and the diversity of Christological expression in Africa are held in dialectical tension, which Pobee sums up as follows:

> On the basis of the Bible that Gospel concerns the person of Jesus Christ and the experience of a living encounter with this One who is eternal hope and who presents humankind with the challenge to change (cf. 1 Corinthians 1:18; 2:2). It is this core which has to be experienced by each individual and community in his/her/ their context, conditioned by time and space. It is when we move from context to the task of communication that the question of contextuality becomes important. Contextualization happens where and when the identity and integrity of the people, situation and circumstances are recognised, respected and engaged in a genuine dialogue with the eternal non-negotiable Gospel of Jesus Christ.
>
> (Pobee 1986: 11)

How, then, does contextuality channel these particular emergent African Christologies? The remainder of this section will first outline key contextual factors, sources, and methods that lend distinctive shape to Christological expression in Africa. Then a brief overview of central images of Jesus will demonstrate some of the Christological developments.

If twentieth-century African theologians sought to divert from contemporary Christological discourse, several composite issues prompted and steered their course. Somewhat as the late mediaeval Church was so far dominated by French concerns that the Holy See was moved to Avignon, likewise today the Church in Africa is captive to the Anglo-sphere of America and Northern Europe. Pobee claimed that:

> Christianity in Africa starts with an assumed definition of the Christian faith which is definitely North Atlantic—intellectually, spiritually, liturgically, organisationally. Missionary preaching in Africa has been so shaped by the North Atlantic cultures and contexts, that the African is unable to see beyond that picture of Christ of the biblical faiths.
>
> (Pobee 1983: 5)

He also laments that '[s]ome have misused the Christian faith to oppress Africans. In the name of bringing "Christian civilization" to the so-called benighted Africans they have oppressed Africans intellectually, physically, spiritually, economically, and culturally' (Pobee 1983: 5).

In sum, African Christians' common experience of domination by Western Christianity in Africa, manifest in theology and in Church polity and practice, influenced their nascent Christologies. For example, because of the appearance of complicity between colonialists and Christian mission workers, Jesus was envisaged as a white European by many Africans, and thus as an alien import into their culture. The message he was deemed to preach was likewise one of obedience to the colonialist regimes. There were thus deep missiological problems connected to the way in which Christian mission came about in Africa in the eighteenth and nineteenth centuries, and the way Christianity was identified with the 'West' in the minds of most colonizers and colonized. The equation of Christianity with Western civilization also generated deep-rooted theological problems. Just as Paul did not want to impose his own Judaism on his Gentile Christian converts, so, as African theologians rightly said, African Christianity did not have to circumscribe itself in what are Western, rather than Christian, theological norms.

Therefore a vital issue arose concerning African Christian identity, as believers sought to interpret Jesus authentically as *African Christians*. This meant overcoming their common experience of straddling two seemingly disparate worlds of Christianity and African culture, often described as African duality or 'spiritual schizophrenia'. Additionally, African women and men confronted the lack of gender inclusiveness characteristic of the modern missionary movement and endeavoured to glean women's perspectives on the person of Jesus. African Christianity needed to be articulated, not in the colonial languages, but in the African tongues, so as to speak with an African voice. African Christology needed to be expressed in culturally fitting words, concepts, and images. Such problems and their solutions have done much to shape contemporary African Christologies (Stinton 2004: 24–44).

Before moving on to the discussion of sources and methods, it must be noted that the contextual factors outlined above pertain primarily to those African Christologies derived from the interface of the modern missionary movement and the rise of African Christianity in the latter half of the twentieth century. Since contexts change and culture is dynamic, some of the currents of thought flow into this new century while others ebb. With Africa now a wellspring of world Christianity in the twenty-first century, there are indications of a new generation of African theologians who are both settled and self-confident in their identity as African Christians. For example, A. E. Orobator writes:

> Many years after my conversion, both my African religious heritage and Christian faith come together in a way that I find meaningful, enriching, and deeply satisfying. Contrary to what some writers believe about African Christians, I do not feel torn between two worlds: I have a strong identity as an African Christian. I am at home as an African Christian.
>
> (Orobator 2008: x–xi)

Thus, riding on the currents of the first few generations of contemporary African theologians, this present generation is well placed to assess and to further channel Christological formulation in light of contemporary contextual factors in Africa and in relation to global discussions of Christology.

Overlapping with the contextual factors, the sources and methods that African Christians employ lend distinctive shape to their Christological reflections. In his early publication on African Christology, cited above, Mbiti advocated four rich sources or 'pillars' for theological reflection in Africa: (1) the Bible; (2) the theology of the older churches, particularly Christian scholarship and tradition from Europe; (3) the traditional African world; and (4) the living experience of the Church, especially the AICs (Mbiti 1972: 52). The 'Final Communiqué' of the 1977 Pan-African Conference of Third World Theologians, held in Accra, Ghana, indicates widespread assent to these sources being constructive for African theology, proposing a nearly equivalent list.

Both proposals begin with the Bible as the basic source for theology and the primary witness of God's revelation in Christ, as emphasized in the section above. While the crucial discussion of biblical hermeneutics in Africa lies beyond the scope of this chapter, one aspect of biblical interpretation is particularly germane to Christological reflection in Africa. Many African theologians contrast the Western tendency to discuss Christology in metaphysical terms with both the biblical and the African tendency to favour concreteness of expression over abstractions. For example, Pobee contends that

> functional terms in the discussion of Christology will be the most apt approach to the subject in Akan society. The process of philosophical abstraction from the concrete biblical texts which has been the chief trend of Western theology is not,

to my mind, terribly effective in Africa, at least if theology is to engage the church as a whole and not just the initiates. This is said in the context of certain views of the semantic nature of abstractions, concrete language, and mythological/metaphoric language, and the different ways in which they relate to thought and knowledge.

(Pobee 1979: 82)

Mbiti's second pillar, the theology of the older European churches, is conspicuously absent from the 'Final Communiqué'. Certainly some African theologians, such as Charles Nyamiti from Tanzania, engage more extensively than others with received Christian tradition from the West. On the whole, however, most African theologians favour the alternative second source in the 'Final Communiqué' list, African anthropology and cosmology.

Closely related to this aspect, the third source is the 'traditional African world', in Mbiti's expression, or 'African traditional religions'. Here, the 'Final Communiqué' sets forth a major presupposition that significantly shapes African theology, including Christology:

The God of history speaks to all peoples in particular ways. In Africa the traditional religions are a major source for the study of the African experience of God. The beliefs and practices of the traditional religions in Africa can enrich Christian theology and spirituality.

(Appiah-Kubi and Torres 1979: 192)

This assertion functions as a watershed, separating various streams of African theology according to degrees of assent or dissent.

The fourth source, shared by both proposals, is the living experience of the Church, particularly the AICs. In this regard, it is worth highlighting African theologians' insistence that Christology encompasses not only formal written expressions, but also informal oral and visual expressions derived from the vital Christian experience presently manifest in Africa. For example, in 1974 Henry Okullu highlighted a fundamental criterion for the development of African theology: namely, that 'it is a function of the Church', not to be found primarily in the books shelved in theological libraries, but rather as lived out in the lives of African Christians. He explained African theology comes from Christian workplaces and homes. It comes from Christian prayer, alive with drum beats and hand claps. It does not come down from on high, but up from below, where Christians make music, perform plays, sing, paint, sculpt, dance, and express their spirituality through their daily lives. Nonetheless, we must listen both to the educated minister and to the raw convert. African theology, says Okullu, comes from African Christian life as a total ecology (Okullu 1974: 53–4).

Finally, the 'Final Communiqué' adds another category of other African realities, including cultural arts, communal life, and the struggle against any form of political, economic, social, or cultural oppression.

Corresponding to these sources, Christological methods in Africa evidence two main approaches: (1) departing from the biblical material about Christ, often reflecting a 'Christology from below' that begins with Jesus of Nazareth, and moving to the African context to discern relevant Christological themes; and (2) drawing upon the African reality, whether aspects of indigenous culture or the contemporary context as the locus for theological formulation. Nyamiti highlights this second category as the most commonly employed in Africa, noting that African Christologies have especially flourished using the 'thematic' or 'functional analogy' approach (Nyamiti 1989: 4).

Depending upon the sources favoured and the methods employed, it has become conventional to distinguish two broad schools of African theology: 'inculturation' and 'liberation' theology. The former category entails theological exploration of African indigenous cultures in an attempt to integrate the African pre-Christian religious heritage with the Christian faith so as to 'ensure the integrity of African Christian identity and selfhood' (Bediako 1996: 1). This is considered the most common and developed approach, which encompasses most African Christologies. The latter category is further subdivided into South African Black theology, arising out of the particular context of apartheid, and African Liberation theology, found throughout independent tropical Africa and broader in scope. Liberation is not restricted to the political and socio-economic realms, but includes freedom from every form of oppression including hunger, disease, ignorance, and the subjugation of women (Nyamiti 1994: 66). Therefore African feminist theologies are often placed within this category. Certainly women's experience has become an important locus for liberation theology: as African women reflect upon various forms of oppression suffered under Western Christianity, African religio-cultural traditions, and contemporary political and socio-economic realities, they offer fresh Christological insights. However, the central theme of liberation does not exhaust African women's Christologies.

Finally, a third paradigm of African theology seeks to move beyond the theme of liberation, deemed outworn in the 'New World Order' of the 1990s, by proposing 'reconstruction' as the more appropriate theological imagery for social transformation in twenty-first-century Africa. While Christology is not prominent in this theological scheme, J. N. K. Mugambi, its key originator, interprets the mission of Jesus as essentially reconstructive rather than deconstructive of Judaism. Drawing upon the Sermon on the Mount as a core text, Mugambi calls for three levels of reconstruction: personal, cultural, and ecclesial (Mugambi 1995: 13).

Although these broad classifications have been instructive in delineating the field of African theology, they definitely defy rigid compartmentalization. In particular, the dichotomy between inculturation and liberation is increasingly called into question, since both facets are intrinsically related to each other and equally necessary. Hence another way to interpret the multiple currents in African Christologies is to take an integrative approach, consistent with the holistic nature of African worldviews, in discerning central themes inherent in these Christologies. While the following outline is neither exclusive nor exhaustive, it offers an overview of the main images of Jesus in

Africa today. Four broad categories of images overlap with one another and each category represents a cluster of related themes (Stinton 2004).

Jesus as Life-Giver

Life is undoubtedly a universal aspiration, yet it stands out as a prime value in indigenous African thought. Therefore African Christologies arise through the confluence of African concepts and biblical affirmations of life, in relation to contemporary realities. Thus a cardinal image of Jesus is life-giver, or the one who fulfils African aspirations for life. A central focus of many African religions, life is understood to originate and have its fullness in God. It is channelled through a hierarchy of powers, some of which can be seen by the naked eye and some which transcend our material vision: down from God, to family and clan members who have attained greater force after death, down to living family, kin and local dignitaries and rulers, all the way down to nature herself.

It is absolutely incumbent upon all to participate in this common life, since the individual is thought to exist only in relation to the community. When these indigenous constructs interact with biblical teaching, Christological portraits of Jesus as the life-giver and the abundant life he brings feature strikingly in Gospel proclamation (e.g., John 10:10; 14:6).

Certain realities in contemporary Africa—bloodshed and bad governance, poverty and preventable disease, opportunism and oppression, crime and corruption, to name but a few—definitely challenge such depictions of Christ's presence and power in Africa. Nonetheless, a widespread, unwavering conviction remains that Jesus Christ is indeed present and active in the everyday realities of life in Africa. There are many images of Jesus as life-giver, providing life, creating life, protecting life, and supplying with life. Amongst these in African Christianity the key image is Jesus the Healer. Here he is understood to renew and rebuild life wherever it is wanting. The image of Jesus the Healer echoes through African sermons, worship, devotion, and imprecation. Jesus the healer is as significant in liturgy and rite as he is in theology. AICs make abundant use of healing services and here Jesus is repeatedly portrayed in the guise of a healer. Where once, in Westernized churches which ignored historical African traditions concerning health and sickness the image of Jesus the healer had been absent, now today it is forcefully present. Jesus heals by imparting integrity and organic 'wellness' to life as a whole, to the community and to the cosmos as well as to the individual. Moreover, that Jesus is healer means he dominates and rises above the evil forces which exist and act in the cosmos. He can beat out the evil forces wherever they are found: in psychological disturbance and in physical illness, in spiritual sickness and in the fragmentation of communities. The image of Christ as healer connects to faith in Christ as redeemer, liberator, and saviour.

African traditional medicine is a hotly debated topic, and so is the portrayal of Christ in the guise of a traditional healer. Some African Christians envisage Jesus as 'nganga', the Bantu term for medicine-man, which Hollywood movies translated as 'witch doctor'. Imagining Jesus as 'nganga' is not universally accepted. People are influenced here by missionary-colonialist aversion to medicine-people. They also worry that it is syncretistic to bind Jesus to the nganga figure. Whether or not in works on paper, in reality very many African people think that, in practice, Jesus performs the same function as the nganga, curing the sick, warding off evil forces, and helping to keep the threads of society from fraying and tearing. This debate runs on and on, and that shows the difficulties and ambiguities of enmeshing the Gospel and African culture in relation to Christ.

Jesus as Mediator

Another fundamental concept in indigenous African thought is that of intermediaries. In the face of problems like crime, sickness, and witchcraft, Africa's indigenous religions look for help to intermediaries. They ask intermediaries to figure out what has brought about the dissonance, and to restore harmony and good relations. The recovery of harmony is channelled through intermediaries. Custom and the forms of political order dictate that high-status individuals are approached indirectly, through an intermediary or third party. This is applied to God: though Africans do pray directly to God, they are also socially inclined to approach God through the mediation of those thought to be closer to him. Specialists and experts are asked to pray on the believers' behalf, functioning as delegates or intermediaries. Mbiti mentions two kinds of intermediaries, human persons, like such as priests, kings, healers, and diviners, and spiritual beings, believed to assist people in establishing closer contact with God. Not all Africans practise what anthropologists have sometimes described in broad strokes as 'ancestor worship'. But very many African societies, perhaps most of them, regard the recently deceased as especially powerful beings. Mbiti calls these 'the living-dead' or 'the ancestors'. Such spirits are perceived as the greatest of intermediaries since they are believed to be close enough to human beings to understand their needs, and close enough to God to accrue spiritual powers.

   Given this heritage, African Christians unsurprisingly interpret Jesus in relation to notions of intermediaries, for example as prophet, priest, lamb, sacrifice, reconciler, and peace-maker. African and biblical traditions converge in the significant, yet controversial, image of Jesus as ancestor. Several critical issues arise in assessing this Christological portrait: methodologically, in the danger of unwarranted generalizations about African beliefs concerning ancestors, given the diversity of ethnic societies. English speakers have translated all the multiple African vernacular words, each of which has its own unique connotations, as 'ancestor'. So-called 'ancestor worship' is a highly varied matter. There are three crucial issues about whether ancestor worship can be used as a way in to the worship of Jesus. One is, who exactly are the ancestors? Were they actually worshipped or were they, in fact, merely venerated? A second question is what status African ancestors can have within Christian belief systems. Are the ancestors analogous to the saints, who are venerated in many Christian traditions? Thirdly, given that Christianity teaches that Jesus is the one and only mediator, what sense can be made of the function of ancestors as mediators?

Despite all these problems, very many African Christians say that the ancestors are an important part of their Christian belief (Pobee 1979; Nyamiti 1984). For example, Kwame Bediako confirms the centrality of ancestors within his Akan heritage and insists that appropriating Jesus as saviour necessarily involves 'making him at home in our spiritual universe' (Bediako 1990: 9). He therefore develops the image of Jesus as ancestor, concluding that 'Jesus Christ is the only real and true Ancestor and Source of life for all mankind, fulfilling and transcending the benefits believed to be bestowed by lineage ancestors' (Bediako 1990: 41–2). Likewise Bénézet Bujo, a theologian from the Democratic Republic of Congo, develops a comprehensive ancestral theology by drawing parallels between ancestral beliefs and biblical teachings, in each case emphasizing that Jesus infinitely transcends the ideal of the God-fearing African ancestors. He thus advocates the image of Jesus as 'Ancestor Par Excellence' or 'Proto-Ancestor'. Four main ancestral functions are delineated: (1) Jesus is the mediator between God and humanity, analogous to the ancestors; (2) he is the founder of a new community of believers, thereby establishing its identity; (3) he continues to participate in the life of that community, in terms of his ongoing presence and power which far exceed that of the ancestors; and (4) he is believed to provide the abundance of life that the ancestors sought for themselves and to transmit to their descendants.

At the same time, some African Christians give forceful and robust criticisms of the very idea of envisaging Jesus as ancestor. The early missionaries tended to deprecate ancestor worship. Modernization separates Christians from their traditions; so does living in cities, a growing reality for many Africans. Some argue that attachment to the ancestors encourages ethnocentrism, which in turn provokes or encourages ethnic conflicts. The strongest objections are of course theological at root. The ancestors, it is said, have a different theological meaning and significance to the meaning and significance of the person of Jesus Christ. They are spirit-forces, not God. So it is claimed that representing Jesus as ancestor or even 'Proto-Ancestor' is to compromise his divinity.

Once again, the heated dispute demonstrates the intricacies of Christological formulation that seeks serious engagement between Gospel and African culture. Since the following two clusters of images are less controversial, they are summarized more succinctly.

Jesus as Loved One

Indigenous African thought, as indicated above, considers the life of the individual to be established and fulfilled only in relation to the life of the community. Mbiti captures this concept in his oft-quoted maxim, 'I am, because we are; and because we are, therefore I am' (Mbiti 1969: 108). So existing is rooted in community. And community itself encompasses living, dead, and those yet to be born. These values have not changed with the coming of modernization and urbanization to Africa. They cannot but affect how African Christians envisage Jesus and the metaphors through which they integrate Christian doctrine.

This third category thus includes many relational metaphors which depict Jesus as family member or as friend. Jesus is seen as brother in a context where brothers provide food, protect other family members, and often assume paternal roles, such as family head. Thus to interpret Jesus as brother is to perceive in Jesus' humanity provision, protection, and headship, that is, intimacy, solidarity, and support. Christians in Africa regard Jesus as the archetypal or universal brother, the brother to all human beings. For African Christians to interpret Jesus as brother is for them to see him as the one who draws all humanity into one ethnic group and clan. It is to see him as the one who overcomes the ethnic enmities which bedevil the continent of Africa.

The Kenyan theologian Anne Nasimiyu Wasike is one of many who present Jesus as mother. This is a common metaphor for Jesus in Africa, drawing upon metaphorical kinships between what motherhood means in Africa and Jesus' own life and teaching. In Africa, a mother is taken as one who nurtures life, and who represents love, kindness, mercy, and compassion. Africa today is being drained of life by economic debt, civil war, and structural adjustment programmes. In this context, Nasimiyu Wasiki calls Jesus the mother to all the faithful—not only women but also men. She claims that, as our mother, Jesus is asking us to nurture all life, not only the lives of our own ethnic group, society, political ideology, economic class, or gender. Jesus' motherhood is not about gender: it is about archetypal, ideal motherhood. Some reject the idea that Jesus could be mother because, historically, he was male. Even so, they are forced to admit that Jesus loves us exactly like a mother loves. So this metaphor is not limited to Africa, but has something to teach all Christians about the feminine aspects of the Triune God. Western Christologies could learn from it.

A final metaphor for Jesus which is very common in contemporary Africa is that of friend. Jesus becomes human and enters into human communities. African Christians embrace him as family member and friend.

Jesus as Leader

Leadership is not one single category in Africa: there are many kinds of leadership. Leadership is a very important foothold for understanding Jesus Christ. We have already discussed various important leadership models, such as healer, family head-ancestor, and brother. Another leadership model comes from the realms of politics and from religion. People think about him analogously on the basis of socio-political and religious leaders. Here are two examples of Jesus as political leader.

Among the Akan people of Ghana, the image of Jesus as king/chief indicates the local belief that traditional leadership expectations are enacted by Jesus. Elucidating the Akan king's role as 'priest/chief/king', combining religious, social, and political leadership, sheds light on the Christology of the New Testament. Hence Akan Christians ascribe traditional vernacular titles, honorifics, symbols, and leadership functions to Jesus, in each case highlighting Jesus' transcendence over human leaders (e.g., 'Osagyefo', traditionally a brave warrior or conquering king who delivers his people in battle). So Akan Christians maintain that these metaphors increase their understanding and deepen their worship of Christ in ways that are meaningful within their cultural context.

Jesus as liberator forms a second significant leadership image that is found throughout the continent. Theologians all over tropical Africa look for liberation from cultural captivity, as well as from political, economic, and social structures that perpetuate the evils of colonialism and neo-colonialism. Cameroonian theologian Jean-Marc Éla is outstanding for his incisive analysis of urgent problems in contemporary Africa, like the oppressive structures of capitalist-driven globalization, as the necessary locus of theology. As also noted above, Jesus as liberator represents, though does not exhaust, African women's Christologies. For example, Ghanaian theologian Mercy Oduyoye integrates biblical and African traditions in elaborating a multi-layered portrait of Jesus as saviour/liberator/redeemer. She then connects the significance of this image to the African context according to the goal of feminist theology, which she identifies to be women and men seeking together to become fully human.

Thus a certain congruence emerges between African Christologies derived from traditional leadership and those advocated in contemporary liberation Christologies. Jesus therefore represents both the fulfilment of leadership expectations in traditional African thought and of current yearnings for liberation in all dimensions of life.

'The River Swells with the Contribution of the Small Streams' (Bateke Proverb)

The foregoing discussion, under the rubrics of the first two African proverbs, has sought to examine twentieth- and twenty-first-century African Christology in terms of its confluence with historic streams of Christology and its divergence, where applicable. Coherence is evidenced in the centrality of Christology to theology, the fundamental content of Christological expression, and the primary place of the Bible in its formulation. Divergence is analysed in terms of contours that channel Christological developments in distinctive ways according to contextual factors in African experience, plus the sources and methods employed. An overview of emergent Christologies illustrates the flow of various currents within the rising swell of Christological formulation across sub-Saharan Africa.

Given the extensive, intricate, Nile-delta-like waterways of Christological reflection throughout Africa, the question of criteria for validity naturally resurfaces. More obvious indicators arise from the section on coherence with Christian tradition, in terms of adherence to the 'elastic circumference' of the biblical revelation of Christ

(Ezigbo 2008: 70) and to the 'non-negotiables' of the humanity and divinity of Jesus. Additionally, one interpretative framework that Bediako proposes for understanding contemporary African theology is likewise constructive in analysing African Christologies. After exploring continuities between the Gospel and Africa's continuing primal religions, Bediako turns to considering discontinuities. Here he finds a range of responses within Africa, which he places on a spectrum of 'Indigenizers', 'Biblicists', and 'Translators'. On one end of the spectrum, those who contend for 'radical continuity' between the Gospel and African culture presuppose the 'foreignness' of Christianity and minimize the newness of the Christian faith in their attempts to revitalize Africa's religious inheritance (e.g., Bolaji Idowu). Hence the efforts towards 'radical indigenization of the Church' find equivalents in any attempts towards the 'radical indigenization of Jesus' that minimize his otherness within Africa. The image of Jesus as traditional healer or *nganga* is illustrative of movement in this direction. On the other end of the spectrum, those who strive for 'radical discontinuity' based on a radical biblicism stress the distinctiveness of the Christian Gospel to such an extent that it virtually precludes any creative engagement between Gospel and African culture (e.g., Byang Kato). Again, the equivalent posture is found in those who object to any Christological formulation in Africa beyond the biblical representation of Christ or that of the ancient Christian creeds.

Between these two extremes is a broad middle ground of 'Translators', where most African theologies lie, according to Bediako. He explains,

> The view here is that Christianity, as a religious faith, is not intrinsically foreign to Africa. On the contrary, it has deep roots in the long histories of the peoples of the continent, whilst it has proved to be capable of apprehension by Africans in *African* terms, as is demonstrated by the vast, massive and diverse presence of the faith in African life. In other words, the eternal Gospel has already found a local home within the African response to it, demonstrating that Christ had effectively become the integrating reality and power linking the 'old' and the 'new' in the African experience.
>
> (Bediako 1996: 6)

Consequently, the task of African theology does not consist in 'indigenizing' Christianity or theology per se, but rather in allowing the Christian Gospel to encounter the African experience, as well as be shaped by it. Bediako further points out that African Christians could proceed with this task without apology to Western traditions of Christianity, since these did not enshrine universal norms. Thus the overall goal of African theology is to discern and explicate the genuinely and specifically *African* contributions—derived from the interface of the African primal tradition and the African experience of the Gospel—to the ongoing development of theology within the universal Church.

In accordance with this interpretative framework, the present chapter has argued that emergent African Christologies reflect this creative interchange between the biblical revelation of Christ and the African experience, both past and present. In other words, the mighty river of Christian tradition does indeed swell with the streams of

Christological reflection flowing within Africa today—as well as other parts of the world. So may they continue to flow until, in Isaiah's great eschatological vision, 'the earth will be full of the knowledge of the Lord as the waters cover the sea' (Isa. 11:9).

Suggested Reading

Bediako (1990); Ezigbo (2010); Mbiti (1972); Mugambi and Magesa (1989); Pobee (1979); Stinton (2004).

Bibliography

Appiah-Kubi, K. and S. Torres (eds.) (1979), *African Theology en Route* (Maryknoll, NY: Orbis Books).

Bediako, K. (1990), *Jesus in African Culture: A Ghanaian Perspective* (Accra: Asempa Publishers); repr. in W. A. Dyrness (ed.), *Emerging Voices in Global Christian Theology* (Grand Rapids, Mich.: Zondervan, 1994), 93–121.

Bediako, K. (1996), 'Understanding African Theology in the 20th Century', *Bulletin for Contextual Theology* 3: 1–11.

Clarke, C. R. (2011), *African Christology: Jesus in Post-Missionary African Christianity* (Eugene, Oreg.: Pickwick Publications).

Coe, S. (1976). 'Contextualizing Theology', in G. H. Anderson and T. F. Stransky (eds.), *Mission Trends No. 3* (Grand Rapids, Mich.: Eerdmans), 19–24.

Éla, J. (1994), 'Christianity and Liberation in Africa', in R. Gibellini (ed.), *Paths of African Theology* (London: SCM Press), 136–53.

Ezigbo, V. I. (2008), 'Rethinking the Sources of African Contextual Theology', *Journal of Theology for Southern Africa* 132: 53–70.

Ezigbo, V. I. (2010), *Re-imagining African Christologies: Conversing with the Interpretations and Appropriations of Jesus Christ in African Christianity* (Eugene, Oreg.: Wipf and Stock).

Jenkins, P. (2006), *The New Faces of Christianity: Believing the Bible in the Global South* (Oxford: Oxford University Press).

Johnson, B. W. (1886), *The New Testament Commentary*, vol. 3: *John* (St. Louis: Christian Publishing Company). <http://ccel.wheaton.edu> (accessed July 27, 2014).

Manus, U. C. (1998), 'African Christologies: The Centre-piece of African Christian Theology', *Zeitschrift für Missionswissenschaft und Religionswissenschaft* 82: 3–23.

Marshall, I. H. (1990), *The Origins of New Testament Christology*, rev. edn. (Leicester: Apollos).

Mbiti, J. S. (1969), *African Religions and Philosophy* (Nairobi: Heinemann).

Mbiti, J. S. (1971), *New Testament Eschatology in an African Background* (Oxford: Oxford University Press).

Mbiti, J. S. (1972). 'Some African Concepts of Christology', in G. F. Vicedom (ed.), *Christ and the Younger Churches* (London: SPCK), 51–62.

Mugambi, J. N. K. (1995), *From Liberation to Reconstruction: African Christian Theology after the Cold War* (Nairobi: East African Educational Publishers).

Mugambi, J. N. K. and L. Magesa (eds.) (1989), *Jesus in African Christianity: Experimentation and Diversity in African Christology* (Nairobi: Initiatives).

Nyamiti, C. (1984). *Christ as our Ancestor* (Gweru: Mambo Press).

Nyamiti, C. (1989), 'African Christologies Today', in J. N. K. Mugambi and L. Magesa (eds.), *Jesus in African Christianity: Experimentation and Diversity in African Christology* (Nairobi: Initiatives), 17–39.

Nyamiti, C. (1994), 'Contemporary African Christologies: Assessment and Practical Suggestions', in R. Gibellini (ed.), *Paths of African Theology* (London: SCM Press), 62–77.

Oden, T. C. (2007), *How Africa Shaped the Christian Mind: Rediscovering the African Seedbed of Western Christianity* (Downers Grove, Ill.: IVP).

Okullu, H. (1974), *Church and Politics in East Africa* (Nairobi: Uzima Press).

Okure, T. (2001), 'The Global Jesus', in M. Bockmuehl (ed.), *The Cambridge Companion to Jesus* (Cambridge: Cambridge University Press), 237–49.

Orobator, A. E. (2008), *Theology Brewed in an African Pot* (Maryknoll, NY: Orbis Books).

Pelikan, J. (1999), *Jesus through the Centuries* (New Haven: Yale University Press).

Pobee, J. S. (1979), *Toward an African Theology* (Nashville: Abingdon).

Pobee, J. S. (1986), 'Contextuality and Universality in Theological Education', in J. S. Pobee and C. F. Hallencreutz (eds.), *Variations in Christian Theology in Africa* (Nairobi: Uzima Press), 1–13.

Pobee, J. S. (1983), 'Jesus Christ—The Life of the World: An African Perspective', *Ministerial Formation* 21: 5–8.

Schreiter, R. J. (1979), *Toward an African Theology* (Nashville: Abingdon).

Schreiter, R. J. (ed.) (1991), *Faces of Jesus in Africa* (Maryknoll, NY: Orbis Books).

Stinton, D. B. (2003), 'African Christianity', in L. Houlden (ed.), *Jesus in History, Thought, and Culture: An Encyclopedia* (Santa Barbara: ABC-CLIO).

Stinton, D. B. (2004), *Jesus of Africa: Voices of Contemporary African Christology* (Maryknoll, NY: Orbis Books).

Taylor, J. V. (1963), *The Primal Vision: Christian Presence amid African Religion* (London: SCM Press).

CHAPTER 28

KENOTICISM IN MODERN CHRISTOLOGY

BRUCE MCCORMACK

INTRODUCTION

KENOTIC Christology in its classical form was a distinctively Lutheran movement which originated in the mid-nineteenth century. There it died a relatively quick death (Loofs 1901), though it lingered much longer in the UK. P. T. Forsyth and H. R. Mackintosh were not the first British theologians to embrace kenoticism but the power and influence of their writings, especially, ensured the survival of the older kenoticism until the years immediately after the Second World War. It was only with the critique advanced by Donald Baillie in 1948 in his widely-read book *God was in Christ* that kenoticism finally fell out of favor (Baillie 1948: 94–8). Though there have been attempts made from time to time to revive the fortunes of the older kenoticism, none has successfully addressed the full range of criticisms that have been brought against it over the years. If, then, the idea of kenosis is to be made fruitful in Christology today, a fresh start will be needed.

ORIGIN OF THE IDEA OF KENOSIS

The idea of kenosis first entered into the stream of Christological reflection through the writings of the apostle Paul. It is to be found in the so-called 'Christ hymn' in Phil. 2:6–11 (beginning with v.5):

> Let the same mind be in you that was in Christ Jesus, who, though he was in the form of God, did not regard equality with God as something to be exploited, but emptied himself, taking the form of a slave, being born in human likeness. And being found in human form, he humbled himself and became obedient to the point of death—even

death on a cross. Therefore God also highly exalted him and gave him the name that is above every name, so that at the name of Jesus every knee should bend, in heaven and on earth and under the earth, and every tongue should confess that Jesus Christ is Lord, to the glory of God the Father.

(NRSV)

The building-blocks of all later *theories* of kenosis are found in the words ἐκένωσεν ('emptied' in v.7) and ἐταπείνωσεν ('humbled' in v.8).

Considered from the standpoint of the history of exegesis and theology, the most basic exegetical decision has had to do with the question of the subject who is said to 'empty' himself in v.7. To be sure, the subject is named 'Christ Jesus' in v.5. But does the hymn envision the 'Christ Jesus' who empties himself as already incarnate? Is 'self-emptying' a human activity which takes place through the course of Jesus' earthly existence? Or does the hymn envision 'Christ Jesus' as not yet incarnate, as performing a divine act that somehow provides the necessary precondition to incarnation? These have typically been understood to be the two basic options where the question of the 'subject' is concerned—all others consisting in modifications of one or the other.

In favor of the first option is the fact that the context in which the 'Christ hymn' is set makes it perform a paraenetic function. 'Let the same mind be in you that was in Christ Jesus.' Paul is saying that the acts most basic to Jesus' way to the Cross—self-emptying and self-humiliation—are to find expression in the lives of believers. He is setting Christ forth as a model to be imitated. Not a few readers of this passage in the modern period, especially, have asked: how could one possibly follow an example set by God? Surely God is able to do what God does because he has powers that far exceed our own. How then could what God does as a precondition to becoming incarnate possibly be imitated by human beings? And if this logic holds, then the only alternative would be to understand the man Jesus as the model we are to imitate and, therefore, as the subject of 'self-emptying', etc.

The preponderance of orthodox theologians have not been persuaded by such arguments. Cyril of Alexandria, Augustine, and Thomas Aquinas understood the subject of the self-emptying to be the λόγος ἄσαρκος—the Word as pre-existent and, therefore, 'without flesh'. Presupposed, virtually without question, was a concept of God in accordance with which God was understood to be simple and impassible. Given these twin commitments, the act of 'self-emptying' undertaken by the Logos could not be understood in terms of a realistically conceived 'composition' or a divestment of anything that is proper to deity. The orthodox solution was to understand 'kenosis' as taking place through addition rather than subtraction; that is, through an assumption of human 'nature' (the 'form of a slave') which preserved the simplicity and impassibility of the divine Person performing this act. What is 'surrendered', on this view, is the 'glory' or recognizability of God. He came to those who were his own but they were not able to recognize him (John 1:11) because he was concealed in the veil of human flesh. The paraenetic argument is not regarded as conclusive because the divine 'emptying' and 'humbling' spoken of in vv.7–8 do have human analogues, even if they are not enacted in the same way. Moreover, the exaltation described in vv.9–11 is understood to secure the divine identity of the subject, since the One who emptied himself is the One exalted—and no mere human could be worshiped as God had he not belonged in some way to the divine identity all along (Bauckham 1998). 'Exaltation' is emergence from concealment; the public declaration by God of an already existing state of affairs.

And so matters stood at the dawn of the Reformation.

REFORMATION-ERA ANTECEDENTS OF THE (OLDER) MODERN KENOTIC THEORY

It was sixteenth-century Lutheran confessional theology which prepared the ground for nineteenth-century kenoticism. To understand why this should be the case requires that we begin where Luther himself did, with the question of the nature of Christ's presence in the Lord's Supper. Confronted by Zwinglian 'memorialism', Luther sternly insisted upon a local, physical presence of the body and blood of Christ in the elements of bread and wine. His Christology was then elaborated with a view towards providing an explanation for how Christ could be locally present at more than one simultaneously occurring Eucharistic celebration. His initial suggestion was that the human 'nature' of Christ obtains through the hypostatic union a share in the ubiquity of the divine 'nature'. But this suggestion, if true, would have proven too much. The so-called 'doctrine of ubiquity' would have made Christ's body to be present everywhere and not just in celebrations of the Lord's Supper. Closer attention to the Christological problem of the relation of Christ's 'natures' to each other and the relation of each to the 'person of the union' was, therefore, a necessity. The name given to this problem historically is that of the *communicatio idiomatum* (the 'communication of properties'). It was with a strong focus on this problem that Luther's followers would construct a Christology which could explain and make credible the desired local, physical presence of Christ in the Supper while *limiting* such presence to the Supper alone.

To Martin Chemnitz goes the credit for creating the Christological solution which was enshrined in the Formula of Concord in 1577. His great work *De duabus naturis in Christo* first appeared in 1570. A second edition—revised and expanded—appeared in 1578. In English translation, the revised work comprised 495 pages of small-print, making it one of the most comprehensive Christologies to have appeared to that point in the history of the Church (Chemnitz 1971). Chemnitz seems to have been the first to divide the 'communication' into three distinct 'genera'. Classically, there had only been two: the communication of the properties of both natures to the person of the union and a communication of works. To these two 'genera' Chemitz added a third, 'the communication of the majesty' (Chemnitz 1971: 265)—that is, the communication of divine attributes like omnipotence, omnipresence, and omniscience to the human nature of Christ.

Chemnitz found the basis for this third kind of 'communication' in a 'communion' or inter-penetration of the 'natures' (Chemnitz 1971: 259). Examined more closely, however, it would be more accurate to say that the divine nature indwells the human nature as fire permeates iron (Chemnitz 1971: 264). This ancient image is very important to Chemnitz for it allows him to say that the 'communication of the majesty' is not an 'essential communication' in the sense that the eternal generation of the Son makes essential to the Son all that is essential to the Father. And yet, just as iron 'possesses' the power of giving off light and heat when permeated by fire without itself becoming fire—iron remains iron and turns cold when fire is removed from it—so it is also with the human nature of Christ (Chemnitz 1971: 290–1). It 'possesses' attributes essential to God without those attributes becoming essential to itself. It is clear why Chemnitz goes to great lengths in explaining this; he is concerned to demonstrate (against Reformed critics) that Lutheran Christology does not violate the 'no confusion' and 'no change' caveats of the Chalcedon Definition (Tanner 1990: 86). On the contrary: he has shown how the natures could remain unimpaired in their original integrity precisely in their communion, so that there is no confusion or 'commingling' (Chemnitz 1971: 269).

There are at least two problems which are unique to Lutheran Christology as devised by Chemnitz. First, the human nature of Christ cannot be withdrawn from the divine nature of the Logos in the way iron can from a fire; the hypostatic union, once it has taken place, is in perpetuity and, therefore, unchanging. For that reason, the distinction between a perpetual 'possession' of divine attributes on the part of the human nature and that which is 'essential' to that nature would seem more nearly rhetorical than real. If the union remains constantly intact (and it does), then 'possession' ought to have been unchanging as well, which would seem to make it 'essential'. The only way to avoid this consequence would be to say that it is not the hypostatic union *as such* which brings about 'possession' but rather the *willed activity* of the divine person in and through the human nature. On this view, the Logos granted to his human nature a share in his divine properties where and when it pleased him to do so. But to put matters that way would render an inter-penetration of natures superfluous to requirements. And, as we shall now see, Chemnitz was fully capable of shifting to the second option when the need arose.

Second, and more importantly, the ancients did not employ the analogy of fire and iron in order to explain how essential divine attributes like omnipresence are made the 'possession' of the human nature; they did not go nearly so far. Their interest lay solely in the question of how immortality was bestowed upon mortal flesh. The idea that the man Jesus 'possessed' essential divine properties would have been unthinkable to them. Thus, the Lutheran 'communication of the majesty' was a *novum* in Christian theological history, without historical precedent. And from the very beginning, it created difficulties which would require those who subscribed to it to try to *limit* its consequences.

To return then to the problem of the uniqueness of Christ's presence in the Supper: the proposed resolution of the difficulties created by the 'communication of majesty' lay in a qualification which effectively undermined it. The Formula of Concord put it this way: 'the fullness [of the essential being of the Logos] shines forth with all of its majesty, power, glory, and efficacy in the assumed human nature, spontaneously and *when and where he wills*' (Tappert 1980: 603). It was by means of the introduction of volition into the question of the real presence of Christ in the Supper that the doctrine of ubiquity was transformed (when necessary) into a doctrine of *multivolenspraesenz*—a local and physical presence of Christ wherever he wills. But this solution looked to a different strand of Chemnitz' thought than his reflections on the communion of natures.

Consistent with this solution was Chemnitz' answer to the question of how Jesus could give evidence of human 'infirmities' (e.g., limited knowledge, hunger, thirst, suffering, etc.). His solution was that the Logos chose not to display the fullness of his majesty through his human nature on every possible occasion but only did so when perform-ing miracles and in those rare moments when, as in the transfiguration, he 'revealed his glory' (John 2:11) to his disciples, who received it as 'the glory of the only-begotten Son of the Father' (John 1:14) (Chemnitz 1971: 491). In all other moments, the Logos 'restrained or held in check, as it were, the radiance of the indwelling fullness of Deity, so that it did not shine forth' (Chemnitz 1971: 490). For Chemnitz, this voluntary restriction was necessary in order that the God-man might take our side, live under the conditions of human life (save for sin), and so be made a 'victim' on our behalf. In principle, at least, the 'state of humiliation' characterized by *a willed non-use* of divine attributes comes to an end with the exaltation—though, as we have seen, the 'state of exaltation' too has its self-imposed limitations.

What we find on this side of Chemnitz' thought is a real kenosis, though not yet a kenosis in the modern sense. For, in the first place, the subject of the self-emptying is the λόγος ἔνσαρκος, not the λόγος ἄσαρκος (as would be the case later). And in the second place, the kenosis is understood in terms of willed non-use of divine attributes in and through the human nature. It does not envision the divestment of anything proper to deity. Still, in this early form of the kenotic theory, the ground was amply prepared for the later development.

The unresolved tensions in Lutheran Christology were scarcely noticed at the time and in one sense, it made little difference whether one argued for an unchanging inter-penetration of natures or an (occasional and incomplete) 'instrumentalization' of the human nature by the Logos. Neither model allowed for a reciprocal 'communication' of human properties to the Logos; commitment to divine simplicity and impassibil-ity made that possibility unthinkable. So the 'traffic' was thought to flow in one direc-tion only: from the divine to the human. The divine was understood to be active and the human was understood to be receptive. And the reason this is a problem is that, in those moments when the activity of the Logos through or upon his human nature is suspended, the man Jesus looks very much like a subject in his own right; a rational agent who is self-activating and self-determining. Should those 'moments' become more expansive, should the man Jesus come to be understood as self-activating in every moment of his life, then the need for an additional genus of 'communication' (from the human to the divine Logos) would become quite pressing if the unity of person were to be maintained. *Or* a way would have to be found to make an end run around the entire problem. It was this last option which was chosen by nineteenth-century kenoticists.

MODERN KENOTICISM

Kenotic Christology was the creation of theological conservatives who were seeking to uphold the theological values resident in classical Lutheran Christology in a rapidly changing situation. To fail to understand this is to see the entire development in the wrong light. However radical some of the moves made might have been, the ultimate goal was conservative in the strict sense of seeking to protect the tradition from erosion and abandonment.

The impetus for such defensiveness was twofold. First, life of Jesus research was steadily eroding confidence in Christological orthodoxy. But it was not so much David Friedrich Strauss' *Life of Jesus Critically Examined* published in 1835 which galvanized the orthodox; it was rather his great two-volume work, *Christliche Glaubenslehre* which appeared in 1840/1841. For in the latter work, Strauss made it his goal to destroy Christian orthodoxy in all of its most important attainments. That was the second and more decisive impetus for the creation of a full-blown kenotic theory.

Strauss' critique was two-pronged. The first was directed to Christological orthodoxy in its historical development. The second was directed to the specifics of the Lutheran Christology on which he had been weaned.

First, the general critique. Once Gregory of Nazaianzen had said (against Apollinarianism) that 'the unassumed is the unhealed', it was no longer possible to think of the human nature of Christ as lacking a human mind. But that then meant what was truly being referred to under the heading of a hypostatic union was not a union of 'natures' but a union of two distinct 'personalities'. For a human nature which is complete in the way insisted upon by Gregory is a human 'personality' by any definition acceptable to modern scientific inquiry—namely, a rational, fully self-conscious, and self-activating individual. To maintain a unity of 'person' on these grounds was an impossibility. For if Jesus Christ had both a divine mind and a human mind, then he knew all things by an immediate act of eternal intuition and he knew some things (not all) as other humans know them, successively. And if he had both a divine will and a human will, then the object of his willing was both the whole world in the totality of its history and particulars in the world in a specific moment of time (Strauss 1841: 112–13). Strauss' point was this: to speak of two natures *in one person* is to imply the existence of a *single* self-consciousness in the one God-human. For what else could the term 'person' mean? But a single self-consciousness cannot emerge out of the union of two such radically different 'personalities'. For either would be canceled out by the other. That was the problem which surrounded the dyothelite position and, for Strauss' money, it was insuperable.

The second prong of Strauss' attack was directed towards problems surrounding the Lutheran doctrine of the 'communication of attributes'. It comprised three arguments. First, he rejected Chemnitz' attempt to distinguish between an 'essential' and a 'personal possession' of the divine attributes. Why? Because 'Divine attributes are nothing other than God himself'. Divine attributes can, therefore, only be proper to a nature and that nature can only be 'divine'. A human being cannot be thought to obtain a 'share' in them without entering into conceptual contradiction. Strauss offers an example. 'To be omnipotent not through Oneself but through something else (through the *unio hypostatica*) is a contradiction, insofar as there lies in the "through Another" a lack of power; and whoever is not essentially divine is not personally divine either, because a divine Person presupposes a divine nature' (Strauss 1841: 132). So either the 'communication of the majesty' is an essential communication or there is no such communication.

The second argument was directed against the seventeenth-century Lutheran distinction between 'effective attributes' of God which are shared with the human nature of Christ and those which are 'at rest' in God alone. To the first class were assigned omnipotence, omniscience, and omnipresence, all of which were thought to be communicated immediately to the human nature in Christ. To the second class belonged such attributes as eternity and infinity. These were said to be communicated to the 'person' and to that extent, were rightly ascribed to the God-human as a composite whole and not to the human nature. This distinction of the attributes anticipates in some ways the distinction which would be employed by the kenoticists, so it is interesting to see what Strauss made of it. In his view, this attempt to save the appearances only made a bad job worse. Ultimately, he thought, no distinction amongst the attributes could be made. All are essential to God. So either all of the attributes are 'communicated' to the human nature or none of them are.

The third argument was lifted straight out of the seventeenth-century Reformed catalogue of complaints against the Lutheran 'genus of majesty'. If it is an inter-penetration of the natures which makes that genus possible, then it should also make possible a 'genus of humility' (i.e., a communication of human properties to the divine nature). Strauss agreed. What he failed to make clear was that the Reformed enjoyed no real advantage on this point. For they too rejected the 'genus of humility'—in spite of the fact that their affirmation of the first genus (i.e., communication of the properties of *both* natures to the 'person') ought to have been sufficient to require its acceptance. But if that be so, then the third argument is applicable to all forms of Chalcedonian Christology and not to Lutheran Christology alone.

The first person to elaborate a full-blown kenotic theory was Gottfried Thomasius in his *Beiträge zur kirchlichen Christologie*, published in 1845. Thomasius was a Professor of Theology in Erlangen and the views set forth in that early work were quickly adopted by several of his colleagues, thus creating a distinctive 'Erlangen school'. The other significant figures belonging to this school were J. C. K. von Hofmann, August Ebrard, and F. H. R. Frank. Others quickly joined the kenotic movement including Wolfgang Gess (who was teaching at the Protestant 'Missionshaus' in Basel when he wrote his most significant work on Christology in 1856).

The starting point of Thomasius' Christological theory lay in a return to the patristic identification of the 'subject' of the self-emptying spoken of in Phil. 2:7 with the λόγος ἄσαρκος. He understood kenosis to consist in a surrender on the part of the pre-existent Logos of precisely those attributes by means of which the 'glory' of God is manifested outwardly to the world God created, namely, omnipotence, omniscience, and omnipresence. This was a kenosis by divestment and Thomasius understood it as an ontological precondition to incarnation.

But there is more to this divestment than first meets the eye. Thomasius was concerned not only with the problem of ubiquity; he was concerned above all with 'omniscience'. Participation in the omniscience of God would have made it impossible for the man Jesus to have experienced the psychological and emotional growth common to all human beings. His self-understanding would have undergone no development. He would have known all things and not known them—which is impossible. And so, as a corollary to his primary account of kenosis, Thomasius posited a surrender on the part of the Logos of his divine consciousness—his divine 'personality' in other words. And he described it in terms of a step back from actuality into a state of potency.

It is clear what Thomasius hoped to achieve with this move. He was seeking to confine the effects of the Lutheran 'genus of majesty' to the 'state of exaltation'. The kenosis was thought to describe the so-called 'state of humiliation' only (i.e., the days of Christ's earthly existence). Thomasius was convinced that participation in the omni-attributes was incompatible with the being of the human nature as human. Left open was the question of how it was possible for the Logos to resume possession and use of his omni-attributes in the 'state of exaltation'. If those attributes are truly destructive of human nature, then that ought to be as true in the 'state of exaltation' as it was in the 'state of humiliation'.

The arch-critic of the Thomasian kenosis theory was Isaak August Dorner, the most significant theologian belonging to the so-called 'mediating school' (which sought to mediate not only between the ancient and the modern worlds but also between Schleiermacher and Hegel). His initial critique of Thomasius' theory appeared in an article-length review of the latter's *Beiträge* (Dorner 1846). He would expand upon it in Part II of the second edition of his *Entwicklungsgeschichte* (Dorner 1853). Already in the review, he made a point which would remain central to his critique in later years. The surrender of divine self-consciousness on the part of the Logos would entail a divestment of that uniquely divine love which is essential to him as God. For how can the Logos love with the love that he 'is' (1 John 4:16) if he is no longer conscious of himself as God? If he cannot, then what has been surrendered is, in fact, the divine essence (Dorner 1846: 42). Moreover, if what is essential to deity has been surrendered, then the Logos is no longer God and the Trinity has been torn asunder.

In its expanded form, Dorner's critique makes three points. First, by depriving the Logos of his divine self-consciousness, Thomasius has made the 'natures' to be equal or essentially the same. But no unity of 'person' can emerge from the uniting of two finite natures (Dorner 1846: 44). Second, by depriving the Logos of the uniquely divine love which is basic to the divine self-consciousness, Thomasius has accomplished what many would have considered impossible. He has made himself guilty of both theopaschitism and subordinationism; theopaschitism because the disruption to the life of the immanent Trinity would impact all of its members, and subordinationism, because the Logos is no longer equal to the Father and the Spirit. If, then, we were to seek a remedy to this problem by means of a distinction between the immanent and the economic Trinity—with an accompanying note of reassurance that it matters not whether the Logos surrenders certain (allegedly) non-essential attributes because the resumption of them would 'heal' and restore the immanent Trinity—we would have overlooked the fact that we had turned the incarnation into a mere *theophany* (Dorner 1853: 1270), an impermanent manifestation of a Logos who had undergone essential change. And, third, Dorner raised a soteriological question (Dorner 1853: 1268). Is it really thinkable that the man Jesus would have been moved to make the sacrifice he finally made had he not continued to participate in that uniquely divine love whose object is the whole world? Would his sense of calling have been sufficient to bring it about? And even if it were, would it have truly been redemptive had that been the case?

In his mature Christology, Thomasius introduced a rather famous distinction which would help to clarify his understanding of kenosis—if not to overcome Dorner's objections to it. He distinguished between 'essential' and 'relative' divine attributes. 'Relative' attributes are those which God 'possesses' only as a consequence of having created the world. Since God was free not to create, these attributes are not necessary to him. The Logos can, therefore, surrender these non-essential attributes without detriment to what he is essentially (love, holiness, etc.). But, of course, making love to be essential to the Logos does bring Dorner's initial criticism back with full force: how could the love of God be present where the divine self-consciousness was not? The best answer Thomasius could give was to say that 'Potency ... is not something empty in itself, completely drained, contentless, as Dorner would have it, but the most completely intensified [reality] which can be conceived; not powerlessness, but a power concentrated in itself, enclosed in itself' (Thomasius 1857: 549). But this hardly constitutes an adequate defense against the charge that Thomasius had replaced incarnation with a theophany. One simply cannot have a real incarnation if the Logos appears in the economy in a radically different form than that in which he appears in the immanent Trinity.

Before departing from mid-nineteenth-century Germany, mention should be made of Wolfgang Friedrich Gess, whose theory was developed through close engagement with that of Thomasius some ten years after it had first appeared. Gess departed from Thomasius at one decisive point. He did not regard the distinction between essential and relative divine attributes as successful. Since the divine self-consciousness of Jesus was extinguished in the 'state of humiliation', the essential attributes which were a function of that consciousness must also have been surrendered—including aseity and self-sufficiency. Moroever, Gess understood kenosis to entail coming under the 'determining power' of the flesh (Bruce 1900: 145). For even without sin, the flesh exercises a power over the soul in the absence of which temptation would be impossible. Thus, Gess posited a more or less complete transformation of the Logos into a human soul (Bruce 1900: 148). To the question of what then distinguished his view from that of Apollinaris, Gess had a ready answer: the Logos did not take the place of a human soul but became a human soul. But, then, that also meant that Gess had completely dispensed with a two-natures theory. To the question of what all of this means for the Trinity, Gess remained consistent by adjusting his doctrine of the Trinity to the demands of his

Christology. In the strictest sense, aseity belongs to the Father alone; the Son and the Spirit share in it only derivatively. If the Son exchanges his aseity and self-sufficiency for radical dependence upon the Father, this leaves untouched the source of triunity in God, namely, the Father, who assumes government of the world during the Son's period of humiliation. The Son only takes up that government again in his exaltation.

With Gess, the older kenoticism had reached its nadir or its full potential, depending upon one's point of view. Certainly, he had made no effort to uphold divine immutability. Thomasius had tried to maintain the essential immutability of God while finding in God genuine affectivity, and a capacity for real interaction with the created world. Gess had simply given up on immutability.

The reason the older kenoticism of Thomasius and Gess died a relatively quick death in Germany had to do with the advent of Ritschlianism. It was, above all, the anti-metaphysical outlook of the Ritschlians which brought an end to all 'speculative theology'—including not only kenoticism but also those 'mediating' theologies which sought to make Hegel (and possibly Schelling) fruitful for Christian theology. Wrestling with the problems bequeathed to later Christian theology by the Chalcedonian Definition was no longer in vogue.

The conditions were rather different in the UK. British theologians were slower to accept the results of biblical criticism in general and life of Jesus research in particular than were their German contemporaries. And it was precisely at the point of the greatest popularity of Ritschlianism that interest in kenoticism grew—suggesting that uneasiness with metaphysics could never become a matter of principle with theologians like Forsyth and Mackintosh. At most, such uneasiness would find expression in an unwillingness to engage metaphysical questions on the grounds that to do so would betray a lack of humility. And so it came about that as late as 1912, H. R. Mackintosh could compose a kenotic theory which, while not differing greatly in content from that of Thomasius in particular, was characterized by a moral and spiritual earnestness and an often poetic style of writing which gave it great appeal.

Neither Forsyth nor Mackintosh was comfortable with the Thomasian idea of a surrender of divine self-consciousness on the part of the Logos—or any attribute, come to that. They preferred to think in terms of 'self-retraction' (Forsyth 1909: 308) or 'self-restraint' (Mackintosh 1912: 465). '[T]o talk of abandonment of this or that attribute on the part of the Eternal Son is a conception too sharp and crude, too rough in shading, for our present problem' (Mackintosh 1912: 477). The Christological problem, as they saw quite rightly, was the 'becoming' of God in the incarnation: how could this take place—how could God make himself to be the subject of a human life—without detriment to his being as God? Faced with this problem, however, Forsyth and Mackintosh hedged their bets. 'We cannot form any scientific conception of the precise process by which a complete and eternal being could enter on a process of becoming, how Godhead could accept growth, how a divine consciousness could reduce its own consciousness by volition. If we knew and could follow that secret we should be God and not man' (Forsyth 1909: 294–5). Mackintosh was more blunt: 'there is no suggestion [here] that it is given to man to watch God as he becomes incarnate' (Mackintosh 1912: 470). Not surprisingly Forsyth and Mackintosh preferred to concentrate their attention on the ethical and psychological dimensions of the problem, rather than the metaphysical. And so, however metaphysical a concept like 'self-retraction' may be, the process of its 'recovery' was spelled out in moral and historical terms.

> [T]he history of Christ's growth is then a history of moral redintegration, the history of recovery, by gradual moral conquest, of the mode of being from which, by a tremendous moral act, he came ... As he grew in personal consciousness he became conscious of himself as the Eternal Son of God, who had disempowered himself to be the son of man by a compendious moral act whereby a God conscious of humanity became a man equally conscious of deity.
>
> (Forsyth 1909: 308)

What has happened here is that the two-natures logic has been abandoned altogether; dyothelitism has been openly rejected (Forsyth 1909: 319; Mackintosh 1912: 470). What we have before us is the conception of God *living and acting humanly*. The historical process by means of which Jesus comes to a conscious awareness of his divinity simply *is* the process by means of which the eternal Son of God recovers his consciousness of his divinity. God has made himself in the incarnation the subject of a human life in a quite literal sense. And the ontological precondition in God for this outcome is said to be the step from the actuality of the Son's deity back into a potentiality in which actuality is 'powerfully condensed' (Forsyth 1909: 303).

The concept of self-retraction is, of course, redolent with ontological significance. Does retraction entail mutation in God? Does it require the abandonment of traditional Christian belief in divine immutability? The fact that the eternal Son is made by self-retraction to be what 'formerly' he was not—namely, the subject of a human life—would seem to make such a conclusion inevitable. Clearly, Forsyth does not want to say this. A *temporary* (time-bound) exercise of self-retraction does not alter the Son of God in his eternal nature, he would say. And yet, the ontological conditions in God which would make such a claim fully coherent remain unexplored. On the face of it, it would seem that Dorner's critique of Thomasius would apply just as readily to Forsyth and Mackintosh. Is this a real incarnation or merely a theophany? What are the consequences for the immanent Trinity and how, then, is it to be related to the economic Trinity? The truth of the matter is this: *if one breaks completely with dyothelitism, the only option left is that of a metamorphosis of a divine agent into a human agent*—with all the attendant problems that creates.

With the idea of the eternal Son 'becoming' the subject of a human life, Forsyth and Mackintosh are reaching forward to the kind of solution to the Christological problem which Karl Barth would one day provide. But there would remain a sizable difference. Barth refused to turn his back on dyothelitism and, with that, on the *logic* (if not the categories) of Chalcedon.

What is needed today is a new kenotic theory—one which will avoid the problems of the older kenoticism by: (a) making kenosis *original* to the being of God so that its concretization in time involves no change in God and, therefore, no split between the immanent Trinity and the economic Trinity, and (b) understanding kenosis in such a way that no divestment of anything proper to God is entailed and no departure from the dyothelitism of the ancient Church is required.

A New Kenotic Theory

As we have seen, the history of exegesis of Phil. 2:6–11 has turned up two major options: either the 'subject' who is said to empty himself is the λόγος ἄσαρκος, that is, the pre-existent eternal Son of God (the ontological view) or he is the man Jesus (the ethical view). We have not considered the second option here since it has not, to this point, generated what most theologians would recognize as a kenotic theory. What is pertinent here is the fact that most readings which focus on that which is done by the man Jesus as the model of Christian behavior have been constructed in studied opposition to the ontological reading, that is to say, they seek to overturn it. The problem is that this goal is attained by stripping the 'Christ hymn' of any ontological significance or even implications. Where that has occurred, the divine ontology which was presupposed by virtually all 'orthodox' readers of Philippians from the fifth century onward is left untouched. That divine ontology found its focus in the twin concepts of divine simplicity and impassibility—and where those concepts were presupposed, discussion of the 'communication of attributes' could never allow for a 'genus of humility' (i.e. a realistic and not simply metaphorical ascription of human properties to the divine 'person')

If now, we were to suspend belief in those twin concepts at the outset (on the grounds that they find no warrant in the biblical witness), we would come to the Christ hymn with a greater openness to the possibility of a 'genus of humility'. A third interpretative model would then present itself. The Christological 'subject' is the divine 'person' (the Logos) acting not through or upon a human 'nature' this time but by means of the acts performed by the man Jesus. The key to this model would be to understand the divine Logos as relating to the man Jesus in a posture of permanent and unbroken *receptivity*. To put it this way is to *reverse* the traditional pattern of 'orthodox' thinking in accordance with which the Logos gives and the man Jesus receives; the Logos acts and the man Jesus is the instrument of that action. Here, the man Jesus acts and the Logos receives those acts as his own. The man Jesus experiences suffering and the Logos takes that suffering up into his own being. The dyothetism proper to the two-natures *logic* is thereby preserved but instead of understanding the extraordinary things done by the man Jesus (e.g., his miracles) as performed by the Logos through him, we are now free to understand them as performed in the power of the Holy Spirit poured out upon him in his baptism in order to equip him for his mediatorial activity. The unity of 'person' is, as traditionally, purchased by making only one of the two 'subjects' active while understanding the other as purely receptive. But the relationship has been reversed.

The receptivity of the Logos simply *is* his 'self-emptying'. And the ontological condition of its possibility in God is an eternal act of 'self-determination' in which the being of the triune God is so completely oriented towards this outcome in time that the identity of the Logos as the second 'person' of the Trinity is formed by it. Seen in this light, not exploiting 'the form of God' refers to willed non-use of the powers shared with the Father and the Spirit. It is not that the triune God does not continue to 'possess' these powers; he deprives himself of nothing proper to deity in that he wills to act 'humanly' (in the power of the Spirit who indwells the man Jesus).

The last-made claim is secured and explained by an understanding of the Trinity along the lines favored by I. A. Dorner and Karl Barth: one divine 'subject' in three 'modes of being'. If the one divine 'subject' has and makes use of, say, omnipotent power in the third 'person', then the one divine 'subject' has and makes use of this power as the 'subject' he is. He does not surrender this power in that he 'elects' not to use it in one of his modes of being.

The criticisms directed against classical kenoticism can all be given satisfying answers on this view. Divine immutability is upheld (though its meaning is no longer controlled by the idea of impassibility). The eternal event in which God is constituted as triune (the divine processions) and the eternal event in which God turns towards the human race in electing grace (the divine missions) is one and the same event; the missions are contained in the processions. Thus, the triune God is 'already', in himself, what he will do in the temporal execution of election. No change takes place in God—no change *can* take place—in that he suffers humanly. And, finally, the coming of the Son of God into this world is a real incarnation and no mere theophany.

SUGGESTED READING

Breidert (1977); Forsyth (1909); Mackintosh (1912); Von Balthasar (1992).

BIBLIOGRAPHY

Baillie, D. M. (1948), *God was in Christ* (New York: Charles Scribner's Sons).

Barth, K. (1956), *Church Dogmatics* IV/1, part 1 (Edinburgh: T. & T. Clark).

Barth, K. (1958), *Church Dogmatics* IV/1, part 2 (Edinburgh: T. & T. Clark).

Bauckham, R. (1998), 'The Worship of Jesus in Philippians 2:9–11', in R. P. Martin and B. J. Dodd (eds.), *Where Christology Began: Essays on Philippians 2* (Louisville: Westminster/John Knox), 128–39.

Breidert, M. (1977), *Die kenotische Christologie des 19. Jahrhunderts* (Gütersloh: Gütersloher Verlagshaus Gerd Mohn).

Bruce, A. B. (1900), *The Humiliation of Christ*, 5th edn. (Edinburgh: T. & T. Clark).

Chemnitz, M. (1971), *The Two Natures in Christ* (Saint Louis: Concordia).

Dorner, I. A. (1846), 'Rezension von G. Thomasius, *Beiträge zur kirchlichen Christologie*', *Allgemeines Repertorium für die theologische Literatur und kirchliche Statistik* 5: 33–50.

Dorner, I. A. (1853), *Entwicklungsgeschichte der Lehre von der Person Christi von den ältesten auf die neueste*; Zweiter Teil, 'Die Lehre von der Person Christi vom Ende des vierten Jahrhunderts bis zur Gegenwart' (Berlin: Verlag von Gustav Schlawitz).

Dorner, I. A. (1994), *Divine Immutability: A Critical Reconsideration* (Minneapolis: Fortress).

Dunn, J. D. G. (1998), 'Christ, Adam, and Preexistence', in R. P. Martin and B. J. Dodd (eds.), *Where Christology Began: Essays on Philippians 2* (Louisville: Westminster/John Knox), 74–83.

Evans, C. S. (2006), *Exploring Kenotic Christology: The Self-Emptying of God* (Oxford: Oxford University Press).

Forsyth, P. T. (1909), *The Person and Place of Jesus Christ* (London: Independent Press).

Gess, W. (1856), *Die Lehre von der Person Christi entwickelt aus dem Selbstbewusstsein Christi and aus dem Zeugnisse der Apostel* (Basel: Bahnmeiers Buchhandlung).

Loofs, F. (1901), 'Kenosis', in *Protestantische Realenzklopedie*, Band 10, 246–63.

McCormack, B. L. (forthcoming), *The Humility of the Eternal Son* (Cambridge: Cambridge University Press).

Mackintosh, H. R. (1912), *The Doctrine of the Person of Christ* (Edinburgh: T. & T. Clark).

Strauss, D. F. (1841), *Die christliche Glaubenslehre in ihrer geschichtlichen Entwicklung und im Kampfe mit der modernen Wissenschaft*, vol. 2 (Tübingen and Stuttgart: C. F. Osiander and F. H. Köhler).

Tanner, N. P. (ed.) (1990), *The Decrees of the Ecumenical Councils*, Volume II: *Trent to Vatican II* (Lanham, Md.: Sheed and Ward).

Tappert, T. G. (ed.) (1980), *The Book of Concord: The Confessions of the Evangelical Lutheran Church* (Minneapolis: Fortress).

Thomasius, G. (1845), *Beiträge zur kirchlichen Christologie* (Erlangen: Verlag von Theodore Bläsing).

Thomasius, G. (1857), *Christi Person und Werk. Darstellung der evangelisch-lutherischen Dogmatik vom Mittelpunkt der Christologie aus*; Zweiter Teil: 'The Person des Mittlers', 2nd expanded edn. (Erlangen: Verlag von Theodor Bläßing).

Von Balthasar, H. U. (1992), *Theo-drama*, vol. 3: *Dramatis Personae. Persons in Christ*, trans. G. Harrison (San Francisco: Ignatius Press), 149–259.

PART VI

IMAGINING
THE SON OF GOD
IN MODERNITY

CHAPTER 29

......

IMAGES OF CHRIST IN POST-ENLIGHTENMENT ORATORIOS

......

CALVIN STAPERT

JESUS asked his disciples, 'Who do people say that the Son of Man is?' A more pointed question followed: 'Who do you say that I am?' Peter answered, 'You are the Christ, the Son of the living God' (Matt. 16:15–16). Jesus' first question and Peter's answer to the second contain the basic ingredients in what would soon become the Church's confession about Jesus' unique person: he is both 'Son of Man' and 'Son of the living God'.

Jesus' identity involves his mission as well as his person. Peter's answer includes a title, 'the Christ', that is, 'the Anointed One'. What he was anointed to do was explicit in his name. An angel instructed Joseph to 'call his name Jesus, for he will save his people from their sins' (Matt. 1:21), and at Jesus' birth an angel announced him to the shepherds as 'a Savior, who is Christ the Lord' (Luke 2:11). His person, his title, and his mission are all wrapped up in an early Christian hymn quoted by Ignatius of Antioch (martyred between 98 and 117 AD) in his *Letter to the Ephesians*:

> Very flesh, yet Spirit too;
> Uncreated, and yet born;
> God-and-Man in One agreed
> Very-Life-in-Death indeed,
> Fruit of God and Mary's seed;
> At once impassable and torn
> By pain and suffering here below;
> Jesus Christ, whom as our Lord we know.
>
> (Staniforth and Louth 1988: 63)

In the early 100s AD, Pliny the Younger wrote to Emperor Trajan that Christians 'were wont to assemble on a set day before dawn and to sing a hymn ... to the Christ, as to a god' (McKinnon 1987: 27). The Church sang not only at dawn but around the

clock—'And from morn to set of sun, through the Church the song goes on', as a versi-
fication of the *Te Deum* puts it. Charles Wesley exclaimed: 'Oh, for a thousand tongues
to sing my great Redeemer's praise'. But before he had written those words, thousands
upon thousands of tongues had sung their great Redeemer's praise for more than sev-
enteen centuries, and thousands upon thousands more would continue to do so in the
nearly three centuries that have elapsed since. Around the clock and through the centuries Christians have sung because Christ accomplished his mission. As Martin Luther
put it in his great Easter hymn:

> Christ lag in Todes Banden
> Für unsre Sünd gegeben,
> Er ist wieder erstanden
> Und hat uns bracht das Leben;
> Des wir sollen frölich sein,
> Gott loben und ihm dankbar sein
> Und singen halleluja.
> Halleluja!
> Christ Jesus lay in death's strong bands
> For our offenses given;
> But now at God's right hand he stands
> And brings us life from heaven.
> Therefore let us joyful be
> And sing to God right thankfully
> Loud songs of alleluia!
> Alleluia!

The Christ to whom Christians have been singing their thanks, praise, and adoration
throughout the centuries is Jesus of Nazareth, identified in the Nicene Creed as the 'only
Son of God', who 'for us and for our salvation ... became incarnate by the Holy Spirit and
the Virgin Mary, and was made human. He was crucified for us under Pontius Pilate; he
suffered and was buried. The third day he rose again.' He is the Christ in the song of the
Church, whether in simple chants, hymns, and chorales, or in elaborate masses, passions, motets, cantatas, and anthems. But during the Enlightenment that changed. The
French *philosophe* Denis Diderot declared: 'Everything must be examined, everything
must be shaken up, without exception and without circumspection' (Gay 1973: 17). Many
responded by questioning the Church's beliefs about Jesus' person and mission.

In the Enlightenment's naturalistic worldview, reason, science, and critical method
were the paths to truth, and the notion of divine revelation was dismissed. However,
Enlightenment naturalism left the door open to the possibility of a creator-god. But such
a god paid no attention to the world it had made. Indeed, given the Enlightenment's
confidence that humans could solve their own problems, the creator-god had no need to
meddle. Jesus, of course, was a problem. There was much in his life that was exemplary,
and his teachings were fine insofar as they expounded a common-sense morality. But
his miracles could not be believed. Most crucially this meant there could be no belief
in the supreme miracles of incarnation and resurrection. Jesus of Nazareth might have

been a good man and a great teacher, but he could not be 'God-and-Man-in-One' whose death and resurrection 'brought new life to us'.

But a rigid naturalistic worldview proved hard to maintain. The Enlightenment's confidence in critical method carried the seeds of its own destruction. As Conrad Donakowski put it, 'The glory and destruction of the Enlightenment was that it showed following generations how to apply critical standards to reason itself' (Donakowski 1977: 12). Romanticism said to the Enlightenment what Hamlet said to Horatio: 'There are more things in heaven and earth than are in your philosophy'—the 'more' being the supernatural that the Enlightenment sought to erase or relegate to irrelevance. Now even Jesus could be viewed not only as the greatest of the world's teachers but as one who in some sense might have been divinely inspired or somehow especially infused with a divine spirit. His miracles could be accepted as myths that embody some kind of spiritual truth. Even his incarnation and resurrection could be accepted if interpreted metaphorically. The story of Jesus' resurrection could be true as a metaphor that points to transformation that happens in people's lives; or it could be true in the sense that his teaching or example or 'spirit' live on. Even Jesus' person could be up-graded above the merely human, albeit to something less than true God and true Man. For example, Schleiermacher saw in Jesus 'a "God-consciousness" that was, in comparison with the God-consciousness of others ... "perfect" and therefore unique in degree, but ... not fundamentally different in kind' (Pelikan 1999: 196).

Romanticism never completely replaced naturalism. Some thoroughgoing naturalists remain, and even ardent romantics have something (often a good bit) of naturalism in their worldview. Their supernaturalism is a 'natural supernaturalism', a 'secularization of inherited theological ideas and ways of thinking' (Abrams 1971: 12). The process of secularization 'has not been the deletion and replacement of religious ideas'. Rather, many Romantics, 'whatever their religious creed or lack of creed, [undertook] to save traditional concepts, schemes, and values which had been based on the relation of the Creator to his creature and creation, but to reformulate them within the prevailing two-term system of subject and object, ego and non-ego, the human mind or consciousness and its transactions with nature' (Abrams 1971: 13).

The waxing and waning of naturalism and romanticism, and their mingling in various proportions, resulted in a variety of images of Jesus, in music no less than in theology or the other arts. Of course the new views of Jesus did not totally displace the old Nicene view of him, but their influence was strong and pervasive. Music that explicitly expresses the Nicene view came to be interpreted by many as referring to someone or something quite other. Even the cantatas, Passions, and *B-minor Mass* of J. S. Bach, arguably the most explicit and vivid of all musical expressions of Nicene Christianity, have been construed to be an expression of a vague (however profound) spirituality. On the other hand, it was hard for new settings of traditional texts to erase the main features of the Nicene view. Therefore the post-Enlightenment oratorio, the genre of sacred music that presented composers with the fewest theological restraints, provided composers with the opportunity to portray Christ in new guises—or affirm the traditional Nicene guise.

Joseph Haydn's *Seven Last Words of Our Savior on the Cross* originated as an orchestral work obviously meant to turn a listener's meditation toward Christ on the Cross. Haydn, a devout Catholic, no doubt intended listeners to focus on the Christ confessed in the Church's creeds. But devoid of words or some other context, music cannot have that kind of specificity. Haydn's early biographer Albert Christoph Dies wrote that it is wrong to suppose that Haydn 'was trying to solve the problem of expressing clearly in instrumental music, without words, the meaning of the words'. He was not trying to go 'beyond the limits of musical art. The idea was to stir the listener's feelings. It was up to the spoken words to guide those feelings in the right direction' (Gotwals 1968: 105–6).

In its original liturgical context, Haydn's music was performed after a reading of Jesus' seven words and the homily that following each of them. The words, both read and preached, lent the music a kind of specificity of meaning it could not have by itself. Other contexts also contributed—the day (Good Friday), the place (the church of Santa Cueva in Cadiz, Spain), and even the décor. As Dies described it, 'The entire church … would be draped with black. A single large lamp in the center' provided the only light. The 'dark, poorly lit church offered the eye no distracting object—Christ on the cross was the single visible object on which it must fix' (Gotwals 1968: 104). But since the work was soon published in its original orchestral form, as well as in string quartet and piano arrangements, it was often performed in situations that offered none of the contexts that guided 'feelings in the right direction'. Although the music clearly and powerfully guides them in the direction of sorrow and love, in such circumstances nothing except the title guides them specifically toward the sorrow and love that flowed down from the 'one Lord Jesus Christ who for us and for our salvation was crucified'. Even if the title turned one's attention to Jesus, there was nothing that necessarily pointed to any particular image of him, Nicene or otherwise. But in addition to the instrumental versions of *The Seven Words*, Haydn later published a version for choir, vocal soloists, and orchestra, thus turning the original instrumental work into an oratorio. Like oratorios generally, it has been performed more frequently in concert than as part of a liturgy. But even though concert performances lack the guidance liturgical contexts provide, its opening prayer brings the Nicene Jesus clearly into view: 'Vater im Himmel … dein Eingeborener, er fleht für Sünder … Wir sündigten schwer; doch allen zum Heil, uns allen, floss deines Sohnes Blut' ('Father in Heaven … your only begotten Son, he pleads for sinners … We have sinned mightily, yet for the salvation of all, all of us, the blood of your Son flowed').

Oratorios about Christ usually focus on one of the central episodes in his life—his birth, Passion and death, resurrection, and ascension. Peter Hawkins says the Passion story 'provides the premier context' for exploring problems that arise from the move from creedal proposition to narrative. 'How', he asks (using terminology of the Athanasian Creed), 'can one represent Christ equal to the Father as "touching" his Godhead but "inferior" to the Father, as touching his Manhood?' (Hawkins 2007: 31). All four Gospels portray Christ's human and divine natures, but in telling the Passion story, they vary in emphasis. Of the three main scenes—Gethsemane, the trials, and Golgotha—Gethsemane most clearly emphasizes Christ's humanity. Therefore in John, where the emphasis on Christ's divinity is more pervasive than in the other Gospels, the 'tortuous experience of the Garden is bypassed altogether; the closest thing we get to it is a rhetorical question in Chapter 12 that gives way immediately to a robust affirmation. "Now my heart is troubled, and what shall I say? "Father, save me from this hour"? No, it was for this reason I came to this hour" ... [12:27]' (Hawkins 2007: 32). But in Gethsemane, Jesus was hesitant to drink the cup from his Father; and as Hawkins succinctly puts it, 'He who hesitates is human' (Hawkins 2007: 30).

Matthew, Mark, and Luke all include the Gethsemane scene. Matthew and Mark especially show Jesus as vulnerably human. On the other hand the 'vision of Jesus at a loss is one that Luke simply cannot abide (Luke 22:39–46)' (Hawkins 2007: 35); so he mollified the anguish. He has Jesus kneeling to pray rather than falling on his face, and although Jesus prays virtually the same prayer as in Matthew and Mark ('remove this cup'), he does it once rather than three times. Luke also adds that an angel from heaven strengthened him (22:43). And when he wrote that Jesus' 'sweat became like great drops of blood', he may have meant it as 'a sign of Jesus' strength, not his anxiety: he is like the athlete preparing for the monumental feat that will lead to victory' (Hawkins 2007: 35). Nevertheless, the Gethsemane scene, on balance, is weighted on the side of Jesus' humanity, even in Luke. That, no doubt, is why Ludwig van Beethoven chose it as the subject for his only oratorio, *Christus am Ölberge*.

No institution or person commissioned *Christus am Ölberge*; the choice of both the genre and subject were Beethoven's. When he began working on it with librettist Franz Xavier Huber, he had recently been engaged by the Theater-an-der-Wien. One of the reasons he took the position was that it provided a choir to work with. Beethoven was eager to show that he was master of all genres, not just the instrumental ones that were the basis for his great reputation. Spurred by the recent success of performances of Haydn's oratorios in Vienna, Beethoven felt challenged 'to establish himself as a composer in all the important genres' (Lodes 2000: 220). But if Beethoven's choice of genre was prompted by professional ambitions, there were deeper reasons for his choice of subject. Gethsemane gave him an opportunity to portray a solitary, heroic victim with whom he could identify. It also provided material suited for proclaiming salvation through brotherly love.

The libretto of *Christus am Ölberge* emphasizes Jesus' humanity. Since it begins *in media res*, it contains nothing of Jesus' walk with his disciples from the Last Supper to the Mount of Olives; thereby it omits Jesus' prophecy about his resurrection (Matt. 26:32 and Mark 14:28). Instead the oratorio begins with a somber orchestral introduction in E♭ minor—the deepest, darkest key in the tonal universe. Jesus is alone, calling to his Father—a Father who is far removed, seemingly unhearing. Later, in his Ninth Symphony, Beethoven would sing of a distant but loving Father: 'über'm Sternenzelt muss ein lieber Vater wohnen' ('beyond the starry firmament a sweet Father must dwell'). But in the oratorio the Father is hardly loving. In the opening recitative of the second scene a seraph sings that Jesus is 'vom Vater ganz verlassen' ('completely abandoned by the Father').

Beethoven greatly amplifies Matthew's description of Jesus as 'sorrowful and troubled' (Matt. 26:37). A tenor, an operatic suffering hero, sings the role of Jesus—not a bass as was traditional in passions. In his first aria he sings: 'Meine Seele ist erschüttert …; Schrecken fasst mich, und es zittert grässlich schaudernd mein Gebein … [U]nd von meinem Antlitz träufet, statt des Schweisses, Blut herab' ('My soul trembles …; fear grips me and shakes dreadfully my shuddering bones … and from my face drips down not sweat, but blood'). In Luke, as noted above, the drops of blood may have been intended to suggest strength. In the oratorio, however, they are not a sign of strength; rather, they suggest exceedingly intense anxiety and anguish.

The appearance of an angel is likewise non-Lucan in its import. In Luke an angel strengthened him (22:43), whereas the seraph in the oratorio, at least at first, is merely a narrator-preacher to the audience. In her opening aria, strongly reminiscent of the Queen of the Night in Mozart's *Magic Flute*, she sings: 'O Heil euch ihr Erlösten! Euch winket Seligkeit, wenn ihr getreu in Liebe, in Glaub' und Hoffnung seid, Doch weh! Die frech entehren das Blut, das für sie floss, sie trifft der Fluch des Richters, Verdammung ist ihr Loos' ('O praise him, your redeemer! Salvation is yours if you remain true in love, faith, and hope. But woe! Those who brazenly dishonor the blood which flowed for them will meet the curse of the judge, condemnation is their lot'). The curse is especially powerful when she is joined by a choir of angels singing 'Verdammung' ('Damnation') for nine and one-half measures (!) on a very loud, high, and highly dissonant chord.

In the following recitative and duet, Jesus asks the seraph if his Father will show mercy. The seraph delivers the Father's message in a slow, stern, chant-like tone accompanied by solemn chords in the brasses: 'Eh' nicht erfüllet ist das heilige Geheimniss der Versöhnung, so lange bleibt das menschliche Geschlecht verworfen und beraubt des ew'gen Lebens' ('The holy mystery of salvation is not fulfilled as long as the human race remains rejected and deprived of eternal life'). Then she describes Jesus' trembling reaction and joins Jesus in a duet. Together they sing of the terror that God pours on Jesus and of the love with which Jesus embraces the world. Jesus, of course, sings in the first person, but the seraph sings in the third person; that is, she is narrating to the audience, not singing in sympathy with Jesus. Or is she? The words keep the seraph in the role of a reporter, but the music, an operatic love-duet, suggests that she is a sympathetic participant in the drama. But even if the seraph offers Jesus a modicum of support, Beethoven's picture of Jesus in the oratorio is that of a lonely, innocently suffering hero, not unlike Florestan, the hero in his opera *Fidelio*. There are close parallels between the Christ of the oratorio and Florestan, the hero of the opera. Allen Tyson calls the Christ of the oratorio an '*Ur*-Florestan' (Tyson 1969: 140). In both oratorio and opera 'a long and somber prelude in the minor depicts the lone figure's plight'. Florestan is lying in the dark and Christ has his face pressed to the ground. Both are facing death, but 'in the oratorio the seraph … cannot offer any escape' (Tyson 1969: 140).

Beethoven clearly identified himself with Christ and Florestan not only in their suffering but also in their isolation. The oratorio is 'suffused with the conception of the solitary hero, one whose isolation is both an effigy of Christ's capacity for endurance and a foreshadowing of his death' (Solomon 2003: 58). The greatest cause of Beethoven's isolation and suffering was his deafness. It is not a coincidence that he composed *Christus am Ölberge* shortly after writing the Heiligenstadt Testament, the letter to his brothers in which he revealed his increasing and irreversible deafness. Barry Cooper has shown that the oratorio 'was conceived only weeks—perhaps only days—after the Heiligenstadt Testament' (Cooper 1995: 22) and points out striking similarities in the language of both. It is obvious that Beethoven saw parallels between Christ's suffering and his own. That he was consciously seeking such parallels is implicit in a remark in the Heiligenstadt Testament: 'The unfortunate may console themselves to find a similar case to theirs' (Beethoven 1802). Although Beethoven was saying that his record of his misfortune might provide consolations for fellow sufferers … he was [also] implicitly seeking accounts of the suffering of others with which to console himself. In doing so he turned … to the supreme suffering of Christ. Here he found a model and example to follow' (Cooper 1995: 22).

Beethoven's Christ was a model and example to follow not only in his suffering but also in his love for humanity. In the second scene, when Peter took up his sword, Jesus rebuked him: 'Ich lehrt' euch blos allein die Menschen alle lieben, dem Feinde gern verzeih'n' ('I taught you only to love all, your enemies to forgive joyfully'). And the seraph joins in: 'Nur eines Gottes Mund macht solche heil'g Lehre der Nächstenliebe kund' ('Only the mouth of God proclaims this holy teaching of love of neighbor'). Then in duet, Jesus and the seraph sing: 'Liebt jene, der euch hasset, nur so gefallt ihr Gott'! ('Love all who hate you, for only so are you pleasing to God'). Beethoven believed he himself fulfilled the 'heil'g Lehre der Nächstenliebe' ('holy teaching of love of neighbor'). In the Heiligenstadt Testament he prayed: 'Gottheit du siehst herab auf mein inneres, du kennst es, du weist, daß menschenliebe und neigung zum Wohlthun drin Hausen' (Beethoven 1802) ('Deity you see into my innermost being, you know it intimately, you know that love of humanity and a fondness of doing good live within'). *Christus am Ölberge*, especially in the context of the Heiligenstadt Testament, expresses a humanistic hope for salvation obtained through following Christ's example in suffering and loving.

Hector Berlioz, like Beethoven, wrote only one oratorio, and he too wrote it not to fulfill a commission but out of his own volition. Also like Beethoven he was very much involved with the libretto—even more so; he was his own librettist. But he came to oratorio very differently than Beethoven. Whereas Beethoven came to both the genre and the subject intentionally, Berlioz came to both almost by accident. He was at a party where everyone was playing cards. Hating card games, he was bored. In a letter to John Ella he wrote that his host told him 'to write a bit of music for my album!' He took up the challenge and wrote a little organ piece that he felt 'had a certain element of rough and naïve mysticism', and 'straight away [he] got the idea of setting to it words of a similar character'. Thus his organ piece 'became the chorus of the shepherds of Bethlehem saying their farewells to the Infant Jesus when the Holy Family is leaving for Egypt'. It was received with great delight. He wrote, 'People stopped their games of whist and brelan in order to hear my holy fabliau. They were amused by the medieval turn in both words and music' (Hunwick 1975: 34).

That happened in 1850. The same year the piece, now titled 'L'Adieu des Bergers', received a concert performance. Over the next few years Berlioz expanded his little 'holy fabliau' into an oratorio. First he prefaced 'L'Adieu' with an overture depicting the shepherds gathering at the manger and followed it with a scene depicting the Holy Family resting in an oasis during their flight from Herod. Then in late 1853, people urged him to add more music, a task he took on readily because, as he wrote his sister, 'the subject delights me' (Rushton 2007: 34). The music he added continued the story of the flight from Herod and told of the Holy Family's reception in Egypt. Finally, in the summer of 1854, Berlioz composed a beginning to the story. He now had a complete three-part oratorio, *L'Enfance du Christ*:

Part I: 'Le Songe d'Hérode'
Part II: 'La fuite en Egypt'
Part III: 'L'arrivée à Saïs'

L'Enfance du Christ contains ingredients from Matthew and Luke: Mary and Joseph, shepherds, a manger, Herod, angels, and the flight into Egypt. But Berlioz omitted key elements from the Gospel accounts, and added much from his own imagination, sparked by such extra-biblical sources as New Testament Apocrypha, the so-called 'infancy gospels', popular novels, and contemporary religious art. He arranged it all into a narrative that can best be called a legend. Indeed he originally subtitled the second scene of Part II 'Légende et pantomime'.

Berlioz had already captured a long ago and far away quality in 'L'Adieu des Bergers'. He characterized its music as having 'a naïve mysticism' and 'a medieval turn in both words and music' (Hunwick 1975: 34). When he later surrounded it with music to create an oratorio, he maintained the same character. 'Stained glass, pictures, manuscript illumination: these metaphors recur throughout the reception history of *L'Enfance du Christ*, and emanate from the composer himself' (Rushton 2007: 37). When he first heard 'La Fuite en Egypt' he characterized it as 'naïve and touching ... rather like the illuminations in old missals' (Rushton 2007: 37). Critic Jacques Gabriel Prod'homme wrote that Berlioz 'had reconstructed himself as a naïve soul of olden times: an engraver, a stained glass painter in an ancient cathedral' (Rushton 2007: 37).

The oratorio begins with the narrator singing, 'Dans la crèche, en ce temps, Jésus venait de naître' ('In a manger, in those days, Jesus had just been born'). Although Berlioz retains the manger from Luke, he is vague about locating the birth in history. 'En ce temps' is hardly more precise than 'once upon a time'. And he added that 'nul prodige encor ne l'avait fait connaître' ('yet no portent had heralded it'). One wonders if he was remembering what he had written about himself just a few years earlier: 'I came into the world quite normally, unheralded by any of the portents in use in poetic times to announce the arrival of those destined for glory' (Berlioz 1975: 31).

Berlioz did not eliminate the supernatural. The opening narration tells us that we are about to hear how 'envoya le Seigneur' ('the Lord sent') a 'céleste avis' ('heavenly message') to Joseph and Mary. But significantly the oratorio contains none of the heavenly messages that identify the baby: an angel's message to Joseph that the child conceived in Mary 'is from the Holy Spirit', and the command to 'call his name Jesus, for he will save his people from their sins' (Matt. 1:20–1); Gabriel's message to Mary that the 'Holy Spirit

will overshadow you, therefore the child to be born will be called holy—the Son of God'
(Luke 1:35); and an angel's announcement to shepherds that 'unto you is born this day in
the city of David a Savior, who is Christ the Lord' (Luke 2:11).

Part I consists of six scenes. The first four deal with Herod. Unlike the Herod in
Matthew, who learned about the birth of the 'king of the Jews' from the wise men (Matt.
1:1–2), Berlioz's Herod has dreams that a child will dethrone him. He consults with
soothsayers instead of chief priests and scribes. The soothsayers, rather than consulting
the Scriptures, consult spirits by means of a exotic dance, filled with 'stylized evocations
of the sinister East' such as a 7/4 meter and a 'whining chromatic oboe melody' that
mark the soothsayers as 'agents of darkness, not of wisdom' (Rushton 2007: 41). They
learn that Herod's dream is true, but 'they know neither the name nor race of Herod's
new-born enemy; and they make no association between him and prophecies of the
Messiah' (Rushton 2007: 41).

The final two scenes of Part I are an idyllic portrayal of the Holy Family in the manger. At his parents' prompting, Jesus gives fresh grass to the lambs and strews flowers
on their straw. In blessing him, Joseph calls him 'divin enfant', the closest the oratorio
comes to referring to him as the Son of God. Then angels (a female choir singing behind
the scene) in a dream tell Mary and Joseph to flee with Jesus to Egypt to escape the mur-
dering Herod. The angels conclude Part I with ethereal hosannas slowly fading away.

Part II begins with the shepherds coming to the manger. They sing their lovely farewell accompanied by reed instruments in a style suggestive of bagpipes. The narrator then describes the Holy Family's arrival at an oasis in the desert. 'In the journey
through the pitiless desert (evoked by pseudo-Matthew) the child points to an oasis,
and causes the palm trees to bend, bringing the fruit within reach, and the ground to
yield fresh water' (Rushton 2007: 42). Berlioz, however, omits these and other miracles
related in his sources.

Part III continues the story of the arduous journey through the desert. When the
family arrives in Saïs, they are footsore, starving, and exhausted. In pseudo-Matthew
'the family, knowing nobody in the town, enters a temple; the pagan idols prostrate
themselves before the son of the true God' (Rushton 2007: 42). Berlioz again omits the
miracle. Instead the family meets with anti-Jewish hostility until they stumble upon an
Ishmaelite family that takes them in, washes their sore feet, feeds them, and refreshes
them with lovely, exotic chamber music for flutes and harp. With regard to the baby
nothing special is noted. When told that his name is Jesus, the Ishmaelite father says,
'quel nom charmant' ('what a delightful name'); he predicts that Jesus will grow up to
help Joseph with his carpentry.

To this point in the story Berlioz has erased, both from his canonical and
non-canonical sources, all but the faintest hint of Jesus' divinity or of his mission. But in
the Epilogue, out of the blue, the narrator explicitly identifies his mission: 'Ce fut ainsi
que par un infidèle/Fut sauvé le Sauveur' ('so it was that by an infidel the Savior was
saved'). He goes on to say that the Holy Family returned to their homeland where the
child will accomplish 'le divin sacrifice/Qui racheta le genre humain/De l'éternel sup-
plice/Et du salut lui fraya le chemin' ('the divine sacrifice which redeemed the human

race from eternal torment and opened to it the way of salvation'). But Berlioz gives no hint what that divine sacrifice would be. Instead, in the final number, the narrator and choir sing: 'Ô mon âme ... briser ton orgueil devant un tel mystère' ('O my soul ... shatter your pride before such a mystery'). But despite the neo-Palestrinian style of the music, when Berlioz 'suddenly seems to have fallen on his knees' (Robertson 1950: 68), he does not accept salvation as God's free gift (Rom. 6:23). In the final lines the choir sings, 'Ô mon cœur, emplis-toi du grave et pur amour/Qui seul peut nous ouvrir le céleste séjour' ('O my heart, fill yourself with solemn and pure love, which alone can open up for us a heavenly destination'). This is the same humanistic hope for salvation that Beethoven had expressed a generation earlier and that Gustav Mahler would express a generation later in his 'Resurrection' Symphony:

> Mit Flügeln, die ich mir errungen,
> in heissem Liebesstreben
> wer' ich entschweben
> zum Licht, zu dem kein Aug' gedrungen!
> With wings I won for myself
> in the ardent striving of love
> will I fly upwards
> to the light which no eye has penetrated

In the mid-1850s, when the first performances of *L'Enfance du Christ* were being given, Franz Liszt, who conducted a performance in 1857, was expressing concern about the direction oratorio was taking. He thought that works were being called oratorios that were not, by his definition, oratorios. The title oratorio, he wrote, 'stems from the earliest origins of the genre'. But now it 'no longer corresponds to biblical subjects'. Oratorios 'no longer relate to worship but to art ... they address themselves more to our imagination than to our faith ... they poeticize their subject without offering it for our adoration ... [and] they stir our feelings ... without creating a mood for real prayer ... without advancing to that more exclusive region of prayer which, by the way, is impossible in the absence of dogma on the one hand and faith on the other' (Munson 1996: 4).

A couple of years earlier, on July 8, 1853, Liszt wrote to Princess Carolyn von Wittgenstein that *Christus*, an oratorio he was planning, 'will be the work by which I shall speak to *you* of my faith' (Williams 1998: 346). When he wrote that, he was on a trip to Lake Lucerne with Richard Wagner and the poet Georg Herwegh, a potential librettist for *Christus*. A few years earlier, Wagner too had been thinking of composing a work on the life of Christ, *Jesus von Nazareth*. It never got beyond a preliminary prose sketch, but from that sketch we can tell that Wagner's Jesus performed no miracles and did not rise from the dead—the crucifixion would be the end. If Liszt discussed his planned *Christus* with Wagner, there must have been sharp disagreements. Just three months before their trip together, Liszt had written to Wagner, 'Your letters are sad; your life is still sadder ... Your greatness is your misery ... and must pain and torture you until you kneel down and let both be merged in *faith*!' He went on: 'I cannot preach to you ... but I will pray to God that He may powerfully illumine your heart ... You may scoff at this feeling as bitterly as you like … Through Christ alone … salvation and rescue come to us' (Hueffer 1889: 273). Wagner replied that he too was a man of 'strong faith'—a faith 'in the future of the human race'. 'I believe in mankind', he wrote, 'and require nothing further' (Hueffer 1889: 277).

Liszt had a hard time finding a suitable librettist, and in the end he compiled the libretto himself. In its final form the work has fourteen numbers divided into three parts:

I *Christmas Oratorio*
  - Introduction: *Rorate coeli*
  - Pastorale and Annunciation of the Angels: *Angelus Domini ad Pastores*
  - *Stabat Mater speciosa*
  - Shepherds' Music-making at the Manger
  - The Three Holy Kings
II *After Epiphany*
  - The Beatitudes
  - The Prayer: *Pater Noster*
  - The Founding of the Church: *Tu es Petrus*
  - The Miracle
  - The Entry into Jerusalem
III *Passion and Resurrection*
  - *Tristis est anima mea*
  - *Stabat Mater dolorosa*
  - Easter Hymn: *O Filii et Filiae*
  - *Resurrexit*

Composition of *Christus* was spread over more than a decade. Liszt began 'The Beatitudes' in 1855 and completed it in 1859. Other matters kept him from working on *Christus* even though his desire to complete it remained as strong as ever. On July 11, 1860, he heard Allegri's *Miserere* and Lotti's *Crucifixus*, which, he wrote, 'put me back … on to the "ascending" slope of my fervent desire to compose religious music. I must soon write the *Stabat mater dolorosa* and the *Stabat mater speciosa* … All this music is moaning, singing, and praying within my soul' (Williams 1998: 506). After he moved to Rome in 1861, he wrote: 'I mean now to undertake the *Oratorio* problem … [T]o me it is the one object in art which I have to strive after, and to which I must sacrifice everything else' (Bache 1894: 33). In 1866, after completing eleven more numbers, he wrote that he had finished the oratorio. But in 1867 and 1868 he added 'Tu es Petrus' and 'O filii et filiae'.

Much about *Christus* suggests Liszt's orthodox intentions and loyalty to the Church. All the texts he chose are directly from Scripture and Catholic liturgy, and he placed a scriptural motto at the head of the work: 'Veritatem autem facientes in charitate, crescamus in illo per omnia, qui est caput: Christus' (Eph. 4:15). Traditional chants of the Church are prominent throughout the oratorio, and he placed Christ's establishment of the Church in the center.

Musically *Christus* is framed by chant melodies. It begins with an instrumental introduction at the head of which Liszt placed the words of the introit for the Fourth Sunday of Advent: 'Rorate Coeli desuper et nubes pluant justum; aperiatur terra et germinet Salvatorem' (Isa. 45:8). The first phrase of the chant is heard alone at the outset, and then throughout the introduction in a neo-Palestrinian point-of-imitation style. Chant melodies also loom large at the end of the oratorio. Like the introduction, the last number, *Resurrexit*, begins with the opening motive of the 'Rorate' chant. Along the way the 'Ite missa est' (from number 10) is heard several times as well as a fugue subject derived from 'Angelus ad pastores' (from number 2). 'The 'Hallelujah' of the *Resurrexit* also makes reference to the 'Hallelujah' incipit of number 13, *O filii et filiae*. The powerful, closing 'Amen' section begins with the incipit of the 'Rorate' chant [thus ending] both this number and the oratorio as they began' (Smither 2000: 242).

Between the chant-filled outer movements, there are seven other movements that incorporate chant melodies. Furthermore, much of the music is in neo-ecclesiastical styles. In addition to the neo-Palestrinian point-of-imitation style already noted, there are the neo-Palestrinian chordal style of *Stabat Mater speciosa*, many passages of modal harmony, and the use of responsorial and antiphonal methods of performance. But there are also sections, and even entire movements, that do not 'smell of the church' (to borrow Frederick the Great's snide comment about fugues). The Pastorale does not 'smell' in the least like a church, even though it is based on a chant melody, 'Angelus ad pastores'. The lilting rhythm Liszt gave it, and his prevalent use of woodwind instruments and drones give the music a rustic, pastoral character that fittingly depicts shepherds watching their flocks by night. Two other instrumental movements, 'Shepherds' Music-making at the Manger' and 'The Three Holy Kings', are distinctly non-ecclesiastical. The former is a pastorale, the latter is a march.

Two of the texted movements largely untouched by ecclesiastical melodies or styles, call for brief comment for theological reasons. 'Tristis est anima mea' is the only aria in *Christus*. It is sung by a baritone soloist representing Christ in Gethsemane. The music is highly chromatic, reminiscent of Wagner's *Tristan und Isolde*. It convincingly expresses the agony of a Christ who is as utterly human as Beethoven's. But unlike Beethoven's, Liszt's human Christ is surrounded in the oratorio by ample witness to his divinity—most importantly by the miracles of Incarnation and Resurrection. But Liszt also represented the miracles Jesus performed during his ministry, choosing the stilling of the storm as the subject for one of the movements in Part II. No doubt he chose this particular miracle because it gave him the opportunity to compose a dramatic storm piece. But it is equally likely that he chose this miracle because it provides a clear allegory of Christ's mission: he came to save the lost and perishing. Most of the movement is an instrumental depiction of a storm of increasing intensity. At the height of the storm the disciples cry out: 'Domine, salva nos, perimus'. Then Jesus speaks and the sea is calmed. Significantly, in the music representing the calm, Liszt incorporated music he had used for the text 'regnum coelorum' in *The Beatitudes*.

Christus has been largely neglected by posterity. According to Paul Merrick, 'the neglect of this work constitutes the greatest injustice suffered by any composer of the nineteenth century' (Merrick 2008: 184). He attributes it to the religious prejudice of 'a secular age [that] could not take seriously a mammoth work devoted ostensibly to religion and the Church' (Merrick 2008: 184–5). If secularists have neglected the work because it is too explicitly grounded in orthodox Christian belief, others have been turned away from it by what composer Edmund Rubbra calls 'the over-publicized legend of Liszt's pianistic (and personal!) prowess' (Watson 1989: 301). For them 'the virtuosic glitter of much of his piano music has cast suspicion on his ability to plumb the depths demanded in a religious work' (Watson 1989: 301). Further, they see his turn from a flamboyant virtuoso to a tonsured cleric as insincere and hypocritical. But despite his earlier lifestyle and his youthful enthusiasm for some heterodox ideas of thinkers like Henri de Saint-Simon and Abbé Félicité de Lamennais, he never renounced his Catholic faith, and entering minor orders late in life was not the hypocritical act it has often been made out to be. This is not to say that there was no dissonance between his life and his faith, or that his thinking was never heterodox. He was a complex person who did some spiritual wandering, but wherever his wanderings took him at times, he never repudiated the Church and her doctrines. In *Christus* we find Liszt's clearest affirmation of his faith, 'even if it was', as Rubbra put it, 'often overlaid with the rich patina of Romanticism' (Watson 1989: 301).

Liszt stated his orthodox intentions regarding *Christus* most directly in a letter to Princess Carolyn concerning a review that reproached the work for being Catholic. In response he wrote: 'I composed my oratorio about Christ as I was taught about Him by my village priest and by the Church of the faithful, the Roman, Catholic, and Apostolic one—but that I would have neither known how, or wished, to compose a work about the Christ of David Strauss' (Williams 1998: 765). And in his criticism of the direction composers were taking oratorio, he wrote that 'they poeticize their subject without offering it for our adoration' (Munson 1996: 4). Ernest Renan was a philosopher who 'poetized' Jesus. His *Vie de Jésus* 'was what he himself called "the poetry of the soul—faith, liberty, virtue, devotion," as this had been voiced by Jesus, the Poet of the Spirit' (Pelikan 1999: 199). In a letter to Olga von Meyendorf, Liszt countered Renan and others who were critical of St. Paul. Paul's role, he wrote, 'was not to sit "weary on the side of the road, or to waste his time in noting the vanity of established opinions". His faith in Our Lord Jesus Christ was not an "opinion"; he preached of Jesus crucified, resurrected, risen into Heaven' (Tyler 1979: 93).

Jesus asked, 'Who do people say that the Son of Man is?' The Enlightenment encouraged new images of the Son of Man. Many composers, like Beethoven and Berlioz, would take up the challenge. Others, like Liszt, would swim against the prevailing current and affirm with the author of Hebrews that 'Jesus Christ is the same yesterday and today and forever' (13:8).

SUGGESTED READING

Cooper (1995); Merrick (2008); Munson (1996); Rushton (2007); Tyson (1969).

BIBLIOGRAPHY

Abrams, M. H. (1971), *Natural Supernaturalism: Tradition and Revolution in Romantic Literature* (New York: W. W. Norton).

Bache, C. (trans.) (1894), *Letters of Franz Liszt II* (New York: Charles Scribner's).

Beethoven, L. von (1802), 'Heiligenstädter Testament'. Wikipedia source. <http://en.wikipedia.org/wiki/Heiligenstadt_Testament> (accessed July 28, 2014).

Berlioz, H. (1975), *The Memoirs of Hector Berlioz*, trans. and ed. D. Cairns (New York: W. W. Norton).

Cooper, B. (1995), 'Beethoven's Oratorio and the Heiligenstadt Testament', *The Beethoven Journal* 10: 19–24.

Donakowski, C. L. (1977), *A Muse for the Masses* (Chicago: University of Chicago Press).

Gay, P. (ed.) (1973), *The Enlightenment: A Comprehensive Anthology* (New York: Simon & Schuster).

Gotwals, V. (trans.) (1968), *Haydn: Two Contemporary Portraits* (Madison: University of Wisconsin Press).

Hawkins, P. S (2007), 'He Who Hesitates is Human: Literary Portrayals of the Gethsemane "Moment"', in C. E. Joynes (ed.), *Perspectives on the Passion: Encountering the Bible through the Arts* (London: T. & T. Clark), 30–41.

Hueffer, F. (trans.) (1889), *Correspondence of Wagner and Liszt I* (New York: Scribner and Welford).

Hunwick, A. (1975), 'Berlioz and "The Shepherds' Farewell": A Misapprehension', *Studies in Music* 8: 32–7.

Lodes, B. (2000), 'Beethoven's Religious Songs, Oratorio and Masses', in G. Stanley (ed.), *The Cambridge Companion to Beethoven* (Cambridge: Cambridge University Press), 218–36.

McKinnon, J. (ed.) (1987), *Music in Early Christian Literature* (Cambridge: Cambridge University Press).

Merrick, P. (2008), *Revolution and Religion in the Music of Liszt* (Cambridge: Cambridge University Press).

Munson, P. (1996), 'The Oratorios of Franz Liszt' (Doctoral dissertation, University of Michigan).

Pelikan, J. (1999), *Jesus Through the Centuries: His Place in the History of Culture* (New Haven: Yale University Press).

Robertson, A. (1950), *Sacred Music* (London: Max Parrish).

Rushton, J. (2007), '"Oratorium eines Zuknftsmusiker"? The Pre-history of *L'Enfance du Christ*', in B. L. Kelly and K. Murphy (eds.), *Berlioz and Debussy: Sources, Context and Legacies—Essays in Honour of François Lesure* (Burlington, Vt.: Ashgate Publishing), 35–51.

Smither, H. (2000), *A History of the Oratorio*, vol. 4 (Chapel Hill: University of North Carolina Press).

Solomon, M. (2003), *Late Beethoven* (Berkeley: University of California Press).

Staniforth, M. and A. Louth (trans.) (1988), *Early Christian Writings* (London: Penguin).

Tyler, W. R. (trans.) (1979), *The Letters of Franz Liszt to Olga von Meyendorff: 1871–1886* (Washington, DC: Dumbarton Oaks).

Tyson, A. (1969), 'Beethoven's Heroic Phase', *The Musical Times* 110: 139–41.

Watson, D. (1989), *Liszt* (New York: Schirmer).

Williams, A. (trans. and ed.) (1998), *Franz Liszt: Selected Letters* (Oxford: Oxford University Press).

··

CHAPTER 30

CHRIST IN CINEMA

The Evangelical Power of the Beautiful

··

ROBERT BARRON

EVEN as a secularist ideology comes increasingly to dominate the culture of the West and as the mainstream Christian denominations (at least in Europe, Canada, the United States, and Australia) continue to lose members and institutional focus, Jesus of Nazareth appears to be alive and well in contemporary cinema. Even the most casual devotee of film will notice a plethora of 'Christ figures' in the movies of the last few decades, including Aslan in the *Narnia* series, Randall Patrick McMurphy in *One Flew Over the Cuckoo's Nest*, Lukas Jackson in *Cool Hand Luke*, John Coffey (notice the initials) in *The Green Mile*, the charming alien in *ET: The Extraterrestrial*, Neo in *The Matrix*, Daniel in *Jesus de Montreal*, Clark Kent in the most recent *Superman* films, Frodo, Aragorn, and Gandalf in the *Lord of the Rings* series, and, for a comic variation on the theme, the Dude—with his long hair, beard, robes, laid-back attitude, pacifism, and, in one scene, a carpenter's belt—in *The Big Lebowski*. Alongside of these more indirect and symbolically evocative presentations, there are also a number of films explicitly about the figure of Jesus, including Franco Zefferelli's multi-part *Jesus of Nazareth*, Martin Scorcese's *The Last Temptation of Christ*, Pier Paolo Pasolini's *The Gospel According to St. Matthew*, George Stevens' *The Greatest Story Ever Told*, and most controversially and lucratively, Mel Gibson's *The Passion of the Christ*. That the person and story of Christ are deep in the cultural DNA of the West goes without saying, but the frequency with which film directors and producers turn to Jesus is one of the clearest indications that Jesus remains disturbingly relevant to our postmodern consciousness.

I have chosen to submit for our consideration three films that include a particularly strong Christ figure, namely, *Babette's Feast*, *The Shawshank Redemption*, and *Gran Torino*. Out of the many I could have picked from, I chose these three for a variety of reasons. First, they are all excellent movies—well-directed, beautifully photographed, and featuring fine acting and writing; second, they all exhibit Christ figures that sneak up on the viewer, asserting themselves subtly; and third, they each illumine a somewhat under-explored theological dimension of the person of Jesus.

BABETTE'S FEAST (1987)

Gabriel Axel's 1987 film adaptation of Isak Dinesen's short story 'Babette's Feast' is about many things—friendship, loss, religious devotion, sensual delight, etc.—but above all it is about the power of Jesus Christ to heal and illumine. The figure of Jesus in this movie is a curious one indeed: a French chef who finds herself living among fiercely puritanical Lutherans in late nineteenth-century Denmark.

The film is set in a remote village nestled at the foot of a mountain at the edge of a Danish fjord, where two sisters—Martine and Philippa—preside over the remnants of a religious community that had been founded by their father, a prim and devout pastor known as 'the Dean'. In a series of flashbacks, we learn that Martine and Philippa were, in their youth, extremely beautiful and had been courted by any number of young men, whose overtures were met with a firm refusal from the girls' father. When Martine was eighteen, she was sought out by a dashing young military officer named Lorens Loewenhielm, but the romance came to nothing, for Lorens knew he could never break through the carapace of piety and other-worldliness that Martine had constructed around herself. And Philippa had been pursued by an even more distinguished suitor, Achille Papin, one of the most celebrated opera singers of his time. While sojourning on the Danish coast, Papin had wandered into the Dean's church and heard Philippa sing. Ravished by the beauty of her voice, Papin commenced to coach the young woman in the hopes of preparing her for the musical stage in Paris. While practicing the 'seduction duet' from Mozart's *Don Giovanni*, Papin took his disciple in his arms and kissed her. Afterward, Philippa asked her father to inform Papin that she would take no further lessons, and the great singer returned, heartbroken, to France.

Some fifteen years later, the sisters were shocked to find a pale and frightened woman on their doorstep, with a note from Achille Papin introducing her. Babette Hersaut had been a *petroleuse* during the recent communard uprising in Paris, had lost both her husband and her son, and was now unable to remain in France. Would the kind sisters, whom Papin had known years before, be willing to take her in? In great generosity of spirit, the sisters took in this forlorn character and in time Babette became their trusted and beloved servant. Because the sisters were suspicious of French cooking (the French, they had heard, ate frogs), they taught Babette how to prepare their customary meal of split cod and ale-and-bread soup. Given their austere religious commitments, they explained, their food had to be as plain and unappetizing as possible.

Returning to the present day, we learn that the sisters want to celebrate the upcoming centenary of their father's birth. Even as they contemplate this glad anniversary, they are saddened that the spirit of the Dean seemed to have faded among his aging followers. Strife, jealousy, and division have replaced the kind fellowship that he has cultivated among them. As the sisters are considering how best to mark the great day, a letter arrives from France for Babette, containing the improbable news that she has won ten thousand francs in the national lottery. The loyal servant begs her mistresses to be allowed to prepare a sumptuous gourmet meal for them and their community in honor of the Dean. Though they are moved by the generosity of the offer, the sisters are reluctant to acquiesce, for they see only spiritual danger in such a sensual affair. But Babette steps forward and with tremendous resolve says, 'Ladies, I have never in twelve years asked you for a favor … because I have had nothing to pray for. But tonight, I have a prayer to make from the bottom of my heart.' The sisters give in and agree to the dinner.

A month before the feast, Babette goes on a journey (her first in twelve years), and upon her return, she announces that the goods necessary for the festivities are on their way. In the course of the next several days, the food, drink, and other accoutrements begin to arrive, and the villagers are flabbergasted, for they never imagined that such culinary extravagence was even possible. But their astonishment is complete when a primaeval-looking turtle arrives, poking his snake-like head out of a greenish-black shell. Concerned that they have countenanced a witch's sabbath, Martine, Philippa, and the other disciples of the Dean agree that they will eat the meal, out of deference to Babette, but that they will neither speak of it nor take any pleasure in it.

The great dinner takes place on Sunday, the Lord's day. The first guest to arrive is ancient Mrs. Loewenhielm, who long ago lost most of her hearing and sense of taste and who thus functions as an apt embodiment of the community's puritanism. The old lady brings as a guest her nephew, General Loewenhielm, the military officer who, so many years before, had courted Martine. Though he has fulfilled all of his professional aspirations, the General is bored and depressed and comes to the dinner only with reluctance. In time, the other members of the Dean's congregation arrive and, after singing two hymns, the diners come to the table. The General, the only member of the company who has not taken a vow against enjoying the dinner, can barely believe it when he sips his first glass of wine: 'Amontillado! And the finest Amontillado that I have ever tasted.' When he takes his first spoonful of the soup, he exclaims, 'the best I have ever had!' But his puzzlement and delight reach their apex when he tastes the main course. He tells his fellow diners that, years before, at the Café Anglais in Paris, he had eaten 'an incredibly recherche and palatable dish' called *Cailles en Sarcophage*, which was the invention of the culinary genius who was the chef of that establishment. Looking about at everyone around the table, he eagerly exclaims, 'But this is *Cailles en Sarcophage*!' As the delicious concoctions are consumed and as the fine wine flows, the conversation becomes freer, the laughter readier. Old resentments seem to melt away and broken friendships are repaired. So moved is he by the entire experience that General Loewenhielm rises and addresses the assembly: 'In our human foolishness and short-sightedness, we imagine that grace is finite. Grace, my friends, demands nothing of but that we shall await it with confidence and acknowledge it in gratitude … Grace takes us all to its bosom and declares general amnesty.' In the wake of this extraordinary oration, the entire place seems suffused with the very Grace of which the General speaks. All during the dinner, a steady snow has fallen, so that when the guests are taking their leave, the entire countryside is blanketed in white. As they set out, they stagger and waver on their feet, some slipping down or falling forward, so that their elbows, backsides, and knees are covered in snow, making them look, for all the world, like gamboling little lambs.

But the film does not end on this gentle note, all things simply reconciled through the mystical power of a meal. The filmmaker shifts our attention to the kitchen, so that we can see the price that was paid to make the Grace-filled repast possible. Babette sits exhausted and pale in the midst of myriad unwashed and greasy pans. More precisely, she sits on the chopping block, where she had butchered the various animals which the happy company had just consumed. Then the one who had, for so many years, maintained silence about her past, speaks up: 'I was once cook at the Café Anglais'. This means little to the sisters, but Babette continues, laying out to them the full extent of her sacrifice. Not only had she lost her husband and son in the uprising, but she had also lost her job, since the gentlemen and aristocrats who had frequented the Café Anglais disappeared after the revolution. Further, she says, 'I have no money'. When the sisters protest that Babette has won ten thousand francs in the lottery, the former master chef explains that she has spent every centime of her winnings on the magnificent dinner.

Christology must always convey a theory of salvation, that is to say, some account of what is fundamentally wrong with humanity and how Jesus saves us from that condition. For the director of *Babette's Feast*, the problem is lifelessness produced by a tragic divorce between body and soul, sensuality and spirituality. And the solution is a figure who comes from a world that has not experienced such a divorce and who willingly sacrifices herself so as to allow those in the fallen world a taste of higher things. Babette, accustomed to the highest and finest, arrived in the forlorn Danish village as an alien, a visitor from another realm. But she freely entered into their lives, emptying herself even to the point of suppressing her skills so as to prepare the simplest and least appetizing meals. Paul said that Christ became poor for our sake so that by his poverty we might become rich. Babette will indeed affect a transformation in the village, but she does not do so right away. Rather, in the manner of Jesus, her saving work is preceded by a long period of preparation during which she humbly identified herself with those she is destined one day to lift up. During these 'hidden years', she was readying herself and her community for the moment of transfiguration.

It is a biblical commonplace that God desires to express his intimacy with his people through a festive meal. In the book of Genesis, God gives the first humans practically free rein in the garden, permitting, even inviting, them to eat of all the trees save one. In the book of Exodus, God commands his people to celebrate a sacred meal on the eve of their liberation from slavery and then to repeat that meal as an emblem of their shared identity. In the book of the prophet Isaiah, we hear that the Lord will host a feast on the summit of his holy mountain, where there will be 'juicy red meats and pure choice wines'. And in the book of Wisdom, God is pictured as a Jewish mother spreading a sumptuous banquet before her people. It is absolutely no accident that Jesus, who is personally identified with the divine Wisdom, picks up and gives radical expression to this theme, offering table-fellowship to all, saints and sinners alike. At the climax of his life, Jesus sat down in table-fellowship with his intimate followers and there spread before them a meal of his own body and blood, effecting thereby the most radical union possible between divinity and humanity. In John's account of the Last Supper, Jesus tells his table fellows: 'I have come that you might have life and have it to the full'. By means of these sacred meals, the God of Israel has been consistently luring his fallen people back to life and communion.

However, in a world gone wrong, there is no communion without sacrifice. An off-kilter state of affairs can only be set right through a painful reconfiguring. This is why Isaiah imagines the savior of Israel to be a suffering, rejected figure. In the Gospel narratives of the Last Supper, there is always a link between the meal that Jesus offered and the sacrifice he would make on the Cross the following day: 'This is my body, which will be given for you' and 'this is my blood which will be poured out for you'. In a world without sin it might be otherwise, but in the actual world, the festive union of God and humanity could take place only through an act of sacrificial love. And so it goes with Babette and her fallen community. She did indeed use a festive meal to bring them together with God and one another, but she paid an enormous price: her many years of humble self-effacing service, her weeks' long labor to prepare the meal, her exhausting evening's labor to cook and present it, and ultimately her expenditure of all the money she had. All of this was summed up in her taking a seat on the chopping block, just as Jesus' was summed up in his being nailed to the Cross.

THE SHAWSHANK REDEMPTION (1994)

Frank Darabont's *The Shawshank Redemption*, a film adaptation of Stephen King's novella, has proven to be one of the most beloved and carefully analyzed movies of the past thirty years. In an interview, Darabont and two of the lead actors—Tim Robbins and Morgan Freeman—opined that *Shawshank* is, at bottom, a story of the liberating power of hope. It is certainly that. But it is also a most compelling presentation of the story of Jesus. Like many other 'Christ figure' films in recent years—*The Green Mile, One Flew Over the Cuckoo's Nest, Cool Hand Luke* come most readily to mind—*The Shawshank Redemption* is set in a prison. These films see the fundamental problem as one of spiritual imprisonment, and they powerfully recover the idea of Jesus as redeemer, which carried in the ancient world the overtone of paying a ransom to buy back the freedom of a hostage. The Council of Trent teaches that sin is a predicament that has implicated the entirety of the human race, a shared dysfunction. It is so pervasive that it amounts to an incarceration. What is required, therefore, is not simply a teacher who can shed light on our suffering, but a liberator, someone powerful enough to foment a general prison break. The well-known hymn text expresses the idea with admirable laconicism: 'O come, O come, Emmanuel, and ransom captive Israel'.

The first clue that Andy Dufresne is a Christ-character (besides his initials, AD) is that he is an innocent man who finds himself unjustly thrown among criminals. John's Gospel describes Jesus as a light shining in the darkness and as the divine Word which has pitched its tent in the midst of a deeply compromised human condition. And all four Gospels present the baptism of Jesus by John. Since the Baptist was offering a ceremonial cleansing from sin, Jesus first great public act was to stand in the muddy waters of the Jordan, in solidarity with the guilty. But his purpose was not simply to express compassion, but rather to get people out of their dreadful condition: 'Behold the Lamb of God who takes away the sin of the world'. What we see in the course of *The Shawshank Redemption* is the process by which the innocent Andy opens up a path to freedom for his fallen brothers. Andy's difference is signaled his first night at Shawshank. As his fellow 'freshmen' inmates collapse in anguish, anger, and despair, Andy, despite the desperation and profound injustice of his own situation, and to the infinite surprise of the veteran prisoners, maintains a Zen-like calm, not uttering a sound. Red, the narrator of the story, remarks that, from the beginning, 'he (Andy) had a quiet way about him, a walk and a talk that just weren't normal around here. He strolled, like a man in a park, without a care or worry. Like he had on an invisible coat that would shield him from this place.' In Shawshank but not of it.

Andy's transcendence of the normal patterns and attitudes appears in connection with the tarring of the roof of the license plate factory on the prison grounds. A number of inmates, including Andy and Red, are chosen by lottery, and they happily take the opportunity to work outside. After hours of laboring in the sun, however, they are exhausted. In the meantime, one of the bored guards is discussing with his fellows how he is being cheated out of an unexpected inheritance through confiscatory taxation. Violating one of the most sacred rules of Shawshank, and taking his life in his hands, Andy approaches the guards without being invited. They stiffen and pull their guns, but Andy stands his ground. The head man grabs Andy by the shirt and dangles him over the edge of the roof, threatening to drop him to his death, but the prisoner (who had been a banker in his previous life) coolly explains that he knows a way for the man legally to keep the entire inheritance. Intrigued, the guard pulls him back, and Andy explains the entire situation, asking in recompense for this invaluable financial advice only that his 'co-workers' be allowed to take a break and share some beers. Red comments: 'we sat and drank with the sun on our shoulders, and felt like free men. We coulda been tarring the roof of one of our own houses. We were the Lords of all Creation.' Andy himself doesn't partake, but only sits against the wall that surrounds the roof and smiles. Like Nurse Ratched and her minions in *One Flew Over the Cuckoo's Nest*, the prison guards represent all of those structures that maintain the integrity of the dysfunctional system, all of those persons, habits, and institutions that keep the fallen world fallen. And like McMurphy in *Cuckoo's Nest*, Andy Dufresne is the courageous and canny fellow who manages, through wit and subtle manipulation, to outmaneuver the keepers of the system. It is very common in contemporary Christology to present Jesus as the wily opponent of the political and religious establishment, the one who, through clever speech and provocative gesture, manages to expose the hypocrisy of the scribes and Pharisees and to undermine the brutality of the Roman occupiers. A direct confrontation of the Shawshank power structure would have been useless, but Andy employed a kind of Aikido, the martial art that uses the momentum of one's opponent against him. This was consistently Jesus' strategy in his struggle with the dark powers that hemmed him in.

Later, Andy petitions the warden, a hypocritical fundamentalist Christian named Norton, to allow him to write to the state government to provide funds for a library at

Shawshank. In a prison setting, freedom matters most of all, and knowledge is a path to spiritual freedom. Norton gives him leave to write, and Andy, over the course of many years, inundates the government with letter upon letter. Finally, to general astonishment, the legislature grants him some money to buy books, magazines, recordings, etc. When the cache arrives, Andy unpacks the boxes and finds, among many other treasures, Mozart's *Le Nozze di Figaro*. Hungry for the music, he immediately turns on the phonograph and plays one of his favorite pieces, the duet between Susanna and the Contessa. Then, knowing full well that he will be punished severely for doing so, he locks the door of his cubicle and brings the PA microphone over to the tiny phonograph speaker and the glorious duet commences to echo all over Shawshank. In the prison yard, the inmates freeze in their places and, with mouths agape, simply take in the impossibly beautiful music. Red sums up their feelings: 'I have no idea to this day what them two Italian ladies were singing about. Truth is, I don't want to know. Some things are best left unsaid. I like to think they were singing about something so beautiful that it can't be expressed in words, and makes your heart ache because of it … It was like some beautiful bird flapped into our drab little cage and made these walls dissolve away, and for the briefest of moments—every last man at Shawshank felt free.' Jesus spoke some of the most lyrical and compelling words ever uttered, and his speech has, across the centuries, set the souls of his listeners free from the constraints of general opinion: *was man sagt*. And he famously upbraided the scribes and Pharisees for storing up knowledge for themselves and allowing no one else access to it. The Andy who unleashes the power of *Le Nozze di Figaro* in the hopeless gray of Shawshank prison is showing this profile of the Christ figure.

One of the consistent themes in *The Shawshank Redemption* is the way in which the prisoners become so accustomed to their lives, so institutionalized, that they cannot imagine a form of life beyond the walls of the prison. Nowhere is this theme more fully on display than in the likeable but tragic character of Brooks, memorably played in the film by the veteran character actor James Whitmore. Acting utterly out of character, Brooks holds a knife to the throat of one of his friends. When he is finally disarmed, he explains, through tears, that he was trying to do something that would guarantee he could stay in prison. The parole board had informed him that he would be released, and Brooks simply couldn't bear the prospect of living in the world outside of Shawshank. Once freed, Brooks tried to make his way at a half-way house and a small grocery store where he served as a bagger, but he found himself frightened and disoriented. Finally, in despair, he hanged himself from one of the rafters in his tiny room. Years later, Andy spoke to Red of the power of hope, and Red reacted angrily: 'Hope is a dangerous thing. Drive a man insane. It's got no place here. Better get used to the idea.' The one who demonstrates an entirely new way of thinking and acting is a threat, not only to the keepers of the established system, but also to most people who are victimized by that system. This helps to explain why the proclaimer of the Kingdom of God was not only harassed and eventually eliminated by the powers that be but also abandoned by the vast majority of his followers, and why the Israelites, liberated from slavery, still hankered after Egypt.

In the course of many years, Andy had also been helping the warden with his taxes and finances. At the prompting of the corrupt Norton, Andy had moved into shadier territory, setting up a series of tax shelters and bank accounts under assumed names, which permitted the warden to siphon off huge amounts of cash with impunity. If he indicated an unwillingness to continue in this vein, the warden would threaten him with brutal retaliation. But Andy was, all this time, contriving a way to undermine and outmaneuver the lord of Shawshank. His plan hinged on successful escape. Many years before, Red had secured a small rock hammer for Andy so that his friend could pursue his hobby of shaping and polishing stones. But Andy had been using that hammer to dig a tunnel from his cell to a sewer pipe, which emptied out five hundred yards from the prison. One stormy night, when the tunnel was complete, Andy made his move, breaking through the sewer pipe with a stone and then, in Red's words, crawling 'through five hundred yards of shit-smelling foulness I can't even imagine. Or just don't want to.' When he emerged from the awful pipe, after his half-mile crawl, Andy spilled into a drainage ditch, pulled off his prison clothes, spread his arms out, and cocked his head to the sky in triumph. For years, Andy had been addressing issues on the surface of life at Shawshank, but finally he entered into the very bowels of the place, into the grime and mud at the foundational level, and worked his way through it to freedom. Christ Jesus brought grace, freedom, and beauty to an imprisoned humanity, but at the end he had to enter into the deepest foundations of the dysfunctional world, which is to say, into death and the fear of death. He did not eschew what is darkest and most painful in the human condition, but rather moved through it to resurrection on the far side. Awash in baptismal water after his journey through the foul tunnel, his arms spread out in the attitude of crucifixion, and looking up to heaven, Andy is an image of the Christ of the Paschal Mystery, the Lord who crawled all the way through sin and death to resurrection.

The Christian imagery becomes even more striking in the scenes depicting the events of the next morning. Roll is called as usual, and the prisoners line up outside their cells, but Andy Dufresne is not there. Annoyed, the guards call out to him, and when he doesn't respond, they inspect his cell directly. To their astonishment, the tiny space is empty; the bird has flown. The infuriated warden arrives, looks in and sees no sign of the escapee. In his frustration, he throws one of Andy's polished stones at a large poster of Raquel Welch affixed to one of the walls of the little cell. The rock goes right through, revealing the tunnel that Andy spent twenty years hollowing out. The camera looks back through the tunnel to the consternated/delighted/puzzled faces of the warden, the guards, and the other prisoners who had crowded in to see what was happening. We see thereby what the faces of the Roman guards, Mary Magdalene, John, and Peter must have looked like when they peered into the empty tomb on Easter morning.

Andy's aikido-like out-maneuvering of the oppressive forces of Shawshank then comes to its fullest expression. Wearing the warden's suit and shoes, and armed with all of the information pertaining to the numerous hidden accounts that Norton had established, Andy makes the rounds of a dozen banks in the area and empties out the funds. Not only does he escape from the penitentiary, but he disempowers the keeper of the place. We will explore this theme much more fully in our discussion of *Gran Torino*, but his is an evocation of the patristic doctrine of the *Christus Victor*, the Christ who released the imprisoned human race and despoiled the devil at the same time.

While he was still behind the walls of Shawshank, Andy dreamed of establishing a new life in the tropical beauty of Zihuatenho, Mexico. Sometime after Andy's escape, Red receives a blank postcard that postmarked from a small town on the Texas/Mexican border, the place, Red concluded, where Andy had crossed into Mexico. When Red is finally paroled, he seeks out a rock that Andy had told him about years before, a rock tucked away near a stone wall in a Maine hayfield. Under that rock is a box in which are a note from Andy and enough cash to allow Red to travel to Mexico. Paul describes Jesus as the 'first fruits of those who have fallen asleep', implying that Christ's resurrection is not simply a boon for him, but rather a signal that those who follow him will experience a like resurrection. The closing of *The Shawshank Redemption* is one of the most beautiful scenes in recent cinema. Having made his way across the United States and through Mexico, Red walks the beach at Zihuatenho. He spies Andy, dressed all in white, working on a boat along the seashore. The two friends smile and then, as the camera pans back to provide a godlike perspective, we see Red dropping his suitcase and enveloping Andy in an embrace. In Matthew's account of the resurrection appearances, an angel speaks to the holy women who have come to the tomb: 'Then go quickly and tell his disciples, "He has been raised from the dead, and he is going before you to Galilee; there you will see him" ' (Matt. 28:7). By the shore of the Sea of Galilee, Jesus met and called his first followers; and Galilee—beautiful and splendid—becomes the place of encounter with the risen Lord. Dressed in white, working on a boat by the sea, at an infinite remove from the gloominess of Shawshank Prison, Andy is a symbol of the risen Christ who, having liberated his friends, invites them to share his life forever.

GRAN TORINO (2009)

Certainly one of the most surprising Christ figures in recent cinema is Walt Kowalski in Clint Eastwood's 2009 film *Gran Torino*. I say surprising, for Walt is probably best known for the scene in which he aims a shotgun and snarls to a group of delinquents: 'Get off my lawn!' Nevertheless, this character, beautifully played by the eighty-year-old Eastwood himself, is an extraordinarily complete embodiment of Christ in his role as conqueror of sin.

The film opens at the funeral of Walt's wife, and the old man is surveying the scene skeptically and critically. Upon seeing his granddaughter exposing her belly-button ring, Walt's eyes narrow and he utters what is only his second line of the film: 'Jesus Christ'. After the choir sings the beatitudes, young Fr. Janovich rises to speak, and he delivers himself of a series of banalities. Disgusted, Walt mutters (and it is his third line of the film), 'Jesus'. A church, the liturgy, the beatitudes, a priest, and two mentions of the sacred name suggest the fundamentally religious theme and purpose of the movie.

At the reception following the funeral, we learn that Walt still lives in a Detroit neighborhood that once had been filled largely with Poles and other whites but that has now gone into economic decline. The formerly tidy and well-kept homes have slid into disrepair, and the Poles have been replaced by Hispanics, Blacks, and Hmong people from Laos and Cambodia. Next door to Walt is a particularly lively Hmong family, one of the younger denizens of which is a teenager named Tao. In one tightly-written scene, we discover that Tao is a decent kid, but is dominated by several of the women in the family. He means well, but he hasn't found his voice, his manhood. Some of the Hispanic gang members in the neighborhood purposely humiliate him, stealing his bicycle and leaving him helpless on the ground. Learning of this, a Hmong gang, led by one of Tao's cousins, decides to recruit him, turning him into a man on their terms. One of the gang-members addresses Tao: 'Spider told me how everyone thinks you're a pushover, how everyone walks over you and shit. I mean, look at you out here, working in the garden like a woman.' Despite the vocal opposition of Tao's sisters and in the face of the boy's own reluctance, the gang draws Tao in, and for his initiation, they give him the assignment to steal the pristine 1972 Gran Torino that is Walt's pride and joy. While rummaging awkwardly and noisily through Walt's garage late one night, Tao is accosted by the old man and runs away.

In the meantime, Walt has managed to become something of a hero among the Hmong, since he had stood up to some obnoxious gang-members who had threatened Tao's family. And this gives him a certain entrée to the Hmong world. In the wake of the attempted robbery, Tao's family commands the young man to give himself to Walt as a sort of servant, and thus begins the unlikely master–disciple relationship which stands at the heart of the film. One of the master's first moves is to help Tao with women. While attending a Hmong gathering—at which he appears a complete fish out of water—Walt notices that a pretty young woman is eyeing Tao. But the young man does not respond and allows her to leave with three other suitors. Outrageously racist but in his own way paternal, Walt says, 'I got the greatest woman who ever lived to marry me. I had to work at it, but I got her. And it was the greatest thing that ever happened to me … But you? You just sit there and watch as Ding Dong and Klick Klack and Charlie Chan walk away with her.' After this bit of romantic instruction, Walt has Tao work around his house, re-attaching gutters, digging up stumps, scraping paint, hanging a screen door. He even has his disciple paint a neighbor's house. Soon, others in the area catch on and approach Walt to get Tao to do things for them. The young man who has been more or less adrift now finds himself an extremely useful contributor to his community, and with satisfaction, Tao looks down at the callouses forming on his hands. When his last day of indentured servitude arrives, Tao eagerly asks Walt what the old man wants him to do and is sincerely disappointed when his master says, 'Take the day off; you've done enough.'

Even after his official time of servitude is up, Tao continues to follow Walt and soak up his wisdom. Like an eager apprentice, Tao asks Walt about the myriad tools in his garage, and like a patient master, the old man names and spells out the purpose of each one: 'Post pole digger, hand spade, tack hammer, putty knife, wire stripper, dry wall saw, tile spacers.' A key moment in the apprenticeship occurs when Walt invites Tao to help him move a large freezer out of the basement of one of Walt's children's house. The old man gives instructions as they place the appliance on a dolly, and then Walt says that he will take the heavy weight on top while Tao pushes from the bottom. When Tao objects to this arrangement, Walt answers with a dismissive slur, but the young man holds his ground: 'You listen, old man. You came and got me because you needed help, so let me help you. Either it's top or I'm out of here.' Walt can barely suppress a smile of satisfaction, as he realizes that the shy, pampered boy is becoming a man.

The funniest episode in the apprenticeship process occurs in a barbershop. Walt is friendly with the neighborhood barber and, for laughs, the two men converse exclusively through outrageous racist slurs: 'Afternoon, Martin, you dumb Italian prick', 'Walt, you cheap asshole, I should have known you'd come in; I was having such a pleasant day', etc. The master brings in his apprentice in order to teach him how to talk like a man. After demonstrating the process a bit more fully, Walt invites Tao to go out and come back in again and greet the barber properly. Imitating Walt to a tee, the boy says, 'Wassup, you old Italian prick?' at which the barber lowers a shotgun barrel to Tao's face and shouts, 'Get out of my shop, you long-haired, faggy little gook!' Tao stiffens with terror, while Walt and the barber throw their heads back and laugh.

From the very beginning of his public ministry, Jesus gathered disciples (*mathetai*, learners) around him. They lived with him at close quarters, watching his moves and listening to his speech. Often, they displayed a gross, even comical, misunderstanding of what Jesus wanted to convey, and the Lord sometimes expressed a profound impatience with their obtuseness: 'How much longer must I endure you?' But all the while, Jesus was shaping their minds and bodies to become the bearers of his way of life. In the Gospel of John, two *mathetai* of the Baptist approach Jesus. The Lord turns on them and asks, 'What do you seek?' Answering a question with a question, they say, 'Where do you stay?' And he replies, simply enough, 'Come and see'. That little exchange discloses the essential dynamic of spiritual apprenticeship. Spiritually immature men come to live in intimacy with a master and thereby absorb his manner of living through their bodies. They 'stay' with the teacher, discovering the source of his spiritual energy. All of this is echoed in the master–disciple relationship between Walt and Tao: a learner comes to see how a master lives, withstands much abuse and sharp correction, and then becomes conformed to his teacher.

But Walt's configuring to Christ becomes especially clear in the last part of the film, when the old man realizes that teaching and modeling will not be enough to save his charge, but rather an act of radical sacrifice. The Hmong gang-members who had tried to recruit Tao earlier have not given up. Just as the young man, with Walt's help, is settling into a job, they approach him and demand that he join their company. When Tao resists, they burn his cheek with a cigarette, and upon seeing the wound, Walt goes into a rage, invading the home of one of the gang-members, dragging him out of his house and onto the front porch and beating him. This in turn leads to a retaliatory act. The gang members spray machine gun bullets through the front window of Tao's family's home and rape his sister. At this point, Walt realizes that the enraged Tao is in serious danger of losing his life. Giving vent to his anger, he will either be gunned down directly or drawn into a cycle of violence from which he will never escape. So after some intense meditation, Walt hatches a plan, which is subtle, ingenious, and very dangerous.

His opening move is, through trickery, to lock Tao in the basement for his own protection. Then he confronts the Hmong gang. Standing in front of the duplex where they live, he calls them out. Though they wave their guns and threaten him, he stands his ground, and the young men are disconcerted by his utter lack of fear. Walt makes sure that all of the gang members are present and accounted for, and he waits until a large contingent of bystanders have assembled. That Walt is played by Clint Eastwood matters enormously at this point, for practically every Eastwood movie comes to its climax with such a scene. Clint the cowboy or Clint the cop faces down a posse of bad guys who have him hopelessly outnumbered and he manages to gun them down. Walt reaches into his coat pocket and mumbles the beginning of the Hail Mary, and the gang-members, convinced that he is going for a pistol, open fire and strike Walt down, in full view of the bystanders. He dies in the attitude of the crucified Jesus, and when the camera comes in on his right hand, we see that it is gripping, not a gun, but a cigarette lighter. In one great act of self-sacrifice, Walt has saved Tao from the cycle of violence and disempowered those who made that cycle possible.

In the Christology of the Church Fathers, Jesus salvific act on the Cross is understood, not so much in Anselm's substitutionary sense, but rather as an act of liberation for sinners and victory over dark powers. The Fathers construe the devil as one who has claimed authority over the human race and Christ as the more powerful agent who has managed to wrest this authority from the dark spirit. What is fascinating for our purpose here is that these early theologians interpret Jesus as a kind of trickster, one who outfoxes the devil, drawing him out by providing an attractive target. In one version of this theory, Jesus' humanity is compared to a tasty bait wrapped around the hook of his divinity. When the devil bites (arranging for the death of Jesus on the Cross), he is 'caught' by the Lord's divinity. In another variation, the devil is seen as a kidnapper who holds the human race in his arms. Jesus offers his perfect humanity in exchange for all the human souls the devil holds. The wicked one willingly surrenders every sinner in order to have this one splendid prize, but when he grasps at Jesus' humanity, he is wrestled to the ground by Jesus' divine power. Walt Kawalski identified the forces that held Tao and indeed the entire neighborhood in their grasp. He then offered himself as a target for their fury, drawing them out into the open, exposing their wickedness. In giving away his life, he was stripping them of power and offering freedom to Tao. In this, he is a splendid contemporary icon of the *Christus Victor*.

CONCLUSION

In the postmodern context, so marked by deconstruction and relativism, it is often difficult to commence an evangelical presentation of the faith with either the true or the good. If we tell people in the contemporary West that they are thinking incorrectly or acting incorrectly, they will typically react with extreme defensiveness, for they are in the grip of what Joseph Ratzinger called 'the dictatorship of relativism'. However, beginning with the beautiful can be much more promising, since the third transcendental is less threatening than the other two. Just look, the evangelist might say, at the Sistine Ceiling or the Sainte Chapelle or the work of Mother Teresa's sisters. The very beauty of those forms can then lure someone toward the good (what is the style of life that made them possible?) and the true (what are the doctrines that undergird such things?). This is why films—the distinctive art form of our time—can prove so evangelically effective. Just look at Babette, at Andy Dufresne, at Walt Kawalski. In doing so, you are, willy-nilly, looking into the face of Christ.

SUGGESTED VIEWING

Babette's Feast (1987); *The Shawshank Redemption* (1994); *Gran Torino* (2009).

CHAPTER 31

IMAGINING CHRIST IN LITERATURE

ROWAN WILLIAMS

BETWEEN THE NARRATABLE AND THE UNNARRATABLE

WITTGENSTEIN's pupil and friend, Con Drury, reports him as saying in 1949 that it would be impossible to decide 'what form' an adequate record of God becoming human should take; we do not have available the criteria that would help us settle what is and is not a plausible or persuasive narrative account of the basic claim (Rhees 1984: 164). Elsewhere, we can find Wittgenstein wrestling with the question of the plurality of the Gospels and their apparent contradictions, concluding,

> might we not say; It is important that this narrative should not be more than quite averagely historically plausible, *just so that* this should not be taken as the essential, decisive thing? … i.e. what you are supposed to see cannot be communicated even by the best and most accurate historian; and *therefore* a mediocre account suffices, is even to be preferred … (Roughly in the way a mediocre stage set can be better than a sophisticated one, painted trees better than real ones—because these might distract attention from what matters).
>
> (Wittgenstein 1980: 31)

If what we are trying to do is to narrate the events around God's appearance in human form, we cannot achieve this by crafting what is humanly the best possible vehicle for such a disclosure, as if the credibility of the claim could be established or enhanced by human skill. What this would mean is that the authority with which we are summoned to believe in God's presence among us would be mixed up with the authority that accrues to a certain level of excellence in performance; we should not be hearing the invitation as it comes from *God*. And this fits closely with Wittgenstein's repudiation—more than once expressed, in various ways—of any idea that God can lie at the end of a chain of reasoning, so that faith in God can be the effect, once again, of a certain quality of human performance.

'Christianity is not based on a historical truth; rather, it offers us a (historical) narrative and says: now believe!' (Wittgenstein 1980: 32). And thus, the detail of the history, as normally understood, is immaterial; it would make no difference, Wittgenstein says, if the Gospel narrative were 'demonstrably false'. The story, the claim, is set forth, and we are invited to say yes or no to it; what the reply will be depends on the life we live and/ or desire to live—or, as Wittgenstein puts it most starkly, on love, whose consequence is a life 'suspended' from above (Wittgenstein 1980: 33). Faith is the acceptance of an absolute imperative: looking around for reasons to obey it is to weaken its imperative character by making my response a matter of acknowledging the sense of what is before me rather than knowing I am judged and changed. It is not difficult to see in all this the scale of Wittgenstein's continuing debt to Kierkegaard, specifically the Kierkegaard of the *Philosophical Fragments*. If the most coherent way for the divine to be present in a human guise is anonymity, so too with the Gospel record. It must have no form or comeliness to commend it, not even the 'comeliness' of historical plausibility (Kierkegaard 1985: 63–71; Rudd 2013: 496–500).

This is a singularly austere approach to the Gospels, equally distant from rationalizing historical criticism and from literalism. The Gospel narrative exists simply as the occasion for an imperative grounded in the claim of God's presence. This is reminiscent of but not quite identical with the neo-Lutheran theology of Wittgenstein's near-contemporary, Rudolf Bultmann. But Bultmann develops his minimalist account of the significance of Gospel history partly as a way of handling the difficulty for the modern consciousness of believing in miracles (Bultmann 1960), while Wittgenstein has no interest at all in making terms with this kind of rationalism, and, as we have seen, concludes that it is important to recognize that we cannot establish in advance what would or would not be an adequate or plausible account of a God-man. If you respond positively to the imperative, problems at *this* level are trivial. But there is some common ground: Bultmann sees the dissociation of the Gospel from historically questionable miracle stories as the gateway to a purified faith, dependent on no proofs drawn from mere matters of fact, and thus a clear witness to the transcendence of God; Wittgenstein's commitment to a proclamation that advances no argument or defence is obviously linked with his belief that rational proofs for God reduce God to one existent among others. For both, the Gospel record is the *occasion* for faith, not the *grounds* for faith.

Wittgenstein's struggles with what to make of the Gospel narrative illustrate the fundamental difficulty of writing about God incarnate. The subject matter has no straightforward analogies: in the words of Con Drury, in conversation with Wittgenstein, 'Novels and plays must indeed be probable, but why should this, the scheme of man's redemption, be probable?' (Rhees 1984: 164). The response 'That doesn't sound very likely' to some narrative about the incarnate God invites the retort, 'Why should it?' And by the same token, 'That sounds just the kind of thing an incarnate God would do/say' is fatuous. Constructing a portrait of the incarnate God on the basis of what such a person might be like is to miss the point. Hence the importance of the 'mediocre' narratives we have in the Bible—not very coherent, not very polished or eloquent. It is a point anticipated by some early Christian authors, defending the stylistic clumsiness of the sacred writers, but Wittgenstein gives it a distinctive twist by allying it to the Kierkegaardian concern to secure the 'anonymity' of the Incarnation. The point may be reinforced by thinking of those early Christian fictions about Jesus, the 'Infancy Gospels', especially the so-called Gospel of Thomas, whose authors clearly begin from asking, 'What would a small child with unrestricted miraculous powers be like?' By projecting what they understand by 'power' and 'miracle' onto the child Jesus, they portray a superbrat combining unrestrained childish whimsy with unrestrained childish malevolence (James 1924: 49–84). Not quite a *gospel* story.

So someone might begin by saying that it is clearly impossible to write fiction about Jesus on the basis of a theological conviction about him; any fiction is *ipso facto* the product of some sort of refusal of faith. Yet this does not seem to be quite the end of the matter. It could be said in reply that if this is a narrative about God's embodiment in a human identity, there must be some analogical element, some way of rendering this as the story of a recognizable human psyche. Jesus grew in wisdom and stature, says Luke's Gospel; he was tempted as we are, says the Letter to the Hebrews. He has an inner history, in other words: he develops as a human subject and he experiences at the very least some kind of awareness of possible diverse choices. Just as significantly, he interacts in a particular way with other subjects, he makes a particular kind of *impression* on them. With any human being, we learn to understand more about who they are partly by looking at how they are seen and heard. If the attempt to write fiction about Jesus might disclose a basic misunderstanding of the nature of faith (imagining what is not imaginable, the inner state of a unique subject), perhaps the *refusal* to contemplate fiction about Jesus might equally disclose a misunderstanding of the nature of what occasions faith—which is not a rootless affirmation, or even a historically indeterminate narrative that could as well be fiction as fact, but something that is presented as grounded in interaction, in the ordinary processes of meeting, understanding, misunderstanding, guessing, trusting, learning.

A basic tension, then, a balancing of risks, is rooted in the Chalcedonian dogma—not to say a version of the iconoclast controversy about whether the humanity of Jesus is capable of being visually represented (Tsakiridou 2013). The incarnate Lord is complete in what is (eternally) his and in what is (historically) ours. To reduce faith to the response to a humanly affecting or impressive or persuasive narrative is to risk reducing God's action to the human scale, to stay with the humanity alone. To isolate Jesus as a human individual from any imagining of him in human interaction or self-relatedness is to risk forgetting that God's solidarity with such human experience—with what it is like to be a finite subject—is the specific vehicle of our liberation; it is to veer towards evoking the divinity alone. We need to hang on to a fundamental fact about the Gospels themselves: they are not the unmediated or 'neutral' record of a human life laid bare for any observer to work over the raw material; nor are they free-floating mythical creations, absolved from connection with actual, local political and interpersonal settings. They are in some measure imaginative essays; they seek to narrate a life that has location, movement, growth, crisis, in a recognizably human way. The Gospels are not in the ordinary sense 'fiction'; but they have something in common with the novelistic enterprise. *Pace* Wittgenstein, they show some concern with plausibility, and their central figure has a history, experiences emotion, and is engaged with and in the life of other agents and subjects. It looks as though the apparently simple Wittgensteinian prohibition isn't so simple after all. In the iconoclast debates, the Morton's fork advanced by the iconoclasts was that in seeking to represent Jesus, you either represented a human being as human, which implicitly denied one wing of the Chalcedonian definition; or you were claiming to represent the utterly invisible and indefinable Godhead, an obvious nonsense and blasphemy. The orthodox response had to (and did) negotiate skilfully between the horns of this dilemma to propose a theory allowing the representation of a humanity suffused by but not cancelled by divine indwelling. The implicit Wittgensteinian question is how such a negotiation could be rendered in narrative form.

I want to look at some of the ways in which writers of fiction have handled the figure of Jesus in their narratives—directly and indirectly. 'Indirect' treatments are important, because one way of dealing with Jesus as a character is to evoke the Gospel narrative through the shape of another narrative. This is not about some dutiful quest for 'Christ-figures' in any and every fiction (a fashion parodied in F. C. Crews' identification of Christological symbolism in *Winnie the Pooh*) (Crews 1964: 53–62). But it is instructive to look at how some texts deliberately foreground a figure onto whom certain expectations are projected, expectations of Christlikeness and saving power, only to display their tragic or tragicomic collapse. Direct treatments have included pious fictionalizing of the Gospel stories and the lives of real or imagined figures around the figure of Christ, from the mid-nineteenth century onwards—from *Ben-Hur* and *A Prince of the House of David* to *The Robe* and *The Big Fisherman* (Theissen 1987). Some of these are at least vigorous and enjoyable stories, but they deal with the underlying theological question mostly by ignoring it, often falling into the Wittgensteinian trap of trying to present an indisputably noble and lovable Jesus acceptable to (especially) Liberal Protestant piety. I have not focused on these works, but have elected to look at another kind of direct narrative, the kind in which the attempt to tell a persuasive and engaging story about Jesus serves as a way of demonstrating that a traditional theological approach is otiose. Show that you can tell a credible story about Jesus without any of the 'anxiety of representation' that Wittgenstein's reflections indicate and you have shown that the theological labour and speculation of the orthodox tradition is unnecessary. And then there is a third category, hard to define with precision: fictions which deploy the figure of Jesus obliquely so as to offer a particular kind of perspective on the world of the novel in question. Like the first style, it generally avoids any attempt to represent the psychology of Jesus; like some works in my second category, it often sketches the figure of the Saviour by inviting us to see it through the eyes of a contemporary. But it has no agenda of demystifying (sometimes the opposite). It leaves open to some extent the question of what more might be or needs to be said about the figure of Jesus, and this enigmatic element brings us back to Wittgenstein's musings: the challenge, the summons to faith, is not bound to any one clearly identifiable element in a historical figure, yet the telling of the whole story somehow proposes the challenge—even if and when the writer has no theological intent or personal commitment. The narrative is a trace of something that escapes being said; yet that in itself invites some sort of speech (Hamilton 1993).

Failing Towards Grace and Incarnation

Deliberately 'failed' representation finds its most extended and sophisticated instance in Dostoevsky's *The Idiot* (Wasiolek 1967; cf. Williams 2008: 47–57). The notoriously chaotic notebooks for that novel have helped nurture the belief that its central character, Prince Myshkin, is meant to be a model, Christlike figure; but it is pretty clear that Dostoevsky's aims changed in the process of composition. He may have started with the goal of depicting a 'perfectly good man', but the demands of writing a credible novel eventually produced a far more interesting result—a figure who is seen by most of those around him as an innocent and a potential saviour (and whose physical appearance recalls the iconography of Christ), but whose own inner confusion or emptiness consistently brings disaster to himself and others. Myshkin is an epileptic (the motif of epilepsy returns in some of the fictions we shall be looking at) and also someone who has no discernible history, no real memory. He cannot settle in any erotic relationship; his lack of a narrative of himself seems to leave him helpless in making decisions and commitments. He does indeed galvanize those around him into new kinds of recognition of themselves, new narratives of themselves, but these have their own ambiguous or destructive dynamic. To call Myshkin a parodic Christ-figure is not quite right—there is too much obvious and tragic pathos about his failure to embody what the narrative on its surface demands of him—but he is certainly an instance of what happens when people are tripped up by their own projection of what they imagine are Christ-shaped gaps in their own well-being and self-knowledge in the direction of an actual human figure. Myshkin is sometimes associated in critical discussion with the strong tradition in Russian Christianity of emphasizing the humiliation, vulnerability, and silence of Christ—the subject of a classic study by Nadezhda Gorodetzky in 1938 (Gorodetzky 1938). This tradition does indeed find some reflection in Dostoevsky, primarily in the silent Christ of Ivan Karamazov's Grand Inquisitor fable; and we shall see something of its impact in the work of another Russian writer. But in *The Idiot*, it works in an almost perverse fashion: Myshkin's helplessness and passivity are like his physical appearance—he *looks* like an icon; and the tempting plausibility of an identification with Christ is thus reinforced. But it is his lack of hinterland or interiority that makes him passive and vulnerable; it is a kind of deficit in 'narratable' human identity.

Although one generally perceptive critic has said that Jesus could not be a novelist's character because his true identity is incapable of change (Holquist 1977: 106–11), this will not quite work in the context of the Gospel stories, which show elements of conflict and decision and of seemingly anguished self-awareness. Myshkin is vulnerable to the chaotic and lethal projection of those around him because he lacks history and memory and the self-awareness that goes with them; in other words, his vulnerability is not the massive, ironic self-constraint associated theologically with the powerlessness of Jesus. The Christ who confronts the Grand Inquisitor is a supremely ironic creation, God being tried and condemned by the Church. It is this irony that is absent in the portrait of Myshkin.

As this suggests, the closer we look at the *kind* of failure Myshkin is, the more certain aspects of the theological picture of Christ come into focus. This is the sense in which one can read *The Idiot* as an oblique Christological statement; if we cannot construct a fiction about a 'perfectly good man', that leaves the question on the table of what we say about the literary figure for whom that goodness is explicitly and uniquely claimed, the Jesus of the Gospels. Is the Gospel story the only successful fiction in this regard? Or must we conclude that a 'successful' narrative cannot be a fiction in the simple sense. What is it that makes the 'success' of the Gospel story unrepeatable (if that is what it is)? How are we to distinguish between what turns out to be a tragically damaging *resemblance* to the Saviour and a truthful representation? I suspect that Dostoevsky would, having written this novel, have agreed that fiction about Christ was not possible and even perhaps have agreed with Wittgenstein that the attempt to depict perfection in a satisfying literary vehicle was doomed, because it would inevitably focus attention on the vehicle not the perfection of the agency that is being evoked. Whatever the conclusion about this, it should be clear that Dostoevsky's narrative of an 'idiot' functions in much the way that Flannery O'Connor's stories do in their gesturing towards grace or holiness or absolution by depicting both its absences and its apes, its failed embodiments.

And while we are in the American South, it is worth glancing at Carson McCullers' masterpiece, *The Heart is a Lonely Hunter* (McCullers 2008), another story of vulnerability and projection. In this case, Singer, the deaf and speechless figure at the novel's centre, is powerless not because of a lack of history (we learn a certain amount about this) but because of enforced silence. He has literally nothing to say to any other character, except for the sign language in which he desperately tries to communicate with his beloved friend Antonapoulos, who is also mute but mentally childlike and self-absorbed; and so Singer cannot establish for himself any conversational space, any presence in the life of others except on their terms. Like Myshkin, he thus becomes a repository for obsessive hopes, fantasies, and unresolvable frustrations and sufferings; and, not surprisingly, he is crushed by this. For a period he attracts a kind of mythology, especially for the four (an obviously significant number) troubled characters who use him as a sort of confessor, 'a home-made God', as one of them reflects: 'Owing to the fact that he was a mute, they were able to give him all the qualities they wanted him to have' (McCullers 2008: 204). His Messianic aura derives from the perception around him that he occupies no space of his own, and allows the needs of others to define him. His name is rich in irony: silent as he is, he draws out the words and music of other people's hearts (McCullers 2008: 51). But what he cannot speak or represent for himself is his own despairing loneliness. As with Myshkin, though in a different vein, his vulnerability is a matter of tragic lack.

McCullers is not in any clear way nudging at a Christological question as we might see Dostoevsky doing; her focus is on isolation in general, and the tragedy of Singer is as much as anything a warning against imagining that there is or could be a selfless listener whose listening will transfigure the grief emptied out into it. McCullers saw her writing as religiously motivated (McCullers 2008: 19); but it is hard to decide whether she is consciously addressing precisely the issues we began with. However, what she does is to focus sharply the ways in which the *image* of Christ can work destructively when the substance is absent. McCullers is not, like Flannery O'Connor, insisting on the absence of grace in the superficially Christianized environment she depicts (Wood 2004; Williams 2005); but the fact is that, in this novel, there is nowhere to 'deposit' the alienation and isolation in which the characters live except in this silent and powerless locus which is Singer. He is—not wholly unlike Myshkin—invited by the narrative to supply a Christlike presence otherwise unknown. The human heart, it seems, is desperate for a listening ear that assures it that it is not alone and not condemned. But when this is identified in a human form, the burden cannot be borne. Singer's silence gives this drama more weight and dignity than the self-pitying protests of the Jesus overwhelmed by human demands whom we meet in the dismal lyrics of *Jesus Christ Superstar*; but the point is not too dissimilar. Identify a Messianic figure and you will kill him by the impossibility of what you ask.

Or, of course, if you identify yourself in some way with the Messianic calling, you will in effect invite killing; and the question is in what way this is salvific or liberating. Patrick White's masterpiece, *Riders in the Chariot* (White 1964), leaves the reader's judgement in suspense as to what exactly has been transacted in the climacteric episodes and whether the astonishingly realized figure of the Jewish contemplative, Mordecai Himmelfarb, has done more than draw down or draw out the latent violence and self-loathing of those around him. We are told of the hints and promptings in his childhood that suggest he has a special vocation; we see him abandoning any thought of such a calling and gradually being drawn back into the mysteries of the Chariot, Ezekiel's vision of the divine glory as reworked in the apocalyptic and mystical literature of Kabbalism. We see him helpless to save those around him as the nightmare of the Final Solution unfolds, and as a humiliated refugee in Australia, where he is subjected to a mock crucifixion by drunken and overwrought workmates. He walks away afterwards 'with the gentle uncertain motion of an eggshell tossed by flowing water'. 'Himmelfarb left the factory in which it had not been accorded to him to expiate the sins of the world' (White 1964: 418), and he dies as a result of the stress and trauma induced. In spite of White's explicit (but heavily ironic) evocation of the idea of 'failed' Messiahship here, Himmelfarb is seen at the end by the alcoholic aboriginal artist, Alf Dubbo, as a Christ taken down from the Cross, being nursed by the other 'riders in the Chariot', the other marginal and disturbed figures who allow the perspective of God to come into the distorted, banal, suffocating world of suburban Australia. Something, we might conclude, has not exactly failed.

As he dies, he dreams of enacting the sacred marriage of Kabbalistic teaching, 'Adam Kadmon, descending from the Tree of Light to take the Bride', the lost Shekhinah, the divine glory, who kisses his wounded hand (White 1964: 430). Between them, the four 'riders' embody that moment of union with the Shekhinah, perpetually marginal, perpetually at risk, subject to almost immeasurable pain and humiliation but not expelled. Mordecai's sense of calling is not an illusion, in spite of all. There is at some level a moment of reconciliation for the world—not achieved by Mordecai or the other 'riders' as individuals, as an aspect of their particular stories, but manifested together. And its unity is discernible as having the shape of the story of the crucifixion of Jesus.

So this is not quite the story of a 'failed' image; more of an image that flickers persistently around certain kinds of human characters, never instantiated in any obvious way in any single one. The specific narrative of any such single character would be a 'failure'; but it would not be simply the chronicle of an absence. White's own theological commitments are no simpler to decipher than McCullers'. He described himself as more sympathetic to Judaism than to orthodox Christianity by the time he was writing this novel (Marr 1991: 357–8), but *Riders* is undeniably pervaded by Christian rhetoric and iconography as well as by the vividly evoked background of Jewish esotericism. Its overall shape suggests that it is in some way a narrative not so much about a tantalizing human dream of the wholly just judge and the wholly compassionate listener as about the persistent unsettling of the moral world by an agency that is terrible and devouring, utterly illuminating, irresistible, and deeply wounding for those who are in its path and become its vehicles. Or, to put it another way, the story is less about a human longing for the Messiah, more about the alarming persistence of 'Messianic' reality in ways that wreak havoc with what we long for. It is in that sense a story one can read in the framework of Wittgenstein's challenges: four lives, four human faces, reminding us that the four living beings upholding the Chariot are also signs of the four evangelists in Christian iconography, whose stories are chaotically at odds with any expectation there might be of how a Messianic destiny would unfold, but which carry a savage imperative to repentance. To borrow an idiom from the late Gillian Rose, this is a narrative that 'fails *towards*' grace and incarnation.

SUBVERSIVE RETELLING

There is a kind of narrative which seeks (explicitly or not) to show the impossibility of a theologically charged depiction of Jesus by the simple expedient of developing a convincing untheological or anti-theological portrait. These alternative and subversive Jesuses are very diverse; but what is interesting is how few could be characterized as 'convincing' portraits if that means 'naturalistic'. The best are most helpfully seen as 'remythologizing' exercises rather than simple demystifications. This is certainly true of the two most substantial twentieth-century examples of subversive narratives of Jesus, Robert Graves' *King Jesus* (Graves 1946) and Nikos Kazantzakis' *The Last Temptation*

(Kazantzakis 1975). Graves uses his narrative to flesh out many of the theories he was developing at the same time to do with poetic inspiration and the roots of mythology, the theories which found their full statement not long after in *The White Goddess* (Graves 1948). This means that the text of the novel is at times grotesquely overprovided with lengthy disquisitions on ancient ritual and myth, all the more awkward given that the novel is supposed to be narrated by an imagined figure several decades later who could have no possible knowledge of most of the conversations related. Graves also makes extensive use of early Christian apocryphal literature, including even the 'Infancy Gospel of Thomas', source of some comically disedifying fictions about Jesus as a small child. The result is a sprawling and densely overloaded work which continues to have a qualified critical reception.

Yet this is to do it far less than justice. The deployment of material from apocryphal sources, particularly the 'Protogospel of James', is often astonishingly skilful and ingenious, there are sections of great imaginative force, and, above all, the figure of Jesus is brilliantly drawn, a tragic hero whose obsessive sense of a mission to end history is sketched compassionately and poignantly. Graves, in a brief 'Historical Commentary' appended to the body of the novel, obliquely grants Wittgenstein's point that, if you accept the premiss of Christian orthodoxy, 'you can afford to disregard' his version, as ordinary criteria of probability do not enter in. He adds, 'Though I reject this premiss, it will be clear that I respect Jesus as having been more uncompromising, more consistent, and more loyal to his God than even most Christians allow' (Graves 1946: 421). Graves sets the whole story against the background of a Jewish world inheriting the divided legacy of the patriarchal reformed religion imposed largely in the eighth and seventh centuries BCE and a mythologically more complex faith, centred upon the Goddess and her consort. Jesus is the issue of a secret marriage, planned by the High Priest, between a Temple virgin of the ancient royal blood and Herod the Great's son, Antipater—a marriage designed to give final legitimacy to the Herodian house and also to bring to birth a royal heir whose horoscope suggests a world-changing degree of power and significance. 'We stand', says the High Priest Simon to Prince Antipater, 'at the cross-roads ... of Time' (Graves 1946: 64).

In the event, Jesus, son of Mary and Antipater, interprets his vocation in the most radical way imaginable: he has come to destroy the cycle of birth and death that is presided over by the Goddess, and his ministry is in part a struggle against her power—though it also involves the proclamation of a Kingdom (as in the New Testament) promising equality and dignity and an intimate relation to God as Father. Forced by Mary of Bethany, who should have been his consort, to use his occult knowledge of the hidden divine Name to raise Lazarus from the dead, Jesus recognizes that the Goddess is winning the struggle. Only his own voluntary death can now bring about the transformation he seeks. His own plans to bring this about go disastrously wrong, and he ends—in a final irony—enduring in his crucifixion the ancient form of sacrificial death designed for the Goddess' human consort. The Christians of the narrator's own day (the last decade of the first century CE) are divided between those who hold to Jesus' ascetic vision and wait for his return and those who, under the malign influence of Paul, have turned the entire story into the history of an incarnate God. The novel implies that Jesus some-how survived crucifixion; but his ultimate fate is unknown.

Without going into the complex matter of Graves' sources for various details of this story, there is no denying that the novel, for all its manifold flaws, is (within its terms) a coherent and imaginatively bold reworking of the history of Jesus and presents at its centre a figure with weight and solidity as a literary and even a psychological con-struct. Somewhere in the background—as in the background of a number of mod-ern fictions—is Albert Schweitzer's image of Jesus 'throwing himself on the wheel of history', inviting apocalyptic disaster so as to force God's hand when his announce-ment of the end had proved mistaken (Schweitzer 2000). But Graves' version gives to this trope a new framework and an ironic and (in the strict sense) tragic flavour. The credibility—and the poignant irony—depends on acceptance of this mythical frame-work; and because the exposition of this is so laboured and over-elaborate, it is hard to see the novel as a whole making quite the imaginative sense it needs to. And it is an understatement to say that Graves' mythical history—dependent as it is on countless brilliant and often perverse hunches and an indiscriminate quarrying of widely diverse kinds of material for supportive detail—is a challenge to any critical reader or anyone with claims to more orthodox anthropological and literary expertise. Perhaps the most useful conclusion one can draw from a reading of *King Jesus* is that a 'counter-narrative' to the canonical one may need a counter-theology, rather than a simply anti-theological agenda (Graves 1946: 30).

The point is well-illustrated by our second major instance of subversive retelling, Kazantzakis' *Last Temptation*. This is another fiction on the heroic scale, turbulent and feverish, cast almost entirely in terms of extremes (floods, sandstorms, thunderstorms, emotional storms, wildly dramatic hallucinations), which makes the notorious penul-timate episode all the more remarkable. Jesus, on the Cross, hallucinates an alternative future in which he is miraculously rescued and settles down with Mary and Martha in Bethany, becoming the contented patriarch of a large family. When his former disciples appear, to reproach him for his betrayal, he initially justifies his embrace of the ordi-nary, even the second-rate, but then acknowledges that he has indeed surrendered his integrity; and this projects him back to the Cross, where he dies in the glad recognition that he has not been unfaithful after all. With his final words, 'it was as though he had said: Everything has begun' (Kazantzakis 1975: 575). Jesus in this novel is initially intro-duced as a tormented youth, struggling with tensions between deliberate sexual priva-tion, political confusion (as a carpenter, he makes crosses for the execution of rebels), and an agonizing sense of God's hand upon him—like a vulture clawing his scalp, a characteristically extreme and savage metaphor. Gradually, he emerges as a charismatic teacher and healer, proclaiming the infinite and indiscriminate love of God; and then the message darkens, as it is rejected and Jesus himself becomes more obviously at risk. He speaks of apocalyptic judgement on the comfortable around him who hear words of love and absolution only as reassuring noises, not as a call to transformation and to economic justice. As he refuses to sanction violent action to bring about the new order, his disci-ples increasingly doubt him; he recognizes that he has to embrace death of his own will in order to 'open the door' of immortality for himself and his friends and break the cycle of violence. As in *King Jesus*, Judas is presented as the disciple most intimate with Jesus, the one entrusted with the task of delivering him to death (though in Graves' novel, Judas tries to circumvent what Jesus plans and inadvertently makes things worse). The hallucination on the Cross is presented as a necessary finishing of business: Magdalene the prostitute has been in love with Jesus since they were children together, but he has refused to consummate their love, although he is initially almost obsessed with her; he must in imagination take that step of sexual self-realization, embrace in thought what he has renounced in fact and so complete his self-sacrifice in full knowledge of what he is surrendering, its goods as well as its ultimate moral inadequacy.

This final hallucination, the 'last temptation' of the title, is probably what the book is most often remembered for (and Scorsese's film of 1988 unhelpfully reinforced this). The presentation of a sexually active Jesus—even in the context of what is clearly a fantasy—was and is profoundly shocking to a good many Christians. But what this focus obscures is the way in which this theme is dealt with throughout the book. Making allowances for Kazantzakis' Lawrentian erotic mysticism and the highly problematic typology of femaleness that goes with it, the essential focus is not so much on sexual activity as such as on the compact made with 'things as they are' that is signalled by marriage and childbearing. The young Jesus, we are told, rejects the possibility of marrying Magdalene because when he contemplates it he feels the claws of God in his scalp, 'two frenzied wings beat[ing] above him, tightly covering his temples' (Kazantzakis 1975: 24); he collapses in what is apparently an epileptic seizure (Graves depicts the young Jesus as having a seizure in a similar moment of trauma, but Kazantzakis makes this a regular occurrence). But this is something felt not just where sex is concerned but whenever he thinks about ordinary human joys. There has to be no compromise with the present moment because of the imperative force of an unknown vocation for the future. In this spirit, Jesus initially heads for a 'monastery' (implausibly situated in Galilee), but comes out again as his vocation unfolds. His journey to his final destiny is a journey, paradoxically, towards an embrace of the present; but in a way that is definitively detached from the comfortable possessiveness of ordinary enjoyment. His capacity to face and fully entertain in imagination the lost alternative of domestic happiness is a sort of index of the degree to which he has embraced the real limits of mortality and, more specifically, his calling to die in a particular way. Here as in *King Jesus*, though very differently expressed, is the Schweitzerian theme again: Jesus in his voluntary death seeks to turn the wheel of history. But Kazantzakis seems to suggest (as of course Schweitzer does in his own way) that in some sense he *succeeds*. Something begins. There is, says Kazantzakis' mature Jesus, a massive conflict and conflagration to come; but it will take his death to provoke it, it cannot be managed or masterminded by human power. 'Love is not unarmed', he says at one point (Kazantzakis 1975: 440); but this is not to say that love's 'arms' are those of the world. They are, it seems, the weapons of radical self-sacrifice in frontal assault on the world of compromise with its gross injustices.

The novel's coherence is not easy to trace. There is too much going on; and the figure of Jesus in its multiple and multiform changes is almost impossible to see whole, especially through the medium of Kazantzakis' fantastically over-rich style. There is also something not quite in focus in the detail: as critics have observed, the setting may notionally be first-century Palestine, but the visual, cultural, and emotional climate is unmistakeably rural Greece, or rather Crete, at some point in the last couple of centuries. Indeed, the novel seems to inhabit a very similar world to that of Kazantzakis' earlier venture into extended theological fiction, *Christ Recrucified*, which is set in the late Ottoman period (Kazantzakis 1954). But the Jesus of the later novel is far more complex than the innocent Christ-substitute, Manolios, in *Christ Recrucified*: Manolios is a heroic scapegoat, with little of Jesus' frenzied struggling with God's call (no vulture claws to contend with). And *The Last Temptation*—to return to our original point in this section—is not so much an anti-theological as a counter-theological, mythically charged narrative. As Kazantzakis explains in his foreword, this is a Jesus who exemplifies spirit's triumph over flesh: he advances towards being in some rather elusive sense an embodiment of God by his unflinching determination to wrestle down his desires—for sexual fulfilment, for posterity, for worldly comfort. But this presupposes that those desires are powerful and persistent. Like the Desert Fathers, Kazantzakis warns his readers to 'expect temptation until their last breath' (Ward 1975: 2; Bien and Middleton 1996); unlike them, he sees those temptations as immensely solid imaginative possibilities that have to be entertained and explored, experienced vicariously. The myth of human struggle that Kazantzakis sketches out for us is of will triumphing over imagination precisely by allowing imagination its full scope. Portraying Jesus in such terms is to help us love and understand him as a fellow human, 'and to pursue his Passion as though it were our own' (Kazantzakis 1975: xi). The patristic theme of the Incarnate Word's embrace of the entirety of human mental or spiritual experience is given a new twist here: Christ must be the exemplar of the process by which spirit consumes flesh while at the same time intensifying the reality of the flesh. He does not, as in the patristic scheme, transform the possibilities of our flesh by his participation in it but calls us to the same bloody struggle and assures us we are not the first to walk this path.

THE DEVIL AS RACONTEUR

One aspect of Kazantzakis' fiction which trails a coat for the orthodox reader is the portrait of the evangelist Matthew, who, as the story unfolds, carefully reconstructs the life of Jesus as it should have been—much to Jesus' alarm and anger. This idea of the unreliable eyewitness is paralleled—but with more conscious irony—in the treatment of Jesus in Mikhail Bulgakov's *The Master and Margarita*—widely and rightly regarded as one of the most remarkable novels of the twentieth century. The narrative shifts between Moscow in the 1930s and first-century Jerusalem on Good Friday, and moves towards an extraordinary weaving together of the stories. The stories related touch on themes of power and magic, truth and illusion, and the nature of political courage. Repeatedly, the conversations in Moscow return, almost obsessively, to the events of Good Friday, described in a continuous but interrupted narrative voice, though this voice is assigned variously to the devil, to the 'Master' of the title (a Moscow writer and intellectual), and to the dreams of a poet confined in a psychiatric clinic. The devil presents this narrative as an eyewitness account, superior to the Gospels ('Precisely nothing of what is written in the Gospels ever actually took place', claims this narrator [Bulgakov 1997: 42]); we have been introduced to the figure of Matthew Levi, who has been following Yeshua (Jesus) and writing down distorted versions of what he says. When a horrified Yeshua catches sight of what he has written, he urges him to burn it, but Matthew refuses.

So whose story is this that we are reading in the Jerusalem sections of the novel? Certainly it is presented as (part of) the suppressed novel of the 'Master': Bulgakov, in one of the complex self-referential twists of the text, ascribes to the Master—or even to Yeshua?—his own self-censorship (Bulgakov 1997: introduction; cf. Milne 2009). But it is also initially the devil's response to the crude anti-religious propaganda of Soviet communism: Jesus really did exist, and the devil was there to see him. Yet the devil is traditionally an unreliable narrator, to put it mildly: is he just lying, or lying about the inaccuracies of the Gospel, is he plagiarizing the Master's novel, is he simply (as in much of the narrative) introducing radical and anarchic uncertainty into the closed world of Stalinist Moscow? Not *just* lying, it seems: the Good Friday story is distributed out between voices that do not share the devil's reputation as a liar; and in any case the devil in this story is more of an uncomfortable truthteller (the tangles are like those you find in Dostoevsky on the same subject). But most decisive is the dramatic and dreamlike sequence at the novel's climax, when Margarita is given the power to decide the fate both of her lover—the Master—and of Pilate who has been sitting in isolation on a mountain top for two millennia, waiting for the conversation with Jesus—which he terminated by crucifying him—to be resumed so that he can again imagine the possibility of absolution for his failure in courage. The Master is told that he can 'finish his novel with one phrase'; and he calls to Pilate, 'You're free! He's waiting for you!' (Bulgakov 1997: 382). Pilate rushes off into the moonlight to continue the unfinished conversation with the one he has killed; but the Master, having set free his 'fictional' creation, opts for another kind of freedom, a gentle eternity of undemanding peace (supervised by the devil), strolling under cherry trees, listening to Schubert. The novel is 'finished' by the release of its main character into the hands of Jesus; finished by the postulating of something unfinishable. The Master's life is frozen 'novelistically' in a timeless happy ending. 'He does not deserve the light, he deserves peace', says Matthew Levi to the devil, on behalf of his (Matthew's) own 'fictional' hero, Yeshua (Bulgakov 1997: 361).

In among all these tightly pleated ironies and paradoxes, what is clear is that the figure of Christ at his trial is more than a fiction—or rather that this fiction is the only real deliverance from the unreal world of Moscow, Jerusalem, Rome, or wherever the ambition of total power is placed. The final choice is between Pilate's restarted conversation and a self-devised happiness, protected from a truth that requires courage. And the bewildered, apparently simple-minded figure who confronts Pilate in the Jerusalem episodes—frightened, confused, and only fluent when he is defending others or sympathizing with his tormentors—is, without any explanation, assumed in the closing pages of the book to be capable of deciding human destinies, more potent than the devil who has thus far been directing events. Yeshua Ha-Notzri, Pilate's prisoner, becomes, improbably, the touchstone of truthfulness; the devil, who wreaks unforgettably comic and occasionally murderous havoc in Moscow, turns out to be his instrument in intruding the touch of reality into the systematic illusion of Moscow and its ideology.

The picture of a 'touchstone' is evoked in a very different register by a novel which is hard to place in the typology we have been using but seems to belong here if anywhere. H. F. M. Prescott's *The Man on a Donkey* (Prescott 1952) is a story about the English Reformation, not the first century; but it briefly depicts Jesus, the 'man on a donkey' of the title, glimpsed going about his business in Yorkshire. As rumours spread that he has been seen by the apparently half-witted priory serving maid, Malle, all parties in the conflicts of the day make attempts to conscript her and make her 'visions' serve their agenda; but she cannot give them anything except cryptic, even frightening, statements: 'There was a great wind of light blowing, and sore pain' (Prescott 1952: 368). For a brief space, about half way through the novel, we are allowed to see what Malle sees—but not only Malle. When Dame Christabel, the formidable prioress of the convent, spots the vagabond workman leaving the priory after drinking companionably with the other labourers in the kitchen, she feels 'strangely and strongly moved against the fellow', suspecting that he is the sort who wants to 'pull down all to be as wretched as they' (Prescott 1952: 358–9). Malle, accompanied by the priest's bastard child, Wat, follows 'the Man' until he goes 'up and out of sight, under the great branches that bowed and swung' (Prescott 1952: 359); and the two clutch each other in ecstasy at the thought that 'that thing which man could never of himself have thought … was true as daylight, here was God in man, here All in a point' (Prescott 1952: 360).

Two things stand out here. The first and more obvious is that 'the Man' comes into the world of 1530s England at an angle: everyone tries to make him serve their ends and to make Malle say something that will endorse what they want, but the visitant is obstinately irrelevant to their priorities. The second is that there is something of a Kierkegaardian quality to this narrative, to the extent that this is a Jesus who does no mighty works and has no miracle or apologetic to confirm his identity. If he is recognizable, it is as the bearer of imperatives that, taken seriously, would unpick the world of the priory and its hierarchy, and also as one who by his presence augments ordinary human joy, especially for the poor and despised. Prescott's theology, here and elsewhere in the book, is unimpeachably orthodox; but this is also a Christology in which the anonymity of incarnation is broken only by the inner assurance or disturbance stirred by 'the Man'. Prescott does not attempt to answer in general terms the question of how anyone might know that the incarnate God has been among them, but we might deduce from her narrative that we cannot expect to find conclusive evidence of this in wonderworking or in exceptional events of any kind. 'We'—the characters in the story and the reader—simply know that the world's terms have been altered as 'the Man' passes through.

The theme of the ambiguity of exceptional works and proofs underlies the last example we shall be examining. Anita Mason's *The Illusionist* (Mason 1983) is about magic and faith: it tells the story of Simon Magus whose attempt to purchase from St Peter the secret of imparting the Holy Spirit wins him a mention in the Acts of the Apostles and whose subsequent career was related in an elaborate set of legends culminating in another (and fatal) confrontation with Peter in Rome in a wonder-working contest. Mason's Simon is a sophisticated manipulator of ritual, hypnosis, and manipulation; Peter—Kepha—is a not very clever and seriously confused figure—though not without dignity—who repeatedly goes over the incomprehensible memories of his association with 'Joshua', who told him years ago that he possessed 'the Key to the Kingdom'. Joshua's declaration is in response to Kepha's confession of faith that he, Joshua, is 'the One Who Is To Come'. Kepha is told to repeat this to no one. Why not, he asks, if it is true? '*Because* it is true', Joshua replies, '… Things must not be said … There is a kind of truth which, when it is said, becomes untrue' (Mason 1983: 127). And this is the Key; Kepha reflects unhappily later on, in the prison cells of King Herod Agrippa, that it is a burden he would gladly shed ('Could you not have given it to someone else?' [Mason 1983: 140]) and can make little or no sense of the tensions in Joshua's vision. He remembers the multiple paradoxes of Joshua's teaching, the still more marked paradoxes of what he sometimes overheard him saying to Mary Magdalene (Mason 1983: 142), the obscure and embarrassing events around the beginnings of the Christian community when Mary declares she has seen Joshua alive. It is evident that this has triggered claims from others that they have seen him; and Kepha is too ashamed to admit that he has had no vision. Meanwhile, Joshua's own stark and compassionate voice, announcing 'an end of placating and pleading, of the anxious counting of faults and the unending rituals to earn favour, and the desperate certainty that no effort would ever be enough' (Mason 1983: 126), has been overlaid by other voices, represented by Joshua's brother, Jacob, and the passionate newcomer, Saul, who elaborate theologies of incarnation and atonement that Kepha half-heartedly adopts.

Much of the force of the novel comes from the constantly sustained tension between Simon's developing philosophy of conscious transgression of every law and the incipient legalism and mythology of the new faith. The enigmatic Joshua stands over against both, and his witnesses, Kepha and—in a rather strained way—Saul, cannot, despite all their confusion and distortion, wholly bury that presence. This is once again a Jesus who does not perform mighty works (though he is able to 'exorcize' Mary Magdalene): in a competition based on supposed miracles, there will always be plausible rivals, like Simon. Intriguingly, Mason's Jesus is shaken and set back by the failure of the Kingdom to come when his disciples have completed their mission to the towns of Judaea—a motif once again drawn directly from Schweitzer's *Quest of the Historical Jesus*, though the consequent decision by Schweitzer's Jesus to force the wheel of history to turn by his self-sacrifice does not feature in the novel. His ultimate word seems to be that it is too difficult and dangerous to recognize his truth. And the novel's ending suggests that he may be right: Simon, who has seen through his own antinomian mythology, concludes that the supreme temptation is to insist on the singleness of truth rather than the unavoidability of paradox. Once you have seen that, you are on the road to death (as Joshua's death was inevitable, Simon says). Magic of one sort or another will always have the advantage over such a vision.

A Certain Energetic Passivity

In one way a de-theologized Jesus, Mason's Joshua in fact crystallizes just the theological conundrum with which we began. If Jesus is indeed the One who is to come, there can be no way of representing this credibly or persuasively; as soon as words and schemes of words are sought to express who he is, we have falsity, power struggles, a new magic, and a new law. Kepha could represent Joshua 'accurately' only by silence, or perhaps by repeating Joshua's paradoxes without any glossing or reconciling. Yet if we are to *live* with such paradoxes, there must be some narrative about how this has been done—how Joshua lived; Kepha's only solid ground of resistance to the mythologies of Saul and Jacob is his memory of a life that makes nonsense of what they are saying. In some way, the 'Key' is a matter of letting Joshua speak his paradoxes and letting other voices fall silent. And this may give us a hint about where a theological response to this variety of narrative experiments might be sought. In the controversy about icons in the Byzantine Church, the final theological formulation proposed that an iconic depiction of Jesus showed neither his divinity nor some supposed 'pure' humanity, but a human individuality activated by the 'energy' of the divine, the humanity sustained and pervaded by the divine person who gives it its integrity and specificity. To a necessarily lesser degree, this is also what the icon of a saint shows and mediates—divine energy working in a human individuality. To put it rather differently, the icon sets out to make us receptive, even passive, to the action of God in Christ and the saints. From that point of view, a theologically defensible fiction involving Jesus is going to be one that in one way or another renders us passive—that is, it does not try to engage us with the wellsprings of action in the character of Jesus. When that is attempted, we are bound into the quest for plausibility, and open ourselves to the implicit criticism of Wittgenstein. What this survey may suggest is not that there can be no theologically defensible representations of Jesus in fiction; rather that such representations will involve finding a narrative technique that manages to depict a credible human interaction, but leaves a surplus of unspoken and unresolved significance in the figure of Jesus, in such a way as not to give us a final 'purchase' on his meaning—in such a way as to draw us into what I have called a certain passivity in his regard. As these examples indicate, there can be 'theologically defensible' versions that are not in themselves designed to articulate a Christological orthodoxy, yet satisfy Wittgenstein's criterion in being stories that conclude with the imperative to believe, to be converted. As with the visual icon, it is important that we are not able to 'get behind' the narrated image. A Mason or a Bulgakov will not deliver a narrative that argues persuasively for Chalcedonian Christology; yet they leave the reader with a sense of what it is to confront a figure both identified with human process and always inexhaustibly engaged in drawing us into an uncontrollable territory not restricted by habitual human experience. Which is arguably what the Chalcedonian definition struggles to define.

Suggested Reading

Bulgakov (1997); Crews (1964); White (1964).

Bibliography

Bien, P. and D. Middleton (eds.) (1996), *God's Struggler: Religion in the Writings of Nikos Kazantzakis* (Macon, Ga.: Mercer University Press).

Bulgakov, M. (1997), *The Master and Margarita*, trans. R. Pevear and L. Volokhonsky (New York: Penguin Classics).

Bultmann, R. (1960), *Jesus Christ and Mythology* (London: SCM Press).

Crews, F. C. (1964), *The Pooh Perplex: A Student Casebook* (London: Arthur Barker).

Gorodetzky, N. (1938), *The Humiliated Christ in Modern Russian Thought* (London: SPCK).

Graves, R. (1946), *King Jesus* (New York: Creative Age Press).

Graves, R. (1948), *The White Goddess* (London: Faber and Faber).

Hamilton, W. (1993), *A Quest for the Post-Historical Jesus* (London: SCM Press).

Holquist, S. (1977), *Dostoevsky and the Novel* (Princeton, NJ: Princeton University Press).

James, M. R. (trans.) (1924), *The Apocryphal New Testament* (Oxford: Oxford University Press).

Kazantzakis, N. (1954), *Christ Recrucified* (London: Faber and Faber).

Kazantzakis, N. (1975), *The Last Temptation*, trans. P. A. Bien (London: Faber and Faber).

Kierkegaard, S. (1985), 'The Contemporary Follower', in H. V. Hong and E. H. Hong (eds. and trans.), *Philosophical Fragments/Johannes Climacus* (Princeton, NJ: Princeton University Press), 55–71.

McCullers, C. (2008), *The Heart is a Lonely Hunter* (New York: Penguin Books).

Marr, D. (1991), *Patrick White: A Life* (London: Vintage).

Mason, A. (1983), *The Illusionist* (London: Abacus Books).

Milne, L. (2009), *Mikhail Bulgakov: A Critical Biography* (Cambridge: Cambridge University Press).

Prescott, H. F. M. (1952), *The Man on a Donkey* (London: Eyre and Spottiswoode).

Rhees, R. (ed.) (1984), *Recollections of Wittgenstein* (Oxford: Oxford University Press).

Rudd, A. (2013), 'Kierkegaard, Wittgenstein and the Wittgensteinian Tradition', in J. Lippitt and G. Pattison (eds.), *The Oxford Handbook of Kierkegaard* (Oxford: Oxford University Press), 484–503.

Schweitzer, A. (2000), *The Quest of the Historical Jesus* (London: SCM Press).

Theissen, G. (1987), *The Shadow of the Galilaean: The Quest of the Historical Jesus in Narrative Form* (London: SCM Press).

Tsakiridou, C. A. (2013), *Icons in Time, Persons in Eternity: Orthodox Theology and the Aesthetics of the Christian Image* (Farnham: Ashgate).

Ward, B. (trans.) (1975), *The Sayings of the Desert Fathers: The Alphabetical Collection* (London: Mowbray).

Wasiolek, E. (ed. and trans.) (1967), *Fyodor Dostoevsky: The Notebooks for The Idiot* (Chicago: University of Chicago Press).

White, P. (1964), *Riders in the Chariot* (New York: Penguin Books).

Williams, R. (2005), *Grace and Necessity: Reflections on Art and Love* (London: Continuum).

Williams, R. (2008), *Dostoevsky: Language, Faith and Fiction* (Waco: Baylor University Press).

Wittgenstein, L. (1980), *Vermischte Bemerkungen/Culture and Value*, trans. Peter Winch (Oxford: Blackwell).

Wood, R. C. (2004), *Flannery O'Connor and the Christ-Haunted South* (Grand Rapids, Mich.: Eerdmans).

CHAPTER 32

··

CHRIST IN ART FROM THE BAROQUE TO THE PRESENT

··

LAWRENCE S. CUNNINGHAM

INTRODUCTION

ONE conspicuous thread of the sixteenth-century Protestant Reformation's theology was a strong aniconic tendency. Many Reformers saw the devotional use of images as a violation of the biblical Decalogue prohibiting both the making of 'graven images' and 'bowing down' or 'serving them' (Exod. 20:4–5). As a result of this reading of Scripture many once Catholic churches now in the hand of the Reform had their sculpture destroyed, their paintings removed, their stained glass windows replaced, and frescos whitewashed over. Such iconoclasm was not universal among the churches of the Reformation but was not infrequent. The Catholic response to this prohibition was stipulated at the twentieth-fifth session of the Council of Trent in 1563 stating that images of Christ, Mary, and the other saints should be 'set up and kept, particularly in churches' and that honor and reverence is due to them because such honor is 'referred to the original'. It is worth noting that the pertinent canons of the Council of Trent referred to the canons of the Second Council of Nicaea which, in the eighth century, decreed the legitimacy of the veneration of icons, a decree that brought about the end of the iconoclast controversy that once divided the Church in the Christian East.

It was inevitable that the Catholic insistence on the legitimacy of the visual arts would shape the work of artists who were employed by their patrons. The flourishing movement of baroque art produced at the end of the sixteenth century and regnant well into the seventeenth derived much of its energy from the Catholic reaction to the Reformation's resistance to the visual arts. Baroque painting had its origins in Rome (mainly under the influence of Caravaggio) with painters like the Spanish-born Jose Ribera (1591–1652) coming to Italy to follow Caravaggio's style. However, soon the influence of Caravaggio became an international phenomenon represented in Spain by Diego Velazquez (1599–1660); in Flanders by Peter Paul Rubens (1577–1640); and in France by Georges de la Tour (1593–1652). The greatest of the seventeenth-century baroque artists—and one who was not a Catholic—was Rembrandt Van Rijn (1606–69).

THE CHRIST OF BAROQUE ART

A contemporary art critic has called Caravaggio de Merisi (1571–1610) the 'master of making strange'. His *The Calling of Saint Matthew* (1600–2) depicts Jesus, bathed in light, somewhat obscured by the figure of Saint Peter pointing towards a table of seated men. Most commentators see the young man, dressed in late Renaissance finery, as Saint Matthew but others have noted the man in shadows at the end of the table with a money bag and coins as the tax collector turned apostle. The vivid juxtaposition of dark and light, characteristic of his work, is called *tenebrism*. Caravaggio sets the scene as if it were taking place in his own city of Rome as he did in his *Supper at Emmaus* where Christ (oddly depicted as young and unbearded—an allusion to his post-resurrection state?) is seated in a Roman trattoria amid typical Roman types.

Many scholars have argued that the settings of Caravaggio's sacred images were inspired by the recommendation of Saint Ignatius of Loyola's *Spiritual Exercises* that encouraged those who meditated on the life of Christ to imagine the scenes as if the person who was meditating were actually there seeing the scene and participating in it. (Ignatius called this meditative practice the 'composition of place'.) Whether or not this was the case it is certainly true, as one of his contemporaries put it, that Caravaggio painted *fra secolo e devoto*—between the sacred and the profane.

Caravaggio's dramatic juxtaposition of light and darkness had a deep impact on painters in the North. The triptych painted by Peter Paul Rubens (1577–1640) between 1610 and 1614 for the Cathedral of Our Lady in Antwerp has a central panel with a vividly bright dead Christ at the center of the painting shedding some of his light on the grieving Mary at the lower left with the muscular figures at top left and bottom right emerging from the darkness. Done between 1612 and 1614 it has a counter point in another panel depicting the raising of Christ on the Cross with the living Christ diagonally depicted in the exact opposite as his deposition shown in the center panel. Both scenes clearly chose influences from the South: the musculature of all the male figures is reminiscent of Michelangelo; the vivid palette reminds us of Venice; and the dramatic chiaroscuro, the dramatic juxtaposition of light and darkness, indicates how much the influence of Caravaggio had traveled.

Diego Velazquez (1599–1660) painted his stunning *Crucifixion* (1632) a year after he returned to his native Spain from studies in Italy. Set against a background of deep black, the figure of Christ stands out in brightness. A small halo of light appears behind his head. Caught at the moment of his death, the figure of Christ sags as his arms create a shallow V under the weight of his body. This powerful rendering of the crucifixion has had a long-standing influence on subsequent popular art. Many a crucifix hanging in classrooms, cells of monks and nuns, and in private homes can claim an ancestry harkening back to this painting. In 1920 the Spanish poet Miguel de Unamuno would compose a lengthy poem *El Cristo de Velazquez* where he would praise the 'white body' of Christ 'like a mirror of the Father of light/the life giving sun'.

The French painter Georges de la Tour (1593–1652) inherited the baroque interest in chiaroscuro via the northern followers of Caravaggio. Unlike Caravaggio or Rubens, his religious paintings do not tend to the dramatic. His *Saint Joseph the Carpenter* (1642), now in the Louvre, depicts the youthful Christ holding a candle at the right of the painting whose light illuminates the face of Christ while shedding some lesser light on the face of Joseph whose body is set in the shadows as he works with a wood drill. Most of the later work of de la Tour took up religious themes inspired, it has been surmised, by his participation in a Franciscan revival held in his native region of Lorraine.

The greater painters of the baroque period were Catholic with the notable exception of the Dutch artist Rembrandt Van Rijn (1606–69). He inherited the technique of chiaroscuro from the painters of the South but is universally praised for his ability to make light seem to emerge from the background of the art work itself rather from some exterior source. A prolific painter of biblical themes, his *Raising of the Cross* (1632) features a Christ, bathed in white light, set at an angle in the frame with a small figure of a man in a blue beret at the bottom left looking up at Christ. Many commentators see that gazing figure as the artist himself. It is instructive to compare the painting with that of Rubens who took on the same topic because Rembrandt sets his scene in a less theatrical setting but, like Rubens, still highlights the body of Christ in light.

Rembrandt was also a prolific maker of etchings (for a period he owned his own print shop) the most famous of which is his 'Hundred Guilder Print' (c.1647) in which Christ emerges from a crowd of the sick to speak to children thus placing into one scene two Gospel topics of Jesus healing and his use of the child as an exemplar of the devoted follower of his teaching. Rembrandt often turned to images of Christ from the Gospels (the circumcision, the presentation in the Temple, the flight into Egypt, etc.) including a striking image of *The Descent from the Cross* (c.1632) which may be considered as a counterpart to his later painting of the *Raising of the Cross* discussed above.

Towards the Modern

While the depiction of Christ in baroque art had its own distinctive style, the themes had a long history behind them. Depictions of the Passion of Christ had roots in the mediaeval interest in the suffering of Christ driven, mainly, by Franciscan inspiration. Scenes from the life of Christ, rooted in the New Testament, served pedagogical ends reinforcing preaching and catechesis. The depiction of a robust bearded male reflected the Renaissance interest in human anatomy while the emphasis on Christ, bathed in light, was intended to *show* the truth about the one who was described as the 'light of the world'. Baroque painting, in short, had its own particular characteristics but it drew upon technical achievements gained in the Renaissance but its spiritual armoire had roots in centuries of artistic reflections on the person and message of Christ. It was an art that emphasized the narrative of Christ's life and death. It served pedagogical and homiletic purposes while its presence in churches and monastic establishments was in obedience to the encouragement of the Catholic reform stipulated by the Council of Trent. The matter was succinctly summarized by Saint Ignatius of Loyola, the founder of the Jesuits, in his eighth rule for 'thinking with the church': 'We ought to praise the ornamentations and structures of churches; also images and their veneration according to what they represent.'

The high art of the European eighteenth and nineteenth centuries was not centrally concerned with depictions of Christ. The reasons for this lack of emphasis are not difficult to explain: patronage had shifted from the Church to the wealthy aristocratic clientele who could afford such art; the central place of religious fervor had become attenuated in the face of Enlightenment critique; the emergent success of science left little room for religious sentiment to find expression. Even a Catholic artist like the Italian sculptor Antonio Canova (1757–1822) who spent much of his career in Rome derived most of his patronage from those who desired classical subjects (or papal tombs!) and portrait sculpture (including one of George Washington for an American client). In his vast oeuvre only an incomplete *Pietà*, of which we only have some scale models in clay and bronze done in the last years of his life, represent an interest in the figure of Christ.

It was in the rise of Romanticism in the late eighteenth century that one finds a renewed preoccupation with the traditional themes of the Gospel depictions of Christ as a central subject of artistic meditation. A small number of the Brotherhood of Saint Luke founded in Germany in 1809 settled in Rome to attempt to recapture the spirit of mediaeval and early Renaissance art. Later called (pejoratively) the 'Nazarenes', their leader Johann Overbeck (1789–1869) brought a large unfinished canvas *Christ's Entry into Jerusalem* which was completed in 1824 and later installed in the Marienkirche in Lubeck but, alas, destroyed by Allied bombs in 1943. Many of the Nazarenes returned to Germany where their influence was felt in religious art and liturgical decoration especially in those places, mainly among the Benedictines, where there was a renewed interest in the liturgy of the Church.

Partially inspired by the Nazarenes, a small number of British artists founded the Pre-Raphaelite Brotherhood with the same desire to rekindle a spiritual sense in art and to resist what they saw as the cold rationalism of neo-classical art trends. These artists were not Catholic but drew on Catholic sources as part of their aesthetic interests. Two paintings of Christ by artists associated with group merit some attention. When John Everett Millias exhibited his *Christ in the Household of his Parents* in 1850 it provoked a huge public scandal because of the naturalism reflected in the Holy Family and the homely setting Millais used to depict the sacred characters at home. Despite the outcry the painting was defended by the contemporary critic John Ruskin who praised its rendering of nature.

By contrast, William Holman Hunt's *The Light of the World*, exhibited in 1854, was an immediate success. Christ, standing in a garden setting looking towards a closed door entangled in vines, held a glowing lamp in his hand which visually alluded to Christ as the 'Light of the World' and the psalmist's assertion that God is a 'lamp unto my feet'. One art historian has argued that it was the single most important depiction of Christ in the English-speaking world in its day (Finaldi 2000: 34). When it was taken on tour to the Commonwealth countries at the beginning of the twentieth century people lined for hours to see it. Hunt himself confessed that he was himself converted to Christianity while in the process of painting it.

In the late 1940s the American artist and illustrator Warner Sallman (1892–1968) did a version of the Hunt painting under the title *Christ at the Heart's Door* inspired, as he said, by the Holman Hunt picture. Sallman, however, was better known for a 1935 painting *The Head of Christ* which has become the best-known rendition of Jesus in Protestant circles in the twentieth century. It has been estimated that hundreds of thousands of versions of that painting as reproductions as small as 'holy cards' have been sold and versions of it are commonly found in churches, parsonages, schools, and other church institutions despite the frequent criticism of the painting's sentimental approach to the figure of Christ.

THE TWENTIETH CENTURY: PROPHETIC THEMES

While the major artists represented in the rise of Impressionism and beyond can be named as occasionally showing interest in the figure of Christ, that interest tends mainly to the tendency of artists to look back on their artistic ancestors to energize their own work. Even Pablo Picasso, as militant an unbeliever as can be imagined, drew some inspiration from the crucified Christ of Velazquez for some studies he did earlier in his career.

If the nineteenth-century Pre-Raphaelites favored a tender alluring figure of Christ, the German-Danish expressionist Emil Nolde (1867–1956) also taught that religious painting could engender deep emotional responses but his *Crucifixion* (1912–13) had nothing of the tender about it. Inspired by Grunewald's late mediaeval *Isenheim Crucifixion*, Nolde's Christ writhes in agony with the onlookers distorted in either grief or hate made all the more vivid by his broad strokes and garish palette. Despite his intense nationalism, Nolde's art was judged by the Nazi regime as 'degenerate' and after 1941 he was forbidden to paint or to exhibit his art by the German government.

In 1938, in response to the Nazi's pogrom known as *Kristallnacht* where Jewish shops in Germany were looted and destroyed, the Russian-French Jewish painter Marc Chagall (1887–1985) painted his *White Crucifixion* (1938) showing a crucified Christ wearing a loincloth modeled on the Jewish prayer shawl (*tallit*) floating over a Jewish town besieged by rioters. At the corner of the painting is a lone figure with a placard saying *Ich bin Jude* (I am a Jew) which Chagall later added to the painting. One of Chagall's most famous paintings (Pope Francis names it his favorite work of art) it is a damning indictment of a 'Christian' people who persecuted Jews in the name of Western values. The *White Crucifixion* is only one of many depictions Chagall made over his artistic career but it is his most famous one.

Of all the modernist masters of the twentieth century no painter was more dedicated to Christian themes in general and the life of Christ in particular than the French painter and print maker Georges Rouault (1871–1958). An early member of the Fauves and deeply influenced by Expressionism, Rouault was a devout Catholic close to such French intellectuals as Leon Bloy and Raissa and Jacques Maritain. At the end of the First World War he began work on a series of prints that he exhibited as a suite only in 1948. Of the 58 sheets in the portfolio, each with an inscription either from Scripture or a phrase from the artist, more than a dozen are devoted to the figure of Christ including three detailing his crucifixion. The title of the entire work is *Miserere et Guerre*. Rouault's art is characterized by dark brush outlines reflecting, perhaps, his early training as a worker in stained glass. His intention was to show the perennial relevance of the life and Passion of Christ. Plate #31 depicts *Veronica's Veil* with the inscription that reads 'And *Veronica with her soft linen still walks the road*' inviting the viewer to imitate the woman who wiped the face of Christ. Plate #35, shows Christ sagging under the weight of his crucified body with the inscription, borrowed from Blaise Pascal, *'Jesus will be in agony until the end of the world'*.

Emil Nolde, a Protestant, Marc Chagall, a Jew, and Georges Rouault, a Catholic, all had this one common inspiration in depicting the crucifixion of Christ, namely, their desire to make a prophetic statement. Nolde did so to evoke a passionate spiritual response against the sterility of academic art; Chagall to render judgment on the anti-Semitism of the putative Christian West; and Rouault to express his deep indignation at the cost of war on the world, especially the world of the forgotten poor.

Of course, these were not the only artists who saw in the person of Christ a way to cry out for social justice. The English pacifist and Catholic convert Eric Gill (1882–1940) produced a prodigious amount of Christian art in his lifetime. He was a controversial person in his own right, not least for his Leeds University War Memorial (1922–3) depicting Christ cleansing the Temple courtyard of the money changers with a whip of cords as pawnbrokers, financiers, politicians, and their wives fled away from the scourge. To underline his message that war was fundamentally driven by greed and cupidity, he carved (Gill was famous for his calligraphy) a line from the prophets (mercifully it was in Latin): *'Go to now, you rich, weep and howl in your miseries, which shall come upon you. Your riches are putrid'*. Despite howls of protest, Gill's memorial was erected near the university library and remains there to this day.

The German-born print maker Fritz Eichenberg (1901–90) fled Germany at the rise of National Socialism. Of a pacifist bent after the horrors of the First World War, he joined the Society of Friends (Quakers) in 1940. Long distinguished as a print maker, he met Dorothy Day in 1949 and from then until his death contributed illustrations for *The Catholic Worker*. Of his many prints, three are conspicuous for their theme of the Christ who is hidden in the poor. *Christ of the Bread Line* depicts a queue of shabby street people with Christ in their midst identifiable by the halo around his head. *Christ the*

Stranger shows Christ with his back to the viewer seated at a round table with a group of indigents sharing a meal. It has lingering echoes of both the Last Supper and the breaking of bread at Emmaus. Finally, there is *Christ of the Homeless* showing Christ under a lamp post that looks similar to a cross, embracing two figures who live on the street. All three of these woodcuts (of which Eichenberg was a master) gain their strength from the artist's capacity to contrast darkness and light thus harkening back to the baroque masters of the chiaroscuro.

TWENTIETH CENTURY: OTHER APPROACHES

The Spanish surrealist Salvador Dali (1904–89), motivated by his return to his childhood Catholic origins, produced three paintings depicting Christ between 1950 and 1955. They rank as some of the most famous and best-loved religious paintings of the twentieth century despite some critics who regard the works as veering close to pure kitsch. *The Crucifixion of Saint John of the Cross* (1951) depicts Christ on the Cross floating against a black background. Inspired by an ink-on-paper sketch attributed to the sixteenth-century Spanish mystic Saint John of the Cross (1542–91), the viewer is looking down on the bowed head of Christ as if looking from a vantage point above Christ while below him is a seascape with fishing boats. Dali actually employed a stunt man to pose in the manner of the figure he wanted and Dali painted on his easel poised above the model in order to fix the exact angle he desired.

Three years later, in 1954, Dali turned again to the subject of the crucifixion in a painting he originally called 'Corpus Hypercubus'. The figure of the Crucified One almost floats in front of a cross consisting of cube forms reflecting the artist's fascination with mathematics in general and geometry in particular. In place of the nails are smaller cube forms, four in number, that also seem to float in front of the body of Christ who is bathed in light. Christ has no crown of thorns and no visible nail points. At the lower left is a portrait of the artist's wife Gala representing Mary (Magdalene?). This 1954 *Crucifixion* (as it is now known) reflects the Dali's fascination with the figure of Christ as he is depicted reflecting the artist's roots in Surrealism and his growing fascination with geometrical forms.

In both crucifixions Dali himself insisted that he would not paint Christ as tortured or twisted in pain but as one who was beautiful after the manner of the beauty of God reflected in the humanity of Jesus. The final painting by Dali taking up the theme of Christ is the 1955 *Sacrament of the Last Supper*. Christ, seated at the center of the table dressed in the robes traditionally seen in resurrection paintings, is surrounded by his disciples (although none are looking at him) in a glassed-in room of five-sided (pentacular) windows. Above the seated Christ is the figure of another man who seems to represent the glorified Christ hovering above the Christ at table. Behind the glassed-in room there is a seascape and distant mountains. Dali himself, commenting on his intentions, later said of this painting that the effect he desired to achieve was a kind of 'mystical realism' for our age similar to that reflected in the great Spanish painters of the baroque age like Zurbaran whose works he had carefully studied over the years.

The English artist Graham Sutherland (1903–80) was an almost exact contemporary of Salvador Dali. A prolific painter, sculptor, and print maker, he was commissioned in the early 1950s to design a tapestry for the English cathedral of Coventry that had been almost totally destroyed in the Second World War. Sutherland worked on the design for most of the decade with the intention of depicting Christ in glory according to the instructions given him by the cathedral authorities. The finished project depicted a hieratic figure of Christ in a mandorla with four arms depicting the traditional symbols of the four evangelists. At the bottom of the piece is a tiny lone figure standing beneath Christ modeled on some images of survivors of the Buchenwald concentration camp that Sutherland had seen after the war. Below that is a square within which is a crucified Christ whose image looks back to the crucifixion of the Isenheim altarpiece. That crucifixion is at roughly eye level with the altar that stands in front of the tapestry. When the design was complete, Sutherland had the tapestry woven in France and then brought back to England. It was installed over a two-day period in 1962 in the apse of the cathedral where it remains to this day. It is one of the largest tapestries in the world measuring roughly 78 by 38 feet. The standard title of the work is *Christ in Glory in the Tetramorph* with the 'tetramorph' indicating the four evangelists and their symbols framing the figure of Christ.

Jacob Epstein (1888–1959), an American-born British citizen, contributed a large outdoor sculpture of *Saint Michael's Victory over the Devil* (1958) attached to the same cathedral at Coventry but four years earlier he executed a large figure of Christ, cast in aluminum, for Llandaff Cathedral in Wales. *Christ in Majesty* (1954) floats in front of a large concrete cylinder which is seated on a large arch that expands over the nave of the cathedral. The figure of Christ looks frontally towards the entrance with his hands extended as if inviting the visitor to enter the church. Earlier in his career Epstein cast a free-standing figure of the resurrected Christ still swathed in burial clothes with one hand gesturing to the wound in his other hand. Of this figure of *Christ* (1917–19) Epstein remarked in his autobiographical memoir that it 'stands and accuses the world of its grossness, inhumanity, cruelty, and beastliness, for the World War ...' (quoted in Finaldi 2000: 194).

The British painter Stanley Spencer (1891–1959) was a devout non-conformist Christian who worshiped regularly in the chapel of his native village of Cookham, a place to which he was devoted. Apart from some time in London studying art and service in the First World War where he saw the horrors of war as an ambulance attendant, Spencer lived most of his life in his native Cookham. Singularly interested in how the person of Jesus would look and act in an English village, he produced paintings of Jesus carrying his Cross through the high street of Cookham as well as a dramatic vision of the final resurrection as he imagined it taking place in the village graveyard. Spencer worked on a huge set of paintings under the working title of 'Christ Preaching at Cookham Regatta' but alas, while this ambitious work had many scenes of the villagers he never finished the work so we do not know how he would have depicted Christ. Three years before his death, Spencer did a 'Deposition from the Cross' (1956) depicting a young, unbearded, and nearly nude Christ being lowered from the Cross by similarly unclothed young men while, on the viewer's left, Mary, in a blue gown is partially depicted with a young man (the apostle John?) restraining her in her grief. Oddly, at the bottom of the painting is a scene of a huge roundish white rock being opened at a rock entrance; hence the full title of the work: *The Deposition and the Rolling Away of the Stone*.

The Vence Chapel designed by Henri Matisse (1869–1954) is arguably the most complete Christian ensemble built by a major artist in the twentieth century. Done at the request of a nun who had once been Matisse's nurse, the artist designed the chapel, all the interior art, the liturgical furnishings, the stained glass windows, and the stations of the Cross, completing the work in 1951 after its actual beginning in 1949. Technically known as the Chapel of Our Lady of the Rosary, it was meant to be the chapel for a woman's high school administered by Dominican nuns. Matisse himself, baptized a Catholic, was in fact an unbeliever who undertook the commission as a favor for the young nurse turned nun who had cared for him so faithfully while he was in poor health.

The figure of Christ appears in an altar crucifix designed by Matisse and in the stations of the Cross which the artist conceived of as a single narrative ensemble as well as a sketched Madonna and Child. What is most striking about the figure of Christ (as well as the other human figures) is that Matisse eschewed giving the faces human figures; thus there are no clear hints that the artist drew on the earlier iconographical tradition of Western religious art. Instead, the face of Christ is depicted only as an ovoid figure without distinguishing facial characteristics. The altar crucifix, for example, has the body of Christ traced out in those perfect lines for which Matisse was a sure master but done only in linear outline. It is almost as if Matisse left us an armature for a later sculptor to supply a full body. One is tempted to think that the faceless Christ of the Matisse stations of the Cross and the altar crucifix are a sign of how the modernist artistic tradition had come to an end with respect to Christ until someone came who could give him a personal identity.

Towards the Present

How fares the figure of Jesus Christ in the world of the visual arts today? The answer to that question is as complex as the situation of Christianity itself. The churches with a strong liturgical tradition still expect an iconography pertinent to their worship. The growth of those churches in the non-Western world will hardly feel a need to imitate an art whose intellectual and cultural and religious roots are in the West. The burgeoning Pentecostal and Evangelical congregations around the world carry with them, typically, a bias against images. Catholic churches in the West went through a mini-period of iconoclasm as older churches, heavily imagistic, were stripped down in favor of more austere church buildings free from the clutter of devotional images and heavily narrative stained glass. That being said, there are some trends that are worth noting.

First, it should be remembered that in the Christian Orthodox and Oriental churches the icon has been a constant. Contemporary icon writers follow a tradition that goes back over a millennium adhering (with regional variations) to a discipline that does not favor innovation but, rather, an attempt to deepen the spiritual value of composing icons that reflect the reality behind them. The traditional maker of icons can be compared to the contemporary musician who plays Bach not by attempting to alter the notes but by attempting to master the composition handed down with deeper refinement.

Icons are an instrument before which one prays and contemplates in order to penetrate into the mystery being depicted. While the tradition of icons is central to Orthodox liturgical and spiritual life it is only in the more recent past that their power has been fully appreciated in the Western Church. It is now not uncommon to see traditional icons of Chris, Mary, saints, and angels used in the churches of the West as part of the visual life of churches, religious houses, and homes. This Western renaissance of transporting icons into liturgical and non-liturgical services has been accompanied by a resurgence of Western artists apprenticing themselves to traditional icon writers in order to learn this spiritual craft.

The Franciscan friar Robert Lentz (1946–) and his one-time student, the Jesuit William Hart McNicholls (1949–) have become extremely popular (and quite controversial) as writers of icons. While both reflect a mastery of the Byzantine style of icon painting, they have been criticized for stepping away from classical iconic forms to portray non-saints (Gandhi, Thomas Merton, etc.) as well as non-traditional images of Christ. Despite that criticism, their popularity is a fair indication of how icons have become a favorite form of artistic representation in Western Christianity.

Second, while this chapter has concentrated on the high culture of art in the mainly European past since the baroque era, it should be noted that in the past century there has been a creative explosion of Christian art coming from the younger churches of Africa, Asia, and elsewhere. That art has been a natural outgrowth of the desire to inculturate the faith in forms native to other cultures possessed of their own artistic vocabulary. Artists, little known in the West, have developed artistic representations of Christ reflective of Asian, Indian, Oceanic, and African cultures. A recent collection of such art made the point by citing the Japanese artist Masao Takenaka: 'Communication through art transcends national and linguistic boundaries … It invites people to respond to the prayers of Christ "that all may be one"' (O'Grady 2001: 8). Takenaka's words preface a collection of Christian art from around the world inspired and supported by the World Council of Churches.

CONCLUSION

Finally, we should say a few words about the function of art depicting the person and work of Jesus Christ. The Eastern tradition of the icon expects the viewer to confront the person of Christ depicted in the icon in order to pass through the image to the person represented. That attitude has been a constant in Orthodox and Oriental Christianity. Many baroque depictions of Christ were intensely narrative in their effort to retell the mysteries of Christ from infancy through the resurrection. Modernist artists harkened back (especially) to the crucifixion in order to speak prophetically to a world of hatred, violence, and the strife of war. Contemporary artists have made some attempts to express the mystery of Christ and his life in ways reflective of our own secular age while artists in the emerging worlds of Christianity attempt the same in a fashion that pays tribute to their own cultures while attempting to plumb the meaning of the One who 'is the image of the invisible God' (Col. 1:15).

SUGGESTED READING

Beckett (2011); Drury (1999); Hall (2011); Harries (2013).

BIBLIOGRAPHY

Beckett, W. (2011), *The Iconic Jesus* (Boston, Mass.: Pauline Publications).
Drury, J. (1999), *Painting the Word: Christian Pictures and Their Meanings* (New Haven: Yale University Press).
Finaldi, G. (2000), *The Image of Christ* (London: The National Gallery Company).
Hall, M. (2011), *The Sacred Image in the Age of Art* (New Haven: Yale University Press).
Harries, R. (2013), *The Image of Christ in Modern Art* (Burlington, Vt.: Ashgate).
O'Grady, R. (ed.) (2001), *Christ For All People: Celebrating a World of Christian Art* (Maryknoll, NY: Orbis Books).

PART VII

THE GRAMMAR OF CHRISTOLOGY: CHRISTOLOGICAL NORMS

CHAPTER 33

....

THE CHRISTOLOGICAL PRISM
Christology as Methodological Principle

....

ROBERT J. WOŹNIAK

Some time ago, Kathryn Tanner developed an interesting idea of how better to read the whole body of various dogmatic disciplines through Christological lenses. Her hermeneutical insight in *Christ the Key* (Tanner 2010), a book which synthesizes her former project *Jesus Humanity and the Trinity* (Tanner 2001), consists of establishing Christology as a material center of theology (cf. also McCord Adams 2006: 1). Tanner interprets the main structure and material content of particular treatises of Christian dogmatic (especially its anthropology, theology of grace, and Trinity) via a Christological prism. It leads to a much broader, and better, articulation of the unity of dogmatic truths from the meaning of Christ's events. Christ's person and work become the hermeneutical key which enlightens all the different parts and puzzles of Christian teaching and its genuine worldview. There is no question in my mind that such a procedure is very classical both in its fundamental aim and origin. The novelty it brings consists in an attempt to create a kind of Christological dogmatic—a material dogmatic which pretends to be a Christological assessment of the theological problematic, a kind of Christ-centered theology (Tanner 2010: vii).

In what follows I try to elevate Tanner's idea into the basic context of theological methodology. My point of view, however, is much more formal than essential. Tanner's use of Christology as the 'meaning middle point' of all theological treatises implies several underlying, tacit methodological presuppositions. I will argue that the so-called Christocentrism of Christian theology has to be understood first of all as a methodological principle. In other words: Theology has to take Christology into account because the methodological axis of Christology is the material organization of the Christ-events together and of their constitutive features. Of course, both of these perspectives, in my opinion, are strictly related and are ordained to each other.

The first steps toward a more complete consideration of a Christological articulation of this methodology will be taken from two preliminary points of view: systematical and historical. Both of these will constitute the background of the main core of my argument.

The Basic Problems of Modern Systematic Theology and Theological Systematization

Systematic or dogmatic theology faces today, in my opinion, three main problems. The first is the issue of the fundamental structure of dogmatic theology, which has undergone a powerful restructuring in the modern age, especially from the seventeenth century and onward. In the attempt to justify its scientific nature, and in its confrontation with the dominion of newly rising empirical sciences, systematic theology has begun to fragment its own body into different treatises. The main idea was to divide the classical exposition of Christian truth into more specialized parts. In this process systematic theology lost its own unity and pre-established sense of totality of revealed truth. Such a state of affairs produced a decentralization of systematic theology: slowly it began to lose its central truth which is a Trinitarian God in his self-donation to human beings. Trinitarian theology was displaced and sometimes was overlapped by different treatises which pretended to describe the essence of Christianity from the standpoint of their fragmented perspective. God, in his mystery, became one of the topics of theology, and in no way was special and privileged.

The second problem is related to the so-called Christocentric character of theology. Christology guaranteed properly, for many centuries, the Christian character of theology. Theology was conceived to be Christian because of its Christological focal point, of its Christ-centered nature. Such a state of affairs led from time to time, *de facto*, to some aberrations which can be characterized as (*pace* Congar 1986) Christomonism. What is peculiar to such a view is an unusual and misleading concentration on Christology which saturates the limits of theology. Christology is treated here as a *telos* of theological reflection, and as its unique topic, as its starting point and ultimate destination and dead end. One may allude here to a famous statement of Rahner, who saw clearly the danger of this monism. According to him most Christians would not notice any difference if the word Trinity were banned and erased from prayer books and handbooks of theology.

The third issue or problem concerns the very nature of Trinitarian theology. Theology in modernity witnesses to the rise of a double Trinitarian orientation in reaction to the aforementioned processes of fragmentation and decentralization. The first orientation is historical and its protagonist is Hegel. His metaphysical project based on Trinitarian consideration of the importance of the dialectic represents probably one of the most accomplished inclusions of Trinitarian dogma into a metaphysical explanation of being. Hegel's systematic thought produced, as its first fruit, an onto-logical identification of God's inner life with history, time, and world. The intrinsic pantheism of Hegel's thought established history as a radical and determinative her-meneutical background for theology. One of the basic statements of theology should be, in such a Hegelian perspective, the acclamation of God's historicity (Murphy 2007: 237 n.): The Trinity is an historical process and 'God's being is in becoming' (Jüngel). God not only appears in his revelation within history, but he produces him-self through and in it. Trinitarian pantheism helps Hegel to refocus all theology and philosophy on the Trinity, nonetheless, at the very same time it introduces a deadly virus into the body. On the other hand, and to a certain degree in contrast and oppo-sition to the Hegelian paradigm, modern theology sees the appearance of a strong tendency to place theological statements out of their historical context. This program was taken up and put into practice especially by various strands of neo-scholastic her-meneutics of doctrine. It consists in *remotio*, in putting God off the stage of history. In such a paradigm, historical revelation is the way to know God in his transcendence, in the historical sphere of his divine existence. It leads to the dissolution of the natural (from a theological perspective) link between revelation and history. In this account, revelation shows divine truth in history but without taking into account the fact that the very existence of history is the main means of revelation. The first and main fact of revelation is that God came into history and became part of it (cf. de Lubac 1974). The neo-scholastic pattern focuses on this ontological question and is interested in an historical constitution of divine mystery. It does not take into account important and intrinsic historical components of the Christian idea of revelation. Both of the above paradigms lead to some internal impasses in systematic theology. Centralizing the totality of doctrine on the Trinity, the historical paradigm mingles divine mystery with history to such an extent that God is only a story; the real meaning of his own divine existence is nothing more than an historical epitome. It produces finally a dis-sociation of both God and history. On the other hand, neo-scholasticism seems to overlook the real value of history in the factual event of revelation. The main problem in both options consists in how to relate God to history. In the first account, God's being is identified with history and is reduced to mere narration (God becomes the story); in the second one, he is transcendent and far from history despite his coming into it, which is considered to be of lesser importance.

To sum up, let us posit a global question: Is there any common denominator of these described attitudes and processes? What is the basic problem in all three men-tioned issues? In my opinion, it is the relationship between Christology and Trinitarian theology. I call this relationship a basic structure of theology. My thesis here is as fol-lows: we will be able to unify fragmented systematic theology, overcome erroneous Christomonism without losing justified Christocentrism, and find a proper and bal-anced articulation of historical principles in systematic theology, but only from the per-spective of a renewed awareness of the basic structure of theology. Now I wish to turn to its description from an historical point of view.

Historical Forms, Varieties, and Mutations of the Basic Structure of Theology

What are the most common historical paradigms of the basic structure of theology? How do different theologies deal with relating Christology and Trinitarian theology in the span of history? There is insufficient space here to present the full argument. I will deal only with the most significant moments of the long story.

A determinative role in this story is occupied by the New Testament. Recent scholarship is unequivocal: what gives the New Testament theology its specificity is, as Bauckham (1999) puts it, the inclusion of Christology into theology. It is precisely this inclusion which grounds the future development of Trinitarian theology. The New Testament doctrine of God is fully centered on Christ-events. This is a fundamental matrix of our classically interpreted basic structure of theology.

The mainstream of ancient Christian thought unifies Christology and Trinitarian faith in one meaningful system of Christian theology. It is characteristic of this period that the developments of Trinitarian and Christological dogma are coextensive not only in time but in the force of the same arguments. Let us consider one of the most representative theological systems of the fourth century, that of Athanasius of Alexandria. It is very well known that his articulation of Christ's divinity is based on soteriology and is its inner moment. Athanasius states that Christ is true God because he is the Savior of humankind. The belief in the divine nature of Christ is interconnected with a firm conviction that he is the unique Savior. What is of transcendent importance here is the moment in which a Trinitarian conviction (Christ is true God) springs from a Christological one (he is the redeemer). Christology is the very center of Trinitarian theology. Their mutual developments are motivated by soteriology. This is true even of later Christology, such as that elaborated after the First Council of Nicaea (325). Further explorations in Christology, which happened especially during the fifth and sixth centuries and are focused on the ontological structure of the Christ composited person, are nothing else than continual efforts to describe the divine mystery from the basic perspective of the Incarnation. They are theological because they are also Christological: incarnate Logos in his human body discloses something of the Trinitarian life. A kind of subordination of Christology to Trinitarian theology is the important mark of this classical model. Christology is taken into account here because it generates specifically Christian theological meaning. There is no theology (especially Trinitarian theology) without Christology; there is no genuine Christology which is not, at the same time, genuine theology.

Early theology does not know a division into treatises. It treats Christian truth in its organic totality and unity where all of the parts are interconnected to each other on the common ground of a basic relationship of Trinitarian faith and Christology. Creation theology can be of help here as a good example. Once again, Athanasius develops his theological account of creation inside the space created by the basic structure (especially in his work *On the Incarnation*). His theology of divine Logos as essentially related to the Father and his description of Logos' relationship with created beings prepares the very space for the new understanding of God's creative work. It is shaped by the same logic which Athanasius discovers to govern God's inner life: the Trinitarian principle of inner unity and plurality is the key to the created realm as well.

It is very significant how Athanasius grasped the unity of theology and articulated its grounding in a basic structure. Athanasius shows that theological elaboration of a singular topic of theology can be achieved fully only when it is put against the broader horizon constituted by the net of the internal connection between different aspects of Christian doctrinal and existential truth. In this theological net (*nexus mysterious*) a basic structure occupies a privileged position. It is important to notice that this Athanasian style can be found in the other ecclesiastical writers of the patristic era, both in the East and West (cf. Basil's *On the Holy Spirit*, or Hilary and Augustine's *De Trinitate*, among others). One can talk here about a theological style of reflection which makes the basic structure central for a theological methodology.

Such a classical model of basic structure developed in and from the struggle for orthodoxy but it is not the only one. Among ancients there were other versions of a basic structure which, in opposition to the classical one, pretended openly to interrupt the natural connection between Christology and Trinitarian theology. One can enumerate amongst them Arianism, Eunomianism, some versions of Monophysitism, and Nestorianism. There is neither necessity nor space here to describe their doctrinal details. Let it be enough to underline that all of these theological systems, operating inside a basic structure, try to disconnect Christology and theology; or, in other words, lead theology back to its pre-Christian status (in its double orientation: Judaization or Hellenization).

A formal distinction of the treatises, even if yet in a truly orthodox shape, appears for the first time in mediaeval theology, especially in the post-Lombardian methodological tradition of *Sentences*. A premodern dissolution of the basic structure, at least a formal one, is grounded in an attempt to group together various theological topics in detailed treatises. We can detect something of it in the most famous among Aquinas' works, his *Summa Theologiae*. Although more recent scholarship has insisted that it is not the most important and representative source of Aquinas' theology, still the *Summa Theologiae* was probably the most studied part of the whole of his system of thought. Thomas introduces Christology only in its third and last part. As is well known, the main structure of the *Summa* is based on the movement from Creator and its inner life (*prima pars*), through the mystery of creation (*secunda pars*), up to the *tertia pars* which describes the universal return of creatures to the Trinitarian God (the classical Neoplatonic *exitus–reditus* outline). Christology is introduced in this last stage of theological inquiry because of its place in the *reditus*: Christ is for all created beings their way back home to the Father. The striking thing is that Christology does not play any important or decisive structural role in the first part of *Summa*, where Thomas focuses largely on God. Aquinas did not have any problems with grasping that the Trinity is disclosed in the Christ-event.

Nonetheless his Trinitarian speculation in the *Summa* seems to be directed more to the task of preparing fully elaborated logical-metaphysical insight into Trinitarian revelation (which obviously is its great merit, cf. McCord Adams 2006: 80–143) than to its Christological exposition (even if it is planned to be a meditative practice). The formal link between Aquinas' Trinitarian theology and his Christology in the *Summa* is not strong enough and seems even a little superfluous. At least, there is no clear and direct genetic or organic interconnection between two treatises and even if such connection exists it points more in the direction from Trinitarian theology toward Christology than the other way round. For Thomas Aquinas the presentation of the doctrinal order of discovery (Christology as the starting point of our Trinitarian knowledge) should be preceded by the speculative order which places the reality itself at the very beginning of its investigation.

> There are two reasons why the knowledge of the divine persons was necessary for us. It was necessary for the right idea of creation. The fact of saying that God made all things by His Word excludes the error of those who say that God produced things by necessity. When we say that in Him there is a procession of love, we show that God produced creatures not because He needed them, nor because of any other extrinsic reason, but on account of the love of His own goodness. So Moses, when he had said, 'In the beginning God created heaven and earth', subjoined, 'God said, Let there be light', to manifest the divine Word; and then said, 'God saw the light that it was good', to show proof of the divine love. The same is also found in the other works of creation. In another way, and chiefly, that we may think rightly concerning the salvation of the human race, accomplished by the Incarnate Son, and by the gift of the Holy Ghost.
>
> (*ST* I, q.32, a.1, ad.3)

Trinitarian theology represents in this option the radical hermeneutical principle for Christology and soteriology (cf. Emery 2010: 419): that without precomprehension of the mystery of the Trinity no comprehension of Christology is possible.

The disconnection of Christology and Trinitarian theology achieved its climax in modern theology. The rudderless theology of modernity was preoccupied with what it for a long time considered as its main task: justification of its own scientific nature in face of other disciplines. A fragmented theology ultimately found its center in rational Christology which seemed to be the most appropriate candidate to occupy the central place in it. Modern ideas of science prompted adequate, that is, empirical modifications of traditional Christology. It was replaced by historical *jesuologie*, which from that time on became the only possible version of rational Christology. If there is any possibility of achieving truly scientific theology it can be realized solely through historical *Lebens-Jesu-Forschung*. Although Christology maintained its position in the very center of the theological *universum*, it was reduced to a mere empirical account of religious experience and an awareness of the concrete historical community. In virtue of this it was trampled within 'limits of the reason alone' *more* Kant. Such empirical mutation produced a situation in which the classical understanding of the fundamental task of theology was forgotten: theology *de facto* ceased to be the science of *Deus sub ratione deitatis*. Rational Christology helped to strip theology from its focus on the divine and rendered Trinitarian theology unnecessary, superfluous, and even dangerous.

Sooner or later, the modern reduction of theology to a rational, historical Christology has to generate a radical opposition. Such opposition rose in anti-liberal theology of the twentieth century, whose preeminent icon is Karl Barth. He restored the centrality of Trinitarian theology grounded in the very event of revelation in Christ. His initial intuition was brought to further completion by the Swiss theologian Hans Urs Von Balthasar. His fundamental theological (theo-phenomenological) insight is probably one of the most complete and radical forms of basic structure. For Von Balthasar, revelation has its main and central point in Christological *Gestalt* (figure). Von Balthasar's *Trilogy* begins with a long treatment of the theo-aesthetical dimension of the figure of revelation, and then it is continued in its dramatic and logical description. The Christological focal point of *Gestalt* is prominently present in all of these treatments and parts of the Trilogy. Von Balthasar produces his Trinitarian theology as a radicalization of the Christological dimension of revelation. Christology is the most decisive part and structure of his doctrine of God. There is no question that such a state of affairs originated in his admiration for patristic theology, whose main strategies he intends to repeat in his own system of thought contextualized by modernity and its philosophical milieu.

It is necessary to underline the fact that the radicalization of the classical form of basic structure in Von Balthasar is connected with his sensitivity to the historical dimension of Christology. It means practically that Von Balthasar mediates the totality of his theology by Christology focused on the meditation of the history of Jesus the Christ. This Irenaean and anti-Gnostic focus on *mysteria perpetrata in carne Christi* culminates in Von Balthasar's treatment of the Paschal mystery. The Christological mediation of Balthasarian theology is focused on it and springs from his meditation on the Paschal mystery. The Cross of Christ and his resurrection give Von Balthasar the basic shape of his doctrinal treatment of God. 'Basically', writes Von Balthasar, 'in Jesus Christ's death, descent into hell, and Resurrection, only one reality is there to be seen: the love of the triune God for the world, a love which can only be perceived through a co-responsive love' (Von Balthasar 1990: 262). Von Balthasar in this way succeeds in implying a classical theological model and, at the same time, in adding to its modern stress on history without producing any dialectical antithesis between them. His reconciliation of the aforementioned dimensions merits being proclaimed as a proper and original radicalization of the basic structure and it is an important achievement on the way to the full articulation of Trinitarian Christology. In the words of Aidan Nichols:

> Balthasar insisted, however, that the manner in which a theology is to be written is Christological from start to finish. He defined theology as a mediation between faith and revelation in which the Infinite, when fully expressed in the finite, i.e. made accessible to man, can only be apprehended by a convergent movement from the side of the finite, i.e. adoring, obedient faith in the God-man. Only thus can theology be Ignatian and produce 'holy worldliness', in Christian practice, testimony

and self-abandonment. Balthasar aimed at nothing less than a Christocentric revolution in Catholic theology. It is absolutely certain that the inspiration for this, derives, ironically for such an ultra-Catholic author, from the Protestantism of Karl Barth.

(Von Balthasar 1990: Introduction, 4–5)

The task mentioned here is still valid for contemporary theology which yet has to struggle to renew its basic structure, recovering it from a long period of neglect in which it has been practically forgotten.

Summarizing this historical sketch one can identify two main models of a basic structure. The classical (and at the same time orthodox) model links Trinitarian theology and Christology so closely that they mutually perpetuate and constitute each other in a kind of *theo*-logical osmotic perichoresis. The second type of basic structure emphasizes and opts for disconnection between the theological doctrine of God and Christology. In such a view theology and Christology can live—to some extent—each in its own independent, isolated intellectual ghetto. It is this mutual ghettoization of Christology and Trinitarian theology which produces an overarching impression of the lack of unity between the topics of theology. Such an impression is dangerous not only from the objective perspective of the credibility of doctrine, but also has disastrous effects in our theological education as well.

CHRISTOLOGY AS AN IN-FORMATIVE PRAXIS

If my argument is plausible, one should concede the great importance to a basic structure for the whole system of Christian theology. Why is a basic structure so fundamental? My personal opinion is that it is due to its structuring, its in-formative potential. This in-formative potential resides in Christology from which springs theology in all its variety. The *basic* structure of theology is basic because it shows the unavoidable origin of all theological reflection, which springs only and always from Christology. In some sense the basic structure, understood in its procedural dimension, enlightens the theological way to knowledge. It shows Christology as the central point for such a way. The Kantian critical question *what can we know?* has in theology a radically Christological character. A classically defined basic structure is the description of the creative, revelatory, heuristic potential of Christology. Without Christology there is no Christian theology at all: this is true not only from material but as well as from a methodological point of view.

That Christology informs theology means that it gives to it its proper Christian form, determining by this donative act its properly Christian content, character, discursive structure, shape, and even existence. The direction of thought, as we could see in the case of the classical basic structure, is this: from Christology to theology. Christology is always the first idea in Christian theology. The basic structure of theology presupposes the formal, methodological priority of Christology in theology; Christology was the starting point of Trinitarian doctrine, which by its own nature is the inner moment of Christological development. Christology is already always the core of the totality of theological reflection.

The fundamental task of Christology consists in offering theology the intellectual instruments which shape it to be properly Christian. Christology is not only a contemplative and speculative exercise; most basically it is also a fundamental methodological rule which enables Christian theology to be itself. In this way Christology identifies Christian theology twice: the first time when it collects and elaborates the basic data and meaning of a Christ-event and then (second) when it forms theology giving it its proper Christian character. One can describe Christology as systematic production of identity of Christian theology in a double sense: material and formal (methodological). There is a real need to distinguish in Christology two main dimensions or levels of meaning. The first one is properly speaking doctrinal: it contains basic, essential material truths about Christ's person and work. But there is another dimension in which Christology offers the necessary tool which identifies theology as Christian. Christology has to be understood from this point of view as a methodological principle of theology.

The in-formative potential of Christology is enclosed and expressed in a very special way in the Chalcedonian ὅρος, which *de facto* is methodological in its character. Like all of the dogmatic statements of the great councils, Chalcedon is, as well and first of all, a heuristic collection of rules which is intended to be a methodological guide as to how to interpret the rich and sometimes equivocal testimony of the written revelation. The Christological linguistic *redoublement* of φύσις and πρόσωπον (one person, two natures formula of the ὅρος) is to save the true orthodox meaning of the revelation effected in Christ (see Larchet 2011). Nonetheless, what is at stake in this statement of the faith is not only Christology. The Chalcedonian formula informs all the main topics of theology: it introduces the most fundamental description of the divine–world relation. Such description is possible because the Chalcedonian definition of faith presents one of the most basic and important theological statements about God, whose transcendence does not exclude true immanence. On this basis, the ὅρος offers a fundamental statement of Christian anthropology too: the human being has to be understood through and inside the hermeneutical horizon of the divine–human relationship. Even more so, some of the Fathers of the Church, of whom Maximus Confessor is probably the most prominent, saw in the ὅρος the essence of the Christian's own theological metaphysics. Christology is treated in this case as a most robust proper theological theory of being *qua* being.

In short: Chalcedon and its dogmatic definition informs and makes explicit the very grammar of Christian theology in the variety of its topics and issues. Even more, Christology itself is this grammar. One can risk affirming that one of the intentions of this council and its definition is to express the conviction that theology (and all its topics) is grounded in Christology. In such a way the Fathers of the council not only propose a solution to the concrete theological dispute of the early fifth century, but implicitly invites us to view theology from the Christological perspective, and to shape its content by putting it into the form pre-established in the Christological matrix. They offer not so much a Christocentric as a Christoformic theology because its first aim is explicitly theological. As Christ is the key to Christianity and its truth, Christology is the master key to theology. What we need is not so much a Christo-*centric* theology as one which is *Christo-formic.*

The Christological rule of faith proposed by the council represents the basic tool or instrument for theology and at the very same time its matrix. In my opinion, there is no doubt that the Chalcedonian ὅρος was and is for the mainstream of orthodoxy the most fundamental rule of thinking, a real center of all possible theology for all and also its starting point. The Chalcedonian doctrinal formula can be recognized as a universal and vast theological pattern of thought. This is why, from a practical point of view, the Christology of Chalcedon is the first point of reference which anyone should consult in the process of doing theology. To put it in a loosely Rahnerian formula, Chalcedon is the *Anfang,* the beginning, not only of every possible Christology, but of theology as well. It offers to all theological sentences their crucial grammar and structure: the theological meaning is already pre-established a priori in Christology.

From the practical point of view, Christological methodology *more* Chalcedon (a dogmatic formula as a universal thought-structure) is the act to be repeated—at least *tacitly* or *a priori*—in every singular and particular theological act. Once again the fundamental dimension here is the essential, organic, and generative mutual relation of Christology and Trinitarian theology, produced and grounded by and in Christology. I would say that the most informative moment of this Christological adventure of ideas is the mutuality (although not symmetry; cf. Bernardi 2012) existing in Christ between radical transcendence and immanence (Rahnerian version: every transcendental moment presupposes a categorial one). This equilibrium, protected and enclosed in the ὅρος, informs, gives existence and shape to proper Christian intellectual and existential οἶκος of truth. Even if it was achieved and formally stated only in the fifth century it was always tacitly presented in ancient παράδοσις.

Briefly, Christology is the very *habitus mentis* of Christian theology both from its very beginning and in virtue of its proper nature. (Saint Bonaventure can be named here as a good example of such a theological approach. The Christological counters of his theological epistemology are explicated especially in *De reductione artium ad theologiam*; see Bonaventure 1996; cf. Rorem 2012.) This is why it offers theology its first hermeneutical tool of reading and understanding revelation and in its light the totality of the cosmos.

Christology as the Prismatic Beryl of Theology

This informative activity of Christology can be best described via the metaphor of a prism, which can be used to refract or break light up into its constituent spectral colors, to reflect light, and also to split light into its component parts with different polarizations. It is like the famous *beryl* described by Cusanus in one of his *opusculi*:

Beryl stones are bright, white, and clear. To them are given both concave and convex forms. And someone who looks out through them apprehends that which previously was invisible. If an intellectual beryl that had both a maximum and a minimum form were fitted to our intellectual eyes, then through the intermediateness of this beryl the indivisible Beginning of all things would be attained.

(Cusanus, De Beryllo, 3; trans. Hopkins 1998: 792–3)

Christology informs theology, gives it its proper sense and shape and is its unifying principle because it works just as does a prism: it makes visible something that was previously invisible. Christology is the exercise in seeing the revealed shape (Von Balthasar's *Gestalt*) of the one who, in his very essence, is invisible.

From this perspective, one can only affirm that Christology is the essential *Gestalt* of revelation because it splits its light (which is its own) into components to allow us to see and to grasp the most important contours of theology and its contents. Theology is grounded in Christology, which is, in turn, subordinated to it and to its formal principle. Christology is not only about how to understand Christ, but first of all it is *the* way in which we can know God and our world, and be moved (or *reduced*) back to our triune Creator. (Bonaventure's famous idea of *reductio* is described by Allard 1969; Delio 2001: 158–69; Ciampanelli 2010: 141–89.) Christology is about seeing through and going back, returning to the Father (cf. John 14:1–12).

The destination of the Christologically informed human gaze goes to the very inner life of God which is presented in Christ in the world. Christ is the only possible icon of the Trinity. The unimaginable richness of divine life resides in him and informs the totality of Christian existence.

SUGGESTED READING

Bauckham (1999); Tanner (2010); Von Balthasar (1990).

BIBLIOGRAPHY

Allard, G.-H. (1969), *La Technique de la 'reductio' chez Bonaventure* (Grottaferrata: Collegio S. Bonaventura).

Ayres, L. (2010), *Augustine and the Trinity* (Cambridge: Cambridge University Press).

Bauckham, R. (1999), *God Crucified: Monotheism and Christology in the New Testament* (Grand Rapids, Mich.: Eerdmans).

Bernardi, P. (2012), *Il logos teandrico. La 'cristologia asimmetrica' nella teologia bizantino-ortodossa* (Rome: Città Nuova).

Bonaventure (1996), *St. Bonaventure on the Reduction of the Arts to Theology*, English and Latin edition prepared by Z. Hayes (New York: Franciscan Institute of St. Bonaventure University).

Ciampanelli, F. (2010), *'Hominem reducere ad Deum'. La funzione mediatrice del Verbo incarnato nella teologia di San Bonaventura* (Rome: Gregorian and Biblical Press).

Coakley, S. (2002), 'What Does Chalcedon Solve and What Does It Not? Some Reflections on the Status and Meaning of the Chalcedonian "Definition"', in S. T. Davis, D. Kendall, and G. O'Collins (eds), *The Incarnation: An Interdisciplinary Symposium on the Incarnation of the Son of God* (Oxford: Oxford University Press), 141–63.

Congar, Y. (1986), *The Word and the Spirit*, trans. D. Smith (San Francisco: Harper & Row).

de Lubac, H. (1974), *Dieu se dit dans l'histoire. La Révélation divine.* Foi vivante 159 (Paris: Cerf).

Delio, I. (2001), *Simply Bonaventure* (Hyde Park, NY: New City Press).

Emery, G. (2010), *The Trinitarian Theology of St Thomas Aquinas*, trans. F. A. Murphy (Oxford: Oxford University Press).

Gioia, L. (2009), *The Theological Epistemology of Augustine's De Trinitate* (Oxford: Oxford University Press).

Hopkins, J. (trans.) (1998), 'De Beryllo (On [Intellectual] Eyeglasses', in Nicholas of Cusa, *Metaphysical Speculations—Six Latin Texts Translated into English* (Minneapolis: Arthur J. Banning Press), 791–838.

Lafont, G. (1996), *Structures et methode dans la 'Somme theologique' de saint Thomas d'Aquin.* Cogitatio fidei 193 (Paris: Cerf).

Larchet, J.-C. (2011), *Personne et nature, La Trinité, Le Christ, L'homme. Contributions aux dialogues interorthodoxe et interchrétien contemporain* (Paris: Cerf).

McCord Adams, M. (2006), *Christ and Horrors: The Coherence of Christology* (Cambridge: Cambridge University Press).

Murphy, F. A. (2007), *God Is Not a Story: Realism Revisited* (Oxford: Oxford University Press).

Norris, R. (1996), 'Chalcedon Revisited: A Historical and Theological Reflection', in B. Nassif (ed.), *New Perspectives in Historical Theology: Essays in Memory of John Meyendorff* (Grand Rapids, Mich.: Eerdmans), 140–58.

Pecorrara Maggi, M. R. (2010), *Il processo a Calcedonia. Storia e interpretazione.* Dissertatio. Series mediolanensis (Milan: Glossa).

Riches, A. (2008), 'After Chalcedon: The Oneness of Christ and the Dyothelite Mediation of his Theandric Unity', *Modern Theology* 24: 199–224.

Rorem, P. (2012), 'Dionysian Uplifting (Anagogy) in Bonaventure's Reductio', *Franciscan Studies* 70: 183–8.

Tanner, K. (2001), *Jesus Humanity and the Trinity* (Minneapolis: Fortress).

Tanner, K. (2010), *Christ the Key.* Current Issues in Theology (Cambridge: Cambridge University Press).

Torrell, J.-P. (2005), *Aquinas's Summa: Background, Structure, and Reception* (Washington, DC: Catholic University of America Press).

Von Balthasar, H. U. (1990), *Mysterium Paschale: The Mystery of Easter*, trans. A. Nichols (Edinburgh: T. & T. Clark).

CHAPTER 34

THE CHRIST OF THE CANONICAL GOSPELS AND THE CHRISTS OF THE APOCRYPHAL GOSPELS

SIMON GATHERCOLE

INTRODUCTION

WHAT is it that makes the four canonical gospels distinctive over against the 'others'? Are the four qualitatively different, or are they simply those gospels which were later identified pragmatically as a potential source of unity, or imposed retrospectively as apostolic through an act of suppressive power by the party which happened to emerge victorious? Are there identifiable differences in content which mark off the canonical gospels on the one hand, from the apocryphal gospels on the other?

In recent times, answers to such questions have been very sceptical about any possible legitimate differentiations. Neither *content*, nor *circumstances of composition*, nor *attestation*, mark the canonical gospels out as distinctive or authentic vis-à-vis their alleged competitors, or so the argument goes. The present essay, because it is part of a theologically oriented volume, will focus on the issue of content. Scepticism about the canonical gospels having anything which makes them especially worthy of canonical status can be illustrated from the work of Pagels, Ehrman, Patterson and Watson.

For Elaine Pagels, for example, it is simply a desire for unity which leads to the exclusion of the now-apocryphal gospels:

> [N]umerous gospels circulated among various Christian groups, ranging from those of the New Testament, Matthew, Mark, Luke, and John, to such writings as the *Gospel of Thomas*, the *Gospel of Philip*, and the *Gospel of Truth*, as well as many other secret teachings, myths, and poems attributed to Jesus or his disciples ...

Those who identified themselves as Christians entertained many—and radically differing—religious beliefs and practices ... Yet by A.D. 200, the situation had changed ... Deploring the diversity of the earlier movement, Bishop Irenaeus and his followers insisted that there could be only one church ...

(Pagels 1979: xxii–xxiii).

Neither Gnostic nor orthodox interpretations of the Jesus tradition are *intrinsically* better than each other:

If we go back to the earliest known sources of Christian tradition—the sayings of Jesus (although scholars disagree on the question of *which* sayings are genuinely authentic), we can see how both gnostic and orthodox forms of Christianity could emerge as variant interpretations of the teaching and significance of Christ.

(Pagels 1979: 148)

In a similar vein, Ehrman declares that the rationale, such as it is, for the fourfold canonical gospel is a political one:

There were lots of gospels ... All of these gospels (and epistles, apocalypses, etc.) were connected with apostles, they all claimed to represent the true teachings of Jesus, and they were all revered—by one Christian group or another—as sacred scripture. As time went on, more and more started to appear. Given the enormous debates that were being waged over the proper interpretation of the religion, how were people to know which books to accept? In brief, one of the competing groups in Christianity succeeded in overwhelming all the others ... This group became 'orthodox', and once it had sealed its victory over all of its opponents, it rewrote the history of the engagement—claiming that it had always been the majority opinion of Christianity, that its views had always been the views of the apostolic Churches and of the apostles, that its creeds were rooted directly in the teachings of Jesus. The books that it accepted as Scripture proved the point, for Matthew, Mark, Luke and John all tell the story as the proto-orthodox had grown accustomed to hearing it.

(Ehrman 2006: 117–18; cf. Ehrman 2003: 248)

Ehrman here maintains, then, (1) that there were a considerable number of gospels sloshing around in the melting pot of earliest Christianity; (2) that the choice of the four New Testament gospels boils down simply to the political triumph of the section of Christianity which championed them; and (3) that what this group did was ultimately to distort historical reality ('it rewrote the history').

Stephen Patterson has raised similar questions, without the rebarbative tone of Ehrman's remarks. He focuses specifically on the portrait of Jesus in the *Gospel of Thomas*, which for most scholars is the closest potential rival to the canonical picture:

[W]e often assume a kind of natural continuity between Jesus and the synoptic tradition's version of what Christianity is all about. But among the earliest followers of Jesus there were clearly other ideas about the meaning and significance of what he said and did ... With its many synoptic parallels, Thomas shows that the synoptic construal of these sayings is not necessarily natural. They could have been, and were, taken in quite a different direction in Thomas Christianity. So who was right about Jesus?

(Patterson 2006: 683)

Patterson does not provide an answer to his question, and so the assumption is that there is nothing intrinsically more (or less) correct about the Synoptic Jesus over against the Thomasine Jesus.

From a different standpoint again, Francis Watson has criticized the view that the canonical gospels and non-canonical gospels are fundamentally different in theological character from each other. Watson instead sees all ancient gospels as legitimate inheritors of the Jesus tradition: 'these gospels all claim apostolic authority, and they all present an image of Jesus rooted in early tradition and shaped by later interpretative developments' (Watson 2013: 341). Nor, he avers, are the canonical and apocryphal gospels as far apart as is sometimes supposed:

It would be difficult to argue on neutral exegetical grounds that differences between the Synoptics and Thomas are more fundamental than differences between the Synoptics and John.

(Watson 2013: 370)

Thus one cannot pit authentic canonical gospels against apocrypha which can be dismissed as 'free invention', for apocrypha too 'are not fictions but renewed attempts to articulate the significance of an already inscribed tradition' (Watson 2013: 370).

The contention in this essay will be that there were sufficiently clear theological reasons for preferring some gospels (i.e., the canonical gospels) over against others. Nor were these merely later, retrospective evaluations: rather, there were theological criteria in operation *even before the composition of any gospels*. These were embedded in the preaching of those who had been closest to the earthly Jesus, namely the apostles: although there were no doubt many who had been impacted by the earthly Jesus (see Meggitt 2010), we do not have any good evidence that they propounded a different message. All the gospels—canonical and apocryphal alike—emerge from a context in which there are already established, though also developing, norms of what constituted authentic apostolic proclamation.

For the purposes of this essay, the corpus of 'others' consists of seven of the best preserved and best known apocryphal gospels: the *Gospel of Peter*, the *Gospel of Truth* (perhaps a homily or discourse on the gospel rather than a 'gospel' proper), the *Gospel of Thomas*, the *Gospel of Philip*, the *Gospel of Mary*, the *Gospel of the Egyptians* from Nag Hammadi (otherwise known as the *Holy Book of the Great Invisible Spirit*), and the *Gospel of Judas*. (For information and bibliography on these gospels, and translations of them, see Meyer 2007 and Ehrman and Pleše 2011.) Others which might have been included, such as the *Egerton Gospel*, the Greek *Gospel of the Egyptians*, and the so-called Jewish-Christian gospels, are excluded as too fragmentary for us to gain an understanding of their outlook. (*Mary* and *Peter* are also fragments, but more substantial ones.) Such a selection means that the treatment here is incomplete; but a complete treatment would not be possible in a single chapter. Nevertheless, the seven listed above are acknowledged by scholars to reflect a great variety of theological viewpoints (including those of Sethian Gnosticism, Valentinianism, as well as other unnamed movements). They comprise a sufficiently large representative sample.

Our argument will draw out four key features of the primitive apostolic gospel: (i) the identity of Jesus as the 'Christ' and the elements integral to that title; (ii) the work of Christ as fulfilling Scripture; (iii) the atoning death of Christ; and (iv) the resurrection. It will be shown that these are four crucial elements in the gospel common to the apostles, a gospel which can then function as a *regula fidei* by which written gospels may be assessed.

The Apostolic Gospels as *regula fidei*

At the beginnings of Christianity, theological criteria emerged by which one might assess true (preached) gospels over against others. One of the earliest documents of the New Testament, Paul's letter to the Galatians, identifies the Judaizing movement consisting of those who have influenced the Galatians as proclaiming 'a different gospel' (Gal. 1:6). In 2 Corinthians, Paul identifies those who 'preach another Jesus' and 'a different gospel' as ψευδαπόστολοι—'false apostles' (2 Cor. 11:4, 13). According to the Synoptic gospels Jesus himself forecast those who would lead the flock astray, pretending to come in his name (Mark 13:5–6). 1 John emphasizes one particular way of distinguishing between true and false messages: 'By this you know the Spirit of God: every spirit that confesses that Jesus Christ has come in the flesh is from God' (1 John 4:2). For the earliest Christians, refusal to do this would have been catastrophic, because—in the Galatian case—the agitators were aiming 'to pervert the gospel of Christ' (Gal. 1:7), and in 1 John the spirit which animates a confession contrary to the incarnational statement above is the spirit of the Antichrist.

One place where we see a summary of the essentials of the Christian gospel in earliest times is 1 Corinthians 15. Although this might appear to be an arbitrary choice of a narrowly Pauline perspective, it is striking that Paul defines the gospel here as the 'ecumenical' gospel of all the apostles. (Some scholars have argued that the language of Paul's definition is uncharacteristic, and therefore evidently indebted to his predecessors: see Thiselton 2000: 1188–9.) After stating that the risen Jesus appeared to all the disciples, and mentioning Peter and James by name, he reports: 'Whether, then, it is I or they, this is what we preach, and this is what you believed' (1 Cor. 15:11). Paul's summary of the gospel here was written *c.*53–57 CE. This gospel can be traced further back, to the time of Paul's proclamation, or 'handing over', of the gospel to the Corinthians (1 Cor. 15.1) in *c.*50 CE, and in fact much earlier still—to when Paul 'received' it (again, 15:1), presumably not long after his conversion, sometime in the 30s CE, even if this formulation did not exist in exactly the same wording (or even the same language). In fact, one can trace this gospel back even further to before Paul's conversion: as he reports in Galatians, when he was converted, the churches of Judaea heard that he was now proclaiming the good news of the faith which he had previously sought to destroy (Gal. 1:23; see Peterson 2005: 7).

As far as its content is concerned, this apostolic message is defined as 'the gospel' (15:1), and Paul underlines its significance as the means by which the Corinthians are 'saved' (15:2), and as 'of first importance' (15:3):

> For what I received I passed on to you as of first importance: that Christ died for our sins according to the Scriptures, that he was buried, that he was raised on the third day according to the Scriptures ...
>
> (15:3–4)

The identity of the saviour ('Christ'), his actions (death for our sins, and resurrection), and their scriptural basis are the key elements.

This same message is reflected in the diverse literature of the New Testament outside Paul and the gospels. Some of the Catholic epistles, as very short documents, do not incorporate all these elements: Jude, for example, explicitly states that it is not covering 'our common salvation'. Others, however, such as Hebrews (e.g. 10:12–13) and 1 Peter (e.g., 3:18), clearly do—as also does Revelation (e.g., 1:5). Paul's claim in 1 Corinthians 15 is not at variance with what we know from elsewhere. So it appears that there are criteria for what constitutes truly Christian proclamation extremely early: probably before any of the gospels—canonical or non-canonical—were written. Chief among these criteria were those positive matters of content identified by Paul in 1 Corinthians 15. There also emerged more 'reactive' criteria when particular errors appeared—as is clear in, for example, Galatians and 1 John.

We can proceed to examine the canonical and apocryphal gospels to see where they position themselves in relation to these four criteria: (a) Jesus' identity as Christ; (b) the scriptural basis for his saving actions; namely (c) his atoning death for sins; and (d) his resurrection.

'CHRIST': JESUS AS ANOINTED BY THE CREATOR GOD OF ISRAEL

Assumed in the fact that Jesus is identified as 'Christ' and acting according to the Scriptures is that Jesus is 'anointed' by the creator God of Israel: the Greek χριστός is a calque of the Hebrew *mashiach* ('Messiah'). The anointing is a unique appointment. Jesus is not just one anointed figure among many prophets, priests, and kings. He is the creator God of Israel's 'son' (2 Sam. 7:14) who as the supreme Davidic king will shepherd the people (Ezek. 37:24), and who brings to fulfilment the divine promise that to Israel's king belong the nations as his inheritance (Ps. 2:8). These are the assumptions of early Christians about Jesus *qua* Messiah (whatever the meanings of these verses in their original OT contexts), reflecting standard assumptions about the Messiah in early Judaism.

Canonical Gospels

These assumptions are widely shared in the New Testament gospels. In Mark, Jesus is identified as 'the Messiah' at the outset (Mark 1:1), and possibly also 'Son of God', though the manuscript tradition is inconsistent here. The voice of God at the baptism identifies Jesus as 'Son' of God (1:11), as again in the transfiguration (9:7), and also in the climactic declaration by the centurion (15:39; cf. also 13:32). The acclamation of Jesus as Messiah by Peter appears at a decisive moment, the turning point in the middle of the gospel (8:29). Matthew echoes some of these points, and also identifies Jesus at the very beginning as 'Messiah, the son of David, the son of Abraham', probably arranging his genealogy (Matt. 1:2–17) in groups of fourteen on the basis of the numerical value of David's name (Hebrew $d + v + d = 4 + 6 + 4$). Luke repeats much of the Markan material and emphasizes this feature of Jesus' identity in the announcement by the angel at the birth: 'to you is born today in the city of David a saviour: he is the Messiah, the Lord' (Luke 2:11). Jesus identifies himself as Messiah in Luke's resurrection narrative (24:26). In John's gospel, Nathaniel rightly identifies Jesus: 'Rabbi, you are the Son of God! You are the king of Israel'! (John 1:48). In conversation with the Samaritan, Jesus identifies himself as Messiah (4:25–6). In the following chapter, we have an extended discourse on Jesus' identity as divine Son (5:17–38). The identity of Jesus in the canonical gospels as the one anointed by his father, the creator God of Israel, needs no longer demonstration.

Apocryphal Gospels

The identity of Jesus as 'Son' of the divine Father is maintained in many apocryphal gospels. The *Gospel of Mary* does not make use of the title, but this cannot be assumed to be significant given the fragmentary nature of the manuscript ('Son of Man' does appear). The *Gospel of Judas* does not, perhaps because of its particular theogony, perhaps by coincidence. The other five in our corpus do refer to Jesus' sonship in some sense. The extent to which Jesus' sonship is understood in these five in relation to the creator God of Israel is patchy, however, and the reluctance or silence about Jesus' relation to the creator God is probably reflected in the absence or infrequency of the 'Christ' title. The *Gospel of Peter* does not contain it, though Jesus is there son of God (3:6; 3:9; 11:46) and king of Israel (3:7; 4:1). The *Gospel of Mary* contains no reference to the 'Christ' title (preferring the more universally comprehensible 'saviour'), nor does *Thomas*, though this may be because of an ambivalence to titles in general. The

Gospel of Judas implies that Jesus is not the son of the disciples' god (34:6–18), and assigns the title 'Christ' to a demonic archon (52:6). The *Gospel of Truth* has it twice. The *Gospel of Philip* has a predilection for the 'Christ' title, because of Valentinian interest both in names and in anointing. In the case of the *Gospel of Philip*, however, Jesus' connection with the creator is severed; the demiurge is a weak figure who created incompetently (75:2–10)—implying a distance between the supreme deity and the act of creation. Similarly in the *Gospel of Truth*, material creation was fashioned by 'error', who thereby made a 'substitute for the truth' (17:14–22). The same interest in anointing is reflected in the Nag Hammadi *Gospel of the Egyptians*, though with an even more negative attitude to the creator (e.g., III 57:16–19). Christ is the child of the Great Invisible Spirit, the supreme being, in the *Gospel of Judas* while Saklas and his demonic minions are the creators of Adam and Eve (52:14–21).

A Sketch of Patristic Assessments

The early Fathers who encountered a distinction between a supreme divine being on the one hand, and the creator and God of Israel on the other, were vehement in their rejections of such a distinction. Above all, it is in patristic responses to Marcion that we find rebuttals of such views. We can note here three of the earliest cases, of Justin (*c*.150 CE), Irenaeus (c.170) and Tertullian (in 207–8).

Justin is the first author to mention Marcion, and criticizes his theology of God and creation on two occasions (*1 Apol.* 26; 58), in the latter place attacking Marcion's teaching that 'the creator God of all heavenly and earthly things, and the one proclaimed beforehand through the prophets—Christ his Son—are to be renounced' (*1 Apol.* 58; cf. *Dial.* 35).

Irenaeus traces this view of Marcion back to a certain Cerdo, who it is said made such a distinction (*AH* 1.27.1). Cerdo's successor, Marcion, also rejected the creator god: Marcion is said to remove references to this god from the Pauline epistles (*AH* 1.27.2).

The importance of the matter is evident in Tertullian, who devotes five books to the refutation of Marcion's view of God:

> So much for skirmishing, as it might be at the first advance, and still at a distance. As from this point I take up the real battle, fighting hand to hand, I see I must even now mark off some front line at which the contest is to be carried on—I mean the Creator's scriptures. In accordance with these I propose to prove that Christ belonged to the Creator, seeing that in his Christ they were afterwards fulfilled …
>
> (*Marc.* 3.5.1; Evans 1972: 179)

Here the interconnection between Creator, Christ, and Scripture is an essential one, worthy of a 'battle' between Tertullian and Marcion: the former regards the views of the latter in this contest as 'heretical madness' (*Marc.* 3.6.1; Evans 1972: 179) berating him for believing in 'that leisured god of yours, who has never either done anything or prophesied anything' (*Marc.* 5.4.3; Evans 1972: 527).

Evaluation

The various options set out in the gospels mentioned above consist of the views: (1) that the 'Christ' title is rejected, and with it Jesus' association with the God of Israel, as in *Judas*; (2) that the title is embraced, but given new content, whereby Jesus is again dissociated or distanced from the creator God, as in *Egyptians, Philip*, and *Truth*. (3) *Thomas, Peter* and *Mary* do not contain the title, but also do not clearly dissociate Jesus from creation as in (1) and (2): indeed, the *Gospel of Peter* embraces the idea that Jesus is the king of Israel. Hence, the position (4) that Jesus is regarded as anointed king of Israel by his Father, the creator God, may well be embraced by the *Gospel of Peter*, as is more clearly the case in the canonical gospels of Matthew, Mark, Luke, and John.

If we were to ask which of these views were more likely to be true to original apostolic preaching about Jesus, it is difficult to imagine that views (1) and (2) were contemplated by the disciples of Jesus and other Christian preachers at the beginning. The reasons why such a move to dissociate Jesus from the creator came about—whether the influence of a form of Platonism, or through extrapolation from Paul's understanding of the Law, or by some other route—are now obscure, but that they were a later development, or distortion, not present at the beginning is clear enough.

'ACCORDING TO THE SCRIPTURES': JESUS AND THE OLD TESTAMENT

Occurring twice in Paul's formula in 1 Corinthians 15 is the adverbial clause 'according to the scriptures', appended both to Jesus' dying and rising.

The Canonical Gospels

It is a commonplace to observe that the canonical gospels see Jesus' coming and activity as the fulfilment of Scripture. The earliest gospel, Mark, after its opening statement of its subject matter in the first verse, declares that John the Baptist came to prepare the way for the Lord (Jesus), in fulfilment of the prophet Isaiah (Mark 1:2–3). Fulfilment of Scripture appears throughout Mark, such as in his teaching in parables (Mark 4:12/Isa. 6:9–10). He is received into Jerusalem on Palm Sunday as one fulfilling Psalm 118 (Mark 11:9–10), and Jesus sees his own rejection as foretold in the same Psalm (Mark 12:10–11), as well as in Zechariah's prophecy according to which God 'will strike the shepherd, and the sheep will be scattered' (Zech. 13:7 in Mark 14:27). The Danielic Son of Man (Dan. 7:13–14) exerts an influence over the whole gospel, in the Son of Man's declaration of authority (Mark 2:10, 28), the rejection of his authority and consequent death (8:31; 9:31; 10:33; 10:45), and the vindication of that authority (Mark 13:26; 14:62). Psalm 22 in particular is reflected in the account of the Passion, both in soldiers' casting lots for Jesus' clothes (Ps. 22:18/Mark 15:24) and in his own cry of dereliction (Ps. 22:1/Mark 15:34). Matthew and Luke have a similar approach, and follow Mark in many of these places. Matthew begins his gospel with a genealogy tracing Jesus' ancestry back to Abraham and David, and adds to Mark an infancy narrative which identifies five scriptural prophecies which Jesus fulfils (see Matt. 1:22–3; 2:5–6; 2:15; 2:17–18; 2:23). Matthew sees Jesus as recapitulating the wilderness wanderings of Israel (Matt. 4:1–11), not abolishing the Law and the prophets but fulfilling them (Matt. 5:17). Scholars have understood various typologies in Matthew, such as Jesus as a new Moses (Allison 1993) and rejected prophet, following the pattern of Jeremiah (Knowles 1993). Matthew makes explicit the analogy between Jesus and Jonah (12:40). Luke's infancy narrative contains a wealth of scriptural allusions, especially in the songs, and—after the main body of the gospel which contains much of the Markan (and Matthean) material—the resurrection narrative emphasizes that both Cross and resurrection were in accordance with, and again *had to* take place in fulfilment of, the whole of Scripture (Luke 24:25–7, 44). The same is true in John's gospel, where Jesus expects his teaching to be understood by a 'teacher of Israel' (John 3:10), and Moses is said to have spoken of Jesus (5:39–47), as is Isaiah (12:37–41). Various OT analogies are employed to explain the saving work of Jesus, such as Moses lifting up the serpent in the desert (3:14) and the provision of manna (6:32–3). As in the Synoptics, the events of the Passion are said particularly to be in fulfilment of Scripture, such as the division of Jesus' clothes (19:23–4/Ps. 22:18), his statement of thirst (19:28; cf: Ps. 22:15; 69:21), the preservation of Jesus' bones (19:36/ Exod. 12:46), and his piercing (19:37/Zech. 12:10).

Apocryphal Gospels

There is a variety of attitudes to the Old Testament in our apocryphal gospels. The *Gospel of Peter*, for example, emphasizes that those involved in the crucifixion of Jesus 'fulfilled all things' (*Gos. Pet.* 5:15). In contrast, the *Gospel of Mary* commands: 'do not give a law as the law-giver did, lest you be constrained by it' (*Gos. Mary* 9:3–4); this is probably 'part of the general polemic employed by some Gnostics against the "orthodox" that the latter are too dependent on, and use too much, the Jewish Law and its demands' (Tuckett 2007: 159). The *Gospel of Thomas*, in saying 52, 'appears to sever the link with the scriptures, contrasting the living Jesus with the twenty-four dead prophets in Israel' (Watson 2013: 608). As fits its deprecation of the creator god, the *Gospel of the Egyptians* presents itself as composed and hidden by Seth, asserting that no one has known the truth since the days of the prophets, apostles, and preachers; the first of these presumably referring to the ignorance of the OT authors (III 68:1–9). No reference is made in the *Gospel of Judas*, the *Gospel of Philip*, or the *Gospel of Truth*, to Jesus as promised in, or acting in fulfilment of, the Old Testament. The most that can be said is that these three gospels have occasional reference to Old Testament characters and themes such as Adam and paradise.

A Sketch of Patristic Assessments

Attempts to undercut the significance of the OT as prophesying Jesus met extensive criticism from the Church Fathers. This is found in various places, such as in Epiphanius' response to the view of Ptolemy, who 'even ventures to insult God's Law which was given through Moses' (*Pan.* 33.2.6; Williams 1997: 198; cf. 33.9.2–13), such is 'the lunacy of this charlatan' (33.8.1; Williams 1997: 204). These criticisms come to particular prominence in responses to Marcion. Justin attacks Marcion's teaching that 'the creator God of all heavenly and earthly things, *and the one proclaimed beforehand through the prophets*—Christ his Son—are to be renounced' (*1 Apol.* 58; Minns and Parvis 2009: 231; cf. *Dial.* 35). Before discussing Marcion, Irenaeus first tackles Cerdo, who according to Irenaeus taught that the Old Testament proclaimed a god other than the Father of Jesus Christ (*AH* 1.27.1). Similarly, Marcion followed in Cerdo's footsteps and 'abolished the prophets and the law' (*AH* 1.27.2; trans. mine; see also 3.12.12). In conjunction with his criticisms of Marcion's understanding of God, Tertullian criticizes his understanding of Scripture with great force and at length. He takes as his subject 'the Creator's scriptures', and states in defiance of Marcion that 'in accordance with these I propose to prove that Christ belonged to the Creator, seeing that in his Christ they were afterwards fulfilled ...' (*Marc.* 3.5.1; Evans 1972: 179).

Evaluation

On this particular point we can return to the argument of Watson: 'It would be difficult to argue on neutral exegetical grounds that differences between the Synoptics and Thomas are more fundamental than differences between the Synoptics and John' (Watson 2013: 370). However, it is legitimate to ask which of several views has the best claim to go back to earliest apostolic preaching: (1) a view according to which Scripture is irrelevant to, or unnecessary for understanding Christ (as apparently in *Truth* and *Philip*); (2) a view in which Scripture is actually unhelpful (as in *Thomas*, and *Egyptians*); or (3) a view in which Jesus' work is seen through the lens of OT Scripture and in fulfilment of it—as in the canonical gospels and the *Gospel of Peter*. To ask the question is to have an instant answer: views (1) and (2) make best sense as later developments, which to the apostles would have seemed fatally compromised.

'For our Sins': Jesus' Atoning Death

In Christian, but also in non-Christian Jewish (see, e.g., Josephus, *AJ* 18.63–4) and Roman sources (Tacitus, *Ann.* 15.44), Jesus is said to have been executed during the principate of Tiberius, when Pilate was prefect of Judaea. As Pagels remarks, however: 'if the sources agree on the basic facts of Jesus' execution, Christians sharply disagree on their interpretation' (Pagels 1979: 72).

Canonical Gospels

The idea that Jesus' death was an atoning sacrifice or redemptive act is prominent across the New Testament, not least in the gospels. Mark and Matthew contain the 'ransom saying', that 'the Son of Man came not to be served but to serve, and to give his life as a ransom for many' (Mark 10:45/Matt. 20:28). All three Synoptic evangelists report Jesus' Eucharistic discourse in which he declares that his body and blood are given for his people (Mark 14:22–5; Matt. 26:26–9; Luke 22:15–20), relating 'blood' to the 'covenant'. Luke's Eucharistic discourse is echoed in Acts, where Jesus is said to have acquired the church of God through his own blood (Acts 20:28). Matthew adds that Jesus sheds his blood 'for the forgiveness of sins' (26:28), such that Jesus' death becomes in Matthew the resolution of the question of how Jesus would 'save his people from their sins' (Matt. 1:21). In John's gospel, similarly, we have an initial statement that Jesus is 'the lamb of God who takes away the sin of the world' (1:29; cf. 1:36). It is unclear here how this will be accomplished, but Jesus later states that his flesh and blood bring eternal life for those who eat and drink them (6:33, 48–51, 53–8), and that he is the good shepherd who lays down his life for his flock (10:11, 15). Caiaphas also unwittingly, yet prophetically, provides an explanation when he states that 'it is better for you that one man die for the people than that the whole nation perish' and that therefore 'Jesus would die for the Jewish nation, and not only for that nation but also for the scattered children of God' (John 11:49–52). Revelation is an integral part of salvation, but 'the cross is not *merely* a revelatory moment ... it is the death of the shepherd for his sheep, the sacrifice of one man for his nation, the life that is given for the world' (Carson 1991: 97).

Apocryphal Gospels

A variety of views on this point appears in our selection of apocryphal gospels. To simplify our Valentinian gospels greatly, the *Gospel of Truth* (even if in quite ambiguous terms; see Thomassen 2008: 154–5) refers to Jesus, on the Cross, as having overcome error and ignorance, and thereby bringing knowledge and life to many;

the Cross is heavily metaphorized, as the tree on which hangs Jesus the fruit, who is knowledge (*Gos. Truth* 18:24–6). The *Gospel of Philip*, again very opaquely, treats the death of Jesus—as one aspect of the activity of Christ—as having accomplished a redemption (*Gos. Phil.* 52:35–53:14; see Thomassen 2008: 93–102). *Peter* seems in some limited sense to attribute saving significance to the death of Jesus inasmuch as the walking cross—but actually not Jesus—claims to have 'preached to those who are asleep' (11:41–2); there is no impression of an atoning sacrifice. In *Thomas* the death of Jesus is important simply as a model of 'taking up one's cross' (*Gos. Thom.* 55). The fragments of the *Gospel of Mary* offer no hint about a meaning of Jesus' death. The death of Jesus in *Judas* is an event of no apparent significance, and indeed Jesus states that he is not really harmed by the crucifixion at all (*Gos. Jud.* 56:8–11; cf. 56:18–21). In the *Gospel of the Egyptians* Jesus is not a passive recipient of a crucifixion; his saving activity (or one aspect of it) consists of him having 'nailed down the powers of the thirteen aeons' (III 64:3–4; trans. mine). Again, *Judas* and *Egyptians*, as Sethian Gnostic compositions, share elements in common: in this case, a lack of any sense of a redemptive death of Jesus.

A Sketch of Patristic Assessments

After 1 John, which insists both on the Incarnation (1 John 4:1–2), and upon Jesus' death as a propitiation and atoning sacrifice (1 John 2:1–2; 4:10), Ignatius and Polycarp also assert, against heretics, the saving death of the incarnate Christ.

Ignatius, writing *c*.110–15 CE, states that he is 'justified' through Jesus Christ, 'his cross and death, and his resurrection and the faith which comes through him' (*Phld.* 8.2; trans. mine). He insists that the Smyrnaeans must understand well the error of heretics who both behave wickedly, and refuse to participate in the Eucharist because of their false understanding of the Cross:

> They keep away from the Eucharist and prayer, because they do not confess that the Eucharist is our saviour Jesus Christ's flesh, which suffered for our sins, and which the Father in his kindness raised.
>
> (*Smyrn.* 6.2; trans. mine)

Ignatius warns against a false understanding of the crucifixion apparently as part of a larger heretical package in his letter to the Tralllians:

> Therefore be deaf whenever anyone speaks to you without Jesus Christ, who is from the family of David, is from Mary, was really begotten, both ate and drank, was really persecuted under Pontius Pilate, was really crucified and died, while those in heaven and on earth and under the earth looked on …
>
> (*Trall.* 9.1; trans. mine)

The importance of this for Ignatius is that 'without him we have no true life' (*Trall.* 9.2; trans. mine; cf. 6.1–2), and the bishop continues to launch attacks against those who say he only '*appeared* to suffer', denouncing them as 'atheists' (10.1).

In a similar vein probably shortly after the death of Ignatius, Polycarp writes (*c*.120 CE):

> For anyone who does not confess that Jesus Christ has come in the flesh is an anti-christ. And whoever does not confess the testimony of the cross is from the Devil.
>
> (Polycarp, *Phil.* 7.1; trans. mine).

Polycarp goes on to explain the Cross, where Jesus 'bore our sins in his body on the tree' (*Phil.* 8.1, citing 1 Pet. 2:24; trans. mine), and 'endured all things for us, so that we might live in him' (8.1; trans. mine).

Evaluation

We are faced from our corpus of gospels with a variety of views of Jesus' death, leaving aside *Mary*, which makes no mention of it: (1) rejection of the idea of the death of the real Jesus (*Judas, Egyptians*); (2) apparent acceptance of the real death of Jesus—as probably in the *Gospel of Thomas*, but with—at least explicitly—limited assessment of its significance; (3) the Valentinian ambiguity about the death of Jesus in the gospels of *Philip* and *Truth*, which may well treat it as a real death, but a death whose significance lies in revelation rather than as an atoning sacrifice for sins; (4) *Peter*'s acceptance of a real death, but again with ambiguity about its role; (5) understanding Jesus' death as a sacrifice or vicarious death, as do the canonical gospels. Certainly John's gospel differs in its emphasis from the Synoptics, although even among the Synoptics Matthew and Mark are perhaps more emphatic about the saving significance of Christ's death than Luke, so that there is some degree of variety across the four canonical gospels. At minimum, there is in Matthew, Mark, Luke, and John a shared understanding of Jesus dying a real physical death, as a vicarious sacrifice for sin(s)—as emphasized in the Apostolic Fathers.

The earliest understanding of Jesus' death among the apostles would have been of a real physical death. As Paul states in 1 Cor. 15:3, the apostolic preaching of the Cross was of an atoning sacrifice, and this makes sense in the light of various factors. One can note, for example, the fact that Christians would have had to respond to Jewish accusations that, having been suspended on a tree, Jesus was cursed according to the Torah. It is interesting that this is not avoided but embraced (e.g. Acts 5:30; 10:39; Gal. 3:13; 1 Pet. 2:24), and thereby provides raw material for understanding Jesus' death as a vicarious bearing of the curse. The sacrificial system provided a ready background against which Jesus' death could be understood, as did Isaiah 53. Jesus' death was immediately understood not as a tragic accident, but as part of the divine plan and as explicable in terms of Scripture. The same can be seen in the Eucharistic words according to which Jesus' death is on behalf of his followers—words which must go back to an early period, given that they are found both in Paul and the Synoptic gospels (1 Cor. 11:23–6/Mark 14:22–5 and parallels).

Jesus' Resurrection on the Third Day

The main controversy over Jesus' resurrection in the second and third centuries was over its physicality, though it is not clear that this is reflected in differences among the various canonical and non-canonical gospels.

Canonical Gospels

All four of the canonical gospels refer to the resurrection as integral to the story of Jesus, though in different ways. Mark does not in his final chapter report the resurrection as extensively as the other evangelists, but nevertheless defines as inevitable and essential not only Jesus' death but also his 'rising after three days' (Mark 8:31; cf: 9:31; 10:33–4). Matthew and Luke repeat the point, both making reference, as Mark does, to the divine plan in the Greek δεῖ, 'it is necessary …' (Matt. 16:21; Luke 9:22). They also narrate the appearances of the risen Jesus (Matt. 28; Luke 24). John similarly speaks of Jesus' resurrection in advance (e.g., John 10:17–18), as well as recounting the various appearances after Jesus' death (John 20–1). Luke and John both insist on the physicality of the resurrection, as Jesus can be touched (Luke 24:39; John 20:27) and eats (Luke 24:41–3; cf. John 21:9–14). All the evangelists make explicit the point that Jesus rises on the third day/after three days (Matt. 12:40; 16:21; 17:23; 20:19; 27:63–4; Mark 8:31; 9:31; 10:34; Luke 9:22; 18:33; 24:7, 21, 46; John 2:19–21).

Apocryphal Gospels

A variety of perspectives on the resurrection appears in our corpus of apocrypha. One can dismiss at the outset the Sethian writings (the gospels of the *Egyptians* and *Judas*) as having no place for a resurrection because they do not have a real death. The *Gospel of Thomas* refers to Jesus as 'the living Jesus' (*Gos. Thom.*, prologue) but it is unclear whether this specifies Jesus as having risen, whether bodily or otherwise. Since Jesus has in some sense a 'cross', however, it may be reasonable to expect that he has therefore died and risen in some sense as well; on the other hand, *Thomas* is negative about a general resurrection (*Gos. Thom.* 51). The *Gospel of Mary* (7:1–9:5) contains a scene which might well be a resurrection appearance, but it is ambiguous, and there is no other hint of resurrection (in what is of course a brief pair of fragments). It is unclear in the *Gospel of Philip* that the death and resurrection are really distinct events (Thomassen 2008: 98): indeed, *Gos. Phil.* 56:16–20 even asserts that Jesus' resurrection *precedes* his death, the converse being an error. The *Gospel of Truth* is similarly ambiguous: there is a statement that Jesus 'put on imperishability' (20:32; cf. 1 Cor. 15:53–4) in a context which may suggest a reference to resurrection, but it is not definite. Famously, the *Gospel of Peter*'s Jesus emerges from the tomb, his head higher than the heavens, led by two angels and followed by a cross. This is a real bodily resurrection, as is evident in the subsequent visit when Mary Magdalene and her friends are told that the tomb is empty: 'he is risen and gone' (13:56; trans. mine), and this takes place on the third day, as is evident from the narration of events from Friday to Sabbath to Lord's day (2:5; 9:34–5; cf. 8:30).

A Sketch of Patristic Assessments

Understandably, early responses to allegedly heretical statements about resurrection are paired with statements about the death of Jesus. Ignatius sees as a touchstone of orthodoxy the confession of 'our saviour Jesus Christ's flesh, which suffered for our sins, and which the Father in his kindness raised' (*Smyrn.* 6.2; trans. mine). Ignatius warned the Trallians against those who deny the death of Jesus; he goes on to add the resurrection as an integral element of the identity of Jesus—'who was also really raised from the dead, when his Father raised him up' (*Trall.* 9.1; trans. mine). We noted above Polycarp's condemnations of those who distort what he regards as the correct understanding of the Incarnation and death of Jesus, and he immediately adds statements about resurrection and judgement: 'And whoever twists the oracles of the Lord towards his own desires and says that there is no resurrection or judgment, he is the firstborn of Satan' (Polycarp, *Phil.* 7.1; trans. mine).

Evaluation

Contrary to what we might expect, we do not find in our gospels clearly varied views of the physicality or otherwise of the resurrection. We do find a lack of clarity on the resurrection, especially in the *Gospel of Truth* and the *Gospel of Philip*, but also in *Thomas*; the silence in the *Gospel of Mary*, at least in our extant fragments, is also tantalizing. The Sethian Gnostic works, *Judas* and the *Gospel of the Egyptians*, are clearer in having no place for a resurrection. The canonical gospels and the *Gospel of Peter*, on the other hand, have a clear sense of Jesus being raised *on the third day*—and raised bodily, because he is no longer in the tomb when disciples arrive (Matt. 28:6; Mark 16:6; Luke 24:3; John 20:6–7; *Gos. Pet.* 13:56).

The resurrection on the third day in the gospels matches with the Pauline kerygma in 1 Cor. 15:4. Moreover, the tension between Jesus' body as both physical and transformed is captured in Paul, the canonical gospels and *Peter*. For Paul, Jesus' risen body is both physical as it is seen publicly with normal vision (1 Cor. 9.1; 15:4–8—contrast, e.g., 2 Cor. 12:1–4), and also glorious (15:43), animated by the Spirit (the meaning of σῶμα πνευματικόν in 1 Cor. 15:44). In Matthew, Jesus escaped from the tomb when the stone still blocked the entrance, and yet he could be grasped (Matt. 28:9). In Luke he eats (Luke 24:42) and yet disappears and reappears (Luke 24:31, 36; cf. Acts 1:3). In John he can be touched (20:27), but can also walk through doors (20:19); as in Luke, it is clear that he makes appearances, rather than remaining with the disciples in his risen state (John 21:14). In the *Gospel of Peter*, he is absent from his tomb, but clearly is risen in an extraordinary form. At risk of over-generalization, the early Christian combination of both physicality and transformation makes good sense against the background of Jewish expectations of resurrection, where, for example, Josephus understands the Pharisees—and with them most of the populace—to believe that resurrection is bodily, but that souls will possess bodies other than those they previously inhabited (*War* 2.162–3). This is apparently also Josephus' own view, according to which souls will be sent into 'pure bodies' at the resurrection (*War* 3.374). The views presented in 1 Corinthians 15, the canonical gospels, and the *Gospel of Peter*, therefore make sense as reflective of earliest understandings, even if the outlandish character of *Peter*'s resurrection narrative stretches, and perhaps even breaks, the limits.

Conclusion

There is in current scholarship a marked tendency to avoid making any evaluation of interpretations of Jesus and his activity, and it is often regarded as a matter of principle that one *cannot* distinguish between good and bad, or better and worse, interpretations. There is an assumption (tacit, or not so tacit) that it is bad form to accuse, say, Valentinus of interpreting Paul less faithfully than did Ignatius.

In one sense a reticence in pronouncing judgement on ancient works is laudable. We are right in one respect to adopt a hermeneutic of charity, and to attempt to understand writings from antiquity on their own terms, not immediately jumping to label them with our own categories. However, most scholars inevitably have a sense that there is a distinction—even if not necessarily always a wide chasm—between legitimate and illegitimate interpretations. We would make very poor examiners of student essays and very poor reviewers of books if we did not think that there was a difference between good and bad interpretations of, say, the theology of the gospel of Matthew.

We have seen above that, as far as the four elements in 1 Corinthians 15 are concerned, the canonical four gospels are a great deal closer than are any of the seven in the apocryphal corpus used in this chapter. Indeed, it is not even that there is a continuum on which all the gospels considered above occupy a position; rather, there is a clear distinction between canonical and non-canonical gospels when they are considered in relation to the four criteria above. Tuckett rightly observes that of course Christian apocrypha shed light on the history of early Christianity. 'However, there is still the question of exactly how early is the "early" Christianity they illuminate' (Tuckett 1998: 19). The present study is a case in point: the apocryphal gospels clearly represent a departure from the earliest apostolic preaching of the gospel in a way that the canonical gospels do not.

SUGGESTED READING

Good translations of the apocryphal gospels, with some introductory material and bibliographies can be found in Meyer (2007) and Ehrman and Pleše (2011). For further material sceptical of the value of apocryphal gospels for understanding Jesus, see Tuckett (1998) and Gathercole (2007, 2015). For a different view, see Hedrick (1988).

BIBLIOGRAPHY

Primary Sources: Translations

Evans, E. (ed.) (1972), *Tertullian: Adversus Marcionem*, 2 vols. (Oxford: Clarendon Press).
Minns, D. and P. Parvis (eds.) (2009), *Justin, Philosopher and Martyr: Apologies*. OECT (Oxford: Oxford University Press).
Unger, D. J. (trans.) (1992), *St Irenaeus: Against the Heresies, Book 1* (Mahwah, NJ: Paulist Press).

Secondary Sources

Allison, D. C. (1993), *The New Moses: A Matthean Typology* (Edinburgh: T. & T. Clark).
Carson, D. A. (1991), *The Gospel according to John* (Grand Rapids, Mich.: Eerdmans).
Ehrman, B. D. (2003), *Lost Christianities: The Battles for Scripture and the Faiths We Never Knew* (New York: Oxford University Press).
Ehrman, B. D. (2006), 'Christianity Turned on Its Head: The Alternative Vision of the Gospel of Judas', in R. Kasser, M. Meyer, and G. Wurst (eds.), *The Gospel of Judas* (Washington, DC: National Geographic), 77–120.
Ehrman, B. D. and Z. Pleše (2011), *The Apocryphal Gospels* (Oxford: Oxford University Press).
Gathercole, S. J. (2007), *The Gospel of Judas: Rewriting Early Christianity* (Oxford: Oxford University Press).
Gathercole, S. J. (2015), 'Early Christian Apocrypha and the Historical Jesus: Other Gospels', in A. F. Gregory and C. M. Tuckett (eds.), *The Oxford Handbook to the Early Christian Apocrypha* (Oxford: Oxford University Press).
Hedrick, C. W. (ed.) (1988), *The Historical Jesus and the Rejected Gospels. Semeia* 44 (Atlanta, Ga.: Scholars Press).
Knowles, M. (1993), *Jeremiah in Matthew's Gospel: The Rejected Prophet Motif in Matthaean Redaction* (London: Continuum).
Meggitt, J. J. (2010), 'Popular Mythology in the Early Empire and the Multiplicity of Jesus Traditions', in R. J. Hoffmann (ed.), *Sources of the Jesus Tradition: Separating History from Myth* (Amherst, Mass.: Prometheus), 55–80.
Meyer, M. W. (ed.) (2007), *Nag Hammadi Scriptures: The International Edition* (New York: HarperCollins).
Pagels, E. H. (1979), *The Gnostic Gospels* (New York: Random House).

Patterson, S. J. (2006), 'The Gospel of Thomas and Historical Jesus Research', in L. Painchaud and P.-H. Poirier (eds.), *Coptica—Gnostica—Manichaica. Mélanges offerts à Wolf-Peter Funk* (Louvain: Peeters), 663–84.

Peterson, J. (2005), 'The Extent of Christian Theological Diversity: Pauline Evidence', *Restoration Quarterly* 47: 1–14.

Thiselton, A. C. (2000), *The First Epistle to the Corinthians: A Commentary on the Greek Text* (Grand Rapids, Mich.: Eerdmans).

Thomassen, E. (2008), *The Spiritual Seed: The Church of the 'Valentinians'* (Leiden: Brill).

Tuckett, C. M. (1998), 'The Gospel of Thomas: Evidence for Jesus?', *Nederlands Theologisch Tijdschrift* 52: 17–32.

Tuckett, C. M. (2007), *The Gospel of Mary* (Oxford: Oxford University Press).

Watson, F. B. (2013), *Gospel Writing: A Canonical Perspective* (Grand Rapids, Mich.: Eerdmans).

Williams, F. (1997), *The Panarion of Epiphanius of Salamis: Book I (Sects 1–46)* (Leiden: Brill).

....

CHAPTER 35

THE DOCTRINAL SIGNIFICANCE OF THE COUNCILS OF NICAEA, EPHESUS, AND CHALCEDON

....

THOMAS G. WEINANDY, O.F.M., CAP.

THIS essay examines the doctrinal significance of the Ecumenical Councils of Nicaea (325), Ephesus (431), and Chalcedon (451). Since the theological controversies surrounding these councils are treated elsewhere in this volume, only the necessary relevant theological and historical background is first provided. Second, there is a theological and doctrinal exegesis of the pertinent statements and creeds. Third, the enduring philosophical, theological, and doctrinal implications are noted. Lastly, a number of the contemporary Christological issues related to these councils are discussed.

INTRODUCTION: THREE INCARNATIONAL TRUTHS

Three incarnational truths governed the patristic and conciliar doctrinal development. While these truths only gradually became fully perceived and clearly formulated, they were, nonetheless, actively present within the faith-life of the early Church and necessarily continue to govern and authenticate, doctrinally, Christology today. The councils, and the theologians who championed them, in conceiving clearly and articulating properly these truths, defended, professed, and advanced a proper understanding of the Incarnation. These truths will direct this present essay so as to guide the reader to follow the doctrinal progress and to track the theological significance of these councils.

The Incarnation demands that the following truths be simultaneously affirmed and preserved:

- It is *truly the Son of God* who is man. This truth focuses on the full divinity of the Son.
- It is *truly man* that the Son of God is. This truth demands that the full and complete humanity be acknowledged.
- The Son of God *truly is* man. This truth affirms that there is an ontological union between the person of the Son and his humanity. Jesus is one being or reality—he *is* the Son of God *existing* as man.

Also, by way of guidance, these three truths are lodged in what came to be known as the communication of idioms, that is, that divine and human attributes are predicated of one and the same person—the divine Son of God. For example, from apostolic times the Church professed that 'God was born of Mary', and that 'God suffered and died on the cross'. Such emphatic claims only possess cognitive truth within the context of the three incarnational statements. Only if Jesus is *truly God* can one assert that *actually* God himself was born and suffered and died. Moreover, only if he is *truly man* can one affirm that he was truly born and suffered and died. Likewise, only if Jesus is God *truly existing* as man can one authentically confess that God *is* the subject of human birth and human suffering and death.

All the early Christological heresies (as well as those throughout the centuries) deny one or more of the three incarnational truths as they manifest themselves within the Church's provocative, yet authentic, profession of the whole truth of the Incarnation as expressed within the communication of idioms. Because of this, the three incarnational truths only become clearly perceived and articulated in the course of defending, endorsing, and cultivating a proper use and understanding of the communication of idioms. Thus, the denial or misuse of the communication of idioms is the hermeneutical key for recognizing Christological error as well as authenticating and adjudicating doctrinal Christological orthodoxy.

The Councils of Nicaea, Ephesus, and Chalcedon, as will be shown, all contribute to explicating and sanctioning the communication of idioms and they do so by properly conceiving, articulating, and validating the three incarnational truths.

THE COUNCIL OF NICAEA

Pre-Nicene Christological Development and Controversy

The Council of Nicaea was the culmination of a long theological and doctrinal trajectory, containing insightful advances, unintentional missteps, and gospel-devastating errors. Flowing from the apostolic proclamation as embodied in the New Testament, the

Christian tradition professed that the man Jesus Christ, as the Son of God, was divine. The question that surfaced early and grew in intensity was: In what manner is Jesus divine and how is one to conceive this divinity in relationship to the one God attested to in both the Old and New Testaments? Does not the divinity of the Son render the oneness of God philosophically and theologically untenable? Various attempts were offered to resolve this seeming conundrum. (For good accounts of this development in Christian thought, see Kelly 1950, 1968; Pelikan 1971; Grillmeier 1975; Behr 2001, 2004; Ayres 2004.)

Diverse forms of adoptionism were proposed, that is, that the man Jesus was adopted by the Father through the indwelling of his Word and so became God's adopted Son. Such proposals were rejected by the Church in that Jesus would simply be, then, another prophet and God's presence in him would not differ in kind from them.

Some, who wished to uphold both the oneness of God and the full divinity of the Son, proposed what is termed modalism, Sabellius (third century) being its chief proponent. Sabellius argued that the Godhead was one and that it expressed itself in different modes in keeping with the economy of salvation. Thus, at times God expressed himself under the mode of fatherhood, at other times under the form of sonship, and again under the guise of the sanctifying Spirit. While such a theological interpretation may confirm the oneness of God, the distinct subjective identities of the Father, the Son, and the Holy Spirit are discarded. These titles possess no ontological depth, but are mere nominal phenomenological expressions of the one undifferentiated Godhead. The early Church realized, in keeping with the scriptural tradition, that each person of the Trinity possesses his own singular ontological integrity and so rejected modalism.

Origen (c.185–c.254), in response to modalism, insightfully argued that since the Father is eternally the Father, the Son must be eternally the Son for to deny his eternity would deny the eternity of the Father. Moreover, Origen grasped that the Father and the Son each possess their own distinct identity or subjectivity and so each is a particular ὑπόστασις or person within the oneness of God. While these insights theologically advanced the Church's understanding of the Son's eternal divinity and the relational distinctiveness of the Father and the Son, the manner in which Origen conceived these proved less than satisfactory.

Origen professed in faith the oneness of God but he, as many before him, conceived this oneness as residing in the Father alone. This being the case, Origen elicited the aid of Platonic emanationism and so proposed that the Son emanated out from the Father and in so doing shared in the Father's divinity and oneness with his own distinct identity or ὑπόστασις. Such emanationism ultimately forced Origen into a theological cul-de-sac. While the eternal Son may share in the Father's divinity and oneness, yet because he emanates out from the Father, who embodies the whole of the Godhead, he is not as divine as the Father is divine. He is derivatively divine within a hierarchy of divinity—a δεύτερος θεός, a secondary God.

Origen wished to uphold and articulate the Gospel and its theological tradition but he employed a philosophical concept, Platonic emanantionism, that threw subsequent endeavors into theological chaos. Some of Origen's followers stressed that the Son was truly God while others emphasized the derivative nature of that divinity and so the Son's lesser divine status to that of the Father.

Arius: The Son is a Creature

Arius (d. 336) brought the theological divergence and episodic doctrinal development to a head (see Williams 2001). He wanted to answer the simple question: Is the Son of God ontologically God or is he ontologically a creature? While the Church's theological tradition professed the divinity of the Son, it did so, according to Arius, in an unacceptable fashion. For Arius, all previous attempts at reconciling the divinity of the Son and the oneness of God failed and the reason that they failed was that it is ontologically impossible to maintain the oneness of God and the divinity of the Son. He rightly refused to continence the notion that the Son is a lesser deity. The Son is either ontologically God or he is not. Moreover, if the Son is God then one must concede that there are two gods (which is contrary to reason and faith).

Further, for Arius, a true notion of God must affirm three necessary and unalterable attributes. God is unoriginate, that is, that he is eternally who he is and originates from no other being. He is, likewise, one and transcendent. Because the Son originates from the Father as begotten he cannot be God. Because God is one and the Son is ontologically distinct from the Father, the Son cannot be God. It is impossible for God to mutate in any manner into two, even by emanation, for such would rend asunder his unoriginate eternal oneness. Because God is unchangeably perfect in his transcendence, the Son cannot be God because he became man and as man underwent and experienced change and human frailty. Arius thus concluded, by the force of logical necessity, that the Son must be created by God. He is the first and supreme of all creatures, but a creature nonetheless. Because the Son was created, there was, for Arius, a time (a 'when') when the Son was not and thus the Father was not eternally the Father.

The Nicene Creed

In the midst of condemnation of and support for Arius and his position, the Emperor Constantine convoked the first Ecumenical Council in 325. When the Fathers of the Council gathered at Nicaea most of them were not wondering: What is the true faith? They recognized that the apostolic faith, as found in Scripture and its subsequent tradition, professed the divinity of Jesus. The question at hand was: How could this be affirmed so as to leave no doubt as to its truth? Moreover, they were confronted by Arius' logic: How could the Son be God and God be one simultaneously?

First the Council Fathers deliberated over a creed that was composed entirely of Scripture quotations for this was the precedent set by earlier synods. However, Arius and his cohorts were all too willing to give assent to statements professing that the Son 'was from the Father' and that he is 'like' the Father. Once Arius had raised the issue of the Son's divinity to the ontological level and having decided that the Son is onto-logically a creature, they could interpret all Scripture citations within that metaphysical framework. Yes, the Son could be 'from the Father' and 'like' the Father; he could even be 'the only begotten of the Father', but he was so as a creature. Those who wanted to assure that the Son was truly divine and that the Scripture passages that referred to the uniqueness of his divinity were properly interpreted realized that reciting Scripture alone was inadequate to the task. At this juncture Nicaea took an extraordinary and unprecedented action. The Fathers commandeered a non-scriptural word that they believed would testify to the Son's full divinity and ensure an orthodox interpretation of Scripture. That word was ὁμοούσιον (homoousion—of the same substance or of the same being).

The Council of Nicaea professed:

> We believe in one God, the Father almighty, creator of all things, visible and invisible, and in one Lord Jesus Christ, the Son of God, the Only-Begotten generated from the Father, that is, from the substance/being of the Father (γεννηθέντα ἐκ τοῦ πατρὸς μονογενῆ, τουτέστιν ἐκ τῆς οὐσίας τοῦ πατρός), God from God, light from light, true God from true God, begotten, not made (γεννηθέντα, οὐ ποιηθέντα), one in substance/being with the Father (ὁμοούσιον τῷ πατρί), through whom all things were created, those in heaven and those on earth …
>
> (Denzinger 2012: # 125)

First, the Council proclaimed that Christians believe in one God who is the Father. Doctrinally the Council asserted, contrary to Arius, that the one God is eternally the Father, and thus, imbedded in this profession, is the profession of the eternal Son, there never was a 'time' when he was not. God would not be eternally the Father if he were not eternally the Father of the Son. To profess in faith the 'Father' is simultaneously to profess in faith the 'Son' (Denzinger 2012: # 126).

Second, the creed states that Christians also believe in one Lord Jesus Christ who is the Son of God. As there is one Father so there is one Son. The reason is that this Son is 'the Only-Begotten' who is 'generated' of the Father. The Council immediately defined the meaning of this generation, that is, that to be generated from the Father is to be from the being/substance of the Father. To be from the being/substance of the Father confirms that the Son is the Only-Begotten for he is what the Father is. The Son is not a different kind being (such as a creature) from the Father. Rather, to be from the being/substance of the Father as the Only-Begotten means that he is 'God from God, light from light, true God from God'. As the Father is God, who like a light enkindles another light, so the Son is true God from the true Father, the source of divine light.

Third, all of the above is founded upon the fact that the Son is 'begotten, not made'. Prior to Nicaea, as witnessed in Arius, 'to be begotten' was assumed by many to be synonymous with 'to be made'. Nicaea made, for the first time, a clear distinction. What is made is of a different nature from that of the maker. Ants make anthills; human beings make houses; God creates/makes the world. However, what is begotten is of the same nature as the one who begets. Ants beget ants; human beings beget human beings; God begets the Son and so the Son, as begotten, is of the same nature as the begetter, God the Father. This is precisely why the Council can now employ its non-biblical word—ὁμοούσιον, one in being/substance with the Father.

It is precisely because the Son is begotten and not made that he is the Only-Begotten of the Father, as from his own substance, and thus truly God from God and so of one being/substance with the Father. The Son is God in the same exact sense as the Father is God. What the Father is the Son is. They are both ontologically God. This is why the Council can declare that the Father, who is the creator of all things, creates through his Son. Since they share one and the same being/substance, they are together one and same Creator God.

Defining ὁμοούσιον

At this juncture a historical question of a doctrinal nature arises. While the Council Fathers clearly professed that the Son is truly God possessing the same nature as the Father, did they satisfactorily address the issue of how the Son can be truly God and yet God remain one? Arius, remember, claimed that to hold that the Son is God and that God is one is metaphysically impossible.

At the time ὁμοούσιον could have been understood in two ways. The first conceived ὁμοούσιον specifying that two or more beings share the same common substance in a generic manner. In this sense, as two copper coins are ὁμοούσιον with one another in that they share the same substance of copper, so the Son is ὁμοούσιον with the Father in that he shares the same common divine substance. This understanding would vindicate Arius' logic for then the Father and the Son would be two distinct realities and so there would be two gods. Some of the Council Fathers may have understood ὁμοούσιον in this manner—content to affirm simply that the Son is truly God.

The second understanding designated that for the Son to be ὁμοούσιον with the Father meant that they are one and the same reality, one and the same being. While it is impossible to determine whether most of the Fathers understood it in this sense, it would appear to be the case since the charge later laid against the Council was not that it professed two gods, but that it had fallen into modalism. Stating that the Son is ὁμοούσιον with the Father could mean not that they were one and the same divine reality, one and the same God, but that they were one and the same 'person' expressed under two different modes—as Father and as Son.

This allegation was based upon a false presupposition. Those responsible for this allegation continued to hold, as exemplified within the Origenist tradition, that the Father embodied the whole of the Godhead—he is God in the strict sense. To say, then, that the Son is ὁμοούσιον with him could easily be construed to mean that he and the Father are one and the same 'person'. The one God is Father/Son. Neither now possesses his own distinct ontological identity.

Athanasius, as the authoritative interpreter of Nicaea, grasped the radical nature of Nicaea's ὁμοούσιον for he appreciated that the Council's declaration demanded a re-conception of God as a trinity of persons. For Athanasius, in keeping with Nicaea, the Father alone does not constitute the one Godhead and from whom the Son comes forth in the begetting. Rather, the one God is the Father begetting the Son. (Obviously, the Holy Spirit must be included within the oneness of God, but that is another story.) The Godhead is now newly conceived. The Father's begetting of the Son is constitutive of the very nature of God's oneness, and contrary to Arius' deduction, it is metaphysically possible to conceive of the Son as God and God as one simultaneously.

Moreover, since the oneness of God is the Father begetting the Son, modalism is, *ipso facto*, excluded. The very term ὁμοούσιον specifies, for Athanasius, that one distinct subject, the Son, is of the same being/substance as another distinct subject, the Father, since nothing can be ὁμοούσιον with itself.

The Fathers of Nicaea, in dogmatically endorsing the ὁμοούσιον, guaranteed both the oneness of God and the differentiation of the distinct identities of divine persons, for the Father and the Son are what the one God is.

For the above reasons the term ὁμοούσιον and the concept it designates is of the utmost theological and doctrinal significance. It is, historically and doctrinally, the most important word and notion within Trinitarian and Christological dogma. It not only definitively defines the being of the Son as God, but it also definitively defines that this same Son is the one who is man, for the question addressed is whether or not the *man* Jesus is the divine Son equal to the Father. Thus, the Council of Nicaea definitely defined the first incarnational truth: It is *truly the Son of God*, identical in divinity with Father, who is man.

THE COUNCIL OF EPHESUS

Prelude to Ephesus

Subsequent to the Council of Nicaea the issue of Christ's full humanity came to the fore. Already at the time of Ignatius of Antioch (d. 107) the Docetists (from the Greek to 'seem' or 'appear') held that, because Christ was fully God, he could not actually take on human flesh since this would be unbecoming of a divine being. Ignatius vigorously responded, arguing that if Christ only 'seemed' or 'appeared' to be man, and thus that his birth, suffering, and death—indeed his whole human life—was a mere charade, then humankind's salvation is a mere pretense possessing no actuality.

Later, Apollinarius (c.310–c.390), in response to adoptionism, wanted to assure that the divine Son was truly ontologically one with his humanity. However, this union entailed that the Son of God united to himself human flesh alone; his divinity assuming the place of the human soul. This guaranteed, Apollinarius argued, the oneness of Christ and the surety of salvation since his divine will governed all that he did.

In order to uphold the full humanity of Christ—soul and body (the second incarnational truth)—Apollinarius was roundly condemned, most authoritatively at the Council of Constantinople (381). Gregory of Nazianzus' (c.330–c.390) soteriological principle expressed the mind of the Church—what was not assumed was not saved.

The issue of Christ's full humanity would surface again at the Council of Chalcedon, but prior to that the nature of the incarnational 'becoming' and ensuing incarnational 'union' became the critical matter at hand. The protagonists, Nestorius (d. 451) and Cyril of Alexandria (d. 444), both held that Jesus was truly the divine Son of God and truly man (body and soul). They radically differed as to the nature of the incarnational union.

Nestorius and Cyril of Alexandria

Nestorius, Patriarch of Constantinople, in response to a request, ruled that it was inappropriate to call Mary *Theotokos*, Mother of God. He reasoned that such a title entailed the erroneous assumption that the Son changed in becoming man and that, as man, he could undergo human experiences, such as birth, suffering, and death. Since God is immutably perfect, he is incapable of changing in 'becoming' man and so incapable of embracing human attributes. Therefore, it was doctrinally incorrect, according to Nestorius, to speak of 'the birth of God' or 'the suffering and death of God'. For Nestorius the whole Christian tradition of the communication of idioms was methodically misguided and theologically misconceived.

In order to protect primarily the divinity of the Son, Nestorius conceived the incarnational union as a 'conjunction' or 'joining' of the two natures so that the Son of God dwells in the humanity by 'good pleasure'. The natures become so closely aligned that they give off one common appearance, what Nestorius termed a 'common πρόσωπον of union', one common personal appearance of both divinity and humanity. This common appearance is to be referred to as 'Christ'. Thus, while Mary cannot be rightfully termed the Mother of God, she can appropriately be designated χριστόκος, Mother of Christ.

For Cyril, Nestorius' denial of Mary as the Mother of God as well as his conception of the incarnational union was anathema. Denying that Mary is the Mother of God was, for Cyril, to deny the reality of the Incarnation. If the Son of God was not born, if he did not suffer and die, then he did not actually come to exist as man. Moreover, since Nestorius thought incarnational union was not an ontological union but a moral union of the two natures, Cyril accused him of espousing two persons/sons. Furthermore, the 'common πρόσωπον of union' (Christ) designated no ontological subject/person, but is merely the term employed to describe the common phenomenological 'appearance' of the two closely conjoined or aligned existing natures.

Cyril's theological starting point was the Council of Nicaea, for it proclaimed that the Son, who was ὁμοούσιον with the Father, was the same Son who 'for us men and for our salvation came down and became man, suffered, and rose again on the third day ...'. He who was eternally God truly came to exist as man for our salvation.

In his attempt to assure that the Son of God truly existed as God and as man, and thus rightly bore the attributes of both, he caused confusion by referring to Jesus as the one person/nature of the Word of God incarnate. Moreover, he spoke of this one person/nature being constituted 'out of two' natures. Nestorius was convinced that this implied that Cyril had ontologically united the two natures so as to form one new nature, a new nature that was neither truly God nor fully man, a *tertium quid* being confusedly composed of a mixture of both divinity and humanity.

In the course of the debate, Cyril more clearly conceived and articulated his position. For Cyril, the incarnational 'becoming' terminated in an incarnational 'is' in that, at Jesus' conception, the humanity simultaneously came into existence and was ontologically united to the one person, the one ὑπόστασις, of the Son so that the Son came to be man. To 'become man', for Cyril, did not mean that the Son of God 'adopted a man' or 'changed into a man'. Nor is the incarnational union the ontological compositional union of natures which would result in the confusion or mixture of natures, causing the mutation of each. For Cyril, 'to become man' meant that the Son of God, remaining who he is as God, 'came to exist as man' and, thus, the incarnational 'becoming' terminated in an incarnational 'is'—the Son of God truly 'is' man. Thus Jesus is one reality/being and the one reality/being that is Jesus is the one Son of God existing as man. This confirmed that both divine and human attributes could rightly be attributed to the one and the same person/subject, the Son of God, for the Son actually existed as God and as man and all that pertained to each were rightfully his. Mary is indeed the Mother of God for the Son of God, who was humanly conceived by the Holy Spirit within her womb, was physically born of her as man. (For a good overview of this controversy, see Weinandy 2003b and McGuckin 2004; the main texts can be found translated in Wickham 1983 and McGuckin 2004.)

The Decree of the Council of Ephesus and the Formula of Union

Both Nestorius and Cyril wrote to Pope Celestine I. A synod in Rome (430) confirmed that Mary is indeed the Mother of God and condemned Nestorius. The Emperor, Theodosius II convoked a council in Ephesus. This became a rather raucous affair in that both factions, those favoring Cyril and those favoring Nestorius, held separate sessions coming, as would be expected, to opposing conclusions. In the end the Council approved, under the authority of the papal legates, Cyril's Second Letter to Nestorius as a true interpretation of the creed of Council of Nicaea—the Son, who is true God, became man and suffered and died for our salvation. This letter stated in part:

> We do not say, in fact, that the nature of the Word underwent a transformation and became flesh or that it changed into a complete man composed of soul and body. Rather, we say that the Word, hypostatically uniting to himself the flesh animated by

a rational soul, became man in an ineffable and incomprehensible manner and was called Son of man, not merely by will or good pleasure or because he only assumed a person [outward appearance]. Furthermore, (we say) that the natures brought together in a real union (are) different and from these two only one Christ and Son results.

(Denzinger 2012: # 250)

Ephesus sanctioned the title 'Mother of God' and the traditional use of the communication of idioms.

Having achieved his theological and doctrinal goal at the Council of Ephesus, Cyril was willing to seek reconciliation with the more moderate 'Nestorians'. In 433 Cyril enthusiastically accepted the *Formula of Union* composed by Theodoret of Cyrus, the leading Antiochene theologian. Cyril agreed to set aside his 'one nature' formula and clearly acknowledged that there are two natures after the incarnational union. The Antiochenes, for their part, agreed that 'Mother of God' is an apt title for Mary and that the communication of idioms was a legitimate expression of the Church's faith in the Incarnation (Denzinger 2012: # 271–3).

With the Council of Ephesus, all three of the incarnational truths have now been sanctioned. Nicaea has authoritatively declared, against Arius, that the Son of God is God as the Father is God and so it is *truly the Son of God* who is man. Apollinarius' denial of the full humanity was found to be contrary to the Gospel. Thus, it is *truly man* that the Son of God is. With the condemnation of Nestorius and the endorsement of Cyril's understanding of the incarnational 'becoming' and ensuing 'hypostatic union' the Council of Ephesus confirmed that the Son of God *truly is* man. In so doing the traditional use of the communication of idioms, which was the catalyst for most of the controversies, was theologically refined and was doctrinally confirmed to be what it was intended to be from apostolic times—a crisp and emphatic declaration of the Church's faith in the total reality of the Incarnation.

These incarnational truths, nonetheless, were affirmed at different times and under diverse theological circumstances. Only at the Council of Chalcedon will all three incarnational truths, together, find their authoritative doctrinal conception and definitive dogmatic expression.

THE COUNCIL OF CHALCEDON

Prelude to Chalcedon

With the death of Cyril in 444, Dioscorus became Patriarch of Alexandria and Eutyches became the chief theologian. Both repudiated the *Formula of Union*. Moreover, Eutyches (378–454) stated that before the Incarnation there were two natures, but after the union there was only one nature. Within this monophysitism (one-naturism) the divinity swallowed up the humanity and thus Christ's humanity became 'heavenly'.

Eutyches did what Nestorius accused Cyril of doing—he conceived the incarnational union as the ontological compositional union of the divine and the human natures, resulting in a third kind of being that is neither fully God nor fully man. Eutyches' Christology was perceived to be a new expression of Docetism and Apollinarianism, and was condemned at the Synod of Constantinople in 448. Appeal was made to Pope Leo the Great, who responded in 449 with his *Letter/Tome to Flavian* (Patriarch of Constantinople) condemning Eutyches. Leo insisted that Christ is one person existing in two natures. In response, the Emperor Theodocius II called a synod in Ephesus in 449 under the leadership of Dioscorus. The papal legates were prohibited from reading Pope Leo's *Tome*. Eutyches was vindicated. This synod came to be known as 'The Robber Synod' for the true faith had been stolen. Pope Leo demanded a new council. When Theodocius unexpectedly died after falling from his horse, the new Emperor, Marcian, being in sympathy with Leo, convoked a council at Chalcedon in 451.

At first the Fathers of the Council did not wish to promulgate a new creed, but simply wanted to re-affirm the Nicene-Constantinopolitan Creed of 381, Cyril's *Second Letter to Nestorius*, and Pope Leo's *Letter to Flavian*. However, the Council came to realize that a new creed was required; one that all could agree upon (see Young 1988).

The Creed of the Council of Chalcedon

The Chalcedonian Creed reads as follows:

> In agreement, therefore, with the holy Fathers [those of the Council of Nicaea], we unanimously teach that we should confess one and the same (ἕνα καὶ τὸν αὐτὸν) Son, our Lord Jesus Christ, the same (τὸν αὐτὸν) perfect in divinity and the same (τὸν αὐτὸν) perfect in humanity, the same (τὸν αὐτὸν) truly God and truly man composed of rational soul and body, one in being/substance with the Father (ὁμοούσιον τῷ πατρὶ) as to the divinity and the same one (τὸν αὐτὸν) in being/substance (ὁμοούσιον) with us as to the humanity, like unto us in all things but sin (Heb. 4:15). Begotten of the Father before the ages as to the divinity and in the latter days, the same (τὸν αὐτὸν), for us and for our salvation was born as to his humanity from Mary the Virgin Mother of God (τῆς θεοτόκου).
>
> [We confess] one and the same (ἕνα καὶ τὸν αὐτὸν) Christ, Son, Lord, only begotten, made known in two natures (ἐν δύο φύσεσιν), without confusion (ἀσυγχύτως), without change (ἀτρέπτως), without division (ἀδιαιρέτως) and without separation (ἀχωρίστως), the difference of the natures never abolished because of the union but the property of each nature being preserved in and in harmony with one Person and one hypostasis (εἰς ἓν πρόσωπον καὶ μίαν ὑπόστασιν συντρεχούσης)—not parted or divided into two Persons (δύο πρόσωπα), but one and the same (ἕνα καὶ τὸν αὐτὸν) Son, only begotten, God the Word, the Lord Jesus Christ, as the prophets of old and Jesus Christ himself have taught us about him and the creed of our Fathers has handed down.
>
> (Denzinger 2012: # 301–2, modified)

While elements from the various documents mentioned above can be found within the Chalcedonian Creed, yet the Creed itself stands as its own profession of faith. Moreover, it must be read through the eyes of Cyril. His teaching is the hermeneutical principle that governs the proper interpretation of Chalcedon. With this in mind, the Christological relationship among the various elements can be grasped and the Creed as a whole can be understood.

First, the Creed conspicuously and markedly repeats the phrases 'one and the same' (three times) and 'the same' (five times). To ascertain who is the 'one and the same' and 'the same' is to discover, doctrinally, the incarnational metaphysics of the Creed. Echoing the voice of Cyril, the Fathers resoundingly professed that he who is 'one and the same' and 'the same' is none other than the one eternal Son/Word. Against Nestorius, there are not two ontological persons/subjects (two 'who's), but only one ontological person/subject (one 'who') the Son of God, our Lord Jesus Christ.

Second, the one and the same person/subject—one and the same 'who'—is ontologically God and ontologically man. The same Son/Word is perfect as to being God and is perfect as to being man. The same Son/Word is one in being/substance (ὁμοούσιον) with the Father (against Arius) and one in being/substance (ὁμοούσιον) with humanity, possessing body and soul (against Apollinarius and Eutyches). The Son/Word is one with the Father since they are one and the same God and he is one with humankind because he is a human being in the same manner as all human beings. Because Jesus is one and the same Son/Word existing as God and man, Mary can truly be designated 'Mother of God' for the one who was born of her as man, this man's identity, was none other than the divine Son of the Father. Thus the Son/Word was not composed 'out of' two natures, which would result in the demise of each, thus resolving Cyril's ambiguity, but he was made known 'in two' natures for he came to exist as man and so revealed himself to be such—the one Son of God incarnate.

Third, Chalcedon, in the above, has clearly defined and so distinguished who it is, the person or subject—the Son/Word of God, and the manner of the Son's/Word's ontological existence, the essence or nature of the Son's existence—as God and as man.

Fourth, the Creed notably defined the mystery of the singular ontological character of the incarnational 'becoming'. To 'become man' means that the Son of God, ontologically, 'comes to be/comes to exist' as man. In 'becoming' man the Son did not change as God or cease to be God, for such would demand that it is not God who is man. Rather, 'to become man' specifies that the Son, remaining who he is as God, assumed a new manner of existence, that is, an existence as man. Thus, the incarnational 'becoming' terminates in an incarnational 'is', a 'becoming' that not only constitutes the ontological unity of both natures, both manners of existing, in the one person of the Son, but also confirms the unaltered existence of the Son's divinity and the ontological bringing into existence of the Son's humanity in the fullness of its integrity.

Fifth, Chalcedon specifies why this is the case. The natures, the particular manners of existence, are not confused or changed, nor are they divided or separated. Such is the essence of the incarnational mystery. While not comprehended, the mystery can be conceived and articulated. The distinct manners of existence are not confused or changed because the incarnational 'becoming', and thus the incarnational unity, is not the onto-logical compositional union of natures whereby they would be metaphysically mixed and mingled so as to constitute a being that is neither ontologically God nor ontologi-cally man, but ontologically a third kind of being. Thus, as Chalcedon affirms, the differ-ence of the two natures, the distinct manners of existence, is in no way removed because of the union precisely because the union is not an ontological compositional union of morphing natures.

Yet, the natures, the distinct manners of existing, are not divided or separated, pre-cisely because they are united and so exist in the one person/subject, the one 'who', of the Son/Word. Each manner of existence, as the Creed insists, is 'preserved and in harmony with the one πρόσωπον and one ὑπόστασιν'. The incarnational act, the 'becoming', while not the compositional union of natures, is the personal uniting, the *hypostically* unit-ing, of the humanity to the person of the Son such that he personally assumes human existence and so, ontologically, comes to live as man. Thus, divine and human existences are united in the one person of the Son. Christ, for Chalcedon, is one reality/being and this one reality/being is the one divine Son existing as a unique historically identifiable man—Jesus.

Sixth, Chalcedon, having properly conceived and fittingly articulated the ontologi-cal nature of the incarnational 'becoming' and so metaphysically defined the mystery that is the Incarnation, simultaneously confirmed the ontological propriety of the communication of idioms. Because the divine Son of God exists as man, the divine Son of God, as man, genuinely was born, thirsted and hungered, suffered, died and rose as man. What had consistently been the catalyst for fostering doctrinal Christological development, often through its very denial, has, through that same doctrinal develop-ment, not simply been vindicated but has been, at Chalcedon, elevated to its rightful place as the supreme theological expression of the authentic reality of the Incarnation and so becomes its ultimate doctrinal guarantee. For Chalcedon, Mary truly *is* the Mother of God.

Seventh, here at the Ecumenical Council of Chalcedon, in its one creed, all three incarnational truths are unambiguously present. The Council Fathers did not sim-ply endorse, but actually doctrinally articulated and definitely defined them. For Chalcedon, it is *truly the Son of God* who is man; it is *truly man* that the Son of God is; and it is the Son of God who *truly is* man.

DOCTRINAL PRINCIPLES AND CONTEMPORARY ISSUES

The creeds and doctrinal statements of the Councils of Nicaea, Ephesus, and Chalcedon are now permanently imbedded within the living Christological tradition of the Church. These persist as guiding doctrinal principles for subsequent Trinitarian and

Christological development (see Weinandy 2006, 2011). By way of concluding this essay, a number of contemporary issues will be briefly discussed in the light of the Councils of Nicaea, Ephesus, and Chalcedon.

Christological Doctrine and Scripture

The New Testament revelation speaks of the one God being the Father, the Son, and the Holy Spirit. The Council of Nicaea's Creed confirmed an essential aspect of this scriptural revelation.

For Arius, the proper name for God was 'ingenerate'—having no origin—thus effacing 'Father' as naming who God essentially is. For Nicaea, conversely, the proper divine names, those that define the very being and essence of God, are those that have been revealed: 'Father', 'Son', and 'Holy Spirit'. These names are not, then, mere descriptive metaphors, but properly designate the ontological identity of the subject to whom they apply. All other divine names—such as Creator, Redeemer, Sanctifier, etc.—flow from, and so are consequent upon, God being the Father, the Son, and the Holy Spirit. This doctrinal judgment is of contemporary significance, since there is presently a theological debate concerning which 'names' are appropriate for rightfully designating God and the persons of the Trinity.

Moreover, over the past hundred years, within some scholarly circles, there has surfaced a tension and even opposition between doctrinal statements and creeds and the sacred Scriptures. The doctrinal definitions, with their philosophical precision and technical terminology, do not, it is claimed, bear the same life-giving appeal of the simple Gospel and may even hinder it.

Such criticism is misguided for it does not recognize and appreciate the invaluable service that doctrine renders the scriptural proclamation. All of the above councils realized that they were providing, in their statements and creeds, an authentic window into the truths of Scripture for what they defined actually arise out of and confirmed, by way of defending and expounding, the authentic Gospel message.

To read the whole of the Bible, especially the New Testament, through the eyes of Nicaea, Ephesus, and Chalcedon, is to read and interpret its message properly—as the various authors and the Holy Spirit intended it to be read and interpreted. Thus, Trinitarian and Christological doctrine does not hinder the life-giving message of the Bible, but actually promotes and fosters its rightful integrity and singular inspiration. These doctrines provide the Church the intellectual freedom and the scholarly assurance to delve more deeply into the unfathomable truths of the Gospel. They also allow individuals of faith to ponder the Scriptures, without fear of error, assured that they are being guided, in communion with the councils, by the Spirit of wisdom and truth. Far from being an oppressive burden heaped upon Scripture's easy yoke the Trinitarian and Christological doctrines, which embody the living faith of the Church, reveal the singular pearls of great price hidden within the treasure-field of Scripture.

Christological Ontology

Today some theologians speak of models of the Trinity and models of the Incarnation. By this they imply that, since both are ultimately unknowable mysteries, one must conceive various ways to express the Trinity and the Incarnation, all of which models may, more or less, approximate the mysteries themselves, but do not intellectually grasp their ultimate metaphysical reality. Thus, Trinitarian and Christological language, and the concepts that inhere within such language, is solely metaphorical or symbolic in nature. Moreover, these models of approximation are conceived within differing historical cultures and so inherently bear within them a provisional conditionality. The final conclusion drawn is that, while all doctrinal and creedal statements may be instructive theological models, they too are formulated within a particular historical culture and philosophical milieu and, as such, they, alongside other models, are not definitive in nature. They are simply part of the revered, but non-binding, Christian tradition.

The conciliar creeds and decrees do not simply propose theological models. Granted that the mysteries of the Christian faith, including the Trinity and the Incarnation, can never be fully comprehended and sufficiently articulated, yet Christians, in faith, do know what the mysteries of faith are for they have been divinely revealed through perceptible deeds and intelligible words. The faithful, even in heaven, may never fully comprehend the mystery of the Trinity, but they do know, even while on earth, the metaphysical reality of that mystery. Similarly, how one and the same Son of God is able to exist simultaneously as God and as man will never be fully grasped, but that Jesus is indeed, nonetheless, the Son of God ontologically existing as man is rationally intelligible and is objectively believed to be metaphysically true.

This essay has emphasized the metaphysical nature of Nicaea's, Ephesus', and Chalcedon's conciliar statements and creeds and so the ontological nature of the mysteries of which they speak. Nicaea's doctrinal definition that the Son is one in being/substance with the Father is ontological in nature. This is ontologically what the one God is: The eternal Father eternally begetting his eternal Son. Nicaea is not simply offering a 'model', however adequate, that can be applied to the Trinity alongside other future models. Nicaea, without making the mystery of the Trinity comprehensible, did clarify more accurately the exact ontological constitution of that mystery.

The Council of Ephesus defined that the ontological identity/subject, the 'who', of the historical man Jesus is the person of the Son of God. Who it is that is ontologically God and man is the one divine Son. This was but a further elaboration and refinement of the incarnational ontology of the Nicene Creed. It professed that the Son, who is consubstantial with the Father, is the same Son 'who for us men and for our salvation came down and became flesh, and made man …'.

The metaphysics of the Incarnation finds its classic definition within the Chalcedonian Creed for here all three incarnational truths, truths that are ontological in nature, are professed with metaphysical care and precision. The mystery of the Incarnation, which will always remain a mystery of faith, is the divine Son of the Father ontologically existing as man. Chalcedon's Creed did not offer one of many possible incarnational models. This Creed emphatically defined the mystery of who the historical and everlasting Jesus *is*.

While these truths may be expressed in multiple ways, the ontological content of these counciliar truths cannot be changed or altered. Future generations and subsequent councils may expand and develop these truths, as did Constantinople I (381) (Denzinger 2012: # 150), Constantinople II (553) (# 421–38), Constantinople III (680–1) (# 550–9), and Nicaea II (787) (# 600–9), but these dogmatic definitions concerning the Trinity and the Incarnation are sacrosanct.

Christology from Above and Below

Some contemporary theologians also speak of two approaches to Christology. The first is a Christology 'from above'. Such a Christology is described as emphasizing the notion that the transcendent Son of God came down to earth and so became man. Christology 'from below' focuses on Jesus' earthly humanity and his historical and cultural conditioning and from within this setting discerns his divinity. In the light of the counciliar Christological tradition, this dichotomy of Christological approaches is ambiguous and is often misconceived and misunderstood.

While it is true that Jesus' disciples came to know who he is through his humanity—his human words and actions—and thus in this sense 'from below', it would be erroneous to claim, as some theologians do, that Jesus himself 'became' God 'from below'. He did not become divine by some form of human openness to the transcendent so that through his prayer and faithfulness to the Father, he became his 'Son'. This would be a contemporary form of 'adoptionism'. While human beings always, by necessity, come to know who Jesus is through his humanity, that is, 'from below', yet, the counciliar tradition demands that the Son of God, ontologically, comes to be man, and so in this sense 'from above'. Having become man, Jesus, epistemologically, reveals who he is as the Son through his humanity and thus human beings come to know him to be the Son through his humanity.

Jesus' Human Self-consciousness and Knowledge

Without entering deeply into the current debate concerning Jesus' earthly self-consciousness and self-knowledge, given the counciliar statements and creeds treated here, the three indispensable incarnational truths are essential for a proper understanding.

Who is conscious and knows himself to be the Son of God is *the divine Son himself*. The manner in which he is conscious of himself and so knows himself to be the Son of God is *in a human manner*, in accordance with his human consciousness and intellect. Again, this is necessitated by the fact that the Son of God *is* man, and thus, as incarnate, he must perceive himself to be the divine Son of the Father within a human mode for that is the manner in which he exists.

For example, as incarnate, the Son would, through his human prayer and reading of scripture, humanly come to know God as his Father. The Son, in humanly perceiving his filial relationship to the Father, would humanly become conscious of himself as the Son and so would humanly know himself to be the Son.

Is Jesus a Human Person?

The councils clearly declared that Jesus is one person, one subject, one 'who'—that of the eternal Son of God. It is sometimes argued today that if such is the case, then Jesus is not a 'human person' and, therefore, he is not fully human. This would be, they hold, contrary to the Council of Chalcedon which demanded that Jesus be ὁμοούσιον with humankind. This position is founded upon a false understanding of the Incarnation.

It is necessary that Jesus be authentically and fully human, as Chalcedon demanded, in order to ensure that it is precisely man that the Son of God is. To insist upon Jesus' humanity while failing to acknowledge that it is the Son who is man is to deprive the humanity of its singular significance—that the identity of this man Jesus is that of the Son of God. To profess that Jesus is a divine person is not, then, to deny anything concerning his humanity. It is merely specifying that, in this unique and unrepeatable instance, the identity of this particular historical man—who this man is—is the Son of God. The Son of God is not only eternally identifiable as God, but he is also, now, temporally identifiable as man.

The Soteriology of Nicaea, Ephesus, and Chalcedon: Jesus as the Definitive and Universal Savior

Despite what might be initially thought, all of the conciliar statements and creeds are of absolute salvific importance. The Council Fathers were not simply engaged in ensuring the truth of Christological doctrine for the sake of doctrinal purity, but to confirm the truth of humankind's salvation. Once again, the three doctrinal truths are central. Only if Jesus is *truly the Son of God* is salvation assured. Only if the Son's salvific words and deeds, particularly his suffering and death, are done *as man* are we guaranteed that they were said and done on humankind's behalf and so are humanly salvific. For the Son of God to speak the good word of the Gospel and enact the human efficacious deeds salvation, he must *be* man.

This is why Nicaea's, Ephesus', and Chalcedon's Christological doctrine necessarily encompasses the truth that Jesus is the definitive and universal Savior. Among all other founders of religion, only Jesus is the Son of God incarnate and as incarnate only did he offer up his holy and innocent human life as a loving sacrifice to the Father out of love for the whole of humankind. He did not provide humankind with religious norms and customs—sacred words and sacred actions—that are to be said and done by human beings after the manner of, for example, Mohammed and Buddha.

Rather, being the Son of God incarnate, Jesus made possible a radically new way of life founded upon a new and singular relationship with his Father. He accomplished this through his life, Passion, death, and resurrection which initiated the outpouring of the Holy Spirit. Through faith human beings do not merely adhere to a set of religious or moral norms, but are personally united, through the indwelling of the Holy Spirit, to the risen Jesus as their Lord and Savior. Living in communion with him as members of his body, the Church, human beings are conformed into Jesus' likeness, and so are adopted children of the Father. The Council Fathers of 325, 431, and 451 have bequeathed to the Church, for all ages, the Gospel truth that in Jesus' name alone is there salvation (Acts 4:12).

Suggested Reading

Ayres (2004); Behr (2001, 2004); McGuckin (2004); Weinandy (2003b, 2006).

Bibliography

Ayres, L. (2004), *Nicaea and Its Legacy: An Approach to Fourth-Century Trinitarian Theology* (Oxford: Oxford University Press).

Behr, J. (2001), *Formation of Christian Theology*, vol. 1: *The Way to Nicaea* (Crestwood, NY: St. Vladimir's Seminary Press).

Behr, J. (2004), *Formation of Christian Theology*, vol. 2: *The Nicene Faith* (Crestwood, NY: St. Vladimir's Seminary Press).

Davis, L. (1988), *The First Seven Ecumenical Councils (325–787): Their History and Theology* (Collegeville, Minn.: Liturgical Press).

Denzinger, H. (2012), *Enchiridion Symbolorum: A Compendium of Creeds, Definitions, and Declarations on Matters of Faith and Morals*, ed. R. Fastiggi and A. Englund Nash (San Francisco: Ignatius Press).

Grillmeier, A. (1975), *Christ in Christian Tradition*, vol. 1: *From the Apostolic Age to Chalcedon (AD 451)* (London: Mowbrays).

Kannengiesser, C. (1992), 'Nicaea, Council', in A. Di Berardino (ed.), *Encyclopedia of the Early Church* (Cambridge: James Clarke & Co.).

Kelly, J. N. D. (1950), *Early Christian Creeds* (London: Longmans).

Kelly, J. N. D. (1968), *Early Christian Doctrines* (London: Adam & Charles Black).

McGuckin, J. (2004), *Saint Cyril of Alexandria and the Christological Controversy* (Crestwood, NY: St. Vladimir's Seminary Press).

Pelikan, J. (1971), *The Christian Tradition: A History of the Development of Doctrine*, vol. 1: *The Emergence of the Catholic Tradition (100–600)* (Chicago: University of Chicago Press).

Pelikan, J. (2003), *Credo: Historical and Theological Guide to Creeds and Confessions of Faith in the Christian Tradition* (New Haven: Yale University Press).

Price R. and M. Gaddis (eds.) (2007), *The Acts of the Council of Chalcedon*, 3 vols. (Liverpool: Liverpool University Press).

Price, R. and M. Whitby (eds.) (2009), *Chalcedon in Context: Church Councils 400–700* (Liverpool: Liverpool University Press).

Tanner, N. (2001), *The Councils of the Church: A Short History* (New York: Crossroad).

Weinandy, T. G. (2003a), 'Cyril and the Mystery of the Incarnation', in T. G. Weinandy and D. Keating (eds.), *The Theology of Cyril of Alexandria: A Critical Appreciation* (London: T. & T. Clark), 23–54.

Weinandy, T. G. (2003b), *Jesus the Christ* (Huntington, Ind.: Our Sunday Visitor Press).

Weinandy, T. G. (2006), 'The Council of Chalcedon: Some Contemporary Christological Issues', *Theological Digest* 53: 345–56.

Weinandy, T. G. (2007), *Athanasius: A Theological Introduction* (Aldershot: Ashgate).

Weinandy, T. G. (2011), 'Trinitarian Christology: The Eternal Son', in G. Emery and M. Levering (eds.), *The Oxford Handbook of the Trinity* (Oxford: Oxford University Press), 387–99.

Wickham, L. (ed.) (1983), *Cyril of Alexandria: Selected Letters* (Oxford: Clarendon Press).

Williams, R. (2001), *Arius*, 2nd edn. (London: SCM Press).

Young, F. (1988), *From Nicaea to Chalcedon: A Guide to the Literature and its Background* (London: SCM Press).

CHAPTER 36

···

NORMATIVE PROTESTANT CHRISTOLOGY

···

KENNETH OAKES

INTRODUCTION

···

PROTESTANT Christology is the spiritual and intellectual task which serves the witness of the Church catholic in its proclamation that Jesus Christ is God for us and with us. While its reflections most directly concern the churches of the Reformations, they are also offered to the Christian communions from which these churches have been estranged historically and are estranged currently. Protestant Christologies can be submitted to and assessed beyond their own confessional boundaries inasmuch as Protestant communions are themselves embodied and living traditions of exegesis and discernment regarding shared matters: the God of the Gospel, Scripture, worship, and the Christian life. It is this extensive common background that explains why many distinctive contours of Protestant theology, including those within Christology, have rich precedents in the Fathers and the Middle Ages. It also helps to account for how originally Protestant theological proposals have at times drifted over or been deliberately incorporated into Roman Catholic teaching and practice.

Within this shared historical and material background, there have developed characteristically Protestant doctrinal accents and commitments. These have affected how Protestant groups view the historical and material background which it shares with both Eastern Orthodoxy and Roman Catholicism. Such Protestant emphases have included the perfect and sufficient work of Christ; free and full grace; alien righteousness; total depravity (understood in terms of extension); the priesthood of all believers; Christian freedom and perfection; and the Gospel's call to peace and love of enemy. Protestant traditions have also been suspicious of mediators, whether metaphysical or ecclesial, in addition to Christ; reifications and abuses of grace; and the usurpation of divine power and privilege by humans or church offices. In terms of their own self-understanding, often couched in polemics against 'scholastic speculation', modern Protestant

Christologies have viewed themselves as recovering the priority of the 'active' and living person over and against consideration of the 'passive' two natures; as intimately linking Christology and soteriology; and as attending to the historical character of the divine being and action in Christ (which comes in both metaphysically modest and bold versions). The final shape of Protestant Christology is thus derived both from its shared roots and from the ways in which its own emphases interpret this common background.

Protestant Christologies have been both diverse and innovative. The churches of the Reformations have put forward a range of Christological proposals, and each church has become associated with particular tendencies within Christology. There has been the Anglican accent on the Incarnation and the healing of human nature; Lutheran stress on the unity of the two natures in the person of the Logos; Reformed emphases on obedience, covenant, and the distinction between the natures; and Anabaptist focus on the words and practices of Jesus and discipleship. The innovative quality of Protestant Christologies can be seen in Lutheran revisions of the traditional *communicatio idiomatum*, Schleiermacher's Christology of perfect God-consciousness, Hegel's historical and concrete unity of the infinite and the finite, the nineteenth-century kenoticists' accounts of Christ as misguided apocalyptic prophet, Bultmann's Jesus as ecclesial *kergyma*, and more contemporary portrayals of Jesus Christ as co-sufferer, liberator, queer, migrant, or disabled.

While the features of distinctly Protestant Christologies are more or less identifiable, the idea of a *normative* Protestant Christology might strain credulity. There is, for instance, the sheer diversity of Protestant communions, each without anything more than denominational or local teaching offices for binding clarifications regarding the proclamation, life, and exegesis of its members. There are also Protestant groups wary of the metaphysical cast of the creeds or their messy political background and there are groups resistant to the imposition of a creed itself, whether as a matter of *sola scriptura* or in defence of personal or academic freedom. Modern Protestant theologians are thus burdened not only with the consideration of what should be held as normative within Christian doctrine, but with questions of normativity itself within church and academic life.

All theologies, including those of the Protestant communions, have operative claims regarding what constitutes the Gospel of Jesus Christ and the forms of ecclesial and civil life which the Gospel elicits. Part of the theological task consists of bringing these tacit normative commitments to light so that they may be critically and constructively assessed. In displaying these normative assumptions Christian theology hopes to purge itself of the dangers of being either an exercise in fantasy or a vehicle for one's own interests. The mission of the Church to the world is also served when the various Protestant communions can clearly and kerygmatically display to others their own normative assumptions and hear back from others their understanding and judgements regarding these assumptions. Finally, theological reflection forms part of the churches' response to divine disclosure, calling, and commission. In discussing what is normative within church life and teaching, Protestant Christologies demonstrate that they are bound to something beyond themselves and the interests and prejudices of its practitioners and are ultimately accountable before their subject matter, which is not an inert object or principle but the living, infinite, and self-communicative God.

In what follows I will briefly rehearse, in a Protestant key, two presuppositions for Christology; the sources, norms, and sphere of Christology; and the person and work of Jesus Christ. The discussions will primarily take place in the register of the assertoric, explanatory, and observatory rather than the apologetic or historical.

PRESUPPOSITIONS

Two presuppositions guide what follows. The first is formal: Christology is an intelligible and identifiable discipline. The positive implication is that Christology concerns the person and work of Jesus Christ in his being and activity for us and with us. The extent to which Christology remains dedicated and committed to Jesus Christ is the extent to which Christology gains its coherence, material content, and distinctive contours as a concrete discipline. The negative implication is that Christology is not an outpost of metaphysics, psychology, politics, or historical research, and so analyses of Christologies past and present best proceed when claims regarding the person and work of Christ remain the subject of analysis.

The same holds true within systematic theology as a whole. Accounts of the person and work of Jesus Christ are not subsets of sacramentology, ecclesiology, soteriology, revelation, the Christian life, or a doctrine of creation. Rather, the reverse is true. Jesus Christ is the light which illuminates, orients, and inspires Christian doctrine, and in the process renders Christian proclamation and teaching Christian. Yet the significance of the person and work of Jesus Christ can only be fully realized when other doctrines are developed to their utmost. There is, then, a mutual conditioning, dependence, and asymmetrical reciprocity between Christology and other doctrinal loci. Christology has a perpetual place of priority within other doctrines and yet these doctrines require their own patient and focused elaboration.

The second presupposition is material and grounds the first: Jesus Christ is God for us and with us. As God for us and with us, Jesus Christ is the unconditioned which conditions all other conditions. He is and provides his own meaning and significance, as infinitely rich and varied as they may be. There exists a perpetual temptation to place Jesus Christ within some larger system, process, or category and in doing so overwhelm Jesus Christ through the imposition of an overarching frame of reference derived from some place or event other than Jesus Christ himself. These frameworks can be naturalist, historicist, political, psychological, or even biblical and yet not be fully Christian. When his meaning and reality are placed within these other frames of reference then Jesus Christ and his work are inevitably seen as the instantiation or illustration of some larger reality, not as God himself for us and with us. The goal and hope of a normative Protestant Christology is that the risen Jesus Christ himself can be heard and followed in our own particular contexts while not becoming a screen for the outplaying of our own whims or partisanships. That he can so quickly become such things means that Protestant Christology will necessarily include a critical task for the sake of allowing Jesus Christ himself to be heard and understood afresh.

SOURCE, NORM, AND SPHERE

In line with the two presuppositions elaborated above, the source and norm of Christology can only be the risen Jesus Christ himself. Put within a more Protestant key, we can say that the source and norm of Protestant Christology is Jesus Christ himself in his self-attestation and revelation through Scripture, the sanctified instrument by which Christ renews and guides his Church. As the risen and exalted Son, Jesus Christ is not a remote, absent, or silent figure, but a living and communicative subject who is present to his Church by the power of the Holy Spirit in its Scripture, sacraments, and ministry of reconciliation. Protestant Christology attempts to heed and follow this self-declaration by an attentive and critical listening to his voice within the whole of Scripture's witness to God's being and act in Jesus Christ. As the self-commissioned means by which Jesus Christ ministers to his Church, the witness of Scripture to Jesus Christ cannot be replaced as the source and norm of Christology. Scripture remains the irreducible *norma normans* of theological reflection. Creeds and confessions can only serve as *norma normata*, with their role being subservient to the identification and description of Jesus Christ as narrated within the NT, and not conceptual enhancements upon it.

The sphere of Christological reflection is the Church, the community established by Jesus Christ which proclaims his good news in its worship and mission. In its responsibility to its source and norm, Jesus Christ himself, Christology dedicates its work to the community which he has justified, sanctified, and sent out into the world as his beloved brothers and sisters. Protestant theology serves this community inasmuch as it seeks to edify church proclamation, life, and mission by critically and constructively measuring it against the self-attestation of Jesus Christ within Scripture. Christology does not invent its sphere anymore than its source and norm, and thus it remains bound first and foremost to the upbuilding of the faith, hope, and love of the Church in its witness and service to the world.

The advent of historical criticism has raised a variety of questions for Christology, one of the most pressing of which has been the relationship between the 'Christ of faith' and the 'Jesus of history'. The Christ of faith refers to the portraits of Jesus Christ as found within the NT and already aglow with the light of post-Easter faith. Whether or not the Gospels are βιοῖ or *vitae*, the NT writings as a whole are seldom interested in giving a laundry list of Jesus Christ's daily activities, but are instead already soaked with profound reflection upon the significance of Christ's life, death, and resurrection; replete with imagery and material from the OT and intertestamental writings; and marked by the specific circumstances of the early communities in which they were circulated, read, and treasured. The Jesus of history, by contrast, could refer either to the historical reality of what Jesus Christ said and did during his life, or to the figure of Jesus as reconstructed by academics according to generally accepted (and shifting) criteria for historical authenticity. While it may be quietly implied or explicitly stated, this second version of the Jesus of history means Jesus shorn of the interpretations and interpolations of his earliest communities of followers and subsequently re-dressed in the conventions of contemporary historians and what passes for history in the modern sense. In the words of Gerhard Ebeling:

> In this situation the phrase 'historical Jesus' is directed not so much, as is funda-
> mental in all historical study, against additions and errors of some kind in the tradi-
> tion; nor even against the legendary Jesus. We could much sooner say, against the
> mythologized Jesus. But even this does not exactly touch the heart of the difficulty.
> Rather the slogan 'historical Jesus' is really directed against the kerygmatic or dog-
> matic Jesus, or, as is also said with a significant change of name, against the 'dogmatic
> Christ' or the 'biblical Christ' or the Christ of faith.

(Ebeling 1963: 291)

Discussion of the adequacy of this distinction and its meaning for Christological reflec-tion has continued unabated since these characteristics of the NT's portrayals of Jesus Christ were pointed out and reflected upon by Martin Kähler in his 1892 *Der sogenannte historische Jesus und der geschichtliche, biblische Christus*. One possible conclusion to the potentially unsettling realization that the NT depictions of Jesus Christ are not examples of modern historiography is to posit the Jesus of history (taken in second sense) as the norm of Christology and the material within the NT which passes the criteria for his-torical authenticity as its source. Once again the tendency here is to place Jesus Christ within some more determinative metaphysical or epistemological framework, which in the case of the tenets of modern historical research would be a kind of methodological naturalism. Methodologies are notoriously prone to becoming metaphysics, and so a great deal of theology's native language and concepts—providence, revelation, divine commissioning, the Spirit's work of sanctifying historical and creaturely media—would be required to prevent viewing the NT as ultimately a failed attempt at history, rather than the *viva vox Christi* for the Church, and then viewing our own reconstructions as historically superior to or more enlightening than Scripture itself.

Nevertheless, inasmuch as Christology presupposes that the Jesus Christ who is risen and present to his Church truly lived, taught, and was crucified and resurrected, it is clear that historical critical research into the life of Jesus, the earliest strata of confession in Jesus, eyewitness testimony and the formation of communal memory, and the origins and transmission of the various Gospel sources and their assemblage and use, are too important to ignore. There is also no reason to deny the undeniable gains in exegetical and theological acuity by increased knowledge of the beliefs and practices of Second Temple Judaism or sociological analysis of the earliest Christian groups. 'The demand that the Bible should be read and understood and expounded historically is, there-fore, obviously justified and can never be taken too seriously. The Bible itself posits this demand' (Barth 1963: 464). Scripture itself issues this demand inasmuch as the inspiration, commissioning, and sanctification of human witnesses and human words is not only part of the reception and proclamation of God's work in Jesus Christ, but one of its goals. Protestant theologians should be confident and generous enough to encourage these historical pursuits, praise their concern for truth telling, and view them as a testament to the attraction of Jesus Christ.

The primary doctrinal issue regarding the 'Jesus of history' and historical criticism more generally is their degree of authority within Christological reflection and the placement and use of their findings in such a way that this degree of authority is recognized. Not all of their historical material will need to be directly and comprehensively inserted into the tasks of doctrinal reflection or preaching (and indeed should not be), but they can be, for instance, of exegetical assistance, which is of genuine interest to theologians, preachers, and laypersons.

CHRIST'S PERSON AND WORK

Protestant Christology has traditionally consisted of discussions of the person and work of Christ (also parsed as his dignity and effects, or being and activity); Christ's threefold office as prophet, priest, and king; and the two states of humiliation (*status exinanitionis*) and exaltation (*status exaltationis*). These discussions might be preceded by an account of the covenant of grace (particularly in the Reformed tradition), and were often followed by the subjective and objective application of salvation and the Church as the means of grace.

As often noted, the division between Christ's person and work is purely heuristic and convenient. As Friedrich Schleiermacher succinctly puts it, the doctrines of Christ's person and work 'are quite different so far as the individual propositions are concerned, but their total content is the same' (Schleiermacher 2011: §92, 376). This division into person and work loses its utility as soon as one imagines oneself to be speaking of different things when describing Christ's person and his work. In Jesus Christ there is the perfect coincident of being and activity. It is Jesus Christ himself who causes us to say this rather than any philosophy of becoming, actualism, or personhood.

Jesus Christ's person cannot be divorced or detached from his work. Jesus Christ serves the Father by offering a life lived in complete self-offering to the children of the Father, even until the acceptance of the Cross as consonant with this self-donation in love and obedience. Yet in this utter disregard for himself, Jesus Christ is and remains supremely himself. His total self-offering is not the dissipation or diminution of his person, but the display and confirmation that he truly is the Son of the Father. Likewise, Jesus Christ's work cannot be divorced or detached from his person. Jesus Christ does not only bring peace, but is himself our peace (Eph. 2:14); he does not only speak the word of God, but is himself the Word (John 1:14); he does not only win our redemption, but is himself our redemption and hope (1 Tim. 1:1). One cannot cling to his work or his benefits without clinging to the very person who won them. There is, then, no way of embracing the majesty or glory of his person without also embracing his lowly work as a servant among the people of Israel and there is no embracing the benefits he has won and bestowed without embracing the broken, crucified, and resurrected body of the majestic and eternal Son.

Person

Jesus Christ is God for us and with us. He is this, however, as a unique mode of being, a distinct manner of subsisting, as one τρόπος ὑπάρξεως of God's self-giving and self-communication to the world. The Father to whom both Israel and the Son pray, who causes his sun to rise and sends his rain on both the righteous and unrighteous, is God. Yet no less God is the Jewish man Jesus who dwelt amongst sinners, the poor, and prostitutes, who was crucified and resurrected, and who now lives in believers and is present to them in Word and sacrament. Yet no less God is the Spirit who hovered over the primordial waters, drove Jesus into the wilderness, is the love and holiness within and amongst believers, and groans with the whole of creation in bondage. Each is not the other and yet each is not without the other. It is not some nondescript divine nature or principle which becomes incarnate, then, but the Son.

Inasmuch as God has given over God's very own self within the economy, and to be known as he truly is, then the relative distinctions between Father, Son, and Spirit are constitutive of the one God of Israel. Neither Jesus Christ nor the Spirit is the temporary mask of some otherwise unknown and general deity. The eternal God is not distorted or changed into something else when acting in the economy. No divine or semi-divine intermediaries are necessary to protect God from creation or creation from God. There is no unknown God locked in the splendid majesty of a remote transcendence. There is but the one threefold God who in his self-giving and self-revelation to his creation has made himself present and known as he truly is: Father, Son, Spirit.

The person of Jesus Christ is primarily identifiable by his relations to the Father and the Spirit. As regards the first term, Jesus Christ is the only begotten Son; the eternal Word who was with God and was God in the beginning; conceived Wisdom (1 Cor. 1:24); and the Image of the invisible God (Col. 1:15; 2 Cor. 4:4). Each stands as a proper name of the Son inasmuch as it expresses that his origin is the unbegotten Father, that he is like the Father in all respects except is not the Father, and that he is equal to the Father in divinity. As regards the second, Jesus Christ is the one conceived by the Spirit, on whom the Spirit rests, and the one whom the Spirit raised from the dead (Rom. 8:11). This Spirit in turn is the Spirit sent out by Jesus Christ and is also identified as his very own Spirit (John 15:26, 20:22; Phil. 1:19; Gal. 4:6). In each instance the persons of the Trinity occupy identifiable relations vis-à-vis the others and are only identifiable in and as these relationships. Jesus Christ is, then, the incarnate Son of the Father, the one both conceived in the womb and raised from the dead by the Holy Spirit, and the sender of this selfsame Spirit.

The doctrine of Christ's two natures is best thought of as subservient to Jesus Christ's personal unity as the one incarnate Word whose life, death, and resurrection is narrated in the Gospels. The life, death, and resurrection of the man Jesus is none other than the life, death, and resurrection of the eternal Son, to follow the logic of 'the crucified Lord of glory' (1 Cor. 2:8) or the tenth anathema of the Second Council of Constantinople (553): 'If anyone does not confess his belief that our Lord Jesus Christ, who was crucified in his human flesh, is truly God and the Lord of glory and one of the members of the Trinity: let him be anathema.' The doctrine of Christ's two natures helps to ensure that statements regarding Jesus Christ are also predicable of the second person of the Trinity inasmuch as Jesus Christ is the incarnate Son and thus fully human as well as divine. That Jesus Christ is truly God and truly human, without any confusion, change, division, or separation of either deity or humanity, means that God can become truly and perfectly human without ceasing to be God and without any curtailment or alteration of either deity or humanity.

The doctrines of the ἀνυπόστασις and ἐνυπόστασις, amongst other things, also aid in asserting the unity of Jesus Christ as the Word made flesh. (Given constraints of space we must bypass the complex history of these doctrines in their late patristic pedigree, their appropriations by the Protestant scholastics, and their modern versions.) The former asserts that the human nature of Jesus Christ exists solely from the goodness, initiative, and prevenience of God. As 'impersonal', Jesus Christ's human nature has no centre of subsistence, existence, or personhood in and of itself apart from the Word's assumption of humanity (taken either as abstract or concrete). Jesus Christ's human nature only exists inasmuch as the Word, forever remaining himself, freely and graciously takes it up into the unity of his person and makes it his very own. There are not, then, two distinct centres of subsistence or existence in Jesus Christ, but only one: the eternal Son. The latter helps to ensure that the human nature fully, truly, and perfectly exists, but only 'in' the personal unity of the divine Word. Within the personal unity of the Word, the divine and human natures need not compete for space, such that one element of either nature (such as soul or νοῦς) would need to replace the other. Instead, the Word has taken up and assumed all of what it means to be human so that all of what it means to be human might be healed and renewed.

The metaphysical cast of the doctrine of the two natures (and the ancient ecumenical creeds more generally) has caused some concern amongst modern Protestant theologians. Yet the creeds and confessions, precisely in their stark and naïve realism regarding the concept of 'nature', are able to ensure that the absolute presence of the divine and human in the man Jesus Christ is not quaint verbiage or psychological projection, but truly expresses the identity and life of this man as both fully God and fully human. The doctrine of the two natures is an ancillary conceptual apparatus which allows us to say clearly and confidently something both simple and wondrous: that Jesus Christ is the Word made flesh. In order to say this, however, it is necessary to sweep away a host of oversimplifications stripped of the astonishing character of this event. Jesus Christ is not simply a blessed and upright man (Ebionism) or a passing theophany (Docetism), neither is he a man become divine (adoptionism), an exalted creature (Arianism), a mixture of deity and humanity (some forms of monophysitism), or an already existing human person assumed by the Son (Nestorianism). He is, rather, God for us and with us in the form of this itinerant and finally crucified and resurrected Jewish peasant. The doctrine of the two natures, along with the traditional *communicatio idiomatum*, conceptually assists the venerable impression that what we can say of the man Jesus Christ we should also be able to say of God himself inasmuch as the life of the man Jesus Christ is none other than the life of the eternal Son.

Work

What follows is a consideration of Jesus Christ's work of reconciliation. This focus should in no way imply that reconciliation exhausts Christ's work such that the whole range of his activity could be handled in this single doctrinal locus. The NT seeps Jesus Christ into the whole of the divine economy. Jesus Christ is an agent within the creation of the world (creation); the very Image of God of which we are secondary images, the final Adam, the heavenly man (anthropology); our salvation and peace with God, the one in whom we are elected, justified, and sanctified (soteriology); the head of the Church, which is his body (ecclesiology); the inaugurator and referent of the Christian practices of baptism and the Lord's Supper (sacramentology); the one who as the first fruits of the resurrection will come to judge the living and the dead (eschatology); the one who teaches us how to pray and live together before the Father (the Christian life); and the one who illumines the Scriptures (exegesis). There seems to be no element of the divine economy outside of his presence and activity.

The sweeping nature of Christ's work is readily reflected in the view, historically in the minority, that the eternal Son would have become incarnate regardless of whether the Fall had occurred or not. The 'incarnation anyway' arguments include Jesus Christ being the crown of creation, the cosmic mediator and king, and the presupposition and completion of humanity. The Incarnation is put forward as the ultimate demonstration of the divine love for humanity, the highest diffusion of goodness, necessary for the revelation of the Trinity and thus of God's identity, or an essential event in humanity's deification. The historically dominant view, however, has been that the Son's Incarnation is a response to the Fall. The reasons given for dismissing the 'incarnation anyway' alternative typically suggest that such a position is so much idle and distracting speculation which downplays the importance of the Cross and repudiates the clear witness of Scripture that Christ came to seek and save the lost (Luke 19:10), to save sinners (Matt. 1:21; 1 Tim. 1:15), and to give his life as a ransom for many (Mark 10:45; Matt. 20:28). In what follows we will only handle this second, more specific aspect of Christ's work.

Within Reformed theology in particular, the 'incarnation anyway' question is sometimes subsumed within the different disagreement regarding infralapsarian and supralapsarian accounts of the eternal divine decrees. The former maintains that the object of the divine predestination is *homo creatus et lapsus*, created and fallen humanity, while the latter holds that it is *homo creabilis et labilis*, humanity not yet created and not yet fallen. This question finally concerns the logical order of the divine decrees of creation, fall, and election and preterition/reprobation rather than whether the Son would have become incarnate regardless of the occurrence of the Fall.

The NT gathers a variety of descriptions and doxologies around the life, death, and resurrection of Jesus Christ and in the process uses concepts, stories, and terms pulled from Jewish, Christian, and Graeco-Roman contexts. This event is named and described as salvation, atonement, reconciliation, new covenant, adoption, deliverance from bondage, restoration, ransom, victory over the powers, new creation, justification, the forgiveness of sin, sacrifice, union with Christ, exchange, and satisfaction. Despite their various linguistic, cultural, and scriptural registers, these descriptions are one in their naming God alone the agent of Christ's reconciling work, humanity alone the benefactor, and Jesus Christ alone its mediator, executor, and bearer.

God alone saves. It is God alone who reconciles the world to himself, who puts to death the 'old man' in Jesus Christ, who forgives sin, who adopts daughters and sons, who frees and releases from the destructive bondage of sin and death, who brings forth his eschatological Kingdom. That humanity is its benefactor means that the goal of Christ's work is the restoration of humanity from its present misery, inhumanity, and rebellion against its Creator and itself. The calling, justification, and sanctification of humanity takes place so that humans may be genuine covenant partners with God and with each other. It is Jesus Christ who in the presence and power of the Spirit executes the Father's desire to bestow his love and forgiveness on his children, who mediates this love and forgiveness, and who bears the Father's good tidings.

The Protestant divines often handled Christ's work according to his one threefold office (*munus triplex*) as prophet, priest, and king (cf. Calvin 2006: 494–503; Schleiermacher 2011: §§102–5, 438–75). As the Messiah, the anointed one of God, Jesus Christ follows in the steps of the prophets, priests, and kings who were anointed in the OT. As prophet, Jesus stands as God's representative before humanity, teaching and interpreting the law, prophesying, and performing miracles. As priest, Jesus Christ is humanity's representative before God, intercedes on our behalf before the Father, fulfils the Law by remaining obedient in life (active obedience), and atones for the sin of humanity by his suffering and death (passive obedience). As king, Jesus Christ rules over his Church, provides for and protects his followers, and seeks out the well-being of his community.

The primary objective of a doctrine of Christ's threefold office is not neat or total classification but descriptive adequacy to the manifold character of Christ's work and its relationship to God's history with Israel. For the sake of this descriptive adequacy older accounts of Christ's threefold office may need to be supplemented or corrected. Traditional accounts of Christ's kingly work, for instance, should be supplemented with the scriptural theme of Jesus Christ's victory on the Cross over the powers and principalities of this world (Col. 2:15). The claim that the crucified and resurrected Jesus Christ is king means that there is none other finally worthy of discipleship and obedience, that true kingship is servanthood for the other, and that the kings of this world are revealed to be pretenders inasmuch as they demand to be served rather than offering to serve.

Likewise, traditional accounts of Christ's priestly work could gain from being attentive to the complex and fluid nature of sacrifice, representation, and the forgiveness of sin within the OT, freed of any lingering Marcionite tendencies, and cognizant of the role of sacrifice as thanksgiving and praise as found in the prophets, the psalms, and Jesus himself. (General theories or sociologies of sacrifice, especially when focused upon the sublimation of violence, or the appeasement and coercion of deity, will be of limited use here, foreign as they are to the complex economy of sacrifice, the banishing of sin, and table fellowship with God as found within Scripture.) They should also be supplemented by the reminder that the work of the priest also consists of gathering together the community's prayers, directing the worship of the people towards God, and pronouncing blessings over the people and in this way follow the cultic framework of Christ's priestly ministry rather than subordinating it to a legal framework. Finally, older accounts of Jesus Christ's prophetic work should be amended by the stress that the bodily nature of his earthly ministry is no less significant or serious than the bodily nature of his resurrection. The signs of the Kingdom are manifested physically, in healings, the exorcism of demons, the feeding of the hungry, and the bodily impact of words of forgiveness and mercy. Even Jesus Christ's sheer presence speaks of the nature of the Kingdom, for in his sovereign freedom he remains physically present in the Father's house, with the lost in table fellowship, and alongside those forgotten or worthless either religiously or politically. His presence among the poor, the oppressed, and the downtrodden is an embodied recognition of their worth, a physical conferring of status, love, and dignity.

While neither *de rigueur* for an account of Christ's work, nor a guarantee of its success, the diversity of office helps prevent reductions of Christ's work to moral influence, sacrifice, or lordship. At its best, then, this way of arranging a doctrine of Christ's work remains materially mobile, deeply rooted and conversant in the history of God's dealings with Israel and the other nations, and comfortable with overlap and incompleteness.

The offices of prophet, priest, and king do not predetermine the work of Jesus Christ, nor do they set up a framework which he necessarily has to fill as mediator. Instead Jesus Christ adopts these offices and makes them his own and in doing so redefines them. The prophets in the OT are commissioned at a specific moment to bring a particular word of God to his people, while from his very inception to his ascension Jesus Christ is himself the Word. The priests represent the people before God, conduct sacrifices, offer prayers, and pronounce blessings on both God and the people. On the great Day of Atonement the high priest enters the Holy of Holies to make atonement for himself, his household, and the whole of Israel (Lev. 16:17). Jesus Christ is a high priest of the order of Melchizedek (Heb. 7:13–17). He does not offer the body and blood of another once a year, but gives over his own body and blood once and for all (Heb. 9:11–28), and acts solely on the behalf of others inasmuch as he himself requires no atoning (Heb. 7:27). Given the tumultuous tradition of the kings of Israel both in the OT and the history of ancient Israel, we should note that the ideal king to come is a just ruler of the people, the hope for peace and posterity in an everlasting dynasty, the deliverer and protector of a suffering people, and the liberator of Israel from foreign oppressors. Jesus Christ is a king whose Kingdom is not of this earth, whose subjects occupy no well-defined territory, whose reign is composed of utter self-giving and love, who bears a crown of thorns and dies cursed on a tree, and who bestows an eternal inheritance upon his adopted children.

Traditionally Jesus Christ's earthly ministry was associated with his prophetic office, the Cross with his priestly office, and his resurrection and ascension with his kingly office. Yet during his earthly ministry Jesus Christ summons the apostles, sends out his ambassadors, authorizes others to speak in his name, and commands the natural elements (kingly work), and yet he also forgives sin and enacts table fellowship with the lost and oppressed (priestly work). Furthermore, his death is also linked to the fate of past prophets (Mark 12:1–9; Matt. 23:34–6), to his implicit claim to kingship (John 19:5), and to his drawing together of his subjects (John 12:32). It seems, then, that there can be no safe separation of Christ's threefold office into discrete moments. Rather Jesus Christ exercises his threefold office simultaneously throughout the course of his life, death, and resurrection, for in each of these instances there is revelation, reconciliation, and lordship.

Jesus Christ's threefold office extends beyond this life, death, and resurrection. As he is a living, acting, and self-communicative subject, the Church does not (and indeed cannot) 'actualize' or 'realize' his presence as it would need to do were he a distant, mute, or absent figure. Instead the risen and exalted Jesus Christ is seated at the right hand of the Father and continues to exercise his threefold office as prophet, priest, and king for the sake of the Church and the world. In his presence and activity within the Church, Jesus Christ remains the interpreter of God for us, bears his scars and intercedes for us before the Father, and provides for his people through the Church's lived proclamation and Lord's Supper. (Barth is perhaps the theologian of the twentieth century who most emphasized the work of the ascended Christ, but it can also be found in the Lutheran and Reformed scholastics and their distinction between the immediate and mediate exercise of Christ's prophetic office in Word and sacrament.)

Jesus Christ's free and gracious work is perfect, sufficient, and unique, and requires no further supplement or enhancement. It is his own free and gracious work inasmuch as it takes place in the face of complete resistance and misunderstanding from both his enemies and his followers; God showed his love for us in that Christ offered himself for us when we were still sinners (Rom. 5:8). Christ's work is perfect and sufficient inasmuch as he fully and willingly accomplishes the whole of the good work the Father set out for him and to which the Spirit led him. It is unique inasmuch as it is completely and utterly the work of this man, the work of the Son of God, and which as such stands as radiant, indestructible, and joyous in and of itself. It is a work which is blessed and glorified by the Holy Spirit who seals and pours it out into our hearts as lives lived in faith, love, and hope. As perfect and sufficient in and of itself, his work encounters us as free, unmerited, and total grace, eliciting in turn sheer and surprised gratitude and joy on our part. Our own work can at most be to speak his words instead of our own, to offer free and bodily witness to the reconciliation which he himself has accomplished, and to pray and labour in his fields while we wait for his coming Kingdom. There is, then, an infinite qualitative difference between his work and our own. There can be at most here a weak and faint resemblance, an ever greater dissimilarity for every yet so weak and fleeting similarity.

While perfect and sufficient, Jesus Christ freely and graciously includes others within his mission. Jesus Christ calls and sends out his apostles, entrusting them with the ministry of reconciliation and giving them promises of being able to perform their own signs and wonders (Mark 16:15–18; Matt. 28:18–20). There is not anything in themselves which make them fit or ready for this service. Christ institutes his Church with those who misunderstand, who fall asleep, who strive for personal glory, and who deny him. This is virtually a guarantee (but not a justification) of the fact that the Church will always be a church of scoundrels, full of resistance to God and others, and replete with misunderstandings of Jesus Christ's message. Thus in order for the Church to be the Church it must remain wholly dependent and constantly renewed by Christ's Holy Spirit and the promise of his presence.

Yet the Church should not be surprised but should even hope and expect to be met by Jesus Christ as it is sent out into the world. It is in the Church's missionary work, in its being called out of itself, that the Church follows and acknowledges the movement and activity of Jesus Christ. No less than in his life, the exalted Christ continues his own work of being present to and among the poor, the oppressed, and the lost, and so it is among the least of these that the Church can expect to find the presence and activity of Jesus Christ and his disciples (whether or not they are known as such). The grace and love of Jesus Christ will always outpace that of the Church, and it is because the Church's hope lies not in itself but in him that the Church can hope for the world. It is because of who Jesus Christ is and what he has done that the Church may be confident and hopeful that his renewing and judging presence will be active and effective even when and where the Church has stumbled and failed. Jesus Christ is God with us and for us inasmuch as he is also with and for the other. Thus Jesus Christ, with all of his beloved children of the world in tow, stands at the door of the Church and knocks, asking the Church to step outside of itself and to join them.

Suggested Reading

Breytenbach (2010); Jenson (1997: 125–45, 165–206); Pannenberg (2004: 277–464); Tanner (2010); Webster (2001: 113–50).

Bibliography

Barth, K. (1963), *Church Dogmatics I/2* (Edinburgh: T. & T. Clark).

Breytenbach, C. (2010), *Grace, Reconciliation, Concord: The Death of Christ in Graeco-Romans Metaphors* (Leiden: Brill).

Calvin, J. (2006), *Institutes of the Christian Religion* (Louisville, Ky.: Westminster/John Knox).

Ebeling, G. (1963), *Word and Faith* (Philadelphia: Fortress).

Jenson, R. (1997), *Systematic Theology*, vol. 1: *The Triune God* (Oxford: Oxford University Press).

Kähler, M. (1964), *The So-called Historical Jesus and the Historic, Biblical Christ* (Philadelphia: Fortress).

Pannenberg, W. (2004), *Systematic Theology*, vol. 2 (London: T. & T. Clark).

Schleiermacher, F. (2011), *The Christian Faith* (Berkeley, Calif.: Apocryphile Press).

Tanner, K. (2010), *Christ the Key* (Cambridge: Cambridge University Press).

Webster, J. (2001), *Word and Church: Essays in Christian Dogmatics* (Edinburgh: T. & T. Clark).

···

CHAPTER 37

WHAT MAKES A CHRISTOLOGY CATHOLIC?

···

GILBERT NARCISSE, O.P.
TRANSLATED BY KENNETH OAKES

CHRISTOLOGY BETWEEN FUNDAMENTAL THEOLOGY AND ECCLESIOLOGY

CATHOLIC Christology refers to the theology of Christ as set out by theologians who belong to the Catholic Church. So it primarily means an ecclesial membership. The root of this membership is not sociological. It is a matter of the deepest mystery of the Church as communion of grace and means of salvation. To say that a Christology is 'orthodox' is to say that it is in agreement with the Church's teaching. This agreement is theological and presupposes being regulated by a norm, dogma, and a certain way of doing theology. These points fall under three areas: fundamental theology, which primarily deals with the presuppositions of any theology, such as revelation, faith, tradition, and theological knowledge; ecclesiology, which spells out the specificity of the Catholic confession; and finally Christology proper, which develops issues related to Christ from the perspective of the two preceding foundations.

SCRIPTURE, TRADITION, AND THE MAGISTERIUM

Throughout its history, the Catholic Church's fundamental theology has described the logic behind its reflections. This reflection issued most recently in Vatican II's constitution *Dei Verbum*, which promulgated the following trilogy: Scripture, Tradition,

Magisterium. This trilogy constitutes the principal source of any Catholic theology. Christology, then, draws on this source for receiving and understanding revelation.

One of the tasks of fundamental theology is to explain the coherence of these three realities. The first question for Christology is, what is it that God reveals in Christ? The answer follows from a consideration of Scripture, Tradition, and the Magisterium. But it is important to note that this does not constitute the whole of theology. Discovering what is revealed is the first step. This step relies on an argument from authority: the authority of Scripture, then of Tradition, then of the Magisterium. These interrelated authorities are, however, not equal. Scripture is the soul of Christology, while Tradition and the Magisterium are at the service of the interpretation of Scripture.

Sacred Scripture

We must emphasize the unique position of Scripture. Strictly speaking, only Scripture is inspired by God. The Second Vatican Council highlights this difference well by saying that Scripture is 'inspired' by the Holy Spirit, while the Church and Tradition are 'guided' by the Holy Spirit. Scripture is a sacred text, the Holy Scriptures. One also speaks of 'sacred' Tradition, but the writings of this Tradition do not have the same degree of authority as Holy Scripture. Sacred Scripture thus has a unique and incomparable place. Scripture is the source and the primary reference for knowing Christ.

The Realism of Scripture in the Tradition

Scripture, however, is the source of Christology to the extent that it places me in real relationship with Christ. Scripture has to be interpreted. One often understands the role of the Tradition and the Magisterium as an exterior or juridical authority, or as a kind of dogmatic framework. But the essential point is truly to meet Christ. The sole aim of the trilogy of Scripture, Tradition, and the Magisterium is to ensure a true and realistic movement from the text to a meaning that places one in relationship with Christ.

Every believer can be in relationship with Christ, by prayer, by an upright life, and, of course, by the direct meditation of Scripture. But to reach Christ in truth, especially with the intention of doing theology and thereby dealing in objective knowledge, requires, according to the Catholic confession, Scripture, Tradition, and the Magisterium all together. In other words, my relation to Christ demands that I open myself to the otherness of Christ, and through that both to the transcendence of God, and also to his intimate and fraternal proximity, the interpersonal immanence of God. This twofold movement of otherness and intimacy is best guaranteed by the otherness of the mediation which Scripture, Tradition, and the Magisterium make when taken together. This trilogy, this way of mediating revelation, was arranged by God precisely because the Holy Spirit wishes to create an absolutely novel intimacy. It is a matter of an interpersonal relation in which every person, the believer and the persons of the Trinity, must meet in truth.

In order to understand Catholic Christology and its concern with orthodoxy it is necessary to move beyond juridical ecclesial considerations. It is not primarily a matter of the legislative power of the Church, Tradition, or dogma, but of a theological (*théologale*) relationship. A theological (*théologale*) relationship is a relationship of the believer with God which recognizes the mystery, gift, and initiative of God to save and to sanctify by means of these mediations, ones which ensure objectivity, truth, universality, and thus reality. This sense of mediation is important for understanding that Christ's humanity is the mediator of revelation in its fullness.

Christ the Fullness of Revelation

In *Dei Verbum* 4 the Second Vatican Council teaches that Christ is the fullness of revelation:

> Then, after speaking in many and varied ways through the prophets, 'now at last in these days God has spoken to us in His Son' (Heb. 1:1–2). For He sent His Son, the eternal Word, who enlightens all men, so that He might dwell among men and tell them of the innermost being of God (see John 1:1–18). Jesus Christ, therefore, the Word made flesh, was sent as 'a man to men'. (3) He 'speaks the words of God' (John 3:34), and completes the work of salvation which His Father gave Him to do (see John 5:36; John 17:4). To see Jesus is to see His Father (John 14:9). For this reason Jesus perfected revelation by fulfilling it through his whole work of making Himself present and manifesting Himself: through His words and deeds, His signs and wonders, but especially through His death and glorious resurrection from the dead and final sending of the Spirit of truth. Moreover He confirmed with divine testimony what revelation proclaimed, that God is with us to free us from the darkness of sin and death, and to raise us up to life eternal. The Christian dispensation, therefore, as the new and definitive covenant, will never pass away and we now await no further new public revelation before the glorious manifestation of our Lord Jesus Christ (see 1 Tim. 6:14 and Tit. 2:13).
>
> (Paul VI 1965)

Christ is fullness first as the consummation of Scripture. He is fullness as the consummation of revelation. This meaning of fullness characterizes the time of revelation. If Christ is fullness, then the time after Christ is nothing but the unfolding of the fullness which is completely present in the person of Christ. The issue, then, is whether this fullness is accessible to all people and in all times. The time of revelation, attested in Scripture, is followed by the time of its transmission. How is the plenitude of Christ accessible then? How do we guarantee that this fullness will be comprehensively present, without being lessened or being mixed with error? This is the role of Tradition.

Tradition: Its Role and Its Agents

In general terms, Catholic theology presupposes Tradition. This is especially true for Christology. It is impossible to develop a Christology without taking into account the first ecumenical councils up until the Council of Chalcedon (451). Several centuries of Tradition were necessary to articulate adequately the Christological reality that Christ is true God and true man. This is the key dogmatic formula. Outside of this Christology, which distinguishes in Christ the person and the two natures, the divine and the human, Christology is no longer 'orthodox'. Once again, it is not a matter of juridical orthodoxy but the maintenance of the fullness in Christ and the theological (*théologale*) relationship of the believer with him.

According to *Dei Verbum* 8, however, Tradition is not limited to dogmatic elaboration:

> This tradition which comes from the Apostles develops in the Church with the help of the Holy Spirit. (5) For there is a growth in the understanding of the realities and the words which have been handed down. This happens through the contemplation and study made by believers, who treasure these things in their hearts (see Luke 2:19, 51) through a penetrating understanding of the spiritual realities which they experience, and through the preaching of those who have received through Episcopal succession the sure gift of truth. For as the centuries succeed one another, the Church constantly moves forward toward the fullness of divine truth until the words of God reach their complete fulfillment in her.
>
> (Paul VI 1965)

It is thus the very life of the Church that allows a deepening of Christology. The Second Vatican Council names as agents of the Tradition the meditation and contemplation of the faithful as well as theological study. It also speaks of the '*sensus fidei*', of an experience of faith which creates in the believer a type of existential proximity with Christ that allows the believer to resist errors in an almost instinctive manner and to bind the believer to the truth. In the Catholic Church, the saints play an important role because of their connection with Christ and because they manifest some aspect of Christ's fullness. One must therefore speak of an ecclesial and spiritual synergy which maintains Christ's fullness through the mediations of Scripture, Tradition, and the Magisterium.

THE ROLE OF THE MAGISTERIUM

The role of the Magisterium should be understood correctly. The Magisterium belongs to the time allocated for the transmission of Christ's fullness. But the Magisterium, meaning the pope along with the bishops in communion with the pope, possesses a precisely defined authority. A Catholic places his or her faith not in the Magisterium, but in the God who is revealed in Christ. It is the theological (*théologale*) character of faith which requires us to maintain the primacy of divine authority. Consequently, the Magisterium does not substitute itself for the fullness of Christ. He is the only real fullness. Rather the Magisterium is at the service of the transmission of this fullness. Even more than the historical compromises made by the Church, erroneous ecclesiological conceptions gave rise to the sense that the 'papacy' was the beginning and end of a Catholic believer's faith. The power of defining a dogma only belongs to the Magisterium for a Christological purpose. It has this power so that it can maintain the fullness of Christ, and do so in accordance with purely pneumatological requirements, such as the specific action of the Holy Spirit in guiding the mission of the successors of the apostles. This Christological and pneumatological reality is thus necessary for understanding the infallibility of a dogma.

However, a certain order exists between Scripture and the Magisterium. The Magisterium is not above Scripture. It is the servant, that is, the authorized guide, which enables all believers to reach Christ in his fullness, in the precise meaning of Scripture. The Catholic Magisterium is not the 'best exegete' in the sense that it could offer the most scientific reading of Scripture. It is the exegete of Scripture in that it exercises a charisma of truth in order to enable Christians to live Christ's fullness, thus to live the fullness of the way of salvation.

REDISCOVERING DOGMA

Another clarification regarding dogma is in order. In the history of the Church, the definition of a dogma is often made in order to refute a heresy. This is almost always the case for the Christology of Christian antiquity. Against Arianism, for example, it was necessary to define Christ's divinity, clarifying that he was '*homo-ousios*', of the same 'substance' of the Father. A concept from philosophy was thereby borrowed to remove the ambiguities regarding the deepest identity of Christ. This process is highly significant. The Council of Nicaea, the first ecumenical council, recognized the necessity of introducing a non-biblical word, 'substance', for clearing up conflicting interpretations of Scripture. The Catholic Church believes that this process enjoys the Holy Spirit's guidance and is therefore willed by God. Furthermore, the fact that a dogma refutes a heresy does not mean that heresy is the cause of dogma. Properly speaking, heresy is not the cause of dogma but its occasion. This is fundamentally different. In this way one avoids a relativistic interpretation of dogma which renders it merely one moment of historical circumstance. Dogma is much more than that. It is a formulation chosen by the Church, by its Magisterium, as nourished by the very life of the Church, so that the mystery being contemplated can be entered more deeply. Dogma is thus both a culmination and a point of departure. It is the culmination of the Church's entire spiritual life, including the diversity of its charisms and in its hierarchal organization, and speaks with clarity on a specific point of revelation. But it is also a point of departure in that it provokes the reflection of believers and theologians who then draw out the consequences of a clear and certain truth. When understood well, dogma is in the service of the understanding of the faith (*l'intelligence de la foi*). We can go further. Dogma does not constitute a detour away from Scripture. It allows one to read Scripture in all its depth. Dogma, however, will never replace Scripture. As such, dogma is often a highly abstract conceptual statement. It is thus always necessary to plunge back into the wealth of Scripture, without, naturally, anachronism and while respecting its literary genres. The affirmation of Christ's lordship, as consubstantial with the Father, is the beginning of numerous and very fertile Christological and Trinitarian developments. From Christ's divinity one will then move to the affirmation of a balance between his humanity and his divinity in accordance with the dogma of the hypostatic union. Dogma exists, then, for rediscovering the theological (*théologal*) meaning and all the theological potentialities that it contains. One can use dogma in fundamentalist or progressive ways and present it as a defense of ecclesial identity. This would be a serious deformation, for dogma would no longer be seen in its intimate link with Scripture and the spiritual life of the community.

Christology primarily responds to this question: what does the revelation of Jesus Christ say to us? It is Scripture read within the Tradition which enables a response. A class on Christology will thus have to examine at length Scripture, the whole of Scripture, and then the givens of Tradition. Each field demands an interpretation which is appropriate to it.

One does not use the same method to study Messianism in Scripture and Christ's divinity in the Tradition. The ideal is to receive revelation by the mutual fertilization of the two, Scripture and the Tradition, on the understanding that the Holy Spirit guides the Church and the believer.

If Christology requires the examination of revelation then it also requires faith. It is only faith, and then the understanding of the faith, which allows one to probe the depths of revelation and thus of Christology. This acceptance of revelation as revelation does not exclude the use of other intellectual means, such as philosophy. But when introduced into dogma, philosophy does not condition what Scripture reveals to us concerning Christ, with all the nuances of which only Scripture is capable.

The key dogmas therefore state that Jesus is God; that Jesus is true God and true man; and that Jesus is a person, the second person of the Trinity, in two natures, human and divine. The big questions concern the being of Christ. They result from the reception of a revelation which finely arranged the work and being of Christ. One grasped who Jesus was by observing his work and, like the disciples, by understanding it in faith. But the inverse is also true. The work of the Holy Spirit in the Tradition allows one to enter into the mystery of the being of Christ and, by this mystery, to know better the meaning and scope of his work. To err on the being of Christ is to err on his work. But not to consider the work of Christ is to contradict the whole of revelation which regards both Christ and what he has done for us human beings.

The Soteriological Motive

Christ's activity is understood as salvific. From ancient times onward, people used a particular argument for what is called the 'soteriological motive'. It consists in this kind of reasoning: if Christ is not like this, then humanity is not saved. For example, if Christ is not God, then humanity is not saved, for only God saves. Or again, if Christ is not 'truly man' then humanity is not saved, for only that which God genuinely assumed in the Incarnation is saved. Incarnation and salvation are thus bound together. This is the realism of the Incarnation.

An open question still remains: is the link between incarnation and redemption necessary? In the Middle Ages the question was posed in this way: if humanity had not sinned, would God have become incarnate? Two different understandings of Christianity can be seen in the possible responses. The first makes the Incarnation primarily about the deification of humanity, its elevation into God, independently of sin. The second maintains that the Incarnation, as the Bible seems to suggest, is linked to soteriology. According to this response, the Cross of the Christ and thus also the Eucharist are central. Naturally, humanity is both saved and deified. But can we establish a certain primacy?

Christology and the Understanding of the Faith

Such a question shows that the revelation we have received generates a multitude of questions which theology must plumb. It is, in fact, essential that Christology confronts different questions, old or new. Christology does not only deal with revelation in terms of arguments from authority, such as that of Scripture, Tradition, and the Magisterium. Christology is the understanding of the faith inasmuch as it develops arguments from reason.

What was discovered in Scripture and in the Tradition, what was formulated in dogmas, must now be dealt with in the form of a demonstration which will allow the intellect, enlightened by faith, to enter more deeply into the mystery by displaying its significance and by offering reasons for it. Naturally, perfect knowledge of God surpasses the light of faith and will only be realized in the hereafter. The same is also true for Christology. St. Thomas Aquinas recognizes that the hypostatic union is an inexhaustible mystery, which means that this union, and along with it the whole mystery of Christ's being and work, will always be only partially understood in this life.

One could give three examples of current Christological questions: the salvation accomplished by Christ; the meaning of the death of Jesus; and the knowledge and consciousness of Jesus. It is not our task to resolve these questions here but simply to indicate how one would handle them within Catholic theology. The presuppositions of fundamental theology were mentioned earlier. The first ecumenical councils are also important for posing these subjects well. One must also take account the current situation of the faith. More than ever before there are interactions with other Christian confessions, especially the Orthodox and Protestant traditions. Mutual influences are recognizable, sometimes in the form of opposition but also often in the form of convergence. There are also interactions with other religions which raise questions regarding the mediation of Christ and the meaning of the Incarnation of God.

THE PROBLEM OF CONTEXTUAL THEOLOGY

These questions lead to reflections on how to proceed within Christology. By beginning with revelation one proposes a Christology 'from above', which is how Scripture proceeds in St. John's prologue or St. Paul's hymn in Philippians. A different procedure begins with the situations of different people and takes them into account when raising Christological questions. This is the method of contextual theology. Christology is placed at the forefront. This can be readily seen in liberation theology's emphasis upon 'following Christ'. More broadly, it is enriching to explore how different cultural situations affect one's understanding of Christ and generate new questions. Contextual theology can be fruitful for Christology but on the condition that it does not become an ideology. It should be more aware of the interaction between its sources of reflection, its context, and revelation and it should clearly lay out the hierarchy among them. Assuming that everything is now merely contextual would warrant philosophical criticism and an analysis of the possible consequences within theology. Catholic theology does not exclude contextual theology but situates it in the wider framework of its fundamental theology.

Contextual theology has also provoked a certain theological pluralism in Catholic theology. This pluralism began developing in the nineteenth century under the influence of various philosophies and different attempts to introduce these philosophies into theology. This poses the basic problem of the place of metaphysics, and in particular the metaphysics of the Thomist tradition, which is not the primary point of reference for many Catholic theologians. The problem of metaphysics has repercussions within Christology concerning the meaning of truth and the universality of salvation. The Magisterium continues to recommend the Thomist tradition while allowing a certain plurality, which has always existed among Catholic theologians. If modern Christologies, under the influence of Protestantism, are often oriented to Christ's work for humanity, the 'pro nobis', it remains important to continue to place the big Christological questions on a solid metaphysical basis so that nothing of Christ's fullness is lost.

The Humanity of Christ as Mediator of Salvation

Soteriology has become an important Christological question within an interreligious context. In Christian antiquity the Church had to assert above all the integrity of Christ's humanity over and against Gnosticism. Gnostic contempt of all things bodily was reflected in its exegesis, for the Old Testament roots Christ in humanity, in the humanity of Adam and then in the humanity of the elected people, and in particular the Messiah but also in the prophetic, priestly, and Wisdom traditions. Christ's humanity is real because of its genealogical roots and because of the real maternity of the Virgin Mary. Salvation from God comes by way of Christ's genuine humanity as the one who lived alongside us and who is now in heavenly glory. St. Thomas Aquinas presents several original ideas as regards the work of Christ's humanity. First of all, it is rare for a theologian to have commented on the entirety of the mysteries of Christ and to do so in a primarily speculative work. This interest in Christ's life stems from the soteriological claim that everything Christ did or suffered brings about our salvation. According to St. Thomas, each action of Christ, including those in his hidden life, is the source of salvation. He even claims that one single action of Christ would be sufficient to save all of humanity due to Christ's infinite love. Consequently, St. Thomas believes that, since the Incarnation, any subsequent grace is communicated to humans by the mediation of Christ's humanity. In this way Christ's humanity is placed at the very heart of revelation and salvation. At the same time, this absolute mediation raises serious issues for interreligious conversation: if Christ's humanity is the mediator of all grace, is this also the case for non-Christians, for other religions, even for non-believers? Here the temptation is to 'contextualize' the humanity of Jesus. It retains its value for Jesus' contemporaries and then for Christian believers. For others, however, salvation comes to them by the Word which reaches each person in the contexts of their religious or existential situations. There is thus a triple reduction: an ecclesiological reduction, as the Church is not the only means of salvation; a Christological reduction, as Christ's humanity is not the only mediator of grace; and at times even a theological reduction, as something beyond the Word, even beyond the one God, can communicate grace and salvation. Discussing these positions would require some extended conversations. On this question the Magisterium of the Church has adopted a specific position such that these reductions are not possible. Stated more specifically, Christological mediation is indissociable from ecclesiological mediation. How, then, should we think about salvation in other religions? This is the pressing concern for contemporary theology of religions, whose research is still ongoing. The Magisterium does not offer the entire solution to the question. This is not its role. It only indicates that potential solutions must respect certain points, which in this case is the irreplaceable and universal role of Christ's humanity for the salvation of human beings. Expecting from the Magisterium a complete solution would be to think of it in a falsely supernatural, almost 'magical' way, as if God directly instilled answers into it. But the Holy Spirit's guidance must be understood within ecclesiology as a whole. The Magisterium reaches a conclusion to the extent that its charisma is nourished by the whole spiritual life and theological activity of the Church. At times the Magisterium can depend too much on certain theological positions from one particular era. This is why the teaching of the Magisterium requires a highly informed interpretation of doctrinal and historical context. Moreover, it is necessary to distinguish carefully what concerns faith and what concerns the understanding of the faith. On the side of the believer, it is faith which saves. The understanding of the faith is, naturally, dependent on faith, but from a soteriological standpoint it remains secondary. Certainly a faulty understanding of the faith can harm faith. But faith and its understanding are not identical. The Magisterium looks after the conditions of faith first, and then looks after its understanding of the faith. But it is necessary never to confuse the various positions of theologians with the position of the Catholic Church. The charisms of the work of theologians and the charisms of the bishops united to the pope are not identical and do not play exactly the same roles. It is, then, legitimate for theologians to look for reasoned solutions within a certain diversity and with hesitations, discussions, and so on. This is yet another indication that the theological task cannot be reduced to arguments from authority.

The Death of Jesus

Understanding the death of Jesus will complete these soteriological reflections. This death is expressed in Scripture and Tradition by four concepts: buying back (redemption), sacrifice, merit, and satisfaction. Each of these concepts is susceptible to being poorly understood. Theologians and spiritual movements have subjected them to deformations far removed from the Christological reality, at times even to the point of being morbid. The best way of rediscovering balance and decontaminating these concepts is to return to the primacy of the love of God, especially to Christ's love in his work of salvation as is well attested in Scripture. It is significant, moreover, that the current Magisterium of the Catholic Church itself is undertaking a refocusing upon Scripture in order to return primacy to charity. The encyclicals of Benedict XVI, but also his Christological writings, are exemplars of this refocusing on Scripture.

Understanding the death of the Christ provides another example of how Christology progresses. A fifth concept, that of substitution, was developed. The history of this concept is interesting, for it shows how a theological idea from another confession was able to be introduced into Catholic theology. The concept of 'substitution' was introduced in the sixteenth century by the theology of the Reformation, starting with Martin Luther. It then underwent various evolutions of meaning up until today. Beginning in the Reformation, the idea will be recovered in both Catholic and Orthodox theology. It is an attempt to deepen the redemptive work of God as work *pro nobis*, for us humans and for our salvation. The evolution of its meaning begins from the death of Christ for the sake of humans beings, so as to merit them grace, to the idea of the death of Christ as taking the place of sinners. Thus the cry of Christ on the Cross, 'why have you abandoned me?', is understood to be the experience of an innocent Christ undergoing condemnation and punishment instead of the sinner. For certain theologians, this substitution would go so far as suffering the punishment of hell, of Christ being substituted for the damned so that humans can escape damnation. In the three great Christian confessions, this concept of substitution is understood with different nuances, at times important ones. Many Catholic theologians, and in particular those from within the Thomist tradition, are still quite far from accepting that this concept is of any importance. The eminent Catholic theologian Hans Urs Von Balthasar, however, made it a key point of his Christology and his soteriology. Here we are in the presence of an open discussion between theologians, almost more in an inter-confessional manner, which has taken place without any significant intervention from the Catholic Magisterium. It is a beautiful example, not necessarily of unity as the accounts are very different, but of an inter-confessional theological liberty which always occurs in the expectation of enrichment. Students of theology, for example, are researching whether St. Thomas has any type of idea of substitution, even if the term itself is not present.

The Knowledge and Consciousness of the Christ

The final topic to cover is that of the knowledge and consciousness of Christ. The theme is both old and modern. The principal question is, how does Christ, according to his humanity, know what he knows? From where does his knowledge come? Fairly early on Christology dealt in depth with the relationship between Christ's two wills, his human will and his divine will, especially in terms of the scene of Christ's agony. There still remained the relationship between his two minds. The question was at first circumvented by replying that Jesus was God and therefore knew everything. But at least as early as the Middle Ages, there were attempts to understand the human mind of Christ. St. Thomas starts out from two different modes of knowing. God knows in an intuitive manner while human beings on earth know in a discursive way. St. Thomas believes that part of Christological doctrine is that Christ enjoyed the beatific vision of blessedness here on earth. He resorts to the Platonic theme of innate ideas to account for the passage from intuition to speech in Christ's humanity. Theologians are still discussing this topic today. Several points are of interest as regards Christological method. First of all, theological reflection is perhaps brought forward, including in St. Thomas. Before discussing Christ's beatific vision it would have been necessary to establish that it was properly revealed. St. Thomas seems to accept it as established teaching. But it is not easy to demonstrate it from either Scripture or even from Tradition. Consequently, the Magisterium of the Catholic Church has not handed down a definitive teaching on this point. At times it avoids adopting a definite position and at other times it repeats the prevailing teaching from an era. But no dogma has been precisely elaborated. Finally, mediaeval scholars did not have modern exegesis at their disposal and this is why no difference is made between pre-Easter Jesus and post-Easter Jesus, at least no difference regarding his human mind.

St. Thomas' introduction of a Platonic theme (innate ideas) is surprising in light of the strictly Aristotelian sense that abstraction is opposed to illumination. St. Thomas' Christology grants increasing importance to Christ's humanity as the mediator of grace, which is due to his better knowledge of Patristic commentaries as well as his own biblical commentaries, especially those on St. Paul. In the same way, St. Thomas grants more importance to Christ's acquired knowledge, just as with all humans in the world. But what is essential comes from the beatific vision. This way of Christological deepening, by using philosophical ideas, is common in Catholic theology. It is sometimes harmful. So a Christology overly dominated by a Stoic conception of humanity will exclude any importance for Christ's affectivity and passions, and will even exclude their very existence in him. It is St. Thomas who will introduce the passions into Christ's humanity in a systematic way. One may thus illustrate the crucial point of the wholeness of Christ's humanity as a Christological and soteriological criterion. Consequently, any genuine development within anthropology can bring about developments in Christology. But the inverse is also true. Christology serves a regulative and indeed critical role for anthropologies. Christology also carries anthropology well beyond what philosophies and the human sciences can think.

Under the influence of modern psychology, the question of Christ's consciousness was also posed: Was Jesus conscious of who he was? How was this knowledge gained? Was Jesus conscious of the significance of his mission? Of the significance of his death? One can squash the question by replying that Christ is God and therefore has full knowledge of his being and work. But an attempt was made to understand better his consciousness within his humanity. Thus this typically Christological question also involves fundamental theology and ecclesiology. The less one attributes to the consciousness of Christ, the more one attributes to the first Christian communities. Revelation then seems to move from God himself in Christ to human conditions, doubtless with the Holy Spirit's guidance but still more dependent on various circumstances. At its extreme, one could even imagine different forms of Christianity. The advantage of the theological claim regarding the beatific vision is that it guarantees the divine origin of revelation. This is the coherence that the Thomist tradition most often defends. Furthermore, if Christ did not enjoy the beatific vision then it would be necessary to say that he has faith (which Scripture never says). Our revelation would thus clear up the 'gray area' of faith, even if Christ's faith were exceptional. Theologians argue for both positions, but the topic loses steam at times inasmuch as it presupposes a high level of reflection as well as theories of knowledge which allow the problem to be properly framed. Other theologians think that the question is inappropriate, for it belongs to the mystery and ineffability of the unique case of the person of the incarnate Word.

The Magisterium remains highly prudent on the theme of Christ's consciousness. It is, however, a serious issue which concerns salvation and the mediation of Christ.

Theologians have thought that Jesus did not have a precise awareness of his mission other than the announcement of the Kingdom and that he did not know of the redemptive significance of his death. On these points, the Magisterium has specified certain limits: Christ was indeed conscious of his being, his divine identity, and the significance of his mission, notably his death for the salvation of humanity. Furthermore, this link between kingship, the Messiah, and the Suffering Servant is revealed and lived by Jesus himself. Thus the whole of Scripture witnesses on behalf of this consciousness by its preparation for the one who came to fulfill it in fullness. It is surprising that the beatific vision of Jesus' earthly humanity was maintained for centuries, at least since St. Thomas, and that most theologians now resolve this question so quickly and so differently. The topic suffers from a lack of theological argumentation, which is doubtless due to the fact that several areas of theology are involved.

Theologians, including at times those in the Thomist tradition, have tried to think about Christ's knowledge and consciousness without invoking the pre-Easter beatific vision. The better explanations look for a solution from the perspective of the charisma of prophecy.

An interesting circular causality is produced. It is Scripture which hands down to us the being and work of Christ. But by his unique charisma of prophecy, Christ would have discovered his identity and the significance of his mission in the reading of Scripture.

The episode of the disciples on the road to Emmaus is rather significant here since Jesus is able to explain everything that concerns him from the Scriptures, meaning the Old Testament. There is a circular causality inasmuch as Christ and the Holy Spirit, as fullness and inspiration, bring about Scripture; and Scripture, the joint fruit of the Holy Spirit and humanity, brings about Christ, his being and his mission. Within these theories we can clearly see how Scripture is at the heart of Christology.

CHRIST'S WITNESSES

Christology is not reducible to the work of theologians. The whole spiritual experience of the Church plays a role. The saints and mystical life have a privileged place. They are the friends of Christ. They are agents in the development of Tradition. By their actions and writings they increase awareness of a part of the faith and their relationship to Christ. The theologian must incorporate these sparks of light and of fire. At times theologians themselves have an intense and conscious mystical life. Sometimes they are in contact with great spiritual masters. But mystical experience is also guided by theology. It does not genuinely produce revelation. St. Catherine of Sienna can talk with Christ. Yet this does not constitute a Christology, for it lacks the objectivity of scholarly procedure. These 'private revelations' do not constitute the first and determinative source of Christology. They are regulated by dogma and by the Church's discernment. But the theologian would be wrong to neglect them. They give a deep sense of mystery and avoid limiting Christ to all too human views or ends. They must be understood as an 'effect of reading' Holy Scripture and manifestations of an inexhaustible fecundity.

CHRISTOLOGY CENTERS THEOLOGY

If Christ is the fullness of revelation, then Christology is at the center of all theological doctrines. In fact, absolute fullness is God and thus the mystery of the Trinity. God is fullness in itself. But Christ is the fullness of revelation. For it is by him that one reaches absolute fullness, both of God and the believer. The doctrine of God is thus linked to Christology, as is the doctrine of the Church. It goes into all the areas of theology. They receive a Christological imprint. This is also true for moral theology, which is nothing other than presenting in detail the imitation of Christ in the communication of his graces. Thus Christology must show how the mystery of Christ is that of his person and, through him, of the other persons of the Trinity.

The doctrine intimately linked to Christology is that of Mariology. It is impossible to have a complete Christology, at least from an evangelical point of view, without reflection on the 'Mother of God' and the entire role of the Mary Virgin in the transmission of his sinless humanity, without reflection on her faith and on her participation in the work of redemption. A Christology without Mariology would introduce serious gaps within ecclesiology. The art of icons and more widely of all Christian art often shows these connections and should nourish the spiritual sense of the theologian.

The theologian does not have the task of making Christ present for spiritual experience. The theologian above all has the task of speaking the truth about Christ. But the theologian has the duty of displaying the presence of Christ in all the different ways provided by God: Christ as prepared in the Old Testament; Christ in the historic time of human beings; Christ in the Eucharistic presence; Christ present in glory. The completeness of these presences is the judge of a Christology.

SUGGESTED READING

Paul VI (1965).

BIBLIOGRAPHY

Paul VI (1965), *Dei Verbum.* <http://www.vatican.va/archive/hist_councils/ii_vatican_council/documents/vat-ii_const_19651118_dei-verbum_en.html> (accessed July 16, 2014).

....

CHAPTER 38

CHRISTOLOGY AND WORLD RELIGIONS

A Systematic Perspective

....

GAVIN D'COSTA

CHRISTOLOGY IN A HISTORICAL CONTEXT: A VERY BRIEF TOUR

THIS chapter will eventually focus on three Christological debates in relation to the world religions. To understand these debates and see their historical context, it will be helpful to outline some earlier related Christological debates with the 'world religions'. 'World religions' is a disputed term for it suggests monolithic stable entities that can be rarely found in history (Masuzawa 2005). But I use it to indicate religions other than what came to be seen as orthodox Christianity, without assuming monolithic and continuous identity. I give some references to further reading to balance the broad brushstrokes of this brief tour. The three themes in Christology that are the subject of this chapter are: the *inculturation* of Christology in fidelity to revelation; the Christian claim that Jesus Christ's self-revelation of God was *unique* and of an entirely new ontological order; that Jesus Christ's death, life, and resurrection was *salvifically efficacious* for the entire world. The latter two points are central tenets of Christian orthodoxy although they have been expressed in numerous ways and by the use of different models. These latter 'expressions' relate to point one, inculturation. The history of heresy may be termed bad inculturation. The history of conciliar dogmatic Christological definitions may be termed appropriate inculturation. This history continues today and it is a history that is always accompanied by intense debate.

Christological reflection developed within the context of the world religions. Initially, this happened in relationship to Christianity's sibling or mother, Judaism. Jesus' status was central to his first Jewish followers and amongst other insights about him they

claimed that he was the Jewish 'Messiah'. Many other Jews disagreed. Some early expli-
cations of Jesus' nature and purpose were expressed through Jewish religious conceptualities: 'Messiah', 'Son of Man', and 'Lord' were titles drawn from the Jewish milieu.
Admittedly, the 'Jewish' milieu was not a hermetically sealed cultural basin but was
already awash with Hellenistic influences (Hengel 1974). But these terms were already
being interpreted, developed, and employed afresh within the New Testament, to proclaim the mystery of the saving life, death, and resurrection of Jesus Christ. The language
was undergoing a conversion, as were the users of that language. Importantly, some new
conceptualizations were rejected. For example, the ideas advanced by the group called
the 'Ebonites' were deemed heretical. While they accepted Jesus as the Jewish Messiah
they stopped short of accepting his divinity. Symbolically they represent a Jewish witness to Jesus as 'Messiah', but not to the divinity also being attributed to Jesus Christ.

To ensure these emerging Christological truths were maintained and explicated and
developed, we find that the early Christian apologists and preachers utilized the most
developed and sophisticated conceptual apparatus closest to hand: Greek philosophy.
That the term ὁμοούσιος should be so crucial in the Nicene Creed (325), a term unknown
in the New Testament, indicates that witnessing to who Christ is knew no cultural or
conceptual bounds in terms of inculturation. However, it was also understood that these
fresh confessions were bound by what was given to the Church in revelation. Saint Paul
puts it forcefully, indicating that something of enormous significance is at stake: 'if anyone preaches a version of the Good News different from the one you have already heard,
he is to be condemned' (Gal. 1:9). This constant interaction with the 'deposit of faith',
generating novel and fresh conceptualities which authentically reflected the previous
ones, was called the 'development of doctrine' (Newman 1846).

By the fourth century most Christians were Gentile and they were clear that their
identity was 'Christian', not Jewish. This relationship always contained elements of
sibling rivalry, given the basic contested claim about the Messiah's arrival. In the early
days of Christianity, the 'Jewish rejection' of their own Messiah was embarrassing for
Jewish Christians trying to preach to Jews and non-Jews. Saint Paul's Jewish reflections in Romans 9–11 were a major theological move out of this impasse: God had a
purpose in the 'reprobate' Jewish 'no' to Christ; so that the Gentiles may be converted.
Only then, would the rest of Israel 'come in'. This bad feeling between siblings, one of
whom had huge political power, had terrifying consequences. The baptized Catholic,
Adolph Hitler, tried to exterminate the Jewish people. While the roots of anti-Semitism
in Hitler's writings are arguably buried within modernity's soil, that soil was in part
watered and even derived from elements of Christian anti-Jewishness (Gilbert 1968;
Flannery 1985). The Christological debate after the Holocaust has centred around
whether Christ's Incarnation superseded and invalidated Judaism or whether Christ's
coming was a fulfilment of the Jewish covenant, not its invalidation. Even this latter
position is criticized, because fulfilment is seen as conceptually making Judaism a religion that needs to become Christian in order to achieve its completion (Ruether 1980;
and Pawlikowski 1994 for a good review of the Christological debate on this point). For
some Jews, this is nothing short of once more trying to eradicate Jewish identity. We see

in this interreligious engagement the complex social and political forces that play upon doctrinal Christological formulations.

Even as it worked out its relationship with Judaism, Christianity simultaneously wrestled with the many mystery religions, cults, and philosophies of the ancient Near East and Mediterranean world (Goodman 2012). The question of what Jesus' life, teachings, death, and resurrection meant was always framed within this interreligious context. It was not just a question of was Jesus the *Jewish* Messiah, because the New Testament also taught he was the *unique* saviour of the world, the God-Man who brought *redemption* to all people. Inherent to the preaching of the Gospel was a move to the ends of the earth, to engage all peoples and nations (Matt. 24:14). Not only was Christ salvifically efficacious; without him, there was no salvation (Acts 4:12). This did not mean God was unknown before Christ. Saint Paul taught that God was known to all humanity by virtue of God's creation: 'Ever since the creation of the world his invisible nature, namely, his eternal power and deity, has been clearly perceived in the things that have been made' (Rom. 1:20). This knowledge served only to judge humanity negatively, for Saint Paul adds in verse 20: 'So they are without excuse'. The Epistle to the Hebrews outlines God's activity before Christ's coming: 'In many and various ways God spoke of old to our fathers by the prophets, but in these last days he has spoken to us by a Son, whom he appointed the heir of all things, through whom also he created the world' (Heb. 1:1). Jesus Christ, given the claim that he created the world and was appointed heir of all things, impacted upon every aspect of human culture, including religious culture.

After the fourth century when Christianity started to become a cosmopolitan, ethnically mixed major world religion, as well as emerging as a type of state religion, its engagement with other religions accelerated. This had a crucial impact on Christological reflection, especially when the consolidated truths of Christology were called into question. Islam uniquely raised a Christological question that Christians had posed to Jews. The Qur'an claimed that Jesus was in the line of great prophets sent by God, that Jesus had been born of the Virgin Mary through God's action and without a human father, and that Muhammad was the last of the prophets, the seal of that teaching tradition. If Christianity had seen Christ as the fulfilment of Judaism, Islam now saw Muhammad's message in the Qur'an as the fulfilment of Jesus' teaching (Robinson 1990). Jesus was a kind of John the Baptist to Muhammad. What was different, without pushing this analogy too far, was the power balance. Islam was as politically and militarily powerful as mediaeval Christianity. Whose Christology would win out seemed at times to be a matter which political and military force might decide, rather than theological debate. Both religions had universal aspirations and a world vision that demanded a response (Daniel 1960). Christ was the centre of this force within Christianity; and the Qur'an was the Muslim centre. Because of this mutual claim over Christ, for centuries most Christians in the East and West would see Islam as a Christian heresy. Scripture could not settle the matter as the Qur'an seemed to teach that Christians had allowed perversions to enter their scripture and Jesus had never departed from the Qur'an teachings. The Qur'an denied Christ's divinity and the Holy Trinity. It saw both as involving idolatry: *shirk*, identifying God with that which is human.

Again, as with Judaism, the modern period has seen a serious re-evaluation of Islam. Christologically, the debates have some parallels. Should Jesus' divinity be reassessed (Küng 2007: 76, 494–7); or more productively, did the Qur'anic denials of the Trinity and Incarnation really engage with the best teachings of those doctrines (Volf 2011); and equally interestingly, what can Muslim Jesuologies teach Christians (Griffiths 1990: 67–134)?

The question asked by Christ: 'who do men say that I am?' was increasingly being played out on a world stage. In answering this question the rule of faith was being established, which did not preclude a development within the answer, but precluded denying answers that had been 'commonly accepted'. As Christian denominations sprouted, first with the great division between the East and West, and later with the massive fragmentation within the Western Latin tradition, 'commonly accepted' became difficult to define. Nevertheless, the ancient Nicene Creed's confession about Christ has united nearly all these groups.

With the discovery of the so-called 'New World' in the sixteenth century, engagement with other religions increased. On another imperial front in the East, the Portuguese missionaries were landing in India and South East Asia and discovering some impressive elements in ancient religions that had pre-existed Christianity. While Judaism and Islam were always implicated in 'Jesus Christ' by virtue of their scripture, Eastern religions had long predated Christianity and had formed within a very different cultural climate altogether.

A Jesuit missionary, Robert De Nobili's encounter with Hinduism caused him to extend the teachings of Hebrews 1:1 regarding the scope of God's activity, but to keep Christ in the same place. God's activity could no longer be confined to Israel or even the best of the Greek philosophers. De Nobili wrote in genuine admiration of some truths he had found in Hindu texts:

> But what is yet more surprising, I discover in these texts even an adumbration of the recondite mystery of the Most Holy Trinity, the Most Gracious and Most High God vouchsafing doubtless even to these far distant lands some inkling of the most hidden secret of our faith through the teaching of some sage living among these people, in much the same way as by a rather mysterious inspiration He deigned to illuminate the sibyls, Trimagistus and certain other masters of human wisdom in our parts of the globe ...
>
> (De Nobili 1972: 4)

De Nobili was drawing on an Augustinian tradition that acknowledged and explained how images and tropes of the Trinity would be found throughout creation, given that God was creator. Augustine, like De Nobili, saw that these vestiges of the Trinity were an indication of the telos within culture and creation that sought Christ, but was constantly thwarted by sin. In the same way that the best Greek philosophers and Israel were seen to be 'preparations' for the coming of Christ, so was the Hindu religion at its perceived best. What we see in this pioneer is a situating of Eastern religions within the

Christological map that had already been established, but still taking into consideration the novelty of these religions.

De Nobili strategically would not mention Christ in his exchanges with Hindus until he perceived that Christ would be properly understood by them. If this were not done, he was worried about Christ's all too easy assimilation into the Hindu pantheon. De Nobili's approach was to be replicated in different ways regarding the best of the religions of the East: Buddhism, Confucianism, Daoism, and so on. Many missionaries were genuinely surprised and delighted at the wisdom they encountered, but it is difficult to find one who thought other than that these religions, like the truths of Greek philosophy, were at best preparations to the truth of Christ. The demonic and all too human elements were rarely ignored, and sometimes singularly emphasized. Nevertheless, a Christology of fulfilment remained present, while still emphasizing the radical discontinuity of Christ inasmuch as he was uniquely the self-revelation of God. This same Christological continuity and discontinuity were present in relation to Judaism.

The next phase of modern European colonialism quite literally reached to the ends of the earth. Most of Europe was ostensibly Christian with governments maintaining varying relationships to the established churches. Joseph Conrad shrewdly observed the twin advance of European colonialism with the 'sword' and often the 'torch' in *Heart of Darkness*. The Middle East was almost entirely under European control and swathes of Asia as well. Through this process, Hinduism (to keep with a single example), was more thoroughly studied, understood, criticized, and also inculturated by some into Christianity. The Indian Christ emerged alongside the European Christ, and inevitably preached slightly differing gospels. Inculturation had an impact on both the Christological questions of uniqueness and efficacy.

But something novel took place which was to mark the modern period. In response to Christianity's missionary activity, some of the major neo-Hindu reformers like Vivekananda, Radhakrishnan, and most influentially, Gandhi, began to present Hindu readings of Jesus Christ (Thomas 1969; Griffiths 1990: 191–246). While Muslims had denied the divinity of Christ, these Hindus affirmed both the divinity and efficacy of Christ. But they questioned why both these aspects should be understood uniquely. For these Hindu reformers, all humans could be like Christ, a man with a fully realized 'God-consciousness', as Radhakrishnan put it. They asked whether the unique claims about Christ could be sustained in the light of unique claims by so many other religions. They asked, and Radhakrishnan did this from the Spalding Chair at Oxford, whether an internal reform of Christianity was required. Could the religions of the world unite to challenge the growing materialism, secularism, and scientism of the West? Their positions would eventually be found in some Christian circles in the West.

For Christians in India there was a complex negotiation in terms of Christology. It is impossible to cover more than a single denomination without excessive generalization. On the one hand there were Christians arguing that Christ should be viewed as a 'guru' (a special teacher of wisdom given great respect within some forms of Hinduism), or as a 'sannyasin' (a renouncer and holy man who has high status within the Hindu Brahmanical tradition), carrying on the veritable traditions of inculturation

(Schouten 2008: 163–99, 229–55). On the other hand there were Catholics arguing that these forms of inculturation would signal the death knell of Catholicism in India as it would allow Christ to become accommodated within the Hindu pantheon. This was De Nobili's concern four hundred years previously. Given that most conversions came from the 'outcastes', 'tribals', or 'scheduled castes' who were at the bottom of hierarchical Brahmanical Hinduism, it is not surprising that many Indian Catholics found these new forms of inculturation alienating. They did not express their own indigenous spirituality. Ironically, many of the pioneers of inculturation were Europeans (Swamis Abhishiktananda and Paramarubhananda, i.e., Fathers Henri le Saux and Jules Monchanin and Bede Griffiths). These Indian Catholics were more interested in Jesus Christ the liberator rather than a Brahmanical sannyasin. Liberation theology was to dominate Indian Christology (Puthanangady 1988; Rajkumar 2010). Of course, that too was a European export of sorts.

I have presented this brief sketch to set the scene for understanding some aspects of the Christological debate in contemporary theology: inculturation; Christ as the unique revelation of God; and the salvific efficacy of the Incarnation. There are many other Christological issues that could be pursued (Kärkkäinen 2003).

INCULTURATION AND CHRISTOLOGY

I will examine one example to clarify some complex issues: Raimundo Panikkar's classic study, *The Unknown Christ of Hinduism* (1st edn. 1964; Panikkar changed his position in the second edition). Panikkar tried to grasp Hinduism on its own terms and *then* asked whether Hinduism anticipates the God-Man, Jesus Christ. Inculturation and missiological proclamation are held carefully in tension. The Christological proclamation is made thorough grounding it thoroughly in classical Hindu texts. Panikkar bears comparison with De Nobili in this move. Panikkar presented an exegesis of the *Brahma Sutra* 1.i.ii, '*janmadi asya yatah*', traditionally rendered: 'Brahman is that whence the origin, sustaining and transformation of this world comes'; in effect, 'Brahman is the total ultimate cause of the world'. This seminal text had been interpreted differently by Hindu philosophical commentators in their *bhasyas*. For Sankara's *Advaita Vedanta*, the problem in interpreting this text was to retain the absoluteness of Brahman, the unconditioned reality. Bridging the gap between Brahman and the conditional reality of the world was and still is a major problem in Advaita philosophy. The followers of Sankara felt that Brahman's unconditioned and absolute nature would be compromised if Brahman was admitted as the cause of the world. They held that this cause was not properly Brahman, but Isvara, the Lord. However, the *Brahma Sutra* text maintained its integrity if it is understood that Isvara, the personal God, was in fact the unqualified absolute Brahman in his personal, qualified aspect. Isvara became the link between the undifferentiated Brahman and the created world. It is at this point in the exegesis that Panikkar suggests that the solution to the antinomy of the One and Many, Brahman and the world, is better solved if we see that Isvara is no other than an anticipation of Christ, the Logos, the Mediator between God and Man (Panikkar 1964: 126). Panikkar is intervening within a Hindu debate regarding the question of the ontological supremacy of Brahman and Isvara.

Panikkar ends his careful exegetical exercise drawing out its very clear theological and missiological rationale. In Hinduism 'Christ has not unveiled his whole face, has not yet completed his mission there. He still has to grow up and be recognised. Moreover, He still has to be crucified there, dying with Hinduism as he died with Judaism and with the Hellenistic religions in order to rise again, as the same Christ (who is already in Hinduism), but then as a risen Hinduism, as Christianity' (Panikkar 1964: 17).

Panikkar's reading has not been criticized for eisegesis or for inadequate indological skills. He has been criticized (and in effect criticizes himself by modifying his argument in the second edition) as advancing a type of spiritual imperialism or colonizing of Hindu scripture. This is a bogus criticism that has often arisen out of the modern Western guilt complex (Sanneh 1987). Some types of reading of other scriptures might be criticized in this fashion, but the early Panikkar's particular approach has significant Christological and missiological value. It underlines a single Christological point: all creation and culture point to Christ and this is thwarted by sin and blindness. By taking seriously the Indian scripture in its own terms, Panikkar is not being a colonial reader. By recognizing there are unresolved questions within the interpretative tradition of Hindu readers, Panikkar tries to do what was done by the early Christians regarding Christ. He sees signs and tropes that point towards Christ. The Christological task is to uncover these, rejoicing that God has moved through all creation and culture, and to purify and baptize them. This does not enforce any meaning onto Hinduism that must be accepted by Hindus, but invites Hindus into theological conversation about who is Christ, and whether his hidden form may be germinally present within their tradition. The neo-Hindu reformers had already done this with Christians as indicated above.

This kind of interreligious traditioned reading process finds an excellent exposition and defence in the work of Alasdair MacIntyre (1990). While MacIntyre is not addressing interreligious dialogue, his arguments relate clearly to differing and sometimes apparently incommensurable traditions. His conviction about traditioned rationality requires a Christological basis for incorporation into theology.

Panikkar's engagement with Hindu scripture raises the inculturation question which has been with Christianity since its beginning. What do religious texts such as the *Upanishads* mean for converts who are in an analogous position to early Jews who became Christians? Not only early Jews, but modern Hebrew Catholics who, as Jews, see their scriptures leading them to Catholicism (Neuhaus 2010: 395–413). Brahmabandhab Upadhyay, the Bengali Brahman, nicely embodies the complexity at stake. He claimed he was both a Hindu and Catholic and proceeded to read his Hindu scriptures religiously as seeing Christ as their promise (Lipner 1999). He is rare compared to thousands of lower caste Hindu converts to Christianity who have no time for Hindu scriptures. They see them as Brahmanical caste-ridden oppressive texts which fail to reflect the love of God they have found in Christ. Panikkar's work shows (in principle) that when Hindus are converted, they are not asked to culturally become Europeans. They might see their scriptures as analogous to the way the Jewish disciples of Jesus saw their scripture leading them to Christ. The analogy is limited: Christians can never be properly Christian and be cut off from their Jewish roots. The relationship with Judaism is *sui generis* and this means that Christology also has a *sui generis* relationship with the history of revelation in Israel. Inculturation of this sort is also clearly missiological, for it can effectively be understood by Hindus so that the challenge of Christ's uniqueness is sensitively explicated. Why did Panikkar's work fall into disrepute even with himself? This leads to the second Christological question.

THE UNIQUENESS OF CHRIST

Panikkar's change of position, complex as it is, can be attributed to many factors, including but not exclusively his own sense of dual or multiple belonging. He called himself a Christian, Hindu, and Buddhist. He was concerned at the political and social implications of fulfilment theology as invoking a spiritual colonialism, the sense that God is bigger than any one single revelation, and the importance of interreligious harmony for the future of the world. All these factors have affected a number of other Christian theologians (see Hick and Knitter 1987) calling into question the uniqueness of Christ.

Another major factor, not present in Panikkar's work, which has seriously affected the Christological debate in the West is the impact of historical criticism on traditional Christological claims and New Testament study. Harnack (and the tradition of Liberal Protestantism) argued that the rule of faith could not be validly used in critical biblical scholarship as it loaded the dice. The scholar had to approach the New Testament with an open historical mind, not with a preconditioned dogmatic viewpoint. Schweitzer had seen the problem that an 'open mind' might simply mean the scholar's mind and prejudices. This debate rumbles on, although New Testament scholarship is much more diverse today and is recognizing the importance of other approaches requiring the rule of faith, canonical reading, and liturgical reading (Ratzinger 1989; Childs 2002). Kant had initiated the questioning as to whether a good moral God could choose to work in such a particular historical fashion (the Incarnation) that only small groups of people would have access to him (Kant 2008). Along with the Western guilt complex, the Holocaust, and the ascendance of science as a master discourse, the uniqueness of Jesus was bound to be questioned. Further, close knowledge of the world religions and friendships with decent if not quite remarkable non-Christian human beings cast a critical spotlight on the notion of 'unique' Christologies. The critics asked: would interreligious relationships be reconfigured for the good if Christians dropped their exclusive/unique claims about Christ? We saw above how these were always central in differing ways in relations to Jews, then Muslims, and later Hindus.

John Hick exemplified nearly all these influences. He argued that the unique saving Incarnation of God in Christ cannot be defended. Hick argued that the doctrine of the Incarnation should be understood 'mythically', as an expression of devotion and commitment by Christians, not as an ontological claim about the unique and exclusive action of God in the particular man, Jesus (Hick 1977: 165–77). He claimed that Christianity would not collapse as a consequence but would be fittingly reborn into the modern world. One might say that Hick saw this as the most appropriate inculturation of traditional Christology. Hick argued that the *solus Christus* teaching, that salvation came through Christ *alone*, was incompatible with the God revealed by Jesus who desires 'all men to be saved' (1 Tim. 2:4). There were many millions who had never heard of Christ through no fault of their own, before and after the New Testament period—the *inculpably ignorant*. It is un-Christian to think that God would have 'ordained that men must be saved in such a way that only a small minority can in fact receive this salvation' (Hick 1977: 122). Finally, Hick argued that it was God, and not Christianity or Christ, towards whom all religions move and from whom they gain salvation. Hick proposed a God-centred revolution away from the Christ-centred or church-centred position that has dominated Christian history. Hick ended up advancing a form of Unitarianism. Incarnation and Trinity are mutually implicated. Ironically the Christological 'problem' had been solved by removing it from the stage.

An important later development in Hick's position came in response to the criticism that his theological revolution was still *theocentric*, thereby excluding non-theistic religions. Eventually, the myth of God incarnate became for Hick the myth of God. I will not follow these later developments as they move away from Christology entirely. Some theologians argued that traditional Christologies did not require such a radical revisioning, as traditional Christologies allowed for those who did not know Christ and for those who were not Christians. For Hick, this minimal revision admitted a problematic reality (the majority of humankind were not Christians—and many were impressively and deeply spiritual), but it denied the implications of the traditional *solus Christus*. Before turning to those alternative Christological positions, let me make some brief observations on Hick.

Hick's notion of 'myth' employs a purely instrumentalist model of language. Take the statement: 'Jesus is divine'. According to Hick it is mythologically true because it evokes 'an appropriate dispositional attitude to its subject matter', such as imitation and devotion, not the claim that Jesus *is* divine. An instrumentalist view replaces a referential view of language. Referential views are rarely exclusive of instrumentalism. Doctrines have always been about practices and practices have always generated further doctrines (Newman 1846; Lindbeck 1984). At best, the instrumentalist view that God *is* acting *in Christ* is emptied of any *sui generis* referential quality so that the Incarnation relates to a general referential quality shared by all claims that God is acting (in Esra, Jane, Muhammad, or Gautama). But this never escapes the question: what is the shape of this reference; whose God and which divine are being advanced and privileged (D'Costa 2000: 24–30)?

Christian language about God is necessarily rooted in the shape of Jesus' life, death, resurrection, the outpouring of the Holy Spirit, and the formation of the Christian community centred on the risen Christ. In theological terms, the Trinity is the foundation of the Church, or another of way of putting it is that Christocentricism, pneumacentricism, and ecclesiocentricism are inextricably related. This in no way implies that God's activity is restricted to the Christian Church, but rather that the manner of narrating these extra ecclesial events will inevitably be shaped by the necessary Christological lens employed. Orthodox Christians do not compromise the Incarnation in acknowledging God's activity in history for such activity is of a different ontological order to the Incarnation. Recall Hebrews 1:1. Hick is in danger of being left with a 'pick and mix' divine, without the control of any authoritative revelation. Like Kant, without any authoritative revelation, Hick ends up with authoritative ethics and principles, and like Kant, with no adequate metaphysical grounding for these ethics. That is not a crime in itself, but it is difficult to see continuity with the Christian tradition in making this move.

There are many different variations to Hick's position with similar Christological conclusions: the English Anglican priest, Alan Race (1983); the American Jesuit Roger Haight (1999); the American Roman Catholic Paul Knitter (2009); and the German ex-Catholic, now Presbyterian, Perry Schmidt-Leukel (2005). I would want to argue that they are all finally theists at best or agnostics at worst. Traditional Christology has been abandoned in terms of the claim regarding uniqueness and universal salvific efficacy (D'Costa 2010). But what of Hick's criticisms of those who have seemingly retained the uniqueness of Christ but somehow circumvented the implications of the *solus Christus*? This takes us to the final Christological issue.

THE SALVIFIC EFFICACY OF CHRIST

Hick argued that modern theologians were not facing up to the implications of the *solus Christus* position in defending traditional Christologies. Is this true? If one examined a limited range of modern Christologies that have defended the unique salvific efficacy of Christ, there is in fact huge diversity to be found. Regarding Hick's dilemma about the majority of humankind being consigned to the fires of hell when unique salvific efficacy is predicated of Christ, I will look at just four types of Christological response.

The first type comes from a certain reading of Augustine and Calvin. Christ's revelation shows us the fallen nature of all humans, who all deserve death as the punishment of sin. Rather than the God of love who is incompatible with the eternal perdition of so many, Christ's revelation exposes the depths of sin showing instead how remarkable it is that any are saved at all (Henry 1991). That any are saved reveals God's love and mercy. Carl Henry argues that salvation is restricted to those who respond to the preaching of the Gospel in this life which is seen as stipulated in the *fides ex auditu* biblical tradition (faith comes from hearing). The concomitant to this is that those who do not hear the Gospel are lost. A variation within this approach proposes that Christ died only for the elect, not for those destined for perdition. This is a distinctly Calvinist position. Neither of the above two positions can be deemed to be incompatible with the justice and mercy of God, as claimed by the likes of Hick. An all loving God, according to Hick, could not consign the majority of people to perdition through no fault of their own. Henry replies to this objection by arguing that God's justice is not compromised because justice actually requires that all be damned and none saved, given the Fall and rebellion of humans. All are justly damned. Further, God's mercy is seen in Christ's death, for the elect-sinners who deserve damnation are actually saved through no merit of their own. We should stand in awe and thanks at God's merciful free undeserved gift of his Son. Henry says that the unevangelized are like the fallen angels, destined for damnation because of their original rebellion.

Henry's position is a working out of a broad set of presuppositions involved in the basically Calvinist/Reform starting point established at the Synod of Dort (1618) and given the delightful mnemonic of TULIP by James Packer (1983: 4). TULIP stands for the five fundamental points established at Dort: Total depravity (justly damned), Unconditional election (some mercifully saved), Limited atonement (Christ only dies for the elect), Irresistible grace (God's sovereignty is paramount), and Preservation of the saints (his restricted saving will must be accomplished). Strange (2014) rigorously applies these axioms.

A second type of response keeps to the *fides ex auditu* requirement, but does not endorse TULIP teachings. Here one finds Catholics, Lutherans, and Orthodox theologians flowering. One might label the position ROSE: 'Resurrection Overcomes Sin in the End'. Here it is argued that Christ's unique atoning death actually wins the salvation of all (usually stated as a hope); and all will come to know him 'somehow'. This kind of 'universalism' is found in the Roman Catholic, Hans Urs Von Balthasar and the Reform giant, Karl Barth, despite both holding a very high Christology which affirms *solus Christus* and *fides ex auditu*. Both are associated with very negative views on other religions, while interestingly both hold to versions of universalism. In this outcome they are bedfellows with Hick—who sees them operating at the other end of the map (Barth 1932–70; Von Balthasar 1990). Von Balthasar and Barth have been criticized for not respecting human freedom adequately, for lacking biblical grounding, and Von Balthasar, for going against the Magisterium. That they are genuinely grounded on profound Christological reasoning is without question: they emphasize the reality of Christ's atoning death as overcoming sin in its ontological root. What is germane for our Christological investigation is that ROSE, like TULIP, affirms a very high Christology, but unlike TULIP has a very different outcome regarding non-Christians.

A third type might be viewed as a ROSE, but one with thorns. It too affirms *solus Christus* and *fides ex auditu*, but not universalism. These positions give greater specification to the conditions for *fides ex auditu*. In universalist ROSE positions, the salvation of the non-Christian is sometimes worked through in a *deus ex machina* fashion as in the pure ROSE position. These positions try to do justice to human freedom while also recognizing Christ's universal efficacy. The ROSEY thorn theologians argue that there will be a chance to respond to the Gospel for all people either at the point of death (Boros 1965), after death in a post-mortem state (Lindbeck 1974), after death in a reincarnation as another person on this earth (Jathanna 1981), or in a type of purgatory (Di Noia 1992: 94–108), or in a type of purgatory/limbo (D'Costa 2000: 161–211).

The above three positions are criticized by those who still hold to the traditional *solus Christus*, but seem to steer away from the *fides ex auditu* requirement. I say 'seem' as there is a serious ambiguity in the major exponent of this fourth Christological position: Karl Rahner. Rahner argues that in Jesus' total abandonment to God, his total 'yes' through his life, death, and resurrection, he is established as the culmination and prime mediator of grace. Christ is the explicit expression of grace which men and women experience implicitly in the depths of their being when for example they reach out, through the power of grace, in trusting love and self-sacrifice or in acts of hope and charity. Rahner attempts to balance the *solus Christus* principle with the doctrine of the *universal salvific will of God* by means of arguing that Christ is the effective cause of all salvation, even for those who do not know him explicitly through no fault of their own. Rahner also argues that Christology and the doctrine of God cannot be separated from the Church because Christ is historically mediated through the Church. This means that Rahner must reconcile membership of the Church as a means of salvation and the possibility that salvific grace is mediated outside the historically tangible borders of the Church. He does this by employing the traditional Catholic teachings regarding the *votum ecclesia* and the related notion of implicit desire. The *votum ecclesia* (a wish or desire to belong to the Church) was understood to count as baptism when for good reason actual baptism could not be administered, but was desired (Rahner 1963). Being run over by a chariot or being eaten by lions on the way to baptism might count as good reasons. Furthermore, given the socio-historical nature of men and women, Rahner argues that grace must be mediated historically and socially. The Incarnation is paradigmatic of this. Therefore, if and when non-Christians respond to grace, this grace must normally be mediated through the non-Christian's religion, however imperfectly. Hence, for Rahner non-Christian religions may be 'lawful religions', analogously to Israel before Christ's Incarnation. Rahner coins the term 'anonymous Christian' (this refers to the source of saving grace that is responded to: Christ), and 'anonymous Christianity' (this refers to its dynamic orientation towards its definitive historical and social expression: the Church).

Rahner's solution had been influential in Catholic circles, despite the incisive criticisms by his fellow Catholic, Von Balthasar (Von Balthasar 1994; see Williams 1986 for a highly nuanced account of this debate). Returning to the 'seems' point, Rahner's own work in other contexts shows that he does hold that salvation *is* the explicit beatific vision. In earlier writings Rahner (1965) developed a complex notion of the pancosmic soul, a communal redemption process *after* death. What is significant is Rahner's ambiguous position on this matter. He both requires explicit faith and the *fides ex auditu* for the beatific vision and simultaneously 'seems' not to require it in his influential anonymous Christian thesis. When pushed, I think Rahner could not hold that the anonymous Christian who has never heard the Gospel is 'saved' in the proper eschatological sense, but is on the road to salvation.

CONCLUSION

There are denominational emphases in Christology, but proposed solutions and themes sometimes cut across denominational lines. There is a small but influential group of theologians who seem to cross the line of traditional Christological orthodoxy. However, most theologians grapple with Christological inculturation with a fidelity to revelation; retain the claim that Jesus Christ's self-revelation of God is *unique* and of an entirely new ontological order, with some emphasizing the epistemological aspect of this claim; and sensitively attend to how Jesus Christ's death, life, and resurrection is *salvifically efficacious* for the entire world. In carrying out these tasks, an important challenge remains: not to efface the Other, to discern God's activity within the world, and to be open to challenges and questions regarding the question: 'who do you say that I am?'

SUGGESTED READING

D'Costa (1986); Dupuis (1977); Griffiths (1990); Kärkkäinen (2003).

BIBLIOGRAPHY

Barth, K. (1932–70), *Die kirchliche Dogmatik*. Evangelisches Buchandlung (Zürich: Zolliken).

Barth, K. (2004), *Church Dogmatics: The Doctrine of God* II/2, trans. G. Bromiley (London: Continuum).

Boros, L. (1965), *The Moment of Truth: Mysterium Mortis* (London: Burns & Oates).

Cheruvally, S. S. (2011), *Jesus Christ: Question and Context of Abhishikrananda* (Delhi: SPCK).

Childs, B. (2002), *Biblical Theology: A Proposal* (Minneapolis: Augsburg Fortress).

Daniel, N. (1960), *Islam and the West: The Making of an Image* (Edinburgh: Edinburgh University Press).

D'Costa, G. (1986), *Theology and Religious Pluralism: The Challenge of Other Religions* (Oxford: Blackwell).

D'Costa, G. (2000), *The Meeting of Religions and the Trinity* (Maryknoll, NY: Orbis Books).

D'Costa, G. (2010), 'Pluralist Arguments: Prominent Tendencies and Methods', in K. J. Becker and I. Morali (eds.), *Catholic Engagement with World Religions* (Maryknoll, NY: Orbis Books), 329–44.

De Nobili, R. (1972), *On Indian Customs*, ed. and trans. S. Rajamanickam (Palayamkottai: Research Institute).

Di Noia, J. A. (1992), *The Diversity of Religions: A Christian Perspective* (Washington, DC: Catholic University Press of America).

Dupuis, J. (1977), *Towards a Christian Theology of Religious Pluralism* (Maryknoll, NY: Orbis Books).

Flannery, A. (1985), *Vatican Council II. The Basic Sixteen Documents: Constitutions, Decrees, Declarations—A Completely Revised Translation in Inclusive Language* (Northport N.Y: Costello).

Gilbert, A. (1968), *The Vatican Council and the* Jews (Cleveland: World Publishing Company).

Goodman, M. (2012), *The Roman World 44 B.C.–A.D. 180*, 2nd rev. edn. (London: Routledge, 2012).

Griffiths, P. (1990), *Christianity through Non-Christian Eyes* (Maryknoll, NY: Orbis Books).

Haight, R. (1999), *Jesus the Symbol of God* (Maryknoll, NY: Orbis Books).

Hengel, M. (1974), *Judaism and Hellenism: Studies in their Encounter in Palestine during the Early Hellenistic Period*, trans. J. Bowden (London: SCM Press).

Henry, C. (1991), 'Is it Fair?', in W. Crockett and J. Sigountos (eds.), *Through No Fault of Their Own? The Fate of Those Who Have Never Heard* (Grand Rapids, Mich.: Baker), 245–56.

Hick, J. (1977). *God and the Universe of Faiths* (London: Collins).

Hick, J. and P. Knitter (1987), *The Myth of Christian Uniqueness: Towards a Pluralistic Theology of Religions* (Maryknoll, NY: Orbis Books).

Jathanna, O. (1981), *The Decisiveness of the Christ Event and the Universality of Christianity in a World of Religious Plurality* (Berne: Herbert Lang).

Kant, I. (2008), *Religion within the Limits of Reason Alone*, trans. T. M. Greene and H. Hoyt (New York: HarperOne).

Kärkkäinen, V. (2003), *Christology: A Global Introduction* (Grand Rapids, Mich.: Baker).

Knitter, P. (2009), *Without Buddha I Could Not be a Christian* (Oxford: Oneworld).

Küng, H. (2007), *Islam: Past, Present and Future* (Oxford: Oneworld).

Lindbeck, G. (1974), 'Fides ex auditu and the Salvation of Non-Christians: Contemporary Catholic and Protestant Positions', in V. Vajta (ed.), *The Gospel and the Ambiguity of the Church* (Minneapolis: Fortress), 91–123.

Lindbeck, G. (1984), *The Nature of Doctrine: Religion and Theology in a Postliberal Age* (London: SPCK).

Lipner, J. (1999), *Brahmabandhab Upadhyay: The Life and Thought of a Revolutionary* (New Delhi: Oxford University Press).

MacIntyre, A. (1990), *Three Rival Versions of Moral Enquiry* (London: Duckworth).

Masuzawa, T. (2005), *The Invention of World Religions, or, How European Universalism Was Preserved in the Language of Pluralism* (Chicago: University of Chicago Press).

Neuhaus, D. (2010), 'Engaging the Jewish People: Forty Years since *Nostra Aetate*', in K. J. Becker and I. Morali (eds.), *Catholic Engagement with World Religions: A Comprehensive Study* (Maryknoll, NY: Orbis Books), 395–413.

Newman, J. H. (1846), *An Essay on the Development of Christian Doctrine* (London: James Toovey).

Packer, J. (1983), 'Introductory Essay', in J. Owen, *The Death of Death in the Death of Christ* (Edinburgh: Banner of Truth), 1–25.

Panikkar, R. (1981 [1964]), *The Unknown Christ of Hinduism: Towards an Ecumenical Christophany* (London: Darton, Longman & Todd).

Pawlikowski, J. (1994), 'Christology in the Light of Jewish-Christian Dialogue', *CTSA Proceedings* 49: 120–34.

Puthanangady, P. (ed.) (1988), *Towards an Indian Theology of Liberation: The Statement Papers and the Proceedings of the Ninth Annual Meeting of the Indian Theological Association* (Bangalore, India: Madras).

Race, A. (1983), *Christians and Religious Pluralism* (London: SCM Press).

Rahner, K. (1963), 'Membership of the Church According to the Teaching of Pius XII's Encyclical Mystici Corporis', in Rahner, *Theological Investigation* (London: Darton, Longman & Todd), 1–88.

Rahner, K. (1965), *Theology of Death* (London: Darton, Longman & Todd).

Rajkumar, P. (2010), *Dalit Theology and Dalit Liberation: Problems, Paradigms and Possibilities* (Farnham: Ashgate).

Ratzinger, J. (1989), 'Biblical Interpretation in Crisis: On the Question of the Foundations and Approaches of Exegesis Today', in R. J. Neuhaus (ed.), *Biblical Interpretation in Crisis* (Grand Rapids, Mich.: Eerdmans), 1–23.

Robinson, N. (1990), *Representation of Jesus in the Qur'an and the Classical Muslim Commentaries* (Basingstoke: Macmillan).

Ruether, R. (1980), *The Theological Roots of Anti-Semitism: Faith and Fratricide* (New York: Seabury Press).

Sanneh, L. (1987), 'Christian Mission and the Western Guilt Complex', *Christian Century* (8 April): 330–4.

Schmidt-Leukel, P. (2005), *Gott ohne Grenzen: eine christliche und pluralistische Theologie der Religionen* (Gütersloh: Gütersloher Verlaghaus).

Schouten, J. (2008), *Jesus as Guru: The Image of Christ among Hindus and Christians in India*, trans. H. Jansen and L. Jansen (Amsterdam and New York: Rodopi).

Smith, W. (1978), *The Meaning and End of Religion: A Revolutionary Approach to the Great Religious Traditions* (London: SPCK).

Strange, D. (2014), *For Their Rock is Not as Our Rock: An Evangelical Theology of Religions* (Leicester: Apollos).

Thomas, M. (1969), *The Acknowledged Christ of the Indian Renaissance* (London: SCM Press).

Volf, M. (2011), *Allah: A Christian Response* (New York: HarperOne).

Von Balthasar, H. U. (1990), *Mysterium Paschale: The Mystery of Easter*, trans. with an introduction by Aidan Nichols (Edinburgh: T. & T. Clark).

Von Balthasar, H. U. (1994), *The Moment of Christian Witness*, trans. R. Beckley (San Francisco: Ignatius Press).

Williams, R. (1986), 'Balthasar and Rahner', in J. Riches (ed.), *The Analogy of Beauty* (Edinburgh: T. & T. Clark), 11–34.

CHAPTER 39

THE PLACE OF CHRISTOLOGY IN SYSTEMATIC THEOLOGY

JOHN WEBSTER

INITIAL OBSERVATIONS

To say that each element of Christian teaching bears some relation to Christology is to state an analytical judgement, to reiterate the inherent and permanent referent of the term 'Christian'. Further reflection, however, prompts two questions: What kind of relation? and What kind of Christology?

What kind of relation obtains between Christological teaching and other doctrinal topics? It may be considered a relation of derivation, such that Christology is the source—cognitive and ontological—from which are drawn all other Christian teachings, whose Christian identity and authenticity are to be ascertained by demonstrable origination from and determination by Christological doctrine. Thus Barth:

> Within theological thinking generally unconditional priority must be given to thinking which is attentive to the existence of the living person of Jesus Christ ... so that *per definitionem* Christological thinking forms the unconditional basis for all other theological thinking ... The only decisions which have any place are those which follow after, which are consistent with thinking which follows him, which arise in the course of Christological thinking and the related investigations, definitions and conclusions.
>
> (Barth 1961: 175)

Another, less straightforwardly deductive conception of the relation between Christology and other doctrines—one which on occasions Barth also maintained—considers Christology not as in and of itself the basis, centre, or starting point of everything else, but rather as a principal part of Christian teaching having wide dispersal across the doctrinal corpus by virtue of the fact that it is an integral element of the doctrine of the Trinity. The formative status and specifying function of Christology in relation to other topics of Christian teaching, that is, arise from the governance of the entire body of Christian divinity by teaching about the triune God. On this account of the matter, it is not Christology per se but a doctrine of God's triune being and his inner and outer works (including the Godhead of the Son and his works in time) which occupies the pre-eminent and commanding place in Christian teaching.

Further: What kind of Christology? A complete Christology comprises two integral parts: teaching about the eternal Son or Word, his deity and the relations which he bears to the Father and the Spirit; and teaching about the Son's temporal mission, especially in the assumption of flesh to redeem lost rational creatures. Where Christology is located in a comprehensive treatment of Christian doctrine, its size, and the relations which it bears to other doctrines, will be determined in part by decisions about the content of each of the two parts, their relative proportions and the priority of one part over the other, as well as by expectations or demands placed on each part.

Any systematic presentation of Christian doctrine adopts a stance on the function and scope of Christology, implicitly or explicitly. The stance is visible both in the way in which the subject-matter of Christian doctrine as a whole is conceived, and in the expository arrangement of its various components. In much modern (and notably, but not exclusively, Protestant) systematic theology these matters have acquired a special prominence, because discrete teaching about the person and work of Christ has often annexed the fundamental role which earlier theologies more naturally recognized in teaching about the Trinity, and so has come to serve as the hallmark of the genuineness, purity, and distinctiveness of Christian doctrine.

To anatomize the matter, we look first at the nature and subject-matter of systematic theology, and then consider the place of Christology in relation to God's inner life ('theology') and God's work towards creatures ('economy').

SYSTEMATIC THEOLOGY

Though the term 'systematic theology' is sometimes used to designate any constructive (rather than simply exegetical or historical) treatment of Christian doctrine, it is best reserved for accounts of Christian teaching which aim at comprehensiveness and coherence, setting forth the content of Christian belief in its entirety with attention to the congruity of its parts. Theological systematization attracts a range of criticisms: dominance by a governing principle abstracted from the range of Christian teaching; reduction of the internal variety of Christian beliefs; over-reliance on deduction in the construction of doctrine; aspirations to finality which accord ill with the incompleteness and liability to revision of temporal knowledge of God. However, systematicity in theology properly derives not from pretensions to perfect understanding but from contemplation of the scope and internal relations of its object. A theological system is not so much a projection as an acknowledgement and reiteration of the order which obtains between the various elements of Christian belief. Well-conducted, it will draw upon resources (intellectual and moral-spiritual) to check the malign bent to total knowledge—most of all, awareness of the ineffability of its object and of the fact that the renovation of human knowledge of God remains unfinished.

From the early Christian era, theological literature has included, alongside the incidental articulation of Christian teaching in exegetical, homiletic, and paraenetic works, more formalized presentations of Christian doctrine whether of its particular elements or of its overall content, in such genres as catechetical manuals or expositions of the Creed. Such works serve the internal didactic and polemical needs of the Church, as well as contributing to its apologetic self-articulation. In the twelfth century systematic schematization received a formative impulse from the topically arranged digest of earlier Christian teaching in Peter Lombard's *Sentences*, which proved very widely influential on later scholastic summas, most of all that of Aquinas. The summa format was largely laid aside by the magisterial Reformers, in favour of exegetical, practical-pastoral, or controversial divinity: Calvin's *Institutes*, for example, is closer in form and rhetoric to Augustine's *Enchiridion* than to a scholastic or modern doctrinal treatise.

Modern forms of systematic theology derive their content and structure from post-Reformation expositions of the theological loci, prepared for didactic, confessional, and controversial purposes. These treatments customarily expounded the articles of Christian belief by beginning with the doctrine of God, followed by material on creation and providence, human nature and sin, the person of Christ and his office and work as redeemer, the nature of salvation and its application by the Holy Spirit, the Church, its sacraments and administration, and the end of all things. This arrangement has proved generally stable, and continues to furnish the basic design of a systematic theology. The genre combines topical analysis with an historical sequence derived from the order of the scriptural materials. Especially in modern variants, it may be prefaced by discussion of the sources of Christian theology and its place in the wider sphere of human enquiry. It may also incorporate material on the moral entailments of Christian teaching, whether as an integral part of the treatment of each topic or as a second treatise on the service of God corresponding to that on the knowledge of God and of God's works.

The character of a systematic theology is a function of a number of factors. (1) A determination of the object or matter (*res*) of Christian teaching, both as a whole and in its various divisions. This will include judgements about which are the principal parts of Christian teaching, about which parts are derivative and how they may be derived, and about which parts may most properly be expected to set the distinctive nature of the system. (2) A judgement about the cognitive principles or sources of Christian teaching and their relative values, and about the ways in which systematic theology gives expression to the matter which these sources communicate. Such sources may be internal (such as Scripture or dogma), or external and ancillary (such as philosophy, history, or aspects of human culture held to be normative). (3) A conception of the end or purpose of systematic theology. This will include answers to such questions as: Is systematic theology a 'positive' science with a given, antecedently established matter of which it is an exposition, or is it critical, reconstructed enquiry? How should contemplative, speculative, didactic, apostolic, and apologetic purposes be ranked in the construction of a system of Christian doctrine? (4) A set of judgements about the ecclesial and extra-ecclesial settings of systematic theology, including judgements of circumstance, that is, determinations about which parts of Christian teaching should receive especial attention in a given set of conditions. (5) A conception of the virtues required of the systematic theologian. Such virtues may be intellectual (exegetical, historical, and conceptual) skills and (if theology is considered to be itself an exercise of religion) moral-spiritual powers.

Decisions about the object, sources, ends, settings, and practitioners of systematic theology exercise a formative influence on the rhetoric of a system of Christian doctrine, in particular upon the ways in which its genre and voice may echo the primary modesty of expression of Christian faith while at the same time striving for conceptual regularity and argumentative clarity. Further, the overall character of a systematic theology will be inscribed in its organization. A system is composed of an orderly arrangement of parts according to a scheme. The design of a systematic theology requires attention to matters of overall sequence: Where are the different elements to be placed? Is the sequence or order of exposition to be a direct transcription of the material order or the order of knowing? Do the various elements simply relate to each other serially, or is there a more complex set of interrelations? Do certain topics require more ample consideration and others more cursory treatment?

These formal questions about location, proportion, and relative influence are of considerable weight in deciding the proper place of Christology in a system of Christian doctrine. They are, however, consequent upon material determination of the object of Christian faith and theology, which is God and the creatures of God. What is the place—location, role, and rank—of Christology in systematic theological exposition of that object?

THEOLOGY AND ECONOMY

Systematic theology has a single but not simple object: God and all things relative to God. 'All things are dealt with in holy teaching in terms of God, either because they are God himself or because they are relative to him as their origin and end' (Aquinas *ST* I, q.1, a.7, corp.). This one complex matter may therefore be divided into (1) God absolutely considered, that is, considered in himself in his inner life as Father, Son, and Spirit (theology); and (2) God relatively considered, that is, considered in his outer works and in relation to his creatures (economy). Systematic theology is enquiry into God and into created realities under the formality of God.

There is a material order in this one complex object according to which theology has preponderance over economy. This is because though it is entirely possible (indeed, necessary) to conceive of the triune God without creatures, it is not possible to conceive of creatures without God. God is from himself and in himself; he is self-subsistent and self-sufficient, and does not receive his being from any other, for he is the first principle and cause of all that is not himself. All other beings, however, are not from themselves; they receive being from him and are sustained by him as they enact the being which they have received. The material priority in systematic theology of God in himself is an acknowledgement of the unqualified priority of the creator over the creature; God is first in being, and so theology precedes economy.

Yet three qualifications must be made. First, to speak of the primacy of theology over economy is to make a distinction, not a separation. The pre-eminence of theology does not mean that economy is an accidental or inessential element of systematic theology. Quite the contrary: consideration of the economy is indispensable because there is not only God in himself but God who of his will and goodness reaches beyond his own being and gives life. A system of theology which failed to treat the economy would not correspond to its object's full range. The material primacy of theology does not eliminate or depreciate all else relative to God; it indicates that theology treats the uncaused cause of all other things, and economy treats those things which are caused.

Second, to say that primacy belongs to God's inner works, not to his economic acts, does not entail that the latter offer no instruction about God's inner being. The outer works of God are *his* works, not some remote operation which is not proper to him, and this continuity of acting subject means that God's economic acts elucidate his inner being, even though they do not exhaust it. God's triune life is not closed in upon itself; it is also communicative or externally relative, and so manifest in acts towards creatures.

Third, the material primacy of theology is not necessarily mirrored in the order of knowing or in the order of exposition adopted in a theological system. The thought that God is the origin of all things—of created being, and of the world's redemption—may arise in our minds as we are moved to reflect on our contingency or on the sheer gratuity of the Christian life. In the order of knowing, we may begin from contemplation of God's outer works which prompt us to trace them to the worker of these works. In systematic theology, what matters is not that the cognitive order reduplicate the material order but that the cognitive order not be allowed to overwhelm the proper material order: first the worker, then the work. Similarly, the order of exposition is a matter of relative indifference. Provided that the material order remains undisturbed, expository arrangements may be invented or adapted according to the requirements of didactic circumstances.

The matter treated in Christology straddles the two subject-domains of systematic theology. Christology considers both the eternal Word, intrinsic to God's inner being, and the Word's temporal mission in creation, providence and supremely in the person and work of Jesus Christ. Because of this, Christology is a distributed doctrine, not restricted to one or other domain; and it is so because it treats one of the triune persons, each of whom is to be considered both immanently and relatively.

If it is properly to reflect the scope and distribution of Christology in a system of Christian teaching, treatment of any particular Christological topic must keep in mind this double matter. No treatment of the doctrine of the Incarnation, for example, may so concentrate upon the historical density of the Word made flesh that it neglects the way in which that history refers back to its antecedent ground in the eternal inner-triune persons and relations. The Word which became flesh is the Word which was 'in the beginning' (John 1:14, 1); the Son who was for a little while made lower than the angels and partook of flesh and blood does so as one eternally begotten of the Father, bearing the very stamp of God's nature (Heb. 2L9, 14; 1:5, 3). To understand the Word made flesh, theological intelligence must consider its *terminus a quo*; systematic Christology connects teaching about Incarnation to the doctrine of the immanent Trinity. Equally, theological investigation of the eternal Word will be incomplete if it neglects the way in which this same Word, possessed of the infinite beatitude and completeness of God's simple being, also has a *terminus ad quem* in his external, relative acts as maker, sustainer, and reconciler of created life. Systematic Christology also considers the work of the Word in time.

The adequacy of a systematic Christology is partly a matter of how these two *termini* are defined and set in relation. In treating the *terminus a quo*, systematic theology is not proposing some abstract, speculative reality unconnected to the history of the Incarnation. It is simply following the rule of Christian faith that the invisible God is infinitely more real than any visible thing, the one by virtue of whom any visible thing has being and effect. The visible reality of the Word in time emerges from his participation in the entire sufficiency and repose of God. In himself the Word lacks nothing, and in his relation to creatures he receives no augmentation, for he is antecedently perfect. To this perfect fulfilment of the processions within the Godhead, in which the Son is eternally begotten of the Father and one from whom the Spirit eternally proceeds, there corresponds the Son's movement towards that which is not God. God's infinite beatitude includes infinite love extended outwards; it is an inner bliss which is causal, limitlessly generous, that by virtue of which created history comes to be.

Again, in treating Christology's *terminus ad quem*, the outward movement of the Word has to be understood as arising from his anterior completeness. It is not the accumulation of properties which extend the Word's identity. In the course of his movement from immanent origin to economic goal, the Word acquires nothing, remains immutable and simple, entirely resolved, and composed. Whatever relations the Word bears to creatures are on his side non-real (that is, non-constitutive). Yet, once more, God's perfect goodness is confirmed in creative causality. Goodness 'is attributed to [God] ... in as much as all desired perfections flow from him as from the first cause' (Aquinas, *ST* I, q.6, a.2, corp.).

By way of initial summary: (1) Christology is a division of the doctrine of the Trinity; (2) as a division of the doctrine of the Trinity, Christology is concerned with both theology and economy, theology first, economy by derivation; (3) Christology is not restricted to one particular locus of a system of Christian teaching, but is widely spread; (4) Christology is not in and of itself the starting point or centre of Christian teaching, but one indispensable element of a complex whole.

A brief exemplification of this arrangement may be found in Aquinas' incomplete *Compendium of Theology*, intended as a summary exposition of Christian teaching structured as a treatment of faith, hope, and love. 'The whole knowledge of faith involves ... two things', Aquinas states at the beginning, 'namely the divinity of the

Trinity and the humanity of Christ' (Aquinas 2009: I.2). Aquinas treats these two topics according to what he takes to be their proper material sequence: the doctrine of the Trinity, followed by the doctrine of the Incarnation. In investigating the divinity, attention to three topics is necessary: 'first, the unity of essence; second, the Trinity of persons; and third, the effects of divinity' (Aquinas 2009: I.2). Once again, the succession of the topics is significant. Only after giving a substantial amount of space to the oneness and the triunity of God (I.3–67) does Aquinas turn to consider the 'effects' or outer works of God in creation, providence, and redemption. Moreover, the treatment of faith in the humanity of Christ and of the restoration of creatures through the Incarnation does not begin until chapter 185, when Aquinas surveys the nature of sin, the nature of the Incarnation, Christ's conception and birth, the Paschal mystery and his exaltation and future work of judgement. The delay in introducing Christological material is, however, merely apparent, and does not indicate that Aquinas considers the incarnate Christ and his work of reparation a negligible matter: a treatment of faith which did not proceed beyond the divine essence and triunity to the effects of God would be Christianly unthinkable. But these effects, including the Incarnation of the Word, are just that: *effects*, only intelligible when their cause is grasped. Christ's humanity and his enactment of his office as Saviour cannot be understood per se, but only as it is 'related to his divinity as an instrument' (Aquinas 2009: I.213). The language of instrumentality, perhaps initially alarming, does not diminish the full reality of the Word's becoming flesh. It simply indicates that this 'becoming' and all that follows from it is 'assumption', that assumption does not compromise the integrity of the two natures, and that the assumed nature is to be understood not from its historical phenomenality, but from the divine person and act of the one who assumes it. 'We … judge the disposition and quality of instruments by their purpose, though also by the dignity of the one using them. Therefore, it is appropriate to esteem the quality of the human nature assumed by the Word of God in accordance with these norms' (Aquinas 2009: I.213, ET altered). Once this is in place, exposition of Christ's person and work follows naturally and completes the sequential treatment of the objects of faith.

We turn to further elaboration of the place of Christology in the two domains of theology and economy.

CHRISTOLOGY AND THEOLOGY

The first domain of Christology is theology. After any formal or prolegomenal matters about the nature, tasks, and cognitive principles of theology have been dealt with (not, of course, without reference to the substance of Christian teaching, including Christology), a system of Christian doctrine opens its material exposition with consideration of the Christian doctrine of God, and it is at this point that Christology receives its first extended treatment: in the course of the explanation of the doctrine of the Trinity, the eternal Son of God enters as an object of reflection.

Three tracts of material are treated in this Christological domain. First, consideration is given to the Son's eternal deity: his consubstantiality with the Father and the Spirit as one who participates in the undivided divine essence, and the properties which are his according to that divine essence. Here systematic theology turns its contemplative gaze and analytical intelligence to the Son's self-subsistent perfection, his infinity, simplicity, immutability, and impassibility as one beyond composition or disintegration, in other words, his entire beatitude. At the same time, systematic theology directs its attention to the Son's omnipotence and omniscience, and his unlimited goodness, wisdom, and justice. This is followed in a second stretch of argument by consideration of the Son's place in the processions which are God's infinite aliveness, that is, the Son's relation to the Father and the Spirit by origin, order, and operation. Here systematic theology gives an account of the eternal generation of the Son—the reality that he is 'begotten of the Father before all worlds, God from God, light from light, true God from true God, begotten not made', and so that the relation of the Son and the Father is wholly natural, consubstantial, and non-sequential rather than external, causal, or temporal. In similar fashion, attention is given to the Son as one from whom with the Father the Spirit proceeds. Treatment of these matters is then concluded, third, by an explanation of the personal property which is his as Son, namely 'filiation', the property of being one begotten by the Father before all worlds.

If it is to occupy its given place in the system of Christian teaching, a presentation of this threefold material needs to keep two thoughts in mind at every point. First, the Son is complete without creatures—not because he does not will to create creatures out of love, but precisely because he creates out of fullness of love rather than out of some indigence by which he is afflicted. Second, therefore, the interior, wholly resolved life of the eternal Son is also fraught with movement beyond itself, willing to direct itself outwards, and in so doing neither completes itself nor is at variance with itself, because the divine Son is supremely good and therefore creative.

In systematic consideration of Christology in the domain of theology, therefore, an account of the missions or external acts of the Son of God will be preceded by an account of the divine procession which is its vital principle. The procession of the Son from the Father is an 'immanent' act, having no external basis or object, but as such it is the uncaused cause of the history of the Incarnation. This is why such a systematic treatment risks distortion if it goes directly to the history of Jesus Christ. His identity as the divine-human agent of that history, as well as the nature, purpose, power, and effect of his acts, cannot be understood in isolation from his eternal relation of origin. The ground of his history, presupposed in each of its episodes and manifest, declared, or confessed in some, is: 'I have come' (see Gathercole 2006). Formally expressed: a divine mission includes within itself and refers to an eternal procession by which the identity of its agent is constituted. Thus the coming of the Son and his reception by creatures has its source and character in the fact that the Son is of one substance with the Father, by whom he is sent and from whom he comes into the world. This coming repeats in outward activity the relation of origin and the oneness of substance proper to Father and Son as eternal divine persons.

The Son's entry into audible, visible, tangible presence is the manifestation of 'that which was from the beginning' (1 John 1:1).

From this, a number of observations about the place of Christology in a system of theology may be drawn. (1) Christology is intrinsic to the doctrine of God, and receives its first treatment in the course of exposition of the doctrine of the Trinity. What is said subsequently about the Son of God relatively considered rests wholly upon what is first said about his eternal deity absolutely considered. One of the finest English divines from the mid-to-late seventeenth century, John Owen, phrases it thus: 'The person of Christ is the next [nearest] foundation of all acceptable religion and worship'; but 'the divine being itself is the first formal reason, foundation and object of all religion' (Owen 1965 [1679]: 44). Again: 'Were he not the *essential* image of the Father in his *own divine person*, he could not be the *representative* image unto us as incarnate' (Owen 1965 [1679]: 78)— and this, because 'God himself is the first and only essential truth' (Owen 1965 [1679]: 79). (2) The first material on the Son's divine essence carries within itself reference to his economic activity. Speaking of Proverbs 8:22f. ('The Lord created me at the beginning of his work …'), Owen writes: 'The eternal personal existence of the Son of God is supposed [presupposed] in these expressions … Without it, none of these things could be affirmed of him. But there is a regard in them, both unto his future incarnation, and the accomplishment of the counsels of God thereby' (Owen 1965 [1679]: 54). (3) A systematic theology will be adequate to its object if it constructs its exposition in a way that makes visible this mutual reference of absolute and relative, procession and mission, inner and outer work. This may be achieved by argumentative devices of anticipation and recapitulation, to ensure both that the full extent of Christology is kept in mind as completely and consistently as possible, and that the loci are not isolated from one another. (4) Christological knowledge is *knowledge by causes*: the visible reality of Jesus Christ becomes an object of understanding only when underlying its invisible principle is kept in mind as that by virtue of which it has phenomenal form. This is because in all its human density that visible form is an effect, that *from* which theological intelligence moves backwards to trace its foundation and source in God's being and will itself, and that *towards* which theological intelligence moves when it considers God's being and will. Christology is therefore only derivatively (yet also necessarily) an historical science. As we shall see shortly, one effect upon Christology of the decline of knowledge by causes or first principles and the prestige of immanent historical explanation has been atrophy of the first domain of Christology and expansion of the second domain, such that the proportions and location of Christological material have undergone extensive alteration.

CHRISTOLOGY AND ECONOMY

The second domain of Christology is economy. Arising from and extending the 'absolute' consideration of the Son of God which is its formative principle, there is a 'relative' consideration of his mission in time and its *telos* in the renewal of creaturely existence.

This second tract of Christological material is no less indispensable than the first; in its absence, systematic Christology would be a fragment.

The necessity of theological study of the Son's acts in time properly does not arise from suspicion that theology remains abstract or merely noumenal until its historical force is registered. Nor is it properly any supposed restriction of human knowledge and experience to the phenomenal realm which necessitates attention to the economy as if it were more immediately available and could be more readily turned to account. Rather, the second Christological domain is a matter for attention because theological intelligence traces the outer movement of God's communicative goodness—that is, God's determination that at the Father's behest the eternal Son should be the giver of life. 'He was in the beginning with God; all things were made through him' (John 1:2f.); 'as the Father has life in himself, so he has granted the Son also to have life in himself' (John 5:26); and so, 'the Son gives life to whom he will' (John 5:21).

Stated in a slightly different register, the hinge between the inner works of God and his economic activity is the divine will. To ground the economy in the divine will is to say that God's external works are not mere indifferent or accidental happenings, but purposive, the fruit of something akin to a decision (though without the deliberative, discursive sequence of a human decision). This divine purpose is eternal, antecedent, wholly spontaneous, and unconditioned by any consequent, 'before the foundation of the world' (Eph. 1:5), arising solely from God and not a response to some reality alongside God (*creatio ex nihilo* is fundamental to the being and history of that which is blessed by the divine purpose). Further, the divine purpose is not the imposition of an alien will, but that by virtue of which creatures come to have life and to flourish. This is because God's will is inseparable from his goodness and wisdom, and so is the gift of life.

God's outer works may be divided into two spheres: that of his work of nature, and that of his work of grace. The first sphere comprises creation and providence, the second the redemption and perfection of creatures. The agent of these works is the undivided Trinity, whose external acts are indivisible, though particular works may be especially appropriated to particular persons. This last point is of some consequence in retaining the correct proportions of Christology in a treatment of the economy. To say that the Son is the agent of redemption is not to concentrate the entirety of God's outer work upon this one person. This is because the Son acts *ad extra* as one who shares in the one divine essence, and so is not a discrete agent. Moreover, attribution of some work to him is *eminent* but not *exclusive* attribution, for in each divine work in time the Father is its fount, the Son its medium, and the Spirit its terminus.

With these preliminaries in mind, what material is treated in the second Christological domain? The Son's work is spread across the two spheres of nature and grace. He is the agent of creation ('in him all things were created', Col. 1:16) and of the providential maintenance and ordering of what has been made ('in him all things hold together', Col. 1:17). This being so, Christological material will have a considerable presence in a systematic account of the bringing into being and preservation of creatures; Christology is not exhausted by the history of redemption.

In the sphere of grace, Christology presents an analysis of the full scope of the Son's divine-human mission. This begins with an account of the act of Incarnation (the conception of Christ; the Word's assumption of human nature and the union of the divine and human natures in Christ's person); his earthly ministry as the herald and agent of the Kingdom of God; his Passion and death in their saving effect; his exaltation in his resurrection, ascension, and heavenly session; his continued operation through the Spirit in calling, sanctifying, and governing the Church and in ruling the course of the world; his future coming as judge and deliverer. Once again, Christology is widely extended, because its matter comprehends the person of the mediator and soteriology in its objective and subjective aspects, as well as ecclesiology and the Christian life. This complex of material may be arranged in various ways: as a relatively straightforward narrative sequence, or through conceptual structures such as the names and titles of the incarnate one (Jesus, Messiah, Christ, Lord, Servant, and so forth), his offices (prophet, priest, and king) or his states (humiliation and exaltation). In practice, most systematic treatments offer some sort of combination of all or most of these various schemes.

In a well-ordered systematic theology, the extensive material on the second domain of Christian teaching will arise naturally from and make appropriate backward reference to the material on the first domain; economy is most fully seen when illuminated by theology, which it in turn illuminates. Some modern systematic theologies have found it difficult to maintain this relation between the two domains, and the corollary placement of Christology. The difficulty arises because well-established principles of modern theological reason, both formal and material, tend to favour a rather different set of arrangements. These principles may be set out schematically as follows (not all modern systematic theologies exhibit any or all of these features, or exhibit them in unmixed form). (1) The differentiating characteristic of the Christian religion is the reference of all its various elements to Jesus Christ. As Schleiermacher puts it, in Christianity 'everything is related to the redemption accomplished by Jesus of Nazareth' (Schleiermacher 1928: 52). (2) The Christology to which all other elements refer is one in which the personal history of Jesus is irreducible, possessing a certain absoluteness which prohibits its resolution into a cause of which it is an external instrument. In a doctrine of the Incarnation, preservation of the integrity of Jesus Christ as unified personal agent takes priority over scrupulous distinction of and ordering of his divine and human natures. (4) In a Christian doctrine of God, God's being is act, and God's act principally understood as external (or externally manifest) operation, in terms of its *terminus ad quem*. (5) In systematic theology, priority is therefore to be assigned to the outer works of God; theology is an extrapolation from economy. (6) The specification of the Christian doctrine of God—its protection from abstraction and from being laden with unbecoming attributes—is to be effected by Christological doctrine rather than by teaching about the immanent Trinity.

Formation of Christology by some or all of these principles may result from various factors, theological and non-theological. Chief among the theological factors is a commitment to a view of divine revelation as embodied divine self-manifestation: in effect, revelation *is* incarnation. One effect of this strong identity between the divine Word and the historical form that it assumes is to close the space between God absolutely considered and God relatively considered. By virtue of the incarnational union of deity and humanity, there is consubstantiality between God's immanent self and God's revealed self, so that 'inner and 'outer' are not simply coherent but identical. Theology cannot 'get behind the back of Jesus to the eternal Son of God' (Torrance 1965: 130). The non-theological factors are more diverse and less easy to specify. They include such matters as: consent to the metaphysical restrictions imposed by Kant's placing of the noumenal beyond the reach of the human intellect; the effects of historical naturalism on interpretation of New Testament Christology; a valorization of history as first reality; a concomitant loss of confidence in the explanation of temporal events, acts, and agents by reduction to their causes.

In their widely varied forms, such principles have made a deep impression on some major systematic Christologies in the last two centuries, though others have been resistant to them. Where they do exercise sway, the result is commonly an expansion of the domain of economy, a corresponding contraction of the domain of theology, and an intensification of expectations surrounding the person and acts of Jesus Christ considered as historical quantities. As the one who constitutes all proper Christian knowledge, he is that reality around which may be ordered an entire account of Christian teaching, of which he is the centre (the metaphor is widely used and informative).

To illustrate the variety of responses to these factors, we may turn briefly to three examples from the history of Protestant systematic theology.

(1)   We look first at a theologian largely (though not entirely) unaffected by these trends, Izaak Dorner, in his *System of Christian Doctrine* (1879–81), a work whose wealth of historical observation, analytical finesse, and spiritual cogency is without equal in the school of 'mediating theology' with which he is usually associated. In treating Christology, Dorner sought to eschew any antithesis of theology and economy. He accomplished this partly by emphasis upon Christ's pre-existence, which he regarded as 'the doctrine of the living, real possibility and necessity of the incarnation', or 'the living potentiality, the productive ground of the possibility of the incarnation ... eternally in God' (Dorner 1882: 284). This directed Dorner's mind to the immanent Trinity, to which teaching about the person of Christ must always be 'conjoined' (Dorner 1882: 284). Yet what the doctrine of the immanent Trinity secures is not so much God's perfection apart from the Incarnation but rather the fact that there is in God 'an eternal self-disposition for incarnation' (Dorner 1882: 285); the Word is principally one who is 'to be incarnate'. Dorner made this move in part because it was for him a rule that 'evangelical piety starts with the world of revelation, and therefore with the revealed Trinity, with historical redemption and justification ... and does not start with the doctrine of the immanent Trinity' (Dorner 1882: 286).

There is more than a hint here that the order of knowing (from economy to theology) is coming to be regarded also as the material order. Yet for all this, Dorner remained clear that systematic reflection 'cannot halt' at this point of departure, and must advance to consider the fact 'that there corresponds to the peculiar and permanent being of God in Christ an eternal determination of the divine essence' (Dorner 1882: 286), a 'ground in God' (Dorner 1882: 297) for the Incarnation such that God's self-communication in Christ is without divine self-detriment or self-realization. This ground is 'the will of perfect self-communication' (Dorner 1882: 293).

(2) With Dorner's slightly younger contemporary, Albrecht Ritschl, matters took on a very different air. In the Christology set out in the third volume of his deeply impressive *Christian Doctrine of Justification and Reconciliation* (1874), Ritschl transposed Kant's separation of noumenal and phenomenal into a severance of theology from economy. The Christological effect of this proved drastic: Christology restricts itself to the effects of Christ in their reception by and formation of the moral existence of community of faith; nothing is gained from speculation about the eternal Son as the cause of those effects and their reception and power to shape. It is the significance of Christ—not his being in himself or his origin in God—which constitutes the proper object of Christological reflection, and that significance is only intelligible to (almost, indeed, constituted by) 'the consciousness of those who believe in him' (Ritschl 1902: 1). Here Ritschl explicitly differentiated himself from classical theology, which starts from an idea of original divine perfection and so fails to envisage 'every part of the system from the standpoint of the redeemed community of Christ' (Ritschl 1902: 5). Ritschl's work is an exemplary instance of how, when detached from its Trinitarian source, Christology may quite quickly collapse into soteriology, and soteriology into analysis of religious fellowship in its experiental and ethical dimensions. Within such a system, the doctrine of God's inner perfection can have very little Christological import: knowledge of God is exhausted in knowledge of his will to enact his love. In a remarkably voluntarist judgement, Ritschl maintained that 'when God is conceived as love, through the revelation of his will to his Son and the community of the Kingdom of God, he is not conceived as being anything part from or prior to his self-determination as love. He is either conceived as love, or simply not at all' (Ritschl 1902: 283). In terms of Christology, the consequence is that Christ's deity is not his immanent essence but purely economically operative: 'the godhead of Christ is not exhausted by maintaining the existence in Christ of the divine nature; the chief point is that in his exertions as man his godhead is manifest and savingly effective' (Ritschl 1902: 393). In short: Christ's origin 'transcends all inquiry' (Ritschl 1902: 451).

(3) A final example is that of Barth, generally judged the most consistently Christocentric modern theologian. The unequalled intellectual grandeur of Barth's achievement in the *Church Dogmatics*, along with its rhetorical,

imaginative, and spiritual force and its descriptive prowess, have combined to convey an impression of originality about his concentration on Christology, an impression which Barth himself did not discourage. However, his indebtedness to the great dogmaticians of the nineteenth century ought not to be understated (Barth himself did not understate it). What was original to Barth was not his Christological concentration so much as his combination of it with classical conciliar incarnational dogma and Reformed teaching about the hypostatic union, and his refusal to concur with the moralization of Christology into the soteriological background to religious-ethical society.

Barth's concentration on Christology is more complex than admirers and critics often allow, and than some of his own programmatic statements about the place and function of Christology suggest (understanding the *Church Dogmatics* requires attention both to Barth's uncompromising enunciations of principles and his often much more nuanced and fine-grained exposition of detail). There are certainly many occasions when he announces the Christological determination of all dogmatic loci: revelation, the being of God in his freedom and his love, the election of humankind, human nature, sin, the Spirit, and more besides. Often the vigour of Barth's statements derives from his resistance to what he considered the corrosive effects of natural theology. Moreover, the fourth volume of the *Dogmatics*, which treats the doctrine of reconciliation by an innovative interlaced account of the person and work of Christ, his natures, offices, and states, and their saving efficacy, is without doubt the point at which Barth's powers are at full stretch. In the details of his exposition, however, Barth rarely reduces all other doctrines to derivatives or implicates of Christology. In part this is because he fears systematic master principles, even dogmatic ones, and seeks to preserve the freedom of the Word of God in dogmatic construction. In part, too, it is because he has a well-developed sense of the range of dogmatics, and an especially strong conviction that, in a dogmatics in which the covenant between God and humanity is of primary import, Christology in the economy must not overwhelm either the freedom of the eternal divine decision or the integrity of the human creature. In addition, Barth remains convinced that Christology and Trinity are inseparable and mutually implicating, and that teaching about the immanent Trinity is of great Christological import (this may be lost from view if Barth's doctrine of reconciliation is detached from his doctrine of the Trinity in *Church Dogmatics* I). Jesus Christ is the name, form, and act of God; yet where those in Ritschl's school (including the theological existentialists with whom Barth engaged in skirmishes in the 1950s whilst writing *Church Dogmatics* IV) took this as permission to set theology proper to one side in favour of an exclusively economic orientation, Barth continued to think that teaching about the eternal Son is essential to identifying the acting subject of revelation and reconciliation. In the overall sweep of his exposition of Christian doctrine, Barth does not allow theology to atrophy, though he is consistently and powerfully attentive to the economy as the sphere of the Son's presence and action.

Conclusion

No element in a system of theology is unrelated to Christology: to contemplate any of its parts is to have one's mind drawn irresistibly to the name and figure of Jesus Christ. Why is this so? Barth judged that it was so because Christian theology

> does not know and proclaim anything side by side with or apart from Jesus Christ, because it knows and proclaims all things only as his things ... For it, there is no something other side by side with or apart from him. For it, there is nothing worthy of mention that is not as such his. Everything that it knows and proclaims as worthy of mention, it does so as his.
>
> (Barth 1956a: 21)

This is, perhaps, stated in an unqualified way; yet there is here something incontestably correct and wholesome, namely, that Jesus Christ is not merely the exponent or symbol of some reality available apart from him, for he is (the term is Hans Frei's) 'unsubstitutable' (Frei 1975: 49). Yet if this conviction—so ample and loving in its dedication to the Word incarnate—is not to occasion over-intensification of one indispensable element of Christology and attenuation of the way in which that element directs attention to God's inner life, systematic theology must specify with some scruple the sense in which God is the formal object of each Christian doctrine, Christology included. In assembling all its various matters into a scheme, systematic theology acknowledges that faith gives assent to many things; but it does so because by those many things faith is conducted to God as first truth. Theology takes things other than God into account as 'effects of the divine working' (Aquinas ST IIaIIae, q.1, a.1, corp.). The breadth and spread of Christology derive from the fact that in it theology considers both God himself as first truth and God's effects. Study of the incarnate Word may not pass too quickly over his phenomenal form; but nor may it terminate there, for it must allow this human history to direct us to the triune God (see Aquinas ST IIaIIae, q.1, a.1, ad1). Yet, again, instruction about this formal object may be had by observation of its extensions or external working: 'we demonstrate something about a cause from its effect' (Aquinas ST I, q.1, a.7, ad1). And so when systematic reflection is directed to God as first truth, the Incarnation is not left behind, because to apprehend this first truth is also to apprehend that the eternal Word participates in God's infinite communicative and creative goodness and is the exemplary cause of God's works in time. When these material—Trinitarian—principles govern the content and proportions of a systematic presentation of Christian teaching, the place, extent, and formative role of Christology will be properly delimited and secured.

Suggested Reading

Aquinas (2009); Barth (1956a); Tanner (2010); Torrance (1965); Weinandy (2011).

BIBLIOGRAPHY

Amberg, E.-H. (1966), *Christologie und Dogmatik. Untersuchung ihres Verhältnisses in der evangelischen Theologie der Gegenwart* (Göttingen: Vandenhoeck & Ruprecht).

Aquinas, T. (2009), *Compendium of Theology* (Oxford: Oxford University Press).

Barth, K. (1956a), *Church Dogmatics* IV/1 (Edinburgh: T. & T. Clark).

Barth, K. (1956b), *Church Dogmatics* I/2 (Edinburgh: T. & T. Clark).

Barth, K. (1961), *Church Dogmatics* IV/3 (Edinburgh: T. & T. Clark).

Barth, K. (1975), *Church Dogmatics* I/1 (Edinburgh: T. & T. Clark).

Dorner, I. A. (1882), *A System of Christian Doctrine*, vol. 3, trans. A. Cave and J. S. Banks (Edinburgh: T. & T. Clark).

Emery, G. (2007), *The Trinitarian Theology of Thomas Aquinas*, trans. F. A. Murphy (Oxford: Oxford University Press).

Fairbairn, A. M. (1893), *The Place of Christ in Modern Theology* (London: Hodder & Stoughton).

Frei, H. (1975), *The Identity of Jesus Christ: The Hermeneutical Bases of Dogmatic Theology* (Philadelphia: Fortress).

Gathercole, S. J. (2006), *The Pre-existent Son: Recovering the Christologies of Matthew, Mark and Luke* (Grand Rapids, Mich.: Eerdmans).

Jenson, R. W. (1997), *Systematic Theology*, vol. 1: *The Triune God* (Oxford: Oxford University Press).

Knitter, P. (1983). 'Theocentric Christology', *Theology Today* 40: 130–49.

McCormack, B. L. (2010), 'Why Should Christology Be Christocentric? Christology and Metaphysics in Paul Tillich and Karl Barth', *Wesleyan Theological Journal* 45: 42–80.

McIntyre, J. (1966), *The Shape of Christology* (London: SCM Press).

MacKinnon, D. M. (1987), 'The Relation of the Doctrine of the Incarnation and the Trinity', in MacKinnon, *Themes in Theology: The Three-Fold Cord. Essays in Philosophy, Politics and Theology* (Edinburgh: T. & T. Clark), 145–67.

Macquarrie, J. (1990), *Jesus Christ in Modern Thought* (London: SCM Press).

Marshall, B. (1987), *Christology in Conflict: The Identity of a Saviour in Rahner and Barth* (Oxford: Blackwell).

Owen, J. (1965 [1679]), *Christologia, or A Declaration of the Glorious Mystery of the Person of Christ*, in *The Works of John Owen*, vol. 1 (Edinburgh: Banner of Truth Trust), 1–272.

Pannenberg, W. (2004), *Systematic Theology*, vol. 2 (Grand Rapids, Mich.: Eerdmans).

Pfleiderer, O. (1890), *The Development of Theology in Germany since Kant* (New York: Macmillan).

Riches, J. (1972), 'What is a "Christocentric" Theology?', in S. W. Sykes and J. P. Clayton (eds.), *Christ, Faith and History*. Cambridge Studies in Christology (Cambridge: Cambridge University Press), 223–38.

Ritschl, A. (1902), *The Christian Doctrine of Justification and Reconciliation III: The Positive Development of the Doctrine* (Edinburgh: T. & T. Clark).

Schleiermacher, F. D. E. (1928), *The Christian Faith* (Edinburgh: T. & T. Clark).

Tanner, K. (2010), *Christ the Key* (Cambridge: Cambridge University Press).

TeSelle, E. (1975), *Christ in Context: Divine Purpose and Human Possibility* (Philadelphia: Fortress).

Torrance, T. F. (1965), 'The Place of Christology in Biblical and Dogmatic Theology', in Torrance, *Theology in Reconstruction* (London: SCM Press), 128–49.

Weinandy, T. (2011), 'Trinitarian Christology: The Eternal Son', in G. Emery and M. Levering (eds.), *The Oxford Handbook of the Trinity* (Oxford: Oxford University Press), 387–99.

Williams, A. (2011), *The Architecture of Theology: Structure, System, and Ratio* (Oxford: Oxford University Press).

AFTERWORD

The Breadth of Christology: The Beautiful Work of Christ

FRANCESCA ARAN MURPHY

THIS great volume contains many dynamic tensions. One concerns the centrality of Christology to systematic theology. For Robert Woźniak, Christology is the necessary prism through which all theological topics are best viewed. The Chalcedonian formula dogmatically instructs us how to read God's immanence and God's transcendence. For John Webster, conversely, thus to foreground Christology risks allowing the economic Trinity to upstage the transcendent Trinity. God's freedom to create must not be granted priority over his freedom to be, lest the sovereignty of God be compromised and God enmeshed in history. A third partner in this lively and fruitful disputation is Bruce McCormack, who seems to conclude his chapter on kenotic Christology by indicating that kenosis will make no sense in its application to Christ until kenosis belongs to our conception of the Trinity. There is, McCormack proposes, an eternal 'self-emptying' by the Logos, because 'the being of the triune God is so completely oriented towards' incarnational kenosis 'that the identity of the Logos as the second "person" of the Trinity is formed by it'. The transcendent Trinity, with its incalculable ontological priority, and the Incarnation, with its inevitable epistemic priority for human beings are doctrinally inseparable: only the love between the Three Persons 'in the Theology' can explain how, 'in the Economy', 'an act of obedience is not necessarily foreign to God himself' (Von Balthasar 1990: 81–2). The chapters by Woźniak, Webster, and McCormack are necessary reading for understanding what is at stake in the most important debate in contemporary systematic theology.

THE PERSON VERSUS THE WORK OF CHRIST?

This handbook has a comprehensiveness which could not have been achieved sixty years ago, when explicitly inter-confessional theology was in its infancy. Today, when many would say that the ecumenical movement has run its course, this volume owes something of its range and completeness to its ecumenical character. This ecumenical character itself springs nonetheless from the fact that the authors do not focus on ecumenicity, saving their attention for the One to whom it is due. The authors you have just read have kept their eyes upon the incarnate, crucified, and risen Lord, when they are not, of course, contemplating the immanent Trinity.

Having been assigned by his editor a chapter on 'the works of Christ in patristic theology', Norman Russell performed his task with exceptional scholarship, and thus observed that 'the distinction between the person of Christ and the work of Christ is a comparatively modern one, going back to the scholastic mindset of the sixteenth-century Protestant Reformers'. No patristic author articulated a distinction between the person and work of Christ. By scholastic times, such a distinction is implicit, in, for instance, Thomas Aquinas' division of the Tertia Pars into Questions 1–26, which probe the ontological constitution of the two natures and the divine Person who unites them, and Questions 27–59, his little 'bios' of Christ, in which he runs through the whole of Jesus' historical life as narrated in the Gospels. Thomas leaves the distinction between the person and work of Christ implicit, and thus he distinguishes the two without partitioning them. In an excess of conceptual clarity the distinction metastasized into a partition whose sole purpose was to provide for tug-of-war between Catholics and Protestants.

In living with this excess of analysis, Catholics and Protestants came to differ about the *works* of Christ. This contestation seemed to set the 'person' of Christ against his 'works'. Perhaps this contestation goes all the way back to Martin Luther himself. According to Brian Lugioyo, Luther's watchword was 'Crux sola est nostra theologia' (*WA* 5: 176) . 'It was the revealed, incarnate God—which the late mediaeval theologians had discarded—that became his starting point. Theology could not begin with the divinity of Christ; it had to begin with his humanity.' Perhaps the dynamic tensions exhibited amongst Woźniak, Webster, and McCormack in this volume has its onset with Luther's watchword. Few of the disagreements in this book are confessional.

The objection of post-Reformation Protestant theology to Catholic or 'ontological' Christologies is that it is all over bar the shouting at the 'Incarnation' event. The 'historicity', or Jesus' ministry as a whole, is thereby lost, some Protestants think. The counter-objection of the Catholics is that the soteriological or 'functional' Christologies of the Protestants so compress the significance of Christ's life into the Passion that the full historicity is dispensed into an event between Father and Son. Classical Protestant objections to the Catholic Christological focus on the *being* of Christ simultaneously contain a rejection of a key aspect of Catholic and Orthodox soteriology, that is, deification. One of the great gains made by Michael Gorman's chapter in this volume is its demonstration that, as Christians understand it, not only the death, and not only one *kind* of work, but the whole breadth of Jesus' life is salvific.

The ancient Catholic–Protestant confessional dispute is not simply about whether to prize the works above the person or vice versa. For no one would prize works which they did not think fit the reality of the case. The dispute has been, rather, about what *kind* of soteriology actually fits the kind of person Jesus was, a soteriology of substitution or a soteriology of deification. The partitioning and contestation between the 'person' and 'work' of Christ came about because of a partitioning and contestation between various of his works. And this partitioning amongst Christ's works itself became a scotoma, which blocked from our view the wholeness and thus the beauty of Christ. The Protestant who offered to remove the mote of 'Incarnationalism' from the Catholic's eye was blinded by the plank of a substitutionary doctrine of atonement which steered him toward Nestorianism; the Catholic who kindly attempted to remove the speck of 'Incarnationalism' from the Protestant's eye was blinkered by a deificatory soteriology which inclined her toward monophysitism. There is no one-sidedness about Christ's works which does not flow from shortsightedness about his person.

This is because Christ does who he is. This is part and parcel of his uniqueness, that is, of his being God the Son. Though only blessed with one nature, human beings have much more trouble being at one with themselves than Christ did. This may surprise students of modern Christological research, which presents Jesus Christ as gamely struggling to wield in unison a divine and a human nature. The unwieldiness is of course not in Christ but in the minds of modern Christologists who, starting by dividing his work from his person, have turned Christ's life into an endless balancing act between the two natures. This is not to say the ancients had it all down pat. But at least the patristic conception of Christ's humanity as the 'instrument' of his divinity integrated the humanity into soteriology without making 'becoming human' the end and goal, rather than the means, of the Trinity's work in the Incarnation.

As creatures, human beings cannot fully be ourselves because we cannot fully *be*. We are not fully and entirely who we are, as God is. When, as Venard notes in his chapter here, the Synoptic Jesus asks, 'Who do you say I am?', he deftly tucks into his question a reminder of the answer: 'I am that I am', of Exodus 3:14. Rowan Williams in this book quite rightly does his best to sidestep his editorial instruction to write about Christ-figures in modern literature: if there is one thing which nineteenth- and early twentieth-century people needed to learn it was that they *cannot* (very easily) be Christ-figures. They had to be instructed by their novelists to stop looking down the well of history and seeing their own face at the bottom, not the face of Christ. The God-man is who he is, and we will not be fully ourselves until we have become the 'deified rational animals' (Norman Russell) who populate Paradise. As for now, our personae are, not just fractured, which comes with being human creatures, but also somewhat warped, which comes with being fallen. The unfallen angels are fractured (they are not, *pace* Calvin, identical to their functions), but unwarped.

Jesus is fully himself, fully at one with all his works and the role that he plays in human salvation, because his mission or sending by the Father *is* his begetting by the Father. As Anatolios reminds us in his chapter, the first move toward subordinationism is imagining that 'there was when he was not', that the Father elected to beget Christ at some moment in a special supernatural pre-temporality. Because Christ is God, it is of Christ's nature and character to be. Christ's begetting *is* his mission or sending, because there is and can be no division between his plenary *being* and his functional role in the theology and in the economy. His ontological begetting and his inner Trinitarian role are one and the same. His extra-Trinitarian role is an extension of who he is in eternity. The human persona of Jesus is the means to the accomplishment of this role. In order to save us, he adopts exactly what has gone wrong with humanity, a persona which partially disguises who he is.

It is no fault in creatures to say that we are given and take up roles and projects, rather than being ontologically identical with them. It is simply what it is to be a creature, one's being not identical to one's nature and character. They would be like that without Adam's fall into sin and death. All that the Fall, and with it 'original death', adds to this disparity, on the one hand, is, since our acting time is finite, a desperation and anxiety about the search for a fitting role, and on the other, the use of roles to lie and deceive. Acting is not in itself untruthful or hypocritical, but it is used manipulatively by concupiscent, fallen creatures. Jesus Christ, the perfect actor of his begotten role, especially scorns hypocrisy and observes that Satan has always lied, because he is 'ontologically untruthful' (John 8:44). The admixture of untruth into our assumption of roles is the mark of our enslavement to demonic structures. The finitude of postlapsarian human life is God's rightful punishment of sin, the deception is demonic.

This is why we find acting and drama so gripping: a rational creature whose nature or character is not identical to his being has constantly to project himself into roles which do not quite equate to his existential reality. And when we add fallenness into the mix, we add the uncertainty about whether other human beings are projecting truthfully or with an aim to deceive. With our projecting roles constantly running ahead of our limping existence (for we are not quite ourselves, cannot quite say, 'I am that I am' with conviction), acting is what we ourselves do all the time. And thus we find the observation of actor playing a role magnetically fascinating: it is to see our anthropological dilemma, as existentially-dependent role-playing animals played out on the instant-video screen.

To take a well-known example, the man Clint Eastwood plays the movie-actor 'Clint Eastwood': he does not so much play 'Dirty Harry' in one movie and 'Walt Kowalski' in another as play 'Clint Eastwood' through all the personae in his movie repertoire. He plays 'Clint Eastwood' even or especially when he is defeating our expectations, and turning the character upside down into a 'Christ figure' (as Robert Barron shows in his chapter). Every movie star has his own filmography, in which the biography of the character he plays is concretized in numerous personae, from young hero or starlet to older man or woman, and this growth and maturation in the actor belongs to the movie itself, and is not extrinsic to it. So the human being plays an invented self, an 'Eastwood', for instance, or a 'Cruise' or 'Weaver', by means of a string of concrete and specific persona.

Dirty Harry or Walt Kowalski is the means by which the human being Clint Eastwood plays his 'Eastwood' role in the cop movies and in *Gran Torino*. The persona is integrally connected to the body of the actor: Javier Bardem 'has the face' for playing villains. Because it is thus bound to the actor's physicality, to his or her features and physique, the human being Clint Eastwood ages over time, and gave his role of 'Clint Eastwood' the persona of Dirty Harry as a young man, and the face of Walt Kowalski as he entered old age. Dirty Harry and Walt Kowalski are *not* personalities: they are instruments for one concrete, specific enactment of the 'Clint Eastwood' role. They are personae, not personalities.

Movies would not be fascinating to us if what they have to show us were unrealistic and unlifelike: over the course of our lives all human persons adopt and play a single 'character' by means of various personae (mother, plumber, professor, dog-lover). Jesus Christ adopts no roles: he *is* what he does. The work of Christ is simply the expression of his person. But he does adopt or assume a human persona (or what the early patristics called a 'flesh') whose specific, concrete humanity is the instrument or means of his soteriological work. Every acting persona is some kind of stereotype, and the New Adam is the acme of all the human personae through which roles are concretized. As the New Adam he recapitulates the human project as a whole.

This is not to say that Jesus' persona is a 'human personality'. It doesn't work to ascribe a human personality to Christ, alongside the *person* of the Logos. As McCormack notes in this handbook, describing Strauss' objections to a 'two-personality' Chalcedonian Christ: 'to speak of two natures *in one person* is to imply the existence of a *single* self-consciousness in the one God-human. For what else could the term "person" mean? But a single self-consciousness cannot emerge out of the union of two such radically different "personalities". For either would be canceled out by the other.' Chalcedonian Christology works only with a single *person*, the agent of the Logos, at work: that agent is begotten by the Father for all time, and for all time plays the role of the one *sent*; he assumes a human persona in order to be sent 'into a far country', into the economy of salvation. A persona is in a sense a disguise, and this is not far from saying that he is disguised in flesh, so long as we recognize that this particular disguise reveals who he is: where do you hide a leaf? In a tree. Jesus has a human *persona*, not a human personality, and it is the physical expression of the being of the second person of the Trinity in a way that a human *personality* could not be.

As Dirty Harry memorably observes, 'a man has to know his limitations'. God knows the limitations and the multivalent structure of the nature God created. The God-man must do his work, carry out his calling, within a nature which is structured between three poles. Three poles to be found in all reality are the actual, the potential, and the privative, or so Aristotle is known to have believed. In one aspect of his works, Christ draws out humanity's potential for deification. He enacts a human character who is fully alive to his own mystery and *knows* himself. In a second aspect of his works, Christ directly addresses the *actuality* of the human situation, by offering atoning sacrifice to God the Father. In a third aspect of his work, he withdraws humanity from the state of *privation* in which it currently languishes, enslaved to the lie and to hypocritical personae. In his work of theosis, Christ deals with human potential in terms of what it positively lacks, in order to fulfill it; in his work of conquest of sin, death, and the devil, Christ deals with human privation, its need for liberation from evil. In his sacrificial or substitutionary works, those works offered to the Father, Christ makes *actual* capital out of his death, by paying the redemptive price *to the Father.*

Russell notes in his chapter that some patristic theologians differed amongst themselves as to whether, by the shedding of his blood, a ransom is being paid to the Father (so Nazianzus) or the devil (thus Nyssa). Some of the Fathers do not conceive of the aspect of the work Christ gives the devil as 'ransoming'. Whatever their emphases, all the Church Fathers at least mention all three corners of Christ's work, the manward, the Godward, and the devilward. For that reason alone, they need to tell us a good deal about 'what' Jesus did in the course of his historical Incarnation: they cannot content themselves with the 'that' of the Incarnation', in the way in which, according to Ziegler in this volume, Rudolf Bultmann was to do in the twentieth century.

This handbook contains several outstanding essays touching upon the modern schism between the 'Jesus of History' and the 'Christ of Faith'. This schism was not only brought about by the rise of modern historical criticism: it was caused by the failure to get hold of what role Christ is playing through his human persona. The 'Jesus of History' has always been projected as some kind of moral teacher, but, effectively, as one who has little to say—barring the mad proclamation that the world is about to end (which it apparently did not do in his lifetime). The crucifixion makes a mess of the 'Jesus of History': this gentle moral teacher makes more sense if he does not die on the Cross (as Schweitzer saw already in 1900). The 'Christ of Faith', on the other hand, is really the resurrected Christ, absent but present in and through the Church (Bockmuehl). The 'Christ of Faith' is in that sense a haloed icon which we might have good reason to be somewhat 'phobic' about (*pace* Nichols): he wears a golden halo and yet his voice is disembodied and he bears no wounds. Or as Ziegler has it, with respect to Martin Kähler, 'The question of how "diaphanous" the earthly man Jesus can become and still be Christologically relevant remains.'

Both the proponents of the 'Jesus of History' and of the 'Christ of Faith' take a pass when it comes to the *Passion and death* of Christ. They do not see the divinity as manifested through the agony of the crucifixion, as Alison Milbank describes the mediaevals as having done in her strikingly beautiful chapter. The Jesus of History and the Christ of Faith are both equally what Schweitzer called 'a puzzle and an enigma' in the sense that we cannot see what this fellow is for, what work he performs. He is, so to say, a 'nowhere man' with no instrumentality, no flesh and blood.

In his chapter, Richard Bauckham proposes that the 'Jesus of Testimony' mediates between the two enigmatic figures, reconciling 'History' and 'Faith'. In modern times, 'History' and 'Faith' are stand-ins for what ancient Christologies (Daley, Louth) called the 'human nature' and the 'divine nature'. Mark Elliott shows how post-Reformation Christologies, both Catholic and Protestant, struggled to hold the two together in a single view. Whereas, as Brian Daley shows, Nestorius was vulnerable to the accusation that his Christ has no unitary substance but merely presents a unitary *Gestalt* in his two natures, our moderns often sought in vain even to achieve this Nestorian nadir. Bauckham's 'Jesus of Testimony' is the Jesus presented to our vision by the Church: he is upheld to us by the Church to touch and see. Philip Ziegler's wonderful, clear chapter reminds us that Bultmann was not a blinkered anti-historicist. He insisted upon the historical 'that' but denied that the historical what, the flow and length, the content, of Jesus' life matters Christologically. By affirming that the only Christ we know anything about is kerygmatic all the way down, Bultmann maintained, in his own way, that the only Christ whom Christians can know and believe in is the Christ of the Gospel. For Bultmann, the Christ of the Gospel is present through his absence, visibly invisible. As Ziegler states, the great Lutheran exegete was happy to put 'Jesus' in inverted commas.

So what is the difference between Bauckham's 'Jesus of Testimony' and Bultmann's 'Christ of Faith'? Are not both equally absent in history but present in the Church? The difference between the two is that we are *reliant upon others*, going back through the chain of witnesses, for our knowledge of the 'Jesus of Testimony', whereas Bultmann's 'Christ of Faith' knows no mediators. Raymond Gawronski points out herein that Christology is all about 'knowing' Christ and that what it means to know Christ has differed from one epoch to another. For Bauckham, knowing Christ is making an historiographically reasonable act of trust in many named witnesses; for Bultmann, Christ is made known to us by an event of faith, not by the bare *that* of his historical humanity, not by the one Bultmann is content to call 'Jesus'. Like Kant, Bultmann had an aversion for dependency.

The two brilliant and complementary pieces by Reynolds, about the Islamic Christ, and by Gathercole, about the Gnostic Christ, both indicate that for Christians there is no credible Christ who is not the Christ of the Church's historical, apostolic, and evidential testimony. The Gnostic Christ is, on Gathercole's showing, the very first 'Jesus of History', the first 'Jesus' constructed outside of, and against, the Church's testimony. There are tendencies both in the Islamic and the Gnostic 'Christ' to duck the Passion and to claim that the death of Jesus is a fiction. This is not solely in order to avoid those tiresome resurrection accounts, along with their tedious tendency to make us wonder what bouncing back from death to life implies about who Christ is. For Gnostics and Muslims, Christ can perform his role and work without dying. It is not central to the human persona he adopts. In these legendary accounts of Jesus' identity, it is not easy to say what Jesus' work or function is. He comes to teach, but not to teach himself. This 'Jesus' is not 'who he is'.

Neither the 'Jesus of History' nor the 'Christ of Faith' enters human history in a 'deathward' direction: the 'work' of the former is to teach, and of the latter to represent the eschatological triumph over death. Neither of these two possible personae has the role or project of 'being toward death': neither of these figures comes in order to reach into death with the entirety of his being. And so, just as neither the Islamic Christ nor the Gnostic Christ is fully divine, so also he is not fully human. To be human after the Fall is to know the deaths of one's friends, one's loved ones, and to die oneself, in absolute helplessness. For an historical, postlapsarian human being to be saved by Christ's work is to be saved from death by death:

if God wished to 'experience' (*zein peira*, cf. Hebrews, 2.18; 4.15) the human condition 'from within', so as to re-direct it from inside it, and thus save it, he would have to place the ... stress on that point where sinful, mortal man finds himself 'at his wit's end' .... this must be where man has lost himself in death without ... finding God .... God has ... to place the emphasis on ... being 'at one's wit's end' ... to bind together the fractured extremities of the idea of man. And this is what we actually find in the identity that holds good between the Crucified and the Risen One.

(Von Balthasar 1990: 13)

In keeping with the nature of the reality into which the actual historical Jesus Christ came to do his work, soteriologies are of three kinds. In the *manward* soteriology, which addresses the fulfillment of human potential, Christ's humanity must make its way deathward, because it is by means of his shed body and blood that he divinizes his followers. In the *Godward* soteriology, which addresses God's actuality, Christ becomes incarnate in the persona of the historical man Jesus in order to offer his death to the Father. In the *devilward* soteriology, which addresses the privations which currently enmesh humanity, Jesus Christ deceives the deceiver with his human persona.

The terms 'manward' and 'Godward' correspond to what Rik van Nieuenhove in his chapter terms 'subjective' and 'objective' views of atonement. I prefer to call 'actual' or 'Godward' what Nieuenhove, in keeping with many commentators, calls 'objective', because the 'repercussions of salvation for the relation between creation and God' is a repercussion in *actuality*, whereas 'the transformative effect on the Christian believer' of Christ's work is, in my opinion, not so much 'subjective' (it strikes me as quite objective) but rather, in the domain of potentiality rather than actuality. It is in and through the mediation of his work that we see Christ for who he is. All three works respond not only to the question, *cur Deus homo?*, but also to the question *cur Deus mortem*? The unifying thread of the three labors is that all orient the human persona of Jesus to death.

POTENTIALITY, PRIVATION, ACTUALITY: RANSOM, THEOSIS, SATISFACTION

Deification is the original 'manward' theory: the work of Christ goes 'to*ward*' human beings. The dramatic vector of Christ's deeds is aimed toward humanity. From its origins in Paul and Irenaeus' words about *anakephalaiosis*, or the recapitulation of humanity in Christ, to its late, cut-price variants, this theory orients Christ's work toward the human. There is a spectrum of manward conceptions of atonement, running from Cyrilline theosis to moral exemplarism. It is not always easy to see where a theory stands on the spectrum. Abelard's theory is said to go beyond moral exemplarism and yield deification if you look hard enough. Exemplarism, or envisaging Jesus as an exemplar of ethical principle, is a much diminished, moralizing version of the original 'manward' soteriology of the patristics and mediaevals, both Western and Eastern. So what Philip Ziegler's chapter ascribes to Schleiermacher, and to thinkers of the caliber of Ernst Renan, that is, conceiving Jesus' work as being an *inspiring* religious-moral teacher, is a kind of 'manward' theory.

In the exemplarism of Kant, as succinctly elucidated in this volume by Kevin Hector, 'doing the moral exemplar', performing the role of exemplar, is not so much *done by* Christ, not acted out by Christ, as it is *detected by us* in him. On Kant's analysis, as 'plausibly' reconstructed by Hector, *we* commit ourselves to Christ out of respect for his moral perfection. Kant seems to render Christ as the passive exponent of moral perfection. We read the moral example off his passive, not to say, lifeless, effigy. Jesus here ceases to be an icon, in the classical sense of a medium and instrument of grace, and becomes a naturalistic portrait. Here 'deification' has been thoroughly stripped out of the 'exemplar' theory: humanity is not so much *acted upon* by Christ (the original meaning of the exemplar theory): rather, on its own volition, humanity takes Christ as its own role model.

As befits the exponent of the rising bourgeoisie of the late eighteenth century, Kant had an aversion to dependency. He would not have us dependent on Christ, or caused or led by him to more virtuous living, because, as he saw it, that would deprive us of our freedom. Hector cites Kant as calling Christ 'an example to be emulated'. The rather bohemian Schleiermacher had no such problems with dependence. His Christ is wholly dependent upon God, indeed, his God-consciousness is measured by the degree of his dependency upon God, and found to be infinite. Schleiermacher's Christ 'is' God to the extent that he is immeasurably dependent upon God. He is the one in whom freedom with respect to God and receptivity with respect to God are not in conflict. He is a 'new Adam' in the sense that this degree of God-consciousness is a new start in human history. His work is then to transmit his receptivity to God, or to make us 'receptive to his receptivity' (so Hector). Schleiermacher's Jesus is thus a causative agent: 'There is', Hector says, 'a transitive property at work here'. No lifeless effigy, Schleiermacher's Jesus must *live* and minister in order thus to influence us toward being receptive to God's love. But need he die in order to provoke such dependency and receptivity? In Schleiermacher's anthropological Christology, Christ's work does not address the human 'issue' of death. *Suffering*, down to the suffering of the Passion, by arousal of love, might assist in making us 'receptive to his receptivity' to God. But, taken not as a psychological fact, but as an ontological reality, not the Passion, but Christ's *death itself* plays no role in Schleiermacher's conception of his work.

In his favor, one may say that, by ascribing absolute dependency to Christ, Schleiermacher reopened the question of whether the incarnate Jesus experienced 'faith'. Joseph Wawrykow tackles in his chapter the fact that many moderns feel that the Christ of the *Summa Theologiae* is not fully human because Thomas Aquinas refuses to ascribe the virtue of 'faith' to him. Wawrykow notes, very astutely, that it is a matter of achieving the *virtue of faith*, not of 'having faith' in a subjective sense. I wonder if, when Thomas is criticized on this matter, they have in mind the distinction Hector articulates, between Kant's Christ as non-dependent, and Schleiermacher's Christ as dependent all the way through. When people criticize Thomas' Christ for his rising above the need for faith in the permanent possession of the beatific vision, are they actually, and merely, siding with Schleiermacher as against Kant? Those who stand against Thomas on this matter are in Schleiermacher's corner when it comes to dependency as a quality without which we are not fully human. And yet, because his human persona has no intrinsic deathward thrust in his vocational task, Schleiermacher's Christ is ultimately not fully man, not one like us. For us, the way in which we approach death is what makes and shapes our human persona; for Schleiermacher's Jesus, not so much. Schleiermacher's Jesus does not know the limitation of death from within, or master it.

In its origins as a conception of Christ's work as theosis, the 'manward' soteriology has two poles: Christ as God acts upon human beings to divinize them; 'God became man so that man could become God', as Athanasius put it. In the classical 'manward' soteriology, and sacramentology, of Eastern and Western mediaevals, the work of Christ is to deify human beings by joining his own divinized humanity to ours. His humanity is the 'instrument' or means of our deification.

The 'manward' soteriology loses its import when detached from Christ's other works. It ceases to show us his person, and becomes the work of a splendid human being, and one whose perfection is, ironically, inimitable. Kant shrank from the conception of human *dependency* on God, avoiding through his rather disembodied conception of Christ as an 'Idea' or moral archetype the very thought of God's healing touch in Christ. And yet, if we sidestep Christ's work as healer, *Pharmakos*, Christ ceases to *act as a cause* upon us. African Christologies today do right to accentuate the patristic image of Jesus as *Pharmakos* of human bodies and souls (Stinton).

Moreover, since as a moralist, Kant continues to consider Christ as *perfect*, his perfection ceases to be imitable. We will not think of him as *acting* as a cause unless, in addition to conceiving his work as fulfilling our human *potential* (for morality and even for godliness), we conceive of human nature as led to *actuality* by the God-man who *is* always already fully actual. God became *man* in order to fulfill our potential; *God* became man because only God could actually do so.

Christ also performs a work which is directed to God. Here the work he does on behalf of humanity is presented, not to human beings, but to God the Father. Anselmian-reparative, sacrificial, and legal-penal conceptions of the atonement are 'Godward': the Father accepts the Son's offering of his sinless life on behalf of sinful humanity. Here again, as with the manward soteriology, there are two poles: this time the dramatic vector moves between the God-man and the Father. As with the manward soteriologies, so with the Godward, there is a spectrum of conceptions, this time running from the Orthodox-Catholic conception of Christ's offering to the Father as a sacrificial satisfaction of the requirements of divine goodness to the Protestant notion of a 'substitution' of Christ for humanity. Going valiantly out to bat for the substitution conception, which, he says, only makes sense when we take the reality of the Fall and original sin into account, Randall Zachman states that, for Calvin, 'Christ reconciles God to us by offering our flesh as the price of satisfaction to God's justice, and by paying the penalty we owed .... the offering of our flesh to God in the death of Christ wipes out our sin in an act of expiation .... the death of Christ clearly offers our flesh to God in a way that appeases God's righteous wrath and makes it possible for God to love us, where before God could only hate us.' In very ably describing the constraints and the freedoms enjoyed by the Catholic Christologist, Gilbert Narcisse notes that substitutionary atonement is an idea which was originally stressed by Protestants, and slowly made its way back to influence Catholic and Orthodox Christians.

The most famous Godward soteriology is that exhibited in Anselm's *Cur Deus Homo*. However annoying Christians find the argument, many are familiar with it. Written, as David Hogg acutely notes, with the intention to evangelize, Anselm's little book may well have been scripted with the intent of persuading Muslims that the persona of Jesus in the Gospels, as the human nature of the incarnate Son of God, makes more sense than the persona of Jesus as an Islamic prophet. Anselm set aside one kind of patristic devil-ward view of Christ's work, within which, as Anselm represents it, the devil had acquired 'rights' over humanity, and justice could be restored only by the reparation to the devil of his due. Anselm notices two problems with the way some Fathers had portrayed 'devilward' atonement. First, that, in justice, nothing is owed to the devil: 'though man deserved to be tormented by the devil, yet the devil tormented him unjustly'. Second, that it leaves *God* out of the frame: 'the devil is said to torment men justly, because *God* in justice permits this, and man in justice suffers it'. Anselm replaces a 'devilward' theory of atonement with a conception in which the God-man makes satisfaction to *God* through his death. He claims it is just that God ordered an innocent man to die in satisfaction because Christ voluntarily undertook this death in obedience. For Anselm, satisfaction for sin is *necessary* because sin infringes God's honor:

> For if Divine wisdom were not to insist upon these things ... there would be, in the very universe which God ought to control, an unseemliness springing from the violation of the beauty of arrangement, and God would appear to be deficient in his management. And these two things are not only unfitting, but consequently impossible; so that satisfaction or punishment must needs follow every sin.
>
> (Anselm 1973: I.VII, VIII–IX, and I.XVI, my italics)

In both of these conceptions, that is, the 'manward' and the 'Godward', the scope of the action is constrained. In the manward conception of Christ's work as deification, God in Jesus acts upon human beings; in the Godward conception of Christ's work as satisfaction, God in Jesus offers the sacrifice of his own body and blood to the Father. There is a sense in which the action could be eternal, or, in any case, extra-historical or a-temporal: God acts upon 'Man' or the God-man sacrifices to God, in one perfect, a-temporal moment in which an essential transaction always already occurs. But this is to say that the action occurs nowhere, and never, or not at any one time, not 'under Pontius Pilate'. Taken by themselves, both the Godward and the manward depictions of Christ's work are 'binary' or 'dualistic', resolving into a struggle between two great actors who have fallen out with one another. Hegel's soteriology, as finely described by Hector, comes down to the resolution of contradiction within God. Taken by themselves, both manward and Godward portrayals of Jesus Christ's role tend toward seeing it as the resolution of contradiction between two opposite poles. This is because there are only two poles in sight!

The temptation of a 'two poles' soteriology is toward conceiving the work of Christ as resolving a contradiction between contraries, and of doing so by eliminating one contrary. Judaism is an obvious culprit, which can be eliminated by Christ's contradiction-resolving work. We find an inclination toward anti-Semitic soteriologies from Luther to Hegel:

> Luther's static dialectic between Law and Gospel (Old Testament and New), continues in a sense the ancient static dialectic of Gnosis, and of Marcion, while Hegel's early writings take us back, via Luther, to this primordially gnostic Anti-Judaism: the Cross … is the 'tearing apart' of Judaism … It is no longer, then, the Cross of Jesus but a 'dialectical situation' (with Marcion, located between the true God and the world-ruler) in which one can only suffer.
>
> (Von Balthasar 1990: 62–3)

Gregory Glazov's contribution to this volume is a gem in itself, and essential to understanding the *objective* meaning of atonement. There are, as Glazov claims, parallels between Jewish suffering and the suffering of Christ which run so deep that to deprecate one is to diminish the other: this is possible because Christ's work really happens in history and in time, not in theory and in some 'bad eternity'. The tendency toward Manicheanism, and thus to the demonization of Judaism, is a liability of any strictly 'two pole' soteriology.

In Godward and manward soteriologies as conceived without a 'third' (the devil), there is a lack of dramatic realism just because there are only two actors on stage. Moreover, there is here, a lack of historical realism. Conceived in a rigidly binary way, as purely manward or as purely Godward, Christ's work seems choreographed, a balletic *pas de deux*, not a realistic, enfleshed, historical narrative. As in pre-Sophoclean tragedy, with just two actors on stage in any scene, or classical Westerns, where the action is driven by the strife of the 'contraries' of a white-hatted and a black-hatted gunman, the action is relatively more ritualized and proportionately less realistic. It's a ritual dance or competition, not yet a drama. Aristotle, the first Westerner to articulate the conception of nature as privation, potentiality, and actuality was a great *realist*. In describing the origins and history of Greek drama, Aristotle asserted with obvious legitimacy that Sophoclean realism brought Greek tragedy to fruition. Before the third character was brought on stage, Greek actors wore costumes. But they did not yet fully adopt a persona, did not really pour a role into the depiction of one human being's fate. Only with the third actor on stage does Greek drama rise to the heights at which it can address the deep human mystery of fallenness and death. Only with the third actor on stage does Greek drama prefigure the Christian mystery.

When Hans Urs Von Balthasar writes that, unlike 'what happened in the Temptations, the entire Passion proceeds without reference to the Devil. The whole story of the Passion passes him by, played out, as it is, between the Father and the Son. What matters in it is the bearing away of the sins of the world (John 1, 29). By that event, the enemy power is "disarmed" (Colossians 2,15) without the appearance of struggle against it' (Von Balthasar 1990: 106–7), it sounds very much as if he, too, wants to reduce Christ's work to a 'binary' form, in which the action is 'played out ... between the Father and the Son'. But one can read this statement otherwise: Christ performs his 'devilward' work, on this analysis, *during the course of his life and teaching ministry*, but not in his Passion and death. Mel Gibson's *The Passion of the Christ* notwithstanding (it portrays the devil as watching in the crowd throughout the spectacle), the canonical Gospels do not place the devil in the Passion and death of Christ. Rather, the 'devilward' work of Christ occurs during his life and ministry. If one removes that 'devilward' work from one's soteriology, then one will have less reason to take the whole historical life of Jesus as soteriologically significant. He does not need his human persona.

If one only has potentiality to be fulfilled and actuality to fulfill it, one's narrative lacks realism and becomes circular. It is by the introduction of a *third* pole, which extends the dynamism of the action between three agents that a story achieves dramatic realism. For Aristotle, the third pole which intervenes between potentiality and actuality is *privation*, the absence of the form. The contrary of actuality is not potentiality, but privation. Potentiality is driven to seek actuality by the positive absence of the Form for which it yearns; that is, it is driven by privation. In American English, 'I want' means only 'I crave', whereas in the Queen's English it continues to connote 'I lack': 'wanting' is still used to mean 'lacking'. A privation is a positive lack of a form, a 'wanting' of a form in both senses.

Considered without a third angle, Christ's work as deification can seem like a parade of great deeds, epiphanies in which he manifests and communicates his divinity. No one deed adds anything to the others. Humanity does not appear urgently to want, in both senses, to escape death. And, considered without a 'Privator' (that is without an active agent of privation, the devil, who wishes intently to thwart human salvation), Christ's work as 'transaction' between Father and Son on the Cross, is an eternally done-deal. In both cases, one has to pile on rhetorical or affective weight to make the whole life of Christ yield a dramatic impetus.

The third kind of soteriology is 'devilward'. Christ comes to defeat the devil, to eliminate the liar's dominion over humanity, and so to rescue humankind from its limitation to death. There's no drama in illuminating and deifying men unless they are in darkness and want immortality. One could say that here the devil has the role of 'privation', since Christian tradition follows Augustine in considering evil as privation. Thomas states that 'the disorder of sin, and evil generally, is not a simple negation, but the absence of something that ought to be there' and that 'Evil is nothing more than the lack of an appropriate good' (Aquinas, *Summa Theologiae* I–II, q.75, a.1 and q.78, a.1). 'Original sin is the lack of original justice' (*ST*, q.82, a.1): this is the state into which the devil has lured and entrapped humanity, one in which the soul is neither directed whole-heartedly toward God, its true good, nor in harmony with its bodily faculties. Postlapsarian humanity is actively trapped in this state of psychosomatic and theological privation by the devil. The devil represents positive privation. That is why there are 'devilward' soteriologies. Without an advertent third, devilward, element, soteriologies easily drift into Manicheanism, either by envisaging an elite corps of humanity retrieving their deity by beaming out of an evil world, or by making the Father exact a demonically punitive reparation from the Son. Soteriology needs a notion of 'privation' so as to avoid the triumph of the devil, in Manicheanism.

Thomas gives 'rescu[ing] man from thraldom' to the devil as a strand in the ex post facto, i.e., historical or material 'necessity' of the Incarnation for human restoration (*ST* III, q.1, a.2). He mentions the devil at least 71 times in qq. 1–59 of the *Tertia Pars*. One feature of the patristic conception of the defeat of the devil upon which modern scholars have poured scorn is the idea that it involved a deceit. As Norman Russell observes, the metaphors of Christ's humanity as a 'mouse-trap' and even the beautiful fish-hook by which the devil was cunningly trapped induce especial revulsion in well-bred writers. And yet, if the devil knows perfectly well that the Incarnation and redemption is in progress, this history looks like ritualized pantomime. In the realistic drama of Sophocles, and any realistic story, it takes the length of the performance for the protagonist to attain certain knowledge of disaster. If the devil has certain knowledge from the outset that Christ is not only human but also divine, then *he* knows the game is up the moment it commences, and it may as well not be played. It's when Sauron *knows* the ring is destroyed that the conflict which he generated is well and truly done. Whose role is concealed behind the persona of Jesus? The devil *wants* to know, as the Gospel temptation scenes indicate.

The biblical objection to the idea that the devil was deceived until the end is posed in the third objection to Thomas' question 'whether it was congruous that Christ should have been born of an Espoused Virgin?' That is, his partisans, the demons cried, 'What have we to do with thee, Jesus of Nazareth? Art thou come to destroy us? I know … thou art the Holy One of God' (Mark 1:23–4). Plus, it looks like the devil had to know, 'by his natural cunning' (*ST* III, q.29, a.1, obj.3). Thomas answers that the marriage of Mary and Joseph fit the circumstances 'for the sake of the new-born child: lest the devil should plot serious hurt against him. Hence, Ignatius says that she was espoused *that the manner of His Birth might be hidden form the devil.*' Gilbert Narcisse has observed that, when Thomas asks whether the events of the Incarnation were congruous, he is asking whether they are beautiful (Narcisse 1997). Thomas thinks the marriage was congruous, or beautiful. But, given that incongruity or just seeming pointless to a given historian is a motive for discounting the reality of an event, Thomas seems also to be inquiring whether it really happened this way. Taking all the facts into account, including the devil's malevolent intentions, it seems historically plausible to Thomas that Mary and Joseph would have married before the baby was born, to conceal the virgin conception of the God-man from the devil (*ST* III, q.29, a.1, rep.). Taking the devil seriously pushes Thomas back into an exploration of Jesus' entire historical life, from conception on. Faith in the 'Jesus of Testimony', which Thomas had in spades, is not the end but the beginning of historical explora-tion of the life of Christ.

Answering the objections about the devil's knowledge, Thomas claims that it 'makes no difficulty' that when the time was right, that is 'afterwards', when 'the time had already come for Christ to make known his power against the devil, and to suffer persecution aroused by him' 'that ... the devil *after a fashion* knew that he was the Son of God' (*ST* III, q.29, a.1, rep.obj.3; my italics). Something which may have happened later does not affect the interpretation of this earlier event. The question comes up again with the tempta-tion. Why on earth, the objector argues, did the devil *ask* Christ if he was the Son of God: surely the demons knew already? Thomas' answer, drawn from Augustine, Hilary, and Ambrose, is psychologically realistic: the demons 'formed a certain conjecture that Christ was the Son of God' from his miracles, but because they could also see human weakness in him 'they did not know for certain' (*ST* III, q.41, a.1, rep.obj.1). Fallen minds can know and blurt out the truth and simultaneously deny it to ourselves. Considering the objection to the miracles, that they would have divulged the 'secret' to the demons, and foreshortened the action (provoking the devil to incite the crucifixion before it was fully prepared), Thomas argues that the demonic 'confessions' exhibited, not 'certainty' but 'a sort of conjectural suspicion that he was the Son of God'. I Corinthians 2:7–8 set-tles the scriptural debate: 'none of the princes of this world knew it, if they had known they would never have crucified the Lord of glory' (*ST* III, q.44, rep.obj.2). The demons' propensity to denial assists the soteriological intent of the Incarnation: 'Christ came to undo the works of the devil, not by mighty deeds but rather by submitting to him and his cohorts, so as to conquer the devil by righteousness, not by might' (*ST* III, q.41, a.1, rep. obj.2). Christ robbed hypocrisy of its power by being fully himself in that very human persona which disguised his identity from the devil.

The devil is to lose his power to make humans into liars like himself. Unless we retain the sense that the devil was provoked *unknowingly* into inciting the crucifixion of the God-man, we lose the recognition that this was a disaster for the devil. And then we lose our insight into the *rescue* from deprivation of the vision of God. Thomas sets the scene for his realistic psychological portrayal of the devil's stupidity in his treatise on angels, where he argues that supernatural things can be obscure to demons (*ST* I, q.58, a.5, rep.). With his Aristotelian belief in the metaphysical and therefore physical, or temporal, pri-ority of the final cause, Thomas fully accepts the chronological requirements of the deifi-cation theory: his Christ is 'full of grace', able to merit for us, and so intrinsically good to go with causing deification in us from the instant of conception. The accounts given in this book by Rik van Nieuenhove and Joseph Wawrykow of how Christ goes about this cannot be bettered (so I will not try here!). Thomas adds, 'there were on our side some obstacles, whereby we were hindered from securing the effect of his preceding merits; consequently, in order to remove such hindrances, it was necessary for Christ to suffer' (*ST* III, q.48, a.1, rep.obj.2).

The time span between birth and Passion was required in order to lure the devil into loss of his stolen goods. Deprived of the freedom to see God, humanity could not achieve the good proper to it. The Passion of Christ is required as our ransom price. We are ransomed *from* privation of the vision of God which the Old Testament patriarchs had been promised, 'congruously merited' and for which they longed (*ST* III, q.2, a.11 rep.; q.14, a.1, rep.), that is, *from* 'slavery' to the devil. The price of releasing the deprived goods is paid not to the thief but to the Father (*ST* III, q.48, a.3, rep. and rep.obj.2).

Thomas' account of Christ's work is certainly not the only possible one, but it is a model account. It shows us the historical 'Jesus of Testimony', reflecting upon every aspect of Jesus' life from conception to death and resurrection, because every aspect of Jesus' life, death, and resurrection is involved in Christ's works, as Thomas conceived it. He integrates the work into the person and thus reflects the beauty of Christ. Thomas Aquinas is not the only 'nose to tail' soteriology, but it is an exemplary one because, within it, Jesus uses every facet of his human and divine natures with which to save us. And it does justice not only to the question, *cur Deus homo?* but also *cur Deus mortem?*

Thomas brushes aside Anselm's notion that God's justice necessarily required this satisfaction: 'God has no one above him, for he is himself the supreme and common good of the entire universe. If then he forgives sin … he violates no one's rights. The man who waives satisfaction and forgives an offence done to himself acts mercifully, not unjustly' (*ST* III, q.47, a.2). Thomas can respect God's joyous anarchism, and not subject him to necessities arising from his own justice and honor, because he does not see the atonement as effected by the interplay of two contraries (justice and injustice). He speaks of humanity as 'contracting a twofold obligation', a double bondage due to sin. One 'obligation' is humanity's bondage to the devil, and the other is 'the debt of punishment according to divine justice'. Both obligations are forms of 'slavery', that is, in Aristotelian terms, of privation of the goal of human nature, the beatific vision. By speaking of a 'double' obligation, Thomas maintains both what is true in the idea that humanity is enslaved to the devil, and in Anselm's view, that payment must ultimately be 'Godward' because God is running the show, and is the 'Form' which humanity wants (*ST* III, q.48, a.4).

Anselm's God-man satisfies by offering God a death of infinite value (Anselm, *Cur Deus Homo*, II.XIV). Although living at a time when the crucifix and painted depictions of the crucifixion had begun to displace the icon of the descent into hell as foci of Western Christian spirituality, Anselm still makes the *death* of Christ the 'satisfaction' offered to God. Abelard shifts the frame to the crucifixion. For him, the work of Christ is 'manward': Christ's death is a pure manifestation of the love of God, and its exemplification of the love of God draws humanity into filial love of God. Even more than Anselm, Abelard lacks the notion of 'privation': humanity is led *to* God, but not *from* peril of loss. Nonetheless, Abelard captures the moment of Christ's crucifixion, as exemplary or formative for those configured to it. Thomas follows Anselm in claiming that Christ pays a penal satisfaction to the Father: 'he was satisfying by his suffering', Thomas writes, and '*God's severity* is thus manifested; he was unwilling to remit sin without punishment' (*ST* III, q.46, a.6 and q.47, a.3, rep.obj.1). That is not so far from Calvin as Zachman describes him here.

Aquinas concurs with Anselm that it was not unjust that God command an innocent man to suffer, since Christ himself wills the suffering (*ST* III, q.47, a.3, rep.obj.1 and 2). But, like Abelard, he shifts the frame from the *death* of Christ to the Passion. When

Thomas says that 'It was not the death of Christ that was the cause of our salvation by way of merit, but only his Passion' (*ST* III, q.50, a.6) he

> reveals a radically different point of view from that of patristic tradition ... For them ... what saves us is the incarnation active in our flesh, and then even including death, which had become its inescapable end. For the Fathers from Irenaeus to Athanasius and ... especially the Cappadocians from Saint Cyril to Saint Maximus, it is not the subjective sufferings of Christ that constituted the decisive element in His passion, but the objective fact that these sufferings led to his death. It is this death ... that was assumed by the Master of Life and had to be overcome for us .... this is what Saint Thomas says at the conclusion of the question .... And yet the transfer of emphasis is undeniable: from the objective event to its subjectivity in the consciousness of Christ.
>
> (Bouyer 1978: 361–2)

Once Thomas had brought the consciousness of the God-man into the frame it was inevitable that the Passion, with its subjective undergoing and 'endorsement' of suffering, should become a key element of the work of Christ. For Thomas, it is not only the death of Christ, but equally that Christ 'suffered out of his love for his Father' (*ST* III, q.47, a.2, rep.obj.1) that speaks for the world's redemption. Because Thomas locates the redeeming power of the atonement in Christ's exemplary, sacrificial love, which illustrates the goodness of God, that is, in a *conscious* act of obedient love for the Father, he is able to depict it not as a transaction, but as an 'economic' *interaction*, in which God's gift of the life of Christ is paid out to God and yet humanity receives its fruits.

HEADING DEATHWARD

Thomas' Christology presents us with the whole Christ, his attention to Christ's historical works only matched by his articulation of the three dimensions of the ontology of the Incarnation—human nature, divine nature, hypostatic union of the two in the person of the Logos. The only lacuna in his soteriology is the death of Christ. It's not a lacuna in a *mediaeval* Christological soteriology to focus on the Passion rather than the death of Christ, as Thomas does. But for moderns to follow him is to fail to face up to and push back against the psychologizing of Christ's person and work which has been an egregious feature of modern Christology.

Thomas' highlighting of the dying of Christ, of his suffering of death is the theological equivalent of what happens in late mediaeval art: what Alison Milbank here calls an 'increasing realism of representation'. It can, as Milbank says, 'be the catalyst for a truly dynamic communication of idioms, in which the two natures are paradoxically juxtaposed. Following Augustine, the Middle Ages loved to dwell on the deformity of Christ's body on the Cross, but in the greatest art, this ugliness of the suffering servant can become beautiful, calling the viewer into the Passion mystery.' Thomas' focus on the Passion at the expense of the death of Christ did not tend toward subjectivism in the sacramental cosmos which he inhabited, but rather toward the elevation of the 'ugliness of the suffering servant' in the beauty of the elevated host in the Corpus Christi liturgy.

But it is difficult to maintain the objectivity of a passion-based soteriology unless the sacramental system of the Church is embedded in a sacramental view of the world. As Nieuenhove would have it, in his chapter about late mediaeval atonement theory, William of Ockham's 'rejection of divine ideas implies the demise of the mediaeval sacramental worldview in which creation is a pointer towards God and makes him present'. Once 'the world has lost its inner intelligibility (the rejection of divine ideas embedded in creation) and its sacramental character' highlighting the Passion of Jesus may tend toward a subjectivization of Christology. Zachman is right to say that once one takes the horror of sin seriously, one can scarcely exaggerate the horror Christ must undergo in order to expiate for it. Nonetheless, once Christ's sacrifice ceases to be integrated into a sacramental worldview (thus, all modern Western Christians) or an ecclesial sacramental system (thus, all Protestant Christians with Luther's rejection of 'the sacrifice of the mass'), the bloody self-sacrifice of the Son to the Father can hardly fail to seem barbaric.

So then we know that this man suffered crucifixion, but we cannot imagine how that crucifixion could be 'for us'. It is barred to non-Gnostics and non-Muslims to imagine that, somehow, Jesus Christ did not suffer all that much. But what for? Many Romantics have dealt with the question by projecting their suffering onto Jesus, and feeling thereby that he identifies with them (since they identify so far with him as to equate him with themselves). Thus as Calvin Stapert says of Beethoven's oratorio *Christus am Ölberge*, 'Beethoven saw parallels between Christ's suffering and his own. That he was consciously seeking such parallels is implicit in a remark in the Heiligenstadt Testament: "The unfortunate may console themselves to find a similar case to theirs" (Beethoven 1802).' Thus subjectivized, Christ's Passion becomes a case of suffering, quite like our own. We need not mock Beethoven and his many fellow Romantics for conceiving Christ through the lens of their own experience: people still need a transcendent object in relation to which to make sense of their life experience.

A world which is unable to conceive of sacramental sacrifice as a meaningful practice will not be iconophobic but rather unable to conceive or imagine an icon. Thus, there are in modern literature, according to Rowan Williams, no simple and direct 'Christ-figures', but rather, 'parodic' figures such as Dostoevsky's Prince Myshkin. It is indeed difficult to see how someone who causes so much damage and destruction could be, in simple terms, a Christ-figure. As Williams says, 'Myshkin's helplessness and passivity are rather like his physical appearance—he *looks* like an icon; and the tempting plausibility of an identification with Christ is thus reinforced. But it is his lack of hinterland or interiority that makes him passive and vulnerable; it is a kind of deficit in "narratable" human identity.'

In the nineteenth century, Goethe had a sacramental, analogical conception of the cosmos and did not believe in Christ; Dostoevsky had no such sacramentology and did believe in Christ (Von Balthasar 1991). Such are the paradoxes of modern Christian faith.

The hard reality of sacrifice is that its precondition is a corpse. Recall Robert Barron's reflection on the bloody slaughter house in Babette's kitchen, the necessary precondition of Babette's *Feast*. To recover the meaning of the work of Christ in a post-sacramental world, without making that work into a projection of our own subjective Gethsemanes, and simultaneously to find in Christ's work the transcendent object which draws out the meaning of our entire life experience, we must understand the goal of Christ's works as giving meaning to death, by becoming a dead body, that most meaningless thing, that thing which signifies nothing. In the parlance of actors, to 'corpse' is to forget the script on stage and fall silent.

In the instrument of the persona of the man Jesus, Christ 'corpsed', falling into the silence of death. In a non-sacramental universe, everything is essentially meaning-less: the only way in which to give that universe meaning is to become the thing in that universe which is most parodically divested of meaning, a human corpse. The human corpse is the most meaningless thing in the world because a *person should* be significant. A dead tree is very sad, and a dead animal can be the source of great grief. But a dead person is itself a contradiction in terms, since there is that in every person which cries out for immortality. Through the instrument of his embodied persona, Christ becomes a lifeless corpse, embodying the end of all 'mortals'. By assuming death into his stereo-typical persona, the New Adam takes death into his life-project.

The fervent, unsystematic Luther surely saw this at times, as did his contempo-rary Holbein, when he painted 'the cadaver of Christ, lying horizontally, putrid blue' (Von Balthasar 1991: 193). Dostoevsky perhaps saw this too when he ascribed to the hero of *The Idiot*, Prince Myshkin, a comprehension of 'Execution, epilepsy, the Holy Saturday picture: the three states of absolute isolation in which he unselfconsiously lives (there is never a word … about the "perfection" of this habitual abandonment … and indifference)' (Von Balthasar 1991: 198). The modern Christ, like his fictional icons, lacks a 'narratable human identity' because the core of his identity enters absurdity and meaninglessness. Only God can do this, in and through an embod-ied human persona. We do not recover sacramentality by reinventing an artistically 'beautiful' sacramental universe and somehow fitting Christ into it. We let Christ rewrite the story through his death. He is not thereby 'unwriting' or erasing the his-tory of the relations between God and creatures, or overwriting it with something else, though he does 'make all things new'. The sacrifice that God *is*, at the heart of his Trinitarian being in love, is expressed through the embodied persona of the 'corpsed' Jesus Christ (McCormack).

The word 'sacrament' ceased to have much meaning for moderns: but 'solidarity' replaced it. Solidarity is to personalist theology what sacramentality was to the cosmic theology of the mediaevals. We think of Christ as offering his sacrificial death in 'soli-darity' with all human beings, with all sinners. The claim that Christ enters death in sub-stitutional solidarity with *all* humanity has raised hackles. In this volume, Gavin D'Costa accuses both Karl Barth and Hans Urs Von Balthasar of universalism because they make such a claim. Ascribing to Barth and Von Balthasar the idea that 'Resurrection Overcomes Sin in the End' D'Costa opines that they teach that

Christ's unique atoning death actually wins the salvation of all (usually stated as a hope); and all will come to know him 'somehow'. This kind of 'universalism' is found in ... Hans Urs Von Balthasar and the Reform giant, Karl Barth, despite both holding a very high Christology .... Both are associated with very negative views on other religions, while interestingly both hold to versions of universalism. In this outcome they are bedfellows with Hick .... Von Balthasar and Barth have been criticized for not respecting human freedom adequately, for lacking biblical grounding, and Von Balthasar, for going against the Magisterium.

Since D'Costa accuses Von Balthasar of 'universalism', which is a heresy for Catholics, and likewise of 'going against the Magisterium' it is at least worth noting, as Narcisse observes, in his wise chapter about Catholic Christological norms, that the debate between proponents of Von Balthasar's substitutionary soteriology and Thomistic opponents 'has taken place without any significant intervention from the Catholic Magisterium. It is a beautiful example, not necessarily of unity as the accounts are very different, but of an inter-confessional theological liberty.'

Since D'Costa gives no argument why we should discount Von Balthasar's explicit statements that universal salvation is a *hope* not a certainty, we cannot analyze, present, or counter an argument which he does not give. We may simply note that, for Von Balthasar, Christ's entrance into death, and isolation from God, means that Christ has *taken* death. He has death covered, has power over it, judging henceforth who goes there and who goes not:

> the desire to conclude from this that all human beings, before and after Christ, are henceforth saved, that Christ by his experience of Hell has emptied Hell, so that all fear of damnation is now without object, is a surrender to the opposite extreme. ... precisely here the distinction between Hades and Hell acquires its theological significance. In rising from the dead, Christ leaves behind him Hades, that is, the state in which humanity is cut off from access to God. But, by virtue of his deepest Trinitarian experience, he takes 'Hell' with him, as the expression of his power to dispose, as judge, the everlasting salvation or the everlasting loss of man.
>
> (Von Balthasar 1990: 177)

Christ rises from the dead as *Judge* of the living and the dead. Those old icons of Christ reigning triumphant from the Cross remain at the center. While Christ 'becomes death' in the persona of Jesus, still, that persona is the expression of his *sending* by the Father, into a 'Far Country' indeed, which sending in turn is identical to his begetting as Son: the fire of divinity is made to burn at the heart of death and it does not burn out or die (Exod. 3). As Von Balthasar writes, 'Inasmuch as the Son travels across the chaos in virtue of the mission received from the Father, he is, objectively speaking, whilst in the midst of the darkness of what is contrary to God, in "paradise", and the image of triumph may well express this .... it is, as Thomas Aquinas underlines, a "taking possession"' (Von Balthasar 1990: 175). This volume would not comprehensively represent the dynamic tensions within early twenty-first-century Christology if it exhibited no signs of flyting between those who think Von Balthasar shows the way forward out of the dilemmas of nineteenth- and early twentieth-century Christology, and those who think that Christian theology does not have to answer Kant, Hegel, and their heirs and should rise above these local and recent disturbances.

Since the Fall, all human beings have been required to cap off their lives with death. And this, precisely, we human beings, whose existence never quite fills out our many roles, cannot do: with our being limping steadily behind our projection of roles for ourselves, we cannot reach forward into death and make something meaningful and personally human with it. Since the Fall, our lives have become a being toward death, and we cannot make sense out of that. We cannot make meaning out of death. But, as rational persons, as signifying animals, what we *do* is to make meaning out of our actions. A meaningless action unmakes us as persons, if it is supposed, as our final act, to cap it all off. As creaturely persons, whose existence is not up to any of our roles, we have to make and construct meaning. We have to write our life into a story through our assumption of roles in the persona of our steadily aging body. But no human life is a story. The narrative arc falters and dies away: there is no rhyme and pattern, too much and too little repetition to become a rounded story. Only He who Is, whose existence *is* his very nature and character, can, through his embodied persona, reach into death and *be himself*, that is, be God in the place of death. Only in God is death beautiful.

Suggested Reading

Aquinas (1981); Von Balthasar (1990).

Bibliography

Anselm (1973), *The Prayers and Meditations of Saint Anselm with the Proslogion*, trans. B. Ward (London: Penguin).

Aquinas, T. (1981), *Summa Theologica*, trans. Fathers of the English Dominican Province (Westminster, Md.: Christian Classics).

Bouyer, L. (1978), *The Eternal Son: A Theology of the Word of God and Christology* (Huntington, Ind.: Our Sunday Visitor Press).

Narcisse, G. (1997), *Les raisons de Dieu. Argument de convenance et esthétique théologique selon saint Thomas d'Aquin et Hans Urs von Balthasar* (Fribourg: Éditions universitaires).

Torrell, J.-P. (1999), *Le Christ en ses mystères. La Vie et l'oeuvre de Jésus selon Saint Thomas d'Aquin*, vol. 2 (Paris: Desclée).

Von Balthasar, H. U. (1990), *Mysterium Paschale: The Mystery of Easter* (Edinburgh: T. & T. Clark).

Von Balthasar, H. U. (1991), *The Glory of the Lord: A Theological Aesthetics*, vol. 5: *The Realm of Metaphysics in the Modern Age* (Edinburgh: T. & T. Clark).

INDEX OF NAMES

SUBJECT INDEX

9 780198 800064